AF323687

THE
DIRECTORY
OF
DISTINGUISHED
AMERICANS

THE DIRECTORY
OF
DISTINGUISHED AMERICANS

Third Edition

published by:
The American Biographical Institute
Main Offices
5126 Bur Oak Circle, Post Office Box 31226
Raleigh, North Carolina 27622 U.S.A.
ISBN Prefix: 934544

Copyright © 1985 by *The American Biographical Institute, Inc.* All rights reserved. *No part* of this publication may be used as a mailing list and/or be reproduced, stored in a retrieval system, or transmitted in any form or by any means, electronic, mechanical, photocopying, or otherwise, without the prior written permission of the publisher.

Library of Congress Catalog Card Number 81-71699
International Standard Book Number 0-934544-36-0

Printed and bound in the United States of America
by
BookCrafters, Chelsea, Michigan, U.S.A.

Table of Contents

Preface

The purpose of this volume is to provide both a directorial listing of individuals who are leaders in many different professions and a portrait, in book form, of Americans who volunteer their time and efforts for the betterment of communities.

Individuals who appear in each edition of *THE DIRECTORY OF DISTINGUISHED AMERICANS* are selected by the Governing Board of Editors of the American Biographical Institute from nominations furnished by mayors, legislators and other public officials; from college and university recommendations; and from lists of outstanding people provided by professional and civic organizations at the local, state, regional and national levels. Uniform selection procedures are followed by the Board according to criteria common to other leading reference works which have national distribution. Each person chosen for listing in the volume is selected, therefore, through standards aimed at genuine reference interest. Purchase of the volume is not a prerequisite for inclusion nor is there a fee for listing.

Included in the pages of this edition is a special section devoted to young Americans between the ages of sixteen and thirty who also have demonstrated dedication toward enriching today's society. These include outstanding students, college and university campus leaders, athletes, promising businessmen and women, club leaders, community volunteers, and more. The young people chosen for inclusion in this volume are setting fine examples for other youths and justifiably deserve recognition.

THE DIRECTORY OF DISTINGUISHED AMERICANS is an everlasting tribute to the following individuals whose lives and deeds will become a part of their community, state and country. The American Biographical Institute is glad to have played a role in nationally recognizing their achievements.

Sincerely,

J.M. Evans
Editorial Director
The American Biographical Institute, Inc.

# The American Biographical Institute

Governing Board of Editors

J.M. Evans
Editorial Director

J.S. Thomson
Editor in Chief

Editorial

K.A. Carpenter

R.L. Jones

E.A. Ledbetter

P.J. Owens

S.R. Penney

H.C. Wood

Communications/Research/Sales

N. D. Avera

S.J. Brown

G.T. Doucet

A.R. Holland

L.M. Kellander

D. Smith

E.C. Williams

ABI BIOGRAPHICAL TITLES

The Directory of Distinguished Americans
International Directory of Distinguished Leadership
Community Leaders of America
Community Leaders of the World
Young Community Leaders of America
Notable Americans
Two Thousand Notable Americans
Personalities of America
Personalities of the South
Personalities of the West and Midwest
Five Thousand Personalities of the World
The Book of Honor
International Book of Honor

Delineative Information

Individual biographical entries in the Third Edition are arranged according to standard alphabetical practice within three distinct categories: 1)*The Directory of Distinguished Americans* Hall of Fame; 2)Biographies of Distinguished Americans; and, 3)Biographies of Distinguished Young Americans. Information within each entry is consistently and uniformly presented using few abbreviations. A Table of Abbreviations is provided on the following pages for the convenience of the reader.

Editors of the Institute make all attempts to edit accurately the information furnished by each biographee. In the rare event of an error by the publisher, the sole responsibility of the publisher will be to correct such in the subsequent edition of the publication.

Editorial evaluation is the ultimate determinant of publication selection. Admission in this series is based on the value of achievement or recognized outreach of endeavor and not on any purchase prerequisite. There is no fee for listing.

All submissions and files at the Institute are maintained in confidence and adequate security.

Nomination sources for the Institute's publications are received through personal recommendations by the Institute's Editorial Advisory Board, Honorary Educational Advisory Board, Research Board of Advisors, and esteemed members of the American Biographical Institute Research Association. Appointees of the aforementioned boards are listed in the latter part of this edition. There are many other sources as well such as nominations furnished by national universities and colleges; professional, service and civic organizations on the local, state and national levels; and many businesses and government officials. Mailing lists have never been bought or sold. Neither nominees nor nominators are placed under any financial obligation whatsoever. Nominees are contacted for their personal submissions of biographical data and it is these credentials that are editorially reviewed by the Institute's Governing Board of Editors.

ABI reference books are used by and provide authoritative guides for business consultants, researchers, reporters, scholars, biographers, librarians, historians and genealogists. The Institute publishes volumes that are regional, national and international in scope. The ABI annually distributes copies of its many titles to public and private libraries and institutions of higher learning. Since establishment in 1967, it has been the aim of the Institute to publish factual, permanent profiles of accomplished, active and dedicated individuals who make substantial contributions to society as a whole. There is no discrimination as to the level of contribution, but only in the effort and involvement in achieving worthwhile endeavors. **Main Offices of Publisher:** 5126 Bur Oak Circle, Post Office Box 31226, Raleigh, North Carolina 27622 U.S.A. **Library Distribution Agent:** BIBLIO Distribution Centre (worldwide), 81 Adams Drive, Post Office Box 327, Totowa, New Jersey 07511 U.S.A. **References:** *The Directory of Directories* and the National Library of Congress Copyright Office.

The Directory of Distinguished Americans
HALL OF FAME

The following individuals are 1984/85 inductees of the Institute's Hall of Fame through *The Directory of Distinguished Americans* series. Overall achievements qualifying these individuals for induction are cited as is the year of induction and residence of each person. Following the main alphabetical entries are the names of those inducted into the Hall of Fame immediately prior to publication of this edition (April 1985). The honor of induction is bestowed upon a select group of individuals each year by the American Biographical Institute. The names of inductees will be featured in all subsequent editions of this publication.

Gertrude Webster Abbott
Contributions to Art and Literature
1984
Sioux Falls, South Dakota

Helen "Missy" Adams
Contributions to Elementary Education
1984
Cumberland, Wisconsin

Daniel R. Appleton, Jr.
Contributions to Optometry
1985
Newburyport, Massachusetts

Karen G. Arms
Outstanding Academic Administration
1984
Kent, Ohio

Simeon Baker
Contributions as Journalist & News Commentator
1984
Brooklyn, New York

Dorothy K. Bidwell
Contributions to Business
1984
San Diego, California

John A. Biggers
Contributions as a Businessman
1984
Sacramento, California

James R. Bilbow
Outstanding Service to the American People
1984
Media, Pennsylvania

Alfred J. Blasco
Contributions to Business and Financial
Consulting Profession
1984
Kansas City, Missouri

Edna L. Gossage Blue
Contributions as a Writer and Civic Leader
1985
Crossville, Tennessee

Ida M. Boodakian
Contributions as a Publisher & Editor
1985
Winchester, Massachusetts

Wilbert C. Bradshaw
Contributions to the Business Profession
1985
Fresno, California

John H. Brookshire
Contributions to International Health
1985
Tampa, Florida

Randy J. Burnworth
Contributions to the Electronics Industry
1985
Tillamook, Oregon

N. M. Camardese
Activities and Community Programs
to Preserve Our Great American Heritage
and Legacy of Freedom for All
1985
Norwalk, Ohio

Julia Elizabeth Dickinson Cane
Contributions to Education
1984
San Antonio, Texas

C. W. Carpenter, II
Contributions to Education and to the
Community
1985
Bloomsburg, Pennsylvania

Eugene S. Chyzowych
Contributions as Physical Education Instructor
1984
South Orange, New Jersey

Eddie-Lou Cole
Contributions to Poetry
1984
Sacramento, California

Richard Bangs Collier
Contributions to Science & Philosophy by
Creating & Expanding the Field of Pleneurethic
1985
Kennewick, Washington

George M. Coriaty
Contributions to Religion
1985
Montreal, Quebec, Canada

Minnie Julia Dahm
Contributions as Archivist, Translator & Researcher
1984
Glendale, Arizona

Yvonne R. Davidson
Contributions to Literature
1985
LaQuinta, California

Jacques M. Delphin
Contributions as a Doctor of Psychiatry
1985
Poughkeepsie, New York

John A. Despol
Contributions as Deputy Labor Commissioner
1984
Sherman Oaks, California

William H. Draper III
Contributions to the Field of Business
1985
Washington, D.C.

Estelle C. Dunlap

Contributions to Education
and Mathematics
1984
Washington, D.C.

Helen E. Dunn

Contributions to the Field of
Education
1985
Peru, Illinois

Iris Daniel Engel

Contributions to the Field of
Music
1984
Orlando, Florida

William Earle Findley

Outstanding Service to the
Community
1984
Pickens, South Carolina

Gerald J. FitzGerald
Contributions to the Field
of Law
1984
Chicago, Illinois

Sharon Fourcard-Bultron
Contributions to the Medical Profession
through Nursing
1985
Pearland, Texas

Annie Belle Freas
Contributions as a Business
and Community Leader
1985
Nashville, Tennessee

Ruth E. French
Contributions to the Field of Education
as an Educator
1985
Proctor, Utah

Edna Garabedian
Contributions to the Field
of Music
1985
Fresno, California

Henry Garcia, Jr.
Contributions as a Business Executive
1985
El Paso, Texas

Arthur R. Getz
Contributions as a Certified Public Accountant
1984
San Francisco, California

Marie T. Giza
Contributions to Education
1985
Baltimore, Maryland

Julius Goodman
Contributions as Nuclear Engineer & Theoretical
Physicist
1985
Fullerton, California

Marita (Rita) Belle Graves
Contributions as a Poet and Artist
1984
Turlock, California

Dora E. Clyburn Gray
Contributions as an Accountant
1985
San Angelo, Texas

Millicent Dickenson Greenaway
Contributions to Early Childhood Education
1984
Newark, New Jersey

E. Hakim-Elahi
Service to the Medical Profession
1984
Jamaica, New York

Kathryn G. Hansen
Contributions to Business and to the Community
1985
Laguna Hills, California

Louise Harris
Contributions to Research and Journalism
1984
Rumford, Rhode Island

V. William Harris
Contributions to Psychology
1985
Tucson, Arizona

Lorene C. Harrison
Outstanding Community Activism
1984
Anchorage, Alaska

Robert H. Heckart
Contributions to Religion and Journalism
1984
Colorado Springs, Colorado

Harry C. Helm
Contributions as an Artist and Poet
1985
Spokane, Washington

Martha M. Saunders Henderson
Contributions as a Museum Director
1985
Willingboro, New Jersey

Gloria T. Hoff
Contributions as a Professor of Physics
1985
Chicago, Illinois

Harry Hong
Contributions to History and Political
Science through Education
1984
Jamestown, North Dakota

G. Turner Howard, Jr.
Contributions as a Surgeon
1984
Knoxville, Tennessee

John Wilfred Howard
Contributions to the Arts
1984
Corinth, Kentucky

John Chih-An Hu
Contributions to Chemistry
1984
Renton, Washington

L. Ron Hubbard
Contributions to Literature
1985
Los Angeles, California

Larry R. Huck
Outstanding Sales Achievements
1985
Bellevue, Washington

Charles F. Jenkins
Contributions to Special Education
1985
Kansas City, Missouri

F. Eileen Kagey
Contributions to Education
1984
Gary, Indiana

Nicolai Kashin
Contributions as a Tax Consultant
and Author
1984
Glendale, California

Robert Gilmore Keene
Outstanding Community Involvement
1984
Bridgehampton, New York

Catherine Earl Bailey Kerr
Contributions to Art & Education
1985
Roswell, New Mexico

Barbara King

Contributions to the Nursing Profession
1984
Alvord, Texas

Joseph Jerone King

Contributions as Economic Consultant
1984
Silverdale, Washington

Nelda R. Knelson

Contributions as an Author of
Children's Books
1985
Dixon, Illinois

L. M. Knill
Contributions to Radiation Biology
1985
Pomona, California

Berthold K. Koester
Outstanding Political Contributions
1984
Phoenix, Arizona

Anna Josephine Kraus
Contributions to Medical Record
Technology
1984
Brookville, Pennsylvania

Shain-dow Kung
Contributions as a Professor
of Biological Sciences
1984
Baltimore, Maryland

Bernard A. Kuttner
Contributions as an Attorney at Law
1984
Roseland, New Jersey

Newlin Landers
Outstanding Contracting and
Community Development
1985
Landers, California

Vernette Landers
Contributions to Education
and to Community
Development
1985
Landers, California

Mary F. K. Lane
Contributions as a Professor
of Psychology
1985
Monterey Park, California

Agnes D. Lattimer
Contributions as a Pediatrician
1985
Chicago, Illinois

James D. Lauter
Contributions to Financial Consulting
1984
Northridge, California

Betty Jean Leasure
Contributions as a Poet
and Author
1985
New Martinsville, West Virginia

Bernard Lesser
Contributions to Management and Guidance
within the Field of
Education
1985
Springfield, New Jersey

Delmore Liggett
Involvement in Education
and Community
1984
Rising Sun, Indiana

Berthe Felder Littell
Contributions as an Insurance
Signatory
1985
Tomball, Texas

Letha Lloyd-Wayne
Contributions as Music Instructor
1984
Concord, California

Edythe Lutzker
Contributions to the Literary Field
1985
New York, New York

Albert A. Magee
Contributions to the Real Estate Profession
1985
Long Beach, California

Hope Marie Maki
Contributions to the
Creative Arts
1984
Pensacola, Florida

Elaine R. Malco
Contributions to Art and Literature
1985
Long Beach, California

Howard G. Malin
Contributions to Podiatry
1984
Martinsburg, West Virginia

Paul F. Massier
Outstanding Research in Engineering
1985
Arcadia, California

Janette E. Matthew-Pemberton

Contributions to the Field of
Education
1985
Rockville, Maryland

Edward C. Maxwell

Contributions to the Legal
Profession
1984
Oxnard, California

James N. McCloud

Contributions to Education
and Mathematics
1984
Pasadena, California

William A. Mills
Contributions as an Accountant
1985
Savannah, Georgia

Virginia Mitchell
Contributions to Business
1984
Cordele, Georgia

Thomas Sanfran Miyada
Outstanding Research in Science
1984
Summit, New Jersey

Martha Annell Moore
Contributions to the Furniture Industry
and to the Community
1985
Memphis, Tennessee

Elbert Raymond Moses, Jr.
Contributions as an Educator
1985
Prescott Valley, Arizona

Raymond Neill
Contributions to the Aircraft Industry
1984
Long Beach, California

Captolia D. Newbern
Contributions as an Educator
1985
Philadelphia, Pennsylvania

Regina Ocwieja
Outstanding Service to the Community
1984
Chicago, Illinois

Wilson R. Ogg
Contributions as a Lawyer, Educator,
and Real Estate Executive
1984
Berkeley, California

Margaret P. Ogilvie
Contributions as a Personal
and Marital
Counselor
1984
Fairfield Glade, Tennessee

Araceli Ortiz
Contributions to the Fields of
Education and Oral
Pathology
1985
Rio Piedras, Puerto Rico

Robert W. Page
Contributions to Engineering and Business
1984
Houston, Texas

Zella J. Patterson
Contributions to Literature
1985
Langston, Oklahoma

Norman Pearson
Contributions as a Consultant Planner
1985
London, Ontario, Canada

S. Macpherson Pemberton
Contributions to Education
1985
Rockville, Maryland

Reginald C. Perry
Contributions as an Educator and Writer
1985
Pine Bluff, Arkansas

George H. Pittman, Jr.
Contributions to the Armed Forces and
Aviation
1985
Melbourne, Florida

Sartell Prentice, Jr.
Contributions as a Profit Sharing and
Management Consultant
1985
Pasadena, California

Alvin A. Price
Contributions to Veterinary Medicine
1985
College Station, Texas

Mark M. Price
Contributions to the Architectural Profession
1984
Washington, D.C.

Panayotis Protopapas
Contributions as a Business Executive
1984
Herndon, Virginia

Sherry Swett Raatz
Contributions as a Civic Leader
1985
Seattle, Washington

A. Guinn Rasbury

Contributions as Corporate
Controller
1984
Houston, Texas

Lee Thornton Rector

Contributions to the Fields of
Medicine and
Poetry
1984
New Smyrna Beach, Florida

Maria L. Reyman

Contributions as an Educator
1985
New Hartford, New York

Charles L. Rhykerd
Contributions as a
Professor of
Agronomy
1984
West Lafayette, Indiana

Ollie Hodrick Ritchey
Contributions to Literature
1985
Bonita, California

Pattie Jayne Ross
Contributions as a Physician
1984
Houston, Texas

Frederic Hull Roth
Contributions to the Field
of Accounting
1984
Rocky River, Ohio

Augusta Rubin
Contributions to Literature
1984
New York, New York

Ann Ruth
Contributions as a Business Executive
1985
Rancho Palos Verdes, California

Grace St. Dawn
Contributions to Literature
1984
Paramus, New Jersey

Margaret T. Savage
Contributions to Microbiology
and Psychology
1984
Westbury, New York

Jack Schwartzman
Contributions to Education, Law and Journalism
1984
Floral Park, New York

Wilhelm Schwarzott
Contributions to Music
1985
San Francisco, California

Robert F. Seng
Contributions as an Oil Company Executive
1984
Oneonta, New York

Shirish K. Shah
Contributions to Education through
Computers and Engineering
Technology
1984
Baltimore, Maryland

Ishaq Shahryar
Contributions to Science
1985
Pacific Palisades, California

Bob R. Shatwell
Exceptional Service to the Community
1984
Tulsa, Oklahoma

Ralph A. Sheetz
Contributions to the Legal Profession
1985
Enola, Pennsylvania

Violet Sheh

Contributions to the Field of
Journalism
1985
Richmond, B.C., Canada

Rama S. Singh

Outstanding Accomplishments in
Microelectronics
1985
Orlando, Florida

Gene S. Sogliero

Contributions to Research Science
and Statistics
1984
Groton, Connecticut

Ruth Staffanson
Contributions to the Bookkeeping Profession
1984
Gresham, Oregon

Gene J. Sterger
Contributions as a Consultant
1984
Waldorf, Maryland

Elsie S. Suyenaga
Contributions to Education and to the
Community
1984
Pearl City, Hawaii

M. N. S. Swamy
Contributions to Engineering
through Education
1984
Lambert, Quebec, Canada

Neva Talley-Morris
Outstanding Accomplishments
in the Legal
Profession
1984
Little Rock, Arkansas

Herbert H. Tarson
Contributions to Education
1984
La Mesa, California

John C. Taylor
Contributions to the Field of Dentistry
and as a Missionary
1985
Herminie, Pennsylvania

Donald M. Telford
Contributions to Education & the Community
1985
Largo, Florida

Barbara Thomas
Outstanding Business Achievements
1984
Bethesda, Maryland

William V. Thomas
Contributions as Roofing Contractor and
Community Volunteer
1984
Alameda, California

Wei-ming Tu
Contributions as a Professor of Chinese
History and Philosophy
1984
Cambridge, Massachusetts

Arthur E. Turner

Contributions to the Field of
Education
1984
Midland, Michigan

Vern W. Urry

Contributions to the Field of
Personnel Research
Psychology
1984
Clinton, Maryland

Aliyah W. M. von Nussbaumer
Contributions as a Research Librarian
1984
Houton, Texas

V. Drexel Waltrip
Outstanding Service to the Community
1985
Martinez, California

Emma B. Wheeler
Contributions as a Representative to the
United States Government
1984
Milford, New Hampshire

Vallie Jo Fox Whitfield
Contributions to Real Estate & Literary Fields
1985
Pleasant Hill, California

Ona Ruth Whitley

Contributions to the Field of
Bacteriology
1985
Monroe, North Carolina

Marion R. Wiemann, Jr.

Outstanding Scientific Achievement
1985
Chesterton, Indiana

Eugen Wierbicki

Outstanding Research in Food
Irradiation
1985
Penllyn, Pennsylvania

Evelyn Williams

Contributions to the Field
of Music
1984
Boca Raton, Florida

Kenneth L. Wright

Contributions to the Field
of Psychology
1984
San Diego, California

Paul M. Yakin

Contributions as a Clinical Psychologist
1985
Chicago, Illinois

Natalie Yopconka

Contributions as an
Applications Analyst
Programmer
1984
Hyattsville, Maryland

Sidney B. Young

Contributions to the Field
of Music
1984
Orangeburg, South Carolina 29115

Bernard M. Zussman

Contributions to the Medical Profession
1984
Memphis, Tennessee

HALL OF FAME
APRIL 1985 INDUCTEES

Fernando G. R. Barbachano
Contributions as a Businessman
1985
Miami, Florida

Charles C. Caro
Contributions to the Field of Microcomputers
1985
Tampa, Florida

Riaya M. Kanso
Contributions to Industrial Development
1985
Atlanta, Georgia

Ralph Reed Payton
Services to the Nation
1985
Carmel Valley, California

BIOGRAPHIES OF
DISTINGUISHED AMERICANS

A

AADAHL, JORG Occupation: Founder and President, Safeware, Inc. Education: M.B.A., M.Sc.M.E. Address: 1707 Monticello Road, San Mateo, California 94402.

ABARBANEL, GAIL Occupation: Director, Rape Treatment Center; Clinical Social Worker. Education: B.A., University of California at Los Angeles, 1966; M.S.W., University of Southern California, 1968. Address: Santa Monica Hospital Medical Center, 1225 15th Street, Santa Monica, California 90404.

ABARBANELL, GAY H Occupation: Financial Advisor. Education: College and Postgraduate Studies. Address: 1181 Hi Point Street, Los Angeles, California 90035.

ABBA, SISTER MARTINA M Occupation: Social Worker; Pastor of Two Churches. Education: B.A. Social Work, M.S.W. Address: Box 760, Kettle Falls, Washington 99141.

ABBASY, IFTIKHARUL HAQUE Occupation: Surgeon. Education: M.B.B.S; F.R.C.S. (C.); Diplomate, The American Board of Surgery; Diplomate, The American Board of Abdominal Surgery. Address: 905 Burr Oak Circle, Oak Brook, Illinois 60521.

ABBOTT, CHARLES FAROUR JR Occupation: Attorney. Education: B.A. Economics; J.D. Law. Address: 3737 Foothill Drive, Provo, Utah 84604.

ABBOTT, DAVID WAYNE Occupation: Marriage and Family Therapist. Education: B.S. Psychology, M.S. Counseling, Ph.D. Therapy. Address: 2838 Goldy Wayt, Sparks, Nevada 89431.

ABBOTT, GERTRUDE WEBSTER Occupation: Professor of Art (Retired); Writer. Education: Doctor of Literature. Address: 2708 Wood Drive, Sioux Falls, South Dakota 57105.

ABBOTT, JOHN DAVID Occupation: Clergyman, Church Administrator. Education: Th.B., D.D. (honorary). Address: 1413 Glendale Drive, Marion, Indiana 46953.

ABBOTT, ROBERT D Occupation: Professor, University of Washington. Education: B.A., M.S., Ph.D. Address: 7357 57 Northeast, Seattle, Washington 98115.

ABDULKAREEM, AMEEN Occupation: Insurance Agent. Education: B.A. Political Science, M.S. Business. Address: 580 White Plains Road, Tarrytown, New York 12591.

ABEL, ERNEST L Occupation: Acting Deputy Director. Education: Ph.D. Address: 106 Ranch Trail West, Williamsville, New York 14221.

ABEL, ROBERT B Occupation: President, New Jersey Marine Sciences Consortium. Education: B.S., M.E.A., Ph.D. Address: 55 Queen Anne Drive, Shrewsbury, New Jersey 07701.

ABEL, ROBERT H Occupation: Writer. Education: B.A., M.A., M.F.A. English. Address: Box 96, 5 Turner Street, Lake Pleasant, Massachusetts 01347.

ABELES, GINA L G Occupation: Freelance Graphic Designer. Education: A.B. Fine Arts, M.A. Social Psychology, Ph.D. Social Psychology. Address: 128 Cabot Street, Newton, Massachusetts 02158.

ABELOFF, ABRAM JOSEPH Occupation: Surgeon. Education: A.B., Columbia University, 1922; M.D., Columbia University, 1926. Address: 150 East 77th Street, New York City, New York 10021.

ABER, MARGERY V Occupation: Professor of Violin, University of Michigan at Stevens Point. Education: B.Mus., Oberlin College; M.A., Columbia University. Address: 511 Michigan, Stevens Point, Wisconsin 54481.

ABERNATHY, SANDRA M Occupation: Assistant Direcctor, Education Research Center. Education: B.S. with honors, University of California at Davis, 1957; M.A.T., New Mexico State University, 1968; Ph.D., New Mexico State University, 1982. Address: Star Route Box 30, Mesilla Park, New Mexico 88047.

ABRAHAMSEN, SAMUEL Occupation: Professor, Brooklyn College. Education: B.A., M.A., University of Oslo (Norway). Address: 4 Washington Square Village, New York, New York 10012.

ABRAM, ALENE JAMES Occupation: Foreign Language Instructor, Consultant. Education: B.A., University of California, 1936; M.A., University of California, 1938; Advanced Study, Claremont Graduate School. Address: 612 Highland Court, Upland, California 91786.

ABRAMS, EDITH L Occupation: Sculptor, Teacher. Education: B.A., Brooklyn College; M.F.A. Sculpture, Pratt Institute. Address: 2820 Avenue J, Brooklyn, New York 11210.

ABRAMS, MARK LEE Occupation: Director of Student Affairs. Education: B.A., M.A. Address: 116 Davis Road, Fairfield, Connecticut 06430.

ABRAMS, MARLENE RAE Occupation: Assistant Regional Attorney, Department of Health and Human Services. Education: J.D., Georgetown University Law Center, 1974; B.S., Boston University, 1971. Address: 3200 North Lake Shore Drive, Chicago, Illinois 60657.

ABRAMS, ROSALIE SILBER Occupation: Maryland State Senator. Education: B.S., M.A. Political Science, The Johns Hopkins University; R.N., Sinai Hospital School of Nursing. Address: 111 Hamlet Hill Road, Baltimore, Maryland 21210.

ABRAMS-SMITH, PAULA Occupation: Child Psychologist. Education: Ph.D., Northwestern University; M.S., National College; B.A., University of Washington. Address: 4828 Bussendorfer Road, Orchard Park, New York 24075.

ABRAMSON, FREDRIC DAVID Occupation: Associate Professor of Management, The American University; Consultant in Business Strategy. Education: A.B., University of Pennsylvania; M.S., University of Rochester; Ph.D., University of Michigan; S.M., Massachusetts Institute of Technology. Address: 21155 Burnham Road, Gaithersburg, Maryland 20879.

ACHESON, LOUIS K JR Occupation: Aerospace Engineer. Education: B.S.E.E., Ph.D. Physics. Address: 17721 Marcello Place, Encino, California 91316.

ACKEN, BRENDA T Occupation: Corporate Officer and Board Member. Education: B.S. Business Administration. Address: 628 Parkway, Bluefield, West Virginia 24701.

ACKERMAN, DIANA FELICIA Occupation: Associate Professor of Philosophy, Brown University. Education: A.B., Cornell University, 1968; Ph.D., University of Michigan, 1976. Address: 89 East Manning Street, Providence, Rhode Island 02906.

ACKERMAN, GERALD MARTIN Occupation: Art Historian; Professor, Art Department, Pomona College. Education: Ph.D., Princeton University, 1963. Address: 360 South Mills Avenue, Claremont, California 91711.

ACKERMAN, JAMES VICTOR Occupation: Vice President of Finance, Director, Ajax Magnethermic Corporation. Education: B.S.B.A with honors, Loyola College of Baltimore, 1970. Address: 508 Sycamore Trail, Cortland, Ohio 44410.

ACKLEN, GERALD G Education: B.S. Address: 1250 Oakview Drive, Grants Pass, Oregon 97527.

ACTON, NORMAN Occupation: Secretary General, Rehabilitation International. Education: B.S. Journalism. Address: Route 5, Box 518, Gloucester, Virginia 23061.

ACZÉL, JÁNOS DEZSÖ Occupation: Mathematician; Professor, University of Waterloo. Education: B.A. 1946, M.A. 1947, Ph.D. 1947, University of Budapest; Habilitation 1952, D.Sc. 1957, Hungarian Academy of Sci. Address: 97 McCarron Circle, Waterloo, Ontario N2L 5M9, Canada.

ADAMCIN, JULIE CAMP Occupation: 4-H Agent; Home Economist. Education: B.S. Home Economics/ Spanish, M.S. Agricultural Education. Address: 2216 West Wagon Wheels Drive, Tucson, Arizona 85745.

ADAMO, JOSEPH ALBERT Occupation: Chairman and Professor, Department of Science, Ocean County College. Education: B.A., M.S., Ph.D. Address: 185 Maple Avenue, Toms River, New Jersey 08753.

ADAMS, CHARLES DeWITT Occupation: Petroleum Engineer. Education: B.S. Petroleum Engineering, University of Texas. Address: 6110 Boca Raton, Corpus Christi, Texas 78413.

ADAMS, DAVID WAYNE Occupation: Semi-Retired. Education: Attended Linn Benton Community College. Address: 42319 Green Mountain Drive, Lebanon, Oregon 97355.

ADAMS, EVELYN I Occupation: Principal, West Logan Grade School. Education: Master's Degree. Address: Box 82, Peach Creek, West Virginia 25639.

ADAMS, GERALD ROBERT Occupation: Professor, Department of Family and Human Development, Utah State University. Education: B.S. Sociology, M.A. Psychology, Ph.D. Human Development. Address: 1685 East 1500 North, Logan Utah.

ADAMS, HOLLY JANE Occupation: Waitress, Tom Tom Restaurant. Address: 42319 Green Mountain Drive, Lebanon, Oregon 97355.

ADAMS, JANET STECKELBERG Occupation: Professor and University Administrator. Education: B.A. 1942, M.A. 1966, Ph.D. 1970, Michigan State University. Address: 2106 West Lane Avenue, Columbus, Ohio 43221.

ADAMS, JERRY L Occupation: Professor of Physics, Roanoke College; Author. Education: B.S., Massachusetts Institute of Technology; M.S., Oklahoma State University; Ph.D., Florida State University. Address: 831 Honeysuckle Road, Salem, Virginia 24153.

ADAMS, S CHARLES Occupation: President and Chief Executive Officer, The Atlantic Companies. Education: J.D., B.C.E., M.S. Address: 2301 South Ocean Drive, #2001, Hollywood, Florida 33019.

ADAMSEN, JOHN RUSSELL Occupation: Sales Training Manager. Address: 12917 58th Avenue Southeast, Snohomish, Washington 98290.

ADAMSON, AGAR Occupation: Professor, Political Science, Head of Department. Education: B.A., M.A., Ph.D. (pending). Address: 94 Main Street, Wolfville, Nova Scotia, Canada BOP 1XO.

ADCOCK, JOY E Occupation: Manager, Interior Design Department, Michigan State University. Education: B.A., Michigan State University. Address: 1624 Dennison, East Lansing, Michigan 48823.

ADDANKI, SOMASUMDARAM Occupation: Nutrition and Diabetes. Education: B.A., M.S., Ph.D., D.A.B.C.C. Address: 1739 Blue Ash Place, Columbus, Ohio 43229.

ADDINGTON, HAROLD W Occupation: Consulting Engineer. Education: Petroleum Engineer.

Address: 2783 South Xanadu Way, Aurora, Colorado 80014.

ADDINGTON-STRONG, JAN MARIE Occupation: Professor of Sociology. Education: Bachelor of Arts, Master of Arts. Address: Fox Den, Morristown, Tennessee 37814.

ADDISON, ANTHONY WILLIAM Occupation: Associate Professor of Chemistry, Drexel University. Education: B.Sc. (honors), Ph.D. Address: 307 Cornell Avenue, Swarthmore, Pennsylvania 19081.

ADE, WALTER FRANK CHARLES Occupation: Retired from Purdue University; Writer, Translator, Researcher. Education: B.A., B.Paed., M.A., M.Ed., M.Sc.Ed., Ed.D., Ph.D. Address: 8021 Schreiber Driver, Munster, Indiana 46321.

ADELMAN, IRMA Occupation: Professor of Agricultural and Resource Economics. Education: B.S. 1950, M.A. 1951, Ph.D. 1955, University of California. Address: 10 Rosemont Avenue, Berkeley, California 94705.

ADESIYAN, HATTIE R Occupation: University Administrator, Teacher. Education: B.Sc., M.Ed., Ph.D. Address: 6735 Magoun, Hammond, Indiana 46324.

ADKINS, GARY WILLIAM Occupation: Writer, Researcher, Research Associate. Education: M.A., Sangamon State University, 1975; B.A., Sangamon State University, 1974; M.A. Creative Writing, Hollins College, 1977. Address: 1831 Seven Pines, Springfield, Illinois 62704.

ADKISSON, GEORGE B J Occupation: Sales Consultant and Public Speaker. Education: Liberal Arts Studies. Address: Post Office Box 59, Itasca, Illinois 60143.

ADLER, CAROL ELLEN Occupation: Poet, Free-lance Writer, Teacher, Editor. Education: B.A. Address: 54 Railroad Mills Road, Pittsford, New York 14534.

ADLER, CAROLE S Occupation: Children's Book Author. Education: B.A., Hunter College; M.S., Russell Sage College. Address: 1350 Ruffner Road, Schenectady, New York 12309.

ADLER, CHARLES SPENCER Occupation: Psychiatrist. Education: B.A., Cornell University, 1962; M.D., Duke University, 1966. Address: 955 Eudora Street, Suite 1607, Denver, Colorado 80220.

ADRIANOWSKA, KAZIMIERA ADRIAN Occupation: Free Lance Writer; Retired News Paper Correspondent. Address: 4841 48th Street, Woodside, New York 11377.

ADROUNIE, V HARRY Occupation: Environmental Consultant. Education: B.S., B.A., Master's Equivalent. Address: 1905 North Broadway, Hastings, Michigan 49058.

AEBISCHER, DELMER W Occupation: Music Consultant, Oregon Department of Education. Education: B.S. 1957, M.S. 1959, Ed.D. 1967; Seattle Pacific College, University of Oregon, University of California at Berkeley. Address: 3945 Kendall Avenue Southeast, Salem, Oregon 97302.

AGARWAL, DWARIKA P Occupation: Director of Physical Metallurgy, Leach and Garner Company. Education: B.Tech. (honors), Ph.D. Address: 13 Stonehedge Lane, Attleboro, Massachusetts 02703.

AGGARWAL, UMA NANDAN Occupation: President, Jensen Tools Inc. Education: M.B.A., M.E., B.Tech. Address: 8527 Via De Viva, Scottsdale, Arizona 85258.

AGGREY, O RUDOLPH Occupation: Consultant, Retired United States Ambassador. Education: B.S., M.S., L.L.D. (hon.). Address: 1257 Delaware Avenue, Southwest; Washington, D.C. 20024.

AGHKADIAN, HELEN R Occupation: Director,

Home Health Agency. Education: R.N., M.A. Address: 16 West 16 Street, New York, New York 10011.

AGIUS, JOSEPH P Occupation: Manager of Management Science and Minicomputers. Education: B.A., M.A. Mathematics. Address: 48 Marlise Drive, Attleboro, Massachusetts 02703.

AGOGINO, GEORGE A Occupation: Professor of Anthropology, Eastern New Mexico University. Education: B.A. 1949, M.A. 1951, University of New Mexico; Ph.D., Syracuse University, 1958; Post Doctorate, Harvard University, 1961-1962. Address: 1600 South Main, Portales, New Mexico 88130.

AGUERO, KATHLEEN R Occupation: Poet. Education: M.A. Creative Writing, Boston University; B.A. English, Tufts University. Address: 244 Ocean Boulevard, Kitty Hawk, North Carolina 27949.

AHERN, MAUREEN Occupation: Director, Thorne-Sagendorph Art Gallery. Education: M.A., State University of New York at Albany, 1972; B.A., University of Massachusetts at Amherst, 1969. Address: RFD 2, Winchester, New Hampshire 03470.

AHLERS, ROLF W Occupation: Professor of Philosophy and Religion, Russell Sage College. Education: Ph.D., M.Div., B.A. Address: 3 Academy Road, Albany, New York 12208.

AHMED, SALEEM Occupation: Agricultural Research and Development, East-West Center. Education: Ph.D. Agronomy and Soils, University of Hawaii, 1965. Address: 781 Eleele Place, Honolulu, Hawaii 96825.

AHRENHOLZ, STEVEN HENRY Occupation: Industrial Hygienist, National Institute for Occupational Safety and Health. Education: B.S. Biology, University of Wisconsin at Stevens Point; M.S. Environmental Health, University of Minnesota at Minneapolis. Address: 5 Orchard Knoll Drive, Cincinnati, Ohio 45215.

AI, STEVEN C Occupation: Executive Vice-President, City Mill Company. Education: B.A., Whittier College, 1976; M.B.A., University of Denver, 1979. Address: Post Office Box 1559, Honolulu, Hawaii 96806.

AIDLIN, SAMUEL SIMEON Occupation: Chairman of the Board, Aidlin Automation Corporation. Education: B.M.E., M.M.E., D.M.E. Address: 5079 Village Gardens Drive, Sarasota, Florida 33580.

AIELLO, JOHN R Occupation: Professor of Psychology, Rutgers University. Education: Ph.D., Michigan State University, 1972. Address: 77 Carson Avenue, Metuchen, New Jersey 08840.

AIKAWA, JERRY KAZUO Occupation: Professor of Medicine, University of Colorado. Education: B.A., University of California, 1942; M.D., Bowman Gray, 1945. Address: 619 South Poplar Way, Denver, Colorado 80224.

AINSLIE, MICHAEL L Occupation: President, National Trust for Historic Preservation. Education: B.A., Vanderbilt University; M.B.A., Harvard University. Address: 3021 Q Street, Northwest, Washington, D.C. 20007.

AIRD, ROBERT B Occupation: Professor of Neurology Emeritus, University of California. Education: B.A., M.D. Address: 80 Summit Avenue, Mill Valley, California 94941.

AISHA, ESHE (MARILYN CARMEN) Occupation: Writer, Teacher. Education: A.A. Liberal Arts, B.S. Social Sciences, M.A. American Studies. Address: 161 French Street, New Brunswick, New Jersey 08901.

AKABAS, SHEILA HELENE Occupation: Professor and Director, Indiana Social Welfare Center,

Columbia University School of Social Work. Education: B.S., M.B.A., Ph.D. Address: 15 Oak Lane, Scarsdale, New York 10583.

AKERA, TAI Occupation: Professor of Pharmacology, Michigan State University. Education: M.D. 1958, Ph.D. 1965, Keio University. Address: 1873 Ridgewood Drive, East Lansing, Michigan, 48823.

ALADJEM, HENRIETTA H Occupation: Author, Editor, *Lupus News.* Address: 25 Gordon Road, Waban, Massachusetts 02168.

ALAM, MOHAMMAD IHTISHAM Occupation: Chemist and Affirmative Action Officer. Education: B.Sc.; M.Sc., Karachi; M.Sc., Toronto; Ph.D., North Texas State University. Address: 11029 Davis Street, Oklahoma City, Oklahoma 73132.

ALBANY, AGNES P Occupation: Family Therapist. Education: M.A. Theology, M.A. Pastoral Counseling. Address: 409 Toland Drive, Fort Washington, Pennsylvania 19034.

ALBERGER, BILL Occupation: Attorney. Education: B.A., M.B.A., J.D. Address: 2532-A South Arlington Mill Drive, Arlington, Virginia 22206.

ALBERT, MIMI A Occupation: Writer, Teacher. Education: M.F.A., Columbia University; B.A., Hunter College. Address: 880 First Street, Sebastopol, California 95472.

ALBERT-HOWARD, FIOZENZA COSSERIA Occupation: Manager, Data Base Administration. Education: Ph.D., Masters in Business Administration, Bachelor of Science. Address: 7027 Fielching Court, Burnaby, Canada V5A 1Y4.

ALBRIGHT, JOHN ROGER Occupation: Systems Engineer, Boeing Military Airplane Company. Education: B.S.E.E.T. Address: 9100 East Harry, Wichita, Kansas 67207.

ALCALA, JOSE RAMON Occupation: Associate Professor of Anatomy. Education: Ph.D. 1972, M.A. 1966, B.A. 1964. Address: 13698 Wales, Oak Park, Michigan 48237.

ALCORN, TROY GENE Occupation: Clergy/ Pastor. Education: B.S., Graduate Work, Industrial College of Armed Forces. Address: 3812 Templeton Gap Road, Colorado Springs, Colorado 80907.

ALDAPE, ALINA A C E Occupation: Investment Executive. Education: B.A., Mexico City Preparatory School, 1970; Departmental Honors in Political Science, 1974; J.D., Stanford University, 1977. Address: 2841 Baker, San Francisco, California 94123.

ALDERMAN, LOUIS CLEVELAND JR Occupation: President, Middle Georgia College. Education: A.A., A.B., M.S., Ed.D. Address: 502 Old Chester Road, Cochran, Georgia 31014.

ALDERMAN, MINNIS AMELIA Occupation: Counselor, Educator, Psychologist, Businesswoman, Executive. Education: A.B. Music and Speech-Dramatics, Georgia State College, 1949; M.A. Guidance, Counseling, Supervision, Murray State University, 1960; Ph.D. Psychology (in progress).

ALDERMAN, SUSANNA EGGER Occupation: Registered Nurse. Education: Diploma Degree in Nursing. Address: 3011 Falling Brook, Kingwood, Texas 77345.

ALDERSHOF, KENT LEROY Occupation: Management Consultant. Education: M.B.A. with high distinction, M.S.E.E., B.S.E.E. Address: 327 Allison Way, Wyckoff, New Jersey 07481.

ALDRICH, THOMAS ALBERT Occupation: Vice President and Corporate Representative, Anheuser-Busch Companies, Inc. Education: B.A. Mathematics, M.S. Business Administration, George Washington University; Graduate, Air War College; Graduate,

Institute of Meteorology, University of Chicago. Address: 1355 Commons Drive, Sacramento, California 95825.

ALESSI, SUSAN INA (CAPERTON) Occupation: Clinical Psychologist in Private Practice. Education: Ph.D. Psychology, State University of New York; M.R.P., University of North Carolina at Chapel Hill; B.A., Oberlin College. Address: 29 Dorchester Road, Buffalo, New York 14222.

ALEXANDER, ANNABELLE M Occupation: Counselor, Marital and Sex Therapist. Education: M.Ed. Counseling and Guidance. Address: 52 Jupiter Way, Gladstone, Oregon 97027.

ALEXANDER, D STEVEN II Occupation: Management Consultant. Education: B.A., M.A. Address: 4158 Balboa Way, San Diego, California 92117.

ALEXANDER, EARL B Occupation: Pedologist (Soils), U.S. Forest Service, San Francisco, California. Education: B.A. 1954, M.S. 1955, Ph.D. 1970, Ohio State University. Address: 1714 Kasba Street, Concord, California 94518.

ALEXANDER, J WESLEY Occupation: Surgeon. Education: M.D., University of Texas Medical Branch, 1953-57. Address: 2869 Grandin Road, Cincinnati, Ohio 45208.

ALEXANDER, JON Occupation: Associate Professor of Political Science, Carleton University. Education: B.A. 1961, M.A. 1962, Southern Illinois University; Ph.D., University of Kansas, 1966. Address: Rural Route #2, Box 2013, Cumberland, Ontario, Canada K0A 1S0.

ALEXANDER, LEELAND NEILL Occupation: Director of Administration and Finance. Education: B.S., 1968. Address: 3714 East 81st Place South, Tulsa, Oklahoma 74137.

ALEXANDER, LUCILLE DILLINGER Occupation: Band and Orchestra Director. Education: B.S. Education, M.A., Ed.D. Music Education, Columbia University. Address: 56 Chestnut, Wayne, New Jersey 08854.

ALEXANDER, ROBERT J Occupation: University Professor, Rutgers University. Education: B.A. 1940, M.A. 1941, Ph.D. 1950, Columbia University. Address: 944 River Road, Piscataway, New Jersey 08854.

ALEXANDER, SAMUEL PRESTON Occupation: Chairman, DISK Corporation. Education: B.Arch. Address: 7000 Auburn Avenue, Apartment 101, Norfolk, Virginia 23513.

ALEXANDER, VIRGINIA T Occupation: Clerk of Trigg County Court. Address: Box 609, Cadiz, Kentucky 42211.

ALFIDI, RALPH J Occupation: Director of Department of Radiology, University Hospitals of Cleveland. Education: M.D. Address: 742 Coy Lane, Chagrin Falls, Ohio 44022.

ALFORD, RANDALL Occupation: Teacher. Education: Ph.D. Foreign Language Education, 1982; M.A., Texas Technical University, 1977; B.A., Texas Technical University, 1975. Address: 8400 Woodlake Drive, North East, #202, Palm Bay, Florida 32905.

ALLARD, MARVEL JUNE Occupation: Professor of Psychology, Worcester State College. Education: A.B., M.A., Ph.D., Michigan State University. Address: 24 Curtis Street, Auburn, Massachusetts 01501.

ALLEGRANTE, JOHN PHILIP Occupation: Associate Professor and Chairman, Department of Health Education Teachers College, Columbia University. Education: B.S., State University of New York; M.S., Ph.D., University of Illinois. Address: 100 East Palisade Avenue, Englewood, New Jersey 07631.

ALLEGRETTI, JOHN JOSEPH Occupation: Retired Owner of A & D Emporium. Education: Public Schools of San Jose, California. Address: 1629 York Street, San Jose, California 95124.

ALLEGRETTI, JOHN MICHAEL Occupation: Manager/Engineer, FMC Corporation. Education: B.S. Human Relations/Organization Behavior, University of San Francisco. Address: 12500 Poppy Lane, San Jose, California 95127.

ALLEN, ANITA F Occupation: President, R. R. Moton Institute. Education: B.A., M.A., Ed.D. Address: 6101 16th Street, Northwest, Washington, D.C. 20011.

ALLEN, ARIS T Occupation: Medical Doctor. Education: M.D. Address: 1323 Magnolia Avenue, Annapolis, Maryland 21403.

ALLEN, BELLE Occupation: President, William Karp Consulting Company, Inc. Address: 900 North Michigan Avenue, Chicago, Illinois 60611.

ALLEN, BETH ELAINE Occupation: Associate Professor of Economics. Education: A.B. Economics and Chemistry, Cornell University, 1974; M.A. 1976, Ph.D. 1978, University of California-Berkeley. Address: Department of Economics, University of Pennsylvania, Philadelphia, Pennsylvania 19104.

ALLEN, CLEO W Occupation: Teacher. Education: B.S., University of South Alabama, 1971; M.S., Alabama State University, 1974. Address: 2258 Downs Court, Mobile, Alabama 36617.

ALLEN, CRAIG ADAMS Occupation: Attorney at Law. Education: Juris Doctor, Ohio State University; B.A. cum laude, Denison University. Address: 615 South Fifth Street, Ironton, Ohio 45638.

ALLEN, DENIS McGEE Occupation: Radcologic Engineer. Education: B.A., M.S.Ed. Address: Star Route 1762, Eagle River, Alaska 99577.

ALLEN, DIOGENES Occupation: Clergy/ Professor. Education: B.A. with honors, University of Kentucky; B.A. with honors, Oxford University; Ph.D., Yale University. Address: 29 Alexander Street, Princeton, New Jersey 08542.

ALLEN, GARY K Occupation: Aerospace Development Engineering/Consulting Structures Specialist. Education: B.S.C.E., M.B.A. Address: 15710 Southeast 46 Way, Bellevue, Washington 98006.

ALLEN, HOWARD P Occupation: President, Southern California Edison Company. Education: A.A., Chaffey Junior College, 1946; B.A. cum laude Economics, Pomona College, 1948; J.D., Stanford University, 1951. Address: Claremont, California.

ALLEN, JACK C JR Occupation: Professor of Geology/Chairman of Department of Geology, Bucknell University. Education: B.S., M.A., Ph.D. Address: 26 South Third Street, Lewisburg, Pennsylvania 17837.

ALLEN, NORMA BRADLEY Occupation: Writer, Lecturer. Address: Route 1, Box 952, Cedar Hill, Texas 87572.

ALLEN, REX WHITAKER Occupation: Architect. Education: A.B. 1936, M.Arch. 1939, Harvard University. Address: 4718 17th Street, San Francisco, California 94117.

ALLEN, WILLIAM THOMAS Occupation: Insurance. Education: B.S.C. Business Administration, University of Iowa; M.S. Management, LaVerne College, 1977. Address: 6052 Hackers Lane, Agoura Hills, California 91301.

ALLENDER, JULIE ANN Occupation: Licensed Psychologist. Education: B.S., M.Ed., Ed.D.. Address: 447 South 8th Street, Lebanon, Pennsylvania 17042.

ALLENTUCH, ARNOLD Occupation: Associate Vice President for Research and Graduate Studies,

New Jersey Institute of Technology. Education: B.S. Mechanical Engineering, M.S. Address: 49 Fairview Street, Huntington, New York 11743.

ALLEY, WILLIAM J Occupation: President and Chief Executive Officer, Franklin Life Insurance Company. Education: J.D., University of Oklahoma. Address: 2014 Illini Road, Springfield, Illinois 62704.

ALLHUSEN, JAMES JOHN Occupation: Banker, BancOhio National Bank. Education: A.B., Colgate Unniversity, 1971; Colorado University School of Bank Marketing, 1977; Rutgers Stonier School of Banking, 1982. Address: 1188 Worthington Heights Boulevard, Worthington, Ohio 43085.

ALLISON, BRENDA DENISE Occupation: Assistant Administrator Central Laborers, Pension Welfare and Annuity Funds. Education: B.S., Certification Corporate Management, Apprentice Pharmacist. Address: 840 East State 6A, Jacksonville, Illinois 62650.

ALLNUTT, FRANKLIN L Occupation: Publisher/Television Producer. Education: B.A. Radio-TV-Film, University of Denver. Address: Box 879, Evergreen, Colorado 80439.

ALLRED, PHILLIP L Occupation: Audiologist in Private Practice. Education: B.S., M.S., Ph.D. Address: 3345 Bent Bough Park, Huntsville, Texas 77340.

ALLS, KATHY Occupation: Speaker, Author. Address: 203 Monarch Bay, South Laguna Beach, California 92677.

ALLUISI, EARL A Occupation: Chief Scientist, Air Force Human Resources Laboratory. Education: B.S., M.A., Ph.D. Psychology. Address: 15211 Sandia, San Antonio, Texas 78232.

ALM, JAMES Occupation: Director of Training and H. R. Development. Education: B.A. English, Cornell University. Address: 6804 Joliet Road #5G, Indian Head Park, Illinois 60525.

ALONZO, RONALD THOMAS Occupation: Vice President, International. Education: B.F.T., B.A. Address: 2335 North 3rd Street, Sheboygan, Wisconsin 53081.

ALOYE, JAMES A JR Occupation: Group Leader Fabricated Metals. Education: B.S. Chemistry. Address: 730 Mimosa Lane, Reading, Pennsylvania 19606.

ALROY, YORAM ADAM Occupation: Industrial Designer. Education: B.I.D. Address: 923 5th Avenue, New York, New York 10021.

AL SAADI, ABDUL A Occupation: Medical Geneticist. Education: B.Sc., M.A., Ph.D. Address: 2325 Adare, Ann Arbor, Michigan 48104.

ALSADI, AKEEL Occupation: Consulting Economist. Education: Ph.D., M.A., B.A., Diploma in Education. Address: 984 Portola Drive, Monterey, California 93940.

ALT, HANSI Occupation: Music Teacher, Educational Composer. Education: Graduate, Vienne Conservatory. Address: 4800 Fillmore Avenue, Alexandria, Virginia 22311.

ALTER, ELEANOR BREITEL Occupation: Attorney. Education: B.A., University of Michigan, 1960; LL.B., Columbia Law School, 1964. Address: 935 Park Avenue, New York, New York 10028.

ALTER, JOHN Occupation: Private Practice Facial Cosmetic Surgery, Head-Neck Surgery, Otolaryngology. Education: B.S., D.O. Address: 3817 Spanish Oaks Drive, West Bloomfield, Michigan 48033.

ALTHOFF, JAMES L Occupation: Construction Executive. Address: 508 North Green Street, McHenry, Illinois 60050.

ALTIER, WILLIAM J CMC Occupation: Management Consultant. Education: B.A., Lafayette College, M.B.A., Pennsylvania State University. Address: R.D. 4, Doylestown, Pennsylvania 18901.

ALTMAN, SHELDON Occupation: Veterinarian. Education: B.S., Biological Science; D.V.M. Address: 5647 Wilkinson Avenue, North Hollywood, California 91607.

ALTMANN, ESTHER NESBIN Occupation: Emeritus Dean of Library Services Retired. Education: B.A. Address: Post Office Box 102, San Marcos, California 92069.

ALTRINGER, PAULETTE B Occupation: Staff Engineer. Education: B.S. Metallurgy, Masters Engineering Administration. Address: 125 Matterhorn Drive, Summit Park, Utah 84060.

AMBACH, GORDON M Occupation: Commissioner of Education and President of the University of the State of New York. Education: B.A., Yale University; M.A., C.A.S., Harvard University. Address: 33 Fiddlers Lane, Box 528, Newtonville, New York 12128.

AMBER, EUGENE LEWIS Occupation: Senior Vice President of Investments, Insurance Company. Education: B.A. Economics, Cornell University, 1948. Address: 152 Main Street, Dalton, Massachusetts 01226.

AMBROSE, JOHN AUGUSTINE Occupation: Research Chemist. Education: B.A., M.S., Ph.D. Address: 3552 Old Chamblee-Tucker Road #3, Doraville, Georgia 30340.

AMES, A E LYN Occupation: Certified Surgical Technologist. Education: B.S./B.A. summa cum laude, University of Riverside; R.N., Pasadena City College; M.B.A. Candidate, California State University. Address: 5020 Laurel Canyon, North Hollywood, California 91607.

AMES, GORDON IAN Occupation: Financial Consultant. Education: B.B.A. Finance, University of Oregon. Address: 150 Ruby Lane, Eugene, Oregon 97404.

AMICK, SHIRLEY M Occupation: Marketing Services Executive. Education: High School Graduate; International World Trade Course. Address: 2927 South Logan Avenue, Milwaukee, Wisconsin 53207.

AMITIN, MARK HALL Occupation: Theatrical Producer/General Manager. Education: Diploma Profound Studies 1976, Doctorate in Theatre 1978, University of Paris. Address: 463 West Street A509, New York, New York 10014.

AMMAN, JOHN C Occupation: Certified Public Accountant. Education: B.S., University of Colorado; M.B.A., Denver University. Address: 5175 Bow-Mar Drive, Littleton, Colorado 80123.

AMMANN, LILLIAN NICHOLSON Occupation: President, Interior Landscape Company. Education: B.A. magna cum laude, Southwestern University, 1968. Address: 603 Mauze, San Antonio, Texas 78216.

AMMANN, THOMAS R Occupation: Police Captain. Education: A.S. 1970, B.S. 1972, M.B.A. 1977. Address: 1368 Pennsbury Drive, Cincinnati, Ohio 45238.

AMMAR, RAYMOND G Occupation: Professor of Physics, University of Kansas. Education: A.B., Harvard University, 1953; Ph.D., University of Chicago, 1959. Address: 1651 Hillcrest Road, Lawrence, Kansas 66044.

AMODEO, JOHN P Occupation: Counselor/Therapist. Education: M.A. Clinical Psychology, Ph.D. Transpersonal Psychology. Address: 324 Summit Avenue, Mill Valley, California 94941.

AMORE, MICHAEL JOSEPH Occupation: Company Comptroller. Education: B.S. Accounting,

M.B.A. Finance, C.P.A., New York State University. Address: 149 Cornell Drive, Commack, New York 11725.

AMPY, FRANKLIN R Occupation: Research and Teaching. Education: B.S., M.S., Ph.D. Address: 5630 16th Street Northwest, Washington, D.C. 20011.

ANAND, RAJEN S Occupation: Professor of Physiology, Research Scientist. Education: D.V.M., Ph.D. Physiology. Address: 8391 Satinwood Circle, Westminster, California 92683.

ANANIA, MICHAEL A Occupation: Writer/Professor of English, University of Illinois. Education: B.A. 1961. Address: 5755 Sunset, LaGrange, Illinois 60525.

ANANIAN, JOYCE L Occupation: Editor/Writer, Guidance Counselor. Education: M.L.S., Simmons College; M.Ed., Boston College; B.A., University of Massachusetts. Address: 204 Church Street, Waltham, Massachusetts 02154.

ANASTASIADIS, SOTIRI SOKRATIS Occupation: Chief Scientist and Chief Engineer. Education: Ph.D. Nuclear Engineering, Ph.D. Mechanical Engineering, M.S., B.S. Mechanical Engineering. Address: 2210 Wilshire Boulevard, No. 379, Santa Monica, California 90403.

ANDEREGGEN, ANTON Occupation: Associate Professor, Lewis & Clark College. Education: B.A., Monmouth College; Ph.D., University of Colorado. Address: 7273 Southwest Nevada Terrace, Portland, Oregon 97219.

ANDERL, STEPHEN Occupation: Retired Catholic Priest. Education: B.A. (mcl), M.Div., Ph.D. Address: 92214 Peters Drive, Apartment 309, Eau Claire, Wisconsin 54703.

ANDERS, MICHAEL FRED Occupation: College Professor, Music. Education: B.S. 1976, M.M. 1979, Lamar University. Address: 400 South West Street, Findlay, Ohio 45840.

ANDERS, SARAH FRANCES Occupation: College Professor, Louisiana College. Education: A.B., M.R.E., M.A., Ph.D. Address: 111 Mary, Pineville, Louisiana 71360.

ANDERSEN, MARK E Occupation: Concert Organist, Vocalist, Flutist. Education: B.A., American Conservatory; M.A., Northeastern Seminary; Ph.D., Paris Conservatory. Address: 3410 Bonneville Drive, Charlotte, North Carolina 28205.

ANDERSEN, ROBERT A Occupation: Associate Professor, Biology. Education: B.S., M.A., Ph.D. Address: 606 South Mitchell, Arlington Heights, Illinois 60005.

ANDERSLAND, ORLANDO B Occupation: Professor of Civil Engineering. Education: Ph.D., M.S.C.E., B.C.E. Address: 901 Woodingham Drive, East Lansing, Michigan 48823.

ANDERSON, ALBERT S Occupation: Physician/President Creation Health Foundation. Education: A.B. Biology, Johns Hopkins University; M.D., New York Medical College. Address: 19 Gallery Centre, Taylors, South Carolina 29687.

ANDERSON, ANN Occupation: Real Estate Securities Broker. Education: A.B. 1926, M.A. 1932, University of Southern California. Address: 231 Alma Real Drive, Pacific Palisades, California 90272.

ANDERSON, B HAROLD Occupation: Professor, Colorado State University. Education: B.S., M.Ed., Colorado State University; Ph.D., Ohio State University. Address: 3316 Canadian Parkway, Fort Collins, Colorado 80524.

ANDERSON, BETH Occupation: Composer/Musician. Education: B.A. Music, 1971; M.F.A. Piano, 1973; M.A. Composition, 1974. Address: 26 Second Avenue #2B, New York, New York 10003.

ANDERSON, DARRELL E Occupation: Professor and Chairman of Department of Counselor Education, University of New Mexico. Education: Ph.D. Psychology, University of Nebraska. Address: 9712 Adm. Emerson Northeast, Albuquerque, New Mexico 87111.

ANDERSON, DAVID ARTHUR Occupation: Public Relations Executive. Education: B.A. Communication Specialist, University of Wisconsin in Madison, 1977. Address: 2922 Holly 204, Durango, Colorado 81301.

ANDERSON, DOROTHEDA REVÁY Occupation: Professor of Dance. Education: A.B. Anthropology 1960, A.M. Education 1961, Stanford University. Address: 536 Woodside Oaks, #3, Sacramento, California 95825.

ANDERSON, DOUGLAS SCRANTON HESLEY Occupation: Investment Banking Executive. Education: A.B., Harvard College, 1951; Certificate Investment Banking, Northwestern University, 1959. Address: 39 Vista Drive, Greenwich, Connecticut 06830.

ANDERSON, ERIC EDWARD Occupation: Clinical Psychologist/Consultant. Education: B.A. summa cum laude, M.A. Theology, Ph.D. Clinical Psychology. Address: 3823 Thomas Avenue South, Minneapolis, Minnesota 55410.

ANDERSON, FRANCES SWEM Occupation: Retired Nuclear Medicine Technologist. Education: Graduate of High School, magna cum; College Certificate (A.R.R.T. & C.N.M.T.). Address: 5757 East Sternberg Road, Fruitport, Michigan 49415.

ANDERSON, G MOFFETT Occupation: Assistant to the President. Education: Completed masters work. Address: 400 Thames Parkway, Park Ridge, Illinois 60068.

ANDERSON, GEORGE D Occupation: Certified Public Accountant. Education: B.A. Economics-Accountancy. Address: 1631 Highland, Helena, Montana 59601.

ANDERSON, GEORGE M Occupation: Director of Pharmacy, Boulder Community Hospital. Education: B.S. Pharmacy. Address: 4750 Ricara Drive, Boulder, Colorado 80303.

ANDERSON, GORDON WOOD Occupation: Physicist/Electronic Engineer. Education: B.E.E., Cornell University; M.S., Ph.D., University of Illinois at Urbana-Champaign. Address: 1320 North Carolina Avenue, Northeast, Washington, D.C. 20002.

ANDERSON, GREGORY LYMAN Occupation: Psychological Intern. Education: Ph.D. Candidate in Counseling Psychology. Address: 421 Boisseuain, Apartment 1B, Norfolk, Virginia 23501.

ANDERSON, J EDWARD Occupation: Professor, Consultant. Education: B.S.M.E., M.S.M.E., Ph.D., Massachusetts Institute of Technology. Address: 1920 South First Street, Minneapolis, Minnesota 55454.

ANDERSON, JACK G Occupation: Business Executive. Education: B.S. Industrial Administration. Address: 28 Winged Foot Road, Dover, Delaware 19901.

ANDERSON, JAMES N Occupation: Principal. Education: B.S., M.S., M.Ed. Science. Address: 3206 Prospect, Houston, Texas 77004.

ANDERSON, JAMES O Occupation: Retail Executive, Federated Department Stores. Education: A.S., B.S., M.S. Address: 621 Mehring Way, Cincinnati, Ohio 45202.

ANDERSON, JAMES WILLIAM Occupation:

Ordained Minister. Education: B.S., Tulane University, 1952; B.D., Austin Presbyterian Seminary, 1955; Th.D., New Orleans Baptist Theological Seminary, 1976. Address: Post Office Box 326, Ponchatoula, Louisiana 70454.

ANDERSON, JEROME TAYLOR Occupation: Biomedical Engineer. Education: B.A. and Postgraduate Studies in Biomedical Engineering. Address: 2525 Ocean Boulevard, #E-5, Corona Del Mar, California 92625.

ANDERSON, JOAN B Occupation: Associate Professor of Economics, University of San Diego. Education: B.A., San Diego State University; M.A., Stanford University; Ph.D., University of California-San Diego. Address: 5422 Drover Drive, San Diego, California 92115.

ANDERSON, JOHN W Occupation: Professor and Chairman of Department of Economics, Bucknell University. Education: A.B., Amherst College, 1956; M.A. 1966, Ph.D. 1967, University of Pennsylvania. Address: 133 South 13th Street, Lewisburg, Pennsylvania 17837.

ANDERSON, JULIA S Occupation: College Professor, Church Musician, William Paterson College. Education: S.M.M., Union Theological Seminary School of Sacred Music; Ed.D., Teachers College, Columbia University. Address: 235 Prospect Avenue 12-E, Hackensack, New Jersey 07601.

ANDERSON, KATHLEEN EASON Occupation: School Counselor. Education: B.A. Education, M.A. Counseling, Principal Certificate. Address: 9573 Telfair Drive, Boise, Idaho 83704.

ANDERSON, LAWRENCE L JR Occupation: President, Anderson Industrial Products, Inc. Education: A.B., Princeton University, 1952; M.A., Columbia University, 1956; M.A. Yale University 1957; M.B.A., New York University, 1966. Address: Post Office Box 684, Meriden, Connecticut 06450.

ANDERSON, LLOYD H Occupation: Architect/Designer. Education: B.Arch. Address: 12791 West Jewell Circle, Lakewood, Colorado 80228.

ANDERSON, LLOYD LEE Occupation: Professor of Animal Science. Education: B.S. 1957, Ph.D. 1961. Address: 1703 Maxwell Avenue, Ames, Iowa 50010.

ANDERSON, MARY ANN Occupation: Principal, Center Elementary School. Education: B.S. Elementary Education, M.A. Educational Administration. Address: 8725 Watt Avenue, Post Office Box 1550, North Highlands, California 95660.

ANDERSON, MAURITZ G Occupation: Professor Biology, Towson State University. Education: B.S., University of Michigan; M.A., Indiana University; Ph.D., Virginia Polytechnic Institute and State University. Address: 18 Maryland Avenue, Towson, Maryland 21204.

ANDERSON, MEL Occupation: President, Saint Mary's College of California. Education: B.A., Saint Mary's College; D.Litt. (honoris causa), St. Albert's College; L.H.D. (honoris causa) Lewis University. Address: Post Office Box 5, Saint Mary's College, Moraga, California 94575.

ANDERSON, PAUL NATHANIEL Occupation: Medical Doctor/Director of Pensore Central Hospital. Education: B.A., M.D. Address: 32 Sanford Road, Colorado Springs, Colorado 80906.

ANDERSON, ROBERT HUNT Occupation: Professor of Chemistry. Education: A.B., Baker University, 1946; M.A. 1948, Ph.D. 1954, Columbia University. Address: 2731 Carlyle Drive, Kalamazoo, Michigan 49008.

ANDERSON, THEODORE WILBUR Occupation: Professor of Statistics and Economics, Stanford University. Education: A.A., B.S., M.A., Ph.D. Address: 746 Santa Ynez Street, Stanford, California 94305.

ANDERSON, TRUDY BOHRER Occupation: Assistant Professor Sociology and Faculty Member of Institute on Aging, East Texas State University. Education: B.A., Creighton University, 1970; M.A., University of Nebraska-Omaha, 1974; Ph.D., University of Nebraska-Lincoln, 1981. Address: 4615 Summerhill Road, Texarkana, Texas 75503.

ANDERSON, WAYNE C Occupation: Vice President Government Relations. Education: B.S., Upsala College. Address: 7 Morgantine Road, Roseland, New Jersey 07068.

ANDERSON, WILLIAM MILLER Occupation: Professor and Assistant Dean, Graduate College. Education: B.M., M.M., Ph.D. Address: 855 Nautilus Trail, Aurora, Ohio 44202.

ANDERSON, WILLIAM PAUL Occupation: University of Dayton Professor. Education: A.B. magna cum laude; B.D. (with distinction) Systematic Theology; Ph.D. Historical Theology; Post-Doctoral Study in Europe. Address: 6355 Noranda Drive, Dayton, Ohio.

ANDRE, THOMAS Occupation: Associate Professor of Psychology. Education: B.S., University of Massachusetts, 1967; M.A. 1970, Ph.D. 1971, University of Illinois. Address: 317 9th Street, Ames, Iowa 50010.

ANDREASSEN, JOHN CHRISTIAN LUDWIG Occupation: Archivist. Education: Ph.B., University of Wisconsin, 1931; M.A., Louisiana State University, 1935. Address: Post Office Box 51, Cleveland, Nova Scotia, Canada.

ANDREWS, GEORGE E Occupation: Evan Pugh Professor of Mathematics, Pennsylvania State University. Education: B.S., M.A., Oregon State University; Ph.D., University of Pennsylvania. Address: R.D. 2, Box 133, Centre Hall, Pennsylvania 16828.

ANDREWS, GEORGE HAROLD Occupation: Professor of Mathematics. Education: A.B., A.M., Ph.D. Address: 74 East College Street, Oberlin, Ohio 44074.

ANDREWS, JAMES WARREN Occupation: Mine Ventilation Engineer. Education: E.M., Colorado School of Mines, 1963. Address: 1942 Mount Zion Drive, Golden Colorado 80401.

ANDREWS, JEAN CAROL Occupation: Logistics & Energy Planner, Tech Writer/Editor. Education: A.B., Brown University; M.A., Columbia University; M.U.R.P., George Washington University. Address: 6800 Granby Street, Bethesda, Maryland 20817.

ANDREWS, LORI E Occupation: Associate Producer. Education: Communications (uncompleted). Address: 601 Panorama Terrace, Birmingham, Alabama 35216.

ANDROLA, RONALD H Occupation: Poet, Artist, Editor. Education: B.A. Address: 1547 West 24th, Erie, Pennsylvania 16502.

ANELLIS, IRVING HENRY Occupation: Mathematician, University of Iowa. Education: Ph.D., Brandeis University, 1977. Address: 209 Holiday Road, Apartment 224, Coralville, Iowa 52241.

ANEMA, DURLYNN C Occupation: University Professor, Author, Executive Director, University of the Pacific. Education: Ed.D., M.S., B.A. Address: 1728 West Vine Street, Lodi, California 95240.

ANGEL, THOMAS M Occupation: Vice President. Education: High School Graduate. Address: 25 Mary Hughes Court, Houma, Louisiana 70363.

ANGILLY, M NATICA Occupation: Director, "Understanding Through the Arts." Education: Training Television Broadcasting, Laney College. Address: 1515 Poplar Avenue, Richmond Heights, California 94805.

ANGILLY, RICHARD W Occupation: Poet; Analyst, Pacific Bell. Education: M.A., University of Rochester; B.A., Union College. Address: 1515 Poplar Avenue, Richmond Heights, California 94805.

ANGIONE, HOWARD F Occupation: Systems Editor, *The New York Times.* Education: B.A., Holy Cross College; M.A., Clark University. Address: 80-47 192nd Street, Jamaica, New York 11423.

ANGUS, FAY D Occupation: Author/Speaker. Education: Convent of the Sacred Heart. Address: 405 North Canon Drive, Sierra Madre, California 91024.

ANNAMALAI, K Occupation: Assistant Professor. Education: Ph.D. Mechanical Engineering. Address: 1115 Austin Avenue, College Station, Texas 77840.

ANNESTRAND, STIG ALVAR Occupation: Manager of Research and Development, Electrical Engineering. Education: M.S.E.E. Address: 5392 Southwest Tree Street, Lake Oswego, Oregon 97034.

ANOVCHI, ABRAHAM Y Occupation: Vice President, Research and Engineering. Education: M.S.E.E., Harvard University. Address: 10 Knollwood Drive, Pittsburgh, Pennsylvania 15215.

ANSBACHER, HEINZ L Occupation: Professor of Psychology Emeritus. Education: Ph.D. Address: 130 East Avenue, Burlington, Vermont 05401.

ANTELL, BEBE S Occupation: Counselor to Parents of Children with Learning Disabilities. Education: B.A., M.A. Address: 930 Ridgewood Road, Millburn, New Jersey 07041.

ANTOINE, ROY W Occupation: Professional Photographer/Businessman. Education: B.S., Purdue University; M.B.A., Harvard University. Address: 92 Main Street, Salem, New Hampshire 03079.

ANTON, MARK J Occupation: Chairman and President, Suburban Propane Gas Corporation. Education: B.A., Bowdoin College. Address: 31 Washington Avenue, Short Hills, New Jersey 07078.

ANTONELL, WALTER JOHN Occupation: Vice President Administration. Education: B.A., M.B.A. Address: RD #3, Still House Road, Freehold, New Jersey 07728.

ANTONOVICH, MICHAEL DENNIS Occupation: Los Angeles County Board of Supervisor, 5th District. Education: Bachelor of Arts 1963, Master of Arts 1967, California State University at Los Angeles; Graduate, Pasadena Police Academy, Reserve Officer School, 1967; Rio Hondo Reserve Officer Advanced Training School, 1978. Address: 3023 San Gabriel, Glendale, California 91206.

ANTONSON, BRIAN A Occupation: Program Head - RAQO, Broadcoast Correspondence Course. Education: Diploma of Technology. Address: 32427 Diamond Avenue, Mission, British Columbia, Canada V2V 1M2.

ANTZELEVITCH, CHARLES Occupation: Senior Medical Research Scientist. Education: B.A., Ph.D. Address: 101 Sylvan Way, New Hartford, New York 13413.

ANWAY, ALLEN R Occupation: Coordinator of Academic Computing. Education: Ph.D. in Physics, University of Chicago, 1968. Address: 1219 North 21st Street, Superior, Wisconsin 54880.

APGAR, B JEAN Occupation: Research in Nutrition. Education: Ph.D. Address: 176 Pearsall Place, Ithaca, New York 14850.

APPEL-MOSESOF, RHODA SARA Occupation: Supervisor, Fine Arts and Media, Board of Education, Newark, New Jersey. Education: B.Sc. 1940, M.Ed. 1949, Rutgers University. Address: 203 Ivy Street, Newark, New Jersey 07106.

APPLE, JACKI Occupation: Intermedia Artist/Writer. Address: 3827 Mentone Avenue, Culver City, California 90230.

APPLEMAN, PHILIP DEAN Occupation: Distinguished Professor English, Indiana University. Education: B.S., Ph.D., Northwestern University; A.M., University of Michigan. Address: 411 East 10th Street, #21A, New York, New York 10009.

AQUINO-BERMUDEZ, FEDERICO Occupation: Professor/Chairman of Department of Puerto Rican Studies. Education: B.S., University of Puerto Rico; M.A., Columbia University; Professional Diploma, Fordham University; Ed.D., University of Massachusetts. Address: 273 Graphic Boulevard, New Milford, New Jersey 07646.

ARAKAWA, AMY Occupation: Assistant Manager, Barney's Catering Service; Management Trainee, First Hawaiian Bank. Education: B.B.A., University of Hawaii, 1983; St. Andrew's Priory, 1979. Address: 94-405 Apowale Street, Waipahu, Hawaii 96797.

ARANDA, JUAN M Occupation: Physician. Education: B.S., M.D. Address: Palma Fala St. 4-A-7, Garden Hills, Puerto Rico 00936.

ARASTEH, A(BDOL) REZA Occupation: Independent Consultant and Writer. Education: B.A. 1948, M.A., 1949, University of Tehran; Ph.D., Louisiana State University, 1953. Address: 7905 Custer Road, Bethesda, Maryland 20814.

ARAYA, PEDRO A Occupation: Senior Corporate Consultant, The Coca-Cola Company. Education: M.S. Industrial and Management Engineering, Columbia University, 1963; Ph.D. Economics and Doctor of Law, University of Chile; B.A. Humanities, University of Chile; B.S. Mathematics, University of Chile; Post Graduate Work in Naval Engineering, Chilean Naval Officers Training Academy; B.S. Mechanical Engineering, B.S. Naval Sciences, Chilean Naval College. Address: Republica de la India 3135, Apartment 1 A, 1425 Buenos Aires, Argentina.

ARBUCKLE, WENDELL SHERWOOD Occupation: Professor Emeritus/Informative Specialist, University of Maryland. Education: B.S.A., Purdue University; A.M., Doctor of Philosophy, University of Missouri. Address: 4602 Harvard Road, College Park, Maryland 20740.

ARCHER, CARL MARION Occupation: Director, Panhandle Bank and Trust Company. Education: University of Texas-Austin. Address: 304 South Endicott, Spearman, Texas 79081.

ARCHER, JUANITA A Occupation: Associate Professor of Medicine/Director of Endocrine Laboratories, Howard University Hospital. Education: B.S., M.S., M.D. Address: 4305 Rouge Avenue, Temple Hills, Maryland 20748.

ARCHER, LLOYD DAN Occupation: Assistant Professor/Director of Media, Fort Valley State College. Education: B.S., M.S., Indiana University. Address: 224 Kingsbury Circle, Warner Robins, Georgia 31093.

ARGOT, JEANNE E Occupation: Professor. Education: M.T. (A.S.C.P.), B.S., M.S., Ph.D. Address: 3806 South Adams, Marion, Indiana 46953.

ARGOW, SYLVIA Occupation: Poet. Education: City University of New York, New York University, Bronx Community College. Address: 2150 Wallace Avenue, Bronx, New York 10462.

ARGUE, JOHN CLIFFORD Occupation: Lawyer.

Education: A.B. Commerce and Finance; LL.B., University of South Carolina. Address: 1314 Descanso Drive, La Canada, California 91011.

ARIALE, JOHN MICHAEL Occupation: Legislative Assistant to Congressman McCollum. Education: B.A. Political Science. Address: 414 4th Street, South East, Washington, D.C. 20003.

ARINOLDO, CARLO G Occupation: Psychologist. Education: B.A. Psychology, M.A. Psychology, Doctorate Psychology. Address: 314 Pond Path, East Setauket, New York 11733.

ARION, WILLIAM J Occupation: Professor, Cornell University. Education: B.S., M.S., Ph.D. Address: 100 Yellow Barn Road, Freeville, New York 13068.

ARIYANTO, MARIANNE JIRGAL Occupation: Professor of Dance. Education: B.S., Northwestern University; M.A., University of California at Los Angeles. Address: 2856 Sumner, Lincoln, Nebraska 68502.

ARKIN, L JULES Occupation: President, Savings and Loan Association. Education: LL.B., University of Miami; Emory University. Address: 250 North Hibiscus Drive, Miami Beach, Florida 33139.

ARKIN, LUCILLE MAESE Occupation: Interior Plantscaping Executive. Address: 785 Westend Avenue, New York, New York 10025.

ARMIJO, JACQULYN D Occupation: A.S.I.D., Interior Design. Education: North Texas State University and University of New Mexico. Address: 509 Chamiso Lane, North West, Albuquerque, New Mexico 87107.

ARMON, NORMA Occupation: Writer/Producer. Education: Ph.D. Address: 1755 Seaview Terrace, Los Angeles, California 90046.

ARMS, DEBORAH LUCAS Occupation: Registered Nurse, Faculty of Franklin University. Education: B.S.N., M.S., Ohio State University. Address: 636 Blacklick Street, Groveport, Ohio 43125.

ARMS, KAREN G Occupation: University Academic Administrator, Kent State University. Education: B.S., M.S., Ph.D. Address: 595 Schocalog Road, Akron, Ohio 44320.

ARMSTRONG, ALMETTA Occupation: Teacher, Highland School. Education: A.B., M.S. Address: Route 2, Box 128, Candor, North Carolina 27229.

ARMSTRONG, CATHERINE A Occupation: Physician/Pediatrician. Education: A.A., B.A., M.D., University of Chicago. Address: 919 North Alameda Street, Carlsbad, New Mexico 88220.

ARMSTRONG, HOWARD W Occupation: Farmer. Education: High School Graduate. Address: Route 1, Ackerly, Texas 79713.

ARMSTRONG, PEG (M) JEAN Occupation: Psychotherapist. Education: B.A., M.A. Address: 118 East French, San Antonio, Texas 78212.

ARMSTRONG-BLEECKER, MARY W Occupation: Speaking and Writing. Education: B.S., Douglas College, Rutgers University; M.A., Ed.D., Columbia University. Address: 674 Duquesne Terrace, Union, New Jersey 07083.

ARNEZ, NANCY LEVI Occupation: Department Chairman, Howard University. Education: B.A., M.A., Ed.D. Address: 3122 Cherry Road, North East, Washington, D.C. 20018.

ARNOLD, DEAN EDWARD Occupation: College Professor of Anthropology. Education: B.A., M.A., Ph.D. Address: 305 Brookside Circle, Wheaton, Illinois 60187.

ARNOLD, ESTHER FRANCES Occupation: Assistant Hospital Administrator. Education: B.S. Foods and Nutrition; Registered Dietitian. Address: 3437 Covey Court, Napa, California 94558.

ARNOLD, STEVEN LELAND Occupation: Physician/Surgeon. Address: 900 Hammond Street #530, Los Angeles, California 90069.

ARONSON, DAVID E Occupation: Clinical Psychologist. Education: Ph.D. Clinical Psychology, 1980; M.A. Psychology, 1977; B.A. Psychology, 1975. Address: 212 Van Evera Road, Tallmadge, Ohio 44278.

ARONSON, SHEPARD GERARD Occupation: Associate Visiting Physician, Bellevue Hospital; Assistant Clinical Professor of Internal Medicine, New York University Medical School; Consultant in Internal Medicine, Institute of Physical Medicine and Rehabilitation of New York University Medical Center; Assistant Attending Physician, New York University Hospital; Attending Physician, New York Infirmary-Beekman Downtown Hospital; Attending Physician, Doctors Hospital. Education: B.A., M.D., Cornell University. Address: 150 East 56th Street, New York 22, New York.

ARORA, PRINCE KUMAR Occupation: Immunologist. Education: Ph.D. Immunology. Address: 9514, Lindale Drive, Bethesda, Maryland 20817.

ARRECHE, CANDY ANN Occupation: Attorney at Law. Education: B.A. 1974, J.D. 1976. Address: Hato Rey Plaza Apartment 19F, Hato Rey, Puerto Rico 00918.

ARSLAN, ORHAN E Occupation: Assistant Professor of Anatomy, Doctor of Veterinary Medicine. Education: B.V.M.S., D.V.M., Ph.D. Address: 1115 Lorraine Road, #139, Wheaton, Illinois 60184.

ARUNKUMAR, KOOVAPPADI A Occupation: Research Professor, University of Kentucky. Education: B.S. 1969, M.Sc. 1971, Ph.D. 1976, Ph.D. 1979. Address: 151 Todds Road, Lexington, Kentucky 40509.

ARZOUMANIAN, ARAM S Occupation: Member of Technical Staff, Dataproducts Corporation. Education: Master's Degree in Electro-Mechanical Engineering. Address: 24326 Caris Street, Woodland Hills, California 91367.

ASBELL, RIVA LEE Occupation: Administrator/ Professor. Education: A.B., C.O. Address: 1810 South Rittenhouse Square, Philadelphia, Pennsylvania 19103.

ASBRIDGE, BERNICE M Occupation: Burleigh County Auditor. Education: High School Graduate. Address: 2707 Hawkens Street, Bismarck, North Dakota 58501.

ASGAR, KAMAL Occupation: Professor, Dentistry University of Michigan. Education: A.B., B.S., Chemical Engineering; M.S., Ph.D. Address: 2240 Belmont, Ann Arbor, Michigan 48104.

ASGHAR, KHURSHEED Occupation: Pharmacologist, National Institute on Drug Abuse. Education: B.Pharm., Ph.D. Address: 8 Bouldercrest Court, Rockville, Maryland 20850.

ASH, FREDERICK M Occupation: Vice President and General Manager. Education: B.S., Ohio State, 1963; M.B.A., Rutgers University, 1982. Address: Aspen 7, New Hope, Pennsylvania 18938.

ASHBERY, JOHN LAWRENCE Occupation: American Author and Critic. Education: Deerfield Academy, 1945; B.A., Harvard College, 1949; M.A., Columbia University, 1951. Address: c/o Georges Borchardt, Inc., 136 East 57th Street, New York, New York 10022.

ASHE, AMELILA H Occupation: Member, New York City Board of Education. Education: Ph.D.

Guidance and Personnel Administration, New York University. Address: 1020 Park Avenue, New York, New York 10028.

ASHMEAD, HARVE DeWAYNE Occupation: President, Albion Laboratories, Inc. Education: B.S., Weber State College; Ph.D., Pacific Institute; Ph.D., Donsbach University. Address: 304 South Mountain Road, Fruit Heights, Utah 84037.

ASHTON, NANCY LYNN Occupation: College Professor, Stockton State College. Education: B.A., M.A., Ph.D. Address: Post Office Box 85, Port Republic, New Jersey 08241.

ASHWORTH, SARA ELIZABETH Occupation: Educational Consultant. Education: Ed.D. Address: 115 Carlton Avenue, Trenton, New Jersey 08618.

ASKEY, RICHARD A Occupation: Professor of Mathematics, University of Wisconsin. Education: B.A., Washington University; M.A., Harvard University; Ph.D. Princeton University. Address: 2105 Regent Street, Madison, Wisconsin 53705.

ASLAM, MUHAMMAD Occupation: Staff Research Associate. Education: Ph.D. Address: 933 Bienville, Davis, California 95616.

ASPEY, WAYNE P Occupation: University Professor of Zoology, Coordinator, General Biology. Education: A.B. Psychology, Ph.D. Zoology, Ohio University; A.M. Psychology, Darmouth College. Address: 3051 Kilcullen Drive, Columbus, Ohio 43220.

ASTA, PATRICIA ELLEN Occupation: Manager of Training and Development, Personal Products Company Johnson and Johnson. Education: B.S. Psychology, M.S. Psychology, M.S. Counseling. Address: 1207 A Lindera Plaza, Cranbury, New Jersey 08512.

ATEN, KENNETH L Occupation: President Mid-Plains Community College. Education: B.A. Education, M.S. Vocational Education. Address: 2121 Beverly Boulevard, North Platto, Nebraska 69101.

ATEN, ROBERT HOLMES Occupation: Director, State and Local Fiscal Research. Education: B.S., M.A., M.A., Ph.D. Address: 4305 Nebraska Avenue, Northwest, Washington, D.C. 20015.

ATHERTON, ARLENE RUTH Occupation: Financial Planner, Investment Advisor. Education: C.F.P. Address: 106 Oka Court, Los Gatos, California 95030.

ATKINS, CHARLES GILMORE Occupation: Associate Dean for Basic Sciences, Ohio University. Education: B.A., Albion College; M.S., Eastern Michigan University; Ph.D., North Carolina State University. Address: 6 Riverview Drive, Athens, Ohio 45701.

ATWATER, P M H Occupation: Author, Designer, Advocate for Near-Death Survivor. Address: 235 Rockingham Drive, Apartment F, Harrisonburg, Virginia 22801.

ATWOOD, DENNIS F Occupation: Chief Financial Officer, Faulkne Hospital. Education: M.B.A., University of Notre Dame, 1972; B.S., Boston College, 1969. Address: 888 Pike Avenue, Attleboro, Massachusetts 02703.

ATWOOD, ROSLYN IRENE Occupation: Field Underwriter. Education: B.A., M.A., M.A. Address: 123 Mayfair, Ocso, California 92054.

ATZ, ANNE L Occupation: Artist. Address: 601 Apalachicola Road, Venice, Florida 33595.

ATZMON, EZRI Occupation: Professor of Education, Jersey City State College. Education: B.S. Equivalency 1951, M.Ed. 1954, Wayne University; Ph.D. Education, University of Michigan, 1958. Address: 165 West End Avenue, New York, New York 10023.

AUDET, HAROLD HUDSON Occupation: Physician. Education: A.B., Colgate; M.D.C.M., McGill University; M.P.H., Tulane University. Address: 2212 Grove Avenue, Richmond, Virginia 23220.

AUFDERHEIDE, ARTHUR C Occupation: Professor, Physician. Education: M.D. Address: 4711 Colorado Street, Duluth, Minnesota 55804.

AUGUSTINE, JANE Occupation: Professor, Writer. Education: A.B. cum laude, Bryn Mawr College; M.A., Washington University. Address: Box 981, Stuyvesant Station, New York, New York 10009.

AULTMAN, LARRY L Occupation: Pastor. Education: B.A., M.Div., Doctor of Ministry. Address: 2201 Oakridge Drive, Gladewater, Texas 75647.

AUST, HAMPTON LEE Occupation: Vice President/Senior Trust Officer. Education: B.S. Address: 137 89th Sunset Beach, Treasure Island, Florida.

AUSTEN, WILLIAM GERALD Occupation: Chief of Surgical Services, Massachusetts General Hospital. Education: B.S., Massachusetts Institute of Technology, 1951; M.D., Harvard Medical School, 1955. Address: 163 Wellesley Street, Weston, Massachusetts 02193.

AUSTGEN, ROBERT JOSEPH Occupation: University Administrator; R C Clergyman. Education: A.B., University Notre Dame, 1955; S.T.L. Gregorian, Rome, 1959; S.T.D. Fribourg, 1963. Address: Post Office Box 200, Notre Dame, Indiana 46556.

AUSTIN, LORA EVELYN Occupation: Medical Technologist/Immune-Serologist. Education: B.A., M.S. Address: 10707 Moorpark Street, Toluca Lake, California 91602.

AUSTIN, SAM M Occupation: Professor of Physics, Research Director. Education: B.S. 1955, M.S. 1957, Ph.D. 1960, University of Wisconsin. Address: 4709 Woodcraft, Okemos, Michigan 48864.

AVEDON, RICHARD Occupation: Photographer. Education: Columbia University. Address: 407 East 75th Street, New York, New York 10021.

AVERILL, ROBERT GUYER Occupation: Sales Manager. Education: Syracuse University, Dartmouth College. Address: 14 Hastings Heights, Northampton, Maine 01060.

AVERY, JIMMIE LYNNE Occupation: Executive Director, Lact-Aid International, Inc. Education: Fine Arts/Psychology, University of Colorado; Fine Arts/Biology, University of Arizona; Art Education, University of Northern Colorado; Painting/Printmaking, Kansas City Art Institute; Painting/Printmaking, University of Denver. Address: Post Office Box 1066, Athens, Tennessee 37303.

AXLINE, STANTON G Occupation: Chief Operating Officer. Education: B.A., Ohio State University, 1956; M.D., Ohio State University, 1960. Address: 845 20th Street #201, Santa Monica, California 90403.

AYCOCK, DON M Occupation: Minister. Education: B.A., M.Div., Th.M., Th.D. Address: Roue 7, Box 128, Franklinton, Louisiana 70438.

AYENGAR, SHANTA Occupation: Physician/Pediatrician. Education: B.Sc., M.B.B.S., D.C.H., M.D., F.A.A.P. Address: 170 North 76th Street #6, Milwaukee, Wisconsin 53213.

AYERS, KENNETH M Occupation: Clinical Coordinator. Education: Certificate of Advanced Graduate Studies. Address: Cathedral Estates, Rindge, New Hampshire 03461.

AZNEER, J LEONARD Occupation: President, University of Osteopathic Medicine and Health and Health Sciences. Education: B.A., M.H.L., Ph.D. Address: 3511 Southwest 27th Street, Des Moines, Iowa 50321.

AZZATO, LOUIS R Occupation: President and C.E.O. Education: B.S. cum laude, Chemical Engineering. Address: 22 Lord William Penn Drive, Morristown, New Jersey 07960.

AZZIZ, NESTOR J Occupation: Professor and Researcher. Education: Doctor of Philosophy. Address: Carr. 351, K4, Miradero, Mayagriz, Puerto Rico.

B

BABB, ALBERT LESLIE Occupation: Professor of Nuclear Engineering and Chemical Engineering, University of Washington. Education: Bachelor of Applied Science, M.Sc., Ph.D. Address: 3237 Lakewood Avenue South, Seattle, Washington 98144.

BABCOCK, MICHAEL W Occupation: Professor of Economics, Kansas State University. Education: B.S., B.A., M.A., Ph.D. Address: 720 Harris, Manhattan, Kansas 66502.

BABCOCK, PATRICIA ANN Occupation: Acting Chairperson of Nursing. Education: B.S.N., M.A., Ed.D. Address: 115 Washington Avenue, Cresterton, Indiana 46304.

BABER, JAMES Occupation: Project Director and Minister. Education: Master in Counseling, Specialist Developmental Education. Address: 2840 Robinson Road, #151, Jackson, Mississippi 39209.

BABICH, ALAN F Occupation: Computer Scientist. Education: B.S. in Physics, M.S. Electrical Engineering, Ph.D. Electrical Engineering. Address: 27341 Osuna, Mission Viejo, California 92691.

BACHKAI, FRANK E Occupation: Counselor Educator. Education: Ed.D. Address: R.D. #3, Lebanon, New Jersey 08833.

BACIGALUPA, ANDREA Occupation: Liturgical Artist. Education: B.F.A., Maryland Institute of Art, 1950. Address: 626 Canyon Road, Santa Fe, New Mexico 87501.

BACKUS, VICTOR J Occupation: Certified Public Accountant. Education: C.P.A. Certificate, College Diploma. Address: 5270 Los Franciscos Way, Los Angeles, California 90027.

BACON, ETHEL FRANCES Occupation: Music Librarian, University of Hartford. Education: B.M., Mus.M. Address: 5 Canborne Way, Suffield, Connecticut 06078.

BACON, H ANITA D Occupation: Counselor and BGS Regional Campus Coordinator, University of Connecticut. Education: B.A., Eastern Connecticut State University, 1968; M.A., University of Connecticut, 1971. Address: 558 Storrs Road, Mansfield Center, Connecticut 06250.

BACON, MADI Occupation: Music Consultant and Voice Teacher. Education: P.H.B. 1927, M.A. 1941, University of Chicago. Address: 1120 Keith Avenue, Berkeley, California 94708.

BACON, VICTORIA LEE Occupation: Coordinator, Counseling Services. Education: B.A., M.A. Address: 54 Lowe Street, Leominster, Massachusetts 01453.

BADALAMENTE, MARIE ANN Occupation: Biomedical Research Scientist. Education: B.A. 1971, M.S. 1973, Ph.D. 1977. Address: 109 Saint Marks Place, Roslyn Heights, New York 11577.

BADGER, BRYANT D Occupation: Ordained Clergyman; Senior Minister, First Christian Church, Disciples of Christ. Education: B.S., M.Div., D.Min. Address: 2105 South Poplar, Casper, Wyoming 82601.

BAEDER, JOHN A Occupation: Artist/Author. Education: Auburn University, 1960. Address: 1025 Overton Lea Road, Nashville, Tennessee 37220.

BAEHR, MELANY E Occupation: Associate Professor, University of Chicago; Adjunct Professor, DePaul University. Address: 5555 South Everett, Chicago, Illinois 60637.

BAER, MAX FRANK Occupation: Organization

Consultant. Education: Ed.D., J.D., M.A., LL.B. Address: 4201 Cathedral Avenue Northwest, Washington, D.C. 20016.

BAGBY, JOSEPH RIGSBY Occupation: Founder and President, National Association of Investments; Author. Education: B.A. Economics, University of Miami, 1959. Address: 125 Brazilian Avenue, Palm Beach, Florida 33408.

BAHNIUK, EUGENE Occupation: Professor. Education: B.S.M.E., M.S., Ph.D. Address: Cairn Lane, Gates Mills, Ohio 44040.

BAIANU, ION C Occupation: Assistant Professor, University of Illinois-Urbana. Education: M.Sc. Biophysics; Ph.D., University of London. Address: University of Illinois at Urbana, 104 DMB/Biotechn. Building, 1302 West Pennsylvania Avenue, Urbana, Illinois 61801.

BAILEY, JAMES D Occupation: Freelance Writer, Public Relations Consultant. Education: B.S. Industrial Education, University of Wisconsin-Stout; M.A. Speech Communications, University of Denver. Address: Bailey's Landing, Route #2, Box 13, Shell Lake, Wisconsin 54871.

BAILEY, STANLEY A Occupation: Sales Manager. Education: B.A. Address: 605 Brookview Way, Costa Mesa, California 92626.

BAILEY, WILLIAM MICHAEL Occupation: Entrepreneur, Financial Services Company. Education: B.A. Accounting, Bellarmine College, 1983. Address: 3322 Dogwood Drive, Louisville, Kentucky 40220.

BAIN, EMILY JOHNSTON Occupation: Artist, Educator. Education: B.A., Northwestern State Louisiana; M.A. Education and Art, Louisiana State University-Baton Rouge; M.A. English, Tulane University, New Orleans, Louisiana. Address: 834 Valley View Drive, Grand Prairie, Texas 75050.

BAIN, WILFRED C Occupation: Retired University Dean. Education: B.A., B.Mus., M.A., Ed.D., D.Mus., D.F.A., Ph.D., LL.D. Address: 2516 Rechter Road, Bloomington, Indiana 47401.

BAINUM, PETER M Occupation: Professor of Aerospace Engineering, Howard University. Education: B.S. Aerospace Engineering, M.S. Aeronautics and Astronautics, Ph.D. Aerospace Engineering. Address: 9804 Raleigh Tavern Court, Bethesda, Maryland 20814.

BAIRD, CLYDE RAY Occupation: Vice President for Administration, Pittsburgh State University. Education: B.A., M.A., Ed.D. Address: Rural Route 5, Pittsburgh, Kansas 66762.

BAJAJ, KAMLESH VIJ Occupation: Real Estate Investment Executive. Education: Masters in Economics (Pb), University of India. Address: 8126 Dinsdale Street, Downey, California 90240.

BAKER, BERNARD ROBERT Occupation: District Court Judge, 4th Judicial District, State of Colorado. Education: B.S. Business Administration, J.D., Indiana University School of Law. Address: 1423 N. Tejan Street, Colorado Springs, Colorado 80907.

BAKER, BETTY LOUISE Occupation: Mathematics Teacher. Education: B.Ed. 1961, M.A. 1964, Ph.D. 1971. Address: 3214 W. 85th Street, Chicago, Illinois 60652.

BAKER, CHESTER B Occupation: Agricultural Economist. Education: B.S., Iowa State University; Ph.D., University of California at Berkeley. Address: 601 East Penn Avenue, Urbana, Illinois 61801.

BAKER, EARL B Occupation: Residential Services Supervisor, Sunland Center. Education: A.A., Chipola Junior College, 1969; B.S. Sociology, Florida A&M University, 1971; M.S. Criminal Justice, Nova

University, 1980. Address: Route 2, Box 88, Grandridge, Florida 32442.

BAKER, LILLIAN Occupation: Author, Historian. Education: Further Studies. Address: 15237 Chanera Avenue, Gardena, California 90249.

BAKER, LLOYD H Occupation: Attorney. Education: LL.B., New York University, 1951. Address: 5 Mulberry Road, Islip, New York 11751.

BAKER, MATTHEW L Occupation: Book Publisher. Education: B.A. Address: 3201 Bemis, #135903, Ypsilanti, Michigan 48197.

BAKER, THERESE LOUISE Occupation: Chairman, Department of Sociology, DePaul University. Education: B.A., Cornell University; Ph.D., University of Chicago. Address: 5540 South Kimbark, Chicago, Illinois 60637.

BAKER, WILLIAM O Occupation: Chairman, Rockefeller University; Chairman, Andrew W. Mellon Foundation. Education: B.S. 1935, Sc.D. 1957, Washington College; Ph.D. Physical Chemistry, Princeton University; D.Eng., Stevens Institute of Technology, 1962; D.Sc., Georgetown University, 1962; D.Sc., University of Pittsburgh, 1963; D.Sc., Seton Hall University, 1965; LL.D., University of Glasgow, 1965; D.Sc., The University of Akron, 1968; D.Sc., The University of Michigan, 1970; D.Sc., Saint Peter's College, 1972; L.H.D., Monmouth College, 1973; D.Sc. Polytechnic Institute of New York, 1973; LL.D., University of Pennsylvania, 1974; L.H.D., Clarkson College of Technology, 1974; D.Sc. Trinity College, 1975; LL.D., Kean College of New Jersey, 1976; D.Sc., Northwestern University, 1976; D.Sc., University of Notre Dame, 1978; D.Eng., New Jersey Institute of Technology, 1978; LL.D., Lehigh University, 1980; LL.D., Drew University, 1981; Sc.D., Tufts University, 1981; Sc.D., New Jersey College of Medicine & Dentistry, 1981; Fairleigh Dickinson University, 1982. Address: Spring Valley Road, Morristown, New Jersey 07960.

BAKI, MOHAMEDUSMAN G Occupation: Senior Civil Engineer. Education: B.S. Civil Engineering, M.S. Public Health, M.S. Env. Engineering. Address: 1736 W. Pratt Boulevard, Chicago, Illinois 60626.

BAKKEN, HAAKON Occupation: Associate Dean, School of Visual Arts, Sheridan College. Education: B.A., University of Wisconsin; M.F.A., Rochester Institute of Technology. Address: 123 Lynn Court, Burlington, Ontario L7T 1B3.

BALA-SUBRAMANIAN, AMMONNI S Occupation: Rongigenologist. Education: M.D. Address: 13992 Route 31 West, Albion, New York 14411.

BALCERZAK, STANLEY P Occupation: Director Division of Hematology and Oncology; Deputy Director, Ohio State University, Comprehensive Cancer Center; Director Hemophilia Program; Associate Chairman, Department of Medicine. Education: B.A., M.D. Address: 1399 Camelot Drive, Columbus, Ohio 43220.

BALDERSTON, JEAN MERRILL Occupation: Psychotherapist, Writer. Education: B.A., M.A., Ed.D. Address: 1225 Park Avenue, New York City, New York 10128.

BALDERSTONE, IRL LA FAYETTE Occupation: Minister, Counselor. Education: B.A. Psychology/Sociology, M.A. Counseling/Guidance, D.D. Religious History. Address: 1310 Mobile Lane, Alamogordo, New Mexico 88310.

BALDWIN, DONALD EDWARD Occupation: Professor, Southern California College. Education: B.A., University of California at Los Angeles; M.A.,

University of Colorado; M.Div., Fuller Seminary; Ph.D., University of Missouri. Address: 203 Wellesley Lane, Costa Mesa, California 92626.

BALDWIN, GARZA JR Occupation: Vice President, Olin Corporation; President, Ecusta Paper & Film Group, Olin Corporation. Education: B.S. 1942, J.D. 1948, Indiana University. Address: 18 Beaverdam Knoll, Asheville, North Carolina 28804.

BALDWIN, JOHN DAVID Occupation: Professor of Sociology. Education: Ph.D. Sociology, Johns Hopkins, 1967. Address: 1159 Palomino Road, Santa Barbara, California 93105.

BALENDRAN, KANDIAH Occupation: General Accounting Manager. Education: B.S., C.P.A., A.C.A. Address: 217 Westwood Court, Woodbury, New Jersey 08096.

BALIUNAS, SALLIE LOUISE Occupation: Research Astrophysicist. Education: M.S., Villanova University; A.M., Ph.D., Harvard University. Address: 92 Van Norden Road, Reading, Massachusetts 01867.

BALKA, DON S Occupation: Associate Professor of Mathematics, Saint Mary's College. Education: B.S. summa cum laude, Missouri Valley College; M.S., Indiana University; Ph.D., University of Missouri. Address: Box 32, LaPaz, Indiana 46537.

BALL, JOHN DAVID Occupation: Clinical Psychologist. Education: M.Ed. School Psychology, Ph.D. Clinical Psychology. Address: 1137 Kings Way Drive, Virginia Beach, Virginia 23455.

BALL, PATRICIA G Occupation: Director of Public Affairs. Education: B.S. Education, Radford College; M.S. Personnel, Ed.D. Psychology, University of Tennessee. Address: 4201 Crosley Road #404, Knoxville, Tennessee 37919.

BALL, ROBERT J Occupation: Professor of Classics, University of Hawaii. Education: Ph.D., Columbia University. Address: Department of European Languages and Literature, University of Hawaii, Honolulu, Hawaii 96822.

BALL, SARA NEE Occupation: Curator, Canadian County Historical Museum. Education: High School Graduate. Address: 400 South 10th, Yukon, Oklahoma 73099.

BALL, WILLIAM Occupation: General Director.

BALLANCE, CHARLEEN SAYLORS Occupation: Training and Education, Management. Education: B.S., M.A. Address: 6945 DeFoe Avenue, Colorado Springs, Colorado 80911.

BALLARD, DANNY J RAMSEY Occupation: Assistant Professor in Health Education. Education: B.S., M.Ed., Ed.D. Address: 2750 Lois Lane, Pocatello, Idaho 83201.

BALLARD, GEORGE SPEIGHTS JR Occupation: Retired Private Investor. Education: A.B., Emory University, 1942; M.B.A., Harvard University, 1942. Address: 3092 Argonne Drive Northwest, Atlanta, Georgia 30305.

BALLARD, JOHN W JR Occupation: President, Safety Federal Savings and Loan Association. Education: B.S., Kansas University. Address: 9311 Buena Vista, Shawnee Mission, Kansas 66207.

BALLARD, MARGUERITE CANDLER Occupation: Hematologist, Centers for Disease Control. Education: A.B., Vassar College, 1942; M.S. 1943, M.D. 1948, Emory University. Address: 3092 Argonne Drive, Northwest, Atlanta, Georgia 30305.

BALLARD, WILLIAM JOSEPH Occupation: Music Director, San Francisco Boys Chorus. Education: B.Mus., M.Mus., Ph.D. Address: 620 Miramar Avenue, San Francisco, California 94112.

BALLOON, JOSEPH LE Occupation: Assistant

Professor of Management. Education: B.S., M.S., Ph.D. Address: 5806 Troy Villa Boulevard, Dayton, Ohio 45424.

BALTAY, CHARLES Occupation: Professor of Physics, Columbia University. Education: B.S., M.S., Ph.D. Address: 21 Hardscrabble Hill, Chappaqua, New York 10514.

BAN, JOHN ROBERT Occupation: Professor of Education. Education: Bachelors, Masters and Doctoral Degrees. Address: 931 West 67th Place, Merrillville, Indiana 46410.

BANAS, PAUL ANTHONY Occupation: Manager, Personnel Research. Education: Ph.D. Address: 5140 Driftwood, Milford, Michigan 48042.

BANDEEM, ROBERT ANGUS Occupation: Chairman, President and Chief Executive Officer, Crown Life Insurance Company. Education: B.A. Economics and Political Science, LL.D. 1975, University of Western Ontario; Ph.D. Economics, Duke University; LL.D., Dalhousie University, 1978; D.C.L., Bishop's University, 1978; LL.D., Queen's University, 1982. Address: 120 Bloor Street East, Toronto, Ontario, Canada M4W 1B8.

BANE, BERNARD MAURICE Occupation: Publisher. Education: Northeastern University, Northeastern University School of Law. Address: 854 Massachusetts Avenue, Cambridge, Massachusetts 02139.

BANERJEE, KALI S Occupation: Visiting Professor, H. Rodney Sharp Professor Emeritus, University of Delaware. Education: Ph.D. Statistics. Address: 1019 Stormont Circle, Baltimore, Maryland 21227.

BANGS, CAROL JANE Occupation: Writer. Education: B.A., M.A., Ph.D. Address: 624 Lincoln Street, Port Townsend, Washington 98368.

BANIK, SAMBHU N Occupation: Chief, Mental Health Center. Education: B.Sc., M.Sc., Ph.D. Address: 8606 Bradmoor Drive, Bethesda, Maryland 20817.

BANKS, SAMUEL ALSTON Occupation: President, Dickinson College. Education: A.B., M.Div., Ph.D., D.Litt. Address: 212 West High Street, Carlisle, Pennsylvania 17013.

BANKS, SARA LYNN Occupation: Professor of Psychology, Rollins College. Education: B.A., M.A., Psy.D. Address: 325 Miami Avenue, Indialantic, Florida 32903.

BANKSTON, GORDON D Occupation: Artist; Cartoonist. Education: Northern Texas State University, three years. Address: 3813 Springdale, Odessa, Texas 79762.

BANKSTON, JESSE H Occupation: Hospital Consultant; Chair, Democratic Party; Member, Board of Elementary & Secondary Education. Education: B.A., M.A., Louisiana State University. Address: 9526 Southmoor Drive, Baton Rouge, Louisiana 70815.

BANNON, KATHLEEN ANGELA Occupation: International Program Officer. Education: B.A. magna cum laude, American University, 1970. Address: 4000 Cathedral Avenue, North West, Washington, D.C. 20016.

BANWART, GEORGE J Occupation: Professor Food Microbiology. Education: B.S., Ph.D. Address: 262 Highgate, Worthington, Ohio 43085.

BARANOV, ANDREY I Occupation: Retired. Education: M.S. Biology. Address: 18 Locke Street, Cambridge, Massachusetts 02140.

BARANOWSKI, FRANK JOHN JR Occupation: Dean. Education: B.A., Education Certificate, M.R.E., M.A.. Address: St. Mary's Preparatory, Post Office Box 5146, Orchard Lake, Michigan 48033.

BARBA, HARRY Occupation: Writer, Publisher, Editor, Teacher. Education: A.B., Bates College, 1944; M.A., Harvard University, 1951; M.F.A., University of Iowa, 1960; Ph.D., 1963. Address: 47 Hyde Boulevard, Ballston Spa, New York 12020.

BARBATO, PETER A JR Occupation: Treasurer. Education: A.S. Accounting, B.S. Accounting. Address: 40 Bradford Road, Tewksburg, Massachusetts 01876.

BARBER, TRIPHY C Occupation: Registered Nurse, Instructor, Author. Education: R.N., M.T., B.S., M.S., Ph.D. Address: 116 Running Deer Drive, Hopkins, South Carolina 29061.

BARBER, VIVIAN K Occupation: High School Learning Disabilities Teacher. Education: B.S. Elementary/Special Education (L.D., E.M.H.). Address: Route 1, Woodlawn, Illinois 62898.

BARBERO, GEORGE J Occupation: Full Professor, Business Law, Iona College. Education: A.B., Catholic University of America, 1950; M.A., University of Notre Dame, 1952; J.D., New York Law School, 1957. Address: 14 Myrtle Boulevard, Larchmont, New York 10538.

BARBIERS, ARTHUR R JR Occupation: Retired Scientist for Upjohn. Education: B.S., B.S., M.A., Bowling Green State University. Address: 7904 Copano Drive, Austin, Texas 78749.

BARCUS, ROBERT A Occupation: College Professor; Clinical Psychologist. Education: B.A., M.A., Ph.D., Ohio State University. Address: 325 West North College Street, Yellow Springs, Ohio 45387.

BARDACH, JOAN LUCILE Occupation: Clinical Psychologist. Education: B.A., M.A., Ph.D., Postdoctoral Certificate Psychology. Address: 50 East 10 Street, New York, New York 10003.

BARDEN, MARK LAWRENCE Occupation: Professor, Murray State University. Education: B.S., M.A. Address: 1310 Divgvid Drive, Murray, Kentucky 42071.

BARDIS, PANOS DEMETRIOS Occupation: Professor, Author, Editor, Poet. Education: B.A., M.A., Ph.D. Address: 2533 Orkney, Toledo, Ohio 43606.

BARDO, JOHN W Occupation: Dean of Liberal Arts, School of Liberal Arts. Education: B.A., M.A., Ph.D. Address: 162 Rolling Oaks, Willow Creek III, San Marcos, Texas 78666.

BARFIELD, KENNY DALE Occupation: Educator; Minister. Education: B.A., David Lipscomb College; M.A., University of Alabama. Address: 2030 Saxton Drive, Florence, Alabama 35630.

BAR-ILLAN, DAVID J Occupation: Concert Pianist. Education: Diploma, Juilliard School of Music. Address: 924 West End Avenue, New York, New York 10025.

BARKER, DOROTHY ERICKSON Occupation: Professor Emeritus, Biological Sciences. Education: B.S., M.S., Ph.D., University of Minnesota. Address: 701-5th Avenue South, St. Cloud, Minnesota 56301.

BARKLEY, OWEN H Occupation: Professional Photographer. Address: 126 North Main Street, Climax, Michigan 49034.

BARLOW, RICHARD G Occupation: Manager, Sun Exploration and Production Company. Education: B.A., Idaho State University; M.A., University of Utah; Ph.D., University of Michigan. Address: 4312 Cobblers Lane, Dallas, Texas 75252.

BARNARD, JANET KAY Occupation: Mathematics Teacher, Parkside Junior High School. Education: B.S. Education, M.S. Education. Address: 404 South Emery, Heyworth, Illinois 61745.

BARNDT, JANE N Occupation: Business Education Teacher. Education: B.S. Business

Education, Bloomsburg University. Address: 317 East Market Street, Perkasise, Pennsylvania 18944.

BARNER, HENDRICK BOYER Occupation: Professor of Surgery, St. Louis University. Education: B.S., M.D. Address: 443 Sherwood Drive, Webster Groves, Missouri 63119.

BARNES, JAMES Occupation: Professor. Education: B.A. magna cum laude, Amherst College, 1954; B.A., New College, Oxford, 1956; Ph.D., Harvard University, 1960; D.H.L., College of Wooster, 1976.

BARNES, JIM W Occupation: Editor, *The Chariton Review*; Professor of English, Northeast Missouri State University. Education: Ph.D., University of Arkansas, 1972. Address: 918 Pine Street, Macon, Missouri 63552.

BARNES, MAGGIE SUE Occupation: Nurse. Education: B.S.N., R.N., A.A. Address: Route 1, Box 9-B, Hermleigh, Texas 79526.

BARNES, MARGARET ANDERSON Occupation: President of Research and Management Com. Education: B.S., M.A., Ph.D. Candidate. Address: Post Office Box 586, Seabrook, Maryland 20706.

BARNES, MELVER RAYMOND Occupation: Retired, Freelance Scientific Research. Education: A.B. Chemistry. Address: Route 1, Box 424, Linwood, North Carolina 27299.

BARNES, MICHAEL D Occupation: Member, U.S. House of Representatives. Education: B.A. 1965, J.D. 1972. Address: 9814 Summit Avenue, Kensington, Maryland 20895.

BARNES, THERESE STIFFLER Occupation: Attorney. Education: B.S., J.D. Address: 44 Polo Drive, Atlanta, Georgia 30309.

BARNES, WENDELL WRIGHT JR Occupation: Senior Counselor for the Deaf, Rehabilitation Service. Education: B.F.A. 1973, M.Ed. 1982, University of Georgia. Address: 2923-11th Avenue, Columbus, Georgia 31904.

BARNETT, EWIN HARVEY III Occupation: Consultant. Education: Computer Science, University of Missouri. Address: Route 1, Box 172, Ashland, Missouri 65010.

BARNETT, JUNE W Occupation: Education: Writer, Lecturer, Instructor. Education: B.S. Retail Merchandising, University of Southern California. Address: 761 Brookside Circle, R.D. #1, Del 255, Elmira, New York 14903.

BARNEY, JAMES EARL II Occupation: Manager, Toxicology Administration, Stauffer Chemical Company. Education: Ph.D. Analytical Chemistry, University of Kansas, 1950. Address: 64 Cold Spring Road, Avon, Connecticut 06001.

BARNEY, NEIL ALLEN Occupation: Podiatrist. Education: B.S., D.P.M. Address: Box 483, Hyannis Port, Massachusetts 02672.

BARNEY, WILLIAM L Occupation: Historian, Professor. Education: B.A., Cornell University; M.A., Ph.D., Columbia University. Address: 407 Westwood Drive, Chapel Hill, North Carolina 27514.

BARNHART, RAY A Occupation: Federal Highway Administrator. Education: B.A., Marietta College; M.A., University of Houston. Address: 400 7th Street, South West, Washington, D.C. 20590.

BARNOFF, ROBERT MARK Occupation: Head, Department of Civil Engineering, Penn State University. Education: B.S., M.S., Ph.D. Civil Engineering. Address: 606 Nimitz Avenue, State College, Pennsylvania 16801.

BAROCAS, HARVEY Occupation: Clinical Psychologist, Psychoanalyst. Education: Ph.D., City University of New York, 1970. Address: 5 Peter Cooper Road, New York, New York 10010.

BARRACK, WILLIAM S JR Occupation: Senior Vice President, Texaco Incorporated; Director, Caltex Petroleum Corporation. Education: B.S. Engineering, University of Pittsburgh. Address: 2000 Westchester Avenue, White Plains, New York 10650.

BARRATT, THOMAS KEATING Occupation: Superintendent, Crawford Central School District. Education: D.Ed., Pennsylvania State University. Address: Route 9, Box 1008, Meadville, Pennsylvania 16335.

BARRER, GERTRUDE Occupation: Artist, Illustrator. Education: Art School, Music School. Address: Rocky Mount Road, Roxbury, Connecticut 06783.

BARRETT, EDWARD C Occupation: Vice President, Finance. Education: B.S. Business Education, C.P.A. Address: 66 Downing Drive, Reading, Pennsylvania 19610.

BARRETT, GERALD V Occupation: Professor and Head, Department of Psychology. Education: Ph.D. Industrial Psychology, 1962; J.D. (in progress). Address: 3088 Highland Drive, Silver Lake, Ohio 44224.

BARRINGER, JOHN PAUL Occupation: President of Two Small Corporations. Education: B.S., Princeton University; Colonel U.S.A.F. Address: 218 Hun Road, Princeton, New Jersey 08540.

BARRON, PAMELA G Occupation: Manager, Media Operations. Education: Cornell University; B.A., City College of New York; M.A., Kent State University. Address: 148 19th Street Northwest, Canton, Ohio 44709.

BARROQUILLO, JIMMIE LEE Occupation: College Administrator. Education: B.S., M.S., Indiana University. Address: 6749 South Cornell Avenue, Chicago, Illinois 60649-1085.

BARRY, ROGER DONALD Occupation: Professor, Chemistry. Education: B.S., Ph.D. Address: 111 Raymbault Drive, Marquette, Michigan 49855.

BARSHAY, MARSHALL E Occupation: Physician. Education: B.A. 1959, M.D. 1963. Address: 1260 15th Street, Suite 816, Santa Monica, California 90404.

BARTA, DOROTHY E Occupation: Fine Artist, Portrait Artist. Address: 3151 Chapel Downs Drive, Dallas, Texas 75229.

BARTA, MARIE LAURA Occupation: Music Educator. Education: Drake University, Sherwood School of Music; St. Olaf College. Address: 223 East North Stret, Manly, Iowa 50456.

BARTEAN, JOHN F Occupation: Vice President of Manufacturing. Education: B.A., B.S.M.E. Address: Route 2, Box 2045A, Boerne, Texas 78006.

BARTLETT, GEORGE WEEKS Occupation: President, Neway Division, Lear Siegler, Incorporated. Education: B.S. Engineering and Business Administration, Massachusetts Institute of Technology, 1943. Address: 330 East Circle Drive, North Muskegon, Michigan 49445.

BARTLETT, LEE A Occupation: Professor of English, Director, Creative Writing Program, University of New Mexico. Education: A.B., University of California-Berkeley; Ph.D., University of California-Davis. Address: 2908 Santa Cruze Southeast, Albuquerque, New Mexico 87131.

BARTLETTE, DONALD L Occupation: Educator, Social Worker, Public Speaker. Education: Ph.D. Education, Ph.B. Social Work. Address: 2602 Ocelot Northeast, North Canton, Ohio 44721.

BARTO, MILAN ANDREW (DOC) Occupation: Hospital Manager. Education: Youngstown College,

LaSalle Extension University. Address: 6351 Wisteria Way, San Jose, California 95129.

BARTOLOMEI, MARGARET MARY Occupation: Vocational Educator/Nursing Consultant. Education: B.S.N. Nursing, M.S. Education, Ph.D. Education. Address: 19442 Rockport Drive, Roseville, Michigan 48066.

BARTON, JERRY LEE Occupation: President, Chairman of the Board. Education: Georgia State University, 1955-1957; Business Administration, University of California, 1967-1968. Address: 1103 Evergreen Road, Anchorage, Kentucky 40223.

BARTON, LAWRENCE Occupation: Associate Professor of Chemistry, Department Head. Education: B.Sc., B.Sc. Hons., Ph.D. Chemistry. Address: 7206 Henderson, St. Louis, Missouri 63121.

BARTON, THOMAS J Occupation: Distinguished Professor. Education: Ph.D., University of Florida, Organic Chemistry. Address: 815 Onyx Circle, Ames, Iowa 50010.

BARUT, ASIM O Occupation: Professor of Physics. Education: Dipl. Sci., Dr. Sci., Dr. hon. causa. Address: 760-12th, Boulder, Colorado 80302.

BARYSHNIKOV, MIKHAIL Occupation: Dancer; Choreographer; Artistic Director. Address: c/o Edgar Vincent Associates, 124 East 40th Street, Suite 304, New York, New York 10016.

BASCUNANA, JOSE LUIS Occupation: Senior Research Engineer. Education: Ph.D. 1968, M.A. Economics 1978. Address: 9104 Cranford Drive, Potomac, Maryland 20854.

BASHFUL, EMMETT W Occupation: Chancellor, Southern University at New Orleans. Education: Ph.D. Address: 5808 Lafaye Street, New Orleans, Louisiana 70122.

BASILIO, JOSEPH S Occupation: Interior Designer. Address: 58 Pine Lane, Watchung, New Jersey 07060.

BASKA, CATHERINE ANN Occupation: School Social Worker. Education: A.A., A.B., M.S.W., S.Sc.D. Address: Grand Tower East, 3520 Laclede Avenue, St. Louis, Missouri 63103.

BASS, MADELINE TIGER Occupation: Poet; Teacher. Education: B.A., Wellesley College; M.A.T., Harvard University; G.S.E.; M.F.A., Columbia University, 1986. Address: 15 Victoria Terrace, Upper Montclair, New Jersey 07043.

BASS, MITCHELL H Occupation: Mortgage Banker. Education: M.B.A., University of Chicago; B.S. Finance, University of Illinois. Address: 206 Honeysuckle Drive, Northbrook, Illinois 60062.

BASSETT, JOHN W JR Occupation: Lawyer. Education: A.B., Stanford University, 1960; J.D., University Texas School of Law, 1964. Address: 602 Rosemary Lane, Roswell, New Mexico 88201.

BASSFORD, FORREST R Occupation: Executive Director, Livestock Publications Council. Education: B.S. Animal Husbandry, Colorado State University. Address: 927 Elmview Drive, Encinitas, California 92024.

BASTURA, BERNARD A Occupation: Museum Curator, Submarine Library/Museum. Education: Grammar and High School. Address: 440 Washington Street, Middletown, Connecticut 06457.

BATE, WALTER JACKSON Occupation: University Professor. Education: B.A. 1939, M.A. 1940, Ph.D. 1942, Harvard University. Address: 3 Warren House, Harvard University, Cambridge, Massachusetts 02138.

BATES, BARBARA JEANNE Occupation: Board of Directors, Global Education Motivators; Library

Consultant. Education: M.S. Address: 3000 Valley Forge Circle, King of Prussia, Pennsylvania 19406.

BATES, CHARLES WALTER Occupation: Personnel Executive. Education: B.A. Economics/Psychology 1975, M.L.I.R. Labor and Industrial Relations 1977, Michigan State University; J.D., William Mitchell College of Law, 1984. Address: 3905 Lancaster Lane North #325, Plymouth, Minnesota 55441.

BATES, JOHN BERTRAM Occupation: Vice President, Research and Development. Education: Ph.D. Colloid Chemistry, 1941. Address: 46701 Betty Hill, Plymouth, Michigan 48170.

BATES, MARY PATRICIA Occupation: Sculptor, Art Professor, Sonoma State University. Education: B.F.A., Colorado State University, 1973; M.F.A., Indiana University, 1981. Address: 243 Arlen, Rohnert Park, California 94928.

BATRA, ROMESH C Occupation: Professor. Education: Ph.D., Johns Hopkins University, Baltimore, 1972. Address: 211 Steeplechase Road, Rolla, Missouri 65401.

BATSON, ESPERANZA ALESANDRINA Occupation: Admissions/Financial Aid Counselor. Education: B.A., M.S. Address: 1156 Troy Avenue, Brooklyn, New York 11203.

BATTERSBY, HAROLD R (ERIC) Occupation: Professor, State University of New York. Education: B.A. Modern Near Eastern Studies, University of Toronto, 1960; Ph.D. Altaic and Uralic Studies, Indiana University, 1969. Address: Box 80, Groveland Station, New York 14462.

BATTERSBY, JAMES LYONS Occupation: Professor of English. Education: B.S., M.A., Ph.D. Address: 472 Clinton Heights Avenue, Columbus, Ohio 43202.

BATTIN, R RAY Occupation: Clinical Neuropsychologist; Audiologist; Director, The Bartin Clinic. Education: B.A. 1948, M.S. 1950, Ph.D. 1959. Address: 3837 Meadow Lake Lane, Houston, Texas 77027.

BATTY, JANE G Occupation: Certified Health Care Safety Professional. Education: B.S., R.N. Address: 10 Sherman Circle, Utica, New York 13501.

BAUDER, GARY L Occupation: Accountant. Education: A.B. Address: 221 Susan, Sturgis, Michigan 49091.

BAUER, ARTHUR A Occupation: Radioactive Waste Disposal, Project Manager. Education: M.S., B.S. Address: 2485 Middlesex Road, Columbus, Ohio 43220.

BAUER, EDWARD ALPHONSE Occupation: Electrical Contractor. Education: A.A. Mechanical Engineering Technology, St. Cloud State University, 1969. Address: 149 Seventh Avenue North, Box 358, Waite Park, Minnesota 56387.

BAUER, JANET GAYE Occupation: Assistant Professor, Section of Operative Dentistry, University of California. Education: B.A. Zoology, University of California at Los Angeles, 1971; D.D.S. 1975, M.S. 1979, Certificate in Medical Education 1979, University of Southern California, School of Dentistry.

BAUGH, L DARRELL Occupation: Estate Planning. Education: B.A., M.S.B.A., C.L.U., Ch.F.C. Address: 92 Caballo Court, Boulder, Colorado 80303.

BAUGHMAN, BARBARA A Occupation: Director, Special Events. Education: B.A., Oglethorpe University. Address: 2479 Peachtree Road, North East #203, Atlanta, Georgia 30305.

BAUM, ARNOLD R Occupation: Education Director; Business Executive. Education: B.S. Business

Management, M.S. Education Administration, Advanced Graduate Studies. Address: Box 213, Callicoon, New York 12723.

BAUM, BERNARD Occupation: Manager, Polymer Science and Technology. Education: B.S., University of Lowell; M.A., Ph.D., Clark University. Address: 44 Kirkwood Road, West Hartford, Connecticut 06117.

BAUM, CARL E Occupation: Senior Scientist in Electromagnetics. Education: B.S. 1962, M.S. 1963, Ph.D. 1969, Caltech University. Address: 5116 Eastern Southeast, Unit D. Albuquerque, New Mexico 87105.

BAUMAN, CAROLINE G Occupation: Physician, Pediatrician. Education: B.A., M.D. Address: Kenilworth Road, Rye, New York 10580.

BAUMRIH, BERNARD STEFAN HERBERT Occupation: Professor of Philosophy, Lawyer. Education: B.A., Ph.D., J.D. Address: 590 West End Avenue, New York, New York 10024.

BAUTSCH, VIRGINIA BELLE Occupation: Secretary, Field & Technical Support/Support Services, Dallas Police Department. Address: 1834 Euclid Street, Dallas, Texas 75206.

BAX, RONALD FRANK Occupation: Engineering Manager. Education: B.A. Physics. Address: 447 Homer Avenue, Palo Alto, California 94301.

BAXTER, BILL L Occupation: Professor of Journalism. Education: M.A., B.A. University of Iowa. Address: 6991 North Beech Tree Drive, Glendale, Wisconsin 53209.

BAXTER, WILLIAM F Occupation: Assistant Attorney General, Antitrust Division, United States Department of Justice. Education: A.B. 1951, J.D. 1956, Stanford University.

BAYAZEED, ABDO FARES Occupation: Petroleum Engineer. Education: B.S. Petroleum Engineering. Address: 1026 South Johnstone, Apartment 8, Bartlesville, Oklahoma 74003.

BAYER, RAYMOND GEORGE Occupation: Senior Engineer, Manager, Tribologist. Education: B.S., M.S. Address: 4609 Marshall Drive, West, New York 13903.

BAYS, JAMES PHILIP Occupation: Professor. Education: B.A., Northwestern University, 1963; Ph.D., Wisconsin University, 1968. Address: 1537 South 13th Street, Niles, Michigan 49120.

BAZANT, ZDENEK P Occupation: Professor of Engineering, Consultant, Northwestern University. Education: Ph.D. Engineering Mechanics, Czechoslovakia Academy of Sciences of Czechoslovakia, 1963. Address: 514 Greenwood, Kenilworth, Illinois 60043.

BAZERMAN, MAX H Occupation: Professor. Education: Ph.D. Address: 996 Centre Street, Jamaica Plain, Massachusetts 02130.

BEACHUM, GRAHAM CARSON Occupation: Retired Colonel Regular, United States Air Force; Assistant Director, Public Works. Education: M.A. Business Administration, B.A. Business G.W.U. Address: 7609 Harps Mill, Raleigh, North Carolina 27609.

BEALL, GRACE R Occupation: College Educator. Education: B.S., M.Ed., Additional Studies. Address: 3232 Crestview, Pineville, Louisiana 71360.

BEAMAN, MARGARINE G GEISTWEIDT Occupation: Metal Broker and Accountant/Consultant. Address: 1406 Wilshire Boulevard, Austin, Texas 78722.

BEAMER, PARKER REYNOLDS Occupation: Pathologist, Director of Resident Training, West Suburban Hospital Medical Center. Education: A.B.

1935, M.S. 1937, Ph.D. 1940, University of Illinois; M.D., Washington University. Address: 1040 Erie Street, Oak Park, Illinois 60302.

BEARD, KENNETH VAN KIRKE Occupation: Associate Professor of Meteorology, Department Atmospheric Science. Address: 2019 Burlison, Urbana, Illinois 61801.

BEARSS, KATHRYN MILDRED Occupation: Nurse Educator, Indiana University. Education: R.N., B.S. Nursing Education, Florida State University; M.A., Ed.D., Columbia University. Address: 5720 West 38th Street, Apartment 5, Indianapolis, Indiana 46254.

BEATTY, MARLENE ROSE Occupation: Student Hygienist, Department of Dental Hygiene, Sheridan College. Education: R.D.H., 1984. Address: 3800 Capitol Avenue, Cheyenne, Wyoming 82001.

BEATY, RETA A Occupation: Physical Therapist. Education: B.S., M.Ed. Address: 901 Kenwood Drive, Abilene, Texas 79601.

BEAUBIEN, RICHARD FROMM Occupation: Transportation Engineer. Education: A.B., B.S.C.E., M.S.C.E. Address: 1685 Ross, Troy, Michigan 48084.

BEAUCHAMP, TOM L Occupation: Professor of Philosophy, Senior Research Scholar. Education: B.A., M.A., Ph.D., Johns Hopkins University. Address: 15112 Georgia Avenue, Rockville, Maryland 20853.

BEAVERS, MARY THOMAS Occupation: Freelance Artist. Address: 1030 North Orange Gove, Avenue 107, Los Angeles, California 90046.

BEAZLEY, CURTIS EDWARD Occupation: Retired Air Force Officer. Education: A.A., East Mississipi Junior College, 1946; B.S., Graduate Studies, Petroleum Geology, Mississippi State University, 1951; B.S., Meteorlogy, Florida State University, 1952; M.P.A., Auburn University, 1980. Address: 3832 Rouse Ridge Road, Montgomery, Alabama 36111.

BECHT, ADELINE CHARLOTTE Occupation: Counselor/Rehabilitation Therapist. Education: Ph.D. Clinical Psychology, University of Oregon, 1982. Address: 9028 Southeast Market Street, Portland, Oregon 97216.

BECHT, JUNE L Occupation: Freelance Writer. Education: B.S. Education, M.A. Education. Address: 1004 Dolores Avenue, St. Louis, Missouri 63132.

BECK, FRANCES Occupation: Psychologist. Education: Ph.D. Address: 319 East 24 Street, New York, New York 10010.

BECK, LOUIS Occupation: Geo. Beck Chemicals/ NC. Education: B.S. Chemistry. Address: 6399 Crossview Road, Cleveland, Ohio 44131.

BECKET, FLORA GRACE Education: B.S., State University of New York. Address: 417 Hvenica Arboles, San Jose, California 95123.

BECKWITH, RODNEY F Occupation: Management Consultant. Education: B.M.E., Cornell University, 1958; M.B.A., Harvard University, 1963. Address: 8 Nolen Lane, Darien, Connecticut 06820.

BECKWITH, SANDRA SHANK Occupation: Judge. Education: B.A. 1965, J.D. 1968. Address: 222 East Central Parkway, Cincinnati, Ohio 45202.

BEDFORD, JAMES WILLIAM Occupation: Toxicologist. Education: B.S., M.S., Ph.D. Address: 1804 Wood Street, Lansing, Michigan 48912.

BEDROSSIAN, AGHAVNI A Occupation: Senior Technical Analyst. Education: Ph.D. Electrochemical Engineering, Columbia University, 1977. Address: 220 Central Park South, New York, New York 10019.

BEDWELL, THEODORE C, JR. Occupation: Physician Major General, United States Air Force (Retired). Education: B.S., M.D., M.P.H. Address: 6218 Hardy Drive, McLean, Virginia 22101.

BEEMSTER, JOSEPH R Occupation: Diector Health, Safety & Productivity. Education: B.A., DePaul University. Address: 6908 West 83rd Street, Bloomington, Minnesota 55438.

BEERE, CAROLE ANN Occupation: Associate Processor, Department of Psychology, Central Michigan University. Education: B.A., M.A., Ph.D. Address: 4472 South Crawford Road, Mount Pleasant, Michigan 48858.

BEHRINGER, SAMUEL JOSEPH JR Occupation: Business Attorney, Simpson and Moran. Education: B.S., Michigan State University, 1970; J.D., University of Detroit, 1973. Address: 333 McKinley Avenue, Grosse Pointe Farms, Michigan 48236.

BEHRMANN, MARION POLLY Occupation: Teacher, Author, Consultant, Lecturer. Education: B.S. Recreation Education, M.S. Special Education. Address: 115 Lake Road, Framingham, Massachusetts 01701.

BEILMAN, MARK EMIL Occupation: Architect. Education: B.S. Architecture, University of Nebraska. Address: 2702 Waunona Way, Madison, Wisconsin 53713.

BEKEY, GEORGE A Occupation: Professor Engineering and Director Robotics. Education: Ph.D. Engineering, University of California, Los Angeles. Address: 4654 Encino Avenue, Encino, California 91316.

BELCHER, LINDA J Occupation: Southwestern Bell Corporation, Network Department. Education: B.A., Soc. S.C. Address: 1913 South Valentine, Little Rock, Arkansas 72204.

BELENCHIA, THERESA AMELIA Occupation: Director of Education, North Mississippi Retardation Center. Education: B.A. Communicative Disorders, M.A. Speech Pathology. Address: 215 Williams Street, Oxford, Mississippi 38655.

BELL, GEORGE A Occupation: Public Relations. Education: B.A. Public Relations. Address: 3830 Underwood Drive, #4, San Jose, California 95117.

BELL, GETHA GINA Occupation: Freelance Writer. Education: Texas Arts and Industries. Address: 2980 Holiday Circle, Buford, Georgia 30518.

BELL, JOHN F Occupation: Professor. Education: B.S., M.F., Ph.D. Address: 465 North West Elizabeth Drive, Corvallis, Oregon 97330.

BELL, LOUISE MATHESON Occupation: Photography. Education: Numerous Courses, Winona School of Photography. Address: 110 South Second Street, Seneca, South Carolina 29678.

BELL, MELANIE MOORE Occupation: University Registrar. Education: B.A., M.P.A. Address: Route 3, Box 271, Cheney, Washington 99004.

BELL, MICHAEL S Occupation: Assistant Director of Cultural Affairs, San Francisco Arts Commission. Education: B.F.A., California Institute of Arts; M.F.A., University of Kentucky. Address: 564 45th Avenue, San Francisco, California 94121.

BELLAN, JOSETTE Occupation: Scientist. Education: Ph.D. Address: 3744 Valley Lights Drive, Pasadena, California 91107.

BELLER, SAM E Occupation: President, Diversified Programs, Inc. Education: B.A., C.L.U., Ch.F.C. Address: 3050 Ann Street, Baldwin, New York 1150.

BELLETTIRIE, GERALD F Occupation: Psychologist. Education: B.A., M.A., Ph.D. Address: 1713 Whitemarsh Lane, Landsdale, Pennsylvania 19446.

BELLINA, JOSEPH H Occupation: Gynecologic Surgeon. Education: M.D., Ph.D. Address: 833 South Carrollton Avenue, New Orleans, Louisiana 70118.

BELLMAN, MARK EMIL Occupation: Architect. Education: B.S. Architect, University of Nebraska. Address: 2702 Waunona Way, Madison, Wisconsin 53713.

BELTON, JOHN A Occupation: Clinical Psychologist. Education: B.A., M.A., M.P.A., Psy.D. Address: 2356 Pennington Road, Trenton, New Jersey 08638.

BELY, JEANETTE LOBACH Occupation: Professor. Education: Ph.D., M.A., B.B.A. Address: 1024 East 93 Street, Brooklyn, New York 11236.

BEMAK, FRED PAUL Occupation: Professor, University Administrator, Organizational Consultant. Education: Ed.D. Address: 35 Gray Street, Amherst, Massachusetts 01002.

BeMILLER, JAMES NOBLE Occupation: Professor, Department of Chemistry and Biochemistry and School of Medicine, Southern Illinois University at Carbondale. Education: B.S. Agricultural Biochemistry, Purdue University, 1954; M.S. Biochemistry, Purdue University, 1956; Ph.D. Biochemistry, Purdue University, 1959. Address: Rural Route 6, Box 436, Murphysboro, Illinois 62966.

BENAROYA, HAYM Occupation: Research Engineer, Policy Studies. Education: B.E., M.S., Ph.D. Engineering. Address: 333 Seventh Avenue, New York, New York 10001.

BENASSI, A LOU Occupation: Attorney. Education: B.S. Finance, University of Illinois; J.D. University of California at Berkeley. Address: 6318 North Mt. Hawley Road, Peoria, Illinois 61614.

BENBOW, RICHARD ADDISON Occupation: Judicial Service Officer, Municipal Court. Education: Ph.D. Clinical Psychology. Address: 7131 Pleasant View, Las Vegas, Nevada 89117.

BENDER, BRENDA ANNE Occupation: Teacher; Adjunct Professor. Education: A.A., B.A., M.Ed., Ph.D. Address: Post Office Box 143, Moore, South Carolina 29369.

BENDER, EILEEN TEPER Occupation: Professor of English. Education: B.S.J., Northwestern University, 1956; Ph.D. English, University of Notre Dame, 1977. Address: 1512 Belmont Avenue, South Bend, Indiana 46615.

BENDER, LESLIE CAROL Occupation: Attorney at Law. Education: B.A., J.D. Address: 3026 St. Paul #82, Baltimore, Maryland 21218.

BENEDEK, ELISSA A Occupation: Director of Training and Research. Education: M.D. Forensic and Child Psychiatrist. Address: 3607 Chatham Way, Ann Arbor, Michigan 48106.

BENEDICT, GARY Occupation: Educator, Administrator. Education: B.E., M.S., Ed.D. Address: 21388 Oakcrest Drive, New Berlin, Wisconsin 53151.

BENFORD, BENJAMIN J II Occupation: Administrative Assistant to Principal, Coach. Education: B.A., Olivet College; M.A., Oakland University. Address: 264 Frazier, River Rouge, Michigan 48218.

BENIS, MAX Occupation: Allergist, Immunologist, Professor. Education: B.S. magna cum laude; M.D. honors. Address: 10500-4 Larwin, Chatsworth, California 91311.

BEN-ISRAEL, ADI Occupation: Professor of Mathematics, H. Fletcher Brown. Education: Ph.D., Northwestern University, 1962; M.Sc., 1959; B.Sc., 1955. Address: 3 Pagoda Lane, Newark, Delaware 19711.

BENJAMIN, RUBY R Occupation: Psychoanalytic Psychotherapist. Education: Ed.D., M.A. Certified Psychoanalytic Psychotherapist. Address: 121 Madison

Avenue, New York, New York 10016.

BENNER, DAVID GORDON Occupation: Professor of Psychology. Education: B.A., McMaster University; M.A., York University; Ph.D., York University. Address: 1206 East Prairie Avenue, Wheaton, Illinois 60187

BENNER, KATHY ANNE Occupation: Registered Nurse, Community Education Coordinator. Education: R.N. Diploma. Address: 528 Bonnie Bell Lane, Birmingham, Alabama 35210.

BENNETT, BERNICE McLEMORE Occupation: Ladies Fashions, Retail Sales, Church School Superintendent. Education: M. Cosmetology. Address: Route 1, Box 82, Duncan, South Carolina 29334.

BENNETT, DENNIS RAY Occupation: Special Feature News Reporter (TV). Education: Virginia State University. Address: 1111 Park Avenue #302, Baltimore, Maryland 21201.

BENNETT, FRANK WEST Occupation: Financial Consultant. Education: Student, George Washington University, University of North Carolina-Chapel Hill; M.A. Economics/Finance, Sussex (England) University of Technology, 1975. Address: Brevard Road, Arden, North Carolina 28704.

BENNETT, GEORGE A Occupation: Nuclear Engineer. Education: B.Ch.E., Syracuse University; M.S.Ch.E., Case Western Reserve University; S.M., Massachusetts Institute of Technology. Address: 27W711 South Lane, Naperville, Illinois 60540.

BENNETT, JOHN M Occupation: Poet, Publisher, Word Artist. Education: B.A., M.A., C.C.L.A.S., C.Phil., Ph.D., I.S. Address: 137 Leland Avenue, Columbia, Ohio 43214.

BENNETT, LAWRENCE A Occupation: Director, Office of Program Evaluation, National Institute of Justice. Education: A.B., M.A., Ph.D. Address: 8380 Greensboro Drive, McLean, Virginia 22102.

BENOIT, PAUL S Occupation: Computer Specialist. Education: B.S. Business Administration. Address: 12007 Aspenwood Lane, Laurel, Maryland 20708.

BENSON, JOAN Occupation: Concert Artist, Adjunct Professor. Education: M.Mus., B.Mus. Address: 2795 Central Boulevard, Eugene, Oregon 97403.

BENT, ALAN EDWARD Occupation: College Professor; Administrator. Education: B.S., M.A., M.A., Ph.D., M.B.A. (in progress). Address: 1004C Celestial Street, Cincinnati, Ohio 45202.

BENTLEY, EDWIN M Occupation: Liability Adjustor, Farmers Insurance. Education: A.A. Pierce Junior College; B.S. Business Administrator. Address: 8101 Langdon Avenue #41, Van Nuys, California 91406.

BENTZEL, CHARLES H Occupation: President, Chief Executive Officer. Education: B.A., B.S., D.C.S. Address: 28637 Dapper Dan, Boerne, Texas 78006.

BENZ, EDWARD J JR Occupation: Associate Professor of Medicine and Genetics. Education: Doctor of Medicine, Harvard University, 1973; Bachelor of Arts, Princeton University, 1968. Address: 57 Cindy Lane, Guilford, Connecticut 06437.

BENZINGER, RAYMOND BURDETTE Occupation: Attorney at Law, Professor of Law. Education: Bachelor of Science, Carnegie Mellon University, 1962; Doctor of Law 1971, Master of Laws, 1973, Georgetown University Law Center. Address: 5509 Ivor Street, Springfield, Virginia 22151.

BERA, FRANCES S Occupation: Sales Representative, Beechcraft West. Education: A.T.P., Commercial Instrument, Pilot. Address: 10420

Briarcliff Way, San Diego, California 92131.

BERALL, FRANK STEWART Occupation: Attorney at Law. Education: B.S., J.D., Yale University; LL.M., New York University. Address: 9 Penwood Road, Bloomfield, Connecticut 06033.

BERENDZEN, RICHARD Occupation: University President. Education: B.S., Massachusetts Institute of Technology; M.A., Ph.D., Harvard University. Address: 3300 Nebraska Avenue, North West, Washington, D.C. 20016.

BERGER, EDMOND L Occupation: Senior Theoretical Physicist. Education: B.S., Massachusetts Institute of Technology, 1961; Ph.D. Princeton University, 1965. Address: 5711 Dearborn Parkway, Downers Grove, Illinois 60516.

BERGER, HOWARD MARTIN Occupation: President, Robotix Corporation. Education: Ph.D., M.S., California State Polytechnic University; B.S., University of Michigan. Address: 2108 Via Fernandez, Palos Verdes Estates, California 90274.

BERGER, LARRY ALLEN Occupation: Financial Planner. Education: B.S. Accounting, C.P.A., C.F.P. Address: 3645 Rosewood Lane, Plymouth, Minnesota 55441.

BERGER, RAYMOND H JR Occupation: Manager, Corporate Planning. Education: B.S. Accounting, University of Maryland; M.S. Finance, George Washington University. Address: 801 Yorkshire Road, Bethlehem, Pennsylvania 18017.

BERGER, SAUL H Occupation: Safety Engineer. Education: B.S. General Management. Address: 24 Michigan Drive, Hicksville, New York 11801.

BERGER, VINCENT F Education: B.S., University of Maryland, 1965; M.S., University of Oklahoma, 1967; Ph.D., University of Oklahoma, 1968. Address: 502 Woodcrest Drive, Mechanicsburg, Pennsylvania 17055.

BERGSTEN, C FRED Occupation: Director, Institute for International Economics. Education: A.B., M.A., Ph.D. Address: 4106 Sleepy Hollow Road, Annandale, Virginia 22003.

BERGT, GREGORY PAUL Occupation: Chemist, Consultant. Education: B.S. Address: 200 Oakwood Circle, Belle Plaine, Minnesota 56011.

BERING, EDGAR ANDREW JR Occupation: Private Practice. Education: A.B., University of Utah, 1927; M.D., Harvard University, 1941. Address: Four Talbottown Lane, Easton, Maryland 21601.

BERK, KAREN MAE Occupation: Administrator. Education: B.A., University of California at Los Angeles. Address: 2280 Hurley, #19, Sacramento, California 95825.

BERKMAN, SYLVIA L Occupation: Retired Professor, Writer. Education: Ph.D., M.A., A.B. Address: 21 Forest, Cambridge, Massachusetts 02140.

BERLA, PETER A Occupation: Advertising Manager, Saab-Scania. Education: B.A., Cornell University. Address: 9 Prospect Avenue, Darien, Connecticut 06820.

BERLIN, STEVEN R Occupation: Financial Executive. Education: M.B.A., University of Wisconsin; B.S. Business Administration, Duquesne University. Address: 230 East 19th Street, Tulsa, Oklahoma 74102.

BERMAR, CLAIRE G Occupation: Writer, Editor, Public Relations. Education: B.A., Barnard College. Address: 52 Riverside Drive, New York, New York 1024.

BERMAN, MARLENE OSCAR Occupation: Professor Neurology and Psychiatry. Education: B.A., M.A., Ph.D. Address: 115 Cotton Street, Newton, Massachusetts 02158.

BERMAN, MURIEL M Occupation: Vice President, Philip I. Berman; Secretary, Philip & Muriel Berman Foundation; Secretary-Treasurer; Member of the Board. Education: Attended University of Pittsburgh and Carnegie Tech University; Music Appreciation and Art History at University of Pittsburgh Graduate School; Comparative Religion and History at Cedar Crest College; Philosophy at Muhlenberg College. Address: 20 Hundred Nottingham Road, Allentown, Pennsylvania 18103.

BERMAN, PHILIP I Education: L.L.D., Ursinus College, 1968; Ph.D., Hebrew University, 1979. Address: 20 Hundred Nottingham Road, Allentown, Pennsylvania 18103.

BERMEO, FRANKLIN Occupation: Assistant School Superintendent. Education: Ph.D. Education, M.A. Lic. Th. Address: 4423 North Ashland Avenue, Lake Shore, South Dakota.

BERNER, JEFF Occupation: Computer Educator, Book Author. Education: B.A. English, Philosophy. Address: Post Office Box 5503, Mill Valley, California 94942.

BERNEY, ROBERT E Occupation: Professor of Economics. Education: B.A., M.A., Washington State University; M.S., Ph.D., University of Wisconsin. Address: North West 1582 Turner Drive, Apartment #11, Pullman, Washington 99163.

BERNS, ELLEN SCHIMMEL Occupation: Professional Interior Designer. Education: Independent Studies in Life Drawing and Pastel: National Academy of Design, New York; Art Students League, 1980-82; Parsons/School of Design, 1978-79; El Centro College, Dallas, Texas, 1975-78; B.A., University of Texas, 1970. Address: 1365 York Avenue, Apartment 35H, New York, New York 10021.

BERNSTEIN, ABRAHAM Occupation: New York State Senator, Attorney. Education: B.S.S., LL.B., J.S.D. Address: 3333 Henry Hudson Parkway, Bronx, New York 10463.

BERNSTEIN, BIANCA L Occupation: Professor, Psychologist, Author, Consultant. Education: B.A., University of California-Berkeley, 1970; M.Ed. 1972, Ph.D. 1975, University of California-Santa Barbara, 1972. Address: 3770 Wedgewood, Birmingham, Michigan 48010.

BERNSTEIN, CHARLES Occupation: Poet, Writer, Essayist. Education: A.B., Harvard College. Address: 464 Amsterdam Avenue, New York, New York 10024.

BERNSTEIN, ISADORE ABRAHAM Occupation: Biochemist, Educator, The University of Michigan. Education: A.B., The Johns Hopkins University, 1941; Ph.D. Biochemistry, Western Reserve University, 1952. Address: 1200 Arlington Boulevard, Ann Arbor, Michigan 48104.

BERNSTEIN, STELLA MAINE Occupation: Co-Owner, P&S Associates. Education: A.A. Address: 717 McCeney Avenue, Silver Spring, Maryland 20901.

BERNSTEN, RICHARD H Occupation: Economist. Education: Ph.D. Address: 17 Woodbridge, Conway, Arkansas.

BERRY, CAROLYN Occupation: Executive Director, Handicapped Activities Unlimited. Education: B.A. Painting, University of Missouri, Columbia, Missouri; C.A. Teaching Credentials, Special Education. Address: 78 Cuesta Vista, Monterey, California 93940.

BERRYMAN, JACK WILLIAM Occupation: Associate Professor; Editor. Education: B.S. Lock Haven State College; M.S. University of Massachusetts. Address: 12924 133rd Place, North East, Kirkland, Washington 98034.

BERRYMAN, KARAN A Occupation: Director of the Library. Education: A.A., Andrew College; B.S., Auburn University; M.S.L.S., University of North Carolina-Chapel Hill. Address: 111 West Harris Street, Cuthbert, Georgia 31740.

BERSTEIN, IRVING A Occupation: Biotechnology Executive and Scientist. Education: Sc.B. Chemistry, Brown University; Ph.D. Chemistry, Cornell University. Address: 42 Buckman Drive, Lexington, Massachusetts 02173.

BERTA, JOSEPH MICHEL Occupation: Professor of Music. Education: B.A., M.A., University of California-Santa Barbara. Address: 55 Ver Planck, Geneva, New York 14456.

BERTANI, CHARLIE L Occupation: Consultant, Labor Management. Address: 1330 Del Norte, Houston, Texas 77018.

BERTRAM, JEAN DE SALES Occupation: Professor of Theatre Arts, Performing Artist. Education: Ph.D., Stanford University, 1963; M.A., University of Minnesota, 1951; B.A., University of North Carolina, 1942. Address: 512 Arballo Drive, San Francisco, California 94132.

BESHOAR, WILMA F Occupation: Investments. Education: Business Graduate, Joliet Junior College. Address: 330 Sunset, LaGrange, Illinois 60525.

BEST, MARY SUE Occupation: Writer, Public Relations. Education: B.A., M.A. Address: 5402 Washington Boulevard, Indianapolis, Indiana 46220.

BESTOR, CHARLES Occupation: Composer, Educator. Education: B.A., Swarthmore College, 1948; B.S., Juilliard School of Music, 1951; M.Mus., University of Illinois, 1952; D.M.A., University of Colorado, 1974. Address: 19 Birchcroff Lane, Amherst, Massachusetts 01002.

BETHEL, LEONARD LESLIE Occupation: Chairperson, Department of Africana Studies, Rutgers University. Education: B.A., M.Div., M.A., D.Ed. Address: 146 Parkside Road, Plainfield, New Jersey 07060.

BETKOSKI, LEONARD ROBERT Occupation: Guidance Counselor. Education: B.A., M.A. Address: 290 Belles Road, Wanamie, Pennsylvania 18634.

BETTS, ERVIN LEE Occupation: Psychologist. Education: Ph.D., New York University; M.A., Baylor University; M.Div., Southwestern Seminary; B.A., University of New Mexico. Address: 25 Garner Street, Norwalk, Connecticut 06854.

BETTS, EUGENE K Occupation: Physician. Education: B.S., Dickinson College, 1964; M.D., The Bowman Gray School of Medicine of Wake Forest University, 1968. Address: 108 Rock Rose Lane, Radnor, Pennsylvnaia 19087.

BETTS, VIRGINIA TROTTER Occupation: Academic Chair, Associate Professor of Nursing. Education: B.S.N., M.S.N., J.D. Address: 4907 Roselawn Circle, Nashville, Tennessee 37215.

BETZAK, IDA Occupation: Artist. Education: New England Conservatory, New York University and American School of Art. Address: 315 West 57 Street, New York, New York 10019.

BEUTLER, LARRY E Occupation: Professor; Psychologist. Education: B.S., M.S., Ph.D. Address: 2249 East Edison, Tucson, Arizona 85719.

BEVAN, MARY VIRGINIA Occupation: Associate Professor; H.P.E.R. Education: A.B. Physical Education/English-Speech, Kansas Wesleyan, 1956; M.S. Physical Education/English, Kansas State University, 1965. Address: 2264 Leland Way, Salina, Kansas 67401.

BEVERSLUIS, LINDA ANNE Occupation:

President, Beversluis, McKee & Associates, Inc. Education: High School Graduate, Eastern Christian High School. Address: 41 Walray Avenue, North Haledon, New Jersey 07508.

BHALLA, AMAR S Occupation: Research Professor. Education. Ph.D. Solid State Science. Address: 1101 West College Avenue, State College, Pennsylvania 16801.

BHANGOO, MAHENDRA S Occupation: Professor. Education: Ph.D. Soil Sciences. Address: 3412 West Palo Alto, Fresno, California 93711.

BHATT, JAGDISH J Occupation: Professor of Geology and Oceanography. Education: Ph.D. Address: 11 Midlands Drive, East Greenwich, Rhode Island 02818.

BHUGRA, SATNAM SINGH Occupation: College Educator. Education: Doctor of Education. Address: 1311 Redleaf Lane, East Lansing, Michigan 48823.

BHUSHAN, BHARAT Occupation: Advisory Engineer. Education: B.S. Mechanical Engineering, M.S. Mechanical Engineering, M.S. Mechanics. Address: 6500 North Pontatoc Road, Tucson, Arizona 85718.

BIAGGIO, MARY KAY Occupation: Associate Professor, Director of Clinical Training, Indiana State University. Education: Ph.D. Psychology. Address: Psychology Department, Indiana State University, Terre Haute, Indiana 47809.

BICKHAUS, JAMES T Occupation: General Manager, Carter Automotive Division, St. Louis, Missouri. Education: B.S.M.E., M.B.A., A.M.P. Address: 13010 Conway Estates Drive, St. Louis, Missouri 63141.

BICKNELL-JOHNSON, MARJORIE R Occupation: Teacher, Mathematics, Santa Clara High School. Education: Bachelor of Arts, Master of Arts, Doctor of Philosophy in Mathematics. Address: 665 Fairlaine Avenue, Santa Clara, California 95051.

BIDDLE, BRUCE JESSE Occupation: Professor Psychology and Sociology, Director Center for Research in Social Behavior. Education: A.B. Mathematics, Ph.D. Social Pschology. Address: 924 Yale Street, Columbia, Missouri 65203.

BIDLAKE, PIERCE W Occupation: Safety Engineer. Education: B.S. Education. Address: 3956 Pawnee, Liverpool, New York 13088.

BIDWELL, DOROTHY KAY Occupation: Officer and Director of Jaycor. Education: A.A. Business, Certification in Legal Assistants. Address: 727 Sapphire Street, #407, San Diego, California 92109.

BIEBER, ROBERT M Occupation: Consultant. Education: Master's Degree, New York University. Address: 26 Forshay Road, Monsey, New York 10952.

BIEGER, ELAINE Occupation: Teacher, Trainer, Reading Consultant. Education: Ph.D. Address: 157 Downey Drive, Tenafly, New Jersey 07670.

BIEHL, FRANCIS W Occupation: Consulting Engineer. Education: B.S.M.E., Marquette University; M.S.M.E., Wayne University. Address: N66 W121659 Ravine Drive, Menomonee Falls, Wisconsin 53051.

BIESENTHAL, W LEROY Occupation: Clergyman. Education: B.A., B.D., Doctor of Letters, Concordia College, 1984. Address: 1102 Cameo Court, St. Louis, Missouri 63131.

BIESTER, JOHN LOUIS Occupation: Retired; Writer. Education: B.S., Beloit College; M.S., Ph.D. Syracuse University. Address: 1737 Arrowhead Drive, Beloit, Wisconsin 53511.

BIGBEE, DANIEL E SR Occupation: Campus Project Coordinator/Information Programs. Education: B.S., M.S., Oklahoma State University; Ph.D., Michigan State University. Address: 521 Birchwood Drive, Lincoln, Nebraska 68510.

BIGG, DONALD M Occupation: Chemical Engineer. Education: Ph.D., University of Massachusetts; M.S., University of Rochester; B.S., Catholic University. Address: 3693 Tillbury Avenue, Columbus, Ohio 43220.

BILEK, FLORENCE R Occupation: Registered Nurse. Education: B.S., C.I.C. Address: 10740 Valley View, Sagamore Hills, Ohio 44067.

BILLET, ARTHUR B Occupation: Honeywell Principal Engineer. Education: Aeronautical Engineering, University of Michigan, 1941. Address: 2322 Via Siena, La Jolla, California 92037.

BILLIAS, GEORGE ATHAN Occupation: Jacob and Frances Hiatt Professor of History. Education: A.B., Bates College, 1948; M.A. 1949, Ph.D. 1958, Columbia University. Address: 23 Minthorne Street, Worcester, Massachusetts 01602.

BILLIG, ROBERT M Occupation: Clinical Psychotherapist. Education: B.A., M.S., M.S.W. Address: 10 Park Terrace, East, New York, New York 10034.

BILLIG, THOMAS C Occupation: Editor, Publisher. Education: B.S.B.A. summa cum laude, Northwestern University, 1956. Address: 3445 Zenith Avenue, South, Minneapolis, Minnesota 55416.

BILLIMEK, THOMAS EWALD Occupation: Professor of Psychology. Education: M.A. Psychology, 1971; B.A. Psychology, 1968. Address: 8914 Melinda Court, San Antonio, Texas 78240.

BILLINGS, CHARLES KELSO JR Occupation: Associate Chairman, Department of Psychiatry. Education: B.A., M.D. Address: 251 Walter Road, River Ridge, Louisiana 70123.

BILLINGS, CHARLES REEMS Occupation: Clinical Psychologist. Education: Ph.D. Psychology, California School of Professional Psychology, Berkeley, California, 1974; M.A. Educational Administration, San Francisco State University, San Francisco, 1971; M.A. Psychology, San Francisco State University, San Francisco, 1967; B.A. Psychology, San Francisco State University, 1965; A.A., College of Marin, Kentfield, California, 1963. Address: 60 East Sir Francis Drake Boulevard, Wood Island Offices, Suite 309, Larkspur, California 94939.

BILON, JOHN J Occupation: Professor and Director, Hotel and Restaurant Management Program, Harrisonburg, Virginia. Education: B.S., M.S., Cornell University. Address: 970 Star Crest Drive, Harrisonburg, Virginia 22801.

BINGHAM, ROBERT EVAN Occupation: Attorney at Law. Education: A.B., Amherst College; J.D., Harvard Law School. Address: 2027 Lyndway Road, Lyndhurst, Ohio 44121.

BINGS, WILLIAM THOMAS Occupation: Executive Vice President. Education: B.S. Commerce; M.B.A., School of Mortgage Banking. Address: 8723 Reichs Ford Road, Frederick, Maryland 21701.

BINSTOCK, ADELAIDE M Occupation: Director, Office of Management Budget. Education: B.A., M.A. Address: 1191 Clubhouse Drive, Aptos, California 95003.

BIRD, MERLE KENDALL Occupation: Director of Employee and Public Relations. Education: B.S.Ed., M.S.Ed. Address: 601 Cress Creek, Crystal Lake, Illinois 60014.

BIRKELAND, CHARLES EVANS Occupation: Professor of Marine Biology. Education: Ph.D. in Zoology. Address: North 28, Casas de Serenidad, Yona, Guam 96914.

BIRKENRUTH, HARRY H Occupation: Vice President, Finance. Education: B.A., M.B.A. Address: 81 Ball Hill Road, Storrs, Connecticut 06268.

BIRKIMER, DONALD LEO Occupation: Technical Director. Education: B.S.C.E., Ohio University; M.S., Ph.D., University of Cincinnati. Address: 1291 Seybolt Avenue, Camarillo, California 93010.

BIRNHOLZ, JASON CORDELL Occupation: Physician; Educator Researcher; Consultant. Education: B.S., Union College; M.D., Johns Hopkins University. Address: 440 Moraine Road, Highland Park, Illinois 60035.

BIRSTEIN, ANN Occupation: Writer. Education: B.A., Queens College. Address: Apartment 27 J West, 1623 Third Avenue, New York, New York 10128.

BISHOP, ROBERT Occupation: Museum Director, New York. Education: Ph.D. American Folk Art Studies. Address: 213 West 22 Street, New York, New York 10011.

BISHOP, ROBERT H Occupation: Investment Broker. Education: B.A. Philosophy, M.A. Higher Education. Address: 321 Bridge Street, Waynesburg, Pennsylvania 15370.

BISHOP, (INA) SUE MARQUIS Occupation: Nursing Educator; Psychiatric Nursing. Education: R.N., B.S.N., M.S.N., Ph.D. Address: 1375 Neitzel Road, Mooresville, Indiana 46158.

BISSELL, RICHARD MERVIN JR Occupation: Self-Employed Consultant. Education: B.A. 1932, Ph.D 1939, M.A. 1949, Yale University. Address: 22 Mountain Road, Farmington, CT 06032.

BITTERMAN, MARY G F Occupation: Director, Institute of Culture and Communication, Honolulu, Hawaii. Education: B.A., M.A., Ph.D., History and Philosophy. Address: 229 Kaalawai Place, Honolulu, Hawaii 96816.

BITTERS, ROBERT GEORGE Occupation: Executive Vice President. Education: Business Administration. Address: 5440 Quakertown Avenue, Woodland Hills, California 91364.

BITTNER, JANET S Occupation: Public Administrator. Education: B.S., Fulbright Study in India. Address: 6417 Dillon Road, Austell, Georgia 30001.

BIXLER, ANDREW L M Occupation: President of Consultant Associates. Education: B.S. Chemical Engineering, 1933; M.S. Chemistry, 1935; Ph.D. Chemistry, 1937. Address: 7301 South 70th East Avenue, Tulsa, Oklahoma 74133.

BLACK, CHARLIE J Occupation: Mathematics Resource Teacher. Education: B.S. Sec. Education, Masters Business and Public Administration. Address: 6435 18th Street North West, Washington, D.C. 20012.

BLACK, LOUIS ECKERT Occupation: President, Avondale Travel Bureau. Education: B.A., College of Wooster; M.A., University of Florida. Address: 3530 St. Johns Avenue, Jacksonville, Florida 32205.

BLACK, PERCY Occupation: Professor of Psychology, Pace University, Pleasantville, New York. Education: B.Sc., M.Sc., Ph.D. Address: 29 Cross Hill Avenue, Yonkers, New York 10703.

BLACK, PERRY Occupation: Professor and Chairman, Department Neurosurgery, Hahnemann University, Philadelphia, Pennsylvania. Education: M.D., C.M. Address: 22 Summit Street, Philadelphia, Pennsylvania.

BLACK, ROBERT P Occupation: Central Banker. Education: B.A., M.A., Ph.D. Address: 10 Dahlgren Road, Richmond, Virginia 23233.

BLACK, WILLIAM ALAN Occupation: Corporate Controller. Education: B.S. Accounting, M.B.A. Accounting. Address: 409 Elizabeth Avenue, Ramsey, New Jersey 07446.

BLACKBURN, JOHN LEWIS Occupation: Retired Consulting Engineer. Education: B.S. Electrical Engineering, University of Illinois, 1935. Address: 21816 8th Place West, Bethell, Washington 98021.

BLACKMAN, FLOYD J Occupation: Banking. Education: B.S. Business Administration. Address: 136 Chillingham Road, Irmo, South Carolina 29063.

BLACKMAN, JESSICA LYNN Occupation: Attorney, Legislative Director. Education: B.A. English/Public Communication, J.D. Address: 1105 Belleview Boulevard, Alexandria, Virginia 22307.

BLACKMAN-WEISS, ALISON Occupation: Freelance Communications Specialist. Education: U.P.A., New York University; B.A., Syracuse University. Address: 135 Willow Street, Brooklyn, New York 112101.

BLACKWELL, ROGER D Occupation: Professor, Department of Marketing, Ohio State University; Consulting Associate and Director of Management Horizons, Incorporated. Education: Ph.D., Northwestern University; M.S., B.S. University of Missouri. Address: 1447 Friar Lane, Columbus, Ohio 43221.

BLAGG, JAMES DOUGLAS JR Occupation: Director, Graduate Program in Allied Health Education. Address: 341 Colonia Boulevard, Colonia, New Jersey 07067.

BLAICH, ROBERT M Occupation: Chiropractic Physician, Researcher, Educator. Education: B.A., B.S., D.C. Address: 2217 North Elizabeth Pueblo, Colorado 81003.

BLAINE, DEVON Occupation: Owner and Founder of Public Relations; Advertising/Marketing Firm, Log Angeles, California. Address: 7309 Franklin, #306, Los Angeles, California 90028.

BLAIR, JOHN R Occupation: Professor of Educational Psychology, Eastern Michigan University, Ypsilanti, Michigan. Education: B.S., M.S., Ph.D. Address: 2329 South Circle Drive, Ann Arbor, Michigan 48103.

BLAIR, STANLEY SCOTT Occupation: Student. Education: B.A. English and French, Gardner-Webb College, Boiling Springs, North Carolina, 1984. Address: 5 Hawkins Lane, Willingboro, New Jersey 08046.

BLAIR, WILLIAM TRAVIS (BUD) Occupation: President, Ohio Chamber of Commerce. Education: B.A., Ohio Wesleyan University. Address: 138 West Cooke Road, Columbus, Ohio 43214.

BLAIS, BERNARD R Occupation: Force Medical Officer. Education: M.D. Address: 15017 Emory Lane, Rockville, Maryland 20853.

BLAKE, BARBARA KING Occupation: Founder, Minister, Hillside Chapel and Truth Center, International, Atlanta, Georgia. Education: Honorary D.D., M.S.W., B.S., Candidate for Ed.D. Address: 1590 Adams Drive, South West, Atlanta, Georgia 30311.

BLAKE, GEORGE ROWLAND Occupation: Professor, University of Minnesota, St. Paul. Education: Ph.D., Ohio State University. Address: 1579 Burton Street, St. Paul, Minnesota 55108.

BLAKE, JAMES JOSEPH, JR Occupation: Executive Director, Public Housing Management. Education: B.S. Economics, Worcester State College, Address: 207 South Meadow Road, Lancaster, Massachusetts 01523.

BLAKE, RUBY M Occupation: Chairman, International Peace Gardens. Education: High School

Graduate. Address: 1575 East Parkway Avenue, Salt Lake City, Utah 84106.

BLAKE, SALLY MIRLISS Occupation: Retired. Education: B.S. Journalism, M.A. Creative Writing. Address: 200 Julia Avenue, Mill Valley, California 94941

BLAKELY, MARTHA CROSS Occupation: Pianist, Accompanist. Education: B.M. Address: 320 Kemp Lane, Chesapeake, Virginia 23325.

BLAKELY, WILLIAM H JR Occupation: Manager, Employee Relations, Engelhard Industries.

BLAKEMAN, BETH R Occupation: News Director, WJYO-FM. Education: B.A. Address: P.O. Box 16233, Orlando, Florida.

BLANCHARD, B EVERARD Occupation: President, Villa Educational Research Associates. Education: B.S., M.S., M.A., Ps.D., D.D., Ph.D. Address: 315 Dee Ct., Bloomingdale, Illinois 60108.

BLANCHET, BERTRAND Occupation: Bishop. Education: B.Sc., L.Th. Address: 172 Sacques Cartier Gasie, Que Can, Gociro.

BLANCK, ANDREW R Occupation: Scientist, Engineer, Businessman. Education: Ph.D., M.A., B.A. Address: 89 Prospect Place, Rutherford, New Jersey 07070.

BLAND-SCHRICKER, LAUREL LeMIEUX Occupation: Educator, Author. Education: A.A, Anchorage Community College, 1966; Ed.B, University of Alaska, 1968; M.A., 1969. Address: 1921 West 17th Street, Kennewick, Washington.

BLANK, FRANKLIN Occupation: Writer. Education: B.B.A., A.A. Address: 5477 Cedonia Avenue, Baltimore, Maryland.

BLANK, GORDON C Occupation: President, Adirondack Community College. Education: B.S., Towson State College; M.Ed., University of Miami; Ed.D, Indiana University. Address: Route 1, Box 267, Summit Lane, Glens Falls, New York 12801.

BLANK, MARION S Occupation: Professor, Psychology. Education: B.A., M.S. Education, Ph.D. Address: 171 Van Nostrand Avenue, Englewood, New Jesey 07631.

BLANK, MARTIN Occupation: Research, Teaching, Editing. Education: Ph.D., Columbia University, 1957; Ph.D., Cantab, 1959. Address: 171 Van Nostrand Avenue, Englewood, New Jersey 07631.

BLANKENSHIP, LYTLE H Occupation: Professor, Wildlife Research Scientist. Education: B.S., Texas A&M University; M.S., University of Minnesota; Ph.D., Michigan State University. Address: P.O. Box 5220, Uvale, Texas 78801.

BLANKSTEIN, MARY FREEMAN Occupation: Violinist, Teacher, Performer. Education: B.S., Juilliard School of Music; M.M., University of Maine. Address: 116-37 Union Turnpike, Forest Hills, New York 11375.

BLANTON, FRED JR Occupation: Lawyer. Education: B.A., LL.B., J.D., M.L. Address: 1912 K.C. Dement Avenue, Fultondale, Alabama 35068.

BLASCO, ALFRED JOSEPH Occupation: Bank Executive. Education: Ph.D., Avila College, 1969. Address: 11705 Central Street, Kansas City, Missouri 64114.

BLASHEK, ROBERT D Occupation: Executive Vice President, Ventura Associates. Education: Business Administration, Ohio State University, 1947. Address: Weavers Hills 10E, Greenwich, Connecticut 06830.

BLASKO, STEFAN Occupation: Retired. District Superintendent of Schools in Slovakia; Slovak Member of Parliament in Prague. Education: State Teacher's College, 1930-35. Address: 60 Crescent Terrace, Belleville, New Jersey 07109.

BLASS, ROSANNE JOHNSON Occupation: Associate Professor of Education, Allegheny College Instruction Center, The Alcazar, Cleveland Heights, Ohio. Education: B.S. Elementary Education, M.S. Curriculum, Ed.D. Curriculum and Instruction. Address: 1413 Grantleigh Road, South Euclid, Ohio 44121.

BLASSINGILLE, BENJAMIN Occupation: Psychiatrist, Neurologist. Education: M.D. Address: 6031 Monticello Drive, Montgomery, Alabama 36117.

BLATT, SIDNEY J Occupation: Professor. Education: Ph.D. Address: 28 Mulberry Road, Woodbridge, Connecticut 06525.

BLATTER, FRANK E Occupation: Executive Vice President, United Banks of Colorado. Education: B.S. Accounting, Graduate School, University of Colorado. Address: 7188 Ammons Street, Arvada, Colorado 80004.

BLAU, FRANCINE D Occupation: Professor of Economics and Industrial Relations. Education: B.S., Cornell University, 1966; M.A. 1969, Ph.D. 1975, Harvard University. Address: 504 East Armory Avenue, Champaign, Illinois 61820.

BLAUER, AARON CLYDE Occupation: Associate Professor, Biology at Snow College for Forrest Services, Ephraim, Utah. Education: M.S. Address: 295 North 300 East Street, Box 16-5, Ephraim, Utah 84627.

BLAUER, HAROLD WOODBURY Occupation: Educator, Elementary Principal. Education: B.S., M.S., Education Specialist. Address: 608 West 21 Street, Burley, Idaho 83318.

BLEJER, HÉCTOR P Occupation: Occupational And Environmental Medicine. Education: B.Sc., M.D., C.M., D.I.H. Address: 4477 Wilshire Bl.-207, Los Angeles, CA 90010.

BLEND, HENRIETTA BORONSTEIN Occupation: Instructional Supervisor. Education: Bachelor of Science in Education, University of Houston; Master of Education, University of Houston; Doctor of Education, Pacific West. Address: 10419 Green Willow Drive, Houston, Texas 77035.

BLEVINS, JOE F JR Occupation: Radio Broadcasting, Operations Manager, WDRV Radio. Education: B.S. Business Administration, Appalachian State University. Address: 1943 East Broad Street, Statesville, North Carolina.

BLISS, S W Occupation: Registered Nurse. Education: R.N.C., C.C.R.N. Address: 135 Lorreta Drive, Dayton, Ohio 45415.

BLOBEL, GÜNTER KLAUS-JOACHIM Occupation: Professor of Cell Biology. Education: M.D., Ph.D. Address: 1100 Park Avenue, New York, New York 10021.

BLOCK, JOSEPH DOUGLAS Occupation: Lawyer and Utility Executive. Education: B.A., Wisconsin University, 1939; J.D., University of Wisconsin, 1941; LL.M., Harvard University, 1946. Address: 920 Park Avenue, New York, New York 10028.

BLOCKER, EUNICE C Occupation: Teacher. Education: M.A. Address: 407 Ruth Street, Lancaster, South Carolina 29720.

BLOMQUIST-HESS, BRITA L Occupation: President, Blomquist, Hess & Associates, Inc. Education: B.S.N., M.S.N. Address: 14 E. Washington Street, Orlando, Florida 32801.

BLOOD, ELIZABETH REID Occupation: Research Scientist. Education: B.S. General Science, M.S. Biology, Ph.D. Ecology. Address: P.O. Box 1355, Pawleys Island, South Carolina 29442.

BLOOM, FREDI BARBARA Occupation:

Probation Officer, Singer, Travel Consultant. Education: B.A., University of Wisconsin-Madison; M.A., John F. Kennedy University. Address: 27 Claus Drive, Fairfax, California 94930.

BLOOM, HERBERT J Occupation: Director Continuing Medical Education, Sinai Hospital of Detroit. Education: D.D.S., M.D., Ph.D. Address: 3066 Middlebelt, Orchard Lake, Michigan 48033.

BLOOM, JANET K Occupation: Writer, Teacher od Eidetic Imagery. Education: B.A., M.F.A. Address: 6425 Broadway 7C, Riverdale, Bronx, New York 10471.

BLOOM, MIRIAM KRASNICK Occupation: Director of a Psychoanalytic Institute; Psychoanalyst in Private Practice, Boulder, Colorado. Education: B.S.; M.A. Psychology, University of Illinois. Address: 2240 Linden Avenue, Boulder, Colorado 80302.

BLOOM, STEPHEN E Occupation: Research, Teacher. Education: B.S., M.S., Ph.D. Address: 600 Warren Road, Ithaca, New York 14850.

BLOSSER, PATRICIA ELLEN Occupation: Professor, Science Education. Education: B.A.. M.A., M.A. Liberal Studies, Ph.D. Address: 2606 Brandon Road, Columbus, Ohio 43221.

BLUE, LEON ROBY Occupation: Cardiologist. Education: B.S., Harding University; M.D., University of Arkansas Medical Science. Address: 16 Country Club, Searcy, Arkansas 72143.

BLUHM, HEINZ Occupation: Professor. Education: B.A., M.A., Ph.D., M.A., Yale University. Address: Boston College, Chestnut Hill, Massachusetts 02167.

BLUM, DOROTHY JEAN SCRIVNER Occupation: Director of Guidance. Education: B.A., Midland College; M.S., University of Nebraska; Ed.D., University of Virginia. Address: 7412 Calico Court, Springfield, Virginia 22153.

BLUM, ROSALIND F Occupation: Psychologist. Education: M.A., Teachers College; Columbia University. Address: 40 West 86 Street, New York, New York 10024.

BLUMBERG, ARNOLD Occupation: Professor of History. Education: B.S., 1947; M.S., 1948; Ph.D. Modern European History, 1952. Address: 3901 Glen Avenue, Baltimore, Maryland 21215.

BLUMBERG, THELMA L Occupation: Psychologist, Author. Education: M.A. Address: 3901 Glen Avenue, Baltimore, Maryland 21215.

BLUMENKRANTZ, STEVEN JAY Occupation: Attorney, Certified Public Accountant, Assistant Professor, Author. Education: B.S., J.D.. Address: R.D. 1, Box 213, Schenevus, New York 12155.

BLUMENTHAL, DANIEL S Occupation: Physician, Medical Educator. Address: B.A., M.D. Address: 445 Clifton Road, Atlanta, Georgia 30307.

BLUMENTHAL, W MICHAEL Occupation: Chairman of the Board of Directors, Burroughs Corporation, 1981. Education: B.Sc. Business Administration, University of California-Berkeley, 1951; M.A. 1953, Ph.D. 1956, Princeton University. Address: Burroughs Corporation, Burroughs Place, Corporate Communications Division, Detroit, Michigan 48232.

BLUMSTEIN, JAMES F Occupation: Professor of Law, Vanderbilt Law School. Education: LL.B., Yale Law School, 1970; M.A. Economics, Yale University, 1970; B.A. Economics. Address: 2113 Hampton Avenue, Nashville, Tennessee 37215.

BLY, JAMES H Occupation: Physicist-Engineer, Design & Technology of Industrial Electron Beam Accelerators & Applications. Education: Physics and Chemistry, University of Chicago, 1940. Address: 56 Fieldstone Drive, Syosset, New York 11791.

BOAM, GARY CARL Occupation: Director Administration, Corporate Planning. Education: B.S., M.S., D.P.A. Address: 111 Terrace Drive, Moscow, Pennsylvania 18144.

BOARD, SALLY ANN Occupation: Retired Registered Dietitian. Education: B.S., Virginia Polytechnic Institute and State University. Address: 902 South East Street, Culpeper, Virginia 22701.

BOCCIO, KAREN CORINNE Occupation: Writer. Education: B.A., Columbia University, 1982. Address: 88-01 80th Street, Woodhaven, New York 11421.

BOCK, LAYEH A Occupation: Poet/Editor/ Freelance Consultant. Education: Ph.D., Stanford University; M.A., University of New Mexico; B.A., Swarthmore College. Address: 642 Aleatrae Avenue #106, Oakland, California 94609.

BODINE, TATIANA KRUPENIN Occupation: Teacher Russian and German, LeMars Senior High, LeMars, Iowa. Education: B.A., Morningside College. Address: 428 Queens Court, Sioux City, Iowa 51104.

BODONYI, RICHARD J Occupation: Professor of Applied Mathematics, IUPUI, Indianapolis, Indiana. Education: B.S. Mathematics, M.S. Engineering, Ph.D. Aerospace Engineering. Address: 308 Thornberry Drive, Carmel, Indiana 46032.

BOECK, LaVERNE DWAINE Occupation: Fermentation Microbiologist, Lilly Research Laboratories, Indianapolis, Indiana. Education: B.S. Biology, M.S. Microbiology, Butler University. Address: 741 Chapel Hill West Drive, Indianapolis, Indiana 46224.

BOEHM, CONSTANCE L Occupation: Supervisor, Mariner Programs. Education: M.A. Education, B.A. Address: 17 Pearl Street, Williamtic, Connecticut 06226.

BOEHME, RICHARD WILLIAM Occupation: Librarian. Education: B.A. 1961, M.A. 1964, M.L.S. 1965. Address: 23 Oriole Avenue, Framingham, Massachusetts 01701.

BOENHEIM, MARION Occupation: Educational Administrator, Professor. Education: B.A. Psychology, M.A. Psychological Counseling, Ed.D. Administration. Address: 13086 Cherry Road, Wilton, California 95693.

BOESE, ROBERT F Occupation: Vice President, Administration and Group Operations. Education: B.A. Business, Texas A&M University. Address: 1320 Jane Avenue, Naperville, Illinois 60540.

BOETTCHER, HAROLD PAUL Occupation: Professor of Electrical Engineering, Milwaukee, Wisconsin. Education: B.S., M.S., Ph.D. Mechanics and Electrical Engineering, P.E. Address: 19285 Lothmoor Drive, Lower, Brookfield, Wisconsin 53005.

BOGARD, SOLOMON Occupation: Senior Court Clerk, New York State Civil Service. Education: B.B.A. Address: 3 Fordham Hill Oval, Bronx, New York 10468.

BOGERT, LILLIAN H Occupation: Guidance Counselor. Education: B.S. Elementary Education, M.A. Student Personnel Services. Address: 573 Lafayette Avenue, Hawthorne, New Jersey 07056.

BOGIN, ABBA Occupation: Councert Pianist & Conductor. Education: Artists Diploma, Curtis Institute of Music. Address: 838 West End Avenue, New York, New York 10025.

BOICE, JOHN DUNNING JR Occupation: Epidemiologist. Education: B.S., M.S., Sc.M., Sc.D. Address: 14612 Woodcrest Drive, Rockville, Maryland 20853.

BOLINO, AUGUST C Occupation: Professor of Economics. Address: 11411 Lund Place, Kensington, Maryland 20895.

BOLLWAGE, J CHRIS Occupation: Traffic Coordinator. Education: B.A. Economics. Address: 1029 North Avenue, Elizabeth, New Jersey 07201.

BOLOGNESI, DARRELL ERCOLE Occupation: Locations Planning Analyst. Education: B.S. Conservation and Natural Resources, University of California; Berkeley; M.P.A., California State University-Hayward. Address: 3790 Painted Pony Road, El Sobrante, California 94803.

BOLOGNESI, MARILYN ROSE Occupation: Computer Software Marketing Representative. Education: B.S. Public Health, University of California-Berkeley; M.B.A. Business Administration (in progress), University of California-Berkeley. Address: 3790 Painted Pony Road, El Sobrante, California 94803.

BOLTON, DOUGLAS JOHN Occupation: Curriculum Supervisor. Education: B.S., M.Ed., Ed.D. Address: North Village Apartments #123, Rochester, New York 14609.

BOLTON, JAMES DENNIS P E Occupation: Senior Manufacturing Engineer. Education: B.S.M.E. 1975, M.S.M.E. 1976, Purdue University. Address: 503 Aurora Street, Lancaster, New York 14086.

BOND, REECE ALEXANDER (ALEC) Occupation: Professor, Chair, English Department. Education: B.A., Murray State University, 1961; M.A., University of Kentucky, 1965; Ph.D., University of Minnesota, 1971. Address: 103 Park Avenue, Marshall, Minnesota 56258.

BOND, ALMA HALBERT Occupation: Psychoanalyst. Education: B.A., M.A., Ph.D. Address: 11 East 87th Street, New York, New York 10128.

BONDURANT, BYRON L Occupation: Professor, Assistant, Chairman, Department of Agriculture Engineering. Education: Bachelor Agricultural Engineer, 1949; M.Sc. Civil Engineering, 1953, University of Connecticut. Address: 265 Franklin Street, Dublin, Ohio 43017.

BONDURANT, CHARLES WITHERS JR Occupation: Professor of Chemistry. Education: B.A., Emory & Henry College; M.S., Ph.D., Virginia Polytechnic Institute and State University. Address: 612 Virginia Avenue, Salem, Virginia 24153.

BONFIELD, PHYLLIS K Occupation: Association Executive. Education: Bachelor of Journalism. Address: 2030 Woodland Road, Abington, Pennsylvania 19001.

BONHOMME, DENISE Occupation: Legal Secretary. Education: Baccalaureat Philosophie, M.A. Literature. Address: 1220 Tasman Drive #420, Sunnyvale, California 94089.

BONSKY, JACK ALAN Occupation: Assistant Secretary, Associate General Counsel, General Tire and Rubber Company. Education: B.A., Ohio University, 1960; J.D., Ohio State University, 1964. Address: 4234 Idlebrook Drive, Akron, Ohio 44313.

BOODEY, CECIL WEBSTER JR Occupation: Professor, Political Science & World Affairs. Education: B.A., M.A., Ph.D. Address: 80 Allen Avenue, Manasquan, New Jersey 08736.

BOOKBINDER, ROBERT M Occupation: Superintendent of Schools. Education: B.A., M.A., Ed.D. Address: R.D. #5, Box 453, East Stroudsburg, Pennsylvania 18301.

BOOKER, LARRY F Occupation: Accountant. Education: B.A. Economics. Address: 2131 Luckner Court, Mobile, Alabama 36618.

BOOKER, REGINALD ALVIS Occupation: Research and Development, Research Chemist. Education: B.S. Chemistry, M.S. Chemistry, Ph.D. Physical Organic Chemistry. Address: Post Office Box 183, Rockland, Delaware 19732.

BOOKOUT, ALICE MAY Occupation: Director, Attitudes Unlimited, Inc. Education: B.S., M.S. Nursing. Address: Route 2 Box 286, Philippi, West Virginia 26416.

BOOKOUT, GARY D Occupation: Counselor. Education: A.B. Biology, Bridgewater College; M.A. Education Administration, West Virginia University. Address: Route 2 Box 286, Philippi, West Virginia 26416.

BOON, DONALD JACKSON Occupation: Private Allergist, Medical Consultant. Education: B.S., M.S., M.D. Address: 4509 Oahu NE, Albuquerque, New Mexico 87111.

BOONE, CLARA LYLE Occupation: Music Publisher, Composer. Education: B.A. Centre College of Kentucky; M.A.T., Radcliffe College. Address: 1719 Bay Street, South East.

BOONE, EMILY C Occupation: Business and Management Consultant. Education: B.A. 1964, M.S.W. 1970. Address: 9206 Walhampton Court, Louisville, Kentucky 40222.

BOOTH, EMILY J Occupation: Marketing/Development Specialist. Education: B.A., Butler University, 1980. Address: 421 South Grant Street, Denver, Colorado 80209.

BOOTH, GEORGE GEOFFREY Occupation: Professor and Chairman, Finance. Education: B.B.A., M.B.A., Ph.D. Address: 102 Downing Road, DeWitt, New York 13214.

BORCHARDT, KENNETH A Occupation: Clinical Microbiologist Consultant, University Professor. Education: B.S. Biology, M.S. Bacteriology, Ph.D. Microbiology. Address: 15 Capilano Drive, Novato, California 94947.

BORDELEAU, WILLIAM F Occupation: Air Show Consultant/Narrator, Continental Sky-0-Rama Air Shows. Education: Mining Engineering. Address: Post Office Box 294, Menomonee Falls, Wisconsin 53051.

BORDEN, CARLA M Occupation: Associate Director, Smithsonian Symposia and Seminars. Education: B.A., Barnard College; M.A., Columbia University. Address: 3822 Davis Place Northwest, Washington, D.C. 20007.

BORDLEY, ROBERT FRANCIS Occupation: Research Scientist; Consultant, Societal Analysis Department, General Motors Research Laboratories, Warren, Michigan. Education: Ph.D., M.S. (Operations Research 1979), M.B.A. 1979, University of California-Berkeley; M.S. Systems Science, B.S. Physics, B.A. Public Policy, Michigan State University. Address: 803 West Fourth Street, Royal Oak, Michigan 48067.

BORER, ANTON JOSEF Occupation: Catholic Priest. Education: B.Phil., B.Theol. Address: 5630 East 17th Avenue, Broomfield, Colorado 80020.

BORIGHT, WALTER E Occupation: Vice Chairman. Education: B.A., M.A. Address: 7 Homestead Terrace, Scotch Plains, New Jersey 07076.

BORJE, ROMY P Occupation: Freelance Editor, Community Leader. Education: A.A., LL.B. Address: 825 South Highland Avenue, Los Angeles, California 90036.

BORKON, ELI L Occupation: Physician. Education: B.S., 1931; Ph.D. Physiology, 1986; M.D. 1937. Address: 14 Pinewood, Carbondale, Illinois 62901.

BOROCHOFF, CHARLES ZACHARY Occupation: President, Designs Unlimited. Education: Atlanta Law School. Address: 3450 Old Plantation Road, Atlanta, Georgia 30327.

BORUM, ELIZABETH ANN Occupation: Psychologist, Psychological Clinic, Concord, California.

Education: B.A. with honors, 1951; M.A., University of California-Berkeley, 1953. Address: 1830 Lakeshore #304, Oakland, California 94606.

BOSHELL, JERRY L Occupation: Orthodontist, Medical College of Georgia, Augusta, Georgia. Education: B.S., D.M.D., Ph.D. Address: 219 Kings Chapel Road, Augusta, Georgia 30907.

BOSLEY, KAREN LEE Occupation: College Professor. Education: A.B., M.A. Address: 9 Old Whaling Lane East, Long Beach, New Jersey 08008.

BOSLEY, NORMAN K Occupation: Associate Professor of Humanities. Education: B.A., Duke University; M.A., Northwestern University. Address: 9 East Old Whaling Lane, Beach Haven, New Jersey 08008.

BOSMAJIAN, HAIG A Occupation: Professor, Speech Communication Department, University of Washington, Seattle, Washington. Education: Ph.D., Stanford University; M.A., University of Pacific; B.A., University of California. Address: 4820 Purdue, North East, Seattle, Washington 98105.

BOSS, LAURA Occupation: Poet; Editor; College Instructor. Education: B.A. summa cum laude; M.A. in English Literature. Address: 7000 Boulevard East #149D, Guttenberg, New Jersey 07093.

BOSTIAN, HARRY E Occupation: Chemical and Environmental Engineer, U.S.E.P.A. Education: B.S. Chemical Engineering; M.Ch.E., Ph.D. Chemical Engineering. Address: 6001 Bagdad Drive, Cincinnati, Ohio 45230.

BOSTLEY, JEAN REGINA Occupation: Member of Religious Order. Education: B.A., College of Our Lady of the Elms; M.L.S., State University of New York-Albany. Address: St. Joseph Central High School Library, 22 Maplewood Avenue, Pittsfield, Massachusetts 01201.

BOSWORTH, MICHAEL F Occupation: Assistant Professor, Wright State School of Medicine. Education: D.O. Address: 1339 Woodland Greens Boulevard, Springboro, Ohio 45066.

BOULTON, SHAUNA D Occupation: Educator. Education: B.S., University of Utah, 1971; M.Ed. University of Utah, 1981. Address: 1516 Glen Arbor, Salt Lake City, Utah 84105.

BOUMA, GERALD DALE Occupation: Professor of Music. Education: B.A. 1967, M.M. 1969, Ed.D. 1982. Address: 615 2nd Street, Southwest, Orange City, Iowa 51041.

BOURGEOIS, DAVID RICHARD Occupation: Project Manager. Education: B.S.E.E. Address: 6 Currier Drive, Framingham, Massachusetts 01701.

BOURGEOIS, MARIE J Occupation: Nursie Administrator. Education: B.S.N.E., M.S.N.E., Ph.D. Address: 8701 Bradmoor Drive, Bethesda, Maryland 20817.

BOUSARD, LORRAINE BETZ Occupation: Assistant Professor. Education: B.S., M.A., Teachers College. Address: 59 Irene Court, Closter, New Jersey 07624.

BOUSFIELD, KENNETH HAROLD Occupation: Engineer. Education: B.S. Civil Engineering. Address: 11538 High Mountain Drive, Sandy, Utah 84092.

BOUTIN, MAURICE Occupation: Associate Professor. Education: Ph.D. Theology, University of Munich. Address: 2835 Goyer, Montreal, Quebec, Canada H3S1H2.

BOWDEN, EDITH FRANKLIN Occupation: Professional Relations Representative, Blue Shield of Florida. Education: High School; Florida State University. Address: 2156 Claremont Lane #D, Tallahassee, Florida 32301.

BOWE, FRANK G Occupation: President, F.B.A., Inc. Education: Ph.D., New York University; B.A., Western Maryland College. Address: 23 Copper Beach Lane, Lawrence, New York 11516.

BOWEN, RAFAEL L Occupation: Director. Education: D.D.S., 1953. Address: 16631 Shea Lane, Gaithersburg, Maryland 20877.

BOWERS, JANETTE L Occupation: Founder, Chairman, Board for the Sunshine House. Education: B.S., Sam Houston University; M.A., Sul Ross State University. Address: Drawer 1440, Alpine, Texas 79830.

BOWERS, MAYNARD C Occupation: University Professor. Education: A.B., M.Ed., Ph.D. Address: 2 Northwood Lane, Marquette, Michigan 49855.

BOWIE, BILL J Occupation: Investor, Business Consultant. Education: Ph.D. Address: P.O. Box 75032, Oklahoma City, Oklahoma 73147.

BOWIE, E J WALTER Occupation: Hematologist. Education: M.A.; D.M. Address: 3495 Hadley Valley Road, North East, Rochester, Minnesota 55904.

BOWLER, JOSEPH JR Occupation: Portrait Artist. Address: 9 Baynard Cove Road, Hilton Head Island, South Carolina 29928.

BOWLING, JOHN KNOX JR Occupation: Advertising Manager, U.S.A. Air France. Education: B.A. Journalism, University of Texas. Address: Hudson Road West, Ardsley on Hudson, New York 10503.

BOWMAN, ROYLESTINE JENKINS Occupation: Education Teacher. Education: B.A. Education, M.A. Education. Address: 698 North Vista Avenue, Rialto, California 92376.

BOYAJIAN, BEN K Occupation: President. Education: B.S., M.S., Ph.D. Address: 309 Alderman Road, Charlottesville, Virginia 22903.

BOYAS, JOHN G Occupation: Vice President, Finance and Administration. Education: B.S. Address: 28 Park Stree, West Caldwell, New Jersey 07006.

BOYCE, GEORGE A Occupation: President, Telecom Resources, Inc. Address: 1061 North March, Mesa, Arizona 85203.

BOYD, DONALD P Occupation: Vice President, Hammermill Paper Company. Education: B.S. Economics, Wharton School. Address: 1620 Wintergreen Lane, Fairview, Pennsylvania 16415.

BOYD, KAY M Occupation: Lacey City Council Member; Manager, Washington Service Corporations, Department of Employment Security, Olympia, Washington. Education: B.A. Liberal Arts, The Evergreen State College. Address: 4716 23rd Avenue, South East, Lacey, Washington 98503.

BOYER-BLOHM, ALTA E Occupation: Preservationist. Education: B.A., William Smith College. Address: 8678 Watkins Glen Road, Lodi, New York 14860.

BOYKAN, MARTIN Occupation: Composer. Education: B.A., Harvard University; M.M., Yale University. Address: 10 Winsor Avenue, Watertown, Massachusetts 02172.

BOYLE, JOHN FRANCIS Occupation: Engineering Management. Education: B.A. 1973, M.E. 1976, M.B.A. 1983. Address: 44 Iroquois Street, Emmaus, Pennsylvania 18049.

BOZYMSKI, EUGENE MICHAEL Occupation: Professor of Medicine, Attending Physician. Education: M.D. Address: 407 Lyons Road, North Carolina 27514.

BRACEWELL, MERVELL L Occupation: Professor of Nursing. Education: B.S.N., M.S.N., M.P.H., Dr.Ph. Address: 1337 Rapides Drive, New Orleans, Louisiana 70122.

BRACKEEN, JOANNE M Occupation: Pianist,

Composer, Band Leader. Address: 104 West 17th Street, New York, New York 10011.

BRADLEY, ELIZABETH OVER Occupation: Retired Educator. Education: B.Sc. in Education; M.A. in Arts. Address: 3872 Sterling Street, Mims, Florida 32754.

BRADLEY, KENNETH ARTHUR JR Occupation. President, WASTE, Incorporated; Forklift Incorporated. Education: B.S. New England College. Address: RFD 3, Dean Avenue, Concord, New Hampshire 03301.

BRADLEY, LAURENCE ALAN Occupation: Clinical Psychologist, Section on Medical Psychology, Bowman Gray School of Medicine, Winston Salem, North Carolina. Education: B.A., Ph.D. in Psychology. Address: 2016 Gaston Street, Winston Salem, North Carolina 27103.

BRADSHAW, JERALD SHERWIN Occupation: Professor of Chemistry. Education: B.S., University of Utah, 1955; Ph.D., University of California, Los Angeles, 1963. Address: 1616 Oaklane, Provo, Utah 84604.

BRADSHAW, LAWRENCE JAMES Occupation: Associate Professor of Art. Education: B.F.A., M.A., Pittsburgh State University; M.F.A., Ohio University, 1967, 1971, 1973. Address: 5607 Howard, Omaha, Nebraska 68106.

BRADY, JOHN ARTHUR Occupation: Communications Executive, Business Consultant. Education: A.A., B.S., M.B.A., Ph.D. Address: 1377 Woodside Drive, San Luis Obispo, California 93401.

BRADY, MARY JO Education: B.S., Indiana State University. Address: 3821 Shannan Road, Portsmouth, Virginia 23703.

BRADY, MAUREEN E Occupation: Fiction Writer. Education: B.S., M.A. Address: R.D. 1, Box 480B, Greenfield Center, New York 12833.

BRADY, RODNEY H Occupation: President, Weber State College. Education: D.B.A., Harvard University; M.B.A., University of Utah; B.S., University of Utah. Address: 4160 Edgehill Drive, Ogden, Utah 84403.

BRADY, WINIFRED B Occupation: Assistant Director, New Jersey State Employment Services. Education: M.B.A., B.S. Address: 19 Spruce Avenue, Bordontown, New Jersey 08505.

BRAHMS, KAREN ALLISON Occupation: Research Consultant, Career Counselor. Education: B.S., The Wharton School, University of Pennsylvnaia, 1975. Address: 85 East End Avenue, Suite 12E, New York, New York 10028.

BRAINERD, CHARLES JON Occupation: Experimental Psychologist. Education: B.S., M.A., Ph.D. Address: Ronning Street, Edmonton, Alberta, Canada.

BRAITO, RITA MURPHY Occupation: Sociologist, Department of Sociology, University of Denver, Denver, Colorado. Education: R.N.; B.S.N.; M.S.; M.A.; Ph.D. University of Minnesota, Minneapolis. Address: 1043 South Clarkson, Denver, Colorado 80209.

BRAMFITT, BRUCE LIVINGSTON Occupation: Research Supervisor. Education: B.S., M.S., Ph.D. Metallurgical Engineering. Address: 16 Pleasant Drive, Bethlehem, Pennsylvania 18015.

BRAMS, MARVIN R Occupation: Economist, Associate Professor of Urban Affairs. Education: B.S., M.B.A., Ph.D. Address: 32 Old Oak Road, Newark, Delaware 19711.

BRANCH, JOHN RUSSELL Occupation: Geologist, Shell Oil Company. Education: B.A., M A.

Address: 4454 Fiesta Drive, New Orleans, Louisiana 70114.

BRAND, EDWARD CABELL Occupation: Chairman of the Board and President, The Stuart McGuire Co. Education: Further Education. Address: 115 Brand Road, Salem, Virginia 24156.

BRANDAO CIONO, WILSON B Occupation: Fine Artist. Education: B.A. Fine Art, M.A. Fine Art. Address: Post Office Box 512, New York, New York 10024.

BRANDES, LISA HETHERINGTON Occupation: Museum Director. Education: B.A., M.P.A. Address: 360 Vernon Street, Oakland, California 94610.

BRANDON, JOHN BRADFORD Occupation: Furniture Design Consultant. Education: Further Studies. Address: 1332 Maxon Road, Attica, New York 14011.

BRANDT, EDWARD NORMAN JR Occupation: Assistant Secretary for Health. Education: B.S. 1954, M.D. 1960, The University of Oklahoma; M.S. 1955, Ph.D. 1963, Oklahoma State University. Address: 12 North Drive, Bethesda, Maryland 20814.

BRANN, EDWARD R Occupation: Senior Editor, Credit Union Magazine; Coordinator, Innovative Ideas Center. Education: B.A., Berea College; M.A., University of Chicago. Address: Post Office Box 383, Madison, Wisconsin 53701-0383.

BRANNAN, RALPH T Occupation: Corporate Management, Information Services. Education: B.S. Physics, Iowa State University. Address: 2132 James Court, Rock Hill, South Carolina 29730.

BRANTL, SISTER CHARLES MARIE Occupation: Chairman, Professor Economics Department. Education: Ph.D., M.A., Fordham University; B.A., Albertus Magnus College. Address: 790 Prospect Street, Connecticut 06511.

BRANTLEY, EDWARD J Occupation: Federal Manager. Education: B.S., M.A., Ed.D. Address: 1643 Roxanna Road, North West, Washington, D.C. 20012.

BRÁS DELGADO, EDGARDO L Occupation: Attorney at Law and Notary Public. Education: B.A. Political Science, J.D. Address: Box 44, Mayaguez, Puerto Rico 00709.

BRASWELL, JAMES A Occupation: College Professor, Music Education, School of Music, University of Georgia, Athens, Georgia. Education: B.M.Ed., East Texas State University; M.M.E., Loyola Univesity; Ph.D., University of Oklahoma. Address: 105 Collier's Creek Road, Watkinsville, Georgia 30677.

BRAZIEL, DELANO R Occupation: CBE Coordinator. Education: B.S., M.Ed., Ed.D. Address: Route 1, Box 359, Pitts, Georgia 31072.

BRECKINRIDGE, DANA W Occupation: Planner. Education: B.S.M.E., M.B.A. Address: 3582 University Avenue, Highland Park, Illinois 60035.

BREDLOW, THOMAS GAYLE Occupation: Designer, Metalworker. Education: B.A. Mathematics, A&M College. Address: 3524 North Olive Road, Tucson, Arizona 85719.

BREE, GERMAINE Occupation: Kenan Professor. Address: 2135 Royal Drive, Winston Scherr, North Carolina 27106.

BREED, ANTHONY GLENN Occupation: Coach, Teacher, Sugar Land Junior High School. Education: B.S. Education, Baylor University. Address: 9330 Synott #408 North, Houston, Texas 77083.

BREGMAN, JACOB I Occupation: Consultant. Education: B.S., M.S., Ph.D. Address: 5630 Old Chester Road, Bethesda, Maryland 20814.

BREMER, RONALD A Occupation: Magazine Editor. Address: Post Office Box 16422, Salt Lake City,

Utah 84116.

BRENDE, JOEL OSLER Occupation: Psychiatrist. Education: B.A., M.D. Address: 8 Hale Hollow Road, Groton du Hudson, New York 10520.

BRENDEL, BETTINA Occupation: Artist and Lecturer. Education: B.A., Hamburg Germany, University of Southern California. Address: 1061 North Kenter Avenue, Los Angeles, California 90049.

BRENDLER, ROBERT ANTON Occupation: Farm Advisor, University of California, Ventura, California. Education: B.S. Agronomy, University of California. Address: 4657 Varsity Street, Ventura, California 93003.

BRENNAN, DEBORAH ANN Occupation: Operations, Marketing Assistant. Education: B.A. Social Work, Penn State University. Address: 69 Providence Avenue, Doylestown, Pennsylvania 18901.

BRESEE, WILMER EDGAR Occupation: Chairman, Board, Oneonta Department Store. Education: A.B., L.H.D., Hamilton College. Address: 160 East Street, Oneonta, New York 13820.

BRETT, PETER D Occupation: Writer. Education: B.Sc. Biology. Address: Post Office Box 697, Ross, California 94957.

BREUDE, JOEL OSLER Occupation: Psychiatrist. Education: B.A., M.D. Address: 8 Hale Hollow Road, Gorton on Hudson, New York 10520.

BREWER, KENNETH W Occupation: Associate Professor of English, Utah State University. Education: Ph.D., University of Utah; M.A., New Mexico State University. Address: 947 Sumac Drive, Logan, Utah 84321.

BREWER, PAUL HUIE Occupation: Financial Advertising Executive. Education: B.A., Louisiana College, 1956. Address: 41 Red Oak Lane, Highland Park, Illinois 60035.

BRICKER, HERSCHEL LEONARD Occupation: University of Maine at Orno Retired. Education: A.B., Coe College, 1928; D.F.A., Colby College, 1977; D.F.A., UMO, 1983. Address: One Middle Street, Farmington, Maine 04938.

BRICKMAN, MIRIAM Occupation: Concert Pianist and Educator. Education: B.A., M.S. Address: 210 Lakeview Place, Riverdale, New York 10471.

BRIDGES, JEAN BOLEN Occupation: Associate Professor of English. Education: A.A., A.B., M.Ed., Ed.S., D.A. Address: Route 2, Forest Drive, Swansboro, Georgia 30401.

BRIGGS, ARTHUR H Occupation: Professor and Chairman, Department of Pharmacology, Internal Medicine. Education: B.A. 1952, M.D. 1956. Address: 707 Serenade, San Antonio, Texas 78216.

BRIGGS, DAVID EUGENE Occupation: Consultant. Education: M.H., Psy.D. Address: Post Office Box 141, Haverford, Pennsylvania 19041.

BRIGGS, EVERETT F Occupation: Nursing Home Administrator. Education: S.T.D., Catholic University, 1932; M.A., Fordham University; L.H.D., Holy Cross College, 1950. Address: Maple Terrace, Lady Lane, Monongah, West Virginia 26554.

BRIGGS, HILTON MARSHALL Occupation: President Emeritus. Education: B.S., M.S., Ph.D. Sc.D. Address: 1734 Garden Square, Brookings, South Dakota 57006.

BRIGGS, PATRICK RAY Occupation: College Professor, The Citadel, Charleston, South Carolina. Education: B.A. Physics; Ph.D. Space Physics. Address: The Citadel, Charleston, South Carolina 29409.

BRIGHT, GEORGE W Occupation: University Professor, University of Calgary, Canada. Education: B.A. 1968, M.A. 1969, Ph.D. 1971. Address: #902, 215 14th Avenue, South West, Calgary, Alberta, Canada T2R 0M2.

BRIGHT, PETER B Occupation: Scientist/ Engineer. Education: B.S. 1960, Ph.D. 1966. Address: 39 Sunset Avenue, Venice, California 90291.

BRILES, JUDITH Occupation: Financial Planner, Author. Education: M.B.A. Address: 130 Fawn Lane, Portola Valley, California 94025.

BRINGS, ALLEN S Occupation: Composer; Pianist; Teacher, Queens College, New York. Education: B.A.; M.A.; Mus. A.D. Address: 199 Mountain Road, Wilton, Connecticut 06897.

BRINK, PATRICIA MARY Occupation: Elementary School Principal. Education: B.A. Elementary Education; M.Ed. Educational Administration. Address: 5813 Willowton Avenue, Apartment C, Baltimore, Maryland 21239.

BRINK, STUART JAY Occupation: Physician. Education: B.S., M.D. Address: 196 Pleasant Street, Newton Centre, Massachusetts 02159.

BRINTON, ROBERT W Occupation: Hotel Executive, Phoenix, Arizona. Education: A.A., B.S., M.B.A. (in progress). Address: 1265 East Inca, Mesa, Arizona 85203.

BRISKIN, MADELEINE Occupation: Associate Professor of Geology, University of Cincinnati. Education: Ph.D. Address: 3346 Sherlock Avenue, Cincinnati, Ohio 45220.

BRITT, JEFFIE LEE Occupation: Retired. Education: B.S., Mississippi State College for Women, 1925. Address: Post Office Box 35, Elaine, Arkansas 72333.

BRIZZOLARA, MARY S Occupation: Professor of Psychology, Department of Psychology, Towson State University, Baltimore, Maryland. Education: B.S., St. Lawrence University, 1956; M.A. Michigan State University, 1960; Ph.D. University of Massachusetts 1963. Address: Five Edgeclift Road, Towson, Maryland 21204.

BROAD, ELI Occupation: Chairman and Chief Executive Officer, Kaufman and Broad, Inc.; Director, Sun Life Insurance Company of America. Education: B.A. Accounting cum laude, Michigan State University, 1954. Address: 10801 National Boulevard, Los Angeles, California 90064.

BROADHEAD, RICHARD Occupation: Physician. Education: M.S., B.S. Address: 3220 Forest Avenue, Murrysville, Pennsylvania 15668.

BROBST, JOYCE E Occupation: Educator. Education: B.S., M.S., M.Ed. Address: 2111 Fairview Avenue, Mt. Penn, Pennsylvania 19606.

BROCK, CHARLES MARQUIS Occupation: Lawyer, Division Counsel, Abbott Laboratories. Education: A.B., Princeton University, 1963; J.D., Georgetown University Law Center, 1968; M.B.A., University of Chicago Business School, 1974. Address: 1473 Asbury Avenue, Winnetka, Illinois 60093.

BROCK, CLARA M Occupation: Software Engineering, Department 62-K9/B177, Sunnyvale, California. Education: B.S. Electrical/Electronic Engineering. Address: 19930 Oakmont Drive, Los Gatos, California 95030.

BROCK, RUTHE EVETTE Occupation: Field Director, Mid-Continent Girl Scouts. Education: B.A. Psychology, B.R.E., M.R.E. (in progress). Address: 2925 East 28th Street, Kansas City, Missouri 64128.

BROCK, WILLIAM ALLEN Occupation: Economist; Consultant; Professor of Economist, University of Wisconsin, Madison, Wisconsin. Education: A.B. University of Missouri, Columbia, 1965; Ph.D. University of California, Berkeley, 1969.

Address: 7949 Deer Run, Cross Plains, Wisconsin 53528.

BROCKHUES, MICHAEL PATRICK Occupation: Psychologist. Education: B.A., M.A., Professional Diploma. Address: Route 2, Box 1050, Chateaugay, New York 12920.

BROCKMAN, TERRY JAMES Occupation: Tax Supervisor. Education: B.S.B.A. Creighton University; J.D. Creighton University. Address: 1010 South 36th Street, Omaha, Nebraska 68105.

BRODY, MYRON ROY Occupation: Sculptor, Educator, Administrator. Education: B.F.A., M.F.A. Address: 1309 West 50th Street, Kansas City, Missouri 64112.

BRODY, STUART MARTIN Occupation: Chemist. Education: B.S. Chemistry. Address: 8 Timberlane Drive, Colonia, New Jersey 07067.

BROEKER, ANNIE B Occupation: Manager of Business Services, Chemicals Division. Education: B.S. Chemical Engineering, University of South Carolina, 1973; M.B.A., University of Houston-Clear Lake. Address: 312 East Tazewell's Way, Williamsburg, Virginia 23185.

BROMIGE, DAVID MANSFIELD Occupation: Professor of English, Sonoma State University. Education: B.A., University of British Columbia, 1962; M.A., University of California-Berkeley, 1964. Address: 626 Monroe, Santa Rosa, California 95404.

BROMKE, ADAM Occupation: Professor of Political Science. Education: M.A., Ph.D. Address: 165 Little John Road, Dundas, Ontario, L9H 4H2 Canada.

BRONSTEIN, ARTHUR J Occupation: Professor of Linguistics, The Graduate School, City University of New York. Education: B.A., M.A., Ph.D. Address: Brokaw Lane, Great Neck, New York 11023.

BRONZAFT, ARLINE L Occupation: College Professor, Herbert H. Lehman College. Education: B.A., M.A., Ph.D. Address: 505 East 79 Street, New York, New York 10021.

BRONZINO, JOSEPH D Occupation: College, Engineering Education, Trinity College. Education: B.S.E.E., M.S.E.E., Ph.D. Electrical Engineering. Address: 6 Wyngate, Simsbury, Connecticut 06070.

BROOK, BENJAMIN N Occupation: Consultant in Management. Education: A.B., M.A., M.S.W., Ed.D. Address: 2542 Avenue San Valle, Tucson, Arizona 85715.

BROOKER, ALAN EDWARD Occupation: Clinical Neuropsychologist, United States Air Force Medical Center, Travis Air Force Base, California. Education: B.A., M.S., Ph.D. Address: 206 Emory Drive, Vacaville, California 95688.

BROOKEY, ROBERT S Occupation: Professor. Education: A.A., B.S., M.S., Ph.D. Address: 246 North Delta Drive, Columbus, Ohio 43210.

BROOKINS, JACOB BODEN Occupation: Artist, Consultant, Designer. Education: B.S., M.S., M.F.A. Address: 431 Cosnino Road, Flagstaff, Arizona 86001.

BROOKINS, OSCAR T Occupation: Professor, Economist, Northeastern University. Education: A.B., M.A., Ph.D. Address: 89 Aspinwall, Brookline, Massachusetts 02159.

BROOKS, BENJAMIN AUGUST Occupation: Hospital Administrator. Education: M.H.A., Baylor University, 1968; B.S., Iowa State University, 1957. Address: 3337 Sparta Road, Sebring, Florida 33870.

BROOKS, DANIEL T Occupation: Attorney. Education: B.S.E. 1963, M.S.E. 1968, LL.B. 1967. Address: 6106 Lorcom Court, Springfield, Virginia 22152.

BROOKS, DAVID MICHAEL Occupation: Vice President Operations and General Counsel. Education: B.A., Hobart College, 1976; M.B.A., Columbia University, 1978; J.D., Washington University, 1981. Address: 15 West 72 Street, Apartment 17F, New York, New York 10023.

BROOKS, JOHN A Occupation: Stock Broker. Education: B.S. Chemical Engineering. Address: 908 Royal St. George, Naperville, Illinois 60540.

BROOKS, MARGUERITE EVE (NAUMANN) Occupation: Research Chemist. Education: B.S. Chemistry. Address: 16 Gunpowder Road, Glen Arm, Maryland 21057.

BROOKS, MARIE Occupation: Director and Instructor, Bedford Stuyvesant Dance Theatre; Founder/Director, The Marie Brooks Dance Theatre, Children's Research Dance Theatre. Address: Marie Brooks Dance Research Theater, 529 West 155th Street, New York, New York 10032.

BROOKS, NANCY S Occupation: Assistant Superintendent, Baltimore County Public Schools. Education: M.S., B.S., Ph.D. Address: 4310 Green Glade Road, Phoenix, Maryland 21131.

BROOKS-GUNN, JEANNE Occupation: Senior Research Scientist. Education: M.A., Harvard University, 1970; Ph.D., University of Pennsylvania, 1975. Address: Educational Testing Service, Princeton, New Jersey 08541.

BROOMAN, ERIC WILLIAM Occupation: Manager of Electrochemical and Inorganic Processes Technology Group, Battelle Memorial Institute, Columbus, Ohio. Education: A.C.T., Dip. Tech. (Hons.); Ph.D. (Cantab.) Metallurgy. Address: 1333 LaRochelle Drive, Columbus, Ohio 43221.

BROOMFIELD, ANN LOUISE Occupation: Comptroller; Office Manager. Education: C.C.A. 1983; A.A. Liberal Arts, Pima College, 1978. Address: Post Office Box 5187, Tucson, Arizona 85703.

BROPHY, MARY O'REILLY Occupation: Research Associate/Adjunct Assistant Professor, State University of New York Upstate Medical Center. Education: B.S., M.S., Ph.D., University of Michigan. Address: 5954 Smith Road, North Syracuse, New York 13212.

BROPHY, ROBERT H III Occupation: Writer/Research Professor. Education: A.B., Fordham University; M.A., Ph.D., University of Michigan. Address: 5954 Smith Road, North Syracuse, New York 13212.

BROSKY, JOHN G Occupation: Judge, Superior Court of Pennsylvania. Education: B.A., LL.B., J.D. Address: 29 Greenview Drive, Carnegie, Pennsylvania 15106.

BROSTOW, WITOLD KONRAD Occupation: Materials Engineer and Educator. Education: M.S. Chemistry, Dr.Sc. Mathematics/Physics, D.Sc. Chemistry. Address: 217 Valley Road, Media, Pennsylvania 19063.

BROTHERS, BARBARA JO Occupation: Psychotherapist. Education: M.S.W. Address: 2514 North Rampart Street, New Orleans, Louisiana 70117.

BROTMAN, ARLENE SANDRA Occupation: Social Worker/Psychotherapist. Education: B.A., M.A., M.S.W. Address: 55 Windsor Avenue, Apartment 212E, Rockville Centre, New York 11570.

BROUDY, HARRY S Occupation: Professor Philosophy of Education Emeritus. Education: A.B., M.A., Ph.D. Address: 406 Sunnycrest Court, Urbana, Illinois 61801.

BROUMAS, OLGA Occupation: Poet; Founder and Associate, Freehand, Inc. Education: B.A. Architecture, University of Pennsylvania; M.F.A.,

University of Oregon. Address: P.O. Box 806, Provincetown, Massachusetts 02657.

BROWN, ALBERTA MAE Occupation: Respiratory Clinician, Inservice Instructor. Education: Certified Respiratory Therapist, A.A., B.S. Address: 1545 North Hancock Street, Orange Wood Estates, San Bernardino, California 92411.

BROWN, ALBERT W Occupation: University Professor of Higher Education, Faculty of Educational Studies, State University of New York-Buffalo. Education: Ph.D. Social Science, Syracuse University, 1952. Address: P.O. Box 184, Stow, New York 14785.

BROWN, ALVIN SANFORD Occupation: Sales Manager. Address: P.O. Box 4754, Panorama City, California 91412.

BROWN, BILL G Occupation: Life Underwriter; After Dinner Speaker. Education: B.S. Address: 2302 Slide Road, Lubbock, Texas 79407.

BROWN, CECILIA DEW Occupation: Registered Pharmacist. Education: B.S. Pharmacy, University of South Carolina. Address: R-5, Box 539, Hartsville, South Carolina.

BROWN, DALE SUSAN Occupation: Manager, President's Committee on Employment of the Handicapped. Education: B.A., Antioch College. Address: Apartment 104, 4570 MacArthur Boulevard, Washington, D.C. 20007.

BROWN, HAROLD PROBERT Occupation: Assistant Dean Emeritus, School of Engineering, Washington University, St. Louis, Missouri. Education: Ph.D., Organic Chemical, University of Nebraska, 1933; M.S., University of Missouri, 1930; B.S., CMSU, 1928. Address: 444 Woodlawn Estates Drive, Kirkwood, Missouri 63121.

BROWN, HERBERT CHARLES Occupation: Wetherill Research Professor Emeritus, Chemistry Department, Purdue University. Education: Ph.D., University of Chicago, 1938. Address: 1840 Garden Street, West Lafayette, Indiana 47906.

BROWN, JOHN LOTT Occupation: President, University of South Florida. Education: Ph.D. Psychology. Address: 1405 Julie Lagoon, Lutz, Florida 33549.

BROWN, KENNETH L Occupation: Associate Professor of Chemistry. Education: B.S., University of Chicago, 1968; Ph.D., University of Pennsylvania, 1971. Address: 2704 Greenbrook Drive, Arlington, Texas 76016.

BROWN, KENNY D Occupation: Chemical Engineer. Education: B.A. Mathematics, B.A. Chemistry, B.S. Chemical Engineering. Address: 7339 Starlawn, Perrysburg, Ohio 43551.

BROWN, LINDA LEE Occupation: Drafting Supervisor. Education: Associate Drafting Technology; B.A. Business Administration. Address: Box 114, Wright, Wyoming 82732.

BROWN, MARY (BETH) OLIVER Occupation: Writer. Education: A.B., Bryn Mawr College; M.F.A., Goddard College. Address: 4421 Chestnut Street, #3, Philadelphia, Pennsylvania 19104.

BROWN, OTHAN Education: B.S., M.A., 6th Year Diploma. Address: Shorefront Park, Norwalk, Connecticut 06854.

BROWN, PAUL EDWARD Occupation: College Administrator, Quincy College. Education: B.S. Accounting, M.B.A. Finance. Address: 3331 West Tower Road, Quincy, Illinois 62301.

BROWN, PAULA MARIE Occupation: Marriage and Family Therapist/Adoption Counselor. Education: B.A. Sociology, M.A. Counseling. Address: 3331 West Tower Road, Quincy, Illinois 62301.

BROWN, SAM C Occupation: Professor and Chairman, University of Missouri, Columbia. Education: B.B.A., M.A., Ph.D. Address: 2718 Bayonne Court, Columbia, Missouri 65213.

BROWN, SAMUEL EDWARD Occupation: Chairman of Science Department, Howaa High School, Wilmington, Delaware. Education: B.S., M.S. Science Education. Address: 4502 Pickwick Drive, Wilmington, Delaware 19808.

BROWN, VIRGINIA Occupation: System Program Manager, Wright Patterson Air Force Base, Ohio. Address: 4360 Pinecastle Court, Dayton, Ohio 45424.

BROWN, W REYNOLD Occupation: Artist. Education: Alhambra High School, Ghoinard Art School. Address: Box 248, Crawford, Nebraska 69339.

BROWN, WALTON LYONNAISE Occupation: Assistant Professor/Post-doctoral Associate, University of Georgia. Education: B.A., M.A./Ph.D., University of Michigan. Address: 160 Dudley Drive, #524, Athens, Georgia 30606.

BROWN, WENDELL Occupation: Lawyer. Education: A.B., University of Hawaii, 1924; J.D., University of Michigan Law School, 1926. Address: 29921 Ardmore, Farmington Hills, Michigan 48018.

BROWN, WILLIAM BOYD Occupation: Certified Public Accountant, Attorney, Professor. Education: B.S. Business Administration, J.D. Address: 2990 Tonkaha Drive, Wayzata, Minnesota 55391.

BROWN, WILLIAM DARREL Occupation: Professional Engineer, On Assignment, Carolina Power and Light Company. Education: B.S.M.E., M.S.N.E. Address: 123, North Humphrey, Oak Park, Illinois 60302.

BROWN, WILLIAM H Occupation: Supervisor Consumer Services (Utility). Address: 1396 River Acres Drive, New Braunfels, Texas 78130.

BROWN, WILLIAM SAMUEL JR Occupation: Professor of Speech and Linguistics, University of Florida. Education: B.S., Edinboro State College; M.A., Ph.D., State University of New York/AB. Address: 1517 Northwest 19th Street, Gainesville, Florida 32605.

BROWN, YVONNE WARREN Occupation: Associate Professor of Accounting, University of Cincinnati. Education: B.A., Howard University; M.B.A., Ohio State University. Address: 4201 Rose Hill Avenue, Cincinnati, Ohio 45229.

BROWNE, ALAN LAMPE Occupation: Staff Research Engineer, GM Research Labs, Warren, Michigan. Education: Ph.D. Northwestern University, 1971; A.B. Harvard University, 1966. Address: 7 Woodland Place, Grosse Pointe, Michigan 48230.

BROWNLEE, PAULA PIMLOTT Occupation: President, Professor of Chemistry, Hollins College. Education: B.A., M.A., D.Phil., Chemistry, Oxford University. Address: P.O. Box 9625, Hollins College, Virginia 24020.

BROYLES, PATRICK JAMES Occupation: United States Department of Agriculture S.C.S. District Conservationist. Education: B.S. Agronomy, M.S. Range Management. Address: 522 South Indiana, Columbus, Kansas 66725.

BROZEN, YALE Occupation: Professor of Business Economics. Education: Ph.D., B.S., A.S. Address: 1101 East 58th Street, Chicago, Illinois 60637.

BRUALDI, RICHARD A Occupation: Professor of Mathematics, University of Wisconsin, Madison. Education: B.A., University of Connecticut, 1960; N.Sc., Ph.D., Syracuse University, 1964. Address: 3191 CTH-P, Mt. Horeb, Wisconsin 53572.

BRUCE, JOHN I Occupation: Director, Center for Tropical Disease, University of Lowell. Education: B.S., Morgan State College, 1953; M.S., Ph.D., Howard University, 1968. Address: 8 Rose Glen Drive, Andover, Massachusetts 01810.

BRUHN, JOHN G Occupation: Dean, School of Allied Health Sciences, University of Texas Medical Branch. Education: B.A., M.A., Ph.D. Address: 7521 Beluche, Galvaston, Texas 77551.

BRUMFIELD, SHANNON MAUREEN Occupation: Speech Language Pathologist. Education: B.A., M.A., Ph.D. Address: 2314 Calhoun, New Orleans, Louisiana 70118.

BRUNALE, VITO JOHN Occupation: Aeronautical Engineering Specialist. Education: A.A.S. 1948, B.S.A.E. 1958, M.S.M.E. 1966, Dr.Sc. 1973. Address: 459 Bronxville Road, Bronxville, New York 10708.

BRUNELLE, PHILIP CHARLES Occupation: Principal Conductor, Minnesota Opera Company; Music Director and Founder, Plymouth Music Series. Education: B.A. Address: 4211 Glencrest Road, Golden Valley, Minnesota 55416.

BRUNER, INEZ W Occupation: Extension Home Economist. Education: Master's Degree Adult Education, Additional Studies. Address: Route 1, Box 201, Porter, Oklahoma 74454.

BRUNNER, REGINA CAROL Occupation: Assistant Profesor of Mathematics, Cedar Crest College. Education: B.A., M.A., M.S., Ph.D. Address: 6439 Tupelo Road, Allentown, Pennsylvania 18104.

BRUSH, DOUGLAS HOWARD Occupation: Advertising Agent, Actor. Education: Graduate, Art School. Address: 7 Sutton Drive, Berkeley Heights, New Jersey 07922.

BRUTON, ROSA A Occupation: Editor; Writer. Education: English/Journalism, Hunter College. Address: 102 Woodland Court, Laurel, Maryland 20707.

BRYAN, JACOB FRANKLIN III Occupation: Chairman of the Board and Chief Executive Officer, Independent Insurance Group, Inc. Education: Graduate, Florida Business University (now defunct); College Degree Equivalent, Private Tutor, 1932. Address: 4255 Yacht Club Road, Jacksonville, Florida 32210.

BRYAN, LESLIE AULLS Occupation: Transportation Economist. Education: B.S., M.S., Ph.D., J.D. Sc.D. Address: 34 Fields East, Champaign, Illinois 61821.

BRYAN, RICHARD R Occupation: Real Estate Development Executive. Education: B.S., M.S. Civil Engineering. Address: 12327 Overcup, Houston, Texas 77024.

BRYANT, EDWARD C Occupation: Education Specialist, United States Navy. Education: B.S., M.S., C.A.G.S., D.Ed. Address: 138 Topsfield Road, Ipswich, Massachusetts 01938.

BRYANT, SYLVIA L Occupation: Editor/ Publisher, Poet, Freelance Writer. Education: D.Lit., World University, 1981. Address: Route 5, Box 498A, Madison Heights, Virginia 24572.

BRZEZICKI, MICHAEL JOSEPH Occupation: Director of Operations. Education: A.A. Address: 35 Toddington Heights, Murfreesboro, Tennessee 37130.

BUBLITZ, WALTER J JR Occupation: Consultant (Retired). Education: B.S., M.S., Ph.D. Address: 1430 Northwest 14th Place, Corvallis, Oregon 97330.

BUCHANAN, JERRY Occupation: Educational Advisor to Various Trade and Technical and Business Schools; Originator and Owner/Writer/Publisher, *Towers Club, USA Newsletter, Towers Club Mail Order Book Store for Entrepreneurs and Self Publishers;* Author, *Writer's Utopia Formula Report.* Address: Box 2038, Vancouver, Washington 98668.

BUCHELE, WESLEY FISHER Occupation: Professor Agricultural Engineering. Education: B.S., Kansas State University; M.S., University of Arkansas; Ph.D., Iowa State University. Address: 239 Parkridge, Ames, Iowa 50010.

BUCHHEIT, LOUISE MARIE Occupation: Assistant Vice President, R. E. Department Manager, Hilltop National Bank. Address: 4051 Powderhorn Green, #6, Alcova Route, Casper, Wyoming 82604.

BUCHTHAL, FRITZ Occupation: Physician, National Institutes of Health, Building 10, Bethesda, Maryland. Education: M.D., Ph.D. Address: 289 El Cielito Road, Santa Barbara, California.

BUCHWALD, HENRY Occupation: Surgeon. Education: M.D., Ph.D. Address: 6808 Margaret's Lane, Edina, Minnesota 55435.

BUCK, JAMES R Occupation: Professor and Chairman, Industrial and Management Engineering. Education: B.S., M.S. in Civil Engineering; Ph.D. in Industrial Engineering. Address: 2353 Cae Drive, Iowa City, Iowa 52240.

BUCKALEW, LOUIS WALTER Occupation: Psychology Professor; Researcher, Alabama A&M University, Normal, Alabama. Education: B.A., M.S., Ph.D. Candidate. Address: 200 Curtis Circle, South East, Huntsville, Alabama 35803.

BUCKHOUT, TERRY SMITH Occupation: Loss Control Representative. Education: B.S. Biology, M.B.A. Management. Address: 137 Evergreen Avenue, Hartford, Connecticut 06105.

BUCKMAN, CHARLES E JR Occupation: President, Blythe-Nelson Midwest, Inc. Education: B.S., Quincy College. Address: 1081 Challdon Court, Naperville, Illinois 60540.

BUCKNER-DOWELL Occupation: Community Development/Social Worker. Education: B.S., M.S.W., A.B.D./S.W. Address: P.O. Box 56355, Washington, D.C. 20011.

BUDD, ISABELLE AMELIA Occupation: Research Economist. Education: B.S. Public Administration, University of Missouri. Address: 2753 McDowell Street, Durham, North Carolina 27705.

BUDIG, RONALD L Occupation: Professor-Safety, Illinois State University, Normal, Illinois. Education: Ph.D. Education and Administration; M.S. Traffic Safety; B.S. Natural Science. Address: 313 Garden Road, Normal, Illinois 61761.

BUEDING, ERNEST Occupation: Research Scientist, Professor of Pharmacology. Education: M.D. Address: 4001 Roundtop Road, Baltimore, Maryland 21218.

BUEKER, KATHLEEN A Occupation: Health Consultant/Writer. Education: R.M., Ph.D. Address: Box 339, Deltaville, Virginia 23043.

BUELL, CHARLES EDWIN Occupation: Consultant for Visually Impaired. Education: B.A., Ed.D., University of California-Berkeley; Master's Degree, University of Michigan. Address: 33905 Calle Acordarse, San Juan Capistrano, California 92675.

BUELL, FREDERICK H Occupation: Poet/ Professor, Department of English, Queens College. Education: B.A., Yale University; Ph.D., Cornell University. Address: 118-65 Metropolitan Avenue, #3-D, Kew Gardens, New York 11415.

BUFORD, THOMAS O Occupation: Educator, Furman University. Education: B.A., B.D., Ph.D. Address: Regent Drive Route #7, Greenville, South

Carolina 29609.

BUHKS, EPHRAIM Occupation: Group Leader, Corporate Research, B. F. Goodrich Research and Development Center. Education: B.S./M.S. Physics, Ph.D. Chemistry. Address: 9960 Applewood Drive, North Royalton, Ohio 44133.

BUJAC, JAMES N JR Occupation: Professional Engineer, Civil Service. Education: B.S. Mechanical Engineering, New Mexico State University, 1953. Address: 10861 Spring Garden Drive, St. Louis, Missouri 63137.

BUJKO, LESTER G Occupation: Manager, Accounting. Education: B.S. Economics 1972, M.B.A. 1983. Address: 4321 North McVicker, Chicago, Illinois 60634.

BULKLEY, DWIGHT H Occupation: Author, Lecturer, Psychobiology. Education: B.A. Address: 6519 40th Avenue, Northeast, Seattle, Washington 98115.

BULL, COLIN B B Occupation: Dean, Ohio State University, Columbus. Education: B.Sc. (Hons., 1st Class); Physics, Birmingham, 1948. Address: 4187 Olentangy Boulevard, Columbus, Ohio 43214.

BULLARD, REUBEN GEORGE Occupation: Professor, Department Chairman, Consultant. Education: Th.B. Theology, M.A. Hist. Geog., A.B. Classics, M.S. Geology, Ph.D. Archgeology and Geology. Address: Box 296, 5310 Madison Pike, Independence, Kentucky 41051.

BULLOCK, JANET MARIE Occupation: Reading Instructor, P. H. Community College; Tutor, JMB's Tutorial Service; Self-Employed. Education: B.A. English, M.S. Reading, Ed.S. Address: 1813 Battle Drive, Greenville, North Carolina 27834.

BULLOCK, WILLIAM J Occupation: Professor and Choral Conductor, Columbus College Music Department. Education: B.M.E., M.A., Ph.D. Address: 3725 Mote Road, Columbus, Georgia 31907.

BUMP, JEROME F A Occupation: Professor of English Literature, University of Texas, Austin, Texas. Education: Ph.D. 1972, M.A. 1966, B.A. 1965. Address: 8910 Currywood, Austin, Texas 78759.

BUNCH, AUSTIN W Occupation: Associate Professor and Coordinator of Special Education, University of Mississippi. Education: B.A.E., Ph.D., University of Mississippi; M.Ed., Georgia State University. Address: 508 Audubon Lane, Oxford, Mississippi 38655.

BUNDY, WAYNE MILEY Occupation: Vice President of Research and Lands. Education: Ph.D. Clay Mineralogy, Indiana University. Address: Box 45 Bissell Road, R.D. 2, Lebanon, New Jersey 08833.

BUNGUM, JOHN L Occupation: Associate Professor of Economics. Education: B.A., Luther College; M.A., University of Iowa; Ph.D., University of Nebraska. Address: 841 Church, St. Peter, Minnesota 56082.

BUNJUN, SEEWOONUNDUN Occupation: Associate Professor of Economics, Department of Economics, East Stroudsburg University. Education: B.A. (Hons.) Economics, M.A. Economics, Ph.D. Economics. Address: 142 Analomink, East Stroudsburg, Pennsylvania 18301.

BUNN, DENNY Occupation: Professional Diver. Education: B.S. Biology and Geography. Address: 4929 Annette Drive, Tallahassee, Florida 32303.

BUNN, ROSEMARY Occupation: High School Teacher. Education: B.S. Criminology, B.A. Education. Address: 4929 Annette Drive, Tallahassee, Florida 32303.

BUNNER, ALAN NEWTON Occupation: Senior

Staff Astronomer, Perkin-Elmer. Education: B.A., M.S., Ph.D., Cornell University. Address: 47 High Ridge Road, Brookfield, Connecticut 06805.

BUNTING, ROGER KENT Occupation: Professor of Chemistry, Illinois State University, Normal, Illinois. Education: B.S., M.S., Ph.D. Address: 1203 Searle Drive, Normal, Illinois 61761.

BUNZA, LINDA HATHAWAY Occupation: Writer and Editorial Consultant. Education: A.B., Bates College, Lewiston, Maine, 1968; M.A., Hartford Seminary Foundation, Hartford, Connecticut, 1971; Ph.D. Candidate, Syracuse University, Syracuse, New York. Address: 14002 North 48th Way, Scottsdale, Arizona 85254.

BURATTI, TERI R Address: 2600 Georgia Avenue #1501, Sanford, Florida 32771.

BURCH, FRANCIS FLOYD Occupation: Clergyman, Educator. Education: B.A. 1956, M.A. 1958, Fordham University; Ph.L. 1957, S.T.L. 1964, Woodstock College; Postgraduate Studies, Tronchiennes, Belgium, 1964-65; Docteur d'universite de Paris, Sorbonne, 1967. Address: 54th and City Line, Philadelphia, Pennsylvania 19131.

BURCHFIELD, JERRY L Occupation: Artist, Writer, Educator, Gallery Owner. Education: B.A. Photography Comm. 1971, M.A. Art 1977. Address: P.O. Box 1502, Laguna Beach, California 92652.

BURCHUM, JACQUELINE ROSENJACK Occupation: Registered Nurse, Regional Hospital, Jackson, Tennessee. Education: A.A. Nursing, B.S.N. Student. Address: Route 3, Old Stage Road, Camden, Tennessee 38320.

BURDETT, JEREMY KEITH Occupation: Associate Professor. Education: A.B., M.A., Ph.D. Address: 1415 East 54th Place, Chicago, Illinois 60615.

BURDZY, EDWARD JAN Occupation: Supervisor Employment and Training. Education: B.A., Bloomfield College; M.A., Montclair State College. Address: R.D. 3, Box 248, Milford, New Jersey 08848.

BURFORD, MARY ANNE Occupation: Chief Technologist, Ob/Gyn, Inc. Education: B.S. Biology, M.T. (A.S.C.P.). Address: 1509 West Buckingham Drive, Muncie, Indiana 47302.

BURGESS, ARTHUR LEE Occupation: Professional Mechanical Engineer. Education: B.A.Ed. Address: 2009-43 Avenue East, #4, Seattle, Washington 98112.

BURGESS, JOSEPH J JR Occupation: Artist, Designer, Orientalist. Education: A.B., Hamilton College; M.A., Yale University. Address: Post Office 2151, Santa Fe, New Mexico 87504.

BURGESS, RICHARD RAY Occupation: University Professor, McArdle Lab for Cancer Research, University of Wisconsin, Madison, Wisconsin. Education: B.S. Chemistry; Ph.D. Biochemistry and Molecular Biology, California Technical University. Address: 10 Knollwood Court, Madison, Wisconsin 53713.

BURGESS, WILLIAM H Occupation: Chairman of the Boards of Directors, International Controls Corporation, TimeLapse Corporation, RHC Corporation. Education: B.B.A., University of Minnesota, 1939; M.B.A., Harvard Graduate School of Business Administration, 1941. Address: 550 Palisades Drive, Palm Springs, California 92262.

BURGET, JOHN E Occupation: Financial Consultant/Investment Banking. Education: Bachelor of Engineering Physics (distinction); M.S. Physics; M.B.A., Harvard Business School. Address: 83 Montgomery Street, Jersey City, New Jersey 07302.

BURHOE, SUMNER OTHNIEL Occupation:

Geneticist, Embryologist, Biologist. Education: B.S., University of Massachusetts, 1925; M.S., Kansas University, 1926; Ph.D., Harvard University, 1937. Address: 9435 Rosehill Drive, Bethesda, Maryland 20807.

BURISH, THOMAS G Occupation: University Professor of Psychology, Vanderbilt University. Education: A.B., University of Notre Dame; M.A., Ph.D., University of Kansas. Address: 625 Brook Hollow Road, Nashville, Tennessee 37205.

BURKE, BARBARA ANNE Occupation: Consulting Psychologist, Probation Officer. Education: B.S.W., Regis College, 1976; M.Ed. Counseling, Boston State College, 1979; Certificate Advanced Graduate Studies in Humanities and Psychology, 1980. Address: P.O. Box 25, Boston, Massachusetts 02112.

BURKE, FRANCE Occupation: Playwright. Education: B.A. English Literature, New York University. Address: 170 Avenue C, New York, New York 10009.

BURKETT, JOHN P Occupation: Economist, Economics Department, University of Rhode Island. Education: B.A., Cornell University; A.A., Ph.D., University of California-Berkeley. Address: A5 Faculty Circle, Kingston, Rhode Island 02881.

BURKHOLDER, WENDELL EUGENE Occupation: Research Entomologist and Professor of Entomology, University of Wisconsin, Madison, Wisconsin; Head of Stored Product Insects Research Lab. Education: Ph.D., University of Wisconsin, 1967; M.Sc., University of Nebraska, 1956; A.B., McPherson College, 1950. Address: 1726 Chadbourne Avenue, Madison, Wisconsin 53705.

BURLAND, BRIAN BERKELEY Occupation: Novelist/Writer. Education: F.R.S.L. Address: Book Essex, Connecticut 06426.

BURMAN, CEARA SUE Occupation: Owner/Administrator, International Language Services. Education: M.A., University of Toledo; B.A., Heidelberg College. Address: 2346 Cedarwood, Maumee, Ohio 43537.

BURNES, CAROL G Occupation: Writing Consultant, Teacher. Education: B.A., M.A. Address: Chestnut Street, Weston, Masachusetts 02193.

BURNETT, HATTIE (ZIESEL) Occupation: Writer. Address: 6804 Greystone Drive, Raleigh, North Carolina 27609.

BURNS, LARRY DeMONT Occupation: Controller. Education: A.A., North Greenville College; B.A. 1967, B.S. 1970, William Carey College; Postgraduate Studies, University of Southern Mississippi, LaSalle Extension University. Address: 500 Hayworth Circle, High Point, North Carolina 27262.

BURNS, MARIETTA JO Occupation: Budget and Accounting Officer. Education: B.B.A., Baylor University, 1962; Graduate Studies, Denver University, 1971-72. Address: 3784 South Quince Street, Denver, Colorado 80237.

BURNS, SANDRA K Occupation: Attorney. Education: B.S., University of Houston, 1970; M.A. 1972, Ph.D. 1975, University of Texas-Austin; J.D., St. Mary's University School of Law. Address: 12126 Forestwood Circle, Dallas, Texas 75234.

BURNS, THOMAS S Occupation: President, N.T.A. Education: B.S.E.E., M.S.E.E., M.B.A., A.M.P. Address: Box 491, Menlo Park, California 94025.

BURNSIDE, OROIN CHARLES Occupation: Professor of Agronomy, University of Nebraska at Lincoln. Education: B.S., M.S., and Ph.D. Address: 6111 Lexington, Lincoln, Nebraska 68505.

BURNWORTH, RANDY JAMES Occupation:

Chief Executive Officer; President, Video Improvement Products Company, Tillamook, Oregon. Education: Machine Technology Degree, 1969. Address: 2715 Fifth Street, Tillamook, Oregon 97141.

BURR, IRVING WINGATE Occupation: Statistician. Education: B.S., Antioch College; M.S., University of Chicago, Ph.D., University of Michigan. Address: P.O. 527, Ocean Park, Washington 98640.

BURRELL, DANIEL WALTER Occupation: Clinical Director. Education: B.A. Psychology, M.S. Rehabilitation Counseling, Ph.D. Counselor Education. Address: 60E Clintwood Court, Rochester, New York 14620.

BURRELL, DAVID BAKEWELL Occupation: Professor of Philosophy/Theology, University of Notre Dame. Education: B.A., University of Notre Dame, 1954; S.T.L., Rome, 1960; Ph.D., Yale University, 1965. Address: Box 402, Notre Dame, Indiana 46556.

BURRILL, MELINDA J Occupation: Associate Professor, California State Polytechnic University. Education: B.S., University of Arizona, 1969; Ph.D., Oregon State University. Address: 149 Stillman Way, Upland, California 91786.

BURRIS, SHARON SUE Occupation: Educational Administration. Education: B.S. in Education, M.S. in Education, Ph.D (in progress). Address: 515 East 6th Street, Metropolis, Illinois 62960.

BURROWES, JOSEPH J Occupation: President, Pakoil Company. Education: B.A., Temple University. Address: 7 North Drexel Avenue, Havertown, Pennsylvania 19083.

BURRUS, CHARLES ANDREW JR Occupation: Research Physicist, AT&T Bell Laboratories, Crawford Hill Laboratory. Education: B.S., Davidson College; M.S., Emory University; Ph.D., Duke University. Address: 62 Highland Avenue, Fair Haven, New Jersey 07701.

BURSTEIN, STEPHEN D Occupation: Neurosurgeon. Education: B.A., University of Michigan, 1954; M.D., State University of New York, 1958. Address: 19 Bridle Path, Roslyn, New York 11576.

BURSUK, LAURA ZELMAN Occupation: Associate Professor of Education, York College-City University of New York. Education: B.A., M.A., Ph.D. Address: York College-City University of New York, Jamaica, New York 11451.

BURTNETT, STEVEN C Occupation: Judiciary. Education: B.S., Iowa State University; J.D., Hastings College of the Law. Address: 16911 Coral Cay, Huntington Beach, California 92649.

BURTOFT, STELLA V Occupation: National President, Ladies Auxiliary, Military Order of the Purple Heart. Education: Business College, Pennsylvania. Address: 9908 48th Avenue, North, St. Petersburg, Florida 33708.

BURTON, LUCILLE PEARSON Occupation: Retired Educator. Education: A.B., M.A. Address: 45 Grail Street, Asheville, North Carolina 28801.

BURTON, ROSS BLAND Occupation: Minister of Education. Education: A.A., B.A., Master of Religious Education. Address: 216 West Auburn, Apartment C, Bolivar, Missouri 65613.

BUSBY, FLORENCE R Occupation: Mayor, Municipal Judge. Address: Box 233, Shubuta, Mississippi 39360.

BUSBY, GERALD Occupation: Composer, Teacher, Pianist. Education: B.A., Yale University, 1960. Address: 222 West 23, New York, New York 10011.

BUSBY, WILLIAM J Occupation: Holistic

Physician, Minister, Organization President. Education: N.D., D.N., D.D., Ph.D. Address: 400 Patterson Street, Sulphur Springs, Arkansas 72768.

BUSCH-VISHNIAC, ILENE J Occupation: Assistant Professor of Mechanical Engineering, University of Texas. Education: Ph.D. Mechanical Engineering, Massachusetts Institute of Technology. Address: 8828 Silverarrow Circle, Austin, Texas 78759.

BUSH, BARNEY F Occupation: Writer/Visiting Writer, North Carolina. Education: B.A. Humanities, Ft. Lewis College; M.A. English, Fine Arts University of Idaho. Address: Thacker's Gap, Herod, Illinois 62947.

BUSH, CYNTHIA JANE Occupation: Inventory Control Clerk. Education: B.S. Business Management (in progress). Address: Post Office Box 622, Cleveland, Tennessee 37311.

BUSH, GARY GRAHAM Occupation: Senior Design Engineer/Magnetic., Intel Corporation, Folsom, California. Education: B.S. Physics, M.S. Physics, M.S.N.E., M.S.E.E., Ph.D. E.E. Address: 5805 Ridgemore Court, Orangevale, California 95662.

BUSH, L RUSS Occupation: Associate Professor of Philosophy of Religion at Southwestern Baptist Theological Seminary, Ft. Worth, Texas. Education: B.A., M.Div., Ph.D. Address: 2105 York, Ft. Worth, Texas 76134.

BUSH, MARTIN H Occupation: Vice President, Wichita State University; Museum Director; Author. Education: M.A., State University of New York-Albany; Ph.D., Syracuse University, 1966. Address: 8201 East Harry #2204, Wichita, Kansas 67207.

BUSH, WENDELL E Occupation: Attorney. Education: A.B., J.D. Address: 3685 Winchester Park Circle, #8, Memphis, Tennessee.

BUSHNELL, JIM L Occupation: Extension Agronomist-Crops. Education: B.S., M.S., Ph.D. Address: 2060 North 1400 East, Logan, Utah 84321.

BUSS, EDWARD G Occupation: Professor, The Pennsylvania State University. Education: B.S., M.S., Ph.D. Address: 1420 South Garner Street, State College, Pennsylvania 16801.

BUSSEMA, KENNETH E Occupation: College Professor/Psychologist, Dordt College, Sioux Center, Iowa. Education: Ed.D. Address: 506 3rd Street, South East, Sioux Center, Iowa 51250.

BUTLER, JACKIE D Occupation: Professor and Turfgrass Specialist. Education: B.S., M.S., Ph.D. Address: 220 South County Road #5, Ft. Collins, Colorado.

BUTLER, PAUL THURMAN Occupation: College Administrator and Professor. Education: Bachelor of Theology; Master of Biblical Literature. Address: 2501 Utica, Joplin, Missouri 64801.

BUTLER, REBECCA BATTS Occupation: Educational Consultant; Workshop and Seminar Conductor. Education: Doctor of Education. Address: 15 Eddy Lane, Cherry Hill, New Jersey 08002.

BUTLER, ROBERT N Occupation: Chairman, Department of Geriatrics and Adult Development. Education: B.A., Columbia University; M.D., Columbia University College of Physicians and Surgeons. Address: 211 Central Park West, New York, New York 10024.

BUTT, LINDA T Occupation: Clinical Coordinator/Nursing Supervisor. Education: B.S.M., Diploma Nursing. Address: 19601 Beallsville Road, Beallsville, Maryland 20839.

BUTTACI, SAL ST JOHN Occupation: Direct Mail Marketing Executive. Education: B.A. Communication Arts, 1965; M.B.A. Management/Marketing, 1981. Address: 100 Maple Street, Garfield, New Jersey 07026.

BUZZATTO, JOHN LEONARD Occupation: USAF/Program Manager, Worldway Postal Center, Los Angeles, California. Education: B.S. Aerospace Engineer, M.S. Operations Research. Address: 15611 Poinsettia Way, West Minster, California 92683.

BYER, MARSHALL Occupation: Mechanical Engineer. Education: S.B. Naval Architecture and Marine Engineering, S.M. Engineering. Address: 921 Vestal Road, Vestal, New York 13850.

BYER, RICHARD I Occupation: President, Richard-Lewis Corporation. Education: B.Sc. Business Administration, Ohio State University. Address: 11 Westwind Road, Yonkers, New York 10710.

BYLER, WILLIAM H Occupation: Independent Researcher (Retired). Education: B.S., A.B., M.A., Ph.D. Address: 5017 Vivienda Way, Sarasota, Florida 33580.

BYRNE, BARBARA Occupation: Lawyer. Education: B.A. Franklint Marshall College, 1975; J.D. Boston University, 1978. Address: Carrolls Ranch, Lamoille, Nevada 89801.

BYRNE, JOHN PATRICK Occupation: Director of Disaster Emergency Services, State of Colorado; President, National Emergency Management Association. Address: 7679 Waverly Mountain, Littleton, Colorado 80127.

BYSIEWICZ, SHIRLEY RAISSI Occupation: Professor of Law. Education: B.A., J.D., M.S.L.S. Address: South Plumb Road, Middletown, Connecticut 06457.

C

CABALQUINTO, LUIS C Occupation: Editor & Free-Lance Writer. Education: B.A. Journalism, M.A. Creative Writing. Address: Post Office Box 618, New York, New York 10009.

CACCAMISE, ALFRED EDWARD Occupation: Head Media Specialist. Education: B.A., Stetson University; M.S.L.S., Syracuse University. Address: Post Office Box 241, DeLand, Florida 32721.

CADY, HENRY LORD Occupation: Professor of Music. Education: A.B., M.A., Ph.D. Address: 24 Minquil Drive, Newark, Delaware 19713.

CAGE, RICHARD HOWARD Occupation: Consulting Statistician. Education: B.S., State University of New York, 1957. Address: 4927 Evergreen Trail, Evergreen, Colorado 80439.

CAHILL, MICHAEL J Occupation: Attorney. Education: B.A. Political Science, University of Chicago; J.D., DePaul University. Address: 61 Community Road, Bayshore, New York 11706.

CAIN, JAMES ALLAN Occupation: Acting Associate Dean. Education: B.Sc., University of Durham (England); M.S., Ph.D., Northwestern. Address: Rural Route 1 Box 788, West Kingston, Rhode Island 02892.

CAIN, JAMES D JR Occupation: U.S. Government Executive. Education: B.A. History; B.S. Political Science; M.S. International Relations; Ph.D. (ABD) Political Science. Address: 8463 Valmora Street, Spring Hill, Florida 33526.

CALDER, ROBERT MAC Occupation: Aerospace Engineer. Education: B.S. Chemical Engineering, M.S. Mathematics and Geology. Address: 530 South 700 East, Kaysville, Utah 84037.

CALDERWOOD, DERYCK DAVID Occupation: Director Human Sexuality Program. Education: B.A., Ph.D. Address: 27 Harvey Drive, Summit, New Jersey 07901.

CALDWELL, STRATTON FRANKLIN Occupation: University Professor. Education: B.S. 1951, M.S. 1953, Ph.D. 1966. Address: 80 North Kanan Road, Agoura, California 91301.

CALHOON, STEPHEN W JR Occupation: Dean of the College. Education: Ph.D., M.S., Ohio State University; B.S., Houghton College. Address: Box 436 CWC, Central, South Carolina 29630.

CALIO, ANTHONY JOHN Occupation: Deputy Administrator. Address: 10112 South Glen Road, Potomac, Maryland 20854.

CALITRI, CHARLES J Occupation: Writer. Education: B.S., M.A., New York University. Address: Hythe A, 1007, Boca Raton, Florida 33434.

CALLAN, PATRICK M Occupation: Education Administrator. Education: B.A., M.A., University of Santa Clara; Graduate Study, University of California, Los Angeles & Irvine. Address: 1020 12th Street, Second Floor, Sacramento, California 95814.

CALLAWAY, HOWARD HOLLIS Occupation: Chairman of the Board. Education: B.S., Military Engineering West Point, 1949. Address: 3131 East Alameda Avenue, #2103, Denver, Colorado 80290.

CALLEO, DAVID PATRICK Occupation: Professor & Director of European Studies. Education: B.A., M.A., Ph.D., Yale. Address: 626 A Stine, Washington, District of Columbia 20002.

CALLEWAERT, DENIS MARC Occupation: University Professor, Professional Consultant, Oakland University, Rochester, Michigan. Education: B.S. cum laude Chemistry, Ph.D. Biochemistry.

Address: 1600 Hosner Road, Oxford, Michigan 48051.

CALVERT, DONALD JOSEPH Occupation: Entomologist. Education: B.S., Ph.D. Address: 1246 Greenway Drive, Richmond, California 94803.

CAMARDESE, NINO MATTEO Occupation: Family Physician, Norwalk, Ohio. Education: B.A., M.D. Address: 244 Benedict Avenue, Norwalk, Ohio 44857.

CAMERON, FLORENCE ELIZABETH Occupation: Speech/Language Pathologist. Education: Bachelor of Arts, Master of Arts, (Mogen Superieur) Degre de Francais. Address: 404 North 16th Street, Beatrice, Nebraska 68310.

CAMERON, ROSALINE BRISKIN Occupation: Professor. Education: B.M. Piano, M.A., Diploma Piano. Address: 104 West 70 Street, 8 East, New York, New York 100023.

CAMERON, VINCENT FRANCIS JR Occupation: Energy Economist. Education: B.S. Economics, University of Massachusetts. Address: 12118 Melody Drive, Northglenn, Colorado 80234.

CAMP, ALBERT TALCOTT Occupation: Consulting Engineer in Defense and Nutrition. Education: B.Eng., Yale University, 1941; M.S. Industrial Management, Massachusetts Institute of Technology, 1956. Address: Route 1, Box 1278, Welcome, Maryland 20693.

CAMP, MARK J Occupation: Associate Professor of Geology, University of Toledo, Toledo, Ohio. Education: B.S. 1970, M.S. 1972, Ph.D. 1974. Address: 856 McKinley, Toledo, Ohio 43605.

CAMP, N HARRY JR Occupation: State Licensed Clinical Psychologist. Address: 7520 South West 105th Lena, Miami, Florida 33156.

CAMPBELL, CHARLES ALTON Occupation: Business Executive, President. Education: B.I.E., Georgia Institute of Technology; M.B.A., Harvard Business School. Address: 10 Canterbury Place, South West, Rome, Georgia.

CAMPBELL, CHARLES GEORGE Occupation: Banker. Education: Graduate, Indiana Business College; University of Chicago, 1923-26. Address: 323 Cherry Street, Mount Carmel, Illinois 62863.

CAMPBELL, CLARICE T Occupation: Speaker, Writer. Retired Professor of History. Education: Ph.D. University of Mississippi; M.A. University of Mississippi and Los Angeles State College; B.S. University of Southern California. Address: Post Office Box 792, Holly Springs, Mississippi 38635.

CAMPBELL, CLIFTON P JR Occupation: Professor Vocational-Technical Education. Education: B.S. 1964, M.Ed. 1968, Ed.D. 1971. Address: 1420 Moorgate Drive, Knoxville, Tennessee 37922.

CAMPBELL, DOUGLAS Occupation: Director of Music, Teacher. Education: Voice, New York City. Address: 501-130 Mount Hope Street, Kitchener, Ontario, Canada N2G 4M6.

CAMPBELL, JANET G Occupation: Free-lance Writer. Education: University of Tulsa, Tulsa, Oklahoma. Address: 6109 Woodbridge Road, Oklahoma City, Oklahoma 73132.

CAMPBELL, JEANNE BEGIEN Occupation: Associate Professor of Art. Address: 3715 Douglasdale Road, Richmond, Virginia 23221.

CAMPBELL, KENNETH F Occupation: Professor. Education: B.A., B.F.A., M.A., M.F.A., Dip.Eth., B.Litt., M.Litt., D.Phil. Address: 628 East Tyler Avenue, Eau Claire, Wisconsin 54701.

CAMPBELL, MILDRED WASSON Occupation: Public Relations and Marketing Representative. Education: Northwestern Oklahoma University.

Address: Post Office Box 340, McCammon, Idaho 83250.

CAMPBELL, ROBERT E Occupation: Clinical Professor of Radiology, Pennsylvania Hospital. Education: B.A., Harvard University, 1953; M.D., University of Pennsylvania, 1957. Address: 121 Orchard Lane, Haverford, Pennsylvania 19041.

CAMPBELL-THRANE, LUCILLE W Occupation: Research Administrator, Ohio State University. Education: B.S. Home Economics, M.Ed., D.Ed. Human Development. Address: 1000 Urlin Avenue, Columbus, Ohio 43212.

CAMPION, CAROL MAE S Occupation: Head Librarian. Education: B.A., M.A., M.L.S. Address: 1041 North Webster Avenue, Scranton, Pennsylvania 18510.

CANDILIS, WRAY O Occupation: Economist. Education: Ph.D. Economics, Georgetown University. Address: 4101 Cathedral Avenue, North West, Washington, District of Columbia 20016.

CANE, ROY D Occupation: Associate Professor of Anesthesia. Education: M.B.B.Ch., F.F.A. (S.A.). Address: 2000 North Orleans, Chicago, Illinois 60614.

CANFIELD, JOAN GILTNER Occupation: Student. Education: State University of Iowa. Address: 4815 Harwood Drive, Des Moines, Iowa 50312.

CANGEMI, JOSEPH PETER Occupation: Professor. Education: Ed.D., Indiana University, 1974; Advanced Graduate Study, Western Kentucky University; Master's Degree, Syracuse University, 1964; B.S., State University of New York, 1959. Address: 1305 Woodhurst Drive, Bowling Green, Kentucky 42101.

CANIZARES, CLAUDE ROGER Occupation: Physics Professor. Education: B.A., M.A., Ph.D. Address: Massachusetts Institute of Technology, Room 37-501, Cambridge, Massachusetts 02139.

CANNADY, CRISS E Occupation: Communications Consultant, ASTO-LA, Los Angeles, California. Education: M.B.A. 1985, M.F.A. 1977, B.A. 1973. Address: 2516 Elm Avenue, Manhattan Beach, California 90266.

CANNON, JESSE L Occupation: Retired Letter Carrier. Education: University of Iowa and SIUE. Address: 2215 Tibbitt Street, Alton, Illinois 62002.

CANNON, VIVIAN F Occupation: Career Education Coordinator. Education: B.A. Education, M.A. Education. Address: 2965 Oro Blanco Drive, Colorado Springs, Colorado 80917.

CANNON, WILLIAM JOHN Occupation: Psychologist Consultant. Education: Ph.D., B.D. Address: 1705 Ritchie Road, Forestville, Maryland 20747.

CANTRELL, JOHN HARRIS JR Occupation: Research Physicist. Education: B.S., Ph.D. Address: 1013 Willow Green, Newport News, Virginia 23602.

CANTRELL, TRUETT VAUGHN Occupation: Retired, United States Air Force. Education: Address: Route 4, Box 277, Palestine, Texas 75801.

CANTÚ, VIRGINIA DOLORES Occupation: Program Specialist-Day Care/Child Development. Education: Bachelor of Music. Address: 1803 East Anderson #2154, Austin, Texas 78752.

CAPORALI, RONALD VAN Occupation: Consultant-Glass Technology. Education: B.S. 1958, M.S. 1964, Ph.D. 1969, Pennsylvania State University. Address: Rural Delivery 1, Box 19, West Sunbury, Pennsylvania 16061.

CAPORALE, LYNN H Occupation: Faculty Member, Biochemistry. Education: Ph.D., University of California-Berkeley; B.S., Brooklyn College of City University of New York. Address: Department of Biochemistry, Georgetown University Medical Center, 4000 Reservoir Road, North West, Washington, District of Columbia 20007.

CAPORASO, JAMES ALBERT Occupation: Professor, Graduate School of International Studies, University of Denver, Denver, Colorado. Education: B.A. Penn State University; Ph.D. University of Pennsylvania; M.A. Villanova. Address: 2250 South Madison, Denver, Colorado 80210.

CAPPAS, ALBERTO OSCAR JR Occupation: Director of Public Information. Education: B.A. in American Studies. Address: 3840 Greystone Avenue, Bronx, New York 10463.

CAPPELLO, EVE Occupation: Behavior Consultant. Education: Ph.D. Psychology. Address: Post Office Box 10578, Marina Del Rey, California 90295.

CAPPON, DANIEL Occupation: Psychiatrist, Professor in Environmental Studies. Education: L.M.S.S.A., L.R.C.P., M.R.C.S., D.P.M., F.R.C.P. Address: 32 York Valley Cres., Willowdale Ontario M2P 1A7, Canada.

CAPPS, RICHARD HUNTLEY Occupation: Professor, Physics Department, Purdue University, West Lafayette, Indiana. Education: A.B., M.A., and Ph.D. in Physics. Address: 2724 Henderson, West Lafayette, Indiana 47906.

CAPPUCI, DARIO TED JR Occupation: Veterinarian/Scientist/Military Officer. Education: A.Sc., B.Sc., D.V.M., M.Sc., Ph.D., M.P.H. Address: 1077 Sanchez Street, San Francisco, California 94114.

CAPUTI, MARIE ANTOINETTE Occupation: Health Care Consultant and Researcher. Education: A.B., M.S.S.W., Ph.D. Address: 5818 Barton Road, Madison, Wisconsin 53711.

CAPUTO, DANIEL V Occupation: Professor of Psychology. Education: Ph.D., B.A. Address: 16-07 150 Street, Whitestone, New York 11357.

CARBONE, GABRIEL Occupation: Principal Chemist. Education: B.S. Address: 1848 - 72 Street, Brooklyn, New York 11204.

CARDEN, DANA HARMON Occupation: Minister and Accountant, Retired. Address: Route 1, Box 398, Elizabethtown, Tennessee 37643.

CARDINALE, KATHLEEN CARMEL Occupation: Senior Vice President. Education: R.N., B.A. Health Education, M.A. Health Sciences. Address: 545 East 14th Street, IE, New York 10009.

CARDINELL, ROBERT H Occupation: Owner-Electric Boat Company. Education: B.S., Michigan State University, 1947; M.B.A., Syracuse University, 1954. Address: Route 1, Box 309, 6 Palm Lane, Mount Dora, Florida 32757.

CARDWELL, MICHAEL STEVEN Occupation: Perinatologist/Obstetrician. Education: B.S., Purdue University; M.D., Indiana University. Address: 2515 Ashmont, Missouri City, Texas 77459.

CAREY, JAMES JOSEPH Occupation: Navy Captain. Education: B.S. Business Administration, Northwestern University, Evanston, Illinois, 1960; M.B.A. (credit) Northwestern University, Chicago, Illinois, 1971-72. Address: Box 62, The Capital Yacht Club, 1000 Water Street, South West, Washington, D.C. 20024 .

CARGILE, PAT K Occupation: Senior Vice President, Marketing Manager. Education: University of New Mexico. Address: 1909 Norht McKinley, Hobbs, New Mexico 88240.

CARLEY, H EDWIN Occupation: Product Development Manager. Education: B.S., M.S., Ph.D.

Address: 11 Callowhill Road, Chalfont, Pennsylvania 18914.

CARLIN, MYRNA LOUISE Occupation: Psychologist. Education: B.S., M.Sc. Address: 4116 Beaconsfield Avenue, Montreal, Quebec, H4A 2H3.

CARLISLE, JAMES PATTON Occupation: Director. Education: B.A., M.Div. Address: 112 Willow Valley Drive, Lancaster, Pennsylvania 17603.

CARLSON, BONNIE LEE Occupation: Marketing Director. Education: University of Baltimore. Address: 742 Youngway, Westminister, Maryland 21157.

CARLSON, ELOF AXEL Occupation: Professor. Education: B.A., New York University, 1953; Ph.D., Indiana University, 1958. Address: 19 Mud Road, Setaket, New York 11733.

CARLSON, ERMA WOOD Occupation: Education: B.S., Minnesota University; B.L.S., Drexel University. Address: 4747 Sunset, La Crescenta, California 91214.

CARLSON, JANE E Occupation: Teacher, The Juilliard School. Education: Bac. Mus., Shenanndoah Conservatory of Music; Professional Diploma, Juilliard Graduate School of West Hartford, Connecticut. Address: 257 West 86th Street, New York, New York 10024.

CARLSON, JOHN GREGORY Occupation: Professor and Chair of Psychology. Education: B.A., Ph.D. Address: 2430 Campus Road, Honolulu, Hawaii 96822.

CARLSON, LEROY T Occupation: Chairman. Education: B.A., University of Chicago; M.B.A., Harvard University. Address: 2 Milburn Park Drive, Evanston, Illinois 60201.

CARLSON, RICHARD LAWRENCE Occupation: Aerospace Company Executive. Education: B.S. Management Engineering. Address: 28 Willie Circle, Tolland, Connecticut 06084.

CARLSON, RICHARD WARNER Occupation: Mortgage Banker. Education: Address: 7956 Avenida Alamar, La Jolla, California 92037.

CARLSON, ROBERT JOHN Occupation: President. Education: B.A., University of Minnesota, 1952. Address: United Technologies Corporation, United Technologies Building, Hartford, Connecticut 06101.

CARLTON, RICHARD N Occupation: Tri-County Director of Special Education, Garfield, Kansas. Education: Doctor of Philosophy. Address: Route 3, Box 31, Larned, Kansas 67550.

CARLTON, WILLIAM W Occupation: Professor, Department Veterinary Pathology, School of Veterinary Medicine, Purdue University, West Lafayette, Indiana. Education: B.S., M.S., D.V.M., Ph.D. Address: 3716 High Acre Place, West Lafayette, Indiana 47906.

CARLUCCI, FRANK V Occupation: Chemist. Education: Ph.D., M.S., B.S. Address: 1371 Thomas Avenue, North Brunswick, New Jersey 08902.

CARMAN, ANNA K Occupation: Manager. Education: B.A., San Angelo College; Hardin Simmons University. Address: Post Office Box 426, Anson, Texas 79501.

CARMODY, DOUGLAS JAMES Occupation: Director. Education: B.S. Engineering, M. Engineering. Address: 1239 Purdue Avenue, Modesto, California 95350.

CARNAHAN, ORVILLE D Occupation: College President. Education: E.D.D., M.Ed., B.S. Address: 2138 West 4620 South, Salt Lake City, Utah 84119.

CARNEY, BARBARA JOYCE Occupation: Executive Search Consultant. Education: M.Ed.,

National College of Education; B.A., University of Los Angeles. Address: 2020 Lincoln Park West, Chicago, Illinois 60614.

CARONE, PATRICK F Occupation: Physician. Education: M.D. Address: 43 Andrew Drive, Massapaqua, New York.

CAROSELLI, PATRICIA ANN Occupation: Vice-President of Production. Education: B.A., Psychology, M.B.A. Marketing. Address: 608 Montana Avenue, Santa Monica, California 90403.

CAROZZI, ALBERT VICTOR Occupation: Professor of Geology, University of Illinois, Urbana, Illinois; International Oil Consultant. Education: M.S., Dr. Sc. Address: 709 West Delaware, Urbana, Illinois 61801.

CARP, GERALD Occupation: Electronics Engineer. Education: B.E.E., M.S.E.E. Address: 8613 Fox Run, Potomac, Maryland 20854.

CARPENTER, ALVIN L Occupation: Pastor. Education: B.A., California Baptist College, 1984. Address: 8471 Diana Avenue, #241, Riverside, California 92504.

CARPENTER, BETTY LOU Occupation: Self-Employed. Education: B.S.B.A. Regis College, Denver, Colorado. Address: 801 South Ellipse Way, Denver, Colorado 80209.

CARPENTER, CHARLES WHITNEY II Occupation: Professor. Education: A.B., Cornell University; M.A., University of Southern California; Ph.D., New York University; M.S.Ed., Bucknell University; Ed.M., Columbia University Teachers' College; Diploma, Industrial College of the Armed Forces. Address: 144 West 4th Street, Bloomsburg, Pennsylvania 17815.

CARPENTER, JOHN RANDELL Occupation: Writer, Editor, Translator. Education: B.A., Ph.D. Address: 1606 Granger Avenue, Ann Arbor, Michigan 48104.

CARPINO, LOUIS A Occupation: Professor of Chemistry. Education: B.S., M.S., Ph.D. Address: 11 Mount Pleasant, Amherst, Massachusetts 01002.

CARR, EDWARD GARY Occupation: Associate Professor of Psychology. Education: B.A., University of Toronto, 1969; Ph.D., University of California, 1973. Address: 28 Rolling Road, Miller Place, New York 11764.

CARR, GEORGE L Occupation: Professor of Physics. Education: B.S., M.Ed., West Maryland College; Ph.D., Cornell University. Address: 2 Gifford Lane, Chelmsford, Massachusetts 01824.

CARR, GLENNA DODSON Occupation: Professor. Education: B.S., M.S., Ed.D. Address: 1546 South West 35th Place, Gainesville, Florida 32608.

CARRAHER, CHARLES E JR Occupation: Teacher. Education: B.A., Sterling College, 1963; Ph.D., University of Missouri-Kansas City, 1967. Address: 2855 College Hill Court, Fairborn, Ohio 45324.

CARREL, LARRY J Occupation: Purchasing Manager. Education: A.A., B.B.A., M.B.A. Address: 16969 Cresta Drive, San Diego, California 92128.

CARRIE, JACQUES F Occupation: Novelist, Short Story Writer, Social Critic. Education: B.S.E.E. Advanced Studies in Communication, Modern Literature and Method Acting. Address: 831 8th Street, Apartment B, Hermosa Beach, California 90254.

CARROLL, CATHERINE AGNES Occupation: Organist-Research. Education: Ph.D., M.M., B.S.M., B.Mus., A.A.G.O. Address: Manhattanville College, New York 10577.

CARROLL, MARTIN HOWARD Occupation:

Optometrist, Cheyenne, Wyoming. Education: A.A. with honor; B.S. with honor; O.D. magna cum laude. Address: 4012 Snyder Avenue, Cheyenne, Wyoming 82001.

CARROLL, ROSEMARY F Occupation: Professor, Department of History, Coe College, Cedar Rapids, Iowa; Attorney at Law. Education: J.D. 1983, Ph.D. 1968, M.A. 1962, B.A. 1957. Address: 439 Crimson Drive, North East, Cedar Rapids, Iowa 52402.

CARROLL, SUSAN ANN Occupation: Speech-Language Pathologist; Program Director, Infant Stimulation Program. Education: B.S. Speech Pathology, 1980; M.S. Speech Pathology, 1982. Address: 3495 Foxcroft Road, Cheyenne, Wyoming 82001.

CARROW, DONALD J Occupation: M.D. Education: B.S., M.D. Address: 2231 Belleair Road, Clearwater, Florida 33546.

CARR-RUFFINO, NORMA J Occupation: Professor of Business. Education: Ph.D., M.B.E., B.B.A. Address: 1600 Holloway, San Francisco, California 94066.

CARSMAN, EVELINE P Occupation: Consultant/ Gerontologist. Education: Ph.D., M.P.H., M.S.L.S., Ph.B. Address: 4582 Shadowhyrst Court, San Jose, California 95136.

CARSTEA, DUMITRU D Occupation: Senior Consultant in Environment, Energy and Natural Resources. Education: B.S. Agricultural Engineer, M.S., Ph.D. Address: 13563 Point Pleasant Drive, Chantilly, Virginia 22021.

CARTER, DEAN Occupation: Professor of Art. Education: A.B., American University, 1947; M.F.A., Indiana University, 1948; Corcoran School of Art; Studio of Zadkine, Paris, France. Address: 1011 Highland Circle, Blacksburg, Virginia 24060.

CARTER, FRANCES T Occupation: Editor, Acteens/GA Products, W.M.U. Education: Assisting Professor 1956-57, Associate Professor 1957-63, Professor 1963-, Samford University School of Education and Department of Home Economics; Instructor Charm Classes, Rocky Ridge Community School. Address: 2561 Rocky Ridge Road, Birmingham, Alabama 35243.

CARTER, GEORGE HERBERT Occupation: Psychiatrist. Education: M.D. Address: 16 Ash Street, Cambridge, Massachusetts 02138.

CARTER, JOSEPH RAY Occupation: Chairman. Education: B.S., Doctor of Business Science. Address: 770 Salisbury Street, Concord 4, Worcester, Massachusetts 01609.

CARTER, MARGARET CAROL Occupation: Human Resources Associate. Education: B.A. Address: 62 Garden Center #212, Broomfield, Colorado 80020.

CARTER, RICHARD BERT Occupation: Historian. Education: B.A. Political Science, Washington State University, Graduate Work Georgetown University Law School. Address: 2180 Elaine Drive, Bountiful, Utah 84010.

CARTER, V L Occupation: Chairman. Education: B.S., M.S., Ed.D., L.L.D. Address: 6500 West 12th, Little Rock, Arkansas 72204.

CARTON, MARY FRANCIS REGIS Occupation: Professor of Religious Studies and Department Chairperson, College of Notre Dame of Maryland. Education: B.A., Hunter College of The City of New York; M.A., Ph.D., The Catholic University of America, Washington, D.C. Address: 4701 North Charles Street, Baltimore, Maryland 21210.

CARTY, CHRISTINE A Occupation: Juvenile Justice Program Director. Education: B.A., University

of Massachusetts; Certificate, School of Business Administration, Harvard University; Certificate, University of Colorado. Address: 2030 East 11th Avenue, Denver, Colorado 80206.

CARVALHO, ANGELINA C A Occupation: Chief Hematology. Education: B.S., M.D. Address: 263 Powell Street, Stoughton, Massachusetts 02072.

CARVALHO, JAIME S Occupation: Assistant Professor of Medicine, Brown University; Research Nephrologist. Education: M.D., Lisbon Medical School, 1964. Address: 263 Powell Street, Stoughton, Massachusetts 02072.

CARVALHO, JOSELY M SOUNIS Occupation: Visual Artist. Education: B.A., Jayme Carvalho de Oliveira. Address: 216 East 18th Street, New York, New York 10003.

CARVALHO, JULIE ANN Occupation: Psychology. Education: B.A., M.D., Ph.D. Address: 11668 Mediterranean Court, Ruston, Virginia 22090.

CARVER, BEVERLY A Occupation: Vice President, Computing Adventures, Ltd. Education: B.A., Ed.M., Ph.D. Address: 3701 East Monterosa #5, Phoenix, Arizona 85018.

CARVER, GEORGE BRYAN Occupation: Police Official. Education: B.A., George Washington University, 1957. Address: Munson Hill Towers, Apartment 802, 6129 Leesburg Pike, Falls Church, Virginia 22041.

CARVER, JULIA Occupation: Professor of Physical Education. Education: Ph.D. Address: 53-126 Halai Street, Hauula, Hawaii 96717.

CARVER, STEVEN H Occupation: Director, Motion Pictures. Education: High School of Music and Art, New York City; M.A. Art and Photography, University of Buffalo, Buffalo, New York; M.A. Art, Film-making, Photography, Washington University, St. Louis, Missouri; American Film Institute, Center for Advanced Studies, Beverly Hills, California. Address: 1010 Pacific Avenue, Venice, California 90291.

CASATI, LAWRENCE W III Occupation: Priest. Education: B.A., M.A. Address: 2126 Elsmere, Dayton, Ohio 45406.

CASE, NORMAN MONDELL Occupation: Associate Professor Anatomy. Education: B.S., M.S., Ph.D. Address: 11635 Vista Lane, Yucaipa, California 92399.

CASE, STUART Occupation: Director of Public Relations. Education: M.A., B.A., Columbia College. Address: Rural Route 1, Box 32A, Hampton, Connecticut 06247.

CASELLA, RUSSELL C Occupation: Theoretical Physicist. Education: B.A., Massachusetts Institute of Technology, 1951; M.S. 1953, Ph.D. 1956, University of Illinois. Address: 1485 Dunster Lane, Potomac, Maryland 20854.

CASEMAN, AUSTIN BERT Occupation: Professor of Civil Engineering. Education: B.S., M.S., Sc.D., C.E., Massachusetts Institute of Technology. Address: 2136 Kodiak Drive, North East, Atlanta, Georgia 30345.

CASEY, EDWIN F Occupation: Cemetery Managing Director. Education: M.B.A., California Coast University. Address: 116 Haddon Road, New Hyde Park, New York 11040.

CASEY, MARY FRANCES Occupation: Theatre/ Music Faculty. Education: B.S., Western Michigan University; M.A., Southwest Missouri State University. Address: 4401 Manner Gate Court, Louisville, Kentucky 40220.

CASH, ROBERT C Occupation: Auditor.

Education: B.S., University of Kentucky, 1974. Address: 1749 Nantucket Drive, Cicero, Indiana 46034.

CASHMAN, SUZANNE B Occupation: Hospital Administration and Research. Education: B.A., M.S., D.Sc. Address: 17 Calvin Road, Newtonville, Massachusetts 02160

CASMIR, FRED L Occupation: Professor of Communication, Pepperdine University, Malibu, California. Education: M.A., Ph.D., Ohio State University; B.A., Lipscomb College. Address: 1967 Hilldale Drive, La Canada, California 91011.

CASSARD, DANIEL W Occupation: Professional International Agri-business Consultant. Education: B.S., Ph.D. Address: 155 McFadden Hut, Brownsville, Texas 78520.

CASSIDY, JACK Occupation: Professor of Education, Writer. Education: A.B., Gettysburg College; M.Ed., Ph.D., Temple Uhiversity. Address: Post Office Box 55, Kemblesville, Pennsylvania 19347.

CASSILL, KARILYN KAY Occupation: Writer/ Artist. Education: B.A., University of Iowa, Graduate Study. Address: 22 Boylston Avenue, Providence, Rhode Island 02906.

CASTANIS, MICHAEL B Occupation: Sculptor. Address: 444 6th Avenue, New York, New York 10011.

CASTENSCHIOLD, RENE Occupation: Executive Engineering Manager. Education: Bachelor of Electrical Engineering. Address: Lee's Hill Road, New Vernon, New Jersey 07976.

CASTOR, WILLIAM STUART JR Occupation: Consulting Chemist. Education: B.S. 1947, Ph.D. 1950, Northwestern University. Address: 111 Schuyler Road, Allendale, New Jersey 07401.

CASTRO, ELIZABETH Occupation: Active in Eli's Enterprises and Foundation; Actress; Model; Writer; Author; Investigator. Education: High School Graduate. Address: 74-02 Metropolitan Avenue, Middle Village, New York 11379.

CASTRO, JAN GARDEN Occupation: Writer, Corporation Director. Education: B.A., University of Wisconsin, 1967; M.A.T., Washington University, 1974. Address: 7420 Cornell, St. Louis, Missouri 63130.

CATALÁ, RAFAEL E Occupation: Poet, Writer, University Professor. Education: B.A., M.A., Ph.D., New York University. Address: Rural Delivery 1, Box 356, Hampton, New Jersey 08827.

CATALFO, ALFRED JR Occupation: Attorney at Law. Education: A.B. 1945, LL.B. 1947, M.A. 1952, J.D. 1969. Address: 450 Central Avenue, Dover, New Hampshire 03820.

CATELLA, GARY C Occupation: Optical Scientist. Education: B.S. Address: 8210 Tulip Lane, Chagrin Falls, Ohio 44022.

CAULFIELD, JANE H Occupation: Assistant Sanctuary Director. Education: B.A., Southern Methodist University, 1960. Address: 385 Old Beaverbrook, Acton, Massachusetts 01718.

CAVANAGH, MARGUERITE EVELYN Occupation: Office Nurse and Endoscopy Assistant. Education: Registered Nurse. Address: 2441 Arlington, Davenport, Iowa 52803.

CAWOOD, BILLIE JEAN Occupation: Supervisor of Instruction. Education: B.A., M.A. Address: Post Office Box 177, Cawood, Kentucky 40831.

CAZEAUX, ISABELLE ANNE MARIE Occupation: Professor of Musicology. Education: B.A., M.A., M.S.L.S., Ph.D. Address: 415 East 72nd Street, New York, New York 10021.

CEBRIK, MELVIN L Occupation: Banking. Education: A.B., M.B.A. Address: 20 Kimberly Court, Ramsey, New Jersey 07446.

CECCONI-BATES, AUGUSTA Occupation: Musician. Education: A.B. 1956, M.A. 1960, Syracuse University. Address: 816 Shaw Drive, Toad Harbor, West Monroe, New York 13167.

CEHELSKY, MARTA Occupation: Policy Analyst. Education: Ph.D., M.A., B.A. Address: 1233 East Street South East, Washington, District of Columbia 20003.

CELLA, EUGENE A Occupation: Certified Public Accountant. Education: B.B.A. Address: 1601 George Road, Wantagh, New York 11793.

CELLINI, WILLIAM QUIRINO JR Occupation: Electrical Engineer. Education: B.S.E.E., Drexel University; M.B.A., University of Pittsburgh; M.S.E.E. Candidate, George Washington University. Address: 2111 Jefferson Davis Highway, 1012-5, Arlington, Virginia 22202.

CELMINS, AIVARS KARLIS RICHARDS Occupation: Mathematician. Education: Dr. rer. nat, Dipl.-Math. Address: 38 Maple Lane, Elkton, Maryland 21921.

CELOTTA, BEVERLY KAY Occupation: Senior Partner. Education: B.A., M.S., Ph.D. Address: 14904 Piney Grove Court, Gaithersburg, Maryland 20878.

CENTERWALL, WILLARD R Occupation: Professor of Pediatrics and Genetics. Education: M.D., M.S., M.P.H. Address: 1047-35th Avenue, Sacramento, California 95822.

CERNEA, MICHAEL M Occupation: Sociologist; Sociology Adviser, The World Bank. Education: Ph.D. Sociology. Address: 5918 Utah Avenue Northwest, Washington, D.C. 20015.

CESSNA, R MICHAEL Occupation: Chiropractic Physician. Education: B.A., D.C. Address: Route 3, Box 539, Rogers, Arkansas 72756.

CEURVELS, WARREN S Occupation: Director of Adult and Continuing Education. Education: B.A., M.A., Ed.D. Address: Rural Route 2, Box 1089, Highlands Lakes, New Jersey 07422.

CHAFFEE, JOHN C Occupation: Faculty. Education: R.D.H., B.A., M.S.H.P. Address: 7711 Ravenridge, St. Louis, Missouri 63119.

CHAGALL, DAVID Occupation: Writer and Publisher. Education: B.A., Pennsylvania State University. Address: 28232 Foothill Drive, Agoura Hills, California 91301.

CHAKRABARTI, SUBRATA KUMAR Occupation: Director of Marine Research, Engineer. Education: B.S. in Mechanical Engineering, M.S. in Mechanical Enginering, Ph.D. Address: 191 East Weller Drive North, Plainfield, Illinois 60544.

CHALMERS, DAVID BAY Occupation: Chairman of the Board, Chief Executive Officer. Education: B.A., Dartmouth College, 1947; Tuck School of Business, Harvard Business School Advanced Management Program. Address: 908 Town and Country Boulevard, Houston, Texas 77024.

CHAMBERS, ROSEMARY Occupation: Coordinator. Education: B.S., M.Ed. Address: 2284 Mammoth Way, Louisville, Kentucky 40299.

CHAMPLIN, ARTHUR K Occupation: Professor of Biology. Education: B.A., M.A., Williams; Ph.D., University of Rochester. Address: 73 First Rangeway, Waterville, Maine 04901.

CHAN, LINDA S Occupation: Dirctor of Research, Planning and Evaluation. Education: Ph.D. in Biostatistics. Address: 8247 La Bajada Avenue, Whittier, California 90605.

CHAN, WAI YEE Occupation: Associate Professor of Pediatrics, Biochemistry and Molecular Biology. Education: B.Sc., Ph.D. Address: 8725 Raven Avenue, Oklahoma City, Oklahoma 73132.

CHANDLER, DIANA L Occupation: Social Worker. Education: B.A., University of Illinois; M.S.W., Western Michigan University. Address: 850 Rosedale #15, Capitola, California 95010.

CHANG, GEORGE CHAO TSI Occupation: Physician and Surgeon. Education: Doctor of Podiatric Medicine. Address: 6416 Terese Terrace, Jamesville, New York 13078.

CHANG, HSIA FEI WANG Occupation: Research Technician. Education: Master of Science. Address: 29 Gregory Street, Waltham, Massachusetts 02154.

CHANG, JOHN H Occupation: Manager of Systems Evaluation. Education: Ph.D., Yale University, 1969. Address: 33 Pheasant Drive, Armonk, New York 10504.

CHANG, WINSTON W Occupation: Professor of Economics. Education: Ph.D., University of Rochester, 1968. Address: 54 Taverly Drive, Williamsville, New York 14221.

CHANOVER, PIERRE E Occupation: Professor. Address: 599 Demott Aveanue, Baldwin, New York 11510.

CHAPEY, ROBERTA Occupation: Aphasiology/ Speech Language Patrology. Education: B.A., M.A., Ed.D. Address: 225 East 66 Street, New York, New York 10021.

CHAPMAN, CARL HALEY Occupation: Professor of Anthropology and Research Professor in American Archology. Education: A.B., University of Missouri, 1939; M.A., University of New Mexico, 1946; Ph.D., University of Michigan, 1959. Address: 211 Edgewood, Columbus, Missouri 65203.

CHAPMAN, HARRY S Occupation: Manager Application Engineering. Education: Bachelor in Chemistry. Address: 603 Hickory Hill, L. Road, Oxford, Pennsylvania 19363.

CHAPMAN, ROBERT GORDON Occupation: Educational/Vocational Counselor. Education: B.A., M.A. Address: 6060 Loma Prieta Drive, San Jose, California 95123.

CHAPPELL, ANNETTE M Occupation: Dean. Education: B.A. 1962, M.A. 1964, Ph.D. 1970, University of Maryland College Park. Address: College of Liberal Arts, Towson State University, Towson, Maryland 21204.

CHAPPELL, LORA L Occupation: Executive Director. Education: Business College. Address: 1104 Ellis Avenue, Jackson, Mississippi 39209.

CHAPPELL, PAUL N Occupation: Sales Representative, Bali Company, New York. Education: Associate Business Administration and Public Administration, 1980; A.B. Economics, University of Georgia, 1982. Address: Post Office Box 453, Sendia, Georgia 30276.

CHAPPELL, WILLIE L (BILL) Occupation: Westernartist, Oil Paintings and Bronzes. Address: Post Office Box 246, South Fork, Colorado 81154.

CHARLTON, GEORGE N JR Occupation: Executive Director. Education: Bachelor of Business Administration, University of Pittsburgh. Address: 1714 Lincoln Avenue, Pittsburgh, Pennsylvania 15206.

CHARNOV, BRUCE H Occupation: College Professor. Education: B.A., M.A., M.B.A., Ph.D., Rabbi. Address: 200 Lexington Avenue, 12-C, Oyster Bay, New York 11771.

CHARY, ERIKA MAGDA Occupation: Artist, Teacher, Pianist. Education: A.R.C.M., L.R.A.M. Address: 6931 Vallon Drive, Palos Verdes Peninsula, California 90274.

CHASE, RICHARD CONANT Occupation: Physicist, ITEK Corporation, Lexington, Massachusetts. Education: B.S., USMA, West Point, New York, 1956; M.S., RPI, Troy, New York, 1962; Ph.D., Northeastern University, Boston, Massachusetts, 1966. Address: 447 Kendall Road, Tewksbury, Massachusetts 01876.

CHASTAIN, GARVIN Occupation: University Professor, Boise State University, Boise, Idaho. Education: Ph.D. Human Experimental Psychology, University of Texas at Austin, 1976. Address: 3500 Tulara Drive, Boise, Idaho 83704.

CHASTEEN, EDGAR RAY Occupation: College Professor, William Jewell College, Liberty, Missouri. Education: M.B.S., M.A., Ph.D. Address: 1702 Magnolia, Liberty, Missouri 64068.

CHATFIELD, RUTH Occupation: Artist. Education: Attended and Graduated from New York School of Applied Design; Attended Art Students League, New York. Address: 6701 Woodcrest Drive, Austin, Texas 78759.

CHATTERJEE, SUNIL KUMAR Occupation: Scientist. Education: M.S., Ph.D. Address: 152 Telfair Drive, Williamsville, New York 14221.

CHATZKY, MICHAEL GARY Occupation: Lawyer. Education: B.S., University of Maryland, 1966; J.D., University of Maryland School of Law, 1969. Address: 5116 Westmont Avenue, San Jose, California 95130.

CHAZANOFF, DANIEL Occupation: Music and Music Education, City School District, Rochester, New York. Education: B.Sc., Ohio State University; M.A.; Ed.D., Columbia University. Address: 114 Penarrow Road, Rochester, New York 14618.

CHAZEN, LEONA Occupation: Fiscal Program Analyst, United States Department of Education, Washington, D.C. Address: 4000 Tunlaw Road, North West, Apartment 1029, Washington, D. C. 20007.

CHEADLE, LOUISE MAXINE Occupation: Concert Pianist, College Teacher. Education: Artist Diploma, Juilliard School of Music. Address: 48 Princeton Avenue Rocky Hill, New Jersey 08553.

CHEKKI, DANESH A Occupation: Professor of Sociology, University of Winnipeg, Manitoba, Canada. Education: M.A., LL.B., Ph.D. Address: 38 Fitzgerald Circle, Winnipeg, Manitoba, Canada R3R 7N8.

CHEN, ALICE W Occupation: Gifted Education, Creativity, Continuing Education, Greece Central School District, North Greece, New York. Education: B.S., M.S., Ph.D. Address: 8 Tartarian Circle, Rochester, New York 14612.

CHEN, CHING-CHIH Occupation: Professor and Associate Dean, Simmons College, Boston, Massachusetts. Education: Ph.D. Address: 1400 Commonwealth Avenue, West Newton, Massachusetts 02165.

CHEN, E EVA Occupation: Quality Assurance Manager, Phones Division, ROLM Corporation, Santa Clara, California. Education: Ph.D. Address: 718 Inverness Way, Sunnyvale, California 94087.

CHEN, HOLLIS C Occupation: Professor of Electrical and Computer Engineering, Ohio State University, Athens, Ohio. Education: B.S.; M.S. and Ph.D. in Electrical Engineering. Address: 1 Ball Drive, Athens, Ohio 45701.

CHEN, KUEN HAI Occupation: Physician. Education: M.D. Address: 51 Warren Road, West Orange, New Jersey 07052.

CHEN, MICHAEL S K Occupation: Manager of Process Evaluation at Air Products and Chemicals, Incorporation, Allentown, Pennsylvania. Education: B.S., Ph.D., in Chemical Engineering. Address: RD 1, Box 140A, Zionsville, Pennsylvania 18092.

CHEN, SOW-HSIN Occupation: Professor of Nuclear Engineering, Massachusetts Institute of Technology, Cambridge, Massachusetts. Education: Ph.D. Physics, McMaster University, Canada, 1964. Address: 1400 Commonwealth Avenue, West Newton, Massachusetts 02165

CHEN, SOW-YEH Occupation: Teaching, Research, Practice; University Teacher. Education: B.M.D., M.S., Ph.D. Address: 828 Hilldale Road, Glenside, Pennsylvania 19038.

CHENG, DAVID K Occupation: Professor of Electrical and Computer Engineering, Syuracuse University, Syracuse, New York. Education: B.S.E.E., S.M., Sc.D. Address: 102 Harpers Court, DeWitt, New York 13214.

CHENNAULT, ANNA CHAN Occupation: President, TAC International, Incorporated, Washington, D.C. Education: Doctor of Letters, Chung-ang University, Seoul, Korea, 1967; Doctor of Laws, Lincoln University, 1970; Doctor of Humanities, Manahath Educational Center, 1970; Doctor of Humanities, St. John's University, 1982; Doctor of Humanities, American University of the Caribbean, 1982. Address: 2510 Virginia Avenue, North West, Washington, D.C. 20037.

CHERNICOFF, DAVID P Occupation: Physician and Associate Professor, Hemotology and Oncology. Education: A.B., D.O. Address: 4165 Ridgeland Lane, Northbrook, Illinois 60062.

CHERNOW, ANN LEVY Occupation: Assistant Professor of Art; Artist. Education: M.A., New York University. Address: 2 Gorham Avenue, Westport, Connecticut 06880.

CHERNOW, BURT Occupation: Artist. Education: B.S. in Art Education, New York University, 1958; M.A. in Higher Art Education, New York University, 1960; Sixth Year of Graduate Work, New York University, 1965-68. Address: 2 Gorham Avenue, Westport, Connecticut 06880.

CHERRY, CLIFFORD B Occupation: Physician. Education: A.B., Stanford University; Riverside Junior College; M.D., Stanford University School of Medicine, 1935. Address: 2400 Beverly Boulevard, Los Angeles, California 90057.

CHERRY, KELLY Occupation: Professor and Permanent Writer in Residence. Address: Engineering Department, University of Wisconsin, Madison, Wisconsin 53706.

CHESS, STEPHEN JOHN Occupation: Chief Surgeon, Buenaventura Medical Clinic, Inc.; Commissioner, Bureau of Medical Quality Administration, State of California. Education: B.S., M.S., M.D., Ph.D. Surgery. Address: 155 Lakewood Avenue, Ventura, California 93004.

CHESSMAN, ELMER F Occupation: Chemistry Teacher; Director of Adult Education. Education: M.S., Northwestern University. Address: 4808 Middaugh, Downers Grove, Illinois 60515.

CHESTER, EMMA L Occupation: Junior High School Science Teacher. Education: B.A. 1970, M.S. 1978. Address: 2353 North College Avenue, Indianapolis, Indiana 46205.

CHEW, MALCOLM CHEE WAN Occupation: Student. Education: B.S. System Science. Address: Post Office Box 32372, University of West Florida, Pensacola, Florida 32514.

CHIANG, FU-PEN Occupation: Professor of Engineering, Department of Mechanical Engineering, State University of New York, Stony Brook, New York. Education: B.S., National Taiwan University; M.S., Ph.D., University of Florida. Address: 27 Cove Lane, Port Jefferson, New York 11777.

CHIANG, JOHN Y L Occupation: Associate Professor of Molecular Pathology. Education: M.S., Ph.D. Address: 1173 Erin Drive, Kent, Ohio 44240.

CHIDA, THOMAS LAWRENCE Occupation: Psychology Intern. Education: M.A. 1982, Doctoral Candidate. Address: 11010 Castolon, Dallas, Texas 75228.

CHIGIER, NORMAN Occupation: Professor, Mechanical Engineering Department, Carnegie Mellon University, Pittsburgh, Pennsylvania. Education: B.Sc., M.A., Ph.D., Sc.D. Address: 5283 Northumberland Street, Pittsburgh, Pennsylvania 15217.

CHILCUTT, DORTHE M Occupation: Art Teacher; Artist. Education: B.S., M.S. University of Wisconsin. Address: 506 South West 15th Street, Okeechobee, Florida 33472.

CHILD, RAWSON DENNIS Occupation: Range Research Scientist. Education: B.S.; M.S.; Ph.D. Address: Route 3, Box 265, Morrilton, Arkansas 72110.

CHILDRES, MARY ROSE Occupation: Secretary; Senior Business Administrator for Continuing Education. Education: Withrow High School; College Conservatory of Music; Business Practice Institute; Kentucky State University; Bluefield State University; West Virginia University; University of Cincinnati: A.S., Secretarial Science; B.S. Administrative Management; Psychology of Human Behaviour. Address: 838 Crowden Drive, Cincinnati, Ohio 45224.

CHILES, JERRY E Occupation: Minister of Education in Baptist Church. Education: B.A., Georgetown College, 1968; M.R.E. 1970, G.S.R.E 1971, Southern Seminary. Address: 614 Valley Drive, Dalton, Georgia 30720.

CHIN, JANET S Occupation: Software Development Manager, Computer Science. Education: B.A. Mathematics, University of Illinois; M.S. Computer Science, University of Illinois. Address: 22047 McClellan Road, Cupertino, California 95014.

CHIN, SUE SUCHIN Occupation: Artist. Education: California College of Arts in Los Angeles; Minneapolis Art Institute and Schaeffer Design Center. Address: Dr. Suchin Associates, Fox Plaza, San Francisco, California 94102.

CHING, JULIA C Occupation: Professor of Religious Studies, Victoria College, University of Toronto, Canada. Education: Ph.D. 1971, M.A. 1960, B.A. 1958. Address: 478 Palmerston Boulevard, Toronto, Canada.

CHINN, GENEVIEVE L Occupation: Professor of Music, Long Island University, Greenvale, New York. Education: Ph.D., M.A., B.S., Columbia University. Address: 199 Mountain Road, Wilton, Connecticut 06897.

CHIRIBOGA, DAVID ANTHONY Occupation: Associate Professor. Education: Ph.D., University of Chicago; A.B., Boston University. Address: Post Office Box 1683, Sausalito, California 94966.

CHISHOLM, WILLIAM DeWAYNE Occupation: Contract Manager. Education: B.S. Chemical Engineering, 1949; B.S. in Industrial Engineering, University of Washington, 1949; M.B.A., Harvard Business School, 1955. Address: 1364 Hercules Avenue, South, Clearwater, Florida 33546.

CHISM, SYLVIA CHARLOTTE Occupation: Assistant Professor, Nursing Department. Education: Diploma, Nursing; Bachelor's Psychology; Master's Science, Nursing; Ph.D. Nursing Administration and Health Services Administration. Address: 1105 Park Avenue, Apartment A, Alameda, California 94501.

CHITRE, NANDKISHORE M Occupation:

International Civil Servant; Physicist. Education: Ph.D. London, 1962. Address: 309 Yoakum Parkway, Alexandria, Virginia 22304.

CHIU, PETER J S Occupation: Drug Research; Pharmacologist, Schering Corporation, Bloomfield, New Jersey. Education: Ph.D., M.S., B.S. Address: 9 Edwin Road, Morris Plains, New Jersey 07950.

CHLARSON, LINDER N Occupation: Composer, Lyricist, Writer. Education: B.A., University of Washington, 1959. Address: 636 East 14 Street, #10, New York, New York 10009.

CHMIELINSKI, EDWARD A Occupation: President and Chief Executive Officer, The Lewis Engineering Company. Education: B.S.M.E., Tulane University, 1950; M.B.A., Colorado University, 1965. Address: 238 Water Street, Naugatuck, Connecticut 06770.

CHOA, RICHARD C Occupation: Civil Engineer, Jacobs Engineering Group, Pasadena, California. Education: M.S.C.E. Address: 724 Topacio Drive, Monterey Park, California 91754.

CHOLMELEY-JONES, EDWARD OWEN NIGAL Occupation: Writer and Artist. Address: Jasup Road, Westport, Connecticut 06880.

CHOU, CHUNG-KWANG Occupation: Research and Teaching in Bioengineering, University Hospital, Seattle, Washington. Education: Ph.D. Address: 11038 15th Avenue, North East, Seattle, Washington 98125.

CHOU, TSU-WEI Occupation: Professor, University of Delaware, Newark, Delaware. Education: M.A., Northwestern University, 1966; Ph.D., Stanford University, 1969. Address: 15 Kenwick Road, Hockessin, Delaware 19707.

CHOUDHURY, DEO CHAND Occupation: Professor of Physics. Education: B.Sc., M.Sc., Ph.D. Address: 90 Gold Street, New York, New York 10038.

CHOUN, ROBERT JOSEPH Occupation: Minister of Education and Professor. Education: B.A., M.R.E., M.A., D.Min., Ph.D. Candidate. Address: 818 Clover Park Drive, Arlington, Texas 76013.

CHOW, GREGORY CHI-CHONG Occupation: Professor of Economics, Princeton University, Princeton, New Jersey. Education: Ph.D. Economics, M.A. Economics, B.A. Economics. Address: 30 Hardy Drive, Princeton, New Jersey 08540.

CHOW, KAO LIANG Occupation: Professor of Neurology, Stanford University, Stanford, California. Education: Ph.D. Address: Apartment 805, 1012 Alma Street, Palo Alto, California 94301.

CHOY, BONG YOUN Occupation: Professor, Contrat Coasta College, San Pablo, California. Education: B.A., M.A., Ph.D. (Honorary). Address: 101 Tamalpais Road, Berkeley, California 94708.

CHRISTENSEN, CHARLOTTE ELSIE Occupation: Instructor, Clothing and Textiles. Education: B.S., Pepperdine University; M.A., California State University, Humboldt. Address: 1096 Rose Drive, Napa, California 94558.

CHRISTENSON, EVELYN CAROL Occupation: Writer, Lecturer. Education: A.A., Bethel College, St. Paul; Student, Moody Bible Institute, Chicago, Illinois. Address: 4265 Brigadoon Drive, Saint Paul, Minnesota 55112.

CHRISTIE, CLARENCE J Occupation: Vice President and Treasurer, Fred. S. James and Company, Incorporated. Education: Graduate, University of Wisconsin. Address: 73 Druid Hill Road, Summit, New Jersey 07901.

CHRISTMAN, EDWARD A Occupation: Radiological Physicist, Rutgers University, New Brunswick, New Jersey. Education: Ph.D. 1977, M.S. 1974, B.S. 1965. Address: 1 Lincoln Place, Apartment 9G, North Brunswick, New Jersey 08902.

CHRISTMAN, LUTHER P Occupation: Vice President, Nursing Affairs, The John L. and Helen Kellogg; Dean, the College of Nursing of Rush University. Education: B.S. Nursing, Ed.M. Clinical Psychology, Ph.D. Sociology and Anthropology. Address: 19141 Loomis Avenue, Homewood, Illinois 60430.

CHRISTOFFERSON, EARL S Occupation: Senior Pastor. Education: A.B., M.Div., Doctor of Ministry (D.Min.). Address: 1486 Thunderbird Avenue, Sunnyvale, California 94087.

CHRISTOPHER, STEVEN L Occupation: Minister of Youth. Education: B.S. in Education, D.C.E. Certificate, L.T.D. Lutheran Teacher Diploma. Address: 4561 Montair D-24, Long Beach, California 90808.

CHRISTOPHERSON, MARIE LUCILLE Occupation: Learning Disabilities Teacher. Education: B.S.Ed., M.S.Ed., Ph.D. Address: 318 Meek, Box 1032, Arkansas City, Kansas 67005.

CHRISTY, JAMES WALTER Occupation: Physicist, Hughes Aircraft. Education: B.S., University of Arizona. Address: 1720 West Niona Place, Tucson, Arizona 85704.

CHROBOT, LEONARD FRANCIS Occupation: President. Education: B.A., M.A., M.Div., Ph.D. Address: Saint Mary's College, Orchard Lake, Michigan 48033.

CHRONIC, HALKA Occupation: Geologist; Writer. Education: M.S., Stanford University; Ph.D., Columbia University. Address: 971 Sixth Street, Boulder, Colorado 80302.

CHU, JU CHIN Occupation: Chairman of the Board, Technology Resources, Incorporated. Education: B.S. in Chemistry, Tsing Hua University; Sc.D. Chemical Engineering, Massachusetts Institute of Technology. Address: 21 Yorktown, Irvine, California 92714.

CHU, RICHARD YUNGDEH Occupation: Professor of History. Education: B.A., Taiwan University; M.A., University of California; Ph.D., Columbia University. Address: 58 Bromley Road, Pittsford, New York 14534.

CHU, YUNG Y Occupation: Basic Research, Chemistry, B.N.L., Upton, New York. Education: B.Sc., Taiwan University; Ph.D., University of California, Berkeley. Address: Garden Lane, Yaphank, New York 11980.

CHUDOMELKA, LaMOND RICHARD Occupation: College Professor. Education: B.S.E., M.S.E., University of Missouri. Address: Box H Beebe, Arkansas 72012.

CHUEY, CARL F Occupation: Associate Professor of Biological Science and Curator of Herbarium. Education: B.S. Youngstown State University, 1966; M.S., Ohio State University, 1969; Ed.D. (Honorary), Ohio Christian College, 1971. Address: 214 Wildwood Drive, Youngstown, Ohio 44512.

CHUNG, DEBORAH DUEN LING Occupation: University Faculty, Carnegie-Mellon University, Pittsburgh, Pennsylvania. Education: Ph.D. in Materials Science, Massachusetts Institute of Technology, 1977. Address: 3812 Henley Drive, Pittsburgh, Pennsylvania 15235.

CHURCH, COLIN BARCLAY Occupation: Federal Government, International Laison, CPSC, Washington, D.C. Education: A.B., Harvard University; M.B.A., Wharton University. Address: 7805 Overhill Road, Bethesda, Maryladn 20814.

CHURCH, IRENE ZABOLY Occupation: President and Chairman of Board, Oxford Peronnel and Temporaries. Education: Graduate of Public Schools 1965. Address: 8 Ridgecrest Drive, Chagrin Falls, Ohio 44022.

CHURCH, LLOYD EUGENE Occupation: Oral Surgery; Research Teaching Administrator. Education: B.A., D.D.S., M.S., Ph.D. Address: 7005 Glenbrook Road, Bethesda, Maryland 20814.

CHURCHILL, ARTHUR C Occupation: College Professor, Defiance College, Defiance, Ohio. Education: B.S. Rhode Island State College, 1934; M.A., American University, 1966. Address: 203 East Sessions, Defiance, Ohio 43512.

CHURCHILL, MELVYN ROWEN Occupation: Professor of Chemistry, State University of New York at Buffalo, Buffalo, New York. Education: B.Sc. 1961, Ph.D. 1964. Address: 670 LeBrun Road, Eggertsville, New York 14226.

CHUTE, PHILLIP BRUCE Occupation: Education: Business Consultant; Author. Education: B.S. Business Administration. Address: 1044 Terrace Drive, Upland, California 91786.

CHWANG, ALLEN T Occupation: Professor, Institute of Hydraulic Research, University of Iowa, Iowa City, Iowa. Education: Ph.D. Address: 139 Penfro Drive, Iowa City, Iowa 52240.

CIABATTARI, JANE DOTSON Occupation: Editor in Chief, DIAL Magazine, Inter-State. Education: B.A., Stanford University, 1968; M.A., San Francisco State University, 1983. Address: 36 West 75th Street, New York, New York 10023.

CIBLEY, LEONARD J Occupation: Physician, Obstetrics, Gynecology. Education: A.B., M.A. Address: 251 Grant Avenue, Newton Centre, Massachusetts 02159.

CICALESE, LOUIS A Occupation: Attorney; Real Estate Developer. Education: Doctor of Jurisprudence, Bachelor of Arts. Address: 193 Tigertail, Los Angeles, California 90049.

CICHON, DONALD J Occupation: Social Science; Educational Research Consultant. Education: M.A., University of Chicago, 1973. Address: 54 Rutland Street, Dover, New Hampshire 03820.

CINADER, BERNARD Occupation: Professor, University of Toronto, Canada; Scientist. Education: B.Sc. 1944, Ph.D. 1948, D.Sc. 1958, University of London, England. Address: 73 Langley Avenue, Toronto, Ontario, Canada M4K 1B4.

CINALLI, ROBERT A Occupation: Owner/ President: Robert A. Cinalli & Associates, a Marketing Agency, Pine Beach, New Jersey. Education: B.A., Upsala College, 1955. Address: 5 Avon Road, Post Office Box 461, Pine Beach, New Jersey 08741.

CIPRIANO, PATRICIA A Occupation: Educator; Consultant. Education: B.A., M.A. Address: 1648 Pacific Avenue, San Leandro, California 94577.

CIRILLO, DAVID J Occupation: Senior Management Development Specialist. Education: B.A., M.A., Ph.D. Industrial Organizational Psychology. Address: 106 Hancock Street, Dorchester, Massachusetts 02125.

CIRILLO, JEANINE M Occupation: Teacher. Education: B.A. Arts Communication. Address: 1920 19th Street, Boulder, Colorado 80302.

CISSIK, JOHN HENRY Occupation: United States Air Force Lt. Colonel; Physiologist, United States Air Force Medical Center, Keesler Air Force Base, Mississippi. Education: B.A., M.A. Zoology, Ph.D. Physiology. Address: 12316 Marlowe Place, Ocean Springs, Mississippi 39564.

CITRENBAUM, CHARLES M Occupation: Clinical Psychologist. Education: B.A., M.A., Ph.D. Address: 402 East Quadrangle, Baltimore, Maryland 21210.

CITRIN, JUDITH Occupation: Transformational Therapist and Counselor. Address: 423 Greenleaf, Wilmette, Illinois 60091.

CLACK, DICK SCOTT Occupation: International Trade. Education: B.S. Wildlife Conservation. Address: Post Office Box 22367, Honolulu, Hawaii 96822.

CLACK, JERRY Occupation: Professor of Classics, Duquesne University, Pittsburgh, Pennsylvania. Education: A.B., Princeton University; M.A., Ph.D., University of Pittsburgh; M.A., Duquesne University. Address: 5920 Kentucky Avenue, Pittsburgh, Pennsylvania 15232.

CLAGUE, ANN F Occupation: Nutritionist and Director of Nutritional Medical Allergy Center. Education: Ph.D. Address: 14601 Atrium Way, Minnetonka, Minnesota 55345.

CLAPP, H JAMES Occupation: Administration and Instruction of Martial Arts. Education: B.S. Political Science, 1970; 6th Degree Black Belt, 1983. Address: 23 Helios Court, Newark, Delaware 19711.

CLARIDGE, LOIS W Occupation: Retired R.N. and Social Worker. Education: Diploma Nursing, Evanston School of Nursing; B.S. Liberal Arts, Northwestern University. Address: Post Office Box 388, Safford, Arizona 85546.

CLARK, ALFRIEDA SORRELS Occupation: Librarian, U.S. Army Engineer Waterways Experiment Station. Education: B.S. Library Science, University of Southern Mississippi, 1957; M.L.S., University of Southern Mississippi, 1980. Address: 206 Enchanted Drive, Vicksburg, Mississippi 39180.

CLARK, CARL R Occupation: Public Administrator. Education: B.A., California Lutheran College, 1970; M.A.M., University of Redlands, 1984. Address: Post Office Box 1118, Wrightwood, California 92397.

CLARK, CHERYL L Occupation: Director, Network Program, DOCS, State Campus, Albany, New York. Education: M.S. Educational Psychology. Address: 431 Plymouth Avenue, Schenectady, New York 12308.

CLARK, HERMAN E JR Occupation: State Farm Insurance Agency. Education: A.A., B.S., University of Southern Mississippi. Address: 326 King, Philadelphia, Pennsylvania 39350.

CLARK, JAMES M Occupation: Real Estate Development and Finance, The Spectrum Group, Kilburn Vacation, Homeshare, Incorporated and Bajan Resorts, Incorporated. Education: B.S., University of the State of New York; M.B.A. Real Estate and Finance, Ph.D. Real Estate, Columbia Pacific University.

CLARK, JAMES ROBERT JR Occupation: Radiologist. Education: B.S. Pharmacy, 1969; D.O., 1977. Address: 621 Garden Road, Dayton, Ohio 45419.

CLARK, JULIA V Occupation: Professor of Science Education, Howard University, Washington, D.C. Education: B.S., M.Ed., Ed.D. Address: 5101 River Road, Bethesda, Maryland 20816.

CLARK, LaVERNE HARRELL Occupation: Author; Photographer; Lecturer. Education: B.A., Texas Woman's University, 1950; M.A., University of Arizona, 1962; Additional Studies, Columbia University. Address: 4690 North Campbell Avenue, Tucson, Arizona 85718.

CLARK, MARY T Occupation: Professor of Philosophy, Manhattanville College. Education: B.A., Manhattanville College; M.A., Ph.D., Fordham

University. Address: Manhattanville College, Purchase, New York 10577.

CLARK, MELVILLE JR Occupation: Physics, Nuclear Engineering, Electrical Engineering. Education: S.B., Massachusetts Institute of Technology; A.M., Ph.D., Harvard University; Additional Studies, University of New Mexico. Address: 8 Richard Road, Wayland, Massachusetts 01778-4099.

CLARK, MERRY MAUREEN Occupation: Editor, *Sunday Woman Magazine.* Education: Bachelor of Journalism Degree, University of Texas. Address: 220 East 54th Street, New York, New York 10022.

CLARK, SCOTT Occupation: Librarian. Education: B.S. Environmental Resources Management, Master of Library Science. Address: Post Office Box 146, Mount Upton, New York 13809.

CLARK, TERRY NICHOLS Occupation: Professor of Sociology, University of Chicago; Senior Study Director, National Opinion Research Center. Education: B.A. Psychology, Bowdoin College, 1962; Univerity of Paris, 1960-61; University of Frankfort, Berlin, Munich, 1962; M.A. Sociology, Columbia University, 1962; Ph.D. Sociology, Columbia University, 1967. Address: 322 Social Science Building, The University of Chicago, 1126 East 59th Street, Chicago, Illinois 60637.

CLARK, WALTER HOUSTON Occupation: Writer and Researcher. Education: B.A., Ed.M., Ph.D. Address: 21 Wildwood Drive, Cape Elizabeth, Maine 04107.

CLARKE, ANGELA WEBB Occupation: Physician. Education: B.S.; M.D. Address: 1703 Civic Center Drive, North Las Vegas, Nevada 89030.

CLARKE, MARGARET A Occupation: Managing Director, Sugar Products Research, Incorporated. Education: Ph.D., M.B.A., B.Sc. Address: Post Office Box 24317, New Orleans, Louisiana 70184.

CLEMENS, EARL L Occupation: Professor of Oboe and Music Education; Performer. Education: B.P.S.M., M.M., 88 Hours Beyond Masters in Performance. Address: 220 West Royal Drive, DeKalb, Illinois 60115.

CLEMENS, T PAT Occupation: Founder, President, T. P. Clemens Laboratory, Inc. Education: B.A. Economics and Management, St. Cloud State University, 1968. Address: 1276 Vildmark Drive, Eagan, Minnesota 55123.

CLEMENTS, MICHAEL REID Occupation: Chief Technical Officer, Amdahl Corporation. Education: A.A., Ricks College; B.E.S., Brigham Young University; Postgraduate, Stanford University. Address: 95 West Sunset Circle, Rexburg, Idaho 83440.

CLEMENTS, SARAH Occupation: Consultant. Education: B.A. Address: 4914 North 34th Street, Arlington, Virginia 22207.

CLEMETSON, C ALAN B Occupation: Professor of Obstetrics and Gynecology, Tulane University School of Medicine, New Orleans, Louisiana. Education: M.A., B.M., B.Ch., Oxford University, England. Address: 314 Country Club Drive, Pineville, Louisiana 71360.

CLEVELAND, CARL S Occupation: President, Cleveland Chiropractic College. Education: B.S., University of Missouri, Kansas City, 1970; Doctor of Chiropractic, Cleveland Chiropractic College, 1975. Address: 1234 West 58th Street, Kansas City, Missouri 64113.

CLEVELAND, CROMWELL COOK JR Occupation: Episopal Priest-Chaplain, Bp. Anderson Foundation. Education: B.A., Centre College

of Kentucky, 1971; M.Div., General Theological Seminary, New York City, 1975. Address: 1011 South Humphrey, Oak Park, Illinois 60304.

CLEVELAND, EMMA WALKER Occupation: College Professor. Education: A.B., Miles College; M.A., New York University. Address: 944 Center Place, South West, Birmingham, Alabama 35211.

CLEVELAND, WILLIAM T Occupation: Social Studies Educator; National Educators Association Director. Education: B.A., M.A., State University of New York-Albany. Address: 290 State Street, Albany, New York 12210.

CLICK, PAULA TAMMIE Occupation: Member of the United States Army. Education: A.A., B.A. magna cum laude, M.A., Marshall University. Address: Route 6, Box 365, Ashland, Kentucky 41101.

CLIFFORD, LEON A Occupation: President, Hudson-Mohawk Development Corporation. Education: A.B. Address: 8607 Teugega Point, Rome, New York 13440.

CLIFT, ANNIE SUE Occupation: Associate Professor of Nursing, University of Tennessee at Martin. Education: B.S.N., University of Tennessee School of Nursing; M.R.E., SWBTS; M.N., Emory University. Address: Route 2, Box 10, Newbern, Tennessee 38059.

CLINE, CHARLES (WILLIAM) Occupation: Professor of English, Poet, Author. Education: A.A., Reinhardt College; B.A., Peabody College; M.A., Vanderbilt University; Litt.D. (hon), World University Roundtable. Address: 9866 South Westnedge Avenue, Kalamazoo, Michigan 49002.

CLINE, JEANNEANE LEWIS Occupation: Assistant Administrator, Hospital. Education: B.S. Nursing; M.S. Psychology, Family Development Nursing. Address: 5733 Walla Avenue, Fort Worth, Texas 76133.

CLINTON, LLOYD DeWITT Occupation: Lecturer. Education: Ph.D., M.F.A., M.A. Address: 3567 North Murray, Shorewood, Wisconsin 53211.

CLOUSE, R. WILBURN Occupation: Professor, Vanderbilt University, Nashville, Tennessee. Education: B.A., M.A., Ph.D. Address: 914 Spain Avenue, Nashville, Tennessee 37216.

COATS, DARYL R Occupation: Student; Graduate Assistant. Education: B.A., M.A. Address: Box 1895, University, Mississippi 38677.

COATS, GARY JOSEPH Occupation: Professor of Architecture, Kansas State University, Manhattan, Kansas. Education: Bachelor of Enviornmental Design, Master of Architecture. Address: 315 North 15th Street, Manhattan, Kansas 66502.

COBB, CAROLYN ANN Occupation: Staff Specialist. Education: B.A., M.A. Address: 6520 Galewood Court, Saint Louis, Missouri 63129.

COBB, SHIRLEY DODSON Occupation: City of Thousand Oaks Writer, Public Relations. Education: B.A. with Distinction, University of Oklahoma. Address: 2481 Brookhill Drive, Camarillo, California 93010.

COBEY, RALPH Occupation: President, Scoopmobile Company. Education: Graduate, Galion Schools; Mechanical Engineering, Carnegie Institute of Technology. Address: 4250 State Route 309, Galion, Ohio 44833.

COCKRELL, MYRTLE BAILEY Occupation: Reading Specialist; Reading Consultant. Education: B.S., M.Ed., C.A.S., D.Ed. Address: 1307 Stonewood Road, Baltimore, Maryland 21239.

CODY, DOUGLAS THANE R Occupation: Physician. Education: M.D., Ph.D. Address: 200 1st

Street, South West, Rochester, Minnesota 55905.

COE, BENJAMIN P Occupation: Executive Director, New York Systems Tug Hill Commission. Education: A.B., Bowdoin College, Brunswick, Maine, 1953; B.S., Ch.E., Massachusetts Institute of Technology, Cambridge, Massachusetts. Address: 314 Paddock Street, Watertown, New York 13601.

COE, RICHARD M Occupation: Professor, Journalist. Education: Ph.D., M.A., B.A. Address: 2001 East Third Avenue, Vancouver, British Columbia, Canada.

COE, WILLIAM CHARLES Occupation: Professor of Psychology. Education: Ph.D., B.S. Address: 2941 Caesar, Clovis, California 93612.

COFFEY, MARILYN J Occupation: Writer and Assistant Professor. Education: M.F.A., Brooklyn College, 1981; B.A., University of Nebraska, 1959. Address: 172 Emerson Place, Brooklyn, New York 11205.

COHEN, ALICE E Occupation: Theatre Artist; Composer; Playwright. Education: B.A., Princeton University. Address: 250 West 77th Street, #103, New York, New York 10024.

COHEN, ANITA M Occupation: Attorney. Education: B.A., University of Pittsburgh, Pittsburgh, Pennsylvania, 1967; J.D., Duquesne University School of Law, Pittsburgh, 1970. Address: 8201 Henry Avenue L-21, Philadelphia, Pennsylvania 19128.

COHEN, BARBARA J TIMMER Occupation: Marine Owner/Manager. Education: B.S. Home Economics Education, Washington State University. Address: 321-73rd Avenue, North East, Olympia, Washington 98506.

COHEN, DARRYL BRANDT Occupation: Attorney, Actor, Model. Education: A.B., University of Georgia; J.D., Mercer University Walter F. George School of Law. Address: 4000 Orchard Lake Court, Atlanta, Georgia.

COHEN, DAVID E Occupation: Associate Publisher, L. A. Weekly. Education: B.A. Intellectual History. Address: 4133 Clayton Avenue, Los Angeles, California 90027.

COHEN, EDWARD Occupation: Construction Engineer. Education: B.S. Engineering 1945, M.S. Civil Engineering 1954, Columbia University. Address: 56 Chestnut Hill, Roslyn, New York 11576.

COHEN, EDWARD LEWIS Occupation: Professor in Mathematics, University of Ottawa, Canada. Education: A.B., Harvard University; S.M., Sc.D., Massachusetts Institute of Technology. Address: Box 136, Station B, Ottawa, Canada K1P 6C3.

COHEN, EVE Occupation: Administrative Law, Judge. Education: B.A., J.D. Address: 9806 Belmar Avenue, Northridge, California 91324.

COHEN, GERALD LEONARD Occupation: Professor of Foreign Languages. Education: Ph.D. in Slavic Linguistics. Address: Route 4, Box 78, Rolla, Missouri 65401.

COHEN, HERBERT A Occupation: Dean of the College, Professor of Psychology, Olney Central College. Education: B.A., M.A., Ed.D. Address: 108 Oakwood Drive, Olney, Illinois 62450.

COHEN, JEFFREY M Occupation: Physics Professor, University of Pennsylvania, Philadelphia. Education: Ph.D., Yale University, 1966. Address: University of Pennsylvania, Philadelphia, Pennsylvania 19104.

COHEN, JOEL RALPH Occupation: Professor of Biology and Health Sciences, Springfield College. Education: B.S., M.S., Ph.D. University of Massachusetts. Address: 14 Inglewood Avenue, Springfield, Massachusetts 01119.

COHEN, MYRON LESLIE Occupation: Biomedical Engineering Consultant. Education: B.S.M.E., M.S.E., Ph.D. Address: 401 Three Corners Road, Guilford, Connecticut 06437.

COHEN, RICHARD STOCKMAN Occupation: United States Attorney. Education: B.B.A., L.L.B. Address: 94 Winthrop Street, Augusta, Maine 04330.

COHEN, ROSALIE AGGER Occupation: Sociologist. Education: B.A., Indiana Central College, Indianapolis, 1951; M.Ed. Administration, Duquesne University, Pittsburgh, 1958; Ph.D. (Mellon Fellow 1965-66), University of Pittsburgh, 1967. Address: 4024 Woodruff Avenue, Lafayette Hill, Pennsylvania 19444.

COHEN, SAMUEL ISRAEL Occupation: Executive Vice President, Jewish National Fund. Education: Ed.D., M.R.E., B.A., Rabbi. Address: 112 Rand Place, Lawrence, New York 11559.

COHEN, STANLEY I Occupation: Author, Engineer. Education: B.S., M.S. Chemical Engineering. Address: 322 Pine Tree Drive, Orange, Connecticut 06477.

COHN, BERTRAM D Occupation: Pediatric Surgeon. Education: B.S., M.D. Address: 8420 Ridge Boulevard, Brooklyn, New York 11209.

COKE, C EUGENE Occupation: Chairman, Coke & Associates Consultants. Education: B.Sc. Honors Chemistry, M.Sc. magna cum laude Organic Chemistry, University of Manitoba; Graduate Student, Yale University; M.A. Physical Chemistry, University of Toronto; Ph.D. Polymer Chemistry, The University of Leeds. Address: 26 Aqua Vista Drive, Ormond Beach, Florida 32074.

COLAIANNIA, LOUIS MARIO Occupation: Dentist. Education: D.D.S. Address: 735 South Nile Way, Aurora, Colorado 80012.

COLBURN, JEAN H Occupation: Teacher, Magruder High School. Education: B.A., M.S. Address: 9907 Tambay Court, Gaithersburg, Maryland 20879.

COLBY, KENNETH A Occupation: Clinical Psychologist. Education: Ph.D. Clinical Psychology, M.A., B.A. Address: 24 Elizabeth Lane, Tolland, Connecticut 06084.

COLE, EDDIE-LOU Occupation: Poet, Poetry Editor. Address: 1841 Garden Highway, Sacramento, California 95833.

COLE, RALPH I Occupation: Education, Management Consultant. Education: B.S. Electrical Engineering, M.S. Physics. Address: 3431 Blair Road, Falls Church, Virginia 22041.

COLEMAN, CARLA SWAN Occupation: Retired. Education: A.B., Bryn Mawr College; M.A., Yale Graduate School; Ph.D., Yale University. Address: 475 Humboldt Street, Denver, Colorado 80218.

COLEMAN, DOROTHY FERN Occupation: Teacher, Centralia City Schools. Education: B.S., M.S., Education, Special Education. Address: 523 North Sycamore, Centralia, Illinois 62801.

COLEMAN, GERALD CHRISTOPHER Occupation: Advertising Agency Executive. Education: A.B. Boston University, 1964; Master of Business Administration, Dartmouth College, The Amos Art School, 1966. Address: 9 Sherry Lane, Darien, Connecticut 06880.

COLEMAN, JAMES SMOOT Occupation: Professor of Political Science and Director, International Studies and Programs. Education: B.A., M.A., Ph.D. Address: 12315 Darlington Avenue, Los Angeles, California 90049.

COLEMAN, JOHN HARROD JR Occupation:

Specialist Municipal Bonds; Vice President, Alstoner Investment. Education: B.A. Honors, University of Florida; Attended The Citadel. Address: 333 North Ocean Boulevard, Deerfield Beach, Florida 33441.

COLEMAN, MARY ANN Occupation: Writer; Poet. Education: B.S. Education, Indiana University, Auburn University. Address: 205 Sherwood Drive, Athens, Georgia 30606.

COLEMAN, MORTON Occupation: Hematologist; Oncologist. Education: A.A., B.A., M.D. Address: 2 Forest Avenue, Rye, New York 10580.

COLEMAN, PAUL D Occupation: Professor; Neurobiologist. Education: A.B., Ph.D. Address: 35 Atkinson Street, Rochester, New York 14608.

COLEMAN, PAUL R Occupation: University Professor. Education: M.A. Music, M.A. Counseling, Ph.D. Curriculum. Address: 3321 West 62nd Place, Indianapolis, Indiana 46208.

COLEMAN, SYLVIA ETHEL Occupation: Research Biologist and Adjunct Assistant Professor, Virginia Medical Center. Education: B.S., M.S., Ph.D. Address: 122 North West 28 Terrace, Gainesville, Florida 32607.

COLIAS, MARY ANN Occupation: Artistic Director, Actor's Center, Incorporated; Owner, Design Ink, Contemporary Cards, Graphics and Advertising. Education: B.A., M.F.A. Drama, Trinity University. Address: 118 East French, San Antonio, Texas 78212.

COLLER, GARY HAYES Occupation: Physician. Education: B.A. 1974, D.O. 1978. Address: 1424 Waukazoo, Holland, Michigan 49423.

COLLIER, GAYLAN J Occupation: Coordinator of Acting; Director. Education: B.A. Drama, Abilene Christian University; M.A. Drama, University of Iowa, 1949; Ph.D. Theatre, University of Denver, 1957. Address: 2616 South University Drive, Fort Worth, Texas 76109.

COLLIER, RICHARD BANGS Occupation: Founder and Director, Pleneurethic International; Author, *Pleneurethic* in 14 Volumes. Education: B.A. Address: Post Office Box 1256, Tacoma, Washington 98401.

COLLINS, CLIFTON SHELL Occupation: Director of Financial Aid. Education: B.A., University of Richmond; B.D., Southeastern Baptist Theological Seminary; M.A., East Carolina University. Address: Post Office Box 101, Murfreesboro, North Carolina 27855.

COLLINS, DAVID RAYMOND Occupation: Author, Teacher, Lecturer. Education: B.S., M.S., Western Illinois University. Address: 3403 45th Street, Moline, Illinois 61265.

COLLINS, DENNIS GLENN Occupation: Assistant Professor, Mathematics Instructor, University de Puerto Rico. Education: B.A., Valparaiso University, Indiana; M.S., Ph.D., Illinois Institute of Technology. Address: 7108 Grand Boulevard, Hobart, Indiana 46342.

COLLINS, DOROTHY SMITH Occupation: Coordinator, Professional Information and Resource Center. Education: B.S. Sociology, M.Ed. Elementary Education, M.L.S. Address: 6267 Rockhurst Drive, San Diego, California 92120.

COLLINS, HENRY E Occupation: Manager, Material Engineering. Education: B.S., Met. Education, Drexel University, 1960; M.S. 1963, Ph.D. 1966 Met. Engineering, Carnegie-Mellon University; M.B.A., Baldwin-Wallace College. Address: 35451 Hanna Road, Willoughby Hills, Ohio 44094.

COLLINS, KATHLEEN Occupation: Writer, Novelist; Teacher. Education: B.A., Barnard; M.A.,

State University of New York, Stony Brook. Address: 7 Salonga Woods Road, Northport, New York 11768.

COLLINS, LINDA G Occupation: Hotel Administrator. Education: C.H.A., Michigan State, Holiday Inn University. Address: 1001 Oak Towers, North Wilkesboro, North Carolina 28659.

COLLINS, ROBERT H III Occupation: President, Getty Synthetic Fuels. Education: B.S.M.E. 1957, M.B.A. 1959, Stanford University. Address: 2387 Kimridge Road, Beverly Hills, California 90210.

COLLINS, RONALD W Occupation: Provost and Vice President for Academic Affairs, Eastern Michigan University. Education: B.S., Ph.D. Chemistry. Address: 1478 Kingwood, Ypsilanti, Michigan 48197.

COLLINS, WILLIAM E Occupation: Research Psychologist, Supervisor Aviation Psychology Laboratory. Education: B.S., St. Peters's College, 1954; M.A. Psychology, Fordham University, 1956; Ph.D. Psychology, Fordham University, 1959. Address: 8900 Sheringham Drive, Oklahoma City, Oklahoma 73132.

COLLINS-MAAT, JOYCE O Occupation: Business Educational Consultant; Minister; Writer; Artist. Education: B.Ph.M. Healing Sciences, A.S. Journalism, Ph.D. Philosophy. Address: 4416 North Racine, Chicago, Illinois 60640.

COLOMBO, JOHN ROBERT Occupation: Editor, Writer, Poet. Address: 42 Dell Park Avenue, Toronto, Canada M6B 2T6.

COLQUITT, BETSY FEAGAN Occupation: Professor of English, Texas Christian University. Education: B.A., Texas Christian University; M.A., Vanderbilt University. Address: 2601 McPherson, Fort Worth, Texas 76109.

COLSTON, FREDDIE C Occupation: Professor, Federal Employee. Education: B.A., Morehouse College; M.A., Atlanta University; Ph.D., Ohio State University. Address: 126 Hazleton Lane, Oak Ridge, Tennessee 37830.

COLVIN, PAMELLA HARRIS Occupation: Social Worker; Freelancer Journalist. Education: B.A. Psychology, Wesleyan College, 1979; M.Ed. Guidance and Counseling, West Georgia College, Carrollton, 1982. Address: #16-3 Brookwood Apartments, Carrollton, Georgia 30117.

COLWELL, RICHARD J Occupation: Teacher. Education: B.F.A.; M.A.; Ed.D. Address: 406 West Michigan, Urbana, Illinois 61801.

COMANOR, WILLIAM S Occupation: Professor of Economics. Education: A.B., Haverford College, 1959; Ph.D., Harvard University, 1964. Address: 1111 Las Canoas Lane, Santa Barbara, California 93105.

COMARR, AVROM ESTIN Occupation: Physician. Education: A.B., M.B., M.D., F.A.C.S., F.I.C.S., D.A.B.U., D.A.B.S.I., A.C.S. Address: 4235 Clubhouse Drive, Lakewood, California 90712.

COMAS, JOAN MURPHREE Occupation: Counselor; Assistant Professor Behavioral Studies. Education: Ph.D., University of Alabama; M.A., University of Alabama; B.A., University of Montevallo. Address: 480 Woodland Hills, Tuscaloosa, Alabama 35405.

COMBS, GERALD FUSON Occupation: Nutrition Administrator, United States Drug Administration. Education: B.S., Ph.D. Address: 10750 Kinloch Road, Silver Spring, Maryland 20903.

COMBS, TRAM Occupation: Poet, Art Critic, Archivist. Education: B.A. Physics, University of California, Certificate; Professor Competence, University of Chicago. Address: 5 Spring Street, New York, New York 10012.

COMFORT, HOWARD Occupation: Professor of

Classics, Emeritus. Education: Haverford College, 1924; Ph.D., Princeton University, 1932. Address: Crosslands 224, Kennett Square, Pennsylvania 19348.

CONARD, CHARLES BRADLEY Occupation: Writer. Education: A.B., Stanford University. Address: 155 Allen, New York, New York 10002.

CONAWAY, JANE E Occupation: Reading Teacher; Supervisor. Education: B.A., M.Ed. Address: 2615 Eastwood, Sandusky, Ohio 44870.

CONDON, DONALD S Occupation: Real Estate Consultant, Investing Development. Education: B.A. Address: 215 Jamaica Lane, Palm Beach, Florida 33480.

CONGER, SYNDY McMILLEN Occupation: Professor of English, Western Illinois University. Education: M.A. English, M.A. German, Ph.D. English. Address: 814 Bobby Avenue, Macomb, Illinois 61455.

CONKLIN, DEBORAH JEANNE Occupation: Area Mental Retardation Specialist. Education: B.A. Psychology, East Carolina University, 1972; M.S. Child Development, East Carolina University, 1973. Address: Rawlwood Arms 1-F, Greenville, North Carolina 27834.

CONLEY, ROBERT J Occupation: Teacher; Administrator; Writer. Education: M.A. English Literature, Midwestern State University, Wichita Falls, Texas. Address: 3830 Garretson, Sioux City, Iowa 51106.

CONLY, JOHN F Occupation: Chairman, Aerospace Engineer. Education: Ph.D. Address: 6478 Bonnie View, San Diego, Californnia 92119.

CONN, JACK T Occupation: Attorney. Education: B.A., LL.B. Address: 7202 Waverly, Oklahoma City, Oklahoma 73120.

CONNAWAY, INA LEE Occupation: Artist-Painting, Sculpture, Graphic, Writer. Education: B.A., George Washington University. Address: Post Office Box 1111, Saint Augustine, Florida 32085.

CONNELL, HAROLD LEE Occupation: Executive Vice President, Pan American Banks Incorporated; Treasurer and Chief Financial Officer. Education: B.A. Honors 1972, Master of Business Administration 1973, University of Florida. Address: 6860 South West 15 Street, Plantation, Florida 33317.

CONNELLEE-CLAY, BARBARA GALBRAITH Occupation: Administrative Staff Member. Education: TheBusiness University of New Mexico; Master of Business Administration. Address: 107 Monte Rey, North Los Alamos, New Mexico 87544.

CONNOLLY, CHARLES B Occupation: Director of Development and Alumni Affairs. Education: A.B., Boston University; M.S., Creighton University. Address: 150 Morrissey Boulevard, Boston, Massachusetts 02125.

CONNOR, JAMES RICHARD Occupation: University Administrator, University of Wisconsin. Education: Ph.D. 1961, M.S. 1954, B.A. 1951. Address: Rural Route 2, Linden Drive, Whitewater, Wisconsin 53190.

CONRAD, JOHN WILFRED Occupation: Professor and Department Chairman. Education: B.S., M.F.A., Ph.D. Address: 3675 Syracuse Avenue, San Diego, California 92122.

CONSTABLE-MARTIN, DORIS-MARIE Occupation: Artist, Art Educator. Education: A.A., Miami-Dade Community College, South Campus, 1971; B.A., University of Miami, Florida; University of North Carolina, Asheville, 1976; M.A. Art, Penland School, Penland, North Carolina, Arrowmont School of Crafts, Gatlinburg, Tennessee; Goddard College, Plainfield, Vermont, 1980. Address: 65 Woodland Road, Asheville, North Carolina 28804.

CONSTANS, H PHILIP JR Occupation: Professor of Educational Leadership. Education: B.S.P.H., M.A.E., Ed.D. Address: 642 Cottonwood, Bowling Green, Kentucky 42101.

CONSTANT, RUTH L Occupation: Entrepreneur-Management Image Consultant. Education: D.Ed., B.S.N., M.S.N. Address: 2206 East Loma Vista, Victoria, Texas 77901.

CONWAY, KEVIN P Occupation: Small Mammal Keeper Leader, President, American Association of Zoo Keepers. Education: B.S. Wildlife Science, Oregon State University. Address: NZP/Conservation and Research Center, Front Royal, Virginia 22630.

COOK, ANN JENNALIE Occupation: Executive Secretary, Shakespeare Association of America; Associate Professor of English, Vanderbilt University. Education: B.A. 1956, M.A. 1959, University of Oklahoma; Ph.D., Vanderbilt University, 1972. Address: 91 Valley Forge, Nashville, Tennessee 37205.

COOK, BLANCHE McLANE Occupation: Art Instruction; Counseling and Portraiture. Education: B.A.; M.A. in Education and Fine Arts. Address: 915 Pleasant Avenue, Yakima, Washington 98902.

COOK, DAVID HALL Occupation: Training Manager. Education: B.B.A., Personnel Management; M.A.Ed., Human Resource Development. Address: 6217 Dana Avenue, Springfieldf, Virginia 22150.

COOK, GEOFFREY ARTHUR Occupation: Writer; Artist. Education: Master's Degree, University of California-Berkeley; Kenyon College and University of California-Berkeley; A.B. Candidate. Address: Post Office Box 4233, Berkeley, California 94704.

COOK, HELGA G Occupation: Executive Assistant. Education: High School and Business Institute Graduate. Address: Mobay Road, Pittsburgh, Pennsylvania 15205.

COOK, J SUE Occupation: Nursing Professor. Education: B.S.N, M.S.N., Ed.D. Address: 924 Dyer Lane, Modesto, California 95350.

COOK, SYBILLA AVERY Occupation: Media Specialist. Education: B.S. Ed., M.A.L.S., M.A. Curriculum and Instruction. Address: 19 North River Drive, Roseburg, Oregon 97470.

COOKS, M LUCILE Occupation: President Delta Zeta National Historical Museum. Education: A.B. and Honorary Doctorate in Public Service, Miami University, Oxford, Ohio. Address: The Ambassador, Apartment 404, 7400 Sun Island Drive, South, South Pasadena, Florida 33707.

COOLE, WALTER A Occupation: College Teacher, Skagit Valley College. Education: B.A., M.A., Brown Belt. Address: 1325 Shirley Place, Mount Vernon, Washington 98273.

COOMBS, LUCILLE C Occupation: Retired Teacher; Social, Church and Community. Education: B.S. Wayne State University, Detroit, Michigan. Address: 1327 Offnere, Apartment 6, Portsmouth, Ohio 45662.

COOPE, PETER GEORGE Occupation: Human Resources Coordinator. Education: B.A. Education, Kentucky Wesleyan College, 1970; M.S. Guidance and Counseling, University of Bridgeport, 1973; C.A.S. Administration and Supervision, Fairfield University, 1978. Address: 26 Maplewood Drive, New Milford, Connecticut 06776.

COOPER, JANE TODD Occupation: Poet, Writer. Education: B.A., Duquesne University; Graudate Work, University of Pittsburgh. Address: 119 Herr Street, Harrisburg, Pennsylvania 17102.

COOPER, JOHN C Occupation: Professor of Religion, Susquehanna University. Education: A.B.;

M.Div.; S.T.M.; M.A.; Ph.D. Address: 718 Picnic Lane, Selins Grove, Pennsylvania 17870.

COOPER, KATHLEEN MARIE Occupation: First Vice President and Senior Economist. Education: Ph.D. Economics, University of Colorado; M.A. Economics, University of Texas at Arlington. Address: 12400 Nedra Drive, Granada Hills, California 91344.

COOPER, LOUISE MITCHELL Occupation: Teacher. Education: M.A. plus 30, Rank I. Address: 2429 LaClede Avenue, Paducah, Kentucky 42001.

COOPER, PATRICIA JEAN Occupation: Author. Education: Ph.D. Address: 4 Maybeck Twin Drive, Berkeley, California 94708.

COOPER, PAUL F Occupation: School District Administrator-Pupil Personnel. Education: A.A., B.A., M.S., Ph.D. Address: 10 James Avenue, East Norwich, New York 11732.

COOPER, RONALD Occupation: Financial Analyst. Education: B.S. Accounting, Johnson C. Smith University, 1980; M.B.A. Finance, Atlanta University, 1984. Address: 17130 Downing Street, #101, Gaithersburg, Maryland 20877.

COOPER, WILLIAM EDWIN Occupation: Professor of Psychology, University of Iowa. Education: Ph.D., Massachusetts Institute of Technology, 1976. Address: 802-34 Benton Drive, Iowa City, Iowa 52240.

COOPERMAN, HASYE Occupation: Author; Educator; University Teacher. Education: B.A., Hunter College; M.A., Ph.D. Columbia University. Address: 334 West 85 Street, New York, New York 10024.

COPELAND, MARGARET LEITCH Occupation: Assistant Professor, Early Childhood. Education: Ed.D., M.Ed., B.S.Ed. Address: 19 East Curlis, Pennington, New Jersey 08534.

COPPERNOLL-BANDER, MARGARET-ANNE M Occupation: Chief, Personnel and Administration. Education: B.A., M.A., Licencees lettres, Ph.D. Address: 15847 Acoma Road, Apple Valley, California 92307.

CORBETT, WILLIAM PAUL Occupation: College Instructor, Northern Oklahoma College. Education: B.S., Clarion State College; M.A., University of South Dakota; Ph.D., Oklahoma State University. Address: Post Office Box 185, Tonkawa, Oklahoma 74653.

CORCORAN, BARBARA A Occupation: Writer. Education: B.A., M.A. Address: Box 4394, Missoula, Montana 59806.

CORCORAN, FRANCIS LEO Occupation: Chairman, Expropriations Advisory Board. Education: Bachelor of Arts; Bachelor of Law. Address: 105 Upton Street, Moncton, N.B., Canada E1E 2Z9.

CORCORAN, MARYA McCLAY Occupation: Professor of Nursing, Chairperson Baccalaureate Nursing Science Courses (Levels I and II). Education: B.S., M.S. Address: 5 Elizabeth Road, Milford, Massachusetts 01757.

CORELLI, JOHN C Occupation: Professor of Nuclear Engineering, Rensselaer Polytechnic Institute. Education: B.S., Providence College, 1952; M.S., Brown University, 1954; Ph.D., Purdue University, 1958. Address: 33 Belle Avenue, Troy, New York 12180.

COREY, ORLIN R Occupation: Publisher/Editor, Anchorage Press, Inc. Education: B.A. 1950, M.A. 1952, Baylor University. Address: 4621 Charles Avenue, New Orleans, Louisiana 70115.

CORLETT, DONNA JEAN N Occupation: Coordinator Elementary Education, Associate Professor. Education: B.A., M.Ed., Ed.D. Address: 1315 Northwest 53rd Street, Vancouver, Washington 98663.

CORLISS, JEAN A Occupation: Public Relations Director, Youngstown Osteopathic Hospital. Education: B.S. Address: 1021 Hartzell, Niles, Ohio 44446.

CORNELIUS, IRA EARL Occupation: Senior Executive Advisor, Advanced Programs. Education: B.A. 1947, Ph.D. 1967, Honor Citation. Address: 1334 West Orangethorpe Avenue, Fullerton, California 92633.

CORNELL, JUDITH Occupation: Member Art Faculty, City College of San Francisco. Education: B.S., Nazareth College, 1967; M.F.A., New York State University, 1969; Ph.D., Columbia Pacific University, 1983. Address: Creative Development, 15 Pearl Street, Sausalito, California 94965.

CORNELL, NANCY VIRGINIA Occupation: Home Base Supervisor, Northern Panhandle Head Start. Education: C.D.A. Address: RD #1, Box 317, Steubenville Road, Toronto, Ohio 43964.

CORNWELL, ANNE CHRISTAKE Occupation: Director, Growth and Development, Department of Pediatrics, FHMC. Education: B.S., M.A., Ph.D. Address: 48 Circle Drive, Hastings-on-Hudson, New York 10706.

CORON, DAVID Occupation: Child Clinical Psychologist, Mental Health Administrator. Education: B.A., M.S., Ph.D. Address: 6200 Fawn, Meadow Victor, New York 14564.

CORRIVEAU, DONALD PAUL Occupation: Psychologist/Researcher. Education: B.A., M.A., Ph.D. Address: 690 County Street, Fall River, Massachusetts 02723.

CORSELLO, LILY JOANN Occupation: Guidance Director. Education: B.A., M.Ed. Address: 4521 Northeast 18 Avenue, Fort Lauderdale, Florida 3334.

CORSON, SAMUEL A Occupation: Professor Emeritus, The Ohio State University. Education: B.S., New York University, 1930; M.S., University of Pennsylvania, 1931; Ph.D., University of Texas, 1942.

CORTINA, RODOLFO J Occupation: Professor, University of Wisconsin-Milwaukee. Education: B.A. 1966, M.A. 1968, Ph.D. 1971. Address: 2976 North Farwell, Milwaukee, Wisconsin 53211.

COSGROVE, THERESA M Occupation: Assistant Director/Curator, Presidio Museum. Education: B.F.A. Address: 6912 Balsam Way, Oakland, California 94611.

COSTAGLIOLA, FRANCESCO Occupation: President, National Capital Chapter, Pearl Harbor Survivors Association; Government Official. Education: B.S.E.E., M.B.A. Address: 307 Gibbon Street, Alexandria, Virginia 22314.

COSTANTINO, MARSHALL U Occupation: Credit Analysis Manager. Education: M.S., South Dakota State University; B.S., University of Florida.

COSTELLO, DAVID F Occupation: Author, Environmental Consultant. Education: A.B., M.S., Ph.D. Address: 4965 Hogan Drive, Fort Collins, Colorado 80525.

COSTEN, MELVA WILSON Occupation: Associate Professor of Music and Worship, Interdenominational Theological Center. Education: B.A., M.A.T., Ph.D. Address: P.O. Box 42497, Atlanta, Georgia 30311.

COSTLEY, BILL Occupation: Educator, Writer. Education: A.B. 1963, M.F.A. 1967. Address: 4 Damien Road, Wellesley Hills, Massachusetts 02181-3416.

COSTON, NEEOMA LEE Occupation: Director of Development and Public Relations, Arthritis Foundation. Education: B.A., Loretta Heights College; A.A., Arapahoe Community College. Address: 3463 West Powers Avenue, Littleton, Colorado 80123.

COTTER, JOHN LAMBERT Occupation: Curator Emeritus, American Historical Archaeology University Museum; Retired Associate Professor, University of Pennsylvania. Education: B.A., M.A., University of Denver; Ph.D., University of Pennsylvania.

COTTINGHAM, JAMES GARRY Occupation: Senior Electrical Engineer. Education: B.S. Address: 10 Cedar Street, Center Moriches, New York 11943.

COTTLE, THOMAS JOSEPH Occupation: Psychologist, Television Commentator. Education: B.A., Harvard University; M.A., Ph.D., University of Chicago. Address: 12 Beaconsfield Road, Brookline, Massachusetts 02146.

COTTON, IRA W Occupation: Management Consultant, Booz, Allen and Hamilton. Education: B.A., Brown University; M.S.E, University of Pennsylvania; D.B.A., GWU. Address: 14 Dairyfield Court, Rockville, Maryland 20852.

COULSON, JOHN CARL Occupation: Real Estate Broker. Education: B.S. Address: 619 Wilshire Avenue, West Lafayette, Indiana 47906.

COURNIOTES, HARRY J Occupation: College President, American International College. Education: B.S., Boston University; I.A., M.B.A., Harvard University; D.C.S., Western Northeast College. Address: American International College, 1000 State Street, Springfield, Massachusetts 01109.

COURTENAY, WALTER ROWE JR Occupation: Professor of Zoology, Florida Atlantic University. Education: B.A., Vanderbilt University, 1956; M.S. 1960, Ph.D. 1965, University of Miami. Address: 1040 Southwest 3rd Street, Boca Raton, Florida 33432.

COURTNEY, A KAAREN Occupation: Associate Professor of Women's Studies and French, Ohio Wesleyan University. Education: B.S.E, Emporia State University; M.A., Ph.D., Ohio State University. Address: 412 Parkview Drive, Columbus, Ohio 43202.

COUSIN, DOROTHY Occupation: Vice President, Manpower and Finance. Education: B.S., M.B.A. (pending). Address: 145 Lindbergh Boulevard, Teaneck, New Jersey 07666.

COUSINO, JOE ANN M Occupation: Professional Sculptor. Education: B.A., University of Toledo; Graduate, University of Southern Illinois, University of Mexico; George Stevens Graduate Scholarship, Pratt Institute. Address: 3717 Indian Road, Toledo, Ohio 43606.

COUSINS, ANN VICTORIA Occupation: Administrative Manager. Education: B.A., M.S. Address: 760 West Lomita #178, Harbor City, California 90710.

COUSINS, LINDA Occupation: Publisher/Editor, The Universal Black Writer Press. Education: B.S. Address: 386 Sterling Place, Brooklyn, New York 11238.

COUTO, ROBERT Occupation: Manager Corporate Communications, Assistant Treasurer, Assistant to the President, Ferrofluidics Corporation. Education: Diploma, Northeast Institute of Industrial Technology, 1965; Attended the University of Rhode Island, Bristol Community College, University of Lowell, University of New Hampshire; Gemologist Diploma, Gemological Institute of America; B.S., Lesley College. Address: 12 Santerre Street, Nashua, New Hampshire 03060.

COVAL, NAOMI MILLER Occupation: Orthodontic Specialist. Education: B.A., New York University, 1939; D.D.S., Columbia University, 1943. Address: 30 Westover Place, Lawrence, New York 11559.

COVAULT, LLOYD R Occupation: Psychiatrist Administrator. Education: B.A., Miami University, Ohio; M.D., Ohio State University. Address: 11096 Darby Creek Road, Orient, Ohio 43146.

COWAN, MARY E Occupation: Forensic Analyst, Trace Evidence, Coroner's Laboratories. Education: B.S. Address: 84 Ennis Avenue, Bedford, Ohio 44146.

COWEN, BRUCE DAVID Occupation: Chief Financial Officer, Vice President. Education: B.S. Address: 922 Gilead Street, Hebron, Connecticut 06248.

COX, ANDREW ANTHONY Occupation: Private Mental Health Practice; Assistant Professor, Psychology and Counseling, Troy State University. Education: B.A., M.Ed., Ed.D. Address: Route 1, Box 119C, Waverly Hall, Georgia 31831.

COX, BILLY R Occupation: Vice Chairman of the Board, Dal-Tile Corporation. Education: LL.D., M.B.A. Address: 28 Victoris, Rowlett, Texas 75088.

COX, DAVID F Occupation: Chiropractor. Education: A.A., B.S., D.C., D.A.B.C.C. Address: 3409 172nd Place, Lansing, Illinois 60438.

COX, GERALDINE V Occupation: Vice President/ Technical Director, Chemical Manufacturers Association. Education: B.S. 1966, M.S. 1967, Ph.D. 1970, Drexel University. Address: 301 North Beauregard Street, #204, Alexandria, Virginia 22312.

COX, GLENDA E Occupation: Legal Administrator. Education: Complete Business Administration Certificate. Address: 906 Twin Falls, Houston, Texas 77088.

COX, MICHAEL H Occupation: Psychologist, Private Practice; Associate Professor. Education: B.S., M.A., Ed.S., Ph.D. 1972, Ph.D. 1984. Address: P.O. Box 355, Vista, California 92083.

COX, MYRON KEITH Occupation: Professor, Quantitative Business Analysis. Education: B.S., Virginia Polytechnic Institute, 1949; B.S., Pennsylvania State College, 1952; M.Sc., Massachusetts Institute of Technology, 1957; E.E., North Carolina State College, 1963; D.Sc., London College, England, 1964.

COX, T VIRGINIA Occupation: Associate Professor of Anthropology, Boise State University. Education: Ph.D. Address: 167 Willoway Drive, Boise, Idaho 83705.

COX, WILLIAM A JR Occupation: Professional Forensic Engineer and Contractor. Education: B.S.M.E., Virginia Polytechnic Institute and State University. Address: 1133 Wye Lane, Virginia Beach, Virginia 23451.

COZAD, JAMES WILLIAM Occupation: Vice Chairman, Standard Oil Company. Education: B.A., B.S., Indiana University. Address: 1205 Central Road, Glenview, Illinois 60025.

CRADDOCK, (JOHN) CAMPBELL Occupation: Professor of Geology, University of Wisconsin. Education: B.A., DePauw University, 1951; M.A. 1953, Ph.D. 1954, Columbia University. Address: 1109 Winston Drive, Madison, Wisconsin 53711.

CRAIG, VERNON EUGENE Address: 323 Ihrig Avenue, Wooster, Ohio 44691.

CRAIN, RICHARD H Occupation: General Manager, Budget Rent-a-Car of Steamboat. Education: B.S. Address: Box 771342, Steamboat Springs, Colorado 80477.

CRAIN, WILLIAM JAMES Occupation: College Professor. Education: A.A.S., B.A., M.A., Ph.D. Address: 2704 West 11th Street, Pueblo, Colorado 81004.

CRANDALL, BLISS H Occupation: President, DHI Computing Service, Inc. Education: B.S., D.Sc. (honorary), Utah State University; M.S., Iowa State

University. Address: 1268 East 700 South, Provo, Utah 84601.

CRANDALL, IRA CARLTON II Occupation: Registered Professional Engineer, President, International Research Associates; Research Consultant. Education: Associate Business Administration, LaSalle University, 1975; B.S. 1954, B.S. 1958, Indiana Institute of Technology; B.S., United States Naval Postgraduate School, 1962; Bachelor of Law, Blackstone School of Law, 1970; M.A., Piedmont University, 1967; Ph.D., University of Sussex, 1964; Doctor of Social Sciences (honorary), Piedmont University, 1968; Doctor of Letters (honorary), Saint Matthew University, 1970; Doctor of Education (honorary), Mount Sinai University, 1972. Address: 5754 Pepperridge Place, Concord, California 94521.

CRANDALL, JOHN D Occupation: Director, Iowa Office of Disaster Services. Education: B.S., U.S. Military Academy, 1958; M.P.A., Drake University, 1981. Address: 670 44th Street, Des Moines, Iowa 50312.

CRANDALL, KATHERINE JUNE Occupation: Vocational Director, Mead School District. Education: B.S., Northern Montana College, 1960; M.S., Washington State University, 1975. Address: Northeast 11614, Monroe Court, Spokane, Washington 99218.

CRAVEN, PATRICIA KOON Occupation: Associate Professor of Nursing, WVWC, West Virginia. Education: R.N., B.S., M.N. Address: 134 Barbour Street, Buckhannon, West Virginia 26201.

CRAVENS, JAMES H Occupation: Pediatrician; President-elect, Illinois Chapter, American Association of Pediatrics. Education: B.S., M.D., F.A.A.P. Address: 62 Lincoln Hill Northeast, Quincy, Illinois 62301.

CRAWFORD, MARY E Occupation: Associate Professor of Psychology, West Chester University. Education: B.S., M.A., P.L.D. Address: Pin Oak Farmhouse, West Chester, Pennsylvania 19380.

CRAWFORD, MYRON LLOYD Occupation: Electronic Engineer. Education: M.S. Address: 7235 Empire, Boulder, Colorado 80303.

CRAWFORD, WILLIAM R Occupation: Psychologist. Education: B.S., M.S., Ed.D. Address: 12310 Hesby Street, North Hollywood, California 91607.

CRAWLEY, BRENDA Occupation: Professor, The University of Kansas; Writer, Consultant. Education: B.A., M.S.W., Ph.D. Address: Meadowbrook T-101 Windsor Place, Lawrence, Kansas 66044.

CRAY, CLOUD LANOR JR Occupation: Grain Processor and Distiller; Chairman of the Board. Education: B.S., Case Institute of Technology, 1943. Address: Potato Hill, Atchison, Kansas 66002.

CREAGER, JOE S Occupation: Professor of Geological Sciences, University of Washington-Seattle. Education: B.S., Colorado College, 1951; Postgraduate Studies, Columbia University, 1952-53; M.S. 1953, Ph.D. 1958, Texas A&M University. Address: 6320 Northeast 157th Street, Bothell, Washington 98011.

CRETARA, DOMENIC ANTHONY Occupation: Artist (Painter); Art Instructor. Education: B.F.A., M.F.A. Address: 23 Grosvenor Park, Lynn, Massachusetts 01902.

CREWE, JENNIFER ELISABETH Occupation: Poet; Editor, Charles Scribner's Sons. Education: B.A., Sarah Lawrence College; M.F.A., Columbia University. Address: 629 West 115th Street, New York, New York 10025.

CREWS, RICHARD L Occupation: President, Columbia Pacific University. Education: M.D. Address:

112 Edgewood Avenue, Mill Valley, California 94941.

CRIARES, NICHOLAS J Occupation: Physician/Surgeon. Education: B.A., M.D., D.Sc., D-O/G, F.A.C.O.G., F.I.C.O.G. Address: 34 Andover Road, Hartsdale, New York 10530.

CRIMMINS, EILEEN M Occupation: Professor, University of Southern California. Education: B.S., M.A., Ph.D. Address: 329 Patrician Way, Pasadena, California 91105.

CRISER, MARSHALL M Occupation: University President, University of Florida. Education: B.S., B.A., J.D., University of Florida. Address: 2151 West University Avenue, Gainesville, Florida 32608.

CRISSIP, MILDRED JUDY Occupation: Medical Assisting Program Director/Instructor. Education: B.A., Certified Medical Assistant (C.M.A.), Clinical (C.), Administrative Specialties. Address: 4199 38th Avenue South, Apartment C, Saint Petersburg, Florida 33711.

CRITTENDEN, LEE JOHN Occupation: Vice President. Education: B.S., Northern Illinois University, 1968.

CROAFF, MARVA J Occupation: Marketing Consultant. Education: B.S., Arizona State University. Address: 2 Commodore Drive #388, Emeryville, California 94608.

CROIS, JOHN HENRY Occupation: Assistant Village Manager. Education: B.A., Elmhurst College; M.A., University of Notre Dame. Address: 10233 Karlov, Oaklawn, Illinois 60453.

CROMER, FRED EUGENE Occupation: Acting Dean, College of Arts and Sciences, University of Alaska. Education: B.S., M.A.T., Ph.D. Address: 10001 Grover, SRA Box 55C, Anchorage, Alaska 99516.

CROMWELL, RUE L Occupation: Professor, Department of Psychiatry, University of Rochester. Education: A.B., M.A., Ph.D. Address: 56 Clintwood Court D, Rochester, New York 14620.

CRONIN, DONALD J Occupation: Attorney-at-Law. Education: B.B. 1951, J.D. 1953, University of Alabama. Address: 5406 Blackistone Road, Bethesda, Maryland 20816.

CROOKE, STANLEY THOMAS Occupation: President, Research and Development, Smith Kline and French Laboratories. Education: B.A. 1966, Ph.D. 1971, M.D. 1974. Address: 511 Hillbrook, Bryn Mawr, Pennsylvania 19010.

CROOKER, BARBARA A Occupation: Writer. Education: B.A., Douglass College; M.S.Ed., Elmira College. Address: 28 Woods Bluff Run, Fogelsville, Pennsylvania 18051.

CROSKERY, ROBERT WILLIAM Occupation: Clergyman/Investor. Education: B.A., B.D., M.Div., D.Min. Address: 319 Compton Hills Drive, Wyoming, Ohio 45215.

CROSS, CHARLOTTE MARIE Occupation: Teaching Assistant in Music, Barnard College. Education: B.A., Goucher College; M.A., M.Phil. Columbia University. Address: 900 West End Avenue, New York, New York 10025.

CROSS, IRVIE K Occupation: Editor and Christian Educator. Education: Th.M., Th.D., D.D. Address: Post Office Box 848, Bellflower, California 90706.

CROSSMON, BRADFORD DEAN Occupation: Professor Emeritus and Consultant. Education: B.S., M.S., M.P.A., Dr.P.A. Address: 1622 Flint Drive, Clearwater, Florida 33519.

CROUCH, ANNE BELLE Occupation: Professor Emeritus of Speech. Education: B.S. 1942, M.R.E. 1947, M.A. 1967. Address: 411 Union Street, Murfreesboro, North Carolina 27855.

CROWNER, RICHARD L Occupation: Medical Technologist, Broward General Medical Center. Address: 201 Southeast 21st Street, Fort Lauderdale, Florida 33316.

CROWNOVER, KENNETH A Occupation: Combustion Engineer/Energy Coordinator. Education: E.E, B.A.H.Y., M.A.H.Y., M.B.A., Ph.D. Candidate. Address: 609 South 4th Street, Gadsden, Alabama 35901.

CRUESS, RICHARD L Occupation: Dean, Faculty of Medicine, McGill University. Education: B.A., Princeton University, 1951; M.D., Columbia University, 1955. Address: 526 Mount Pleasant Avenue, Montreal, Quebec H3Y 3H5.

CRUM, LAWRENCE A Occupation: Professor of Physics, Department of Physics, University of Mississippi. Education: B.S., M.S., Ph.D. Address: 103 Lakeway Drive, Oxford, Mississippi 38655.

CRUSE, IRMA R Occupation: Free-lance Writer; Graduate Student. Education: A.B., University of Alabama; M.A., Samford University; M.A. (in progress). Address: 136 Memory Court, Birmingham, Alabama 35213.

CRUZ, JOSE QUINENE Occupation: President, University of Guam. Education: Ed.D. Address: 153 Asucena Avenue, Barrigada Heights, Guam 96913.

CRYAN, JOHN R Occupation: Professor, Early Childhood Education. Education: B.A., M.S., Ph.D. Address: 5822 North Main Street, Sylvania, Ohio 43560.

CUA, ANTONIO S Occupation: Professor of Philosophy, Catholic University of America. Education: A.B., M.A., Ph.D. Address: Catholic University of America, Washington, D.C. 20064.

CUARON, ALICIA VALLADOLID Occupation: President, Cuaron, Silvas & Associates, Inc. Education: B.A., M.A., Ed.D. Address: 1000 South Monaco Street, Denver, Colorado 80224.

CUCIN, ROBERT LOUIS Occupation: Plastic Surgeon. Education: B.A., Cornell University; M.D., Cornell University Medical College. Address: 425 East 58th Street, New York, New York 10022.

CUE, NELSON Occupation: Professor of Physics, State University of New York. Education: Ph.D. Address: 25 Grounds Road, Albany, New York 12205.

CUELLAR, ROBERT A Occupation: Executive/ Management Consultant. Education: B.A., M.A., Doctoral Studies. Address: 1517 Montana Avenue, El Paso, Texas 79902.

CULBERTSON, JOHN DENNIS Occupation: Counselor. Education: B.S., M.S., Ph.D. Address: 1886 Westmoreland Avenue, Florence, South Carolina 29501.

CULLIGAN, JOHN W Occupation: Chairman of the Board and Chief Executive Officer, American Home Products Corporation. Education: Attended Seton Hall University, Utah University, University of Chicago, Philippine University. Address: 685 Third Avenue, New York, New York 10017.

CULLISON, THOMAS P Occupation: Chairman, Department of Business. Education: B.S., M.B.A., D.B.A. Candidate. Address: 13058 North Surrey Circle, Phoenix, Arizona 85029.

CULP, MILDRED L Occupation: Personal Marketing Executive; Author. Education: B.A., Knox College, 1971; A.M. 1974, Ph.D. 1976, The University of Chicago. Address: Seattle Tower, Suite 2404, Seattle, Washington 98101.

CULP, PAULA N Occupation: Musician, Minnesota Orchestra. Education: B.M.E., M.M.E. Address: 4210 Abbott South, Minneapolis, Minnesota 55410.

CULVER, ROBERT ELROY Occupation: Osteopathic Physician. Education: B.S., University of Toledo, 1951; D.O., Chicago College Osteopathic Medicine, 1959; Intern, Sandusky (Ohio) Memorial Hospital, 1960. Address: 5517 Corduroy Road, Oregon, Ohio 43616.

CUMMINS, J DAVID Occupation: Professor of Insurance, Wharton School. Education: B.A., M.A., Ph.D. Address: 8225 Weymouth Drive, Pennsanken, New Jersey 08109.

CUMMINGS, W DEAN Occupation: Director, Real Life Ministries. Education: B.S. Address: 7 Northway Drive, Taylors, South Carolina 29687.

CUNNINGHAM, FREDERICK E Occupation: Corporate President; Engineer. Education: S.B., S.M., Massachusetts Institute of Technology, 1963. Address: 118 Webb's Hill Road, Stamford, Connecticut 06903.

CUNNINGHAM, KEITH A II Occupation: Mining/Distribution Executive; President/Chief Executive Officer. Education: B.A., Michigan State University. Address: 12208 Meadow Creek Court, Potomac, Maryland 20854.

CUNNINGHAM, LARRY L Occupation: Librarian. Education: B.A., M.A. Address: 2915 Wedgewood Drive, Columbus, Indiana 47201.

CUNSOLO, RONALD S Occupation: Professor of History, Nassau Community College. Education: B.A., New York University; M.A., University of Chicago; Ph.D., New York University. Address: 30 Bright Street, Westbury, New York 11590.

CURCIO, FRANCES RENA Occupation: Assistant Professor of Education, Chairman Department of Education. Education: Ph.D., New York University, 1981. Address: 1111 Tompkins Avenue, Staten Island, New York 10305.

CURRAN, DANIEL J Occupation: Director of Criminal Justice, St. Joseph's University. Education: B.A., St. Joseph's University, 1973; M.A., Temple University, 1978; Ph.D., University of Delaware, 1980.

CURRELLEY, LORRAINE RAINIE Occupation: Poet; Writer; Founder/Director, Growing Theatre, Inc., and Poets Cafe, Inc. Address: Post Office Box 562, College Station, New York, New York 10030.

CURREY, RICHARD A Occupation: Author, *Crossing Over: A Vietnam Journal*. Education: M.S., Howard University. Address: Post Office Box 1402, Los Lunas, New Mexico 87031.

CURRUN, WARD SCHENK Occupation: Professor of Economics, Trinity College. Education: B.A., Trinity College; M.A., Ph.D., Columbia University. Address: 6 Stoner Drive, West Hartford, Connecticut 06107.

CURRY, LINDA WILSON Occupation: Business Development Executive. Education: B.S., M.S., Ph.D. (in progress). Address: 2808 Elm Avenue, Manhattan Beach, California 90266.

CURTIN, LEO V Occupation: Consultant in Feed and Nutrition. Education: B.S., M.S., University of Illinois; Ph.D., Cornell University. Address: 500 Willowmere Lane, Ambler, Pennsylvania 19002.

CURTIS, A KENNETH Occupation: President, Gateway Films; President, Christian History Institute. Education: B.A., Gordon College; M.Div., Gordon College-Conwell; Ph.D., Walden University. Address: Box A, Lansoace, Pennsylvania 19446.

CURTIS, GARY ROGER Occupation: Translator, Teacher, Minister. Education: B.A., Grinnell College; Bachelor of Theology, The Way College of Biblical Research-Indiana. Address: 206 South Main, New Knoxville, Ohio 45871.

CURTIS, JACKIE J Occupation: Surgeon, University Hospital, Columbia, Missouri. Education: B.A., M.D. Address: 1033 Bourn, Columbia, Missouri 65201.

CURTIS, MICHAEL R Occupation: Professor of Political Science, Department of Political Science. Education: B.Sc. 1951, Ph.D. 1958. Address: 294 Western Way, Princeton, New Jersey 08540.

CURTIS, NEVIUS MINOT Occupation: President and Chief Executive Officer, Delmarva Power and Light Company. Education: B.A., M.B.A. Address: 1912 Academy Place, Wilmington, Delaware 19806.

CURTIS, ROBERT EDMUND Occupation: Superintendent of Schools. Education: B.S., M.Ed., University of Rochester; Ed.D., Cornell University. Address: 123 Artillery Drive, Gettysburg, Pennsylvania 17325.

CURTIS, ROBERT J Occupation: Financial Consultant, Certified Public Accountant, C.M.A. Education: B.B.A., M.B.A. Address: 21 Ivanhoe Drive, Robbinsville, New Jersey 08691.

CURTRIGHT, THOMAS LYNN Occupation: Theoretical Physicist, Physics Department, University of Florida. Education: B.S., M.S., Ph.D. Address: 2440 Northwest 38th Street, Gainesville, Florida 32605.

CURVIN, KENYA JOYCE Occupation: President, Wildcat Mapping, Inc.; Vice President, Scissortail Oil Corporation; Secretary/Treasurer, GBK Company; Consultant, GADSCO, Inc.; Owner, M. W. Galaxy Music Company. Address: 3764 River Oaks Drive, Norman, Oklahoma 73069.

CUTHBERTSON, KATHRYN JEAN Occupation: Associate Professor, Wichita State University. Education: B.A., M.A. Address: 2029 North Woodlawnn #515, Wichita, Kansas 67208.

CUTLER, ROLAND M Occupation: Author, Screen Writer, Attorney. Education: B.A., LL.B. Address: 753 North Kings Road, Los Angeles, California 90069.

CUTLER, VIRGINIA F Occupation: Retired Professor. Education: B.S., University of Utah; M.S., Stanford University; Ph.D., Cornell University. Address: 1173 Princeton Avenue, Salt Lake City, Utah 84105.

CUTTER, ELIZABETH PARSONS Occupation: Psychologist, Texas Department of Corrections. Education: B.S., Wilkes College; M.S., The Pennsylvania State University. Address: Post Office Box 904, Gatesville, Texas 76528.

CYPESS, RAYMOND H Occupation: Director Diagnostic Laboratory; Chairperson, Department of Preventive Medicine. Education: D.V.M., Ph.D. Address: 123 Renwick Drive, Ithaca, New York 14850.

CZAMANSKI, STAN Occupation: University Professor, Cornell University. Education: Ph.D., University of Pennsylvania, 1963. Address: 102 Regency Lane, Ithaca, New York 14850.

CZARNEZKI, JOSEPH J Occupation: Wisconsin State Senator. Education: B.S., M.A., University of Wisconsin-Milwaukee. Address: 7004 West Van Beck Avenue, Milwaukee, Wisconsin 53220.

D

DACE, TISH Occupation: Dean of Arts and Sciences, Southeastern Massachusetts University. Education: A.B., M.A., Ph.D. Address: Southeastern Massachusetts University, North Dartmouth, Massachusetts 02747.

DACKAWICH, S JOHN Occupation: Professor, California State University. Education: B.A., University of Maryland; Ph.D., University of Colorado. Address: 1459 West Sample, Fresno, California 93710.

DACKOW, SANDRA KATHERINE Occupation: Professor, Slippery Rock University; Musician. Education: Bachelor of Music, Master of Music, Eastman School of Music. Address: 1220-B Shetland Drive, Lakewood, New Jersey 08701.

DACRE, JACK CRAVEN Occupation: Research Toxicologist, U.S. Army Medical Bioengineering Research and Development Laboratory. Education: B.S., M.S., University of New Zealand; Ph.D., D.Sc., University of London. Address: 8218 Yellow Springs Road, Frederick, Maryland 21701.

DAGER, EDWARD Z Occupation: Professor of Sociology, University of Maryland. Education: B.A., M.A., Ph.D. Address: 4 Bentana Way, Rockville, Maryland 20850.

DAHBANY, AVIVAH Occupation: School Psychologist, Franklin Township Public Schools. Education: B.A., M.S., Advanced Graduate Study, Clinical School of Psychology. Address: 1425H Oak Tree Drive, North Brunswick, New Jersey 08902.

DAHLIN, CYNTHIA JEAN Occupation: Management Consultant, American Management Systems, Inc. Education: B.A., Wellesley College; Master of Public Policy, Harvard University. Address: 1832 North Ode Street, Arlington, Virginia 22209.

DAHLIN, ROSALIE JULE Occupation: Artist-Designer. Education: Minneapolis School of Art and Design; Walker Arts. Address: 7361 Landaw Drive, Bloomington, Minnesota 55438.

DAHLMAN, STANLEY MILLER Occupation: Provost, Montgomery College. Education: B.A., Ph.D. Address: Post Office Box 25, Germantown, Maryland 20874.

DAHM, MINNIE JULIA Occupation: Archivist, Translator, Researcher, Dardt College. Education: A.B., William Penn College; Library Science, Cedar Falls, Iowa. Address: 8080 North 51st Avenue, Maplewood Apartment #106, Glendale, Arizona 85302.

DAINES, DELVA Occupation: Professor, Brigham Young University. Education: B.S., M.S., Ed.D., Postdoctoral Studies. Address: 227 MCKB, Brigham Young University, Provo, Utah 84602.

DALAL, FRAM R Occupation: Director, Clinical Chemistry, Temple University Hospital. Education: Ph.D., B.S. (Technology), B.S. Address: 7619 Mountain Avenue, Elkins Park, Pennsylvania 19117.

DALE, JOHN CERTER Occupation: President, Jack Dale Associates, Inc. Education: B.S., U.S. Naval Academy. Address: 38 Theo Lane, Towson, Maryland 21204.

DALE, MARCIA L Occupation: Associate Dean, School of Nursing University of Wyoming. Education: B.S., M.N., Ed.D. Address: 827 Evergreen, Cheyenne, Wyoming 82009.

DALE, STANLEY J Occupation: Gartner Group, Inc. Education: B.B.A., Pace University; M.B.A., Iona College. Address: Post Office Box 291 Valley Cottage, New York 10989.

DALLIN, LEON Occupation: Professor of Music, California State University. Education: B.Mus., M.Mus., Ph.D. Address: Post Office Box 2400, Seal Beach, California 90740.

DALLMAN, ELAINE G Occupation: Self-Employed. Education: Ph.D., M.A., B.A. Address: Post Office Box 60550, Reno, Nevada 89506.

D'ANCONA, MIRELLA LEVI Occupation: Professor of Art History. Education: M.A., Ph.D., Archives and Paleography. Address: 360 East 72nd Street, New York, New York 10021.

DANALD, RUTH M Occupation: Professor, Purdue University. Education: B.A., M.A., A.B.D. Address: 11 New Durham Estates, Westville, Indiana 46391.

DANATOS, STEVEN CLARK Occupation: Corporate Tax Manager, J. M. Huber Corporation. Education: B.S., Montclair State; M.B.A., Fairleigh Dickinson University. Address: 52 Avenue C, Lodi, New Jersey 07644.

DANCA, JOHN ARTHUR Occupation: Associate Professor Student Development/Psychotherpist. Education: B.A., De Paul University; M.A., Governors State University; C.A.S., Northern Illinois University; Ed.D., Northern Illinois University. Address: 1588 Timber Trail, Wheaton, Illinois 60016.

DANE, HENRY LAWRENCE Occupation: Creative Independent. Education: Master's Degree, Anthropology and Philataly, Boston University, 1976. Address: 57 Hutchinson Street, Winthrop, Massachusetts 02152.

DANESE, ARTHUR E Occupation: Mathematician, State College. Education: A.B., A.M., Ph.D. Address: James Place H-5, Fredonia, New York 14063.

DANG, HARBANS SINGH Occupation: Chief Financial Officer. Education: M.A. (Economics), M.B.A. Address: 29628 Norma Drive, Warren, Michigan 48093.

DANHOF, JOHN BENJAMIN Occupation: Pastor, Trinity Presbyterian Church. Education: B.S., B.D., Th.M., D.Min. Address: 3702 West Michigan, Midland, Texas 79703.

DANIEL, RICHARD LEE Occupation: Deputy 11, Marshal, Businessman, Institute Self Defense. Address: Post Office Box 1265, Palm Springs, California 92263.

DANIEL, SUSAN M Occupation: Broker Dealer Specializing in Mutual Funds. Education: B.A., M.P.A. Address: 305 N. Street, Southwest, Washington, D.C. 20024.

DANIELS, CRAIG E Occupation: Professor of Psychology, Director Stress Research Center, University of Hartford. Education: B.S.Ch.E., M.Ed., Ph.D. Address: 546 Bloomfield Avenue, Bloomfield, Connecticut 06002.

DANIELS, LORI G Occupation: Student. Education: A.S. (in progress), Phillips College. Address: 3925 Wesgate Drive, Columbus, Georgia 31907.

DANN, JACK Occupation: Writer. Education: B.A. Political Science, State University of New York-Binghamton. Address: 71 Mill Street, Johnson City, New York 13790.

DANNER, GEORGIA LOUANNE Occupation: Executive Director, Chamber of Commerce, Chillicothe, Missouri. Education: M.P.A., B.S. Political Science. Address: 2633 North Fair, Chillicothe, Missouri 64601.

DANSBY, GLORIA F Occupation: College Administrator, St. Philip's College. Education: B.A., M.A., Ed.D. Address: 118 Applin, San Antonio, Texas 78210.

DANSEREAU, FRED E Occupation: Associate Professor, School of Management, State University of New York at Buffalo. Education: B.S. cum laude, St. Joseph's University; M.A., University of Illinois; Ph.D., University of Illinois. Address: 60 Groton Drive, Williamsville, New York 14221.

DANTZIC, CYNTHIA MARIS Occupation: Professor of Art, Department Chairman, Brooklyn Campus, Long Island University. Education: M.F.A., Pratt Institute; B.F.A., Yale University. Address: 910 President Street, Brooklyn, New York 11215.

DARDEN, DONNA K Occupation: Professor of Sociology, University of Arkansas. Education: B.A., M.A., Ph.D. Address: 1645 Appleburg, Fayetteville, Arkansas 72701.

DARLEY, SANDRA C Occupation: Pre-Law Student; First Vice Chairman, College Republican Federation of Virginia. Education: Attended Randolph-Macon Woman's College. Address: 5713 Hawthorne Lane, Portsmouth, Virginia 23703.

DARZYNKIEWICZ, ZBIGNIEW D Occupation: Research Professor. Education: M.D., Ph.D. Address: 37 Meadow Lane, Chappaqua, New York 10514.

DAS, MUKUNDA B Occupation: Professor of Electrical Engineering, Penn State University. Education: Ph.D. (London); M.Sc., B.Sc. Honors, Dacca University. Address: 1380 Circleville Road, State College, Pennsylvania 16801.

DAS GUPTA, AARON Occupation: Research Mechanical Engineer, U.S. Ballistic Research Laboratory. Education: Ph.D., Virginia Polytechnic Institute and State University; M.S., New Mexico State University; B.S., I.I.T. Address: 104 John Street, Perryville, Maryland.

DASGUPTA, SUNIL P Occupation: Research. Education: B.Sc. Honours, M.Sc., Ph.D. Address: 104 Simca Lane, Wilmington, Delaware 19805.

DATHAK, DEV S Occupation: Professor, Ohio State University. Education: M.S. Economics, M.B.S., D.B.A. Marketing Finance. Address: 7739 Strathmoore Road, Dublin, Ohio 43017.

DATZ, ISRAEL MORTIMER Occupation: Independent Consultant/OPS Research. Education: B.S., City College of New York. Address: 700 Americana Drive, Annapolis, Maryland 21403.

DATZ, RUTH ELIZABETH Occupation: Vocal Music Teacher, Conductor. Education: B.S.Mus.Ed., M.A.Mus.Ed. Address: 1564 Barrington, Ann Arbor, Michigan 48103.

DAVENEL, GEORGE F Occupation: Professor Emeritus. Education: M.S. Arts. Address: 45-14 156 Street Flushing, New York 11355.

DAVID, JON R Occupation: Management Consultant. Education: Undergraduate, Queens College; Graduate, Columbia; B.A., Ph.D. Address: 63 Hamilton Avenue, Tappan, New York 10983.

DAVIDSON, JOAN G Occupation: Management Trainer/Consultant. Education: B.S.Ed., M.A., Postgraduate Courses. Address: 121 Buckingham Drive, Santa Clara, California 95051.

DAVIDSON, JOELINE DILLARD Occupation: G.S.M.T., A.S.M.T., Manager Clinical Laboratory. Education: B.S. Medical Technology Certification, B.M. Address: Post Office Box 1786 LaGrange, Georgia 30241.

DAVIDSON, JUDITH A Occupation: Assistant Professor of Sport History, Head Field Hockey Coach. Education: B.S., University of New Hampshire; M.Ed., Boston University; Ph.D., University of Massachusetts. Address: 1106 Yewell Street, Iowa City, Iowa 52240.

DAVIDSON, REETA LINDSEY Occupation:

Director of Youth Music and Education. Education: (in progress) B.A. Music, B.A. Elementary Education. Address: Penson Hills 15, Livingston, Alabama 35470.

DAVIES, BETTILU DONNA Occupation: Author of 5 Published Books. Education: Diplomas from Pontiac Business Institute and Institute of Childrens' Literature. Address: 1911 Burton, Beloit, Wisconsin 53511.

DAVIES, CHARLOTTE E Occupation: University Professor of Geriatric Nursing, Towson State University. Education: B.S., M.S., Ph.D. Address: 2605 East Jappa Terrace, Baltimore, Maryland 21234.

d'AVIS, LUIS M Occupation: Physician and Surgeon. Education: M.D. Address: 8417 North Christiana, Skokie, Illinois 60076.

DAVIS, ANN E Occupation: Professor of Sociology, Miami University. Education: B.A., M.S. Social Work, Ph.D. Sociology. Address: 788 West Sharon Road, Cincinnati, Ohio 45240.

DAVIS, BARBARA SNELL Occupation: Educator. Education: B.S., M.S. Address: 7293 Beechwood Drive, Mentor, Ohio 44060.

DAVIS, BOB J Occupation: Educator. Education: B.B.A., M.B.A., J.D. Address: 1111 East Grant, Macomb, Illinois 61455.

DAVIS, BRUCE ALLEN Occupation: Psychologist. Education: A.B., M.B.A., Drury College; M.S., Southwest Missouri State University. Address: 1240 South Saratoga, Springfield, Missouri 65804.

DAVIS, CAROLE J Occupation: Clinical Psychologist. Education: Ph.D. Address: 441 West Allens Lane, Philadelphia, Pennsylvania 19119.

DAVIS, CLAUDE-LEONARD Occupation: Attorney. Education: B.A. Journalism, J.D. Address: 365 Westview Drive, Athens, Georgia 30606.

DAVIS, DONALD JAMES Occupation: Bishop of Diocese of Northwest Pennsylvania. Address: 308 Frontier Drive, Erie, Pennsylvania 16505.

DAVIS, DUSTIN P Occupation: Professor, Frostburg State College. Education: B.S., Northland College; M.F.A., University of Wiconsin. Address: Route 3, Box 350, Frostburg, Maryland 21532-1099.

DAVIS, DWIGHT DOUGLASS Occupation: Education Specialist, Research and Development. Education: B.S., M.Ed., Mississippi College; Ph.D., Florida State University. Address: 825 Bayshore Drive #1205, Pensacola, Florida 32507.

DAVIS, ELAINE CARSLEY Occupation: Educator. Education: LL.B., Ph.D. Address: 3800 Menlo Drive, Baltimore, Maryland 21218.

DAVIS, EURAL N JR Occupation: Social Worker. Education: B.A., M.S.W. Address: 2400 South Loop, West #1417, Houston, Texas 77054.

DAVIS, EVELYN M Occupation: Musician, Artist. Education: Secretarial Training; Private Student of Organ and Piano; Attended Special Art Classes, Drury College; Various Music Seminars and Workshops. Address: Route 2, Box 405, Rogersville, Maryland 65742.

DAVIS, FRANCES VINSON Occupation: Artist. Education: B.A., M.A. Address: 3231 South Utica Avenue, Tulsa, Oklahoma 74105.

DAVIS, JESSE DUNBAR Occupation: Lawyer. Education: LL.B. Address: 3231 South Utica, Tulsa, Oklahoma 74105.

DAVIS, JOHN CLARENCE JR Occupation: Chief Executive Officer, Media Ministries. Education: B.Sc. 1958, Ph.D. 1960, Metropolitan University of California; Master's Degree, Kingdom Bible Institute; Northwestern University Certificate in Communications and University of Tennessee

Research, 1959-. Address: 1728 Fair Drive, North East, Knoxville, Tennessee 37918.

DAVIS, KENNETH E Occupation: Field Claims Representative. Education: A.A. Degree, B.S. Address: 8102 Langdon Avenue, #45, Van Nuys, California 91406.

DAVIS, POLLY ANN Occupation: Professor and Chairman, Department of History and Political Science, East Texas Baptist College. Education: Ph.D., University of Kentucky; M.A., University of Mississippi; B.A. Blue Mountain College. Address: North Grove, East Texas Baptist College, Marshall, Texas 75670.

DAVIS, REBA J Occupation: Program Coordinator, Home Economic Education, University of Arkansas. Education: B.S., M.S., Ed.D. Address: 1812 Greenvalley, Fayetteville, Arkansas 72701.

DAVIS, RICHARD R Occupation: Electro/Optic Engineering Specialist. Education: B.S., M.Ed., Idaho State University; Ph.D., Columbia Pacific University. Address: Box 1127, APO San Francisco, California 96555.

DAVIS, RUTH GARDEMAL Occupation: Educator, Librarian. Education: Bachelor of Music Education. Address: 401 South Lawrence, Roby, Texas 79543.

DAVIS, THOMAS G Occupation: Administrative Accountant. Education: B.B.A, North Texas State University. Address: 5718 Galaxie, Garland, Texas 75042.

DAVIS, ZINDA LYNN Occupation: Department of Defense-Secretary. Education: High School and Business School. Address: 8015 West Point Drive, Springfield, Virginia 22153.

DAVITT, JOHN MONTGOMERY Occupation: Pharmacologist/Toxicologist, U.S. Food and Drug Administration. Education: B.S. 1959, M.S. 1963. Address: 703 Midland Road, Silver Spring, Maryland 20904.

DAVY, PHILIP SHERIDAN Occupation: President, Davy Engineering Company. Education: B.S., M.S. Address: 1230 King Street, La Crosse, Wisconsin 54601.

DAWKINS, CECIL Occupation: Writer. Education: B.A., University of Alaska; M.A., Stanford University. Address: Box 2114, Taos, New Mexico.

DAWSON, HANES MOORE Occupation: Oil Executive. Education: B.S., University of Oklahoma. Address: 529 South Poplar Way, Denver, Colorado 80224.

DAY, LUCILLE ELIZABETH Occupation: Author/Educator. Education: A.B., M.A., Ph.D., University of California-Berkeley. Address: 109 Monte Vista Avenue, Oakland, California 94611.

DAY, RONALD E Occupation: Bank Officer, Information Management. Education: B.A., M.B.A. Address: 2 Bigham Road, North Reading, Massachusetts 01864.

DAYRINGER, RICHARD Occupation: Professor, Department of Medical Humanities and Department of Family Practice, Southern Illinois University School of Medicine. Education: A.A., Southwest Baptist College; A.B., William Jewell College; M.Div., Midwestern Baptist Theological Seminary; Th.D., New Orleans Baptist Theological Seminary. Address: 3221 Dorchester, Springfield, Illinois 62708.

DAYTON, WILBER T Occupation: Professor of Biblical Literature, Wesley Biblical Seminary. Education: A.B., B.D., M.R.E., Th.D., M.A. Address: 1912 Hamilton Boulevard, Jackson, Mississippi 39213.

D'AZZO, JOHN J Occupation: Professor of Electrical Engineering, Air Force Institute of Technology. Education: B.E.E., M.S.E.E., Ph.D. Address: 3923 Winthrop Drive, Dayton, Ohio 45431.

DEADY, GENE MARTIN Occupation: Professor Emeritus. Education: B.S., M.A., Ph.D. Address: California State University. Address: 4 Lakewood Way, Chico, California 95926.

DEAL, BORDEN Occupation: Author. Education: B.A. Address: 1851 Datura, Sarasota, Florida 33579.

DEAL, GEORGE EDGAR Occupation: Consultant and Educator. Education: B.S. Business, M.S. Business, Doctor of Business Administration. Address: 6245 Park Road, McLean, Virginia 22101.

DEAL, PATRICIA LOU EISENBISE Occupation: Public School District Administrator. Education: M.A., B.S. Address: 8401 Woodlawn Avenue, Southwest, Tacoma, Washington 98499.

DEAL, STEVEN L Occupation: Chiropractor. Education: B.A., D.C. Address: 311 Kirkwood Boulevard, Davenport, Iowa 52803.

DEAL, SUSAN STRAYER Occupation: Poet, Teacher. Education: B.A., Kearney State College; M.A., University of Nebraska. Address: 311 Kirkwood Boulevard, Davenport, Iowa 52803.

DEAL, THERRY N Occupation: Director, Continuing Education/Public Services, Georgia College. Education: Ph.D. Child Development, University of North Carolina-Greensboro. Address: 321 North Wayne Street, Milledgeville, Georgia 31061.

DEALY, JOHN FRANCIS Occupation: Lawyer; Distinguished Professor, Georgetown University. Education: B.S., Fordham College; LL.B., New York University School of Law. Address: 11504 West Hill Drive, Rockville, Maryland 20852.

DEAN, ALBERTA LaVAUN Occupation: Registered Nurse. Education: Diploma, Hurley Medical Center. Address: 276 Dayton Road, Dayton, Indiana 47941.

DEAN, LLOYD Occupation: Pastor, Morehead United Pentecostal Church, Counselor, Rowan County Senior High School, Morehead, Kentucky. Education: B.S., M.A. Guidance. Address: Route 6, Box 498, Morehead, Kentucky 40351.

DEAN, MAUDELL MAPP Occupation: Vocal Concert Artist, Music Teacher. Education: B.A., Jackson State University; Roosevelt University. Address: 7627 South Constance, Chicago, Illinois 60649.

DEAN, PETER Occupation: Artist. Education: B.S., University of Wisconsin. Address: 2 Spring Street, New York, New York 10012.

DEANE, WALTER JOHN Occupation: Retired School Teacher, Anchorage School District, Retired U.S. Air Force (Lt. Col.). Education: B.S. Elementary Education, M.A. Social Science, Hofstra College. Address: 2526 Sprucewood Street, Anchorage, Alaska 99508.

DEAN, WILLIAM DENARD Occupation: Professor of Religion, Gustavus Adolphus College. Education: B.A., Carleton College, 1959; M.A. 1964, Ph.D. Theology 1967, University of Chicago. Address: 918 South Washington Avenue, St. Peter, Minnesota 56082.

DEANIN, RUDOLPH D Occupation: Professor of Plastics, University of Lowell. Education: A.B., M.S., Ph.D. Organic Chemistry. Address: Box 466, 42 South Chelmsford Road, Westford, Massachusetts 01886.

DEATON, FAE ADAMS Occupation: Social Worker/Therapist. Education: B.A.Mus., B.S.Ed., M.S.W. Address: 1176 Pickett Road, Norfolk, Virginia 23502.

DEATON, GEORGE C Education: B.S., Louisiana State University and Southwestern University. Address: 1615 Enterprise Boulevard, Lake Charles, Louisiana 70601.

DeBAKEY, LOIS Occupation: Writer, Lecturer, Communication Expert, Educator, Baylor College of Medicine. Education: B.A., M.S., Ph.D., Tulane University, New Orleans, Louisiana.

DeBAKEY, MICHAEL E Occupation: Cardiovascular Surgeon. Education: B.S., M.D., M.S. Address: 1200 Moutsund Avenue, Houston, Texas 77030.

DeBAKEY, SELMA Occupation: Professor of Scientific Communication. Education: B.A., Newcomb College, Tulane University; Graduate Study. Address: 1200 Moutsund Avenue, Houston, Texas 77030.

deBERNARDI, JOSEPH MARIO Occupation: Author, Lecturer, Consultant, Professor, NCR Corporation. Education: B.A., M.S.F.S., M.B.A., D.B.A. Address: 1700 South Patterson Boulevard, Dayton, Ohio 45479.

DeBOER, A JOHN Occupation: Agricultural Economist, Winrock Internation. Education: B.S., Ph.D. Address: 4 Ironwood, Conway, Arkansas 72032.

DeBOER, ROY J Occupation: School Principal. Education: B.A., M.Ed. Address: 3528 South East Pine Tree Drive, Port Orchard. Washington 98366.

deBOURBON, CHARLES LOUIS Occupation: Real Estate Broker. Education: Secondary School, Haarlem, Netherlands. Address: Rural Route 4, Stouffville, Ontario, Canada.

DEBREU, GERARD Occupation: Professor of Economics and Mathematics, University of California-Berkeley. Education: D.Sc., Universite de Paris, 1956. Address: Department of Economics, University of California, Berkeley, California 94720.

DE BRUIN, HENDRIK CORNELIS Occupation: Associate Director for Instruction, University of New Mexico. Education: B.A., M.Ed., Ph.D. Address: 1811 Mariyana, Gallup, New Mexico 87301.

DE BUSSY, CARVEL Occupation: University Professor. Education: B.A., M.A., Ph.D. Address: 3801 Connecticut Avenue Northwest, Washington, D.C. 20008.

DeCELLES, CHARLES EDOUARD Occupation: Professor, Religious Studies, Marywood College. Education: B.A. Philosophy, M.A. Theology, M.A. Religion, Ph.D. Theology. Address: 923 East Drinker Street, Dunmore, Pennsylvania 18509.

DECHARIO, TONY H Occupation: Symphony Orchestra Manager. Education: B.A. Music, M.S. Music. Address: 199 Oak Lane, Rochester, New York 14610.

DECHERT, CHARLES RICHARD Occupation: Professor of Politics, Catholic University of America. Education: Ph.D. Social and Political Philosophy, Catholic University of America. Address: 1308 Perry Street, North East, Washington, D.C. 20017.

DeCICCO, BENEDICT THOMAS Occupation: Professor of Microbiology, Catholic University of America. Education: B.A., M.S., Ph.D., Rutgers University. Address: 12505 Caswell Lane, Bowie, Maryland 20715.

DECKER, ERWIN L Occupation: Business Executive-Engineer, Fuller Company. Education: B.S.M.E., M.S.M.E., Lehigh University. Address: 847 Church, Catasauqua, Pennsylvania 18032.

DECKER, JEAN CAMPBELL Occupation: Treasurer, Corporate Director, Consultant. Education: B.A., University of Chicago. Address: 885 Smith Street, Glen Ellyn, Illinois 60137.

DECKERT, CURTIS KENNETH Occupation: Certified Management Consultant. Education: A.A., B.S.M.E., M.S.M.E., M.B.A. Address: 18061 Dermel Place, Santa Ana, California 92705.

DeCRAENE, JANET KAY Occupation: Teacher for the High Potential Student. Education: B.S., University of Wisconsin. Address: Route 3, Box 89, River Falls, Wisconsin 54022.

DEEB, RICHARD J Occupation: Deeb Construction Company. Education: B.S., Civil Engineering, Notre Dame. Address: 701 58th Street, North, St. Petersburg, Florida 33710.

DeFIGUEIREDO, MARIO PACHECO Occupation: Food Executive. Education: S.B. Chemistry, Massachusetts Institute of Technology; S.M., Master of Business Administration, University of Chicago; Ph.D. Food Science & Technology, Massachusetts Institute of Technology. Address: 1887 Schoettler Valley Drive, Chesterfield, Missouri 63017.

DeFOREST, GRAY MORROW Occupation: Financial Executive, Certified Public Accountant. Education: B.S. Accounting. Address: 45 Columbus Place Stamford, Connecticut 06907.

DeGHETTO, KENNETH ANSELM Occupation: Engineering Company Executive, Foster Wheeler Corporation. Education: B.S., U.S. Merchant Marine Academy; B.M.E., Rensselaer Polytechnic Institute. Address: 42 Cornell Drive, Livingston, New Jersey 07039.

DeGIDIO, SANDRA FAY Occupation: Free Lance Writer, Lecturer, Consultant. Education: B.A., M.A. Address: 230 North Central Avenue, Wayzata, Minnesota 55391.

deGRAVEL, ROBERT EVARIST Occupation: Corporate President. Education: B.S., University of Southwestern Louisiana. Address: Post Office Box 1376 La Mesa, California 92041.

deGROAT, WILLIAM C Occupation: Pharmacologist, Department of Pharmacology, Medical School, University of Pittsburg. Education: B.S., M.S., Ph.D. Address: 6357 Burchfield Avnue, Pittsburgh, Pennsylvania 15217.

DEHN, JAMES T Occupation: Physicist, Ballistic Research Laboratory. Education: Ph.D., M.S., M.A., M.B.A., Th.L., Ph.L. Address: 1244 Grafton Shop Road, Bel Air, Maryland 21014.

DE HODGINS, OFELIA CANALES Occupation: Staff Engineer, Materials Scientist, IBM Corporation. Education: M.S. Physics, M.S. Materials Science, M.S. Engineering Physics. Address: 612 Granite Springs Road, Yorktown Heights, New York 10598.

DEKKER, HARRIETT Occupation: Psychologist, Director Supportive Services, ARI. Education: B.A., Queens College; M.A., New York University. Address: 41 Londonderry Drive, Greenwich, Connecticut 06830.

DeLAURI, IRMA WOODARD Occupation: Principal. Education: M.S. Elementary Education and Administration. Address: 214 Bellhaven Road, Portsmouth, Virginia 23707.

DE LA VEGA, ENRIQUE MIGUEL Occupation: Free-lance Architectural Sculptor. Education: M.F.A., Los Angeles County Otis Arts Institute. Address: 4507 Atoll Avenue, Sherman Oaks, California 91423.

DeLAY, ROGER L Occupation: Development Program Manager, Animal Products, American Cyanamid Company. Education: B.S., M.S., Ph.D. Address: 9 Oaken Lane, Hamilton Square, New Jersey 08619.

DELCO, WILHELMINA RUTH Occupation: Texas State Representative. Education: B.A. Fish University. Address: 1805 Astor Place, Austin, Texas

78721.

DELGADO, RAMON L Occupation: Associate Professor of Theatre, Montclair State College. Education: B.A. cum laude, M.A., M.F.A., Ph.D. Address: 16 Forest Street, Montclair, New Jersey 07042.

DEL GIORNO, BETTE J Occupation: Science Consultant Fairfield Public Schools. Education: B.A., University of Connecticut; M.A., Trinity College; Ph.D., University of Connecticut. Address: 96 Inwood Road, Trumbull, Connecticut 06611.

D'ELIA, CHRISTOPHER FRANCIS Occupation: Associate Professor, University of Maryland. Education: Ph.D. Zoology, Georgia; A.B. Biology, Middlebury College. Address: Post Office Box 3, Solomons, Maryland 20688.

DELISLE, JAMES R Occupation: Assistant Professor of Special Education, Kent State University. Education: B.S., M.Ed., Ph.D. Address: 519 Earl Avenue, Kent, Ohio 44240.

DELL, MARGARET, A Occupation: Doctor, Nutrition Analyst. Education: B.S., M.S., Ph.D., D.N. Address: Box 685 Manahawkin, New Jersey 08050.

DELONG, ROBERT M Occupation: Assistant Head Nurse, Adult Psychiatry. Education: Registered Nurse, Diploma in Nursing. Address: 5104 Pennway Street, Philadelphia, Pennsylvania 19124.

DeLONG, RUSSELL T Occupation: Technical Writer/Editor. Education: B.S.E.E., University of California-Los Angeles. Address: 103 Turtle Dove, Universal City, Texas 78148.

DEL PADRE, FRANCES P Occupation: Child Life Coordinator/Adjunct Faculty, Department of Education and Training, Baystate Medical Center. Education: B.S., M.Ed. Address: 165 Farnsworth Street, Chicopee, Massachusetts 01013.

DELPHIN, JACQUES M Occupation: Medical Doctor of Psychiatry; Supervising Psychiatrist, Dut. County Department of Mental Hygiene; Attending Physician, St. Francis Hospital. Education: B.S., M.D. Address: 8 Garfield Place, Poughkeepsie, New York 12601.

DEMAS, JEAN V Occupation: Lawyer, Real Estate Company Executive. Education: B.A., Northwestern University, DePaul University, 1982; Member Illinois Bar, 1982; Member U.S. District Court, Illinois, 1982. Address: 6842 North Kostner, Lincolnwood, Illinois 60646.

de MAZIA, VIOLETTE Occupation: Educator, Lecturer, Writer. Education: B.A., Merion State. Address: Box 93, Merion Station, Pennsylvania 19066.

deMATTIES, NICK Occupation: Artist. Education: B.A., M.S. Address: 2337 North 10th Street, Phoenix, Arizona 85006.

DEMBY, EMANUEL HARRY Occupation: Psychologist, President. Education: Ph.D. Psychology, B.S.S. Address: 50 East 42nd Street, New York, New York 10017

DEMILLE, LESLIE B Occupation: Artist. Address: 1721 Orchard Drive, Santaana, California 92707.

DE MELLO, AGUSTIN EASTWOOD Occupation: Science Writer; Concert Artist. Education: B.A., B.S., M.S., Ph.D., D.Sc. Address: Post Office Box 78, Ventura, California 93002.

DEMOREST, MARGARET SCOTTIE Occupation: Mayor, City of Wooster. Education: Bachelor of Science in Elementary Education. Address: 128 West Henrietta, Wooster, Ohio 44691.

DEMPSEY, PAUL STEPHEN Occupation: Associate Professor of Law and Director of the Transportation Law Program, University of Denver College of Law. Education: LL.M. summa cum laude International Law, George Washington University; J.D., School of Law, University of Georgia; A.B.J. with honors, School of Journalism, University of Georgia. Address: 2073 Dahlia Street, Denver, Colorado 80207.

DENGERINK, HAROLD A Occupation: Professor of Psychology, Washington State University. Education: B.A., Calvin College; M.S., Ph.D., Kent State University. Address: Northwest 1835 Turner Drive, Pullman, Washington 99163.

DE NICHOLAS, ROBERT P Occupation: Director of County and Municipal Government. Education: B.B.A., Upsala College, 1961. Address: 48 Gallaway Lane, Willingboro, New Jersey 08046.

DENLINGER, ELMER L Occupation: Chiropractic Physician Specializing in Nutrition. Education: B.A., D.C., F.A.C.C. Address: 25909 Lake Drive, Elkhart, Indiana 46514.

DENNER, MELVIN W Occupation: Chairman, Division of Science and Math, Indiana State University. Education: B.S., M.S., Ph.D. Address: 100 South Peerless, Evansville, Indiana 47712.

DENNISON, BOBBY Occupation: Associate Professor of Industrial Education and Technology, East Central University. Education: B.S., M.Ed., D.Ed. Address: R.R. 4, Ada, Oklahoma 74820.

DENNISON, LAURA H Occupation: Poet/ Teacher. Education: M.Ed., M.A., Teachers College, Columbia University. Address: 45 West 10 Street, 5H, New York, New York 10011.

DENNO, KHALIL I Occupation: Professor, New Jersey Institute of Technology. Education: Ph.D., M.E.E., B.S.C. Address: 68 Ridgeway Avenue, North Orange, New Jersey 07052.

DENNY, DAVID A Occupation: Professor of Education, State University College, Oneonota, New York. Education: B.S., M.A.E., Ed.D. Address: R.D. #1, Box 156, Maryland, New York 12116.

DENSEN-GERBER, JUDIANNE Occupation: Psychiatrist, Consultant. Education: B.A., cum laude, Bryn Mawr College; B.L., Columbia University Law School; D.Med., New York University Medical School; Rotating Internship, French Hospital; Psychiatric Residency, Bellevue and Metropolitan Hospital; J.D., Columbia University Law School; D.Sc., Honorary Degree, Lebanon Valley College. Address: 817 Fairfiew Avnue, Bridgeport, Connecticut 06604.

DENTON, AHELA I Occupation: Executive Director, National Association of Physical Therapists, Inc. Education: A.A.M.A., C.A.E. Address: 1325 South Hills Drive, West Covina, California 91793.

DEONIER, D L (DICK) Occupation: University Professor, Entomologist, Miami University. Education: B.S. 1959, M.S. 1961, Ph.D. 1966. Address: Post Office Box 545, Oxford, Ohio 45056.

DERBYSHIRE, CAROLINE Occupation: Associate Director for Education, Massachusetts General Hospital. Education: A.B., Harvard University; Ed.M., Boston University School of Education; C.A.S., Harvard Graduate School of Education. Address: Boston, Massachusetts.

DERICK, DOROTHY BOSK Occupation: Vice President, The Northern Trust Company. Education: A.B., Mount Holyoke College; S.M. Management, Massachusetts Institute of Technology. Address: 830-A Forest Avenue, Evanston, Illinois 60202.

DERRICK, HOMER Occupation: United States of America Banker and Insurance Executive. Education: University of South Carolina, American Institute of Banking. Address: 314 Overhill Drive, Lexington, Virginia 24450.

DERRICOTTE, TOI Occupation: Writer, Master Teacher, New Jersey State Council on Arts, Poet-in-the-School. Education: M.A., New York University. Address: 237 Runnymede Road, Essex Fells, New Jersey 07021.

DERRY, MICHAEL L Occupation: Management Consultant. Education: B.A., Northern Michigan University. Address: 6480 Westmoor, Birmingham, Michigan 48010.

DeRUTH, JAN Occupation: Artist. Education: Art Studies, Lehjng, New York; Ruskin Art School, Oxford, Great Britain. Address: 1 West 67 Street, New York, New York 10023.

DESAI, CHANDRAKANT S Occupation: Professor, Department of Civil Engineering and Engineering Mechanics, University of Arizona. Education: Ph.D., University of Texas. Address: 6776 North Harran Drive, Tucson, Arizona 85704.

DESAI, SURESH A Occupation: Dean, School of Business Administration, Montclair State College. Education: M.A., Ph.D., University of California-Los Angeles; M.A., Ph.D., LL.B., Gujarat University, India. Address: 108 Osborne Street, Glen Ridge, New Jersey 07028.

DESAI, VEENA BALVANTRAI Occupation: Obstetrician and Gynecologist. Education: M.D., M.R.C.O.G., F.A.C.O.G., D.A.B.O.G., F.A.C.S., F.I.L.S. Address: 12 Harborview Drive, Rye, New Hampshire 03870.

DE SANTIS, VINCENT P Occupation: Professor Emeritus of History, University of Notre Dame. Education: B.S., Ph.D. Address: Box 562, Notre Dame, Indiana 46556.

DeSEYN, DONNA E Occupation: Science Teacher, Central School. Education: B.S., M.S. Address: 5 Tamarack Drive, Canadaigua, New York 14424.

DeSILVA, HEMA NIHAL Occupation: Director, Section of Neonatology, Saint Francis Hospital, Medical Center. Education: M.B.B.S., D.C.H., F.A.A.P. Address: 71 Glenwood Drive, Windsor, Connecticut 06095.

DeSOMOGYI, AILEEN ADA Occupation: Retired Librarian. Education: B.A., M.A., A.L.A., Certificate in Archival Principles, M.L.S. Address: 9 Bonnie Brae Boulevard, Toronto, Ontario M4J 4N3.

desRIOUX, DEENA Occupation: Artist, Designer, Exhibitions Coordinator, Ward-Nasse Gallery. Education: Rhode Island School of Design; Brown University; La Sorbonne, Paris. Address: 251 West 19th Street, New York, New York 10011.

DETERS, DAVID H Occupation: Adult Basic Education Instructor/Counselor. Education: B.A. Spanish (Honors), University of Iowa; M.A., Community College Counseling, University of Iowa; M.A. Spanish, University of Iowa; M.Div. magna cum laude Ministry, Dubuque Theological Seminary. Address: 1306 Orange, Muscatine, Iowa 52761.

DETJEN, GUSTAV HEINRICH HUGO JR Occupation: Publisher/Editor. Education: Attended Pace College. Address: 154 Laguna Court, St. Augustine Shores, Florida 32086.

DEUEL, THEODORE NORMAN Occupation: Partner, Real Estate Investment Banker. Education: A.A., Diablo Valley College; B.S.E.E., Stanford University; M.B.A., University of Santa Clara. Address: 4335 Marina City Drive, 944 ETS, Marina Del Rey, California 90291.

DEVEAU, ROGER JOSEPH Occupation: Consultant/Educator. Education: D.Ed., M.B.A., B.S. Address: 5 Sisson Brook Lane, Westport, Massachusetts 02790.

DEVINS, LINDA CLARIECE Occupation: Professional Artist, Juror. Address: Route #1, Box 42E, Mary Esther, Florida 32569.

DeVITO, ALBERT KENNETH Occupation: Publisher/Editor/Music Educator. Education: B.S., M.A., Mus.D. (Honorary), Ph.D. Address: 361 Pin Oak Lane, Westbury, New York 11590.

deVOLT, ARTISS C Occupation: Harpist. Education: N. Z. Conservatory of Music. Address: Box 202, Sea Island, Georgia 31561.

DE VRIES, ADRIAAN Occupation: Research Scientist, Physical Chemist, Liquid Crystal Institute, Kent State University. Education: B.S. 1952, D.R.S. 1957, Ph.D. 1963. Address: 722 Beryl Drive, Kent, Ohio 44240.

DeVRIES, DEBORAH A D Occupation: Director, I.O.E.A. Program, Langley Air Force Base, Arizona. Education: Ed.D., University of Southern California; M.S.Ed., University; B.A. History, University of California at Los Angeles. Address: 4840 Christine, Glendale, Azrizona 85308.

deVRIES, RIMMER Occupation: Bank Economist, Morgan Guaranty Trust Company. Education: B.S., M.A., Ph.D. Address: R.D. 3 Hill and Dale Road, Lebannon, New Jersey 08833.

DEWEY, PATRICIA PARKER Occupation: Owner/President Northern Neck Tidewater Broadcasting Company. Education: Bachelor of Music, University of Mississippi. Address: 6211 Garnett Drive, Chevy Chase, Maryland 20815.

DeWITT, SUSAN PIERSON Occupation: U.S. Trustee for the Northern District of Illinois. Education: A.A., B.S., J.D. Address: 505 North Lake Shore Drive #4912, Chicago, Illinois 60611.

DEWITZ, ARDEN VON Occupation: Professional Artist and Teacher. Education: B.A. Address: 5132 White Oak Avenue, Encino, California 91316.

DEWSBURY, DONALD ALLEN Occupation: Professor/Comparative Psychologist, Department of Psychology, University of Florida. Education: A.B., Bucknell University; Ph.D., Michigan State University. Address: 840 North West 20th Street, Gainesville, Florida 32603.

DHARMARAJAN, SANGIAHNADAR Occupation: Professor of Aerospace Engineering, San Diego State University. Education: Bachelor of Engineering, M.S., Ph.D. Address: 5215 College Garden Court, San Diego, California 92115.

DHILLON, HARPAL SINGH Occupation: Engineer/President of Corporation, EER, Inc. Education: Ph.D. Operations Research; B.S. Mechanical Engineering (Honors). Address: 132 North Ithaca Court, Sterling, Virginia 22170.

DIAMAN, NICKOLAS ANTHONY Occupation: Novelist. Education: B.A., University of Southern California. Address: 2950 Van Ness Avenue, San Francisco, California 94l09.

DIAMOND, DAVID J Occupation: Nuclear Engineer, Brookhaven National Laboratory. Education: Ph.D., M.S., B.S. Address: 4 Settlers Path, Port Jefferson, New York 11777.

DIAMOND, DOROTHY B Occupation: Author, Editor. Education: B.A., Wellesely College; M.S., Columbia School of Journalism. Address: 9 Old Farm Lane, Hartsdale, New York 10530.

DIAMOND E FAYE Occupation: Co-Owner-Chairman of the Board of Metroplex Sign Manufacturing Company. Education: High School Education. Address: 609 Country Club Drive, Cleburne, Texas 76031.

DIAMOND, HARVEY J Occupation: President,

Chief Executive Officer, Plasti-Vac, Inc.; Chairman of the Board, Diamond Supply, Inc. Education: B.S., University of North Carolina. Address: Post Office Box 5543, Charlotte, North Carolina 28225.

DIAMOND, SONDRA Occupation: Psychologist. Education: B.A., M.Ed. Address: 9325 Academy Road, Philadelphia, Pennsylvania 19114.

DIAMOND, WALTER H Occupation: Editor, Economist, Author. Education: A.B., Syracuse University; Attended American Institute of Banking. Address: 9 Old Farm Lane, Hartsdale, New York 10530.

DIAS, JERRY RAY Occupation: Chemistry Professor and Researcher. Education: B.S. with honors Chemistry, S.J.S.U., 1965; Ph.D., A.S.U., 1970. Address: 10001 West 93rd Street, Overland Park, Kansas 66212.

DIBENEDETTO, ANTHONY T Occupation: Vice President for Academic Affairs, Professor Chemical Engineering, University of Connecticut. Education: B.S. Chemical Engineering, City University of New York, 1955; M.S. 1956, Ph.D. 1960, Chemical Engineering, University of Wisconsin. Address: 1 Brookside Lane, Mansfield, Connecticut 06250.

DI BERARDINO, MARIE ANTOINETTE Occupation: Professor of Physiology. Education: B.S., Chestnut Hill College; Ph.D., University of Pennsylvania. Address: 3300 Henry Avenue, Philadelphia, Pennsylvania 19129.

DiBIANCA, RICHARD PAUL Occupation: Manager, Travel Agency; Student, Colgate University. Education: B.A. Biology, B.A. Religion, Colgate University. Address: 3 North Osborne Avenue, Margate, New Jersey 08402.

DiBIANCA, VINCENT FRANK Occupation: Management Consultant, The DiBianca-Berkman Group; University Lecturer. Education: B.S., Drexel University; Master's Degree, Bucknell University. Address: Amwell Road, Hopewell, New Jersey 08525.

DiCHELLO, JOHN JOSEPH Occupation: Associate Publisher, Connecticut Business Review. Education: A.B. English, Providence College. Address: 1460 Shepard Avenue, Hamden, Connecticut 06518.

DICKASON, ROBERT HART Occupation: Physician/Surgeon. Education: B.S. Biology, Baldwin-Wallace College; Graduate Courses, Case Western Reserve University, Ccollege of Medicine; Summer Preceptorships, Lorain Community Hospital, Green Cross Osteopathic Hospital; D.O., Chicago College of Osteopathic Medicine, 1975; Resident General Surgery, Riverside Osteopathic Hospital, 1976-80; Fellow Colon and Rectal Surgery, William Beaumont Hospital, 1980-81; Board Eligible General Surgery, American Board of Osteopathic Surgeons; Degree in Business (in progress), Detroit College of Business; Additional Studies. Address: 9672 Waterway, Grosse Ile, Michigan 48138.

DICKERSON, DEBORRAH ANNE Occupation: Vice-President, Disk Corporation. Education: College Studies. Address: 3412 Colonial #G-4, Norfolk, Virginia 23518.

DICKERSON, DOROTHY M Address: Route #1 Seminole, Oklahoma 74840.

DICKERSON, RALPH THORNTON Occupation: Reservation Sales Agent, United Airlines. Education: B.S., McPherson College. Address: 2994 Colorado Boulevard, Denver, Colorado 80207.

DICKERSON, WILLIAM R Occupation: Attorney at Law. Education: B.A. in Accounting, California State University; J.D., University of California-Los Angeles. Address: 5006 Los Feliz Boulevard, Los Angeles, California 90027.

DICKEY, CHARLES D JR Occupation: Retired Chairman of the Board, Scott Paper Company. Education: B.A., Yale University. Address: 649 Dorset Road, Devon, Pennsylvania 19333.

DICKINSON, JUNE G Occupation: Chief, Division of Nutrition, Prince George's County Health Department. Education. A.B. Speech, B.S. Home Economics. Education: M.S. Food and Nutrition, Registered Dietitian (R.D.). Address: 7201 Beacon Terrace, Bethesday, Maryland 20817.

DICKINSON, WILLIAM LOUIS Occupation: U.S. Representative, R-Alabama. Education: B.A., Law Degree, University of Alabama. Address: 3535 North Glebe Road, Arlington, Virginia 22207.

DiCOLA, LEE J Occupation: Vice President Finance, Treasurer. Education: B.S. Business Administration. Address: 3020 Scott Street, Cuyahoua Falls, Ohio 44223.

DiDIO, LIBERATO J A Occupation: Dean, Graduate School, Medical College of Ohio. Education: M.D., D.Sc., Ph.D. Address: 3563 Edgevale Road, Toledo, Ohio 43606.

DiDOMENICO, ANGELO S Occupation: Teacher of Mathematics. Education: B.A., Clark University; M.A., Boston College. Address: 23 Taft Street, Milford, Massachusetts 01757.

DIEMER, EMMA LOU Occupation: Composer, Musician, Professor, Department of Music, University of California. Education: B.M., M.M., Yale School of Music; Ph.D., Eastman School of Music. Address: 2249 Vista de Campo, Santa Barbara, California 93101.

DILL, ELLIS HAROLD Occupation: Dean of Engineering, Rutgers University. Education: B.S.C.E., M.S., Ph.D., University of California of Berkeley. Address: 436 Brentwood Drive, Piscataway, New Jersey 08854.

DILLARD, ANNIE Occupation: Writer. Education: B.A., Hollins College; M.A., Hollins College. Address: c/o Blanche Gregory, 2 Tudor City Place, New York, New York 10017.

DILLARD, LESTER BADGETT Occupation: Executive Vice President, The Southern Baptist Theological Seminary. Education: B.S.B.A., B.D.R.E., M.R.E., Ed.D. Address: 610 Upland Road, Louisville, Kentucky 40206.

DILLEHAY, RONALD CLIFFORD Occupation: Social Psychologist, Department of Psychology, University of Kentucky. Education: A.B., Ph.D., University of California of Berkeley. Address: 1848 McDonald Road, Lexington, Kentucky 40503.

DILLER, JAMES G Occupation: Plastic Surgeon. Education: A.B., M.D. Address: 4235 Secor Road, Toledo, Ohio 43623.

DILLINGHAM, MARJORIE CARTER Education: Ph.D Spanish, Florida State University. Address: 2109 Trescott Drive, Tallahassee, Florida, 32312.

DILLON, MILLICENT G Occupation: Writer. Education: A.B. Physics, M.A. English. Address: Post Office Box 18243, San Francisco, California 94118.

DILLON, ROBERT M Occupation: Architect/Building Research. Education: B.A., M.A. Architecture. Address: 811 Arrington Drive, Silver Spring, Maryland 20901.

DILLON, ROBERT WILLIAM SR Occupation: Professor of English Language and Literature, Department of English, California University of Pennsylvania. Education: A.B. cum laude, M.A., Ohio University; Ph.D. magna cum laude English Language Literature, Ohio University. Address: Post Office Box 524, 970 Wood Street, California, Pennsylvania 15419.

DILSAVER, DONNA BOLTON Occupation:

Utility Executive. Education: B.A. Sociology, Friends University. Address: 304 Stratford Road, Wichita, Kansas 67206.

DILSAVER, PAUL L Occupation: Author/College Instructor, Carroll College. Education: B.A., M.A., M.F.A. Address: 704 Breckenridge, Helena, Montana 59601.

DiMANNO, PAUL FRANCIS Occupation: President of Crest Paper Products. Education: B.A. Address: 2 Lisa Court, Hamilton Square, New Jersey 08690.

DiMASCIO, ANGELO JOHN Occupation: Engineering Executive Aerospace, Naval Air Systems Command. Education: B.S.M.E., M.S.E.M, Drexel Technical; D.B.A., George Washington University. Address: 4466 Dale Boulevard, Woodbridge, Virginia 22193.

DIMMICK, CAROLYN REABER Occupation: Supreme Court Justice, Temple of Justice, Olympia, Washington. Education: B.A., J.D., LL.D. honors. Address: Temple of Justice, Olympia, Washington 98504.

DINAN, THOMAS E Occupation: Regional Sales Manager. Education: B.S. Sociology, M.S. Social Sciences. Address: 102 Victoria Park Drive, Liverpool, New York 13088.

DINBERG, MICHAEL DAVID Occupation: Commissioned Officer, United States Public Health Service. Education: A.S. Engineering Science, B.S.I.E., O.R. Address: 1901 Stanley Avenue, Rockville, Maryland 20851.

DINCULEANU, NICOLAE Occupation: Professor of Mathematics. Education: Ph.D. Mathematics. Address: 610 North West 22 Street, Gainesville, Florida 32603.

DINGLI-ATTARD DE BARONI INGUANEZ, MARCEL V Occupation: Heraldic Consultant, Author. Education: B.Phil. 1976, Ph.D. 1977. Address: 865 Twyman Road, Independence, Missouri 64050.

DINIC, CARL J Occupation: Personal Investments. Education: B.S., University of California-Berkeley. Address: 262 Ridge Road, Douglas Manor, Long Island, New York 11363.

DINSMORE, KAREN E Occupation: Associate Professor, University of Nebraska (on leave). Education: B.S., Kent State University; M.A., Eastern Michigan University; Ph.D., University of Nebraska. Address: 5639 Kugler Mill Road, Cincinnati, Ohio 45236.

DiPIETRO, JOSEPH Occupation: President, Sclavo Inccorporated. Education: B.S., M.S., Ph.D. Address: 163 Montclair Avenue, Montclair, New Jersey 07042.

DiSALVO, ARTHUR F Occupation: Chief, Public Health Laboratory. Education: M.D. Address: 100 Morningside, Columbia, South Carolina 29210.

DISHMAN, RODNEY KING Occupation: Associate Professor, University of Georgia; Sport Psychologist. Education: B.S., M.S., Ph.D. Address: 211 Tawnyberry Drive, Athens, Georgia 30606.

DISQUE, ELWOOD JOHN Occupation: Professor Emeritus. Education: A.B., Dickinson College. Address: 57 Jima Court, Fort Myers, Florida 33908.

DITTMAN, JUNE R Occupation: Teacher of Gifted/Talented Grades 2-6, Russell School. Education: B.S., Baylor University. Address: 1001 Central Boulevard, Brownsville, Texas 78520.

DITTRICH, THOMAS STAYTON Occupation: Advertising Manager. Education: B.A., Indiana University, 1979. Address: 104 Rowland Road, Fairfield, Connecticut 06430.

DiVINCENTI, MARIE P Occupation: Graduate Program Director. Education: Diploma, B.S.N.E., M.S.N.E., Ed.D. Address: 1039 Royal Street, New Orleans, Louisiana 70116.

DIWAN, ROMESH KUMAR Occupation: Chairman, Economics Department. Education: Ph.D. Address: 6 Bolivar Avenue, Troy, New York 12180.

DIXON, FRED W Occupation: Attorney; Pharmacist. Education: Pharm.D., J.D. Address: 130 Waddington, Birmingham, Michigan 48009.

DIX, ROBERT W Occupation: Newspaper Cartoonist. Education: High School and Correspondence Art Course. Address: 35 Amherst Street, Manchester, New Hampshire 03032.

DIXON, JO-ANN C Occupation: Human Performance Specialist. Education: A.A., B.A. Sociology. Address: 29 High Street, Glen Ridge, New Jersey 07028.

DIXON, LAWRENCE P Occupation: Insurance/Bond Broker. Education: B.S., Fordham University. Address: 35 Bunkerhill Drive, Huntington, New York 11743.

DIXON, ROBERT MORTON Occupation: Research Soil Scientist, Reversing of Worldwide Desertification. Education: B.S., M.S., Kansas State University; Ph.D., University of Wisconsin. Address: 1231 East Big Rock Road, Tucson, Arizona 85718.

DIZER, JOHN T Occupation: Dean, Technology of Business, Mohawk Valley Community College. Education: Ph.D. Industrial Engineering; M.S., B.S. Engineering. Address: 10332 Ridgecrest Road, Utica, New York 13502.

DOBIN, RUBIN REOUVAIN Occupation: Rabbi, Organization Executive Head. Education: Ordination, B.A., M.A., D.D. Address: 17720 North Bay Road, Suite 8D, Miami, Florida 33160.

DOBINSKY, PAUL S Occupation: President, Dobinsky Insurance Agency, Incorporated. Education: A.B., Washington University. Address: 404 Marford Drive, Creve Coeur, Maryland 63141.

DOBSON, JAMES GORDON JR Occupation: Cardiovascular Physiologist, Department of Physiology, University of Massachusetts Medical School. Education: B.S., M.A., Ph.D. Address: 55 Lake Avenue North, Worcester, Massachusetts 01605.

DOCKETT, DOSHIA C M Occupation: Head of Music Department, Jamaica Plain High School. Education: B.M., M.Ed., Ed.D. Address: 113 Wellington Hill Street, Mott, Missouri 02130.

DODD, CHARLES G Occupation: President, Connecticut Technology Consultants, Incorporated. Education: B.S. Chemical Engineering, Rice University; M.S. and Ph.D. Physical Chemistry, University of Michigan. Address: 581-B North Trail, Stratford, Connecticut 06497.

DODD, FRANK POTTER Occupation: Insurance Agent and Broker. Education: B.A., Wesleyan University; C.P.C.U. Address: One Starhaven Avenue, Middletown, New York 10940.

DODD, THOMAS FRANCIS Occupation: Marketing Manager. Education: B.A. Chemistry, M.B.A. Marketing. 521 Piermont Avenue, Rivervale, New Jersey 07675.

DODGE, DEXTER ARTHUR Occupation: Investment Counselor. Education: B.S. in B.A. Address: 19 Elmwood Road, Marblehead, Massachusetts 01945.

DODGE, DONALD W Occupation: Technical Director, Polymer Products Research and Development. Education: Ph.D. Chemical Engineering. Address: 330 Brockton Road, Wilmington, Delaware 19898.

DOHERTY, GEORGE WILLIAM Occupation: Psychologist. Education: B.S., Pennsylvania State University; M.S., Mississippi State University. Address: Post Office Box 607, Ely, Nevada 89301.

DOLAN, SUSAN M Occupation: Counselor, Women's Services, Women's Center. Education: M.A. Marriage and Family Counseling, B.A. Child Development. Address: 752 Seneca, Box 11493, Tahoe Paradise, California 95708.

DOLE, CHARLES H Occupation: Sailing Coach, University of Hawaii. Education: A.B. 1936, M.B.A. 1938. Address: 2333 Kapiolani, Apartment 3501, Honolulu, Hawaii 96826.

DOLGIN, STEPHEN MARK Occupation: Social Security Claims Examiner, Social Security Western Program Service Center and Active Army Reservist. Education: B.A., M.S.W., M.B.A. Address: 27808 Huntwood Avenue #1 Hayward, California 94544.

DOLGUN, ALEXANDER M Occupation: Program Office. Education: B.Sc., M. Address: 12704 Deep Spring Drive, Potomac, Maryland 20854.

DOLL, RONALD C Occupation: Author, Professor Emeritus. Education: B.A., Columbia College; M.A. and Ed.D., Columbia University. Address: 1081A Argyll Circle, Lakewood, New Jersey 08701.

DOLLITZ, GRETE F Occupation: Broadcasting, Teaching. Education: B.A. Address: 2305 Norman Avenue, Richmond, Virginia 23228.

DOLNICK, LEE A Occupation: Vice-President and General Manager, WLSN Radio Division, The Hearst Corporation. Education: B.S., University of Wisconsin/Madison. Address: 4909 North Ardmore, Milwaukee, Wisconsin 53217.

DOLPH, RICHARD MICHAEL Occupation: Associate Professor, Memphis State University; Principal Horn, Memphis Symphony Orchestra. Education: B.M., Curtis Institute; M.A., University of Pennsylvania. Address: 2085 Kingsrow, Cordova, Tennessee 38018.

DOLPHIN, WARREN DEAN Occupation: Professor of Zoology, Executive Officer Biology, Iowa State University. Education: B.S., West Chester State College; Ph.D., Ohio State University. Address: 1925 Hunziker Drive, Ames, Iowa 50011.

DOMINGUE, GERALD J Occupation: Professor of Bacteriology, Immunology, and Urology, Tulane University School of Medicine. Education: B.S., University Southwestern Louisiana; Ph.D., Tulane University. Address: 729 Dumaine Street, New Orleans, Louisiana 70116.

DONAHUE, TROY Occupation: Actor. Education: High School. Address: 1022 Euclid Street, Santa Monica, California 90403.

DONALD, JANET GAIL Occupation: Director and Associate Professor. Education: B.A. Psychology, M.A. Psychology, Ph.D. Educational Theory. Address: 479 Strathcona Avenue, Westmount, Quebec, Canada H3A 2K6.

DONCASTER, BARBARA WEISS Occupation: Professional Artist. Address: S.R. 62, Box 25, Great Barrington, Massachusetts 01230.

DONEGAN, CHARLES EDWARD Occupation: Professor of Law, Southern University Law School. Education: B.S.C., M.S.I.R., J.D., LL.M. Address: 10837 Flintwood Avenue, Baton Rouge, Louisana 70811.

DONER, RICHARD BYRON Occupation: Chairman of the Board and President. Education: B.S., Indiana Institute of Technology. Address: 11510 Brigadoon Court, Fort Wayne, Indiana 46804.

DONLON, MICHELE LYNN Occupation: Vocational Training Coordinator. Education: B.A. Education, M.S. Education. Address: 18479 Stone Hollow Drive, Germantown, Maryland 20874.

DONOVAN, MARY SUDMAN Occupation: Historian. Education: B.A., Mills College; M.A., University of Louisville; M.Phil, Columbia University. Address: 5920 Grandview Drive, Little Rock, Arkansas 72207.

DONOVAN, PATRICIA BURNS Occupation: Guidance Counselor. Education: B.S., St. Joseph's University; M.A., Villanova University, 1976. Address: 1321 Illinois Avenue, Cape May, New Jersey 08204.

DOOLEY, THOMAS J Occupation: Research Chemist, Polychrome Corporation. Education: B.S., M.A., Ph.D. Address: 975 Teaneck Road, Teaneck, New Jersey 07666.

DOORNBOS, ROY JR Occupation: President, Recreation Management Corporation. Education: B.S., Central Michigan University; M.S., University of Northern Colorado; Ed.D., University of Northern Colorado. Address: 51361 Truemper Way, #6, Fort Wayne, Indiana 46815.

DOPUCH, NICHOLAS Occupation: Professor of Accounting and Finance, Washington University. Education: B.S., M.S., Ph.D. Address: 614 Audubon, Clayton, Missouri 63105.

DORAN, TIMOTHY PATRICK Occupation: Educator, Anthony S. Andrews School. Education: B.A., Le Moyne College, 1971; M.A.T., University of Alaska. Address: Anthony S. Andrews School, St. Michael, Alaska 99659.

DORIOT, NINA RUTH Occupation: Retired. Address: 3082 Marquette Avenue, Muskegon, Michigan 49442.

DORN, GORDON H Occupation: Director of Purchases. Education: High School, Technical School, Draftsman. Address: W142 N6769 Washington, Menomonee Falls, Wisconsin 53051.

DORNER, SHARON A Occupation: Business Educator. Education: Ed.D, Rutgers University, 1982; M.A. 1970, M.A. 1978, Montclair State College. Address: 28 College Avenue, Upper Montclair, New Jersey 07043.

DORNSIFE, SAMUEL J Occupation: Interior Designer Specializing in Historic Restoration. Education: High School, Honorary Doctor of Fine Arts. Address: 974 Hollywood Circle, Williamsport, Pennsylvania 17701.

DORRELL, JEAN T Occupation: Professor. Education: B.S., M.S. Address: Box 632, Vidor, Texas 77662.

DORSET, GERALD Occupation: Poet, Librarian. Education: B.A., M.F.A., M.L.S., Ph.D. Address: 45 Tudor City Place, New York, New York 10017.

DOSSETT, BETTY JO Occupation: Social Insurance Representative, Retired. Education: B.S. Science, M.S. Education. Address: 209 South 24th Avenue, Hattiesburg, Mississippi 39401.

DOTY, CAROLYN HOUSE Occupation: Novelist. Education: B.F.A. Painting, University of Utah, M.F.A. Creative Writing, University of California of Irvine. Address: 307 East 76th Street #5, New York, New York 10021.

DOUGLAS, MICHAEL HANAU Occupation: Software Engineering and Educational Counsulting, Laboratory Data Products, Digital Equipment Corporation. Education: M.S. Biological Chemistry, M.S. Computer Science. Address: 46 Edgewood Road, Southboro, Massachusetts 01772.

DOULIS, THOMAS JOHN Occupation: Professor of English/Novelist, Department of English, Portland

State University. Education: B.A., LaSalle College; M.A., Stanford. Address: 2236 North East Regents Drive, Portland, Oregon 97212.

DOW, FREDERICK W Occupation: Professor of International Management, U.S. International University. Education: B.S., M.S., A.M., Ph.D. Address: 5080 Carlsbad Boulevard, Carlsbad, California 92008.

DOW, HELEN JEANNETTE Occupation: Professor of Art History, Department of Fine Art, University of Guelph. Education: B.A., University of Toronto; M.A., Ph.D., Bryn Mawr. Address: 406-89 Raymond Street, Guelph, Ontario N1H 3S5, Canada.

DOW, MARGUERITE RUTH Occupation: Professor of English and Drama, Faculty of Education, University of Western Ontario. Education: B.A., B.Ed., M.A., University of Toronto. Address: 1231 Richmond Street Apartment 909, London, Ontario N6A 3L9, Canada.

DOWDELL, JOHN L Occupation: President, The Dowdell Corporation. Education: A.B., Stanford University; M.B.A., Stanford Graduate School of Business. Address: 1266 Norfolk Way, Sacramento, California 95831.

DOWE, CARLTON I Occupation: Fire Chief. Education: Associate Degree Fire Technology, Associate Degree Fire Administration, Associate Fire Arts. Address: Estate Thomas #14-53, St. Thomas, Virgin Islands 00801.

DOWNER, CHARLES W Occupation: Investment Banker. Education: B.A., Harvard University; M.B.A. Address: 125 Pearl Street, Boston, Massachusetts 02110.

DOWNS, ROBERT C S Occupation: Writer/ Professor, English Department, Penn State University. Education: A.B., Harvard University; M.F.A., University of Iowa. Address: R.D. Box 365 Pennsylvania Furnace, Pennsylvania 16865.

DOYLE, JAMES A Occupation: Health Services and Private Counseling. Education: Ph.D., Litt.D., M.P.H., B.S. Psychology and Public Health. Address: 1202 Village Lane, Winter Park, Florida 32792.

DOYLE, PETER THOMAS Occupation: Vice President Finance. Education: B.A. Address: 3430 Cloudcroft Drive, Malibu, California 90265.

DOYLE, ROBERT J Occupation: Engineering. Education: B.S., M.E.A. Address: 3431 Arcadia Drive, Ellicott City, Maryland 21043.

DOYLE, WILLIAM FRANCIS Occupation: Engineer. Education: S.B., S.M. Candidate, Massachusetts Institute of Technology. Address: RR-2, Woodstock, Connecticut 06281.

DOZOIS, GARDNER R Occupation: Writer/ Editor. Education: High School Diploma. Address: 401 South Quince Street, Philadelphia, Pennsylvania 19147.

DRACHMAN, DAVID A Occupation: Professor and Chairman, Department of Neurology, University of Massachusetts Medical Center. Address: 111 Barrett's Mill Road, Concord, Massachusetts 01742.

DRAGON, PAUL K Occupation: Computer Design Engineer, Business Executive. Education: A.S. Electronics Technology, Hillsborough Community College; A.A. Architecture and Mathematics, St. Petersburg Junior College. Address: 2180 Bridle Path, Melbourne, Florida 32935.

DRAGUN, JAMES Occupation: Soil Chemist. Education: B.S., M.S., Ph.D. Address: 3114 Harvard, Royal Oak, Michigan 48072.

DRAIME, DOUGLAS Occupation: Poet/ Playwright. Address: 1253 North East 6th Street, Grants Pass, Oregon 97526.

DRAKE, THOMAS LEE Occupation: Coordinator, Product Safety. Education: B.S., Southwest Texas State University, 1971; M.S., University of Houston CLC, 1979. Address: 2931 Alexander Circle, Flossmoor, Illinois 60422.

DRAPER, E LINN JR Occupation: Engineering, Nuclear. Education: B.A., B.S., Ph.D. Address: 1190 Dowlen, Beaumont, Texas 77706.

DRAPER, WILLIAM H III Occupation: President and Chairman, U.S. Export-Import Bank. Education: B.A., Yale University; M.B.A., Harvard University. Address: 3122 P Street, Northwest, Washington, D.C. 20007.

DRENCHKO, ELIZABETH MAE K Occupation: Teacher, Chemistry, Physics, Laboratory Technology, Piscataway High School. Education: B.Sc. Chemistry, M.Ed., Ed.D. Address: 624 Hillsborough Road, Belle Mead, New Jersey 08854

DRIEVER, STEVEN L Occupation: Associate Professor of Geography, Department of Geosciences, University of Missouri. Education: B.A. with distinction, University of Virginia; M.S. Geography, Northwestern University; Ph.D. Geography, University of Georgia. Address: 5106 West 49th Street, Roeland Park, Kansas 66205.

DRISCOLL, NANCY J Occupation: Area Director, Department of Social Services. Education: A.B. Regis College; M.S.W., Boston College. Address: 276 Chestnut Street, Clinton, Massachusetts 01510.

DROLL, MARIAN CLARKE Occupation: Speech Writer/Special Assistant, White House Office of Planning and Evaluation. Education: B.A. Address: 305 University Place, Grosse Pointe, Michigan 48230.

DRONET, VIRGIE M Occupation: Head of Science Department, Lake Arthur High School, Visiting Lecturer at McNeese State University. Education: B.S., M.Ed., Ed.S., McNeese State University; Ed.D., East Texas State University. Address: Post Office Box 674, Lake Arthur, Louisiana 70549.

DROSTE, W CLAIRE Occupation: Speech Pathology and Audiology. Education: M.S. Address: 714 East Union, Litchfield, Illinois 62056.

DROWN, EUGENE A Occupation: Consultant, Forest Engineer. Education: Ph.D. Public Administration. Address: 5624 Bonniemae Way, Sacto, California 95824.

DROZDZIEL, MARION J Occupation: Chief Engineer, Aerospace, Structures and Weights. Education: B.S. Aerospace Engineering, B.S. Mechanial Engineering, M.S. Mechanical Engineering. Address: 152 Linwood Avenue, Tonawanda, New York 14150.

DRUCKER, HERBERT Occupation: Director, Business Information Services. Education: B.S. Mathematics. Address: 8504 Red Wing Lane, Lanham, Maryland 20706.

DRUGER, STEPHEN DAVID Occupation: Physicist, Research in Chemical Physics, Departmet of Chemistry, Northwestern University. Education: Ph.D., University of Rochester; A.M., University of Rochester; B.S. Brooklyn College. Address: 4820 Greenleaf, Skokie, Illinois 60077.

DRUMMOND, OLIVER LEE Occupation: Chief of Police. Education: B.S., California State University-Long Beach, 1974; Advanced Graduate Certificate, Pacific Christian College, 1979; Ph.D. Candidate, Newport University. Address: 425 North Irwin Street, Hanford, California 93230.

DRYHURST, GLENN Occupation: Chairman, George Lynn Cross Research Professsor of Chemistry, University of Oklahoma. Education: B.Sc., A.R.I.C., Ph.D. Address: 223 Crest Court, Norman, Oklahoma

73071.

DUBES, MARGARET JOANNE Occupation: Nutritionist. Education: B.A., M.S. Address: 7515 Lawndale, Omaha, Nebraska 68134.

DUBIN, JAMES M Occupation: Partner, Paul, Weiss, Rittard, Wharton and Barrsir. Education: B.A., University of Pennsylvania; J.D., Columbia Law. Address: One Madison Place, Harrison, New York 10528.

DUBNER, RONALD Occupation: Neurobiologist, National Institutes of Health. Education: D.D.S, Ph.D. Address: 11806 Milbern Drive, Potomac, Maryland 20854.

DuBOFF, LEONARD DAVID Occupation: Law Professor, Lewis and Clark Law School; Lawyer. Education: A.A.S., B.E.S., J.D. Address: 12440 Southwest Iron Mt., Portland, Oregon 97219.

DuBOIS, DONNA M Occupation: Medical Record Administrator, Saint Mary Medical Center. Education: A.S., 1981. Address: 2202 West 85th Avenue, Merrillville, Indiana 46410.

DuBOIS, NELSON F Occupation: Professor, Educational Psychology. Education: B.A., M.A., Ph.D. Address: 148 East Street, Oneowta, New York 13820.

DuBOIS, ROCHELLE H Occupation: Adjunct English Teacher, Union College; Writer for Women Sense; Editor for Merging Media. Education: B.A., University of Illinois; M.F.A., University of Iowa; Ph.D., Columbia Pacific University. Address: 59 Sandra Circle A-3, Westfield, New Jersey 07090.

DuBROFF, RICHARD EDWARD Occupation: Electrical Engineer, Phillips Petroleum Company. Education: B.S., M.S., Ph.D. in Electrical Engineering. Address: Rural Route 2, Box 142D, Bartlesville, Oklahoma 74003.

DUDLEY, MARGARET JOYCE Occupation: Assistant Principal. Education: B.A., M.Ed. Address: 9417 Album, El Paso, Texas 79925.

DUEWEL, WESLEY L Occupation: International Missionary Leader. Education: A.B., Th.B., M.Ed., Ed.D., D.D. Address: 617 Horton, Greenwood, Indiana 46142.

DUERR, J STEPHEN Occupation: Engineering Consultant. Education: B.S., M.S., Ph.D., Metallurgy, Massachusetts Intitute of Technology. Address: 9 Schenic Falls Road, Long Valley, New Jersey 07853.

DUFF, ANN SHELDON Occupation: Grant Coordinator, Minnitonta Public Schools. Education: B.A., University of Minnesota, M.A. Address: 2830 Maplewoods Road, Wayzata, Minnesota 55391.

DUFFEY, GEORGE HENRY Occupation: Professor of Physics, South Dakota State University. Education: B.A., Cornell College; A.M., Ph.D., Princeton University. Address: 628 11th Avenue, Brookings, South Dakota 57006.

DUGGAN, ROBERT W Occupation: Investor. Education: Attended the University of California-Santa Barbara and the University of California-Los Angeles. Address: 3969 Cuervo Avenue, Santa Barbara, California 93110.

DUKE, JAMES B Occupation: Vice President, Sales and Marketing. Education: Bachelor of Aerospace Engineering, S.M. Address: 43 Coleman Avenue West, Chatham, New Jersey 07928.

DUKE, JUNE LABER Occupation: Director of College Events. Education: R.N., B.A. Address: 2508 Long Quarter Court, Lutherville, Maryland 21093.

DULEY, ALVIN J Occupation: Retired Professional Educator. Education: B.S., Brigham Young University; M.A., Arizona State University; B.S., Marian College. Address: 953 Meadow Creek Lane, Fond du Lac,

Wisconsin 54935.

DULSKI, KATHIE A Occupation: Newspaper Publishing Company Manager. Address: 2149 Heather Lane, Palatine, Illinois 60074.

DUMESNIL, CARLA DAVIS Occupation: Head Designer, IDEAS. Education: B.S., M.A. Address: 361 South 1300 East, Salt Lake City, Utah 84102.

duMOUCHEL, ANNE MARIE MARCHELLE Occupation: Executive Administrative Assistant. Education: Bachelor of Arts in History and Political Science. Address: 125 D Larchmont Acres, Larchmont, New York 105238.

DUNCAN, ARTHUR WILLIAM Occupation: Vocational School Administrator. Education: M.A., B.A. Address: 6 Brown Road, Montrose, Colorado 811401.

DUNCAN, BERT LOGAN Occupation: Retired Liberal Protestant Clergyman. Education: A.B., William Jewell College; Th.M., South Baptist Theological Seminary; Postgraduate, University of Chicago; University of Virginia and Indiana University. Address: 2531 East 7th Street, Bloomington, Indiana 47401.

DUNCAN-JOHNSON, CONTANCE CATHARINE Occupation: Research and Clinical Psychologist, National Institute of Mental Health. Education: Ph.D. Psychology, A.M. Psychology, B.A. Mathematics. Address: 4513 Gretna Street, Bethesda, Maryland 20814.

DUNLOP, DAVID W Occupation: Teacher/ Economist, Health Management Program, School of Management, Boston University. Education: Ph.D. Economics, Michigan State University; M.A., B.S., University of California-Berkeley. Address: 1800 R Street North West #609, Washington, D.C. 20009.

DUNN, ERAINA BURKE Occupation: District Community Coordinator, School District 147, Washington School. Education: B.A., Wilberforce University. Address: 15221 Lincoln Harvey, Illinois 60416.

DUNN, HELEN ELIZABETH Occupation: School Teacher, Counselor. Education: B.S. Education, M.A. Counseling, Bradley University. Address: 2604 Rock Street, Peru, Illinois 61354.

DUNN, HENRY HAMPTON Occupation: Editor. Education: High School, College Studies. Address: 10610 Carrollwood Drive, Tampa, Florida 33618.

DUNN, IMA CHARLENE Occupation: Educational Administrator. Education: A.A., B.A., M.Ed., Ed.D. Address: 131 West Routt, Pueblo, Colorado 81004.

DUNN, ROSALIE A Occupation: Health Scientist Administrator, National Heart, Lung and Blood Institute, National Institutes of Health. Education: A.B., M.A., Ph.D. Address: National Heart, Lung and Blood Institute, National Institutes of Health, Bethesda, Maryland 20205.

DUNN S THOMAS Occupation: Consultant. Education: B.S.M.E., M.S.M.E., Ph.D. Address: 1131 Beaumont Circle, Vista, California 92083.

DUNN, STEPHEN Occupation: Poet/Teacher, Stockton State College. Education: M.A. in Creative Writing, Syracuse University. Address: 445 Chestnut Neck Road, Port Republic, New Jersey 08241.

DUNSING, MARILYN M Occupation: Director, School of Human Resources and Family Studies, University of Illinois. Education: M.B.A., Ph.D., University of Chicago.

DUNSTONE, JOHN J Occupation: Professor of Psychology, Research Psychologist, Psychology Department, University of Scranton. Education: B.S., M.S., Ph.D. Address: 14 Sunset Road, RD #2, Moscow,

Pennsylvania 18444.

DUNWORTH, JAMES RICHARD Occupation: Panama Canal Pilot, Panama Canal Commission. Education: B.S., U.S. Merchant Marine Academy, 1958; J.D., Hastings College of Law, 1973. Address: PSC Box 2140, APO Miami 34002.

DUPREE, KATHRYN JOYCE Occupation: Physician Assistant. Education: A.B., A.B., B.S. Address: 2212 I Street, North West, Apartment 109, Washington, D.C. 20037.

DURANTE, MARY P Occupation: Dental Hygiene, Sheridan College. Education: A.G.S., A.S. Dental Hygiene. Address: Box 482 Ranchester, Wyoming 82839.

DURANTY, LAWRENCE Occupation: Business Executive. Education: M.B.A., Ph.D. Address: 53 Aspen Way, Rolling Hills Estates, California 90274.

DURNEY, CARL H Occupation: Professor of Electrical Engineering, University of Utah. Education: B.S., M.S., Ph.D. Address: 4688 Wallace Lane, Salt Lake City, Utah 84117.

DURYEA, ELIAS J Occupation: Professor of Health Education, The University of New Mexico. Education: B.S., M.S., Ph.D. Address: Department of H.P.E.R., The Unversity of New Mexico, Albuquerque, New Mexico 87131.

DUSHKIND, DONALD STANFORD Occupation: Forensic Psychologist and Family Mediator. Education: B.S.S., College of the City of New York, 1945; M.A., State University of Iowa, 1946; Ph.D., New York University, 1959. Address: 120 San Gabriel Drive, Fairfax, California 94930.

DUTTON, DENNIS LEE Occupation: Computer Consultant and Programmer. Education: B.S., A.S. Address: 717 West 15th, Spokane, Washington 99203.

DUTZ-KOHOUT, ELFRIEDE I Occupation: Assistant Chief, Laboratory Services, Professor of Pathology. Education: M.D., F.A.C. Pathology, F.C. Pathology, F.A.C. Microbiology, F.A.C. T.M. Address: 4306 Oxford Circle West, Richmond, Virginia 23221.

DUVEEN, HENRY J Occupation: Investment Advisor. Education: B.A. Liberal Arts. Address: 58 Milford Lane, Suffern, New York 10901.

DWORSKI, SYLVIA Occupation: Retired College Professor, Emeritus. Education: B.A., M.A., Ph.D. Address: 70 Byron Place, New Haven, Connecticut 06515.

DWYER, JANE E Occupation: Director of Religious Education/Psychological Examiner. Education: B.A., M.Ed. Address: 15 Turkey Hill Road, Merrimack, New Hampshire 03054.

DWYER, MAUE R Occupation: Assistant to Dean of Student Affairs. Education: B.A., M.A. Address: 526 Oakwood, St. Louis Missouri 63119.

DYBAS, LINDA K Occupation: Associate Professor of Biology. Education: B.A., Knox College; M.A., California State University; Dr. Human Biology, University Ulm, West Germany. Address: 159 West First Street, Galesburg, Illinois 61401.

DYBEK, STUART JOHN Occupation: Writer/ Professor of English, Western Michigan University. Education: M.F.A., Iowa University; M.A., Loyola University. Address: 320 Monroe, Kalamazoo, Missouri 49007.

DYCKMAN, THOMAS R Occupation: Professor, Cornell University. Education: Ph.D., University of Michigan. Address: 402 Winthrop Drive, Ithaca, New York 14850.

DYE, CHARLES MYRON Occupation: Professor Department of Educational Foundations, Director Graduate Studies in Education, The University of Akron. Education: B.A., M.A., Ph.D. Address: 2999 Chamberlain Road, Akron, Ohio 44313.

DYE, DAVID A Occupation: Educator and Attorney. Education: B.A. 1972, J.D 1976, U.M.K.C. Address: 6220 Harrison, Kansas City, Missouri 64110.

DYER, SHARON ELLEN Occupation: Science/ Technology Policy, General Accounting Office, Science/Technology Policy Group. Education: M.P.A., B.A. Address: 4201 South 31st Street, Apartment 418, Arlington, Virginia 22206.

DYKES, MARIE DRAPER Occupation: Associate Provost for Academic Programs, Wayne State University. Education: B.S.N., M.S.N., Ph.D. Address: 19419 Bretton Drive, Detroit, Michigan 48223.

DYKES, MARY HELEN Occupation: Assistant Secretary-Treasurer, BOBS Candies. Education: B.A., Manhattanville College. Address: 3509 Old Dawson Road, Albany, Georgia 31707.

DZIADYK, BOHDAN Occupation: Botany and Ecology Educator/Professor, Augustana College. Education: B.A., M.S., Ph.D. Address: 3319 Second Street Court, East Moline, Illinois 61244.

E

EAKIN, THOMAS CAPPER Occupation: Sports Promotion Executive. Education: B.A. History, Denison University. Address: 2729 Shelley Road, Shaker Heights, Ohio 44122.

EAKINS, PAMELA S Occupation: Sociologist, Center for Research on Women, Stanford University. Education: Ph.D. Address: Center for Research on Women, Stanford University, Stanford, California 94305.

EALEY-JONES, JUANITA YVONNE Occupation: Entrepreneur and Business Executive. Education: B.A. Business Administration; A.A. Computer Language. Address: 2843 Hillcrest Drive, Los Angeles, California 90016.

EANEMAN, JAMES MICHAEL Occupation: Northern San Mateo County District Manager, Pacific Gas and Electric Company. Education: B.S., Chicago State College, 1968; M.B.A., Pepperdine University, 1980. Address: 517 Jackson Street, Albany, California 94706.

EARL, LEWIS H Occupation: Manager, Chamber of Commerce. Education: A.B., Texas Tech University, 1939; J.D., Georgetown University, 1950. Address: 601 West Main, Post, Texas 79356.

EARLY, GERALD L Occupation: Cardiovascular and Thoracic Surgeon. Education: B.A., Central Methodist College; M.A., University of Missouri; M.D., University of Missouri-Kansas City. Address: 2520 Grand Avenue, Kansas City, Missouri 64108.

EARNEST, ROBERT C Occupation: Marketing Executive. Education: B.S., Mount Union College, 1960; M.B.A., Indiana University, 1966. Address: 9633 Marston Lane, Gaithersburg, Maryland 20879.

EASA, SAID M Occupation: Associate Professor of Civil Engineering. Education: B.Sc., Cairo, 1972; M.Eng., Hamilton, 1976; Ph.D., Berkeley, 1981. Address: 315 Hodder Avenue, Thunder Bay, Ontario, Canada P7B 5E1.

EASTMAN, ANN HEIDBREDER Occupation: Director, Public Affairs Programs, Arts and Sciences; Director, Scholarly Publishing. Education: B.A. Address: 716 Burruss Drive, Northwest, Blacksburg, Virginia 24060.

EATON, JoANNE WALTON Occupation: Professor of Literature and Rhetoric. Education: B.A. 1975, J.D. 1978, West Virginia University. Address: Apartment 999, 14 Concord Avenue, Cambridge, Massachusetts 02138.

EATON, LUCY ELLEN Occupation: Retired, Writer/Poet. Education: Honorary Doctorate, H.L.D. Address: 101 8th Avenue, Castlegar, British Columbia, Canada V1N 1M7.

EATON, RICHARD BEHRENS Occupation: Judge of the Superior Court (Retired). Education: A.B. 1934, J.D. 1938, Stanford University. Address: 1520 West, Redding, California 96001.

EBERLY, ROBERT EDWARD SR Occupation: Banker and Independent Gas Producer. Education: B.S. Chemistry, Penn State University. Address: 56 Charles Street, Uniontown, Pennsylvania 15401.

EBERSPACHER, WARREN A Occupation: President, Historical Aircraft Corporation. Education: B.A.E., University of Minnesota, 1952; M.B.A., Pepperdine University, 1972. Address: Post Office Box 2218, Durango, Colorado 81301.

EBERT-FLATTAU, PAMELA Occupation: Science Policy Analyst, National Science Foundation. Address: 4532 Van Ness Street Northwest, Washington, D.C. 20016.

EBISUZAKI, YUKIKO Occupation: Chemistry Faculty Member, North Carolina State University. Education: B.S., M.S., Ph.D. Address: Department of Chemistry, North Carolina State University, Raleigh, North Carolina 27695-8204.

EBY, LAWRENCE THORNTON Occupation: Principal Associate Research and Development/ Chemist. Education: B.S. Ch.E. 1938, M.S. 1939, Ph.D. 1941. Address: 102 South Kennicott Avenue, Arlington Heights, Illinois 60005.

ECHOLS, DAVID LORIMER Occupation: Assistant Commissioner, N.Y.S. Dept. of Social Services. Education: B.A. Political Science. Address: 414 Parker Avenue, Buffalo, New York 14216.

ECK, CARYLL LORIMER Occupation: Associate Professor of Nursing Education. Education: Registered Nurse, B.S. Education. Address: RD 1, Box 437, Williamsport, Pennsylvania 17701.

EDELSTEIN, ROSE MARIE HUBLOU Occupation: Associate Director of Nursing and Staff Development. Education: Bachelor of Science in Nursing, M.A.Ed., Ed.D. Address: 10 Grande Pasco, San Rafael, California 94903.

EDEN, JAMES GARY Occupation: Professor, University of Illinois. Education: B.S., M.S., Ph.D. Address: 1801 Stratford Drive, Champaign, Illinois 61821.

EDGAR, THOMAS E Occupation: Professor. Education: Ed.D., M.A., B.Ed., B.S. Address: 419 South Garfield, #3, Pocatello, Idaho 83204.

EDGEMON, CONSTANCE (CONNIE) KAY Occupation: Clinical Staff Psychologist, Big Spring State Hospital. Education: B.A., Pan American University, Texas; M.A., Chapman College, California. Address: 2007 Runnels, Big Spring, Texas 79720.

EDMUNDS, DALE C Occupation: Commercial Banking. Education: A.B., Dartmouth, 1975; M.B.A., Sloan School, Massachusetts Institute of Technology, 1977. Address: 332 Walnut Street, Wellesley Hills, Massachusetts 02181.

EDMUNDS, ROBERT LARRY Occupation: Vice President, Secretary and Treasurer, Avondale Mills. Education: B.S. Business Administration, Auburn University. Address: 20 Lake Louise Drive, Sylacauga, Alabama 35150.

EDWARDS, DOUGLAS PHILLIP Occupation: Director of Admissions. Education: B.A. Art Education, Pepperdine University; M.A. Higher Education Administration, Villanova University. Address: 229 Bailey Road, Rosemont, Pennsylvania 19010.

EDWARDS, JO BETH STELL Occupation: Media Coordinator, ENMU. Education: B.S., M.Ed. Address: East Star Route, Box 171, Portales, New Mexico 88130.

EDWARDS, LEILA SCELONGE Occupation: Associate Dean of the Graduate School, Northwestern University. Education: Ph.D., M.S., M.A., B.A. Address: 2519 Orrington Avenue, Evanston, Illinois 60201.

EDWARDS, WALTER HARRISON JR Occupation: Chairman of the Board, W.H. Edwards Eng. Co. (Retired). Education: B.S., Indiana University. Address: 2856 Jamieson Lane, Indianapolis, Indiana 46268.

EDWARDS, WARD Occupation: Research Institute Director, Professor. Education: B.A. Psychology, Swarthmore, 1947; M.A. 1950, Ph.D. 1952, Harvard. Address: 11466 Laurelcrest Road, Studio City, California 91604.

EDWARDSON, JOHN R Occupation: Agronomist, University of Florida. Education: B.S.,

M.S., Ph.D. Address: 2721 Southwest 3rd Place, Gainesville, Florida 32607.

EFFEL, LAURA Occupation: Attorney. Education: B.A. 1971, J.D. 1975. Address: 111 Third Avenue, New York, New York 10003.

EGAN, MARY JOAN Occupation: Associate Professor of English. Education: B.A., Alabama; M.A., Ph.D., Catholic University of America. Address: 417 Summit Street, Grove City, Pennsylvania 16127.

EGERTON, JOHN R Occupation: Research Veterinary Parasitologist. Education: B.S. 1951, M.S. 1951, Ph.D. 1953. Address: R.D. 2, Box 209, Neshanic Station, New Jersey 08853.

EGLI, DAN Occupation: Clinical Psychologist, Private Practice. Education: Ph.D. Address: R.D. #5, Box 192, Muncy, Pennsylvania 17756.

EHRLICH, BERNARD HERBERT Occupation: Attorney and Counsellor at Law. Education: A.B. 1946, LL.B. 1949, J.D., M.A. 1950, George Washington University. Address: 507 Bonifant Street, Silver Spring, Maryland 20910.

EHRLICH, GEORGE E Occupation: Vice President, Pharmaceuticals Division, Ciba-Geigy Corporation. Education: A.B., Harvard University, 1948; M.B., M.D., Chicago Medical School, 1952. Address: 2223 Delancey Place, Philadelphia, Pennsylvania 19103.

EHRSAM, ELDON EDWARD Occupation: Ops Research Analyst. Education: B.S. Physics, M.S. System Management. Address: 3087 Fairleard, Santa Ynez, California 93460.

EINSELEN, KENNETH LEE Occupation: Miami County Highway Engineer, Miami County Courthouse. Education: B.S.C.E. 1976, M.S.C.E. 1977, Purdue University. Address: Route 1, Box 104, Amboy, Indiana 46911.

EISELE, ROBERT H Occupation: Playwrite/Screenwriter/Professor. Education: B.A., M.F.A. Address: 404 North Sweetzer Avenue, Los Angeles, California 90048.

EISENHART, CHARLES R Occupation: Councilman, Town of Queensbury; President Emeritus of Adirondack Community College. Education: Ph.B., M.A., Ed.D., Hum.D. (honoris causa). Address: 238 Bay Street, Glens Falls, New York 12801.

EISSMANN, ROBERT F Occupation: Plant Manager. Education: Electrical Engineering Courses, Pratt Institute and Clemson A&M. Address: 266 Paterson Avenue, Little Falls, New Jersey 07424.

EIZENSTAT, STUART E Occupation: Attorney. Education: A.B., University of North Carolina; LL.B., Harvard Law School. Address: 9107 Brierly Road, Chevy Chase, Maryland 20815.

EKVALL, SHIRLEY M Occupation: Associate Professor/Nutritionist. Education: B.S., M.S., Ph.D. Address: 549 Tohatchi Drive, Cincinnati, Ohio 45215.

EL-AHRAF, AMER MOHAMED EL-MAHDY Occupation: Professor and Chairman, Department of Health Science and Human Ecology. Education: D.V.M., M.P.H., Dr. P.H. (with distinction). Address: 140 Pinehurst Court, San Bernardino, California 92407.

ELDEFRAWI, MOHYEE ELDIN Occupation: Professor of Pharmacology. Education: B.Sc. Agriculture, Ph.D. Toxicology. Address: 8403 Topping Road, Pikesville, Maryland 21208.

ELIAS, HANS G Occupation: Consultant, The Dow Chemical Co. Education: Dipl.-Chemistry, Dr.rer.nab., Habilitation. Address: 4009 Linden, Midland, Michigan 48640.

ELIASON, PHYLLIS MARIE Occupation: Missionary. Education: B.A. Psychology, M.Ed. Guidance Counseling. Address: Post Office Box 20217, Main Facility, Guam 96921.

ELIOT, LANCE BRIAN Occupation: Professor and Consultant. Education: B.A. in C.I.S., M.B.A. in M.I.S., Ph.D.-A.B.D. in M.I.S. Address: 2619 Monogram, Long Beach, California 90815.

ELIZABETH, PAMELA H Occupation: Assistant Professor of Psychology. Education: B.S., M.A., Ed.D. Address: 580 Route 244, PO252, Alfred Station, New York 14803.

ELKIND-SAVATSKY, PAMELA DEE Occupation: Professor of Sociology. Education: A.B. 1965, M.A. 1972, Boston University; Ph.D. Northeastern University, 1979. Address: East 407 27th, Spokane, Washington 99203.

ELLENBOGEN, GEORGE Occupation: Chairman, Department of English; Poet. Education: B.A., McGill; M.A., University De Montreal; Ph.D., Tufts University. Address: 22 Lewis Road, Belmont, Massachusetts 02178.

ELLIOTT, JOYCE Occupation: Professor, Chowan College. Education: B.A., University of Kansas; M.F.A., Yale School of Drama; Ed.D., Columbia University. Address: Route 1, Box 36, Sunbury, North Carolina 27979.

ELLIOTT, MARY MARGARET DRAKE Occupation: Writer, Retired Librarian. Education: Bachelor of Arts, Albion College; Master of Science, University of Michigan. Address: 1530 Nelson Street, Muskegon, Michigan 49441.

ELLIS, JACQUELYNNE LOUISE Occupation: Associate Professor, Nursing. Education: R.N., Harrisburg Polyclinic Medical Center, B.S. Elizabethtown College. Address: 1201 Arthur Road, Montoursville, Pennsylvania 17754.

ELLIS, RANDALL POOR Occupation: Assistant Professor of Economics. Education: B.A., Yale University; M.S., London School of Economics; Ph.D., Massachusetts Institute of Technology. Address: 54 Carleton Street, Newton, Massachusetts 02158.

ELLIS, RONALD J Occupation: Manager Systems Development. Education: M.B.A., University of Southern California, 1978; B.A., California State University-Fullerton, 1974.

ELLIS, WILLIAM A Occupation: Semi-retired. Education: Doctor of Osteopathy. Address: 2202 Rosedale Lane, Arlington, Texas 76011.

ELLISON, CRAIG WILLIAM Occupation: Professor of Urban Ministries and Counseling. Education: B.A. 1966, M.A. 1969, Ph.D. 1972, Post-Doctoral Course 1975-76. Address: 81 Front Street, Nyack, New York 10960.

ELLISON, RICHARD PERHAM Occupation: President, Boat America Corporation. Education: B.A., Trinity College, 1952. Address: 5009 North 25th Street, Arlington, Virginia 22207.

ELLOIE, LOUIS LEON JR Occupation: Professor of Psychology. Education: B.A., M.A. Address: 9516 Caminito Toga, San Diego, California 92126.

ELMAN, HOWARD LAWRENCE Occupation: Aerospace Engineer-Operations Research. Education: S.B., Massachusetts Institute of Technology; Masters, University of Oklahoma; Partial Ph.D. Studies, Rensselaer Polytechnic Institute. Address: 4 Kingfisher Drive, Smithtown, New York 11787.

ELMEGREEN, DEBRA MELOY Occupation: Astronomer. Education: A.B. Astrophysics, Princeton University, 1975; A.M. 1977, Ph.D. 1979, Harvard University. Address: 9 Haymont Terrace, Briarcliff Manor, New York 10510.

ELROD, JULIA A Occupation: Fellow in Neonatology. Education: B.A. Biology, M.D. Address: 10900 West 65 Terrace, #201, Shawnee, Kansas 66203.

ELROD, RACHEL E Occupation: Registered Nurse Instructor. Education: R.N., B.S., M.S. Address: 770 Troy Court, Aurora, Colorado 80011.

ELSAYED, ELSAYED A Occupation: Chairman, Department of Industrial Engineering. Education: B.Sc. Mechanical Engineering, M.Sc. Mechanical Engineering, Ph.D. Industrial Engineering. Address: 11 Center Lane, East Brunswick, New Jersey 08816.

ELTERICH, G JOACHIM Occupation: Professor, Department of Agricultural Economics. Education: Diploma, Agricultural University of Bonn; M.S., University of Kentucky; Ph.D., Michigan State. Address: 145 Timberline Drive, Newark, Deleware 19711.

ELTON, DAVID JOHN Occupation: Assistant Professor of Civil Engineeirng, The Citadel. Education: B.S., M.S., Ph.D. Address: Civil Engineering Department, The Citadel, Charleston, South Carolina 29409.

ELY-CHAITLIN, MARC ERIC AUGUSTUS R Occupation: Proponent for the Advancement of the Doctrine of Legitimacy and of Restoration of the Law. Address: Post Office Box 7075, Laguna Niguel, California 92677.

EMBODEN, WILLIAM Occupation: Author of Approximately 200 Papers and 4 Books; Research Fellow in Ethnobotany, Harvard University; Research Associate, Natural History Museum, Los Angeles; Professor of Biology, California State University-Northridge. Education: B.S., Purdue University, 1957; M.A., Indiana University, 1961; Ph.D., University of California-Los Angeles, 1965. Address: Department of Biology, California State University, North Ridge, California 91330.

EMERSON, SHIRLEY ARMSTRONG Occupation: Director, Bridge Counseling Association; Faculty Member, University of Nevada at Las Vegas Counseling and Education Psychology Department. Education: B.A., Rice University; M.A., Ph.D., University of Michigan. Address: 4240 Woodcrest Road, Las Vegas, Nevada 89121.

EMMEN, DENNIS R Occupation: Electric Utility Executive. Education: B.B.A., University of Minnesota. Address: 808 Glemway, Fergus Falls, Minnesota 56537.

EMMERICH, ANDRE Occupation: Art Dealer, Author. Education: B.A., Oberlin College, 1944; Graduate studies, New School for Social Research. Address: Business: 41 East 57th Street, New York, New York 10022.

ENDEMANN, CARL T Occupation: Writer. Education: Litt.D.h.c., F.R.C. Lecturer, Prof. W.O. University. Address: 1969 Mora Avenue, Calistoga, California 94515.

ENDLER, HENRY C Occupation: Division Manager. Education: B.A., M.A., University of Redlands. Address: 4860 San Gabriel Court Northeast, Salem, Oregon 97305.

ENDRIZZI, JOHN E Occupation: Professor, University of Arizona. Education: B.S., M.S., Ph.D. Address: 2335 East 9th Street, Tucson, Arizona 85719.

ENG, JOE YOOK Occupation: Transportation Engineer/Architectural Designer. Education: M.S. Transportation Engineering. Address: 412 12th Avenue, San Francisco, California 94118.

ENGEL, IRIS DANIEL Occupation: Owner/Director of Iris Daniel Engel School of Music. Education: B.A., Stetson Univiversity, School of Music, 1936. Address: 726 Vassar, Orlando, Florida 32804.

ENGEL, PETER A Occupation: Research Engineer. Education: B.E., M.S., Ph.D. Address: 1004 Murray Hill Road, Binghamton, New York 13903.

ENGELBERG, LOUIS Occupation: Rabbi, The Taylor Road Synagogue. Education: B.A., M.A., D.D. D.H.L. Address: 3485 Blanche Road, Cleveland Heights, Ohio 44118.

ENGELHARDT, SISTER M VERONICE Occupation: School Psychologist, Member of Religious Order. Education: Bachelor of Science in Education, M.A., Ph.D. Address: 302 East Linebaugh Avenue, Tampa, Florida 33612.

ENGLE, RAPHAEL Occupation: President, Ray Engle and Associates. Education: M.A. Address: 4726 La Villa Marina, Marina Del Ray, California 90292.

ENGLISH, RAYMOND HERMAN Occupation: Architect. Education: B.A.Ed., University of Washington-Seattle, 1971. Address: 4411 Southwest 100th Street, Seattle, Washington 98146.

ENSTROM, RONALD E Occupation: Materials Scientist. Education: S.B., S.M., Sc.D., Massachusetts Institute of Technology. Address: 81 Sycamore Lane, Skillman, New Jersey 08558.

EPSTEIN, HARRY H Occupation: Rabbi of Ahavath Achim Synagogue. Education: B.A., M.A., Ph.D., D.D. Address: 2545 Arden Road, Atlanta, Georgia 30327.

EPSTEIN, MARVIN M Occupation: Executive, Engineering and Construction Company. Education: B.A., University of Michigan (with honors), 1951. Address: 4161 Hadleigh Road, University Heights, Ohio 44118.

ERB, RANDALL JAY Occupation: Chief Executive Officer. Education: Ph.D. Biopharmaceutics, Purdue University. Address: 109 Tamiami Court, West Lafayette, Indiana 47906.

ERDMANN, ROBERT L Occupation: Metabolic Analyst. Education: B.S., M.A., Ph.D. Address: 2308 Fairglen Drive, San Francisco, California 95125.

ERICKSON, KAREN L Occupation: Professor of Chemistry. Education: B.S., Ph.D. Address: 2 Thayer Pond, North Oxford, Massachusetts 01537.

ERKKILA, BARBARA H Occupation: Author-Editor. Education: Attended Boston University. Address: Post Office Box 96, Lanesville, Massachusetts 01930.

ERLENMEYER—KIMLING, L Occupation: Professor, Director of Developmental Behavioral Studies. Education: B.S. magna cum laude; Ph.D. Address: Business-722 West 168th Street, New York, New York 10032.

ERNSTEN, CLETE P SR Occupation: Industrialist. Education: High School. Address: 201 East Prairie Street, Cuero, Texas 77954.

ERSKINE, BRUCE ALAN Occupation: Professor, Memphis State University; Musician. Education: B.A., M.M., State University of New York at Stony Brook. Address: 1250 West Perkins Road, Memphis, Tennessee 38117.

ESCANDON, RALPH Occupation: Spanish Professor. Education: Ph.D. Address: 280 Washburn, Angwin, California 94508.

ESCHENROEDER, ALAN Occupation: Consulting Scientist. Education: B.M.E., Ph.D., Cornell University. Address: 13 Dover Street, Concord, Massachusetts 01742.

ESKRIDGE, CHRIS W Occupation: Professor, University of Nebraska. Education: B.S., Brigham Young University; M.A., Ph.D., Ohio State University. Address: 4007 Teri Lane, Lincoln, Nebraska 68502.

ESON, MORRIS E Occupation: Professor.

Education: Ph.D. Address: 14 Holmes Dale, Albany, New York 12203.

ESPARZA, TOMMY Education: B.S., M.S., Ph.D. Address: 811 South 16th Avenue, Edinburg, Texas 78539.

ESSENWANGER, OSKAR M Occupation: Supervising Research Physicist and Adjunct Professor, Environmental Science. Address: 610 Mountain Gap Drive, Huntsville, Alabama 35803.

ESSEX, DUANE A Occupation: Senior Test Engineer. Education: B.S., M.S., Iowa State University. Address: 2728 Carole Circle, Des Moines, Iowa 50322.

ESTEP, WILLIAM R JR Occupation: Distinguished Professor of Church History, Southwestern Baptist Theological Seminary. Education: B.A., Th.M., Th.D. Address: 1 York Drive, Fort Worth, Texas 76134.

ETCHESON, DENISE ELENE Occupation: Airport Designer/Planner. Education: Master of Architecture/ Urban Design, University of Washington. Address: 10911 Northeast 37th Place, Bellevue, Washington 98004.

ETHEREDGE, ROBERT FOSTER Occupation: Lawyer. Education: A.B. 1946, LL.B. 1949, University of Alabama. Address: 3748 Locksley Drive, Birmingham, Alabama 35223.

ETHERIDGE, ROBERT FILES Occupation: Dean of Students and Vice President for Student Affairs. Education: B.A., B.S., Southern Illinois University, 1949; Ed.D., Michigan State University, 1958. Address: 1 Iveswood Drive, Oxford, Ohio 45056.

ETTER, DAVE Occupation: Poet and Freelance Writer. Education: B.A., University of Iowa. Address: Post Office Box 413, Elburn, Illinois 60119.

ETTINGHAUSEN, ELIZABETH S Occupation: Art Historian. Education: Ph.D. Address: 24 Armour Road, Princeton, New Jersey 08540.

ETTL, DOROTHY A Occupation: Extension Clothing Specialist, Cooperative Extension, Washington State University. Education: B.S., University of California-Davis; M.S.H.E., Texas Tech University; Ph.D., University of Minnesota, St. Paul, Minnesota. Address: Northwest 340 North Street, Pullman, Washington 99163.

ETU, PAUL DAVID Occupation: Psychologist. Education: M.S. Clinical Psychology, Marquette University. Address: Box 54, RD#4 Stephanie Lane, Glens Falls, New York 12206.

ETZEL, BARBARA COLEMAN Occupation: Professor of Psychology, Department of Human Development, University of Kansas. Education: A.A., B.A., M.A., Ph.D. Address: J. B. Ranch, Route 1, Box 82-E, Oskaloosa, Kansas 66066.

EVANS, FREDERICK JOHN Occupation: Psychologist/Director of Research. Education: Ph.D., University of Sydney, N.S.W., Australia. Address: 36 Knickerbocker Drive, Belle Mead, New Jersey 08502.

EVANS, JO BURT Occupation: Rancher. Education: B.A., Mary Hardin-Baylor College; M.A., Trinity University. Address: Post Office Box 283, Junction, Texas 76849.

EVANS, LOUISE Occupation: Clinical Psychologist, Lecturer. Education: B.S., M.S., Ph.D. Address: 727 South Beverly Glen Boulevard, Los Angeles, California 90024.

EVANS, RICHARD P Occupation: Minister. Education: B.B.A., Th.M. Address: 1054 Dutch Mill Drive, Manchester, Missouri 63011.

EVANS, SUSAN IRENE Occupation: Teacher, Secondary Level. Education: B.A., Slippery Rock State College; M.Ed., St. Bonaventure University. Address: 33 Berva Drive, Bradford, Pennsylvania 16701.

EVANS, THEDA Occupation: Artist, Lecturer, Musician. Education: B.A. Address: Green Hill EE120-1001 City Avenue, Philadelphia, Pennsylvania 19151.

EVANS, WAYNE CANNON Occupation: Advertising and Public Relations. Education: B.A., M.S., University of Utah. Address: 1246 Gilmer Drive, Salt Lake City, Utah 84105.

EVENSON, MERLE A Occupation: Professor. Education: B.S., M.S. (2), Ph.D. Address: 6009 Piping Rock Road, Madison, Wisconsin 53711.

EVERETT, GRAHAM L Occupation: Publisher. Education: B.A. Address: Business-Box 555, Port Jefferson, New York 11777.

EVERETT, WADE HOWELL Occupation: Law Student, Mercer University. Education: B.B.A. Accounting, Kennesaw College. Address: 2050 Old Clinton Road, Apartment Q2, Macon, Georgia 31211.

EVERS, LaFONDA A Occupation: Library Director. Education: B.S., Certificate Act. Dir. Address: 1001 Park Terrace, Paxton, Illinois 60957.

EVOLA, PHILLIP A Occupation: Theatrical/ Commercial Designer. Education: B.A., St. Mary of the Plains College, 1971; M.F.A., Goodman School of Drama, 1974. Address: 95 Third Place, Brooklyn, New York 11231.

EWALD, HENRY THEODORE JR Occupation: President, H. T. Ewald Foundation. Education: B.A., Yale University; Bachelor of Laws, Detroit College of Law. Address: 284 Moross Road, Grosse Pointe, Michigan 48236.

EWING, DAVID L Occupation: Research, Hahnemann University. Education: B.S., M.S., Ph.D. Address: 88 South Spring Lane, Phoenixville, Pennsylvania 19480.

EWY, DONNA HOHMANN Occupation: Director, Youth Programs YWCA; Author. Education: Doctorate in Education. Address: 1315 Norwood, Boulder, Colorado 80302.

EYSMAN, HARVEY A Occupation: Attorney, Self-Employed. Education: Physics, Massachusetts Institute of Technology, 1961; J.D. 1964, L.L.M. 1966, Brooklyn Law School. Address: 15 Park Circle, Great Neck, New York 11024.

EZELL, JAMES KENNETH Occupation: Private Investigator/Insurance Consultant. Education: B.B.A. Accounting, University of Houston, 1953. Address: 1219 Ship Wheel Lane, Gillette, Wyoming 82716.

F

FABRIKANT, CRAIG S Occupation: Clinical Psychologist. Education: B.S. 1974, M.A. 1977, Ph.D. 1983. Address: 37 Oakdene Avenue, Teaneck, New Jersey 07666.

FABRY, JOSEPH B Occupation: Director, Institute of Logotherapy. Education: J.D., University of Vienna. Address: 315 Carmel Avenue, El Cerrito, California 94530.

FACINELLI, JIM W Occupation: Agricultural Education Instructor; Director Vocational Education. Education: M.Ed., CSU; B.S., University of Wyoming. Address: 11 Sunset Rim, Cody, Wyoming 82414.

FACUSSÉ, ALBERT SHUCRY Occupation: Attorney at Law. Education: Law, Loyola University, 1943; J.D., 1968. Address: 6731 Manchester Street, New Orleans, Louisiana 70112.

FAGEN, RICHARD R Occupation: Educator, Author. Education: B.A., Yale University, 1954; M.A., Stanford University, 1959; Ph.D., Stanford University, 1962. Address: Department of Political Science, Stanford, California 94305.

FAIR, DOUGLAS M Occupation: Chiropractor. Education: D.C., B.A., M.A. Address: 120 North Scott, St. Francis, Kansas 67756.

FAIRHURST, CARL W Occupation: Scientist and Teacher. Education: M.S., Ph.D. Address: 2316 Overton Road, Augusta, Georgia 30909.

FALCONI, ALINA D Occupation: Personnel Officer. Education: B.S. Management. Address: 2715 South Kolin, Chicago, Illinois 60623.

FALES, DeCOURSEY JR Occupation: Professor of History, Emerson College. Education: A.B. 1941, M.A. 1947, Ph.D 1957, Harvard University. Address: 11 Hilliard Street, Cambridge, Massachuchetts 02138.

FALK, MOWRY W Occupation: General Agent, Insurance and Investments. Education: High School Graduate. Address: 7003 North Fox Point, Peoria, Illinois 61614.

FANCHER, EDWIN CRAWFORD Occupation: Psychoanalyst-Psychologist. Education: M.A. Address: 40 Fifth Avenue, New York, New York 10011.

FARABAUGH, MARTIN P Occupation: Associate Dean, Faculty of Professional Studies, Edinboro University. Education: M.Ed., University of Pittsburgh; Doctor of Philosophy, Catholic University. Address: R.D. 4, 108 Valley View Drive, Edinboro, Pennsylvania 16412.

FARAGHER, THOMAS JAMES Occupation: Chairman of the Board, Texas Commerce Bank. Education: B.B.A. University of Washington, 1963; M.B.A., Stanford University, 1975. Address: 13732 Hughes Lane, Dallas, Texas 75240.

FARAH, TAWFIC E Occupation: President, Middle East Research Group, Inc. Education: Ph.D. 1975. Address: 2611 North Fresno Street, Fresno, California 93703-1897.

FARBER, DANIEL A Occupation: Professor of Law, Law Center. Education: B.A., M.A., J.D. Address: 3144 5th Avenue, South, Minneapolis, Minnesota 55408.

FARHO, JAMES H JR Occupation: Mechanical Engineer. Education: B.S.M.E. Address: 701 Willow Street, Cranford, New Jersey 07016.

FARION, MARTA Occupation: Attorney. Education: B.A., M.A., J.D. Address: 6133 North Forest Glen, Chicago, Illinois 60646.

FARISON, JAMES B Occupation: Professor of Electrical Engineering, The University of Toledo, Ohio. Education: B.S.E.E., University of Toledo; M.S.E.E., Ph.D., Stanford University. Address: 2314 Secor Road, Toledo, Ohio 43606.

FARNSWORTH, SUSAN STEELE HIGGINS Occupation: Head, Farnsworth and Associates Communication Consulting Firm. Education: Bachelor of Journalism. Address: 9737 Southwest 135th Terrace, Miami, Florida 33176.

FARQUHAR, BETTY MURPHY Occupation: Artist, Poet. Education: Certificate Administration Assistant, German Business School, 1942; Secretarial Diploma, Nixon Clay College, 1950; Art Studies at Mexico American Cultural Exchange Institute and under Private Teachers. Address: Post Office Box 127, Marion, Texas 78124.

FARRELL, MARGARET C Occupation: Member of Religious Order; Registered Nurse. Education: B.A., B.S., M.S. Address: 1 Hickory Trace Drive, Justice, Illinois 60458.

FARRELL, MARY L Occupation: Teacher, Coordinator. Education: B.S., Mount Mercy College; M.A., University of Iowa. Address: 1511 Derwen Drive, Iowa City, Iowa 52240.

FARRELL, SAMUEL DENISON Occupation: Businessman. Education: B.A., M.A., M.Th. Address: 3333 Broadway, Apartment D32C, New York, New York 10031.

FARRELL, THOMAS GEORGE Occupation: Attorney. Education: A.B. Arts and Letters, Pennsylvania State University, 1954; J.D., Southwestern University School of Law, 1970. Address: 2329 West 231st, Torrance, California 90501.

FARRIS, JEROME Occupation: United States Circuit Judge. Education: B.S., M.S.W., J.D., LL.D. (Hon.). Address: 1908-34th Avenue, South, Seattle, Washington 98144.

FARRIS, MARTIN T Occupation: University Professor, College of Business, Arizona State University. Education: B.A. 1949, M.A. 1950, University of Montana; Ph.D., Ohio State University, 1957. Address: 6108 East Vernon, Scottsdale, Arizona 85257.

FEAVER, GEORGE ARTHUR Occupation: Professor of Political Science. Education: B.A. (Hons), University of British Columbia; Ph.D., University of London. Address: 4776 West 7th Avenue, Vancouver, B.C. Canada V6T 1C6.

FEDDERSON, YVONNE LIME Occupation: Co-Founder and President, Childhelp USA/International. Address: 6463 Independence Avenue, Woodland Hills, California 91367.

FEDDOES, SADIE CLOTHIL Occupation: Banker/Consultant. Education: Bachelor of Professional Studies. Address: 291 New York Avenue, Brooklyn, New York 11216.

FEDERHAR, DAVID BERNARD Occupation: School Psychologist. Education: B.A. 1972, M.A. 1975, Ph.D. 1983, University of Arizona. Address: 7580 East LaCienega, Tucson, Arizona 85715.

FEDERICO, PAT-ANTHONY Occupation: Research Psychologist. Education: B.A. cum laude, University of St. Thomas, 1965; M.S. 1967, Ph.D. 1969, Tulane University. Address: 4493 Pescadero Avenue, SAn Diego, California 92017.

FEHER, GEORGE Occupation: Physicist/Biophysicist, University of California. Education: Ph.D., University of California, 1954. Address: 2710 Bordeaux Avenue, LaJolla, California 92037.

FEHRMAN, KENNETH R Occupation: Interior Designer and Educator. Education: M.A. Textiles, B.A. Art/Design. Address: 4112 California Street, San

Francisco, California 94118.

FEINBERG, GARY H Occupation: Assistant Labor Relations Director, Montgomery Ward. Education: B.A., University of Pennsylvania; J.D., State University of New York School of Law. Address: 5671 Vantage Point Road, Columbia, Maryland 21044.

FEINBERG, WALTER Occupation: Professor of Education, University of Illinois. Education: A.B., M.A., Ph.D. Address: 1704 Henry, Champaign, Illinois 61821.

FEINDT, MARY CLARISSA Occupation: Licensed Land Surveyor and Land Title Abstracter. Education: A.B., Albion College; B.S., M.S., University of Michigan. Address: Post Office Box 18, Charlevoix, Michigan 49720.

FEINGOLD, RUSSELL D Occupation: State Senator; Attorney. Education: B.A. with Honors, University of Wisconsin-Madison; Oxford University (First Class Honors in Final Honors School of Leon Feingold) 1912-1980; Jurisprudence (Law); Juris Doctor with Honors, Harvard University Law School. Address: 3705 Lynn Street, Middleton, Wisconsin 53562.

FEINSTEIN, ALAN SHAWN Occupation: Author and Publisher. Education: B.S., M.S. Address: 41 Alhambra Circle, Cranston, Rhode Island 02905.

FEIST, MARIAN JEAN Occupation: Retired as Director of Nutrition at Good Samaritan Hospital; Currently R. D. at Large. Education: B.S. in Foods and Nutrition. Address: 2331 Deblin Drive, Cincinnati, Ohio 45239.

FEITLER-KARCHIN, BARBARA JOAN Occupation: Director, Career Planning and Placement. Education: B.A., Case Western Reserve University; M.S., Indiana University. Address: 3392 Fox Hill Road, Aurora, Illinois 60505.

FELDMAN, DAVID LEWIS Occupation: College Professor, Political Science, Moorhead State University. Education: Ph.D., University of Missouri, 1979; M.A., University of Missouri, 1975; B.S., Kent State University, 1973. Address: 811 10th Avenue, South, Moorhead, Minnesota 56560.

FELDMAN, GARY G Occupation: Hospital Administrator. Education: B.S. Business Administration, University of Virginia; M.A., Ph.D., University of North Carolina-Chapel Hill.

FELDMAN, HARRY A Occupation: Educator, Professor and Chairman, Upstate Medical Center. Education: M.D. Address: 704 Crawford Avenue, Syracuse, New York 13224.

FELDMAN, ROBIN Occupation: Assistant Manager. Education: B.A. with honors. Address: 330 Third Avenue, New York, New York 10010.

FELDMAN, WALTER Occupation: Artist and Professor. Education: B.F.A., M.F.A., M.A. Address: 107 Benevolent Street, Providence, Rhode Island 02906.

FELDMAR, GABRIEL G Occupation: Neuropsychologist, Professor, Editor, Administrator. Education: Ph.D. Psychology. Address: 37 Eden Lane, Levittown, New York 11756.

FELDSTEIN, RONALD F Occupation: Associate Professor of Slavic Linguistics, Indiana University. Education: M.A., Ph.D., Princeton University. Address: 603 Plymouth Road, Bloomington, Indiana 47401.

FELSEN, JUDITH EDNA Occupation: Psychologist, Psychotherapist and Consultant. Education: Ph.D., M.A., B.A. Address: 220-55 46 Avenue 10K, Bayside, New York 11361.

FELTHOUSE, TIMOTHY R Occupation: Research Chemist, Monsanto Company. Education: B.S., Ph.D. Address: 12425 Dunedin Lane, #l02, Saint Louis, Missouri 63146.

FELTON, JUDITH R Occupation: Psychoanalyst. Education: Ph.D. Address: 159 Valley Road, Princeton, New Jersey 08540.

FEMMINELLA, FRANCIS X Occupation: Professor of Sociology and Education. Education: A.B., A.M., M.S.S., Ph.D. Address: Grandview Terrace, Selkirk, New York 12158.

FENIMORE, GEORGE W Occupation: Senior Vice President and Secretary, Litton Industries, Incorporated. Education: B.S. Finance and Business Administration, Northwestern University; J.D., Harvard Law School.

FENSKE, VIRGINIA E Occupation: Retired Public Welfare Administrator. Education: A.B., University of Illinois, 1931; M.A., University of Chicago, 1941. Address: 920 Fenske Drive, Olympia, Washington 98506.

FENTON, JULIA ANN Occupation: Artist. Education: B.A., Millsaps College, 1959. Address: 397 Emory Drive, Northeast, Atlanta, Georgia 30307.

FEREBEE, CAROLYN J Occupation: Director of Community Schools Program, Greenville City Schools. Education: Bachelors, Masters Educational Specialists. Address: 1704 Battle Drive, Greenville, North Carolina 27834.

FERGUS, PATRICIA MARGUERITA Occupation: Retired College Professor and Writer. Education: B.S., M.A., Ph.D. Address: 1235 Yale Place #201, Minneapolis, Minnesota 55403.

FERGUSON, BOB L Occupation: Photographer. Education: Certified Professional Photographer. Address: Rural Route 1, Box 34, Freetown, Indiana 47235.

FERGUSON, JUANITA YVONNE Occupation: Assistant Director, Adult Education, West Virginia Department of Education. Education: B.S. Home Economics; M.A. Home Economics Education; M.S. Vocational, Technical Education. Address: #1 Timmy Court, Milton, West Virginia 25541.

FERGUSON, LARRY S Occupation: Artist. Education: B.F.A., University of Nebraska-Lincoln, 1977. Address: 1402 William, Omaha, Nebraska 68108.

FERGUSON, SUSAN L Occupation: Owner, Cinderella School of Professional Development. Address: 317 Court, North East, Salem, Oregon 97301.

FERNANDEZ, JUAN A Occupation: Executive Vice President, COO. Education: B.S.; M.B.A., Doctoral Student, University of Louisville. Address: 3917 Ashridge Drive, Louisville, Kentucky 40222.

FERRARI, MICHAEL R Occupation: University Administration and Professor of Management. Education: B.A., M.A., Doctor of Business. Address: 1746 West Rahn Road, Dayton, Ohio 45459.

FERRARIO, CARLOS MARIA Occupation: Chairman, Department of Cardiovascular Research, Cleveland Clinic Foundation. Education: M.D. Address: 12111 New Market Street, Chesterland, Ohio 44026.

FERRARIS, FRED Occupation: Writer. Address: 620 South 43rd Street, Boulder, Colorado 80303.

FERRARO, MARGUERITE M Occupation: Teacher. Education: B.S., M.S. Address: Mark Twain School, Yonkers, New York 10704.

FERRIER, RICHARD B Occupation: Associate Professor of Architecture. Education: B.Arch., Texas Technical University, 1968; M.A., University of Dallas, 1973. Address: University of Texas, Arlington, Texas.

FEST, THORREL B Occupation: Professor Emeritus, University of Colorado and Management Consultant. Education: B.A., Northern Iowa University; M.Ph., Ph.D., University of Wisconsin. Address: 1546 Sunset Boulevard, Boulder, Colorado

80302.

FETTERMAN, DAVID M Occupation: Senior Administrator and Anthropologist. Education: B.S. History 1976, B.A. Anthropology 1976, University of Connecticut, both Summa Cum Laude; M.A. Anthropology 1977, M.A. Education 1979, Ph.D. Anthropology 1981, Stanford University. Address: 3208 Alameda de las Pulgas, Menlo Park, California 94025.

FIEDLER, JEAN F Occupation: Writer. Education: B.A. Address: 69-23 Bell Boulevard, Bayside, New York 11364.

FIELD, JULIA ALLEN Occupation: Conceptual Planner, Futurist. Education: A.B. cum laude, Harvard University, 1960; Postgraduate Studies, Pius XII Art Institute, 1961; Master Degree Program, Harvard Graduate School of Design, 1965; Doctoral Program, Institute for Advanced Studies, Walden University, 1983. Address: 3551 Main Highway, Miami, Florida 33133.

FIELDER, BETTY ANN Occupation: Mental Health Administrator/Psychologist. Education: B.A. Psychology; M.A. Social Psychology. Address: Carolina Mill Lane, Carolina, Rhode Island 02812.

FIELDS, CLYDE DOUGLAS Occupation: President, Basic American Health Care Management. Education: B.S., B.A. 1963; M.B.A. 1968. Address: 3044 Golfview Drive, Greenswood, Indiana 46142.

FIELDS, PAUL R Occupation: Research Chemist, Argonne National Laboratory. Education: B.S. Address: 7308 North California Avenue, Chicago, Illinois 60645.

FIENE, RICHARD JOHN Occupation: Psychologist. Education: B.A., M.A., Ph.D. Address: 1800 Pineford Drive, Middletown, Pennsylvania 17057.

FIERER, JOSHUA A Occupation: Professor and Chairman, Department of Pathology, University of Illinois, College of Medicine. Education: B.A., M.D. Address: 565 North Minnesota Avenue, Morton, Illinois 61550.

FILIPPONE, ELLA F Occupation: Executive Administrator. Education: Ph.D. Address: 25 Holmesbrook Road, Basking Ridge, New Jersey 07920.

FILLER, SUSAN M Occupation: Musicologist. Education: B.A., University of Illinois, 1969; M.M., Northwestern University, 1970; Ph.D., Northwestern University, 1977. Address: 441 West Barry, Chicago, Illinois 60657.

FILLMORE, ALBERT JAMES Occupation: Associate Director, Detroit Community Music School. Education: B.M., M.M., M.A. Address: Post Office Box 781, Owosso, Michigan 48867.

FINCKE, GARY W Occupation: Writing Program Director. Education: Ph.D., Kent State University; M.A., Miami University; B.A., Thiel College. Address: 401 North Ninth Street, Selinsgrove, Pennsylvania 17870.

FINE, ALBERT S Occupation: Chief Dental Research Laboratory and Associate Professor Histology Cell Biology. Education: B.A., M.A., Ph.D. Address: 2928 West 5th Street, Brooklyn, New York 11224.

FINGER, MARTHA ADAMS Occupation: Professor of Art/Artist. Education: B.F.A., Master in Art Education. Address: 6852 Simca Drive, Jacksonville, Florida 32211.

FINGERHUT, BRUCE M Occupation: Book Publisher. Education: B.A. 1965; M.A. 1969. Address: 2118 Renfrew Court, South Bend, Indiana 46601.

FINIGAN, GLORIA A Occupation: Field Service Technician. Education: B.S., Eastern Illinois University; A.S., Lincoln Land Community College. Address: 2301 Cahokia Drive, Springfield, Illinois 62702.

FINK, MARTIN RONALD Occupation: Aerospace Engineer. Education: B.S. 1952, M.S. 1953, Massachusetts Institute of Technology; M.S. Address: 183 Woody Lane, Fairfield, Connecticut 06430.

FINKELSTEIN, RICHARD A Occupation: Microbiologist; Professor and Chairman, University of Missouri. Education: B.S., University of Oklahoma, Norman, Oklahoma, 1950; M.A., University of Texas, Austin, Texas, 1952; Ph.D., University of Texas, Austin, Texas, 1955. Address: 3207 Honeysuckle Drive, Columbia, Missouri 65201.

FINKELSTEIN, SHELDON SY Occupation: Director of Health Fitness, of a Local Health Club. Education: B.A. Psychology and Sociology 1977, B.A. Education 1978, M.A. Guidance and Counseling 1979, The University of Michigan. Address: 700 South Blackbird Roost #132, Flagstaff, Arizona 86001.

FINN, WILLIAM F Occupation: Obstetrician/Gynecologist. Education: B.A., Holy Cross College, 1936; M.D., Cornell University Medical College, 1940. Address: 3 Aspen Gate, Manhasset, New York 11030.

FINNEGAN, JAMES J Occupation: Poet-Editor-Businessman. Education: B.S.B.A., M.B.A., University of Missouri. Address: 740 Leland, St. Louis, Missouri 63130.

FINNEY, MARY CREWS Occupation: Civic Worker. Education: Student, Florida State University, University of South Carolina, Duke University. Address: 15 Blue Ridge Drive, Liberty, South Carolina 29657.

FINNEY, WILLIAM BERT II Occupation: Librarian, American College of Traditional Chinese Medicine. Education: B.A., M.A. Sociology. Address: 2247 Clement Street, San Francisco, California 94121.

FIORENTINO, CARMINE Occupation: Lawyer. Education: Hunter College, 1951; Columbia Broadcasting School, 1952; Blackstone School of Law, 1954; John Marshall Law School, 1957; Famous Writers School, 1962. Address: 2164 Medfield Trail, Northeast, Atlanta, Georgia 30345.

FIRESIDE, HARVEY F Occupation: Professor of Politics. Education: A.B. 1952, M.A. 1955, Harvard University; Ph.D., New School for Social Research, 1968. Address: 105 Valentine Place, Ithaca, New York.

FIRKUSNÝ, RUDOLF Occupation: Concert Pianist. Education: Conservatory of Music, University of Brno, Master Music Academy. Address: Staatsburg, New York 12580.

FISH, JEFFERSON M Occupation: Professor and Chairperson, Department of Psychology, St. John's University. Education: B.A., M.S., Ph.D. Address: 17 Polo Road, Great Neck, New York 11023.

FISHER, ADA MARKITA Occupation: Physician, Martin Marietta Energy Systems, Inc. Education: B.A. Biology, Secondary Education Teacher Certification, M.D., Family Residency Certification, M.P.H. Address: Post Office Box 3614, Durham, North Carolina 27702.

FISHER, CHARLES HAROLD Occupation: Research Professor and Consultant. Education: B.S., M.S., Ph.D. Address: 2553 South Clearing Road, Salem, Virginia 24153.

FISHER, JOHN COURTNEY Occupation: Consultant in Laser Medicine and Surgery. Education: B.Sc., M.Sc., D.Sc., Harvard University. Address: 417 Palmtree Drive, Bradenton, Florida 33507.

FISHER, KENNETH LEE Occupation: Artist, Sculptor-Painter. Education: Master of Fine Arts 1971, Bachelor of Fine Arts 1969, Bachelor of Science 1968, University of Oregon, Eugene, Oregon. Address: 1656

South East Clatsop, Portland, Oregon 97202.

FISHER, RHODA LEE Occupation: Child Clinical Psychologist. Education: M.A., Ph.D., University of Chicago; B.Mu.Ed., DePaul University. Address: 4855 Armstrong Road, Manlius, New York 13104.

FITZGERALD, DESMOND GERALD Education: A.B., Harvard University; M.A., Columbia University. Address: 94 Zaccheus Mead Land, Greenwich, Connecticut 06830.

FITZGERALD, JANET A SR Occupation: President and Professor of Philosophy. Education: Ph.D., M.A., B.A. Address: 1000 Hempstead Avenue, Rockville Centre, New York 11570.

FITZGERALD, LAURIE ANN Occupation: Organization Development Consultant. Education: B.S., M.Ed., Ph.D. (in progress). Address: 2215 Race, Denver, Colorado 80205.

FITZGERALD, LYNNE M L Occupation: Ph.D. Candidate. Education: B.A., University of Miami; M.S., Biscayne College. Address: 12300 Southwest 68 Avenue, Miami, Florida 33156.

FITZGERALD, S JANET ANN Occupation: President of Molloy College and Philology Professor. Education: Ph.D., M.A., B.A. Address: 1000 Hempstead Avenue, Rockville Centre, New York 11570.

FITZSIMONS, AGNES MARIE Occupation: President, Our Lady of Lourdes Regional Medical Center. Education: Masters Nursing Education. Address: Post Office Box 4027-C, Lafayette, Louisiana 70502.

FLACCUS, EDWARD Occupation: Professor of Biology. Education: B.S., Haverford College, 1942; M.S., University of New Hampshire, 1952; Ph.D., Duke University, 1959. Address: 110 Putnam Street, Bennington, Vermont 05201.

FLAHERTY, DOUGLAS ERNEST Occupation: Professor, Poet. Education: B.S., Merrimack University; M.A., Massachusetts University; M.F.A., Iowa University. Address: 3263 Shorewood Drive, Oshkosh, Wisconsin 54901.

FLAHERTY, ROSE IZZO Occupation: Educator-Reading Specialist. Education: B.S.Ed., M.S.Ed., Ed.D. Address: 10 Orchard Street, Glen Head, New York 11545.

FLAHERTY, THOMAS FRANCIS Occupation: Chairman, Education Department, Providence College. Education: B.A., M.A.T., Ph.D. Address: 12 Kimberly Ann Drive, Greenville, Rhode Island 02828.

FLAKE, JANICE L Occupation: Professor. Education: B.S., M.A., Ph.D. Address: 1065 Merritt, Tallahassee, Florida 32301.

FLANNIGAN, SANDRA F Occupation: English Teacher. Education: B.S., Taylor University; M.Ed., National College of Education. Address: 1342 South Finley, Lombard, Illinois 60148.

FLATT, DOWELL E Occupation: Chairman, Bible Department, Freed-Hardeman College. Education: M.A., M.A., M.Th., Th.D. Address: 211 Sand Road Circle, Henderson, Tennessee 38340.

FLATT, WILLIAM P Occupation: Dean and Coordinator, College of Agriculture. Education: B.S., University of Tennessee; Ph.D., Cornell University. Address: 110 Broomsedge Trail, Athens, Georgia 30605.

FLAX, ROBERT LEWIS Occupation: Psychotherapest/Educator. Education: B.A., M.A., Ph.D. Address: 29-49 137 Street, Flushing, New York 11354.

FLEISCHMANN, ERNEST MARTIN Occupation: Executive Director, Los Angeles Philharmonic. Education: Bachelor of Commerce; Bachelor of Music;

Postgraduate Study. Address: c/o Los Angeles Philharmonic, 135 North Grand Avenue, Los Angeles, California 90012.

FLEMING, MARTIN Occupation: Economist. Education: B.S., M.A., Ph.D. Address: 144 Butman Road, Lowell, Massachusetts 01852.

FLEMING, SHELDON JOHN Occupation: Attorney at Law. Education: B.S., California State University, 1980; J.D., Pepperdine University School of Law, 1983. Address: 14001 Howland Way, Tustin, California 92680.

FLETCHER, BRADY JONES Occupation: Career and Vocational Specialist. Education: B.A. Mathematics, M.A. Education, Specialist Guidance, Dr. Counselor Education. Address: 1 Waterway Court, Rockville, Maryland 20853.

FLETCHER, CHARLES THOMAS Occupation: Governor of Utah. Education: B.S. Address: 1700 North 1450 East, Provo, Utah 84604.

FLETCHER, JANE H Occupation: Director of Student Services. Education: M.Ed., B.A. Address: 904 Maikai Street, Haliimaile, Hawaii 96787.

FLETCHER, JANIE ROSE FOSTER Occupation: Texas A&M Extension. Education: B.S., M.S. Address: 2328 Glenwood, Denton, Texas 76201.

FLETCHER, JESSE C Occupation: University President, Hardin-Simmons University. Education: Ph.D., B.B.A., M.Div., Litt.D. Address: Post Office Box 3778, Abilene, Texas 79604.

FLETCHER, STANLEY M Occupation: Research Agricultural Economics; Assistant Professor, Georgia Experimental Station. Education: B.S., M.S., Oklahoma State University; Ph.D., North Carolina State University. Address: 107 McEthel Drive, Griffin, Georgia 30223.

FLICKINGER, BONNIE GORDON Occupation: Lecturer. Education: Buffalo Seminary, Member cum laude Society, 1950; Undergraduate Study, Vassar College, 1950-51. Address: c/o Rainbow Lectures, 31 Nottingham Terrace, Buffalo, New York 14216.

FLINN, ROBERTA J Occupation: Operator Manager to Wholesale Distributors. Address: 30213 South Candlelight Court, Canby, Oregon 97013.

FLORSHEIM, STEWART JAY Occupation: Director, Technical Communications. Education: M.A., San Francisco State University; B.A., Syracuse University. Address: 319 Lexington Street, San Francisco, California 94110.

FLOURNOY, DAYL J Occupation: Clinical Microbiologist. Education: A.B., B.S., M.A., Ph.D., M.T. (A.S.C.P.), S.M. (A.S.C.P.). Address: 10305 Fawn Canyon, Oklahoma City, Oklahoma 73104.

FLORIANI, LAWRENCE P Occupation: Orthopedic Surgeon. Education: B.S., M.D. Address: 49 Chimney Ridge Drive, Convent Station, New Jersey 07961.

FLOYD, HENRY BASCOM III Occupation: President, Floyd Engineering Company, Consulting Engineer and Land Surveyor. Education: B.S.C.E., The Citadel, 1949; M.S.I.M., Georgia Technical College, 1966. Address: 4017 Dobbs Drive, Huntsville, Alabama 35802.

FLY, ANDERSON BILLY Occupation: President and General Manager, Marine Metals, Inc. Education: B.S., Texas Technological College, 1951. Address: 136 Bayrock Circle, Post Office Box 30400, Amarillo, Texas 79120.

FLY, CLAUDE LEE Occupation: Professional Consultant/Agriculture. Education: B.S., M.S., Ph.D. Address: 415 South Howes Street, Fort Collins, Colorado 80521.

FOBES, JAMES L Occupation: Research Psychologist. Education: Ph.D. Psychology. Address: 667 Lighthouse Avenue, Suite 302, Pacific Grove, California 93950.

FOLLAIN-GRISELL, VERA S Occupation: Adminstrator. Education: Ph.D. Candidate. Address: 1205 Prospect Avenue, Takoma Park, Maryland 20912.

FOLLETT, RONALD F Occupation: National Program Leader, Agricultural Research Service. Education: B.S., Colorado State University, 1961; M.S., Colorado State University, 1963; Ph.D., Purdue University, 1966. Address: 1824 Busch Court, Fort Collins, Colorado 80525.

FOLTA, JEANNETTE RUTH Occupation: Professor, Chairperson Sociology Department, University of Vermont. Education: R.N., B.S., Boston University; Ph.D., University of Washington. Address: R.D. #2, Snake Mount Road, Weybridge, Vermont 05753.

FONTANA, JOSEPH B Occupation: Dentist. Education: D.D.S. Address: 1 Lakeview Drive, Peekskill, New York 10566.

FONTENOT, MARTIN M JR Occupation: Quality Control Manager. Education: B.S., M.S. Chemistry, Master of Engineering (Environmental). Address: 9024 Staring Court, Baton Rouge, Louisiana 70810.

FORAKER-THOMPSON, JANE Occupation: Professor of Criminal Justice, Boise State University. Education: Ph.D. Candidate Political Science, Stanford University, Palo Alto, California, 1970-74. Address: 3510 Forsythia Drive, Boise, Idaho 83703.

FORAN, MARGARET ELLEN Occupation: Assistant Superintendent, Bureau of Institutional Schools. Education: B.A. Social Work, M.A. Special Education, Doctoral Degree (in progress). Address: 25 Atlanta Street, Worcester, Massachusetts 01604.

FORAN, RAYMOND EDWARD Occupation: Electrical Engineer. Education: B.A. Physics, M.S. Electrical Engineering. Address: 5035 Stenton Avenue, Philadelphia, Pennsylvania 19144.

FORCHHEIMER, LUDWIG L Occupation: Ophthalmologist, Private Practice. Education: M.D., F.I.C.S. Address: 136-10 72nd Avenue, Flushing, New York 11367.

FORD, JOHNNY Occupation: Mayor. Education: Master of Business Administration. Address: 1 Lake Shore Drive, Tuskegee, Alabama 36083.

FORER, LOIS G Occupation: Judge, Court of Common Pleas, Pennsylvania. Education: A.B. honors, J.D., Northwestern University. Address: 2401 Pennsylvania Avenue, Philadelphia, Pennsylvania 19130.

FORGIONNE, GUISSEPPI A Occupation: University Professor, School of Business, California Polytechnic Institute. Education: B.S., M.A., M.B.A., Ph.D. Address: 1678 North Woodbend Drive, Claremont, California 91711.

FORKEL, CURT EMIL Occupation: Mechanical Engineer. Education: B.S.M.E., University of Texas; M.S.M.E., University of Idaho. Address: 2306 Koro Avenue, Idaho Falls, Idahoo 83401.

FORKNER, CLAUDE E Occupation: Physician, Educator, Foundation President. Education: A.B., M.A., M.D. Address: 130 Interlake Avenue, Deland, Florida 32724.

FORMAN, RUTH LOVE Occupation: Elementary School Teacher. Education: B.S., Alabama A&M University, Huntsville, Alabama. Address: 3012 Wenonah Circle, Birmingham, Alabama 35211.

FORNOFF, FRANK J Occupation: Senior Examiner, Educational Testing Service. Education: A.B., University of Illinois; M.Sc., Ph.D., Ohio State University. Address: 338 Franklin Avenue, Princeton, New Jersey 08540.

FORSBERG, CARL E Occupation: Professor of Music, University of Central Arkansas. Education: B.M., B.S., M.A., Ph.D. Address: 5 Salem Road, Conway, Arkansas 72032.

FORSHEY, CHESTER G Occupation: Pomologist, Researcher, Hudson Valley Laboratory. Education: B.Sc., Ph.D., Ohio State University. Address: 3 Circle Drive, Hyde Park, New York 12538.

FORSYTH, LOUISE BIRNIE Occupation: Educational and Public Relations Consultant. Education: B.S., M.A. Address: 75 Monroe Road, Quincy, Massachusetts 02169.

FORTH, CATHERINE MARY Occupation: Computer Graphics Scientist. Education: B.S. Biology, M.S. Biology, M.S. Computer Science. Address: 2493 Hilltop Road, Schenectady, New York 12309.

FORTIN, DENISE H Occupation: Assistant Director of Personnel, The Memorial Hospital. Education: A.S., B.S., M.B.A. (in progress). Address: 108 Holmes Road, North Attleboro, Massachusetts 02760.

FOSTER, CHERYL A Occupation: Social Caseworker. Education: A.B., Salve Regina College, 1966. Address: 18 Gunning Court, Middletown, Rhode Island 02840.

FOSTER, LINDA NEMEC Occupation: Poet; Teacher of Creative Writing. Education: B.A., Aquinas College; M.F.A., Goddard College. Address: 427 West Pere Marquette, Big Rapids, Michigan 49307.

FOSTER, MAE E Occupation: Logistician, Naval Oceanographic Office, Bayst Louis, N.S.T.L. Education: B.S. Business Administration. Address: Route 2 Box 521, Picayune, Mississippi 39466.

FOSTER, MARY HELEN Occupation: Community Leader, Patriotic Organizations and The Woman's Club of York. Education: Honor Graduate, Thompson Business College, 1931. Address: Wyndham Drive, York, Pennsylvania 17403.

FOTH, EDWARD C Occupation: Administrator, Master of Science of Taxation Program. Education: Ph.D., Michigan State University. Address: Route 1 Box 459, Genoa, Illinois 60135.

FOUAD, FETNAT M Occupation: Medical Research-Hypertension; Radiology. Education: M.D. Address: 3162 Rumson Road, Cleveland Heights, Ohio 44118.

FOULKES, FRED KLEE Occupation: Professor of Management Policy, Boston University. Education: A.B., Princeton University; M.B.A., D.B.A, Harvard University. Address: 50 Follen Street, Cambridge, Massachusetts 02138.

FOURCARD-BOULTRON, SHARON LYNNE Occupation: Assistant Head Nurse, Oncology Unit. Education: Bachelor of Science in Nursing, McNeese State University. Address: 1014 West Brompton Drive, Houston, Texas 70601.

FOWLER, BETTY JANMAE Occupation: Metabolic Technician. Education: B.A., Eastern Washington University, 1984. Address: North 7105 G Street, Spokane, Washington 99208.

FOWLER, CHARLES WINSOR Occupation: Research Biologist. Education: B.A., M.A., Ph.D. Address: 16300 164th Avenue, North East Woodinville, Washington 98072.

FOWLER, RONALD MONROE Occupation: School Administrator/Funeral Director. Education: B.S., M.Ed. Address: 3402 Pinewood Drive, Loris, South Carolina 29569.

FOX, DENAMAE DAWSON Occupation: College Director. Education: B.A., M.A., Ph.D. Address: 13850 East Marina, #207, Aurora, Colorado 80114.

FOX, LAURETTA EWING Occupation: Retired Associate Professor. Education: B.S., Westminster College, 1931; M.S. 1932, Ph.D. 1934, University of Illinois; Post-Doctoral Studies, Vanderbilt University School of Medicine. Address: 1410 Southwest 35th Place, Gainesville, Florida 32608.

FOX, ROBERT R Occupation: Writer/Arts Administration. Education: M.A. English. Address: Route 4, Pomeroy, Ohio 45769.

FOX, STEPHEN CARY Occupation: Internist, Medical Oncologist. Education: B.A., M.S., Boston University, 1974. Address: 915 Charleston Greene, Malvern, Pennsylvania 19355.

FOX, THOMAS G Occupation: Professor of Economics. Education: B.A., M.A., Ph.D. Economics. Address: 611 Old Farm Lane, State College, Pennsylvania 16803.

FOX-BAKER, JACK Occupation: Diplomate, American Board of Psychiatry and Neurology. Education: M.D. Address: 311 Camden Suite 211, San Antonio, Texas 78215.

FRANCE, KEVIN E Occupation: Buyer. Education: Associate of Business Management, Associate of Marketing and Finance. Address: 3617 Orchard Drive, Hammond, Indiana 46323.

FRANCE, VICTOR Occupation: Physicist; Professor, Physics Department, Brooklyn College. Education: B.S., M.A., Ph.D. Address: 50 Craigie Street, Somerville, Massachusetts 02143.

FRANCIS, DEBBIE LOU Occupation: Owner, R. H. Francis Company, Business for Nationwide Finance Adjusting and Investigations. Education: Sorbonne, Paris, 1975; A.A., San Antonio College, 1979; B.A. (in progress), University of Texas-San Antonio.

FRANCIS, RAYMOND LLEWELLYN III Occupation: Band Director. Education: B.A. Music Education. Address: Apartment G-1, Summer Army, Sumter, South Carolina 29150.

FRANCOEUR, ROBERT THOMAS Occupation: University Professor, Author/Lecturer. Education: Ph.D., University of Delaware; A.C.S., American College of Sexologist; M.S., University of Detroit; M.A., St. Vincent College, Latrobe, Pennsylvania. Address: 2 Circle Drive, Rockaway, New Jersey 07866.

FRANK, BILLY HULSEY Occupation: Attorney, Executive Director, Senior Citizens Legal Services. Education: B.S., LL.B., J.D., M.S. Address: 2039 Sunset Cliffs, San Diego, California 92107.

FRANK, EDWARD JOSEPH Occupation: Work Experience Coordinator, Associate Professor. Education: A.A.A. Nursing, B.S. Business Administration, Ed.M., M.S. Education, Ed.D. (A.B.D.). Address: 6619 Jewett Holmwood Road, Orchard Park, New York 14127.

FRANK, ELLEN RYAN Occupation: Operations Research/Management Consultant. Education: B.S. Psychology, M.A. Psychology, Ph.D. Applied Research. Address: 246 West 11th Street, New York, New York 10014.

FRANK, MARION HUSIK Occupation: Clinical/Consulting Psychology. Education: M.A., Columbia University; Ed.D., Temple University. Address: 402 West Mount Airy, Philadelphia, Pennsylvania 19119.

FRANK, STUART M Occupation: Director, Kendall Whaling Museum. Education: B.A., Wesleyan University, 1970; M.A.R., Yale University, 1972; M.A., Brown University, 1981; Ph.D. Candidate, Brown University. Address: Kendall Whaling Museum, Box 297, Sharon, Massachusetts 02067.

FRANK, WILLIAM A Occupation: Professor of Philosophy, Benedictine College. Education: B.A., M.A., Ph.D. Address: 1118 Laramie, Atchison, Kansas 66002.

FRANKLIN, PAULA ANNE Occupation: Psychologist, Researcher, Teacher, Writer. Education: B.Sc. History (honors), M.A. Psychology, Ph.D. Psychology. Address: 3946 Clover Hill Road, Baltimore, Maryland 21218.

FRANKLIN, ROSE MARIE T Occupation: Researcher. Education: Ph.D. Sociology. Address: 68 South Highland Avenue, Ossining, New York 10562.

FRASER, KAREN R Occupation: Thurston County Commissioner, Thurston County Courthouse. Education: B.A. Sociology 1966, M.P.A. 1969, University of Washington. Address: 6710 Sierra Drive Southeast, Lacey, Washington 98503.

FRAZE, DENNY T Occupation: Professor and Chairman of Art, Amarillo College. Education: B.F.A., University of Texas-Austin; M.F.A., University of Colorado. Address: 2219 South Hayden, Amarillo, Texas 79109.

FREAS, ANNIE BELLE H Education: Business Administration, Martin College. Address: 3003 Natchez Trace, Nashville, Tennessee 37215.

FREDERICKS, MARCEL Occupation: Professor Medical Sociology, Loyola University of Chicago. Education: School Certificate, Cambridge; Matriculation, London; B.S., M.A., Ph.D., Loyola University; Post-Doctoral Studies, Harvard University. Address: 7853 North Kilbourn, Skokie, Illinois 60076.

FREEDMAN, DAVID NOEL Occupation: Dirctor, Program on Studies in Religion, University of Michigan. Education: Student, College City of New York, 1935-38; A.B., University of California at Los Angeles, 1939; B.Th., Princeton Theological Seminary, 1944; Ph.D., Johns Hopkins University, 1948; Litt.D., University Pacific, 1973; Sc.D., Davis and Elkins College, 1974. Address: Post Office Box 7434, Ann Arbor, Michigan 48107.

FREEDMAN, ROSELYN L Occupation: University Professor of Speech Communication. Education: A.B. English, M.F.A. Theatre Arts, Ph.D. Rhetoric/Speech. Address: 1530 Quarrier Street East, Charleston, West Virginia 25311.

FREEDMAN, STUART C Occupation: Professor of Management, University of Lowell. Education: Ph.D. Organizational Behavior. Address: 1 Greenock Lane, Nashua, New Hampshire 03062.

FREEL, MARLIN J Occupation: Executive; Owner. Education: B.S., University of Southern California. Address: 1429 Avenida Colina, San Dimas, California 91773.

FREEMAN, LANNY ROSS Occupation: Geological Engineer. Education: B.S. and M.S. Geological Engineering, Ph.D. Geology, University of Texas. Address: 1502 Skyline, Portland, Texas 78374.

FREEMAN, MARY JAYNE Occupation: Coordinator, Project W.H.O.L.E. Education: M.R.E., M.Div., D.D. Address: 1715 Northwest 46th Street, Miami, Florida 33142.

FREEMAN, PAUL DOUGLAS Occupation: Music Director and Conductor. Education: Eastman School of Music, Study Board; Germany, Other Studies. Address: 996 Carolwood Drive, Victoria, British Columbia, Canada V8X 3V2.

FREEMAN, WILLIAM T Occupation: Writer. Address: 205 Orange Street, Waterbury, Connecticut 06704.

FREI, GUENTHER H Occupation: Professor,

Department of Mathematics, University of Laval. Education: M.S., Ph.D. Address: 2019 Dickson, Sillery, Quebec G1T 1C6.

FREILICHER, MELVYN S Occupation: Novelist, Magazine Editor, College Instructor. Education: B.A., Brandeis University; Doctoral Candidate, University of California-San Diego. Address: 4641 Park Boulevard, San Diego, California 92116.

FREY, MARSHA L Occupation: Associate Professor of History, Department of History, Kansas State University. Address: 1729 Denholm Drive, Manhattan, Kansas 66502.

FRICON, TERRI M Occupation: President, Chairman, The Fricon Entertainment Company, Incorporated. Education: B.A. Music, University of Miami. Address: 8825 Ashcroft Avenue, Los Angeles, California 90048.

FRIEDEN, LEX Occupation: Executive Director, National Council for the Handicapped. Education: B.S., M.A. Address: 504 West Taylor Run Parkway, Alexandria, Virginia 22314.

FRIEDHOFF, ARNOLD JEROME Occupation: Professor of Psychiatry; Director of Millhauser Laboratories. Education: New York University School of Medicine. Address: 550 First Avenue, New York, New York 10016.

FRIEDMAN, ALAN WARREN Occupation: Professor of English, Department of English, University of Texas-Austin. Education: Ph.D., University of Rochester. Address: 1908 Stamford Lane, Austin, Texas 78712.

FRIEDMAN, NORMAN Occupation: Professor of English and Private Practice of Psychotherapy. Education: A.B. 1948, A.M. 1949, Ph.D. 1952, Harvard University, M.S.W., Adelphi University, 1978. Address: 33-54 164 Street, Flushing, New York 11358.

FRIEDMAN, RICHARD N Occupation: Lawyer. Education: B.A., University of Miami, 1962; J.D., University of Miami School of Law, 1965; LL.M. Taxation, Georgetown University Law Center, 1967. Address: 100 North Biscayne Boulevard, #616, Miami, Florida 33132.

FRIEL, JOHN J Occupation: Research Scientist, Homer Research Laboratories, Bethlehem Steel Corporation. Education: B.A., Ph.D. Geology, University of Pennsylvania; M.A., Temple University. Address: 3 Oakhurst Drive, Center Valley, Pennsylvania 18034.

FRITSCH, ALBERT JOSEPH Occupation: Public Interest Researcher. Education: B.S., M.S., Ph.D. Chemistry, S.T.L. Theology. Address: 863 Bennett Avenue, Lexington, Kentucky 40508.

FROMME, ARNOLD Occupation: College Professor of Music, Jersey City State College. Education: Ph.D., New York University; M.M., B.M., Manchester School of Music. Address: 4 Janet Lane, Berkeley Heights, New Jersey 07922.

FRONING, GLENN W Occupation: Professor, Food Science and Technology, University of Nebraska. Education: B.S., University of Missouri, 1953; M.S., University of Missouri, 1957; Ph.D., University of Minnesota, 1961. Address: 7420 Whitestone Drive, Lincoln, Nebraska 68583-0919.

FRY, CHARLES L JR Occupation: Associate Professor of Psychology. Education: B.A., Harverford College, Ph.D., University of Rochester. Address: Route 1, Box 51, Scottsville, Virginia 24590.

FRYE, ALVA L Occupation: Senior Vice President of Technology, Aladdin Industries. Education: B.S. Chemical Engineering, Iowa State College, 1943. Address: 6210 Bridlewood Lane, Brentwood, Tennessee 37027.

FRYE, GARY W Occupation: Psychologist. Education: B.A., M.A. Psychology. Address: 9 Edward Court, Newark, Delaware 29702.

FUENTES, MARTHA AYERS Occupation: Author/Playwright. Education: B.A. English. Address: 102 Third Street, Belluair Beach, Florida 33535.

FUHRER, LARRY Occupation: Chairman, President, The Centre Capital Group, Incorporated, Private Investment Banking Group. Education: M.A., Northern Illinois University; A.B. Psychology and Religion, Taylor University, Upland, Indiana, 1961. Address: 521 Iroquois, Naperville, Illinois 60540.

FUHRER, WILHELMINE E Occupation: Licensed Public Accountant. Education: Private Secretarial Studies. Address: 6452 Cr. 35, Auburn, Indiana 46706.

FUIS, FRANK JR Occupation: Consulting Engineer, Artist, Author. Education: B.S. Engineering. Address: 52 Pine Road, Norris, Tennessee 37828.

FUKUSHIMA, TAKASHI Occupation: Professor of Economics, Department of Economics, State University of New York-Albany. Education: Ph.D. Economics. Address: 60 Alden Court, Delmar, New York 12054.

FULCHER, CLAIRE E Occupation: President, Team Associates; Psychologist, Private Practice. Education: B.A., M.A., Ed.D. Address: 85 Kennedy Drive, Bridgeport, Connecticut 06606.

FUMENTO, ROCCO L Occupation: Professor of English and Film, English Department, University of Illinois-Urbana. Education: B.S., M.F.A. Address: 307 South Garfield Avenue, Champaign, Illinois 61821.

FUNG, BING-MAN Occupation: Professor of Chemistry, University of Oklahoma. Education: Ph.D., 1967. Address: 1528 Homeland, Norman, Oklahoma 73069.

FUNK, GARY LLOYD Occupation: Senior Control Systems Engineer, Principal Engineer, Phillips Petroleum. Education: B.S., Rose-Hulman Institute of Technology; M.S., Purdue University; Ph.D., University of Pittsburgh. Address: 600 South 6th, Fairfax, Oklahoma 74637.

FUNN, COURTNEY HARRIS Occupation: Director of Library/Media Services. Education: B.A., M.A., M.L.S. Address: 213 Harry Truman Drive, #12, Largo, Maryland 20772.

FURMAN, EVELYN EDITH LIVINGSTON Occupation: Retail Store, Museum, Rentals and Mining. Education: Milton College; University of Colorado. Address: 815 Harrison Avenue, Leadville, Colorado 80461.

FURNAS, DAVID W Occupation: Plastic Surgeon. Education: A.B. 1952, M.S. 1955, M.S. Pharmacy 1957, University of California-Berkeley. Address: 2501 Blue Water Drive, Corona del Mar, California 92625.

FURNESS, EDNA L Occupation: Free-Lance Writer, Translator, Professor Emeritus. Education: B.A., B.E., M.A., Ph.D. Address: 725 South Alton, Denver, Colorado 80231.

FURST, LILIAN RENÉE Occupation: University Professor of Literature. Education: Ph.D., Cambridge, England; B.A. honors, Class 1, Manchester. Address: 7654 Royal Lane, Dallas, Texas 75230.

FYE, PAUL M Occupation: President/Oceanographer, Woods Hole Oceanographic Institution. Education: B.A., Albright College, 1935; Ph.D., Columbia University, 1939; 6 Honorary Degrees. Address: P.O. Box 309, Woods Hole, Massachusetts 02543.

FYE, RODNEY WAYNE Occupation: Real Estate Executive. Education: Graduate, Chillicothe Business

College, 1948; Bachelor of Science, Brigham Young University, 1959; Master of Science, San Francisco State University, 1964; Secondary Teaching Certificate, University of Utah, 1962. Address: Post Office Box 15308, San Francisco, California 94115.

G

GABBARD, BESSIE FLANNERY Occupation: Chairperson, Board of Governors of the Phi Delta Kappa Educational Foundation. Education: B.S., B.E., M.Ed. Address: 26953 North Lewisburg Road, North Lewisburg, Ohio 43060.

GABLE, EDWARD BRENNAN JR Occupation: Director, Carriers, Drawback and Bonds Law Division, U.S. Customs Service. Education: B.S., Villanova University; J.D., Georgetown University. Address: 10428 Kardwright Court, Gaithersburg, Maryland 20789.

GABLEHOUSE, CHARLES JOHN Occupation: Aviation Editor, Public Relations. Education: Fordham University; College of William and Mary; Hoffstra College. Address: 82 Paulison Avenue, Passaic, New Jersey 07055.

GABRIELE, GUY F Occupation: Marketing Consultant. Education: M.B.A., Rensselaer Polytechnic Institute. Address: 812 Vincente Way, Santa Barbara, California 93105.

GABRIEL, BILLIE LUCILLE BURKLE Occupation: President/Owner, Computer Industry; Consultant, Computer Industry. Education: B.S., Memphis State University; Real Estate Sales License, Lumbleau Real Estate School; M.B.A. Studies. Address: 2888 Bayshore Drive, Newport Beach, California 92663.

GABRIEL, RONALD L Occupation: Management. Education: B.S., M.B.A., Ph.D. Address: Post Office Box 34844, West Bethesda, Maryland 20817.

GAER, ERIC W Occupation: Vice President, Advertising Agency. Education: B.A., California State University-Northridge, 1970. Address: 21040 Avenue San Luis, Woodland Hills, California 91364.

GAGNON, LEONARD C (SANDY) Occupation: Associate Professor of Animal Science, Animal/Range Sciences Department, Montana State University. Education: B.S., M.S. Address: 3190 Stuckey Road, Bozeman, Montana 59715.

GAINES, EDYTHE J Occupation: Commissioner. Education: B.A., M.A., C.A.S., Ed.D., LL.D. Address: 275 Kenyon Street, Hartford, Connecticut 06105.

GAINES, SYLVIA TAYLOR Occupation: Executive Director, State University of New York at Old Westbury. Education: Ph.D., M.S., B.A., P.P.N. Address: 46 Third Avenue, Westbury, New York 11590.

GAJEWSKI, FERDINAND JOHN Occupation: Pianist/Musicologist. Education: S.B., The Juilliard School; A.M., Ph.D., Harvard University. Address: 30 Westbrook Road, Westfield, New Jersey 07090.

GALAT, KAREN R Occupation: Attorney/ Supporter of Rights of Hearing Impaired. Education: B.A. cum laude, State University of New York at Albany; J.D. cum laude, Suffolk University Law School. Address: 5 Bacon Street, Winchester, Massachusetts 01890.

GALBRAITH, LILYAN KING Occupation: Professor, Home Economics Education (Retired). Education: B.S., M.S., West Virginia University; Ed.D., Pennsylvania State University. Address: 47 Water Street, Smithfield, Pennsylvania 15478.

GALE, HOYT RODNEY Occupation: Scientific Research, Writing and Publication. Education: A.B., Harvard University, 1926; Ph.D. Geology and Paleontology, Stanford University, 1929; M.A. Economics, University of California at Los Angeles, 1936. Address: 823 St. Clair Street, Costa Mesa, California 92626.

GALL, SALLY M Occupation: Author/Editor. Education: B.A., Radcliffe College; M.A., Ph.D., New York University. Address: 29 Bayard Lane, Suffern, New York 10901.

GALLAGHER, ANNA HELEN Occupation: Consultant in Nursing Education/Administration. Education: B.S., M.S., Ed.D. Address: 952 Agate Street, San Diego, California 92109.

GALLAGHER, JOAN S Occupation: Immunologist, University of Cincinnati Medical Center. Education: B.S., M.S., Ph.D. Address: 3340 Ferry Road, Bellbrook, Ohio 45305.

GALLAGHER, JOHN J Occupation: Consultant, Systems Ecology. Education: B.A., Ph.D. Address: 952 Agate Street, San Diego, California 92109.

GALLEGO, JOSE MIGUEL Occupation: Chemist. Education: B.S., 1977. Address: 250 Quintard Avenue, Apartment 96, Chula Vista, California 92011-4924.

GALLINGTON, ROGER W Occupation: Consulting Engineer/Scientist. Education: B.S. 1960, M.S. 1961, Ph.D. 1969, University of Illinois. Address: 23913 6th Avenue South, Seattle, Washington 98188.

GALLYEN, CHARLES A II Occupation: Iredell County Fire Marshal. Education: A.A., Mitchell College; B.T., Appalacian State University. Address: 107 Kimball Street, Statesville, North Carolina 28677.

GALVIN, G TIMOTHY Occupation: Real Estate Sales Manager. Education: B.A., M.P.A., University of Southern California. Address: 24 Wildwheat, Irvine, California 92714.

GAMAL, IRWIN "IRV" BERT Occupation: Internal Consultant. Education: A.A., B.A., M.A. Address: 28075 Klamath Court, Laguna Niguel, California 92677.

GANAS, PERRY S Occupation: Professor Physics, California State University. Education: B.Sc., University of Queensland, 1961; Ph.D., University of Sydney, 1968. Address: 11790 Radio Drive, Los Angeles, California 90064.

GANDEVIA, VINAY D Occupation: Executive Director. Education: B.A. (Hons.), D.A.S.S., C.A.G.S., D.S.Sc. Address: 12 Harborview Drive, Rye, New Hampshire 03870.

GANS, BRUCE MICHAEL Occupation: Writer, College Professor. Education: B.A. English; M.F.A. Fiction Writing. Address: 1123 Columbia, Chicago, Illinois 60626.

GANSER, CARL J Occupation: Education, College of Business and Economics, University of Wisconsin. Education: Ph.D., M.B.A., B.Ed. Address: 212 Park Street, Fort Atkinson, Wisconsin 53538.

GANT, MARGI C Occupation: Budget and Management Analyst. Education: M.S. Personnel and Guidance; M.S. Education; B.A. History. Address: 1401 Patricia Drive #503, San Antonio, Texas 78213.

GANTZ, ANN CUSHING Occupation: Artist/ Educator. Education: B.F.A., Newcomb College; Tulane University. Address: 4654 Edmondson, Dallas, Texas 75209.

GAPOSHKIN, PETER JOHN ARTHUR Occupation: Computer Programmer/Head Office Services Committee, Experience Unlimited. Education: B.Sc. Mathematics, Massachusetts Institute of Technology, 1961; Ph.D. Physics, University of California at Berkeley, 1971. Address: 1442A Walnut 371, Berkeley, California 94709.

GARABEDIAN, EDNA MAE Occupation: Chairman, Professor of Voice and Opera, University of Connecticut; Professional Concert and Opera Singer. Address: 3338 Lowe Avenue, Fresno, California 93702.

GARCIA, GREGORY M Occupation: School Psychologist, Educational Consultant. Education: B.A. Philosophy and Theology; M.A., Post Graduated in Clinical Psychology. Address: 1293 Sherwood Drive, Vineland, New Jersey 08360.

GARCIA, HENRY JR Occupation: Partner, Island Mercantile; Chairman of the Board, The El Paso Graphics Group, Inc.; Chairman of the Board, Omarco, Inc.; Editor, *The Luminario*. Address: 1607 Opossum Circle, El Paso, Texas 79927.

GARCIA, JOSE JOEL Occupation: Assistant Professor of Health Policy and Law, University of California-Berkeley. Education: B.A. Political Science (with high honors), University of California at Berkeley, 1969. Address: 3826 Lyon Avenue, Oakland, California 94601.

GARCIA, KAY WELLING Occupation: Director, Office of Continuing Education for the Health Professional, Montana State University. Education: B.S., Montana State University, 1968; M.T. (A.S.C.P.), 1969. Address: 105 Valley Drive, Bozeman, Montana 59715.

GARCÍA-CASTRO, JOSÉMIGUEL Occupation: Director Medical Genetics; Associate Professor of Pediatrics, Medical Genetics, School of Medicine University of Puerto Rico. Education: Bachelor of Science, Master of Science. Address: GPO Apartado 1764, San Juan, Puerto Rico 00936.

GARCIA OLIVERO, CARMEN SYLVIA Occupation: Consultant, Drug Addiction Prevention and Treatment; Executive Director, Advocacy Program of Mental Health Services; President/Director, Institute of Psycho-Legal Services and Research, Inc. Education: Bachelor of Science, Master in Social Work, Doctorate in Social Work. Address: San Julian Street 421, Urbannizacion Sagrado Corazon, Rio Piedras, Puerto Rico 00926.

GARCIA-PALMIERI, MARIO R Occupation: Medical Doctor. Education: B.S. magna cum laude, University of Puerto Rico, 1947; M.D., University of Maryland, 1951. Address: Box DG, Caparra Heights Station, San Juan, Puerto Rico 00922.

GARDNER, LARRY A Occupation: Chairman of Department of Religion and Philosophy, Capital University. Education: B.A., M.Div. Th.M., Th.D. Address: 911 Pleasant Ridge Avenue, Columbus, Ohio 43209.

GARDNER, NORD A Occupation: Business Development Director. Education: B.A., M.S., M.P.A. (course work). Address: 2995 Bonnie Lane, Pleasant Hill, California 94523.

GARDNER, ROBIN PIERCE Occupation: Nuclear Engineering Educator, North Carolina State University. Education: B.Ch.E. 1956, M.S. Chemical Engineering 1958. Address: 805 Ivanhoe Drive, Raleigh, North Carolina 27609.

GARDNER, WALTER H Occupation: Professor Emeritus, Washington State University; Past President, Soil Science Society of America; President, American Association for the Advancement of Science. Education: B.S., M.S., Ph.D. Address: Northeast 1505 Upper Drive, Pullman, Washington 99163.

GARMHAUSEN, WINONA M Occupation: Writer/Consultant Arts Administration. Education: B.S.Ed., M.F.A., Ph.D. Address: Route 6, Box 90K, Santa Fe, New Mexico 87505.

GARNER, CHARLES WILLIAM Occupation: University Administrator and Professor, Rutgers University. Education: B.S., M.Ed., D.Ed. Address: 12 James Avenue, Kendall Park, New Jersey 08824.

GARNETT, W LESLIE Occupation: University Professor of English (Retired). Education: B.A., M.A., Ph.D. Address: 1912 Graslon Drive, Iowa City, Iowa 52240.

GARRETT, CAROL A Occupation: Speech-Language Pathologist. Education: A.A., B.S., M.Ed. Address: 723 Custer Drive, Lynchburg, Virginia 24502.

GARRETT, NORMAN LAWRENCE Occupation: Professor/Psychologist. Education: A.A, A.B., M.A., Doctoral Degree. Address: 804 North Citrus Avenue, Los Angeles, California 90038.

GARRETT, VIRGINIA BONNER Occupation: Attorney-at-Law. Education: Associate Degree, South Georgia College; J.D., Woodrow Wilson College of Law, 1972; LL.M., Woodrow Wilson College of Law. Address: 3230 McKown Road, Post Office Box 337, Douglasville, Georgia 30133.

GARRISON, JUANITA Occupation: Co-ordinator of Southeastern Cancer Study Group, University of Kentucky Medical Center. Education: Diploma, School of Nursing. Address: 1773 Blue Licks Road, Lexington, Kentucky 40504.

GARRISON, WILLIAM LLOYD Occupation: Executive Director. Education: B.A., M.S.W., M.S. Management. Address: 29375 Cedar Road, Mayfield Heights, Ohio 44124.

GARSIDE, COLLEEN Occupation: Night Manager/Program Director at Central State University. Education: B.S., Weber State College; M.Ed., Central State University. Address: 1132 North Ross, Oklahoma City, Oklahoma 73107.

GARVIN, JAMES LEO Occupation: Curator, New Hampshire Historical Society. Education: A.Eng 1963, B.A. 1967, M.A. 1969, Ph.D. 1983. Address: R.F.D. #4, Box 228A, Concord, New Hampshire 03301.

GARZIA, RICARDO F Occupation: Senior Engineering Consultant. Education: B.S.E.E., M.S.E.E. Address: 509 Vosello Avenue, Akron, Ohio 44313.

GASSNER, JULIUS STEPHEN Occupation: Professor, University of Albuquerque. Education: A.B. 1937, M.A. 1940. Address: Post Office Drawer G, Corrales, New Mexico 87048.

GAST, AARON EDWARD Occupation: President, United Presbyterian Foundation. Education: B.A., M.Div., Ph.D. Address: 2 Haddon Place, Fort Washington, Pennsylvania 19034.

GATES, ANN MARIE DONOHOE Occupation: Epidemiological Researcher in Nutrition. Education: B.S., M.S.P.H., R.D. Address: 124 Pinecrest Avenue, West Columbia, South Carolina 29169.

GAUNCE, AVANELLE GRAVLEY Occupation: Teacher of the Profoundly Handicapped. Education: B.A. 1976, Master's Degree 1981, Education Specialist 1983. Address: Post Office Box 195, Pauline, South Carolina 29374.

GAUNCE, JAMES RICHARD Occupation: Elementary Principal. Education: B.A., Asbury College; M.A., Western Carolina; Ed.S. Address: Post Office Box 195, Pauline, South Carolina 29374.

GAUS, PAULA J Occupation: Professor of Education. Education: B.A., M.A., Ph.D. Address: 122 Seth Low Mountain Road, Ridgefield, Connecticut 06877.

GAVLOCK, EUGENE HARLAN Occupation: Drinking Water Equipment Executive. Address: 132 Hampshire Road, Waterloo, Iowa 50701.

GAY, MARILYN FANELLI MARTIN Occupation: Television Talk Show Hostess, Producer, Writer. Education: Attended University of California-Berkeley, University of Oregon. Address: 2400 East Pleasant Valley Road #98, Oxnard, California 93030.

GAY, ORA D Occupation: President, Downtown

Council of Minneapolis. Education: B.A., University of Illinois; C.P.A. Address: 6450 York Avenue South, No. 218, Edina, Minnesota 55435.

GAYLIN, SHELDON Occupation: Physician/Psychiatrist; Professor, Cornell University. Education: M.D., Western Reserve of Case Western Reserve University; Ph.D., University of Chicago. Address: 192 Fox Meadow Road, Scarsdale, New York 10583.

GEARY, ALICE J Occupation: Rehabilitation Counselor Supervisor. Education: M.Ed., B.A. Address: 3278 January, St. Louis, Missouri 63139.

GEARY, BARBARA ANN Occupation: Concert Pianist. Education: B.A. French, M.M. Piano, Indiana University. Address: 2545 South Birmingham Place, Tulsa, Oklahoma 74114.

GEER, JAMES FOOSHE Occupation: Certified Public Accountant. Education: B.B.A., Georgia Southern College, 1981. Address: 875 Franklin Road, Apartment #16-1631, Marietta, Georgia 30067.

GEHRING, DENISE HILARIE Occupation: Assistant Manager of Naturalist Services, Toledo Area Metroparks. Education: B.A. Biology. Address: 5360 Dubois Streeet, Toledo, Ohio 43615.

GEHRING, EDWIN FRANCIS Occupation: Attorney at Law, Beekeeper. Education: B.A., J.D. Address: 5360 Dubois Street, Toledo, Ohio 43615.

GEHRY, FRANK O Occupation: Architect. Education: B.Arch., University of Southern California, 1954. Address: 1002 22nd Street, Santa Monica, California 90403.

GEIGER, LOREN DENNIS Occupation: Band Director/Music Teacher, Orchard Park Central Schools. Education: B.M. 1968, M.M. 1970. Address: 15 Park Boulevard, Lancaster, New York 14086.

GEILING, JAMES WILLIAM Occupation: Manager of Engineering, Pennsylvania Power and Light Company. Education: B.S. Mechanical Engineering, Bucknell University; Executive Program in Business Administration, Columbia University. Address: 935 Donald Drive, Emmaus, Pennsylvania 18049.

GELLERT, MAX E Occupation: Chairman/Chief Executive Officer, ELDEC Corporation. Education: B.S.E.E., Massachusetts Institute of Technology, 1948; M.S.E.E., University of Pennsylvania, 1951. Address: 2301 Fairview Avenue East, #PH1, Seattle, Washington 98102.

GELMAN, MARTIN L Occupation: Physician. Education: M.D. Address: 164 State Street, Framingham, Massachusetts 01701.

GELTRICH-LUDGATE, BRIGITTA GISELA Occupation: Faculty Trainer/Researcher/Writer. Education: Dissertation on Germanic Folklore/Linguistics. Address: 24665 Cabrillo Street, Carmel, California 93923.

GEN, MARTIN Occupation: Owner/Executive Director. Education: B.A., Pace University; Syracuse University. Address: 2 Summit Road, Cranford, New Jersey 07016.

GENN, MORDECAI Occupation: Registered Representative, Merrill Lynch. Education: B.A. English and American Literature 1968, B.R.E. History and Biblical Literature 1968, Ordination Rabbinic Jurisprudence 1971, M.S. Educational Administration 1971, Yeshiva University; M.A. Modern Hebrew Literature 1975, Ph.D. Near Eastern Language and Literature 1978, Brandeis University. Address: Post Office Box 1341, Daytona, Florida 32015.

GENTRY, WANDA MARKHAM Occupation: Administrative Assistant to President and Chairman of Board, Tennessee Natural Gas Lines, Inc., and Nashville Gas Company. Address: 104 Trout Valley, Hendersonville, Tennessee 37075.

GEORGE, JOHN ANTHONY Occupation: Adviser/Consultant. Education: B.S., M.B.A. Address: 107 Cherry Valley Road, Pittsburgh, Pennsylvania 15221.

GERBER, DAISY Occupation: Director/Producer. Education: B.A., M.F.A., University of California-Los Angeles. Address: 9617 Oak Pass Road, Beverly Hills, California 90210.

GERBER, H C Occupation: Banker, Realtor, Rancher. Address: 14 West Oak Avenue, Colorado Springs, Colorado 80906.

GERRINGER-BUSENBARK, ELIZABETH JACQUELINE Occupation: Systems Analyst/Consultant. Education: M.Div., Ph.D. (with honors). Address: 533 Sutter, Suite 411, San Francisco, California 94102.

GERSHATOR, DAVID Occupation: Writer/Poet. Education: B.A., Community College of New York; M.A., Columbia University; Ph.D., New York University, 1967. Address: 171 Dean Street, Brooklyn, New York 11217.

GERSHOWITZ, SONYA Z Occupation: Administrative Director CHAI Management. Education: R.N., M.A. Nursing Administration. Address: 2307 Hidden Glen Drive, Owings Mills, Maryland 21117.

GESELL, MERLE FRANCES Occupation: Attorney (Retired). Education: B.A., Newcomb College; L.L.B., Tulane University. Address: 5335 St. Charles Avenue, New Orleans, Louisiana 70115.

GETTLE, JUDY A Occupation: Director of Women's Services/Clinical Mental Health Counselor. Education: B.A., M.Ed. Address: 158 South Linwood Avenue, Pittsburgh, Pennsylvania 15205.

GETTLES, JANICE I Occupation: Realtor. Education: High School Graduate; Ohio School of Real Estate. Address: 751 North Pennsylvania Avenue, Wellston, Ohio 45692.

GETZ, ARTHUR R Occupation: Certified Public Accountant. Education: B.S. Business Administration. Address: 316 Durant Way, Mill Valley, California 94941.

GETZ, WILL R Occupation: Animal Scientist. Education: B.S., M.S., Ph.D. Address: 302 North St. Joseph, Morrilton, Arizona 72110.

GEWALD, ROBERT M Occupation: President, Robert M. Gewald Management Inc. Education: B.A., M.A., Hon. Ph.D. Address: 58 West 58th Street, New York, New York 10019.

GHEITH, MOHAMED A Occupation: Professor/Director of Special Extension Programs for Mid East, Boston University. Education: B.Sc. (Hons), Cairo University; M.S., Ph.D., University of Minnesota. Address: 271 Forest Street, Arlington Heights, Massachusetts 02174.

GHERING, M VIRGIL Occupation: Faculty Member/Librarian, St. Thomas Institute; Member of Religious Order. Education: A.B. Centennial, Michigan University; M.S., Marquette University; Ph.D. Candidate, Fordham University; Ph.D., St. Thomas Institute. Address: 2335 Grandview Avenue, Cincinnati, Ohio 45206.

GHETTI, BERNARDINO Occupation: Professor of Pathology (Neuropathology) and Psychiatry. Education: M.D. Address: 1124 Frederick S. Drive, Indianapolis, Indiana 46260.

GHOSH, SUBIR Occupation: Educator, Researcher, Department of Statistics, University of California-Riverside. Education: Ph.D. Address: 257

West Big Springs Road, Apartment-A, Riverside, California 92507.

GIAMBERTONE, PAUL Occupation: Sculptor. Education: Beaux Arts Institute of Design; College of the City of New York. Address: 400 East 20th Street #5F, New York, New York 10009.

GIANNINI, A JAMES Occupation: Psychiatrist in Private Practice. Education: B.S., M.D., Post-Doctoral Certificate. Address: Post Office Box 2169, Youngstown, Ohio 44504.

GIANNINI, DAVID Occupation: Poet/Freelance Teacher. Address: Wendling Farm, Williamstown, Massachusetts 01267.

GIANNINI, MATTHEW C Occupation: Attorney at Law. Education: B.S. Biology, J.D. Address: 7377 Elmland Drive, Poland, Ohio 44514.

GIBBS, JOHN G Occupation: Acquisitions Editor, John Knox Press. Education: A.B., M.Div., Th.M., Ph.D. Address: 4111 Tahoe Court, Stone Mountain, Georgia 30083.

GIBSON, G RUTH Occupation: College/ University Professor, Georgia State University. Education: B.S. Secondary Education, Ed.S. Counseling, M.E.D. Counseling, Ph.D. Educational Leadership. Address: 1185 Winterberry Court, Lawrenceville, Georgia 30245.

GIBSON, GARY E Occupation: Scientific Research. Education: B.S., Ph.D. Address: 60 Fernwood Road, Larchmont, New York 10538.

GIBSON, GEORGE HORNER Occupation: Vice President and Dean of College, St. Lawrence University. Education: B.A., M.A., Ph.D. Address: 16 Hillside Road, Canton, New York 13617.

GIBSON, JOHN MILTON Occupation: Architect. Education: B.S.Arch., University of Cincinnati, 1954. Address: Rural Route 2, Box 381, Shelbyville, Indiana 46176.

GIBSON, ORPHA RAY Occupation: Professor of Education, School of the Ozarks. Education: Educational Doctorate. Address: Route 1 Box 100, Blue Eye, Missouri 65611.

GIBSON, P J (PATRICIA JOANN) Occupation: Playwright/Poet, Instructor (Writing). Education: B.A., Keuka College; M.F.A., Brandeis University. Address: 400 West 43rd Street #14L, New York, New York 10036.

GIBSON, WELDON BAILEY Occupation: Senior Director, SRI International. Education: Graduate, Washington State University, 1938; M.B.A. 1940, Ph.D. 1950, Stanford University. Address: 593 Gerona Road, Stanford, California 94305.

GIDDINGS, C BLAND Occupation: Cellist and Nuclear Physician. Education: B.S. Chemistry, Brigham Young University, 1938; M.D., University of Cincinnati, 1947; Ph.D. Biochemistry, 1943. Address: 1820 East Jensen Street, Mesa, Arizona 85203.

GIDDINGS, J CALVIN Occupation: Professor, University of Utah. Education: B.S., Brigham Young University, 1952; Ph.D., University of Utah, 1954. Address: 3978 Emigration Canyon, Salt Lake City, Utah 84108.

GIER, DONALD A Occupation: Soil Scientist. Education: Ph.D. Soil Morphology, Genesis and Classification. Address: 507 North 11st, Marysville, Illinois 66508.

GIES, FREDERICK JOHN Occupation: Professor and Dean, College of Education and Behavioral Sciences, Northwestern State University. Education: B.A., DePaul University, 1960; M.Ed. 1964, Ed.D. 1970, Missouri University. Address: 815 Woodyard, Natchitoches, Louisiana 71457.

GIESTING, WALTER E Occupation: President, Unitech International. Education: B.S.C., Xavier University, 1940; G.R.B., University of Texas, 1971. Address: 10115 Parkwood Drive, Cupertino, California 95014.

GIESY, JOHN PAUL Occupation: Professor of Aquatic Toxicology, Michigan State University. Education: B.S. 1970, M.S. 1971, Ph.D. 1974. Address: 2355 Bravender, Williamston, Michigan 48895.

GIFFORD, ERNEST M JR Occupation: Professor of Botany, University of California. Education: B.A., Ph.D. Address: 1023 Ovejas Avenue, Davis, California 95616.

GIFFORD, RAY W JR Occupation: Physician, the Cleveland Clinic Foundation. Education: M.D. Address: 3479 Glen Allen Drive, Cleveland Heights, Ohio 44121.

GILBERT, BERNADETTE MARIE Occupation: Teacher Facilitator, Chicago Effective School. Education: B.A., M.S.Ed. Address: 8336 South LaSalle Street, Chicago, Illinois 60620.

GILBERT, JOHN ANDREW Occupation: Associate Professor of Engineering Mechanics, Department of Civil Engineering, University of Wisconsin-Milwaukee. Education: B.S. 1971, M.S. 1972, Polytechnic Institute of Brooklyn; Ph.D., Illinois Institute of Technology, 1975. Address: 4770 North 40th Street, Milwaukee, Wisconsin 53209.

GILBERT, LYNN TENDLER Occupation: Management Consultant. Education: B.A. Mathematics. Address: 11 Sigma Place, Riverdale, New York 10471.

GILBERT, VIRGINIA L Occupation: Assistant Professor of English at Alabama A & M University, Writer, Photographer. Education: B.A., Iowa Wesleyan College; M.F.A., University of Iowa. Address: 1500 Sparkman Drive #37G, Huntsville, Alabama 35805.

GILBO, PATRICK F Occupation: Public Affairs, American Red Cross. Education: B.A., M.S.Ed. Address: 2759 Greenway Boulevard, Falls Church, Virginia 22042.

GILES, BARBARA A Occupation: Writer, Psychologist. Education: Ph.D., Master of Education, Master of Communications. Address: Post Office Box 155, Black Mountain, North Carolina 28711.

GILL, ROBERT MONROE Occupation: Associate Professor of Political Science, Radford University. Education: B.A., Washington and Lee University; M.A., Ph.D., Duke University. Address: 1228 Preston Street, Radford, Virginia 24141.

GILLAN, MARIA MAZZIOTTI Occupation: Cultural Affairs Coordinator, Poetry Center Director. Education: B.A., Seton Hall; M.A., New York University; Ph.D. Candidate, Drew University. Address: 40 Post Avenue, Hawthorne, New Jersey 07506.

GILLESPIE, JOANNA BOWEN Occupation: Independent Scholar, Affiliated with Center for Research on Women at Stanford University. Education: B.A., B.Mus., M.Mus., Ph.D. Address: 163 Beaumont Avenue, San Francisco, California 94118.

GILLIAM, PAULETTE MARIE Occupation: Owner and President, ReelPro. Education: B.S., M.A. Address: 301 West T Street, Apartment F-20, Tumwater, Washington 98501.

GILLIES, PATRICIA A Occupation: Senior Public Health Biologist. Education: A.B., M.S. Address: 7060 East Butler, Fresno, California.

GILL-THOMPSON, NORMA N Occupation: Certified Enterostomal Therapist, Worldwide Ostomy Center, Inc. Education: Student at R. B. Turnbull, Jr., M.D. School of Enterostomal Therapy, The Cleveland

Clinic Educational Foundation in 1958; Birmingham General Hospital in 1970; Dale Carnegie Course in 1974; Spanish Courses at Berlitz School of Language in 1979, Lakeland College in 1980, and at Greensburg Vocational School in 1982; Leadership Course, The Cleveland Clinic Foundation; Certified, International Association for Enterostomal Therapy, 1981. Address: Akron, Ohio.

GILMAN, BENJAMIN A Occupation: Member of Congress, United States of America. Education: B.S., Wharton School of Business and Finance, University of Pennsylvania, 1946; LL.B., New York Law School, 1950. Address: Post Office Box 358, Middletown, New York 10940.

GILMAN, DAVID A Occupation: Professor and Educational Consultant, Indiana State University. Education: B.S., M.A., Ph.D. Address: 500 Garden Dale Road, Terre Haute, Indiana 47803.

GILMAN, RICHARD CARLETON Occupation: College President, Occidental College. Education: B.A., Dartmouth College; Ph.D., Boston University. Address: 1852 Campus Road, Los Angeles, California 90041.

GILROY, PAULA JEAN Occupation: Elementary Counselor, Pleasant View School. Education: B.S. Education; M.S. Counseling. Address: 613 West Maple Street, Red Lion, Pennsylvania 17356.

GIMMESTAD, MICHAEL JON Occupation: Assistant Dean, College of Education, University of Northern Colorado. Education: B.A., St. Olaf College; M.S., Indiana University; Ph.D., University of Minnesota. Address: 5220 27th Street, Greeley, Colorado 80634.

GINN, JOHN CHARLES Occupation: Newspaper Publisher, Communications Company. Education: B.Jour., University of Missouri, 1959; M.B.A., Harvard University, 1972. Address: Route 14 Box 57, Anderson, South Carolina 29621.

GINTAUTAS, JONAS Occupation: Physician/ Researcher. Education: M.D., Ph.D. Address: Post Office Box 9011, El Paso, Texas 79982.

GIOMI, THELMA S Occupation: Clinical Psychologist. Education: B.A., M.A., Ph.D. Address: 713 Manzano Northeast, Albuquerque, New Mexico 87110.

GIRDNER, LINDA K Occupation: Professor of Family Studies, University of Illinois. Education: Ph.D., American University. Address: 808 Kerr, Apartment 206, Urbana, Illinois 61801.

GIRION, BARBARA MICHELLE Occupation: Author of Books for Young People. Education: B.A., Montclair State College. Address: 25 Wildwood Drive, Short Hills, New Jersey 07078.

GIRSH, FAYE JOAN Occupation: Clinical and Forensic Psychologist. Education: B.A., Temple University; M.A., Boston University; Ed.D., Harvard University. Address: 2600 Torrey Pines Road, A36, La Jolla, California 92037.

GITTELSON, ABRAHAM J Occupation: Educational Administrator. Education: B.S.S., B.R.E., M.A. Address: 970 Northeast 172 Street, North Miami Beach, Florida 33162.

GIVAN, GUY VAN Occupation: Ceramic Engineer, QC and RD. Education: B.S. 1969, M.S. 1970. Address: 2239 Concord, Wheelersburg, Ohio 45694.

GIVEN, BARBARA KNIGHT Occupation: Associate Professor, George Mason University. Education: A.A., B.S., M.Ed., Ph.D. Address: 3113 Shadeland Drive, Falls Church, Virginia 22044.

GIVENS, DOUGLAS RANDALL Occupation: Professor of Anthropology/Chairman of the Department of Behaviorial Science, St. Louis Community College. Education: B.A., M.A., Ph.D. 1984. Address: 2342 Emert Avenue, Granite City, Illinois 62040.

GLADUE, BRIAN ANTHONY Occupation: Psychobiologist/Sexologist/Biopolitics. Education: Ph.D. Address: 630-B, Main Street, Port Jefferson, New York 11777.

GLASER, PATRICIA L Occupation: Lawyer. Education: B.A., LL.B. (J.D.). Address: 1711 Manzanita Park Avenue, Malibu, California 90265.

GLASER, R BONNIE Occupation: Psychologist. Education: B.A., M.A., Ph.D. Address: 1140 Grizzly Peak Boulevard, Berkeley, California 94708.

GLASS, ALABAMA ("BAMA") Occupation: Owner/Manager, Bama's Drive Up Liquors. Education: B.S.C.E. Address: 12357 West 67th Avenue, Arvada, Colorado 80004.

GLASSER, JULIAN Occupation: President, Chemical and Metallurgical Research, Inc. Education: B.S. Chemistry; M.S. Chemistry; Ph.D. Physical Chemistry. Address: 3400 Glendon Drive, Chattanooga, Tennessee 37411.

GLAZE, DIANA G Occupation: School Principal. Education: B.S., M.A., Ed.Sp., E.A.D. Address: The Landing, S222, Greenville, South Carolina 29615.

GLAZER, BARBARA L Occupation: Psychotherapist, Teacher, Consultant. Education: B.A., M.S. Address: 6310 Eastmont Court, Carmichael, California 95608.

GLEASON, WILLIAM C Occupation: Engineering Consultant. Education: B.S.C.E. Address: 7498 River Road, Baldwinsville, New York 13027.

GLEIMER, ANITA Occupation: Director of Sales and Marketing. Education: B.A., Florida Atlantic University. Address: Post Office Box 14854, North Palm Beach, Florida 33408.

GLESNE, RONALD L Occupation: President (Manufacturing Agent), Glesne Sales, Inc. Education: B.Sc., University of Iowa, 1957. Address: 1470 Cherry Place, Mound, Minnesota 55364.

GLICK, JACOB Occupation: Educator, Violist, and Viola d'Amore Player. Education: High School Graduate. Address: Bennington College, Bennington, Vermont 05201.

GLICK, MILTON DON Occupation: Dean of Arts and Science, University of Missouri-Columbia. Education: A.B., Ph.D. Address: 1001 Hulen, Columbia, Missouri 65203.

GLIEBERMAN, HERBERT A Occupation: Lawyer, Author, Broadcaster. Education: Doctor of Jurisprudence. Address: 180 East Pearson Street, Chicago, Illinois 60611.

GLOCK, MARVIN D Occupation: Professor Emeritus, Cornell University. Education: B.A., M.S., Ph.D. Address: 101 Homestead Terrace, Ithaca, New York 14850.

GLOVER, BETTY S Occupation: Musician/ Professor, College-Conservatory of Music, University of Cincinnati. Education: B.M., M.M. Address: 8791 Cottonwood Drive, Cincinnati, Ohio 45231.

GLUCK, LOUISE ELISABETH Occupation: Author, Teacher. Address: Creamery Road, Plainfield, Vermont 05667.

GMEINDEL, THOMAS JAMES Occupation: Attorney, Parliamentary Consultant. Education: B.S., J.D. Address: 881 Laurel Avenue, St. Paul, Minnesota 55104.

GODT, HENRY CHARLES JR Occupation: Technology Appraisal Manager. Education: B.S. 1950, M.S. 1951, Ph.D. 1984, University of Michigan.

Address: 12410 Ballas Meadows Drive, Des Peres, Missouri 63131.

GODWIN, PAUL MILTON Occupation: Chairman, Department of Academic Studies, School of Music, Belmont College. Education: B.A., Arkansas Technical University, 1964; M.A. 1969, Ph.D. 1972, Ohio State University. Address: 15459 Old Hickory Boulevard, Nashville, Tennessee 37211.

GOETHERT, BERNHARD HERMANN Occupation: Dean Emeritus, Professor of Aerospace Engineering, University of Tennessee Space Institute. Education: Master of Science in Mechanical Engineering, Master of Science in Aeronautics, Doctor of Philosophy in Aeronautics. Address: Manchester, Tennessee 37355.

GOLANY, GIDEON S Occupation: Professor of Urban and Regional Planning, Department of Architecture, Pennsylvania State University. Education: B.A. 1956, M.A. 1962, Ph.D. 1966, Hebrew University; M.S., Technion, College of Architecture and Town Planning, 1965; Dip.Compreh.Pl., Institute of Social Studies, 1965. Address: 292 Douglas Drive, State College, Pennsylvania 16801.

GOLD, IVAN Occupation: Writer/Teacher. Education: B.A., Columbia University; B.A. Honors, University of London. Address: 96 Bay State Road, Boston, Massachusetts 02215.

GOLD, PHIL Occupation: Professor of Medicine, McGill University; Professor of Physiology, McGill University; Senior Investigator, Montreal General Hospital Research Institute; Director, McGill University Medical Clinic of The Montreal General Hospital; Physician-in-Chief, The Montreal General Hospital. Education: B.Sc. Physiology (honors) McGill University, 1957; M.Sc., McGill University, 1961; M.D. 1961, C.M. 1961, McGill University; Ph.D. Physiology, McGill University, 1965. Address: 5705 Parkhaven, Montreal, Quebec, Canada H4W 1X6.

GOLD, RAYMOND Occupation: Physicist, Westinghouse Hanford. Education: B.S., M.S., Ph.D. Address: 1982 Greenbrook Boulevard, Richland, Washington 99352.

GOLDBERG, BARBARA JACOBY Occupation: Co-Coordinator of the Returning Students Program, University of Maryland. Education: B.S., University of Pittsburgh; M.A., University of Pittsburgh. Address: 12809 Deep Spring Drive, Potomac, Maryland 20854.

GOLDBERG, BARRY Occupation: Public Relations. Education: B.A., Community College of New York, 1969. Address: 139 Massachusetts Avenue, Congers, New York 10920.

GOLDBERG, HARVEY Occupation: Vice President and Chief Financial Officer. Education: B.S. Accounting, Brooklyn College. Address: 19798 Greenbriar Drive, Tarzana, California 91356.

GOLDBERG, LORRAINE H Occupation: Clinical Psychologist/Psychoanalyst. Education: Ph.D. Address: 4170 North Marine Drive, Chicago, Illinois 60613.

GOLDBLATT, BARRY L Occupation: Marketing Executive. Education: B.S. 1967, M.B.A. 1968, University of Southern California. Address: 42 Phelps Avenue, New Brunswick, New Jersey 08901.

GOLDEN, CHARLES J Occupation: Professor of Medical Psychology. Address: 856 Parkwood Lane, Omaha, Nebraska 68132.

GOLDEN, LINDA LORRAINE Occupation: Professor of Marketing, University of Texas. Education: B.S.B.A., M.A., Ph.D. Business, University of Florida. Address: 5712 Fairlane Drive, Austin, Texas 78731.

GOLDEN, MARILYN SCHEER Occupation:

Program Management Engineer. Education: B.A. Address: 1111 Bruckner Circle, Mountain View, California 94040.

GOLDFARB, I JAY Occupation: Certified Public Accountant. Education: B.A. Address: 16004 Sabana West, Encino, California 91436.

GOLDMAN, HARVEY S Occupation: Rabbi. Education: A.B., M.A., D.M. Address: 271 Tallowood, Westerville, Ohio 43081.

GOLDSMITH, BARBARA Occupation: Author/Social Historial. Education: B.A., D.Lit., D.H.L. Address: c/o Morton L. Danklow, 598 Madison Avenue, New York, New York 10022.

GOLDSTEIN, J JEFFY Occupation: Chemical Sales to Dry Cleaners. Address: 4604 Kemper Street, Rockville, Maryland 20853.

GOLDSTEIN, J RICHARD Occupation: New Jersey State Commissioner of Health. Education: B.A., M.D., M.Arch. Address: 141 Nathan Drive, North Brunswick, New Jersey 08902.

GOLDSTEIN, RICHARD JAY Occupation: Mechanical Engineer; Educator, Department of Mechanical Engineering, University of Minnesota. Education: B.S., Cornell University, 1948; M.S. 1951, Ph.D. 1959, University of Minnesota. Address: 520 Janalyn Circle, Golden Valley, Minnesota 55416.

GOLLAND, JEFFREY H Occupation: Psychoanalyst and Professor of Education, Baruch College. Education: A.B., Brandeis University, 1961; A.M. 1962, Ph.D. 1966, New York University. Address: 145 Fourth Avenue, New York, New York 10003.

GOLLOB, HARRY F Occupation: Professor of Psychology, Department of Psychology, University of Denver. Education: B.A., University of Denver, 1960; M.S. 1962, Ph.D. 1965, Yale University. Address: 2558 East Cresthill Avenue, Littleton, Colorado 80121.

GOMES, WAYNE REGINALD Occupation: Education/University Administrator, University of Illinois. Education: B.S., M.S., Ph.D. Address: 2402 Provine Circle, Urbana, Illinois 61801.

GÓMEZ, NÉLIDA Occupation: Professor, Consultant. Education: M.B.A. Address: 312 32nd Street, Villa Neravez, Rio Piedras, Puerto Rico 00927.

GOMMI, JULIUS V Occupation: Process Engineering Specialist, Pulp and Paper Industry, Weyerhaeuser Company. Education: Bachelor of Chemical Engineering, P.I.N.Y., 1961; Master of Mechanical Engineering, R.P.I., 1969. Address: 25804 214 Avenue Southeast, Maple Valley, Washington 98038.

GOMOLL, ALLEN W Occupation: Cardiovascular Pharmacologist; Research Fellow, Bristol-Myers Pharmaceutical Research and Development Division. Education: B.S., College of Pharmacy, University of Illinois, 1955; M.S. 1958, Ph.D. 1961, College of Medicine, University of Illinois. Address: 6001 O'Hara Drive, Evansville, Indiana 47711.

GONTANG, AUSTIN J Occupation: Consultant in Health and Sport Psychology. Education: M.A.; M.S., Ph.D. Candidate. Address: 2903 29th Street, San Diego, California 92104.

GONZÁLEZ, CRISTINA Occupation: Assistant Professor of Spanish, Purdue University. Education: B.A.; A.M.; M.A., University of Oveido, 1973; M.A., Indiana University, 1977; Ph.D., Indiana University, 1981. Address: 3332 Peppermill Drive, West Lafayette, Indiana 47906.

GONZALEZ, JOSÉ GAMALIEL Occupation: Artist/Arts Administrator. Education: B.F.A., M.F.A. Candidate. Address: 567 West 18th Street, Chicago, Illinois 60616.

GONZALEZ, RAFAEL C Occupation: Professor, University of Tennessee. Education: B.S.E.E., M.E., Ph.D. Address: 11642 South Monticello Drive, Knoxville, Tennessee 37922.

GOOCH, BRAD D Occupation: Writer/Teacher. Education: B.A. 1973, M.A. 1977, Columbia University Address: 222 West 23 Street, #410, New York, New York 10011.

GOOD, THOMAS L Occupation: Professor, Department of Curriculum and Instruction, University of Missouri; Research Associate, Center for Research in Social Behavior, University of Missouri-Columbia. Education: A.B., University of Illinois, 1965; C.I.C. Traveling Scholar, University of Michigan, 1966; M.S. 1967, Ph.D. 1968, Indiana University. Address: 112 Parkhill, Columbia, Missouri 65201.

GOODALE, TONI KRISSEL Occupation: Development Consultant, TKG Associates. Education: A.B. cum laude, Smith College, 1963; Student, University of Geneva, 1962-63; Postgraduate Studies, Hunter College, 1964-65. Address: 3 West 51st Street, New York, New York 10019.

GOODGLASS, HAROLD Occupation: Research Psychologist. Education: B.A. 1939, M.A. 1948, Ph.D. 1951. Address: 131 Sewall Avenue, Brookline, Massachusetts 02146.

GOODHEER, WIL C Occupation: Professor at Abilene Christian University and European Missions Consultant. Education: M.A., B.A., Candidate for Doctor of Misciology. Address: Route 1, Box 364, Abilene, Texas 79601.

GOODMAN, HERBERT I Occupation: President, Gulf Oil Trading Company. Education: B.S., University of Pittsburgh; M.B.A., A.M., Harvard University. Address: 5710 Tecumseh Circle, Houston, Texas 77057.

GOODMAN, LESTER Occupation: Consultant. Education: B.S., M.S., Ph.D., P.E. Address: 4853 Cordell Avenue, Bethesda, Maryland 20814.

GOODMAN, SEYMOUR E Occupation: Professor of Management Information System, Management and Policy, University of Arizona. Education: B.S., M.S., Columbia University; Ph.D., California Institute of Technology. Address: MIS/BPA, University of Arizona, Tucson, Arizona 85721.

GOODMAN, YETTA M Occupation: Professor of Education, College of Education, University of Arizona. Education: B.A. 1952, M.A. 1956. Address: 5649 East 10th Street, Tucson, Arizona 85713.

GOODRICH, BILLY G Occupation: District Controller. Education: Associate Accounting. Address: 3863 Windyre Drive, Memphis, Tennessee 38115.

GOODWIN, DONALD W Occupation: Professor and Chairman of Psychiatry, Kansas University Medical Center. Education: M.D., 1964. Address: 6130 Morningside Drive, Kansas City, Missouri 64113.

GOODYEAR, NELSON Occupation: President, California Christian University (Inactive); Real Estate Investor; Biographical Writer on Goodyear Family. Education: B.A. Languages, Columbia University, M.A. Secondary Education, Ph.D. Public Administration. Address: 15111 Bushard Sp. 23, Westminster, California.

GORDON, CYRUS H Occupation: Director, Center for Ebla Research, New York University. Education: A.B., M.A., Ph.D. Address: 130 Dean Road, Brookline, Massachusetts 02146.

GORDON, GRISELDA Occupation: Assistant to the Vice President for Academic Affairs, Director of Special Programs, Western Michigan University. Education: B.S., M.A. Address: 42818 North 30th Street, PawPaw, Michigan 49079.

GORDON, JEAN T Occupation: Director of Planning and Research, Motlow State Community College. Education: M.A., B.S. Sociology. Address: Tropez, Arrington, Tennessee 37388.

GORDON, MARILYN Occupation: Director/Founder, The Northeast Bronx Poets and Writers Forum, Parkchester Library; Author, *The Flaming Spirit, A Treasury of Poetry and Thought*; Editor/Publisher, Contributor, *The Northeast Bronx Poets and Writers Forum Anthology*, Volume I. Education: B.A., New York University. Address: 2153 Westchester Avenue, Bronx, New York 19462.

GORDON, NEIL R Occupation: Treasury Services Manager, Centronics Data Computer Corporation. Education: B.S., Pennsylvania State University. Address: 16 Belknap Drive, Andover, Massachusetts 01810.

GORDON, SHELLEY A Education: B.S., Texas Tech University.

GORNEY, SONDRA K Occupation: Public Relations Executive. Education: B.A. Address: 270 West End Avenue, New York, New York 10023.

GORSUCH, RICHARD L Occupation: Director of Research, Professor of Psychology, Fuller Theological Seminary, Graduate School of Psychology. Education: A.B., M.A., Ph.D., M.Div. Address: 3367 Ellington Villa Drive, Altadena, California 91001.

GOTH, JOHN WILLIAM Occupation: Metals Company Executive. Education: B.S. Metallurgy, South Dakota School of Mines; M. Engineering Metallurgy, McGill University; Advanced Management Program, Harvard University. Address: 41 Sawmill Lane, Greenwich, Connecticut 06877.

GOTH, MAJA JULIA Occupation: Professor of German, Wellesley College. Education: Staatsexamen; Ph.D. Address: Fiske House, Central Street, Wellesley, Massachusetts 02181.

GOTHSCHECK, BEATRICE Occupation: General Directress. Education: M.A. Theology. Address: 12, Frontenac E., St.-Bruno, Quebec Canada H3V 1B4.

GOTT, JIMMIE C Occupation: Park Manager. Education: A.A., B.A. Address: 230 Central Street Saugus, Massachusetts 01906.

GOTTFRIED, IRA S Occupation: President, Gottfried Consultants, Inc. Education: M.B.A., University of Southern California; B.B.A., City College of New York. Address: 12118 La Casa Lane, Los Angeles, California 90049.

GOTTLIEB, DAVID GEORGE Occupation: Foundation Director. Education: B.A., J.D. Address: 232-S.W. 28th Avenue, Delray Beach, Florida 33445.

GOULANDRIS, GEORGE C Occupation: University Director of Management Information Systems. Education: Ph.D., M.B.A., M.Ch.E. Address: 16 Ravine Road, Greak Neck, New York 11023.

GOULD, HELEN GRACE Occupation: Real Estate Broker/Co-Owner, Louis H. Gould Realty. Education: B.A., University of Texas. Address: 2404 Martin, Wichita Falls, Texas 76308.

GOULD, JANICE SANDRA CALDWELL Occupation: Stock Broker. Education: B.A. Address: 1307 East Detroit, Indianola, Iowa 50125.

GOUNARD, BEVERLEY ELAINE Occupation: Psychologist in Private Practice. Education: B.A. 1964, M.A. 1968, Ph.D. 1971. Address: 38 Idlewood Drive, Tonawanda, New York 14150.

GOVINDJEE Occupation: Professor of Biophysics and Plant Biology. Education: B.Sc. 1952, M.Sc. 1954, University of Allahahad; Ph.D., University of Illinois, 1960. Address: 2401 South Boudreau, Urbana, Illinois

61801.

GOYAL, SATISH CHANDRA Occupation: Professor of Civil Engineering, Tri-State University. Education: B.Sc., Agra; C.E., Roorkee; M.S., University of California-Berkeley. Address: 42451 Ravina Court, Northville, Michigan 48167.

GRABURN, NELSON HAYES HENRY Occupation: Professor and Chairman of Department of Anthropology, University of California. Education: B.A.; M.A. (Cantab); M.A., McGill University; Ph.D., University of Chicago. Address: 12 Wilson Circle, Berkeley, California 94708.

GRADDICK, CHARLES H Occupation: Judge/Lawyer. Education: B.S. Business Management Administration, Indiana University Northwest; J.D., Valparaiso University. Address: 910 North Vermillion, Gary, Indiana.

GRAEBE, ANNETTE MULVANY Occupation: Director, University Information Center, Southern Illinois University-Edwardsville. Education: B.A., M.A. Address: 208 Yorktown Drive, Collinsville, Illinois 62234.

GRAEBNER, LINDA S Occupation: Director of Marketing, Crown Advanced Films. Education: M.B.A., Stanford University; B.S., Purdue University. Address: 16 Humphrey Place, Oakland, California 94610.

GRAFTON, ROBERT B Occupation: Computer Scientist. Education: Sc.B. Engineering; Ph.D. Applied Mathematics, Brown University. Address: 5131 Portsmouth Road, Fairfax, Virginia 22032.

GRAHAM, CHARLES JOHN Occupation: President, Hamline University. Education: A.B., M.A., Ph.D. Address: 830 Simpson Street, St. Paul, Minnesota 55104.

GRAHAM, FLORINE R Occupation: Director of College Relations, New River Community College. Education: B.S., M.S., Radford University; Ed.D., Virginia Polytechnic Institute and State University. Address: Post Office Box 884, Radford, Virginia 24141.

GRAHAM, FRANCIS GLENN Occupation: Astronomer. Education: B.A. 1975, M.S. 1981, University of Pittsburgh. Address: 417 Franklin Street, East Pittsburgh, Pennsylvania 15112.

GRAHAM, JOSEPH M Occupation: Thoracic, Cardiovascular Surgeon. Education: B.S. Zoology; M.D. Address: 1365 Crest Drive, Joplin, Missouri 64801.

GRAHAM, LOLA A Occupation: Poet and Photographer. Education: Teacher's Certificate. Address: 225-93 Mt. Hermon Road, Scotts Valley, California 95066.

GRANT, CLAUDE D Occupation: Arts Administrator and Publisher. Education: B.A., Hunter College; M.A. Program, Long Island University/Mercy College. Address: 1783 Bussing Avenue, Bronx, New York 10466.

GRANTHAM, JOSEPH M JR Occupation: Chairman of the Board and President, Independent Financial Investments; Chairman of the Board and President, Carolina Hotels Inc. Education: B.S. Business Management and Real Estate. Address: Magnolia Road, Pinehurst, North Carolina 28374.

GRASSELLI, JEANNETTE G Occupation: B.S. 1950, D.Sc. (Honorary) 1978, Ohio University; M.S., Case Western Reserve University, 1958. Address: 150 Greentree Road, Chagrin Falls, Ohio 44022.

GRASSER, JEFF A Occupation: Dental Student. Education: B.S. Address: 2147 Exeter Place, Cordova, Tennessee 38018.

GRAVELLE, WILLIAM DAVID Occupation: Research Biologist. Education: M.S. Agronomy, Virginia Polytechnic Institute and State University; B.S. Plant Science, University of Delaware. Address: 2228-D Renault Drive, St. Louis, Missouri 63146.

GRAVES, WILLIAM LESTER JR Occupation: Educator/Symphony Conductor. Education: B.S.Ed., M.M.Ed., Ed.D. Address: 1421 College Street, Columbus, Mississippi 39701.

GRAY, ELIZABETH DODSON Occupation: Feminist Theologian and Writer. Education: B.A., B.Divinity. Address: Four Linden Square, Wellesley, Massachusetts 02181-4709.

GRAY, GEORGE W Occupation: Deputy Fire Chief. Education: A.A., B.A. Address: 3518 Rubin Drive, Oakland, California 94602.

GRAY, INA TURNER Occupation: Executive Director, Pi Gamma Mu, International Honor Society in Social Science. Education: B.S., Central Methodist College; M.A., Scarritt College. Address: 1701 Winfield Street, Winfield, Kansas 67156.

GRAY, MILDA MARIA Occupation: Registered Dental Hygienist. Education: B.A., University of California at Los Angeles; R.D.H., Northwestern University. Address: 38 Mission Bay Drive, Corona Del Mar, California 92625.

GRAY, RALPH D Occupation: Professor of History, Department of History, Indiana University; Editor, *Journal of the Early Republic*. Education: B.A., Hanover College; M.A., University of Delaware; Ph.D., University of Illinois. Address: 1724 West 73rd Place, Indianapolis, Indiana 46260.

GRAY, THOMAS W Occupation: Corporate Buyer, International Harvester. Education: B.S., Additional Study M.B.A. Program, Tougaloo College. Address: 150 Brookside Drive, Glendale Heights, Illinois 60139.

GRAYBEAL, NORMAN DWAIN Occupation: Assistant Principal, Robert D. Edgren High School. Education: B.S., M.A., M.S., Ph.D. Address: PSC Box 5059, APO San Francisco 96519-0006.

GREEN, CLIFFORD SCOTT Occupation: Judge, United States District Court. Education: B.S., J.D., Hon LL.D., Temple University. Address: 2311 North 50th Street, Philadelphia, Pennsylvania 19131.

GREEN, CYNTHIA ANNE Occupation: Professor. Education: B.S., M.S., Ed.D. Address: 901 Kenwood Drive, Abilene, Texas 79601.

GREEN, DAVID THOMAS (Deceased) Occupation: International Evangelist; Security Consultant. Education: Three Honorary Doctor of Divinity Degrees. Address: 1176 Milwaukee Avenue, Chicago, Illinois 60622.

GREEN, FELICE J Occupation: Director of Reading Clinic/Associate Professor of Education, University of North Alabama. Education: B.S., M.A., Ed.D. Address: 104 Oak Drive, Tuscumbia, Alabama 35674.

GREEN, LARRY H Occupation: Research Physicist. Education: Ph.D. Address: Post Office Box 15012, Panama City, Florida 32406.

GREEN, LINDA L Occupation: Chairperson Fine Arts Division and Drama Department, Spelman College. Education: B.S., Southern Illinois University; M.A., St. Louis University; Ph.D., Bowling Green State University. Address: 404 Summit North Drive Northeast, Atlanta, Georgia 30324.

GREEN, MARY S Occupation: Associate Professor in Mathematics, George Fox College. Education: A.B., Masters. Address: 1339 Northwest Viewmont Drive, Dundee, Oregon 97115.

GREEN, ROSE B Occupation: Professor Emeritus of English, Poet, Critic. Education: B.A., College of New Rochelle; M.A., Columbia University; Ph.D.,

University of Pennsylvania. Address: 308 Manor Road, Philadelphia, Pennsylvania 19128.

GREEN, RUTH CUMMINGS Occupation: Elementary School Teacher. Education: B.S.Ed. plus 67 hours. Address: 500 West 31st Avenue, Bellevue, Nebraska 68005.

GREEN, SIDNEY Occupation: Pharmacologist. Education: B.A., Dillard University; Ph.D., Howard University. Address: 15722 Allanwood Drive, Silver Spring, Maryland 20906.

GREEN, THEODIS GUY Occupation: College Professor. Education: Associate B.S., M.S., Ed.D. Address: 244 North Lincoln, Langston, Oklahoma 73050.

GREENBERG, FRANK JOSEPH SR Occupation: Nontraditional Experimental Educational Researcher, Lecturer, Writer, Administrator, Biblical Archaeologist. Education: B.A., B.B.A., B.D. LL.B., Ed.M., Ed.D., D.CO., Ph.D. Address: 14 Lindsey Street, Dorchester, Massachusetts 02124-1399.

GREENBERG, JOANNE Occupation: Writer. Education: B.A., American University. Address: 29221 Rainbow Hill Road, Golden, Colorado 80401.

GREENBERG, JOEL S Occupation: Management Consultant, Econ, Inc. Education: B.E.E., M.E.E. Address: 145 Parkside Drive, Princeton, New Jersey 08540.

GREENBERG, JOHN L Occupation: Research Fellow in History, R.A. Millikan Memorial Library. Education: B.A., M.A., Ph.D. Address: 551 South Wilson Avenue, Pasadena, California 91106.

GREENBERG, JUDITH LYNN Occupation: Director of Preventive Service Program; Psychotherapist. Education: B.A. with distinction Elementary Education, University of Michigan, 1967; M.A. Social Work, University of Chicago School of Social Service Administration, 1970; D.S.W., Adelphi University School of Social Work in progress, 1979-present. Address: 210 West 89 Street, Apartment 1C, New York, New York 10024.

GREENBERGER, STEVEN L Occupation: Vice President Taxes, Avis Inc. Education: B.B.A. Accounting, Adelphi University; J.D. Brooklyn Law School. Address: 1981 Bayberry Avenue, Merrick, New York 11566.

GREENBLATT, IRA J Occupation: Executive Vice President, The HIG Corporation. Education: A.B., Cornell University; J.D., New York University. Address: 400 East 54th Street, New York, New York 10022.

GREENE, ADELE S Occupation: Management Consultant. Education: New York University; Juilliard School of Music, New School of Social Research. Address: 30 West 60 Street, New York, New York 10023.

GREENE, ETHEL J Occupation: University Professor, Northeastern Illinois University. Education: B.E., M.E., Ed.D. Address: 9720 Morgan Street, Chicago, Illinois 60643.

GREENE, TIMOTHY J Occupation: Assistant Professor, Virginia Polytechnic Institute. Education: B.S. Aerospace Engineering, M.S.I.E., Ph.D., Purdue University. Address: 308 Mulberry Drive, Blacksburg, Virginia 24060.

GREENE, VICTOR R Occupation: Historian, Professor of History, History Department, University of Wisconsin-Milwaukee. Address: 4869 North Woodburn Street, Whitefish Bay, Wisconsin 53217.

GREENE, WILLIAM H Occupation: President, Livingstone College. Education: B.A., M.A., Ph.D. Address: 630 West Monroe Street, Salisbury, North Carolina 28144.

GREENSPAN, BARNEY Occupation: Child Psychoanalyst. Education: Ph.D. Address: 17307 Lomond Boulevard, Shaker Heights, Ohio 44120.

GREENSPAN, PATRICIA S Occupation: Fellow, National Endowment for the Humanities; Visiting Scholar, University of Bristol. Education: A.B., Barnard College; A.M., Ph.D., Harvard University. Address: 3003 Van Ness Street, Northwest, Washington, D.C. 20008.

GREER, DONALD M Occupation: Associate Professor and Head, Divison of Plastic and Reconstructive Surgery, University of Texas. Education: M.D., University of Cincinnati, 1962. Address: Box 4509, Route 4, Boerne, Texas 78006.

GREER, JERRY STONE Occupation: Consulting Economist, Charles T. Main, Inc. Education: S.B. Civil Engineering, S.B. Economics, S.M. Management. Address: 157 Osgood Street, Andover, Massachusetts 01810.

GREER, RACHEL D Occupation: Professor. Education: B.S.E., M.S.E., Ed.D. Address: Route 1, Box 144, Sherrill, Arkansas 72152.

GREFRATH, RICHARD WARREN Occupation: Librarian, University of Nevada Library. Education: B.A., New York University; M.A., Temple University; M.L.S., University of Maryland. Address: 635 Cardinal Way, Reno, Nevada 89509-1230.

GREGG, LINDA ALOUISE Occupation: Poet, Teacher. Education: B.A., M.A. Address: 21 Valley Street, Northampton, Massachusetts 01060.

GREGOR, ARTHUR Occupation: Poet/Professor. Education: B.S. in E.E. Address: 131 West 78 Street, New York, New York 10024.

GREGORY, CALVIN LUTHER Occupation: President, Insurance Agency Placement/Service. Education: A.A., B.A., M.Div., M.R.E., D.D., Ph.D. Address: 3307 Big Cloud Circle, Thousand Oaks, California 91359.

GREIG, LAURIE M Occupation: Researcher/Student. Education: B.A., M.Ed., Ph.D. (in progress). Address: 7627 40th Northeast, Everett, Washington 98205.

GREINER, MAURICE Occupation: Director of Training and Safety. Education: M.I.F.E., Q.A.A., Association of Administrative Assistants. Address: 21 Stanford, Pocatello, Idaho 83201.

GREIST, MARY C Occupation: Dermatologist, Private Practice. Education: B.A., Valparaiso University, 1969; M.D., Indiana University, School of Medicine, 1973. Address: 1175 Princeton Place, Zionsville, Indiana 46077.

GRESSAK, ANTHONY R JR Occupation: Executive Vice President, Silco Corporation. Education: A.A., Utah State University, 1967. Address: 17775 Nearbank Drive, Rowland Heights, California 91798.

GRETCHEN, HARRIS Occupation: Independent Account Representative. Education: Graduate, Vocational Technical School. Address: 5230 13th Avenue, South, Minneapolis, Minnesota 55417.

GREY, JERRY Occupation: Aerospace Scientist/Engineer. Education: B.M.E., M.S. Engineering Physics, Ph.D. Aeronautics. Address: 1 Lincoln Plaza, 25-O, New York, New York 10023.

GREYTAK, DAVID EDWARD Occupation: Professor of Economics. Education: B.A., M.A., Ph.D. Address: 103 Burlingame Drive, Syracuse, New York 13203.

GRIEBLING, KAREN JEAN Occupation: Teacher, University of Texas at Austin. Education: D.M.A. (in progress), University of Texas; M.M., University of

Houston; B.M., Eastman School of Music. Address: 4606 Avenue H, Austin, Texas 78751.

GRIESINGER, DONALD WILLIAM Occupation: Professor of Management, Claremont Graduate School; Chairman of Faculty of Management, Graduate Management Center; Consultant. Education: B.S., University of Southern California, 1954; M.S., University of California-Los Angeles, 1960; Ph.D., University of California, 1970. Address: 2230 Edinboro Avenue, Claremont, California 91711.

GRIFFIN, MICHAEL JAMES Occupation: Marketing/Advertising. Education: B.S. Education, Indiana University, 1971. Address: 1059 Chestnut, Chesterton, Indiana 46304.

GRIFFIN, PAULA YARDLEY Occupation: Sales, Management Trainer. Education: B.A. Address: 9 High Acres Drive, Poughskeepsie, New York 12603.

GRIFFITH, BENJAMIN FRANKLIN JR Occupation: President, Data-Com Inc. Address: 6130 Shetland Drive, New Orleans, Louisiana 70114.

GRIFFITH, CAROLE LOTSTEIN Occupation: Communications Consultant. Education: B.A., Fairleigh Dickinson University. Address: 302A Washington Valley Road, Basking Ridge, New Jersey 07920.

GRIFFITH, JAMES C Occupation: Dentist. Education: D.D.S. Address: Route 2 Box 32, Meridian, Mississippi 39301.

GRIFFITH, REBECCA RUNYAN Occupation: English Teacher, Plano East Senior High School. Education: B.A. English and French; Currently pursuing M.A. Humanities. Address: 3400 Custer, #1070, Plano, Texas 75023.

GRIFFITH, WANDA I Occupation: Assistant Professor of Sociology. Education: B.A. 1973, M.A. 1974, Ph.D. 1977, Washington State University. Address: 2440 Olive, Denver, Colorado 80207.

GRIGGS, IONE QUINBY Occupation: Newspaper Columnist. Education: Studied at Northwestern University. Address: Hotel Wisconsin, 720 North 3rd Street, Milwaukee, Wisconsin.

GRIM, PATRICK Occupation: Philosopher. Education: A.B., University of California at Santa Cruz; B.Phil., St. Andrews University; A.M.; Ph.D., Boston University. Address: 115 Beach Street, Port Jefferson, New York 11777.

GRIMES, LLOYDENA V Education: Master's Degree Nursing and Administration. Address: 1650 Southwest Filmont Avenue, Portland, Oregon 97225.

GRITTA, RICHARD DAVID Occupation: Professor of Finance, School of Business, University of Portland. Education: B.B.A, University of Notre Dame; M.B.A., Indiana University; Ph.D., University of Maryland. Address: 6790 Southwest Larkspur Place, Berverton, Oregon 97005.

GRIZZLE, JESSY W Occupation: Assistant Professor and Research Assistant Professor of Electrical Engineering, Coordinated Sciences Laboratory, University of Illinois. Address: Coordinated Science Laboratory, University of Illinois, Urbana, Illinois 61801.

GRODBERG, MARCUS GORDON Occupation: Director of Research, Colgate-Hoyt Labs. Education: A.B., M.S. Address: 111 Hyde Street, Newton, Massachusetts 02161.

GROFF, WARREN H Occupation: Director of Research and Development. Education: B.S.Ed., Millersville State College, 1955; M.Ed., The Pennsylvania State University, 1961; Ed.D. 1967, Postdoctoral 1971, Temple University; Postdoctoral, University of Pennsylvania, 1967. Address: 497 Edgewood Road, Mansfield, Ohio 44907.

GRONER, DENNIS MARK Occupation: Psychologist; Insurance Company Executive. Education: Ph.D. Industrial Psychology, University of Minnesota. Address: 2 Bear Brook Court, Livingston, New Jersey 07039.

GRONOWICZ, ANTONI Occupation: Author. Education: Ph.D. Address: 128 Brookmoor Road, Avon, Connecticut 06001.

GROSS, BERTRAM M Occupation: Professor-at-Large, Saint Mary's College of California. Education: B.A. 1933, M.A. 1935. Address: 1382 Camino Perul, Moraga, California 94536.

GROSS, JAMES D Occupation: Director of Laboratories, St. Mary's Hospital. Education: B.S. with honors in Biology, University of Chattanooga, 1951; M.D., Vanderbilt University Medical School, 1955. Address: 54 Sunset Drive, Streator, Illinois 61364.

GROSS, THOMAS L Occupation: Physician, Researcher. Education: B.A., M.D., University of Illinois. Address: 29581 Wellington, North Olmsted, Ohio 44070.

GROSSMAN, ELIZABETH GREENWELL Occupation: Architectural Historian. Education: Bachelor of Arts, Master of Arts, Ph.D. Address: 77 Everett Avenue, Providence, Rhode Island 02906.

GROSSMAN, ELLEN S Occupation: U.I. Claims Examiner. Education: B.S. Education with Specialization in Fine Arts. Address: 332 North Forest Avenue, Rockville Centre, New York 11570.

GROTHAUS, CLARENCE EDWARD Occupation: Professor of Chemistry Emeritus. Education: A.B., Greenville College; M.A., Ph.D., University of Kansas. Address: 135 West Marsile, Bourbonnais, Illinois 60914.

GROVES, GRATIA BAILEY Occupation: Writer and Lecturer. Education: A.B., M.A., Honorary Ph.D. Address: 6830 Huntdale Street, Long Beach, California 90808.

GROVES, RUTH C Occupation: Head High School Librarian (Retired). Education: B.S., M.A. Library Science. Address: 5831 Pea Ridge Road, Huntington, West Virginia 25705.

GRUB, PHILLIP DONALD Occupation: Professor, The George Washington University. Education: B.A. Economics (highest honors), B.A. Business Education (highest honors), Eastern Washington State University; M.B.A., The George Washington University; Doct.B.A., The George Washington University. Address: 2342 South Rolfe Street, Arlington, Virginia 22202.

GRUBBS, RANDALL LEE Occupation: Attorney. Education: B.S. 1966, M.A. 1967, J.D. 1972. Address: 2849 Colleen, Garland, Texas 75043.

GRUBER, ROSALIND H Occupation: Director/ Counseling Psychologist. Education: M.A. Counseling, Suffolk University. Address: 2150 Route 6A, West Barnstable, Massachusetts 02668.

GRUBERG, MARTIN Occupation: Professor of Political Science, Political Science Department, University of Wisconsin. Education: B.A., Ph.D. Address: 1660 Westhaven Drive, Oshkosh, Wisconsin 54901.

GRUNDSTEIN, NATHAN DAVID Occupation: Professor, Weatherhead School of Management, Case Western Reserve University. Education: B.A. 1935, M.Sc. 1936, Ohio State University; J.D. (LL.B.), The George Washington University College of Law, 1951; Ph.D., The Maxwell School of Syracuse University, 1943. Address: 2872 Washington Boulevard, Cleveland Heights, Ohio 44188.

GRUNDY, JOHN OWEN Occupation: City Historian and Chairman of the Historical Districts Committee. Education: D.H.L., Jersey City State College. Address: 54 Park Street, Jersey City, New Jersey 07304.

GRYGUTIS, BARBARA ZION Occupation: Artist. Education: B.F.A, M.F.A. Address. 273 North Main Avenue, Tucson, Arizona 85705.

GUALTIERI, JOSEPH PETER Occupation: Artist, Museum Director. Education: Graduate of Art Institute of Chicago. Address: 60 Warren Street, Norwich, Connecticut 06360.

GUBBINS, KEITH E Occupation: Director, School of Chemical Engineering and T. R. Briggs Professor of Engineering, Cornell University. Education: Ph.D. Chemical Engineering, King's College. Address: 523 Highland Road, Ithaca, New York 14850.

GUDAS, LINDA J Occupation: Nurse Practitioner/Full time Ph.D. Student at Tufts University. Education: B.S., M.S., Boston University. Address: 208 Fuller Street #8, Brookline, Massachusetts 02146.

GUELDNER, SARAH HALL Occupation: Nurse Educator. Education: B.S.N., M.N., D.S.N. Address: 155 Tamarack Drive, Athens, Georgia 30605.

GUENTHER, CHARLES JOHN Occupation: Teacher, Poet, Translator. Education: A.A., B.A., M.A., L.H.D. (hon.). Address: 2935 Russell Boulevard, St. Louis, Missouri 63104.

GUESMAN, KIMBERLY JO Occupation: Registered Nurse, Critical Care Nurse Clinician. Education: B.S., M.S. (in progress). Address: Apartment 205, 5426 Fifth Avenue, Pittsburgh, Pennsylvania 15232.

GUFFIN, GILBERT LEE Occupation: Consultant/Executive Director, Samford University. Education: A.B., Bh.D., Th.M., Th.D. Address: 3605 Ratliff Road, Birmingham, Alabama 35210.

GUIDROZ-GREEN, FAY THRASHER Occupation: Chief, Psychology Service. Education: M.Ed., McNeese State University; M.A., Ph.D. 1970, Louisiana State University. Address: 210 South College, Woodbury, Tennessee 37190.

GULA, ROBERT JOHN Occupation: Teacher and Director of Studies, Groton School. Education: B.A. Address: Farmers Row, Groton, Massachusetts 01450.

GULLION, GORDON W Occupation: Wildlife Management Research/Education. Education: B.S., University of Oregon-Eugene, 1948; M.A., University of California-Berkeley, 1950. Address: 605 Slate Street, Cloquet, Minnesota 55720.

GUMPORT, RICHARD I Occupation: Professor, University of Illinois, Department of Biochemistry; Biochemist. Education: B.S. 1960, Ph.D. 1968, University of Chicago. Address: 2009 South Anderson Street, Urbana, Illinois 61801.

GUNSHOR, RUTH Occupation: Painter, Instructor. Education: Brooklyn Music and Art School, 1957; Education Alliance Art School, 1959. Address: 3820 Lyme Avenue, Brooklyn, New York 11224.

GUPTA, AARON DAS Occupation: Senior Mechanical Engineer, U.S. Army. Education: B.Tech. (Hons.), I.I.T.; M.Eng., N.S.T.C.; Ph.D., Virginia Polytechnic Institute. Address: 104 John Street, Perryville, Maryland 21005.

GUPTA, GOPAL D Occupation: Manager, Engineering Science and Technology Department. Education: Ph.D., 1970; M.S., 1968; Mech.Engr., Lehigh University. Address: 50 Timberhill Road, East Hanover, New Jersey 07936.

GUPTA, RAGHUVIR K Occupation: Accounting. Education: Graduate in Commerce, C.P.A. Address: 101 Central Avenue, Morris Plains, New Jersey 07950.

GUPTA, SURENDRA M Occupation: Associate Professor of Industrial Engineering, Northeastern University. Education: B.E.E.E., M.B.A., M.S.I.E., Ph.D. Address: 63 Trayer Road, Canton, Massachusetts 02021.

GUPTA, VENU G Occupation: Professor of Psychology, Kutztown University of Pennsylvania. Education: B.A., M.A., M.Ed., Ph.D. Address: 744 Highland Avenue, Kutztown, Pennsylvania 19530.

GUPTA, VIRENDRA PRAKASH Occupation: Research Physicist. Education: M.S., A.S.I.N.P., Ph.D. Address: 2072 Beth Street, Pocatello, Idaho 83201.

GURASH, JOHN T Occupation: Chairman of the Board and Director, CertainTeed Corporation; Chairman of the Board and Director, Household International, Inc. Education: Loyola University. Address: 456 South Orange Grove B1, Pasadena, California 91105.

GUTHREY, EVELYN MAY Occupation: Registered Nurse, Doctor of Law, Legal Consultant. Education: A.A., B.S.N., J.D. Address: 1201 Sheridan Road, Concord, California 94518.

GUTHRIE, RICHARD ALAN Occupation: Physician, Professor and Director of Kansas Regional Diabetes Center. Education: M.D. Address: 4967 North Hillcrest, Wichita, Kansas 67220.

GUTSCHICK, WILLIAM C Occupation: Manager Corporate Methods and Procedures/Forms Control and Design. Education: B.S. Business Management. Address: 900 West Rand Road, Arlington Heights, Illinois 60004.

GUY, MATTHEW JOEL Occupation: Gastroenterologist. Education: M.D., M.Ed.; Sc.D. Address: 1401 Ocean Avenue, Brooklyn, New York 11230.

H

HAAKE, ROBERT Occupation: Minister. Education: B.M.Sc., M.M.Sc., Doctor of Metaphysical Science. Address: 15319 Daphne Avenue, Gardena, California 90249.

HAAS, MAY V Occupation: Greenhouse Floriculturist; Collector of Horticulture Books. Education: Attended Carnegie Library School. Address: R.D. #2, Box 334, Birdsboro, Pennsylvania 19508.

HAAS, MERRILL W Occupation: Petroleum Consultant. Education: B.A.. Address: 1D910 Wickwild, Houston, Texas 77024.

HABERMAN, REX Occupation: State Senator, Nebraska. Address: 436 West 11th Street, Imperial, Nebraska 69033.

HACKMAN, HELEN ANNA HENRIETTE Address: 230 South Illinois Street, Box 227, Pittsfield, Illinois 62363.

HACKNEY, HOWARD SMITH Occupation: County Executive Director of A.S.C.S., Farmer. Education: B.S. Wilmington College. Address: 2003 Inwood Road, Wilmington, Ohio 45177.

HACKWORTH, THEODORE J JR Occupation: Denver City Councilman, Chairman Denver Regional Council of Governments. Education: B.A., University of Denver. Address: 3955 West Linvale Place, Denver, Colorado 80236.

HADDEN, STUART T Occupation: Consultant Chemical Engineer Thermodynamics. Education: B.S.E. Chemical Engineering, B.S.E. Mathematics, N.I.A. Mathematics, D.E.S. Chemical Engineering. Address: 36 Tealwood Drive, Creve Coeur, Missouri 63141.

HADDOCK, JAY LAMAR Occupation: Research Soil Scientist, Consultant. Education: B.S., Brigham Young University; M.S., Massachusetts State College; Ph.D., Iowa State University. 188 North 300-E, Logan, Utah 84321.

HADLEY, NEIL F Occupation: Professor, Arizona State University. Education: Ph.D. Address: 321 La Diosa, Tempe, Arizona 85282.

HADLOCK, DENNIS EDWARD Occupation: Senior Research Scientist, Battelle Northwest Labs, Richland. Education: B.S. Physics, M.S. Physics. Address: 1324 Farrell Lane, Richland, Washington 99352.

HAFNER, ARTHUR WAYNE Occupation: Director, Library and Archival Services, American Medical Association, Chicago. Education: Ph.D., M.S., M.A., B.S.. Address: 3523 Maple Leaf Drive, Glenview, Illinois 60025.

HAFTER, MONROE Z Occupation: Professor of Spanish, University of Michigan. Education: Ph.D., Harvard University, 1956. Address: 1325 Brooklyn Avenue, Ann Arbor, Michigan 48104.

HAGAN, PAUL W Occupation: Priest. Education: B.M.E., M.S.M.T. Address: 1031 Kem Road, Marion, Indiana 46952.

HAGE, JERALD Occupation: Professor and Chairman, Department of Sociology, University of Maryland. Education: Ph.D. Address: 5406 Wilson Lane, Bethesda, Maryland 20814.

HAGEMAN, RICHARD H Occupation: Professor Emeritus Plant Physiology, Department of Agronomy, University of Illinois. Education: B.S., M.S., Ph.D. Address: 1302 East McHenry Street, Urbana, Illinois 61801.

HAGER, HELLMUT W Occupation: Professor, The Pennsylvania State University. Education: Ph.D., University of Bonn, Germany. Address: 318 East Prospect Avenue, State College, Pennsylvania 16801.

HAGERTY, GAIL Occupation: Burleigh County State's Attorney, Burleigh County Courthouse. Education: J.D., University of North Dakota. Address: 1318 North 3rd, Bismarck, North Dakota 58501.

HAGEY, WALTER R Occupation: The Pennsylvania Bible Society, President. Education: Certificate of Proficiency, University of Pennsylvania; Graduate, Peirce Junior College, 1929; Certificate of Proficiency, University of Pennsylvania, Wharton School, 1936; LL.B., LaSalle Extension University, 1938; Audited Courses, Temple University Law School; S.T.B., Temple University School of Theology, 1943; Attended Rutgers University Stonier Graduate School of Banking, 1951; LL.D., Muhlenberg College 1963. Address: 510 East Lawn Avenue, Lansdale, Pennsylvania 19446.

HAGGAH, FAHMY MAHMOUD Occupation: Senior Engineer, Materials Engineering, EG&G Idaho, Inc. Education: B.S. 1970, M.S. 1980. Address: 724 Saturn Avenue #8, Idaho Falls, Idaho 83402.

HAHN, ELSA M Occupation: Secretary to Vice President, Advertising Director. Education: Attended Milwaukee Technical College. Address: 1129 North Jackson Street, 909C, Milwaukee, Wisconsin 53202.

HAIM, MARC ALAN Occupation: President, R.H. Belan Company, Inc., Lake Success, New York. Education: B.A., Colgate University, Virginia, 1970; M.B.A., Columbia University, Virginia. Address: 4 Pinebrook Court, Dix Hills, New York 11746.

HAISCH, BERNHARD MICHAEL Occupation: Astrophysicst, Lockheed Palo Alto Research Lab, California. Education: Ph.D., University of Wisconsin-Madison; B.S., Indiana University. Address: 847 San Ramon, Moss Beach, California 94038.

HAJJAR, DAVID PHILLIP Occupation: Scientist; Professor, Cornell Medical College, New York. Education: Ph.D. Biochemistry; M.S., B.A., Biochemistry. Address: 1161 York Avenue, Apartment 3D, New York, New York 10021.

HAKIM, PETER Occupation: Vice President for Research and Evaluation, Inter-American Foundation. Education: A.B., Cornell University; M.S., University of Pennsylvania; M.P.A., Princeton University. Address: 1724 Euclid Street, Washington, D.C. 22036.

HALABY, SAMIA A Occupation: Artist, Painter, Lecturer, New York. Education: B.S., University of Cincinnati; M.A., University of Michigan; M.F.A., University of Indiana. Address: 103 Franklin Street, New York, New York 10013.

HALE, DEAN EDWARD Occupation: Social Work Administration, Eugerb, Oregon. Education: B.A.S.W., University of Pennsylvania-Shippensburg. Address: 2101 Hawkins, Eugerb, Oregon 97405.

HALE, HELENE H Occupation: Councilwoman and Realtor, Hilo, Hawaii. Education: B.S., M.A. Address: 262 Anela Street, Hilo, Hawaii 96720.

HALE, JAMES RUSSELL Occupation: Educator, Clergyman, Gettysburg, Pennsylvania. Education: A.B., B.D., S.T.M., Ed.D. Address: 153 S. Hay Street, Gettysburg, Pennsylvania 17325.

HALL, DAVID Occupation: Clergyman and Consultant Advisor, Washington, D.C. Education: Ph.D., D.D., M.Div., B.S., B.A. Address: 1338 K Street Southeast, Washington, D.C. 20003.

HALL, GENE E Occupation: Acting Director, R&D Center for Teacher Education, University of Texas-Austin. Education: Ph.D., M.S., Syracuse University; B.S., Castleton College. Address: 1004 Castle Ridge Road, Austin, Texas 78746.

HALL, HARBER HOMER Occupation: Real Estate Development, Bloomington, Illinois. Education: Attended University of Miami. Address: 203 North Main, Bloomington, Illinois 61701.

HALL, JAMES W Occupation: President, Empire State College/State University of New York. Education: Ph.D., M.A., M.S.M., B.Mus. Address: 173 Phila Street, Saratoga Springs, New York 12866.

HALL, JAMES WILLIAM Occupation: Minister, Southern Baptist Convention. Education: B.S., B.A., Th.M., D.D. Address: 1209 Hustonville Road, Danville, Kentucky 40422.

HALL, JOE B Occupation: Head Basketball Coach, University of Kentucky. Education: A.B., U.K., 1955; M.A., Colorado State University, 1964. Address: 713 Beechmont Avenue, Lexington, Kentucky 40502.

HALL, LISA L Occupation: Government Executive. Education: M.B.A., B.A. Address: 620 East Adams, Springfield, Illinois 62704.

HALL, PEARL REGINA Occupation: WXVI Radio, Account Executive. Education: B.A., Huntingdon College, 1976. Address: Post Office Box 341, Montgomery, Alabama 36101.

HALL, SUE HAMMACK Occupation: Vice President, Sea Island Bank. Education: Associate Degree in Business Administration. Address: 124 Holly Drive, Statesboro, Georgia 30458.

HALL, WILFRED McGREGOR Occupation: Chairman of the Board and Chief Executive Officer, The C.T. Main Corporation, Boston, Massachusetts. Education: B.S. Civil Engineering, University of Colorado, Hon.D. English, Tufts University. Address: Penthouse D, The Fairfield, Prudential Center, Boston, Massachusetts 02199.

HALLFORD, DENNIS M Occupation: Professor of Animal Science, New Mexico State University. Education: B.S., Tarleton State University; M.S., Ph.D., Oklahoma State University. Address: 1135 Calle del Encanto, Las Cruces, New Mexico 88005.

HALLINAN, NANCY Occupation: Writer: Novels, Short Stories; Teacher. Education: B.A., Vassar College; Columbia University. Address: 276 Riverside Drive, New York, New York 10025.

HALLMAN, LEON C Occupation: Professor, Stephen F. Austin State University, Nacogdoches, Texas. Education: B.B.A., M.A., Ph.D. Address: 3502 Windsor, Nacogdoches, Texas 75961.

HALLOCK, JOHN WALLACE JR Occupation: Attorney, State Legislator. Education: B.A., Loyola University; J.D., Chicago-Kent College of Law. Address: 123 North Vale, Rockford, Illinois 61107.

HALLUM, ROSEMARY N Occupation: Writer, Teacher, Workshop Leader. Education: Ph.D., M.A., B.A., General Elementary and Secondary Teaching Credentials. Address: 1021 Otis Drive, Agameda, California 94501.

HALQUIST, CARL J JR Occupation: Pastor. Education: B.A. in Bible. Address: 2730 Breton Southeast, Grand Rapids, Michigan 49506.

HALSEY, JAMES ALBERT Occupation: Music Industry Impresario. Education: Graduate, Independence High School, 1948; Independence Junior College, 1950. Address: 3225 South Norwood, Tulsa, Oklahoma 74135.

HALSTEAD, DIANNE CLAIRE Occupation: Director Microbiology and Immunology; Assistant Professor Department of Microbiology. Education: M.S. Microbiology, Ph.D. Microbiology, Research Virology (Herpes Viruses). Address: 156 Springhouse Road, Allentown, Pennsylvania 18104.

HALSTEAD, HELEN LUCILE Occupation: Nursing Educator. Education: B.S.N., M.Ed., Ph.D. Address: 5540 Porter, Wichita, Kansas 67204.

HAMBLIN, MAREE B Occupation: Fiction Writer. Education: B.S., Postgraduate Studies. Address: 503 Sixth Street, Monett, Missouri 65708.

HAMER, IRVING S Occupation: Headmaster, Park Heights Street Academy, Baltimore, Maryland. Education: Ed.D. Harvard University. Address: 6018 Pimlico Road, Baltimore, Maryland 21209.

HAMILTON, DENNIS HARRY Occupation: Teacher, Greenbay, Wisconsin. Education: B.S. in Education. Address: Route 1, Box 271, Shawano, Wisconsin 54166.

HAMILTON, HARLAN B Occupation: College Professor, Jersey City State College. Education: B.A., M.A., Ed.D. Address: 170 East 83 Street, Apartment 3L, New York, New York 10022.

HAMILTON, PAULA H Occupation: Library Director. Education: B.A. Art History, M.L.S. Library Service. Address: 7110 South West Burlingame Avenue, Portland, Oregon 97219.

HAMILTON, R MARGARET WHITSON Occupation: Associate Professor of Education Emeritus, Frostburg State College, Maryland. Education: B.S., M.Ed. Address: 203 Columbia Street, Cumberland, Maryland 21502.

HAMILTON, VERA E Occupation: Instructor, Bliss College. Education: B.S. Business Administration. Address: 1382 East Livingston, Columbus, Ohio 43205.

HAMILTON, WILLIAM E JR Occupation: Robotics Research, GM Research Labs, Warren, Michigan. Education: B.S. Electrical Engineering, M.S. Electrical Engineering, Ph.D. Address: 1346 West Fairview, Rochester, Michigan 48064.

HAMILTON-KEMP, THOMAS ROGERS Occupation: Associate Professor, University of Kentucky. Education: Associate of Arts, State Catharine College, 1962; Bachelor of Arts, University of Kentucky, 1964; Ph.D. in Chemistry, University of Kentucky, 1970. Address: 868 Laurel Hill Road, Lexington, Kentucky 40504.

HAMM, CATHARINE MARGARET Occupation: Travel Editor. Education: B.A., McPherson College. Address: 5919 Robinson Lane, North, 43, Overland Park, Kansas 66202.

HAMMACK, HENRY EDGAR Occupation: Professor of Theatre Arts, Texas Christian University, Fort Worth, Texas. Education: B.A. 1956, M.A. 1962, University of Washington; Ph.D., Tulane University, 1967. Address: 3205 Lamesa Place, Fort Worth, Texas 76109.

HAMMACK, ROBERT DEAN Occupation: District Executive, Saint Louis Area. Education: B.A. English, M.A. English. Address: 21 Saint Theresa Lane, Bridgeton, Missouri 63044.

HAMMOND, KARLA MARIE Occupation: Analyst/Documentation and Training Services, Hartford, Connecticut. Education: B.A. English, Goucher College; M.A. English, Trinity College. Address: Rural Route #4, 12 West Drive, East Hampton, Connecticut 06424.

HAMMOND, RUSSELL I Occupation: Retired University Professor and Dean. Education: B.A. 1929, M.A. 1934, Ed.D. 1942, Columbia University. Address: 816 South 17th Street, Laramie, Wyoming 82070.

HAMPTON, MARGARET Occupation: Associate Professor of German, Earlham College. Education: B.A., M.A., Ph.D. Address: 1002 Woolman Drive, Richmond, Indiana 47374.

HANCOCK, JOYCE ANN Occupation: Adjunct Professor of English, Kentucky State University.

Education: B.A., M.A., Ph.D. Address: 1005 Letcher Avenue, Frankfort, Kentucky 40601.

HANEY, DAVID N Occupation: Biochemist/Biotechnology. Education: Ph.D., M.S., B.A. Address: 5 Breyerwood Court, Hortonville, Wisconsin 54944.

HANGER, ROBERT E Occupation: Virginia District Sales Manager, Armor Research Company, Charlottesville, Virginia. Education: Honorary Degree, Alderson-Broaddus College. Address: 3405 Indian Spring Road, Charlottsville, Virginia 22901.

HANLEY, MARY B Occupation: Owner of Hanley, Secretarial Services. Education: Attended Foothill College, DeAnza College, College of San Mateo, Arizona State University. Address: 1806 Higdon Avenue, #3, Mount View, California 94041.

HANNAHS, JAMES R Occupation: President, Midwest Testing Laboratories. Education: B.S. Welding Engineering 1967. Address: 8598 Industry Park Drive, Piqua, Ohio 45356.

HANOVER, PAUL N Occupation: Professional Speaker, Space Programs. Education: Bachelor of Electrical Engineering, Electronics. Address: 3551 Winslow Drive, Tucson, Arizona 85715.

HANRAHAN, LINDA L Occupation: Professor. Education: B.A., M.A., Ph.D. Address: Post Office Box 397, Arcata, California 95521.

HANSCH, THEODOR W Occupation: Educator, Physicist, Stanford University. Education: Ph.D., 1965. Address: 1510 Oak Creek Drive 405, Palo Alto, California 26304.

HANSON, LAWRENCE Occupation: Artist, College Professor. Education: B.A. 1959, M.F.A. 1962, University of Minnesota. Address: 1321½ Railroad Avenue, Bellingham, Washington 98225.

HANSON, MARY JANE Occupation: Elementary Teacher, Barton Open School, Minneapolis, Minnesota. Education: B.S. 1968, M.Ed. 1975, University of Minneapolis. Address: 1601 Colorado Avenue South, Minneapolis, Minnesota 55416.

HANTGAN, GEORGE Occupation: Endowment Consultant, Tenafly, New Jersey. Education: B.A., M.P.A., M.S.S.W. Address: 188 St. Micholas Avenue, Englewood, New Jersey 07631.

HANTON, MICHAEL Occupation: Public and Personnel Relations Consultant. Education: A.B. 1951, M.A. 1955, Indiana University; Graduate, U.S. Air Force Air War College, Air University.

HARALSON, MABLE KATHLEEN Occupation: Government Official (Executive Assistant), South Carolina Water Resources Commission. Education: B.S. Health Education, University of South Carolina, Columbia, 1974; M.P.H. Community Health Education, University of Tennessee-Knoxville, 1976. Address: Post Office Box 515, Abbeville, South Carolina 29620.

HARBESON, JOHN W Occupation: Professor of Political Science; Director International Studies. Education: Ph.D., Wisconsin University, 1970; M.A., Chicago University, 1962; B.A., Swarthmore University, 1960. Address: 1020 Park Avenue, Racine, Washington 53403.

HARBET, SHELIA C Occupation: Associate Professor, California State University. Education: H.S.D., M.S., B.S.E. Address: 29854 N. Violet Hills Drive, Canyon Country, California 91351.

HARD, ARNE M Occupation: Chairman of the Board, Hawkeye Savings and Loan Association, Boone, Iowa. Education: American Institute of Business. Address: 1128 Country Club Drive, Boone, Iowa 50036.

HARDAWAY, EVELYN R Occupation: Data Processing Manager. Address: Post Office Box 656, Katy, Texas 77449.

HARDEN, OLETA ELIZABETH Occupation: Professor of English, President of the Faculty, Wright State University. Education: B.A. English, M.A. English, Ph.D. English. Address: 2618 Big Woods Trail, Fairborn, Ohio 45324.

HARDEN, R JOYCE Occupation: Assistant Professor Speech Pathology. Education: B.A. 1949, M.A. 1967, Ph.D. 1972. Address: 6924 Valhalla Road, Fortworth, Texas 76116.

HARDIN, CAROLYN MYRICK Occupation: College Teacher/Physiologist. Education: A.A., B.A., M.A., Ph.D. Address: 2503 Hawthorne Drive, Bettendorf, Iowa 52722.

HARDING, FANN Occupation: Assistant to the Director, Division of Blood Diseases and Resourses, National Heart, Lung and Blood Institute, Maryland. Education: A.B. Biology, Coker College, Hartsville, Maryland, 1951; M.S. Anatomy, Medical College of South Carolina, Charleston, 1954; Ph.D. Anatomy, Medical College of South Carolina, Charleston, 1958. Address: 5306 Bradley Boulevard, Bethesda, Maryland 20814.

HARDWICK, JOHN L Occupation: College Faculty, Business and Economics. Education: A.B., M.B.A. Address: Box 02004, Detroit, Michigan 48202.

HARDY, CAROLE MORGAN Occupation: State Coordinator of Educational Field Services, Criminal Justice. Education: B.A., Wayne State University; M.A., Metropolitan Collegiate Institute, England. Address: 1033 Rockcrest Drive, Marietta, Georgia 30062.

HARDY, E VERNEDA Occupation: O.R. Supervisor, Nurse. Education: B.S. Occupational Education. Address: 605 Saint Louis Street, Pinckneyville, Illinois 62274.

HARDY, MARIE PAULA Occupation: Professor of English, Head of Education Department, Member of Religious Order. Education: B.S., B.A., Saint Mary College, 1962; M.A., University of Nebraska, 1969; Ph.D., University of Illinois, 1972. Address: Saint Mary College, Leavenworth, Kansas 66048.

HARFORD, CAROL V Occupation: President, Wolf Trap Foundation, Vienna, Viriginia. Address: 823 South 26th Place, Arlington, Virginia 22202.

HARGROVE, BARBARA J Occupation: Seminary Professor. Education: B.S., M.S., Ph.D., Colorado State University. Address: 2685 South Vine Street, Denver, Colorado 80210.

HARGROVE, LOGAN E Occupation: Scientific Officer (Physicist), Office of Naval Research. Education: B.S. 1956, M.S. 1957, Ph.D. 1961. Address: 1536 Scandia Circle, Reston, Virginia 22090.

HARJO, JOY Occupation: Poet/Screenwriter. Education: M.F.A., University of Iowa; B.A. University of New Mexico. Address: Post Office Box 9463, Denver, Colorado 80209.

HARKINS, DOROTHY WHITE Occupation: Professor of Physical Education, Eastern Kentucky University. Education: B.S., M.S., Ed.D. Address: 123 Westwood, Richmond, Kentucky 40475.

HARMAN, ESTELLE KARCHMER Occupation: Director, E.H.A.W., Inc. Education: A.A., B.A., M.A. Address: 522 North LaBrea Avenue, Los Angeles, California 90036.

HARMELINK, HERMAN III Occupation: Clergyman, Professor, Author. Education: B.A., B.D., M.A., M.Div., S.T.M., M.Phil. Address: 70 Hooker Avenue, Poughkeepsie, New York 12601.

HARMON, VERDELL T Occupation: Administrator Workmen's Compensation. Education: Currently Enrolled in Degree Program at Notre Dame of Maryland. Address: 98 Padonia Road, Timonium, Maryland 21093.

HARPAVAT, GANESH L Occupation: Manager/Scientist. Education: Ph.D. Mechanics and Aerospace, M.B.A. Address: 921 Angela Drive, Lewisville, Texas 75067.

HARRAL, HARRIET BRISCOE Occupation: Mayor's Aide; Director of Training. Education: B.A., M.A., Baylor University; Ph.D., University of Colorado. Address: 925 Alhambra North, Jacksonville, Florida 32207.

HARRELL, STEWARD HAVENS Occupation: Pastor, South Rosemary Baptist Church. Education: Diploma, Oak City High School, Oak City, North Carolina. Address: Route 2, Box 409A, Roanoke Rapids, North Carolina 27870.

HARRINGTON, JOSEPH F Occupation: Educator. Education: B.S., M.A., Ph.D. Address: 119 Holmes Avenue Stroghton, Maryland 02072.

HARRIS, ARLO DEAN Occupation: Professor of Chemistry, California State College. Education: B.Sc. Chemistry, University of Dayton, 1961; Ph.D. Inorganic Chemistry, Tulane University, New Orleans, Louisiana, 1964; Post-doctoral Fellowship, University of California, Berkeley, 1964-65; Participant, C.A. Coulson School for Theoretical Chemistry, Oxford University, England, 1970. Address: 3488 North D Street, San Bernardino, California 92405.

HARRIS, AURAND Occupation: Playwright. Education: A.B., University of Kansas City, Missouri; M.A. Northwestern University. Address: c/o Anchorage Press, Box 8067, New Orleans, Louisiana 70182.

HARRIS, CARL VERNON Occupation: Professor of Classical Languages, Wake Forest University. Education: B.A., Wake Forest University; B.D. and S.T.M., Yale University; Ph.D., Duke University. Address: Wake Forest Apartments 6C, Winston-Salem, North Carolina 27106.

HARRIS, JAMES H Occupation: Physician, Scientist: Pathology, Neuropathology. Education: A.A., B.S., Ph.D., M.D. Address: 550 Oak Knoll, Perrysburg, Ohio 43551.

HARRIS, JANA N Occupation: Director, Writers in Performance, MTC. Education: B.S. Mathematics, M.F.A. Creative Writing. Address: Route 2 Box 331, Ringoes, New Jersey 08551.

HARRIS, JOSEPH DONALD Occupation: Marketing Promotion; Art Financial Aid Director. Education: B.A.A., M.B.A. Address: 5035 North 39th Drive, Phoenix, Arizona 85019.

HARRIS, JOSEPH E Occupation: Professor of History, Howard University. Education: B.A., M.A., Ph.D. Address: 10726 Kinloch Road, Silver Spring, Maryland 20903.

HARRIS, KENNETH PHILIP Occupation: Radio, Television Promotion Manager. Address: High Knoll Cottage, Point Shares, Bermuda.

HARRIS, LOUISE Education: Brown University, A.B. Economics. Address: 395 Angell Street, Apartment 111, Providence, Rhode Island 02906.

HARRIS, PAULETTE PROCTOR Occupation: Faculty Member, Augusta College. Education: B.A. Med., Ed.D., University of South Carolina. Address: 2707 West Terrace Drive, Augusta, Georgia 30909.

HARRIS, PHYLLIS IRENE Occupation: Special Education Teacher/Counselor. Education: B.S. Biology/Psychology, M.S. Special Education, M.S. Occupational Education. Address: 7729 South Cregier Avenue, Chicago, Illinois 60649.

HARRIS, RANSOM BAINE Occupation:

Professor of Philosophy, Executive, International Scholarly Society, Old Dominion University, Norfolk, Virginia. Education: B.A., M.A., B.D., Ph.D. Address: 4037 Windymille Drive, Portsmouth, Virginia 23703.

HARRIS, R WESLEY Occupation: President, Union Frondenberg, USA Company. Education: B.S., M.S. Industrial Engineering Management. Address: 30 Willow Drive, Olney, Illinos 62450.

HARRISON, DOROTHY G Occupation: Computer Center Director, Independent Computer Consultant. Education: B.A., M.S., M.Ln. Address: 310 Cedar Creek Drive, Athens, Georgia 30605.

HARRISON, FRANK RUSSELL Occupation: University Professor, University of Georgia. Education: B.A., M.A., Ph.D. Address: 310 Cedar Creek Drive, Athens, Georgia 30605.

HARRISON, JOE F Occupation: Executive Vice President, Chamber of Commerce, Stamford, Texas. Education: B.S. Biological Sciences. Address: 506 Dodson Drive, Stamford, Texas 79553.

HARRISON, LORENE C Occupation: Retired. Education: A.B. Address: 1200 I Street, #315, Anchorage, Alaska 99501.

HARRISON, SHIRLEY M Occupation: Teacher, Lecturer, Writer, Loyola University, New Orleans. Education: B.S., M.S.W., Ph.D. Address: 2840 Jefferson Avenue, New Orleans, Louisiana 70115.

HARRISON, YVONNE E Occupation: Director, Pharmaceutical Research Coordination, Hoffman-La Roche, Inc., Nutley, New Jersey. Education: B.S. 1959, M.S. 1970, Ph.D. Pharmacology 1972, Howard University. Address: 17 Clearview Road, East Brunswick, New Jersey 07110.

HARROLD, WILLIAM EUGENE Occupation: Professor of English. Education: B.A., Wake Forest University, 1959; M.A. 1962, Ph.D. 1967, University of North Carolina-Chapel Hill. Address: 1982 North Prospect, 2A, Milwaukee, Wisconsin 53202.

HARSAGHY, FRED JOSEPH Occupation: Educator. Education: B.A. 1948, M.P.A. 1953, Ph.D. 1965, New York University; M.S. Library Science, Columbia University, 1954. Address: Box 8897, New Fairfield, Connecticut 06810.

HART, JAMES HARLAN Occupation: Emergency Medicine Physician. Education: B.S. 1963, M.D. 1968. Address: Rural Route #2, Williamsport, Indiana 47993.

HART, MARGIE RUTH Occupation: Publisher; Candidate State Assembly, 61st. Education: Attended Greenville (South Carolina) Technical School, Barstow College. Address: 36832 Colby Avenue, Barstow, California 92311.

HARTIGAN, MARYELLEN K Occupation: Public Relations Staff Member, Senior Sales Promotion Representative. Education: B.S. Journalism. Address: Clarendon Hills, Illinois 60514.

HARTING, JAMES J Occupation: President, Health Resources. Education: B.A. 1965, M.S.W. 1969. Address: 34 Windsor Drive, Belleville, Illinois 62223.

HARTJE, ROBERT GEORGE Occupation: Professor of History, Director of American Studies. Education: B.A., M.A., Ph.D, Vanderbilt University. Address: 2140 Saint Paris Pike, Springfield, Ohio 45504.

HARTMAN, NANCY L Occupation: Medical Doctor. Education: M.D., M.S., B.A., A.A. Address: Post Office Box 98, Roslyn, New York 11576.

HARTMAN, RONALD J Occupation: Pharmacist, Pharmacy Owner. Education: B.S.Ph. Address: 503 1st Avenue, South East, Mapleton, Minnesota 56065.

HARTMAN, SHIRLEY A Occupation: President, Richmond Children's Theatre, Inc.; Vice President,

Home Meals Delivery; Trustee, First United Methodist Church, Richmond, Kentucky. Address: Route 2, Box 104, Richmond, Kentucky 40475.

HARTZOG, CHERYL DELK Occupation: Animal Care Specialist, Graphologist, Genealogist, Notary Public for South Carolina. Education: American Institute of Banking Basic Certificate, 1972; Firefighting Technology Certificate, 42-Hour Phase I, 1975; Certified Graphologist, 1980; North American Student Animal Science Association Certificate, Animal Care Specialist/Veterinarian Assistant; Radiological Monitoring Certificate; Additional Studies. Address: 120 Old Salem Road, Post Office Box 127, Hilda, South Carolina 29813.

HARTZOG, DANIEL EDWARD Occupation: Construction Project Manager. Education: Drafting I Certificate; Teachers Certificate; Jobsite Supervision Certificate; Construction Motivation Seminar Certificate, Human Reltions/Construction Personnel Management; 42-Hour Phase I Certificate; Multimedia System Instruction First Aid to the Injured Certificate; Radiological Monitoring Certificate. Address: Post Office Box 127, Hilda, South Carolina 29813.

HASNER, ROLF KAARE Occupation: Food Equipment Manufacturing Company Executive. Education: Graduate, Norwegian Military Academy, 1939; M.B.A., University of Chicago, 1947. Address: Bobolink Lane, Greenwich, Connecticut 06930.

HASSENGER, ROBERT LEO Occupation: College Professor/Writer. Education: B.A., University of Notre Dame; Ph.D., University of Chicago. Address: 186 Spring Street, Saratoga Springs, New York 12866.

HATAJACK, FRANK JOSEPH Occupation: Commercial Diver/Welder. Education: B.S. Geological Engineering, Michigan Technological University. Address: 78 Schill Avenue, Kenner, Louisiana 70065.

HATCHER, CHARLES ROSS JR Occupation: Cardiac Surgeon, Director. Education: B.S. magna cum laude, M.D. cum laude. Address: 1105 Lullwater Road, Atlanta, Georgia 30307.

HATFIELD, CORDELIA M Occupation: Legal Assistant. Address: 2521 Old Lake Shore Drive, St. Joseph, Michigan 49085.

HATTIKUDUR, UMESH RATNAKAR Occupation: Senior Research Engineer, Dupont Company. Education: Ph.D., Northwestern University, Evanston, Illinois. Address: 307 Windsor Road, Greenville, North Carolina 27834.

HATTON, BARBARA R Occupation: Educator. Education: B.S., M.A., M.E.A., Ph.D. Address: 1855 Wallace Road, Atlanta, Georgia 30331.

HAUCK, RICHARD HENRY Occupation: Chemist, Physics Instructor, U.S.-N.O.C.C. Education: B.Sc.Ed., M.Ed. Address: 112 South Market Street, Mechanicsburg, Pennsylvania 17055.

HAUER, ANN Occupation: Educator. Education: Master's Degree Elementary Education Administration. Address: 2600 Mercury Lane, Bismarck, North Dakota 58501.

HAUGHT, ALMA JENNINGS Occupation: Clerk of Superior Court, Jury Commissioner Probate Registrar and Court Administrator, Arizona. Education: Northern Arizona University, 1946-1948; Arizona State University, 1948-49. Address: 810 West Dewey, Coolidge, Arizona 85228.

HAUKENESS, HELEN Occupation: Short Story Writer, Editor. Education: A.B. English. Address: 100 Bank Street, New York, New York 10014.

HAULSEE, ANNE LOUISE Occupation: Administrative Director, The Executive Club Development Group; Career Effectiveness Consultant.

Education: M.A. Sociology, West Virginia University; B.A. Sociology, Roanoke College. Address: 205 Yoakum Parkway, #1511, Alexandria, Virginia 22304.

HAUSER, MARIANNE Occupation: Writer and Lecturer. Education: M.A., Sorbonne, Paris. Address: 2 Washington Square Village, #13M, New York, New York 10012.

HAUSMANN, WERNER KARL Occupation: Director of Quality Assurance. Education: M.S. Chemical Engineering, D.Sc. Chemistry. Address: 4610 Sandringham Drive, Columbus, Ohio 43220.

HAVASI, GEORGE Occupation: Anesthesiologist. Education: M.D. Address: Post Office Box 50060, Amarillo, Texas 79159.

HAVERLAND, ELOISE K Occupation: Management Development Representative. Education: B.A., University of Rhode Island; M.A., University of Chicago. Address: 338 North Benton, Palatine, Illinois 60067.

HAWES, EVANS C Occupation: Environmental Consultant. Education: B.S., University of Montana; M.S., Yale University. Address: 3 Olde Town Way, Post Office Box 326, Newbury, Maryland 01950.

HAWK, ROBERT STEVEN Occupation: Library Administrator, Akron-Summit County Public Library. Education: B.S., Wright State University; M.S.L.S., University of Kentucky. Address: 1643 Tanglewood Drive, Akron, Ohio 44313.

HAWKINS, JASPER STILLWELL Occupation: Architect and Land Planner, Phoenix, Arizona. Education: Bachelor of Architecture, U.S.C, 1955. Address: 5332 North 24th Street, Phoenix, Arizona 85016.

HAWKINS, JOSEPH ELMER JR Occupation: Professor Emeritus, Otorhinolaryngology, Kresge Hearing Research Institute, University of Michigan Medical School. Education: A.B., Baylor University; Ph.D., Harvard University; B.A., M.A., D.Sc., Oxford University. Address: 4004 East Joy Road, Ann Arbor, Michigan 48105.

HAY, BETTY JO Occupation: Full Time Volunteer, Mental Health Association and Education. Education: B.A., S.M.U. Address: 7236 Lupton Circle, Dallas, Texas 75225.

HAY, BEVERLY REED Occupation: Assistant Professor, Voice; Professional Singer, Soprano. Education: B.A., M.M., University of South Carolina; D.M. (in progress), Indiana University. Address: 734 Watson Street, Memphis, Tennessee 38111.

HAY, ROBERT PETTUS Occupation: University Professor of History, Marquette University. Education: B.S., Middle Tennesse State University, 1962; Ph.D., University of Kentucky, 1967. Address: 2146 Laura Lane, Waukesha, Wisconsin 53186.

HAY, WILLIAM WINN Occupation: Director, University of Colorado Museum. Education: B.S., S.M.U., 1955; M.S., Illinois, 1958; Ph.D., Stanford University, 1960. Address: 2045 Windcliff Estes Park, Boulder, Colorado 80517-0783.

HAYES, GWENDOLYN D Occupation: Cosmetogist, Make-up Artist; Modeling Teacher. Education: High School Diploma; Attended Cape Fear Beauty Institute. Address: 7041 Media Drive, Fayetteville, North Carolina 28304.

HAYES, J T Occupation: Traffic Accident Reconstruction Specialist; New Mexico State Police Officer. Education: University of New Mexico Engineering Student. Address: 7025 Prairie Court, North East, Albuquerque, New Mexico 87109.

HAYES, JACK Occupation: Associate Professor, Texas Tech Medical School. Education: Ph.D.,

University of Texas at Houston. Address: 2801 19th Street, Lubbock, Texas 79410.

HAYES, JOSEPH Occupation: Composer-Teacher. Education: Bachelor of Music in Composition. Address: 17160 Kentucky, Detroit, Michigan 48221.

HAYES, MARTHA B Occupation: Cosmetologist Instructor. Address: Post Office Box 0844, Fayetteville, North Carolina 28302.

HAYES, NANCY DIANE Occupation: Student. Education: B.S. Agricultural Economics (in progress), Texas A&M University . Address: 811 Itasca, Plainview, Texas 79072.

HAYNES, MARION ELVIN Occupation: Author, Trainer, Consultant. Education: B.S., Arizona State University; M.B.A., New York University. Address: 5223 Imogene Street, Houston, Texas 77096.

HAYREH, SOHAN S Occupation: Professor of Ophthalmology, University of Iowa Hospitals and Clinics. Education: M.D., Ph.D., F.R.C.S. (Edin.), F.R.C.S. (Eng.). Address: 600 River Street, Iowa City, Iowa 52240.

HEACOX, JOHN L Occupation: Teacher; Coorinator Distributive Education. Education: B.S. Education, Master's Degree in Marketing, Additional Studies. Address: 115 Linda Drive, Sikeston, Missouri 63801.

HEAD, GEORGE L Occupation: Safety Educator, Risk Management. Education: Ph.D. Applied Economics, University of Pennsylvania. Address: 361 Barker Circle, West Chester, Pennsylvania 19380.

HEAD, WILLIAM IVERSON SR Occupation: Superintendent Acetate Yarn Department, Chemicals Division, Eastman Kodak. Education: B.S. Textile Engineering, Georgia Institute of Technology, 1950. Address: 2026 Bruce Street, Kingsport, Tennesee 37664.

HEALY, JOHN J Occupation: Senior Staff Economist, General Motors Corporation. Education: B.A. 1966, M.B.A. 1968, St. John's University. Address: 30-12 44 Street, Long Island City, New York 11103.

HEAPS, RICHARD A Occupation: Psychologist, Professor, Education Psychology. Education: B.S., M.A., Ph.D. Psychology. Address: 688 South 630 East, Orem, Utah 84058.

HEARD, DOLAN Occupation: U.S. Air Force Management Consultant. Education: B.S. Sociology, B.S. Criminology. Address: 3321 Brookwood Drive, Montgomery, Alabama 36116.

HEATH, JEFFREY A Occupation: General Manager, Executive Search. Education: M.B.A. Finance, Pace University, 1978; B.S. Psychology, Manhattan College, 1975. Address: 9 Old Millwood Road, Chappaqua, New York 10514.

HEATHERLY, JAMES P Occupation: Business Systems Manager. Education: B.A. English, M.B.A. Marketing, DePaul University. Address: 16527 Craig Drive, Oak Forest, Illinois 60752.

HEBALD, CAROL Occupation: Writer, Professor. Education: M.F.A., University of Iowa, 1971; B.A., City College of CUNY, 1969. Address: EE105 Bristol Terrace, Lawrence, Kansas 66044.

HEBBEN, NANCY Occupation: Clinical Neoropsychologist/Psychologist. Education: A.A., B.A., M.A., Ph.D., Clinical Psychology. Address: 93 Longwood Avenue, Brookline, Maryland 02146.

HECHT, CONRAD G Occupation: Director of Special Education. Education: Mus.B., Mus.M. Address: 16 Lindron Avenue, Smithtown, New York 11787.

HECK, MELVIN RALPH Occupation: State Government Executive, North Dakota. Education: B.A., M.A., M.B.A., Ph.D. Address: 300 Second Street, Northeast, Mandan, North Dakota 58554.

HECKART, ROBERT H Occupation: Clergyman, Lecturer, Educator, Author. Education: Th.B., B.A., M.A., B.D., Th.M., D.D. Address: 2022 Condor Street, Colorado Springs, Colorado 80909.

HECKMAN, JOHN J JR Occupation: Chairman, John Heckman Enterprises, Inc. Education: M.B.A., Chicago University. Address: Post Office Box 15577, Lakewood, Colorado 80215.

HEDAHL, GORDEN O Occupation: University Theatre Educator, Department of Theatre, University of Wisconsin-Whitewater. Education: B.S. 1968, M.A. 1972, University of North Dakota; Ph.D., University of Minnesota, 1980. Address: 679 Walton Drive, Whitewater, Wisconsin 53190.

HEDBERG, FLOYD C Occupation: Chairman, Department of Music, Washburn University. Education: B.M., Washburn University; M.M.Ed., University of Kansas; Ed.D., University of Northern Colorado. Address: 3111 Munson, Topeka, Kansas 66604.

HEDGLEY, DAVID R JR Occupation: Research Mathematician. Education: B.S., M.S.: Biology/Chemistry, Mathematics. Address: Post Office Box 1674, Lancaster, California 93539.

HEDTKE, DELPHINE L Occupation: Educator, Author, LaHaute Couture and Theatre Costume Designer and Speaker. Education: B.S., Master's Degree, Ph.D. Address: 1661 Western Avenue, North, Saint Paul, Minnesota 55117.

HEESELER, EDGAR CARLTON Occupation: Investment Banker-Public Finance. Education: B.S.C. in Finance, Master of Business Administration Finance, Hofstra University. Address: 2225 Jones Avenue, Wantagh, New York 11793.

HEGINBOTHAM, ERLAND HOWARD Occupation: United States Senior Professional Staff. Education: Bachelor of Arts in Economics. Address: 8502 Wilkesboro Lane, Potomac, Maryland 20854.

HEHL, LAMBERT Occupation: Circuit Judge. Education: J.D. Degree, Chase College of Law, Northern Kentucky University, 1952. Address: 46 Madonna Drive, Fort Thomas, Kentucky 41075.

HEICKLEN, JULIAN P Occupation: Chemist. Education: B.Ch.E., Cornell University, 1954; Ph.D., University of Rochester, 1958. Address: 2008 Park Forest Avenue, State College, Pennsylvania 16801.

HEIER, DOROTHY R Occupation: Professor of Music. Education: B.S.M., M.M., Ed.D. Address: 680 Ramapo Valley Road, Oakland, New Jersey 07436.

HEILEMAN, JOHN P Occupation: Physician. Education: B.S., Arizona State University, 1951; M.D., Loyola University, 1955. Address: 5449 Calle Del Medio, Phoenix, Arizona 85018.

HEILIG, MARGARET C Occupation: Director of Health Services, Delaware County Community College. Education: B.A., M.S.W., A.A.S. Nursing, R.N. Address: 605 Mason Avenue, Drexel Hill, Pennsylvania 19026.

HEIM, WERNER G Occupation: Professor of Biology, The Colorado College. Education: Ph.D. 1954, M.A. 1952, B.A. 1950, University of California. Address: 1010 Jupiter Drive, Colorado Springs, Colorado 80906.

HEIMERICKS, GARY W Occupation: Director, Division of Finance, Department of Social Services. Education: B.S. in Government, 1973; Masters in Public Administration, 1977. Address: Route 2, Box 27, Holts Summit, Missouri 65043.

HEIMLICH, HENRY JAY Occupation: Professor Advanced Clinical Sciences and Director of The

Heimlich Institute. Education: M.D. Address: 17 Elmhurst Place, Cincinnati, Ohio 45208.

HEIN, MARGARET A Occupation: Vice President Compliance, Trust and Special Credits, Alaska Statebank. Education: B.A., University of Illinois Chicago, 1974; J.D., University of Puget Sound, 1977. Address: 1500 Demeure Place, Anchorage, Alaska 99508.

HEINEN, JAMES A Occupation: Professor of Electrical Engineering and Computer Science. Education: B.E.E. 1964, M.S. 1967, Ph.D. 1969, Marquette University. Address: 820 Menomonee River Parkway, Wauwatosa, Wisconsin 53213.

HEINLEN, DAN L Occupation: Director of Alumni Affairs. Education: B.S. Social Welfare, The Ohio State University, 1960. Address: 2981 East Powell Road,, Westerville, Ohio 43081.

HEINZE, RUTH-INGE Occupation: Research Associate. Education: Ph.D. 1974, M.A. 1971, B.A. 1969, University of California-Berkeley. Address: 2321 Russell #3A, Berkeley, California 94705.

HEIRMAN, DONALD N Occupation: Electrical Engineer Specializing in Electromagnetic Compatibility. Education: Bachelor and Master of Science, Electrical Engineering. Address: 143 Jumping Brook Road, Lincroft, New Jersey 07738.

HEISE, GEORGE A Occupation: Professor of Psychology, Indiana University. Education: Ph.D., Harvard University, 1952; B.A., Swarthmore College, 1944. Address: 2369 Browncliff, Bloomington, Indiana 47401.

HEIST, JOHN ARTHUR Occupation: Vice President Human Resourcs. Education: B.S. Economics, M.A. Education Administration. Address: 26333 North Hickory Road, Countryside Lake, Mundelein, Illinois 60060.

HEITMAN, BETTY G Occupation: Co-Chairman, Republican National Committee. Education: B.S., Texas Woman's University, 1949. Address: 655 Waverly Drive, Baton Rouge, Louisiana 70806.

HEIZER, WILLIAM DAVID Occupation: Professor of Medicine, University of North Carolina. Education: B.A., M.D. Address: Route 4, Box 532, Chapel Hill, North Carolina 27514.

HELFAND, ABRAHAM Occupation: Education/ Administrator. Education: B.B.A., M.A., Professional Diploma. Address: 2399 Maple Street, Seaford, New York 11783.

HELFET, STEPHEN CLARK Occupation: Biologist. Education: M.S. Biology 1978, B.S. Fish and Wildlife Biology 1976. Address: 6225 Hott Springs Drive, Arlington, Texas 76017.

HELFFERICH, FRIEDRICH G Occupation: Professor of Chemical Engineering, Pennsylvania State University. Education: Dipl. Chem. 1949, 1952; Dr. rer. nat. 1955. Address: 1845 Woodledge Drive, State College, Pennsylvania 16803.

HELFORD, PAUL QUINN Occupation: Marketing and Programming Director. Education: B.A.E., University of Illinois; M.A., Northeastern Illinois University. Address: 9410 Madison, Eugene, Oregon 97402.

HELGANZ, BEVERLY B Occupation: Manager. Education: A.A., B.A. Address: Post Office Box 1825, Jacksonville, Florida 32201.

HELLER, JANET RUTH Occupation: Instructor of English. Education: B.A. (Honors), M.A., University of Wisconsin. Address: 701 North Eddy Street, Sandwich, Illinois 60548.

HELM, HARRY C Education: B.A., E.W.U.; Postgraduate Studies, University of Washington.

Address: North 2121 Hemlock, Spokane, Washington 99205.

HELMKER, JUDITH A Occupation: Teacher/ Author. Education: B.S.Ed. 1960, M.A. 1968, Ed.S. 1970. Address: 2300 Wellington Drive, Owosso, Michigan 48867.

HELWEG, ARTHUR WESLEY Occupation: Associate Professor, Western Michigan University. Education: B.S., M.A., Ph.D. Address: 810 Weaver Avenue, Kalamazoo, Michigan 49007.

HENDEE, WILLIAM R Occupation: Professor and Chairman, Department of Radiology, University of Colorado Health Sciences Center. Education: Ph.D., University of Texas, 1962. Address: 4248 North 109th Road, Lafayette, Colorado 80026.

HENDERSON, CAROL MORNER Occupation: Associate Dean/Professor College of Nursing, University of Southern Alabama. Education: B.S.N., M.A., Ed.D. Address: 2904 Starlit Drive West, Mobile, Alabama 36609.

HENDERSON, CHARLES DELANO Occupation: Assistant Principal. Education: B.S., M.S. Address: 4208 Charleston Street, Houston, Texas 77021.

HENDERSON, EDGAR C Occupation: Napa County Superintendent of Schools. Education: B.A. Speech/English, M.A. Educational Administration. Address: 269 Monte Vista Drive, Napa, California 94558.

HENDERSON, ELIZABETH BAKER Occupation: Handweaver and Potter, Handbuilt Ceramics. Education: B.A., Michigan State University, 1933; A.M., University of Chicago, 1942. Address: Old Road to Bloomfield, Newark, New Jersey 07104.

HENDERSON, GLENN V JR Occupation: Professor. Education: B.B.A., M.B.A., D.B.A. Address: 27 Highview Circle, Denton, Texas 76205.

HENDERSON, THOMAS ASBURY Occupation: Band and Orchestra Director. Education: B.S., Master's Degree, Music Education. Address: 98 20 Westfield Road, Birmingham, Alabama 35217.

HENDLER, NELSON HOWARD Occupation: Doctor of Medicine, Clinical Director of Mensana Clinic. Education: B.A., Princeton University; M.D., M.S., University of Maryland School of Medicine. Address: 5 Grenadier Court, Owings Mills, Maryland 21117.

HENDRICK, HAL W Occupation: Chairman, Human Factors Department. Education: Ph.D., Purdue University, 1966; M.S., Purdue University, 1961; B.A., Ohio Wesleyan University, 1955. Address: 831 East Ocean Avenue, Long Beach, California 90801.

HENDRICKS, NATHANIEL Occupation: Real Estate Broker. Education: M.A., Columbia University. Address: 325 State Street, Brooklyn, New York 11217.

HENDRICKSON, CLIFFORD C JR Occupation: Superintendent of Schools. Education: B.S., West Chester State University; M.Ed., Ed.D., Temple University. Address: 235 Beatrice Avenue, Hatboro, Pennsylvania 19040.

HENDRICKSON, NOREJANE JOHNSTON Occupation: Professor of Home and Family. Education: B.Sc., Mansfield State University; M.A. with distinction, Michigan State University; Ph.D., Ohio State University. Address: 1121 Mercer Drive, Tallahassee, Florida 32312.

HENDRIX, ALBERT RANDEL Occupation: Director-North Mississippi Retardation Center. Education: B.S, M.S., University of Mississippi; Doctorate, University of Southern Mississippi. Address: Route 4, Box 350, Oxford, Mississippi 38655.

HENISCH, HEINZ K Occupation: Professor of

Physics, Professor of the History of Photography. Education: B.Sc., Ph.D., D.Sc. Address: 346 West Hillcrest Avenue, State College, Pennsylvania 16803.

HENKEN, BERNARD SAMUEL Occupation: Clinical and School Psychologist. Education: B.S., Harvard University; M.S., Purdue University, D.S., Calvin Coolidge College. Address: 118 Waverly Avenue, Melrose, Massachusetts 02176.

HENLEY, GORDON B JR Occupation: Zoo Director, Ellen Trout Zoo. Education: B.S., M.S., Biology. Address: Post Office Drawer 190, Lufkin, Texas 75902-0190.

HENNING, JAMES SCOTT Occupation: Physician, Southern California Permanente Medical Group. Education: A.B. Liberal Arts, Gonzaga University, 1966; Attended University of California, Los Angeles, 1967-68; M.S. Clinical Psychology, University of California at Los Angeles, 1970; Ph.D. Clinical Psychology, University of Wisconsin, Milwaukee, 1974; Certification Series, Mental Health Administration, University of Southern California, Department of Public Health, 1981-. Address: Southern California Permanente Medical Group, Downey, California 90242.

HENRY, KAREN HAWLEY Occupation: Attorney, Partner, Littler, Mendelson, Fastiff, and Tichy. Education: B.S., M.S., J.D. Address: Post Office Box 379, Diablo, California 94528.

HENRY, MARVIN A Occupation: Chairman, Department of Secondary Education, Indiana State University. Education: B.S., M.S., Ed.D. Address: 21 Crescent Drive, Terre Haute, Indiana 47802.

HENRY, QUINN Occupation: Part-time Instructor, Dalton Junior College. Education: B.S.A., M.Ed. Address: 3060 Underwood Road, Northeast, Dalton, Georgia 30720.

HENSLER, MARY E Occupation: Civic Leader. Education: B.A., Studies toward M.A. Address: 605 Western Avenue, Juliet, Illinois 60435.

HENZL, ELIZABETH MARY Occupation: Adult Religious Education. Education: B.A. Education, M.A. Education, Ed.D., M.A. Religious Studies. Address: West 2911 Fort Wright Drive, Spokane, Washington 99207.

HEPLER, MERLIN JUDSON JR Occupation: Associate Broker, Realty World, Apex Realty. Education: B.S. General Business, University of Idaho. Address: Route 1, Box 119, Troy, Idaho 83871.

HEPPENHEIMER, THOMAS A Occupation: Author. Education: Ph.D. Aerospace Engineering, University of Michigan, 1972. Address: 11040 Blue Allium Avenue, Fountain Valley, California 92708.

HEPWORTH, JANICE C Occupation: Director Special Programs and Continuing Education, Associate Research Professor. Education: B.A., University of Pennsylvania; M.A., Ph.D., University of Colorado. Address: 471 South Garfield Street, Denver, Colorado 80209.

HERD, RICHARD M Occupation: Oral Maxillofacial Surgeon. Education: A.B. Chemistry, D.D.S. Address: 6825 Creekside Lane, Indianapolis, Indiana 46220.

HERMAN, BARBARA RITA Occupation: Advertising Executive. Education: A.B., Syracuse University; M.B.A., Pace University. Address: 52 Maple Avenue, South, Westport, Connecticut 06880.

HERMAN, CLARK S Occupation: Labor Relations Consultant. Education: B.S. Industrial Relations, Cornell University, 1945; J.D., Seton Hall. Address: 19 Bellevue Avenue, Rumson, New Jersey 04460.

HERMAN, JOHN ALLEN Occupation: President, Industrial Business Association of Minnesota. Education: Studies in Journalism, University of Minnesota. Address: 6192 65th Street, South, Cottage Grove, Minnesota 55016.

HERMAN, MELVIN J Occupation: Physician. Education: M.D. Address: 16 Fir Drive, Great Neck, New York 11024.

HERNANDEZ, ERNEST JR Occupation: Computer Consultant and Publisher of Computer Books. Education: A.A. Psychology, B.A. Sociology, M.A. Sociology, Ph.D. Sociology. Address: 22386 Sunlight Creek, El Toro, California 92630.

HERNANDEZ, FONT LUZ SOFIA Occupation: Professional Singer. Education: University Studies. Address: Cond. Doral Plaza, Apartment 17 H, Guaynato, Puerto Rico 00657.

HERNDON, ANN SCOTT Occupation: Staff Accountant with Price Waterhouse. Education: B.S. Accounting and Insurance. Address: 4600 Jackson Boulevard, #113, Columbia, South Carolina 29209.

HEROUX, EVA D Occupation: Director of Development, Rhode Island Hospital. Education: A.S.B.A., B.S.B.A., M.B.A. Address: 156 Grove Street, Woonsocket, Rhode Island 02895.

HERRON, ROBERT LANE Occupation: Author, Books and Articles. Education: Attended College and Night Courses. Address: 709 Madison Avenue, Northeast, Albuquerque, New Mexico 87110.

HERSHBERGER, CHARLES L Occupation: Molecular Biologist, Eli Lilly and Company. Education: B.S. Chemistry, Ph.D. Biochemistry. Address: Rural Route 1, Box 343, New Palestine, Indiana 46163.

HERSHEY, DANIEL Occupation: Gerontologist and Professor of Chemical Engineering. Education: B.S., M.S., Ph.D. Address: 726 Lafayette Avenue, Cincinnati, Ohio 45220.

HERSHEY, ROBERT LEWIS Occupation: Consulting Engineer/Management Consultant. Education: Ph.D. Engineering, Catholic University of America, 1973. Address: 1255 New Hampshire Avenue, Northwest, Washington, D.C. 20036.

HERTING, DAVID C Occupation: Nutritional Biochemist, Research/Development. Education: B.S. Chemistry, M.S., Ph.D. Biochemistry. Address: 2778 Nichols Street, Spencerport, New York 14559.

HERZER, HARRY B III Occupation: Aerospace Education Specialist/Adjunct Associate Professor. Education: A.B., B.S., M.S., Ed.D. Address: 1905 Taylor Avenue, Fort Washington, Maryland 20744.

HESBURGH, THEODORE MARTIN Occupation: President, University of Notre Dame. Education: Ph.B., Gregorian University, Rome; S.T.L., S.T.D., Catholic University of America. Address: University of Notre Dame, Notre Dame, Indiana 46556.

HESKETH, HOWARD E Occupation: Professor, Consultant. Education: B.S., M.S., Ph.D. Chemical Engineering. Address: Route 4, Carbondale, Illinois 62901.

HESSELGRAVE, PAUL ARMOUR Occupation: Research Chemist. Education: B.S. Chemistry. Address: 2462 Gallup Drive, Santa Clara, California 95051.

HESTER, JAMES FRANCIS JR Occupation: Fastener Manufacturing Company Executive. Education: B.S. Commerce, De Paul University, 1951. Address: 1701 Habberton Street, Park Ridge, Illinois 60068.

HEYMAN, STEVEN RONALD Occupation: Clinical Psychologist. Education: B.A., M.A., Ph.D. Address: 1910 Garfield, Laramie, Wyoming 82070.

HEYN, ANTON NICOLAAS JOHANNES Occupation: Professor Emeritus, Louisiana State University Research Science. Education: Bachelor of Science, Master of Science, Ph.D., Utrecht University, Netherlands, 1931. Address: 2263 Killdeerstreet, New Orleans, Louisiana 70122.

HEYWARD, ADRIENNE V Occupation: Associate Staff Manager. Education: Bachelor of Arts, Bethune-Cookman College. Address: 4540 Strangford Avenue, Charlotte, North Carolina 28215.

HEYWOOD, PHOEBE ANN GREGORY Occupation: Classroom Teacher/Music Director, Director of Church Music, Singer. Education: B.A. Sociology, Wheaton College, 1960; M.A. Education 1969, M.A. Music 1978, California State University at Los Angeles. Address: 1340 North Citrus Avenue, Los Angeles, California 90625.

HIATT, DIANA BUELL Occupation: Associate Professor. Education: Ed.D., M.S., B.S. Address: 18403 Wakecrest Drive, Malibu, California 90265.

HIBBARD, JUDITH HOFFMAN Occupation: Assistant Professor. Education: B.S. 1974, M.P.H. 1975, University of California-Los Angeles; Dr.P.H., University of California-Berkeley, 1982. Address: 1867 Fircrest Drive, Eugene, Oregon 97403.

HIBBE, DOUGLAS WARREN Occupation: Legislative Counsel, National Fraternal Congress of America. Education: B.S. 1948, J.D. 1951, New York University. Address: 130 South Ellsworth, Naperville, Illinois 60540.

HICHENS, WALTER W Occupation: State Senator. Education: Prep School, Agricultural and Technical Institute. Address: 424 State Road, Eliot, Maine 03903.

HICKS, JEFFREY LOUIS Occupation: Psychologist. Education: B.A. 1967, M.A. 1969, Ph.D. 1972, University of Oregon. Address: 1707 Sweetbriar Lane, Eugene, Oregon 97405.

HIEB, MARIANNE Occupation: Art Therapist. Education: B.A., M.F.A. Address: 14 Baily Road, Yeadon, Pennsylvania 19050.

HIGDON, BETTINA PEARSON Occupation: Retired Director, Cullman County Public Library Region. Education: A.B. 1941, M.A. 1960, Alabama College; Double A, University of Alabama-Tuscaloosa, 1971. Address: Post Office Box 325, Cullman, Alabama 35056-0325.

HIGDON, JOHN FRANCIS Occupation: Clinical Psychologist. Education: B.S., M.A., Ph.D. Address: 1952-B Waterfront Drive, North, Columbia, Missouri 65202.

HIGGINBOTHAM, SARA P Occupation: Director, Education Department. Education: B.S. Nursing, M.S. Personnel Counseling. Address: Route 2, Box 155, Gadsden, Alabama 35903.

HIGBY, WAYNE Occupation: Artist-Professor of Ceramic Art. Education: B.F.A., University of Colorado; M.F.A., University of Michigan. Address: R.D. #1, Box 261, Alfred Station, New York 14803.

HIGLE, J ALEXANDER Occupation: Transportation Analyst. Education: B.S., M.S., M.P.A. Address: Box 49, R.D. #1, Valley Falls Road, Melrose, New York 12121.

HILBERRY, CONRAD A Occupation: Teacher and Writer. Education: B.A., Oberlin College, 1949; Ph.D., University of Wisconsin, 1954. Address: 1601 Grand Avenue, Kalamazoo, Michigan 49007.

HILDEBRAND, VERNA LEE Occupation: Professor, Researcher, Writer. Education: Ph.D., Texas Woman's University; B.S., M.S., Kansas State University. Address: 308 Michigan #8, East Lansing, Michigan 48823.

HILDEBRANDT, DARLENE MYERS Occupation: Information Scientist. Education: M.A. Library and Information Science. Address: 32606 7th Avenue, Southwest, Federal Way, Washington 98023.

HILFERTY, JOANNE K Occupation: Deputy Commissioner, Quality Assurance and Finance Division. Education: A.B., Brown University; M.P.A., Woodrow Wilson School, Princeton University. Address: 375 Washington Avenue, Albany, New York 12206.

HILFSTEIN, ERNA Occupation: Historian of Science, Educator. Education: B.A., M.A., Ph.D. Address: 1523 Dwight Place, Bronx, New York 10465.

HILL, GEOFFREY MICHAEL Occupation: Psychotherapist, Lecturer, Writer. Education: A.A., B.A., M.A. Address: 2513 South Deegan Drive, Santa Ana, California 92704.

HILL, JAMES L Occupation: Chairman, Division of Arts and Sciences. Education: B.S., M.A., Ph.D. Address: 2408 Greenmount Drive, Albany, Georgia 331705.

HILL, LOWELL D Occupation: L. J. Norton Professor of Marketing. Education: B.S. Agricultural Education, Iowa State University, 1951; M.S. Agricultural Economics, Michigan State University, 1961; Ph.D. Agricultural Economics, Michigan State University, 1963. Address: 1002 Silver, Urbana, Illinos 61801.

HILL, STEPHEN LAURENCE Occupation: Student. Education: High School Diploma. Address: 2601 Homewood Avenue, Florence, South Carolina 29501.

HILL, THOMAS BOWEN JR Occupation: Attorney-at-Law. Education: A.B., LL.B., LL.D (honorary). Address: 1831 Hillwood Drive, Montgomery, Alabama 36101.

HILL, TOMMIE ANN Occupation: Assistant Professor of Mathematics. Education: B.A. Mathematics, M.S., Ed.D. Mathematics Education. Address: 1106 Carlton Street, Clearwater, Florida 33515.

HILLEBRANDT, INA S Occupation: President, Hillebrandt Consultants, Inc. Education: A.B. Anthropology. Address: 64 Musket Ridge Road, Wilton, Connecticut 06897.

HILTON, HART DALE Occupation: Vice President and General Manager, Connell and Chaffin Commercial Interiors. Education: B.S. Engineering, University of Southern California; Diploma International Relations. Address: 1 South Orange Grove Boulevard, #6, Pasadena, California 91105.

HINDIN, RUSSELL Occupation: Managing Director, Investment Banking Firm. Education: B.S. International Finance, University of Southern California. Address: 8530 Wilshire Boulevard, Beverly Hills, California 90211.

HINDMAN, TIMOTHY W Occupation: Student. Education: B.S. in Mechanical Engineering (in progress). Address: HC 70, Box 45, Hay Springs, Nebraska 69347.

HINDS, SALLIE A Occupation: Sims Township Treasurer. Education: College Studies. Address: 767 Crescent Drive, Point Lookout, Augres, Michigan 48703.

HINSON, DERL J Occupation: General Manager of 4-County Electric Power Association. Education: B.S. Agricultural Economics. Address: Chanticleer Apartments T-52, 1123 6th Street, North, Columbus, Mississippi 39701.

HINSON, PEGGY MILDRED Occupation: Educator. Education: B.S. Education, Auburn

University, 1958; Medical Administration and Supervision, Georgia State University, 1978. Address: 3312 Gail Drive, Columbus, Georgia 31907.

HIRAHARA, PATRICIA DIANE Occupation: Public Relations Agent, Japan Trade Center. Education: B.A., California State University-Fullerton. Address: 601 North Dwyer Drive, Anaheim, California 92801.

HIRSCHBERG, BESSE BRYNA Occupation: Social Worker/Consultant for Community Relations. Education: B.A. Address: 2 Stuyvesant Oval, New York City, New York 10009.

HISCOE, HELEN B Occupation: Professor, Michigan State University. Education: A.B., Vassar College; M.S., Brown University; Ph.D., University of California-Los Angeles. Address: 1817 Walnut Heights Drive, East Lansing, Michigan 48823.

HISSEM, FRANK T Occupation: President, Photographic Corporation Services. Education: B.S. Farm Operations. Address: 236 Van Scoyoc, Avilla, Indiana 46710.

HITCHCOCK, HUGH WILEY Occupation: Professor. Education: B.A., M.Mus., Ph.D. Address: 1192 Park Avenue, New York, New York 10128.

HITCHINS, DIDDY R M Occupation: University Professor, University of Alaska. Education: B.Sc. Social Sciences, M.A. Government, Ph.D. Government. Address: University of Alaska, Anchorage, Alaska 99508.

HOADLEY, WALTER E Occupation: Senior Research Fellow, Hoover Institution, University of California-Berkeley. Education: A.B. 1938, M.A. 1940, Ph.D. 1946, Economics. Address: c/o Bank of America, Room 4970, Post Office Box 37000, (Department #9996), San Francisco, California 94137.

HOARD, CHARLES MASON JR Occupation: District Business Manager, Continental Cablevision. Education: B.G.S., University of Kansas; M.A., The Ohio University. Address: 9124 MacArthur Court, Des Plaines, Illinois 60016.

HOARD, DONA Occupation: Managment Consultant. Education: A.B., Vassar College; M.P.A., University of Pittsburgh. Address: 5412 Proctor, Oakland, California 94618.

HOBACK, FLORENCE KUNST Occupation: Psychiatrist. Education: M.D. Address: 2658 3rd Avenue, Huntington, West Virginia 25702.

HOBBS, NILA A Occupation: Computer Systems Analyst. Education: B.S. Mathematics (high distinction), 1971; M.B.A., Colorado State University, 1973. Address: 1037 Parkview Drive, Fort Collins, Colorado 80525.

HOBSON, DONALD L Occupation: Judge of Recorder's Court. Education: B.S. History, Eastern Michigan University; M.A., Michigan State University; J.D., Detroit College of Law. Address: 2136 Bryanston Crescent, Detroit, Michigan 48207.

HOCHBERG, FREDERICK GEORGE Occupation: Accountant. Education: B.A., University of California-Los Angeles, 1937. Address: 6760 Hill Park Drive 505, Los Angeles, California 90068.

HOCHHAUSER, MARK Occupation: Psychologist, Education Coordinator. Education: B.A., M.S., Ph.D., University of Pittsburgh. Address: 3344 Scott Avenue North, Golden Valley, Minnesota 55422.

HOCKENBERRY, RONALD K Occupation: Teacher, Concert Pianist. Education: B.S., West Chester University; M.S., Pennsylvania State University. Address: 105 Runnymede Avenue, Wayne, Pennsylvania 19087.

HODGKIN, JOHN E Occupation: Physician. Education: B.S., M.D. Address: 1330 Crestmont Drive, Angwin, California 94508.

HOEFT, DONALD C Occupation: Elementary Principal. Education: B.S., Wisconsin State University-Oshkosh; M.S., University of Wisconsin-Madison. Address: 510 Bluff Avenue, Sheboygan, Wisconsin 53081.

HOEHN, MARGARET MAIER Occupation: Researcher, Parkinson's Disease; Neurologist. Education: B.A., M.D., F.R.C.P.S. (C); F.A.A.N., F.A.C.P. Address: 3535 Cherry Creek North Drive, Denver, Colorado 80209.

HOFF, GLORIA THELMA ALBUERNE Occupation: Associate Professor of Physics. Education: D.Sc., University of Havana, 1984; Ph.D., University of Chicago, 1965. Address: 5634 South Blackstone Avenue, Chicago, Illinois 60637.

HOFFER, ANITA P Occupation: Assistant Professor of Anatomy, Director of Research in Urology, Brigham and Women's Hospital. Education: B.A., Harvard University; M.S., Ph.D., Harvard Medical School. Address: 14 Welland Road, Brookline, Massachusetts 02146.

HOFFLEIT, E DORRIT Occupation: Astronomer. Education: A.B. 1928, M.A. 1932, Ph.D. 1938, Radcliffe College. Address: 255 Whitney Avenue, New Haven, Connecticut 06511.

HOFFMAN, BYRON JAY Occupation: Physician. Education: B.S., Duke University; M.D., Emory University. Address: 1148 Springdale Road, Northeast, Atlanta, Georgia 30306.

HOFFMAN, EDWARD ARNOLD Occupation: Pastor, Evangelist of Church of God. Education: High School Diploma. Address: Post Office Box 86, Reedley, California 93654.

HOFFMAN, GARY P Occupation: Engineering Supervisor. Education: B.S.A.E. Address: 173 South Estate Drive, Webster, New York 14580.

HOFFMAN, HOWARD TORRENS Occupation: Multi-Industry Executive. Education: B.S.E.E., M.S.E.E., Ph.D. Management Science. Address: 5545 Stresemann, San Diego, California 92122.

HOFFMAN, JANET LOUISE Occupation: Elementary Physical Education Teacher. Education: B.S. Elementary Education, Howard Payne University. Address: Post Office Box 245 Somerset, Texas 78069.

HOFFMAN, JEAN L Occupation: Retired. Education: M.S., Florida State University; A.B., Samford University. Address: 928 Hillcrest Avenue, Birmingham, Alabama 35235.

HOFFMAN, NANCY YANES Occupation: Medical Journalist, Essayist, Writer, Associate Professor of English. Education: B.S., M.A. Address: 77 Southern Parkway, Rochester, New York 14618.

HOFFMAN, ROBERT JOSEPH Occupation: Herbalist, Arch Priest. Education: Dr. Wholistic Therapy; Priest, Church of Antioch. Address: 380 Oak Spring Road, Paradise, California 95969.

HOFFNUNG, AUDREY S Occupation: Associate Professor. Education: B.A. cum laude, Brooklyn College, 1949; M.A., Columbia University Teacher's College, 1950; Ph.D., City University of New York, 1974. Address: 3282 Woodward Street, Oceanside, New York 11572.

HOGAN, JOSEPH T Occupation: Podiatrist. Education: B.A., D.P.M. Address: 118 Clifton Boulevard, Binghamton, New York 13903.

HOGAN, RICHARD MICHAEL Occupation: Priest (Catholic). Education: B.A., M.A., Ph.D. Address: 7301 Bass Lake Road, Crystal, Minnesota 55428.

HOGUE, MONTEZ Occupation: Insurance Consultant. Education: Studied Public Administration and Business. Address: 1138 East 229th Street Dr. S. 6C, Bronx, New York 10466.

HOKAMA, YOSHITSUGI Occupation: Professor of Pathology, Researcher-Teacher. Education: A.B., M.A., Ph.D., University of California-Los Angeles. Address: 274 Polohiwa Place, Honolulu, Hawaii 96817.

HOLBROOK, JAY MACK Occupation: Publisher/ Author. Education: B.S., M.A., M.A. Address: 57 Locust Street, Oxford, Massachusetts 01540.

HOLCOMB, LILLIAN P Occupation: Psychologist. Education: Ph.D., M.A.T., B.A. Address: Post Office Box 1797, Honolulu, Hawaii 96806.

HOLCOMBE, BILL MORGAN Occupation: Director, University of South Carolina-Salkehatchie/ Walterboro. Education: B.S., M.A., Ph.D. Address: 100 Hayne Street, Walterboro, South Carolina 29488.

HOLIAN, GAIL CONCA Occupation: Assistant Professor of English Literature. Education: B.A., Georgian Court College, 1970; M.A. English Literature, St. John's University, 1972. Address: 65 Washington Street, Red Bank, New Jersey 07701.

HOLLAND, JAMES R Occupation: Real Estate Executive. Education: B.F.A., Ohio University; Advanced Graduate Studies, University of Missouri School of Journalism. Address: 226 South Hamel Drive, Beverly Hills, California 90211.

HOLLAND, MARJORIE M Occupation: Assistant Professor of Biology. Education: Ph.D., University of Massachusetts-Amherst; Five-College Ph.D., 1977. Address: 112 Warren Street, New Rochelle, New York 10801.

HOLLINGER, MARY BEAN Occupation: Oceanographer. Education: B.S., Saint Mary's College of Maryland, 1971. Address: 3131 Bayside Road, Huntingtown, Maryland 20639.

HOLLINGSWORTH, PAUL M Occupation: Professor of Education and Chairman of Curriculum and Instruction Department. Education: B.S., M.A., Ed.D. Address: 1601 Byrd Drive, Sparks, Nevada 89431.

HOLLINSHEAD, ARIEL C Occupation: Professor, Department of Medicine, George Washington Medical Center. Education: Ph.D., D.Sc. Address: 3637 Van Ness Street, North West, Washington, D. C. 20008.

HOLLOWAY, ERNEST L Occupation: President, Langston University. Education: B.S., M.S., Ed.D. Address: Post Office Box 666, Langston, Oklahoma 73050.

HOLM, JAMES B Occupation: Manager, Human Resoures. Education: M.B.A. Address: 2720 Ross Avenue, Ammon, Idaho 83401.

HOLMBERG, BRANTON KIETH Occupation: Management and Organization Development Consultant. Education: B.A. 1962, M.Ed. 1964, Ed.D. 1970. Address: 910 Yew Street, Bellingham, Washington 98226.

HOLMGRAIN, FLOYD H JR Occupation: Executive Director, National Academy of Opticianry, Educational Organization for Opticians. Education: B.S., M.A., Ed.D. Educational Administration. Address: 12208 Lisborough Road, Mitchellville, Maryland 20715.

HOLTZ, ITSHAK J Occupation: Artist (Fine Art). Education: Attended Bezalel Art Academy (Jerusalem, Israel), Art Students League (New York City), and National Academy of Design (New York). Address: 66 Fort Washington Avenue, New York, New York 10032.

HONAMAN, NANCY Occupation: Registrar and Director of Continuing Education, Franklin and Marshall College. Education: A.B., Mt. Holyoke College; M.A., Pennsylvania State University. Address:

465 Hawthorne Drive, Lancaster, Pennsylvania 17603.

HONEA, FRANKLIN IVAN Occupation: Chemical Engineer, Fossil Energy Synthetic Fuels Process Research and Plants. Education: Ph.D., Ch.E., University of Denver, 1969; M.S.M.E., University of Southern California, 1962; B.S.M.E., University of California at Berkeley, 1955. Address: 2615 5th Avenue North, Grand Forks, North Dakota 58201.

HONG, HARRY C Occupation: Chairman and Professor of History and Political Science. Education: B.A., B.A., M.A., Ph.D. Address: 250-18th Avenue North East, Jamestown, North Dakota 58401.

HONIGS, DAVID EARL Occupation: Assistant Professor of Chemistry. Education: B.S. Chemistry, Kansas State University; Ph.D., Indiana University. Address: H-106, 18115 36th West, Lynnwood, Washington 98037.

HOOD, ROGER WILLIAM Occupation: Orthopaedic Surgeon. Education: B.A. Chemistry, Southern Illinois University; M.D., Loyola-Stritch School of Medicine. Address: 10248 Walmer, Overland Park, Kansas 66212.

HOOKS, E JAMES Occupation: Chairman Department of Theatre, Teaching Professor, University of Florida. Education: B.S. Education, M.A. Theatre, Ph.D. Theatre. Address: 752 Northwest 22 Street, Gainesville, Florida 32603.

HOOKS, JANET MONTGOMERY Occupation: Professor Emeritus, Economics, Eastern Illinois University. Education: B.A., Mount Holyoke College; M.A., Bryn Mawr College; Ph.D., University of Illinois. Address: 708 La Sell Drive, Champaign, Illinois 61820.

HOOPER, JERE MANN Occupation: Vice President, Trusthouse Forte, Inc. Education: B.A., Vanderbilt University, 1955. Address: 5141 Marlborough Drive, San Diego, California 92116.

HOOVER, LARRY ALLAN Occupation: Data Processing Management/Deputy Director. Education: A.A., B.S., M.S. Address: 801 Croydon Street, Sterling, Virginia 22170.

HOPE, DAVID M Occupation: Vice President, Financial Affairs, Southwestern Adventist College. Education: B.A.A., M.Ed. Address: 1207 Honeysuckle Drive, Keene, Texas 76059.

HOPFINGER, ANTON J Occupation: Director, Department Medicinal Chemistry. Education: B.S. Mathematics and Physics, Ph.D. Physical Chemistry. Address: 1780 Wilson Drive, Lake Forest, Illinois 60045.

HOPKINS, BARBARA P Occupation: Corporation President. Education: Associate of Arts, B.S. Botany, Graduate Work in Public Relations and Journalism. Address: Post Office Box 49813, Los Angeles, California 90049.

HOPKINS, JEAN HUMMER Occupation: Operating Room Supervisor. Education: B.S.N. Address: 8012 Bueno Vista Drive, West Jordan, Utah 84084.

HOPSTETTER, ROBERT A Occupation: Accountant. Education: B.S. Business Administration-Accounting. Address: 22 Lehman Street, Lebanon, Pennsylvania 17042.

HORAK, PENELOPE Occupation: Engineer, Consultant, President EFI. Education: B.S. Engineering Science, M.P.A. honors, M.P.H. honors. Address: Post Office Box 695, Winfield, Illinois 60190.

HORMELL, SIDNEY JAMES Occupation: Minister, Communications Consultant. Education: B.S., Ph.D., University of Illinois; B.D., Louisville Presbyterian. Address: 527-4 Pepeekeo Street, Honolulu, Hawaii 96825.

HORN, JOHN L Occupation: Psychologist, Professor. Education: B.A., M.A., Ph.D. Address: 196 South Corona Street, Denver, Colorado 80209.

HORN, JOHN STEPHEN Occupation: President, California State University-Long Beach. Education: A.B. with great distinction, M.P.A., Ph.D. Address: 3944 Pine Avenue, Long Beach, California 90807.

HORN, MARION J R Occupation: President-U.S. Mortgage and Trust Company. Education: B.S. Business and English. Address: 2964 Candlelight Way, Lexington, Kentucky 40502.

HOROVITZ, ISRAEL Occupation: Playwright. Education: Diploma, Royal Academy Dramatic Art; M.A., City University of New York. Address: 146 West 11th Street, New York, New York 10011.

HOROWITZ, LARRY LOWELL Occupation: Electrical Engineer. Education: S.B., S.M., Ph.D. Address: 244 Wood Street, Lexington, Massachusetts 02173.

HORTON, FRANK Occupation: U.S. Congressman. Education: B.A., Louisiana State University, 1941; LL.B., Cornell University Law School, 1947.

HORVÁTH, JOHN Occupation: Poet, Teacher. Education: B.A., George Peabody College of Vanderbilt University; M.A., Florida State University. Address: English Department, Purdue University, West Lafayette, Indiana 47907.

HORVATH, RALPH S Occupation: Professor of Electrical Engineering, Michigan Technical University. Education: Ph.D. Address: Route 1, Box 412A, Baltic, Michigan 49905.

HOSTLER, CHARLES WARREN Occupation: President, Pacific Southwest Capital Corporation. Education: A.A., B.A., M.A., M.A., Ph.D. Address: Post Office Box 9976, San Diego, California 92109.

HOULIHAN, KATHLEEN Occupation: Professor of Linguistics, University of Minnesota. Education: B.A. Highest Honors Spanish 1969, Ph.D. Linguistics 1975, The University of Texas-Austin. Address: 1209 Grand Avenue, Saint Paul, Minnesota 55105.

HOUSEL, JERRY WINTERS Occupation: Lawyer. Education: B.A., University of Wyoming, 1935; J.D., 1936; Ph.D., American University, 1941. Address: 1203 Sheridan Avenue, Cody, Wyoming 82414.

HOUSEMAN, CHRISTINE ELIZABETH Occupation: Educator, Composer, Lecturer, Musician. Education: Scholarships and Master Classes. Address: 6448 North College Avenue, Indianapolis, Indiana 46220.

HOUSLANGER, NEAL P Occupation: Podiatrist. Education: B.A., D.P.M., F.A.A.F.S., F.A.S.P.D. Address: 23 Bruno Lane, Dix Hills, New York 11746.

HOWARD, DAVID M Occupation: General Director, World Evangelical Fellowship. Education: A.B., Wheaton College, 1949; M.A. Theology, Wheaton Graduate School, 1952. Address: 823 Anchor Court, Bartlett, Illinois 60103.

HOWARD, JOHN WILFRED Occupation: Commercial Artist. Education: College Credits in Art, Certificates, B.A., F.O.A. Address: RR#2, Corinth, Kentucky 41010.

HOWARD, LINDA DURIAN Occupation: Sculptor. Education: M.A., Hunter College. Address: 11 Worth Street, New York City, New York 10013.

HOWARD, LORRAINE H Occupation: Associate Dean of Students and Professor. Education: B.S., Ed.M., Ph.D. Address: 1724 Lee Ann Court, San Luis Obispo, California 93401.

HOWARD, MARY Y TATUM Occupation: Psychologist and Coordinator of Educational and Vocational Consulting. Education: B.A., West Virginia State College; M.A., University of Missouri-Kansas City; Ph.D., University of Minnesota. Address: 110 North 32 Avenue, Saint Cloud, Minnesota 56301.

HOWARD, WALTER E Occupation: Professor of Wildlife Biology, Vertebrate Ecologist. Education: A.B., M.S., Ph.D. Address: 24 College Park, Davis, California 95616.

HOWELL, EUGENIA DONALSON Occupation: Retired Dean of Students. Education: B.A., M.A. Address: Post Office Box 236, Graham, Texas 76046.

HOWELL, JAMES B III Occupation: Sales Consultant, Asgrow Seed Company, Subsidiary of Upjohn Company. Education: B.S., Rutgers University; M.B.A., University of Delaware. Address: Sayres Neck, Cedarville, New Jersey 08311.

HOWELL, ROGER JR Occupation: Professor of History. Education: A.B., Bowdoin College; B.A., M.A., D.Phil., Oxford University. Address: 16 Cleaveland Street, Brunswick, Maine 04011.

HOWLETT, PHYLLIS L Occupation: Athletic Administrator. Education: Bachelor's Degree. Address: 1309 Oak Hill Road, L.B.S., Barrington, Illinois 60010.

HOYER, STENY HAMILTON Occupation: U.S. Congressman and Attorney at law. Education: B.S., University of Maryland, College Park, 1963; J.D., Georgetown Law Center, Washington, D.C., 1966. Address: 6621 Lacona Street, Berkshire, Maryland 20747.

HOYE, ROBERT EARL Occupation: Professor of Systems Science. Education: A.B., M.S., Ph.D. Address: 2238 Wynnewood Circle, Louisville, Kentucky 40222.

HSIA, H T Occupation: Chemical Engineer. Education: B.S., M.S., Ph.D., M.B.A. Address: 2 Dutch Road, Somerset, New Jersey 08873.

HSU, MING-TEH Occupation: Nuclear Engineer, Bechtel Power Corporation. Education: Ph.D. Nuclear Engineering, University of Maryland, 1974. Address: 513 Lyons Way, Placentia, California 92670.

HU, JOHN CHIH-AN Occupation: Boeing Specialist Engineer, Certified Professional Chemist, Inventor and Author. Education: B.S., National Central University, China; M.S., Postgraduate Study, Organic Chemistry, University of Southern California. Address: 16212 122 Southeast, Renton, Washington 98055.

HU, TEH-WEI Occupation: Professor of Economics. Education: Ph.D. Address: 1171 Smithfield Street, State College, Pennsylvania 16801.

HUANG, CHUNG L Occupation: Researcher, Agricultural Economist. Education: Ph.D. Address: 1432 Dauset Drive, Griffin, Georgia 30223.

HUANG, FREESIA L Occupation: Research Biochemist, Cancer Research. Education: Ph.D. Address: 11213 Korman Drive, Potomac, Maryland 20854.

HUBBARD, HARVEY HART Occupation: Noise Control Engineering. Education: B.S. in Electrical Engineering, University of Vermont, 1942. Address: 23 Elm Avenue, Newport News, Virginia 23601.

HUBBARD, ISABEL JANICE Occupation: Educator Public School. Education: B.S. 1957, M.S. 1979, University of Wisconsin. Address: 5321 Namekagon Lane, Madison, Wisconsin 53704.

HUBBARD, MARGARET ELEANOR Occupation: Public Affairs/News Director. Address: 52 Park View Avenue, Warwick, Rhode Island 02888.

HUBBARD, MARYJOANNE C Occupation: Clinical Psychologist; Police Psychologist. Education: B.A., M.S., Ph.D. Address: 1313 Rosario Circle, Placentia, California 92670.

HUBBS, RONALD M Occupation: Retired Chairman, The St. Paul Companies, Inc. Education: B.A., University of Oregon; LL.D., Mitchell College of Law; LL.D., Macelester College. Address: 689 West Wentworth, Saint Paul, Minnesota 55118.

HUBER, WALTER G Occupation: Retired Judge. Education: B.A. 1930, J.D. 1932, University of Nebraska. Address: Box 530, Blair, Nebraska 68008.

HUBLEY, CECIL ERNEST FRANCIS Occupation: Association Executive. Address: 34 Metcalf Street, Saint John, New Brunswick, Canada, E2K 1J8.

HUDGENS, THOMAS A Occupation: Airline Consultant; Lecturer; World Government. Education: Attended Vanderbilt University. Address: 43 Sunset Drive, Englewood, Colorado 80110.

HUDIK, MARTIN FRANCIS Occupation: Hospital Administration. Education: B.S. Mechanical and Aerospace Engineering; Bachelor Police Administration; M.B.A. Address: 2116 South 51 Court, Cicero, Illinois 60650.

HUDSON, CLARA M Address: 2002 Southeast Pyramid Road, Port St. Lucie, Florida 33452.

HUDSON, FREDERIC MINER Occupation: President, The Fielding Institute. Education: Ph.D., Columbia University. Address: 2112 Santa Barbara Street, Santa Barbara, California 93105.

HUDSON, H DON Occupation: Veterinarian. Education: A.A. 1962, B.S. 1968, D.O.M. 1970.

HUDSON, MICHAEL W Occupation: Vice President, State Bank of Oxford. Education: Graduate, American Institute of Banking; Attending Purdue University. Address: Rural Route 1, Box 116, Pine Village, Indiana 47975.

HUEBNER, DONALD F Occupation: Treasurer-Corporate Executive. Address: 1104 Linden Lane, Mount Prospect, Illinois 60056.

HUEBNER, RICHARD ALLEN Occupation: Executive Director-Kappa Sigma Fraternity. Education: Bachelor of Business Administration, University of Wisconsin-Madison. Address: 2700 Leeds Lane, Charlottesville, Virginia 22901.

HUFF, WYNELLE JEAN Occupation: Dean, School of Nursing. Education: Ph.D. Address: 1769 Southeast 114th Place, Portland, Oregon 97216.

HUGABOOM, WILLIAM T Occupation: Senior Vice President-Broadway Bank. Education: M.B.A., New York University. Address: Business-100 Hamilton Plaza, Paterson, New Jersey 07505.

HUGHBANKS, WOODARD MONROE Occupation: Professor of Eduction, Pastor. Education: B.A., M.S., Ed.D. Address: 1204 Glendale Road, McPherson, Kansas 67460.

HUGHES, PAULA ANN Occupation: Associate Dean-Grad. School of Mgmt. Education: B.S., M.B.A., Ph.D. Address: 211 University Drive, Richardson, Texas 75081.

HUGHES, SAMUEL THOMAS JR Occupation: Assistant Dean, Graduate Studies in Nursing. Education: B.S.N., M.S.N.Ed., Registered Nurse. Address: 7031 Westlake Avenue, Dallas, Texas 75214.

HUGHES, WILLIAM J Occupation: Member, U.S. Congress. Education: A.B., J.D. Address: 1019 Wesley Road, Ocean City, New Jersey 08226.

HULLEY, CLAIR MONTROSE Occupation: Professor Industrial Engineering. Education: B.S., M.E. Address: 11560 Deerfield Road, Cincinnati, Ohio 45242.

HUMENICK, SHARRON SMITH Occupation: Associate Professor of Nursing. Education: B.S.N., M.P.H., Ph.D. Address: 1017 Sheridan, Laramie, Wyoming 82070.

HUMMEL, FRED EDWARD Occupation: Consultant; Mining, Metallurgical, Mechanical and Petroleum Engineer. Education: B.S. Metallurgy, South Dakota School of Mines and Technology; M.E. Metallurgy. Address: 338 Bonita Drive, Ojai, California 93023.

HUMPHERYS, A GLEN Occupation: Museum Director. Education: Ph.D., M.A., B.S. Address: 274 East 6790 South, Midvale, Utah 84047.

HUMPHREY, DORIS D Occupation: College Professor. Education: Ph.D., Ed.S., M.B.E., B.S. Address: 8504 Capricorn Drive, Cincinnati, Ohio 45249.

HUMPHRIES, JEAN ROPES Occupation: Professor. Education: B.A., University of Miami, 1950; M.S., Florida State University, 1955; Ph.D., Louisiana State University, 1963. Address: 1311 Alhambra Circle, Coral Gables, Florida 33134.

HUNG, YUNG-TSE Occupation: Professor of Civil Engineering. Education: B.S.C.E., M.S.C.E., Ph.D. Sanitary Engineering. Address: 27906 Lincoln, Bay Village, Ohio 44140.

HUNSAKER, DON II Occupation: Professor of Biology, San Diego State University. Education: B.S., M.A., Ph.D. Address: 1540 Savin Drive, El Cajon, California 92021.

HUNSBERGER, DONALD R Occupation: Professor of Conducting and Ensembles, Conductor Eastman Wind Ensemble. Education: B.M., M.M., D.M.A. Address: 160 Alpine Drive, Rochester, New York 14618.

HUNT, ALEXANDRA Occupation: Opera and Concert Singer. Address: 170 West 74th Street, New York, New York 10023.

HUNT, BERNICE K Occupation: Psychotherapist, Author, Gerontologist. Education: B.A., M.S. Address: 8 Ledgewood Commons, Millwood, New York 10546.

HUNT, MARK A Occupation: Museum Director, Kansas Museum of History. Education: M.A. Historical Museum Training. Address: 1720 Willow Avenue, Topeka, Kansas 66606.

HUNT, MARY LOU Occupation: Counselor; Consultant, Individual Development Center, Inc. Education: M.A. Psychology 1954, B.A. Psychology 1954, Stanford University. Address: 2001 Killarney Drive, Bellevue, Washington 98004.

HUNT, MICHAEL O Occupation: Professor and Director, Wood Research Laboratory. Education: B.S., University of Kentucky; M.F., Duke University; Ph.D., North Carolina State University. Address: 126 Ivy Hill Drive, West Lafayette, Indiana 47906.

HUNT, WAYNE PHILIP Occupation: Clinical Psychologist. Education: B.S., Mars Hill College; M.S., The Johns Hopkins University; Ed.D., The George Washington University. Address: 9 Chandelle Road, Baltimore, Maryland 21220.

HUNTER, BERTRAM HARRY JR Occupation: Interior Designer. Address: 5336 North Colonial #101, Fresno, California 73304.

HUNTLEY, WILLIAM ROBERT Occupation: Administrative Librarian. Education: B.A., University of North Carolina, 1951; Graduate Studies, George Washington University, Catholic University. Address: 4215 Flam Street, Fort Washington, Maryland 20744.

HURDLE, BESSIE Occupation: Executive Director, Berks Co. Welfare Rights Organization. Education: Special Education, Reading Area Community College; Advanced Clerical Practice. Address: 343 South 4th Street, Reading, Pennsylvania 19602.

HURLEY, MAUREEN VIOLA Occupation: Poet, Photojournalist, Visual Artist. Education: A.A. Art,

B.A. Art, M.A. English. Address: 7491 Mirabel Road, Forestville, California 95436.

HURT, BILLY G Occupation: Minister, First Baptist Church. Education: Ph.D. Theology, Southern Seminary, Louisville, Kentucky. Address: 8 Breckenridge Boulevard, Frankfort, Kentucky 40601.

HURWITZ, T ALAN Occupation: Associate Dean. Education: B.S., M.S., Ed.D. Address: 100 Holley Brook Drive, Penfield, New York 14526.

HUSEMANN, ROBERT W Occupation: Chief Engineer. Education: B.A. Mathematics, B.S.M.E., Valparaise University. Address: 12802 Teaberry Road, Silver Spring, Maryland 20906.

HUSTON, JAMES ALVIN Occupation: Dean of the College, Lynchburg College. Education: A.B. honors, A.M., Indiana University; Ph.D., New York University. Address: 300 Langhorne Lane, Lynchburg, Virginia 24501.

HUSTON, THOMAS L Occupation: Manager, Health Care. Education: B.A., M.Div., M.A. Address: 1561 Cohasset Avenue, Lakewood, Ohio 44107.

HUTCHCROFT, SALLY ANN Occupation: Junior High Language Arts Teacher. Education: B.A., University of Wisconsin; M.A., Bradley University. Address: 301 East North Street, Knoxville, Illinois 61448.

HUTCHINS, JAMES NELSON Occupation: Regional Director, Cargo Services. Education: Student, University Complutense de Madrid, 1973-74; University de Los Andes, Bogota, Columbia, 1975-76;

A.B., University of Scranton, 1976. Address: 532 Brookhaven Road, Brookhaven, Pennsylvania 19015.

HUTCHINS, JEANNE B Occupation: Government Official, Legislature, Town of Brighton. Education: B.A., Wells College; Masters of Public Administration, State University of New York. Address: 75 Indian Spring Lane, Rochester, New York 14618.

HUTSON, JANET KERN Occupation: Vocational Cosmetology Teacher. Education: Masters equivalency 1977. Address: 215 South Sixth Street, Denton, Maryland 21629.

HUTT, MAX LEWIS Occupation: Consulting Psychologist. Education: A.B., M.S., L.H.D. Address: 21 Regent Drive, Ann Arbor, Michigan 48104.

HUTTENSTINE, MARIAN L Occupation: Professor and Consultant. Education: B.S., M.Ed., Ph.D. Candidate. Address: K-1 Woodland Trace, Tuscaloosa, Alabama 35405.

HUZAR, ELEANOR GOLTZ Occupation: Professor of History, Michigan State University. Education: Bachelor of Arts, University of Minnesota, 1943; Master of Arts, 1945, Doctor of Philosophy, 1948, Cornell University. Address: 289 Gunson Street, East Lansing, Michigan 48823.

HUZURBAZAR, VASANT SHANKAR Occupation: University Professor of Statistics. Education: B.A. with honors, Bombay University; B.A., Banaras; Ph.D., Cambridge University. Address: 3755 East Buchtel Boulevard, #206, Denver, Colorado 80210.

I

IAKOVIDIS, SPYROS E Occupation: Professor of Classical Archeology and Curator of University Museum, University of Pennsylvania. Education: Ph.D.. Address: 525 South 46th Street, Philadelphia, Pennsylvania 19143.

IACOVIDES, TASOS I Occupation: Engineering. Education: M.S.. Address: 28 John Street, New City, New York 10956.

IBA, PEGGY ANN Occupation: Consumer Relations Representative. Education: B.S., Montana State University, 1969. Address: 1 Sussex Court, Glendive, Montana 59330.

IBERALL, ARTHUR S Occupation: Visiting Scholar, Crump Institute for Medical Engineering. Education: B.S., D.Sc. Address: 4675 Willis Avenue, Sherman Oaks, California 91403.

IGL, RICHARD F Occupation: Lawyer. Education: B.A. 1946, M.A. with honors 1947, J.D. 1950. Address: 9800 Yoakum Drive, Beverly Hills, California 90210.

IGO, JAMES PRENTICE Occupation: Chiropractor. Education: Doctor of Chiropractic, Cleveland Chiropractic College, 1974. Address: 623 Plaza Drive, Marshall, Missouri 65340.

IGO, LOUIS DANIEL Occupation: Lawyer; Legal Educator, Los Angeles Community College District; Naval Officer. Education: B.S., Missouri Valley College, 1963; J.D., University of Tulsa, 1967. Address: 16552 Sell Circle #19, Huntington Beach, California 92649.

IHLER, GARRET M Occupation: Professor and Department Head, Medical Biochemistry, Texas A&M University. Education: M.D., Ph.D. Address: 1115 Langford, College Station, Texas 77840.

IKEDA, TATSUYA Occupation: Patent Attorney, American Hoechst Corporation. Education: B.E., University of Tokyo, 1963; M.S., University of Wisconsin, 1968; Ph.D., Massachusetts Institute of Technology, 1972; J.D., Suffolk University, 1981. Address: 4 Appletree Lane, Leominster, Massachusetts 01453.

IKI, DANIEL H Occupation: Electronic Media Consultant. Education: Electronic Engineering Technology. Address: 1055 Ala Napunan Street #206, Honolulu, Hawaii 96818.

ILEY, MARTHA STRAWN Occupation: Coordinator Cultural Arts Program, Central Piedmont Community College. Education: B.A., M.A., M.Mus., M.Ed., Ed.D. Address: 6100 Creola Road, Charlotte, N.C. 28226.

IMAD, AZMI PHILIP Occupation: Director of Safety and Radiation Safety Officer, University of Colorado. Education: B.S., M.Sc., University of London, 1966. Address: Campus Box 375, University of Colorado, Boulder, Colorado 80309.

INFANTE, ISA Occupation: Professor of Political Science, Jersey City State College. Education: B.A., University of California, 1973; M.A., Yale University, 1975; Ph.D. University of California, 1977. Address: 1861 Kennedy Boulevard, #206, Jersey City, New Jersey 07305.

INGIS, GAIL Occupation: Interior Designer. Education: Student, Brooklyn College, 1953; Graduate Interior Architecture and Design 1973, B.F.A. 1980, New York School of Interior Design; Postgraduate, Pratt Institute. Address: 39 Clairmont Drive, Woodcliff Lake, New Jersey 07675.

INGLE, JAMES HOBART Occupation: Engineering Technician and Office Manager. Education: Associate Applied Science Civil Engineering. Address: Star Route Box 447, Gwinn, Michigan 49841.

INGRAM, TERRENCE N Occupation: Environmental Leader, Insurance Agent. Education: B.S. Address: 8384 North Broadway, Apple River, Illinois 61001.

INSOLIA, ANTHONY E Occupation: Editor and Senior Vice President,*Newsday*. Education: B.A., New York University. Address: 333 Grand Central Avenue, Amityville, New York 11701.

INSTONE, JOHN C Occupation: President and Chief Executive Officer, SGL Industries, Inc. Education: B.S., Drexel University. Address: 465 Pelham Road, Cherry Hill, New Jersey 08034.

INTRIERI, MICHAEL F Occupation: Educational Administration and Counseling, Stamford High School. Education: B.A., M.A., Ed.D. Address: Argentine Way, Silvermine, Norwalk, Connecticut 06850.

IOANNOU, SUSAN Occupation: Poet, Freelance Writer and Editor; Associate Editor, *Cross-Canada Writers' Quarterly*. Address: 36 Elvaston Drive, Toronto, Ontario, Canada M4A 1N3.

IODICE, RUTH GENEVIEVE WORK Occupation: Poet, Writer, Editor, Educator, Homemaker. Education: B.A., Indiana State University; Graduate Studies, University of Chicago, University of California. Address: 22 Avon Road, Kensington, California 94707.

IPES, THOMAS PETER Occupation: Marriage and Family Therapist. Education: B.A., M.Div., D.Min. Address: 6700 Concord Drive, Newburgh, Indiana 47630.

IRSFELD, JOHN HENRY Occupation: Professor of English, University of Nevada. Education: B.A. 1959, M.A. 1966, Ph.D. 1969, University of Texas Austin. Address: 3605 Briarglen Lane, Las Vegas, Nevada 89108.

IRVINE, DAVID JAMES Occupation: Educator, New York State Education Department. Education: B.A.A., M.A., Ph.D. Address: 45 Preston Road, Delmar, New York 12054.

IRWIN, JOHN BARROWS Occupation: Retired Astronomer. Education: B.S. 1933, Ph.D. 1946, University of California-Berkeley. Address: 2744 North Tyndall Avenue, Tucson, Arizona 85719.

IRZA, SUSAN M Occupation: Health Administration. Education: B.A., M.P.A. Address: 5849 South West 22nd Terrace, Topeka, Kansas 66614.

ISAACS, GREGORY SULLIVAN Occupation: Conductor, Southeast Symphony Orchestra, West Coast Opera. Education: B.M., Miami University; M.M., Indiana University. Address: 2098 Mound Street, Hollywood, California 90036.

ISAACS, LESLIE THOMAS Occupation: Electrical Engineer, Douglas Aircraft Company. Education: B.S.E.E., University of Arizona, 1950. Address: 5132 Cambridge Avenue, Westminster, California 92683.

ISAAK, G EUGENE Occupation: Lawyer. Education: B.S.B.A., J.D., LL.M. Address: 425 East Yvon Drive, Tucson, Arizona 85704.

ISHII, THOMAS KORYU Occupation: Professor, Marquette University. Education: B.S., M.S., Ph.D., Dr. Engrg. Address: 6601 West Carolann Drive, Brown Deer, Wisconsin 53223.

ISSARI, MOHAMMAD ALI Occupation: Mass Media Consultant. Education: B.A., M.A., Ph.D. Address: 4454 Seneca Drive, Okemos, Mississippi 48864.

ISSAWI, CHARLES Occupation: Professor, Princeton University. Education: B.A., M.A., Oxford

University. Address: 97 Castle Howard Court, Princeton, New Jersey 08540.

IUNGERICH, LINDA JEAN Occupation: Homemaker. Education: High School Diploma. Address: 20833 Highway 52, Fort Morgan, Colorado 80701.

IVANOFF, JOANNE M Occupation. Consulting Psychologist, Private Practice. Education: B.S., M.S., Ph.D. Address: 929 North Astor #1102, Milwaukee, Wisconsin 53202.

IVANOFF, JOHN M Occupation: Professor Educational Psychology, Marquette University; Consulting Psychologist. Education: B.E., M.A., Ed.D. Address: 929 North Astor, Milwaukee, Wisconsin 53202.

IVERSON, JANICE Occupation: Member of Religious Order, Mother of God Priory; Coordinator of Cardiac Rehabilitation, Instructor, H.P.E.R. Center, South Dakota State University. Address: Mother of God Priory, Watertown, South Dakota 57201.

IVES, JANE H Occupation: Professor of International Business, Suffolk University. Education: B.A., M.Sc., Ph.D. Candidate. Address: 25 Elmore Street, Newton, Massachusetts 02159.

J

JACKS, ELIN BECKMAN Occupation: Psychotherapist and Business Consultant. Education: B.A., University of Arkansas, 1964; M.S.S.W., University of Texas Arlington, 1973. Address: 2020 Monaco, Arlington, Texas 76010.

JACKSON, EDWINA LOWERY Occupation: English Advanced Placement Instructor. Education: B.A., M.A. Address: 725 West Quincy Road, Seneca, South Carolina 29678.

JACKSON, ELMER MARTIN JR Occupation: Newspaper Columnist, Owner Commercial Shop. Education: B.A., St. John's College. Address: 219 Claude Street, Wardour, Annapolis, Maryland 21401.

JACKSON, HERBERT CROSS Occupation: Professor. Education: B.A., Th.M., M.A., Ph.D. Address: 1927 Tomahawk Road, Okemos, Michigan 48864.

JACKSON, LORRAINE MORLOCK Occupation: Research Scientist. Education: B.Sc., M.Ed., Ph.D. Address: 911 Ashton Road, Cornwell Heights, Pennsylvania 19020.

JACKSON, NANCY A Occupation: Nurse Educator, West Virginia Wesleyan College. Education: B.S.N., M.N.Ed., Ph.D. Address: 507 Haymond Highway, Clarksburg, West Virginia 26301.

JACKSON, RODNEY NEWLAND Occupation: Chief Cytotechnologist, Histotechnologist, Medical Photographer, Section Head, Passavant Memorial Hospital. Education: Attended Lincoln College, Illinois Wesleyan University, Illinois State University-Normal, Millikin University. Address: 429 Pendik Road, Jacksonville, Illinois 62650.

JACKSON, RONALD A Occupation: Director of Counseling, Counseling Center, Susquehanna University. Education: B.A., Johns Hopkins University; Ph.D. Temple University. Address: 300 West Snyder Street, Selinsgrove, Pennsylvania 17870.

JACKSON, RONALD FREDERICK Occupation: Veterinarian. Education: D.V.M. Address: 311 Oglethorpe Boulevard, Saint Augustine, Florida 32084.

JACOBS, ABIGAIL C Occupation: Toxicologist, Biochemist. Education: B.S., Ph.D. Address: Silver Spring, Maryland 20901.

JACOBS, EDWARD J Occupation: Director, Human Resources Management, College of Saint Mary. Education: B.A., Yeshir University; M.A., Southern Methodist University; Ph.D., International College. Address: 8540 Cuming Street, Omaha, Nebraska 68114.

JACOBS, FRANCIS A Occupation: Professor of Biochemistry, Department of Biochemistry and Molecular Biology, University of North Dakota. Education: B.S., Ph.D. Address: 1525 Robertson Court, Grand Forks, North Dakota 58201.

JACOBS, JEROME F Occupation: Podiatrist. Education: Doctor Podiatric Medicine. Address: 5223 Pine Tree Drive, Miami Beach, Florida 33141.

JACOBS, MALCOLM M Occupation: Building Contractor. Education: Refrigeration Engineer. Address: 360 Vallejo Drive #117, Millbrae, California 94030.

JACOBS, STANLEY B Occupation: Engineering Manager, Stone and Webster Engineering Corporation. Education: B.Ch.E., Rensselaer Polytechnic Institute, 1958. Address: 32 Spring Lane, Sharon, Massachusetts 02067.

JACOBS, STEVE A Occupation: Research Chemist. Education: B.S. Chemistry, Ph.D. Analytical Chemistry. Address: 757 Story Drive, Fairfield, Ohio 45014.

JACOBSEN, STEPHEN C Occupation: Professor/ Researcher, University of Utah. Education: B.S., M.S., Ph.D. Address: 300 South, 1240 East, Salt Lake City, Utah 84102.

JACOBSON, BERT HANS Occupation: Professional Football Coach. Education: B.S., M.S., Ph.D. Address: 1815 Mansfield, Stillwater, Oklahoma 74074.

JACOBSON, GARY VICTOR Occupation: Chief Financial Officer. Education: B.B.A., M.S. Address: 111 Mayo Road, Wellesley, Massachusetts 02181.

JACOBSON, JAY STANLEY Occupation: Plant Physiologist. Education: B.S., M.A., Ph.D. Address: 420 Sheffield Road, Ithaca, New York 14850.

JAEGER, BRENDA K Occupation: Fine Artist. Education: B.A., Eastern Washington University, 1972; M.A.T., Whitworth College, 1975. Address: Box 2152, Longview, Washington 98632.

JAEGER, DONNA M Occupation: Administrative Analyst, San Diego Police. Education: B.A., M.A. Address: Post Office Box 3064, San Diego, California 92103.

JAEGER, SHARON ANN Occupation: Fulbright Professor; Co-editor, Sachem Press; Editor, Intertext. Education: B.A. summa cum laude, M.A., D.A. Address: Post Office Box 100014, Anchorage, Alaska 99510.

JAFFE, IRA S Occupation: Associate Professor of Film, University of New Mexico. Education: A.B., M.F.A., Ph.D. Address: 1331 Park Avenue Southwest, Albuquerque, New Mexico 87102.

JAHN, PAULA H S Occupation: Library Clerk, Hobart College. Education: Studies in Germany. Address: 295 Hamilton Street, Geneva, New York 14456.

JAIN, SAGAR CHAND Occupation: Professor and Chairman, Department of Health Policy and Administration, University of North Carolina. Education: B.A. 1950, M.A. 1952, A.M. 1960, Ph.D. 1964. Address: 1520 Crestwood Lane, Chapel Hill, North Carolina 27514.

JAKO, GEZA J Occupation: Surgeon, Professor, Government Advisor. Education: M.D. Address: 169 East Emerson Street, Melrose, Massachusetts 02176.

JAMES, A EVERETTE JR Occupation: Professor and Chairman, Department of Radiology, Vanderbilt Medical Center. Education: Sc.M., J.D., M.D. Address: 519 Belle Meade Boulevard, Nashville, Tennessee 37205.

JAMES, GEORGE ALFRED Occupation: Assistant Professor of Philosophy, North Texas State University. Education: B.C.E., M.A., M.Phil., Ph.D. Address: 2501 West Oak Street #45, Denton, Texas 76201.

JAMES, ROBERT BLEAKLEY JR Occupation: Attorney at Law. Education: LL.B., Catholic University, 1951. Address: 7411 Galanis Drive, Annandale, Virginia 22003.

JAMES, WARREN E Occupation: Musician (Flutist, Composer, Record Producer). Education: M.A., Ph.D., Ohio State University. Address: 114 West North College Street, Yellow Springs, Ohio 45387.

JAMISON, DARLENE MARY Occupation: University Administrator, University of Alabama in Birmingham. Education: B.A., M.A., University of Missouri, Kansas City. Address: 3586 Rockhill Road, Birmingham, Alabama 35223.

JAMISON, MAGGIE JENKINS Occupation: Retired Teacher. Education: A.B., M.A. Address: 1210 Goff Avenue, Orangeburg, South Carolina 29115.

JAMISON, SUSAN CLAPP Occupation: Adjunct

Professor, Library Director. Education: B.A., M.A., M.A., M.L.S. Address: Box 324, Odessa, Delaware 19730.

JAMME, ALBERT JOSEPH Occupation: Research Professor, The Catholic University. Education: S.T.D., Doctor of Oriental Philology and History. Address: 1624 21st Street, Northwest, Washington, D.C. 2009.

JANDES, KENNETH MICHAEL Occupation: School Principal. Education: B.S.Ed., M.Ed., Ed.D. Address: 6671 Wheatfield Street, Woodridge, Illinois 60517.

JANIAN, PAULETTE Occupation: Attorney at Law. Education: B.A., J.D. Address: 3190 South Fowler, Fresno, California 93725.

JANOS, LUDVIK Occupation: Professor of Mathematics, California State University, Fullerton. Education: Doctor Degree, Charles University, Pragyue, Czechoslovakia, 1950. Address: 501 Juanita, La Habra, California 90631.

JANOVICI, ROBERT Occupation: Zoning Administrator. Education: B.A., University of California-Los Angeles, 1965; J.D., University of San Diego, School of Law, 1968. Address: 2126 Mayall Street, Chatsworth, California 91311.

JANOWITZ, PHYLLIS W Occupation: Assistant Professor of English, Cornell University. Education: B.A., M.F.A., University of Massachusetts-Amherst, 1970. Address: One Lodge Way, Ithaca, New York, 14850.

JANOWITZ, TAMA Occupation: Writer/Novelist. Education: B.A., Barnard College, 1977; M.A., Hollins College, 1979; M.F.A., Columbia University, 1985. Address: c/o Cutrone, 463 West Street, #707A, New York, New York 10014.

JANSON, PHILIP Occupation: Sociologist/Gerontologist. Education: B.A., M.A., Ph.D. Address: 344 Larchmont, San Antonio, Texas 78209.

JAOUNI, KATHERINE COOK Occupation: Research Microbiologist, Scientist Administrator; Member Board of Directors, Graduate Women in Science, Inc. Education: B.S., College of William and Mary, 1949; M.S. 1952, Ph.D. 1957, George Washington University. Address: 515 Bradford Drive, Rockville, Maryland 20850.

JARAMILLO, MARI-LUCI Occupation: Associate Dean, College of Education, University of New Mexico. Education: B.A., M.A., Ph.D. Address: 2301 Artesanos Court Northwest, Albuquerque, New Mexico 87108.

JARMON, CHARLES Occupation: Professor, Howard University. Education: Ph.D., State University of New York at Buffalo. Address: 1789 Verbena Street, Washington, D.C. 20012.

JAROSLAWICZ, ISAAC MORDECHAI Occupation: Investment Banking. Education: Yeshiva University, Brooklyn College. Address: 16 East 65th Street, New York, New York 10021.

JASKOT, SHEILA ELIZABETH Occupation: Local Origination Manager, Group W Cable. Education: Bachelor of Arts, Stephens College, 1981. Address: 3904 South Providence Road, Columbia, Missouri 65201.

JASSER, RONALD M Occupation: Sales and Marketing Manager. Education: A.A.S., B.S. Address: 7 Wilmington Drive, Melville, New York 11747.

JAUHAR, PREM P Occupation: Research Geneticist, Research Consultant. Education: M.S., Ph.D. Address: 230 West Campus View Drive, Riverside, California 92507.

JAY, HILDA LEASE Occupation: Adjunct Staff, University of Connecticut. Education: B.S., Indiana University, 1945; M.S., Danbury State College, 1960; Ed.D., New York University, 1970. Address: Post Office Box F, Sandy Hook, Connecticut 06482.

JEFFREY, LOUIS P Occupation: Directory of Pharmacy Services, Rhode Island Hospital. Education: B.S. 1953, M.S. 1955, D.Sc. 1979, Massachusetts College of Pharmacy and Allied Health Sciences. Address: 19 Old Oak Drive, Warwick, Rhode Island 02886.

JEHU, JOHN PAUL Occupation: Attorney. Education: LL.B., Cornell Law School. Address: 49 Dove Street, Albany, New York 12210.

JENKINS, CHARLES FRANKLIN Occupation: Teacher, Special Education (Homebound). Education: A.A., B.A., M.A., Ed.S., Ed.D. Address: 1608 Poplar, Kansas City, Missouri 64127.

JENKINS, FRANK G Occupation: School Administrator. Education: B.S., M.A., Dissertation (in progress), George Washington University. Address: 6509 Red Top Road, Chillum, Maryland 20783.

JENKINS, JOHN A Occupation: Associate Director, Fine Arts Center; Professor of Music and Dance, University of Massachusetts. Education: B.M., M.M., M.A., Ph.D., University of Michigan. Address: 265 Northeast Street, Amherst, Massachusetts 01002.

JENKINS, LLOYD GARY Occupation: Senior Account Executive. Education: B.S. Political Science, Rutgers University, 1963. Address: 38 Museum Way, San Francisco, California 94114.

JENNINGS, LEE W Occupation: Managing Partner (Certified Public Accountant), Peat, Marwick, Mitchell. Education: B.S., M.B.A. Address: 1110 North Lake Shore Drive #27S, Chicago, Illinois 60611.

JENNINGS, MADELYN PULVER Occupation: Senior Vice President, Personnel and Administration, Gannett Company, Inc. Education: B.A. Address: 2500 East Avenue, Rochester, New York 14610.

JENNINGS, VINNIE CLARK Occupation: Retired Accountant, United States Navy; Community Leader. Education: College Studies. Address: Route 2, Box 1000, Orangeburg, South Carolina 29115.

JENSEN, HELEN Occupation: Musical Artist's Manager, Agent, Business Owner. Education: High School Diploma. Address: 19029 56th Lane Northeast, Seattle, Washington 98155.

JENSH, RONALD P Occupation: Faculty Member, College of Allied Health Sciences, Thomas Jefferson University. Education: B.A. 1960, M.A. 1962, Bucknell University; Ph.D., Jefferson Medical College, 1966. Address: 230 East Park Avenue, Haddonfield, New Jersey 08033.

JEREMIAH, LESTER EARL Occupation: Research Scientist, Meat Science Section, Canada Agricultural Research Station. Education: B.Sc., Washington State University, 1965; M.Sc., University of Missouri, 1967; Ph.D., Texas A&M University, 1971. Address: Rural Route 1, Olive, Alberta, Canada T0C 0Y0.

JEWELL, JAMES EARL Occupation: Lighting Designer. Education: B.A., M.F.A. Address: 749 Rhode Island Street, San Francisco, California 94107.

JEWELL, NICHOLAS PATRICK Occupation: Professor/Biostatistician. Education: B.Sc. honors, Ph.D., University of Edinburgh. Address: 8 Parkside Drive, Piedmont, California 94611.

JHIRAD, ELIJAH E Occupation: Assistant Corporation Counsel. Education: B.A., Barrister at Law. Address: 85-15, 139th Street, Briarwood, New York 11435.

JIMÉNEZ, FRANCISCO Occupation: Division Director of Arts and Humanities and Professor of Spanish, University of Santa Clara. Education: B.A., M.A., Ph.D. Address: 624 Enos Court, Santa Clara,

California 95051.

JOCHUM, SISTER MARY JUDE Occupation: Supertintendent of Schools, Diocese of Wheeling-Chas. Education: B.Ed., Duquesne University; M.A., St. John College of Cleveland. Address: 2260 Marshall Avenue, Wheeling, West Virginia 26003.

JOFFE, WILLIAM I Occupation: Roman Catholic Priest. Education: B.A., M.A., M.A., D.Min. Address: 7319 Maxon Road, Harvard, Illinois 60033.

JOHANSON, DONALD CARL Occupation: Director, Institute of Human Origins. Education: Ph.D., University of Chicago. Address: 1435 Campus Drive, Berkeley, California 94708.

JOHNSON, ALICE LORETTA Occupation: Speech Pathologist. Education: B.A., M.A., D.Ed., Columbia University. Address: 14809 Channel Lane, Santa Monica, California 90402.

JOHNSON, BRUCE CHRISTOPHER Occupation: Associate Librarian/Senior Cataloger, University of Maryland Health Sciences Library. Education: B.Mus., M.A., M.S.L.S., Ph.D. Candidate. Address: 5720 Thunder Hill Road, Columbia, Maryland 21045.

JOHNSON, CLARENCE JR Occupation: Professor, Fort Valley State College. Education: B.S., Alcorn State University; M.S., Mississippi State University, Ph.D., Cornell University. Address: 307 Troutman Avenue, Fort Valley, Georgia 31030.

JOHNSON, DARRYL ARTHUR Occupation: Student and Musician. Address: 2421 Tempest Drive, Birmingham, Alabama 35211.

JOHNSON, DEANE H Occupation: County Extension Agent, Staff Chairman, 4-H. Education: B.S. Agricultural Education, M.S. Extension. Address: 554 Northwest Pennsylvania Avenue, Chehalis, Washington 98532.

JOHNSON, DOUGLAS ALAN Occupation: Corporate Responsibility Activist. Education: B.A. cum laude, Macalester College. Address: 3629 Blaisdell, Minneapolis, Minnesota 35409.

JOHNSON, EVELYN BRYAN Occupation: Chief Flight Instructor. Education: Tennessee Wesleyan College, University of Tennessee. Address: Box 667, Jefferson City, Tennessee 37760.

JOHNSON, FRANCIS WILLARD Occupation: Clergyman (Lutheran). Education: B.A., B.Div., M.Div., D.Min. Address: 606 Yorkshire Drive, Washington, Illinois 61571.

JOHNSON, GRANT WILLIAM Occupation: Psychologist. Education: B.A., M.A., Ph.D. Address: 5806 North 37 Drive, Phoenix, Arizona 85019.

JOHNSON, H WAYNE Occupation: Professor, University of Iowa. Education: B.S., M.A., M.A. Address: 915 Talwrn Court, Iowa City, Iowa 52240.

JOHNSON, JOHNNY R Occupation: Engineering Specialist. Education: B.S.E.E., Louisiana Technical University, 1951; M.S. 1953. Ph.D. 1959, Auburn University. Address: 3029 Santa Fe Trail, Fort Worth, Texas 76116.

JOHNSON, JORENE KATHRYN Occupation: Urbanist. Education: B.F.A., Pratt Institute; M.P.A., University of Cincinnati. Address: 5200 Race Road, Cincinnati, Ohio 45247.

JOHNSON, JUDI FORD Occupation: Miss America 1969. Education: B.S. cum laude, University of Illinois, 1973. Address: 1062 Castlehill Drive, Rockford, Illinois 61107.

JOHNSON, KRAIG NELSON Occupation: Retail Merchandising Executive. Education: B.A. honors, Eckerd College; M.I.M., American Graduate School of Interntional Management. Address: 14527 Catalina Circle, Seminole, Florida 33542.

JOHNSON, LESLIE CAROLE Occupation: Editor/Publisher. Education: B.A. Journalism, University of Minnesota. Address: 5644 Morgan Avenue South, Minneapolis, Minnesota 55419.

JOHNSON, LESTER B JR Occupation: Professor of Engineering Technology. Education: B.S., M.S., Ph.D. Address: 1905 Fitzgerald Street, Savannah, Georgia 31405.

JOHNSON, LLOYD JR Occupation: Manager, Meter Reading, Unitro Illuminating Company. Education: A.S. Urban Professional Assistance, B.S. Sociology. Address: 27 McLean Street, Stratford, Connecticut 06497.

JOHNSON, MALCOLM C JR Occupation: Publishing Consultant. Education: A.B., Dartmouth College; M.S., University of Illinois. Address: 65 Larchwood Avenue, West Long Branch, New Jersey 07764.

JOHNSON, MICHAEL Occupation: Engineer, Statistician. Education: B.Sc., University of Bristol, 1956; Registered Professional Engineer. Address: 3012 Nth 32nd Street #22, Phoenix, Arizona 85018.

JOHNSON, NICHOLAS Occupation: Writer, Lecturer, Educator. Education: B.A.. LL.B. Address: Box 1876, Iowa City, Iowa 52244.

JOHNSON, PATRICIA M Occupation: Poet, Speaker, Seminar Leader. Education: H.S., Breckenridge High School, 1942; University of Minnesota Summers Arts Study Center, 1979. Address: 732 Garfield Avenue, North Mankato, Minnesota 56001.

JOHNSON, PAULA KATHLEEN Occupation: Customer Service, Alco Discount. Education: Oklahoma Christian College. Address: 603 Maple, Ottawa, Kansas 66067.

JOHNSON, PENNY DEE Occupation: Professor of Voice, Performer. Education: B.Mus., M.Mus. Address: 921A Pyrtle Drive, Salem, Virginia 24153.

JOHNSON, PHILIP R Occupation: Executive, Travel Industry. Education: B.A. honors, University of Sussex. Address: 7607 South Fieldstone Lane, Salt Lake City, Utah 84121.

JOHNSON, ROBERT LELAND Occupation: Attorney at Law. Education: Yale University, 1955; J.D., University of Denver, 1958; B.A., University of Denver, 1962; Human Development Certificate, The Institutes for the Achievement of Human Potential, 1978. Address: 534 Pearl Street #306, Denver, Colorado 80203.

JOHNSON, SAMMYE LaRUE Occupation: Assistant Professor of Journalism, Trinity University. Education: B.S.J. cum laude 1968, M.S.J. summa cum laude 1969, Northwestern University. Address: 2906 Spring Bend, San Antonio, Texas 78209.

JOHNSON, TERESA MARIE Occupation: Pulmonary Clinician/Registered Nurse. Education: Diploma Nursing 1974, A.A. Gerontology 1977, B.S.N. Candidate. Address: 1844 Bremen Avenue, Granite City, Illinois 62040.

JOHNSON, VINCENT ARNOLD Occupation: Professor of Biological Sciences, Biology Department, Saint Cloud State University. Education: B.Sc., M.Sc., Ph.D., University of Nebraska. Address: 1608 Washington Memorial Drive, Saint Cloud, Minnesota 56301.

JOHNSON, VIRGIL A Occupation: Leader Wheat Research, U.S.D.A. Agricultural Research Service. Education: B.Sc. 1948, Ph.D. 1952, University of Nebraska. Address: 3849 Dudley, Lincoln, Nebraska 68503.

JOHNSON, WILLIAM G Occupation: Professor of

Economics, Senior Research Associate. Education: B.S., University of Pennsylvania, 1956; M.A., Temple University, 1968; Ph.D., Rutgers University, 1971. Address: 28 Cross Road, DeWitt, New York 13224.

JOHNSON, WILLIAM I Occupation: Chairman Department of Mathematics, Ambassador College. Education: B.S., North Texas State University; M.Ed., Texas Christian University; Ed.D., Texas Tech University; A.A., Ambassador College. Address: Route 2, Box 517, Big Sandy, Texas 75755.

JOHNSTON, ADA CLARA Occupation: Instructor. Education: M.Ed. Address: 1005 6th Avenue, Marianna, Florida 32446.

JOHNSTON, KEITH P Occupation: Assistant Professor, Department Chemical Engineering, University of Texas. Education: B.S. M.S. Ph.D. Address: 2400 Barton Hills, Austin, Texas 78704.

JOHNSTON, RUTH LeROY Occupation: Retired Nosologist. Education: B.A., Bob Jones University, 1945; R.R.A., Emory University, 1953. Address: 100 Paradise Harbour Boulevard, North Palm Beach, Florida 33408.

JOHNSTON, WARREN E Occupation: Professor, Chairman, Department of Agricultural Economics, University of California-Davis. Education: B.S., University of California-Davis; M.S., Ph.D., North Carolina State University. Address: 625 Rutgers Drive, Davis, California 95616.

JOINER, THOMAS WITHERINGTON Occupation: Assistant Professor of Music, University of Georgia. Education: Bachelor of Music, Master of Choral Music, Bachelor of Music, Address: 210 Ferncliff Drive, Athens, Georgia 30602.

JOLLY, NAOMI EDWINER Occupation: Multilingual Translator. Education: B.A., University of Missouri-Columbia. Address: Post Office Box 8541, Kansas City, Missouri 64114.

JONAS, HANS Occupation: Alvin Johnson Professor Emeritus of Philosophy. Education: D.Phil., Marburg University, Germany; D.H.L. h.c.; D.L.L. h.c.; D.Theo. h.c. Address: 9 Meadow Lane, New Rochelle, New York 10805.

JONAS, SARAN Occupation: Professor of Clinical Neurology, New York University School of Medicine. Address: 60 East End Avenue, New York, New York 10028.

JONES, BERNARD L Occupation: Safety/Fire Manager. Education: B.S. Safety Engineering. Address: 121 15th Avenue, Lewiston, Idaho 83501.

JONES, BERNARD WALTER II Occupation: Corporation President, Accountant. Education: B.S. Business Administration, M.A. Economics, Ph.D. Candidate Business Administration. Address: 8 Oakdale Drive, Springfield, Illinois 62707.

JONES, CALVIN PAUL Occupation: Historian, Consultant, Educator. Education: Bachelor of Arts, Master of Arts, Ph.D. Address: Rural Free Delivery, Number 2, Waddy, Kentucky 40076.

JONES, CLARA P Occupation: New Mexico Secretary of State. Address: 228 Crestview Drive Southwest, Albuquerque, New Mexico 87105.

JONES, CLAUDELLA ARCHAMBEAULT Occupation: Director of Professional Activities, Division of Burn Surgery. Education: Diploma, Mercy School of Nursing, 1959; Special Student, University of Michigan, 1964-72; Management by Objectives, University of Michigan, 1968. Address: 914 Lincoln Road, Ann Arbor, Michigan 48104.

JONES, DAVID EDWIN Occupation: Assistant Professor. Education: B.A., Los Angeles State College, 1963; Ph.D., Kent State University, 1973. Address:

6219 Mary Ellen Avenue, Van Nuys, California 91401.

JONES, DEE WALKER Occupation: Public Relations Director, Swedish Hospital Medical Center. Education: B.A. Journalism. Address: 19095 35th Avenue Northeast, Seattle, Washington 98155.

JONES, EDITH IRBY Occupation: Physician. Education: M.D. Address: 3402 South Parkwood Drive, Houston, Texas 77021.

JONES, ELVIS C Occupation: Professor, Frostburg State College. Education: B.A., M.A. Psychology. Address: 222 McCulloh, Frostburg, Maryland 21532.

JONES, ERIC WYNN Occupation: Veterinarian. Education: B.R.C.V.S., Ph.D. Address: P.O. 1935, Starkville, Mississippi 39759

JONES, HATTIE ELIZABETH RUSSELL Occupation: Professor, Chowan College. Education: B.S., M.Ed. Address: 605 Union Street, Murfreesboro, North Carolina 27855.

JONES, HELEN-LEE Occupation: Assistant Professor of Art, Mount Saint Mary's College. Education: B.A., M.F.A. Address: 174 Highland Road, Chambersburg, Pennsylvania 17201.

JONES, JAMES ALONZO Occupation: College Professor, Minister. Education: B.A., Diploma in Theology, M.S.Ed., Ed.S., Ed.D. Address: 627 Locust Lane, Brownsburg, Indiana 46112.

JONES, JAMES EDWARD Occupation: Professor of Art Education, Morgan State University. Education: M.F.A., B.F.A., Diploma. Address: 2930 Silverhill Avenue, Baltimore, Maryland 21207.

JONES, JOHN EDWIN Occupation: Director of Education. Education: B.S., M.S., C.A.S., Ph.D. Address: P.O. Box 184, Owego, New York 13827.

JONES, JOHN HARDING Occupation: Doctor of Philosophy with Vocational Rehabilitation Therapy, Veterans Administration Medical Center. Education: B.F.A., Rochester Institute of Technology; M.Photo., Brantridge College, England; M.B.A., Pepperdine University; Ph.D., Kentucky Christian College; D.Litt., University of London; D.H.Ed. (Honorary), St. John's University. Address: 8774 Tyrone Avenue, Panaroma City, California 91402.

JONES, JUANITA B Occupation: Author, Retired Educator and Administrator. Education: M.A., Credential Supervision. Address: 22770 De Berry Street, Grand Terrace, California 92324.

JONES, MARGARET O Occupation: Travel Agent. Education: Graduate, Viking International School of Travel, 1978. Address: 2503½ Thomas Avenue, Dallas, Texas 75201.

JONES, MEADE BARNER Occupation: President, The Valley Forge Historical Society. Education: Attended The College of William and Mary. Address: Yellow Springs Road, Paoli, Pennsylvania 19301.

JONES, MILDRED JOSEPHINE Occupation: Real Estate Broker. Education: Attended Howard College, 1946-47. Address: 3024 Biltmore Avenue, Montgomery, Alabama 36109.

JONES, PATRICIA Occupation: Senior Computer Systems Analyst. Education: B.S., M.A. Address: 5907 Old Richmond Avenue, Richmond, Virginia 23226.

JONES, ROBERT L Occupation: University Professor, Pennsylvania State University, College of Medicine. Education: D.Ed. (Ph.D.), M.S., B.S. Address: 214 East High Street, Hummelstown, Pennsylvania 17036.

JONES, ROBERT LEWIS Occupation: Management Consultant. Education: B.A., M.A.E., Ph.D. Address: 2027 East Rice Drive, Tempe, Arizona 85283.

JONES, ROBERT NOBLE Occupation:

Accountant/Statistician. Education: B.A., University of Nebraska; M.A., University of Northern Colorado. Address: 605 Union Street, Murfreesboro, North Carolina 27855.

JONES, ROLAND LEO Occupation: Teacher/Performer, Violin, Viola; Member, Highland String Quartet. Education: B.A., University of Michigan. Address: 3004 South Kearney, Denver, Colorado 80222.

JONES, THOMAS EVAN Occupation: Author, Lecturer, Consultant. Education: D.S.Sc., New School for Social Research; Ph.D., Johns Hopkins University. Address: 1648 Cottle Avenue, San Jose, California 95125.

JONES, WILLIAM FRANK Occupation: Associate Professor of Philosophy. Education: B.S. Business, B.A. Philosophy, M.A. Philosophy, Ph.D. Philosophy. Address: 146 Redwood Drive, Richmond, Kentucky 40475.

JONTRY, RICHARD I Occupation: Psychologist/Consultant. Education: B.B.A., M.A., Ph.D. Address: P.O. Box 70, New London, Pennsylvania 19360.

JORDAN, GARY BLAKE Occupation: Electronic Engineer in Electronic Warfare. Education: B.S.E.E., Ph.D. Electrical Engineering, Doctorate Electrical Engineering. Address: 1012 Olmo Court, San Jose, California 95129.

JORDAN, GARY PHILLIP Occupation: Policeman, Martial Arts Instructor. Education: College Studies. Address: 43 West 143rd Street, Dixmoor, Illinois 60426.

JORDAN, LETITIA CUNNINGHAM Occupation: Banker. Education: B.S. Accounting. Address: 201 Rugby Avenue, Rochester, New York 14619.

JORDAN, PAUL M Occupation: Dean of Students. Education: B.A., M.A. Address: Route 1 Box 64C, Diamond, Missouri 64840.

JORDAN, R BRUCE Occupation: University Professor. Education: B.A. Public Administration, M.B.A. Management, Stanford University. Address: 110 41st Street, Apartment 705, Oakland, California 94611.

JOSEFOWITZ, NATASHA Occupation: Adjunct Professor, College Human Service, San Diego State University. Education: M.S.W., Ph.D. Address: 2235 calle Guaymas, La Jolla, California 92037.

JOSHI, MADAN M Occupation: Soil Microbiologist/Plant Pathologist, DuPont Experimental Station. Education: Ph.D. Address: 2036 Floral Drive, Wilmington, Delaware 19180.

JOST, FRANZ A Occupation: Marketing Executive. Education: Master Business Administration, B.S. International Economics, University of Illinois. Address: 11043 North Saint Andrews Way, Scottsdale, Arizona 85254.

JOYCE, ROSEMARY ENYART Occupation: Real Estate Broker. Education: Attended Northwestern University. Address: 579 Patrick Henry Square, Oak Brook, Illinois 60521.

JUAREZ, SUSANA PATRICIA Occupation: Nurse, Nurse Educator. Education: B.S.M., M.S.N. Address: Route 1 Box 1494, Del Valle, Texas 78617.

JUDD, WILLIAM ROBERT Occupation: Professor and Consultant. Education: A.B. Geology, Graduate Study Civil Engineering. Address: 200 Quincy Street, West Lafayette, Indiana 47906.

JUMONVILLE, FELIX JOSEPH JR Occupation: University Professor, Real Estate Broker. Education: B.S., M.S., Ed.D. Address: 8816 Whitaker Avenue, Sepulveda, California 91343.

JUN, JONG SUP Occupation: Professor of Public Administration, Department of Public Administration, California State University-Hayward. Address: 5600 Trail Side Court, Castro Valley, California 94546.

JUNEMANN, EDNA JULIA Occupation: Poet/Writer. Education: B.A. Address: 144-41 Sanford Avenue #5E, Flushing, New York 11355.

JUNG, LYNNETTE C Occupation: Chief, Mental Health Clinic, United States Air Force Regional Medical Center, Clark Air Force Base. Education: M.S.W. Address: 505 2nd Avenue North, Glasgow, Montana 59230.

JURICH, JULIE ANN Occupation: Family/Child Therapist. Education: B.S., Ohio State University, 1968; M.S., M.E.I., Pennsylvania State University, 1970; Ph.D., Kansas State University, 1978. Address: 3225 Park Circle, Manhattan, Kansas 166502.

JUROE, BONITA B Occupation: Director, Stepparents Institute of California; Co-Author, *Successful Stepparenting*, 1985; President, Women's Ministries in the Evangelical Free Church of Orange; Co-Founder, National Stepparents Day. Education: B.S., California State University-Fullerton, 1984; A.A., Santa Ana Junior College, 1979. Address: 563 Kensington Road, Orange, Califonria 92669.

JUST, RICHARD E Occupation: Professor of Agriculture and Resource Economics, University of California-Berkeley. Education: B.S. Agricultural Economics, M.A. Statistics, Ph.D. Agricultural Economics. Address: 838 Indian Rock, Berkeley, California 94707.

K

KABALKA, GEORGE W Occupation: Professor of Chemistry, Consultant. Education: B.S., Ph.D. Address: 7124 Cresthill Drive, Knoxville, Tennessee 37919.

KAGAN-KANS, EVA Occupation: Professor. Education: B.A., M.A., Ph.D. Address: 2014 Georgetown Road, Bloomington, Indiana 47401.

KAGEY, F EILEEN Occupation: Teacher. Education: B.S., M.S. in Education. Address: 3040 West 39th Place, Gary, Indiana 46408.

KAHANA, BOAZ Occupation: Professor, Chairperson, Clinical Psychologist, Cleveland State University. Education: B.A. 1955, M.A. 1957, Ph.D. 1967. Address: 4421 University Parkway, University Heights, Ohio 44118.

KAHANA, EVA F Occupation: Professor of Sociology, Department of Sociology, Case Western Reserve University. Education: M.A. Psychology, City College of New York, 1965; Ph.D. Human Development. Address: 4421 University Parkway, University Heights, Ohio 44118.

KAHN, LISA MARGARETE Occupation: Professor. Education: M.S., Ph.D. Address: 4106 Merrick, Houston, Texas 77025.

KAHN, SY M Occupation: Professor of English and Drama. Education: B.A., M.A., Ph.D. Address: 3725 Monitor Circle, North, Stockton, California 95209.

KAISER, CHRISTOPHER BARINA Occupation: Theological Educator, Western Theological Seminary. Education: A.B., M.Div., Ph.D. Address: Western Theological Seminary, Holland, Michigan 49423.

KALECHOFSKY, ROBERTA D Occupation: Writer, Publisher, Editor. Education: B.A., M.A., Ph.D. in English Literature. Address: 255 Humphrey Street, Marblehead, Massachusetts 01945.

KALIKOW, THEODORA J Occupation: Dean College of Arts and Sciences, University of Northern Colorado. Education: A.B., Sc.M., Ph.D. Address: 1601 Reservoir Road, Greeley, Colorado 80631.

KALVINSKAS, JOHN JOSEPH Occupation: Project Manager/Chemical Engineer. Education: B.S. Chemical Engineering 1951, M.S. Chemical Engineering 1952, Massachusetts Institute of Technology; Ph.D. Chemical Engineering 1959, California Institute of Technology.

KALWINSKY, CHARLES KNOWLTON Occupation: Government Executive. Education: B.A., University of Pennsylvania; M.B.A., Fairleigh Dickenson. Address: 13 Oakleaf Lane, Toms River, New Jersey 08753.

KAMAKAWIWOOLE, REYNOLDS N JR Occupation: Police Officer. Education: Police Science. Address: Post Office Box 821, Honokaa, Hawaii 96725.

KAMERICK, JOHN J Occupation: President Emeritus, Professor of History, University of Northern Iowa. Education: B.A., M.A., Ph.D. Address: 1893 Pinehurst Court, Waterloo, Iowa 50701.

KAMIMOTO, DAVID ROSS Occupation: University Admissions Counselor. Education: B.A., University of California-Berkeley; M.S., San Francisco State University. Address: 115 Felix Street #8, Santa Cruz, California 95060.

KAN, HSIN-CHIA Occupation: Research Chemist. Education: Ph.D. in Materials Science. Address: 28 Bent Oak Trail, Fairport, New York 14450.

KANE, KATHERINE Occupation: Poet and Playwright. Education: B.A. English Literature,

Manhattanville College; M.F.A., University of Iowa. Address: 20 Oak Road, Katonah, New York 10536.

KANFER, FREDERICK H Occupation: Professor of Psychology, Department of Psychology, University of Illinois. Education: Attended Cooper Union School of Technology; B.S. cum laude, Long Island University; M.A. 1952, Ph.D. 1953, Indiana University. Address: Department of Psychology, University of Illinois, 603 East Daniel Street, Champaign, Illinois 61820.

KANTEN, ANNE I Occupation: Assistant Commissioner, Department of Agriculture. Education: B.S., Olaf College. Address: 2045 Christianson, St. Paul, Minnesota 55118.

KANTOFF, JOYCE Occupation: Probation Officer. Education: B.S. Sociology. Address: 1100 South Hamilton, Chicago, Illinois 60612.

KAPLAN, HAROLD M Occupation: Professor Medical Physiology, Southern Illinois University. Education: A.B., A.M., Ph.D. Address: 106 North Almond, Carbondale, Illinois 62901.

KAPLAN, LAURA KAY Occupation: Advertising Executive. Education: B.F.A., Drake University. Address: 5200 West 98th Street, Bloomington, Minnesota 55437.

KAPLAN, ROBERT B Occupation: Professor Applied Linguistics, University of Southern California. Education: B.A., Willamete University, 1952; M.A. 1957, Ph.D. 1963, University of Southern California. Address: 30303 Canado Drive, Rancho Palos Verdes, California 90274.

KAPLAN, SANFORD S Occupation: Geologist, Oil/Gas Exploration and United States Navy Reserve. Education: A.B. 1971, M.S. 1976, Ph.D. 1981. Address: 11761 East Asbury Place, Aurora, Colorado 80014.

KAPP, SANDRA LILLIAN Occupation: Registered Nurse. Education: R.N. Address: 2923 Moon Lake Drive, West Bloomfield, Michigan 48033.

KAPRAL, FRANK ALBERT Occupation: Professor Medical Microbiology and Immunology. Education: B.S. Bacteriology, Ph.D. Medical Microbiology. Address: 873 Clubview Boulevard, Worthington, Ohio 43085.

KAPROV, SUSAN LEE Occupation: Artist. Education: B.A., M.A., Dartmouth College. Address: 149 Willow Street, Brooklyn Heights, New York 11201.

KAPUSTA, LORRIE JANET Occupation: Television Broadcaster; President, Prime Entertainment Network, Inc. Address: 35916 South Valley Court, Apartment 41208, Farmington Hills, Michigan 48018.

KARDOS, LASZLO A Occupation: Medical Technologist, Clinical Laboratory Director. Education: Medical Technology. Address: 1717 Cliffside, Wichita Falls, Texas 76302.

KARLIN, GARY LEE Occupation: Insurance Executive; Consultant, Estate Planning. Education: University of Chicago. Address: 1497 Lake Shore Court, Barrington, Illinois 60010.

KARMEL, A MATTHEW Occupation: Research Engineer. Education: Ph.D., Princeton University. Address: 20754 Kennoway Circle, Birmingham, Michigan 48010.

KARPEN, MARIAN JOAN Occupation: Financial Executive. Education: A.B., Vassar College, 1966; Postgraduate, Sorbonne (Paris); M.B.A. Program, New York University Graduate School of Business, 1974-77. Address: 233 East 69th Street, New York, New York 10021.

KARPILOW, BABETTE Occupation: Therapeutic Recreational Specialist, Theater Therapist. Education: Certified T.R.S. Address: 215 14th Avenue East,

Seattle, Washington 98112.

KARRENBAUER, BEVERLY W Occupation: Administrator, Dade County Public School. Education: B.S., M.Ed., Post-Graduate Administration. Address: 1040 Northeast 82nd Street, Miami, Floria 33138.

KARUHIJE, HARRIETT F Occupation: Assistant Professor of Nursing Education. Education: B.Sc. Ed., M.A., M.Ed. Nursing Education, Ed.D. Address: 108 West 23rd Street, Chester, Pennsylvania 19013.

KARWOSKI, RICHARD C Occupation: Artist and Professor of Art. Education: B.F.A., M.A. Address: 28 East 4th Street, New York, New York 10003.

KASBERG, LOIS ARLENE Occupation: Occupancy Technicial II. Education: Business School Diploma. Address: 1115 Church Street, Redlands, California 92374.

KASPERBAUER, JAMES C Occupation: Professor. Education: B.A., University of Nebraska (Omaha); M.A., Central Michigan University; Ed.D., Memphis State University. Address: 2576 Tigrett Cove, Memphis, Tennessee 38119.

KASS, EDWARD HAROLD Occupation: Physician. Education: A.B. 1939, M.S. 1941, University of Kentucky; Ph.D., University of Wisconsin, 1943; M.D., University of California, 1947; M.A. (hon.), Harvard University, 1958; D.Sc. (hon.), University of Kentucky, 1962. Address: Todd Pond Road, Lincoln, Massachusetts 01773.

KASSER, JUDITH Occupation: Executive Director, Jewish Family and Children's Services. Education: A.B., Temple University; M.S.S., Bryn Mawr College. Address: 32 Emerson Place, Boston, Massachusetts 02114.

KAST, GLORIA E Occupation: International Library Consultant. Education: A.B., M.A. Address: 4600 Robertson Avenue, Sacramento, California 95821.

KATSH, ABRAHAM I Occupation: President Emeritus, The Dropsie University (Retired); Professor Emeritus of Hebrew Culture and Education, New York University (Retired). Education: B.S. 1931, M.A. 1932, Doctor of Jurisprudence 1936, New York University; Doctor of Philosophy, Dropsie College, 1944. Address: 45 East 89th Street, New York, New York 10028.

KATSUTANI, MICHELE A Occupation: Assistant Director. Education: B.A. Psychology. Address: 846 Puapana Place, Makawao, Hawaii 96768.

KATZ, ARNOLD Occupation: Professor of Economics. Education: A.B., Hamilton College; Ph.D., Yale University. Address: 4350 Lydia Street, Pittsburgh, Pennsylvania 15207.

KATZ, (ELAINE) E MARCIA Occupation: Associate Professor of Nuclear Engineering. Education: B.S., M.E., M.S., Ph.D. Address: 1431 Cherokee Trail-106, Knoxville, Tennessee 37920.

KATZ, ELIA J Occupation: Novelist, Editor, TV Producer. Education: B.A., Johns Hopkins University. Address: Post Office Box 471, Bronx, New York 10458.

KATZ, J LAWRENCE Occupation: Professor of Biophysics and Biomedical Engineering, Chairman Department of Biomedical Engineering. Education: B.S., M.S., Ph.D. Address: 838 Maxwell Drive, Schenectady, New York 12309.

KATZ, MYER Occupation: Businessman, Historian, Biologist, Educator. Education: B.E., B.A., M.A. Address: 1525 State Street, La Crosse, Wisconsin 54601.

KATZ, RICHARD JON Occupation: President/ Creative Director. Education: Associate, Applied Science. Address: 635 Madison Avenue, New York City, New York 11577.

KATZ, STEVEN R Occupation: Novelist, Poet, Screenwriter, Teacher. Education: B.A. honors, Cornell University; M.A., University of Oregon. Address: 3060 8th Street, Boulder, Colorado 80302.

KATZ, WILLIAM LOREN Occupation: Historian/ Lecturer. Education: B.A., Syracuse University, 1950; Attended New York University, 1952. Address: 231 West 13th Street, New York, New York 10011.

KAUFER, GERALD IRA Occupation: General/ Vascular Surgeon. Education: M.D., University of Pittsburgh School of Medicine. Address: 1574 Tiffany Drive, Pittsburgh, Pennsylvania 15241.

KAUFFMAN, GEORGE B Occupation: University Professor, Chemist, Historian of Science, Author. Education: B.A. honors, University of Pennsylvania, 1951; Ph.D., University of Florida, 1956. Address: 3881 East Pico Avenue, Fresno, California 93726.

KAUFMAN, ALAN S Occupation: Professor, University of Alabama. Education: A.B. 1965, M.A. 1967, Ph.D. 1970. Address: 5407 Woodhill Circle, Tuscaloosa, Alabama 35405.

KAUFMAN, BEL Occupation: Writer, Lecturer. Education: B.A. magna cum laude, Hunter College; M.A. (1st Class), Columbia University. Address: 1020 Park Avenue, New York City, New York 10028.

KAUFMAN, FRANK A Occupation: U.S. District Judge. Education: A.B. summa cum Laude, Dartmouth College, 1937; LL.B. magna cum laude, Harvard University, 1940. Address: U.S. Courthouse, Baltimore, Maryland 21201.

KAUFMAN, MICO Occupation: Sculptor. Education: Academy Fine Arts, Rome. Address: 23 Marion Drive, Tewksbury, Massachusetts 01876.

KAUFMAN, NADEEN LAURIE Occupation: College Professor, University of Alabama. Education: B.S. Education, M.A. Psychology, Ed.D. Learning Disabilities. Address: 5407 Woodhill Circle, Tuscaloosa, Alabama 35405.

KAUR, INDERJIT Occupation: Counsel. Education: B.A., M.A. Address: 219 Amhurst Southeast, Albuquerque, New Mexico 87106.

KAWABATA, MINORU Occupation: Artist/ Painter. Address: 463 West Street, New York, New York 10014.

KAY, BRUCE G Occupation: Director of Pharmacy Services. Education: B.A., B.S., M.S. Address: 750 Kensington Court, Westbury, New York 11590.

KAY, STANLEY ROBERT Occupation: Clinical Psychologist. Education: B.A. 1968, M.A. cum laude 1970, Ph.D. 1980, Psychology. Address: Kirkwood Road, R.F.D. 2, Mahopac, New York 10541.

KAYE, ALAN S Occupation: Professor, Director Phonetics Laboratory. Education: Ph.D. Address: Post Office Box 32, Atwood, California 92601.

KAYS, JAMES W Occupation: Investment Executive and Chairman of the Board. Education: B.S. Business Administration, University of Oregon, 1948. Address: 2085 Sunrise Boulevard, Eugene, Oregon 97405.

KAZAKIA, JACOB Y Occupation: Associate Professor. Education: Ph.D. in Applied Mechanics. Address: 420 Garretson Road, Bridgewater, New Jersey 08807.

KEARNEY, MICHAEL JOHN Occupation: Banker. Education: B.S., E.E., M.B.A. Address: 2515 Peachtree Lane, Northbrook, Illinois 60062.

KECK, GWENDOLYN ODESSA Occupation: Public Relations/Marketing. Education: B.S. Address: 12489 East Amherst Circle, Aurora, Colorado 80014.

KEDDLE, DAVID GLEN Occupation: Director, Chi Medical Library. Education: A.A. Business and

Librarianship. Address: 1687 Tuscany Lane, Holt, Michigan 48842.

KEEFE, CAROLYN B Occupation: Associate Professor and Director of Forensics, Department of Speech Communications Theatre, West Chester University. Education: A.B., Oberlin College; M.A., Temple University; M.A., Villanova University; Ed.D., University of Pennsylvania. Address: Hershey's Mill, 5 Hershey's Drive, West Chester, Pennsylvania 19380.

KEEL, SALLIE C Occupation: Mail Order Business Supervisor. Education: B.S., M.L.S. Address: 1035 West Rock Spring Road, Greenville, North Carolina 27834.

KEENE, ROBERT GILMORE Occupation: Rare Book Dealer. Address: Montauk Highway, Bridgehampton, New York 11932.

KEENE-BURGESS, RUTH FRANCES Occupation: Chief, Inventory Management Division, Crane Army Ammunition Activity. Education: Bachelor of Science Mathematics, Arizona State University, 1970; Master of Science Management Science, Fairleigh Dickinson University, 1978. Address: 4916 West Pinchot Avenue, Phoenix, Arizona 85031.

KEENEY, WILLIAM ECHARD Occupation: Faculty Member, Center for Peaceful Change, Kent State University. Education: A.B., B.D., S.T.M., Ph.D. Address: 826 Mae Street, Kent, Ohio 442409.

KEHL, RANDALL H Occupation: Captain, United States Air Force (Judge Advocate), Special Assistant, U.S. Attorney. Education: B.S., J.D., M.B.A. Address: 2051 Steeple Drive, Anchorage, Alaska 99507.

KEIL, LUCY GUTHRIE Occupation: International Accounting Manager. Education: Master of Accountancy, Bowling Green State University; Master Divinity, Union Theological Seminary; B.A., Stanford University. Address: 426 Wallace, Bowling Green, Ohio 43402.

KEIMACH, BRAD M Occupation: Orchestra and Opera Conductor. Education: B.M., Juilliard School of Music, 1975. Address: 250 West 77th Street, New York, New York 10024.

KEISER, JOYCE B Occupation: Child Psychologist. Education: B.S. Psychology, M.Ed. Special Education, Additional Studies. Address: 50 Highlands Drive, Richboro, Pennsylvania 18954.

KEITH, LINDA GABBERT Occupation: Certified Public Accountant, Lecturer. Education: B.A. Accounting, Washington State University. Address: 8325 Spurgeon Creek Road, Southeast, Olympia, Washington 98503.

KELLEHER, DIANA L Occupation: Vice President Marketing, Vitamin Manufacturer. Education: M.B.A, University of Chicago; B.S. Finance, Drexel University. Address: 13423 Contour Drive, Sherman Oaks, California 91423.

KELLER, LEROY ANDERSON JR Occupation: Loan Officer. Education: B.S. in Commerce, M.B.A. Address: 4611 North Lakefront Drive, Glen Allen, Virginia 23060.

KELLER, MINNIE B Occupation: Retired Professional Nurse, Associate Professor. Education: R.N., B.S.N., M.S. Address: Apartment 306C, 824 Lakeview Drive, Parkersburg, West Virginia 26104.

KELLER, PAUL DUDLEY Occupation: Surgeon. Education: B.S., Utah State University, 1934; M.D., University of Oregon Medical School, 1939.

KELLEY, JEAN ANN Occupation: Assistant Dean, Graduate Programs. Education: Diploma in Nursing, M.A., Ed.D. Address: 4766 Overwood Circle, Birmingham, Alabama 35222.

KELLEY, MARYELLEN R Occupation: College Professor Business Management and Labor Relations.

Education: B.A., Brandeis University; M.C.P., Harvard University; Ph.D., Massachusetts Institute of Technology. Address: 1514 Beacon Street #48, Brookline, Massachusetts 02146.

KELLEY, WILLIAM N Occupation: Chairman, Department of Internal Medicine, University of Michigan. Education: M.D. Address: 521 Hillspur Road, Ann Arbor, Michigan 48105.

KELLOGG, BRUCE MICHAEL Occupation: Real Estate Investor/Realtor. Education: B.S.E.E., M.B.A. Address: Post Office Box 18966, San Jose, California 95158.

KELLY, DOROTHY HELEN Occupation: Doctor of Pediatrics. Education: B.S.N., Fitchburg State College, 1966; B.S. 1968, M.D. 1972, Wayne State University. Address: 39 Drummer Road, Acton, Massachusetts 01720.

KELLY, JOHN LOVE Occupation: Vice President Director of Public Relations and Communications. Education: B.S., St. Peters College. Address: 21 Furnace Woods Road, Cortlandt, New York 10566.

KELLY, KATHLEEN WILLIAMS Occupation: Administrative Secretary. Address: 2821 Embassy Row, Apartment 814, Speedway, Indiana 46224.

KELLY, LEO J Occupation: Callaway Professor of Special Education. Education: B.S., M.A., Ed.D. Address: Route 8, Box 31, Lot 32, Valdosta, Georgia 31602.

KELLY, LILY MARCIA Occupation: Clincal Psychologist, Professor, Howard University. Education: B.S., Pittsburgh University; M.S., Ph.D., University of Georgia. Address: 301 G Street Southwest, #129, Washington, D.C. 20024.

KELLY, MARGARET R Occupation: Retired Educator, Writer of Genealogy. Education: B.A. Address: 402 Fayetteville Avenue, Bennettsville, South Carolina 29512.

KELLY, NANCY JEAN MONROE Occupation: Medical Technologist. Education: B.S., M.T., M.A. Address: 100 Walnut Circle, Bristol, Tennessee 37620.

KELLY, RITA MAE Occupation: Professor. Education: Ph.D., Political Science. Address: 1335 East Ellis Drive, Tempe, Arizona 85282.

KELLY, VELTA M Occupation: Program Administrator, University of Cincinnati. Education: B.S Personnel Administration, M.Ed. Business/Adult Education; Associate Degree General Business. Address: 6281 Robison Road, Cincinnati, Ohio 45213.

KEMLER, R LEONARD Occupation: Physician. Education: B.A. 1939, M.D. 1943, Yale University. Address: 65 Norwood Road, West Hartford, Connecticut 06117.

KEMP, DOROTHY ELIZABETH WALTER Occupation: Professor of Music. Education: B.S. Education, College of Music in Cincinnati and University of Cincinnati Teachers College, 1948; M.A., Eastern Kentucky University; Additional Studies. Address: 4559 Hamilton Avenue, Cincinnati, Ohio 45223.

KEMPER, MARLYN J Occupation: Local Government Documents Librarian, Broward County Main Library. Education: Bachelor of Arts, Master of Arts in Anthropology, M.L.S. in Library Science. Address: 2845 Northeast 35th Street, Fort Lauderdale, Florida 33306.

KEMPNER, WALTER Occupation: Physician, Professor Emeritus of Medicine. Education: M.D., Heidelberg, Germany, 1926. Address: Box 3099, Duke University Medical Center, Durham, North Carolina 27710.

KENAGA, EUGENE E Occupation: Ecologist, Pesticide-Wildlife Consultant. Education: B.S., M.A.,

Ph.D. Address: 1281 North Wagner Road, Essexville, Michigan 48732.

KENDALL, KATHLEEN E Occupation: Chairperson and Associate Professor, Department of Communications, State University of New York-Albany. Education: B.A., Oberlin College; M.A., University of Southern Mississippi; Ph.D., Indiana University. Address: R.D. #1, New Salem South Road, Voorheesville, New York 12186.

KENDRICKS, JAMES W Occupation: President Financial Institution. Education: J.D., University of California-Los Angeles, 1971. Address: 4966 North Grand Avenue, Covina, California 91724.

KENN, CHARLES WILLIAM Occupation: Consultant on Hawaiian History, Language, Activities. Education: A.B., University of Hawaii; Graduate Certificate, Whittier College. Address: 45-028 Lilipuna Road, Kaneohe, Hawaii 96744.

KENNEDY, GAY L Occupation: Executive Director, Social Service Non-Profit Organization. Education: B.S. Accounting. Address: 6020 North Flora, Fresno, California 93710.

KENNEDY, JEANNE D Occupation: Director of Community Relations. Education: A.B. Mathematics, Smith College. Address: 623 Mirada Avenue, Stanford, California 94305.

KENNEDY, WILLIAM S Occupation: Publisher and Editor, *Reflect*. Education: Attended William and Mary College. Address: 3306 Argonne Avenue, Norfolk, Virginia 23509.

KENNERLY, RAYMOND GRADY II Occupation: Data Processing and Management Consultant. Address: 6302 Merna Lane, Lanham, Maryland 20706.

KENNY, JOHN EDWARD Occupation: Senior Computer Analyst. Education: A.A.S. Data Processing. Address: 212 McKinley Avenue, Kenmore, New York 14217.

KENT, JACK Occupation: Author/Illustrator. Address: 103 West Johnson, San Antonio, Texas 78204.

KENYON, KAREN BETH Occupation: Author, *Sunshower*, 1981; Instructor, MiraCosta College, U.C.S.D. Education: B.A. Address: 3440 Dorchester Drive, San Diego, California 92123.

KERAN, DOUGLAS CHARLES Occupation: Natural Resource Educator/Consultant. Education: B.S. Wildlife Biology, M.A. Biology. Address: Route #7, Box 14, Brainerd, Minnesota 56401.

KERN, EDITH Occupation: Author, Critic/Doris Silbert Professor in the Humanities Emeritus, Smith College. Education: Ph.D. Address: 1025 5th Avenue, New York, New York 10028.

KERR, CATHERINE EARL BAILEY Occupation: Artist, Teacher; Owner, Kerr International School of Art for the Handicapped. Address: 1412 West Hendricks, Roswell, New Mexico 88201.

KERR, WENDLE LOUIS Occupation: Pharmaceutical Education. Education: B.S., M.S., Pharmacy. Address: 236 Hutchinson Avenue, Iowa City, Iowa 52240.

KERRI, KENNETH DONALD Occupation: Professor of Civil Engineering. Education: B.S.C.E., M.S. Sanitation Engineering, Ph.D.C.E. Address: 5839 Shepard Avenue, Sacramento, California 95819.

KERSTEN, TIMOTHY WAYNE Occupation: Professor of Economics. Education: B.A., California State University, 1967; M.A. 1971, Ph.D. 1973, University of Oregon. Address: 1705 14th Street, Los Osos, California 93402.

KESSEL, JOHN HOWARD Occupation: Professor of Political Science, Ohio State University. Education: B.A., Ohio State University, 1950; Ph.D., Columbia University, 1958. Address: 223 Derby Hall, 154 North Oval Mall, Columbus, Ohio 43210-1373.

KESSELRING, JOHN PAUL Occupation: Vice President, Alzeta Corporation. Education: B.S., University of Michigan, 1961; M.S. 1962, Ph.D. 1968, Stanford University. Address: 401 Preston Drive, Mountain View, California 94040.

KESSLER, CAROLYN L Occupation: Professor, Bicultural Bilingual Studies, University of Texas at San Antonio. Education: B.A., St. Mary-of-the-Woods College; M.S., Ph.D., Georgetown University. Address: 2500 Jackson Keller #208, San Antonio, Texas 78230.

KESSLER, MARY EMELINE Occupation: Registered Nurse, Operating Room Supervisor. Education: Diploma R.N., 1954. Address: 6117 Manton Avenue, Woodland Hills, California 91367.

KESSLER, MICHAEL G Occupation: Assistant Chief Auditor Investigator. Education: A.A., B.S., M.B.A., St. Johns University; C.A.G.S., Pace University. Address: 20 Stone Lane, Staten Island, New York 10314.

KESSLER, MINUETTA Occupation: Concert Pianist, Educator, Composer. Education: L.A.B. Graduate and Postgraduate Diploma in Piano, Juilliard School of Music. Address: 30 Hurley Street, Belmont, Massachusetts 02178.

KETCHUM, WILLIAM C JR Occupation: Author, Attorney. Education: B.A., Union College; J.D., Columbia University. Address: 241 Grace Church Street, Rye, New York 10580.

KETTNER, DAVID A Occupation: Artist/Educator, Philadelphia College of Art. Education: B.F.A., Cleveland Institute of Art; M.F.A., Indiana University. Address: 106 Cliff Terrace, Wyncote, Pennsylvania 19095.

KEYES, DANIEL Occupation: Professor, Author, Playwright. Education: B.A., M.A., Brooklyn College. Address: Ohio University, Athens, Ohio 45701.

KEYS, CHRISTOPHER B Occupation: Professor of Psychology, Psychology Department, University of Illinois. Education: B.A., Oberlin College; M.A. and Ph.D., University of Cincinnati. Address: 533 North Cuyler, Oak Park, Illinois 60302.

KEYSERLING, MARY DUBLIN Occupation: Consulting Economist, Writer, Speaker. Education: B.A. honors, Ph.D. Candidate. Address: 2610 Upton Street, Northwest, Washington, D.C. 20008.

KHALIL, MUHAMMAD AHSAN KHAN Occupation: Research Scientist. Education: B.Sc., M.Sc., A.I.F.C., Ph.D. Address: 17 Diefenbaker Street, St. John's, Newfoundland, A1A 2M2.

KHAN, ALIMA Occupation: Student. Education: B.S. Address: Calle Uroyan, AD4, Mayaguez, Puerto Rico 00709.

KHAN, IQBAL M Occupation: Researcher. Education: Ph.D. Physiology, Reproductive Endocrinology. Address: 1453 West Flournoy, Chicago, Illinois 60607.

KHANDELWAL, UMESH C Occupation: Occupational Safety/Health Engineer. Education: Bachelor of Technology in Mechanical Engineering. Address: 3378 Avenida Simi, Simi Valley, California 93063.

KHARADIA, VIRABHAI CHELABHAI Occupation: Professor of Economics and Department Chairman. Education: Master of Commerce, Master of Science, Ph.D. Address: Rural Route 4, Maryville, Missouri 63368.

KHOSLA, MAHESH C Occupation: Cardiovascular Research, Cleveland Clinic. Education: B.Sc. honors, M.S. honors, Ph.D. Address: 7415

Warwick Lane, Chesterland, Ohio 44026.

KIAMIE, DON ALBERT N Occupation: Accountant. Education: B.S., Fordham University, 1965; M.B.A., New York University, 1967. Address: 4 North 3rd Street, Quarry Acres, Peekskill, New York 10566.

KIBLER, D BURKE III Occupation: Attorney. Education: B.A. cum laude 1947, LL.B. 1949, University of Florida. Address: 2113 Fairmont Avenue, Lakeland, Florida 33803.

KIDD, MARINA VON LINSOWE Occupation: Senior Systems Consultant. Address: 8016 Hatwick Way, Sacramento, California 95828.

KIDWELL, MICHELE ANNE FALIK Occupation: Certified Historian. Education: B.A. Address: 495 West End Avenue, New York City, New York 10024.

KIEF, PAUL A Occupation: Lawyer. Education: B.A. 1957, LL.B. 1957, University of Minnesota. Address: Box 212, Bemidji, Minnesota 56601-0212.

KIERSTEAD, FRED DAVID JR Occupation: College Professor. Education: B.A., M.Ed., Ph.D. Address: 15819 Stonehaven Drive, Houston, Texas 77059.

KIERULFF, STEPHEN Occupation: Clinical Psychologist. Education: Ph.D. Psychology. Address: 358 South Bentley Avenue, Los Angeles, California 90049.

KIHNE, JOHN FRANKLIN Occupation: Industrial Arts Instructor. Education: B.S. Education. Address: 1202 3rd Street Northeast, Mandan, North Dakota 58554.

KILBOURN, GARY LYNN Occupation: Advertising Sales and Marketing. Education: B.A. Address: 5782 Magnolia Avenue, Rialto, California 92376.

KILBURN, LARRY ALAN Occupation: Superintendent of Public Works, Village of Arcade. Education: B.S. Civil Engineering. Address: 26 Maple Avenue, Arcade, New York 14009.

KILDUFF, JANE M Occupation: Manager. Education: A.A. Business Management. Address: 20 Center, Keyport, New Jersey 07735.

KILLMAN, J RUSSELL Occupation: Clergyman. Education: B.A., Th.B., B.D., D.D., F.R.G.S. Address: 3922 Community Avenue, La Crescenta, California 91214.

KILPATRICK, BEVERLY AVIS Occupation: Owner/Account Executive. Education: Bachelor's Degree. Address: 1708 Plaza De San Joaquin, Modesto, California 95350.

KILPATRICK, CHARLES O Occupation: Editor/Publisher. Education: B.A. Address: 2019 East Lawndale Drive, San Antonio, Texas 78209.

KILSBY, MARY ELLEN G Occupation: Senior Minister. Education: B.A., Pomona College; Rel.M., M.Div., D.Min., Claremont. Address: 470 Blaisdell Drive, Claremont, California 91711.

KIM, EUISHIN EDMUND Occupation: Professor of Radiology and Medicine. Education: M.D. Address: 7715 Moondance, Houston, Texas 77071.

KIM, HARRY HYUNKIL Occupation: Housing Program Assistant. Education: Ph.D., M.A., B.A. Address: 4239 North East 74th Street, Seattle, Washington 98115.

KIM, YONG CHOON Occupation: Professor. Education: B.A., B.D., Th.M., Ph.D. Address: 58 Parkwood Drive, Kingston, Rhode Island 02881.

KIM, YOUNSUK ERNEST Occupation: Professor. Education: Ph.D. Address: 102 East Madison Avenue, Cresskill, New Jersey 07626.

KIMBALL, W WAYNE JR Occupation: Artist.

Education: B.A., Southern Utah State College, 1968; M.F.A., University of Arizona, 1970. Address: 1328 East Harvest Street, Mesa, Arizona 85203.

KIMMELMAN, BURT J Occupation: Professor. Education: Ph.D. Address: 33-41 71st Street, Jackson Heights, New York 11372.

KIMMONS, KEITH DE WAYNE Occupation: Psychological/Vocational Counselor. Education: A.A. Sociology, B.A. Psychology, M.A. Counseling/Psychology. Address: 25227 Avenida Dorena, Newhall, California 91321.

KING, CAROL SOUCEK Occupation: Vice President, Editor-in-Chief, Designers West Magazine. Education: B.A., M.F.A., Ph.D. Address: 60 El Circulo Drive, Pasadena, California 91105.

KING, DAVID F Occupation: Deputy Director, Northern New Hampshire Mental Health and Developmental Services. Education: B.A. Psychology, M.A. Sociology. Address: 36 Florence Street, Dover, New Hampshire 03820.

KING, JOHN THEODORE III Occupation: Executive Assistant. Education: A.B., Princeton University, 1940. Address: 27 Warrenton Road, Baltimore, Maryland 21210.

KING, JOSEPH JERONE Occupation: Executive Consultant. Address: Ioka Beach Hood Canal, 11655 Ioka Way, North West, Silverdale, Washington 98383.

KING, LIS SONDER Occupation: Public Relations Executive. Education: School of Fine Arts. Address: 30 Dundee Court, Mahwah, New Jersey 07430.

KING, ROSALIE ROSSO Occupation: Chairman and Professor. Education: Ph.D., Ed.M., B.S. Address: 5075 West Mercer Way, Mercer Island, Washington 98040.

KING, S MacCALLUM Occupation: Vice President of Technical Services, Certified Professional Agronomist and Soil Scientist. Education: B.S.A., M.S., Ph.D., M.B.A. Address: 36 Pine Avenue, Lake Zurich, Illinois 60047.

KING, TIMOTHY L Occupation: Aviation Insurance Consultant. Education: B.S. Address: 760 South Brevard Avenue, Cocoa Beach, Florida 32931.

KINNEY, GORDON D Occupation: Educational Consultant, Seattle Breakers Hockey Club, Inc. and Cascade Job Corp Center. Education: B.S. Education. Address: 7519-South Taft Street, Seattle, Washington 98178.

KINNEY, JANICE L Occupation: Publicist, Northwest Chamber Orchestra. Education: B.A. Spanish. Address: 23814½ Yale Avenue East, Seattle, Washington 98102.

KINNEY, MARJORIE S Occupation: Senior Vice President. Education: L.H.D., West Coast University, 1982. Address: 450 North Roxbury Drive, Beverly Hills, California 90210.

KINNISON, ROBERT RAY Occupation: Senior Research Statistician. Education: B.A., Pomona College; Ph.D., University of California-Los Angeles. Address: 700 North Montana Place, Kennewick, Washington 99336.

KINSELLA, JAMES J SR Occupation: Business Venture Enterprises. Education: Business. Address: 2010 North Atlantic, Peoria, Illinois 61603.

KINTALA, CHANDRA MOHAN RAO Occupation: Computer Science Research. Education: Ph.D. Address: 253 Farragut Road, North Plainfield, New Jersey 07062.

KINTZELE, JOHN A Occupation: Attorney at Law. Education: B.A., L.L.B. Address: 2040 Clermont Street, Denver, Colorado 80207.

KIPLINGER, CHRISTINA LOUISE Occupation:

Writer. Education: G.E.D., Degree in Non-Fiction Writing. Address: 1320-B Beckett Avenue, Cambridge, Ohio 43725.

KIPNIS, IGOR Occupation: Harpischordist, Fortepianist, Clavichordist. Education: A.B., Harvard University, 1952. Address: 20 Drummer Lane, West Redding, Connecticut 06896.

KIRBY, CHARLES WILLIAM JR Occupation: Principal. Education: A.A., Little Rock University. Address: 58 Amelia, Toronto Ontario M4X 1E1, Canada.

KIRBY, J AUBREY Occupation: President. Education: B.Arch. Address: 460 Archer Road, Winston-Salem, North Carolina 27106.

KIRBY, PAULA M Occupation: Instructional Designer. Education: B.S., M.S., Ph.D. Address: 2404 Buchenhorst Road, State College, Pennsylvania 16801.

KIRCHMAN, MARGARET MARY Occupation: Professor. Education: B.S., M.A., Ph.D, O.T.R., F.A.O.T.A. Address: 903 South Ashland Boulevard, Chicago, Illinois 60607.

KIRCHNER, JOHN HOWARD JR Occupation: Executive Director. Education: Ph.D., Northwestern University, 1964; A.B.P.P., 1977. Address: 300 East 30 Street South, Newton, Iowa 50208.

KIRILLOFF, LESLIE H Occupation: Faculty. Education: B.S.N., Ph.D. Address: 3329 Fawnway Drive, Murrysville, Pennsylvania 15668.

KIRK, NORMAN A Occupation: Writer. Education: A.A. Address: 14 Bayfield Road, Wayland, Massachusetts 01778.

KIRKENDALL, LESTER A Occupation: Principal. Education: Washburn College, Kansas State College, Columbia University Teachers College. Address: 12705 South East River Road, Portland, Oregon 97222.

KIRKHAM, JAMES ALVIN Occupation: Corporation President. Education: High School Diploma. Address: Route #1, Box 35, Greenwood, Indiana 46142.

KIRKLAND, ELEANOR R Occupation: Professor. Education: Ph.D., University of California-Berkeley; M.A., California State University at Los Angeles. Address: 8707 Mohawk Way, Fair Oaks, California 95628.

KIRKLAND, VIRGIL WAYNE Occupation: Manager. Education: B.S.E.E. Address: 17232 El Cajon Avenue, Yorba Linda, California 92686.

KIRKORIAN, DONALD G Occupation: Associate Dean. Education: Ph.D., Northwestern University, 1972; M.A. 1966, B.A. 1961, San Jose State University. Address: 1655 Rockville Road, Suisan City, California 94585.

KIRKPATRICK, ANNE HELENE Occupation: Teacher. Education: B.A. 1959, M.S. 1966, Syracuse University. Address: 300 North Bellinger Street, Herkimer, New York 13350.

KIRKPATRICK, PHILLIP HUGH Occupation: Supervisory Education Specialist. Education: B.A. 1956, M.S. 1962. Address: 1922 Cumberland Avenue, Petersburg, Virginia 23805.

KIRKSEY, AVANELLE Occupation: Professor. Education: Ph.D. Address: 400 North River Road, Apartment 1708, West Lafayette, Indiana 47906.

KIRSCHENBAUM, NEAL Occupation: Psychologist, Professor of Psychology. Education: Bachelor of Arts, Advanced Professional Certificate, Master of Arts, Master of Science, Ph.D. Education: 6524 North Drake, Lincolnwood, Illinois 60645.

KIRSHNER, CYRUS Occupation: Professor. Education: B.S., Ed.M., Ph.D. Address: 7053 Ethel Avenue, North Hollywood, California 91605.

KISSANE, SHARON FLORENCE Occupation: President. Education: B.A., M.A., Ph.D. Address: 15 Turning Shores, South Barrington, Illinois 60010.

KIST, GERALDINE F Occupation: Vice President. Education: R.N., B.S.N., M.A. Address: 11908 Ballentine, Overland Park, Kansas 66213.

KISTLER, MARIANNE Occupation: Garden Writer. Education: Liberal Arts. Address: 1517 Nimitz Avenue, Ridgecrest, China Lake, California 93555.

KITADA, SHINICHI Occupation: Research Biochemist. Education: M.D., M.S., Ph.D. Address: 478 Landfair Avenue #5, Los Angeles, California 90024.

KITCHEN, ANDREW R Occupation: Dancer, Songwriter, Television Producer, Owner Television Modeling Workshop. Education: Associate's Degree. Address: 5114 South Kimbark, Chicago, Illinois 60615.

KITTNER, SABRA CORBIN Occupation: Media Specialist. Education: A.B. 1944, M.Ed. 1966, Western Maryland College; Post-Graduate Studies, Catholic University, Johns Hopkins University. Address: 94 Willis Street, Westminister, Maryland 21157.

KITTO, FRANKLIN CURTIS Occupation: Media Center Supervisor. Education: M.A. 1980, B.A. 1978, Brigham Young University. Address: 8892 Flatiron Drive, Sandy, Utah 84092.

KIZER, DAVID L Occupation: Professor, Department of Physical Education and Sport, Central Michigan University. Education: B.A., M.A., Ed.D. Address: 4630 South Mackenzie, Mount Pleasant, Michigan 48858.

KIZZIER, DONNA L Occupation: Assistant Professor of Business, Kearney State College. Education: B.S. 1972, M.S. 1978, Ed.D. 1985. Address: 2010 West 35th Street, Kearney, Nebraska 68847.

KLABIN, DON Occupation: Architect. Education: B.A., Brandeis University, 1969; M.Arch., Harvard University, 1973. Address: 4 Longfellow Place - #804, Boston, Massachusetts 02114.

KLANFER, KARL Occupation: Consulting Chemical Engineer. Education: Chemical Engineer, M.S., F.C.I.C. Address: 18 Colgate Road, Marblehead, Massachusetts 01945.

KLAPERMAN, GILBERT Occupation: Rabbi, Attorney. Education: B.A., Rabbi, D.H.L., D.D., J.D. Address: 64 Muriel Avenue, Lawrence, New York 11509.

KLARE, NANCY C Occupation: Administrative Assistant. Education: Burdett College. Address: 419 Franklin Street, Reading, Massachusetts 01867.

KLASS, SHEILA SOLOMON Occupation: Professor. Education: B.A., M.A., M.F.A. Address: 330 Sylvan Avenue, Leonia, New Jersey 07604.

KLECKNER, WILLARD RICHARDS Occupation: Consultant and College Instructor. Education: B.S., M.B.A., LL.B., Ph.D. Address: 15 Colonial Road, Lake Telemark, New Jersey 07842.

KLEIN, ANDREW MARC Occupation: Supervisor Special Education. Education: B.S., M.A. Address: 504 Bean Blossom Drive, Lancaster, Pennsylvania 17603.

KLEIN, CARL F Occupation: Manager. Education: B.S.E.E., M.S.E.E. Address: 5740 South Lochleren Lane, New Berlin, Wisconsin 53151.

KLEIN, LAWRENCE R Occupation: Resident Vice President Investments. Education: B.A., M.B.A., C.F.P. Address: 715 Arroyo Oaks Drive, Westlake Village, California 91632.

KLEIN, MINNIE FRANCES Occupation: Professor. Education: B.S., M.S., Florida State University; Ed.D., University of California at Los Angeles. Address: 928 23rd Street, Santa Monica, California 90403.

KLEIN, PHILIP ALEXANDER Occupation: Professor. Education: B.A., M.A., Ph.D. Address: 719 South Sparks Street, State College, Pennsylvania 16801.

KLEIN, THEODORE ULMER Occupation: President. Education: B.S., M.A. Address: 39 East 10 Street, New York, New York 10003.

KLEINBAUM, RICHARD NATHAN Occupation: Management/Development Consultant. Education: B.A. History/English, M.A. U.S. Political History. Address: 760 Iglehart, St. Paul, Minnesota 55104.

KLEINMAN, SEYMOUR Occupation: Professor, Ohio State University. Education: Ph.D. Address: 2051 Iuka Avenue, Columbus, Ohio 43201.

KLETT, WILLIAM GREGORY Occupation: Chief Psychologist, Veterans Administration Medical Center. Education: B.A., M.A., Ph.D. Address: Box 387, St. Joseph, Minnesota 56301.

KLEVEN, ESTHER SCHAFFER Occupation: Medical Technologist, Director Laboratory Services, Southwest Washington Hospitals. Education: B.S. Medical Technology, M.A. Management and Supervision Services. Address: 3607 Northeast 105th Street, Vancouver, Washington 98665.

KLIEN, WOLFGANG JOSEF Occupation: Architect/Developer. Education: Dipl. Ing., Technical University. Address: 214 East Griswold Road, Phoenix, Arizona 85020.

KLIGERMAN, MORTON M Occupation: Professor. Education: B.S., M.D., M.Sc., M.A. Address: 2122 Delancey Street, Philadelphia, Pennsylvania 19103.

KLIMENKO, MICHAEL Occupation: Professor. Education: B.D., Ph.D., Friedrich-Alexander University, Erlangen, Germany. Address: 578-C Hahaione Street, Honolulu, Hawaii 96825.

KLIMESZ, HENRY ROMAN Occupation: Professor. Education: B.S., B.A., M.Econ., M.B.A., M.A. Address: 63 Lodges Lane, Bala Cynwyd, Pennsylvania 19004.

KLINE, NANCY Occupation: Writer. Education: B.A., Barnard University; M.A., Columbia University; Ph.D., Tufts University. Address: 34 Cypress Street, Brookline, Massachusetts 02146.

KLOSOWSKI, JEROME M Occupation: Associate Scientific Consultant, Silicone Chemistry. Education: B.S., M.A. Mathematics 1965, Central Michigan University; M.S. Chemistry, Wayne State University, 1966. Address: 2029 Briar, Bay City, Michigan 48706.

KMETEC, EMIL P Occupation: Biochemist; Professor of Biochemistry, Wright State University. Education: Ph.D. Address: 2172 Crabtree Drive, Beavercreek, Ohio 45431.

KNAUF, JANINE B Occupation: Educator, Accounting Professor. Education: S.B., M.B.A., M.Ph., C.P.A. Address: 12 Springwood Lane, Pittsford, New York 14534.

KNEBEL, FLETCHER Occupation: Writer. Education: A.B., Miami University. Address: 1119 Kaumoku Street, Mariners Ridge, Honolulu, Hawaii 96825.

KNELSON, NELDA RIFE Occupation: Author of Children's Books. Address: 2016 West First Street, Dixon, Illinois 61021.

KNEPPER, EUGENE ARTHUR Occupation: Real Estate Syndicator. Education: B.C.S. Address: 283 Tomahawk Trail, South East, Cedar Rapids, Iowa 52403.

KNIGHT, ARTHUR WINFIELD Occupation: Writer. Education: B.A., M.A., San Francisco State University. Address: Post Office Box 439, California, Pennsylvania 15419.

KNIGHT, KIT MARIE Occupation: Writer. Education: B.A. Address: Post Office Box 439, California, Pennsylvania 15419.

KNIGHT, SUSAN S Occupation: Assistant Manager, Advertising and Sales Promotion. Education: B.A. Address: 1938 Lake Avenue, Wilmette, Illinois 60091.

KNOLL, SHARON R Occupation: Greene County Supervisor. Education: Ed.S., M.S., B.S., Indiana State University. Address: Rural Route 1, Box 468, Linton, Indiana 47441.

KNOOP, FLOYD C Occupation: Assistant Professor. Education: Ph.D. Address: 208 Bellevue Boulevard South, Bellevue, Nebraska 68005.

KNOWLES, MARYELLEN SHANK Occupation: Special Education Director, Clinton Community Schools. Education: A.A., B.S., M.A., C.A.S., Ed.D. Address: 1045 8th Avenue North, Clinton, Iowa 52732.

KNOWLTON, EDGAR COLBY JR Occupation: Professor of European Languages. Education: A.B. 1941, A.M. 1942, Harvard University; Ph.D., Stanford University, 1959. Address: 1026 Kalo Place, Honolulu, Hawaii 96826.

KNUDSEN, A BRUCE Occupation: Scientist. Education: B.S., M.S., Ph.D. Address: 1010 West 1300 South, Salt Lake City, Utah 84104.

KO, WEN H Occupation: Professor, C.W.R. University. Education: Ph.D. Electrical Engineering. Address: 1356 Forest Hills Boulevard, Cleveland, Ohio 44118.

KOBERT, NORMAN Occupation: Engineering Consultant. Education: B.S.I.E., M.B.A., D.C.S. Address: 1611 South Ocean Drive, Fort Lauderdale, Florida 33316.

KOCH, FRAN Occupation: Director. Education: B.S., M.S. Address: Route 1, Box 62 C, Troy, Texas 76579.

KOCHAKIAN, CHARLES D Occupation: Professor Emeritus. Education: A.B., 1930, A.M., 1931, Ph.D., 1936. Address: 3617 Oakdale Road, Birmingham, Alabama 35223.

KOCHEN, MANFRED Occupation: Research in Information Sciences, The University of Michigan. Education: B.S., Massachusetts Institute of Technology, 1950; M.A. 1951, Ph.D. 1955, Columbia University. Address: 2026 Devonshire, Ann Arbor, Michigan 48104.

KOCOT, S LAWRENCE Occupation: Assistant Director. Education: B.A., M.P.A., 1985. Address: 67 Butterfield Terrace, Amherst, Massachusetts 01002.

KOCZAK, MICHAEL J Occupation: Professor. Education: Ph.D., M.S., University of Pennsylvania; B.S. Poly Institute of New York. Address: 1216 Foulkrod Street, Philadelphia, Pennsylvania 19124.

KOEHLER, G STANLEY Occupation: Professor. Education: B.A., Ph.D., Princeton University; M.A., Harvard University. Address: 54 Hills Road, Amherst, Massachusetts 01002.

KOEHLER, LYLE PETER Occupation: Director, Tutorial and Referral Services. Education: B.A. 1966, M.A. 1968. Address: 2996 Gilbert, Cincinnati, Ohio 45206.

KOELLING, LYNNE M Occupation: Private Music Teacher. Education: B.A. Music Education. Address: 8 Airport Drive, Milford, Iowa 51351.

KOENIG, ROBERT AUGUST Occupation: Clergyperson. Education: B.S. cum laude, University of Wisconsin-Superior, 1955; M.A. 1965, Ph.D. 1973, University of Minnesota-Minneapolis; M.Div. magna cum laude, San Francisco Theological Seminary, 1969.

Address: 1020 West Cedar Street, Chippewa Falls, Wisconsin 54729.

KOESTER, BERTHOLD KARL Occupation: Attorney. Education: Doctor of Jurisprudence. Address: 6201 East Cactus Road, Scottsdale, Arizona 85254.

KOETZLE, THOMAS F Occupation: Chemist. Education: Ph.D., Harvard University, 1970. Address: 35 Arista Drive, Dix Hills, New York 11746.

KOGA, ROKUTARO Occupation: Research Physicist. Education: Ph.D. Physics, 1974. Address: 8005 Stewart Avenue, Los Angeles, California 90045.

KOH, HAN SHIL Occupation: Director of Research, World Institute of Technology. Education: LL.D., Ed.D., Ph.D. Law. Address: 13908 Bethpage Lane, Silver Spring, Maryland 20906.

KOHN, ALAN ROBERT Occupation: Psychologist. Education: B.S., M.S., M.A., Ph.D. Address: 13 Oak Road, Delmar, New York 12054.

KOHN, EUGENE Occupation: Conductor, Metropolitan Opera, New York. Education: Private Training. Address: 2109 Bway, New York, New York 10023.

KOHOUTEK, FRANK LEO JR Occupation: Educator. Education: B.S., M.Ed. Address: 121 Colfax Avenue Southwest, Wadena, Minnesota 56482.

KOLASA, KATHRYN M Occupation: Professor and Chairperson, Food, Nutrition and Institution of Management, School of Home Economics, East Carolina University. Education: B.S. Home Economics/Communication Arts 1970, Ph.D. Food Science 1974, Michigan State University. Address: 101 Queen Anne, Greenville, North Carolina 27834.

KOLBET, LORI L Occupation: Assistant Professor of Psychology, Department of Psychology, University of Nevada. Education: B.A., Whitworth College; Ph.D., Brown University. Address: Department of Psychology, University of Nevada, Las Vegas, 4505 Maryland Parkway, Las Vegas, Nevada 89154.

KOLLIGIAN, GREGORY SCOTT Occupation: Managing Director, Selame Design. Education: B.A., Harvard University, 1953. Address: Deer Run Road, Lincoln, Massachusetts 01773.

KOLMAN, LAURENCE STEVEN Occupation: Filtration Executive. Education: M.A./L.S., B.A. Address: 3 Ludi Lane, Monsey, New York 10952.

KOLVOORD, PHILIP A Occupation: Attorney. Education: B.A., LL.D., University of Virginia. Address: 15 Upper Main Street, Essex Junction, Vermont 05452.

KOMOSA, ADAM ANTHONY Occupation: Retired Lieutenant Colonel, United States Army; University Professor Emeritus. Education: A.A., B.A., M.A., Ph.D. Address: Route 1, Box 294, Columbia, Kentucky 42728.

KOMP, RICHARD J Occupation: Scientist, Photovoltaics, Other Solar Energy. Education: B.S., Loras College; Ph.D., Wayne State University. Address: Route 2, English, Indiana 47118.

KONDO, SADAO Occupation: Trading Company Executive. Education: Graduate, Communication Academy, Japan, 1942. Address: 1507 San Vicente Boulevard, Santa Monica, California 90402.

KONDRASUK, JOHN NORTON (JACK) Occupation: Education Consultant. Education: B.S., M.A., Ph.D, Psychology. Address: 4187 Southwest Greenleaf Drive, Portland, Oregon 97221.

KONECKY, EDITH Occupation: Fiction Writer. Address: 511 East 20 Street, New York, New York 10010.

KONG, ERIC SIU-WAI Occupation: Research Scientist. Education: B.A., M.Sc., Ph.D. Address: 936

Bluebonnet Drive, Sunnyvale, California 94086.

KONG, JIN AU Occupation: Professor of Electrical Engineering. Education: Ph.D. 1968. Address: 72 Hillcrest Avenue, Lexington, Massachusetts 02173.

KONICK, MARCUS Occupation: Emeritus Associate Dean of Arts and Sciences. Education: B.S. Education, M.A., Ph.D. Address: 1214 North Hillview Street, Lock Haven, Pennsylvania 17745.

KONO, TOSHIHIKO Occupation: Concert Cellist, Appearing in Recitals, Chamber Music and Symphony Orchestras, Radio Television, Festival Concerts; Cellist, American Symphony Orchestra; Resident Artist and Member, Acadia String Quartet, Bar Harbor Festival, Maine; Leader, Kono Trio. Education: LL.B., Kyoto University; Attended Mannes College of Music, Stanford University. Address: 400 West 43rd Street, New York, New York 10036.

KOONTZ, THOMAS W Occupation: Poet, Editor, University Professor. Education: B.A., University of Miami, Ohio; M.A., Ph.D., Indiana University. Address: R.R. 2 Box 110, Daleville, Indiana 47334.

KOPFLER, JUDITH HALL Occupation: Gestalt and N.L.P. Psychoeducational Therapist. Education: B.S., Master's Degree Special Education, Certified Gestalt Therapist, Certified N.L.P. Practitioner, Ph.D. Candidate. Address: 1412 Broadmoor Drive, Slidell, Louisiana 70458.

KOPLO, HARVEY ALAN Occupation: Owner, Fort Imports; Technical Producer, Crystal Radio. Education: B.A. Work, Culture, and Society, Sangamon State University. Address: Rural Route 11 Box 217, Springfield, Illinois 62707.

KORMES, JOHN WINSTON Occupation: Attorney. Education: B.A., University of Michigan, 1955; J.D., University of Michigan Law School, 1959. Address: 1070 Edison Avenue, Philadelphia, Pennsylvania 19116.

KORPAL, CHARYL ELAINE Occupation: Marketing and Distributive Education Teacher/Coordinator. Education: B.S. Education, Mankato State University. Address: 503 North Broad Street, Mankato, Minnesota 56001.

KOSHKIN, NAOMI Occupation: Consultant Dietitian, Author. Education: B.S. Home Economics. Address: 13855 Sheri Hollow Lane, Houston, Texas 77082.

KOTECHA, MAHESH K Occupation: Managing Vice President, International Ratings, Standard and Poor's Corporation. Education: B.S., Harvey Mudd College, 1970; M.S., Massachusetts Institute of Technology, Sloan School of Management, 1972. Address: 118 Edgars Lane, Hastings-on-Hudson, New York 10706.

KOTKER, ZANE Occupation: Writer. Education: B.A., Middlebury College; M.A., Columbia Universtiy. Address: 45 Lyman Road, Northampton, Massachusetts 01060.

KOTLOWITZ, ROBERT Occupation: Vice President. Education: B.A. Address: 54 Riverside, New York, New York 10024.

KOZBERG, DONNA WALTERS Occupation: Eastern Region Director. Education: Master of Rehabilitation Counseling, Master of Fine Arts. Address: 714 Woodland Avenue, Westfield, New Jersey 07090.

KOZBERG, RONALD P Occupation: Director of Rehabilitation. Address: 714 Woodland Avenue, Westfield, New Jersey 07090.

KRABBE, JOAN LOUISE Occupation: Dean of Education. Education: M.A. Communication Arts. Address: 2495 Sir Martin Drive, Hamilton, Ohio 45013.

KRAMER, EMMANUEL MARTIN Education: Master's Degree, Temple University, 1952. Address: 503 Laverock Road, Glenside, Pennsylvania 19038.

KRAMER, FREDERICK C Occupation: Men's Photographer. Education: Master's Degree, University of Vienna, 1932. Address: 446 Sandy Lane, Wilmette, Illinois 60091.

KRAMER, MARY ALBERT Occupation: Professor. Education: B.S.N., M.S.N.E., Ph.D. Address: 342 Oakland Avenue, Pittsburgh, Pennsylvania 15213.

KRAMER, IRVING Occupation: Art Director. Education: Art/Advertising. Address: 132 Belmill Road, Bellmore, New York 11710.

KRANTZ, MARY ELISE Occupation: Program Administrator. Education: B.A., M.A. Address: Notre Dame Institute, Middleburg, Virginia 22117.

KRANTZ, MARILYN Occupation: Freelance Writer. Education: Attended Temple University, 1948. Address: 1383 Kimberly Drive, Philadelphia, Pennsylvania 19151.

KRAPF, NORBERT Occupation: College Professor, English Department, C. W. Post College of Long Island University. Education: M.A., Ph.D. English, University of Notre Dame. Address: 219 Main Street, Roslyn, New York.

KRATZBERG, G CLAUDINE Occupation: College Teacher. Education: B.S. Home Economics Education, M.H.Ec. Address: 1100 North Meridian #7, Newberg, Oregon 97132.

KRAUS, ANNA J Occupation: Director. Education: A.A., M.P.H., M.S. Address: 1719-38th Street, Northwest, Canton, Ohio 44709.

KRAUSE, MARCELLA MASON Occupation: Educator. Education: B.S., M.A., Ph.D. Address: 5615 Estates, Oakland, California 94618.

KREDA, SALLIE P Occupation: Public Relations. Address: 345 East 56, New York, New York 10022.

KREGLEWSKI, ALEKSANDER Occupation: Senior Research Scientist. Education: Doctorate Chemistry. Address: 1221 Airline Drive, College Station, Texas 77840.

KREIS, SIEGFRIED RICHARD Occupation: Teaching Assistant. Education: B.A., M.S.Ed., Baylor University. Address: 3400 Brookmeade, Rolling Meadows, Illinois 60008.

KRETSCHMAR, WILLIAM EDWARD Occupation: Attorney-at-Law. Education: Bachelor of Science, Bachelor of Laws. Address: Box A, Venturia, North Dakota 58489.

KREWSON, JAMES W Occupation: Architect. Education: B.S., M.A., Ph.D. Address: 838 Country Club Drive, Hannibal, Missouri 63401.

KRIBBS, JAYNE K Occupation: Associate Dean. Education: B.A., M.A., Ph.D. Address: 7 Yale Road, Marlton, New Jersey 08053.

KRISHNAN, PALANIAPPA Occupation: Assistant Professor and Research Agricultural Engineer, Oregon State University. Education: B.Tech. (honors), M.S., Ph.D. Address: 3930 Northwest Witham Hill Drive #81, Corvallis, Oregon 97330.

KRISHNAN, PARAMESWARA Occupation: Professor. Education: Ph.D., M.A., Cornell University; M.S., B.S., Kerala University. Address: 3217 104 A Street, Edmonton, Alberta Canada T6J 4A1.

KRITCHER, KAREN MARIE Occupation: Nursing Student. Education: A.S. Address: 178 U.S. 31 North, Petoskey, Michigan 49770.

KROESEN, JILL ANNE Occupation: Artist. Education: B.A., M.F.A. Address: 24 Fifth Avenue #1412A, New York, New York 10011.

KROLL, STEVEN LAWRENCE Occupation: Writer. Education: A.B., Harvard College, 1962. Address: 64 West 11 Street, New York, New York 10011.

KRONENFELD, JENNIE J Occupation: Professor. Education: B.A., University of North Carolina, 1971; M.A. 1973, Ph.D. 1976, Brown University. Address: 920 Walters Lane, Columbia, South Carolina 29209.

KRUDOP, JAMES D Occupation: Administrator. Education: B.S., M.A., Ph.D. Address: 1213 First Avenue, Bellwood Andalusia, Alabama 36420.

KRYSTUFEK, ZDENEK Occupation: Professor of Political Science and Jurisprudence. Education: J.D., Ph.D., J.S.M. Address: 805 29 Street, Boulder, Colorado 80303.

KUBE, WAYNE R Occupation: Professor Chemical Engineering. Education: B.S., M.S. Address: 630 Boyd Drive, Grand Forks, North Dakota 58201.

KUBILUS, NORBERT J Occupation: Officer. Education: M.S., Rensselaer Polytechnic Institute; Sc.B., Seton Hall University. Address: Post Office Box D402, Landing, New Jersey 07850.

KUBLY, DON JR Occupation: President. Education: B.E.A. Address: 215 La Vereda Road, Pasadena, California 91105.

KUBY, LOLETTE BETH Occupation: Writer. Education: Ph.D. Address: 2250 Par Lane #801, Willoughby Hills, Ohio 44094.

KUCERA, THOMAS J Occupation: Chemical Consultant. Education: B.S., M.S., Ph.D. Address: 3126 Thayer Street, Evanston, Illinois 60201.

KUCHAR, ROMAN V Occupation: Professor. Education: M.A., University of Heidelberg; B.M., University of Colorado; M.L.S., Pratt Institute; Ph.D., Ukrainian Free University of Munich. Address: 2402 Canal Boulevard, Hays, Kansas 67601.

KUCHERA, THOMAS JOHN Occupation: Lawyer, North Dakota Legislator. Education: B.A., College of St. Thomas; M.A., George Washington University; J.D., University of North Dakota School of Law. Address: 525 South 6th Street, Grand Forks, North Dakota 58201.

KUDO, AKIRA Occupation: Research Scientist and Professor. Education: B.Sc., M.Sc., Ph.D., Doctor of Engineering. Address: 1838 Beattie Avenue, Ottawa, Ontario Canada K1H 5R8.

KUEHN, DAVID L Occupation: Chairman Department of Music, California State University-Long Beach. Education: B.M., M.S., D.M.A.; Diplomas L.G.S.M. (London), A.R.C.M. (London). Address: 156 College Park Drive, Seal Beach, California 90740.

KUHN, K KUHN Occupation: Professor. Education: B.A., M.A., Ph.D. Address: 3909 Spruce Street #174, Philadelphia, Pennsylvania 19104.

KUHN, PHILIP HOWARD Occupation: Assistant Professor. Education: B.A., University of Maryland, 1964; M.S. 1972, Ph.D. 1976, University of Wisconsin. Address: 641 Whitham, B1, A8, Fayetteville, Arizona 72701.

KUMAR, KRISHNA Occupation: Physics Educator/Research. Education: B.Sc., M.Sc., M.S., Ph.D. Address: 1248 North Franklin, Cookeville, Tennessee 38501.

KUMKE, SHERRIE M Occupation: Senior Consumer Affairs Associate. Address: 6892 Brian Michael Court, Springfield, Virginia 22153.

KUMM, ROBERT Occupation: Jazz Researcher, Journalist. Address: Post Office Box 298, Staten Island, New York 10314.

KUNG, SHAIN-DOW Occupation: Professor. Education: B.Sc., M.A., Ph.D. Address: 8415 Maymeadow Court, Baltimore, Maryland 21207.

KUNTZMAN, RONALD Occupation: Vice President. Education: Ph.D., George Washington University, 1962. Address: 12 Augustine Avenue, Ardsley, New York 10502.

KUPPLER, KARL JOHN Occupation: Hospital Administrator. Education: B.S. cum laude, Alleghany College; M.H.A., Ohio State University. Address: 281 Corriedale Drive, Cortland, Ohio 44410.

KURIANSKY, JUDITH B Occupation: Psychologist. Education: Ph.D. Address: 8 Thomas Street, New York, New York 10007.

KURIAKONE, MIRA BOGVNOVIĆ Occupation: Scientist. Education: Chemical Technology. Address: 432 Atwood Street, Pennsylvania 15213.

KURTZ, ARTHUR DIGBY Occupation: Composer and Teacher. Education: Master's Degree in Music, Study in France. Address: 685 Oakwood, Webster Groves, Missouri 63119.

KURTZ, MAX Occupation: Consulting Engineer. Education: B.B.A., City College of New York, 1940. Address: 33-47 91 Street, Flushing, New York 11372.

KURTZKE, JOHN FRANCIS Occupation: Neurologist. Education: B.S., St. John's University, 1948; M.D., Cornell University, 1952. Address: 7509 Salem Road, Falls Church, Virginia 22043.

KURZMAN, DAN Occupation: Author. Education: A.B., University of California; Diploma, Sorbonne, Paris. Address: c/o H. Knopf, 187-Boulevard, Apartment 9H.

KUSHNICK, STEPHEN A Occupation: Psychologist. Education: B.S. 1958, M.S. 1961, Ph.D. 1963. Address: 3312 Norwood Road, Shaker Heights, Ohio 44122.

KUTTNER, PAUL Occupation: Publicity Director. Education: Bryanston College. Address: 37-26 87th Street, Jackson Heights, New York 11372.

KUWAYAMA, GEORGE Occupation: Sensor Curator, Far Eastern Art. Education: B.A., William College; M.A., University of Michigan. Address: 1417 Comstock, Los Angeles, California 90024.

KUYKENDALL, RUTH JANE Occupation: Real Estate Broker. Education: College Studies. Address: 261 Ponce de Leon Avenue, Venice, Florida 33595.

KWAIN, WEN-HWA (TONY) Occupation: Scientist-in-Charge. Education: B.Sc., M.Sc., Ph.D. Address: 54 Drake Street, Sault Ste., Marie, Ontario PGA 5A7 Canada.

KYLES, CALVIN E Occupation: Manager Product Information/Product Marketing. Education: B.B.A., Texas Southern University. Address: 2085 Teakwood Manor Drive, Florissant, Missouri 63031.

L

LAAKSO WALSH, LIISA LYDIA JOHANNA Occupation: Physician, Radiologist, Assistant Professor. Education: B.S., D.O. Address: 1237 Dartmouth, Flossmoor, Ilinois 60422.

LACH, BENJAMIN Occupation: Editor Education: B.A., B.S., B.B.A. Address: 8 Verndale Street, Brookline, Massachusetts 02146.

LACHS, ANNE Occupation: Executive Director, A.A.M.H. Education: B.A., M.A., C.S. Address: 18 Darby Road, East Brunswick, New Jersey 08816.

LACHS, JOHN Occupation: Professor of Philosophy, Vanderbilt University. Education: B.A., M.A., Ph.D. Address: 2005 Maplemere Drive, Nashville, Tennessee 37215.

LACKMAN, CONWAY LEE Occupation: Economist. Education: B.A., M.S., Ph.D. Address: 7 Sherman Circle, Somerset, New Jersey 08873.

LACY, ELSIE HALSEY Occupation: Educator, Writer. Education: College Equivalent. Address: Route 1, Post Office Box 24, Grassy Creek, Kentucky 41435.

LACY, NORRIS J Occupation: College Instructor, Department of French, University of Kansas; Editor. Education: A.B., M.A., Ph.D. Address: 1904 Countryside, Lawrence, Kansas 66044.

LADD, EVERETT CARLL Occupation: Professor and Author. Education: A.B. magna cum laude, Bates College, 1959; Ph.D., Cornell University, 1964. Address: 86 Ball Hill Road, Storrs, Connecticut 06268.

LADENSON, MARK L Occupation: Professor of Economics, Department of Economics, Michigan State University. Education: B.A., University of Wisconsin; M.B.A., University of Chicago; Ph.D., Northwestern University. Address: 230 Oxford Road, East Lansing, Michigan 48823.

LADIN, EUGENE Occupation: Management/ Financial Consultant. Education: B.B.A., M.B.A. Address: 170 Spring Lake Hills Drive, Altamonte Springs, Florida 32714.

LAFFERTY, JUDY ANN Occupation: Psychologist/ Analyst, Department of Social Service, Quality Control. Education: M.S. Counseling, Ph.D. Psychology. Address: 2339 North Catalina Street, Los Angeles, California 90027.

LAGUNA, ASELA RODRIGUEZ De Occupation: Associate Professor of Spanish, Rutgers University. Education: M.A. 1970, Ph.D. Comparative Literature, University of Illinois. Address: 207 39th Street, Union City, New Jersey 07087.

LaHARRY, NORMAL Occupation: Pharmacist. Education: B.S. Chemistry, Tougaloo College, 1951; Graduate School, Howard University, 1956; College of Pharmacy, Xavier University, 1958; Attended Texas Southern University and University of Illinois. Address: 601 East 32nd Street, Chicago, Illinois.

LAINO, JOSEPH FRANCIS II Occupation: Educator/Director of Career and Co-op. Education, Agawam Public Schools. Education: M.A., M.Ed., B.A. (with honors), A.A. Address: 135 Magnolia Terrace, Springfield, Massachusetts 01108.

LAKE, OLIVER EUGENE Occupation: Musician. Education: Four Years of College Music. Address: 163 Adelphi 81, Brooklyn, New York 11205.

LAKSHMANAN, VAIKUNTAM IYER Occupation: Manager, Mineral Processing and Hydrometallurgy. Education: M.Sc., Ph.D., M.R.I.C., M.I.M.M. Address: 3921 Selkirk Place, Mississauga, Ontario L5L 3L5 Canada.

LAMB, HELEN KEITHLEY Occupation: Poet.

Education: B.A., Drake University. Address: 819 Humboldt, Manhattan, Kansas 66502.

LAMBERT, CLINTON E JR Occupation: Certified Clinical Nurse Specialist, Adult Psychiatric Mental Health Nursing, Dwight David Eisenhower Army Medical Center. Education: B.S., B.A., B.S.N., M.S.N. Address: 120 Dresden Court, Martinez, Georgia 30907.

LAMBERT, HANCEL DANIEL III Occupation: Student. Education: High School. Address: Route #1, Box 119, Mount Crawford, Virginia 22841.

LAMBERT, VICKIE ANN Occupation: Professor of Nursing, School of Nursing, Medical College of Georgia. Education: B.S.N., M.S.N., D.M.Sc. Address: 120 Dresden Court, Martinez, Georgia 30912.

LAMBERT-CAHILL, MARGARET A Occupation: Assistant Director of Admissions/Educational Consultant, St. George's University School of Medicine. Education: B.A., Boston College, 1974. Address: 61 Community Road, Bay Shore, New York 11706.

LAMBIN, HENRY J Occupation: Psychologist. Education: B.A., M.A., Ph.D. Address: 1218 West Norwood Street, Chicago, Illinois 60660.

LAMBRINOS, JAMES Occupation: Professor, Union College. Education: B.A., M.A., Ph.D. Address: 9 Yorkshire Terrace, Clifton Park, New York 12065.

LAMM, MICHAEL E Occupation: Professor and Chairman of Pathology, Case Western Reserve University and University Hospitals Cleveland. Education: M.D., M.S. Address: 2856 Glengary Road, Cleveland, Ohio 44120.

LAMOUTTE, SYLVIA M Occupation: Musician. Education: B.A. (with honors) 1958, M.A. (with honors) 1960, New England Conservatory of Music. Address: 267 San Jorge Street, Apartment 12-C, Santurce, Puerto Rico 00912.

LANCASTER, CECILE ELIZABETH Occupation: Missionary Teacher to Japan (Retired). Education: B.A., Howard Payne University; M.A., Baylor University. Address: 7135 Tanager, Houston, Texas 77074.

LANCASTER, EMANUEL LEO Occupation: Associate Professor of Music, School of Music, University of Oklahoma. Education: B.M.E., Murray State University; M.S., University of Illinois; Ph.D., Northwestern University. Address: 3923 Pine Tree Circle, Norman, Oklahoma 73069.

LANCASTER, IVIE WADE III Occupation: Associate Professor Marketing, University of Alabama. Education: B.B.A., Kent State University; M.B.A., Texas Christian University; Ph.D., University of Oklahoma. Address: 3916 River View Road, Birmingham, Alabama 35243.

LAND, WILLIAM E Occupation: Director Quality Assurance, Narda Corporation. Education: B.S.I.E., M.B.A., D.B.A. Address: 3560 Mount Pleasant Court, San Jose, California 95148.

LANDAZURI, COLLEEN ANN Occupation: Public Health Nurse, Supervisor/Program Director of Prenatal Education and Assessment Program. Education: B.S.N., Marquette University. Address: 3368 North 44th Street, Milwaukee, Wisconsin 53216.

LANDERS, SHARON L Occupation: Policy Advisor and Lawyer. Education: B.S., J.D. Address: 320 West 83rd Street, New York, New York 10024.

LANDERS, VERNETTE TROSPER Occupation: Author, Retired School Counselor, Volunteer Clerk-in-Charge. Education: A.B. with honors; M.A. 1935; Ed.D. 1953; Educational Credentials, State of California. Address: 905 Landers Lane, Landers, California 92284.

LANDGARTEN, HELEN BARBARA Occupation:

Director and Professor, Graduate Division of Art Therapy, Loyala Marymount University. Education: B.F.A., University of California-Los Angeles; M.A., Goddard College; A.T.R.; M.F.C.C. Address: 2427 Arbutus, Los Angeles, California 90049.

LANDRESS, HARVEY J Occupation: Social Agency Executive. Education: B.A., M.A., M.S.W. Address: 1301 West Missouri Avenue, Dade City, Florida 33525.

LANDY, EUGENE E Occupation: Clinical Psychologist. Address: 2300 Century Hill Apartments, Century City, California.

LANE, BENSONETTA TIPTON Occupation: Attorney. Education: B.A., New York University; M.Ed., University of Massachusetts; J.D., University of Virginia. Address: 3750 Will Lee Road, College Park, Georgia 30349.

LANE, GEORGE ASHEL Occupation: Scientific Research in Chemistry, Dow Chemical. Education: A.B., Grinnell College; Ph.D., Northwestern University. Address: 3802 Wintergreen Drive, Midland, Michigan 48640.

LANE, HELEN HUGHES Occupation: Lecturer, Public Relations Consultant. Education: B.A., Emerson College; M.A., Columbia University. Address: 1208 Marine Way, North Palm Beach, Florida 33408.

LANE, JOSEPH MICHAEL Occupation: Orthopaedic Surgeon. Education: A.B., Columbia University; M.D., Harvard University. Address: 180 East End Avenue, New York, New York 10028.

LANE, KATHERINE A Occupation: Counseling Psychologist, University of California-Davis, Counseling Center. Education: Ph.D. Counseling Psychology. Address: 1730 Fremont Court #1, Davis, California 95616.

LANE, STANLEY GWIN Occupation: Clergyman, Prison Chaplain (Juvenile). Education: B.A., M.Div., Post-Graduate Clinical Pastoral Education. Address: 2313 Black Road, Joliet, Illinois 60435.

LAND, ANTON Occupation: Plant Biologist/ Professor Emeritus, Michigan State University. Education: Dr. Nat. Sci. Address: 1538 Cahill Drive, East Lansing, Michigan 48823.

LANGE, JEANNE S Occupation: Director, Program in Extracorporeal Technology. Address: 5890 Sugar Bush Drive, Tully, New York 13159.

LANG, KATHERINE A Occupation: Counseling Psychologist, University of California-Davis Counseling Center. Education: Ph.D. Counseling Psychology. Address: 1730 Fremont Court #1, Davis, California 95616.

LANGER, SANDRA LOIS Occupation: Art Historian/Critic, Sloan College Art Department, University of South Carolina. Education: B.A., M.A., Ph.D., New York University. Address: 3300 Heyward Street, Columbia, South Carolina 29205.

LANGHOUT-NIX, NELLEKE Occupation: Artist, Curator, Gallery Owner. Education: M.F.A., Academy of Visual Arts. Address: 2312 North 43rd Street, Seattle, Washington 98103.

LANGLEY, REBECCA J Occupation: Executive Assistant, State of Arkansas Land Office. Address: Route 3, Box 182, Hot Springs, Arkansas 71913.

LANGLOIS, AIMÉE Occupation: Associate Professor, Humboldt State University. Education: B.A. 1965, M.A. 1967, Ed.D. 1975. Address: 425 Bayside Road #A, Arcata, California 95521.

LANGSAM, WALTER CONSUELO Occupation: President Emeritus and Distinguished Service Professor, University of Cincinnati. Education: B.S., M.A., Ph.D. Address: 1071 Celestial Street, Cincinnati, Ohio 45202.

LANGSTON, DEWEY FRANCIS Occupation: Acting Dean, College of Education and Technology, Eastern New Mexico University. Education: B.A. 1943, M.Ed. 1948, Director of Physical Education 1950, Doctor of Physical Education 1952. Address: 1500 West 17th Lane, Portales, New Mexico 88130.

LANIER, GENE DANIEL Occupation: Professor of Library Science, East Carolina University. Education: B.S., East Carolina University; M.S. Library Science, Ph.D., University of North Carolina-Chapel Hill. Address: 526 Westchester Drive, Greenville, North Carolina 27834.

LANKFORD, PAULETTE GLAZENER Occupation: Director of Technology, Humana, Inc. Education: B.S. Medical Technology, Ph.D. Pathology, Master of Business Administration. Address: Route 2, Rockwood Lane, Mt. Washington, Kentucky 40047.

LANNES, WILLIAM JOSEPH III Occupation: Substation Engineering Manager (Electrical Engineer). Education: M.S.E.E., Naval Postgraduate School; B.S.E.E., Tulane University. Address: 7 Kings Canyon Drive, New Orleans, Louisiana 70114.

LANT, JEFFREY LADD Occupation: Management Consultant, Writer. Education: B.A. summa cum laude, University of California-Santa Barbara, 1969; M.A. 1970, Ph.D. 1975, Harvard University; Certificate of Advanced Graduate Studies, Higher Education Administration, Northeastern University, 1976. Address: 50 Follen Street, #507, Cambridge, Massachusetts 02138.

LANTZ, JOANNE B Occupation: Professor and Chairperson, Department of Psychological Sciences, Indiana-Purdue University. Education: B.S., Indiana Central University; M.S., Indiana University; Ph.D., Michigan State University. Address: 6108 Crofton Drive, Fort Wayne, Indiana 46815.

LANYON, E JEAN Occupation: Fine Artist and Poet Laureate for the State of Delaware. Education: Certificate, Choinard Art Institute; B.A., Goddard College. Address: 4 East Cleveland Avenue, Newark, Delaware 19711.

LANZKRON, ROLF WOLFGANG Occupation: Engineer. Education: C.P.A., 1948; B.S.E.E., Milwaukee School of Engineering, 1953; Math.E.Eng.D. 1956, M.S.E.E. 1955, University of Wisconsin. Address: 35 Gardner Road, Brookline, Massachusetts 02146.

LAPOMARDA, VINCENT ANTHONY Occupation: Clergyman, Historian. Education: A.B., A.M., S.T.L., Ph.D. Address: Holy Cross College, Worcester, Massachusetts 01610.

LAO, Y J Occupation: Professor, East Carolina University. Education: B.S., M.S., Ph.D. Chemical Engineering. Address: 300 Wesley Road, Greenville, North Carolina 27834.

LAREY, BERT BETHEL Occupation: Attorney at Law. Education: LL.D. (J.D.), Vanderbilt University. Address: 2600 Locust, Texarkana, Arkansas 75502.

LARGEN, MARY ANN Occupation: Director of Governmental Affairs, National Coalition Against Sexual Assault. Education: B.A., University of Maryland. Address: 955 South Columbus Street, Arlington, Virginia 22204.

LARIMORE, LEON Occupation: Pastor, Third Avenue Baptist Church. Education: A.B., M.D., Southern Baptist Theological Seminary; D.D., Campbellsville College. Address: 1041 Eastern Parkway, Louisville, Kentucky 40217.

LaROCQUE, EUGENE P Occupation: Roman Catholic Bishop, Alexandria-Cornwall. Education: B.A. (Y.W.D.); M.A. (Laval). Address: 1800 Montreal Road,

Cornwall, Ontario K6H 1G2, Canada.

LARROWE, VERNON L Occupation: Senior Research Engineer. Education: B.S., University of Kansas, 1950; M.S., University of Illinois, 1951; Ph.D., University of Michigan, 1964. Address: 1219 Share Avenue, Ypsilanti, Michigan 48197.

LARSEN, ERNEST A Occupation: Representative; Assistant Director, Anoka A.U.T.I. Education: B.S. Vocational Education. Address: 7229 153rd Lane, Anoka, Minnesota 55303.

LARSEN, IVA MAY Occupation: Assistant Professor. Education: M.A., B.S.Ed. Business Education. Address: 1017 Northwest Seventh Street, Madison, South Dakota 57042.

LARSEN, JEAN M Occupation: Associate Professor, Brigham Young University. Education: B.S. 1953, M.S. 1960, Brigham Young University; Ph.D., University of Utah, 1972. Address: 2678 North 880 East, Provo, Utah 84604.

LARSEN, LENA SCHULTZ Occupation: Selling-Buying Seeds and Grain, Agricultural Supply Company. Address: Rural Route 2, Post Office Box 107M, Clinton, Wisconsin 53525.

LARSON, JACQUELINE FAY Occupation: Media Specialist. Education: B.S., M.S. Address: 213 North Campbell, Beloit, Kansas 67420.

LASBURY, LEAH B Occupation: Community Worker. Education: B.A., Rollins College, 1936; B.S., Simmons College, 1937. Address: Post Office 777, Englewood, Florida 33533.

LASHLEY, VIRGINIA S Occupation: Professor of Computer and Information Systems, Coordinator of Instructional Computing, Glendale College. Education: B.A. Mathematics, University of Kansas; M.A. History, Occidental College; Ph.D. Education-Instructional Technology, University of Southern California. Address: 1240 San Marino Avenue, San Marino, California 91108.

LASKA, VERA O Occupation: Professor at Regis College, Author, Lecturer, Columnist. Education: Ph.D., University of Chicago. Address: 50 Woodchester Drive, Weston, Massachusetts 02193.

LASKIN, LEE B Occupation: Attorney and New Jersey State Senator. Education: LL.B., Rutgers University, 1961. Address: Pams Path, Cherry Hill, New Jersey 08034.

LATONDRESS, HAZEL JANET Occupation: Nursing Administration. Education: R.N., B.S. Address: 5107 Maple Ridge Drive, Kalamazoo, Michigan 49008.

LAU, LAWRENCE J Occupation: Professor of Economics, Department of Economics, Stanford University. Education: B.S. (great distinction), Stanford University, 1964; M.A., University of California, 1966; Ph.D., University of California, 1969. Address: 524 Gerona Road, Stanford, California 94305.

LAUDER, GEORGE VARICK Occupation: Director Public Affairs, Central Intelligence Agency. Education: B.A., Yale University; J.D., University of Virginia. Address: 5260 Partridge Lane, Northwest, Washington, D.C. 20016.

LAUER, JAMES L Occupation: Research Professor of Mechanical Engineering, Rensselaer Polytechnic Institute. Education: B.S. Chemistry, M.S. Chemistry, Ph.D. Physics, Post-Doctoral Mechanical Engineering. Address: 7 North East Lane, Ballston Lake, New York 12019.

LAUREANO-COLON, JUAN A Occupation: Executive Director and Founder, Christian Homes and Center of Puerto Rico and Latin America. Education: A.A., Kansas Community College, 1977; B.S.

Chemistry, Kansas Newman College, 1979; B.Min. 1979, Master of Theology 1982, International Bible Institute and Seminary, 1979; Ordained Baptist Minister, 1979. Address: Urb. Jordines de San Lorenzo, 2, A-15, San Lorenzo, Puerto Rico 00754.

LAURIE, MARY S Occupation: Administrative-Office Services. Education: Attended McKee Vocational and Technical High School. Address: 604 Quincy Avenue, Staten Island, New York 10305.

LAURIE, RAYMOND F Occupation: Administrator, Adult Probation/Volunteer Program. Education: M.Ed. Psy. Counseling, Georgia State University; B.A., University of California-Northridge. Address: 506 Hascall Road Northwest, Atlanta, Georgia 30309.

LAUSON, S KENT Occupation: Orthodontist and Real Estate Syndicator. Education: D.D.S., University of Iowa; M.S. Orthodontics, St. Louis University; Certificate in Periodontics, U.S.A.F. Address: 4282 B South Fairplay Circle, Aurora, Colorado 80014.

LAVALLEE, DAVID K Occupation: Professor and Chairman, Chemistry Department, Hunter College. Education: Ph.D., University of Chicago, 1971. Address: 97 Cleveland Drive, Croton-on-Hudson, New York 10520.

LAVENDER, EULA MAE TAYLOR Occupation: Owner, Handcrafts by Lavender; Artist, Handcrafter. Address: 1930 Highway 9, Black Mountain, North Carolina 28711. **LAW, BEULAH ENFIELD "BOO"** Occupation: Nurse, Educator. Education: Teaching Certificate; R.N. Address: 7603 Winterberry Place, Bethesda, Maryland 20817.

LAW, SALLY E Occupation: Financial Planner. Education: A.A., Columbia College, 1963; Postgraduate Studies, American University, 1972. Address: 5300 Mohican Road, Bethesda, Maryland 20816.

LAW, THOMAS M Occupation: Deputy to the Chancellor for Special Programs, State University of New York. Education: B.S. Industrial Education summa cum laude, Saint Paul's College, 1950; M.A. Industrial Education, New York University, 1953; Ed.D. Development of Human Resources, Cornell University, 1962. Address: State University of New York, Office of Special Programs, State University Plaza, Albany, New York 12246.

LAWER, BETSY Occupation: Vice President in Charge of Marketing Division, Director, The First National Bank of Anchorage. Education: B.A. Economics, Duke University, 1971; Graduate Studies, California State University-Sacramento.

LAWHON, TOMMIE C M Occupation: Associate Professor, North Texas State University. Education: Ph.D., M.S. H.O.E.C. Ed., B.S. Address: 2810 Carmel, Denton, Texas 76205.

LAWRENCE, ARLENE WHITE Occupation: Bishop, President, General Superintendent, Pillar of Fire. Education: A.A., B.A., M.A. Address: Box 163, Willow Road, Belle Mead, New Jersey 08502.

LAWRENCE, ARLINE BERYL Occupation: Professional Writer. Education: High School Diploma; National Penwoman, Arts and Letters. Address: Post Office Box 474, Willow Creek, California 95573.

LAWRENCE, JAMES STAVA Occupation: Clinical Psychologist. Education: Ph.D. Clinical Psychology, 1977. Address: 4949 Creek Haven Road, Cottage Grove, Wisconsin 53527.

LAWSON, ARCHIE DAVID Occupation: Physician's Assistant. Education: Certified Physician's Assistant (P.A.). Address: 206 Harding Street, Florence, Alabama 35630.

LAWSON, KENNETH RAY Occupation:

Instructor/Adjunct Professor. Education: A.B., Eastern Kentucky University; M.A., University of Dayton; Ed.D., Virginia Polytechnic Institute and State University. Address: 773 Northeast 9th Street, Apartment G, Crystal River, Florida 32629.

LAYCOCK, FRANK Occupation: Professor of Psychology, Oberlin College. Education: A.B., M.A., Ph.D., University of California-Berkeley. Address: 172 Shipherd Circle, Oberlin, Ohio 44074.

LAZARUS, CAROL NUNES Occupation: Clinical Psychologist. Education: Ph.D., Adelphi University, 1978. Address: 225 Wellington Road, Garden City, New York 11530.

LAZOVICK, PAUL B Occupation: Vice President, Management Assistance Inc. Education: B.E.E., M.S.E.E. Address: 4 Temple Terrace, Lawrenceville, New Jersey 08648.

LEACH, JOHN ROBERT JR Occupation: Manager, Computer Store. Education: B.S. Recreation. Address: 3618 Castle Terrace, Silver Spring, Maryland 20904.

LEACH-CLARK, MARY A Occupation: Teacher, Counselor. Education: B.S., University of Kansas, 1954; M.Ed., Wichita State University, 1978. Address: 951 South Bleckley #209, Wichita, Kansas 67218.

LEAHY, JOHN T Occupation: Marketing Agent. Education: Attended Iona College. Address: 7009 Beachmont Drive, Sykesville, Maryland 21784.

LEARNARD, JAMES MICHAEL Occupation: Insurance Agent, United Insurance Company of America. Education: A.A., Florida Junior College, 1968. Address: Route 1, Box 117, Green Street, Graniteville, South Carolina 29829.

LEASURE, BETTY JEAN Occupation: Homemaker. Education: Attended West Liberty State College, West Virginia Northern Community College. Address: 552 Kappel Street, New Martinsville, West Virginia 26155.

LEAVITT, JOSEPH Occupation: Executive Director, Baltimore Symphony. Education: B.A., American Union University; Further Studies at New England Conservatory of Music, Boston University, and Manhattan School of Music. Address: 1110 Hampton Garth, Towson, Maryland 21204.

LEBEDEFF, DIANE A Occupation: Judge, Civil Court of the City of New York. Education: B.A. 1965, J.D. 1968, University of Michigan. Address: 111 Centre Street, New York, New York 10013.

LEBRA, TAKIE SUGIYAMA Occupation: Professor of Anthropology, University of Hawaii. Education: M.A., Ph.D. Address: 3625 Woodlawn Terrace Place, Honolulu, Hawaii 96822.

LeCOMPTE, DOROTHY J (DORY) Occupation: Podiatric Physician and Surgeon. Education: B.S., Temple University, 1961; D.P.M., Ohio College of Podiatric Medicine, 1979. Address: Post Office Box 1776, Lynnwood, Washington 98046-1776.

LeCOMPTE, GARÉ Occupation: Private Practice, Stress Disorders, Association Executive. Education: B.A., University of Washington; M.A., Ph.D., American University; Ph.D., Case Western Reserve University. Address: Post Office Box 1776, Lynnwood, Washington 98046-1776.

LeCOMPTE, PEGGY L Occupation: Educator, Television Host. Education: B.S. Language Arts. Address: 212 Bunker Hill Road, Belleville, Illinois 62221.

LEE, AMY H Occupation: Principal Engineer. Education: M.S. Mechanical Engineering. Address: 2200 West Iowa Street, Chicago, Illinois 60622.

LEE, BRAD Occupation: Writer, Owner of Brad Lee Publications. Education: B.S. Economics, New York University; M.A. Sociology, The New School. Address: Box 8, Forest Hills, New York 11375.

LEE, DAVID ISOM Occupation: Minister, McKendree United Methodist Church. Education: B.S., Jacksonville State University; M.Div., Asbury Theological Seminary. Address: Route 1 Box 64, Danville, Alabama 35619.

LEE, ELEANOR M Occupation: State Senator. Education: B.A., Evergreen State College. Address: Post Office Box 66274, Burien, Washington 98166.

LEE, JAMES WIDNER Occupation: Engineer, Morton Thiokol, Inc. Education: B.S. Aerospace Engineering; Certificate in Archaeology. Address: 1004 Appalachee Road, Huntsville, Alabama 35801.

LEE, JOHN EDWARD JR Occupation: Administrator, Edonomic Research Service, U.S. Department of Agriculture. Education: B.S., M.S., Auburn University; Ph.D., Harvard University. Address: 8217 Chivalry Road, Annandale, Virginia 22003.

LEE, KAREN ANNE Occupation: Certified Public Accountant, Tax Accountant. Education: B.S. Business Administration; M.S.T. (in progress), Bentley College. Address: 111 South Main Street, Newton, New Hampshire 03858.

LEE, NELDA S Occupation: Fine Arts Appraiser/ Dealer in Investment Art; President, Nelda Lee, Inc. Education: A.A. Art, Tarleton State University, 1961; B.A. Fine Arts, North Texas State University, 1963; Graduate Work in Fine Arts, Texas Tech University and San Miguel de Allende Art Institute. Address: 2610 East 21 Street, Odessa, Texas.

LEE, PALI JAE KEALOHALANI'KILOA Occupation: Author, Researcher. Education: University of Hawaii, University of Michigan. Address: c/o Koko, Atherton Halau, Bishop Museum, Honolulu, Hawaii.

LEE, PAULINE W Occupation: Director of the Library. Education: Bachelor of Arts, Master of Arts in Library Science. Address: Post Office Box 456, Grambling, Louisiana 71245.

LEE, RICHARD M Occupation: Psychologist, Psychophysiologist. Education: Ph.D., University of Maryland, 1966. Address: 3041 Moon Lake, West Bloomfield, Michigan 48033.

LEE, RONALD DEMOS Occupation: Professor of Demography and Economics. Education: B.A., M.A., Ph.D. Address: 2933 Russell Street, Berkeley, California 94705.

LEE, SIDNEY PHILLIP Occupation: Senator, United States Virgin Islands. Education: B.S., M.S. Chemical Engineering. Address: Chateau Pierre, Christiansted, St. Croix, Virgin Islands.

LEE, THOMAS HENRY Occupation: Professor of Electrical Engineering, Massachusetts Institute of Technology. Education: B.S. 1946, M.S. 1950, Ph.D. 1954. Address: 44 Chestnut Street, Boston, Massachusetts 02108.

LEE, WILLIAM DAVID Occupation: Professor of English, Southern Utah State College. Education: M.A., Idaho State University, 1971; Ph.D., University of Utah, 1973. Address: Box 62, Paragonah, Utah 84760.

LEE, WILLIAM JOHNSON Occupation: Attorney, Administrator, State Medical Board of Ohio. Education: Attended University of Akron, Denison University, Harvard University Graduate School of Engineering; J.D., Ohio State University Law School. Address: 4893 Brittany Court West, Columbus, Ohio 43229.

LEE, WILLIS LeGRAND Occupation: Physicist (Consultant). Education: D.Sc., Ph.D. Address: 1879

North Marlowe Street, Thousand Oaks, California 91360.

LEE-MERROW, SUSAN W Occupation: Management Consultant, Writer. Education: B.A. Address: 31422 Brae Burn Avenue, Hayward, California 94544.

LEEDS, DONALD S Occupation: Educator. Education: A.B., A.M., Ed.D. Address: 9 Ferland Lane, Aberdeen, New Jersey 07747.

LEENHOUTS, LILLIAN SCOTT Occupation: Architect. Education: Layton School of Art; B.S. Architecture, University of Michigan. Address: 1204 East Concordia Avenue, Milwaukee, Wisconsin 53212.

LEES, MARGRIT HAMILTON Occupation: Artist, Writer and Genealogist. Education: Certified Genealogy Teacher. Address: 2666 Rutherford Drive, Hollywood, California 90068.

LEESON, JANET CAROLINE Occupation: President, Leeson's Party Cakes, Inc. Education: Prairie State College, 1975. Address: 6713 West 163rd Place, Tinley Park, Illinois 60477.

LeFAIVRE, DENIS Occupation: Physical Oceanography. Education: B.Sc., M.Sc., Ph.D. Address: 2420 Che. du Foulon, Sillery, Que, Canada G1T 1X7.

LEFEBRE, FREDERICK H Occupation: Financial Services. Address: 48 Cuesta Way, Walnut Creek, California 94596.

LEFEBVRE, D'ARGENCÉ, RENÉ-YVON MARIE MARC Occupation: Museum Director, Asian Art Museum of San Francisco. Education: Licencie-es Lettres, Sorbonne, 1952; Chinese 1950, Japanese 1951, Finnish 1952, Brevete de l'Ecole Nationale des Langues Orientales Vivantes. Address: 16 Midhill Drive, Mill Valley, California 94941.

LEFFERT, LILLIAN WEINER Occupation: Director of Publications, State University of New York College of Technology. Education: B.S. Journalism, B.S. Business Administration. Address: 17 Barley Mow Run, New Hartford, New York 13413.

LEFKOWITZ, LOUIS H Occupation: Physician/ Obstetrician/Gynecologist. Education: B.A., M.D. Address: 6 East Place, Suffern, New York 10901.

LEHMAN, CLEO J Occupation: Nurse, Fairmont General Hospital. Education: B.S.N., M.S.N. Address: 208 Jefferson Street, Bridgeport, West Virginia 26330.

LEHMAN, DENNIS D Occupation: Professor of Chemistry, Department of Chemistry, Northwestern University. Education: B.Sc., M.Sc., Ph.D. Address: 3940 Elm Lane, Wadsworth, Illinois 60087.

LEHMAN, HYLA BEROEN Occupation: Lecturer and Performing Artist. Education: B.S.E., Drake University; M.A., University of Iowa; International Graduate Program, Athens, Greece. Address: 4347 Eaglemere Court Southeast, Cedar Rapids, Iowa 52403.

LEHMANN, ARNOLD O Occupation: Music Professor (Retired). Education: B.A., B.Mus., M.A., Ph.D. Address: Route 4 Box 271, Watertown, Wisconsin 53094.

LEHMANN, M DRUE Occupation: Associate Professor of Clinical Speech Pathology. Education: B.S., M.A. Address: 680 Overland #1, Cincinnati, Ohio 45226.

LEIBHARDT, EDWARD Occupation: Research Scientist. Education: B.A. 1954, Ph.D. 1959, Northwestern University. Address: 9416 West Bull Valley Road, Woodstock, Illinois 60098.

LEIDING, JAMES H Occupation: Sociologist. Education: B.S., M.A., Ph.D. Address: R.D. 3, Kunkletown, Pennsylvania 18058.

LEIGH, JAMES HENRY Occupation: University Educator, Texas A&M University. Education: B.B.A.,

M.B.A., Ph.D. Address: 2809 Hillside Drive, Bryan, Texas 77802.

LEIN, ALLEN Occupation: Professor, University of California. Education: Ph.D. Address: 8653 Dunaway Drive, La Jolla, California 92037.

LEIPHOLZ, HORST H E Occupation: University Professor, University of Waterloo. Education: Engineering Graduate, Diploma Mathematics, Dr.-Ing., Docent. Address: 401 Warrington Drive, Waterloo, Ontario, Canada N2L 2P7.

LEIPOLD, WAYNE H Occupation: Technical Services Department Head, Phelps Dodge Corporation. Education: B.S., M.S.E.E. Address: Post Office Box 682, Pirtleville, Arizona 85626.

LEKBERG, BARBARA HULT Occupation: Sculptor/Teacher, Philadelphia College of Art. Education: B.F.A., M.A., Honorary D.F.A. Address: 911 Stuart Avenue, Mamaroneck, New York 10543.

LELCHIK, ALAN Occupation: Writer; Visiting Professor, Amherst College. Education: M.A., Ph.D. English. Address: R.F.D. 2, Canaan, New Hampshire 03741.

LELE, PADMAKAR PRATAP Occupation: Professor of Experimental Medicine, Massachusetts Institute of Technology. Education: M.D., D.Phil., Oxon. Address: 21 Squire Road, Winchester, Massachusetts 01890.

LEMEGA, ROMAN W Occupation: Clinical Psychologist, North Jersey Developmental Center. Education: B.A., M.A. Address: 3 Midwood Drive, Florham Park, New Jersey 07932.

LEMKE, CORRINE L Occupation: Financial Aid Grant Coordinator, Moorhead State University. Education: B.A. Philosophy. Address: 128 Pierce Trailer Court, Moorhead, Minnesota 56560.

LENAGHAN, MICHAEL J Occupation: Director of External Affairs, National Headquarters of American Red Cross. Education: Ed.D., Virginia Polytechnic Institute and State University; B.S.F.S., M.A., Georgetown University. Address: 8418 Lynwood Place, Chevy Chase, Maryland 20815.

LENKEY, SUSAN V Occupation: Art Historian; Rare Book Librarian Emerita, Stanford University; Visiting Professor on Ecclesiastical Art, St. Patrick's Seminary. Education: Ph.D. Art History. Address: 274 San Luis Drive, Menlo Park, California 94025.

LENT, ROBERT W Occupation: Associate Professor and Staff Psychologist, Student Counseling Bureau, University of Minnesota; Adjunct Professor, Department of Psychology, University of Minnesota. Education: B.A. summa cum laude, State University of New York-Albany, 1975; M.A. 1977, Ph.D. 1979, The Ohio State University. Address: 3609 13th Avenue South, #2, Minneapolis, Minnesota 55407.

LENTES, DAVID EUGENE Occupation: Corporate Executive. Education: B.B.A. Accounting. Address: Post Office Box 141561, Spokane, Washington 99214.

LENTINI, GERARD F Occupation: Professor and Chairman, Department of Educational Leadership, West Georgia College. Education: B.S., M.Ed., Ed.D. Address: 123 Melody Drive, Carrollton, Georgia 30117.

LEONARD, MARILYNN R Occupation: Strategic Planning Manager, Solid State Operations; Marketing Manager, Display Devices Operations. Education: Doctorate. Address: 4131 Northeast Wistaria Drive, Portland, Oregon 97212.

LEONARD, NELS JR Occupation: Professor of Music at West Liberty State College; Oboist; Classical Guitarist. Education: A.B., M.M., Ph.D. Address: 15 Crestview Drive, Wheeling, West Virginia 26003.

LEONARD, PETER Occupation: Musician/ Conductor. Education: B.Mus., M.Mus. 1974, The Juillard School of Music. Address: Box 4057, Shreveport, Louisiana 71134.

LEONBERG, STANLEY CURTIS JR Occupation: Neurologist, South Jersey Medical Center. Education: B.S., M.D. Address: 232 East Main, Moorestown, New Jersey 08057.

LEONE, PATRICIA BUDER Occupation: Systems Engineer, Lockheed. Education: B.S., S.M. Address: 32 Holmes Drive, San Jose, California 95127.

LEONG, LINCOLN Occupation: Certified Business Counselor. Education: C.B.C. Address: 751 Clay Street #B, San Francisco, California 94108.

LEOPOLD, IRVING HENRY Occupation: Senior Vice President, Allergan Pharmaceuticals, Inc. Education: M.D., D.Sc. Address: 1484 Galaxy Drive, Newport Beach, California 92660.

LEPPARD, GARY GRANT Occupation: Research Scientist, National Water Research Institute. Education: B.A. (Dist.), B.A. (Hons.), M.A., M.Sc., M.Phil. Ph.D. Address: 226 Simon Drive, Burlington, Ontario, Canada L7N 1X9.

LERCH, JAMES S Occupation: Freelance Adult Educator. Education: B.S. Chemical Engineering, M.Ed. Adult Education Leadership. Address: 16 East 44th Street, Wilmington, Delaware 19802.

LERMAN, CHARLES A Occupation: Educator/ Consulting Psychologist, University of Southern California. Education: Ph.D., M.S., B.A. Address: 519 South Barrington #4, Los Angeles, California 90049.

LERNER, MAX Occupation: Professor, Columnist, Writer, Lecturer. Education: B.A., Yale University; A.M., Washington University; Ph.D., Brookings University. Address: 25 East End Avenue, New York, New York 10028.

LERNER, SHELDON Occupation: Plastic Surgery. Education: A.B., M.D. Address: 3399 First Avenue, San Diego, California 92103.

LeROUX, EDGAR JOSEPH Occupation: Ecologist. Education: B.A., Carleton University, 1950; M.Sc. 1952, Ph.D. 1954, Honorary D.Sc. 1973, McGill University. Address: 27 Keppler Crescent, Nepean, Ontario K2H 5Y1, Canada.

LeROY, HAROLD M Occupation: Artist, Writer, Lecturer. Education: M.F.A. Address: 1916 Avenue K, Brooklyn, New York 11230.

LESCH, BARBARA E Occupation: University Administrator, Sonoma State University. Education: B.A., Brooklyn College, 1968; M.A., University of Maryland, 1970; Ph.D., University of Wisconsin, 1979. Address: 8945 Old Redwood Highway, Cotati, California 94928.

LESCOE, RICHARD JOHN Occupation: M.D., J.D. Education: B.S., M.D., J.D. Address: 3400 West Lomita #300, Torrance, California 90505.

LESLIE, HENRY A Occupation: President and Chief Executive Officer, Union Bank and Trust Company. Education: B.S., LL.B. (J.D.), S.J.D. Address: 3332 Boxwood Drive, Montgomery, Alabama 36111.

LESLIE, ROBERT CAMPBELL Occupation: Emeritus Professor of Pastoral Psychology and Counseling, Pacific School of Religion. Education: A.B., S.T.B., Ph.D. Address: 646 Santa Rosa Avenue, Berkeley, California 94707.

LESSENBERRY, ROBERT ADAMS Occupation: Retail Executive. Education: B.A., Centre College of Kentucky, 1950. Address: 913 South Green Street, Glasgow, Kentucky 42141.

LESSER, LORYN SARI Occupation: Certified Clinical Mental Health Counselor. Education: M.A.

Counseling; Ph.D. Counseling, 1984. Address: 3655 B Old Court Road, Suite 19, Baltimore, Maryland 21208.

LESSICK, MIRA LEE Occupation: Nursing. Education: R.N., B.S.N., M.S., Doctoral Student, University of Texas-Austin. Address: 4520 Bennett Avenue, Apartment 202, Austin, Texas 78751.

LESSIN, ANDREW RICHARD Occupation: Certified Public Accountant, Accounting Executive. Education: B.B.A., Hofstra University, 1965. Address: 2760 Lindenmere Drive, Merrick, New York 11566.

LESTER, WILLIAM ALEXANDER JR Occupation: Professor of Chemistry, University of California-Berkeley. Education: B.S. Chemistry, M.S. Chemistry, Ph.D. Chemistry. Address: 4433 Briar Cliff Road, Oakland, California 94605.

LEUKEFELD, CARL GEORGE Occupation: Commissioned Officer, U.S. Public Health Service. Education: Doctorate, Masters, Bachelors. Address: 13 Sussex Road, Silver Spring, Maryland 20910.

LEVENDOSKY, CHARLES L Occupation: Poet, Editor, Columnist. Education: B.S. Physics, B.A. Mathematics, M.A. Education. Address: 1621 West Odell, Casper, Wyoming 82604.

LEVETOWN, LEWIS D Occupation: Vice President of Personnel. Education: B.B.A. Business Administration; M.A. Educational Administration. Address: 12 Coolidge Avenue, White Plains, New York 10606.

LEVI, DORIS J Occupation: Educational Administrator. Education: Ed.D., Nova University; A.P.C., Loyola University; M.S.L.S., Atlanta University. Address: 3532 White Chapel Road, Baltimore, Maryland 2l215.

LEVIN, A LEO Occupation: Director, Federal Judicial Center. Education: B.A., LL.D. (Hon.), Yeshiva University; J.D., University of Pennsylvania; LL.D. (Hon.), New York Law School. Address: 1520 H Street, Northwest, Washington, D.C. 20005.

LEVIN, ALVIN IRVING Occupation: Behavioral Psychologist. Education: B.M.Ed., University of Miami, 1941; M.A., California State University, 1955; Ph.D. (with honors), University of California at Los Angeles, 1968. Address: 8612 Jellico Avenue, Northridge, California 91325.

LEVIN, BETSY Occupation: Dean and Professor of Law, University of Colorado Law School. Education: LL.B., Yale Law School, 1966; A.B., Bryn Mawr College, 1956. Address: 3782 Wonderland Hill Avenue, Boulder, Colorado 80302.

LeVINE, BERNARD Occupation: Safety Consultant. Education: C.S.P., H.S.P. Address: 2280 East 22nd Street, Brooklyn, New York 11229.

LEVINE, MYRON L Occupation: Optometrist. Education: B.S., D.D., Pacific University. Address: 10587 Holman Avenue, Los Angeles, California 90024.

LEVINE, STUART Occupation: Editor, Professor, Department of English, University of Kansas. Education: A.B., Harvard University; M.A., Ph.D., Brown University. Address: 1846 Barker, Lawrence, Kansas 66044.

LEVINGER, JEFFREY EMMET Occupation: Author. Education: B.S. Mathematics, Massachusetts Institute of Technology, 1963. Address: 300 Sussex Street, San Francisco, California 94131.

LEVITT, LYNN Occupation: Associate Professor Psychology, Human Resources Development Center, New York Institute of Technology. Education: B.A. Mathematics, B.S. Psychology, M.S. Psychology, Ph.D. Psychology. Address: 6 Parkside Drive, Apartment 1-V, Carle Place, New York 11514.

LEVITT, SEYMOUR HERBERT Occupation:

Professor and Head, Department Therapeutic Radiology, University of Minnesota. Education: M.D. Address: 6413 Cherokee Trail, Edina, Minnesota 55435.

LEVY, DAVID S Occupation: Director of Financial Aid. Education: B.A. History, M.A. Psychology, Occidental College. Address: 3522 Henrietta Avenue, La Crescenta, California 91214.

LEWANDOWSKA, SISTER M THEODOSETTE Occupation: Archivist of Holy Family College and of the Sisters of the Holy Family of Nazareth. Education: Bachelor of Arts, Marywood College, 1944; Master of Arts cum laude, Villanova University, 1950. Address: Grant and Frankford Avenues, Philadelphia, Pennsylvania 19114.

LEWIS, ALEXANDER LEONARD Occupation: Member, Senior Citizens Advisory Commission, State of Hawaii; President, Leahi Hospital Auxiliary. Education: A.B., B.D., M.D., Johnson C. Smith University; M.S., Columbia University. Address: 94-412 Noholoa LP, Miliani, Hawaii 96789.

LEWIS, CHERIE S Occupation: Tax Advisor and Journalism Educator. Education: B.A., Michigan; M.S., Boston University; Ph.D. Candidate, University of Minnesota. Address: 3104 Fourth Street, Suite 106, Santa Monica, California 90405.

LEWIS, GLEN EDWARD Occupation: Management Consultant. Education: B.A., California State College, 1967; M.A., Indiana University of Pennsylvania, 1968; Ph.D., Cornell University, 1976. Address: Post Office Box 67, Jones Mills, Pennsylvania 15646.

LEWIS, GREGORY E Occupation: Vice President for Administration, Fisk University. Education: B.S., M.S., C.P.A. Address: 1809 Morena Street, F-1, Nashville, Tennessee 37208.

LEWIS, JAMES MICHAEL Occupation: Plant Engineer. Education: B.S.E.T., Purdue University, 1979. Address: 0811-CR28, Corunna, Indiana 46730.

LEWIS, LORAINE RUTH Occupation: Teacher of Migrant Children, Kindergarten through Second Grade. Education: B.S.L., B.S. Education. Address: 1914 Highland Drive, Prosser, Washington 99350.

LEWIS, LOUISE MILLER Occupation: Director, Art Gallery; Professor, Art History. Education: B.A., University of California-Berkeley, 1963; M.A. French 1966, M.A. Art History 1972, University of New Mexico. Address: 18111 Nordfioff Street, Northridge, California 91330.

LEWIS, SEYMOUR A Occupation: Public Accountant. Education: B.Sc. Accounting. Address: 412 Old Manor Road, Columbia, South Carolina 29210.

LEWIS, THEODORE G Occupation: Computer Scientist and Author. Education: B.S., M.S., Ph.D. Address: 4400 Sulphur Springs Road, Corvallis, Oregon 97330.

LEXA, ROBERT CAROL Occupation: Executive Vice President. Education: B.B.A., J.D. Address: 7694 Oak Hill Drive, Chesterland, Ohio 44026.

LI, GEORGE S Occupation: Scientist. Education: Ph.D. Organic Chemistry. Address: 1069 Riverview Drive, Macedonia, Ohio 44056.

LI, TIEN-YI Occupation: Mershon Professor, The Ohio State University. Education: B.A. 1937, M.A. 1946, Ph.D. 1950. Address: 4532 Kipling Road, Columbus, Ohio 43220.

LIANG, WINSTON W Occupation: Research and Development Manager. Education: Sc.D. Materials Engineering, M.S. Metallurgy, B.S. Chemical Engineering. Address: 330 Carriage Hill, Naperville, Illinois 60565.

LIANIDES, SYLVIA PANAGOS Occupation: Professor Anatomy and Physiology, West Valley College. Education: B.S., Ph.D. Physiology, Tufts University School of Medicine. Address: 19643 Montauk Drive, Saratoga, California 95070.

LIAO, WEI-CHI Occupation: Medical/ Pharmaceutical Scientist. Education: Ph.D., Rutgers Pharmacy School. Address: 84 Warwick Street, Iselin, New Jersey 08830.

LIBACKYJ, ANFIR Occupation: Professor Theology, St. Sophia Seminary. Education: M.Sc., M.Div., Ph.D. Address: 84-22, 107 Avenue, Jamaica, New York 11417.

LIBERMAN, ARTHUR L Occupation: Patent Attorney. Education: LL.M., J.D., M.S.Che., B.S.Che., A.B. Address: #1 Scenic Drive, Highlands, New Jersey.

LIBMAN, ROBERT H Occupation: Physician and Attorney. Education: M.D., J.D. Address: 901 South Ashland, Number 1109, Chicago, Illinois 60607.

LICHTENBERG, BYRON K Occupation: Space Flight Consultant. Education: Sc.B., Brown University; M.S., Sc.D., Massachusetts Institute of Technology. Address: 48 Leighton Road, Wellesley, Massachusetts 02181.

LIDICKER, WILLIAM Z JR Occupation: Professor of Zoology, Curator of Mammals, Museum of Vertebrate Zoology, University of California-Berkeley. Education: B.S., M.S., Ph.D. Address: Museum of Vertebrate Zoology, University of California, Berkeley, California 94720.

LIE, KIAN JOE Occupation: Research Professor, University of California. Education: M.D., Ph.D., D.T.M. & H. Address: 30 Lansdale, San Francisco, California 94127.

LIEBERMAN, STEPHEN JACOB Occupation: Orientalist, Dropsie College. Education: B.A., University of Minnesota, 1963; Ph.D., Harvard University, 1972. Address: 7400 Haverford Avenue, Apartment E-309, Philadelphia, Pennsylvania 19151.

LIEBERSON, STANLEY Occupation: Sociologist, University of California. Education: M.A., Ph.D. Address: 560 Valle Vista Avenue, Oakland, California 94610.

LIEBLEIN, SEYMOUR Occupation: Manager of Technical Report Services. Education: B.Mech.Eng., M.Aero.Eng. Address: 3400 Wooster Road, #320, Rocky River, Ohio 44116.

LIENHART, DAVID A Occupation: Geologist. Education: B.A., M.S. Address: 7229 Longfield Drive, Cincinnati, Ohio 45243.

LIFCHITZ, MAX Occupation: Assistant Professor of Music, Columbia University. Education: B.M., M.S., M.M. Address: 862 West End Avenue, New York, New York 10025.

LIFF, CAROL A Occupation: Teacher, Kindergarten, Cambridge Public Schools. Education: B.A., M.Ed. Address: 19 Douglas Road, Lexington, Massachusetts 02173.

LIGHT, ROBERT MERWIN Occupation: Broadcasting Association Executive. Address: 1800 North Highland Avenue, Suite 609, Hollywood, California 90028.

LIGHTCAP, EDWARD JOHN Occupation: Financial Auditor. Education: B.B.A., University of Iowa, 1976; Student, DePaul University, University of Portland. Address: 12375 Mount Jefferson Terrace, Lake Oswego, Oregon 97034.

LIGHTSTONE, RONALD Occupation: Vice President. Education: A.B., Columbia University, 1959; J.D., New York University School of Law, 1962. Address: 15 West 81 Street, New York, New York

10024.

LIJPHART, AREND N M N Occupation: Professor of Political Science, University of California. Education: B.A. 1958, M.A. 1959, Ph.D. 1963. Address: 7010 Via Valverde, La Jolla, California 92037.

LIM, HENRY C Occupation: Professor of Chemical Engineering, Purdue University. Education: B.S., M.S.E., Ph.D. Address: 100 Spinning Wheel Court, West Lafayette, Indiana 47906.

LIM, LUCY Occupation: Executive Director/Curator, Chinese Culture Center. Education: M.A., Ph.D. Candidate. Address: 1661 Leavenworth Street, San Francisco, California 94109.

LIM, TOH-WOON Occupation: Periodontist. Education: D.M.D., Ph.D., S.T.D. Address: 9515 Butternut Drive, Crystal Lake, Illinois 60014.

LIN, ALICE LEE LAN Occupation: Physicist. Education: M.A. Physics, George Washington University, 1974; A.B. Physics, University of California-Berkeley, 1963. Address: 28 Hallett Hill Road, Weston, Massachusetts 02193.

LIN, HAN-SHENG Occupation: Professor of History, Sonoma State University. Education: B.A., M.A., Ph.D. Address: 119 Westridge Drive, Petahuma, California 94952.

LIN, JUIYUAN WILLIAM Occupation: Certified Public Accountant, Vice President, Associate. Education: M.B.A., Illinois State University. Address: 1921 Washington, Wilmette, Illinois 60091.

LIN, MING C Occupation: Senior Scientist and Adjunct Professor of Chemistry, Naval Research Laboratory. Education: Ph.D. Chemistry. Address: 8897 McNair Drive, Alexandria, Virginia 22309.

LIN, PING-WHA Occupation: Professor, Project Manager, Tri-State University. Education: Ph.D. Address: 506 South Darling Street, Angola, Indiana 46703.

LIN, RAY Y Occupation: University Professor, University of Cincinnati. Education: B.S., M.S., Sc.D., Massachusetts Institute of Technology. Address: Post Office Box 21008, Cincinnati, Ohio 45221.

LINDEBORG, RICHARD A Occupation: Chief Editor and Head of Publications, U.S. Forest Products Laboratory. Education: B.A., M.S. Address: 2921 Monroe Street, Madison, Wisconsin 53711.

LINDAHL, THOMAS J Occupation: Assistant Provost Academic Affairs, University of Minnesota-Waseca. Education: B.S., University of Wisconsin; M.Ed., University of Illinois; Ph.D., Iowa State University. Address: 711 8th Avenue Northeast, Waseca, Minnesota 56093.

LINDHOLM, JOHN C Occupation: Professor of Engineering. Education: B.S. Business Administration 1949, B.S.M.E. 1949, M.S.M.E. 1956, Ph.D. 1961. Address: 744 Elling Drive, Manhattan, Kansas 66502.

LINDLEY, JANE ANN Occupation: Government Administrator, Library of Congress. Education: B.A., Butler University; M.L.S., University of Maryland. Address: 2435 May Place, Fort Washington, Maryland 20744.

LINDSAY, LARRY L Occupation: Park Naturalist, Toledo Metro-Parks. Education: B.S., M.Ed. 1984. Address: 12750 Sager, Swanton, Ohio 43558-9440.

LINDSEY, BARBARA ANN Occupation: Consultant, Publisher/Editor. Education: University of Palm Beach, Indian River Junior College. Address: Buchanan House Suite 504, 2301 South Jefferson Davis, Arlington, Virginia 22202.

LINDSEY, CHARLES A Occupation: Doctor of Chiropractic. Education: Doctor of Chiropractic, Ph.D. Address: 605 Ivy Street, Ellisville, Mississippi 39437.

LINDSTROM, ANITA INGER Occupation: Psychologist. Education: Ph.D. Address: 17349 Boswell Place, Granada Hills, California 91344.

LINDVIG, ELISE KAY Occupation: School Psychologist. Education: B.A. Psychology/Education, M.S. Clinical Psychology. Address: Post Office Box 2999, Nogales, Arizona 85628.

LINGHAM, MARCELLA ERMA Occupation: Professor, Rutgers University. Education: B.S.Ed., M.Ed., Ed.D. Address: 119 South Peach Street, Philadelphia, Pennsylvania 19139.

LINGLE, CHARLES PHILLIP Occupation: Engineer. Education: B.S. Agro, Massachusetts Institute of Technology, 1957; M.B.A., California State University, 1974. Address: 736 Gould Avenue 19, Hermosa Beach, California 90254.

LINIGER, WERNER Occupation: Research in Mathematics. Education: M.S., Ph.D. Address: 703 Fieldstone Court, Yorktown Heights, New York 10598.

LINN, ROBERT L Occupation: Professor, University of Illinois. Education: B.A., University of California-Los Angeles; M.A., Ph.D., University of Illinois. Address: 1902 South Anderson, Urbana, Illinois 61801.

LINNELL, ALBERT P Occupation: Professor of Physics and Astronomy, Michigan State University. Education: B.A., College of Wooster, 1944; Ph.D., Harvard University, 1950. Address: 1918 Yuma Trail, Okemos, Michigan 48864.

LINNES, JOANNE C Occupation: Teacher, E.S.L.; Author, *Welcome to the World*. Address: 1248 20 Street Northwest, Rochester, Minnesota 55901.

LIPMAN, DANIEL GORDON Occupation: Director of Research, Creative Research Institutes, Inc. Education: M.D., Ph.D. Address: 20104 Hob Hill Way, Gaithersburg, Maryland 20879.

LIPPERT, FELICE M Occupation: Consultant. Education: B.A. Home Economics. Address: Sousa Drive, Sands Point, New York 11050.

LIPPINCOTT, JAMES ANDREW Occupation: Professor, Northwestern University. Education: A.B., A.M., Ph.D. Address: Department of Biochemistry, Molecular Biology and Cell Bilogy, Northwestern University, Evanston, Illinois 60201.

LIPPMANN, GORHAM JAMES Occupation: Executive Director, American Boat and Yacht Council. Education: B.S. Naval Architecture and Marine Engineering. Address: 314 Ocean Avenue, Amityville, New York 11701.

LIPSCHULZ, JLSE HEMPEL Occupation: Professor of French, Andrew W. Mellon Professor in the Humanities, Vassar College. Education: Baccalaureat es lettres, Licence es lettres, Diploma d'Etudes Superieures, University de Paris; Diploma de Estudios Hispanicos, University of Madrid; M.A., Harvard University; Ph.D., Radcliffe University. Address: 11 Park Avenue, Poughkeepsie, New York 12603.

LIPTON, WILLIAM LAWRENCE Occupation: Futurist. Education: B.S., New York University; A.A.S. Real Estate, M.B.A. Accounting, Pace University. Address: Post Office Box 134, Harrington, Maine 04643.

LISHMAN, ROBERT C Occupation: Library Supervisor, Memphis City Schools. Education: B.S., M.A., Memphis State University. Address: 8199 Farmington East, Southaven, Mississippi 38671.

LIT, JOHN Occupation: Professor, Wilfrid Laurier University. Education: B.Sc., Hong Kong; D.Sc., Laval. Address: Wilfrid Laurier University, Waterloo, Ontario N2L 3C5, Canada.

LITTELL, BERTHA FELDER Occupation: Signatory, Kansas City Title Insurance Company; Licensed Real Estate Agent; Writer; Songwriter. Address: 1003 Surrey Court, Tomball, Texas 77375.

LITTELL, JEFFREY D Occupation: Owner, Real Estate Mangement and Brokerage Company. Address: 18662 MacArthur Boulevard, Suite 200, Irvine, California 92715.

LITTLE, RICHARD R Occupation: President, Quest National Center. Education: B.A., Findlay College, 1984. Address: 89 Ormsbee, Westerville, Ohio 43018.

LITTLE, SCOTT E Occupation: Independent Oil Producer; Partner, The Quintin Little Company. Education: B.S.B., Oklahoma Christian College. Address: Post Office Box 1509, Ardmore, Oklahoma 73401.

LITTLE, WARREN MASTERS Occupation: Museum Administration, Higgins Armory Museum. Education: A.B., Ed.M., Ed.D. Address: 106 Dover Road, Wellesley, Massachusetts 02181.

LITVAK, ISAIAH A Occupation: Professor, Faculty of Administrative Studies, York University. Education: B.Comm., McGill University, 1957; M.S., Columbia University, 1959; Ph.D., Columbia University, 1964. Address: 193 Dunvegan Road, Toronto, Ontario M5P 2P1, Canada.

LITVIN, WILLIAM TREFFERT Occupation: Painter/Sculptor. Education: B.S., M.A. Address: 383 Union Street, Brooklyn, New York 11231.

LITWOK, EVELYN Occupation: Businesswoman, Psychologist. Address: 207 West 102nd, New York, New York 10025.

LITZENBERG, KERRY K Occupation: Professor/ Educator. Education: B.S., M.S., Ph.D., Purdue University. Address: 1604 Austin, College Station, Texas 77840.

LIU, STEPHEN C Y Occupation: Professor of Microbiology, Eastern Michigan University. Education: Ph.D., University of Minnesota. Address: 2901 Pebble Creek Road, Ann Arbor, Michigan 48104.

LIU, YUEN CHOU Occupation: Nurse. Education: B.S.N., M.S.N., Ph.D. Address: 2704 36th Place, Northwest, Washington, D.C. 20007.

LIVERMORE, JILL DIANE Occupation: Shop Manager, Sette Publishing Company. Education: B.F.A. Printmaking, Arizona State University. Address: 1418 South Grandview, Tempe, Arizona 85281.

LIVINGSTON, PAMELA A Occupation: Image Consultant, Corporate Identity Specialist. Education: B.A., Adelphi University; Post-Graduate Work at New York University and Columbia University. Address: 108 South Rockburn Street, York, Pennsylvania 17402.

LIZUT, NONA MOORE PRICE Occupation: Administrator, Health Services Division, New Mexico Health and Environment Department. Education: Completed One Year of College. Address: 1408 Santa Rosa Drive, Santa Fe, New Mexico 87501.

LLOYD, D H Occupation: Writer/Producer. Education: B.S. Address: 1239 East 10th, Long Beach, California 90813.

LLOYD, WILLIAM K II Occupation: Assistant Principal. Education: B.A. Economics; M.A. and Professional Diploma, Guidance and Administration. Address: 741 Cottage Street, Uniondale, New York 11553.

LO, CHIN T Occupation: Professor of Chinese, University of Hawaii. Education: B.A., M.A., Ph.D. Address: 1612 Kanalui Street, Honolulu, Hawaii 96816.

LOBERG, ROBERT W Occupation: Artist. Education: A.A., City College of San Francisco; B.A.,

M.A., University of California. Address: 2020 Vine Street, Berkeley, California 94709.

LOCK, WILLIAM ROWLAND Occupation: Educator/Professor of Musician. Education: B.M., M.M., D.M.A., A.R.C.T. Address: 13967 Whiterock Drive, La Mirada, California 90638.

LOCKHART, AILEENE SIMPSON Occupation: Professor, Texas Woman's University; Editor. Education: B.S., M.S., Ph.D., D.Sc. Address: 610 Northridge Drive, Denton, Texas 76201.

LOCKHART, BARBARA DAY Occupation: Professor, Temple University. Education: B.S., M.A., Michigan State University; Ed.D., Brigham Young University. Address: 511 East Mill Road, Flourtown, Pennsylvania 19031.

LOCKLAIR, DAN STEVEN Occupation: Composer/Recitalist/Professor of Music, Wake Forest University. Education: S.M.M., Union Theological Seminary; D.M.A., Eastman School of Music. Address: 921 South Main Street, Winston-Salem, North Carolina 27101.

LOCKWOOD, DAVID JOHN Occupation: Physicist. Education: B.Sc., M.Sc., Ph.D., D.Sc. Address: Physics Division, National Research Council, Ottawa, Ontario K1A 0R6, Canada.

LOEB, GLADYS E Occupation: Chairman, Gladys E. Loeb Foundation. Education: High School Graduate. Address: 2002 Forest Hill Drive, Silver Spring, Maryland 20903.

LOEB, JUDY Occupation: Professor of Art, Eastern Michigan. Education: B.F.A., M.F.A., Tyler School of Art, Temple University. Address: 3286 Alpine Drive, Ann Arbor, Michigan 48104.

LOEW, RALPH WILLIAM Occupation: Clergy, Author. Education: A.B., Capital University; M.Div., Hamma School of Theology. Address: 342 Depew Avenue, Buffalo, New York 14214.

LOEWY, OLIVIA ROCHELLE Occupation: Psychotherapist/Consultant. Education: Ph.D., M.A., Educational Psychology. Address: 11233 Blix Street, North Hollywood, California 91602.

LOFSTROM, MARK D Occupation: Public Relations Officer, Arts Administrator. Education: B.A., Carleton College, 1976. Address: 3350 Sierra Drive, #504, Honolulu, Hawaii 96816.

LOFTUS, DANIEL P Occupation: Account Executive. Education: B.S. Psychology, M.S.W., M.B.A. Address: 123 Circle Drive, RD 2, Moscow, Pennsylvania 18444.

LOFTUS, ELIZABETH Occupation: Professor of Psychology, University of Washington. Education: M.A., Ph.D., Stanford University. Address: 1221 22nd Avenue East, Seattle, Washington 98112.

LOISELLE, ROBERT H Occupation: Psychologist. Education: B.A., Ph.D. Address: 1485 Fredricksburg Drive, Boardman, Ohio 44512.

LOMEN, DAVID O Occupation: Professor of Mathematics, University of Arizona. Education: B.A., M.S., Ph.D. Address: 6945 East Blue Lake Drive, Tucson, Arizona 85715.

LONDON, BILLIE LEE Occupation: Organizational Development Consultant. Education: B.S., M.S. Address: 160 Oakdale Drive, Aptos, Louisiana 95003.

LONDON, HERBERT I Occupation: Dean, New York University; Director, Hudson Institute. Education: B.A., M.A., Ph.D. Address: 2 Washington Square Village, New York, New York 10012.

LONDON, SHIRLEY L Occupation: Social Worker. Education: B.A., M.S., 3rd Year Postmaster's Certificate. Address: 444 East 82nd Street, New York,

New York 10028.

LONEY, GLENN M Occupation: Professor of Theatre. Education: A.B., University of California; M.A., University of Wisconsin; Ph.D., Stanford University. Address: 3 East 71st Street, New York, New York 10021.

LONG, HOMER J Occupation: University Administrator. Education: B.S., M.Ed., Ed.D. Address: Route 9, Box 470 F, Springfield, Missouri 65804.

LONG, RICHARD L JR Occupation: Engineering Educator, Department of Chemical Engineering, New Mexico State University. Education: B.A., Ph.D. Chemical Engineering, Rice University. Address: Box 3850, Las Cruces, New Mexico 88003.

LONG, ROBERT EMMET Occupation: Author, Writer. Education: B.A., Ph.D., Columbia University; M.A., Syracuse University. Address: 254 South Third Street, Fulton, New York 13069.

LONG, THEODORE LOUIS Occupation: Psychotherapist/Administrator. Education: B.A., M.S.W., M.S.B.A. Address: 125 West Marquette Avenue, South Bend, Indiana 46617.

LONG, VALDA ELOISE Occupation: Nurse (Retired). Education: Attended Gordan Keller School of Nursing; Bachelor's Degree in Religion. Address: Box 133, Route 1, Ona, Florida 33865.

LONGO, PHILLIP ANTHONY Occupation: Management Consultant to Financial Institution. Education: A.A. Finance; Graduate, Colorado School of Banking. Address: 1113 South Palm Avenue, San Gabriel, California 91776.

LONGOBUCCO, ARDEN ANNE Occupation: Medical Social Worker. Education: B.A. Address: 42 Richmond Avenue, Worchester, Massachusetts 01602.

LONGSTAFF, THOMAS RICHMOND WILLIS Occupation: College Professor, Colby College. Education: B.A., M.Div., Ph.D. Address: 39 Pleasant Street, Waterville, Maine 04901.

LOONEY, GERALD L Occupation: Medical Director, Memorial Hospital. Education: B.A. 1959; M.D., Johns Hopkins University, 1963; M.P.H., Harvard University, 1968. Address: 2519 Southwest 34th Street, Topeka, Kansas 66611.

LOPER, CARL RICHARD JR Occupation: Professor of Metallurgical Engineering, University of Wisconsin-Madison; Professional Engineer. Education: B.S., M.S., Ph.D., Metallurgical Engineering. Address: 4730 La Fayette Drive, Madison, Wisconsin 53705.

LOPEZ, MARY GARDNER Occupation: Administrative Social Worker; Writer. Education: B.S., M.S., M.B.I.A. Address: 105-11 Ditmars Boulevard, East Elmhurst, New York 11369.

LoPRESTI, PETER LIBORIO Occupation: University Professor. Education: B.S., M.A., Ph.D. Address: 4499-B Via Marisol #233, Los Angeles, California 90042.

LORENZ, ELLEN-JANE Occupation: Free-lance Composer, Lecturer, Author. Education: B.A., M.S.M., Ph.D. Address: 324 Oak Forest, Dayton, Ohio 45419.

LORENZ, MARIAN J Occupation: Leader/ Teacher, Preschool Program. Education: B.S., M.S. Address: 156 Monell Avenue, Islip, New York 11751.

LORET DE MOLA, MARIA M Occupation: Director, Marketing Information and Support. Education: B.S., M.S. Mathematics. Address: 380 Prospect Avenue, Hackensack, New Jersey 07601.

LORIMER, CRAIG GORDON Occupation: Professor of Forestry, University of Wisconsin-Madison. Education: B.A., Colby College, 1972; Ph.D., Duke University, 1976. Address: 4501 Gregg Road, Madison, Wisconsin 53705.

LORNE, SIMON M Occupation: Attorney. Education: A.B., Occidental College, 1967; J.D. magna cum laude, Michigan Law School, 1970. Address: 612 South Flower Street, Los Angeles, California 90017.

LOS, CORNELIS ALBERTUS Occupation: Economist. Education: Ph.D., Columbia University; M.Phil.; Doctorandus, Candidatus. Address: 108 Erie Street, Jersey City, New Jersey 07302.

LOSCHEN, LESLIE R Occupation: Professor of Business Administration, California State University. Education: A.B., M.B.A., Ph.D. Address: 21 Gaucho Drive, Rolling Hills Estates, California 90274.

LOSEY, ALBA ELIONOR Occupation: Painter, Fine Arts, Celestial Scope. Education: Liberal Arts. Address: 80 North Craig Avenue, Pasadena, California 91107.

LOSIN, EDWARD THOMAS Occupation: Senior Research Scientist. Education: B.S. Chemistry, A.M. Chemistry, Ph.D. Chemistry. Address: 10000 North Sheridan Drive, Mequon, Wisconsin 53092.

LOUGHLIN, MARY ANNE ELIZABETH Occupation: Television Producer/Anchor. Education: Bachelor of Science, Florida State University, 1977. Address: 2344 DeFoors Ferry Road, Northwest, Atlanta, Georgia 30318.

LOVE, MICHAEL Occupation: Design Management/Construction. Education: Traphagew School of Design, Pratt Institute, University of Miami. Address: 440 East 79th Street, New York, New York 10021.

LOVE, ROBERT WILLIAM JR Occupation: Executive Medicine/Physician Surgeon. Education: A.B., M.D. Address: Post Office Box 2714, Reston, Virginia 22090.

LOVELADY, JOE RENDER Occupation: Pastor. Education: B.A., Master of Theology, Master of Divinity, Doctor of Ministry. Address: 6730 Manchester, New Orleans, Louisiana 70126.

LOVETT, JUANITA PELLETIER Occupation: Clinical Psychologist. Education: B.A., M.Phil. M.S., Ph.D. Address: 166 Woodland Avenue, Summit, New Jersey 07901.

LOW, JOHN HENRY Occupation: International Banker. Education: B.S.E., Princeton University, 1976. Address: 64 East 86th Street, New York, New York 10028.

LOWE, DONALD R Occupation: College Professor, University of Georgia. Education: B.M.E., M.M.E., Wichita State University. Address: 170 Gibbons Way, Athens, Georgia 30605.

LOWEN, MARILYN N Occupation: Educator, Poet. Education: B.A., Bennington and Goddard Colleges; M.A., City University of New York. Address: 286 South Street, Apartment 16A, New York, New York 10002.

LOWEN, SHARON ANNE Occupation: Classical Indian Dance, Concert Performer. Education: B.A., M.A., University of Michigan. Address: 1705 McIntyre Drive, Ann Arbor, Michigan 48105.

LOWMAN, SISTER PATRICIA Occupation: Professor of History, Bellarmine College. Education: B.S., M.A., Creighton University; Ph.D., St. Louis University. Address: 1243 East Burnett Street, Louisville, Kentucky 40217.

LOY, WILLIAM GEORGE Occupation: Professor of Geography, University of Oregon. Education: Ph.D. Address: 2683 Elinor Street, Eugene, Oregon 97403.

LU, KUO HWA Occupation: Professor, Oregon Health Sciences University. Education: Ph.D. Address: 11780 Southwest Terra Linda, Beaverton, Oregon 97005.

LUBINSKI, ROSEMARY B Occupation: Associate Professor of Communicative Disorders. Education: B.S., M.A., Ed.D. Speech Pathology. Address: 30 Parkwood Drive, Amherst, New York 14226.

LUCAS, AUBREY KEITH Occupation: President, University of Southern Mississippi. Education: B.S. Education and History (with honors) 1955, M.A. Psychology of Reading 1956, University of Southern Mississippi; Ph.D. Administration of Higher Education, Florida State University, 1966

LUCAS, GLENN E Occupation: Associate Professor of Nuclear Engineering, Department Chemical and Nuclear Engineering, University of California-Santa Barbara. Education: B.S. Nuclear Engineering, University of California-Santa Barbara; M.S. Nuclear Engineering 1975, Sc.D. Nuclear Engineering 1977, Massachusetts Institute of Technology. Address: 618 Andamar Way, Goleta, California 93117.

LUCAS, STANLEY JEROME Occupation: Physician, Radiologist. Education: B.S., M.D. Address: 6760 East Beechlands, Cincinnati, Ohio 45237.

LUCIANO, ROBERT A Occupation: Consulting Engineer, President, Robert A. Luciano Associates. Education: B.S.M.E. 1963, M.S. 1966, New Jersey Institute of Technology. Address: R.D. #2, Bissell Road, Lebanon, New Jersey 08833.

LUCKE, THOMAS W Occupation: National Park Service. Education: B.A. History, M.A. History, J.D. Law. Address: 2504 South Tulane, Ft. Collins, Colorado 80525.

LUDWIG, DORENE MARIE Occupation: Artistic Director and President, American Living History Theater. Education: M.F.A., University of California-Los Angeles; B.A., University of South Florida. Address: 1647 North Martel Avenue, Los Angeles, California 90046.

LUE-HING, CECIL Occupation: Director, Research and Development. Education: B.S. Civil Engineering, M.S. Sanitary Engineering, D.Sc. Environment and Sanitary Engineering. Address: 6101 North Sheridan Road, Apartment 40B-East, Chicago, Illinois 60660.

LUGINBYHL, ROBERT IVAN Occupation: Electrical Engineer. Education: B.S.E.E. Address: Box 779, Stinnett, Texas 79083.

LUM, JEAN L J Occupation: Dean and Professor of Nursing, University of Hawaii. Education: B.S. Nursing, University of Hawaii, 1960; M.S. Nursing, University of California, 1961; M.A. 1969, Ph.D. 1972, University of Washington. Address: School of Nursing, University of Hawaii at Manoa, Honolulu, Hawaii 96822.

LUM, ROBERT SING GHUN Occupation: Airport Architect. Education: B.Arch. 1972, Master Urban and Regional Planning 1975. Address: 801 East Leslie Drive, San Gabriel, California 91775.

LUNA, BARBARA CAROLE Occupation: Management Consultant. Education: A.B. Physics and Math, Wellesley College; M.S. and Ph.D. Applied Mathematics and Financial Analysis, Harvard University. Address: 18026 Rodarte Way, Encino, California 91316.

LUNA, DENNIS R Occupation: Attorney. Education: B.S. Petroleum Engineering, 1968; M.S. Petroleum Engineering, 1969; M.B.A., 1971; J.D., 1974. Address: 18026 Rodarte Way, Encino, California 91316.

LUND, DALE A Occupation: Associate Director of Research, Gerontology Program and Research Assistant Professor, University of Utah. Education: B.S. Psychology; M.S. Sociology; Ph.D. Medical Sociology, 1979. Address: 2666 East 2980 South, Salt Lake City, Utah 84109.

LUND, DARYL B Occupation: Professor and Chairman, Food Science Department. Education: B.S. Mathematics, M.S. Food Science, Ph.D. Food Science/Chemical Engineering, University of Wisconsin-Madison. Address: 541 Caromar Drive, Madison, Wisconsin 53711.

LUND, STEVE Occupation: Research Administration. Education: B.S., Clemson College; M.S., Ph.D., University of Wisconsin at Madison. Address: 1201 Southwest 23rd, Pendleton, Oregon 97801.

LUNDE, DAVID ERIC Occupation: Professor of English, English Department, State University College; Poet, Writer. Education: B.A., Knox College; M.F.A., University of Iowa Writer's Workshop. Address: 252 King Road, Forestville, New York 14062.

LUNDQUIST, CARL H Occupation: President, Christian College Consortium. Education: B.A., B.D., Th.M., Th.D., D.D., LL.D. Address: 1900 North Asbury, St. Paul, Minnesota 55113.

LUNG, JIA-LING F Occupation: Operation Research Specialist. Education: B.A., M.S., Ph.D. Address: 6720 Bedford Avenue, Los Angeles, California 90056.

LUNT, OWEN RAYNAL Occupation: Director, Laboratory of Biomedical and Environmental Sciences, University of California at Los Angeles. Education: B.A., Brigham Young University; Ph.D., North Carolina State University. Address: 1200 Roberto Lane, Los Angeles, California 90077.

LUNTZ, MAURICE H Occupation: Ophthalmologist. Education: M.D., F.R.C.S., F.A.C.S. Address: 180 East End Avenue, New York, New York 10128.

LUPIN, E RALPH Occupation: Self-Employed Physician; Consultant, National Medical Enterprises, Inc.; Medical Director and Chairman, American Provider Organization, Inc.; President, LaMothe House, Inc.; President, E. R. Lupin, Inc.; Member, Lloyd's of London Underwriting Sydicate. Education: B.S., Loyola University of the South, 1952; M.D., Louisiana State University, 1956. Address: 1021 Chartres Street, New Orleans, Louisiana 70116.

LUSTES, HERBERT S Occupation: Psychiatrist. Education: M.D. Address: 700 Suburban Square Building, Ardmore, Pennsylvania 19003.

LUTTRELL, GWENDOLYN W Occupation: Geologist, U.S. Geological Survey. Education: B.A., Wellesley College; Attended University of New Mexico. Address: 9408 Byeforde Road, Kensington, Maryland 20895.

LUTZ, ALFRED C Occupation: Owner, A & C Services. Education: A.A. high honors, B.A., M.B.A. President's Scholar. Address: 233 East Avenue, Park Ridge, Illinois 60068.

LUTZ, ARTHUR LEROY Occupation: Professor Emeritus of Physics, Wittenberg University. Education: B.S., Capital University, 1931; M.S. 1936, Ph.D. Physics 1943, The Ohio State University. Address: 1605 Shelby Drive, Springfield, Ohio 45504.

LUTZ, CAROL RICHARDS Occupation: Private Law Practice. Education: A.A. high honors, B.A., J.D. honors. Address: 233 East Avenue, Park Ridge, Illinois 60068.

LUTZ, JUNE LOUISE Occupation: Genealogist. Address: 1433 Elderwood Court, Northwest, Grand Rapids, Michigan 49504.

LUTZ, WILLIAM L Occupation: United States Attorney, District of New Mexico. Education: B.S., J.D.,

University of Texas. Address: 2713 Casa del Norte Court, Northeast, Albuquerque, New Mexico 87112.

LUZA, RADOMIR V Occupation: Professor of History, Tulane University. Education: M.A., Ph.D., J.D. Address: 839 Roseland Parkway, Harahan, Louisiana 70123.

LYDEN, EDWARD FRANCIS XAVIER Occupation: Consulting Geologist-Environmental. Education: B.S. Geology, Columbia University; Post Graduate Studies, Princeton University, Rutgers University, and University of Maine. Address: 14 Coldbrook Road, Hampden, Maine 04444.

LYDOLPH, PAUL E Occupation: Associate Professor and Professor of Geography, Chairman of Russian and East European Studies Committee, University of Wisconsin-Milwaukee. Education: Bachelor of Arts, State University of Iowa, 1948; Master of Science 1951, Doctor of Philosophy 1955, University of Wisconsin; Postdoctoral Studies, University of California.

LYLE, JEROLYN ROSS Occupation: Economist. Education: B.A., M.A., Ph.D. Address: 5512 Center Street, Chevy Chase, Maryland 20815.

LYLE, KENNETH CURTIS Occupation: Professor of English Literature. Education: B.A. English, M.A. Philosophy. Address: 132-11 Foch Boulevard, New York, New York 11420.

LYNCH, CHARLES ALLEN Occupation: Chairman of the Board and Chief Executive Officer. Education: B.S. Industrial Administration. Address: 210 Park Lane, Atherton, California 94025.

LYNN, VERNE L Occupation: Engineer. Education: B.S. Physics, Tufts University, 1951. Address: 5350 North 37th Street, Arlington, Virginia 22207.

LYON, CATHRYN C Occupation: Manager Technical Information Services, Institute for Defense Analysis. Education: B.A. in S.S., M.P.A., University of Northern Colorado. Address: 6806 Westcott, Falls Church, Virginia 22042.

LYONS, ARTHUR W Occupation: Psychologist, Moravian College. Education: B.A., M.S., D.A. Address: 1509 Main Street, Bethlehem, Pennsylvania 18018.

LYONS, CHARLES A Occupation: Chancellor, Fayetteville State University. Education: B.A., M.A., Ph.D. Address: 1303 Yaupon Drive, Fayetteville, North Carolina 28301.

LYONS, CHERIE ANN Occupation: Staff Development Specialist, Writer. Education: B.S. English Education, M.A. Secondary Education, Ph.D. (in progress). Address: 8041 Lamar Street, Arvada, Colorado 80003.

LYONS, GEORGE W C Occupation: Educator, Minister. Education: A.B., Doctoral Degree. Address: 1206 West 89th Street, Los Angeles, California 90044.

LYTLE, ROBERT BRUCE JR Occupation: Architectural Consultant, Professor Emeritus. Education: B.S., U.S.M.M.A.; B.Arch., The University of Michigan. Address: 2222 Fuller Road #701A, Ann Arbor, Michigan 48105.

M

MAAHS, JAN Occupation: Student. Education: Animal Science. Address: Route 13, Lincoln, Nebraska 68527.

MAASKE, MARVIN L Occupation: Region Superintendent of Schools. Education: B.A., M.A. in Mathematics; C.A.S in Education Administration; Ed.D in Education Administration. Address: 1542 West Stephenson Street, Freeport, Illinois 61032.

MACBETH, LOUISE Occupation: Clinical Psychologist. Education: B.A., M.A., Ph.D. Address: 1748 South Garth, Los Angeles, California 90035.

MacCORQUODALE, PATRICIA LEE Occupation: Sociologist. Education: B.A., Carelton College; M.S., Ph.D., Wisconsin-Madison. Address: 2008 East Copper, Tucson, Arizona 85719.

MacDONALD, KENNETH DANIAL Occupation: Appliance Distribution. Education: Student. Address: 873 Chestnut Street, Waban, Masschusetts 02168.

MacDONALD, MARY THOMAS Occupation: Int. Architecture and Design. Education: M.A., B.A. Address: 1925 Brickell Avenue, Miami, Florida 33129.

MACE, SHARON ELIZABETH Occupation: Physician. Education: B.S., M.D. Address: 8243 Merrie Lane, Chesterland, Ohio 44026.

MACERA, CAROLINA A Occupation: Associate Professor. Education: Ph.D., 1982, M.S., 1980, University of California, Berkeley. Address: 505 Saluda Avenue, Columbia, South Carolina 29205.

MACHLUP, MARILYN RUTH Occupation: Child Development Specialist; Lay Child Psychoanalyst. Education: B.S. Nursing, 1953; M.A. Education, 1961; Certificate in Child Analysis, 1972. Address: 2906 Washington Boulevard, Cleveland Heights, Ohio 44118.

MACIUSZKO, JERZY J Occupation: Professor. Education: Ph.D., C.W.R.U.; M.S. Library Science; M.A., University of Warsaw. Address: 133 Sunset Drive, Berea, Ohio 44017.

MACKARA, WARREN FREDERICK Occupation: Associate Professor. Education: A.B., 1969, Rutgers; Ph.D., 1976, Texas A&M. Address: 1026 Pagel Court, Johnson City, Tennessee 37601.

MACKENZIE, KENNETH DONALD Occupation: Professor. Education: B.A., Ph.D., University of California at Berkeley. Address: 502 Millstone Drive, Lawrence, Kansas 66044.

MacKENZIE, NORMAN HUGH Occupation: Professor. Education: B.A., M.A., Rhodes University; Ph.D., University of London. Address: 416 Windward Place, Kingston, Ontario, K7M 4E4 Canada.

MACKEY, THOMAS S Occupation: Consultants. Address: 1210 Sunset Lane, Texas City, Texas 77590.

MacKINNON, GEORGE E Occupation: United States Circuit Judge. Education: L.L.B. Address: 11333 Willowbrook Drive, Potomac, Maryland 20854.

MACNEE, ALAN B Occupation: Professor of Electrical Engineering. Education: S.B., S.M. 1943; Sc.D. 1948, Massachusetts Institute of Technology. Address: 1911 Austin Avenue, Ann Arbor, Michigan 48104.

MACPHERSON, BARRY LEE Occupation: Psychologist. Education: A.A., B.A., M.A. Address: 515 - 35th Street, Newport Beach, California 92663.

MacVEIGH, ROBERT CHARLES Occupation: Assistant Corporate Controller. Education: B.A., Accounting, 1953; M.A, Economics, 1958. Address: 335 Crestline, Cincinnati, Ohio 45205.

MADDEN, CAROLYN Occupation: Director. Education: M.S., B.S. Address: Route 1 Box 351, Saranac Lake, New York 12983.

MADDEN, SARA LEE Occupation: Teacher; Department Chairperson. Education: B.S. in Business Administration/Education, University of Wichita, Kansas. Address: 3503 Harpers Ferry Drive, Stockton, California 95209.

MADDEN, THOMAS J Occupation: President. Education: B.S., Temple University; M.A., University of Pennsylvania. Address: 5 East 22nd Street, New York, New York 10010.

MADDISON, SHIRLEY E Occupation: Research Microbiologist. Education: Ph.D. Address: 4 Westchester Square, Decatur, Georgia 30030.

MADDOX, IRENE NEWCOMB Occupation: Concert Flutist. Education: B.A., M.M. Address: 4508 Carriage, Charlotte, North Carolina 28205.

MADEJ, SUE BATTAGLIA Occupation: Clinical Nursing Director. Education: B.A., M.A., M.S. Address: 1115 Granite Drive, Bethlehem, Pennsylvania 18017.

MADER, EILEEN LOUISE LLOYD Occupation: Assistant Headmistress. Education: A.A., B.A., Graduate Work in Art. Address: 2320 Pinneberg Avenue, Rockville, Maryland 20851.

MADEY, RICHARD Occupation: Professor. Education: Ph.D., University of California at Berkeley. Address: Box 123, Kent, Ohio 44240.

MADGETT, JOHN P III Occupation: President, Wellspring Corporation; Wellspring Energy Corporation; Wellspring Financial Corporation; Wellspring Propertes; Wellspring Offshore Service. Education: B.A. in Math and Physics, Carleton College, 1962; B.S., E.E. Columbia University, 1963; M.B.A. in Financial Management Science, Stanford University, 1965. Address: 4601 Golf Terrace, Edina, Minnesota 55424.

MADRID, PATRICIA A Occupation: District Judge. Address: 2219 Vista Larga, North East Albuquerque, New Mexico 87106.

MAGARGAL, LARRY ELLIOT Occupation: Ophthalmologist. Education: A.B., 1965, M.D., 1969. Address: 9601 Milnor Street, Philadelphia, Pennsylvania 19114.

MAGLIO, JOHN F Occupation: Senior Systems Analyst. Education: B.S., M.S. Address: 12 Phillips Street, Marblehead, Massachusetts 01945.

MAGNES, GERALD DONALD Occupation: Dentist. Education: B.S., D.D.S. Address: 4625 Grove Street, Skokie, Illinois 60076.

MAGNUSON, WINIFRED M Occupation: Retired. Education: Northwestern University. Address: 705 Thorn Street, Mountain Home, Arkansas 72653.

MAGOCSI, PAUL ROBERT Occupation: Associate Professor. Education: B.A., M.A., Rutgers; B.A., M.A., Princeton University. Address: 424 Brunswick Avenue, Toronto, Ontario, Canada M5R 2Z4.

MAGRUM, VIRGINIA MARY Occupation: Counselor, Teacher, Accountant. Education: M.S. in Education. Address: LaVerna Heights, Savannah, Missouri 64485.

MAHER, MARY FRANCES Occupation: Attorney. Education: B.S., M.A., J.D., Ph.D. (in progress). Address: 1501 Maple Avenue, #305 Evanston, Illinois 60201.

MAHESH, VIRENDRA B Occupation: Regents Professor. Education: Ph.D., D.Phil. Address: 2911 Sussex Road, Augusta, Georgia 30909.

MAHMOUDI, HODA Occupation: Assistant Professor. Education: B.A., 1972, M.A., 1973; Ph.D., 1979. Address: 3581 East Millstream Lane, Salt Lake

City, Utah 84109. ..

MAHONEY, JOËLLE K D Occupation: Astrologer. Education: Associate Arts, Baccalaureate Arts, M.B.A. in Progress. Address: "Morningstar," Long Pond, Pennsylvania18334.

MAHTAB, M ASHRAF Occupation: Associate Professor Mining Engineering, H. K. School of Mines, Columbia University. Address: 605 West 113 Street, No. 42, New York, New York 10025.

MAIBACH, MICHAEL CHARLES Occupation: Government. Education: B.A., 1982, California State University; B.A., 1975, Northern Illinois University. Address: 3101 New Mexico Avenue Northwest, Washington, District of Columbia 20016.

MAIBENCO, HELEN CRAIG Occupation: Professor of Anatomy, Rush Medical College. Education: B.S., Wheaton College; M.S., DePaul University; Ph.D., University of Illinois. Address: 1324 South Main Street, Wheaton, Illinois 60187.

MAIERSPERGER, WALTER P Occupation: USAF ROTC, Aero Eng Ret, Pilot Ret. Education: B.M.E.. State University of New York, 1939. Address: 25420 Telarana Way, Carmel, California 93921.

MAIN, TOM TALMAGE Occupation: Petroleum Consultant. Education: A.A., Tyler Junior College; B.B.A., The University of Texas-Austin; M.S., Texas Technological College-Lubbock. Address: 4564 Arcady, Dallas, Texas 75205.

MAIONE, DOROTHY M Occupation: Director. Education: B.A., M.S., M.A. Address: 206 Walberta Road, Syracuse, New York 13219.

MAITZEN, DOLORES ANN Occupation: Teacher Educator. Education: B.S., Illinois State University; M.S., Chicago State University. Address: 3702 East Dahlia Drive, Phoenix, Arizona 85032.

MAJKA, LORRAINE C Occupation: Research Associate. Education: Ph.D., M.A., B.A. Address: 468 West Melrose #550, Chicago, Illinois 60657.

MAJOR, CECIL E Occupation: Store Manager, Food Lion Stores, Incorporated. Education: B.S. Business Administration. Address: 2504 Crofton Way, Apartment C, Columbia, South Carolina 29206.

MAJUMDAR, DALIM K Occupation: Consulting Engineer. Education: B.S., 1957, M.S., 1960, Ph.D., 1964. Address: 1224 Cardinal Lake Drive, Cherry Hill, New Jersey 08003.

MAKEPEACE, JAMES M Occupation: Professor, Author, Consultant, Researcher. Education: Ph.D., M.S., B.S.. Address: 1001 Meadow Lane, Saint Joseph, Minnesota 56374.

MAKI, HOPE MARIE Occupation: Artist, Sculptor, Cartoonist, Illustrator. Education: Self Taught in Art, Art Instruction Incorporated, 2 years, Commercial Art; Minnesota Home Course; Graduated from High School; Teacher Certificate from Florida. Address: 3985 Langley Avenue, Pensacola, Florida 32504.

MAKK, A B Occupation: Fine Arts: Painter. Education: Academia de Belas Arts, Sao Paulo, Brazil; cum laude, University of Hawaii, Honolulu, Hawaii; McGeorge School of Law, Sacramento, California. Address: 1515 Laukahi Street, Honolulu, Hawaii 96821.

MAKK, AMERICO IMRE Occupation: Artist. Education: Graduate, 1974, University of Hawaii. Address: 1515 Laukahi Street, Honolulu, Hawaii 96821.

MAKK, EVA HOLUSA Occupation: Fine Arts: Painter. Education: Private Tutors and Schools in Uganda, Kenya, Tanganyika, Madagascar; Academy of Fine Arts, Paris, France; summa cum laude, Academy of Fine Arts, Rome, Italy. Address: 1515 Laukahi Street, Honolulu, Hawaii 96821.

MAKOW, DAVID Occupation: Physicist. Education: Dipl.Eng., D.Sc. Address: 13 Davidson Crescent, Ottawa, Ontario, Canada KWG M2.

MAKULOWICH, GAIL SHINER Occupation: Medical Writer. Education: B.A., 1979, University of Colorado. Address: 18413 Stone Hollow Drive, Germantown, Maryland 20874.

MAKULOWICH, JOHN S Occupation: Financial Planning. Education: B.A., M.A. Address: Post Office Box 30, Germantown, Maryland 20874-0030.

MALATESTA, BEVERLY ANN Occupation: Publications Director. Education: B.A., Brandeis University. Address: 54 Hancock Street, Watertown, Massachusetts 02172.

MALIN, HOWARD GERALD Occupation: Podiatrist. Education: A.B., B.Sc., M.A., M.Sc., S.H., D.P.M. Address: 210 Shenandoah Road 2D, Martinsburg, West Virginia 25401.

MALINAK, EDWARD M Occupation: Associate Professor. Education: B.A., M.A., Michigan State University; Ph.D., University of Kentucky. Address: 35 Summit Street, Fairport, New York 14450.

MALLIN, DEA ZUCKERMAN Occupation: Professor. Education: B.A., M.A. Address: 2200 Benjamin Franklin Parkway, Philadelphia, Pennsylvania 19136.

MALLORY-BARKLEY, BARBARA Z Occupation: Psychologist. Education: B.A., M.A. Address: 411 Marrett Road, Lexington, Massachusetts 02173.

MALMER, REYNOLD WILLIAM Occupation: Assistant Executive Director/Communications, American Optometric Association. Education: B.A., University of Minnesota. Address: 77 Heatherbrook Lane, Kirkwood, Missouri 63122.

MALONEY, GARY LEE Occupation: Psychologist, Reality Therapist, Lecturer. Education: M.S. in Psychology, Emporia State College, 1975. Address: 1050 North Edgemoor, Wichita, Kansas 67208.

MALPIEDE, RONALD JOSEPH Occupation: Doctor of Chiropractic. Education: A.A., A.B., D.C. Address: 4834 West Maplewood Place, Littleton, Colorado 80123.

MALSKY, RANDOLPH JOSEPH Occupation: Psychology. Education: B.A., M.S., Ph.D. Address: 29 Fiore Court, St. James, New York 11780.

MAMMUCARI, DARLENE R BOYD Occupation: Coordinator. Education: B.S., M.A. Address: 612 West Saint Andrews Drive, Media, California 19063.

MAMPRE, VIRGINIA ELIZABETH Occupation: Owner, Mampre Media International. Education: B.A., Speech/Theater/Education, University of Iowa; M.S., Indiana University; Harvard Executive Management Programs. Address: 5123 Del Monte, Houston, Texas 77056.

MANCINI, FRANK TOM Occupation: Public Accountant. Education: B.S.E., University of South Dakota. Address: 7665 West Ontario Place, Littleton, Colorado 80123.

MANCUSO, JOSEPHINE T Occupation: Chairman for Health and Physical Education. Education: B.S. Education; M.A. Physical Education; Secondary Education. Address: 18W113 Willow Lane, Westmont, Illinois 60559.

MANDEL, DAVID SCOTT Occupation: Law Student, Cornell Law School. Education: A.B. Political Science, magna cum laude, Brown University. Address: 1225 Hohlfelder Road, Glencoe, Illinois 60022.

MANDEL, JACK K Occupation: Assistant Professor. Education: B.B.A., 1969, M.B.A., 1975,

Address: 4402 South Othello Street, Seattle, Washington 98118.

MARTIN, GARY A Occupation: Author, Lecturer, Counselor, Doctor. Education: B.S., M.S., D.N., Ph.D., Th.D. Address: 7104 East Dreyfus, Scottsdale, Arizona 85254.

MARTIN, GARY RUNNING BEAR Occupation: Psychologist. Education: M.A. Developmental Psychology. Address: Post Office Box 41 Flint, Fall River, Massachusetts 02723.

MARTIN, GEORGE KEITH Occupation: Attorney. Education: B.A., University of Virginia; J.D., Howard University School of Law. Address: 715 Spottswood Road, Richmond, Virginia 23220.

MARTIN, HENRY LAWRENCE Occupation: Chaplain, United States Navy. Education: A.B., M.Div., Th.M., D.Min. Address: 9514 Meadow Grove Court, Burke, Virginia 22015.

MARTIN, JAMES M Occupation: Senior Administator, Health and Safety. Education: B.S. Letters and Science. Address: 653 Wilwood, Rochester, Michigan 48063.

MARTIN, JANE MARIE Occupation: Director, Diagnostic Evaluation Services. Education: M.Ed. Educational Administration, B.S. Special Education. Address: 62 Barham Avenue, Quincy, Washington 02171.

MARTIN, JESSE LEE Occupation: Manager, Engineering Methods. Education: B.E.E. 1963, B.I.E. 1968, M.S. 1973. Address: 2688 Buckboard Road, Birmingham, Alabama 35244.

MARTIN, JOANNE Occupation: University Professor, Stanford University. Education: B.A., Smith College; Ph.D., Harvard University. Address: Graduate School of Business, Stanford University, Stanford, California 94305.

MARTIN, JOHN L Occupation: Speaker, Maine House of Representatives. Education: B.A. Address: Post Office Box 250, Eagle Lake, Maine 04739.

MARTIN, ROBERT LEO Occupation: Assistant Professor of Speech and Drama, Director of Broadcasting. Education: B.S.E., M.S. Address: Post Office Box 579, Alva, Oklahoma 73717.

MARTIN, TRUMAN GLEN Occupation: Professor of Animal Genetics, Purdue University. Education: B.S., Texas A&M University, 1949; M.S. 1951, Ph.D. 1954, Iowa State University. Address: 2025 Robin Hood Lane, West Lafayette, Indiana 47906.

MARTIN, WILLIAM COLLIER SR Occupation: Health Care Administrator. Education: B.S. Address: 3225 Pursell Drive, Pensacola, Florida 32506.

MARTINEZ, ELENA Occupation: Social Worker. Education: M.A., 1974. Address: 3925 North Claremont College, Chicago, Illinois 60618.

MARTINEZ, JOHN S Occupation: President, Physics International Company. Education: Ph.D., University of California-Berkeley; B.Ch.E., Rensselaer Polytechnic Institute. Address: Post Office Box 1695, San Leandro, California 94577.

MARTINEZ, JULIO A Occupation: Associate Librarian. Education: Ph.D., University of California-Riverside, 1980. Address: 5642 Hamill Avenue, San Diego, California 92120.

MARTINICH, ALOYSIUS P Occupation: Associate Professor of Philosophy. Education: B.A., University of Windsor, Ontario; M.A., Ph.D., University of California-San Diego. Address: 6823 Williamette Drive, Austin, Texas 78723.

MARTINSON, EARL H Occupation: Management Consultant, Data Systems Consultant. Education: B.A. Address: South 4106 Lamonte, Spokane, Washington 99203.

MARTNER, HILDEGARDE M Occupation: Senior Partner, The Martner Company. Address: Post Office Box 292, Brookfield, Connecticut 06804.

MARUSIN, STELLA LUCIE Occupation: Consultant. Education: Ph.D. Address: 16 East Willow Road, Prospect Heights, Illinois 60070.

MARVELLE, JOHN D Occupation: Educational Consultant, Specialist Microcomputers. Education: Ed.D., University of Massachusetts; M.Ed., B.A., Bridgewater State College. Address: 8 Kingsley Road, Norton, Massachusetts 02766.

MARWAH, JOE Occupation: Professor/Scientist. Education: B.Sc., Ph.D. Address: 7595 Carlisle Road, Terre Haute, Indiana 47802.

MARYOTT, RICHARD M Occupation: D.O.D., Equipment Specialist (Electronic). Education: Associate in Technology. Address: 40-A Ekolu Place, Wahiawa, Hawaii 96786.

MARZOLF, STANLEY S Occupation: Distinguished Professor of Psychology Emeritus. Education: Ph.D. Address: 806 Hester Avenue, Normal, Illinois 61761.

MASKER, WARREN E Occupation: Molecular Biologist. Education: Ph.D., University of Rochester; B.S., Lehigh University. Address: 103 Viola Road, Oak Ridge, Tennessee 37830.

MASON, CARROLL A Occupation: President, March Enterprises. Education: B.S., M.P.A. Address: 12611 Easthampton Drive, Midlothian, Virginia 23113.

MASON, CHARLES PERRY Occupation: Professor. Education: B.S., University of Rhode Island, 1954; M.S., University of Wisconsin-Madison, 1958; Ph.D., Cornell University, 1961; Marine Biological Laboratory, Woods Hole, Massachusetts, Summer 1959.

MASSENGALE, MARTIN A Occupation: Chancellor, University of Nebraska, Lincoln. Education: B.S., M.S., Ph.D. Address: 6701 Everett Street, Lincoln, Nebraska 68506.

MASSENGILL, ELLEN WEBB Occupation: Library Resources Specialist, High School. Education: B.S., M.S., M.L.S. Address: 510 East 6th Littlefield, Texas 79339.

MASSETTI, CECILIA ANN Occupation: Psychologist, Instructional Consultant. Education: B.S., M.A. Psychology, M.A. Educational Administration. Address: 8256 Road 26, Madera, California 93637.

MASSIER, PAUL F Occupation: Manager of Energy Conversation Tasks. Education: B.S. Mechanical Engineering, University of Colorado; M.S. Mechanical Engineering, Massachusetts Institute of Technology. Address: 1000 North First Avenue, Arcadia, California 91006.

MASTERS, LANCE ALAN Occupation: Professor/Consultant. Education: B.A. honors Economics, M.B.A., M.A., Ph.D. Executive Management. Address: 2619 Kayjay Street, Riverside, California 92503.

MASTERSON, JAMES FRANCIS Occupation: Psychiatrist, Doctor of Medicine. Education: M.D.; Jefferson Medical School, 1951; Intern, Philadelphia General Hospital, 1952; Resident, New York Hospital (Payney Whitney Clinic), 1952-55. Address: 921 Grant Avenue, Pelham Manor, New York 10803.

MASTRIA, ERNEST Occupation: Private Practice, Clinical Psychology. Education: Psy.D., Rutgers University. Address: 146 Berkshire Road, Hasbrouck Heights, New Jersey 07604.

MATCHETTE, PHYLLIS L COLLIER Occupation: Editor, Director of Communications. Education: A.B.

Journalism, University of Kansas. Address: 7405 El Monte, Prairie Village, Kansas 66208.

MATEJKA, MICHAEL G Occupation: Journalist. Education: Bachelor's Degree in History, Illinois State University. Address: 1406 West Oakland, Bloomington, Illinois 61701.

MATEJKO, ALEXANDER JAN Occupation: Professor, University of Alberta. Education: Ph.D. Docent. Address: 7623 119th Street, Edmonton, Alberta, Canada T6G lW4.

MATHENY, THOMAS HARRELL Occupation: Attorney. Education: B.A., Southeastern Louisiana University; J.D., Tulane University. Address: Post Office Box 221, Hammond, Louisiana 70404.

MATHEWS, NADENE Occupation: Editor. Education: B.A., Willametta University; M.A., University of Wisconsin; City College of New York. Address: 1750 Broadway, San Francisco, California 94109.

MATHEWSON, KENT II Occupation: Educator, Geographer. Education: B.A. Geography, 1970; M.A. Geography, 1976; Ph.D. Geography, 1985. Address: 945 Edgewater Court, Madison, Wisconsin 53715.

MATHIS, JOSEPH C Occupation: Manager, Economics and Research/Agricultural Economics. Education: B.S., Graduate Studies, Cornell University. Address: Indian Hill Road, Manlius, New York 13104.

MATIJEVIC, EGON Occupation: Professor of Chemistry and Chairman. Education: B.S., Ph.D., Dr.Habil. Address: 94 Market Street, Potsdam, New York 13676.

MATLACK, ARDENA LAVONNE Occupation: Kansas State Legislator, 93rd District. Education: Bachelor of Music Education, Wichita State University, 1969. Address: 615 Elaine, Clearwater, Kansas 67026.

MATLACK, DON Occupation: Attorney at Law, Washburn University School of Law, Topeka, Kansas. Education: J.D., Kansas State University, Manhattan, 1957; B.S. Business Administration, 1951. Address: 615 Elaine, Clearwater, Kansas 67026.

MATLOFF, GREGORY L Occupation: Educational Technology Specialist. Education: Ph.D., M.S., New York University; B.A., Queens College of City University of New York. Address: 121 Vanderbilt Avenue, Brooklyn, New York 11205.

MATSUMOTO, SHIGEMI E Occupation: Opera Singer. Education: B.A. Address: 60 Riverside Drive #1D, New York, New York 10024.

MATSUOKA, SHIRO Occupation: Head of Plastics Research and Development. Education: Ph.D. Mechanical Engineering, Princeton University. Address: 161 Thackeray Drive, Millington, New Jersey 07946.

MATSUYAMA, WAYNE S Occupation: Optometrist. Education: Doctor of Optometry. Address: 98-1358 Hoohonua Street, Pearl City, Hawaii 96782.

MATTER, EDITH ANN Occupation: Associate Professor of Religious Studies. Education: A.B., M.A., M.Phil., Ph.D. Address: 3909 Spruce Street, Box 200, Philadelphia, Pennsylvania 19104.

MATTHEWS, NORMA R Occupation: President, Washington Intelligence Bureau, Inc. Education: Attended Southeastern University. Address: 2346 Hunter Mill Road, Vienna, Virginia 22180.

MATTHEWS, WILLIAM P Occupation: Poet, College Instructor. Education: B.A., Yale University; M.A., University of North Carolina. Address: 245 Avenue C #10-D, New York, New York 10009.

MATTHEWS-EVANS, DEBORAH Y Occupation: Clinical Psychologist. Education: B.A., M.A., Ph.D.

Address: 11700 Old Columbia Pike, Silver Spring, Maryland 20904.

MAUE-DICKSON, WILMA Occupation: Manager, Educational Services, Continuing Medical Education and Nursing, Allied Health Education. Education: B.A., M.A., Ph.D. Address: 8330 South West 138th Street, Miami, Florida 33158.

MAUPIN, STEPHANIE Z Occupation: Educator, Foreign Language. Education: B.S.Ed., University of Missouri-Columbia; M.A.T., Webster University. Address: 5006 East Concord Road, Saint Louis, Missouri 63128.

MAURER, BRUCE LESLIE Occupation: Assistant Director II, Department of University Recreational and IM Sports. Education: B.S., University of Illinois, 1969; M.S., University of Washington, 1970; Ph.D., The Ohio State University, 1972. Address: 7727 Strathmoore Road, Dublin, Ohio 43017.

MAURISSEN, JACQUES PAUL JEAN Occupation: Toxicologist. Education: M.A. Psychology; M.S., Ph.D. Toxicology. Address: 534 Woodcock Road, Midland, Michigan 48640.

MAUST, EZMA M Occupation: Music Instructor. Education: Certificate, Sherwood Music School; A.A., Butte College; B.A., Chico State University. Address: 887 Rita Lane, Paradise, California 95969.

MAUZY, THAMES L Occupation: State Representative; Owner, Home Furnishings Market. Education: Anthony Wayne College. Address: 1025 County Club Lane, Warsaw, Indiana 46580.

MAVROS, DONALD O Occupation: Executive Director. Education: B.F.A. Address: Post Office Box 547, Unionville, New York 10988.

MAX, ELIZABETH Occupation: Associate Professor of Curriculum and Instruction. Education: B.S. Theatre, M.L.S., Ed.D. Address: 817-C North Burdick, Stillwater, Oklahoma 74075.

MAXSON, LINDA ELLEN RESNICK Occupation: Professor, University of Illinois. Education: B.A., M.A., Ph.D. Genetics. Address: 612 West Washington, Urbana, Illinois 61801.

MAXWELL, EDWARD CREIGHTON Occupation: Rancher. Education: LL.B., University of Illinois, 1926. Address: Post Office Box 5586, Oxnard, California 93031.

MAXWELL, THOMAS JAMES Occupation: Anthropologist, Professor. Education: Ph.D. 1962, M.A. 1953, B.H., U.N.M. de San Marcos. Address: 3268 Luther Avenue, Thousand Oaks, California 91360.

MAY, AVIVA RABINOWITZ Occupation: Educator, Musician, Folk-Singer, Composer, Writer. Education: A.A., Oakton Community College, 1978; B.A. Psychological Musical Method/Piano Pedagogy, Northeastern Illinois University, 1979. Address: 410 South Michigan Avenue, Chicago, Illinois.

MAY, JANIS SUSAN Occupation: Writer. Address: 10453 Foxton Ste. C, Dallas, Texas 75238.

MAY, JOHN R Occupation: Business Executive. Education: B.S. Address: 10 Pritten Hill Road, Brookfield, Connecticut 06805.

MAYE, MAMIE ELLENE Occupation: Instructor of Music. Education: B.S., M.A., Educational Specialist. Address: 7909 Manchester, Apartment 6, Kansas City, Missouri 64138.

MAYER, BEATRICE C Occupation: Director, Consolidated Foods Corporation. Education: B.A. Chemistry, University of North Carolina; Graduate Studies, University of Chicago. Address: 175 East Delaware Place, Apartment #7403, Chicago, Illinois 60611.

MAYER, CHARLES EDWARD Occupation:

Electrical Engineer. Education: B.S.E.E., M.S.E., Ph.D., University of Texas-Austin. Address: 4512 A, Speedway, Austin, Texas 78751.

MAYER, JAMES MOERS Occupation: Professor of Chemistry, University of Washington. Education: Ph.D., California Institute of Technology, 1982; A.B., Harvard University, 1978. Address: 2214 10th Avenue, East, Seattle, Washington 98102.

MAYER, ROBERT ANTHONY Occupation: Director, International Museum of Photography at George Eastman House. Education: M.A., New York University; B.A., Faircloth Dickinson University. Address: 4 Greenwood Street, Rochester, New York 14608.

MAYESKI, FRAN E Occupation: Director Curriculum and Instruction. Education: B.S., M.B.A. Address: 11 Skyline Drive, Kearney, Nebraska 68847.

MAYESKI, JOHN K Occupation: Library Director. Education: B.S., M.A.L.S., M.B.A. Address: 11 Skyline Drive, Kearney, Nebraska 68847.

MAYFIELD, GRACE BIRGE Occupation: Flight Instructor, A.S.E., A.M.E.L. Instrument. Education: B.A., M.A. Address: 2616 South Sheridan Boulevard, Denver, Colorado 80227.

MAYFIELD, JULIAN H Occupation: Writer-in-Residence, Harvard University. Address: 2031 Brooke Drive 521, Suitland, Maryland 20747.

MAYNARD, JO HELEN Occupation: Real Estate. Address: 88 Virginia, Unite #31, Seattle, Washington 98101.

MAYO, VERNA DEL MARIE Occupation: Professor of Biology, Anderson College. Education: A.B., M.S., Doctoral Candidate, Indiana University. Address: 1013 Imel Drive, Anderson, Indiana 46012.

MAYO, WILLIAM T JR Occupation: Research Manager, Philips Ultra Sound, Inc. Education: Ph.D. Electrical Engineering. Address: 2900 D South Greenville, Santa Ana, California 92704.

MAYOR, ROBERTA ADRIAN Occupation: Educational Administrator, Hawaii School Systems. Education: M.A., B.A. Address: 2332 Ahamoa Street, Pearl City, Hawaii 96782.

MAYS, VICKIE M Occupation: Assistant Professor of Psychology. Education: Ph.D. Address: 2027 Preuss Road, Los Angeles, California 90034.

MAZUR, DEBORAH J Occupation: Administrator Human Services. Education: B.S. Address: 27663 Ryan Road, Warren, Michigan 48092.

MAZUR-STEWART, MARIANNE E Occupation: Educator. Education: B.S., M.Ed., Ed.S., Ph.D. Address: 541 Independence, Waterville, Ohio 43566.

MAZZOLA, GERARDO Occupation: Hand Craft Wrought Iron Sculpture. Education: High School, Extra-curricular Courses at Local Colleges. Address: 201 Jackson Road, Newton, Massachusetts 02158.

MAZZOLA, MICHAEL LEE Occupation: Professor. Education: A.B., LeMoyne College, 1962; M.A., Middlebury College, 1964; Ph.D., Cornell University, 1967. Address: 115 Tilton Park Drive, DeKalb, Illinois 60115.

McALISTER, NEIL HARDING Occupation: Physician, Writer. Education: M.D. Address: 22 Renfield Circle, Whitby, Ontario, Canada LlP lB4.

McANALLY, DON Occupation: Editor. Address: 4409 Indiana Avenue, La Canada, California 91011.

McANINCH, MYRENE Occupation: Director, Accreditation Program for Psychiatric Facilities, J.C.A.H. Education: Ph.D. Psychology. Address: 850 North DeWitt Place, Chicago, Illinois 60611.

McARTHUR, BARBARA J Occupation: Professor, Epidemiologist. Education: R.N., B.S.N., M.S., M.S., Ph.D. Address: 26500 Summerdale Drive, Southfield, Michigan 48034.

McARTHUR, ELDON DURANT Occupation: Project Leader and Supervisor, Research Geneticist. Education: A.S., Dixie College; B.S., M.S., Ph.D., University of Utah. Address: 555 North 1200 East, Orem, Utah 84067.

McAULEY, LAWRENCE Y JR Occupation: Manager. Education: B.S.M.E. Address: 11581 Blythe Street, North Hollywood, California 91605.

McBEE, JOE DAVID Occupation: Head of Serials and Binding Department, University of the South. Education: Bachelor's Degree Business Administration, Master's Degree Education/Administration and Supervision. Address: Box 127, Sewanee, Tennessee, 37375.

McBRIDE, VICKIE DARLENE Occupation: Registered Nurse. Education: B.S. Nursing. Address: 3101 Granger, Medine, Ohio 44256.

McCABE, DONALD LEE Occupation: Physician, General Practice and Psychiatry. Education: D.O., Doctor Social Science. Address: 3221 Greenwood Avenue, Sacramento, California 95821.

McCAIN, MARY ELOISE Occupation: Attorney, Agency Legal Specialist. Education: J.D., B.A. Address: 1134 Woodland Drive, Wilson, North Carolina 27893.

McCALLA, MARY ELLEN Occupation: Artist, Educator. Education: B.S., Memphis State University, 1966; Teacher's Certificate, 1967. Address: 264 Scenic Ridge Road, Kalispell, Montana 59901.

McCARTHY, JOHN FRANCIS JR Occupation: Vice President and General Manager, Electro-Mechanical Division, Northrop Corporation. Education: Ph.D., M.S., B.S. Address: 19171 Via del Caballo, Yorba Linda, California 92686.

McCARTHY, MARY ELLEN Occupation: Speech Pathologist. Education: B.A. Address: 717 Bolivar Drive, San Jose, California 95123.

McCARTHY, ROBERT J Occupation: Lawyer; Partner, McCarthy & Schwartz. Education: J.D., University of Chicago School of Law, 1972; Graduate magna cum laude, University of Santa Clara, 1969. Address: 354 Santa Clara Avenue, San Francisco, California 94127.

McCARTNEY, ROBERT C Occupation: Law. Education: A.B., Princeton University, 1956; J.D., Harvard Law School, 1959. Address: 9843 Woodland Road, North, Pittsburgh, Pennsylvania 15237.

McCASLAND, IMA JEAN Occupation: Retired Banker. Education: Attended Sherman Business College, Kilgore Junior College; Graduate, Southwestern Graduate School of Banking at Southern Methodist University, 1974. Address: 603 Newell Avenue, Dallas, Texas 75223.

McCASLIN, LEON Occupation: Attorney at Law. Education: B.S., L.L.B., LaSalle University. Address: 1096 Briar Lane, Yuba City, California 95991.

McCAULEY, RANDALL PAUL Occupation: Professor and Chairman, Department of Criminology. Education: B.S., M.S., Ph.D. Address: 4620 Lucerne Road, Indiana, Pennsylvania 15701.

McCLAIN, DANIEL J Occupation: Design Director, National Audubon Society. Address: 297 Park Street, New Canaan, Connecticut 06840.

McCLEAVE, MILDRED M Occupation: Designer, Formal Wear and Costumes. Education: Attended Chatham County Training School; North Carolina Practical Nursing License, Lincoln Hospital School of Nursing, 1954; License, University of North Carolina School of Public Health Educational Programme for Waivered Nursing Home Administrators, 1971;

Accreditation, Medical Record Personnel of the American Medical Record Association, 1974; Numerous Certificates. Address: 913 Borders Terrace, Greensboro, North Carolina 27401.

McCLOUD, JAMES N Occupation: Educator, Mathematics. Education: A.A., B.S.M.E., M.S.M.E. Address: 340 South Sierramadre Bl #18, Pasadena, California 91107.

McCLUNG, NORVEL MALCOLM Occupation: Professor. Education: A.B., M.S., Ph.D. Address: 2701 Varsity Place, Tampa, Florida 33612.

McCLUSKY, MILDRED B Occupation: Consultant, Die Casting Company. Education: Public Schools. Address: 50 Hardwick Drive, Syracuse, New York 13209.

McCOIN, JOHN M Occupation: Supervisory Social Worker. Education: A.A., Wingate Junior College, 1955; B.S., Appalachian State Teachers College, 1957; M.S.S.W., Richmond Professional Institute, 1962; Ph.D., University of Minnesota, 1977. Address: 310-B Kiowa Street, Leavenworth, Kansas 66048.

McCOMB, CARLY L Occupation: Occupational Therapist. Education: M.S. Occupational Therapy, Bachelor's Degree. Address: 2854 East 90th Street, #1507, Tulsa, Oklahoma 74137.

McCOMIE, VAL THEODORE Occupation: Assistant Secretary General, Organization of American States. Education: B.A. Address: 5936 Searl Terrace, Bethesda, Maryland 20816.

McCONKEY, DALE D Occupation: Professor, Management Consultant. Education: B.S., M.B.A. Address: Post Office 1746, Madison, Wisconsin 53701.

McCONNELL, ALBERT LYNN Occupation: Depty G-2; Deputy Director of Intelligence. Education: B.A., M.A. Address: Quarters 149-B, Fort Clayton, Republic of Panama.

McCONNELL, J DOUGLAS Occupation: Vice President, Marketing. Education: Ph.D. in Business Administration, Stanford University; B.A., University of Melbourne. Address: 4174 Oak Hill Avenue, Palo Alto, California 94306.

McCONOMY, RICHARD JOSEPH Occupation: Lawyer. Education: B.A., Bachelor of Civil Law. Address: 400 Kensington Avenue, Montreal, Quebec, H3Y 3A2.

McCOUL, VICKY JEAN Occupation: Author, Journalist. Education: B.A. Political Science, University of California-Santa Barbara. Address: 124 Ralston Street, #1A, Reno, Nevada 89503.

McCOY, LLOYD O Occupation: Writer, Real Estate. Education: B.S.; M.Ed.; Additional Studies, North Texas State University, Texas Tech University. Address: Post Office Box 5233, Abilene, Texas 79608.

McCRAW, SAMMY TIMOTHY Occupation: Cost/Schedule Planning Specialist. Education: B.A. Economics, M.S. Operations Management, M.B.A. Business Administration. Address: 3204 Needham Drive, Dublin, Ohio 43017.

McCRICKARD, RUBY ASHWELL Occupation: Director Nursing Service, Assistant Administrator. Education: Doctor of Philosophy Candidate, M.S.N., B.A., Diploma in Nursing. Address: Route 1, Box 483, Rustburg, Virginia 24588.

McCUEN, W J BILL Occupation: Commissioner of State Lands. Education: B.S.E., M.S.E. Address: Post Office Box 269, Hot Springs, Arkansas 71901.

McCULLOUGH, KENNETH DOUGLAS Occupation: Program Specialist. Education: Bachelor of Arts, University of Delaware, 1966; Master of Fine Arts, University of Iowa, 1968. Address: 534 South Lucas Street, Iowa City, Iowa 52240.

McCULLOUGH, LOYCE R J Occupation: Registered Nurse. Education: R.N., B.S., M.S. Address: 7705 Shelton Road, Austin, Texas 78725.

McCULLOUGH, ROSE VERNIE Occupation: Editor, Author, Speaker. Address: 5263 Crestview, Indianapolis, Indiana 46220.

McCURDY, DONALD W Occupation: Professor, University of Nebraska. Education: B.S., M.Ed., M.S., Ed.D. Address: 7901 East Avon Lane, Lincoln, Nebraska 68505.

McCURDY, JOHN ANDREW JR Occupation: Physician. Education: A.B., Duke University, 1967; M.D., Wake Forest University, 1971. Address: 3126 Mapu Place, Kihei, Hawaii 96753.

McDANIEL, MARJORIE WYVONNE Occupation: Librarian, Canadian High School. Education: B.B.A., Texas Tech University-Lubbock; M.Ed., Earl Texas State University. Address: Box 52 Canadian, Texas 79014.

McDANIEL, SHANNON KAYE Education: B.S. Interior Design, Texas Woman's University, 1981. Address: 4401 Windsor Parkway, Dallas, Texas 75205.

McDERMOTT, PAMELA McCLURE Occupation: University Faculty Member. Education: Ed.D., M.Ed., A.B. Address: 218 North Tenth Avenue, Pocatello, Idaho 83201.

McDERMOTT, PATRICIA L Occupation: Attorney/State Legislator. Education: Attended Creighton University; B.A. Political Science, Idaho State University, 1958; J.D., George Washington University, 1961; L.L.M., Georgetown University Law Center, 1964. Address: 218 North Tenth Avenue, Pocatello, Idaho 83201.

McDONALD, ARLINE M Occupation: Assistant Professor. Education: M.S., Ph.D. Address: 1219 Hull Terrace, Evanston, Illinois 60202.

McDONALD, JULIE J Occupation: Writer. Education: B.A. Address: 2802 East Locust, Davenport, Iowa 52803.

McDOWELL, ALMA SUE Occupation: Senior Internal Auditor. Education: B.S. Address: 5402 East 20th Place, Indianapolis, Indiana 46218.

McELLHENNEY, JOHN G Occupation: Ordained Deacon. Education: A.B. Address: 525 Parkview Drive, Wynnewood, Pennsylvania 19096.

McELROY, COLLEEN J Occupation: Writer; Professor of English, University of Washington. Education: B.S., M.A., Kansas State University; Ph.D., University of Washington. Address: 5233 15th North East, #201, Seattle, Washington 98105.

McELROY, JOSEPH PRINCE Occupation: Teacher. Education: Ph.D. Address: 77 Hudson Street, New York, New York 10013.

McELWAIN, JUANITA M Occupation: Assistant Professor, Director of Music Therapy. Education: Ph.D., M.M., M.M.E., B.M.E. Address: 2010 West Beech Street, Portales, New Mexico 88130.

McELYEA, LOU A Occupation: Automated Systems Consultant. Education: B.S. Business Administration; M.B.A. Systems Management. Address: 806 Bailey, Campbell, Missouri 63933.

McFADDEN, JAMES PATRICK Occupation: Editor, *The Daily Intelligence*. Address: 23 Countryside Drive, Doylestown, Pennsylvania 18901.

McGEE, MARK G Occupation: Professor, Saint Mary's College. Education: B.A. summa cum lade; Ph.D. Psychology. Address: 1104 Gilmore Avenue, Winona, Minnesota 55987.

McGEE, MARY ELLEN Occupation: College Administrator. Education: B.S., M.S. Address: 2817

Long Lake Drive, Roswell, Georgia 30075.

McGHEE, ROSA M Occupation: Retired Educator; Founder/President, Chattanooga Branch, A.S.A.H. Education: A.B., Knoxville College; M.S., University of Tennessee. Address: 1019 East 8th Street, Chattanooga, Tennessee 37403.

McGILL, SCOTT DOUGLAS Occupation: Director of Data Processing, City of Colorado Springs. Education: B.S., Allegheny College, 1968; B.S., New York University, 1971; M.A., University of Nebraska, 1972. Address: 4529 Misty Drive, Colorado Springs, Colorado 80907.

McGINN, DAVID F Occupation: Eastern Zone Sales Manager, Furniture Sales Executive. Education: A.A., Mason City Junior College, 1968; B.A. Radio and Television, Mankato State College, 1976. Address: 2646 Clearview Avenue, New Brighton, Minnesota 55112.

McGINTY, OMA VALJEAN Occupation: Public Relations and Real Estate Executive, Counselor. Education: Ph.D. Candidate. Address: 255 North El Cielo Drive, Suite 369, Palm Springs, California 92262.

McGONIGLE, PAUL JOHN Occupation: Broadcasting Executive. Education: Attended Ohio Wesleyan University, University of Virginia, North Carolina State University. Address: 3723 West Townley Avenue, Phoenix, Arizona 86021.

McGOVERN, PATRICK EDWARD Occupation: Archaeologist/Archaeometrist. Education: A.B., Cornell University; M.Div., Faith Seminary; Ph.D., University of Pennsylvania. Address: 4823 Beaumont Avenue, Philadelphia, Pennsylvania 19143.

McGOWN, LINDA BAINE Occupation: Assistant Professor of Chemistry, Oklahoma State University. Education: B.S. Chemistry, Ph.D. Chemistry. Address: 410 North Manning, Stillwater, Oklahoma 74075.

McGOWAN, MICHAEL JAMES Occupation: Scientist. Education: B.A. 1976, M.A. 1978, University of Kansas; Ph.D., Oklahoma State University, 1980. Address: Rural Route 4, Box 331, Greenfield, Indiana 46140.

McGRAIN, PRESTON Occupation: Consulting Geologist. Education: A.B. 1940, M.A. 1942, Indiana University. Address: 1221 Providence Road, Lexington, Kentucky 40502.

McGRATH, SYLVIA FREEMAN WALLACE Occupation: Associate Professor of History, Stephen F. Austin State University. Education: Doctor of Philosophy, University of Wisconsin, 1966; Master of Arts, Radcliffe University, 1960; B.A., Michigan State University, 1959. Address: 216 North Mound Street, Nacogdoches, Texas 75961.

McGREGOR, D SCOTT Occupation: Private Consultant. Education: B.S., M.B.A., Ph.D. Address: 1569 East Stonemoor Court, Salt Lake City, Utah 84121.

McGUIRE, DANIEL T Occupation: Director, Agency Head, Nebraska Wheat Board. Education: B.A. Journalism, University of Nebraska, 1976. Address: 3925 B Street, Lincoln, Nebraska 68510.

McGURN, BARRETT Occupation: Writer, Lecturer. Education: A.B. 1935, Litt.D. (hon.) 1958, Fordham University. Address: 5229 Duvall Drive, Westmoreland Hills, Maryland 20816.

McHENRY, JAMES O'NEAL Occupation: Chief United States Pretrial Officer. Education: B.S., M.Ed., Ed.D. Address: 17191 Pennington Drive, Detroit, Michigan 48221.

McILHANY, STERLING FISHER Occupation: President, I.F.O.T.A., Inc. Education: B.F.A. with high honors, University of Texas, 1953; 2 Diplomas, State University of New York, 1961, 1963. Address: 6376 Yucca Street, Los Angeles, California 90028.

McILRATH, THOMAS JAMES Occupation: Professor, University of Maryland. Education: Ph.D., Princeton University, 1966; B.S., Michigan State University, 1960. Address: 5944 Westchester Park Drive, College Park, Maryland 20740.

McILVAIN, JESS H Occupation: Architect, Consultant. Education: Bachelor of Architecture. Address: 6012 Woodacres Drive, Bethesda, Maryland 20816.

McINTIRE, LARRY VERN Occupation: E. D. Butcher Professor and Chairman of Chemical Engineering. Education: B.Ch.E., M.S., Cornell University, 1966; Ph.D. Princeton University, 1970. Address: 2216 Quenby, Houston, Texas 77005.

McINTYRE, ROBERT ALLEN JR Occupation: President, Chief Executive Officer, MDM Products. Education: B.A., B.S., M.S., Ph.D. Address: 616 Farmdale Road, Franklin Lakes, New Jersey 07417.

McINTYRE, ROOSEVELT Occupation: Pastor. Address: 1624 Taylor Street, North West, Washington, D.C. 20011.

McKAMEY, DAWN L Occupation: Student. Education: A.A., Michigan Christian College. Address: Route 1 Box IVY-1, New Palestine, Indiana 40163.

McKAY, ROXANE Occupation: Consultant Paediatric Cardiothoracic Surgeon. Education: M.D., B.A., F.R.C.G., M.R.C.S., L.R.C.P. Address: The Coach House, 27 Knowsley Road, Cressington Park, Liverpool L19 0PF, England.

McKEE, KATHLEEN ROWE Occupation: Account Executive, Corporate Communications. Education: B.A., Villanova University; M.A., University of Pennsylvania. Address: 53 Englewood Road, Clifton, New Jersey 07012.

McKEE, MOLLY T Occupation: Manager, Project and Purchasing. Education: B.A. Sociology; B.A. Anthropology; Master's Work, Sociology. Address: 811 Ninth Street, Boulder, Colorado 80302.

McKENNA, JOHN D Occupation: President, ETS, Inc. Education: B.S., M.Ch.E., M.B.A. Address: 4118 Chaparral Drive, Southwest, Roanoke, Virginia 24018.

McKENZIE, HORACE HOUSTON Occupation: Lawyer, McKenzie, McRae & Vasser. Education: Admitted to Practice in the Supreme Court of the United States and All Lower Courts. Address: 604 East Main Street, Prescott, Arkansas 71857.

McKNIGHT, ROBERT ALLEN Occupation: Executive Secretary, Scottish Rite Masonry, Valley of Columbus; Partner, Prime Asset Management. Education: B.A. Journalism, M.A. Business Communication, Ohio State University. Address: 4540 Tetford Road, Columbus, Ohio 43220.

McKUEN, ROD Occupation: Author, Composer, Performer. Address: Post Office Box G, Beverly Hills, California 90213.

McLAIN, MYRTLE GRACE Occupation: Psychiatric Nurse Consultant. Education: B.S., M.S. Address: 8830 Piney Branch Road #705, Silver Spring, Maryland 20903.

McLANE, BETTIE L Occupation: Health Services Administrator. Education: Diploma in Nursing. Address: 845 Kensington Road, Coshocton, Ohio 43812.

McLAUGHLIN, DOROTHY C Occupation: Sociologist, Consultant. Education: B.A. Address: Post Office Box 36524, Dallas, Texas 75235.

McLAUGHLIN, RENATE Occupation: Professor of Mathematics. Education: A.M., Ph.D. Address: 1432 Duffield Road, Lennon, Michigan 48449.

McLEOD, MARILYNN HAYES Occupation: Reading Supervisor, Marlboro County Schools. Education: B.A., M.Ed., Educational Specialist in Educational Administration. Address: Post Office Box 38, Clio, South Carolina 29525.

McLEOD, PEDEN B Occupation: Attorney. Education: A.B., J.D. Address: 512 Hampton Street, Walterboro, South Carolina 29488.

McLEVIE, ELAINE M Occupation: Dean of Communications and Fine Arts, Grossmont College. Education: Ph.D., M.A. with honors, B.A. Address: 9100 Brier Road, La Mesa, California 92041.

McLURE, CHARLES E JR Occupation: Deputy Assistant Secretary for Tax Analysis. Education: B.A. 1962, M.A. 1964, Ph.D. 1966. Address: 250 Yerba Santa Avenue, Los Altos, California 94022.

McMAHAN, JOHN JULIA Occupation: President, Las Cruces Retired Teachers Association; Secretary, Las Cruces Committee on Aging. Education: B.S., M.A., Additional Studies. Address: 2501 Chaparral Street, Las Cruces, New Mexico 88001.

McMAHON, BERNICE G Occupation: Writer. Education: B.A., S.U.I. Address: 903 14th Street, Hermosa Beach, California 90254.

McMANUS, EDWARD JOSEPH Occupation: Chief Judge, U.S. District Court, Northern District of Iowa. Education: B.A. 1940, J.D. 1942, University of Iowa. Address: Post Office Box 4815, Cedar Rapids, Iowa 52407.

McMULLIN, MARY JO Occupation: Acting Director of Nursing. Education: Nursing. Address: Route 2, Lamonte, Missouri 65337.

McNABB, BETTY WOOD Occupation: Health Records Analyst and Consultant. Education: B.A., M.A., United States Air Force Air War College. Address: 1265 Capri Drive, Panama City, Florida 32405.

McNABB, MARIAN Occupation: Musician, Professor of Music. Education: Mus.B., S.M.M. Address: 2828 Connecticut Avenue, Northwest, Washington, D.C. 20008.

McNAMARA, EDWARD CHARLES Occupation: Executive Director, Central Massachusetts EMS Corporation. Education: B.S., Education, R.E.M.T. Address: 51 Newell Hill, Sterling Junction, Massachusetts 01565.

McNAMARA, JOSEPH DONALD Occupation: Chief of Police. Education: B.S., John Jay College; M.P.A., D.P.A., Harvard University. Address: Post Office 270, San Jose, California 95112.

McNANAMY, EVE W Occupation: Clinical Psychologist, Independent Private Practice. Education: Ph.D. Address: 6640 Southwest 71st Lane, South Miami, Florida 33143.

McNEAL, RALPH L SR Occupation: President, North Street Capital Corporation. Education: B.S. Business Administration/Accounting. Address: 42 WeeQuahic Avenue, Newark, New Jersey 10625.

McNEELY, DORA LÓPEZ Occupation: Educator (Second Grade). Education: B.A., Texas Western College, 1952. Address: 1828 Cliff Drive, El Paso, Texas 79902.

McNEESE, MARSHA D Occupation: Assistant Professor of Radiotherapy; Physician. Education: M.D. Address: 4033 Woodfin, Houston, Texas 77025.

McNITT, RUTH M Occupation: Vice President, Advertising. Education: B.S. Home Economics, Michigan State University. Address: 2217 North Fremont, Chicago, Illinois 60614.

McNUTT, ANNE S Occupation: Dean of Instruction. Education: Ph.D., George Peabody College; M.A., B.S., East Tennessee State University. Address: 1011 Highland Road, Brentwood, Tennessee 37027.

McPHAIL, JOHN D Occupation: Director, Well Being Health Improvement Program. Education: B.S., M.A. Address: 4567 Keweenaw, Okemos, Michigan 48864.

McPHERSON, MELVILLE PETER Occupation: Administrator. Education: B.A. 1963, M.B.A. 1968, J.D. 1969. Address: 4601 Chevy Chase Boulevard, Chevy Chase, Maryland 20815.

McQUEEN, SANDRA M Occupation: Educator, Special Education Department Chairperson. Education: B.A., M.A., Ph.D. (in progress). Address: 2172 Lenox Road Northeast, Atlanta, Georgia 30324.

McQUILLEN, DENIS F Occupation: Vice President of Engineering, Head of Research and Development. Education: B.S.M.E., M.S.M.E. Address: 33 Springwood Drive, Lawrenceville, New Jersey 08648.

McREYNOLDS, NEIL L Occupation: Vice President Corporate Relations. Education: B.A. Journalism, University of Washington, 1956. Address: 14312 Southeast 45th Street, Bellevue, Washington 98006.

McWHORTER, GENEVA MARSHALL Occupation: Professor. Education: Master of Education. Address: Route 2, Box 64, Towa Park, Texas 76367.

MEADOWS, PATRICIA BLACHLY Occupation: President and Director, D-Art Visual Art Center, Dallas, Texas. Education: Bachelor of Arts, University of Texas, 1960. Address: 4505 San Carlos, Dallas, Texas 75205.

MEANEY, JOSEPH T Occupation: Assistant Superintendent. Education: B.S., M.S., S.E.A., Ph.D. Address: 3599 Pleasant Avenue, Hamburg, New York 14075.

MEARA, MARGARET ANN SPAGNOLO Occupation: Principal, King William High School. Education: B.Sc., M.Ed. Address: 2320 Dorking Road, Richmond, Virginia 23236.

MECH, RAYMOND ANDREW Occupation: Music Professor, Voice Teacher, Director I.S.U. Chorale, Indiana State University; Director, Motet Choir, Central Presbyterian Church. Education: B.S., State University of New York; Master of Music, University of Rochester. Address: 7140 Williamsburg Lane, Terre Haute, Indiana 47802.

MECH, WILLIAM P Occupation: Professor of Mathematics, Director University Honors Program. Education: B.A., M.S., Ph.D. Address: 1178 Ironside, Boise, Idaho 83706.

MECHEM, KIRKE LEWIS Occupation: Composer. Education: B.A., Stanford University; M.A., Harvard University. Address: 49 Marcela Avenue, San Francisco, Louisiana 94116.

MEDENBACH, MILTON H Occupation: Retired Educator, Superintendent Emeritus, Valley Forge Military Academy and Junior College. Education: A.B., The John Hopkins University; Dipl., Konsulerakademie, Vienna, Austria; Ped.D., Gettysburg College. Address: 15 Fariston Road, Wayne, Pennsylvania 19087.

MEDIN, MYRON JAMES JR Occupation: City Administrator. Education: B.A., St. Olaf College; M.P.A., University of Michigan. Address: 8737 Greeley Drive, Kansas City, Kansas 66109.

MEECE, DAVID CHARLES Occupation: Information Center, Office Automation Consultant. Education: B.A. Mathematics, Campbellsville College; M.B.A., Indiana Central University. Address: 1531 Maria Lane, Plainfield, Indiana 46168.

MEGILL, VIRGIL GLEN JR Occupation: Professor of Communication, Toccoa Falls College. Education: A.B., College of Emporia; M.Div., United Theological Seminary, Dayton, Ohio; M.A., New York University; Ed.D. Candidate, Teachers College, Columbia University. Address: 1 Terrace St. C-14, Gainesville, Georgia 30501.

MEHAFFEY, COY R Occupation: Custodial Supervisor, Buncombe County Schools. Education: B.S. Business Administration cum laude. Address: Route 1 Box 90, Arden, North Carolina 28704.

MEHRA, NIRMAL Occupation: Faculty Research Officer. Education: B.Ed., M.A. History, M.A. Education, Doctorate Education. Address: 39 Westbrook Drive, Edmonton, Alta, Canada T6J 208.

MEHTA, M PAUL Occupation: Dean, School of Education and Human Services, Minot State College, Minot, North Dakota. Education: Ed.D., M.A., University of Montana; M.A., B.A., Punjab University, India. Address: 4 Glacial Court, Minot, North Dakota 58701.

MEHTA, RAGHU N Occupation: Physician, Health Care Specialist. Education: R.A., Medical College, Uttar Pradesh, Government's Board of Indian Medicine, Lucknow, 1944; D.M.R.D., Queen's University, Canada, 1952; M.Ed., University of Maryland, 1957; C.H.A., University of Saskatchewan, 1965; Certification in Management of Alcoholism, Laurentian University, Canada. Address: 65 Park Street, Caribou, Maine 04736.

MEHTA, VED PARKASH Occupation: Author. Education: B.A., Pomona College, 1956; B.A. Hons. Modern History, Oxon, 1959; M.A., Harvard University, 1961; M.A., Oxford, 1962. Address: 1035 Fifth Avenue, New York, New York 10028.

MEIJER, PAUL HERMAN ERNST Occupation: Professor of Physics, Catholic University of America; Physicist, National Bureau of Standards. Education: Doctorate in Physics, University of Leyden, Netherlands, 1951. Address: 1438 Geranium Street, Northwest, Washington, D.C. 20064.

MEINKE, DEAN LEE Occupation: Professor of Educational Psychology. Education: B.A., M.Ed., Ph.D. Address: 3664 Indian Road, Toledo, Ohio 43606.

MEIS, PATTIE MORELAND Occupation: Principal, Executive Vice President and Media Director, Strong/Hill/Meis/Rozier, Inc. Advertising Agency. Education: B.B.A., University of Oklahoma, 1954. Address: 6313 North Warren, Oklahoma City, Oklahoma 73112.

MEISTER, RONALD WILLIAM Occupation: Attorney. Education: B.A. summa cum laude 1967, J.D. 1970, Yale University. Address: 21 Stuyvesant Avenue, Larchmont, New Mexico 10538.

MEJER, ROBERT LEE Occupation: Professor of Art/Gallery Director. Education: B.S., M.F.A. Address: 2009½ Spring, Quincy, Illinois 62301.

MELLERT, LUCIE A Occupation: Writer, Public Relations and Office Management Consultant. Education: Attended West Virginia University, Mason College of Music and Fine Arts. Address: 1017 West Virginia Avenue, Dunbur, West Virginia 25064.

MELLICHAMP, JOSEPHINE WEAVER Occupation: Writer. Education: A.B., Emory & Henry College, 1943; Graduate Studies, Emory University. Address: 1124 Reeder Circle, Northeast, Atlanta, Georgia 30306.

MELLINGER, MICHAEL V Occupation: Project Manager, Ecologist. Education: Bachelor of Arts, Bloomsburg State College, 1967; Doctor of Philosophy, Syracuse University, 1972. Address: 122 Bafer Drive, Exton, Pennsylvania 19341.

MELLO, HENRY GOULART Education: A.B., M.D., M.P.H. Address: 33 Balboa Avenue, Vallejo, California 94591.

MELINK, BERTHA Occupation: Opera Coach. Education: B.A. Address: 110 West End Avenue, New York, New York 10023.

MELTON, GARY B Occupation: Professor, University of Nebraska. Education: B.A., University of Virginia; M.A., Ph.D., Boston University. Address: 3301 North 73rd Street, Lincoln, Nebraska 68507.

MELTON, IRA B Occupation: Vice President and Director, Consolidated Consultants Inc., C.C.I. Funds Inc, C.C.I. Realty Inc.; Vice President, Mortgage Investments, Inc.; Vice President and Treasurer, Specialized Training Institute, Inc.; Vice President and Director, Peachstone Development Corporation; Director, Shallowford Arms, Inc.; Member, Austin Realty Company; Partner, Warren I-20 Association. Address: 613 Dogwood Road, Pine Lake, Georgia 30072.

MENDEL, EDWARD Occupation: Electronics Executive. Education: B.S., United States Naval Academy, 1950; M.S.E., University of Michigan, 1960. Address: 418 University Avenue, Los Altos, California 94022.

MENDELL, TITUS CARLOS RENATOS Occupation: Training Manager, Michigan Employment Security Commission. Education: Bachelor of Arts, University of Michigan. Address: 22045 West Eight Mile, Apartment 113, Detroit, Michigan 48219.

MENDELS, JOSEPH Occupation: Physician, Professor. Education: M.B., Ch.B., M.D. Address: 37 Greenhill Lane, Philadelphia, Pennsylvania 19151.

MENDELSON, PHILIP LEE Occupation: Vocational Support Services Team Leader. Education: Adanced Graduate Specialist, Master of Education, Bachelor of Science. Address: 19213 Bonmark Court, Germantown, Maryland 20874.

MENDELSON, RALPH R Occupation: Consultant. Education: B.S. in Mechanical Engineering, University of Michigan, 1939. Address: 16015 Van Aken Boulevard, #203, Shaker Heights, Ohio 44120.

MENDENHALL, RODGER EUGENE Occupation: Hospital Administrator. Education: Master of Science Hygiene. Address: 90 Lynn Rae Circle, Centerville, Ohio 45450.

MENDIRATTA, VEENA BHATIA Occupation: Telecommunications Systems Engineer. Education: Ph.D., M.S., B.Tech. Civil Engineering. Address: 758 Chateaux North, Oak Brook, Illinois 60521.

MENKES, JOSHUA Occupation: Section Head of Policy Sciences, National Science Foundation. Education: Ph.D. Address: 7510 Alaska Avenue, N.W., Washington, D.C. 20012.

MENKIN, PETER A Occupation: Editor-Manager. Education: Attended Trade School, College Preparatory School. Address: Post Office Box 9144, San Rafael, California 94912.

MENON, I ARAVINDAKSHAN Occupation: Research/Teaching. Education: Ph.D. Address: 27 Kingslake Road, Willowdale, Ontario, Canada M2J 3E2.

MENOR, RICKY ANTHONY Occupation: Physician. Education: B.A. Biology, M.D. Address: 1235 Granville Avenue, Apartment 4, Los Angeles, California 90025.

MERCER, SUSAN O Occupation: Associate Professor, Graduate School of Social Work. Education: D.S.W., M.S.S.W. Address: 3216 Hazy Ridge Court, Little Rock, Arkansas 72207.

MEREDITH, DONALD C Occupation: Writer. Education: A.A. Address: 2832 Gough Street, San

Francisco, California 94123.

MERENSKI, J PAUL Occupation: Professor, University of Dayton. Education: B.S.B.A., M.B.A., Ph.D. Address: 416 Falcon Drive, New Carlisle, Ohio 45344.

MERKATZ, RUTH B Occupation: Clinical Nurse Specialist, Women's Health. Education: R.N., B.S.N., M.S.N. Address: 89 Greenhaven Road, Rye, New York 10580.

MERLISS, REUBEN Occupation: Physician. Education: B.A., M.D. Address: 12821 Beverly Hills, California 90210.

MERRELL, VERNON C Occupation: College Instructor/Lecturer. Education: B.S., M.S.A. Address: 805 Hill Street, Copperas Cove, Texas 76522.

MERRIAM, DANIEL FRANCIS Occupation: Endowment Distinguished Professor of Geology, Chairman Department of Geology, Wichita State University. Education: B.S., M.S., Ph.D., University of Kansas; M.Sc., D.Sc., University of Leicester. Address: 5918 East 10th Street, Wichita, Kansas 67208.

MERRICK, ROBERT A JR Occupation: Attorney. Education: B.A., Princeton University, 1973; J.D., Northwestern University, 1977; Ph.D., Northwestern University, 1981. Address: 2244 North Maplewood, Chicago, Illinois 60647.

MERRIFIELD, JOHN T Occupation: Engineer, Pilot, Consultant. Education: M.S. Astronautical Engineering. Address: Post Office Box 1458, Lancaster, California 93534.

MERRILL, THOMAS SELFRIDGE Occupation: Clinical Psychologist. Education: B.A., M.Ed., M.D. Address: 120 Maono Place, Honolulu, Hawaii.

MERRITT, SHARON L Occupation: Associate Professor, Graduate Program, Medical-Surgical Nursing Specialiation. Education: B.S.N., M.S.N., Ed.D. Address: 14611 Lake Trails, Chesterfield, Missouri 63017.

MESKELL, UNA Occupation: Mental Health Nurse Specialist. Education: B.A., M.S. Address: 3235 Grand Concourse, Bronx, New York 10468.

MESNARD, D DEAN Occupation: Life Insurance Salesperson. Education: B.S., Millikin University; C.L.U., Ch.F.C., American College. Address: 3236 Green Lake Court, Decatur, Illinois 62521.

MESSINA, ANTOINETTE J Occupation: Educational Consultant, Financial Advisor. Education: B.A., M.B.A., M.A., Ed.D. Address: 44 Gales Drive, New Providence, New Jersey 07974.

MESSNER, PATRICIA MARILYN Occupation: Musician, Sport Instructor, Coach. Education: Diploma, Secondary School. Address: Box 666 Rural Route #5, Gloucester, Ontario, Canada.

METCALF, JACK Occupation: State Senator, 10th District; Educator. Education: B.A., B.Ed. Address: 3273 Saratoga Road, Langley, Washington 98260.

METRES, PHILIP JOHN JR Occupation: Clinical Psychologist. Education: B.A. Psychology, Holy Cross College, 1964; M.A., 1971; Ph.D. Professional Psychology, 1975. Address: 49 Cambridge Lane, Lincolnshire, Illinois 60015.

METZ, JERRED M Occupation: Writer, City Administrator. Education: Ph.D. Literature, University of Minnesota, 1972. Address: 2318 Albion Place, St. Louis, Missouri 63104.

METZGER, ERIKA ALMA Occupation: Professor of German. Education: M.A., Ph.D. Address: Department of Modern Languages and Literatures, 910 Clemens, S.U.N.Y.A.B., Buffalo, New York 14260.

MEUSER, FRED W Occupation: President. Education: B.A., B.D., M.A., S.T.M., Ph.D. Address:

2402 Berwick Boulevard, Columbus, Ohio 43209.

MEYER, ANN J Occupation: Professor, Chair Department H.D.E.V., California State University-Hayward. Education: Ph.D. Address: 5670 Cabot Drive, Oakland, California 94611.

MEYER, KATHERINE Occupation: Associate Professor, Department of Sociology, The Ohio State University. Education: A.B., Trinity College; M.A., Ph.D., University of North Carolina-Chapel Hill. Address: 653 Glenmont Avenue, Columbus, Ohio 43214.

MEYER, MELVIN BERNARD Occupation: Director of Traffic Engineering and Parking. Education: B.S. Civil Engineering. Address: 1414 34th Street Southeast, Cedar Rapids, Iowa 52403.

MEYER, NANCY J Occupation: Senior Finance Officer. Education: B.A., C.F.A. Address: 17606 Southeast 60th, Issaquah, Washington 98027.

MEYERKORTH, MARGARET A Occupation: Certified Public Accountant. Education: B.A. Business Administration. Address: 1855 Taft Street, Concord, California 94521.

MEYERS, JUDITH K Occupation: Coordinator of Media Services, Lakewood Board of Education. Education: B.A., M.A., Ad.M., Ed.D. Address: 25570 Lake Road, Bay Village, Ohio 44140.

MICHAELSON, LOUIS W Occupation: Professor Creative Writing, Science Fiction. Education: B.A., M.A., Ph.D. Address: 1406 Lakeshore Drive, Ft. Collins, Colorado 80525.

MICHELL, GEORGIE ANN Occupation: Attorney. Education: A.B., University of California-Berkeley; J.D., University of California, Hastings College of the Law. Address: 1080 Brown Avenue, Lafayette, California 94549.

MICHELSON, DAVID TODD Occupation: Training Design. Education: B.A. Economics, Dickinson College. Address: 11629 Kiowa Avenue #6, Brentwood, California 90049.

MICKELSEN, OLAF Occupation: Specialist Human Nutrition and Its Relation to Disease. Education: B.S., Rutgers University, 1935; M.S., Ph.D., University of Wisconsin, 1939. Address: Rural Route 1, Lula, Georgia 30554.

MIGDALOF, BRUCE HOWARD Occupation: Director Department of Metabolism/Xenobiologist, The Squibb Institute for Medical Research. Education: B.A., Cornell University; M.S., Purdue University; Ph.D., University of Pittsburgh. Address: 156 Richardson Road, Robbinsville, New Jersey 08691.

MIGL, DONALD RAYMOND Occupation: Doctor of Optometry/Optometrist. Education: O.D. 1980, B.S. 1970, B.S. 1978, University of Houston. Address: 2600 Pinecrest Drive, Nacogdoches, Texas 75961.

MIGLIARO, MARCO WILLIAM Occupation: Consulting Electrical Engineer, Ebasco Services Inc. Education: B.E.E., Pratt Institute. Address: 14 Crest Lane, Fanwood, New Jersey 07023.

MIHALOW, PAULA J Occupation: Teacher. Education: A.A., B.A., M.A. Address: Post Office Box 87, Placentia, California 92670.

MILER, GEORGE G JR Occupation: President, George Miler, Inc. Education: B.S., Clemson University; M.S., Florida Institute of Technology. Address: 305 Sasanqua Drive, Greenville, South Carolina 29615.

MILHOUSE, PAUL WILLIAM Occupation: Bishop-in-Residence. Education: A.B., B.A., Th.D., D.D., S.T.D., H.L.D., D.D. Address: 2213 Northwest 56 Terrace, Oklahoma City, Oklahoma 73112.

MILLER, BOB W Occupation: Professor and Director of Community College Programs. Education: B.A., M.A., Doctorate. Address: 316 Circle View Drive, South Hurst, Texas 76053.

MILLER, DALE E Occupation: Company Officer/Manager. Education: Master of Archaelogy, B.A. Address: 1537 38th Avenue, Seattle, Washington 98122.

MILLER, DAVID L Occupation: Professor of Philosophy Emeritus, University of Texas-Austin. Education: B.A., College of Emporia; Ph.D., University of Chicago. Address: 1413 Ethridge Avenue, Austin, Texas 78703.

MILLER, GEORGE D III Occupation: Dean of Student Affairs. Education: M.A. Marriage and Family Couseling. Address: 3102 Chatham, Endwell, New York 13760.

MILLER, GEORGE J Occupation: Paleontologist/Lecturer. Education: B.S., California State University; L.B., M.S., Idaho State University. Address: BSR 762, Julian, California 92036.

MILLER, JAN D Occupation: Professor of Metallurgy, University of Utah. Education: B.S., M.S., Ph.D. Address: 1886 Atkin Avenue, Salt Lake City, Utah 84106.

MILLER, JANE RUTH Occupation: Poet. Education: M.F.A., M.A., B.A. Address: 535 Commercial Street, Provinceton, Massachusetts 02657.

MILLER, JIM WAYNE Occupation: Teacher, Western Kentucky University; Writer. Education: A.B. English, Berea College, 1958; Ph.D. German, Vanderbilt University. Address: 1512 Eastland Drive, Bowling Green, Kentucky 42101.

MILLER, JOAN M Occupation: Associate Professor of Humanities. Education: B.A., Ph.L., Ph.D. (A.B.D.), Graduate Religious Studies. Address: 1418 Pearce Park, Erie, Pennsylvania 16502.

MILLER, JOSEPH Occupation: Chairman, Fortune Assurance Company, Inc. Education: B.A. Address: 1913 Delancey Street, Philadelphia, Pennsylvania 19103.

MILLER, MARILYN F Occupation: Pastor. Education: B.S., M.Div., D.Min. (in progress). Address: 6956 Robb, Arvada, Colorado 80004.

MILLER, RALPH H Occupation: Professor, California State Polytechnic University-Pomona. Education: B.A. 1967, M.A. 1969, Ph.D. 1979, San Jose State University. Address: 1725 Finecroft Drive, Claremont, California 91711.

MILLER, RAYMOND WOODRUFF Occupation: Professor of Soil Science, Utah State University. Education: B.S., M.S., Ph.D. Address: 487 East 600 South, Logan, Utah 84321.

MILLER, STEVE K Occupation: Co-Proprietor, Red Ozier Press; Lecturer on the Book Arts. Education: B.A., University of Wisconsin. Address: 530 West 25th Street, New York, New York 10001.

MILLER, THELMA KAY Education: B.A., Central Washington University. Education: B.A., Central Washington College of Education, 1939; Post-Graduate Study, Washington State University, University of Washington, Kinman Business University; Nurse's Training, St. Luke's Hospital. Address: 103 South Mill, Colfax, Washington 99111.

MILLER, WARREN E Occupation: Professor of Political Science, Department of Political Science, Arizona State University. Education: B.S. 1948, M.S. 1949, University of Oregon; Ph.D., Syracuse University, 1954. Address: 8814 North 86th Street, Scottsdale, Arizona 85258.

MILLER, WESTON P III Occupation: Physician/Surgeon, General Vascular-Thoracic. Education: B.S., Louisiana State University. Address: 101 North East Street, Abbeville, Louisiana 70510.

MILLER, WILBUR R Occupation: Associate Dean, University of Missouri. Education: B.S.Ed., M.Ed., Ed.D. Address: 2201 Danforth Court, Columbia, Missouri 65201.

MILLIE, HAROLD R Occupation: Petroleum Trade Specialist. Education: B.A., Claremont Men's College; M.A., Claremont Graduate School. Address: 5152 Manning Place, Northwest, Washington, D.C. 20016.

MILLIGAN, ALICE JUNE Occupation: Business Owner and Educator. Education: A.A., B.S. Address: 8225 N. Central Avenue #11, Phoenix, Arizona 85020.

MILLIGAN, BETTY L Occupation: Executive Director, Crime Stoppers of Houston. Education: B.A., Western New England University. Address: 15943 Windom Drive, Webster, Texas 77598.

MILLMAN, LAWRENCE B Occupation: Teacher/Writer. Education: M.A., Ph.D., Rutgers University. Address: Box 1217, Montpelier, Vermont 05602.

MILLS, EARL S Occupation: Director of Research and Planning, Executive Director TRACS, Liberty Baptist College. Education: Ed.D. Address: 1434 Nelson Drive, Lynchburg, Virginia 24502.

MILLS, SHERRY RAE Occupation: Executive Director, Colorado Arts for the Handicapped. Education: B.M.E., M.Ed., Administrative Certificate. Address: 2220 Glenwood Circle, Colorado Springs, Colorado 80909.

MILLS, WILBUR D Occupation: Lawyer. Education: Attended Hendrix College, Harvard Law School. Address: 1600 Eads Street, Arlington, Virginia 22202.

MILLS, WILLIAM A Occupation: Partner, International Accounting Firm of Haskins and Sells (Retired). Education: B.S., C.P.A. Address: 802 East 41st Street, Savannah, Georgia 31401.

MILLSAPS, ELIZABETH A (BETTY) Occupation: Account Executive, Jacqueline Schaar Associates. Education: B.A., University of Wyoming; M.A., University of Redlands. Address: Post Office Box 1742, Redlands, California 92373.

MILNE, GEORGE RICHARD ALOYSIOUS Occupation: Manufacturing Company Official. Education: Attended University of Cincinnati; N.O.M.A. Graduate Fellow Certificate in Management Administrative Services; B.S. Business and Commerce, University of Louisville, 1963. Address: 9635 Greentree Drive, Carmel, Indiana 46032.

MILSPAW, YVONNE J Occupation: Education Director, Historical Society of Dauphin County. Education: B.A., Mary Washington College of University of Virginia; M.A., Ph.D., Indiana University. Address: 1917 Felker Road, Middletown, Pennsylvania 17057.

MILTON, DAVID SCOTT Occupation: Writer. Address: Star Route 3, Box 101, Tehachapi, California 93561.

MIN, AN—SIK Occupation: Professor. Education: Ph.D., University of Iowa. Address: 5124 Clinton Drive, Erie, Pennsylvania 16509.

MINCER, JACOB Occupation: Professor of Economics, Economics Department, Columbia University. Education: Ph.D. Address: Riverside Drive, New York City, New York 10027.

MINCHEFF, EDISON ELAINE Occupation: Engineering Executive, Vice President. Education: B.S.M.E., University of Kansas, 1949. Address: 3244

South Evanston, Tulsa, Oklahoma 74105.

MINER, CAROL SPALDING Occupation: Director of Continuing Education. Education: B.A., University of Louisville; M.A., Pepperdine University. Address: 2487 Cypress, Spring Road 2, Florida 32073.

MINER, VALERIE J Occupation: Novelist, University Instructor. Education: B.A., M.A. Address: Mass Communications, 301 Campbell Hall, University of California at Berkeley.

MINIC, HELEN GREER Occupation: Lawyer. Education: B.A., J.D. Address: 250 Liberty, Fairhope, Alabama 36532.

MINISTER, KRISTINA Occupation: Director, Oral History Center, Inc. Education: B.F.A., Ohio University, 1958; M.A., Columbia University, 1962; Ph.D., Northwestern University, 1977. Address: 1144 West Orangewood Avenue, Phoenix, Arizona 85021.

MINNERS, HOWARD A Occupation: Science Advisor, A.I.D.; Assistant Surgeon General, U.S.P.H.S. Education: A.B., Princeton University, 1953; M.D., Yale School of Medicine, 1957; M.P.H., Harvard School of Public Health, 1960. Address: 4700 Locust Hill Court, Bethesda, Maryland 20814.

MINNICH, LEONARD LORRAINE Occupation: Regional Sales Manager, Abex Corporation. Education: High School Diploma. Address: R.D. #3 Mallard Drive, Delmar, Maryland 21875.

MINUI, MORTEZA Occupation: Psychiatrist. Education: B.S., M.D. Address: 1576 Kirkway Drive, Bloomfield Hills, Michigan 48013.

MITAL, ANIL Occupation: Engineering Educator, University of Cincinnati. Education: Bachelor of Engineering, 1974; Master of Science Industrial Engineering, 1976; Ph.D. Industrial Engineering, 1980. Address: 937 Gawain Circle, West Carrollton, Ohio 45449.

MITCHELL, C WAYNE Occupation: Speaker, Trainer. Education: Business Administration, Eastern Maine Vocational Technical Institute. Address: 693 East 135th, Punce South, Glenpool, Oklahoma 74033.

MITCHELL, CHRISTINE I Occupation: Nurse. Education: B.S.N., M.S., M.T.S. Address: 42 Browning Road, Somerville, Massachusetts 02145.

MITCHELL, DANIEL R Occupation: Professor, Chairman Department of Theology, L.B.C. Education: B.A., M.Div., S.T.M., Th.D. Address: 102 Wooldrige Circle, Lynchburg, Virginia 24502.

MITCHELL, JO BENNETT Occupation: Director, Alaska/NW Extension Center, San Francisco Theological Seminary. Education: B.A., M.A. Address: 1020 University Street #501, Seattle, Washington 98101.

MITCHELL, LeROY WILLIAM Occupation: Certified Public Accountant, Partner. Education: B.B.A., M.B.A., A.B.D. Address: 1083 Warburton Avenue, Yonkers, New York 10701.

MITCHELL, MADELEINE E Occupation: Professor of Nutrition. Education: B.Sc., M.S., Ph.D. Address: Northeast 430 Oak #3, Pullman, Washington 99163.

MITCHELL, RUSSELL H Occupation: Physician (Dermatology). Education: M.D., F.A.A.D, F.A.C.P. Address: Rural Route #2, Box 99, Leesburg, Virginia 22075.

MITCHELL, TERENCE R Occupation: Professor of Management and Psychology, School of Business, University of Washington-Seattle. Education: B.A., Graduate Diploma of Public Administration, M.A., Ph.D. Address: 2514 Magnolia Boulevard, West, Seattle, Washington 98199.

MITCHELL, ULYSS STANFORD Occupation:

Minister, Counselor, World Affairs. Education: A.B., Th.B., M.A., Th.D. summa cum laude. Address: 33 Linda Avenue #2111, Oakland, California 94611.

MITCHELL, VIRGINIA S Education: Address: 501 Bag Street, North Cordile, Georgia 31015.

MIYADA, THOMAS SANFRAN Occupation: Scientific Researcher; Member, E.U.P.C. Education: Sc.D., Ph.D. Address: Post Office Box 430, Summit, New Jersey 07901.

MIYAHIRA, RICHARD S Occupation: Certified Professional Code Administrator. Education: B.S.A.E., M.P.A. Address: 721 Lawnwood, Oxnard, California 93030.

MOCK, HARMON ROY Occupation: Transit Analyst, Mass Transit Administration. Education: B.Arch., University of Kansas. Address: 4 East 39 Street, Baltimore, Maryland 21218.

MOGULL, ROBERT G Occupation: Professor of Business Statistics and Economics, School of Business, California State University. Education: B.A., M.S., M.A., Ph.D. Address: School of Business, California State University, Sacramento, California 95819.

MOHAN, BRIJ Occupation: Dean. Education: M.S.W. 1960, Ph.D. 1964. Address: 1573 Leycester, Baton Rouge, Louisiana 70808.

MOHN, CHERI A Occupation: Artist. Education: A.B. Address: 12691 South Avenue, North Lima, Ohio 44452.

MOHR, RUTH ANN Occupation: Assistant Professor, Academic Coordinator, Chapman College. Education: B.S.N., M.P.H. Address: 2367 Glendon Avenue, Los Angeles, California 90064.

MOLINA, ANN T Occupation: Coastal Zone Management Coordinator. Education: B.B.A. Address: 90 Mohala Place, Pukalani, Hawaii 96788.

MOLLENHAUER, BERNARD Occupation: Writer. Education: Hon. Ph.D., University Extension. Address: 3614 Third Avenue, San Diego, California 92103.

MOLO, WALTER J JR Occupation: Elementary School Superintendent, Pleasantdale School District #107. Education: B.S. 1948, M.S. 1949, University of Illinois; Ed.D., Loyola University-Chicago, 1970. Address: 7450 South Wolf Road, LaGrange, Illinois 60525.

MOMIYAMA, NANAE Occupation: Artist, Art Lecturer. Education: Bunka Gakuin College, Tokyo Women's College. Address: Post Office Box 44, Glenville Station, Greenwich, Connecticut 06830.

MONAHAN, LEONARD FRANCIS Occupation: Singer, Composer, Musician, Producer. Education: B.S. Psychology and Philosophy. Address: 4-9967-US-A20, Delta, Ohio 43515.

MONCRIEFFE, HYACINTH Occupation: Registered Nurse; Poet; Author; Performer, Viceroy Productions. Education: Master of Professional Human Services. Address: Post Office Box 615, Brooklyn, New York 11216.

MONDY, NELL I Occupation: Professor. Education: Ph.D., Cornell University, 1953; M.A., Texas University, 1945; B.S. 1943, B.A. 1943, Quachita University. Address: 126 Honness Lane, Ithaca, New York 14850.

MONGEAU, CARMEN A Occupation: Guidance Counselor. Education: B.A., M.A. English, M.A. Counseling. Address: 207 Aronimink Drive, Newtown Square, Pennsylvania 19073.

MONROE, KARLTON LEE Occupation: Bank Director, Community Leader. Education: Attended William and Mary College. Address: Box 155, Round Hill, Virginia 22141.

MONROE, KRISTEN RENWICK Occupation: Visiting Assistant Professor. Education: Ph.D., M.A., A.B. Address: 3 J Magie, Faculty Road, Princeton, New Jersey 08540.

MONTASSER, ALI S Occupation: Financial Operations Analyst, The World Bank. Education: B.A. Corporate Finance and Economics, University of South Florida. Address: 2129 Florida Avenue, Northwest, #605, Washington, D.C. 20008.

MONTGOMERY, OLIVE W Occupation: International Real Estate Broker. Education: Attended Oxford School, Hartford School of Music, Smith College. Address: 1114 2nd Avenue South, Tierra Verde, Florida 33715.

MONTGOMERY, WENDELL C Occupation: Professional Nutritional Consultant. Education: B.S., M.S., D.N. Address: 4666 Quaker Trace Road, Eaton, Ohio 45320.

MONTGOMERY, YVONNE WASHINGTON Occupation: Placement Director. Education: Bachelor of Science Music Education, Master Science Student Personnel Administration. Address: 18 Shady Creek, Guthrie, Oklahoma 73099.

MONTHAN, DORIS BORN Occupation: Free-lance Writer. Education: University of Arizona, New York University, Columbia University. Address: Post Office Box 1698, Flagstaff, Arizona 86002.

MOODY, ARNOLD JR Occupation: Research Plant Pathologist. Education: B.S., M.S., Ph.D. Address: 301 Charlotte Avenue, Colonial Heights, Virginia 23834.

MOODY, ERNEST L Occupation: Resource Conservationist. Education: B.S. Agronomy, Virginia State University. Address: 3309 25th Avenue, Temple Hills, Maryland 20748.

MOORE, ANN MADDOX Occupation: Manager, Oil and Gas Royalty Interest and Investment; Artist. Education: Bachelor of Fine Arts, University of Texas; Teachers Certificate Art, Pan American University. Address: 111 West Eire, McAllen, Texas 78501.

MOORE, ANNABELLE FISHER Occupation: Associate Professor, University of Alaska-Anchorage. Education: B.S., M.S. Address: 3435 Rosella Street, Anchorage, Alaska 99504.

MOORE, CLARA L Occupation: Speech, Language Pathologist. Education: M.S., Florida State University, 1974. Address: 401 North U Street, Pensacola, Florida 32505.

MOORE, DAN TYLER Occupation: Writer, Association Executive. Education: B.S., Yale University, 1932. Address: 2564 Berkshire Road, Cleveland Heights, Ohio 44106.

MOORE, GIBBS BERRY Occupation: Vice President, Valley Division, Eastern Associated Coal Corporation. Education: Attended Fairmont State College, West Virginia University School of Mines. Address: Grandview Road, Route 9, Box 300, Beaver, West Virginia 25813.

MOORE, GWEN Occupation: Assistant Professor of Sociology, Russell Sage College. Education: A.B., Bucknell University; M.A., Ph.D., New York University. Address: 45 Union Avenue, Delmar, New York 12054.

MOORE, LYNN Occupation: Entrepreneur; Marketing, Sales, Promotion, Small Business Specialist, Moore Efficiency. Address: 3804 North Wasington Street, Westmont, Illinois 60559.

MOORE, MARTHA A Occupation: Vice President and Treasurer, Fortner Furniture Company, Inc. Address: 4088 Walnut Grove Road, Memphis, Tennessee 38117.

MOORE, MICHAEL D Occupation: Health Care Administrator. Education: A.S. Business Administration, B.S. Business Administration, Master of Health Administration. Address: 1825 Platte Drive, Lafayette, Indiana 47905.

MOORE, NANCY RYDER Occupation: Artist, Teacher, Pianist. Education: B.M. magna cum laude; M.M.; A.R.C.M., University of London. Address: 1 Haverhill Place, Dewitt, New York 13214.

MOORE, OLA M Occupation: Federal Manager. Education: Master's Degree in Studies in Aging. Address: 2169 Kessler Court, Dallas, Texas 75208.

MOORE, RICHARD Occupation: College Teacher, New England Conservatory; Poet; Critic. Education: B.A., Yale University; M.A., Trinity College. Address: 81 Clark Street, Belmont, Massachusetts 02178.

MOORE, RUDOLPH Occupation: Publisher, Educational Materials. Education: B.A., M.A., Ph.D. Address: Post Office Box 20587, Phoenix, Arizona 85036.

MOORE, SONIA Occupation: Artistic Director, Stanislavski Theatre; Director, Sonia Moore Studio of the Theatre, Inc.; Author, Lecturer. Education: Attended University of Kiev, University of Moscow, 1918-20; Drama Stusio, Solovzov Theatre, Kiev, 1919-20; Studio of Moscow Art Theatre, 1920-23; Diploma, Alliance Francaise, Paris, 1927; Instituto Interuniversitario Italiano, Rome, 1928; Degrees, Reale Conservatorio de Musica, Santa Cecilia, 1939; Reale Accademis Filarmonica, 1939. Address: 485 Park Avenue, New York, New York 10022.

MOORE, TERRY LOCKLIN III Occupation: Engineer, Project Management. Education: B.S. Civil Engineering, M.S. Administration. Address: 155 Butternut Lane, Stamford, Connecticut 06903.

MOORE, WILMA C Occupation: Professor. Education: B.S., M.Ed. Address: 612 Orchard Drive, Lake Charles, Louisiana 70605.

MOOREHEAD, GEORGE A Occupation: Physician (Dermatologist). Education: B.S. Pharmacy, M.D. Specialist in Dermatology. Address: Estate Wintberg 373, Charlotte Amalie, St. Thomas, Virgin Islands 00801, Post Office Box 3668.

MOORE-WEST, MAGGI LOUISE Occupation: Medical Sociologist/Program Evaluator. Education: B.A., U.N.H.; M.S.W., Smith College; Ph.D., Bryn Mawr College. Address: Post Office Box 1404, Corrales, New Mexico 81048.

MOORMAN, WILLIAM J Occupation: Agronomist. Education: Student, University of Kansas, Kansas State University. Address: 810 Fallwood Drive, Columbus, Mississippi 39702.

MOOZ, ELIZABETH DODD Occupation: Research Scientist, Philip Morris, U.S.A., Research Center. Education: B.A., Hollins College; Ph.D., Tufts University. Address: 100 Gun Club Road, Richmond, Virginia 23221.

MORAN, MARGUERITE KATHERINE Occupation: Vice President and Director, Technical and Business Information, M&T Chemicals, Inc. Education: B.S., M.L.S. Address: 13 Longfellow Drive, Colonia, New Jersey 07067.

MORAN, MARLENE JUNE Occupation: Assistant Food Service Director. Education: Food Service Supervisor Certificate. Address: 34 Walnut Avenue, Bethlehem, West Virginia 26003.

MORAN, PETER W Occupation: Clinical Psychologist. Education: Ph.D. Clinical Psychology, M.A. Applied Psychology, B.A. Natural Sciences. Address: 19 Jeffrey Keating Road, Fitchburg,

Massachusetts 01420.

MORAY, JOHN E Occupation: Director of Research, Cosray Research Institute. Education: B.S., M.S. & T., University of Utah. Address: 1919 Hubbard Avenue, Salt Lake City, Utah 84108.

MOREHOUSE, JAMES E Occupation: Management Consultant. Education: B.S.I.E., M.S.I.E., Purdue University. Address: 6033 North Sheridan 37A, Chicago, Illinois 60660.

MORENG, ROBERT EDWARD Occupation: College Professor, Colorado State University. Education: B.S., M.S., Ph.D. 1950, University of Maryland. Address: 6221 North County Road 15, Fort Collins, Colorado 80524.

MORGAN, ANDREW L Occupation: Urological Surgeon. Education: B.A., M.D. Address: 4022 Nuuanu Pali Drive, Honolulu, Hawaii 96817.

MORGAN, BARBARA A Occupation: Real Estate Broker. Education: High School. Address: 703 Bullock Place, Lexington, Kentucky 40508.

MORGAN, CLYDE NATHANIEL Occupation: Physician, Dermatology. Education: B.S., M.D., F.A.A.F.P., A.C.S. Address: 1718 Cedarcrest Drive, Abilene, Texas 79601.

MORGAN, EDMUND JOSEPH JR Occupation: Physician. Education: M.D. cum laude, Tufts Medical School, 1948. Address: 1023 Bernardston Road, Greenfield, Massachusetts 01301.

MORGAN, GARY B Occupation: Professor. Education: A.B., N.M. Highlands; M.A., Colorado State University. Address: Box 5012, Greeley, Colorado 80631.

MORGAN, MARK PATRICK Occupation: Attorney at Law. Education: B.A. 1976, J.D. 1979, DePaul University. Address: 2650 North Central, Flossmoor, Illinois 60422.

MORGAN, MARSHAL CHARLES Occupation: Physician. Education: B.S., M.D. Address: 662 Hampton Ridge Road, Akron, Ohio 44313.

MORGAN, ROBERT EARLE Occupation: Professor French and Mathematics, Gardner-Webb College. Education: A.B., Lenior Rhyne College, 1956; M.Ed. 1961, Ph.D. 1971, University of North Carolina. Address: Post Office Box 903, Boiling Springs, North Carolina 28017.

MORGAN, ROBERT R Occupation: Poet, Educator. Education: B.A., University of North Carolina, 1965; M.F.A., University of North Carolina-Greensboro. Address: 105 North Wood Road, Freeville, New York 13068.

MORGAN, WALTER CLIFFORD Occupation: Professor. Education: B.Sc., M.Sc., Ph.D. Address: 1610 First Street, Brookings, South Dakota 57006.

MORI, RICHARD ALAN Occupation: Lawyer, Greater Boston Chamber of Commerce. Education: B.S., J.D. Address: 43 Stone Street, Beverly, Massachusetts 01915.

MORITZ, MILTON EDWARD Occupation: Audit and Security Manager. Education: Attended University of Maryland, Florida State University. Address: 7723 Avondale Terrace, Harrisburg, Pennsylvania 17112.

MORITZ, TIMOTHY BOVIE Occupation: Physician (Psychiatrist). Education: M.D. Address: 2829 Hyland Park Road, Fayetteville, Arkansas 72701.

MORLOK, EDWARD K Occupation: U.P.S. Foundation Professor of Transportation and Chairman Graduate Group in Transportation, University of Pennsylvania. Education: B.E., Yale University; Ph.D., Northwestern University. Address: 460 Fox Chase Lane, Media, Pennsylvania 19063.

MORONEY, EDWARD FRANCIS PIUS Occu-

pation: Organist-Choirmaster, Accompanist, Conductor, O.L.J., M.M.L.J. Education: Mus.B., B.Ed., F.R.C.C.O. (C.H.M.), A.R.C.O. (C.H.M.), A.R.C.T. Address: 1, Elliotwood Court, Willowdale, Ontario, Canada M2L 2P8.

MOROSO, MICHAEL J Occupation: Aerospace Engineer/Scientist. Education: B.S.M.E., University of Wisconsin. Address: 964 Lansing Lane, Costa Mesa, California 92626.

MORRICE, RUTH-MADELYN FILL Occupation: Writer, Artist, Educational Consultant, Counselor. Education: B.A. 1942, M.A. 1943, Doctoral Work 1945-47, Boston University; Doctoral Work, University of California, S.J.S.U., Others, 1964-74. Address: 3508 Trevis Way, Carmel, California 93923.

MORRIS, ALVIN L Occupation: Consulting Meteorologist. Education: B.S., University of Chicago; M.S., U.S. Navy Postgraduate School. Address: 15759 Sunshine Canyon, Boulder, Colorado 80302.

MORRIS, CATHY G Occupation: Degree Program Assistant, The University of Georgia, School of Music. Address: Route 4, Box 376B, Winder, Georgia 30680.

MORRIS, CECIL ARTHUR Occupation: Chairman Mathematical Sciences Department, Director Computer Services, Cumberland College. Education: B.A., Pfeiffer College; M.A., Appalachian State University; Ph.D., Virginia Polytechnic Institute and State University. Address: Route 3, Box 911, Williamsburg, Kentucky 40769.

MORRIS, IRVING Occupation: Teacher, Library Media Certificate, L. D. Brandeis High School. Education: B.A., M.L.S. Address: 21-15 34th Avenue (2D), L.I.C., New York 1106.

MORRIS, LESLIE A Occupation: Rare Book Librarian. Education: B.A. History, Northwestern University; A.M. Library Science, University of Chicago; M.A. Bibliography and Textual Criticism, University of Leeds. Address: 326 Circle Drive, Wichita, Kansas 67218.

MORRIS, ROBERT EARL Occupation: Corporation Chairman. Education: Order of the British Empire; Kentucky Colonel. Address: 17 Talcott Notch Road, Farmington, Connecticut 06032.

MORRIS, RONALD GEORGE Occupation: Industrial Sales. Education: B.S., Purdue University, 1961. Address: 10907 Silkwood, Houston, Texas 77031.

MORRISON, JOY S Occupation: Editor. Education: B.A. Journalism, University of Wisconsin. Address: 1015 East Elm, Pocatello, Idaho 83201.

MORRISON, MINION K C Occupation: Associate Professor and Chairman, Department of Afro-American Studies. Education: B.A. 1968, M.A. 1969, Ph.D. 1977. Address: 118 Ferris Avenue, Syracuse, New York 13210.

MORROCCO, JOHN THOMAS Occupation: Director Sales and Marketing. Education: B.S. Marketing, M.B.A. Address: 220 LaCava Road, Bristol, Connecticut 06010.

MORROW, FRANK S JR Occupation: Producer, Alternative News Magazine, Television Program, Public Access Television; Writer on U.S. Power Structure. Education: B.A. Speech, M.A. History, Ph.D. Communications. Address: 66 UT Trailer Park, Austin, Texas 78703.

MORSE, RICHARD JAY Occupation: Vice President Human Resources, The Bekins Company. Education: B.A., M.A. Address: 60 Glenflow Street, Glendale, California 91206.

MORTMAN, HARRIETTE C Occupation: Superintendent. Education: B.A., M.A. Address: 21 Arbor Lane, Merrick, New York 11566.

MORTON, BONNIE S Occupation: Committee Member, National Federation of Music Clubs. Education: B.A., M.A. Address: 2 Palm Club, 1431 South Ocean Boulevard, Pompano Beach, Florida 33062.

MOSBACKER, WANDA BATH Occupation: Director, Associate Dean and Professor of Professional Development Emeritus; Member College Advisory Board; Consultant. Education: Commercial Engineer, M.Ed., Additional Studies. Address: 2106 Harrison Avenue, Cincinnati, Ohio 45214.

MOSCOSO, CARLOS G Occupation: Consultant, Tropical Agricultural Sciences. Education: B.Sc., M.Sc., D.Sc. Address: Post Office Box 1746, Plant City, Florida 33566.

MOSEBAR, THELMA IRENE Occupation: Manager, Medical Laboratory. Education: B.S. Bacteriology, 1970; Medical Technology, 1971; M.A. Management, Specialty Health Care Administration, 1983. Address: 5301 20th Avenue Southeast, Lacey, Washington 98503.

MOSELEY, LAURICE CULP Occupation: Businesswoman. Education: Extension Course, Institute Air University. Address: 2543 Wildwood Drive or Post Office Box 11388, Montgomery, Alabama 36111.

MOSER, NORMAN C Occupation: Professional Writer/Teacher; Actor; Author, *El Grito del Norte and Other Stories*. Address: 2110 9th Street #B, Berkeley, California 94710.

MOSIER, MARTHA FIKE Occupation: Associate Professor of Business, Abilene Christian University. Education: B.S., Southwestern State University; M.Ed., University of Oklahoma. Address: 402 College Drive, Abilene, Texas 79601.

MOSS, LYNDA (SUSAN) Occupation: Senior Residential Retail Marketing Representative, Tifton District, Georgia Power Company. Education: A.A., Abraham Baldwin Junior College; B.S.H.E., University of Georgia. Address: 1206 North College Avenue, Tifton, Georgia 31794.

MOSS, MIKE Occupation: Market Technician. Address: 706 Yarmouth Court, San Diego, California 92109.

MOSSTON, MUSKA Occupation: Educational Consultant. Education: B.A., M.A., City College of New York; Ed.D., Temple University. Address: 115 Carlton Avenue, Trenton, New Jersey 08618.

MOTT, DAVID E W Occupation: Supervisor of Test Development, Testing Service, Division of Research, Evaluation and Testing, Virginia Department of Education, Richmond, Virginia. Education: B.A. Psychology, Vanderbilt University, 1967; M.A. Experimental Psychology, The American University, 1972; Ph.D. General Psychology, Virginia Commonwealth University, 1979. Address: 2821 Ellwood Avenue, Richmond, Virginia 23221.

MOTTO, ANNA LYDIA Occupation: Professor and Director, Classics, University of South Florida. Education: B.A., Queens College, City College of New York, 1946; M.A., New York University, 1948; Ph.D., University of North Carolina, 1953. Address: 11712 Davis Road, Tampa, Florida 33617.

MOULTON, SUSAN GENE Occupation: Department Chairperson, Associate Professor of Art, Stanford University. Education: B.A. magna cum laude, University of California-Davis; M.A., Ph.D., Stanford University. Address: 7736 Elphick Road, Sebastopol, California 95472.

MOUNTZOURES, HARRY L Occupation: Writer. Education: B.A. English, Wesleyan University. Address: 29 Old Black Point Road, Niantic, Connecticut 06357.

MOUZAKITIS, CHRIS M Occupation: Assistant Professor, School of Social Work and Course Planning. Education: B.S., M.S.W., Ed.D. Address: 6438 Tauler Court, Columbia, Missouri 21045.

MOVCHAN, JULIAN G Occupation: Physician, General Medical Practice. Education: M.D., Lviv Medical Institute, Ukraine. Address: Post Office Box 133, Macedonia, Ohio 44056.

MOYA, AURY Occupation: Director. Education: Bachelor of Education; Postgraduate Studies. Address: Siena 307, College Park, Rio Piedros, Puerto Rico.

MRAK, EMIL M Occupation: Chancellor Emeritus, University of California-Davis. Education: B.S., M.S., Ph.D., University of California. Address: 602 Cordova Place, Davis, California 95616.

MUELLER, GARY ALFRED Occupation: Mathematician/Computer Programmer, United States Geological Survey. Education: B.S. Mineral Engineering Physics 1972, B.S. Mineral Engineering Mathematics 1973, Colorado School of Mines; B.S. Electrical Engineering/Computer Science with honors 1975, M.S. Electrical Engineering (in progress), University of Colorado. Address: 340 Iris Street, Broomfield, Colorado 80020.

MUIR, RUTH B Occupation: Patient Representative. Education: B.A., Rollins College; M.A., University of Iowa. Address: 6 Glendale Court, Iowa City, Iowa 52240.

MULHAUSER, KAREN Occupation: Executive Director, Citizens Against Nuclear War. Education: B.A. Biology, Antioch College. Address: 319 7th Street Northeast, Washington, D.C. 20002.

MULLEN, PHILIP E Occupation: Artist/Professor, University of South Carolina. Education: B.A., M.A., Ph.D. Address: 1611 Hollywood Drive, Columbia, South Carolina 29205.

MULLER, JEAN F Occupation: Tumwater City Council Member. Education: B.A. Business, The Evergreen State College. Address: 701 Irving Street, Tumwater, Washington 98502.

MULLER, SYLVIA RUTH BARBUSH Occupation: Pianist, Organist, Choirmaster, Vocalist; Teacher of Piano, Organ and Choral Music; Northwest Indiana Symphony Pianist and Composer. Education: B.M. 1957, M.M. 1961, Sherwood School of Music. Address: 108 North Road, Schererville, Indiana 46375.

MULLIGAN, KATHLEEN M Occupation: High School Assistant Principal. Education: B.A., M.A. Address: 290 Double Creek Parkway, Freehold, New Jersey 07728.

MULLING, EMORY W Occupation: Division Human Resource Manager. Education: B.A. Address: 3093 Rockaway Road, Atlanta, Georgia 30341.

MUNI, SANT NARAYAN Occupation: Discourses on Indian Philosophy and Culture. Education: Masters of Art, Literature and Philosophy. Address: Hindu Temple, Post Office Box 56, Monroeville, Pennsylvania 15146.

MUNN, KATRINA J Occupation: Instructor, Piano and Organ; Organist/Choir Director; Choral Society Accompanist. Education: B.S., Diploma in Piano, Julliard School. Address: Box 244, Bradford, Vermont 05033.

MUNNERLYN, MARGARET R Occupation: Elementary Education Teacher. Education: B.S., M.Ed., Additional Studies toward A.A. Address: 2254 Rushing Drive, Mobile, Alabama 36617.

MUNSON, NORMA FRANCES Occupation: Biologist, Nutritionist. Education: B.A., M.A., Ph.D. Address: 206 West Maple Avenue, Libertyville, Illinois

60048.

MUNTER, PAMELA OSBORNE Occupation: Clinical Psychologist. Education: A.A., B.A., M.A., M.A., Ph.D. Address: 1970 Southwest Pheasant Drive, Beaverton, Oregon 97006.

MUNZER, JEAN G Occupation: Hypnotist. Education: B.A., Douglass College. Address: 10 Pequot Path, Oakland, New Jersey 07436.

MURAYAMA, MAKIO Occupation: Biochemist. Education: Ph.D., University of Michigan. Address: 5010 Benton Avenue, Bethesda, Maryland 20814.

MURDOCK, HAZEL STEWARD Occupation: Administrative Assistant. Education: A.B., M.A. Address: 413 Hitt Street, Columbia, Missouri 65201.

MURNANE, GEORGE T Occupation: Insurance Broker. Education: University of Minnesota, American College, Chartered Life Underwriters, CLU Certifications. Address: 2812 Benton Boulevard, Minneapolis, Minnesota 55416.

MURPHY, DENNIS PERRY Occupation: Executive Vice President, Cummings Corporation. Education: Attended Elkins Institute of Electronics. Address: 306 South Schaefer, Appleton, Wisconsin 54915.

MURPHY, ELISABETH ANNE Occupation: Teacher of Deaf. Education: B.A., MacMurray College, 1973. Address: 1104 West White, Marion, Illinois 62959.

MURPHY, FRANCES L II Occupation: Associate Professor, Area Head of Journalism, State University College-Buffalo. Education: B.A., B.S., M.Ed. Address: 91 Deerfield, Buffalo, New York 14215.

MURPHY, JAMES M Occupation: Financial Management and Planning Executive. Education: Business. Address: 9 Court of Lagoon View, Northbrook, Illinois 60062.

MURPHY, JOYCE ANITA Occupation: Personnel Director. Education: Business Administration, Address: Rural Route 1, Box 157, Harrisburg, South Dakota 57032.

MURPHY, RUSSELL G Occupation: Law Professor. Education: B.A, University of Massachusetts; J.D., Suffolk University. Address: 85 Ripley Street, Newton, Massachusetts 02159.

MURPHY, SHEILA ELLEN Occupation: Management Development Specialist. Education: Ph.D., M.A., B.A. Address: 3701 East Monterosa Street #5, Phoenix, Arizona 85018.

MURPHY, SOLBRITT ELISABET Occupation: Director, Bureau, Maternal, Child Health. Education: M.D., M.P.H. Address: 15-A King Court, Selkirk, New York 12158.

MURPHY, THOMAS DEE Occupation: Minister, Counselor, Pastor. Education: B.S., University of Arkansas; Master of Divinity, Doctor of Minister, Luther Rice Seminary. Address: Post Office Box 455, Folkston, Georgia 31537.

MURPHY, WALTER YOUNG Occupation: President. Education: B.A., M.Div., Emory University; LL.D., Bethune College; D.D., LaGrange College. Address: 1102 Vernon Road, LaGrange, Georgia 30240.

MURRAY, BARBARA BATEMAN Occupation: Professor of Business. Education: Ph.D., M.A., M.B.A. Address: 33742 York Ridge Drive, Farmington Hill, Michigan 48018.

MURRAY, JOAN Occupation: Television News Broadcaster. Education: Address: 4525 Valley Ridge Avenue, Los Angeles, California 90008.

MURRAY, JOHN P Occupation: Director of Youth and Family Policy, The Boys Town Center. Education: Ph.D. Address: 5607 Leavenworth Street, Omaha, Nebraska 68106.

MURRAY, KAY L Occupation: Executive/Deputy Commissioner. Education: B.S. Public Administration, 1976. Address: 1145 East Hyde Park Boulevard, Chicago, Illinois 60615.

MURRAY, MAUREEN Occupation: Member of Religious Order; Provincial Leader of School Sisters of Notre Dame. Education: B.A. History, M.A. English. Address: Good Counsel Hill, Mankato, Minnesota 56001.

MURRAY-JACOBY, F CATHERINE Occupation: Writer. Education: Convent Sacred Heart of Mary. Address: 401 Peruvian Avenue, Palm Beach, Florida 33480.

MURRELL, SAM EDWIN JR Occupation: Lawyer. Education: J.D. Address: 3041 Westchester, Orlando, Florida 32803.

MURTY, KATTA GOPALAKRISHNA Occupation: Professor, University of Michigan. Education: Doctor of Philosophy, University of California-Berkeley. Address: 3311 Alton Court, Ann Arbor, Michigan 48105.

MUSSER, JEAN WILMER Occupation: Poet, Therapist, Counselor. Education: B.A., Smith College; M.A., Case Western Reserve University; M.Ed., University of Puget Sound. Address: 3408 North 25th, Tacoma, Washington 98406.

MUSSLEWHITE, JOYCE C HOLTER Occupation: Art Specialist, Realtor. Education: B.S.B., M.A.Ed. Colorado University. Address: Route 3, Box 480-A, Loveland, Colorado 80537.

MUSTARD, MARTHA JEAN Occupation: Professor of Tropical Botany. Education: Ph.D., M.S., B.S. Address: 1204 Placetas Avenue, Coral Gables, Florida 33146.

MUTH, ERIC P Occupation: Licensed Optician. Education: Ph.D. Address: 25 Parkland Place, Milford Connecticut 06460.

MUUSS, ROLF E Occupation: Professor, Author, Psychologist, Chairman Department of Sociology and Anthropology, Director Special Education, Goucher College. Education: Ph.D, University of Illinois, 1957; M.Ed. Western Maryland College, 1954; Attended Central Missouri State College, University of Hamburg, Germany; Teaching Diploma, Paedagogische Hochschule, Flensburg, 1951. Address: 1540 Pickett Road, Lutherville, Maryland 21093.

MYERS, JESSE J Occupation: Construction Executive, Lawyer. Education: B.S., J.D. Address: 341 South Shefford, Wichita, Kansas 67209.

MYERS, LUEBURDA JAMISON Occupation: Educator. Education: B.S., M.Ed., Additional Studies. Address: 333 Holcomb Drive, Shreveport, Louisiana 71103.

MYERS, MARY L Occupation: Minister, Teacher, Writer, Poet. Education: Business Administration, Doctor of Divinity. Address: 3427 Denson Place, Charlotte, North Carolina 28215.

MYERS, PHILLIP SAMUEL Occupation: Professor of Mechanical Engineering. Education: B.S. Mathematics and Commerce, B.S. and Ph.D. Mechanical Engineering. Address: 3210 Oxford Road, Madison, Wisconsin 53705.

MYERS, ROBERT EUGENE Occupation: Curriculum Coordinator. Education: Ed.D., M.A., A.B. Address: 2846 Northwest Angelica Drive, Corvallis, Oregon 97330.

MYERS, SHIRLEY S Occupation: Interior Designer and Consultant. Education: B.A., M.A. Address: 235 Pacific, Solana Beach, California 92075.

MYREN, RICHARD A Occupation: Professor, School of Justice, The American University, Washington, D.C. Education: J.D., B.S. Address: Route 1, Box 394, Purcellville, Virginia 22132.

N

NADIR, ZAKEE Occupation: H.R.S./Contract Manager, Performing Poet. Education: Student, College. Address: 159 Ashford Street, Brooklyn, New York 11207.

NADLER, BEVERLY Occupation: Director, Stop Smoking Center and Weight Loss Center; Lecturer; Author; Consultant. Education: Fashion Institute of Technology, 1954; Continuing Education, Queens College, 1956-58; Certification as Metabolic Technician, International Health Institute, 1978. Address: 177-31 Edgerton Road, Jamaica Estates, New York 11366.

NADLER, GERALD Occupation: Professor and Chairman of Department. Education: B.S.M.E., M.S.I.E., Ph.D. Address: 221 Tranquillo Road, Pacific Palisades, California 90272.

NAGATA, KENNETH M Occupation: Research Associate. Education: B.A. Botany, 1968; M.A. Geography, 1980. Address: 1655 Makaloa 1203, Honolulu, Hawaii 96814.

NAGLEE, DAVID INGERSOLL Occupation: College Professor. Education: B.A., B.D., M.A., Ph.D. Address: 804 Piney Woods, LaGrange, Georgia 30240.

NAGLEE, ELFRIEDE K Occupation: Clinical Supervisor. Education: Philadelphia General Hospital. Address: 804 Pineywoods Drive, LaGrange, Georgia 30240.

NAGY, MARTIN W Occupation: Executive Director, Community Arts Center. Education: B.F.A. Address: 3616 Mapleway Drive, Toledo, Ohio 43615.

NAKAMOTO, TETSUO Occupation: Assistant Professor of Physiology. Education: D.D.S., M.S., Ph.D. Address: Department of Physiology, Louisiana State University Medical Center, 1100 Florida Avenue, New Orleans, Lousiana 70119.

NAPLES, JOHN D Occupation: Physician, Gynecologic Surgeon. Education: A.B., Canisius College, 1955; M.D., Georgetown University, 1959. Address: 58 Dan Troy Drive, Williamsville, New York 14221.

NAPOLI, JOSEPH CHARLES Occupation: Psychiatrist, Administrator, Educator. Education: B.A., Fordham College, 1968; M.D., Georgetown University, 1972. Address: 2185 Lemoine Avenue, Fort Lee, New Jersey 07024.

NAQVI, ISHRAT HUSAIN Occupation: University Professor, Physicist Astronomer. Education: Ph.D. Nuclear Physics. Address: 3949-17th Avenue, Regina, Saskatchewan S4S 0B7 Canada.

NARVAEZ, AMALIA LOUISA Occupation: Teacher. Education: B.A. 1970, M.A. 1973, M.S. Guidance and Counseling 1983. Address: 86 Division Avenue, Spring Valley, New York 10977.

NASH, ROYSTON H Occupation: Music Director, Conductor. Education: L.R.A.M., A.R.A.M., A.R.C.M., B.Mus. Address: 87 Hinckley Circle, Osterville, Massachusetts 08655.

NASH-MORGAN, LEONORA ELIZABETH Occupation: Physician. Education: Bachelor of Arts, Master of Arts, Doctor of Medicine. Address: 3700 14th Street, Moline, Illinois 61265.

NATALINI, JOHN JOSEPH Occupation: Chairman and Teacher of Biology. Education: B.S., M.S., Ph.D. Address: 1860 Chestnut, Quincy, Illinois 62301.

NATHAN, LEONARD E Occupation: Teacher, Writer. Education: B.A., M.A., Ph.D. Address: 40 Beverly Road, Kensington, California 94707.

NATHAN, RONALD G Occupation: Director, Medical Psychology; Associate Professor. Address: 8467 Indian Hills Boulevard, Shreveport, Louisiana 71107.

NATHANIEL, ALVITA KAY Occupation: Registered Nurse, Facilitator for West Virginia Health Right; Part-time Staff Nurse. Education: B.S., M.S. Nursing. Address: 1033 Valley Road, Charleston, West Virginia 25302.

NATTKEMPER, C DON Occupation: Attorney-at-Law. Education: B.S., J.D., Indiana University. Address: 75 Monterey Avenue, Terre Haute, Indiana 47803.

NAUMER, JANET N Occupation: Director, Library, Media Center. Education: B.A., Pennsylvania State University; M.A., University of Denver; Ph.D., University of Colorado. Address: 33368 Tule Oak Drive, Porterville, California 93257.

NAVAJAS-SOUFFRONT, EMMA D Occupation: Director, Puerto Rico Federal Affairs Administration. Education: J.D. Address: 8101 Connecticut Avenue, Apartment N-402, Chevy Chase, Maryalnd 20815.

NAZARENO, JOSE P Occupation: Pathologist, Acupuncturist. Education: M.D. Address: 1445 Carnegie Drive, Binghamton, New York 13903.

NEAL, PATSY A Occupation: Art Critic, Educator, Writer. Education: B.A., M.A., Doctoral Candidate, University of Texas-Austin. Address: 522 Woodcrest, San Antonio, Texas 78209.

NEAL, STERLING Occupation: Chief of Police, Cuyahoga Bureau Joint Investigation. Education: Case Western Reserve University, 1970; M.E.D.C., 1976. Address: 9203 Bessemer Avenue, Cleveland, Ohio 44104.

NEEL, H BRYAN Occupation: Surgeon, Scientist, Educator. Education: B.S., M.D., Ph.D. Address: 828 Southwest Eighth Street, Rochester, Minnesota 55902.

NEEPER, RALPH ARNOLD Occupation: Computer Specialist. Education: B.S. Psychology, 1963; M.S. Photogrammetry, Purdue University, 1972. Address: 13530 Delaney Road, Woodbridge, Virginia 22193.

NEHER, LESLIE IRWIN Occupation: Retired Professional Engineer. Education: B.S. Electrical Engineering, Purdue University. Address: 113 East South A Street, Gas City, Indiana 46933.

NEIDELL, NORMAN S Occupation: President, Zenith Exploration Company, Inc. Education: Ph.D., Cambridge, 1964; B.A., New York University, 1959. Address: 13054 Taylorcrest, Houston, Texas 77079.

NEIDERT, KALO EDWARD Occupation: University Professor. Education: B.S.B.A., M.S.B.A., Washington University; University of Minnesota. Address: 2300 Balsam Street, Reno, Nevada 89509.

NELSON, ALAN JAN Occupation: Film Production Company President. Education: B.S., M.S. Address: 6356 Ventura Canyon, Van Nuys, California 91401.

NELSON, ARNOLD B Occupation: Head, Department of Animal and Range Sciences, New Mexico State University. Education: B.S., M.S., Ph.D. Address: 2010 Crescent Drive, Las Cruces, New Mexico 88005.

NELSON, JOHN FRANKLIN Occupation: Professor and Chairman Department of Oral Diagnosis, Baylor College of Dentistry. Education: B.S., D.D.S., M.Ed. Address: #4 Wendram Bluff, Iowa City, Iowa 52240.

NELSON, MARGARET R Occupation: Lawyer. Education: B.A. magna cum laude, Brigham Young University, 1973; J.D., J. Reuben Clark Law School,

Brigham Young University, 1976. Address: 210 West 800 South, Orem, Utah 84058.

NELSON, NEIL D Occupation: Biotechnology Program Leader, Research Plant Physiologist, Forest Sciences Laboratory. Education: B.S., Iowa State University; M.S., Ph.D., University of Wisconsin. Address: 7014 Firetower Road, Rhinelander, Wisconsin 54501.

NELSON, RALPH ERWIN Occupation: President. Education: Ph.D., Columbia Pacific University, 1984; M.H.S., The University of Sarasota, 1983. Address: Post Office Box 11255, Bradenton, Florida 34282-1255.

NELSON, RICHARD KENT Occupation: Professor. Education: B.A., M.B.A., C.P.A. Address: 15 Daisy Lane, Orchard Park, New York 14127.

NELSON, RUSSELL GENE Occupation: Senior Research and Development Engineer. Education: B.S.E.E., M.E.E. Address: 708 Stoneledge, Friendswood, Texas 77546.

NELSON, SUSAN BLOUROCK Occupation: Executive Director, National Association of Private Schools for Exceptional Children. Education: B.A., M.Ed., Ph.D., University of Maryland. Address: 8038 Inverness Ridge Road, Potomac, Maryland 28054.

NELSON, VIRGINIA L Occupation: Retired Philatelic Journalist. Address: 501 South Oak Street, Hillsboro, Illinois 62049.

NELSON, WERNER L Occupation: Senior Vice President/Agronomist, Potash and Phosphate Institute. Education: B.S. 1937, M.S. 1938, University of Illinois; Ph.D., Ohio State University, 1940. Address: 1800 Happy Hollow Road, West, Lafayette, Indiana 47906.

NELSON-HUMPHRIES, TESSA Occupation: Professor, Writer. Education: B.A., M.A., Ph.D. Address: York Cottage, Williamsburg, Kentucky 40769.

NEMCHIN, ROBERT G Occupation: Industrial Safety and Health. Education: B.A. Biology, 1959; M.S. Biochemistry, 1965. Address: 4426 Rockcrest Drive, Fairfax, Virginia 22032.

NEPO, MARK Occupation: Poet, Professor. Education: D.A. English, B.A. Theatre. Address: 116 Horizon View Drive, East Greenbush, New York 12061.

NES, WILLIAM R Occupation: W.L. Obold Professor of Biological Sciences. Education: B.A. 1946, Ph.D. 1950. Address: 10 Tanglewood Circle, Rose Valley, Pennsylvania 19086.

NESBIT, PHYLLIS S Occupation: District Judge, Baldwin County. Education: B.S. Chemistry, Juris Doctor. Address: 302 Creek Drive, Fairhope, Alabama 36532.

NESBITT, JOHN ARTHUR SR Occupation: Professor Recreation Education Program, The University of Iowa; President Special Recreation, Inc. Education: B.A. Journalism, Michigan State University, 1955; M.A. Therapeutic Recreation 1961, D.Ed. Recreation 1968, Teachers College, Columbia University. Address: 362 Koser Avenue, Iowa City, Iowa 52240.

NeSMITH, VERA C Occupation: Retired Administrator. Education: Further Study. Address: 1912 Weber Street, Orlando, Florida 32803.

NESS, HOWARD L Occupation: Professor of Accounting. Education: B.B.A., M.B.A., J.D. Address: 2365 Goodard Road, Toledo, Ohio 43606.

NESS, LARRY DEAN Occupation: Director, Irrigation Systems, Lindsay International Sales Corporation. Education: A.A., Austin State Junior College; B.S. Agricultural Engineering, North Dakota.

Address: 14131 Prestonwood Forest Drive, Houston, Texas 77070.

NETI, SUDHAKAR Occupation: Associate Professor of Mechanical Engineering. Education: Ph.D. Mechanical Engineering; M.S. Mechanical Engineering. Address: 3524 Moravian Court, Bethlehem, Pennsylvania 18017.

NETTLESHIP, PATRICIA SHARYN Occupation: Chairman of the Board, North Pacific Investment Group. Education: Stephens College, University of Missouri, Harvard Graduate School of Business.

NEUCKS, HOWARD C Occupation: Physician, Radiation Oncologist. Education: B.A., M.D. Address: 2024 Cureton Drive, Urbana, Illinois 61801.

NEUHAUS, JAY J Occupation: Dentist. Education: B.S., City College of New York, 1972; D.D.S., N.Y.U.C.D., 1975. Address: 8 Gramercy Park, New York, New York 10003.

NEUMANN, GERWIN W W Occupation: Neurological Surgeon. Education: M.D. Address: 37 Woodridge Road, Wayland, Massachusetts 01778.

NEUMANN, JOACHIM PETER Occupation: Associate Professor of Metallurgical Engineering, University of Alabama. Education: Diplom-Ingenieur, Ph.D. Address: 12109 Northwood Lake, Northport, Alabama 35476.

NEUSNER, JACOB Occupation: University Professor. Education: A.B., Harvard College, 1953. Address: Brown University, Providence, Rhode Island 02912-1826.

NEVIUS, FRANKLIN CHALMERS JR Occupation: Finance and Planning Director. Education: Bachelor of Science in Chemical Engineering, Princeton University. Address: #9 North Forbes Park, Makati, MM, Philippines.

NEVLING, HARRY REED Occupation: Personnel Director. Education: A.A. Business, B.A. Business Administration Economics. Address: 1432 Brookfield Drive, Longmont, Colorado 80501.

NEWBERG, ALAN Occupation: Professor and Chairman, Department of Art, Eastern Montana College. Education: B.A., M.A., M.F.A. Address: 925 Burlington Avenue, Billings, Montana 59102.

NEWBERN, CAPTOLIA DENT Occupation: Minister, Educator, Lecturer, Writer, Ecumenical Affairs Participant. Education: B.S.Ed., B.Mus., M.S.S.W., Ed.D., M.Div., D.Min. Address: 5833 Cobbs Creek Parkway, Philadelphia, Pennsylvania 19143.

NEWBORG, BARBARA C Occupation: Physician. Education: A.B., Swarthmore College; M.D., John Hopkins School of Medicine. Address: Box 3385, Duke University Medical Center, Durham, North Carolina 27710.

NEWBY, JOHN M Occupation: President, Central Wesleyan College. Education: Ph.D. Address: Post Office Box 408, CWC, Central, South Carolina 29630.

NEWBY, JOHN R Occupation: Principal Research Metallurgist. Education: M.S. Metallurgical Engineering; Metallurgical Engineer; B.A. Chemistry. Address: 100 Marymont Court, Middletown, Ohio 45042.

NEWCOMB, MARY JANE Occupation: Coordinator of Institutional Research, Cleveland Chiropractic College. Education: D.C., Cleveland Chiropracic College, 1946; B.S. Education, University of Kansas, 1963; M.A. English, Kansas State University, 1964; Ph.D. Education, University of Kansas, 1970. Address: 8504 Booth, Raytown, Missouri 64138.

NEWELL, DONALD LEWIS Occupation: Investment Consultant, Real Estate Broker. Education:

B.S. Business Administration, M.B.A. Address: Post Office Box 108, Unity, Maine 04988.

NEWKIRK, JOHN BURT Occupation: Professor and Corporation President. Education: D.Sc., Bachelor of Metallurgical Engineering, M.S. Address: 24400 Snow Valley Road, Evergreen, Colorado 80439.

NEWKIRK, NATE A Occupation: Management Consultant. Education: B.B.A., M.B.A. Address: 1550 Oak Hills Drive, Colorado Springs, Colorado 80919.

NEWLIN, JANINE JORDAN Occupation: Kitchen and Bath Design Consultant. Education: B.A., Chatham College; Kitchen Design Diplomas; N.K.B.A. and S.C.K.D. Address: 42 Whippoorwill Road, Chappaqua, New York 10514.

NEWMAN, DEAN G Occupation: Vice President, Human Resources and Communications. Education: B.A., Simpson College, 1950; M.B.A., Stanford University, 1952. Address: 6028 Berne Circle, Edina, Minnesota 55436.

NEWMAN, HARRY Occupation: Chief Financial Officer. Education: B.B.A., M.B., C.P.A. Address: 55 Charles Lindbergh Boulevard, Mitchel Field, New York 11553.

NEWMAN, M D Occupation: Businessman, Rancher. Education: M.B.A., B.A., College of William & Mary. Address: Amwell Road, R.D. #1, Box 43, Hopewell, New Jersey 08525.

NEWSOME, TERESA I Occupation: Instructor, University of Kentucky. Education: B.A. Psychology, M.A., M.S. Address: 1889 Courtland Drive, Lexington, Kentucky 40505.

NEWTON, WALLACE BERKELEY Occupation: Banker. Education: B.S., M.B.A., Virginia Polytechnic Institute. Address: 12303 Ashton Glen Court, Richmond, Virginia 23233.

NEZU, ARTHUR MAGUTH Occupation: Clinical Psychologist, Professor, University Administrator. Education: B.A., M.A., Ph.D. Address: 452 Churchill Road, Teaneck, New Jersey 07666.

NG, KWANG J Address: 759 Ash Court, Fairfield, California 94533.

NG, REBECCA LEN Occupation: Optometrist. Education: O.D., B.S. Address: 25236 Arcadian, Misson Viego, California 92691.

NGUYEN, VIETSON V Occupation: Mathematician. Education: University of Wisconsin, University of Chicago. Address: 23-04 30 Drive, Astoria, New York 11102.

NGUYEN-VAN-HUY, PIERRE Occupation: Professor. Education: Ph.D. Address: 47-22 163 Street, Flushing, New York 11358.

NIAGER, PAUL DAVID Occupation: Counselor. Education: B.A. Psychology; Advanced Studies Certificate, Biblical Studies. Address: 4620 Forest Lane, Chattanooga, Tennessee 37343.

NICEWANGER, WILLIAM B Occupation: President, Business Telephone Systems of America, Inc. Education: B.S.E.E. 1963, M.B.A. 1965. Address: 324 East Sycamore, Columbus, Ohio 43206.

NICHOLS, MARY WILLIAMS Occupation: Artist/Owner, In-House Gallery. Education: B.S., Northwestern Oklahoma State University; Master's Degree, University of Maryland. Address: 2809 Northwest 63rd, Oklahoma City, Oklahoma 73116.

NICHOLSON, JOAN MARTIN Occupation: Senior Liaison Officer, U.N. Environment Programmes. Address: 5508 39th Street, North West, Washington, D.C. 20015.

NICHOLSON, JOSEPH M Occupation: Professor of Music. Education: B.Mus., T.W.C.; M.M.E., N.T.S.U.; D.M.A., U.M.K.C. Address: Route 5, Box 462-3, Springfield, Missouri 65803.

NICHOLSON, ROSEMARY T Occupation: District Manager, Social Security Administration. Education: Attended Georgia State University, Edison Community College. Address: 1311 Southeast 34th Street, Cape Coral, Florida 33904.

NICHOLSON, THEODORE ROOSEVELT Education: M.B.A. Management Marketing, 1984; B.A. Political Science, 1969. Address: 6511 Ross Street, Philadelphia, Pennsylvania 19119.

NICKERSON, SCOTT PHILLIP Occupation: Student. Education: B.S.E.E., Norwich, 1984. Address: 73 Skylark Road, Portland, Maine 04103.

NICOL, BETTY LOU Occupation: State President, Ohio Federation of Republican Women. Education: B.S. Education. Address: 12696 S.R. 38, Marysville, Ohio 43040.

NIEDERJOHN, RUSSELL JAMES Occupation: Professor of Electrical Engineering and Computer Science. Education: B.S.E.E., M.S.E.E., Ph.D., University of Massachusetts. Address: 2545 Brookside Parkway, New Berlin, Wisconsin 53151.

NIEDZIELSKI, HENRY Z Occupation: Educator, Professor Linguistics. Education: B.A. 1959, M.A. 1963, Ph.D. 1964, University of Connecticut. Address: 419 Keoniana 904, Honolulu, Hawaii 96815.

NIELSEN, KAREN E JACOBSEN Occupation: Reading Coordinator, DoDDS Mediteranean. Education: B.S., M.Ed., Ed.D. (Secondary Certificate). Address: 97 Avde de San Luis 9°A, Madrid 33, Spain.

NIELSON, VEIGH J Occupation: Management Consultant. Education: B.S., University of Utah; M.B.A., Harvard University. Address: 2100 Skyline Drive, Bartlesville, Oklahoma 7406.

NIEMEYER, GROVER CHARLES Occupation: Film Historian. Education: B.A., M.A., Ph.D. Address: 1616 18 Northwest Washington, D.C. 20009.

NIESSEN, RICHARD Occupation: Associate Professor of Apologetics, Christian Heritage College. Education: B.A., Th.B., M.A., Ph.D. Candidate. Address: 10457 Ken Lane, Santee, California 92071.

NIGRO, ARMAND M Occupation: Professor of Religious Studies, Gonzaga University.

NIKITINE, ANDRÉ V Occupation: President, Shopping Center Management. Education: M.B.A. Business, B.A. Economics. Address: 2305 Laurel Street, Cond. Park Boulevard, Apartment 412, S.J., Puerto Rico 00913.

NIKKEL, VERNON LLOYD Occupation: Protective Structures and Institutional Turf Products Manufacturing Company Executive. Education: Bachelor of Music Education, Bethany College, 1950; M.S., Emporia State College, 1961. Address: Box 67, 230 South Weaver, Hesston, Kansas 67062.

NILSSON, PATRICIA JOAN KALKOWSKI Occupation: Assistant Professor, School of Nursing, Creighton University. Education: R.N., B.S.N., M.S. Address: 609 South 93 Street, Omaha, Nebraska 96114.

NIMBERG, GERALD Occupation: Financial and Investment Counselor. Education: M.B.A. Finance, C.F.P. Financial Planning. Address: 408 Queen Anne Road, Cherry Hill, New Jersey 08003.

NINOS, VALERY Occupation: College Student. Address: 450 Caracas Drive, Merritt Island, Florida 32953.

NIP, WAI-KIT Occupation: Associate Professor of Product Science and Technology. Education: B.S. 1962, M.S. 1965, Ph.D. 1969. Address: 1615 Wilder Avenue #304, Honolulu, Hawaii 96822.

NIRENBERG, KENNETH C Occupation: Data

Processing Manager. Education: B.A. Economics, Brandeis University. Address: 12812 Poquoson Drive, Austin, Texas 78727.

NISBETT, SUSAN ISAACS Occupation: Journalist, Dance Critic. Education: B.A., M.Phil. Address: 837 West Huron, Ann Arbor, Michigan 48103.

NISSENSON, NORMA Occupation: Clinical Psychologist. Education: B.S., M.A. Psychology, Northwestern University. Address: 966 Princeton Avenue, Highland Park, Illinois 60035.

NIST, JOAN STIDHAM Occupation: University Professor. Education: B.A., M.A., Ed.D. Address: 620 Florence Drive, Auburn, Alabama 36830.

NIXON, FRANK EDWIN Occupation: Newspaper Executive. Education: Further Studies. Address: 1005 Bay Vista Drive, Tarpon Spring, Florida 38589.

NIXON, GERALD EUGENE Occupation: Controller, Part-time College Instructor. Education: A.A., B.S. Accounting, C.P.A. Address: 3804 N.E. 140th Street, Edmond, Oklahoma 73034.

NIXON, ROBERT PLEASANTS Occupation: Retired Executive. Education: A.B., Duke University, 1935. Address: 630 Elm Drive, Bluffton, Indiana 46714.

NJOKU, ENI GERALD Occupation: Research Scientist. Education: B.A., M.S., Ph.D. Address: 744 Magnolia Avenue, Pasadena, California 91106.

NOBES, LEON D Occupation: Assistant Professor Emeritus, Western Michigan University. Address: 2033 Crozier Avenue, Muskegon, Michigan 49441.

NOBLE, FRANCES E Occupation: Author, Retired Professor. Education: B.A., M.A., Ph.D. Address: 2915 North East Center Avenue, Fort Lauderdale, Florida 33308.

NOBLE, JAMES V Occupation: Lawyer. Education: Attended University of New Mexico, 1940-43; LL.B. 1949, J.D. 1968, University of Colorado. Address: 615 East Barcelona, Santa Fe, New Mexico.

NOBLE, WESTON HENRY Occupation: Professor of Music, Luther College. Education: B.A., Luther College, 1943; M.M., University of Michigan, 1953. Address: 602 Mound, Decorah, Ioa 52101.

NOBLE, YVONNE YOLANDA Occupation: Teacher, Counselor. Education: B.S., M.E. Address: Route 2, Box 236, Luverne, Alabama 36049.

NOBLES, BEVERLY B Occupation: Banker. Education: A.A., B.B.A., B.A. Address: 7365 Eastover Drive, Walls, Mississippi 38680.

NOCITA, FRANK EDWARD Occupation: Licensed Psychologist. Education: Ph.D. Address: 3808 Riverside Drive, Suite 202, Burbank, California 91505.

NOEL, ROGER A Occupation: University Lecturer. Education: M.A., Ph.D., Licence. Address: 7329 Princeton, St. Louis, Missouri 63130.

NOHE, B Occupation: Health Care Management. Education: B.A., M.P.H. Address: 20 Springs Road, Bedford, Massachusetts 01730.

NOKES, MARY TRIPLETT Occupation: Teacher, Counselor. Education: M.A. Education. Address: 41235 North West 57, Oklahoma City, Oklahoma 73112.

NOLEN, MAYE ETTA Occupation: Assistant Professor of Nursing. Education: R.N., B.S., M.S. Nursing. Address: 1508 Park Circle, Oklahoma City, Oklahoma 73111.

NOLEN, MILTON WAYNE Occupation: Pastor. Education: B.A., M.Div. D.Min. Address: 173 Sylvan Road, Walnut Creek, California 94596.

NOLL, RHONA S Occupation: College Professor. Education: B.A., M.S. Education, Ph.D. Address: 477 F.D.R. Drive, New York, New York 11002.

NONG Occupation: Artist, City Official.

Education: LL.B. Address: 999 Green Street, No. 2701, San Francisco, California 94018.

NORBACK, CRAIG T Occupation: Author, Book Producer. Education: B.S., Washington University, 1967. Address: 1013 Hughes Drive, Hamilton Square, New Jersey 08690.

NORDBY, EUGENE JORGEN Occupation: Orthopedic Surgeon. Education: A.B., M.D. Address: 6234 South Highlands, Madison, Wisconsin 53705.

NORMAN, CHARLES H Occupation: Radio Station Owner. Education: B.A. Address: 4400 Lindell, St. Louis, Missouri 63108.

NORMAN, JOHN E Occupation: Senior Staff Landman. Education: B.S.B.A., M.B.A. Address: 2710 South Jay Street, Denver, Colorado 80227.

NORRELL, OLIVER LEWIS III Occupation: Attorney-at-Law. Education: B.A. Speech Communication, J.D. Address: 10221 Sauna Drive, Richmond, Virginia 23236.

NORRIS, JOHN HART Occupation: Lawyer. Education: B.A., Indiana University, 1964; J.D., University of Michigan, 1967. Address: 1325 Buckingham Street, Birmingham, Michigan 48008.

NORTHRUP, DONALD Occupation: Bank Vice President, Attorney. Education: B.A., Tufts University, 1963; B.C., J.D., Northwestern University. Address: 47 Lovell, Melrose, Massachusetts 02176.

NORTON, ALAN PAUL Occupation: Executive Management Consultant. Address: 59 Huntford Road, Calgary, Alberta, T2K 348.

NORVELL, JOHN EDMONDSON III Occupation: Professor, Chairman, Oral Roberts University. Education: B.S., University of Charleston; M.S., West Virginia University; Ph.D., Ohio State University. Address: 9909 South Kingston Avenue, Tulsa, Oklahoma 74137.

NOVAK, DENNIS E Occupation: Physician. Education: B.A., M.D. Address: 1001 West Lacey Road, Post Office Box 780, Forked River, New Jersey 08731.

NOVACK, RICHARD M Occupation: Corporate Officer, Engineer. Education: Civil Engineering, University of Massachusetts. Address: 24775 Hilltop Drive, Beachwood, Ohio 44122.

NOVICK, DAVID Occupation: Vice President and Area Manager, Civil Engineering Consultants. Education: B.S. 1948, M.S. 1954, Columbia University. Address: 30 Cherry Lane, Wynnewood, Pennsylvania 19102.

NUCCI, ANNAMARIA Occupation: Physician, Musician. Education: M.D., Ph.D. Address: 5 Westview Court, Cedar Grove, New Jersey 07009.

NUMAJIRI, SATORU SAM Occupation: Senior Scientist, Head of Resynthesis, Chemist. Education: B.A. Biology, B.A. Chemistry, M.A. Chemistry. Address: 2821 Southgate Drive, Fort Worth, Texas 76133.

NUMANO, ALLEN STANISLAUS M Occupation: Industrial Designer, Violinist, B & W Artist. Education: Attended St. Joseph's College, Colombo, Ceylon; Oxford and R. C. of Music, London, England. Address: Post Office Box 2266, Santa Barbara, California 93120.

NUNAMAKER, ROBERT ROYAL Occupation: Chief Engineer. Education: B.S.M.E., Georgia Institute of Technology, 1957. Address: 2592 Orinda, San Jose, California 95121.

NUNLEY, CHARLES EUGENE Occupation: Superintendent, Arlington Public Schools. Education: B.S., M.Ed., Ed.S., Ed.D. Address: 3907 Chesterbrook Road, Arlington, Virginia 22207.

NUREYEV, JAIME M LEE Occupation: Private Investigator. Education: A.A., Masters Criminal

Justice. Address: 11750 Southwest 22 Court, Davie, Florida 33325.

NUSS, SHIRLEY A Occupation: Sociologist, Consultant, Author, Lecturer. Education: B.A. 1969, M.A. 1975, Ph.D. 1975, University of Colorado. Address: 4327 West Buena Vista, Detroit, Michigan 48238.

NUSSEL, EDWARD JOSEPH Occupation: Associate Dean, University of Toledo. Education: B.S. Education, M.Ed., Ed.D. Address: 3309 Cheltenham, Toledo, Ohio 43606.

NYE, BERNARD C Occupation: Dean Business Division, Columbus Technical Institute. Education: B.Sc., Ph.D., The Ohio State University; M.Sc., Bowling Green State University. Address: 315 East Dunedin Road, Columbus, Ohio 43214.

NYLAND, LAWRENCE L Occupation: Superintendent of Schools. Education: Ph.D. Educational Administration. Address: 2507 Rd. 60, Pasco, Washington 99301.

NYLES, ROBERT DAVID Occupation: Psychologist. Education: B.A., University California, 1949; M.A., University of London, 1955; Ph.D., 1956. Address: Box 621, Inverness, California 94937.

O

OATES, ELAINE Occupation: Educational Media Center Librarian. Education: B.S., North Carolina A&T State University; M.S.L.S., Atlanta University; Ph.D., Kansas State University. Address: 2250 Holly Hall #389, Houston, Texas 77054.

OBER, STUART ALAN Occupation: President of Securities Investigations, Inc. Education: B.A., Wesleyan University; License, The Sorbonne, University of Paris; M.B.A., City University of New York. Address: Post Office Box 888, Woodstock, New York 12498.

OBERT, CHARLES FRANK Occupation: Banker. Education: Attended Ohio State University. Address: 6498 Creekside Trail, Solon, Ohio 44139.

OBICHERE, BONIFACE IHEWUNWA Occupation: Professor of History, University of California; Editor and Founder, *Journal of African Studies*. Education: B.A., M.A., D.Phil. Address: 973 Keniston Avenue, Los Angeles, California 90019.

O'BRIEN, DANIEL WILLIAM Occupation: Lawyer, Business Executive. Education: B.S.L., LL.B. Address: 685 Linwood Avenue, St. Paul, Minnesota 55105.

O'BRIEN, G PETER Occupation: Investment Banker. Education: A.B., Colgate University, 1967; M.B.A., Columbia Business School, 1971. Address: 41 Leonard Avenue, Riverside, Connecticut 06878.

O'BRIEN, GENE R Occupation: Marketing Communications. Education: B.S.E.E., New Jersey Institute of Technology, 1962; M.B.A., Rutgers University, 1967. Address: Post Office Box 101, Princeton Junction, New Jersey 08550.

O'BRIEN, LAWRENCE FRANCIS Occupation: Commissioner, National Basketball Association. Education: LL.B., Northeastern University. Address: 860 United Nations Plaza, New York, New York 10017.

O'BRIEN, PAMELA RENEÉ Occupation: Area Coordinator. Education: A.B., M.A. Address: 2605 South Indiana, Chicago, Illinois 60616.

O'BRIEN, ROBERT T Occupation: Professor and Chairman, Department of Biology, New Mexico State University. Education: B.S., M.S., Ph.D. Address: 2901 Karen Drive, Las Cruces, New Mexico 88001.

OCKERMAN, HERBERT W Occupation: Professor, Ohio State University. Education: B.S., M.S., University of Kentucky; Ph.D., North Carolina State University. Address: 4250 Kendale Road, Columbus, Ohio 43220.

O'CONNELL, AGNES ANNE NAHMIE Occupation: Educator, Researcher, Author. Education: A.B., M.S., PhD. Address: 50 Inglewood Lane, Matawan, New Jersey 07747.

O'CONNELL, DANIEL CRAIG Occupation: Jesuit Priest, Professor of Psychology. Education: A.B. 1951, Ph.L. 1952, A.M. 1953, S.T.M. 1960, St. Louis University; Ph.D., University of Illinois, 1963.

O'CONNELL, JOHN (SEAN) Occupation: Catholic Priest, Doctoral Student. Education: B.A.; A.C.P. Diploma (London); M.Ed.Sc.; F.C.P. (London); Student, University of California-Los Angeles. Address: Box 887, Toyopa Drive, Pacific Palisades, California 90272.

O'CONNOR, EDWARD GERARD Occupation: Sales Executive. Education: B.S. Business. Address: 634 Dudley Road, Edgewood, Kentucky 41071.

OCWIEJA, REGINA Occupation: Vice President, Polish Roman Catholic Union of America. Address: 4256 South Mozart Street, Chicago, Illinois 60632.

ODELL, GEORGE V Occupation: Professor of Biochemistry, Department of Biochemistry, Oklahoma State University. Address: Department of Biochemistry, Oklahoma State University, Stillwater, Oklahoma 74074.

O'DESKY, RICHARD NEIL Occupation: Senior Associate, National Occupational Medical Associates; Director, Division of Occupational Medicine, Cincinnati, Ohio. Education: B.S. Civil Engineering, University of Toledo, 1970; M.D., University of Health Sciences, College of Osteopathic Medicine, 1978; M.S. Community and Industrial Medicine, The University of Cincinnati, 1984; Internship Certificate, The Brentwood Hospital, Cleveland, Ohio, 1979; Residency Certificate Occupational Medicine, The University of Cincinnati, Institute of Environmental Health, Department of Occupational Medicine. Address: 2351 Madison Road, Cincinnati, Ohio 45208.

ODOM, MARJORIE MORGAN Occupation: Secondary School Librarian. Education: B.A. Library Science, 1964; M.A. Education, 1979. Address: Post Office Box 8374, San Antonio, Texas 78208.

O'DONNELL, ARLENE CAROL Occupation: Environmental Scientist. Education: B.S. Zoology, Environmental Science; M.S. Civil Engineering and Urban/Environmental Policy. Address: 17 Walnut Street, Medford, Massachusetts 02155.

O'DONNELL, ROBERT DANIEL Occupation: United States Air Force Officer (Colonel), Psychologist. Education: B.S., St. Joseph's College; M.A.; Ph.D., Fordham University. Address: 6990 Peters Pike, Dayton, Ohio 45414.

O'DOWDY, DANNY MICHAEL Occupation: Artist. Education: M.F.A. Address: 4224 Ocean Drive, Corpus Christi, Texas 78411.

ODVARKO, JAROSLAVA Occupation: Doctor of Chiropractic. Education: D.C. Address: 1546 Brown Street, Bettendorf, Iowa 52722.

OFSOWITZ, PAULA JOYCE Occupation: Computer-System Programmer. Education: Programming Certificate, Control Data Institute. Address: 485 Northlake, San Jose, California 95117.

OGATA, JEFFERY MORIMASA Occupation: Attorney. Education: B.A. Economics, J.D. Address: 1258 Pebblewood Drive, Sacramento, California 95833.

OGG, WILSON REID Occupation: Curator in Residence. Education: B.A. 1949, LL.B., J.D., University of California-Berkeley. Address: 1104 Keith Avenue, Berkeley, California 94708.

O'HAIR, MADALYN MAYS Occupation: Lawyer. Education: B.A., J.D. Address: Post Office Box 2117, Austin, Texas 78768.

O'HARA, MORGAN Occupation: Artist. Education: M.A. Address: 273 Green Street, San Francisco, California 941.

OHMAN, JOHN M Occupation: Attorney, Shareholder. Education: B.S.B.A., Creighton University; J.D. Address: 190 Fieldstream, Idaho Falls, Idaho.

OHRENSTEIN, ROMAN A Occupation: Professor of Economics, Rabbi, Lecturer. Education: M.A. Economics, Ph.D. Economics, M.H.L. Address: 28-74 208 Street, Bayside, New York 11300.

OIEN, ARTHUR CARLISLE Occupation: Educator, Historian. Education: B.A., Concordia College; M.A., University of Minnesota, 1954. Address: 220 Bedford Street, Bridgewater, Massachusetts 02324.

OISTEANU, VALERY Occupation: Writer. Education: Master's Degree Chemistry; Attended School of Broadcasting. Address: 170 2nd Avenue, New

York City, New York 10003.

OJO, FRANK Occupation: Reporter/Supervisor, Texas State University. Education: Associate Degree Public Affairs. Address: 3201 Wheeler Avenue, Apartment 174, Houston, Texas 77004.

OKAGBAA, OBITOR GEOFFREY Occupation: University Professor, University of Cincinnati. Education: B.S. Engineering, M.S., Ph.D. Engineering. Address: 2075 Clifton Avenue, Cincinnati, Ohio 45219.

OKOYE, RENEÉ L Occupation: Occupational Therapist. Education: B.S., M.S.H.S. Address: 59 Ford Drive West, Massapegua, New York 11758.

OKRAH, PETER O Occupation: Student, Trainee in Oceanography. Education: College Student. Address: 1377 Singing Trees, Memphis, Tennessee 38116.

OLDS, GLENN ALVERO Occupation: President, Alaska Pacific University. Education: A.B., Willamette University, 1942; B.D., Garrett Theological Seminary, 1945; M.A., Northwestern University, 1945; Ph.D. Philosophy, Yale University, 1948. Address: 4101 University Drive, Anchorage, Alaska 99508.

OLDS, SALLY WENDKOS Occupation: Author. Education: B.A., University of Pennsylvania. Address: 25 North Washington Street, Port Washington, New York 11050.

O'LEARY, PATRICIA FRANCES Occupation: Consultant, Division of Health Sciences. Education: B.S.N., M.P.H. Address: 200 Barington Hills Road, Chapel Hill, North Carolina 27514.

OLGAS, KASSIE ANN Occupation: Registered Nurse. Education: B.S. 1961. Address: 22 South Taylor Street, Manchester, New Hampshire 03103.

OLIVER, LORENE H Occupation: Retired Elementary Principal. Education: B.S. Education, M.E. Address: 901 Foch, Ranger, Texas 76470.

OLIVER, MARVIN E Occupation: Professor of Education. Education: Ph.D., Ed.M., B.Ed., B.S. Address: 210 6th Street, Cheney, Washington 99004.

OLLING, GUSTAV J Occupation: Professor, Chairman, Bradley University. Education: B.S., M.S., M.A. Ph.D. Address: 2901 North Bigelow, Peoria, Illinois 61606.

OLM, KENNETH W Occupation: University Professor. Education: B.A. Economics, Pomona College; M.A. Economics, University of New Mexico; Ph.D. Management, University of Texas. Address: 2706 Macken, Austin, Texas 78703.

OLMSTED, MAXINE BLAKEMORE Occupation: Investigator and Chairman Scholarship Program for Artes Bellas. Education: B.A. Drama. Address: 8531 North 11th Avenue, Phoenix, Arizona 85021.

OLSEN, DAGNE B Occupation: State Representative. Education: B.S. Education. Address: R.R. 1, Manvel, North Dakota 58256.

OLSEN, RICHARD G Occupation: Professor. Education: B.S., M.S., Ph.D. Address: 2255 Street, Route 56, London, Ohio 43140.

OLSON, JAMES ALLEN Occupation: Professor and Chairman, Department of Biochemistry and Biophysics, Iowa State University. Education: B.S., Ph.D. Address: 2409 Timberland Road, Ames, Iowa 50010.

OLSON, JANET LEE M Occupation: Corporate Controller. Address: 10720 South Laramie, Oaklawn, Illinois 60453.

OLSON, JOHN M Occupation: Private Attorney, State Senator. Education: B.A., J.D., University of North Dakota. Address: 1835 North 21st Street, Bismarck, North Dakota 58501.

OLSON, MARLIN L Occupation: Associate Professor. Education: Ph.D. Candidate. Address: 3936 Honeybrook, Grandville, Michigan 49418.

OLSON, OSCAR E Occupation: Biochemist. Education: B.S., M.S., Ph.D. Address: 1625 Elmwood Drive, Brookings, South Dakota 57006.

OLSON, TOBY Occupation: Novelist, Poet, Associate Professor of English. Education: B.A., Occidental College; M.A., Long Island University. Address: 329 South Juniper Street, Philadephia, Pennsylvania 19107.

O'MEARA, SARA ELIZABETH Occupation: Chairman of the Board, Child Help U.S.A./ International. Address: 5425 Shirley Avenue, Tarzana, California 91356.

O'NEAL, RUTH Occupation: Associate Professor of Pediatrics, Bowman Gray School of Medicine. Education: A.B., Transylvania University, 1939; M.D., Medical College of Virginia, 1943; M.S. Pediatrics, Mayo Foundation Fellow in Pediatrics, 1948. Address: 445 Springdale Avenue, Winston-Salem, North Carolina 27104.

O'NEILL, PATRICIA M Occupation: School Psychologist. Education: M.A. Clinical Psychology, Ph.D. School Psychology. Address: 75 Miles Avenue, Albertson, New York 11507.

O'NEILL, RICHARD T Occupation: Professor of Chemistry, Department of Chemistry, Xavier University. Education: B.S., Loyola University; M.S., Ph.D., Carnegie Institute of Technology. Address: 6249 Beech View Circle, Cincinnati, Ohio 45207.

OOSTING, MARY ROBINSON Occupation: Tapestry Artist. Education: B.A., University of Tennessee. Address: 857 South Oak Street, Ukiah, California 94582.

OPENSHAW, CALVIN R Occupation: Practice General and Thoracic Surgery. Education: B.S. 1942, M.D. 1944, M.S. Surgery 1952. Address: 1824 North Main Street, Hutchinson, Kansas 67502.

OPENSHAW, DALE KIM Occupation: Assistant Professor of Family and Human Development, Director Marriage and Family Therapy, Utah State University. Address: 1152 East Mountain Road, Logan, Utah 84321.

OPLER, EDMOND Occupation: Chairman, World's Finest Chocolate, Inc. Address: 3501 North Adams Road, Oak Brook, Illinois 60521.

OPLER, LEWIS A Occupation: Research Psychiatrist. Education: Ph.D., M.D. Address: 106 New England Drive, Stamford, Connecticut 06903.

OPPENHEIM, GARRETT Occupation: Psychotherapist, Hypnotherapist. Education: Bachelor of Arts, Master of Arts, Doctor of Philosophy. Address: Box 56, Tappan, New York 10983.

OPPENHEIM, JEAN REEVE Occupation: Mathematics Teacher. Education: B.A., Cornell University; M.A., Wesleyan University; Ed.D., Columbia University. Address: 560-19 Main Street, New York, New York 10044.

ORAZIO, JOAN P Occupation: Certified Financial Planner. Education: B.S., C.F.P. Address: 17 Wilder Road, Suffern, New York 10901.

OREFFICE, PAUL F Occupation: President and Chief Executive Officer, The Dow Chemical Company. Education: B.S. Chemical Engineering, Purdue University. Address: 2030 Dow Center, Midland, Michigan 48640.

OREL, HAROLD Occupation: University Distinguished Professor of English, English Department, University of Kansas. Education: B.A., U.N.H., 1948; M.A. 1949, Ph.D. 1952, University of Michigan. Address: 713 Schwarz Road, Lawrence,

Kansas 66044.

ORENSTEIN, MORTON H Occupation: Attorney. Education: B.A., J.D. Address: 1530 Euclid Avenue, Berkeley, California 94708.

ORLAND, HENRY Occupation: Professor, Writer, Conductor, Composer. Education: Ph.D., M.M., B.M. Address: 21 Bon Price Terrace, St. Louis, Olivette, Missouri 63132.

ORLANS, F BARBARA Occupation: Executive Director. Education: Ph.D. Address: 7106 Laverock Lane, Bethesda, Maryland 20817.

ORLICH, MARGARET ROBERTA Occupation: Administrator, University of Minnesota. Education: B.S., M.A., Ed.D. Address: 421 Anderson Road, Duluth, Minnesota 55811.

ORLIK, PETER BLYTHE Occupation: Broadcast Educator, Michigan University; Consultant. Education: B.A., M.A., Ph.D. Address: 1411 East Maple, Mount Pleasant, Michigan 48858.

ORMROD, JEANNE ELLIS Occupation: Assistant to the Vice President for Academic Affairs, Office of Academic Affairs, University of Northern Colorado. Education: A.B., Brown University; M.S., Ph.D., Pennsyvlania State University. Address: 2324 21st Avenue, Greeley, Colorado 80631.

ORNSTEIN, ALLAN C Occupation: Professor. Education: Ph.D. 1971. Address: Loyola University, 820 North Michigan, Chicago, Illinois 60611.

O'ROURKE, JAMES SCOFIELD IV Occupation: United States Air Force Officer, Professor of Public Affairs, Defense Information School. Education: B.B.A., M.S., M.A., Ph.D. Address: 1044 Selkirk Lane, Indianapolis, Indiana 46260.

ORR, ARLENE Occupation: Dental Assistant, Office Manager. Education: Further Studies. Address: 49 East 156th Street, Harvey, Illinois 60426.

ORR, JOAN MELTON Occupation: Nurse Educator, Chairperson. Education: B.S. Nursing, M.S. Psychiatric Nursing. Address: Route 3, Box 271, Philippi, West Virginia 26416.

ORR, WENDELL E Occupation: Associate Professor of Music. Education: B.S., B.M., M.Mus. Address: 7197 Elmland, Poland, Ohio 44514.

ORRICK, ROSALIE KOTRLA Occupation: Educator, Gate Coordinator. Education: B.S. Education, M.E.D., Southwest Texas State University. Address: 9751 Mango Lane, Fontana, California 92335.

ORSZULAK, RICHARD STEWART Occupation: Chief Accountant, Hagman's, Inc. Education: B.S.B.A., Pittsburgh State University, 1979. Address: Post Office Box 1795, Pittsburgh, Kansas 66762.

ORTHNER, DENNIS K Occupation: University Professor, University of Georgia. Education: B.A., M.A., Ph.D. Address: 8615 Woodledge Lane, Roswell, Georgia 30076.

ORTMANS, KAY Occupation: Director of Well-Springs Foundation Teacher, Lecturer, Counselor. Education: Royal Academy of Music, Dalcroze School of Eurhythmics. Address: 11667 Alba Road, Ben Lomond, California 95005.

ORTOLANI, MINOT HENRY Occupation: Director. Education: B.S. History, Stonier Graduate School of Banking. Address: 81 Huntington Court, Williamsville, New York 14221.

ORY, MARCIA GAIL Occupation: Medical Sociologist, Gerontologist. Education: Ph.D. 1976, M.P.H. 1981. Address: 9810 Parkwood Drive, Bethesda, Maryland 20814.

ORZANO, JOSEPH E JR Occupation: IBM Manager of National Languages. Education: A.B., Duke University. Address: 27 Londonderry Drive,

Greenwich, Connecticut 06830.

OSBORN, JOSEPH P Occupation: Education. Address: 169 Prospect Street, Garfield, New Jersey 07026.

OSBORN, LESLIE ANDREWARTHA Occupation: Researcher, the Ultimate Prevention of War. Education: M.B., B.S., M.D. Address: 5158 North 83rd Street, Scottsdale, Arizona 85253.

OSBORN, MICHAEL M Occupation: Professor and Chairperson. Education: B.A., M.A., Ph.D. Address: 459 Meadowcrest Cl., Memphis, Tennessee 38117.

OSBORN, PRIME F III Occupation: Chairman of the Board (Retired). Education: J.D., 1939; LL.D. (Honorary), 1970, 1982. Address: 5005 Yacht Club Road, Jacksonville, Florida 32210.

OSBORNE, CHARLES E Occupation: Professor and Assistant Dean of Medical School. Education: B.S. and M.S. Education, Ed.D. Address: 2505 Manchester, Springfield, Illinois 62701.

OSBORNE, J SCOTT III Occupation: Researcher, Department of Anthropology, Michigan State University. Education: B.A., M.A., Ph.D. Address: Department of Anthropology, Michigan State University, East Lansing, Michigan 48823.

O'SHEA, JOHN J Occupation: Controller, Global Marine, Inc. Education: B.S., Fordham University, 1969. Address: 1111 Fleetwood Place, Houston, Texas 77079.

O'SHEA, LYNNE Occupation: Director of Communications. Education: B.A. Political Science, B.J. Makreting Communications, M.A. Communications Research, Ph.D. International Communications. Address: 3720 North Lake Shore Drive, Chicago, Illinois 60613.

OSIGWEH, CHIMEZIE A B Occupation: University Professor. Education: Ph.D. 1982, M.L.H.R. 1981, M.A. 1980, B.Sc. 1978. Address: Post Office Box 932, Kirksville, Missouri 63501.

OSNER, JOY W Occupation: Revenue Agent. Education: B.S. Accounting. Address: 665 Washington Boulevard, Abilene, Texas 79601.

OSTERLING, ALLEN W Occupation: Consulting Engineer. Education: B.S.C.E., B.S.M.S.&T., M.B.A. Address: 173 Ramblewood Road, Moorestown, New Jersey 08057.

OSTERMAN, SUSAN Occupation: Poet. Education: A.B., Barnard College; M.A., City College of New York; M.A., Teachers College, Columbia University. Address: 610 West 115 Street #94, New York, New York 10025.

OSTRANDER, THOMAS W Occupation: Investment Banker. Education: A.B., University of Michigan, 1972; M.B.A., Harvard University, 1976. Address: 420 East 79th Apartment 6A, New York, New York 10021.

OSTROM, BARBARA DIANE Occupation: Interior Designer. Education: M.S. Interior Design, Pratt Institute; B.F.A., New York University; Certificate, New York School of Interior Design; Certificate, Traphagen School of Fashion. Address: 28 Hopper Farm Road, Upper Saddle River, New Jersey 07458.

OSWALD, JAMES O Occupation: Director, Institutional Advancement. Education: B.S.Ed., B.A., M.A. Address: 306 Washington Boulevard, Orrville, Ohio 44667.

O'TOOLE, EDWARD THOMAS Occupation: Microbiologist, Educator. Address: Thornton Ridge Road, Riderwood, Maryland 21139.

OTOOLE, LELA Occupation: Dean Emeritus,

Oklahoma State University. Education: B.S.Ed., B.S., M.S., Ph.D. Address: 1820 Arrowhead Place, Stillwater, Oklahoma 74074.

OTTAWAY, LOIS M Occupation: Assistant Director, Volunteer Representation MAP International. Education: B.S. Journalism, M.S. Journalism. Address: 201 North President #3A, Wheaton, Illinois 60187.

OTTO, ALBERT DEAN Occupation: Mathematics Department Chairperson, Illinois State University. Education: B.A. 1961, M.S. 1962, Ph.D. 1965, Mathematics, University of Iowa. Address: 1012 Barton Drive, Normal, Illinois 61761.

OTTO, ELEANOR Occupation: Poet Musician, Actess. Education: A.B. Address: 400 West 43 Street, New York, New York 10036.

OTTO, KLAUS Occupation: Staff Scientist, Research in Physical Chemistry. Education: Verdiplom, Diplom, Dr.rer.nat. Address: 35173 West Six Mile Road, Livonia, Michigan 48152.

OUIMET, ALFRED JOSEPH JR Occupation: Chemical Editor, Chemical Abstracts Service. Education: B.A. 1953, Ph.D. 1962, University of Connecticut. Address: 1655 Doone Road, Upper Arlington, Ohio 43221.

OVERBY, GEORGE ROBERT Occupation: President of Freedoms University. Address: 5927 Windhover Drive, Orlando, Florida 32819.

OVERHOLSER, J HOMER HAROLD Occupation: President, National Golf Products, Inc. Education: Aeronautical Engineering. Address: 4961 Palomar Drive, Tarzana, California 91356.

OVESEN, ELLIS Occupation: Writer/Artist. Education: M.A. cum laude, University of Wisconsin. Address: Box 482, Los Altos, California 94022.

OWEN, GARNET Occupation: Writer. Education: B.S., James Madison University; M.A., Duke University. Address: 5834 East Oak Street, Scottsdale, Arizona 85257.

OWEN, JOHN E Occupation: Professor, Writer. Education: B.A., Duke University, 1943; M.A. 1946,

Ph.D. 1949, University of Southern California. Address: 5834 East Oak Street, Scottsdale, Arizona 85257.

OWEN, NORMAN LLOYD Occupation: Owner, Learning Horizons. Education: Ed.D., Stanford University, 1970. Address: 5924 Highplace Drive, San Diego, California 92120.

OWEN, THOMAS LLEWELLYN Occupation: Senior Investment Executive. Education: A.B., M.B.A. Address: 251 East 32nd Street, New York, New York 10016.

OWEN, TOBIAS CHANT Occupation: Astronomer. Education: B.A., University of Chicago, 1955; B.S., 1959; M.S., 1960; Ph.D., University of Arizona, 1965. Address: 6 Ivy Lane, Setauket, New York 11733.

OWENS, ALFONZO BENJAMIN III Occupation: Dentist. Education: A.B. Biology, Lafayette College; D.M.D., University of Pennsylvania. Address: 221 Union Avenue, Mount Vernon, New York 10553.

OWENS, ALFRED Occupation: Fld. Office Manager and Tax Consultant. Education: B.S. Accounting, Johnson C. Smith University. Address: 2201 Severn Avenue, Apartment F101, Metairie, Louisiana 70001.

OWENS, MAUREEN Occupation: Director, Community Health Education. Address: 1600 Haddon Avenue, Camden, New Jersey 08103.

OWINGS, BENJAMIN F Occupation: International Geophysical Consultant. Education: B.S. Physics. Address: 3400 Kipling, Wheat Ridge, Colorado 80033.

OZAWA, TERUTOMO Occupation: Professor of Economics, Colorado State University. Education: M.B.A. Management, Ph.D. Economics, Columbia University. Address: 684 Heather Court, Fort Collins, Colorado 80525.

OZOLS, LIA Occupation: Medical Technoloist. Education: B.S., Univ. of Minnesota. Address: 2012 West 68th Street, Minneapolis, Minnesota 55423.

P

PACHUT, JOSEPH F JR Occupation: Associate Professor of Geology, I.U.P.U.I. Education: B.A., State University of New York; Ph.D., Michigan State University. Address: 8924 Sunburst Circle, Indianapolis, Indiana 46227.

PAGE, DREW ERNEST Occupation: Writer, Former Musician. Education: College and Private Music Studies. Address: 1412 Cottonwood Place, Las Vegas, Nevada 89014.

PAGE, THOMAS L Occupation: Manager, Applied Ecology Section. Education: B.A., M.A., Ph.D. Address: 1725 Birch, Richland, Washington 99352.

PALADE, GEORGE E Occupation: Medical Doctor. Education: M.D. Address: 22 Coachmans Lane, Woodbridge, Connecticut 06525.

PALADINO, ALBERT E Occupation: General Partner, Advanced Technology Ventures. Education: Sc.D., B.S., M.S. Address: 26 Berrian Road, New York, New York 10804.

PALLISTER, JANIS L Occupation: University Professor. Education: Ph.D., University of Minnesota, 1964. Address: 211 State Street, Bowling Green, Ohio 43402.

PALLMANN, ALBERT J Occupation: Professor Earth and Atmosphere. Education: Ph.D. Physical Sciences. Address: 9 Middlesex Drive, St. Louis, Missouri 63144.

PALLMANN, MARGOT SIMONS Occupation: Director, Actuarial Science Program. Education: Ph.D. Mathematics, A.M., M.A., B.A. Address: 9 Middlesex Drive, Saint Louis, Missouri 63144.

PALM, ANN Occupation: Educator, Author, Philosophy of Science, Integrative Science. Education: Ph.D. Physical Chemistry/Physics. Address: 1771 Highland Place, Berkeley, California 94709.

PALMER, BLAINE CHARLES Occupation: Director Human Resources. Education: B.S. Business Administration. Address: 5221 Aztec Drive, Ogden, Utah 84403.

PALMER, BONITA ANN Occupation: Church Volunteer. Education: A.B., M.D. Address: 3667 A 20th Street, San Francisco, California 94110.

PALMER, JANE JOLLIFFE Occupation: Virginia Teachers Association, Retired. Education: B.A., College of William and Mary. Address: 320 South Maple Avenue, Purcellville, Virginia 22132.

PALMER, ROSEYLEE KATHRYN Occupation: Chairman, Fine Arts Division. Education: A.A., B.S., M.A. Address: 1409 Marigold, Borger, Texas 79007.

PALMER, WILLARD A Occupation: Music Editor, Composer, Lecturer. Education: B.S., Doctor of Humanities, Doctor of Music. Address: 9602 Winsome Lane, Houston, Texas 77063.

PALOMBO, THOMAS A Occupation: Missionary, Poet, Writer. Education: College Equivalent. Address: 2845 Waterbury Avenue, Bronx, New York 10461.

PALUMBO, LOUIS ALEXANDER JR Occupation: Catholic Priest, Educator, Theologian. Education: B.D., S.T.L., S.T.D., D.D., Ph.D. Address: 5 Beckwith Street, Cranston, Rhode Island 02910.

PAMILLA, JEANNE ROSE Occupation: Orthopedic Surgeon. Education: B.S., St. John's University; M.D. Address: 520 East 72 Street, New York City, New York 10021.

PANSKY, BEN Occupation: Professor of Anatomy. Education: B.A., M.S., Ph.D., M.D. Address: 2809 Manchester, Toledo, Ohio 43606.

PAOLI, SYLVIA LEE Occupation: Attorney. Education: B.A., M.M., J.D. Address: 8121 Barrington Drive, La Mirado, California 90638.

PAOLUCCI, ANNE Occupation: President, Council on National Literatures. Address: Post Office Box 81, Whitestone, New York 11357.

PAOLUCCI, HENRY Occupation: Professor, Government and Politics. Education: Ph.D. 1961, M.A. 1948, Columbia University; B.S.S., The City College of New York 1942.

PAPAGEORGIOU, JOHN C Occupation: Professor and Chairperson, Management Sciences Department. Education: B.S., Dipl. Tech. Sc., Ph.D. Address: 14 Putney Road, Wellesley, Massachusetts 02181.

PAPALIA, JOHN A Occupation: Researcher, Therapeutic Value of Royal Jelly. Education: Doctor of Music. Address: 263 East 10th, New York City, New York 10009.

PAPROCKI, WAYNE JOSEPH Occupation: Realtor and Professor. Education: B.A.Ed., M.S.Ed., C.A.S. Address: 3856 Rutgers Lane, Northbrook, Illinois 60062.

PAQUET, JEAN-GUY Occupation: Rector, Universite Laval, Canada. Education: B.Sc. Physics, 1959; M.Sc. Aeronautics, 1960; Ph.D. Electrical Engineering, 1963. Address: 1517 rue Commerciale/Saint-Romuald, Quebec G1W 1Z6, Canada.

PARCELL, RAYMOND E JR Occupation: Corporate Staff Executive, Hughes Aircraft. Education: E.E., Virginia Polytechnic Institute and State University; M.B.A., Columbia University. Address: 1500 Esplanade, Redondo Beach, California 90277.

PARIS, GERMAINE Occupation: Actress, Model, Published Author, Poet. Education: B.A. Address: Post Office Box 141, Haverford, Pennsylvania 19041.

PARK, JOE CHARLES Occupation: Professor of Education, College of Education, University of Wisconsin. Education: Ph.D., Northwestern University. Address: Route 3, Whitewater, Wisconsin 53190.

PARKENING, TERRY ARTHUR Occupation: Associate Professor of Anatomy. Education: Ph.D., M.A., B.S. Address: 619 Reynaldo, Dickinson, Texas 77539.

PARKER, BARRETT Occupation: Lecturer, Writer. Education: A.B., Haverford College; M.A., Harvard University. Address: 57 McKeen Street, Brunswick, Maine 04011.

PARKER, BARRY RICHARD Occupation: Professor of Physics. Education: B.A., M.Sc., Ph.D. Address: 750 Fairway Drive, Pocatello, Idaho 83201.

PARKER, DOUGLAS JAMES Occupation: Art Director, Bostonia Magazine. Education: Boston University, B.F.A. 1966, M.F.A. 1968. Address: 10 Lenox Street, Brookline, Massachusetts 02568

PARKER, E CAMILLE KILLIAN Occupation: Ophthalmologist. Education: M.D. Address: 2500 East Broadway, Logansport, Indiana 46947.

PARKER, EDWARD A Occupation: Textbook Editor. Education: B.B.A. 1969, M.B.A. 1970. Address: 5291 Belleview Road, Cincinnati, Ohio 45242.

PARKER, GEORGE D Occupation: Associate Professor of Mathematics, Department of Mathemtics, Southern Illinois University. Address: Department of Mathematics, S.I.U., Carbondale, Illinois 62901.

PARKER, GORDON ARTHUR Occupation: Chemist, Chemistry Department, University of Toledo. Education: B.S., University of Michigan, 1958; M.S. 1962, Ph.D. 1966, Wayne State University. Address: 217 Smith Street, Milan, Michigan 48160.

PARKER, JUDITH K Occupation: Science Laboratory Manager, Maryville College. Education: B.S., M.A. Address: 53 Forest Knoll, Fenton, Missouri 63026.

PARKER, LUCY T Occupation: Clinical Director, Psychologist, Senior Consultant. Education: Ed.D., Ph.D., Ed.M., B.S. Address: 11 Riverview Terrace, Dover, Massachusetts 02030.

PARKER, PAMELA J Occupation: Wildlife Biologist. Education: M.F.S., Yale School of Forestry; Ph.D., Yale University. Address: Chicago Zoological Society, Brookfield, Illinois 60513.

PARKER, W DALE Occupation: Executive, Engineer, Personnel Manager, Political Advisor, Author, Lecturer, Self-Ordained Minister, Columnist. Education: Attended University of Virginia, University of Delaware, California Western University, University of California, Stetson University. Address: Post Office Box 246, Boone, North Carolina 28607.

PARKINSON, WILLIAM CHARLES Occupation: Professor of Physics. Education: B.S.E., M.S., Ph.D. Physics, University of Michigan. Address: 1600 Sheridan Drive, Ann Arbor, Michigan 48104.

PARMALEE, PATTY LEE Occupation: Writer, Athlete. Education: Ph.D. 1970. Address: 2680 Broadway, New York, New York 10025.

PARMELEE, HAROLD JAMES (JIM) Occupation: Paper Tester, Paper Mill; Rental Property Owner. Education: High School Diploma. Address: 419 East Franklin Street, Marshfield, Wisconsin 54449.

PARR, CAROLYN MILLER Occupation: Special Counsel to Assistant Attorney General. Education: J.D., Georgetown University; M.A., Vanderbilt University; B.A., Stetson University. Address: 13640 Glenhurst Road, Travilah, Maryland 20878.

PARR, JERRY S Occupation: Assistant Director, U.S. Secret Service. Education: B.A., Vanderbilt University. Address: 13640 Glenhurst Road, Gaithersburg, Maryland 20878.

PARRINO, GEORGE Occupation: Director, The San Antonio Art Institute. Education: M.F.A., Yale University, School of Art and Architecture, 1970; B.F.A., Cooper Union Art School, 1964. Address: 355 East Terra Alta, San Antonio, Texas 78209.

PARRISH, CHARLES EDWIN Occupation: Historian, Army Corps of Engineers. Education: B.A. History, University of Louisville, 1964. Address: 8608 Cool Brook Court, Louisville, Kentucky 40291.

PARRISH, JOYCE T Occupation: Administrative Secretary, Kentucky State University. Education: Business School Diploma. Address: Route #6, Frankfort, Kentucky 40601.

PARSELL, LLOYD E Occupation: Supervisor of Pupil Assignment and Administration, Roanoke County Public Schools. Education: A.B., Morris Harvey College; M.Sc. Education Administration, Radford University. Address: 2029 Governor Drive, Roanoke, Virginia 24019.

PARSON, ERWIN RANDOLPH Occupation: Regional Outreach Director. Education: M.A., Ph.D. Address: 316 Pemaco Lane, Uniondale, New York 11553.

PARTAIN, C LEON Occupation: Radiology/Nuclear Medicine. Education: B.S.N.E., M.S.N.E., M.D., Ph.D. Address: 211 High Lea Road, Brentwood, Tennessee 32027.

PARTIN, ALLEN J Occupation: Member Technical Staff. Education: B.S. Psy. Address: R.R. #1, Box 655, Idaho Springs, Colorado 80452.

PARTLOW, HARRY A Occupation: Manager Industrial Hygiene, Safety and Compliance Review.

Education: B.S. Chemical Engineering. Address: 1143 Chajeaugay, Naperville, Illinois 60540.

PASSET, CHARLES JEFFREY Occupation: Podiatrist. Education: D.P.M. Address: 63-57 108 Street, Forest Mills, New York 11375.

PATCH, MARLENA B Occupation: Corporate Executive Vice President, Patch Associates, Baltimore, Maryland. Education: B.A., University of California, 1967. Address: Route 2, Box 239-T, Waldorf, Maryland 20601.

PATE, ARTIE THOMAS JR Occupation: Minister and University Professor. Education: B.A., Doctor of Education. Address: 4644 Tara Drive, Nashville, Tennessee 37215.

PATE, DAVID S Occupation: Solar Trainer. Address: 2059 Huntington Avenue, Alexandria, Virginia 22303.

PATE, LARRY EUGENE Occupation: University Professor. Education: B.A., M.S., University of California-Irvine; Ph.D., University of Illinois. Address: 3217 Saddlehorn Drive, Lawrence, Kansas 66044.

PATEL, JASHU Occupation: Library Educator. Education: B.A., M.L.S., Ph.D. Address: 65 West 146th Street, Riverdale, Illinois 60627.

PATHAK, DEV S Occupation: Professor and Chairman of Pharmaceutical Administration, Professor of Marketing, The Ohio State University. Education: M.Com. 1964, LL.B. 1965, Gujarat University; M.S., Southern Illinois University, 1966; M.B.A. 1969, D.B.A. 1972, Michigan State University. Address: 7739 Strathmoore Road, Dublin, Ohio 43017.

PATON, DAWNA LISA Occupation: Project Manager Marketing and Sales. Education: B.S. 1977, M.S. 1979, Massachusetts Institute of Technology. Address: 27 Micer Lane, Wellesley, Massachusetts 02181.

PATON, N EMERSON JR (PAT) Occupation: Chairman, Chief Executive Officer, Paton and Associates, Marketing, Advertising, and Public Relations. Education: B.A., University of Missouri, 1953. Address: 2101 Condolea Circle, Leawood, Kansas 66209.

PATRAY, BOBBIE Occupation: President, Eagle Forum of Lexington; Advisory Board Member, Committee for Life; Kentucky Alliance for Exploited and Missing Children. Address: 3389 Carriage Lane, Lexington, Kentucky 40502.

PATRICK, CHARLOTTE A Occupation: Associate Professor of Speech Communications. Education: B.A., University of Wyoming, 1965; M.A., University of Wyoming, 1967. Address: Post Office Box 941, Powell, Wyoming 82435.

PATRICK, H HUNTER JR Occupation: Lawyer, Judge. Education: B.A., 1961; J.D., 1966, University of Wyoming. Address: Post Office Box 941, Powell, Wyoming 82435.

PETRY, BELA Occupation: Professor of Architecture, Architect, Artist. Education: Dipl. Profl., Academy Fine Arts, Budapest, 1927; Reg. Arch., Architectural Academy, Vienna. Address: 331 Sandspur Road, Maitland, Florida 32751.

PATSCH, JOSEF R Occupation: Associate Professor of Medicine, Baylor College of Medicine. Education: M.D. Address: 4814 O'Meara, Houston, Texas 77035.

PATTEN, JACQUELINE LaVETTA Occupation: Director, Career Planning, Long Island. Education: B.S. Psychology, Sociology, Photography; M.S. Education. Address: 1239 Ward Avenue, Bronx, New York 10472.

PATTEN, MAURINE D Occupation: Registered (Licensed) Psychologist, Private Practice; Consultant.

Education: B.S., M.S., Ed.D. Address: 540 Fairway Lane, Sycamore, Illinois 60178.

PATTEN, RONALD JAMES Occupation: Dean, School of Business Administration. Education: B.A. 1957, M.A. 1959, Ph.D. 1963. Address: 39 Storrs Heights, Storrs, Connecticut 06268.

PATTERSON, ALBERT C Occupation: President, Fleet Information. Education: A.B. English Literature. Address: 90 Commonwealth Avenue, Boston, Massachusetts 02116.

PATTERSON, DONALD MAYO Occupation: Residential Resale Specialist, Goodman Segar Hogan Residential Sales Corporation. Education: B.S., United States Naval Academy, 1974. Address: 3558 Campion Avenue, Virginia Beach, Virginia 23462.

PATTERSON, FLOYD GUYTON JR Occupation: President, Computer Software Manufacturing Company. Education: B.A., M.S., M.S., Sc.M. Address: 1090 Marcia Road, Memphis, Tennessee 38117.

PATTERSON, JAMES W Occupation: Professor and Chairman, Pritzker Department of Environmental Engineering, Illinois Institute of Technology. Education: B.S. Civil Engineering, M.S. Sanitary Engineering, Ph.D. Environmental Engineering. Address: 1540 North State Parkway, Chicago, Illinois 60610.

PATTERSON, MARJORIE D Occupation: Editor, Mid American Shelflist. Education: Attended Park College. Address: 207 Walnut Hill Road, Westchester, Pennsylvania 19380.

PATTERSON, MICHAEL MILTON Occupation: Director of Research, Researcher, College of Osteopathic Medicine, Ohio University. Education: B.A., Grinnell College; Ph.D., University of Iowa. Address: 88 Wonder Hills Drive, Athens, Ohio 45701.

PATTERSON, PATRICIA T Occupation: Clinical Coordinator. Education: B.S. 1970, M.N. 1975. Address: 55 Arnold Street, Washington, Pennsylvania 15301.

PATTERSON, PEGGY J Occupation: Owner, Realtor, Patterson Realty, Inc. Education: Southwestern College. Address: 14 Pine Road, Otto, North Carolina 28763.

PATTERSON, RICHARD NORTH Occupation: Novelist. Education: B.A., Ohio Wesleyan University, 1968; J.D., Case Western Reserve University, 1971. Address: 2400 Pacific Avenue, San Francisco, California 94115.

PATURIS, E MICHAEL Occupation: Attorney. Education: B.S., J.D. with honors. Address: 2732 North Radford Street, Arlington, Virginia 22207.

PAUL, AILEEN Occupation: Writer, Public Relations Specialist. Education: B.A. Address: 2562 Avenida de Isidro, Santa Fe, New Mexico 87501.

PAULSEN, JOSEPH CHARLES Occupation: Publisher. Address: 420 Lexington Avenue, New York City, New York 10017.

PAULSON, WILLIAM LEE Occupation: Surrogate Justice, North Dakota Supreme Court. Education: B.A., Valley City State College; LL.B., J.D., University of North Dakota. Address: 361 College Street Southwest, Valley City, North Dakota 58072.

PAULUS, NORMA J Occupation: Secretary of State, Oregon. Education: LL.B., Willamette University, 1962. Address: 3090 Pigeon Hollow Road, South, Salem, Oregon 97302.

PAVLIDES, MILLER HARRY Occupation: Public Accountant. Education: Attended Yale University, Ohio University, New Mexico University. Address: 3117 Silver Southeast, Albuquerque, New Mexico 97106.

PAWLOVICH, KAREN J Occupation: Financial Analyst. Education: Masters in Communication Research. Address: 5923 Bois Ile, Haslett, Michigan 48840.

PAXTON, JUANITA WILLENE Occupation: Director, Counseling Center. Education: A.B., M.A., Ed.D. Address: 1203 Lester Harris Road, Johnson City, Tennessee 37601.

PAYNE, DANIEL FRANKLIN Occupation: President, Founder, American Television Network. Education: M.B.A., Ph.D. Address: Post Office Box 1211, Glendale, California 91209.

PAYTON, RALPH REED Occupation: Founder, President, Black Raven Mining and Refineries. Address: Post Office Box 126, Carmel Valley, California 93924.

PEACHEY, CHRISTINE Occupation: Volunteer. Address: 912 East North, Magnolia, Arkansas 71753.

PEAKE, LUISE EITEL Occupation: Musicologist. Education: B.A., University of Tennessee; M.M., Chicago Musical College; Ph.D., Columbia University. Address: 516 Santee Avenue, Columbia, South Carolina 28205.

PEARDON, PATRICIA CAMERON Occupation: Artist/Actress. Address: 305 Riverside Drive, New York, New York 10025.

PEARSON, LENA M Occupation: Beautician. Address: 2437 Carlton Place, Riverside, California 92507.

PEARSON, NORMAN Occupation: Consultant Planner and University President. Education: B.A., M.B.A., Ph.D., D.B.A. Address: Post Office Box 5362, Lundon, Ontario, Canada.

PECKENPAUGH, ANGELA JOHNSON Occupation: Lecturer in English, U.W.-Whitewater. Education: B.A. English, M.A. Contemporary Literature, M.F.A. Writing. Address: 2513 East Webster Place, Milwaukee, Wisconsin 53211.

PECKHAM, CHARLES W SR Occupation: Clergyman, Gerontologist, Social Worker, Educator. Education: B.A., Master of Divinity, Master of Sacred Theology, Ed.D. Address: 689 North Street, Route 741, Lebanon, Ohio 45036.

PECORA, PETER JOHN Occupation: Assistant Professor, Graduate School of Social Work, University of Utah. Education: B.A. Psychology, M.S.W., Ph.D. Social Welfare. Address: 2010 Highland View Circle, Salt Lake City, Utah 84109.

PEDERSEN, K GEORGE Occupation: University President. Education: B.A., M.A., Ph.D. Address: 6565 Northwest Marine Drive, Vancouver, B.C., Canada V6T 1A7.

PEEPLES, AUDREY RONE Occupation: Executive Director. Education: B.A., University of Illinois; M.A., Northwestern University. Address: 9339 South Hayne, Chicago, Illinois 60620.

PELTON, SHERWIN C Occupation: Lawyer. Education: B.B.A., LL.B., LL.M. Taxation, S.J.D. Address: 8877 North Malibu Drive, Bayside, Wisconsin 53217.

PEMBERTON, ROBERT LINWOOD Occupation: Artist-in-Residence. Education: B.F.A. Theatre. Education: B.F.A. in Theatre. Address: 2712 East Franklin Street, Richmond, Virginia 23223.

PEMBERTON, SHERRY L Occupation: Student. Address: Route 2, Box 394A, La Follette, Tennessee 37766.

PENA, LYDIA M Occupation: Associate Professor of Art. Education: B.S., M.Ed., M.A., Ph.D. Address: 3101 West Hillside Place, Denver, Colorado 80219.

PENDER, MICHAEL R Occupation: Civil

Engineer. Education: A.B., M.S.C.E., Dartmouth College. Address: 148 Poplar Street, Garden City, New York 11530.

PENLAND, PATRICIA R Occupation: Professor and Consultant. Education: Ph.D., M.L.S., A.B. Address: Box 79007, Pittsburgh, Pennsylvania 15216.

PENTA, BONNIE LOUISE Occupation: Educator. Education: B.S. Education, Adaptive Physical Education. Address: 2923 Moon Lake, West, Bloomfield, Michigan 48033.

PEPLAU, HILDEGARD ELISABETH Occupation: Professor Emeritus, Rutgers University. Education: Nursing Diploma, B.A., M.A., Ed.D. Address: 118 Shunpike Road, Madison, New Jersey 07940.

PERCIA, VALERIE CHASE Occupation: Speech Language Pathologist, Consultant. Education: B.A., St. John's University; M.Ed., Bridgewater State College. Address: 46 Kendall Hill Road, Sterling Jet, Massachusetts 01565.

PEREIRA, TERESINKA P Occupation: Professor of Spanish and Portuguese, Department of Spanish and Portuguese, University of Colorado. Education: Ph.D., University of New Mexico, 1972. Address: Department of Spanish and Portuguese, University of Colorado, Boulder, Colorado 80302.

PEREZ, ROSANNE C Occupation: Chairman and Professor, Department of Pediatrics, Family and Women's Health Nursing. Education: Ed.D., M.S.N., B.S.N. Address: 8254 Shadow Circle, Indianapolis, Indiana 46260.

PERKEY, DONALD J Occupation: Associate Professor. Education: B.A., B.S., Ph.D. Address: 224 Warren Avenue, Berwyn, Pennsylvania 19312.

PERKINS, JAMES ARTHUR Occupation: President, Chatfield Brass Band and Free Music Lending Library, Attorney. Education: B.A., L.L.B. Address: 322 Winona Street, Chatfield, Minnesota 55923.

PERLMAN, DANIEL Occupation: Professor of Family Science and Psychology, University of British Columbia. Education: Ph.D. Social Psychology, Claremont Graduate School, 1971. Address: 3493 West 23rd, Vancouver, B.C. Canada V6S 1K2.

PERLMAN, EILEEN E Occupation: Investor. Address: 6401 Cellini, Coral Gables, Florida 33146.

PERRIN, ARNOLD S Occupation: Editor, Publisher, Wings Press. Education: B.E., Plymouth College, 1965. Address: R.F.D. 2, Box 730, Belfast, Maine 07915.

PERRENOD, DOUGLAS ARTHUR Occupation: Aviation Consultant; Aerospace Maintenance Officer, United States Air Force Reserve. Education: Attended Florida Institute of Technology; Student, California State University; B.A. Astronomy, University of South Florida. Address: Box 4361, Downey, California 90241.

PERRY, CHARLES D Occupation: Professor, Classic, University of Alabama. Education: B.A., DePauw University; M.A., University of Michigan. Address: 1102 Riverside Drive, Tuscaloosa, Alabama.

PERRY, EUGENE A Occupation: Southern Baptist Minister. Education: B.A., B.D., M.Div., M.R.E., M.A., D.Min. Address: 306 South 3rd Street, Tonkawa, Oklahoma 74653.

PERRY, MARK STEVEN Occupation: Interior Architect. Education: B.A. Interior Architecture, University of Oregon. Address: 1010 Tennessee Street, San Francisco, California 94017.

PERRY, RONALD W Occupation: Professor of Public Affairs. Education: B.Sc. 1971, M.A. 1973, Arizona State University; Ph.D., University of Washington, 1975. Address: 1297 East Alameda,

Tempe, Arizona 85282.

PERTELESI, ELENA M Occupation: Secretary, A.T.T. Communications. Address: 912 Constant Avenue, Peekskill, New York 10566.

PESCHAU, DAVID F Occupation: Vice President, General Manager, Broadcast Television Station. Education: Graduate, Luther College. Address: 2531 Sherwood Drive, La Crosse, Wisconsin 54601.

PESEK, BORIS PETER Occupation: Professor of Economics, University of Wisconsin. Education: B.A., Coe College, 1952; M.A., University of Chicago, 1953; Ph.D., University of Chicago, 1956. Address: 12928 North Colony Drive, Mequon, Wisconsin 53092.

PESKE, PATRIC O Occupation: Child Study Psychologist. Education: B.A., M.A. Address: Box 7149, Flint, Michigan 48507.

PETACCIA, MARIO AUGUSTUS Occupation: Interviewer. Education: B.A. Address: 441 Tomlinson, R.D. E-8, Philadelphia, Pennsylvania 19116.

PETERS, BETH Occupation: Actress. Address: Post Office Box 38641, Los Angeles, California 90038.

PETERS, DAVID L Occupation: Business Manager. Education: B.A. Psychology, M.A. Management. Address: 632 Wakefield Downs, Wales, Wisconsin 53183.

PETERS, DENNIS G Occupation: Herman T. Briscoe Professor of Chemistry, Department of Chemistry, Indiana University. Address: 1401 Nancy Street, Bloomington, Indiana 47401.

PETERS, DIANE P Occupation: Artist, Designer. Education: Del Mar College, University of Oklahoma. Address: 531 Chamberlain Street, Post Office Box 3808, Corpus Christi, Texas 78404.

PETERS, JERRY LEON Occupation: Professor, Purdue University. Education: B.S., M.S., Ph.D. Address: 3138 State Road 26, West Lafayette, Indiana 47906.

PETERS, LARRY DEAN Occupation: Gallery Director, Curator. Education: B.F.A. 1962, M.F.A. 1965. Address: 801 Fillmore, Topeka, Kansas 66606.

PETERS, MARGOT McCULLOUGH Occupation: Professor and Writer. Education: B.S., M.A., Ph.D. Address: 511 College Street, Lake Mills, Wisconsin 53551.

PETERS, ROBERT MICHAEL Occupation: Accountant, Faculty and Consultant. Education: B.A., M.B.A., M.A., M.S., Ph.D. Address: 181 Tenneyson Drive, Wheater, Illinois 60187.

PETERS, SALLY ANN Occupation: Writer, Scholar. Education: Ph.D., Florida State University; M.A., University of South Florida; A.B., Temple University. Address: 116 Mount Vernon Street, Middletown, Connecticut 06457.

PETERSEN, NEIL F Occupation: Supervisor, Petroleum Geochemistry, Superior University. Education: B.A., Hofstra University, 1964; M.S., University of Pennsylvania, 1967. Address: 21315 Park Bluff, Katy, Texas 77450.

PETERSEN, NORMAN WILLIAM Occupation: Captain, United States Navy; Director of Programs and Comptroller. Education: B.S.E.E., University of New Mexico, 1956; M.S., U.S.N.P.G.S., 1962. Address: 1143 Greenway Road, Alexandria, Virginia 22308.

PETERSEN, RONALD L Occupation: Radio Broadcasting, Cable Television. Address: 1020 South Megregor, Carthage, Missouri 64836.

PETERSON, BENJAMIN Occupation: Visual Artist, Educator. Education: A.B., B.F.A., M.F.A. Address: 109 Brainerd Road #7, Boston, Massachusetts 02134.

PETERSON, DAVID L Occupation: Facilities

Project Engineer. Education: M.E. Mechanical Design. Address: 730 East Mission Lane, Phoenix, Arizona 85020.

PETERSON, DONALD A Occupation: Publisher, Alliance Review; President, WFAH/WDJQ. Address: 1084 Glamorgan, Alliance, Ohio 44601.

PETERSON, EDWARD N Occupation: History Professor, University of Wisconsin-River Falls. Education: Ph.D. Address: 936 West Maple, River Falls, Wisconsin 54002.

PETERSON, JOHN BURL Occupation: Distribution Manager for American Breeders Service. Education: B.S. 1947, M.S. 1948, Agriculture, University of Missouri. Address: 1954 Melrose Street, Madison, Wisconsin 53704.

PETERSON, LoANN C Occupation: Physician, Pathologist. Education: M.D. Address: 4649 East Lake Harriet Parkway, Minneapolis, Minnesota 55409.

PETERSON, MARY K Occupation: Reading Coordinator, Director of Chapter 1. Education: B.S. Education, M.S. Education. Address: R.D. 1, Box 424 D, Franklin, Pennsylvania 16323.

PETERSON, OTIS GRANVILLE Occupation: Physicist, Technical Manager, Los Alamos National Laboratory. Education: Ph.D. Solid State Physics, University of Illinois, 1965. Address: 220 Kimberly, Los Alamos, New Mexico 87544.

PETERSON, RALPH MAX Occupation: Chief Forester, U.S.D.A. Forest Service. Education: B.S.C.E. University of Missouri; Master Public Administration, Harvard University. Address: 10742 Marlborough Road, Fairfax, Virginia 22030.

PETRACK, KENNETH MICHAEL Occupation: Director, Regional Public Affairs, Western U.S.; President, Freeman, Teilmann, and Petrack, Inc., International Public Relations. Address: Public Affairs, Headquarters, Sixth U.S. Army, Presidio of San Francisco, California 94129.

PETRONKO, MICHAEL ROMAN Occupation: Clinical Psychologist. Education: Ph.D. Address: R.D. #2, Longview Road, Lebanon, New Jersey 08833.

PETTERSON, SYLVIA ROYSENE Occupation: Physician. Education: B.S. 1966, M.D. 1970. Address: 2430 Deer Creek, CC Boulevard #707, Deerfield Beach, Florida 33441.

PETTIGREW, THOMAS FRASER Occupation: Professor of Social Psychology. Education: B.A. Psychology, University of Virginia; M.A., Ph.D. Social Psychology, Harvard University. Address: 524 Van Ness Avenue, Santa Cruz, California 95060.

PETTINATI, HELEN MARIE Occupation: Assistant Director of Research/Research Psychologist. Education: B.S., Drexel University, 1973; Ph.D., The Medical College of Pennsyvlania, 1979. Address: 568 Fernwood Lane, Fairless Hills, Pennsylvania 19030.

PETTIS, JOYCE O Occupation: Assistant Professor. Education: B.S., M.A., Ph.D. Address: 2104 Pendleton Street, Greenville, North Carolina 27834.

PETTY, GREGORY CHARLES Occupation: Associate Professor. Education: B.S., M.S. Ph.D. Address: 1917 Northwood Drive, Knoxville, Tennessee 37923.

PETTYJOHN, SHIRLEY ANN Occupation: Attorney, Real Estate Executive. Education: B.Sc., University of Louisville, 1974; J.D., University of Louisville Law School, 1977. Address: 6924 Norlynn Drive, Louisville, Kentucky 40228.

PETZEL, THOMAS PAUL Occupation: Professor of Psychology, Department of Psychology, Loyola University. Education: B.A., M.S., Ph.D. Address: 3004 North 78th Court, Elmwood Park, Illinois 60635.

PFEIFER, LUANNE Occupation: Journalist. Education: B.S. Address: 3224 Malibu Cyn. Road., Malibu, California 90265.

PHELAN, JAMES Occupation: Associate Professor of English, Department of English, Ohio State University. Education: B.A., Boston College; M.A., Ph.D., University of Chicago. Address: 424 Oakland Park Avenue, Columbus, Ohio 43214.

PHELAN, JAMES B Occupation: President, Insurance Marketing Associates. Education: B.A. Address: 11720 Conover Road, Versailles, Ohio 45380.

PHIBBS, CLIFFORD M JR Occupation: Clinical Associate Professor of Surgery. Education: B.S. Zoology, M.D., M.S. Surgery. Address: 9613 Upton Road South, Bloomington, Minnesota 55431.

PHILLIPPE-BARRY, JAMIE Occupation: Director of Development, Louisville Ballet Company. Education: M.A.T., University of Louisville; B.A. Psychology, Butler University. Address: 1294 Willow Avenue, Louisville, Kentucky 40204.

PHILLIPS, CLAUDIA SUENETTE Occupation: R.N. Director of Nurses, Parkview Convalescent Unit. Education: A.A. Nursing, University of Tennessee-Martin. Address: 30 Harrison Court, Martin, Tennessee 38237.

PHILLIPS, D HOWARD Occupation: Director, The Aerospace Corporation. Education: Bachelor's Degree Electrical Engineering, Master's Degree Nuclear Engineering, Ph.D. Electrical Engineering. Address: 917 Dune Street, El Segundo, California 90245.

PHILLIPS, DOW I Occupation: Science and Policy Administration. Education: B.S. Chemistry, Ph.D. Chemistry. Address: 3733 Jocelyn Street, Northwest, Washington, D.C. 20015.

PHILLIPS, GLENN ALLEN Occupation: Instructor, Private Business College. Education: B.A., Additional Studies, University of Northern Iowa. Address: 244 Drinkward Northwest, Cedar Rapids, Iowa 52405.

PHILLIPS, JILL META Occupation: Novelist, Researcher, Critic, Historian. Education: High School Diploma. Address: 851 North Garsden Avenue, Covina, California 91724.

PHILLIPS, JOHN G Occupation: Chairman of the Board. Education: B.S., University of Arkansas, 1948. Address: 2524 St. Charles Avenue, New Orleans, Louisiana 70130.

PHILLIPS, TEDDY S Occupation: Band Leader, Writer, Producer. Education: Music. Address: 6252½ Nita Avenue, Woodland Hills, California 91367.

PHILLIPS, THOMAS WILLIAM Occupation: Manager, Public Relations. Education: B.A. Journalism, M.B.A. Address: 39 Pheasant Ridge Road, West Redding, Connecticut 06896.

PHILLIPS, WILLIAM GEORGE Occupation: Chairman and Chief Executive Officer, International Multifoods Corporation. Education: A.B., C.P.A. Address: 2610 West Lafayette Road, Excelsior, Minnesota 55331.

PHOENIX, NAOMI B Occupation: Educator. Education: B.A., M.A., Ph.D. Address: 2028 South 7th Street, Camden, New Jersey 08104.

PHUTELA, RAMESH C Occupation: Research Associate. Education: B.Sc., M.Sc., Ph.D. Address: 2732 Benvenue Avenue #1, Berkeley, California 94705.

PIANTADOSI, JEANETTE KEMCHICK Occupation: Vice President Marketing. Education: Bachelor of Arts Sociology, Master of Education Student Development. Address: 247 Selby Ranch Road #6, Sacramento, California 95825.

PIASECKI, FRANK NICHOLAS Occupation: Executive, President and Chairman of the Board, Piasecki Aircraft Corporation. Education: Honorary Doctor of Aeronautical Sciences, Pennsylvania Military College, 1953; Honorary Doctor of Aeronautical Engineering, New York University, 1955; Doctor of Science Degree, Alliance College, 1970. Address: Tunbridge and Andover Roads, Haverford, Pennsylvania 19041.

PICKING, ROBERT BOYD Occupation: Founder and Principal, Robert Picking, Architect, Urban Planner and Engineer. Education: B.A. Structural Engineering, Lehigh University; M.Arch., Yale University School of Architecture; Attended Duke University, Technical (Hogskolan) University (Sweden). Address: 105 Greenbay Road, Lake Bluff, Illinois 60044.

PIEKARSKI, KONSTANTY Occupation: Educator. Education: Doctoral Degree. Address: 42 Murray Hill Court, Kitchener, Ontario, Canada N2E 1N9.

PIERCE, E R C Occupation: Educator. Education: B.A., M.A. Address: 4822 Creekmoor Drive, San Antonio, Texas 78220.

PIERCE, HAZEL BESSLEY Occupation: Professor of English, Kearney State College. Education: B.A., M.A., University of Illinois; Ph.D., University of Nebraska. Address: 1023 West 22nd Street, Kearney, Nebraska 68847.

PIERCE, HELENE J Occupation: Social Editor. Education: Attended Wisconsin Academy, University of Michigan, Henry Ford Community College. Address: 7319 Yinger, Dearborn, Michigan 48126.

PIETARILA, KATHRYN FRICKE Occupation: Certified Social Worker, Early Childhood Education. Education: B.A. Sociology, William Woods College, 1971; M.S.W., University of Kansas. Address: 613 Sheridan Drive, Corpus Christi, Texas 78412.

PIETRZAK, LAWRENCE MICHAEL Occupation: Research Engineer. Education: B.S., University of Detroit, 1965; M.S. 1966, Professional Engineer 1967, Massachusetts Institute of Technology. Address: 5218 Parejo, Santa Barbara, California 93111.

PIKUNAS, JUSTIN Occupation: Professor of Psychology and Director Child and Family Center, University of Detroit. Education: Ph.D. Address: 8761 West Outer Drive, Detroit, Michigan 48219.

PILCER, SONIA H Occupation: Writer. Education: B.A. Address: 172 West 79 Street, New York, New York 10024.

PIMENTEL, DAVID D Occupation: Associate Professor, Arizona State University. Education: B.S. Education, Massachusetts College of Art; M.F.A., Rochester Institute of Technology. Address: 335 East Palmcroft, Tempe, Arizona 85282.

PINKETT, HAROLD THOMAS Occupation: Consulting Archivist and Historian. Education: A.M., University of Pennsylvania; Ph.D., American University. Address: 5741 27th Street, Northwest, Washington, D.C. 20015.

PINKIN, JAMES E Occupation: President, Corporate Mailings, Inc. Education: B.S. Accounting/Marketing; M.B.A. Finance, C.P.A. Address: 20 Barchester Way, Westfield, New Jersey 07090.

PINKNEY, DOVE SAVAGE Occupation: Medical Technologist, Hematology. Education: B.A., Additional Studies. Address: 5601 Coliseum Street, Los Angeles, California 90016.

PINO, JOHN A Occupation: Science Advisor. Education: B.S. 1944, Ph.D. 1951, Rutgers University. Address: 1515 South Jefferson Davis Highway, Arlington Virginia 22202.

PINSKER, SANFORD S Occupation: Professor of English and Chairman of Department, Franklin and Marshall College. Education: B.A., Washington and Jefferson College; Ph.D., University of Washington. Address: 700 North Pine, Lancaster, Pennsylvania 17604.

PINSKY, LAWRENCE M Occupation: Senior Vice President, Information Services. Education: B.A. Mathematics, M.S. Computer Science, M.B.A. Finance. Address: 53 Nassau Drive, Great Neck, New York 11021.

PINTER, JOSEPH KALMAN Occupation: Chairman, Department of Bible and Theology, Professor of Theology, Appalachian Bible College. Education: B.A. Bob Jones University, 1951; Th.M. 1955, Th.D. 1964, Dallas Theological Seminary. Address: 103 Connor Street, Beckley, West Virginia 25801.

PIOQUINTO, RONALD Occupation: Psychiatric Social Work Supervisor. Education: B.A., Hofstra University; M.S.W., Fordham University. Address: 285 Syosset-Woodbury Road, Woodbury, New York 11797.

PIRKLE, ESTUS W Occupation: Pastor, Evangelist. Education: B.A., B.D., M.R.E., Th.M., D.D. Address: Post Office Box 80, Myrtle, Mississippi 28650.

PIRSCH, CAROL McBRIDE Occupation: State Senator/Supervisor Community Relations. Address: 4223 Aurora Drive, Omaha, Nebraska 68134.

PISEL, GARY H Occupation: Airline Pilot, Artist's Agent. Education: B.S. Physics, Coe College. Address: 2935 200th S.E., Issaquah, Washington 98027.

PISTONE, RICK Occupation: Poet, Dramatist. Education: 149-05 Centreville Street, Ozone Park, New York 11417.

PITCHER, VIRGINIA GRIFFITH STEIN Occupation: Oral Historian. Education: Postgraduate Certificate. Address: 472 Henkel Circle, Winter Park, Florida 32789.

PITTMAN, GEORGE HENRY JR Occupation: Assistant Director of Aviation, Melbourne (Florida) Airport Authority. Education: B.S., United States Military Academy-West Point. Address: 1490 Country Club Drive, Northeast, Palm Bay, Florida 32905-4402.

PITTMAN, JAMES EUGENE JR Occupation: Consultant, Entrepreneur. Address: 155 Madison Street, Oceanside, California 92056.

PITTS, DONALD L Occupation: Attorney, Bishop. Education: B.S. Political Science. Address: 313 G Street, Beckley, West Virginia 25801.

PITTS, WILLIAM L Occupation: Professor. Education: B.A. 1960, M.Div. 1963, Ph.D. 1969. Address: 717 Ivy Ann, Waco, Texas 76710.

PIZZURRO, JOSEPH P Occupation: Medical Doctor. Education: B.S. 1959, M.D. 1963. Address: 104 Fox Hedge Road, Saddle River, New Jersey 07458.

PLATT, NAOMI DORNFELD Occupation: Professor, Kingsborough Community College, The City University of New York. Education: B.S.Ed., M.S.Ed., Ed.D. Address: 1009 Willow Brook Road, Staten Island, New York 10314.

PLEETS, WILBUR LAWRENCE Occupation: Industrial/Business Development Specialist. Education: A.A., B.S. Address: Post Office Box 64, Fort Yates, North Dakota 58538.

PLETTA, DAN H Occupation: Engineer, University Distinguished Professor Emeritus, Virginia Polytechnic Institute and State University. Education: B.S., M.S., C.E. Address: 1414 Highland Circle, Blacksburg, Virginia 24060.

PLOTNICK, ROBERT N Occupation: Law Librarian, Director Paralegal Institute, Law Library,

Connecticut Institute for Paralegal Studies. Education: B.A., University of Bridgeport; J.D., New York Law School. Address: 40 Caprice Drive, Stamford, Connecticut 06902.

POBO, KENNETH GEORGE Occupation: English Instructor, English Department, University of Tennessee-Knoxville. Education: Ph.D. English. Address: 2751 Jersey #4, Knoxville, Tennessee 37919.

PODEST, MABEL FRANCES Occupation: Director, Luna County Work Activity Center. Education: B.A., New Mexico State University; M.S.W., Arizona State University. Address: Route 1, Box 109, Deming, New Mexico 88030.

POE, GERALD D Occupation: Director of Bands, University of Florida. Education: B.M., M.M., D.M.A. Address: 1716 Northwest 21st Street, Gainesville, Florida 32605.

POEHNER, RAYMOND G Occupation: Former Assistant Manager and Consumer Credit Officer, Security Pacific National Bank. Education: Attended Public and Military Schools, Workshops. Address: 6674 Water Street, Gulf Breeze, Florida 32561.

POELLMAN, MICHAELLA Occupation: Member of Religious Order, Reading Specialist, Educator. Education: M.A. Reading Specialist. Address: 3221 South Lake Drive, Milwaukee, Wisconsin 53207.

POHL, HERBERT ACKLAND Occupation: Director, Pohl Cancer Research Laboratory. Education: A.B., Ph.D. Address: 515 Harned Avenue, Stillwater, Oklahoma 74075.

POINDEXTER, HILDRUS A Occupation: Professor. Education: A.B., M.D., A.M., Ph.D., M.S.P.H. Address: 9507 Piscataway Road, Clinton, Maryland 20735.

POKLUDA, SANDRA JEAN Occupation: Director, Outreach Department, Mexia State School. Education: B.B.A., M.Ed. Address: 1102 North Red River, Mexia, Texas 76667.

POL, LOUIS G Occupation: Associate Professor of Marketing/Sociology, Memphis State University. Education: B.A., M.A., Ph.D. Address: 2104 Westchester Drive, Apartment #5, Memphis, Tennessee 38134.

POLACHEK, SOLOMON WILLIAMS Occupation: Professor. Education: Bachelor of Arts, Doctor of Philosophy. Address: 4509 Forest Lane, Binghamton, New York 13903.

POLAHA, JEROME M Occupation: Attorney. Education: A.A., Syracuse University; B.A., University of Nevada, 1964; J.D., George Washington University, 1968. Address: 115 Green Ridge Drive, Reno, Nevada 89509.

POLL, ROBERT E JR Occupation: Partner. Education: M.B.A., Indiana University; B.A., Kenyon College. Address: 70 East Schiller, Chicago, Illinois 60610.

POLLACK, ROBERT H Occupation: Professor of Psychology and Director of Graduate Training, University of Georgia. Education: B.S. Psychology, City College of New York; M.A., Ph.D. Psychology, Clark University. Address: 190 Gatewood Place, Athens, Georgia 30606.

POLLAN-COHEN, SHIRLEY Occupation: Poet; Performing Poet; Poetry Workshop Facilitator and Consultant; Coordinator, Bronx Poets and Writers Alliance; College Administrative Assistant. Education: B.A. (in progress). Address: Jerome Avenue Station, Post Office Box 627, Bronx, New York 10468.

POLLARD, CHARLES L Occupation: Mortician. Education: B.S., M.S. Address: 1625 East College, Guthrie, Oklahoma 73044.

POLLOCK, LESLIE S Occupation: City Planner. Education: B.Arch. 1966, Master Urban Planning 1968, University of Illinois. Address: 104 9th, Wilmette, Illinois 60091.

POLOMÉ, EDGAR C Occupation: Professor of Germanic and Oriental Languages and Linguistics, University of Texas-Austin. Education: M.A., Louvain, 1943; Ph.D., Brussels, 1949. Address: 3403 Loyola Lane, Austin, Texas 78723.

POLOUJADOFF, MICHEL E Occupation: Distinguished Hooker Visiting Professor. Education: Ingenieur ESE, M.S., Ph.D. Address: 144 Flatt Avenue, Hamilton, Ontario Canada L8P 4N3.

POMEROY, MAHLON WALTER Occupation: Nursing Home Administrator. Education: B.A., B.D., M.Div., M.A., Ph.D. Address: 504 Brown Street, Wauconda, Illinois 60084.

PONDER, HENRY Occupation: President, Fisk University. Education: B.S., M.S., Ph.D. Address: Fisk University, 17th Avenue North, Nashville, Tennessee 37203.

PONTECORVO, GIULIO Occupation: Professor of Economics. Education: A.B., M.C.S., Ph.D. Address: 178 Parrott Road, West Nyack, New York 10994.

POPE, ALEXANDER H Occupation: Los Angeles County Assessor. Education: A.B. Political Science, 1948; J.D., 1952. Address: 800 West 1st Street #2205, Los Angeles, California 90012.

POPOVICS, SANDOR Occupation: Professor of Civil Engineering. Education: Ph.D. Civil Engineering, Purdue University. Address: 283 Congress Avenue, Lansdowne, Pennsylvania 19050.

POPPINO, KATHRYN BERRY Occupation: Editor Reports and Proposals. Education: B.A. English, Oberlin College; M.A. Education, State University of New York-Albany. Address: 1027 Hickory Road, Schenectady, New York 12309.

PORATH, PEARL B Occupation: Writer, Reporter, Council Member. Education: University of Wisconsin, University of Miami. Address: 421 Pierce Street, Black River Falls, Wisconsin 54615.

PORGES, STEPHEN WILLIAM Occupation: Professor of Psychology, University of Illinois. Education: B.A., Drew University, 1966; M.A. 1968, Ph.D. 1974, Michigan State University. Address: 1407 Grandview, Champaign, Illinois 61820.

PORRECA, ANTHONY GABRIEL Occupation: Professor, The Ohio State University. Education: Doctorate. Address: 4088 Mountview Road, Upper Arlington, Ohio 43220.

PORTER, JEAN HASLER Occupation: Consultant. Education: B.A., University of Buffalo; M.L.S., State University of New York. Address: 3739 Hartland Road, Gasport, New York 1467.

PORTER, PARA BEATRICE Occupation: Counselor, Diagnostician. Education: B.S., M.S., North Texas State University; Ph.D., Baylor University, 1960. Address: 1616 South 9th Street, Waco, Texas 76706.

PORTER, REGINA Occupation: Editor and Founder, Loft Press, Inc. Education: A.A. Address: Jennijill Loop, Warrensburg, New York 12885.

PORTER, WILLIAM LANSING Occupation: President, Energy Company. Education: B.A. Address: 2266 Hidden Glen Drive, Marketta, Georgia 30067.

PORTWOOD, CHARLES STERLING Occupation: Advanced Information Systems President. Education: B.S. Chemical Engineering, University of Kansas, 1964; M.S. Nuclear Engineering 1969, PhD. Business Administration 1972, University of California-Berkeley. Address: 2611 Ala Wai Boulevard, Honolulu, Hawaii 96815.

POSEY, CHARLES R II (BOB) Occupation: Meteorological Data Automation Consultant/Systems Analyst. Education: B.A. Zoology, B.S. Meteorology, M.S. Meteorology. Address: 915 West St. Louis Street, Lebanon, Illinois 62254.

POSNER, BEN Occupation: Management Consultant; College Administrator, College of the Virgin Islands. Education: B.S., University of Arizona-Tucson; M.A., George Washington University; Ph.D., American University. Address: Post Office Box 9296, St. Thomas, U.S. Virgin Islands 00801.

POTEET, JAMES ALLEN Occupation: Professor of Special Education, Ball State University. Education: M.A., Michigan State University, 1959; Ph.D., Purdue University, 1970. Address: 8325 North Pennsylvania, Indianapolis, Indiana 46240.

POTENTE, EUGENE JR Occupation: Interior Designer. Education: Ph.B., Marquette University. Address: 6634 Third Avenue, Kenosha, Wisconsin 53140.

POTTS, BERNARD Occupation: Attorney. Education: A.B.A., LL.B., J.D. Address: 3206 Midfield Road, Pikeville, Maryland 21208.

POUND, WINSDON N Occupation: Educator (Retired). Education: B.S., M.A., C.A.G.S., Ed.D. Address: Route 2, Box 65, Pulaski, Virginia 24301.

POWELL, DIANE KEARNY Occupation: Retired Lawyer, Writer. Education: LL.B. 1940, LL.M. 1942. Address: 1500 Massachusetts Avenue, Northwest, Washington, D.C. 20005.

POWELL, WILLIAM COUNCIL Occupation: President, Granite Diagnosticoluc. Education: M.B.A., Wake Forest University; B.S. Address: 1616 Rockinwood Avenue, Burlington, North Carolina 27215.

POWER, KATHRYN R Occupation: Therapist, Consultant. Education: M.A., M.Th. Psychology/Religion. Address: 10301 South Cedar Lake Road, Minnetonka, Minnesota 55343.

POWER, SEAN DAVID Occupation: Jazz Dancing Teacher. Education: Further Studies. Address: 775 South James Road 3-B, Columbus, Ohio 43227.

POWERS, ARTHUR GEORGE Occupation: International Lawyer, Poet, Writer. Education: A.B., Shriner College, 1967; J.D., Harvard Law School, 1975. Address: 585 Commonwealth Avenue, Newton Centre, Massachusetts 02159.

POWERS, RICHARD F Occupation: President, Insight, Inc. Education: B.A., M.A., Ph.D. Address: 8608 Victoria Road, Springfield, Virginia 22151.

POWERS, THOMAS LYNWOOD Occupation: History Educator. Education: B.A., Ph.D. Address: U.S.C.-Sumter, 200 Miller Road, Sumter, South Carolina 29150.

POZNIAK, RICHARD ALEXANDER Occupation: Director, Department of Public Relations. Education: B.S., Emerson College; Postgraduate, Wharton School. Address: 11 Chester Road, Billerica, Massachusetts 01866.

PRADIER, JEROME MARTIN Occupation: United States Air Force Officer, Assistant Professor of Philosophy. Education: M.S. Management, M.A. Philosophy. Address: Quarters 4504A, United States Air Force Academy, Colorado 80840.

PRADO, GERALD M Occupation: Executive. Education: B.A., M.B.A., C.P.A. Address: 205 Overlook Drive, McMurray, Pennsylvnaia 15317.

PRASAD, ANANDA S Occupation: Physician, Professor, Director, Hematology Division. Education: M.B., B.S., Patna University; Ph.D. Medicine, University of Minnesota, 1953. Address: 4710 Cove Road, Orchard Lake, Michigan 48033.

PRESLEY, MERGIE M Occupation: Retired. Education: B.A., Philander Smith College; M.S., Tennessee State University. Address: 1004 Southeast Front Street, Haynesville, Louisiana 71038.

PRESS, MICHELLE Occupation: Editor. Education: B.A. English Literature, The New School for Social Research. Address: 584 Chapel Street, New Haven, Connectivut 06511.

PRESSER, LEON Occupation: President of Softool Corporation. Education: B.S.E.E. 1961, M.S.E.E. 1964, Ph.D. 1968. Address: 974 North Kellogg, Santa Barbara, California 93111.

PRESTON, DONALD G Occupation: Senior Vice President, Manager. Education: A.B., Center College of Kentucky; M.B.A., University of Kentucky. Address: 14001 Wolcott Drive, Tampa, Florida 33624.

PRESTON, FREDERICK W JR Occupation: Banker, Southeast Bank Corporation. Education: B.A. 1967, M.B.A. 1973. Address: 5201 Southwest 74 Street, Miami, Florida 33143.

PRESTON, FREDERICK WILLARD Occupation: Surgeon, Retired Professor of Surgery. Education: B.A., Yale University, 1935; M.D., Northwestern University, 1940; M.S., University of Minnesota, 1948. Address: 755 Via Airosa, Santa Barbara, California 93110.

PREVOTS, HAIMA Occupation: Professor, Museum Director. Education: B.A. 1955, M.S. 1960. Address: 5219 Massachusetts Avenue, Bethesda, Maryland 20816.

PRICE, ALAN ROGER Occupation: Associate Vice President for Research, University of Michigan. Education: B.S. Chemistry, Ph.D. Biochemistry. Address: 1450 Covington, Ann Arbor, Michigan 48103.

PRICE, ALVIN A Occupation: Director of Biomedical Science, Texas A&M University. Education: A.S., B.S., M.S., D.V.M. Address: 1203 Walton Drive, College Station, Texas 77840.

PRICE, MARK MICHAEL Occupation: President. Education: University of Detroit. Address: 4960 Sentinel Drive, Bethesda, Maryland 20816.

PRICE, RICHARD LEE Occupation: Judge, Justice. Education: B.A., Roanoke College; J.D., New York Law School. Address: 577 Grand Street, New York, New York 10002.

PRICHARD, ELLA WALL Occupation: Board of Directors, National Federation of Parents for Drug Free Youth. Education: B.A., Baylor University, 1963. Address: 5252 Greenbriar, Corpus Christi, Texas 78413.

PRITIKIN, ROLAND I Occupation: Brigadier General, I.L.A.N.G. (Retired). Education: M.D. Address: 1211 Talcott Building, Rockford, Illinois 61101.

PRITZKER, PAUL EDWIN Occupation: Consulting Engineer. Education: Registered Professional Engineer. Address: 11 Young Road, Weston, Massachusetts 02193.

PROCHNOW, HERBERT VICTOR Occupation: Secretary, Federal Advisory Council of the Federal Reserve System. Education: B.A., M.A., LL.D.

PROCOPE, ERNESTA G Occupation: Commercial Insurance Brokerage. Education: College Studies, Honorary Doctoral Degrees, Morgan State University, Adelphi University. Address: 2-18 Parsons Boulevard, Malba, Long Island, New York 11357.

PROCTOR, CLAUDE O JR Occupation: Translator, Consultant. Education: M.A. Government, B.G.E. Geography. Address: 1712 McCoy Place, Georgetown, Texas 78626.

PROCTOR, ROBERT S Occupation: Vice President Manufacturing. Education: M.S. Mechanical Engineering, Oregon State University. Address: 6 Linda Juta, Tiburon, California 94920.

PROCUNIER, KERI L Occupation: Executive Director, Agnews State Hospital. Education: B.A. Pol./Psychology, M.S. Administration, Ph.D. Address: 3500 Zanker Road, San Jose, California 95134-2299.

PRODAN, JAMES CHRISTIAN Occupation: Assistant Professor of Music, University of North Carolina-Greensboro. Education: B.S., Ohio State University; M.M., Catholic University; D.M.A., Ohio State University. Address: 1814 Dunleith Way, Greensboro, North Carolina 27408.

PROSSER, HAROLD LEE Occupation: Sociologist, Writer. Education: A.A. English, B.S. Sociology, M.S.Ed. Social Science. Address: 1313 South Jefferson Avenue, Springfield, Missouri 65807.

PROVDA, LOIS J Occupation: Educational Therapist, Private Preacher. Education: Ph.D. Address: 208 South Lasky Drive, Beverly Hills, California 90212.

PRUNSKIS, JOSEPH Occupation: Roman Catholic Priest; Director of Information, American Lithuanian Council. Education: Doctor in Canon Law. Address: 6135 South Austin Avenue, Chicago, Illinois 60638.

PRY, ROBERT HENRY Occupation: Executive. Education: Ph.D. 1951, M.S. 1949, Rice University; B.S., Texas A&I, 1947. Address: 21038 Andover Road, Kildeer, Illinois 60047.

PSUTY, NORBERT PHILLIP Occupation: Director, Center for Coastal and Environmental Studies. Education: B.S., Wayne State University, 1959; M.S., Miami University, 1960; Ph.D., Louisiana State University, 1966. Address: 19 Green Hills Road, East Brunswick, New Jersey 08816.

PUDERBAUGH, HOMER L Occupation: Professor of Architecture, University of Nebraska-Lincoln. Education: B.Arch., M.S. Address: 1201 "J", Lincoln, Nebraska 68508.

PUDNOS, STANLEY H Occupation: Executive Vice President, Insurance Brokers Association of New Jersey. Education: City College of New York, 1952. Address: 37 York Street, Old Bridge, New Jersey 08857.

PULFER, LESLIE LOUIS Occupation: Assistant Administrator. Education: B.A., A.A. Address: 1504 South 7th, Pekin, Illinois 61554.

PUNNETT, AUDREY FRANCES Occupation: Psychologist. Education: B.A., M.S., Ph.D. Address: 5100 North Sixth Street, Suite 135, Fresno, California 93710.

PURI, MADAN L Occupation: Professor of Mathematics. Education: D.Sc. 1975, Ph.D. 1962, M.A. 1950. Address: 1302 Winfield Road, Bloomington, Indiana 47401.

PURISCH, ARNOLD D Occupation: Clinical Neuropsychologist. Education: Ph.D. Address: 4408 Fir Avenue, Seal Beach, California 90740.

PURPURA, ANTHONY G Occupation: Medical Doctor. Education: B.A., Colgate University; M.D., George Washington University. Address: 3 Helena Road, Staten Island, New York 10304.

PURTLE, VIRGINIA S Occupation: Associate Dean A&S, Professor of Sociology, College of Arts and Sciences, Louisiana State University. Education: B.S., M.S., Ph.D. Address: 412 LSU Avenue, Baton Rouge, Louisiana 70808.

PUTNAM, LINDA L Occupation: Professor/Researcher, Department of Communication, Purdue University. Education: B.A., M.A., University of Wisconsin; Ph.D., University of Minnesota. Address: 157 Ivy Hill Drive, West Lafayette, Indiana 47906.

PUYEAR, ROBERT BREWER Occupation: Manager, Materials Technology, Monsanto Company. Education: B.S. Ch.E., University of Missouri-Rolla; M.S., Purdue University; Address: 226 River Valley Drive, Chesterfield, Missouri 63017.

PYFER, JEAN L Occupation: Chairman of Physical Education Department, Texas Woman's University. Education: B.S., M.S., P.E.D. Address: 1815 Creek, Denton, Texas 76201.

PYLE, DAVID BURTON Occupation: Management Analyst. Education: A.A., B.A., M.P.A. Address: 748 Jacob Court, Napa, California 94558.

PYSICK, RALPH W Occupation: Realtor and Insurance Salesman. Education: B.S. Business, University of Minnesota; Chartered Life Underwriter, Society of Chartered Life Underwriters; Graduate, Realtor Institute, National Association of Realtors. Address: 301 Lewis Avenue South, Watertown, Minnesota 55388-0728.

PYSZKOWSKI, IRENE S Occupation: Assistant Professor, Division of Education, St. John's University. Education: Ph.D. Address: 89-73 Street, Brooklyn, New York 11209.

Q

QUAAS, LEROY M Occupation: City Engineer. Education: B.S.C.E., Valparaiso University, 1964. Address: 1333 East Donner Drive, Tempe, Arizona 85282.

QUAGLIANO, ANTHONY J Occupation: Educator, Writer, Poet. Education: B.A., University of Chicago; Ph.D., University of Hawaii. Address: 509 University Avenue, #902, Honolulu, Hawaii 96826.

QUANDT, ELIZABETH Occupation: Artist. Education: B.F.A., M.F.A. Address: 920 McDonald Avenue, Santa Rosa, California 95404.

QUANSTROM, WALTER ROY Occupation: General Manager Environmental Affairs and Safety, Standard Oil Company. Education: B.S., Bethany Nazarene College, 1964; Ph.D., University of Oklahoma, 1968. Address: 353 South Stewart, Lombard, Illinois 60148.

QUARTEY, SAMUEL F Occupation: Podiatrist-Surgeon. Education: Bachelor of Science, Master of Science, Doctor of Podiatric Medicine. Address: 2 Eastwood Court, West Berlin, New Jersey 08901.

QUEBBEMAN, ROBERT CHRISTIAN Occupation: Conductor, Minot Symphony; Associate Professor, Minot State College. Education: A.Mus.D., The University of Michigan. Address: 1303 Tuxedo Road, Minot, North Dakota 58701.

QUIDD, DAVID ANDREW Occupation: Paralegal. Education; Bachelor of Arts in Political Science, The University of New Orleans. Address: 1141 Papworth Avenue, Metairie, Louisiana 70005.

QUIGLEY, JOHN M Occupation: Professor of Economics and Public Policy. Education: B.S., United States Air Force Academy; M.Sc., University of Stockholm. Address: 875 Hilldale, Berkeley, California 94708.

QUILLEN, JAMES H Occupation: Member, U.S. House of Representatives. Education: Honorary LL.D., Milligan College, Tennessee, 1978. Address: 1601 Fairidge Place, Kingsport, Tennessee 37664.

QUINER, MARK Occupation: Lawyer. Education: B.S. General Business, J.D., University of Wyoming. Address: 3334½ Alexander, Cheyenne, Wyoming 82001.

QUINN, GEORGE Occupation: Student. Education: A.A., Attending U.S.M. Address: Route 2, Box 345, Natchez, Missouri 39120.

QUINN, JAMES I Occupation: Composer/Professor of Humanities, Loop College. Education: B.M., M.M., Ph.D. Address: 4 Aberdeen Road, Hawthorn Woods, Illinois 60047.

QUINN, JAMES J Occupation: Partner, Coopers and Lybrand. Education: B.S. Accounting, Fordham University, 1951. Address: 110 Kensington Road, Garden City, New York 11530.

QUITTMAN, STEPHEN ASHLEY Occupation: Psychologist. Education: B.A., Columbia University, 1964; Ph.D., Adelphi University, 1969. Address: 20 Aberdeen Drive, West Nyack, New York 10994.

QURAISHI, MOHAMMED SAYEED Occupation: Entomologist-Toxicologist. Education: Ph.D. Address: 19813 Cochrane Way, Gaithersburg, Maryland 20879.

QURESHI, ABDUL MAJID Occupation: Project Leader, Product Process Development. Education: Bachelor in Pharmacy, Master Pharmaceutical Science. Address: 13 Gifford Road, Somerset, New Jersey 08873.

QUTUB, MUSA Y Occupation: Professor, Northeastern Illinois University; Consultant. B.A. Geology, M.S. Hydrology, Ph.D. Water Resources. Address: 720 Madelyn Drive, Des Plaines, Illinois 60016.

R

RAAD, VIRGINIA Occupation: Concert Pianist-Musicologist. Education: Doctorate, University of Paris, France. Address: 60 Terrace Avenue, Salem, West Virginia 26426.

RAATZ, SHERRY SWETT Occupation: First Vice Regent, Rainier Chapter, N.S.D.A.R.; Membership Chairman, Seattle-King County Chapter, Freedoms Foundation at Valley Forge. Education: B.A. Creative Dramatics and Drama (cum laude), University of Washington. Address: 7500 27th Northeast, Seattle, Washington 98115.

RABIL, MITCHELL J Occupation: Attorney. Education: B.S., Wake Forest University, 1953; J.D., Georgetown University, 1961. Address: 524 Main Street, Riverton, New Jersey 08077.

RABON, WILLIAM J JR Occupation: Architect. Education: B.S., B.A., M.A. Address: 2324 Madison Road, Cincinnati, Ohio 45208.

RABORG, FREDERICK A JR Occupation: Free Lance Writer, Poet, Playwright. Education: B.A. English Literature, Graduate Studies. Address: Post Office Box 2835, Bakersfield, California 93303.

RACH, RANDOLPH CARL Occupation: Microwave Tube Engineer. Education: B.S. with honors in Physics and Mathematics. Address: 9 Hudson Street, Watertown, Massachusetts 02172.

RACHETER, DONALD PAUL Occupation: Chairman, Department of Political Science, Central College. Education: B.A. with distinction, Michigan; M.A., Ph.D., Iowa. Address: 1013 Main, Pella, Iowa 50219.

RACHLIN, HARVEY BRANT Occupation: Author. Education: B.A., Hofstra University, 1973. Address: 252 Robby Lane, New Hyde Park, New York 11040.

RADER, CHARLES P Occupation: Research Chemist. Education: B.S. Chemistry, M.S., Ph.D. Address: 2457 Greenhaven Drive, Akron, Ohio 44313.

RADER, STEVEN PALMER Occupation: Attorney. Education: B.A., J.D. Address: 113 South Harvey Street, Washington, North Carolina 27889.

RADEWAGEN, FRED Occupation: Director, Washington Office, Government of American Samoa. Education: B.A., Northwestern University, 1966; M.S.F.S., Georgetown University, 1968. Address: 103 East Luray Avenue, Alexandria, Virginia 22301.

RADFORD, RICHARD FRANCIS JR Occupation: Author. Education: B.A. with honors. Address: 31 Harvard Street, Brookline, Massachusetts 02146.

RADINSKY, STEPHEN HARRIS Occupation: Diagnostic Radiologist. Education: A.B., D.O. Address: 12267 Winrock, Creve Coeur, Missouri 63141.

RADLAUER, RUTH SHAW Occupation: Author and Editor of Children's Books. Education: B.A., University of California-Los Angeles. Address: Post Office Box 1637, Whittier, California 90609.

RADNER, EPHRAIM Occupation: Senior Vice President, Finance and Administration. Education: B.A., University of Massachusetts; M.B.A., Harvard Business School. Address: 116 Douglas Road, Belmont, Massachusetts 02178.

RAFTOPOULOS, DEMETRIOS D Occupation: Professor of Mechanical Engineering. Education: B.S.C.E., M.C.E., Ph.D. in Engineering Mechanics. Address: 2091 Morocco Road, Ida, Michigan 48140.

RAGAN, CONNIE SEABOURN Occupation: Visual Artist (Painter, Printmaker). Education: Bachelor of Fine Arts. Address: 2605 Southwest 99, Oklahoma City, Oklahoma 73159.

RAGHEB, MAGDI Occupation: University Teaching and Research. Education: M.Sc., Ph.D. Nuclear Engineering and Computer Science. Address: 401 Edgebrook Drive, Champaign, Illinois 61820.

RAGLAND, LeANITA S Occupation: Advertising Representative. Education: B.A. Visual Arts. Address: 5470 Watercress Place, Columbia, Maryland 21045.

RAI, SHAMBHU K Occupation: Attorney-at-Law; Real Estate Syndication. Education: LL.M., New York University School of Law; LL.B., Sagar, India. Address: 23861 Pebble Beach Place, Laguna Niguel, California 92677.

RAITHEL, FREDERICK J Occupation: Information Systems Specialist. Education: B.A. Philosophy, M.A. Library and Information Science. Address: 501H Columbia Drive, Columbia, Missouri 65201.

RAJ, HARKISAN D Occupation: Professor. Education: B.S. with honors, M.S., Ph.D. Address: 16251 Gentry Lane, Huntington Beach, California 92647.

RAJAGOPAL, RANGASWAMY Occupation: Editor-in-Chief/College Professor, Department of Geography, University of Iowa. Education: B.Sc., M.Eng., Ph.D. Address: 343 Koser Avenue, Iowa City, Iowa 52240.

RAJENDRA, KUNWAR Occupation: Engineer, City Planner, University Professor. Education: Ph.D. Address: 5244 Bluehaven Drive, East Lansing, Michigan 48823.

RAJANDER, ROBERT ANTON Occupation: City Planning Commissioner and Retired Educational Administrator. Education: B.V.E. and Master's Degree Educational Administration. Address: 153 Raleigh Drive, Vacaville, California 95688.

RAKICH, CHRISTA MARTIN Occupation: Musician and Educator. Education: B.Mus., B.A., M.Mus. Address: 552 Storrs Road, Mansfield Center, Connecticut 06250.

RAMEY, JOHN HENRY Occupation: Associate Professor of Social Work, University of Akron. Education: B.A. Philosophy, M.A. Social Administration, Ohio State University. Address: 463 Moreley Avenue, Akron, Ohio 44320.

RAMEY, RAY R Occupation: Vice President, Lane Company, Inc. Education: B.S., University of Virginia. Address: 1922 Tabby Lane, Altavista, Virginia 24517.

RAMICK, CHARLES CONRAD Occupation: Technical Consultant. Education: A.A., B.A., M.S. Address: 410 Park Drive, Glenwood, Illinois 60425.

RAMIREZ, SUSAN ELIZABETH Occupation: Professor, De Paul University. Education: B.A., M.A., Ph.D. 1977. Address: 2908 North Spaulding, Chicago, Illinois 60618.

RAMIREZ DE ARELLANO, DIANA Occupation: Writer, Educator. Education: B.A., M.A., Ph.D. Address: 23 Harbor Circle, Centerport, New York 11721.

RAMLER, WARREN J Occupation: Senior Vice President, Construction of Accelerators. Education: B.S., M.S., Electrical Engineering. Address: 15 Buckingham Drive, Prestbury, Aurora, Illinois 60504.

RAMSEY, DAVID MORGAN Occupation: Associate Professor. Education: A.A., B.A., M.A., Ph.D. Address: 1024 East 12th Street, York, Nebraska 68467.

RAMSEY, MARYLOU Occupation: College Professor. Education: B.A. Psychology, M.A. Counseling, Ed.D. Counseling and Administration. Address: 15 Westway, Clinton, New Jersey 08809.

RAMSEY, WILLIAM L Occupation: Director,

Webster University. Education: Bachelors of Arts and Science, Master's Degree, Doctoral Degree. Address: 15322 Golden Rain Drive, Chesterfield, Missouri 63107.

RANDALL, DUDLEY (FELKER) Occupation: Author. Education: B.A., Wayne University, 1949; M.A.L.S., The University of Michigan, 1951. Address: 12651 Old Mill Place, Detroit, Michigan 48238.

RANDALL, PHILLIP M Occupation: Director, Training and Development. Education: B.A., M.A., Ph.D. Address: 1230 Avenue of the Americas, New York, New York 10020.

RANDAZZO, ARLENE Occupation: Opera Singer. Education: Attended High School of Performing Arts, Henry St. Settlement. Address: 221 West 82nd Street, New York, New York 10024.

RANDLER, KAREN R Occupation: Poet, Educational Consultant for the Gifted. Education: A.B., M.A. Address: 2450 Warring #31, Berkeley, California 94704.

RANK, ARVILLA C Occupation: Independent Living Coordinator for Hearing Impaired. Education: B.S., M.S., M.S. Address: 6358 South 20th Street, Milwaukee, Wisconsin 53221.

RANKAITIS, SUSAN Occupation: Artist. Education: B.F.A., University of Illinois, 1971; M.F.A., University of Southern California, 1977. Address: 707 East Hyde Park Boulevard, Inglewood, California 90302.

RANKIN, KELLY DAVID Occupation: Coordinator of Physical Education/Athletics, Vancouver Public Schools. Education: B.S. Elementary Education, 1962; M.S. Administration, 1965; Educational Specialist Elementary Education, 1970; Ed.D. Physical Education, 1975. Address: 6220 Montana Lane, Vancouver, Washington 98661.

RANKIN, MERTHA S Occupation: Educator, Co-Ed-Y Sponsor, Mississippi C. Social Studies. Education: B.S. Social Science, M.S. Social Science. Address: Route 3 #328, Magee, Mississippi 39111.

RANKINE-GALLOWAY, HONORA M F Occupation: University Professor. Education: B.A., College of New Rochelle; M.A., Ph.D., University of Pennsylvania. Address: 123 West 93rd Street, New York, New York 10025.

RANNEY, JAMES LARRY Occupation: Director of Elementary Curriculum, Peoria Public Schools. Education: B.S., Eureka College; M.A., Bradley University; M.A., Southern Illinois University. Address: 109 Coventry Lane, East Peoria, Illinois 61611.

RANSON, GUY H Occupation: Professor Emeritus, Real Estate Investments. Education: B.A., Hardin-Simmons University; M.A., University of Kentucky; Ph.D., Yale University. Address: 115 Irvington Drive, San Antonio, Texas 78209.

RAO, K L SESHAGIRI Occupation: Professor of Religious Studies, University of Virginia. Education: B.A., M.A., Ph.D. Address: 1907 Swanson Drive, Charlottesville, Virginia 22901.

RAPP, JAMES A Occupation: Director, Marketing Services. Education: B.A. English. Address: 509 Mandeville Street, New Orleans, Louisiana 70117.

RAPPAPORT, MARGARET M Occupation: Psychologist. Education: B.A., M.A. Ph.D. Address: 509 East Sedgwick Street, Philadelphia, Pennsylvania 19119.

RASMUSSEN, ROBERT G Occupation: President and Junior Consultant, Practice Management Association. Education: B.S. Accounting, Business Management and Economic Minors. Address: 259 East 1950 South, Bountiful, Utah 84010.

RASS, REBECCA RIVKA Occupation: Writer, Journalist, College Professor. Education: B.A., M.F.A. Address: 319 Broadway, New York, New York 10007.

RATCLIFF, BRUCE EPHLIN Occupation: President, Ratcliff Hoist Company and Ratcliff Company. Education: B.A. Economics, San Francisco State University, 1967. Address: 1308 Sunnyslope Avenue, Belmont, California 94002.

RATLIFF, DAVID W Occupation: Financial Broker. Education: B.B.A. in Accounting. Address: 1298 Kingsbury, Abilene, Texas 79602.

RATLIFF, GERALD LEE Occupation: Associate Professor of Theatre. Education: B.A. magna cum laude, Georgetown University, 1967; M.A., University of Cincinnati, 1970; Ph.D., Bowling Green State University, 1975. Address: 361 Crestmont Road, Cedar Grove, New Jersey 07043.

RAU, CHARLES A JR Occupation: Consulting Engineer. Education: B.S., Lafayette College; M.S., Ph.D., Stanford University. Address: 130 Croyden Way, Woodside, California 94062.

RAVELING, DENNIS G Occupation: Professor, University of California-Davis. Education: B.A., Ph.D., Southern Illinois University; M.A., University of Minnesota. Address: 504 Del Oro, Davis, California 95616.

RAWLINGS, CHARLES ADRIAN Occupation: Professor, Electrical Engineering, Southern Illinois University; Consultant. Education: B.S.E.E., M.S., Ph.D. Address: 1430 East Walnut Street, Carbondale, Illinois 62901.

RAWLINS, JACK P Occupation: Professor of English. Education: B.A., University of California-Berkeley, 1968; M. Phil., Ph.D., Yale University, 1972. Address: 332 West Frances Willard Avenue, Chico, California 95926.

RAWLINS, JOSEPH T Occupation: Professional Musician/Teacher. Education: A.A., University of Florida; B.M., M.M., D.M.A., Louisiana State University. Address: 8339 Pilgrim Road, Pensacola, Florida 32504.

RAWLS, BARBARA WATSON Occupation: Senior Consultant. Education: A.B., Stanford/Smith; M.A., Stanford University; M.B.A., Wharton School of Finance and Commerce. Address: 1754 Cedar Lane, Villanova, Pennsylvania 19085.

RAY, AJIT KUMAR Occupation: Consultant and Advisor, Fundamental Research Institute; Reviewer Applied Mechanics Reviews, U.S.A. Education: B.Sc., Asutosh Memorial School, 1944; M.Sc., Gold Medalist and University Prizeman, Calcutta University, 1947; D.Sc. Mathematics, Humboldt School, Gottin, 1955. Address: 318-A, 2767 Innes Road, Gloucester, Ottawa, Ontario, Canada.

RAY, DAVID EUGENE Occupation: Writer, Teacher, Editor. Education: B.A., M.A., University of Chicago. Address: 5517 Crestwood Drive, Kansas City, Missouri 64110.

RAYBIN, JUDITH A Occupation: Investor Relations Manager. Education: B.S., Tufts University; M.B.A., Wharton School of Business and Finance. Address: 226 Funston Avenue, San Francisco, California 94118.

RAYBURN, B J Occupation: Manufacturing Company Executive. Education: B.S. Mechanical Engineering, U.S. Air Force Institute, 1955. Address: 1610 Woodstead Court, The Woodlands, Texas 77380.

RAYMOND, ARTHUR Occupation: Director, Indian Program Development, University of North Dakota. Education: B.A., A.M., Ph.D. Address: 2111

University Avenue, Grand Forks, North Dakota 58201.

READ, DWIGHT W Occupation: Professor, Department of Anthropology, University of California at Los Angeles. Education: B.A., M.A., Ph.D. Address: 1147 Beverwil Drive, Los Angeles, California 90035.

READE, CHARLES FALKINER JR Occupation: Chairman and Chief Executive Officer, International Merchant of Metals and Minerals. Education: B.B.A. Finance, University of Miami, 1965; Attended Harvard University Graduate School of Business, 1971. Address: 18 First Street, Rumson, New Jersey 07760.

REAGAN, STUART A Occupation: Investment Officer. Education: A.B. (W.H.D.), M.A., M.P.A. Address: 531 Menominee Trail, Frankfort, Kentucky 40601.

RECHARD, PAUL A Occupation: President, Engineering Consulting Firm. Education: B.S. Civil Engineering, M.S. Civil Engineering, Professional Degree of C.E. Address: 316 Stuart, Laramie, Wyoming 82070.

RECHCIGL, JOHN EDWARD Occupation: Research Assistant working on Ph.D. in Agronomy. Education: B.S. Plant Science, M.S. Agronomy. Address: 11 Wharton Street, Blacksburg, Virginia 24060.

RECHT, NADYNE M Occupation: Real Estate Broker-Owner. Education: Real Estate Courses. Address: 6853 Woodcrest Drive, Fort Wayne, Indiana 46815.

RECK, WALDO EMERSON Occupation: Vice President Emeritus, Wittenberg University; Writer. Education: A.B., Wittenberg College, 1926; M.A., University of Iowa, 1946; LL.D., Midland College, 1949. Address: 61 Hedgely Road, Springfield, Ohio 45506.

REDAY, LADISLAW Occupation: Writer. Education: B.S., Massachusetts Institute of Technology. Address: 359 Via Lido South, Newport Beach, California 92663.

REDD, FRANK JACKSON Occupation: Vice Commander, Air Force Space Technical Center. Education: B.S., United States Military Academy at West Point; M.S., Stanford University; Ph.D., Brigham Young University. Address: 2219 Stockton Loop, Albuquerque, New Mexico 87118.

REDDEN, HARRAL A JR Occupation: Insurance and Real Estate Broker. Education: B.A., Ursinus College. Address: 18 Center Street, Rumson, New Jersey 07760.

REDDINGTON, CHARLES L Occupation: Professor of Art. Education: Artists' Diploma, B.F.A., M.F.A. Address: 504 Hulman, Terre Haute, Indiana 47802.

REDDY, GUNDA Occupation: Research Toxicologist, Health Effects Research Division, U.S. Army Medical Bioengineering Research and Development Laboratory. Education: M.Sc., Ph.D. Address: 5636 Single Tree Drive, Frederick, Maryland 21701.

REDELSHEIMER, ARTHUR C Occupation: Professional Engineer (California). Education: B.S., De Paul University; M.B.A., Indiana University; Ph.D., Western. Address: 5258 Krenning Street, San Diego, California 92105.

REDENBAUGH, M KEITH Occupation: Plant Biology Scientist, Plant Genetics, Inc. Education: B.A., University of California; Ph.D., State University of New York College Environmental Science and Forestry. Address: Plant Genetics, Inc., 1930 5th Street, Davis, California 95616.

REDMAN, JOHN JAMES Occupation: Deputy Auditor, Consumer Affairs, Franklin County Auditor's Office; Night School Director, Bliss College. Education: A.B. Address: 1403-A West Third Avenue, Columbus, Ohio 43212.

REDMAN, WILLIAM W JR Occupation: North Carolina Senator, Real Estate Businessman, Retired Member of the Military. Education: B.S., Embry-Riddle Aeronautical University. Address: Route 2, Box 43, Statesville, North Carolina 28677.

REDMOND, JOHN D Occupation: Director, Health Cost Consulting, Blue Cross/Blue Shield. Education: B.S. Business Administration, Columbus College, 1970; M.B.A., Georgia State University, 1975; M.B.A., Columbus College, 1977. Address: 3942 Tifton Drive, Columbus, Georgia 31907.

REDMOUNT, MELVIN B Occupation: Director of Planning. Education: B.S.Ch.E., M.Ch.E. Address: 310 Jackson Avenue, Ridgway, Pennsylvania 15853.

REED, RODNEY J Occupation: Professor, Graduate School of Education, University of California. Education: B.A., Clark College; M.A., University of Michigan; Ph.D., University of California-Berkeley. Address: 6623 Glen Oaks Way, Oakland, California 94611.

REEDY, JOHN JOSEPH Occupation: University Professor. Education: B.S., N.S., M.S., Ph.D., M.Ed. Address: 914 Oneida Street, Lewiston, New York 14092.

REEP, ROBERT GREGG Occupation: Director, Community Development. Education: B.A. Political Science. Address: 212 East Central, Warren, Arizona 71671.

REEPMEYER, MARIE CHRISTINA Occupation: Librarian. Education: A.A., B.A. Sociology, Master's Degree Library Science. Address: 12 MacDonald Circle, Menands, New York 12204.

REESE, (MRS) LEE FLEMING Occupation: Retired Teacher, Writer, Lecturer, Editor. Education: A.A., B.A., M.A. Address: 4872 Old Cliffs Road, San Diego, California 92120.

REESE, STEVE E Occupation: Pharmaceutical Marketing. Education: B.S., M.S., Pharmacy. Address: 27 Tracey Drive, Lawrenceville, New Jersey 08648.

REEVES, JERRY D Occupation: Physician, Pediatric Hematologist, Director of Medical Education. Education: B.A., M.D. Address: 5310 Kilkenny Road, Vacaville, California 95688.

REEVY, WILLIAM ROBERT Occupation: Clinical Psychologist. Education: B.A., Stanford University; Ph.D, Pennsylvania State University. Address: 730 Crestview Drive, Durham, North Carolina 27712.

REGAN, HELENE Occupation: Second Vice President, International Banking Specialist. Education: Baruch College, Brandeis Study Group. Address: 4 Lexington Avenue, New York, New York 10010.

REGAN, LYNNDA M Occupation: Strategic Planning Manager. Education: B.S., Purdue University; P.M.D., Harvard University. Address: 108 Monticello Drive, Monroeville, Pennsylvania 15146.

REGAT, JEAN-JACQUES Occupation: Sculptor, Moralist, Lithographer. Education: B.A. Fine Arts/Anthropology cum laude; Latin American Seminar, Independent Study Affiliated Membership, University of Alaska. Address: 518 Pearl Drive, Anchorage, Alaska 99502.

REGAT, MARY EILEEN Occupation: Sculptor, Moralist, Lithographer. Education: Latin American Seminar, Independent Study Affiliated Membership, University of Alaska. Address: 518 Pearl Drive, Anchorage, Alaska 99502.

REGNIER, CLAIRE N Occupation: President, Metro Consultants, Inc. Education: B.S. Journalism cum laude, Trinity University. Address: 7772 Woodridge, San Antonio, Texas 78209.

REHAK, JAMES R Occupation: Orthodontist. Education: B.S., D.D.S., M.S. Address: 859 Nelsons Walk, Naples, Florida 33940.

REHM, DOROTHY A Occupation: Association Executive, Director Special Clinical Projects and Programs. Education: B.S., M.A. Address: 2983 Marion Avenue, Bronx, New York 10458.

REICH, BERNARD Occupation: Professor, Consultant, Lecturer. Education: B.A., M.A., Ph.D. Address: 13800 Turnmore Road, Wheaton, Maryland 20906.

REICH, JACK E Occupation: Chairman of the Board and Chief Executive Officer, American United Life Insurance Company. Education: Attended Purdue University. Address: 7404 North Pennsylvania Street, Indianapolis, Indiana 46204.

REICH, MICHAEL Occupation: Electronics Engineer. Education: B.E.E.E., City College of the City University of New York; M.S.A., George Washington University, Washington, D.C. Address: 749 Piney Wood Circle, California, Maryland 20619.

REICHENBACH, BRUCE R Occupation: Professor of Philosophy, Augsburg College. Education: B.A., Wheaton College; M.A., Ph.D., Northwestern University. Address: 707 West County Road B-2, Roseville, Minnesota 55113.

REID, FRANCES K Occupation: Filmmaker/ Cinematographer. Education: B.A. Address: Post Office Box 5353, Berkeley, California 94705.

REID, RANDALL CLYDE Occupation: College Professor and Novelist. Education: B.A., M.A., Ph.D. Address: 1530 Hillside Drive, Reno, Nevada 89503.

REID, SARALOU (SALLY) L Occupation: Media Specialist, Supervisor. Education: B.S., M.S., and Ed.D. Address: 2045 Menominee Drive, Oshkosh, Wisconsin 54901.

REID, SHERRI JO Occupation: Tax Preparer and Consultant Enrolled to Practice before IRS Classes in Tax Electronics. Education: Attended Iowa State Bar Tax Schools and Iowa State University. Address: Route 1, Box 27, Onslow, Iowa 52321.

REILLY, MARY LOU Occupation: Educator, Businesswoman. Education: B.S. Education, B.A. History, M.S. Education, Ph.D. Curriculum and Instruction Education. Address: 5381 Eagan Court, Rohnert Park, California 94928.

REINHARDT, MADGE Occupation: Publisher, Novelist, Playwright. Education: B.A. Address: 1803 Venus Avenue, St. Paul, Minnesota 55112.

REIS, JOAN S Occupation: Lecturer on Music History, University of Cincinnati. Education: B.M. Violin, M.M. Musicology. Address: 1815 Taft Road, Cincinnati, Ohio 45206.

REISDORF, SHIRLEY CARMAN Occupation: Swimming Instructor and Special Olympic Coach. Education: A.S., Recreation (Theraputic). Address: Route #11, 18596 Sarasota Road, Southeast, Fort Myers, Florida 33908.

REISINGER, GEORGE LAMBERT Occupation: Partner/Managing Vice President. Education: B.S., Business Administration. Address: 7924 Deertrail, Parker, Colorado 80134.

REISS, ALVIN H Occupation: Writer, Editor, Educator. Education: B.A., M.A. Address: 110 Riverside Drive, New York, New York 10024.

REMBIESA, PETER JOHN Occupation: Physicist, The Citadel. Education: Ph.D. Address: Post Office Box 78, Charleston, South Carolina 29409.

RENNER-TANA, PATTI L Occupation: Author (Poet) and College Professor. Education: M.A. in English. Address: 462 West Beech Street, Long Beach, New York 11561.

RENNICK, ROBYN AVERY Occupation: Headmistress, Private School for Dyslexics. Education: B.A. English and Theatre. Address: 3915 Woodgreen Way, Tallahassee, Florida 32308.

RENZETTI, CLAIRE M Occupation: Assistant Professor and Assistant Chairperson, Department of Sociology. Education: B.A.A.S. 1977, M.A. 1979, Ph.D. 1981, University of Delaware. Address: 6482 Morris Park Road, Philadelphia, Pennsylvania 19151.

REPLOGLE, ELEANOR Occupation: Restorer of Oriental Rugs and Tapestries. Education: Attended Omaha Nebraska Technical College, 1927. Address: 6821 Brookside Road, Kansas City, Missouri 64113.

REPPERGER, DANIEL WILLIAM Occupation: Research Electrical Engineer. Education: B.S.E.E., M.S.E.E., Ph.D., P.E. Address: 711 Kirkwood Drive, Vandalia, Ohio 45377.

RESSMAN, RICHARD B Occupation: Orthopaedic surgeon. Education: B.S., M.D. Address: 901 Detroit Street, Denver, Colorado 80206.

REST, FRIEDRICH O Occupation: Associate Pastor, Author. Education: A.B., B.D., D.D. Address: 827 West Merriweather Street, New Braunfels, Texas 78130.

RESTON, JAMES BARRETT Occupation: Author, Newspaperman. Education: B.S., University of Illinois, 1932; Address: 1804 Kalorama Square, Northwest, Washington, D.C. 20008.

REUM, ROBERT C Occupation: Purchasing Agent. Address: 2302 Trillium Trail, Rockford, Illinois 61108.

REUMAN, ROBERT EVERETT Occupation: Professor of Philosophy. Education: B.A., Middlebury College; M.A., Ph.D., University of Pennsylvania. Address: Marston Avenue, Waterville, Maine 04901.

REVANKAR, NAGESH S Occupation: Professor of Economics, Department Chairman, Department of Economics, State University of New York. Address: 186 Fruitwood Terrace, Williamsville, New York 14221.

REYMAN, MARIA LANDOLFI Occupation: Instructor of English, Utica Free Academy. Education: B.A., M.A. Address: 4 Hughes Lane, New Hartford, New York 13413.

REYNOLDS, ANNE W Occupation: Development Office, Hollins College. Address: Development Office, Hollins College, Virginia 24020.

REYNOLDS, BEATRICE KAY Occupation: College Professor. Education: B.A., University of Maine; M.A., Ohio University; Ph.D., Pennsylvania State University. Address: 15 Northshire, Victoria, Texas 77904.

REYNOLDS, CLAYTON Occupation: Physician and Endocrinologist. Education: Bachelor of Science, Doctor of Medicine, C.M., F.R.C.P.(C), F.A.C.P., M.S., L.F., Bachelor of Arts Address: 39744 Country Club Drive, Palmdale, California 93550.

REYNOLDS, DOUGLAS ROBERTSON Occupation: History Professor, Chinese and Japanese History, Georgia State University. Education: Doctor of Philosophy, Columbia University, 1976. Address: 613 Clairmont Circle, Decatur, Georgia 30033.

REYNOLDS, THOMAS MORGAN Occupation: Electronic Industry Manager. Education: B.S.B.A., Roosevelt University. Address: 1605 East Central, Arlington Heights, Illinois 60005.

RHEE, SUSAN BYUNGSOOK Occupation: Counselor, College of DuPage. Education: M.S.

Counseling Psychology. Address: 3605 Buckthorn Lane, Downers Grove, Illinois 60515.

RHEINSTEIN, PETER HOWARD Occupation: Physician; Attorney; Acting Director, Office of Drugs, U.S. Food and Drug Administration. Education: B.A., M.S., Michigan State University; M.D., Johns Hopkins University; J.D., University of Maryland. Address: 621 Holly Ridge Road, Severna Park, Maryland 21146.

RHETT, WILLIAM Occupation: Consultant in International Marketing. Education: M.B.A., Harvard Business School; A.B., Hamilton College. Address: Post Office Box 141, Moraga, California 94556.

RHIM, JOHNG S Occupation: Career Researcher/Physician. Education: M.D. Address: 8309 Melody Court, Bethesda, Maryland 20817.

RHOME, FRANCES DODSON Occupation: Director, Institute for Humanities Research/IUPUI; Professor of English. Education: B.A., M.A., Ph.D. Address: 4774 Stansbury Lane, Indianapolis, Indiana 46254.

RHYE, PATSY GAIL Occupation: Language Arts Teacher, Gifted Coordinator. Education: B.A., M.A., English and Secondary Education. Address: Box 62, Saint Thomas, Providence, Kentucky 42450.

RICARDI, LEON JOSEPH Occupation: Head, Milstar Technical Advisory Office, Massachusetts Institute of Technology. Education: B.S. Electrical Engineering, M.S. Electrical Engineering, Ph.D. Electrical Engineering. Address: 750 West Sycamore Avenue, El Segundo, California 90245.

RICE, ALICE MARIE Occupation: Office Manager, The Compton Company. Address: 2265 Westmeade Drive, Southwest, Decatur, Alabama 35603.

RICE, CHARLES AUBREY Occupation: Sales Engineer. Education: Attended Numerous Advanced Courses and Seminars at Institutions including Harvard University, Memphis State University, Browning Power Transmission School, Fafnir Bearing School. Address: 2265 Westmeade Drive, Southwest, Decatur, Alabama 35603.

RICE, EARL CLIFTON Occupation: Professor of Math Emeritus, Central State University. Education: M.A., Ph.D. Address: 808 Myrtle Drive, Edmond, Oklahoma 73034.

RICE, JAMES T Occupation: Vice President-Executive Director, Seaboard System Railroad. Education: B.S., University of Richmond; M.B.A., University of North Florida. Address: 1471 Satsuma Road, Jacksonville, Florida 32223.

RICE, LINDA TILLMAN Occupation: Administrative Assistant. Education: Attending Florida Junior College. Address: 1471 Satsuma Road, Jacksonville, Florida 32223.

RICE, ROSE ANNE Occupation: President, Rice Manufacturing Company. Education: M.F.A., University of Washington and The Art Center School. Address: Post Office Box 8422, Van Nuys, California 91409.

RICE, WILLIAM DAVID Occupation: President of Advertising Agency. Education: B.S., University of Utah, 1942. Address: 1435 Military Way, Salt Lake City, Utah 84103.

RICE, WILLIAM YNGVE Occupation: Chairman of the Board, Town North National Bank. Education: B.B.A., Baylor University Address: 1308 Inverness, Longview, Texas 75601.

RICH, MARIA F Occupation: Executive Director, Central Opera Service, Metropolitan Opera. Education: Baccalaureate. Address: 57 West 58 Street, New York, New York 10019.

RICH, MICHAEL Occupation: Owner, Fairview Hotel. Education: 12 years. Address: 1362 West 37th, Erie, Pennsylvania 16508.

RICHARD, EDWARD H Occupation: President and Chairman of the Board, Magnetics International, Inc.; Director of Public Utilities, City of Cleveland and Northeastern Ohio. Education: B.A., Antioch College. Address: #2 Bratenahl Place, Bratenahl, Ohio 44108.

RICHARDS, EARL FREDERICK Occupation: Professor of Electrical Engineering. Education: B.S., M.S., Ph.D., Electrical Engineering. Address: 8 Hyer Court, Rolla, Missouri 65401.

RICHARDS, RONALD E Occupation: Flight Commander/Instructor Pilot RF-4C. Education: B.S. Economics, United States Air Force Academy, 1972; M.S. Economics, University of Pittsburgh, 1973. Address: #1 St. Botolphs Green, Elton, Petersborough, United Kingdom PES 65H.

RICHARDSON, BARBARA DRUMMOND Occupation: Director Employment and Training Administration. Education: Bachelor of Science Business Education, Master's Degree in Personnel Services. Address: 120 Lynch Drive, Greenville, South Carolina 29605.

RICHARDSON, CHARLES RAY Occupation: News Director. Education: B.S., M.S., M.A. Address: 1465 Clinton Street, Abilene, Texas 79603.

RICHARDSON, E ROSS Occupation: Historical Researcher. Education: B.S. Social Science, M.A. Public Administration, 77 Seminar Hours Law. Address: Post Office Box 512, Wilberforce, Ohio 45384.

RICHARDSON, GILBERT P Occupation: Professor; President, American Association for Study of the U.S. in World Affairs. Education: Attended Mexico City College, David Lipscomb College, George Peabody College of Vanderbilt University, American University, Allied Officers School of the U.S. Air University.

RICHARDSON, JODY Occupation: Attorney. Education: Bachelor of Journalism 1971, Juris Doctor 1980, U.T. Address: 8100 Cambridge #1, Houston, Texas 77054.

RICHARDSON, JOHN V JR Occupation: Associate Professor, University of California-Los Angeles. Education: B.A., M.L.S., Ph.D. Address: 5522 Village Green, Los Angeles, California 90016.

RICHMAN, LARRY LEON Occupation: Publishing Executive. Education: B.A. Spanish/Linguistics, M.A. Instructional Science, Brigham Young University; Ph.D. Religion, Clayton Theological Institute. Address: Post Office Box 11307, Salt Lake City, Utah 84147.

RICHMOND, JOHN Occupation: Attorney-at-Law. Education: B.S. 1928, M.S. 1934, University of California-Berkeley; LL.B., Oakland College of Law, 1942; Ph.D., Hamilton State University (Honorary), 1973. Address: 1611 Bonita Avenue, Berkeley, California 94709.

RICHTER, JOLYNNE Occupation: Graduate Assistant, Master Tutor, Forensics Coach, Division of Humanities, Division of Education, Learning and Counseling Services Centers, Western State College of Colorado. Education: B.A. English Education, Colorado State University, 1974; M.A. Communication Arts 1984, M.A. Education 1984, Western State College of Colorado. Address: Post Office Box 86, Cripple Creek, Colorado 80813.

RICHTER, ROBERT Occupation: Independent Film Producer. Education: B.A., M.A., M.F.A. Candidate. Address: 330 West 42nd Street, New York, New York 10036.

RICKARD, LARRY D Occupation: President/ Broker, Continental Real Estate and Realty School of Kansas. Education: Bachelor's and Master's Degrees, Business. Address: Post Office Box 18552, Hillcrest, 115 South Rutan, Wichita, Kansas 67218.

RIDDELL, ALICE MARY Occupation: Director. Education: B.A., M.S., Queens College, City University of New York; P.D. (Post-Masters), St. John's University. Address: 65-25 160 Street, Flushing, New York 11365.

RIDDLE, PAXTON W Occupation: Executive Vice President, Michigan Association of the Professions. Education: B.A., M.P.S. Address: 2457 Wild Blossom Drive, East Lansing, Michigan 48823.

RIEDER, RONALD FREDERICK Occupation: Public Relations Consultant. Education: B.A., B.Jour. Address: 7240 Ranchito Avenue, Van Nuys, California 91405.

RIEKEHOF, LOTTIE L Occupation: Professor of Sign Communication. Education: B.A., M.A., Ph.D. Address: 3800 North Fairfax Drive, Arlington, Virginia 22203.

RIES, MARTIN Occupation: Artist and Teacher. Education: M.A. Art History. Address: 36 Livingston Road, Scarsdale, New York 10583.

RIFKIN, SANDRA A Occupation: Interior Designer. Education: St. Mary's Hall-Bergman Art Institute. Address: 3864 South Quince, Denver, Colorado 80237.

RIFKIN, VIVETTE RAVEL Occupation: President and Founder of Educational Tape Recording for the Blind. Address: 9906 South Campbell, Chicago, Illinois 60642.

RIGG, MARGARET R Occupation: Professor of the Visual Arts, American Calligrapher. Education: B.F.A. Study, 1945-49; B.A., 1951; M.F.A. Study, 1963; M.A., 1955; Studies with Edmund Lewandowski, Florence Kawa, Tsustomu Yoshida, Kim KeeSung, Kim Hahn, Mathias Goeritz, Corita Kent, George Thomson. Address: The Keep, 2960 58th Avenue, South, St. Petersburg, Florida 33712.

RIGGS, FRED W Occupation: Professor. Education: B.A., University of Illinois, 1938; M.A., Fletcher School of Law and Diplomacy, 1941; Ph.D., Columbia University, 1948. Address: 3920 Lurline Drive, Honolulu, Hawaii 96816.

RIGGS, KARL ALTON JR Occupation: Geologic Consultant and Educator. Education: B.S. with honors 1951, M.S. 1952, Ph.D. 1956, Iowa State University Address: 109 Grand Ridge Drive, Starkville, Mississippi 39759.

RIGOR, BENJAMIN MORALES SR Occupation: Professor and Chairman of Anesthesiology, University of Louisville, Kentucky. Education: B.S., M.D. Address: 6801 Shadwell Place, Prospect, Kentucky 40059.

RIKHOFF, JEAN M Occupation: Founder and Editor, *The Loft Review*. Education: B.A. English, Mt. Holyoke College; M.A. English, Wesleyan University Address: 42 Sherman Avenue, Glens Falls, New York 12801.

RILES, WILSON C Occupation: Educational Consultant. Education: B.A., M.A. Address: 4246 Warren Avenue, Sacramento, California 95822.

RILEY, ANTHONY GAINES JR Occupation: Certified Public Accountant. Education: B.S., Virginia Polytechnic Institute; M.B.A., Clemson University. Address: 238 East 27th, Littlefield, Texas 79339.

RILEY, DONALD C Occupation: Consultant, Sales and Marketing. Education: B.B.A., M.B.A., Ph.D., University of Wisconsin. Address: 40 Central Park South, New York, New York 10019.

RILEY, HELENE M Occupation: University Professor, Writer, Researcher. Education: B.A., N.T.S.U., 1970; M.A. 1973, Ph.D. 1975, Rice University. Address: 61 Loomis Place, New Haven, Connecticut 06511.

RILEY, HERBERT PARKES Occupation: Emeritus Professor of Botany, University of Kentucky. Education: A.B. 1925, A.M. 1929, Ph.D. 1931, Princeton University. Address: 1023 Cooper Drive, Lexington, Kentucky.

RILEY, MONICA Occupation: Professor of Biochemistry, State University of New York-Stony Brook. Education: B.A., Ph.D. Address: 4 Woodbine Avenue, Stony Brook, New York 11790.

RIMROTT, ULRICH A Occupation: Supervisor, Technical Communications. Education: Dipl.Ing., M.E., T.H. Darmstadt, Germany; M.S. E.Mch., Pennsylvania State University. Address: 1718 North Forge Mountain Drive, Valley Forge, Pennsylvania 19481-0252.

RINALDI, NICHOLAS M Occupation: Professor. Education: B.A., Shrub Oak, 1957; M.A., Ph.D. English 1963, Fordham University. Address: 190 Brookview Avenue, Fairfield, Connecticut 06432.

RINALDO, MATTHEW J Occupation: Congressman. Education: B.S., Rutgers University, M.B.A., Seton Hall University; D.P.A., New York University. Address: 142 Headley Terrace, Union, New Jersey 07083.

RINES, ALICE R Occupation: Associate Professor, Graduate Education in Nursing. Education: B.S., M.A., Ed.D. Address: 106 Ridge Road, Rutherford, New Jersey 07070.

RINGERWALE, JOAN MAE Occupation: Professor of Music, Dordt College. Education: M.M., Eastman School of Music, Doctor of Musical Arts in Performance, University of Iowa. Address: 591 8th Street, Northeast, Sioux Center, Iowa 51250.

RINGSDORF, WARREN MARSHALL JR Occupation: Nutrition Researcher and Counselor. Education: A.B., D.M.D., M.S. Address: 728 Sussex Drive, Birmingham, Alabama 35226.

RIOTTE, JULES CHARLES E Occupation: Curator Lepidoptora, B. P. Bishop Museum. Education: M.A. Address: Post Office Box 19000-A, Honolulu, Hawaii 96819.

RIPLEY, REBECCA ANN Occupation: Senior Employment Representative, Middle South Services. Education: B.A., M.S. Educational Psychology, University of Wisconsin-Milwaukee. Address: 45 West Park Place, New Orleans, Louisiana 70124.

RIPPLE, WAIVE B Occupation: Consultant. Education: A.B., Ph.D. School Administration. Address: Post Office Box 64, West Lafayette, Ohio 43845.

RISCH, JAMES E Occupation: Attorney and President Pro Tem, Idaho State Senate. Education: B.S. Forestry, Doctorate in Law, University of Idaho-Moscow. Address: 5400 South Cole Road, Boise, Idaho 83709.

RISLEY, ROD ALAN Occupation: Director Alumni Affairs, Phi Theta Kappa. Education: A.A., San Jacinto College; B.B.A., San Houston State. Address: 306 Shady Lane, Canton, Mississippi 39046.

RITCEY, GORDON MALCOLM Occupation: Head Solution Purification Section. Education: B.Sc. Address: 258 Grandview Road, Nepean, Ontario, Canada K2H 8A9.

RITCHEY, KENNETH WILLIAM Occupation: Superintendent, Montgomery County Board of Mental Retardation and Developmental Disabilities. Education: B.S. Education, M.Ed. Mental Retardation,

M.S. Educational Administration. Address: 454 West Hudson Avenue, Dayton, Ohio 45406.

RITCHIE, GISELA F Occupation: Associate Professor. Education: M.A., Free University of Berlin; Ph.D., University of Michigan. Address: 1206 Farmstead, Wichita, Kansas 67208.

RITCHIE, JOHN JR Occupation: Executive Director, Virginia Housing Development Authority. Education: B.A., University of Virginia; J.D., Harvard Law School. Address: 2234 Monument Avenue, Richmond, Virginia 23220.

RITTER, WILLIAM ALLEN Occupation: Vocational Agriculture Instructor. Education: B.S., M.S., University of Illinois. Address: Rural Route #1, Xenia, Illinois 62899.

RITTERSHOFER, HELEN BROWN Occupation: Writer, Poetess, Public Speaker, Club Woman. Education: Teachers Life Certificate; A.B. 1926, M.A. 1928, University of Michigan. Address: 3092 Glacier Way, Ann Arbor, Michigan 48105.

RITZ, V EUGENE Occupation: Municipal Consultant. Education: A.B., DePauw University; Graduate Studies, Indiana University. Address: 209 Columbia Avenue, Tipton, Indiana 46072.

RIVENES, JAMES DIXON Occupation: President, Rivenes and Associates. Education: B.A., University of Washington. Address: 44 Riverside Drive, Bozeman, Montana 59715.

RIVERA, EZEQUIEL R Occupation: Professor/ Biologist, University of Lowell. Education: B.S. 1964, M.S. 1967, Ph.D. 1970. Address: 17 Old Stage Road, Chelmsford, Massachusetts 01824.

RIZZA, JOSEPH PADULA Occupation: President, California Maritime Academy. Education: B.A., M.A. Political Science. Address: Post Office Box 1392 C.M.A. Vallejo, California 94590.

ROACHE, PATRICK M JR Occupation: Manager, Division of Motors, City of Newark, New Jersey. Education: B.S. Address: 170 Binnacle Road, Brick, New Jersey 08723.

ROADEN, ARLISS L Occupation: President Higher Education Administration. Education: A.B., M.S., Ph.D. Address: Box 5007, T.T.U., Cookeville, Tennessee 38505.

ROARK, JACQUELYN DEVORE Occupation: Director of Admissions. Education: B.S., Lander College; M.Ed., Clemson University. Address: 100 Gracemont Drive, Greenwood, South Carolina 29646.

ROBBINS, RUBY LUCILLE COY Occupation: Registered Professional Nurse, Director of Volunteers. Education: Graduate, Bethel School of Nursing; Registered Nurse, Colorado and California. Address: 1109 Broadway, Chillicothe, Missouri 64601.

ROBBINS, SUSAN PAULA Occupation: Assistant Professor of Social Work. Education: B.A. 1974, M.S.W. 1976, D.S.W. 1979. Address: 1714½ California Street, Houston Texas 77006.

ROBBINS, WAYNE L Occupation: Vice President for Development. Education: B.S., B.D., M.Div., M.Ed., Ed.D. Address: 500 Plantation Court, V-2, Nashville, Tennessee 37221.

ROBERSON, CAROLYN A Occupation: Teacher, Discipline Counselor. Education: B.S., M.A. Special Education, Additional Studies. Address: 1021 South LaFayette, Chicago, Illinois 60628.

ROBERT, ROBERT Occupation: Ph.D. in Theology Student. Education: M.A. Theology. Address: 12 Frontenac East, Saint-Bruno, Quebec, Canada H3V 1B4.

ROBERTS, ANNE B Occupation: Attorney, Partner, O'Donnell and Gordon. Education: B.A. magna cum laude, J.D. 1976, University of California-Los Angeles. Address: 3012 Oakhurst Avenue, Los Angeles, California 90034.

ROBERTS, BEAUFORT G SR Occupation: Teacher of Biological Science. Education: B.A., Paine College; M.S.T., Georgia Southern College. Address: Post Office Box 552, Sylvania, Georgia 30467.

ROBERTS, CATHERINE Occupation: Scholar, Writer. Education: A.B. 1938, Ph.D. 1943, University of California. Address: 1215 Queens Road, Berkeley, California 94708.

ROBERTS, ELIZABETH H Occupation: Podiatrist, Author, Lecturer. Education: D.P.M. Address: 210 West 90th Street, New York, New York 10024.

ROBERTS, GERTRUD HERMINE KUENZEL Occupation: Concert Harpsichordist-Composer. Education: Bachelor of Arts, Piano and Composition, University of Minnesota, 1928. Address: 4723 Moa Street, Honolulu, Hawaii 96816.

ROBERTS, ISABEL NIECE Occupation: Gynecologist. Education: B.A., Barnard College; M.D., Medical College of Pennsylvania. Address: 101 Orlando Boulevard, Indialantic, Florida 32903.

ROBERTS, JOAN ILA Occupation: Social Psychologist/Professor, Child and Family Studies. Education: B.A., University of Utah; M.A., Doctorate, Columbia University Address: 235 Waring Road, Syracuse, New York 13224.

ROBERTS, JOHN A Occupation: Engineering Manager. Education: B.S.M.E. Address: 66 Westchester Drive, Picayune, Mississippi 39466.

ROBERTS, JOHN D Occupation: United States Magistrate. Education: B.S., Hampden-Sydney College; LL.B., Washington and Lee University. Address: Box 46, 701 C Street, Anchorage, Alaska 99513.

ROBERTS, KATHLEEN JOY DOTY Occupation: Educator. Education: Certificate of Advanced Study, Education Administration; M.S. Special Education; B.A. Address: 52 Hicksville Road, Massapequa, New York 11758.

ROBERTS, MARKLEY Occupation: Economist, AFL-CIO. Education: A.B., M.A., Ph.D. Address: 4931 Albemarle Street Northwest, Washington, D.C. 20016.

ROBERTS, MODDIE DECKER Occupation: Principal, W. A. Fountain Junior High School. Education: A.B., M.A., M.S., Ed.D. Address: 1124 Fountain Drive Southwest, Atlanta, Georgia 30314.

ROBERTS, PATRICIA L Occupation: Professor of Education, California State University-Sacramento. Education: Ed.D., University of the Pacific. Address: 6000 J Street, Sacramento, California 95819.

ROBERTS, SUSAN CAROL Occupation: Lecturer, Education, Barry University. Address: Barry University, 11300 Northeast 2nd Avenue, Miami Shores, Florida 33161.

ROBERTSON, DAVID WAYNE Occupation: Medicinal Chemist/Scientist. Education: B.S.S.S. Chemistry and Biology, M.S. and Ph.D. Chemistry. Address: 3712 Ivory Way, Indianapolis, Indiana 46227.

ROBERTSON, GEORGE WILBUR Occupation: Consulting Agrometeorolgoist. Education: B.Sc., University of Alberta, 1939; M.A., University of Toronto, 1948. Address: Post Office Box 1120, Kemptville, Ontario, Canada K0G 1J0.

ROBINSON, CHARLOTTE H Occupation: Artist, Writer. Education: Attended Art Students League, New York University. Address: 6324 Crosswood Drive, Falls Church, Virginia 22044.

ROBINSON, ELMER Occupation: Director, NOAA/GMCC Mauna Loa Observatory. Education: B.A. 1947, M.A. 1948, University of California-Los

Angeles. Address: 327 Ohukea, Hilo, Hawaii 96720.

ROBINSON, GUNER SUZEK Occupation: Director, Advanced Technology Laboratory, Northrop Corporation. Education: B.S. and Ph.D. Electrical Engineering. Address: 27146 Travis Lane, Palos Verdes, California 90274.

ROBINSON, MAUDE ELOISE Occupation: Nurse-Educator. Education: R.N., B.A., B.S.N., M.S., M.P.H., Ph.D. Address: 260 65th Street, Apartment 5J, Brooklyn, New York 11220.

ROBINSON, PATRICIA JONES Occupation: Data Collector, Middle Georgia Regional Assessment Center, State Department of Education. Address: 1810 Crystal Lake Circle, Macon, Georgia 31206.

ROBINSON, SHERMAN Occupation: Associate Professor, Department of Agriculture and Resource Economics, University of California-Berkeley. Address: 3009 Hillegars Avenue, Berkeley, California 94705.

ROCHE, GEORGE CHARLES III Occupation: President, Hillsdale College. Education: B.S. History, M.A. History, Ph.D. History. Address: 189 Hillsdale Street, Hillsdale, Michigan 49242.

ROCHE DE COPPENS, PETER G Occupation: Professor of Sociology and Anthropology, Psychotherapist, Consultant. Education: B.S., M.A., M.S.W., PhD. Address: 244 Analomink Street, East Stroudsburg, Pennsylvania 18301.

ROCHELLE, MIMI Occupation: Cosmotologist and Executive Vice President, The Enchanted Carousel, Inc. Address: 3410 San Martin Circle, Palm Springs, California 92262.

RODERICK, WAJDA WALKER Occupation: Author, Investor. Education: B.S., Murray State University, 1960; M.S., Illinois State University, 1963; Graduate Studies, University of Illinois; Educational Specialist, Michigan State University. Address: 1045 Whitman Drive, East Lansing, Michigan 48823.

RODERIQUES-ANDRADE, MARLENE Occupation: School Adjustment Counselor. Education: Bachelor of Arts in Education, Master of Education, C.A.S. Guidance-Psychological Services. Address: 51 Shawmut Avenue, New Bedford, Massachusetts 02740.

RODGERS, JOSEPH JAMES JR Occupation: Professor of Romance Languages, Chairman Department of Languages and Linguistics, Lincoln University. Education: B.A. summa cum laude, Morehouse College; Certificat d'etudes, Certificat de phonetique, Universite de Grenoble; Woodrow Wilson Fellow, Harvard University; M.A., University of Wisconsin, 1965; Ph.D. French, University of Southern California, 1969; Additional Studies. Address: Oxhaven Apartments, E-38, Conowingo Circle, Oxford, Pennsylvania 19363.

RODGERS, MARY COLUMBRO Occupation: Professor of English, University of the District of Columbia; Chancellor, the American Open University. Education: B.A., M.A., Ph.D., Ed.D., D.Litt. Address: 3916 Commander Drive, College Heights Estates, Hyattsville, Maryland 20782.

RODKIEWICZ, CZESLAW MATEUSZ Occupation: Professor, The University of Alberta, Canada. Education: Dip. Ing., Master of Science, Doctor of Philosophy. Address: 8528-190 Street, Edmonton, Alberta, Canada T5T3X9.

RODMANN, DOROTHY P Occupation: Personnel Manager. Education: B.A. Economics, Graduate Work Economics. Address: 8428 Georgian Way, Annandale, Virginia 22003.

RODRIQUEZ, CAROL HAVLIK Occupation: Resource Teacher, Library Media Specialist. Education: B.A. English Literature, G.I.A. Diploma, Gemologist. Address: 615 Water Street, Apartment #203, Golden, Colorado 80401.

RODRIGUEZ DE LAGUNA, ASELA Occupation: Associate Professor of Spanish/Director, First National Public Conference on Images and Identities: The Puerto Rican in Literature. Education: B.A., M.A., Ph.D. Address: 207 39th Street, Union City, New Jersey 07087.

ROE, BRUCE A Occupation: Professor, Chemistry Department, University of Oklahoma. Address: 2822 Walnut Road, Norman, Oklahoma 73069.

ROE, CLAUDE L Occupation: Executive Director, Copeland Oaks/Crandall Medical Center. Education: B.D., S.T.M., D.Min. Address: 1-504, 800 South 15th Street, Sebring, Ohio 44672.

ROEHL, JERRALD J Occupation: Attorney. Education: B.A., J.D. Address: 4000 Aspen Northeast, Albuquerque, New Mexico 87110.

ROESSLER, DAVID M Occupation: Scientist, General Motors Research Laboratories. Education: B.Sc., Ph.D. Address: 22610 Oak Court, Hazel Park, Michigan 48030.

ROFFMAN, RICHARD H Occupation: Public Relations Counsellor, Practicing Attorney, Radio and Television Broadcaster. Education: LL.B., D.J., City College of New York. Address: 697 West End Avenue, New York, New York 10025.

ROGERS, BEN C Occupation: Pastor, Melrose Baptist Church; Christian Life Commission Virginia Baptist Association. Education: B.S. Social Work, Florida State University; Master of Divinity, Southern Seminary. Address: 2035 Governor Drive Northwest, Roanoke, Virginia 24019.

ROGERS, BRIEN B Occupation: Vice President, Goulds Pumps, Inc. Education: B.A., M.B.A. Address: 4990 Route 89, Romulus, New York 14541.

ROGERS, CAROL J Occupation: Independent Systems Consultant. Education: Diploma, Minneapolis Public Schools, 1958; Certificate Data Entry, IBM, 1960; Diploma Modeling, Estelle Compton Institute, 1964; Certificate Professional Procedural Charting and Analyzation, 1975. Address: 3305 Shores Boulevard, Wayzata, Minnesota 55391.

ROGERS, CHARLES H Occupation: Investor, Banker, Farmer. Education: Attended Emory University. Address: 503 Latimer Street, Hazlehurst, Georgia 31539.

ROGERS, JOSEPH WILSON Occupation: Professor of Sociology, New Mexico State University. Education: B.A. 1949, M.A. 1959, Ph.D. 1965. Address: 306 Capri Arc, Las Cruces, New Mexico 88005.

ROGERS, RUSSELL R Occupation: Professor/Consultant. Education: B.A., M.A., M.H.R.D., Ph.D. Address: 900 Long Boulevard #816, Lansing, Michigan 48910.

ROGERS, VERN C Occupation: President, Consulting Engineering Firm. Education: B.S. Physics, M.S. Mechanical Engineering, Ph.D. Nuclear Engineering. Address: 747 West 3500 South, Bountiful, Utah 84010.

ROGOFF, ARNOLD M Occupation: Book Dealer, Publisher, Management Consultant. Education: Attended University of Missouri, Boston University; B.S., Harvard College, 1951. Address: 1040 Erica Road, Mill Valley, California 94941.

ROID, GALE HAROLD Occupation: Director of Research, Author, Consultant. Education: A.B., Harvard University, 1965; M.A. 1967, Ph.D. 1969, University of Oregon. Address: 186 East Kelly Road, Newbury Park, California 91320.

ROJAS, DAHLIA Z Occupation: Nursing Care Coordinator. Education: M.S. Nursing. Address: 219 East Railroad, San Juan, Texas 78589.

ROKUSEK, H JAMES Occupation: Professor and Department Head, Department of Business and Industrial Education, Eastern Michigan University. Education: B.S., M.S., Ph.D. Address: 1726 Collegewood, Ypsilanti, Michigan 48197.

ROLEN, SUSAN SIMONTON Occupation: Instructional Supervisor. Education: B.A., M.A. Education. Address: 103 Timber Ridge, Peachtree City, Georgia 30269.

ROMAIN, MARGARET A Occupation: Public Accountant, Self-Employed. Education: Attended Youngstown State University, LaSalle Extension University, Pennsylvania State University, Alliance College. Address: 125 Koehler Drive, Post Office Box 27, Sharpsville, Pennsylvania 16150.

ROMAN, PAUL Occupation: Dean of the Graduate School, Drexel University. Education: D.Sc., Ph.D. Address: Drexel University, Philadelphia, Pennsylvania 19104.

ROMANO, GERALDINE Occupation: Member of Religious Order. Education: B.A. Education, M.A. Counselor. Address: 1383 Pleasant Street, Schenectady, New York 12303.

ROMETO, LORRAINE K Occupation: Director of Television, Wissahickon High School. Education: B.A., M.Ed., Ed.D. Address: 2011 Birchwood Drive, Norristown, Pennsylvania 19401.

ROMTVEDT, DAVID W Occupation: Writer. Education: M.F.A., University of Iowa; B.A., Reed College. Address: P.O. Box 484, Port Townsend, Washington 98368.

RONDESTVEDT, CHRISTIAN S Occupation: Research Chemist, DuPont Company. Education: Ph.D. Address: 2547 Deepwood Drive, Wilmington, Delaware 19180.

RONNE, EDITH M Occupation: Lecturer and Writer on Antarctican Affairs. Education: B.A., George Washington University, 1940. Address: 6323 Wiscasset Road, Bethesda, Maryland 20816.

ROOT, WILLIAM PITT Occupation: Author/Professor, English Department, University of Montana. Education: B.A., M.F.A. Address: 201 Kensington, Missoula, Montana 59801.

ROPER, WILLIAM EDWARD Occupation: Mechanical Engineer. Education: B.S.M.E. 1965, M.S. 1966, University of Wisconsin; Ph.D., Michigan State University, 1969; Graduate, Federal Executive Institute, 1978; Graduate, Federal Executive Development Program, 1979-80. Address: 9339 Boothe Street, Alexandria, Virginia 22309.

RORABOUGH, DONALD THOMAS Occupation: Project Manager, Materials Engineering. Education: Bachelor of Science Metallurgical Engineering, Master of Science Materials Engineering, Postgraduate Studies Business. Address: Post Office Box 477, Netcong, New Jersey 07857.

ROSARIO, PARA HARPER Occupation: Manager Governmental Affairs. Education: B.S. Business Administration, Bluefield State College; M.Ed. Candidate, Springfield College. Address: 185 Shell Street, Bridgeport, Connecticut 06605.

ROSE, COLIN PENFIELD Occupation: Physician, Researcher. Education: B.Sc., M.D., Ph.D., F.R.C.P. (c). Address: 3778 Cote des Neiges, Montreal, Quebec, Canada H3H 1V6.

ROSE, HELEN CARLOTTA Occupation: Interior Designer, Community Planner for the Speech and Hearing Handicapped. Education: B.A., M.A., L.H.D., Emerson College. Address: 150 Bradley Place, Palm Beach, Florida 22480.

ROSE, PHYLLIS Occupation: Writer, Educator. Education: B.A., Radcliffe College; M.A., Yale University; Ph.D., Harvard University. Address: 74 Wyllys Avenue, Middletown, Connecticut 06457.

ROSE, S JANE Occupation: Attorney, Securities and Exchange Committee. Education: J.D., M.A., B.A. Address: 59 East 75th Street, New York, New York 10021.

ROSE, SUSAN ANN Occupation: Professor of Psychiatry, Albert Einstein College of Medicine. Education: Ph.D. Address: 18 Floral Drive, Hastings-on-Hudson, New York 10706.

ROSEN, BERNARD Occupation: Vice President. Education: M.E.E., Polytechnic Institute of New York. Address: 1200 Patlen Drive, Los Altos, California 94022.

ROSEN, GERALD Occupation: Novelist, Sonoma State University. Education: B.S.E.E., M.B.A., M.A., Ph.D. Address: 489 Utah Street, San Francisco, California 94110.

ROSEN, HERBERT I Occupation: Chairman of the Board, Skippers, Inc. Education: B.A., University of Washington. Address: 9110 Northeast 36th, Bellevue, Washington 98004.

ROSEN, LOUIS Occupation: Director, Clinton P. Anderson Meson Physics Facility. Education: B.A., M.S., Ph.D., Honorary Doctor of Science Degree. Address: 1170 41 Street, Los Alamos, New Mexico 87544.

ROSEN, STANFORD Occupation: Podiatrist/Surgeon. Education: B.S., D.P.M. Address: 226 Reston Drive, Tuscaloosa, Alabama 35406.

ROSENBAUM, MORTIMER Occupation: Attorney. Education: B.S., J.S. Address: 2104 Willow Street, San Diego, California 92016.

ROSENBERG, MORRIS Occupation: Professor of Sociology, University of Maryland. Education: B.A., Brooklyn College; M.A., Ph.D., Columbia University. Address: 10113 Ashburton Lane, Bethesda, Maryland 20817.

ROSENBERG, TERRY JEAN Occupation: Assistant Professor of Sociology/Anthropology, Ohio Wesleyan University. Education: B.A., University of Chicago; Ph.D., M.A.; Antioch College. Address: 77 West Lincoln Avenue, Delaward, Ohio 43015.

ROSENBLUM, HAROLD Occupation: Senior Staff Consultant, Singer Company, Link Simulation Systems Division. Education: Bachelor of Chemical Engineering, Master of Electrical Engineering. Address: 1310 Webster Street, Orlando, Florida 32804.

ROSENBLUM, MARTIN JACK Occupation: Admissions Specialist/Academic Advisor, University of Wisconsin-Milwaukee. Education: B.S., University of Wisconsin, 1969; M.A. 1971, Ph.D. 1980, University of Wisconsin-Milwaukee. Address: 2521 East Stratford Court, Shorewood, Wisconsin 53211.

ROSENBROOK, WILLIAM JR Occupation: Senior Research Chemist. Education: B.A., University of Nebraska-Omaha. Address: 15440 West Fair Lane, Libertyville, Illinois 60048.

ROSENCRANZ, ARMIN D Occupation: Executive Director, The Pioneer Fund. Education: A.B., Princeton University, 1958; J.D. 1962, Ph.D. 1970, Stanford University. Address: Post Office Box 33, Inverness, California 94937.

ROSENFELD, LEONARD S Occupation: Professor Emeritus, University of North Carolina School of Public Health; Consultant, Health Care. Education: M.S., M.D., M.P.H. Address: 1309

Arboretum Drive, Chapel Hill, North Carolina 27514.

ROSENMAN, RAY H Occupation: Cardiologist and Senior Research Physician, SRI International. Education: A.B., M.D., University of Michigan. Address: 76 Calhoun Terrace, San Francisco, California 94133.

ROSENQUIST, CHARLES D Occupation: School Psychologist, Pendleton, Oregon. Education: B.A., University of Northern Iowa, 1951; M.A. 1962, Ed.S. 1966, Ed.D. 1968, University of Northern Colorado. Address: 105 Northwest 6, Pendleton, Oregon 97801.

ROSENTHAL, ALAN S Occupation: Physician/Scientist, Merck and Company, Inc. Education: M.D. Address: 35 Dug Way, Watchung, New Jersey 07060.

ROSENTHAL, DAVID H Occupation: Author, Translator. Education: Ph.D. Comparative Literature. Address: 785 West End Avenue, New York, New York 10025.

ROSENTHAL, JOHN P Occupation: Investment Banker. Education: A.B., Harvard College; M.B.A., Harvard Business School. Address: 1112 Park Avenue, New York, New York 10128.

ROSENTHAL, MIRIAM FREUND Occupation: Writer, Lecturer, National Historian Hadassah. Education: B.A., M.A., Ph.D. Address: 515 South Lexington, Saint Paul, Minnesota 55116.

ROSENTHAL, NEIL B Occupation: Psychotherapist, Keynote Speaker, Author. Education: M.B. Behavioral Science. Address: 950 South Cherry Street, Ste. G-4, Denver, Colorado 80471.

ROSEVEAR, RUTH F Occupation: Nutrition Consultant. Education: A.B., Cornell University. Address: 527 McAlpin Avenue, Cincinnati, Ohio 45220.

ROSLER, MARTHA R Occupation: Artist, Educator. Education: B.A., M.F.A. Address: 53 Pearl Street, Brooklyn, New York 11201.

ROSOW, IRVING Occupation: Sociologist. Education: A.B., M.A., Ph.D. Address: 81 Seal Rock Drive, San Francisco, California 94121.

ROSS, BILLY E Occupation: Professor and Coordinator Ed.D. Program in Educational Leadership. Education: B.S., West Virginia Institute of Technology; M.S., Marshall University; Ed.D., University of Tennessee. Address: 1204 Blatty Place, Newark, Delaware 19702.

ROSS, CHARLES F Occupation: Podiatrist. Education: B.S., Columbia University College of Pharmaceutical Sciences, 1968; Attended Hofstra University; D.P.M., California College of Podiatric Medicine. Address: 1661 Aladdin Avenue, New Hyde Park, New York 11040.

ROSS, CHARLOTTE P Occupation: Executive Director, Suicide Prevention Center. Address: 445 Virginia, San Mateo, California 94402.

ROSS, FRANK HOWARD III Occupation: Financial Consultant. Education: B.S. Engineering. Address: 536 Eton Drive, Barrington, Illinois 60010.

ROSS, JOAN M Occupation: Artist, Chairman Art and Science Department, Educator. Education: B.S., Postgraduate Studies. Address: Rural Route 1 Box 94, Highland Lakes, New Jersey 07422.

ROSS, JOHN MUNDER Occupation: Psychologist, Educator, Author. Education: B.A., M.A., Ph.D. Address: 277 West End Avenue, New York, New York 10023.

ROSS, MARY ANN Occupation: Field Support Coordinator, Micro Data Base Systems. Education: B.S., M.S., Ph.D., Purdue University. Address: 40 La Rosa Court, Lafayette, Indiana 47905.

ROSS, PATTI JAYNE Occupation: Physician. Education: B.A. Zoology, M.D. Address: 12214 Drakemill, Houston, Texas 77077.

ROSS, SHARON J Occupation: Professional Artist/Gallery Owner. Address: 330 Farallone, Tacoma, Washington 98466.

ROSS, STANLEY RALPH Occupation: Writer, Producer, Composer. Education: D.D. Address: 451 Beverwil Drive, Beverly Hills, California 90212.

ROSSMAN, ROBERT HARRIS Occupation: Productivity Improvements. Address: 3413 Spring Lake Terrace, Fairfax, Virginia 22030.

ROSTVOLD, GERHARD N Education: A.B., M.A., Ph.D. Economics, Stanford University. Address: #7 Wildbrook, Irvine, California 92714.

ROTH, FREDERIC HULL Occupation: Certified Public Accountant, Business Executive. Education: A.B., Wooster College, 1935; M.B.A., Harvard Graduate Business School, 1937. Address: 20661 Avalon Drive, Rocky River, Ohio 44116.

ROTH, PAUL A Occupation: Assistant Professor of Classics. Education: B.A., Brown University; M.A., Ph.D., Bryn Mawr College. Address: 1732 Marques Street, Honolulu, Hawaii 96822.

ROTH, ROSEMARY ANN Occupation: Assistant Director of Nursing. Education: R.N. 1968, B.S. 1975, M.S.N. 1979. Address: 237 Forgham Road, Rochester, New York 14616.

ROTH, THOMAS J Occupation: District Financial Manager, Sperry Corporation; Retired Lieutenant Colonel, United States Army. Education: B.G.E., University of Nebraska; Postgraduate, U.S.A. Command and General Staff College, 1968. Address: 7618 Leith Place, Alexandria, Virginia 22307.

ROTH, WILLIAM DAVID Occupation: Professor. Education: B.A., Yale College; Ph.D., University of California-Berkeley. Address: 144 Lancaster Street, Albany, New York 12210.

ROTHENBERG, JEROME Occupation: Writer (Poet), Department of Visual Arts, University of California-San Diego. Education: M.A., University of Michigan, 1953. Address: 1026 San Abella, Encinitas, California 92024.

ROTHENBERG, ROBERT D Occupation: Assistant Professor, Certified Public Accountant, Lawyer, Author. Education: B.B.A., J.D. Address: Box 350 A, TSR, Delhi, New York 13753.

ROTHMAN, BARRY K Occupation: Attorney at Law. Address: 9200 Sunset Boulevard, Los Angeles, California 90069.

ROTHMAN, JULIUS L Occupation: English Professor, Nassau Community College. Education: B.S.S., M.A., Ph.D. Address: 373 Moore Avenue, Oceanside, New York 11530.

ROTHMAN, ROSALIND W Occupation: Associate Professor, Southern Connecticut State University; Director, Total Learning Center, Eastchester, New York. Education: M.A. Early Childhood, M.A. Special Education, Ed.D. Special Education. Address: 14 Channing Place, Eastchester, New York 10709.

ROTUNDA, DONALD T Occupation: Writer. Education: M.A., Ph.D., London School of Economics. Address: 1297 New Britain Avenue, West Hartford, Connecticut 06110.

ROULAC, STEPHEN E Occupation: President, Stephen Roulac and Company. Education: B.A., Pomona College; M.B.A., Harvard University; J.D., Boalt School of Law; Ph.D., Stanford University. Address: 157 Beach Road, Belvedere, California 94920.

ROUSE, JOHN RATCLIFFE Occupation: Fine Arts Consultant and Appraiser. Education: B.A., Bethel

College. Address: 115 South Rutan, Wichita, Kansas 67218.

ROUSH, MILDRED J Occupation: Nutritionist. Education: B.S., Ohio State University; M.A. and Professional Diploma, Columbia University. Address: 2889 Neil Avenue, #411B, Columbus, Ohio 43202.

ROUSSEL-PESCHE, ANNETTE Occupation: Professor Emerita of Music, Pianist. Education: B.A., Carnegie Mellon University. Address: 37 East 8th Avenue, Clarion, Pennsylvania 16214.

ROUTSON, RONALD C Occupation: Staff Soil Scientist. Education: B.S. Agriculture, Ph.D. Soil Physical Chemistry. Address: Route 1, Box 1351, Benton City, Washington 99320.

ROVEN, MILTON D Occupation: Podiatrist/Foot Specialist. Education: D.P.M., Dip. A.B.A.F.S. Address: 68 Marlborough Road, Brooklyn, New York 11226.

ROVIARO, SUSAN ELIZABETH Occupation: Certified Clinical Psychologist. Education: B.A., University of Massachusetts; M.A., Ph.D., University of Kansas. Address: 812 Colorado Street, Manhattan, Kansas 66502.

ROWE, HERBERT J Occupation: Senior Vice President, Electronic Industries Association. Education: B.S. Marketing, B.S. Management, University of Illinois. Address: 1451 Highwood Drive, McLean, Virginia 22101.

ROWE, MARIELI D Occupation: Executive Director, The National Telemedia Council. Education: B.S., Graduate Studies. Address: 1001 Tumalo Trail, Madison, Wisconsin 53711.

ROWE, ROBERT D Occupation: Economist. Education: Ph.D. Economics. Address: 2680 South Jersey, Denver, Colorado 80222.

ROWLAND, HOWARD RAY Occupation: University Administrator. Education: B.J., M.S., Ph.D. Address: Route 2, Box 125, St. Joseph, Minnesota 56374.

ROWLETT, KAREN L Occupation: Professional Writer; Owner, Rowlett and Associates, Professional Writers. Education: B.A. Journalism, Valparaiso University. Address: 3826 Farmbrook Court, #457, Dallas, Texas 75234.

ROWLETT, RALPH MORGAN Occupation: Archaeologist, University of Missouri. Education: B.A., Marshall University, 1956; Ph.D., Harvard University, 1968. Address: "Hollywell Hill," Route 5, Fulton, Ohio 65251.

ROWLEY, MARGARET NELSON Occupation: Professor and Chairperson, Department of History, Atlanta University. Education: A.B., Hunter College; M.A., Ph.D., Columbia University. Address: 2965 Baker Ridge Drive, Northwest, Atlanta, Georgia 30318.

ROWLEY, PEGGY DAHL Occupation: President and Founder, Bay Arts Council. Education: Bay City Junior College. Address: Post Office Box 1115, Bay City, Michigan 48706.

ROWLEY, RICHARD FAY Occupation: Pastor, Northminster Presbyterian Church. Education: A.B., M.Div., S.T.D., D.Min. Address: 6207 East Sunny Drive, Tucson, Arizona 85712.

ROX, FRANK F Occupation: Senior Vice President, Flight Operations, Delta Air Lines, Hartsfield Atlanta International Airport. Education: J.D. cum laude, University of Georgia, 1950. Address: 3840 Randall Ridge Road, Northwest, Atlanta, Georgia 30327.

ROY, JEAN H Occupation: Nurse Educator and Administrator. Education: B.S. Nursing, M.A. Sociology, Ed.D. Education. Address: Route 1, Box 61, Philippi, West Virginia 26416.

ROYCE, JAMES E Occupation: Director and Professor, Alcohol Studies, Seattle University. Education: B.A., M.A. Philosophy, Ph.D. Psychology, S.T.L. Address: Seattle University, Seattle, Washington 98122.

ROYSTON-JAKES, PENNY JANE Occupation: Instructor, Vocational Business Computers. Education: B.S., Montana State University; M.Ed., University of Montana. Address: 3001 Mack Smith Lane, Stevensville, Montana 59870.

ROZENDAAL, JAMES W Occupation: Certified Public Accountant. Education: M.B.A., B.S., C.P.A. Address: 1194 Manchester Road, Chico, California 95926.

RUBEL, BEATRICE Occupation: Educator, Artist, Designer, Lecturer, Psychic. Education: B.A., A.A.S. Address: 20-55-42nd Street, Astoria, Queens, New York 11105.

RUBEN, ALAN MILES Occupation: Professor of Law, Cleveland-Marshall College of Law, Cleveland State University; Labor Abritrator. Education: A.B. 1953, M.A. 1956, J.D. 1956, University of Pennsylvania. Address: 9925 Lakeshore Boulevard, Bratenahl, Ohio 44108.

RUBIN, DOROTHY M Occupation: Professor of Education, Trenton State College; Writer. Education: B.A. English; M.Ed, Rutgers University; Ph.D., Johns Hopkins University. Address: 917 Stuart Road, Princeton, New Jersey 08625.

RUBIN, EMANUEL Occupation: Director, Ball State University School of Music. Address: 2008 Forest, Muncie, Indiana 47304.

RUBINOW, JAY ELLIOTT Occupation: State Trial Referee. Education: A.B., Harvard University, 1933; LL.B., Harvard Law School, 1937. Address: 49 Pitkin Street, Manchester, Connecticut 06040.

RUBY, LAURA Occupation: Artist, Instructor in Art, Art Department, University of Hawaii. Education: B.A. English, University of Southern California; M.A. English, San Francisco State College; M.F.A., University of Hawaii. Address: 509 University Avenue, #902, Honolulu, Hawaii 96826.

RUBY, ROBERT HOLMES Occupation: Physician, Surgeon. Education: B.S., Whitworth College, 1943; M.D., Washington University, 1945; Diplomate, American Board Abdominal Surgery; Intern, Woman's Hospital, Detroit, 1945-46; Resident, St. Louis County Hospital, 1949-53. Address: 1022 Ivy Street, Moses Lake, Washington 98837.

RUCKER-HUGHES, WAUDIEUR ELIZABETH Occupation: Executive Director, OIC Vocational Skills Academy. Education: B.S., M.A., Educational Administration. Address: 8907 Delano Drive, Riverside, California 92503.

RUDAVSKY, ALEXANDER BOHDAN Occupation: President/Director Hydro Research Science, Professor of Civil Engineering, San Jose State University. Education: Dr. Ing., Franzius Institute Hydraulic Laboratory, Germany. Address: 4004 Twyla Lane, Campbell, California 95008.

RUDD, HOWARD FREDERICK, JR Occupation: Chairperson and Professor of Management, California State College. Education: Master's Degree, Doctorate, Business Administration; B.S. Mechanical Engineering. Address: 2807 Sunset Avenue, Bakersfield, California 93304.

RUDENBERG, F HERMANN Occupation: Neurophysiologist. Education: S.B., S.M., Ph.D. Address: 3327 Avenue Q½, Galveston, Texas 77550.

RUDIN, A JAMES Occupation: Rabbi; Director Interreligious Affairs, American Jewish Committee.

Education: Attended Wesleyan University; B.A. with distinction, George Washington University; M.A., Rabbinical Ordination, Hebrew Union College-Jewish Institute of Religion, 1960.

RUDMAN, MARK Occupation: Free-lance Writer. Education: B.A., New School, Seminar College; M.F.A., Columbia University. Address: 817 West End Avenue, New York, New York 10025.

RUDNIK, MARY CHRYSANTHA Occupation: College Administrator, Nun, Director Public Relations Development. Education: M.A. Library Science, Rosary College, 1962; Ph.D., DePaul University, 1958. Address: 3800 West Peterson Avenue, Chicago, Illinois 60659.

RUDNYCKYJ, JAROSLAV BOHDAN Occupation: Professor Emeritus of Slavic Studies. Education: Master of Arts, 1934, Doctor of Philosophy 1937, Dr. habil. 1941. Address: 5790 Rembrand Avenue, #404, Montreal, H4W 2V2 Canada.

RUDNYTSKY, ROMAN VICTOR Occupation: Concert Pianist and University Professor of Piano. Education: B.S., M.S., Juilliard School of Music. Address: 6072 Applecrest Court, Youngstown, Ohio 44512.

RUDOFF, ALVIN Occupation: Professor Emeritus, San Jose State University. Education: B.A. 1949, M.A. 1960, University of Southern California; Ph.D., University of California-Berkeley. Address: 1772 Dalton Plae, San Jose, California 95124.

RUDY, DOROTHY L Occupation: Professor of English, Montclair State College. Education: B.A., Queens College; A.M., Columbia University. Address: 161 West Clinton Avenue, Tenafly, New Jersey 07676.

RUESINK, WILLIAM GUST Occupation: Head Economic Entomology, Illinois Natural History Survey. Education: Ph.D. Entomology, Michigan State University. Address: 1 Bellamy Court, Champaign, Illinois 61821.

RUETZ, JULIANNE M Occupation: Assistant Professor of Journalism, Colorado State University. Education: Bachelor of Philosophy, M.A., University of Denver. Address: 1705 Heatheridge Road, Fort Collins, Colorado 80526.

RUGGERI, ROGER BENJAMIN Occupation: Musician, Bassist, Annotator, Composer. Education: B.M., Eastman School of Music, 1961. Address: 3533 North Shepard Avenue, Shorewood, Wisconsin 53211.

RUGGIERO, ROBERTA E Occupation: Founder and Director, The Hypoglycemia Research Foundation, Inc. Education: High School Diploma. Address: 9100 Southwest 54 Place, Cooper City, Florida 33328.

RUHL, CAROL LYNNE Occupation: Editor, Lecturer, Secretarial Administration and Word Processing. Education: B.B.A., Westminster College; M.Ed., Indiana University of Pennsylvania. Address: 373 Walnut Lane, Mason, Ohio 45040.

RULON, PHILIP REED Occupation: Professor of History, Northern Arizona University. Education: B.A. History, Washburn University, 1963; M.A. History, Kansas State Teachers College, 1965; D.Ed. History/Higher Education, Oklahoma State University, 1968; Post-doctoral Visitor, University of Texas. Address: Northern Arizona University, Flagstaff, Arizona 86011.

RUMMEL, ROBERT W Occupation: Aviation Consultant. Education: Attended Curtis Wright Technical Institute. Address: Post Office Box 7330, Mesa, Arizona 85206.

RUNGE, VAL M Occupation: Radiologist. Education: B.S. Chemistry, B.S. Biology. Address: 605 Country Club Lane, Nashville, Tennessee 37205.

RUNYON, DEBRA DARLEY Occupation: Group Secretary. Education: B.S. Health and Physical Education, M.S. Education. Address: 2194 Briarcliff Road, Northeast, Apartment 5, Atlanta, Georgia 30329.

RUPERT, HOOVER Occupation: Professor of Religion, Florida Southern College. Education: A.B., M.A., S.T.B., M.Div., D.D., L.H.D. Address: 210 Lake Hollingsworth Drive, Lakeland, Florida 33803.

RUPPEL, EARL G Occupation: Research Plant Pathologist. Education: B.S., University of Wisconsin-Milwaukee, 1958; Ph.D., University of Wisconsin, 1962. Address: 2721 Meadowlark Avenue, Fort Collins, Colorado 80526.

RUSCH, WILBERT H SR Occupation: Professor Emeritus Biology and Geology, Concordia College. Education: B.Sc., M.Sc., Sp.Sc., Hon. LL.D. Address: 2717 Cranbrook Road, Ann Arbor, Michigan 48104.

RUSKE, LYNNAE CAROL Occupation: Major, United States Marine Corps. Education: B.A. Environmental Biology, University of Colorado, 1971; M.A., Central Michigan University, 1984. Address: 35 Canterbury Square, #101, Alexandria, Virginia 22304.

RUSNAK, JAMES EUGENE Occupation: Computer Scientist. Education: B.A., C.D.P. Address: 2948 Sunset Circle, Sioux City, Iowa 51104.

RUSS, LAWRENCE Occupation: Writer/Attorney. Education: B.A. magna cum laude, M.F.A., J.D. Address: 245-49 Unquowa Road, Fairfield, Connecticut 06430.

RUSSELL, ALLEN STEVENSON Occupation: Adjunct Professor, Metallurgical and Materials Engineering Department, University of Pittsburgh. Education: B.S., M.S., Ph.D., The Pennsylvania State University. Address: 929 Field Club Road, Pittsburgh, Pennsylvania 15238.

RUSSELL, BEVERLY A Occupation: Editor, Author, Lecturer. Education: G.E.E., London University, 1951. Address: 236 Piermont Avenue, Piermont, New York 10968.

RUSSELL, JAYRENE F Occupation: Attorney at Law. Education: B.A. Political Science, J.D. Address: Post Office Box 3, Highfalls, North Carolina 27259.

RUSSELL, RALPH TIMOTHY Occupation: Vice President, Insurance Company. Education: B.S. Accounting, M.B.A., C.P.C.U. Address: 117 West Rosette Avenue, Foley, Alabama 36535.

RUSSO, JOHN FRANCES Occupation: State Senator, 10th District of New Jersey. Education: B.A., LL.B. Address: 488 Madison Avenue, Toms River, New Jersey 08753.

RUSSO, PETER JOHN Occupation: Business/Corporate Controller, Gerber Scientific, Inc. Education: B.B.A., Niagara University, 1968. Address: 63 Colony Road, South Windsor, Connecticut 06074.

RUST, NICHOLAS CREGG Occupation: Training Officer. Education: B.A., University of the Pacific; M.A., University of Arizona. Address: 2969 Smoke Tree Circle, Stockton, California 95209.

RUTHERFORD, JAMES WILLIAM Occupation: Mayor, City of Flint, Michigan. Education: B.S. 1960, M.S. 1964, Michigan State University. Address: 1713 Chelsea, Flint, Michigan 48506.

RUTMAN, ROANNE CLINE Occupation: Associate Administrator. Education: B.S., M.A. Address: 12680 Verwood Drive, Florissant, Missouri 63033.

RUTSALA, VERN Occupation: Professor of English, Lewis and Clark College; Writer. Education: B.A., Reed College; M.F.A., University of Iowa. Address: 2404 Northeast 24th Avenue, Portland,

Oregon 97212.

RUTTENBERG, HAROLD JOSEPH Occupation: Chairman, Chief Executive Officer, AVM Corporation. Education: B.A., University of Pittsburgh. Address: 307 South Dithridge Street, #814, Pittsburgh, Pennsylvania 15213.

RYDER, GEORGIA ATKINS Occupation: Academic Dean, Arts and Letters. Education: B.S., Mus.M., Ph.D. Address: 5551 Brookville Road, Norfolk, Virginia 23502.

RYDER, HARL E Occupation: Professor of Economics, Brown University. Education: B.S. 1960, M.S. 1961, University of Illinois; Ph.D., Stanford University, 1967. Address: 171 Laurel Avenue, Providence, Rhode Island 02906.

RYAN, MICHAEL RUSSELL Occupation: Minister of The Gospel. Education: B.A. Public Administration, University of Southern California, 1973; M.A., Grace Graduate School, 1979; M.Div., Talbot Seminary, 1984. Address: 52 Chenery, San Francisco, California 94131.

RYKER, KENNETH WILTON Occupation: Educator, Researcher, Writer. Education: A.A., B.G.E., M.B.A. Address: 448 Meadowhill Drive, Benbrook, Texas 76126.

RZEMINSKI, PETER JOSEPH Occupation: Assistant Executive Director, Human Resources, St. Francis Hospital. Address: 14317 Medina Drive, Orland Park, Illinois 60462.

RZEWNICKI, JANET C Occupation: Treasurer, State of Delaware. Education: B.S., University of Delaware; Certified Public Accountant. Address: 125 Westgate Drive, Wilmington, Delaware 19808.

S

SABATELLA, JOSEPH J Occupation: Professor of Art and Dean of College of Fine Arts, University of Florida. Education: B.F.A. 1954, M.F.A. 1958, University of Illinois. Address: 2510 Northwest 30th Terrace, Gainesville, Florida 32605.

SABATINI, DAVID DOMINGO Occupation: Scientist, New York University Medical Center. Education: M.D., Ph.D. Address: 77 Wellington Avenue, New Rochelle, New York 10804.

SABBAGH, HAROLD ABRAHAM Occupation: President, Analytics, Inc. Education: B.S.E., M.S.E.E. 1958, Ph.D. 1964, Purdue University. Address: 2634 Round Hill Lane, Bloomington, Indiana 47401.

SABEL, MICHAEL I Occupation: Physicist, Professor of Physics, Brooklyn College. Education: B.A., Swarthmore College, 1959; M.A. 1962, Ph.D. 1964, Harvard University. Address: 15 Pickwick Terrace, Rockville Centre, New York 11570.

SABEY, BURNS R Occupation: Professor and Researcher, Colorado State University. Address: 3505 Canadian Parkway, Ft. Collina, Colorado 80524.

SACHAR, ABRAM L Occupation: Chancellor, Brandeis University. Education: Ph.D. Address: 66 Beaumont Avenue, Newtonville, Massachusetts 02160.

SACHTLEBEN, CARL HENRY Occupation: Director of Libraries, Western Michigan University. Education: A.B., B.S. Library Science, M.A. Address: 34268 CR 653, Paw Paw, Michigan 49079.

SACK, EDGAR A Occupation: Senior Vice President, General Instrument Corporation. Education: B.S., M.S., Ph.D., Carnegie Mellon University. Address: 57 Margo Lane, Huntington, New York 11743.

SACKETT, SAMUEL JOHN Occupation: Public Relations. Education: A.B., A.M., Ph.D. Address: 6100 North Brookline Avenue, Number 28, Oklahoma City, Oklahoma 73112.

SADKER, DAVID Occupation: Professor, American University. Education: B.A., City College of the City University of New York; M.A.T., Harvard University; Ed.D., University of Massachusetts. Address: 8608 Carlynn Drive, Bethesda, Maryland 20817.

SADLER, ERNEST ELMORE Occupation: Operations Vice President, Unisen, Inc. Education: B.A. 1959, M.S. 1961, University of Massachusetts. Address: 405 South West Street, Anaheim, California 92805.

SADLO WILSON, KATHRYN R Occupation: Concert Performer, Writer and Director State Productions. Education: B.M., M.M. Voice Performance. Address: 304 South First Street, Dundee, Illinois 60118.

SAGE, GEORGE H Occupation: Professor of Physical Education and Sociology, University of Northern Colorado. Education: B.A., M.A., University of Northern Colorado; Ed.D., University of California-Los Angeles. Address: 1933-26th Avenue, Greeley, Colorado 80631.

SAGER, MARTHA CORCORAN Occupation: Chairman of Biology Department and Professor of Biology, American University. Education: Ph.D., Catholic University/America. Address: 1528 Briarcliff Road, Arnold, Maryland 21012.

SAGER, ROBERT J Occupation: Professor of Earth Sciences, West Los Angeles College. Education: B.S., Wisconsin State University; M.S., University of

Wisconsin; J.D., Western State University. Address: 840 Catalina, Laguna Beach, California 92651.

ST CLAIR, J WALTON JR Occupation: President/ Chief Executive Officer, Wilmington Savings Fund Society, FSB. Education: B.A. Economics, 1951; M.B.A. Finance, 1958. Address: 4011 Springfield Lane, Greenville, Delaware 19807.

ST DAWN, GRACE Occupation: Author, Poet, Lecturer, Lyricist. Education: Honorary Doctor of Humane Letters, Doctor of Divinity. Address: 340 Elliot Place, Paramus, New Jersey 07652.

ST JOHN, JUDITH BROOK Occupation: Plant Physiologist, U.S.D.A., A.R.S. Education: B.S., Ph.D. Address: 3306 Sellman Road, Adelphi, Maryland 20783.

ST JOHN, RICHARD A Occupation: President, Accountant. Education: A.B. Geology; M.B.A. Address: 2918 Austin Bluffs Parkway, Colorado Springs, Colorado 80907.

SAJJADI, PETER S Occupation: Director of Human Resources, Engineering and Construction Group, Dravo Corporation. Education: B.S. Political Science, B.S. Industrial Psychology, M.B.A. Industrial Management. Address: 258 Rutledge Drive, Bridgeville, Pennsylvania 15017.

SALADINI, VINCENT ROCCO Occupation: Educator. Education: B.S., M.A. Address: 11 Pilgrim Drive, Clifton, New Jersey 07013.

SALAMONE, FRANK A Occupation: Anthropologist. Education: B.A., M.A., Ph.D. Address: 23 West Street, White Plains, New York 10605.

SALANS, LESTER B Occupation: Director, National Institute of Arthritis, Diabetes, Digestive and Kidney Diseases. Education: B.A., M.D. Address: 3214 Pickwick Lane, Chevy Chase, Maryland 20815.

SALCUDEAN, MARTHA Occupation: Professor. Education: B.Eng. 1956, Postgraduate 1962, Ph.D. 1969. Address: 157 Heath Street, Ottawa, Ontario, Canada.

SALIBELLO, COSMO Occupation: Doctor of Optometry. Education: O.D., B.A. Biology, B.Mgt.E. Address: 9260 South Wet Cutter Place, Beaverton, Oregon 97005.

SALINAS-SNYDER, CYNTHIA MARIE Occupation: Consumer Consultant, Home Economist. Education: B.S. Home Economics, Southwest Texas State University. Address: 1500 Sam Houston F-9, Harlingen, Texas 78550.

SALISBURY, BART R Occupation: Research Consultant, University of Washington. Education: B.A. 1979, M.A. 1981, Ph.D. 1984. Address: 11525 40th Avenue Northeast, Seattle, Washington 98125.

SALLIE, ARNETHA Occupation: Certified Public Accountant and Fashion Counselor. Education: Accounting and Business Law. Address: 2002 Flagler Street, McKeesport, Pennsylvania 15132.

SALMON, CHARLES GERALD Occupation: Professor, Structural Engineering. Education: B.S.E. Civil Engineering; M.S.E. Civil Engineering; Ph.D. Address: 614 South Segoe Road, Madison, Wisconsin 53711.

SALOUKAS, BILL I Occupation: Personnel and Executive Recruitment. Address: 1000 River Road, Belmar, New Jersey.

SALSBURY, BARBARA G Occupation: Consumer Specialist; Vice President, Salsbury Enterprises; Author; Lecturer. Education: Attended El Camino College, Gardena, California, 1956-58. Address: 651 West 40 North, Orem, Utah 84057.

SALT, GEORGE WILLIAM Occupation: Professor of Zoology, University of California. Education: B.A., M.A., Ph.D. Address: 310 12th Street, Davis, California

95616.

SALTER, PAUL SANFORD Occupation: Dean, College of Arts and Sciences. Education: Ph.D., University of North Carolina; M.A., Indiana University; B.S.E., Massachusetts State College. Address: 5518 West 15th Street, Topeka, Kansas 66604.

SALVADOR, SAL Occupation: Jazz Musician, Educator, Composer, Columnist. Address: 1697 Broadway, New York, New York 10019.

SALVADORI, MAX Occupation: Professor Emeritus of History, Smith College. Education: Licencie es Sciences Sociales, University of Geneva, 1929; Doctor of Political Sciences, University of Rome, 1930; Litt.D. (Hon.), American International College, 1959. Address: 36 Ward Avenue, Northampton, Massachusetts 01060.

SALVO, EMILIA B Education: Licenza Tecnica. Address: 852 Miller Avenue, South San Francisco, California 94080.

SALYER, PAULINE A Occupation: Artist, Author, Editor, Real Estate Broker. Education: Attended Hills Business College, Oklahoma City University, University of Oklahoma. Address: 3111 Northwest 19th Street, Oklahoma City, Oklahoma 73107.

SALZMAN, DAVID ELLIOT Occupation: Executive Vice President, Telepictures Corporation. Education: B.A., Brooklyn College, 1965; M.A., Wayne State University, 1967. Address: 31640 Saddletree Drive, Westlake Village, California 91361.

SALZMANN, ZDENEK Occupation: Professor of Anthropology, University of Massachusetts. Education: M.A. 1949, Ph.D. 1963, Indiana University. Address: 25 Chapel Road, Amherst, Massachusetts 01002.

SAMKO, MICHAEL R Occupation: Clinical Psychologist. Education: Ph.D. Address: 2885 Hope, Carlsbad, California 92008.

SAMMARCO, PATRICIA E Occupation: Zoo Keeper. Address: Lincoln Park Zoo, 2200 North Cannon Drive, Chicago, Illinois 60614.

SAMPLE, DOROTHY E Occupation: President, Woman's Missionary Union, Southern Baptist Convention. Education: A.B. high distinction, University of Michigan, 1966; M.A., 1967; Ph.D., 1976; B.A. summa cum laude, Free Will Baptist Bible College, 1961; Th.D., Toledo Bible College and Seminary, 1973. Address: 3119 Prospect Street, Flint, Michigan 48504.

SAMPSON, J FRANK Occupation: Artist; Teacher of Fine Arts. Education: B.A., Concordia College, Moorhead, Minnesota; M.F.A., University of Iowa, Iowa City, Iowa. Address: 1912 Columbine, Boulder, Colorado 80302.

SAMPSON, MARCELLA A Occupation: Director, Career Planning and Placement. Education: B.S. Business Administration. Address: 536 Dayton Street, Yellow Springs, Ohio 45387.

SAMS, BARBARA DUKE Occupation: Director of Advertising and Public Relations. Address: 7806 Lieber Road, Indianapolis, Indiana 46260.

SAMUELSEN, ROY Occupation: Professional Bass-Baritone, Professor of Music, Indiana University. Education: B.S., M.M. Music. Address: 2012 Montclair Avenue, Bloomington, Indiana 47401.

SANCHEZ, MARIA ANNA Occupation: Patient Education Specialist. Education: B.S.N., E.T. Address: 1726 Tarlton, Corpus Christi, Texas 78415.

SanCLEMENTE, ADELE M Occupation: Optometrist. Education: Simmons College; Massachusetts College of Optometry. Address: 50 Water Street, Medford, Massachusetts 02155.

SAND, PAUL M Occupation: Justice of North Dakota Supreme Court. Education: LL.B., J.D. Address: 1022 North 8th Street, Bismarck, North Dakota 58501.

SANDERS, GILBERT OTIS Occupation: Psychology and Education. Education: B.A., Oklahoma State University; M.S., Troy State University; Ed.D., The University of Tulsa. Address: 5404 North West 65th Street, Oklahoma City, Oklahoma 73132.

SANDERSON, CAROL J Occupation: Photographer; Journalist for Elementary Schools. Education: Teacher's Certificate, State of Kansas. Address: Rural Route 1, Howard, Kansas 67349.

SANDERSON, GLEN C Occupation: Secretary, Wildlife Research; Illinois Natural History Survey; Wildlife Biologist. Education: B.S., A.M., University of Missouri; Ph.D., University of Illinois. Address: 711 South State Street, Champaign, Illinois 61820.

SANDLER, MARION O Occupation: Savings and Loan Executive. Education: B.A. Economics; Postgraduate, Business Administration; M.B.A. Banking and Finance. Address: 1970 Broadway, Suite 1000, Oakland, California 94612.

SANDOR, EDWARD P JR Occupation: Associate Professor of Music, University of Georgia. Education: B.M.E., Ph.D., Ohio State University; M.M.E., University of Illinois. Address: 111 Winterberry Lane, Athens, Georgia 30606.

SANDOVAL, JULIAN Occupation: Financial Consultant. Education: B.S. Business Administration. Address: 908 Mitchell, Laramie, Wyoming 82070.

SANDSTROM, BODEN Occupation: Sound Engineer. Education: A.M.L.S., B.A., M.S. Address: 19 Logan Circle, Washington, D.C. 20005.

SANFORD, G MARSHALL Occupation: Teacher of Social Studies, Norwalk High School. Education: B.A. History, M.S. Secondary Education. Address: 27 Turney Road, Redding Ridge, Connecticut 06876.

SANFORD, LESLIE McHENRY JR Occupation: United States Naval Officer. Education: B.S. Psychology, B.A. Engineering 1968, Virginia Polytechnic Institute; University of West Florida, 1977. Address: 359 Calle Navarro, Camarillo, California 93010.

SANNELLA, JOSEPH L Occupation: Director of Research. Education: A.B. Biochemical Science, M.S. Chemistry, Ph.D. Biochemistry, M.B.A. Finance. Address: 2803 West Woodbridge, Muncie, Indiana 47304.

SANSONE, MARLEEN B Occupation: Artist, Arts Lobbyist. Education: M.A., Goddard College; B.A. Address: 46 Stevens Street, East Haven, Connecticut 06512.

SANTORO, STEVEN J Occupation: Principal Maintainability Engineer. Address: 418 Pleasant Street, Tewksbury, Massachusetts 01876.

SARAFIAN, ARMEN Occupation: President, University of LaVerne. Education: A.B., M.A., Ph.D. Address: Post Office Box 1624, Glendora, California 91740.

SARGENT, ALICE G Occupation: Organization Consultant and Trainer. Education: Ed.D., University of Massachusetts, 1974; M.Ed., Temple University; M.A., Brandeis University; B.A., Oberlin College. Address: 4819 Dexter Terrace, Northwest, Washington, D.C. 20007.

SARGENT, J McNEIL Occupation: Printmaker/ Artist. B.A., University of California, 1977. Address: 519 Stratford Court, #D, Del Mar, California 92014.

SARGENT, ROBERT GEORGE Occupation: Professor of Engineering, Syracuse University. Education: B.S.E., M.S., Ph.D. Address: 130 Remington

Avenue, Syracuse, New York 13210.

SARGOT, SUSAN H Occupation: Manager Pharmacist. Education: B.S. Pharmacy. Address: 63 1/2 South Wade Avenue, Washington, Pennsylvania 15301.

SARID, AKSEL Occupation: Research Institute Director. Education: B.A. Health, Medicine and Society, 1978; M.S. Studies of the Future, 1983; M.P.H., 1984. Address: 1914 Wyndale #2, Houston, Texas 77030.

SARKAR, ANIL K Occupation: Writer, Research Director. Education: M.A., Ph.D., D.Litt. Address: 818 Webster Street, Hayward, California 94544.

SARNO, MARK J Occupation: Optometrist in Private Practice and Director, Optometric Technician Program. Education: A.A. with honors, 1978; B.S., 1978; O.D. cum laude, 1978. Address: 6807 Sandwater Trail, Pinellas Park, Florida 33565.

SARNO, RONALD ANTHONY Occupation: Director of Development. Education: B.A., M.A., M.Div. Candidate, Ph.D. Address: 52 Charles Street, Little Ferry, New Jersey 07643.

SARNOFF, LILI-CHARLOTTE Occupation: Artist (Sculptor). Education: Graduate of Reinmann Art School. Address: 7507 Hampden Lane, Bethesda, Maryland 20814.

SASLAW, LEONARD DAVID Occupation: Chemist and Toxicologist. Education: B.S., M.S. Biochemistry, Ph.D. Chemistry. Address: 425 G Street Southwest, Washington, D.C. 20024.

SASLOFSKY, HARRY Occupation: Vice President of Sales and Marketing. Education: M.B.A. Address: 7608 Brentwood Road, Philadelphia, Pennsylvania 19151.

SATHRE, ROGER C Occupation: Supervisor, Special Needs Programs. Education: B.B.A., M.S., University of Minnesota; M.Ed., University of Idaho. Address: 10680 Hollandale Drive, Boise, Idaho 83709.

SATO, EUNICE N Occupation: Long Beach City Council Woman. Education: B.A., M.A. Address: 2895 Easy Avenue, Long Beach, Califonria 90810.

SATO, IRVING SHIGEO Occupation: Director, National/State Leadership Training Institute on the Gifted and Talented. Education: B.Ed., M.S.Ed. Address: 1744 Via Del Rey, South Pasadena, California 91030.

SATRE, WENDELL JULIAN Occupation: Chairman of the Board and Chief Executive Officer, Washington Water Power Company. Education: B.S.E.E., Honorary Doctor of Science, University of Idaho, 1978. Address: West 39 - 33rd Avenue, Spokane, Washington 99203.

SAUER, MARY-LOUISE STEINHILBER Occupation: Community Leader. Education: B.M.E. Address: 830 West 58th Terrace, Kansas City, Missouri 64113.

SAUGET, CLYDE RAYMOND Occupation: Director of Product Development. Education: A.A., B.S., M.B.A., Ph.D. Business Administration. Address: 1351 Graff Avenue, San Leandro, California 94577.

SAUL, GEORGE BRANDON II Occupation: Professor Emeritus of English, University of Connecticut; Writer and Composer. Education: A.B. 1923, A.M. 1930, Ph.D. 1932, University of Pennsylvania. Address: 136 Moulton Road, Storrs, Connecticut 06268.

SAVAGE, PATRICIA WERNER Occupation: Coordinator of Aftercare and Geriatrics. Education: B.A. Psychology, M.S.W. Address: R.R. #2, Box 1014, Cresco, Pennsylvania 18326.

SAVAGE, XYLA RUTH Occupation: Manager of Forms Design and Graphics. Education: B.A.,

Oklahoma University; Postgraduate, U.S.D.A. Graduate School. Address: 12901 Chalfont Avenue, Fort Washington, Maryland 20744.

SAVARD, LORENA BERUBE Occupation: Marketing and Sales Manager, Integral Computer Systems. Education: A.S. Accounting, A.S. Management, D.P. Courses. Address: R.F.D. #1, Box 172, Putnam, Connecticut 06260.

SAVINI, DORIS DIANA Occupation: Librarian, Community Christian School. Education: B.A. Psychology. Address: 9048 Southeast Pine Cone Lane, Hobe Sound, Florida 33455.

SAVITZ, FRIEDA Occupation: Artist, Instructor. Education: B.S. Art, New York University, 1957; Attended Hans Hofmann School, Cooper Union; Honorary Diploma, Universitai delle Arti, 1981; Master of Painting honoris causa, Accademia Italia, 1983; Appointment, Accademice d'Europa, 1983. Address: 109 West Clarkstown Road, New City, New York 10986.

SAVO, DOMINICK S Occupation: Product Manager. Education: B.S. Chemical Engineering, M.S. Physical Chemistry, M.M. Business Management. Address: 102 Blackstone, LaGrange, Illinois 60525.

SAVVAS, MINAS Occupation: Professor, San Diego State University; Poet; Critic. Education: B.A., M.A., University of Illinois; Ph.D., University of California. Address: Department of English and Composition Literature, San Diego State University, San Diego, California 92182.

SAWICKI, JAMES A Occupation: Military Historian; Writer. Address: 14703 Dunbar Lane, Woodbridge, Virginia 22193.

SAWYER, CAROL ANNE Occupation: Associate Professor, Michigan State University. Education: Ph.D., M.S., B.S., R.D. Address: 1642 Melrose, East Lansing, Michigan 48823.

SAWYER, HOWARD J Occupation: Physician. Education: Graduate, Cooley High School, Detroit, Michigan, 1943-47; B.A. Philosophy, Wayne State University, 1948-52; Naval Aviator, United States Naval Air Training Command, 1952-53; M.D., Wayne State University, 1958-62; 30 Hours toward M.Sc. Industrial Hygiene, Wayne State University, 1969-72. Address: 7072 Edinborough Drive, West Bloomfield, Michigan 48033.

SAWYER, PATRICIA ROYSTON Occupation: National Co-Chairperson, Senior Adult Theatre Program, American Theatre Association; Speech and Drama Consultant. Education: B.S., Clark University. Address: 1 Tapiola Court, Rockville, Maryland 20850.

SAWYER, WILLIAM DALE Occupation: Dean, School of Medicine, Wright State University. Education: M.D. cum laude, Washington University, 1954. Address: 5583 Hugh Drive, Dayton, Ohio 45459.

SAX, BORIA Occupation: Freelance Writer and Lecturer. Education: B.A. Philosophy, University of Chicago, 1971; M.A. German 1978, Ph.D. German and History 1983, State University of New York. Address: 25 Franklin Avenue, #2F, White Plains, New York 10601.

SAXTON, VERNON CAROLE Occupation: Special Education Teacher. Education: B.S., M.S., Additional Studies. Address: 1287 West Avenue, Buffalo, New York 14213.

SAYLE, JO ANN Occupation: Child Examiner, Vanderburgh County Health Department. Education: B.S. Address: 4137 Kensington Avenue, Evanston, Indiana 47710-3742.

SAYLES, RONALD LYLE Occupation: Supervisor Computer Operations. Education: B.S. Secondary

Education. Address: 4278 North 53rd Street, Milwaukee, Wisconsin 53216.

SAZ, HOWARD J Occupation: Professor of Biology, University of Notre Dame. Education: B.S. City College of New York, 1948; Ph.D., Western Reserve University, 1952. Address: 17453 Arbor Drive, South Bend, Indiana 46635.

SBORDONE, ROBERT J Occupation: Clinical Psychologist, Clinical Neuropsychologist. Education: B.A., M.A., Ph.D. Address: 13412 Donegal Drive, Garden Grove, California 92644.

SCAER, ROBERTA M Occupation: Medical Writer. Education: B.A. high distinction; M.S.S. Address: 1320 Oak Court, Boulder, Colorado 80302.

SCAGLIONE, CECIL FRANK Occupation: Senior Vice President of Media Relations, Berkman and Daniels, Inc. Education: Ryerson Technological Institute; Davenport Fellow, University of Missouri. Address: 3911 Kendall Street, San Diego, California 92109.

SCANDURA, JOSEPH M Occupation: Professor. Education: A.B., M.A., Ph.D., H.M.A. Address: 1249 Greentree Lane, Norberth, Pennsylvania 19072.

SCHACHTER, GUSTAV Occupation: Professor of Economics, Northeastern University. Education: Ph.D., M.B.A., B.S., D.S.H.C. Address: 15 Thatcher Street, Brookline, Massachusetts 02146.

SCHAEFER, FRANK WILLIAM III Occupation: Parasitologist; Microbiologist. Education: B.A., M.S., Ph.D. Address: 2 Amherst Place, Fairfield, Ohio 45014.

SCHAEFER, PATRICIA Occupation: Librarian, Assistant Director, Muncie Public Library. Education: Bachelor of Music; Master of Music; Master of Arts in Library Science. Address: 405 South Tara Lane, Muncie, Indiana 47304.

SCHAEFFER, JURGEN R Occupation: Professor of Agronomy and Genetics, Montana State University. Education: Diploma of Agriculture, Doctor of Agriculture. Address: 4959 Hallelujah Lane, Belgrade, Montana 59714.

SCHANBERG, SYDNEY H Occupation: Columnist, New York Times. Education: B.A., Harvard University, 1955. Address: c/o New York Times, 229 West 43rd Street, New York, New York 10036.

SCHARPF, LEWIS GEORGE JR Occupation: Technical Director, Specialty Chemicals Company. Education: B.S., M.S., Ph.D. Address: 35 Lewis Point Road, Fair Haven, New Jersey 07701.

SCHAUER, NANCY R Occupation: Attorney. Education: A.B., J.D. Address: 4316 Marina City Drive #633CTN, Marina Del Rey, California 90292.

SCHAUMBERG, GENE D Occupation: Professor of Chemistry. Education: B.S., Ph.D. Address: 2655 Bennett Ridge Road, Santa Rosa, California 95404.

SCHEEREN, FRED A Occupation: Certified Financial Planner. Education: B.A. Sociology, C.F.P. Address: 217 Concord Street, Clarksburg, West Virginia 26301.

SCHEERENBERGER, RICHARD CHARLES Occupation: Director, Central Wisconsin Center for the Developmentally Disabled. Education: B.S., M.Ed., Ph.D. Address: 5205 Comanche Way, Madison, Wisconsin 53704.

SCHEIN, LORRAINE SANDRA Occupation: Branch Librarian, Long Island Center Library. Education: B.A., Adelphi University, 1954; M.S., New York University, 1959; M.S. Library Science, Long Island University, 1967. Address: 117 Admiral Lane, Hicksville, New York 11801.

SCHELAR, VIRGINIA M Occupation: Consultant. Education: B.S., M.S., M.Ed., Ph.D. Address: 5702 Baltimore Drive #282, California 92041.

SCHELL, JOHN W Occupation: Director, Institute of Advanced Technology. Education: Ph.D. (pending). Address: 8373 Knollwood Street, Allison Park, Pennsylvania 15101.

SCHENDEL, WINFRIED G Occupation: Sales Manager, New York Life Insurance Company. Education: B.S. Electrical and Industrial Engineering. Address: 13802 West 20th Place, Golden, Colorado 80401.

SCHENK, ROY U Occupation: Chemist, Research and Development; Writer. Education: B.S., M.S., Ph.D., Cornell University, 1954. Address: Post Office Box 9141, Madison, Wisconsin 53715.

SCHERER, CLARENCE H Occupation: Water Superintendent. Education: B.S., M.S. (Chemistry and Biology). Address: 1012 Melody Lane, Amarillo, Texas 79108.

SCHERTLE, ALICE MARGUERITE Occupation: Author of Children's Books. Education: B.S. cum laude, University of Southern California. Address: 1210 North Cypress Street, La Habra Heights, California 90631.

SCHIAMBERG, LAWRENCE B Occupation: Professor, Michigan State University. Education: Ph.D., University of Illinois, Urbana, Illinois. Address: 3596 West Arbutus, Okemos, Michigan 48864.

SCHIAVI, ROSEMARY F Occupation: Educator, Syracuse University. Education: A.A.; B.A.; M.S.; Ed.D. Candidate, Syracuse University. Address: 237 Stafford Avenue, Syracuse, New York 13206.

SCHICK, HARRY L Occupation: General Partner, First Manhattan Company. Education: A.B., M.S. Address: 215 East 68th Street, New York, New York 10021.

SCHIFFMAN, SONDRA (SANDY) H Occupation: Interior Designer. Address: Post Office Box 861, Tarzana, California 91356.

SCHIMMEL, WILLIAM MICHAEL Occupation: Composer, Performer, Conductor, Educator. Education: B.M.; M.S.; D.M.A., The Juilliard School. Address: 345 East 65 Street, Apartment 4RE, New York, New York 10028.

SCHIPMAN, HENRY C JR Occupation: Writer, Artist, Museum Owner. Education: High School Graduate, Attended College. Address: 644 West Court, Las Cruces, New Mexico 88005.

SCHIRMEISTER, BARBARA F Occupation: Interior Designer (ASID), Color Consultant. Education: B.A., Parsons School of Design. Address: 15 Beechcroft Road, Short Hills, New Jersey 07078.

SCHIRMEISTER, CHARLES F Occupation: Attorney. Education: B.A., LL.B. Address: 15 Beechcroft Road, Short Hills, New Jersey 07078.

SCHLEGEL, ROBERT PHILIP Occupation: President, Intelligent Images Incorporated. Education: B.Sc., A.M.P. Address: 3723 Crystal Drive, Beulah, Michigan 49617.

SCHLEGELMILCH, REUBEN ORVILLE Occupation: Technical Director, Research and Development, U.S. Coast Guard. Education: B.S.E., M.S.E., S.M. Industrial Management, Ph.D. Electrical Engineering (pending). Address: 8415 Frost Way, Annandale, Virginia 22003.

SCHLENK, HERMANN Occupation: Professor, Biochemistry. Education: B.S., M.S., Dr.rer.nat. Address: 801 16th Avenue, North East, Austin, Minnesota 55912.

SCHLESINGER, STEPHEN C Occupation: Special Assistant to the Governor of New York. Education: A.B. 1964, LL.B. 1968, Harvard University. Address:

53 West 71st Street #3A, New York, New York 10023.

SCHLOSS, IRA J Occupation: Director, Corporate Research and Development. Education: M.B.A. Industrial Psychology, M.B.A. Management, B.A. Psychology. Address: 4 Lewis Lane, Port Washington, New York 11050.

SCHMALL, VICKI L Occupation: Gerontology Specialist. Education: B.S. Home Economics and Health Education; Ph.D. Gerontology and Family Life. Address: 835 Marylhurst Circle, West Linn, Oregon 97068.

SCHMIDT, BENJAMIN EARL Occupation: Instructor Lapidary and Jewelry Crafts, Adult Evening School, Baltimore City. Education: B.S., Dakota State University, 1927; M.A., Columbia University, 1935; Postgraduate Work at University of Minnesota 1928-39, University of Maryland 1940-50. Address: 1315 Windemere Avenue, Baltimore, Maryland 21218.

SCHMIDT, CARL HOWARD JR Occupation: President, Carl H. Schmidt Company. Education: Bachelor of Chemical Engineering, University of Detroit. Address: 7375 Creek View Court, West Bloomfield, Michigan 48033.

SCHMIDT, JAMES A Occupation: Director of Financial Aid/Education. Education: B.S., M.S., Ph.D. Address: 1321 Macombo Road Southwest, Ft. Myers, Florida 33907.

SCHMIDT, JOYCE D Occupation: Director, Creative Arts in Education, National Youth Theater Institute, National Theater Arts Institute, Theatre Arts in Deaf Education, Artist in Corrections. Education: B.S., Boston University, 1959. Address: 46 Mansfield Road, New London, Connecticut 06320.

SCHMIDT, MIA Occupation: Poet, Teacher of Creative Self-Expression. Education: Certificate, Institute for Human Excellence, 1977. Address: General Delivery, Saint Mary's City, Maryland 20686.

SCHMIDT, ROBERT R Occupation: Safety Engineering Manager. Education: B.S. Business Administration, Indiana University. Address: 3923 101st St. Court, North West, Gig Harbor, Washington 98335.

SCHMIDT, STEPHEN C Occupation: Professor of Agriculture Marketing and Policy, University of Illinois. Education: D.Sc., University of Budapest, Hungary; Ph.D., McGill University, Montreal, Canada. Address: 20 Greencroft, Champaign, Illinois 61821.

SCHMIEDER, ROBERT WILLIAM Occupation: Physicist/Marine Scientist, Sandia National Laboratories. Education: A.B. 1963, B.S. 1963, M.A. 1965, Ph.D. 1968. Address: 4295 Walnut Boulevard, Walnut Creek, California 94596.

SCHMITT, CAROLYN SUE (JARRETT) Occupation: Vocational Counselor. Education: B.S.Business Administration, University of Charleston, 1962; B.S. Liberal Studies, University of the State of New York, 1978; B.A. Social Science, Thomas A Edison State College, 1979; M.A. Education/Manpower Administration, University of Redlands, 1974; Postgraduate Studies. Address: 538 North Pampas Avenue, Rialto, California 92376.

SCHMITT, CARVETH JOSEPH RODNEY Occupation: Internal Auditor. Education: A.A., San Bernardino Valley College, 1962; B.S. Business Administration, University of Riverside, 1970; M.A. Education/Manpower Administration, University of Redlands, 1975; Bachelor of Science Liberal Studies, University of the State of New York, 1977; Bachelor of Arts Social Sciences, Edison State College, 1978; Postgraduate Studies. Address: 538 North Pampas Avenue, Rialto, California 92376.

SCHMITT, JAMES ANTHONY Occupation: Mathematician. Education: B.A. Mathematics, M.S., Ph.D. Address: 437 Maitland Street, Bel Air, Maryland 21014.

SCHMUECKLE, JEAN Z Occupation: Advertising Agency Executive. Education: University of Pennsylvania, 1936; Charles Morris School of Advertising, 1938. Address: Overlook Valley Farm, Rushland, Pennsylvania 18956.

SCHNEEBAUM, TOBIAS Occupation: Director of Research and Documentation, Asmat Museum of Culture and Progress. Education: Masters in Cultural Anthropology. Address: 463 West Street, New York, New York 10014.

SCHNEEMAN, PETER H Occupation: Associate Professor of English and Comparative Literature, Pennsylvania State University. Education: B.A., M.A., Ph.D. Address: 313 East Curtin Street, Bellefonte, Pennsylvania 16823.

SCHNEIDER, CLAIRE Occupation: High School Teacher, Poet, Publisher. Education: B.A. Liberal Arts; Graduate Credits in French Education, Brooklyn College. Address: 1655 Flatbush Avenue, Brooklyn, New York 11210.

SCHNEIDER, FREDERICK R Occupation: Professor of Law, Northern Kentucky University. Education: B.A., Luther College, 1961; J.D., University of Chicago, 1964. Address: 8643 Empire Court, Cincinnati, Ohio 45231.

SCHNEIDER, JUDITH A Occupation: Financial Systems Analyst/Accountant. Education: B.S. Business Administration. Address: 19111 Bella, Cleveland, Ohio 44119.

SCHNEIDERS, SANDRA MARIE Occupation: Associate Professor of New Testament and Spirituality. Education: B.A. Sociology, M.A. Philosophy, S.T.L. Theology, S.T.D. Address: 1717 Oxford, Berkeley, California 94709.

SCHNEITER, GEORGE MALAN Occupation: Golf Professional, Builder, Developer. Education: B.S. Business, University of Utah. Address: 8968 South 1300 East, Sandy, Utah 84070.

SCHOCKET, ELINOR H Occupation: Accountant. Education: B.A. Address: 36-23 Ferry Heights, Fairlawn, New Jersey 07410.

SCHOENER, EUGENE PAUL Occupation: Professor of Pharmacology, Wayne State University. Education: B.S., City College of New York; M.S., Rutgers University; Ph.D., Rutgers University. Address: 18324 New Hampshire, Southfield, Michigan 48075.

SCHOENFELD, CLARE A Occupation: System Liaison. Education: B.S.B.A. summa cum laude, Boston College; M.B.A. with high distinction, Babson College. Address: 429 East 52nd Street, #24D, New York, New York 10022.

SCHOENWOLF, GARY CHARLES Occupation: Assistant Professor, University of Utah School of Medicine. Education: B.A., M.S., Ph.D. Address: 2280 East 900 South, Salt Lake City, Utah 84108.

SCHOFIELD, MIRIAM N Occupation: Public Health Nurse Supervisor I. Education: Sc.B. Nursing, M.A. Guidance and Counselling. Address: 10915 Southwest 177 Terrace, Miami, Florida 33157.

SCHOLES, ROBERT T Occupation: President, The Bioresearch Ranch, Inc. Education: B.S., D.T.M.&H., M.D. Address: Box 117, Rodeo, New Mexico 88056.

SCHOLL, SHARON LYNN Occupation: College Professor, Jacksonville University. Education: B.M., M.Mus.Ed., Ph.D. Address: 6854 Howalt Drive,

Jacksonville, Florida 32211.

SCHOLZ, ROBERT VICTOR Occupation: Associate Professor of Music (Choir Director, Voice Teacher), St. Olaf College. Education: B.A., St. Olaf College, 1961; M.M. Musicology 1967, D.M.A. Choral Conducting 1968, University of Illinois. Address: 704 St. Olaf Avenue, Northfield, Minnesota 55057.

SCHORZMAN, MARK HEWIT Occupation: Consultant in Industrial Hygiene. Education: B.S. 1961, M.S.P.H. 1975, University of Washington. Address: 3419 South Nucla Way, Aurora, Colorado 80013.

SCHRAMM, DAVID N Occupation: Chairman, Department of Astronomy and Astrophysics. Education: Ph.D. Address: Post Office Box 500, Batavia, Illinois 60510.

SCHREIBER, RON Occupation: Writer, Editor, Teacher. Education: B.A., Wesleyan College; M.A., Ph.D., Columbia University. Address: 9 Reed Street, Cambridge, Massachusetts 02140.

SCHREINER, ROBERT NICHOLAS Occupation: Project Management. Education: B.S., Capital University. Address: 30520 Via Rivera, Rancho Palos Verdes, California 90274.

SCHREMPF, DAVID W Occupation: Insurance Industry Executive, CIGNA International Corporation. Education: B.A., M.B.A. Address: 1114 Club House Road, Gladwyne, Pennsylvania 19035.

SCHROEDER, JANICE JONES Occupation: Director, Buffalo Native American Bilingual Program. Education: B.S., M.Ed., Ph.D. (in progress). Address: 75 Palmer Avenue, Kenmore, New York 14217.

SCHROEDER, RITA MOLTHEN Occupation: Doctor of Chiropractic. Education: D.C., Palmer School of Chiropractic; D.C., Cleveland College of Chiropractic. Address: 9870 North Millbrook, Fresno, California 93710.

SCHROY, JERRY M Occupation: Chemical Engineer. Education: Ch.E., University of Cincinnati, 1963. Address: 5 Springlake Court, Ballwin, Missouri 63011.

SCHUBERT, DONALD KEITH Occupation: Clinical Psychologist. Education: Ph.D. Address: 215 Euclid Avenue #214, Long Beach, California 90803.

SCHUETTER, DOUGLAS J Occupation: Telemarketing Consultant. Education: B.S., M.B.A. Address: 409 East Raymond, Danville, Illinois 61832.

SCHULER, RICHARD JOSEPH Occupation: Roman Catholic Priest, Musicologist. Education: B.A., College of St. Thomas, 1942; Ordained Priest, St. Paul Seminary, 1945; M.A., Eastman School of Music, 1950; Ph.D., University of Minnesota, 1963. Address: 548 Lafond Avenue, St. Paul, Minnesota 55103.

SCHULER, WILLIAM G Occupation: Insurance Executive. Education: University of Mississippi; Biarritz American University; Ursinus College. Address: 168 Erie Avenue, Souderton, Pennsylvania 18964.

SCHULTES, JEFFREY L Occupation: Airport Administrator. Education: B.S. Air Commerce, Florida Institute of Technology, 1976. Address: 2506 Lowman Drive, Bloomington, Illinois 61701.

SCHULTZ, PHILIP A Occupation: Poet, Novelist, English Professor at New York University. Education: M.F.A. Creative Writing, B.A. English. Address: 78 Charles Street, New York, New York 10014.

SCHULTZ, ROY A Occupation: Veterinarian. Education: B.S., D.V.M., M.S. Address: R.R. 1, Box 46, Avoca, Iowa 51521.

SCHULZE, ERWIN F C Occupation: Consulting Engineer, Vice President of Purchasing. Education: B.S.M.E. Address: 14027 East Willard Drive, Novelty, Ohio 44072.

SCHULZE, JOHN H Occupation: Professor, University of Iowa. Education: B.S., M.F.A. Address: 5 Forest Glen, Iowa City, Iowa 52240.

SCHULZINGER, MARK Occupation: Clinical Psychologist. Education: B.S., M.A. Address: 601 East Delmar, Springfield, Missouri 65807.

SCHUM, MARY LOUISE Occupation: Interior Designer. Education: B.F.A. Address: 41 South "D" Street, Hamilton, Ohio 45012.

SCHUMACHER, FREDERICK R Occupation: Tax Attorney. Education: A.B., Princeton University, 1952; J.D., Cornell University Law School, 1957. Address: 1401 Treasure Lane, Santa Ana, California 92705.

SCHUMAN, KAY E Occupation: Western Regional Math Consultant. Education: B.S., University of Minnesota; M.A., California State University. Address: 6614 North Locan, Clovia, California 93612.

SCHURTER, KENNETH L Occupation: Business Manager. Education: B.S., M.B.A. Address: 5407 Three Oaks Circle, Houston, Texas 77069.

SCHUSTERMAN, CHARLES Occupation: President, Samson Resources Company. Education: B.S. Petroleum Engineering, University of Oklahoma, 1958. Address: 2142 Forest Boulevard, Tulsa, Oklahoma 74114.

SCHWAB, GEORGE Occupation: Educator/Author. Education: Ph.D., M.A., B.A. Address: 140 Riverside Drive, New York, New York 10024.

SCHWAB, GLENN ORVILLE Occupation: Professor of Agriculture Engineering. Education: Ph.D. Address: 3737 Summitview, Powell, Ohio 43065.

SCHWAN, LEROY BERNARD Occupation: Teacher of Art. Education: B.S., University of Minnesota; M.Ed., University of Minnesota. Address: 1826 North 24th Street, Quincy, Illinois 62301.

SCHWARTZ, ALLAN BRADLEY Occupation: Chemical Engineer. Education: B.Ch.Eng., M.S. Address: 910 Chelten Parkway, Cherry Ill, New Jersey 08034.

SCHWARTZ, CAROL HALPERT Occupation: Associate Dean/Associate Professor, Schools of Business, Adelphi University. Education: B.A., Ph.D. Address: Adelphi University, Garden City, New York 11530

SCHWARTZ, DONALD Occupation: Chancellor, University of Colorado. Education: Ph.D. Chemistry and Fuel Science. Address: 21 Sanford Road, Colorado Springs, Colorado 80906.

SCHWARTZ, DOROTHY R Occupation: Associate Director of Grants-Making Organization, Maine Humanities Council. Education: A.B., M.A.T., Smith College; M.Ed., University of Southern Maine. Address: 5 Atwood Lane, Brunswick, Maine 04011.

SCHWARTZ, DOUGLAS W Occupation: President, Archaeologist, School of American Research. Education: B.A., University of Kentucky; Ph.D., Yale University. Address: School of American Research, Post Office Box 2188, Santa Fe, New Mexico 87504.

SCHWARTZ, GORDON FRANCIS Occupation: Professor of Surgery, Jefferson Medical College. Education: A.B., Princeton University; M.D., Harvard Medical School. Address: 1805 Delancey Place, Philadelphia, Pennsylvania 19103.

SCHWARTZ, LLOYD Occupation: Poet, Music Critic, Teacher, University of Massachusetts. Education: B.A., Queens College; Ph.D., Harvard University. Address: 27 Pennsylvania Avenue, Somerville, Massachusetts 02145.

SCHWARTZ, MARK W Occupation: Research

Biochemist, Clinical Systems. Education: B.A., Grinnell College; Ph.D., Arizona State University. Address: 5 Holt Road, Newark, Delaware 19711.

SCHWARTZ, MICHAEL Occupation: Educator/Administrator, President of Kent State University. Education: B.S. Psychology, M.A. Industrial Relations, Ph.D. Sociology. Address: 1100 East Main Street, Kent, Ohio 44240.

SCHWARTZ, PEPPER J Occupation: Author/Professor, Department of Sociology, University of Washington. Education: Ph.D., Yale University; M.A., Washington University; B.A., Washington, University. Address: Department of Sociology, University of Washington, Seattle, Washington 98195.

SCHWARTZ, PHILIP CHARLES Occupation: President, Ludwig Industries, Inc. Education: B.B.A. Address: 133 Middleton Street, Brooklyn, New York 11206.

SCHWARTZ, ROBERT J Occupation: Vice President, Shearson/American E; President, Trust for Balanced Investment. Education: Ph.D. Address: 30 West 95th Street, New York, New York 10025.

SCHWARTZ, ROSALIE FEINMAN Occupation: Reading Specialist. Education: Ph.D. Address: 2455 Haring Street, Brooklyn, New York 22345.

SCHWARTZ, SHEILA R Occupation: Professor/Author, State University College. Education: Ed.D. Address: 5 Spies Road, New Paltz, New York 12561.

SCHWARTZ, THOMAS D Occupation: Attorney at Law. Education: B.A., J.D. Address: Route 6, Box 126-1, Carbondale, Illinois 62901.

SCHWARTZMAN, JACOB Occupation: Professor English, Nassau Community College; Attorney, State of New York; Editor, *Fragments* Magazine. Address: 1066 Hancock Avenue, Franklin Square, New York 11010.

SCHWARZOTT, WILHELM Occupation: Concert Pianist, Chamber Music Performer. Education: Certificate, Vienna Academy, 1938; Diploma, Royal Music Conservatory, Oslo, Norway, 1939; M.A. Equivalent, University of Denver, 1957; Additional Studies. Address: 1882 11th Avenue, San Francisco, California 94122.

SCHWEBEL, ANDREW I Occupation: Professor of Psychology, Ohio State University. Education: B.A., Antioch College; M.S., Ph.D., Yale University. Address: 4123 Kendra Court, Columbus, Ohio 43220.

SCHWEITZER, VANESSA GAYL Occupation: Otolaryngologist; Clinical Assistant, Professor, University of Michigan; Senior Staff, Henry Ford Hospital. Education: M.D., University of Michigan. Address: Apartment 2B, 4817 Sandstone Pass, Ypsilanti, Michigan 48197.

SCHWEMM, JOHN B Occupation: Chaiman and President, R. R. Donnelley and Sons Company. Education: B.A., Amherst College; J.D., University of Michigan. Address: 2 Turvey Lane, Downers Grove, Illinois 60515.

SCHWESINGER, EDMUND A JR Occupation: Partner. Education: B.A., M.B.A. Address: 94 Cutler Road, Greenwich, Connecticut 06830.

SCHWOERER, LOIS G Occupation: Professor, History Department, George Washington University. Education: Ph.D., Bryn Mawr College. Address: 7213 Rollingwood Drive, Chevy Chase, Maryland 20815.

SCHYCKER-BAILEY, NANCY Occupation: Educator. Education: A.A., B.A., M.A., Ph.D. Address: 14737 Calkin, Hacienda Heights, California 91745.

SCHYDOLOWSKY, DANIEL M Occupation: Professor of Economics. Education: LL.B., M.A., Ph.D. Address: 23 Philbrick Road, Brookline, Massachusetts 02146.

SCILEPPI, JOHN A Occupation: Associate Professor of Psychology/Author, Marist College. Education: Ph.D., M.A. Social Psychology, Loyola University. Address: 39 Delafield Street, Poughkeepsie, New York 12601.

SCITOVSKY, ANNE A Occupation: Chief, Health Economics Department, Palo Alto Medical Foundation. Education: M.A. in Economics. Address: 161 Erica Way Menlo Park, California 94025.

SCLAFANI, CHARLES CARLO Occupation: Professor, Westchester Community College. Education: B.A., M.A. Address: 56 Atlantic Avenue, Hawthorne, New York 10532.

SCOTT, ALICE SMITH Occupation: Assistant Superintendent. Education: B.S., East Carolina University; M.S., University of North Carolina; Ph.D., North Carolina State University. Address: Post Office Box 375. Pink Hill, North Caroloina 28572.

SCOTT, CYNTHIA ANN Occupation: Anesthetist. Education: Degree in Anesthesia, Degree in Nursing. Address: 8820 Southwestern #320, Dallas, Texas 75206.

SCOTT, ELDRED H Occupation: Director and Consultant, Ross Valve. Education: B.A. Address: 815 Rivenoak Road, Birmingham, Michigan 48008.

SCOTT, J NORMAN Occupation: Associate, Jase Associates. Education: B.S.M.E. Address: 91 Holyoke Road, Richboro, Pennsylvania 18954.

SCOTT, JERRY D Occupation: Sales Representative, Horace Mann Insurance. Education: B.S., M.Ed., M.S., Ed.D. Address: Route, Afton, Tennessee 37616.

SCOTT, JOHN BROOKS Occupation: Vice-President, ITT Research Institute. Education: B.S., M.A., University of Arizona. Address: 407 Halsey Road, Annapolis, Maryland 21401.

SCOTT, JOHN FREDRIK Occupation: Associate Professor of Art History, University of Florida. Education: Ph.D. Address: 1506 North West 46 Terrace, Gainesville, Florida 32605.

SCOTT, JUANITA FULLER Occupation: Rehabilitation Counselor, State of Colorado. Education: B.A. Psychology and Sociology, M.A. Rehabilitation Counselor and Psychology. Address: 5303 Tucson Way, Denver, Colorado 80239.

SCOTT, MILDRED CAROLYN Occupation: Businesswoman. Address: Skyline Farms, White Oak, West Virginia 25989.

SCOTT, ROBERT KEITH Occupation: Nurse Anesthesia Student, Part-time Registered Nurse. Address: 5412 Manzonita Drive, Panama City, Florida 32401.

SCOVELL, WILLIAM MARTIN Occupation: Professor, Biomedical Researcher. Address: 1206 Bourgogne Avenue, Bowling Green, Ohio 43402.

SCREPETIS, DENNIS Occupation: Consulting Engineer. Education: Professor's License, New Jersey and New York. Address: 2200 North Central Road, Fort Lee, New Jersey 07024.

SCROGGIE, WAYNE LEE Occupation: Cost Management. Education: M.B.A., B.A. Business Administration. Address: 1702 11th Avenue South #205B, Seattle, Washington, 98134.

SCRUGGS, ROBERT GORDON Occupation: Housing Officer. Education: B.S. Business Administration, A.A.S. Business Administration. Address: Post Office Box 18626, Raleigh, North Carolina 27619.

SCULLY, MARLAN ORVIL Education: Ph.D Physics, M.S. Physics, B.S. Engineering Physics and Mathematics. Address: Route 1, Box 8, Estancia, New

Mexico 87016.

SEABOURN, BERT D Occupation: Artist. Education: Certificate in Art, Oklahoma State University. Address: 6105 Covington Lane, Oklahoma City, Oklahoma 73132.

SEAL, ASHER F SR Occupation: Vice President, Treasurer, Board of Directors, Arjay International Corporation; President, Chairman of the Board, RHS Enterprises; Consultant. Education: Attended University of Kentucky-Lexington, Western University, Bowling Green University, George Washington University, American University, U.S.D.A. Graduate School; Graduate, National Academy of Broadcasting. Address: 910 Gazelle Trail, Casselberry, Florida 32708.

SEARLES, JERRY LEE Occupation: Television Executive, Financial Counsultant, Philanthropist. Address: 1704 Maryland Avenue, Saint Paul, Minnesota 55106.

SEARS, ELIZABETH CLINE Occupation: Broadcaster. Education: B.A. summa cum laude in English. Address: 711 West 9th Street, Wichita, Kansas 57203.

SEARS, FREDERICK M Occupation: Research Scientist, Fiber Optics, Bell Laboratories. Education: Ph.D., University of California-Berkeley; B.S., M.S., Massachusetts Institute of Technology. Address: 161 Dunellen Avenue, Piscataway, New Jersey 08854.

SEATOR, LYNETTE HUBBARD Occupation: Professor, Illinois College. Education: B.S., M.A., Ph.D. Address: 1609 Mound Avenue, Jacksonville, Illinois 62650.

SEBEOK, THOMAS A Occupation: Regents Fellow, Smithsonian Institution. Education: B.A., University of Chicago; M.A. and Ph.D., Princeton University. Address: 1104 Covenanter Drive, Bloomington, Indiana 47401.

SECRIST, DOLLY ALVAREZ Occupation: Executive Staff Assistant. Education: B.A. Address: 306 Berkshire Way, Placentia, California 92670.

SEELEY, T TALBOT Occupation: Psycho Neuro Endocrinology and Psychiatry. Education: B.A., M.D. Address: 4622 Green Tree Lane, Irvine, California 92715.

SEESTADT, HAROLD ANDREW Occupation: Resident Secretary Marine Insurance. Education: B.S. Banking and Finance, New York University. Address: 24456 Conifer, Farmington Hills, Michigan 48018.

SEETO, DEWEY Q Occupation: Economist. Education: Ph.D., M.A., B.S. Address: 2 Balceta Avenue, San Francisco, California 94127.

SEGAL, DAVID R Occupation: Professor of Sociology, University of Maryland. Education: B.A. Harpur College; M.A., Ph.D., University of Chicago. Address: 9007 Gettysburg Lane, College Park, Maryland 20740.

SEGAL, LORE Occupation: Writer; Professor of English, University of Illinois. Education: B.A. English, University of London. Address: 280 Riverside Drive, New York, New York 10025.

SEGER, RONALD E Occupation: Management Consultant, A. T. Kearney, Inc. Education: B.S., University of Maine. Address: 15 Walnut Place, Wilton, Connecticut 06897.

SEGRE, BERYL GAY Occupation: Assistant Professor, Coordinator, Public Health, Health Education Program, Dillard University. Education: M.S.W., M.P.H. Address: 2326 Upperline Street, New Orleans, Louisana 70115.

SEGUIN, MAURICE KRISHOLM Occupation: Professor, University of Laval, Canada. Education:

B.A., B.Sc., M.Sc., Ph.D. Address: Suite 7584, Pav. Lemieux, University of Laval, Quebec, Canada 6lK 7P4.

SEIBEL, GEORGE H Occupation: Quality Assurance Specialist (Retired). Address: 96-C-36, Route #1, Eastaboga, Alabama 36260.

SEIBERT, JANET LOOS Occupation: Advocate for Home Health Care. Education: B.Sc. Nursing Education, Registered Nurse. Address: 4827 Bellann Road, Columbus, Ohio 43220.

SEIDE, ROCHELLE K Occupation: Professor of Medical Genetics, Attorney at Law. Education: B.S. Microbiology, M.S. Immunology, Ph.D. Human Genetics. Address: 1377 Mockingbird Drive, Kent, Ohio 44240.

SEIDEN, JEAN TRAGER Occupation: Interior Designer/Consultant. Education: B.A. Address: 11100 Rosemont Drive, Rockville, Maryland 20852.

SEIDMAN, JEROME MARTIN Occupation: Professor Emeritus of Psychology, Montclair State College. Education: B.S., M.S., Ph.D. Address: 81 Brookdale Gardens, Bloomfield, New Jersey 07003.

SEIDMAN, ROBERT J Occupation: Screenwriter/Novelist. Education: B.A., Williams College; M.A., Worcester College, Oxford. Address: 577 Broadway, New York, New York 10012.

SEIPOS, ANDREW GEORGE Occupation: Real Estate Broker, Sales. Education: Architecture, New York University, Cooper Union. Address: 661 Cardium Street, Sanibel Island, Florida 33957.

SELAME, JOSEPH Occupation: Principal/Design Director, Selame Design. Education: Bradley College; U.S. Engineers School of Photography. Address: 33 Cutler Lane, Chestnut Hill, Massachusetts 02167.

SELDITCH, ALAN DANIEL Occupation: Environmental Management Engineer. Education: Student, Saint Lawrence University, 1944-46; B.S., University of Southern California, 1948; B.S. Environment Sciences 1981, M.S. 1982, Ph.D. 1983, Heed University; B.A. Law, Thomas Jefferson University, 1982; Postgraduate, Los Angeles City College, LaSalle University. Address: 6267 #E Joaquin Murieta, Newark, California 94560.

SELENKE, WILLIAM MICHAEL Occupation: Research Biomedical Scientist; Inventor. Education: M.S. Medical Microbiology; Ph.D. Environmental Health. Address: 18 Gambier, Cincinnati, Ohio 45218.

SELIGMAN, BARNARD Occupation: Professor, Pace University. Education: Ph.D., M.A., B.S. Address: 2 Washington Square Village, New York, New York 10012.

SELL, GEORGE ROGER Occupation: Professor of Mathematics and Associate Director of the Institute for Mathematics and Its Applications, University of Minnesota. Education: Ph.D. Address: University of Minnesota, Minneapolis, Minnesota 55455.

SELLERS, FRED COURT Occupation: Certified Public Accountant. Education: Attended University of Houston. Address: 11601 Green Oaks Street, Houston, Texas 77024.

SELTZER, RONNI LEE Occupation: Physician, Psychiatric Practice. Education: M.D., Chicago Medical School; B.A., Syracuse University. Address: 200 Old Palisade Road, Fort Lee, New Jersey 07024.

SELTZER, VICKI LYNN Occupation: Physician. Education: M.D., B.S. Address: 36 Bacon Road, Old Westbury, New York 11568.

SEMAAN, KHALIL I Occupation: Professor of Arabic, State University of New York. Education: Ph.D. Address: 713 Country Club Road, Binghamton, New York 13903.

SEMINACK, STEPHEN JOSEPH Occupation:

Accountant. Education: B.S. Marketing, St. Joseph's College; M.B.S., Drexel University. Address: 5627 Miriam Road, Philadelphia, Pennsylvania 19124.

SEMKOW, JERZY Occupation: Conductor. Education: Master Conservatories of Crakow and Leningrad. Address: 13993 West 20th Place, Golden, Colorado 80401.

SEMONOFF, RALPH P Occupation: Attorney. Education: A.B., Brown University; LL.B. (M.C.L.) Harvard Law School. Address: 40 Lowden Street, Pawtucket, Rhode Island 02860.

SEN, ASHISH K Occupation: Professor, School of Urban Planning, University of Illinois. Education: Ph.D. Address: 2557 Farwell, Chicago, Illinois 60645.

SEN, SUBHA Occupation: Research in Cardiovascular Diseases. Education: Ph.D., D.Sc. Address: 540 Edinborough Drive, Bay Village, Ohio 44140.

SENNETT, JOHN PATRICK Occupation: Editor/ Student. Education: B.A. English, B.S. Electronic Engineering, University of Wisconsin. Address: 553 West Oakdale #317, Chicago, Illinois 60657.

SERDAKOWSKI, JOSEPH ALAN Occupation: President, Chemical Engineering Consultants. Education: B.S.Ch.E., M.B.A. Address: 274 Moosehorn Road, East Greenwich, Rhode Island 02818.

SERRANI, THOM Occupation: Mayor, City of Stamford. Education: B.A., Sacred Heart University. Address: 113 Knickerbocker Avenue, Stamford, Connecticut 06901.

SESSIONS, JOHN TURNER JR Occupation: Physician. Education: M.D. Address: 700 Morgan Creek Road, Chapel Hill, North Carolina 27514.

SESTINA, JOHN E Occupation: Certified Financial Planner. Education: B.S., University of Dayton. Address: 4145 Mumford Court, Columbus, Ohio 43220.

SETIK, RAYMOND Occupation: Senator, Federated States of Micronesia. Address: Post Office Box 37, Truk, E.C.I 96942.

SETTE, LISA M Occupation: Director, Sette Publishing Company. Education: B.F.A. Fine Arts, Arizona State University. Address: 407 South Roosevelt Street, Tempe, Arizona 85281.

SEVARINO, ANGELO PAUL Occupation: Lawyer/Insurance Executive. Education: B.A. Psychology, M.A. in Educational Psychology, J.D. Address: 24 White Avenue, West Hartford, Connecticut 06119.

SEVAYEGA, DINA MARIA Occupation: Director, Educational Opportunity Program. Education: B.S., M.S., Ed.D. Address: 161 Snyder Hill Road, Ithaca, New York 14850.

SEVIER, JOHN C Occupation: Retired Educator.

SEVIGNY, CORINNE KERNAN Occupation: President, Horizon Realties, Inc. Education: Milton Academy, Milton, Massachusetts. Address: 370 Wood Avenue, Westmount, Quebec, Canada 43Z 1Z2.

SEVIGNY-McCONOMY, PIERRETTE Occupation: Lawyer. Education: Bachelor of Civil Law, Bachelor of Arts, Class I Certificate, Education Faculty, McGill University. Address: 400 Kensington Avenue, Montreal, Quebec H3Y 3A2.

SEWELL, WILLIAM G III Occupation: Electronics Engineer. Education: B.S.E.E., Ph.D. Address: 35 Tonset Court, Schaumburg, Illinois 60193.

SEYMOUR, RAYMOND BENEDICT Occupation: Author, Lecturer. Education: B.S., M.S., University of New Hampshire; Ph.D., University of Iowa. Address: 111 Lakeshore Drive, Hattiesburg, Mississippi 39901.

SHACHTMAN, TOM Occupation: Writer/TV

Producer. Education: B.S., M.F.A. Address: 12 West Tenth Street, New York, New York 10011.

SHAEVITZ, ROBERT MYRL Occupation: President and Chief Executive Officer, RMS Properties Corporation. Education: B.Sc. Business with Real Estate minor. Address: 65 Baywood Lane, Lake White, Waverly, Ohio 45690.

SHAFER, PAULINE M Occupation: President, Land Development Company. Education: B.S. Accounting and Business Administration. Address: 43 Green Ridge Road, Mechanicsburg, Pennsylvania 17055.

SHAFFER, DIANA LOUISE Occupation: Artist/ Educator. Education: B.A., Mt. Holyoke College; M.F.A., Cranbrook Art Academy. Address: 1015 Arch Adams #220, Fort Worth, Texas 76107.

SHAFFER, HOWARD J Occupation: Psychologist. Education: B.A., University of New Hampshire; M.S., Ph.D., University of Miami. Address: 171 Summer Street, Andover, Massachusetts 01810.

SHAH, GIRISH POPATLAL Occupation: Data Processing Professional; Scientist, Tymshare Inc. and Donnell Douglas Company. Education: M.S. Engineering, University of California-Berkeley, 1965; B.Tech. Engineering, Indiana University of Technology, Bombay, India, 1963. Address: 4048 Twyla Lane, Campbell, California 95008.

SHAH, HASMUKH SANKALCHAND Occupation: Director, Operations Planning at Mack Trucks, Inc. Education: M.S.I.E., M.B.A., West Virginia University. Address: 6411 Tupelo Road, Allentown, Pennsylvania 18104.

SHAH, SHIRISH K Occupation: Professor of Science and Chairperson, Computer Systems and Engineering Technology, Community College of Baltimore. Education: Ph.D., University of Delaware. Address: 5605 Purlington Way, Baltimore, Maryland 21212.

SHAHRYAR, ISHAQ M Occupation: President, Solec International, Inc. Education: B.S. Physical Chemistry, M.A. Political Science, University of California-Santa Barbara. Address: 1132 Tellem Drive, Pacific Palisades, California 90272.

SHAMSID-DEEN, ABDUR-RAHIM Occupation: Imam (Leader), American Muslim-Mission. Education: King Abdel Aziz University, Saudi Arabia. Address: 113 West Desert Drive, Phoenix, Arizona 85041.

SHANHOUSE, BILL Occupation: Sculptor. Education: Attended Northwestern University, Hofstra University, Corcoran School of Art; B.S.E.E., United States Naval Academy. Address: 10708 Great Arbor Drive, Potomac, Maryland 20854.

SHAPIRO, ELI Occupation: Professor of Management, Sloan School, Massachusetts Institute of Technology. Education: A.B., A.M., Ph.D. Address: 180 Beacon Street, Boston, Massachusetts 02116.

SHAPIRO, HAROLD BENJAMIN Occupation: Vice President of Finance and Treasurer, Diversified, Inc. Education: B.S., B.A., M.S. Accounting. Address: 12631 Conway Club Court, St. Louis, Missouri 63141.

SHAPIRO, LINDSAY STAMM Occupation: Assistant Chairman, Department of Environmental Design, Parsons School of Design. Education: B.A., Barnard College; M.Arch., Columbia University. Address: 560 Riverside Drive, New York, New York 10027.

SHARDA, BAM DEV Occupation: Associate Professor, University of Utah. Education: Ph.D. Address: 8395 South 1575 East, Sandy, Utah 84092.

SHARKEY, PAUL W Occupation: Clinical Assistant Professor of Psychiatry and Human

Behavior, University of Mississippi School of Medicine. Education: A.A., Pasadena City College; B.A. in Philosophy with high honors, California State University-Los Angeles, Ph.D. in Philosophy, University of Notre Dame.

SHARMA, MAHINDAR N Occupation: Senior Environmental Engineer, Lake County Health Department, Division of Environmental Health. Education: M.S.C.E., B.Ch.E., P.E. Address: 230 Old Mill Grove Road, Lake Zurich, Illinois 60047.

SHARMA, RAJENDRA M Occupation: Doctor of Medicine, Newcomb Hospital. Education: M.D. Address: 319 North Eighth Street, Vineland, New Jersey 08360.

SHARMA, RAVINDRA NATH Occupation: Head Librarian, The Pennsylvania State University. Education: B.A. with honors, M.A. in History, M.L.S., Ph.D. Address: 147 Ridgewood Drive, Freedom, Pennsylvani 15042.

SHARP, MARY SIMMONS Occupation: Registered Nurse, Head Nurse, Relief Supervisor. Education: A.A. Nursing. Address: Route 1, Box 288A, Dyer, Tennessee 38330.

SHARP, SHARON BARTS Occupation: Special Assistant to the Governor on Women, Office of the Governor, State of Illinois. Education: Attended Holy Cross Central School of Nursing; A.A.S. in Journalism, Harper Community College. Address: 1306 West Cedar Lane, Arlington Heights, Illinois 60005.

SHASTEEN, DAN M Occupation: Businessman. Education: High School Diploma; Attended Southern Illinois University. Address: 13 Mockingbird Lane, Carterville, Illinois 62918.

SHASTEEN, JAMES H Occupation: Business Executive. Education: Associate Degrees. Address: 14 Mockingbird Lane, Carterville, Illinois 62918.

SHATWELL, BOB R Occupation: Administrator, Tulsa County; Insurance Businessman. Education: Student, Will Rogers University, Tulsa University, University Center at Tulsa; Graduate, American Institute of Business and Law.

SHAW, DANNY WAYNE Occupation: Educator, Consultant. Education: Ph.D., Ed.S., M.A., B.S.E. Address: 1999 Church Place, Trenton, Michigan 48183.

SHAW, DAVID T Occupation: Professor, Department of Electrical and Computer Engineering. Education: Ph.D., M.S., B.S. Engineering. Address: 247 Cottonwood Drive, Williamsville, New York 14221.

SHAW, GEORGE BERNARD Occupation: President, Shaw, Weiss & De Naples, Consulting Engineers; Associate Professor, Civil Engineering and Engineering Mechanics, University of Dayton. Education: A.S. Mechanical Engineering, B.S. Civil Engineering, M.S. Civil Engineering. Address: 14 West First Street, Dayton, Ohio 45402.

SHAW, GEORGE KENTON Occupation: Pastor, Wayside Church of the Bible Covenant. Education: High School Diploma. Address: R.D. #5, Box 5203, Mercer, Pennsylvania 16137.

SHAW, GEORGE WILLIAM II Occupation: Microsystems Analyst. Education: A.A. Data Processing, A.A. Business Administration. Address: 18944 Rainier Avenue, Hayward, California 94541.

SHAW, WALTER THOMAS Occupation: Assistant Controller, Roytex, Inc. Education: B.S. Accounting, Rutgers University. Address: R.R. #1, Box 448, Oakridge, New Jersey 07438.

SHEAD, WILLIAM CARROLL Occupation: Attorney at Law. Education: J.D., South Texas College of Law. Address: 202 Kolb, Pasadena, Texas 77017.

SHEARER, CHARLES EDWARD JR Occupation:

Lawyer/Financial Planning. Education: J.D., A.B., A.S. Address: 6101 Walhonding Road, Bethesda Maryland 20816.

SHEARER, RUTH E Occupation: Professor of Education/Psychology, Alderson Broaddus College. Education: B.A., Western Maryland College; M.Ed., Ed.D., Columbia University. Address: Broaddus Knolls, Philippi, West Virginia 26416.

SHEBILSKE, WAYNE L Occupation: Study Director, National Academy of Sciences. Education: B.A., M.S., Ph.D. Address: 10020 Chestnut Wood Lane, Burke, Virginia 22015.

SHECTER, PEARL Occupation: Artist/Consultant. Education: F.F.A., M.F.A., Columbia University. Address: 60 East 9th Street, New York, New York 10003.

SHEDD, CARRIE McDONALD Occupation: Teacher/Educator, Writer/Authur, School of Business, Tuskegee Institute. Education: B.S. in Elementary Education, M.S. in Education Administration Supervision, Ph.D. Studies. Address: Post Office Box 516, Tuskegee Institute, Alabama 36088.

SHEEHAN, DANIEL E Occupation: Catholic Archbishop of Omaha. Education: D.D., J.C.D. Address: 110 North 62, Omaha, Nebraska 68132.

SHEEHAN, ROBERT JAMES II Occupation: Vice President, Regis J Sheehan and Associates, Management/Economic Consultants. Education: A.B., M.A. Economics. Address: 1606 Wrightson Drive, McLean, Virginia 22101.

SHEEHY, THOMAS D Occupation: Director, Manufacturing Resource Planning. Education: Master's Degree Business Administration, Bachelor's Degree Business Administration. Address: 40 C3 Whitney Rodge, Fairport, New York 14450.

SHEFFIELD, JAMES EDWARD Occupation: Chief Judge, Circuit Court, Richmond, Virginia. Education: B.A. Political Science, University of Illinois, 1955; LL.B., Howard University School of Law, 1963. Address: 800 East Marshall Street, Richmond, Virginia 23219.

SHEFTEL, HARRY B Occupation: Retired Economist, Office of Management and Budget, Executive Office. Education: A.B., Clark University; M.A., American University. Address: 5813 3rd Place Northwest, Washington, D.C. 20011.

SHEH, VIOLET MAE Occupation: Journalist. Education: Attended Mun Yew School of Chinese Studies, Toishan, China. Address: 10251 Aintree Crescent, Richmond, B.C., Canada V7A 3T9.

SHELLEY, LOUISE I Occupation: Professor, School of Justice, American University. Education: B.A., Cornell University; M.A., Ph.D., University of Pennsylvania. Address: 4538 Cathedral Avenue Northwest, Washington, D.C. 20016.

SHELTON, BESSIE ELIZABETH Occupation: Educator, Educational Media Associate, Musician. Education: B.A., M.S., Specialized Diplomas. Address: Post Office Box 187, Cumberland, Maryland 21502.

SHELTON, DAVID L Occupation: Professor of Theatre, Actor, Director. Education: A.B., M.F.A., Ph.D. Address: 2321 Southwest 39 Way, Gainesville, Florida 32607.

SHELVER, JANET WERNER Occupation: School Psychologist and Consultant. Education: Ed.D., Northern Illinois University; Ed.S., Purdue University. Address: 2216 South Western Avenue, Sioux Falls, South Dakota 57105.

SHEPARD, NEIL Occupation: Assistant Professor of Creative Writing, Rider College. Education: B.A., University of Vermont; M.F.A., Colorado State University; Ph.D., Ohio University. Address: 879

Lawrence Road, Lawrenceville, New Jersey 08648.

SHEPPARD, NAOMI KATE (TAYLOR) Occupation: Associate Professor, Psychiatric Nursing. Education: Associate of Arts, Diploma Nursing, Bachelor of Arts. Sociology, M.S. Nursing, Postgraduate Studies. Address: 3813 Loop Drive, Temple, Texas 76502.

SHEPPARD, WALTER LEE JR Occupation: Consulting Engineer. Education: B.Chem., Cornell University, 1932; M.S., University of Pennsylvania, 1933. Address: 923 Old Manoa Road, Havertown, Pennsylvania 19083.

SHERIDAN, EDWARD PATRICK Occupation: Professor and Chairman, Division of Psychology, Northwestern University Medical School. Education: B.A., M.A., Ph.D. Address: 666 North Lake Shore Drive, 1605, Chicago, Illinois 60611.

SHERIDAN, PATRICK M Occupation: President and Chief Executive Officer. Education: B.A., University of Notre Dame; M.B.A., University of Detroit. Address: 6628 Walnutwood Circle, Baltimore, Maryland 21212.

SHERMAN, A ROBERT Occupation: Psychology Professor and Clinical Psychologist, Department of Psychology, University of California-Santa Barbara. Education: B.A., Columbia University, 1964; M.S. 1966, Ph.D. 1969, Yale University. Address: 961 Crown Avenue, Santa Barbara, California 93111.

SHERMAN, FRANCES BUCK Occupation: Artist, Photographer, Writer. Education: College Studies. Address: 4331 San Jose Lane, Jacksonville, Florida 32207.

SHERMAN, JEROME KALMAN Occupation: Professor of Anatomy, Medical College, University of Arkansas. Education: A.B., Brown University, M.S., Western Reserve University; Ph.D., University of Iowa. Address: 3012 North Grant, Little Rock, Arkansas 72207.

SHERMAN, KENNETH I Occupation: Electrical Engineer. Education: B.S.E.E. Address: Route 2, Box 38, Pevely, Missouri 63070.

SHERMAN, PATRICIA ANN Occupation: Assistant Professor Physical Education, Men's and Women's Division I-A, Head Tennis Coach, East Carolina University. Education: B.S., M.A., Ph.D., Physical Education. Address: 112 Greene Way Apartments, Greenville, North Carolina 27834.

SHERREN, ANNE TERRY Occupation: Professor of Chemistry, North Central College. Education: B.A., Ph.D. Address: 10 South 108 Meadow Lane, Naperville, Illinois 60565.

SHERRILL, ANNE HUMMEL Occupation: History Professor, History Department, Mills College. Education: B.A., University of Arizona, 1952; M.A. 1956, Ph.D. 1966, University of California-Berkeley. Address: 156 Texas Street, San Francisco, California 94107.

SHERRY, PAUL H Occupation: Executive Director, Community Renewal Society. Education: Ph.D., M.Div., B.A. Address: Belden Stratford Hotel, 2300 North Lincoln Park West, Chicago, Illinois 60614.

SHERTZER, BRUCE ELDON Occupation: Professor of Education, Purdue University. Education: B.S., M.S., Ed.D. Address: 1620 Western Drive, West Lafayette, Indiana 47906.

SHETLER, FREDERICK CHARLES Occupation: Chief Engineer, WRID. Address: 977 Oak Street, Indiana, Pennsylvania 15701-1020.

SHEVLIN, KATHLEEN MARY Occupation: Social Work Administrator and Educator, Georgetown University Medical Center. Education: A.B., M.S.S.W.,

Ph.D. Address: 4301 Massachusetts Avenue, Northwest, Washington, D.C. 20016.

SHICHI, HITOSHI Occupation: Professor of Biomedical Sciences, Oakland University. Education: Ph.D. Biochemistry. Address: 4455 Pine Tree Trail, Bloomfield, Michigan 48013.

SHIELDS, HENRY RICHARD Occupation: Business Executive, Tax Consultant. Education: A.B., Brooklyn College; LL.B., J.D., New York University; M.B.A., Harvard University. Address: 98 Cutter Mill Road, Great Neck, New York 11021.

SHIELDS, THOMAS C Occupation: Attorney/Partner, Hopkins and Sutter. Education: A.B., Georgetown University, 1963; J.D. cum laude, University School of Law, 1966. Address: 756 Arlington Road, Riverside, Illinois 60546.

SHILLING, WINONA SIMMS Occupation: Counselor/Recruiter. Education: B.A. English, M.S. Educational Counseling (in progress). Address: 2502 Cypress, Norman, Oklahoma 73069.

SHILLINGSBURG, MIRIAM JONES Occupation: Professor of English. Education: B.A., M.A., Ph.D. Address: Box 2932, Mississippi State, Mississippi 39762.

SHIMIZU, IRIS M Occupation: Mathematical Statistician. Education: B.S.E., M.S., Ph.D. Address: 8513 Montpelier Drive, Laurel, Maryland 20708.

SHINE, CAROLYN R Occupation: Curator, Costume, Textiles, Tribal Arts. Education: B.A., Bryn Mawr College. Address: 250 Greendale, Cincinnati, Ohio 45220.

SHIPMAN, HARRY L Occupation: Astrophysicist. Education: B.A. Astronomy, Harvard University, 1969; M.S. 1970, Ph.D. Astronomy 1971, California Institute of Technology. Address: 346 Old Paper Mill Road, Newark, Delaware 19711.

SHIRAS, VIRGINIA ECHOLS Occupation: Home Health Nursing Coordinator. Education: B.A. Social Science, B.S. Nursing, M.A. Education. Address: 3 Rosemont, Little Rock, Arkansas 72204.

SHIREY, MARK STEVEN Occupation: Engineer. Education: B.S., M.Engr., M.B.A., Dip.Theo. Address: 2302 West Adams Street, Santa Ana, California 92704.

SHIRLEY, JOHN L Occupation: Psychotherapist, Clinical Hypnotherapist, Sexologist. Education: Doctor of Psychology, Doctor of Human Sexuality. Address: 15221 Preston Road, #2026, Dallas, Texas 75248.

SHIVELY, JOE E Occupation: Educational Researcher. Education: B.S. 1967, M.S. 1968, Ph.D. 1970, Purdue University. Address: 513 Dabney Drive, Charleston, West Virginia 25314.

SHLAES, JOHN B Occupation: Director of Planning, Edison Electric Association Executive. Education: B.S. Advertising. Address: 5629 Cambeth Road, Bethesda, Maryland 20814.

SHNEIDMAN, J LEE Occupation: Professor of History, Adelphi University. Education: B.A., M.A., Ph.D. Address: 161 West 86, New York, New York 10024.

SHOBER, R PHILIP Occupation: Teacher Education, College Faculty, Ohio Wesleyan University. Education: B.S., M.A., B.D., Ph.D. Address: 571 Clear Run Road, Delaware, Ohio 43015.

SHOKEIR, MOHAMED H K Occupation: Professor and Head-Physician, University Hospital, Saskatoon, Canada. Education: M.B., B.Ch., D.Ch. (Orth.), M.S., Ph.D., F.C.C.M.G. Address: 108 Riel Crescent, Saskatoon, Canada S7J 2W6.

SHORE, HERBERT Occupation: Author, Dramatist, Educator. Education: B.A., M.A., Ph.D. Address: 4091 West 8th Street, Los Angeles, California

90005.

SHORTER, KATIE M Occupation: Principal. Education: Master of Administration, Bachelor of Education. Address: 27600 Chardon Road, Willoughby Hills, Ohio 44092.

SHOTWELL, J RALPH Occupation: Executive Director, International Council of Community Churches. Education: B.A., B.D., M.Div. Address: 7761 Foresthill Lane, Palos Heights, Illinois 60430.

SHOUP, PAUL C Occupation: Vice President Commercial Bank. Education: B.B.A., M.B.A. Address: 101 Shore Club, St. Clair Shores, Michigan 48080.

SHRIME, GEORGE P Occupation: President/Chief Executive Officer, Micro Star, Inc. Education: Ph.D. Electrical Engineering, Northwestern University. Address: 9611 Milltrail, Dallas, Texas 75238.

SHRUM, (ALYCE) JANET Occupation: Associate Professor of Education and Director Guidance. Education: A.B., M.S., Ed.S. Address: 210 South Main, Sullivan, Indiana 47882.

SHUBIK, MARTIN Occupation: Seymour Knox Professor of Mathematical Institutional Economics. Education: B.A., M.A., A.M., Ph.D. Address: 140 Edgehill Road, New Haven, Connecticut 06511.

SHULL, LEO Occupation: Publisher, *Show Business*; Producer. Address: 1501 Broadway, Penthouse Tower, New York, New York 10036.

SHULMAN, DEBRAH ANNE ROTH Occupation: School Psychologist, Head School Based Drug Education/Prevention Program. Education: A.B., Ph.D. Address: 5193 Duane Drive, Fayetteville, New York 13066.

SHULTZ, FRED T Occupation: Consulting Geneticist and Biologist. Education: A.B. Biological Science, Stanford University, 1947; Ph.D. Genetics, University of California-Berkeley, 1952. Address: 19443 Marna Lane, Sonoma, California 95476.

SHULUASS, MOSES A Occupation: Professor of Jewish History. Education: Rabbi, Ph.D., D.H.L. (h.c.). Address: 2733 West Greenleaf Avenue, Chicago, Illinois 60645.

SHUMATE, MINERVA Occupation: Insurance Underwriter, Supervisor. Education: B.A. Address: Post Office Box 477, Hudson, Ohio 44236.

SHUMWAY, SPENCER THOMAS Occupation: Industrial Distributing Company Executive. Address: 11002 Maumee Drive, Granger, Indiana 46530.

SHUPERT, ANN E Occupation: Personnel Manager. Education: M.B.A., Butler University, 1976; B.A. Sociology, Hanover College, 1971. Address: 9333 North Meridian, Indianapolis, Indiana 46280.

SHUR, IRENE G Occupation: Professor, West Chester University. Education: Ed.D. Address: 981 North Penn Drive, West Chester, Pennsylvania 19380.

SHURTLEFF, WILLIAM ROY Occupation: Author. Education: B.A., B.Sc., M.A., Stanford University. Address: Post Office Box 234, Lafayette, California 94549.

SHUSMAN, EUGENE L Occupation: Pharmacy Executive/Businessman. Education: B.Sc. Address: 1550 Cherry Lane, Rydal, Pennsylvania 19046.

SHUSTER, MALCOLM DAVID Occupation: Engineer and Educator, Business and Technological Systems, Inc. Education: S.B. Physics, Massachusetts Institute of Technology, 1965; Ph.D. Physics, University of Maryland, 1971; M.S. Electrical Engineering, Johns Hopkins University, 1982. Address: Post Office Box 431, Glenn Dale, Maryland 20769.

SICARD, RAYMOND EDWARD Occupation: Research Scientist and Educator, Amherst College. Education: A.B. Biology, M.S. Zoology, Ph.D. Biological Sciences. Address: 290 Edgell Road, Framingham, Massachusetts 01701.

SICILIANO, THOMAS ALBERT Occupation: Coordinated Procurement/Parts Engineer. Education: B.A. Mathematics, St. Michael's College, 1955. Address: 13804 Freiburg Street, Whittier, California 90602.

SICOLI, M L CORBIN Occupation: Professor and Psychologist, Cabrini College. Education: B.S., M.S., M.S., Ph.D. Address: 404 Darlington Drive, West Chester, Pennsylvania 19380.

SIDOTI, DANIEL ROBERT Occupation: Brand Development Manager, Anheuser-Busch Company, Inc. Education: B.A., Union College; M.S., Stevens Institute of Technology. Address: 500 Wellshire, Ballwin, Missouri 63011.

SIEDEL, GEORGE J Occupation: Professor. Education: B.A., College of Wooster, 1967; J.D., University of Michigan, 1970; D.C.L.S., Cambridge University, 1971. Address: 2103 Devonshire Road, Ann Arbor, Michigan 48104.

SIEFKER, CAROL A Occupation: Psychotheologist, Cognitive Psychotherapist, Psychomedia Specialist. Education: B.A. Psychology, M.A. Psychology. Address: 5 Bryant Crescent 2K, White Plains, New York 10605.

SIEGEL, BEN Occupation: Professor. Education: B.A., M.A., Ph.D. Address: 239 Monterrey Drive, Claremont, California 91711.

SIEGEL, LAWRENCE S Occupation: Physician and Surgeon. Education: B.S., University of North Dakota, 1933; M.D., Rush Medical College, 1936. Address: 6010 Wilshire Boulevard, Los Angeles, California 90036.

SIEGEL, RACHEL JOSEFOWITZ Occupation: Clinical Social Worker, Private Practice. Education: B.S., M.S.W. Address: 203 Forest Drive, Ithaca, New York 14850.

SIEGEL, RITA SUE Occupation: Recruiter, Design Professions. Education: M.I.D., B.I.D., Pratt Institute. Address: 60 West 55 Street, New York, New York 10019.

SIEGEL, RUTH VIVIAN Occupation: Lawyer and Educational Consultant. Education: J.D., A.B., State University of New York; Ed.M., Columbia University; B.A., Ithaca College. Address: R.D. #1, Brooktondale, New York 14817.

SIEGEL, STEPHEN B Occupation: President and Chief Executive Officer. Address: 405 East 54th Street, New York, New York 10022.

SIERACKI, LEONARD MARK Occupation: President, Research and Development Company (Tritec). Education: Bachelor Aerospace Engineering 1963, Master Mechanical Engineering 1970, Catholic University of Washington, D.C.; M.B.A., Johns Hopkins University, 1977. Address: 9421 Kilimanjaro Road, Columbia, Maryland 21045.

SIGLER, LOIS OLIVER Occupation: Educator. Education: B.S., East Tennessee University, 1944; M.S., The University of Tennessee, 1952; Postgraduate Studies, The University of Tennessee and Memphis State University. Address: 4785 Rollilng Meadows Drive, Memphis, Tennessee 38128.

SIKS, GERALDINE B Occupation: Professor of Drama, Author, Playwright. Education: M.A. Speech, Northwestern University. Address: 1754 Northeast 90th Street, Seattle, Washington 98115.

SILBERT, MIMI HALPER Occupation: Co-President, Delancey Street Foundation in San Francisco and New York; President, Delancey Street Foundation in New Mexico. Education: B.A. English, University of Massachusetts, 1963; M.A. Counseling and

Psychology 1965, Ph.D. Criminology and Psychology 1968, University of California-Berkeley. Address: 2563 Divisadero Street, San Francisco, California 94115.

SILCOX, GORDON BRUCE Occupation: Executive Recruiting Consultant. Education: A.B., Princeton University; M.B.A, Wharton School of Finance and Commerce. Address: 3811 Dalebrook Drive, Dumfries, Virginia 22026.

SILVER, DAVID MAYER Occupation: Associate Vice President for Graduate Studies and Research, Butler University. Education: A.B., Butler University, 1937; M.A. 1938, Ph.D. 1940, University of Illinois. Address: 8230 North Illinois Street, Indianapolis, Indiana 46260.

SILVERMAN, FAYE ELLEN Occupation: Composer. Education: B.A., Barnard College; M.A., Harvard University; D.M.A., Columbia University. Address: 1000 East Joppa Road, Apartment 207, Baltimore, Maryland 21204.

SILVERMAN, JACK H Occupation: Chairman, Martin, Sturtevant, Silverman and Marshall, Inc. Education: A.B., Johns Hopkins University, 1954. Address: 444 East 82nd Street, New York, New York 10028.

SILVERTON, JOHN SAUNDERS Occupation: Plastic Surgeon. Education: M.B., B.S., St. Bartholomew's Hospital Medical College, 1967. Address: 1803 West March Lane, Suite B, Stockton, California 95207.

SIMINI, JOSEPH PETER Occupation: Certified Public Accountant and Communicator, Writer/Publisher. Education: B.S. Mathematics, B.B.A. Accounting, M.B.A. Policy and Administration, D.B.A. Address: 2 Mountain Springs Road, San Francisco, California 94114.

SIMIU, EMIL Occupation: Research Engineer, National Bureau of Standards. Education: Ph.D., Princeton University, 1971. Address: 6031 Valerian Lane, Rockville, Maryland 20852.

SIMMONS, CHESTER R Occupation: Commissioner, United States Football League. Education: A.B. Address: 18 Daffodil Lane, Cos Cob, Connecticut 06870.

SIMMONS, S DALLAS Occupation: President, Saint Paul's College. Education: B.S., M.S., North Carolina Central University; Ph.D., Duke University. Address: Saint Paul's College, Lawrenceville, Virginia 23868.

SIMMONS, WILLIAM WILSON Occupation: Consultant. Education: B.S.E.E. Address: 56 Husten Lane, Greenwich, Connecticut 06830.

SIMMS-MACHARIA, GREGORY F Occupation: President, New Educational Methods, Inc. Education: B.M., University of Kansas, 1950; Certificate, University of Paris, University of Perugia, Vienna Academy of Music. Address: 17 Lee Avenue, Trenton, New Jersey 08618.

SIMON, JOHN A Occupation: Professor of Biochemistry and Nutrition. Education: B.Sc., M.S., Ph.D. Address: 16215 White Star, Houston, Texas 77062.

SIMON-MILLER, FRANCOISE LOUISE Occupation: Product Manager, Abbott Laboratories; Adjunct Professor of Marketing, University of Chicago. Education: Doctor of Philosophy, Yale University, 1980; Master of Business Administration, Northwestern University, 1983. Address: 2760 Hampton Parkway, Evanston, Illinois 60201.

SIMONE, CHARLES B Occupation: Physician, Oncologist/Immunologist, Author, Inventor. Education: M.M.S., M.D. Address: 16 Balsam Court,

Lawrenceville, New Jersey 08648.

SIMONE, CHERYL LUCILLE Occupation: Supervisor. Education: B.A., M.A., M.Ed. Address: 294 Glenn Avenue, Lawrenceville, New Jersey 08648.

SIMONS, ANNEKE PRINS Occupation: Professor, Jersey City State College; Artist. Education: B.A., Vassar College; M.A.T., Harvard University; Ph.D., Pennsylvania State University. Address: 265 Liberty Avenue, Jersey City, New Jersey 07307.

SIMPSON, BARBARA JEAN Occupation: Court Intake Officer, North Carolina Department of Correction, Adult Probation and Parole. Education: A.A. Address: 210 Bell Air Street, Beaufort, North Carolina 28516.

SIMPSON, ERVIN PETER YOUNG Occupation: Ordained Minister, Educational Ministries (Retired). Education: B.A., M.A., University of New Zealand; B.D.; Th.M.; Th.D.; M.Div. Address: Box 82, Alderson-Broaddus College, Philippi, West Virginia 26416.

SIMPSON, JANET YVONNE Occupation: Social Service Coordinator and Consultant. Education: M.S.W., B.S.W. Address: 1717-H Vestawood Court, Birmingham, Alabama 35216.

SIMPSON, MARY MICHAEL Occupation: Episcopal Priest, Psychotherapist, Canon Counselor. Education: B.A., B.S., Certificate of Psychotherapy, S.T.M. Address: 1047 Amsterdam Avenue, New York, New York 10025.

SIMPSON, RUSSELL GORDON Occupation: Attorney at Law. Education: B.A., Yale University, 1951; J.D., Boston University, 1956; Harvard Law School, 1961. Address: 76 Brook Hill Road, Milton, Massachusetts 02187.

SIMS, PAUL K Occupation: Geologist. Education: B.S. 1940, M.S. 1942, University of Illinois; Ph.D., Princeton University, 1950. Address: 1315 Overhill Road, Golden, Colorado 80401.

SINCLAIR, JAMES BURTON Occupation: Professor of Plant Pathology. Education: B.Sc., Ph.D. Address: 408 Abours Drive, Savoy, Illinois 61874.

SINGER, CYNTHIA K Occupation: Licensed Embalmer and Funeral Director. Education: R.N., Associate of Mortuary Science. Address: 1629 Polk, Chillicothe, Missouri 64601.

SINGER, EVELYN J T Occupation: Dean, School of Nursing, Florida State University. Education: B.S.N., M.S.N., Ph.D. Address: 2637 Vasser Road, Tallahassee, Florida 32308.

SINGER, JEANNE Occupation: Composer, Pianist, Lecturer. Education: B.A. magna cum laude, Barnard College, 1944; Artist Diploma, National Guild of Piano Teachers, 1954. Address: 64 Stuart Place, Manhasset, New York 11030.

SINGER, SARAH BETH Occupation: Poet and Teacher. Education: B.A. Address: 38 Stephan Marc Lane, New Hyde Park, New York 11040.

SINGH, RAMA SHANKAR Occupation: Pediatrician, Neonatologist. Education: M.B.B.S., M.D., F.A.A.P. Address: 9912 South Kilpatrick, Oak Lawn, Illinois 60453.

SINGHAL, VIVEK K Occupation: Corporate Director of Strategic Planning, Consolidated Foods. Education: M.S.E.E., M.B.A. Address: 6104 Washington Street, Downers Grove, Illinois 60516.

SINGLETARY, REBECCA L Occupation: Director of Special Gifts and Planned Support, Attorney. Education: A.A., B.A., M.A., J.D. Address: Post Office Box 7576, Rocky Mount, North Carolina 27802.

SINGLETON, "J" ARTHUR Occupation: Social Science Teacher, Bayside High School. Education: B.S. Social Science and Secondary Education, M.S.

Secondary Guidance and Counseling Education. Address: Post Office Box 5428, Virginia Beach, Virginia 23455.

SINHA, DEVENDRA P Occupation: Veterinarian. Education: M.S., D.V.M., Ph.D. Address: 696 Stow Place, Reynoldsburg, Ohio 43068.

SINHA, KUMARES G Occupation: Professor and Head Transportation Engineering, Purdue University. Education: B.S., Jadaupur University, India, 1961; M.A. 1966, Ph.D. 1968, University of Connecticut. Address: 2224 Miami Trail, West Lafayette, Indiana 47906.

SINOTO, YOSIHIKO H Occupation: Chairman, Department of Anthropology, Bernice Pauahi Bishop Museum. Education: D.Sc. Address: 2367 Aina Lani Place, Honolulu, Hawaii 96822.

SINZER, JOSEPH FRANCIS Occupation: C. Richard Pace Professor. Education: B.A., M.A., Ph.D. Address: 365 Ridgewood Avenue, Glen Ridge, New Jersey 07028.

SIPE, GEORGE EMERY IV Occupation: Interior Design Showroom Manager. Education: B.A. English, Pennsylvania State University, 1972. Address: 12 Divisadero, San Francisco, California 94117.

SISLER, HARRY H Occupation: Professor. Education: M.Sc., Ohio State University, 1936; Ph.D., University of Illinois, 1939. Address: 6014 Northwest 54th Way, Gainesville, Florida 32606.

SITLINGTON, PATRICIA L Occupation: Associate Professor, Department of Special Education, Indiana University. Education: B.A. Mathematics, M.Ed. Educational Psychology, Ph.D. Special Education. Address: 112 Hampton Court, Bloomington, Indiana 47401.

SIU, JENNIFER JEAN Occupation: Assistant Director, Intramural Recreation. Education: B.A. Physical Education, M.A. Athletic Administration. Address: 969 Hilgard Avenue #306, Westwood, California 90024.

SIVINSKI, JACEK STEFAN Occupation: Food Irradiation/Isotope Utilization. Education: B.S.M.E., Iowa State University. Address: 9825 Hannett Place Northeast, Albuquerque, New Mexico 87112.

SIZEMORE, WILLIAM CHRISTIAN Occupation: President, Alderson-Broaddus College. Education: B.A., B.D., M.S.L.S., Adv.M.L.S., Ph.D. Address: Alderson-Broaddus College, Greystone, Philippi, West Virginia 26416.

SJOBERG, LEIF T Occupation: Professor of Scandinavian Studies and Comparative Literature, State University of New York-Stony Brook. Education: F.K., F.M., F.L., Fil.Dr.h.c., Uppsala University. Address: 50 Morningside Drive, New York, New York 10025.

SJOGREN, C STEVEN Occupation: President, Home Federal Savings and Loan Association. Education: B.B.A., M.B.A. Address: 2853 Soland Drive, Rockford, Illinois 61111.

SKEAN, CHARLES THOMAS Occupation: Clinical Social Worker, Children's Services. Education: M.S.W. Address: 202 8th Street, Kenova, West Virginia 25530.

SKEETER, SHARYN JEANNE Occupation: Assistant Professor, Emerson College; Poet/Writer. Education: B.A. Romance Languages, Master of Business Administration. Address: 30 Charles Street, Lexington, Massachusetts 02173.

SKIDMORE, JAMES ALBERT JR Occupation: Chairman, President and Chief Executive Officer, Science Management Corporation. Education: Bachelor of Economics, Muhlenberg College. Address: 641 Ocean, Sea Girt, New Jersey 08750.

SKINSNES, OLAF KRISTIAN Occupation: Professor of Pathology, Department of Pathology, Zhongshan Medical College. Address: Department of Pathology, Zhongshan Medical College, Guangzhou, Guangdong, China.

SKOTHEIM, TERJE A Occupation: Physicist, Brookhaven National Laboratory. Education: Ph.D. Address: 248 Durkee Lane, East Patchogue, New York 11772.

SKROWACZEWSKI, STANISLAW Occupation: Conductor, Composer. Education: Diploma, Faculty Philosophy, University of Lwow, 1945; Diploma Faculties Composition and Conducting, Academy of Music of Lwow, 1945; Attended Conservatory at Krakow, 1946; L.H.D., Hamline University 1963, Macalaster College 1975, University of Minnesota 1979. Address: Post Office Box 700, Wayzata, Minnesota 55391.

SLACK, MICHAEL L Occupation: Attorney. Education: B.S. Aerospace Engineering, M.S. Aerospace Engineering, J.D. Address: 11620 Audelia Road, #718, Dallas, Texas 75243.

SLAPPEY, MARY McGOWAN Occupation: Writer, Artist. Education: A.B., George Washington University, 1947; J.D., International School of Law, 1977; D.Lit., World University, 1981; Honorary Certificate, Corcoran School of Art. Address: 4500 Chesapeake Street Northwest, Washington, D.C. 20016.

SLATKIN, MURRAY Occupation: President, Felmore Corporation. Education: A.B., J.D. Address: Stevenson, Maryland 21153.

SLAVENS, THOMAS PAUL Occupation: Professor of Library Science, School of Library Science, University of Michigan. Education: A.B., M.Div., A.M., Ph.D. Address: 3745 Tremont Lane, Ann Arbor, Michigan 48105.

SLAVOV, ATANAS VASILEV Occupation: Writer. Education: Ph.D. Theory of Literature, Post Doctoral Degrees in Folklore and Folk Arts. Address: Post Office Box 34096, Bethesda, Maryland 20817.

SLAVOV, EUGENIA MARGARET Occupation: Professor of Languages and Literature, University of Delaware. Education: D.Lit. Address: 719 Fiske Lane, Neward, Delaware 19711.

SLEDD, MARY GLENN Occupation: Business Instructor. Education: B.A. Vocational Education, M.A. Business. Address: 1233 Madison Street, Paducah, Kentucky 42001.

SLEDGE, ANDREA CELINE Occupation: Assistant Professor, Coordinator Graduate Program in Reading, Herbert H. Lehman College. Address: 30 Park Avenue, Mount Vernon, New York, New York.

SLEITH, BARBARA ANN BALKO Occupation: Special Educator. Education: B.S.Ed., M.Ed.Sp.Ed., Supervisor Certificate. Address: R.D. #2, Box 115, West Newton, Pennsylvania 15089.

SLEMON, GORDON R Occupation: Dean of the Faculty of Applied Science and Engineering, University of Toronto. Education: B.A.Sc., M.A.Sc., D.I.C., Ph.D., D.Sc. Address: 40 Chatfield Drive, Don Mills, Ontario M3B1K5, Canada.

SLIWINSKI, EDWARD ROBERT Occupation: Engineering Consultant. Education: B.C.E., M.C.E., P.E. Address: 26-34 213th Street, Bayside, New York 11360.

SLOAN, BLAINE F Occupation: Professor of International Law and Organization, Pace Law School. Education: A.B., LL.B., Nebraska University; LL.M., Columbia University. Address: 23 Hall Road, Briarcliff Manor, New York 10510 and Fox Hill-Forbes Park,

Fort Garland, Colorado 81133.

SLOVICK, ROBERT JOHN   Occupation: Manager of Computer Switching, Western Union. Education: Diablo Valley College. Address: 301 Pantano Circle, Pacheco, California 94553.

SLOWINSKI, DAVID ALLEN   Occupation: Software Engineer, Cray Research, Inc. Education: B.S. Computer Science, 1976; M.S. Computer Science, 1980. Address: Route 5 Box 583, Chippewa Falls, Wisconsin 54729.

SMALL, SHEILA ELIZABETH   Occupation: Assistant Professor of Nursing. Education: R.N., B.S., M.S.N. Address: Route 1, Box 368, Clarksburg, West Virginia 26301.

SMALLWOOD, DAVID M   Occupation: Agricultural Economist. Education: B.S., M.E., Ph.D., North Carolina State University. Address: 5913 Flanders Street, Springfield, Virginia 22150.

SMARIO, THOMAS MICHAEL   Occupation: Poet. Education: A.A., Laney College; Attended University of California. Address: 11900 Southeast Foster Place, Portland, Oregon 97266.

SMEALLIE, PETER HENRY   Occupation: National Academy of Sciences. Education: B.A. Urban Studies. Address: 2700 Q Street Northwest, Washington, D.C. 20007.

SMEDLEY, RONALD FRANK   Occupation: Personnel Manager. Education: B.A. Psychology, M.S.I. Psychology. Address: 13609 East Sunset Drive, Whittier, California 90602.

SMELTZER, SUSAN   Occupation: Pianist, Artist, Sculptor. Education: B.M., Oklahoma City University, 1963; M.M., University of Southern California, 1967; Postgraduate Studies, Akademie fur Musik. Address: 8102 Tavenor, Houston, Texas 77075.

SMILARDO, MARGARET   Occupation: Hotel Manager. Education: High School Diploma. Address: 720 North Third Street, Milwaukee, Wisconsin 53203.

SMILEY, WILLIAM ABDO   Occupation: Certified Public Accountant, Realtor, Investor. Education: B.A. Business and Teaching; Graduate Work. Address: 2408 Margaret Drive, Newport Beach, California 92663.

SMIT, CHRISTIAN J B   Occupation: Associate Dean and Director, University of Georgia. Education: B.Sc., H.E.D., Ph.D. Address: 196 Deertree Drive, Athens, Georgia 30605.

SMITH, ADELL E   Occupation: Consultant, Upward Mobility Women and Minorities. Education: B.A. Psychology, M.B.A. Address: 4435 Crestland Drive, St. Louis, Missouri 63121.

SMITH, ALBERT E   Occupation: Executive Vice President, Fidelity Bank and Trust Company; Certified Public Accountant, Partner-Lutz, Smith and Company. Education: B.S., Rutgers University; C.P.A. Address: 104 Covered Bridge Road, Cherry Hill, New Jersey 08034.

SMITH, ALBERT J   Occupation: Professor of Biology, Wheaton College. Education: B.A., Wheaton College; B.D., Northern Baptist Theological Seminary; M.S., Northern Illinois University; Ph.D., University of Chicago. Address: 26W331 Parkway, Winfield, Illinois 60190.

SMITH, ANDREW V   Occupation: President, Pacific Northwest Bell Telephone Company. Education: B.S. Electrical Engineering, Oregon State University. Address: 9060 Northeast 41st Street, Bellevue, Washington 98004.

SMITH, ARTHUR COOKE JR   Occupation: Ophthalmologist. Education: B.A., M.D. Address: 1362 Upper Coleman Avenue, Elmira, New York 14903.

SMITH, BERTHA J   Occupation: Faculty Member and Activities Director. Education: B.S. Education. Address: 4435 Crestland Drive, St. Louis, Missouri 63121.

SMITH, CAMERON OUTCALT   Occupation: Venture Capital Management. Education: B.A. Art History, Princeton University, 1972; M.Sc., Pennsylvania State University. Address: Great Elm South, Sharon, Connecticut 06069.

SMITH, CAMILLE M   Occupation: Assistant Professor, University of Florida, Music Department. Education: B.M.Ed., M.M., Ph.D. Address: 2635 Southwest 35th Place, #702, Gainesville, Florida 32608.

SMITH, CHARLES FOSTER   Occupation: Certified Public Accountant. Education: B.S., University of South Carolina, 1940. Address: 3400 North Kings Highway, Myrtle Beach, South Carolina 29577.

SMITH, CHARLES LeROY   Occupation: Research Scientist, Lecturer in Geography, Center for Strategic Technology, Texas A&M University. Education: B.S., Kansas State University; M.S., University of Alabama; Ph.D., University of Georgia. Address: 1009 Braeswood, Bryan, Texas 77801.

SMITH, CLYDE CURRY   Occupation: Professor of Ancient History and Religion. Education: A.B. cum laude Physics, 1951; M.S., University of Miami, Ohio, 1951; D.B. 1954, M.A. 1961, Ph.D. 1968, University of Chicago. Address: 939 West Maple Street, River Falls, Wisconsin 54022.

SMITH, CORINNE ROTH   Occupation: Associate Professor and School Psychologist, Syracuse University. Education: Ph.D. Address: 14 Bovington Lane, Fayetteville, New York 13066.

SMITH, CORNELIA MARSCHALL   Occupation: Emeritus Professor and Chairman of Biology, Baylor University; Researcher. Education: B.A., Baylor University; M.A., University of Chicago; Ph.D., Johns Hopkins University. Address: 801 James, Waco, Texas 76706.

SMITH, DAVID B D   Occupation: Professor, University of Southern California. Education: Ph.D. Address: 1311 South Brass, Lantern Drive, La Habra, California 90631.

SMITH, DORENE CARTER   Occupation: Free-Lance Artist, Part-time Proof Clerk. Education: Individualized Studies Degree, Frank Phillips College; Associate of Art (in progress). Address: 137 Abilene Street, Borger, Texas 79007.

SMITH, DOROTHY B   Occupation: Hemodialysis Nurse. Education: Licensed Nurse, Medical College of Virginia. Address: 2004 Del Rio Drive, Richmond, Virginia 23223.

SMITH, DOROTHY M   Occupation: Hotel Manager. Education: B.S., M.S. magna cum laude in Chemistry, University of Wisconsin. Address: 11449 Airlane Drive #B, Bridgeton, Missouri 63044.

SMITH, ELEANOR GAINES   Occupation: Counselor, Instructor Piano and Organ. Education: Attended Hartt School of Music. Address: 118 Torcon Drive, Torrington, Connecticut 06790.

SMITH, ELTON O JR   Occupation: Clergyman, Superintendent of Susquehanna Conference Free Methodist Church. Education: B.A., Roberts Wesleyan College; M.Div., Asbury Theological Seminary. Address: 210 Longmeadow Drive, Syracuse, New York 13205.

SMITH, EPHRAIM PHILIP   Occupation: Dean of the College of Business. Education: B.S., Providence College; M.S., University of Massachusetts; Ph.D., University of Illinois. Address: 22325 Rye Road, Shaker Heights, Ohio 44122.

SMITH, ERIC PARKMAN Occupation: Assistant Treasurer, Maine Central Railroad Company (Retired). Education: A.B. 1932, M.B.A. 1934, Harvard University. Address: Academy Lane, Concord, Massachusetts 01742.

SMITH, GAIL PRESTON Occupation: Consultant in International Research, Corning Glass Works. Education: B.S., Geneva College, 1934; M.A., Syracuse University, 1936; Ph.D., University of Michigan, 1941. Address: 75 Caton Road, Corning, New York 14830.

SMITH, GARY RICHARD Occupation: Professor, Brigham Young University. Education: B.A. 1954, B.A. 1959, Ed.D. 1970. Address: 990 East 2680 North, Provo, Utah 84604.

SMITH, GEORGE P II Occupation: Professor of Law, Catholic University. Education: B.S., J.D., Indiana University; LL.M., Columbia University. Address: 2500 Q Street Northwest, #521, Washington, D.C. 20007.

SMITH, GERARD P Occupation: Professor of Psychiatry. Education: M.D. Address: 65 Ogden Avenue, White Plains, New York 10605.

SMITH, HAROLD F Occupation: Librarian. Education: A.B., A.M., A.M.L.S., Ph.D. Address: 206 Summer, Parkville, Missouri 64152.

SMITH, HOKE LaFOLLETTE Occupation: President, Towson State University. Education: A.B., M.A., Ph.D. Address: 209 Churchwarden's Road, Baltimore, Maryland 21212.

SMITH, HORTON Occupation: Judge of the Superior Court. Education: J.D., LL.B., B.A. Address: West 941 King County Court House, Seattle, Washington, 98104.

SMITH, HOWARD WESLEY Occupation: Professor of Aerospace Engineering, University of Kansas. Education: B.S., M.S., Ph.D. Address: 1612 Crescent Road, Lawrence, Kansas 66044.

SMITH, IAN CORMACK PALMER Occupation: Research in Biophysics, National Research Council. Education: B.Sc., M.Sc., Ph.D. Address: 550 Rivershore Crescent, Ottawa, Ontario, Canada K1J 7Y7.

SMITH J B Occupation: Lecturer in Music, Humboldt State University. Education: B.M.E., Baylor University; M.M., University of Illinois. Address: 546 24th Street, Arcata, California 95521.

SMITH, JAMES BERNARD Occupation: Field Claim Manager, Allstate Insurance Company. Education: B.A. Business Administration, M.B.A., Ph.D. Business Administration. Address: 1028 Bushard Drive, Escondido, California 92025.

SMITH, JAMES G Occupation: Educator. Education: B.S.E.E., M.S.E.E., Ph.D. Address: 2604 Sunset, Carbondale, Illinois 62901.

SMITH, LAWRENCE N Occupation: President and Chief Executive Officer, Essex Financial Group, Inc. Education: B.S. Address: 826 Riverview Drive, Suffolk, Virginia 23434.

SMITH, MARK A Occupation: Professor, University of Maryland. Education: B.S. Civil Engineering, M.S., Ph.D. Address: 9348 Cherry Hill Road #523, College Park, Maryland 20740.

SMITH, MERYL COULSON Occupation: Educator (Retired), Private Vocal and Piano Teacher, Church Choir Director, Soloist. Education: B.A., Southwestern Oklahoma State University, 1940. Address: Rural Route 2, Box 8, Leedey, Oklahoma 73654.

SMITH, NAN S Occupation: Assistant Professor of Art, University of Florida; Artist. Education: B.F.A., Temple University; M.F.A., Ohio State University. Address: 4409 Northwest 27th Terrace, Gainesville, Florida 32605.

SMITH, PAUL A Occupation: Consulting Psychologist. Education: Ph.D. Psychology, University of Central California, 1982. Address: 6105 Glenhurst Way, Citrus Heights, California 95621.

SMITH, PHILIP ALAN Occupation: Public Relations. Education: B.A. Address: 9518 Rockport Road, Vienna, Virginia 22180.

SMITH, RAYMOND K Occupation: Retired Educator. Education: M.Ed. Address: Post Office Box 70, Hahnville, Louisiana 70057.

SMITH, RHONDA ROSE Occupation: Registered Nurse, Health Educator. Education: B.S.N., M.P.H. Candidate, University of Michigan. Address: 653 Van Buren Street, Fostoria, Ohio 44830.

SMITH, RICHARD ALLAN Occupation: Computer Scientist. Education: Bachelor's Degree, Computer Science and Information Processing. Address: 1390 Market Street, #907, San Francisco, California 94102.

SMITH, RICHARD K Occupation: Coordinator of Clinical Services, Consuelo Vocational and Transitional Facility. Education: M.S. Rehabilitation Counseling, California State University. Address: Box 227, Pineville, Pennsylvania.

SMITH, ROBERT E JR Occupation: Professor, Purdue University. Education: B.A., M.F.A., Ph.D. Address: 520 Terry Lane, West Lafayette, Indiana 47906.

SMITH, ROBERT EARL Occupation: Space Scientist, Marshall Space Flight Center. Education: Ph.D. Atmospheric Science. Address: 125 Westbury Drive, Huntsville, Alabama 35802.

SMITH, ROBERT ELLIS Occupation: Newsletter Publisher, Author. Education: B.A., Harvard College; Georgetown University Law Center. Address: Post Office Box 15300, Washington, D.C. 20003.

SMITH, ROCH C Occupation: Professor and Head of the Department of Romance Languages, University of North Carolina at Greensboro. Education: B.A. 1962, M.A.T. 1965, University of Florida; M.A. 1970, Ph.D. 1971, Emory University. Address: Department of Romance Languages, University of North Carolina at Greensboro, Greensboro, North Carolina 29412.

SMITH, RODGER CHAPMAN Occupation: Consultant, Chemical Marketing/Technology. Education: B.S., University of Massachusetts. Address: 24 East Street, South Hadley, Massachusetts 01075.

SMITH, SAMUEL H Occupation: Dean of the College of Agriculture, The Pennsylvania State University. Education: B.S., Ph.D. Address: 1108 Kay Street, Boalsburg, Pennsylvania 16827.

SMITH, SHARON M Occupation: Personnel Assistant. Education: A.A., B.A. Psychology (in progress). Address: 601 Pico Avenue, San Mateo, California 94403.

SMITH, STANLEY R Occupation: Tennis Professional. Education: B.A. Business Finance, University of Southern California. Address: 1095 Lighthouse, Hilton Head Island, South Carolina 29928.

SMITH, STEPHEN D Occupation: Safety Engineer. Education: B.S.Ed., Miami University; M.S., Central Missouri State University. Address: 12401 West Okeechobee Road, Box 19, Hialean Gardens, Florida 33016.

SMITH, THEODORE C Occupation: President, Yaskawa Electric America. Education: B.S., M.B.A. Address: 925 South Beverly Place, Lake Forest, Illinois 60045.

SMITH, TOM E Occupation: President and Chief Operating Officer, Food Lion Stores, Inc. Education: A.B. Business Administraton, Catawba College, 1964.

Address: 620 Catawba Road, Salisbury, North Carolina 28144.

SMITH, TROY ALVIN Occupation: Aerospace Engineer, Professional Engineer. Education: B.C.E., The University of Virginia, 1948; M.S.E. Civil Engineering 1952, Ph.D. Engineering Mechanics 1970, The University of Michigan. Address: 2406 Bonita Drive, Southwest, Huntsville, Alabama 35801.

SMITH, WARREN WILLIAM Occupation: Specialist in Internal Medicine. Education: M.D., New York University College of Medicine. Address: 2348 Johnston Road, Columbus, Ohio 43220.

SMITH, WILLIAM II (BILL) Occupation: Supervisor of Engineering, Denver Public Schools. Education: B.S., Tuskegee Institute; Postgraduate Studies, Washington University. Address: 102 South Balsam Street, Lakewood, Colorado 80226.

SMITH, WILLIAM F Occupation: Professor of Psychology. Education: A.B., Northeastern University; M.S., University of Massachusetts; Ph.D., Michigan State University. Address: 1401 12th Avenue South, St. Petersburg, Florida 33705.

SMOLANOFF, MICHAEL L Occupation: President, Real to Reel Productions. Education: B.M., M.S., Ph.D. Address: 14A La Bonne Vie Drive, East Patchogue, New York 11772.

SMOLLEN, WILLIAM JOHN Occupation: Treasurer, Dart International. Education: C.P.A., B.S. Address: 3044 Arrowhead Drive, Los Angeles, California 90068.

SNIDER, CLIFTON M Occupation: Professor at California State University, Writer. Education: B.A., M.A., California State University-Long Beach. Address: 1246 Appleton Street, Long Beach, California 90802.

SNOWDEN, LILLIAN R Occupation: Operating Accountant, Community Activist. Education: B.S.B.A., A.S.B.A. Address: Post Office Box 23576, L'Enfant Station, Washington, D.C. 20026.

SNYDER, DARL EVERETT Occupation: Director of International Development, University of Georgia. Education: B.Sc., M.A., Ed.D. Address: 160 Snapfinger Drive, Athens, Georgia 30605.

SNYDER, HUGH C Occupation: Free-Lance Consultant. Education: Attended University of Toledo, Bowling Green State University, Ohio University. Address: Post Office Box 124, Perrysburg, Ohio 43551.

SNYDER, JOHN JOSEPH Occupation: Optometrist. Education: A.B., University of California-Los Angeles, 1931; B.S. 1948, O.D. 1949, Los Angeles College of Optometry. Address: 735 Luring Drive, Glendale, California 91206.

SOCRATES, PHILIP OWENS Occupation: Typesetter/Editor. Education: B.A., University of North Carolina-Chapel Hill; M.A., Harvard University; Ph.D., Oxford University. Address: 132 Trotter Street, Roxboro, North Carolina 27573.

SODER, DEE ANN Occupation: Vice President of Human Resources Development. Education: B.S. with special distinction, M.S., Ph.D. Address: 1200 Springfield, New Providence, New Jersey.

SOGLIERO, GENE SANDRA Occupation: Senior Research Scientist/Statistician. Education: M.A. Mathematics, Brown University; Ph.D. Mathematical Statistics, University of Connecticut. Address: 324 Thames Street, #5, Groton, Connecticut 06340.

SOKOL, MARSHALL D Occupation: Financial Management Consultant. Education: B.A., M.Ph., Ph.D. Candidate. Address: 60 Hoags Cross, New Castle, New York 10562.

SOLARI, JOSEPH P Occupation: Manager of Marketing Development. Education: B.A., Williams College; M.B.A., Indiana University. Address: 5246 Wiltonwood Court, Indianapolis, Indiana 46254.

SOLBERG, RUELL FLOYD JR Occupation: Research and Development Engineer. Education: B.S. Mechanical Engineering, M.S. Mechanical Engineering, University of Texas; M.B.A., Trinity University. Address: 5906 Forest Cove, San Antonio, Texas 78240.

SOLBRIG, INGEBORG HILDEGARD Occupation: University Teaching, Research and Committee Work. Education: Bachelor of Arts, San Francisco State University, 1966; Master of Arts 1966, Ph.D. Humanities and German Literature 1969, Stanford University. Address: 1126 Pine Street, Iowa City, Iowa 52240.

SOLIMAN, KARAM F A Occupation: Professor and Director of Basic Pharmacy Science Division. Education: B.Sc., M.S., Ph.D. Address: 2414 Blarney Drive, Tallahassee, Florida 32308.

SOLOMON, EZRA Occupation: Dean Witter Professor of Finance, Stanford University. Education: A.B. Economics, Ph.D. Address: 775 Santa Ynez Street, Stanford, California 94305.

SOLOMON, JACK Occupation: Business Manager. Education: B.S., Massachusetts Institute of Technology; Ph.D. Chemistry, Columbia University. Address: 590 Forest Avenue, Rye, New York 10580.

SOLOMON, MARIAN AUDREY Occupation: Computer Systems Management. Education: Ph.D., M.S., B.S. Address: 7911 Hillside Avenue, Los Angeles, California 90046.

SOLOMONS, HOPE C Occupation: Psychologist, College of Nursing, University of Iowa. Education: B.A., A.M., Ed.D. Address: 319 Mullin Avenue, Iowa City, Iowa 52240.

SOLOWAY, ALBERT H Occupation: Dean, College of Pharmacy, The Ohio State University College of Pharmacy. Education: B.S. Chemistry, Ph.D. Organic Chemistry. Address: 1209 Clubview Boulevard, North, Worthington, Ohio 43085.

SOLTERO, EUGENE ANDRE Occupation: President, Soltero Oil Company. Education: B.S.E., Cooper Union; M.S. Industrial Management, Massachusetts Institute of Technology. Address: 7127 Hillgreen, Dallas, Texas 75214.

SOMASUNDARAN, PONISSERIL Occupation: La Von Duddleson Krumb Professor, Columbia University. Education: B.Sc., B.E., M.S., Ph.D. Address: 748 Broadway Avenue, Nyack, New York 10960.

SOMERS, JAMES L Occupation: Vice President, Marketing Services. Education: B.S.I.E., M.S.I.E., Ph.D. Address: 1903 89th Place, Kenosha, Wisconsin 53140.

SOMMERS, FREDERIC TAMLER Occupation: Harry Austryn Wolfson Professor of Philosophy, Brandeis University. Education: B.A., Yeshiva, 1944; Ph.D., Columbia University, 1955. Address: 185 Davis Avenue, Brookline, Massachusetts 02146.

SONN, GEORGE FRANK Occupation: Marketing Director. Education: B.S.Ch.Eng., M.S.Ch.Eng. Address: 141 Mundy Avenue, Edison, New Jersey 08820.

SORENSON, CARL W W Occupation: Special Projects, Norwegian Society of Texas. Education: B.S. Printing and Journalism, South Dakota State University. Address: 837 Evergreen Hill Road, Dallas, Texas 75208.

SORENSEN, JACKI F Occupation: Chairman of the Board, Choreographer. Education: B.A. Social Science, Graduate Studies Exercise Physiology. Address: 18907 Nordhoff, Northridge, California 91328.

SORRELLS, RICK D Occupation: Buyer, Southwestern Bell Telephone. Education: B.A. Biology. Address: 2624 Lancrest, Dallas, Texas 75228.

SORRENTINO, FRANK MICHAEL Occupation: Professor, Author. Education: B.A., M.A., Ph.D. Address: 545 East 14th Street, New York, New York 10009.

SOTIS, SHIRLEY BURCH Occupation: Business Manager. Education: B.S. Allied Health and Sciences. Address: 2670 Dalto Court, Oceanside, New York 11572.

SOTO, ROGELIO ROY Occupation: Personnel Officer. Education: Higher Accounting. Address: 94-581 Holaniku Street, Mililani Town, Hawaii 96789.

SOUBY, ARMAND MAX Occupation: Consultant on Synthetic Fuels. Education: B.S.Ch.E. magna cum laude, Vanderbilt University. Address: 103 Nichols, San Marcos, Texas 78666.

SOUDER, PAUL CLAYTON Occupation: Chairman, Michigan National Outstate Banks. Education: B.A., DePauw University; Attended Harvard Graduate School of Business Administration, Rutgers University Graduate School of Banking. Address: 2800 Maurer Road, Charlotte, Michigan 48813.

SOUDER-JAFFERY, LAURA M T Occupation: Researcher. Education: M.A. Sociology, Ph.D. American Studies. Address: Post Office Box 1651, Agana, Guam 96910.

SOULE, SAMUEL DAVID Occupation: Physician. Education: M.D., Ph.G. Address: 1152 Center Drive, St. Louis, Missouri 63117.

SOUTAS-LITTLE, ROBERT Occupation: Professor and Chairman, Michigan State University. Education: B.S., M.S., Ph.D. Address: 2402 Holett Road, Okemos, Michigan 48864.

SOUTH, MARY LOU Occupation: Health Care Administrator. Education: M.A., University of Redlands; B.A., Iowa State University. Address: 120 Fey Drive, Burlingame, California 94010.

SOUTHALL, MITCHELL B Education: B.A., M.A., M.F.A., Ph.D. Address: 918 Breedlove, Memphis, Tennessee 38107.

SOWELL, WENDELL LORAINE Occupation: Private Forensic Scientist. Education: B.S. Chemistry 1947, M.S. Biological Sciences 1955, Auburn University; LL.B., Jones Law School, 1960; Ph.D. Preventive Medicine and Public Health/Toxicology, University of Oklahoma, 1967. Address: Route 4, Box 669, Athens, Alabama 35611.

SOWERS, MIRIAM R Occupation: Artist. Education: Attended Miami University. Address: Symbolic Art Studios, 3020 Glenwood Northwest, Albuquerque, New Mexico 87107.

SOZA, SHARON ELIZABETH Occupation: Writer, Micro-Computer Consultant, Independent Software Vendor, Networker. Education: M.S., Ph.D. Computerizing Civil Procedure (in progress), Columbia Pacific University; B.S. Chemistry, Lamar State College Technology, 1968. Address: 349 North Oregon, Post Office Box 81, Yreka, California 96097.

SPACHNER, SHELDON A Occupation: President, Technical Development Enterprises. Education: B.S. Physics, M.S. Physics, Ph.D. Metallurgical Engineering. Address: 17 Country Village Way, Media, Pennsylvania 19063.

SPALLA, DENNIS JOSEPH Occupation: Real Estate Developer. Education: B.A., University of Michigan, 1963; J.D., Wayne State University Law School, 1967. Address: 440 Vinewood Lane, Plymouth, Minnesota 55441.

SPANIER, THOMAS A Occupation: President, Sullivan Industries. Education: B.S., University of California-Berkeley; M.B.A, Harvard Business School. Address: 459 Ridge Road, Novato, California 94947.

SPANN, BETTYE J Occupation: Director. Education: B.S., M.A. Address: 632 North 24 Street, East St. Louis, Illinois 62205.

SPANO, PATRICIA ANN Occupation: Associate Professor. Education: A.B., M.A., University of Southern California. Address: 3419 Ethel Avenue, Columbus, Georgia 31906.

SPARLING, VIRGINIA VAUGHT Occupation: Professional Volunteer. Education: B.A. Zoology, M.S.W. Social Work, M.Ed. Education, Honorary Doctorate of Humanities. Address: 3271 Evergreen Point Road, Bellevue, Washington 98004.

SPECKMAN, JOHN NICHOLAS Occupation: Director of Admissions, Jacksonville University. Education: B.A., M.Ed. Address: 3625 Hedrick Street, Jacksonville, Florida 32205.

SPECTOR, AUDREY F Occupation: Nursing Programs Director, Southern Regional Education Board. Education: M.S.N. Address: 101 Alden Avenue Northwest, Unit E, Atlanta, Georgia 30309.

SPEER, ALLEN PAUL III Occupation: Professor of Political Science. Education: B.S. Social Science, M.A. Political Science. Address: Box 537, Banner Elk, North Carolina 28604.

SPENCE, EMILY HUMES Occupation: Educator. Education: B.S., Trenton State College. Address: 112 Carroll Drive, Carlisle, Massachusetts 01741.

SPENCE, RICHARD JAMES Occupation: Child Care Program Administrator. Education: B.S. Psychology, M.S. Guidance Counseling, C.A.S. Counseling and Psychology. Address: 207 Victory Avenue, Schenectady, New York 12307.

SPENCE, SHARON LLOYD Occupation: Film Production Manager, Director. Education: B.S.S. Speech, Northwestern University. Address: 1201A Central, Evanston, Illinois 60201.

SPENCE, WARREN ANDREW Occupation: Electrical Engineer. Education: B.S., M.S., Worcester Polytechnic Institute. Address: 112 Carroll Drive, Carlisle, Massachusetts 01741.

SPENCER, ALAN Occupation: Audio-Visual, Entertainment, and Film Producer; Genealogist. Education: B.S.Ed., Ohio University, 1963; M.A., Central Michigan University, 1966.

SPERBER, PHILIP Occupation: President, REFAC International, Inc. Education: B.S., J.D. Address: 30 Normandy Heights Road, Convent Station, New Jersey 07961.

SPETHMANN, DOROTHY MARIE Occupation: Assistant Professor of Education. Education: B.S. Elementary Education, College Misericordia; M.A. Education, University of South Dakota. Address: 904 Northwest 5th Street, Madison, South Dakota 57042.

SPEZIALE, JOHN ALBERT Occupation: Chief Justice, Connecticut Supreme Court. Education: B.A. 1943, J.D. 1947, Duke University. Address: 278 Wind-Tree, Torrington, Connecticut 06790.

SPEZZANO, VINCENT E Occupation: Senior Vice President of Communications, Gannett Company, Inc. Education: B.A. Journalism and English. Address: 855 South Atlantic Avenue, Cocoa Beach, Florida 32931.

SPIES, HAROLD GLEN Occupation: Research Institution Administrator, Biomedical Research. Education: Ph.D. Address: ORPRC, 505 Northwest 185th Avenue, Beaverton, Oregon 97006.

SPILLANE, RICHARD JEROME Occupation: Management Training Official, Alcoholism Counselor.

Education: B.S.C., Loyola University, 1957; Postgraduate, California American University, 1959; M.S. Management, 1983. Address: 320 Wisconsin, Oak Park, Illinois 60302.

SPILLER, ELLEN BRUBAKER Occupation: Instructor, Lee College. Education: B.S., University of Texas-Austin, 1954; M.A. English 1965, M.A., College Teaching, University of Hawaii Central Campus. Address: 211 Rue Orleans, Baytown, Texas 77520.

SPINKS, JOHN L Occupation: President, Environment Emissions Engineering Company. Education: B.S.M.E., University of Kentucky. Address: 26856 Eastvale Road, Rolling Hills, California 90274.

SPIRO, ROBERT H JR Occupation: National Executive Director, Reserve Officer Association of the U.S. Education: B.S., Ph.D., D.Sc. Address: 5103 Heritage Lane, Alexandria, Virginia 22311.

SPISELMAN, DAVID Occupation: Management Consultant. Education: M.B.A., New York University; M.A., New School; B.A., Boston University. Address: 330 East 39th Street, #32-F, New York, New York 10016.

SPIVACK, BARBARA J Occupation: Director of Student Services. Education: B.A. Education; M.A. Student Personnel Administration. Address: 310 Stanmore Road, Baltimore, Maryland 21212.

SPIVACK, HENRY ARCHER Occupation: Employee Benefits Consultant, Financial Plans. Education: B.B.A. Address: 18 Cornell Place, Englishtown, New Jersey 07726.

SPIVEY, BILL G Occupation: Chief Staff Development Officer. Education: B.A. Prelaw, M.S.W. Social Service Administration. Address: 1811 Winne, Helena, Montana 59601.

SPOHN, PEGGY WEEKS Occupation: Deputy Director, Office of Community Investment. Education: M.A. Address: 1741 Harvard Street, Northwest, Washington, D.C. 20009.

SPRADLEY, DON DELOY Occupation: Real Estate Broker. Education: B.S., Kansas State College. Address: 1411 Waggoner Drive, Arlington, Texas 76013-1473.

SPRAFKIN, BENJAMIN R Occupation: Social Work Consultant and Social Work Educator. Education: B.A., M.A., Graduate Degrees in Psychology and Social Work. Address: 1901 Walnut Street, Philadelphia, Pennsylvania 19103.

SPRAGENS, WILLIAM CLARK Occupation: Professor of Political Science, Bowling Green State University. Education: A.B. Journalism, M.A. Journalism, Kentucky; Ph.D., Michigan State University. Address: 607 Lafayette Boulevard, Bowling Green, Ohio 43402.

SPRAGUE, NANCY E Occupation: Educator. Education: B.S. Education, Pennsylvania State University; M.S. Reading Education, Marywood College; M.S. Administration, University of Scranton. Address: Hilltop Drive, RD #3, Tunkhannock, Pennsylvania 18657.

SPRATT, JOHN STRICKLIN Occupation: General Surgeon. Education: B.S., M.D., M.S.P.H. Address: 2206 Bell Tavern Court, Louisville, Kentucky 40207.

SPREITER, JOHN R Occupation: Professor of Mechanical Engineering, Aeronautics and Astronautics. Education: B.Aero.E., Minnesota; M.S., Ph.D., Stanford University. Address: 1250 Sandalwood Lane, Los Altos, California 94022.

SPRING, LEONARD HARRY Occupation: Business Executive/Marketing and Advertising. Education: B.S., M.S. Address: 390 First Avenue, New York, New York 10010.

SPRINGBORN, ROBERT JOHN Occupation: Executive Vice President, Treasurer and Secretary of Springborn Group, Inc. Address: 93 Yorktown Drive, Springfield, Massachusetts 01108.

SPROULL, FREDERICK ANTHONY Occupation: Assistant Professor of Nursing Health, Natural Sciences; Lawyer. Education: Ph.D. Biology, J.D. Address: 302 Brilliant Avenue, Pittsburgh, Pennsylvania 15215.

SPURLOCK, JACK M Occupation: University Research Administrator, Educator, Consultant at Georgia Institute of Technology. Education: B.Ch.E., M.S.Ch.E., Ph.D. Address: 293 Indian Hills Trail, Marietta, Georgia 30067.

SQUILLACE, ALEXANDER PAUL Occupation: Investment Advisor, Investment Management Group, Inc. Education: B.S. Business Administration, Ohio State University; Chartered Financial Analyst. Address: 2009 East 52nd, Sioux Falls, South Dakota 57103.

SQUIRE, JAMES R Occupation: Executive Consultant, Publishing, Education. Education: A.B., M.A., Ph.D., D.Litt. Address: 43 Round Hill Road, Lincoln, Massachusetts 01773.

SQUIRES, WILLIAM ALLEN Occupation: Carbon Dioxide Distributor. Education: B.A., University of Pennsylvania; Temple University School of Law. Address: 33 Willow Circle, Longmeadow, Massachusetts 01106.

SRIVASTAVA, BHARTENDU Occupation: Scientific Services, Research/Meteorologist. Education: B.Sc.; M.Sc., Allahabad; Ph.D., Saskatchewan. Address: 64 Longsword Drive, Scarborough, Ontario, Canada M1V 3A3.

STAAL, DENNIS R Occupation: Controller. Education: B.S. Address: 3512 Powderhorn Drive, Rapid City, South Dakota 57702.

STABLES, JEAN B Occupation: Senior Information Scientist. Education: B.A., M.S. Address: 181 River Road, Nutley, New Jersey 07110.

STACY, DORIS A Occupation: Director of Counseling, Young Women's Christian Association; President, Milwaukee Board of School Directors; President, City of Milwaukee Library. Education: B.S., M.S., University of Wisconsin-Madison. Address: 3164 North 51 Boulevard, Milwaukee, Wisconsin 53216.

STACEY, RONALD LEE Occupation: Vice President. Education: B.A., M.B.A. Address: 127 Scottsdale Drive, Coraopolis, Pennsylvania 15108.

STACZEK, JAMES JOHN Occupation: Consultant. Education: Associate Industrial Technology. Address: 417 Forest Drive, Rossford, Ohio 43460.

STAGL, JOHN M Occupation: Second Vice President. Education: B.A., M.B.A. Address: 500 Kegworth, Severna Park, Maryland 21146.

STALLINGS-ROBERTS, VIOLA PATRICIA Occupation: Administrative Analyst. Education: B.S., M.B.A. Address: 2101-C Grant Avenue, Redondo Beach, California 90278.

STAMBAUGH, JOHN E JR Occupation: Medical Oncology. Education: M.D., Ph.D. Address: 119 White Horse Circle Pike, Haddon Heights, New Jersey 08035.

STANDEFER, EDWIN MILES JR Occupation: Vice President. Education: B.A., Memphis State College; L.W.B., University of Memphis. Address: 3573 Monessen, Memphis, Tennessee 38128.

STANDISH, NORMAN WESTON Occupation: Laboratory Director. Education: Ph.D. Purdue University. Address: 3098 Huntington Road, Shaker

Heights, Ohio 44120.

STANIEC, MARY M Occupation: City Planner (Real Estate Broker). Education: B.A. Public Administration and Political Science. Address: 5707 North New Hampshire, Chicago, Illinois 60631.

STANKIEWICZ, RAYMOND Occupation: Authority in Plastics Technology. Education: Graduate Studies, American Western University; M.S. Address: 866 Bohemia Parkway, Bohemia, New York 11716.

STANKOVICH, IVAN D Occupation: Consulting Engineer, Lecturer. Education: Graduate, Military College, U.S.S.R., 1948; Diploma Mechanical Engineering, Institute of Technology, U.S.S.R., 1959; Postgraduate Study, University of California-Berkeley, 1967-68. Address: 324 San Carlos Avenue, Piedmont, California 94611.

STANLEY, FRANK JOSEPH Occupation: Data Processing Consultant. Education: A.S. 1972, A.A. 1973, B.A. 1982. Address: 7743 Arbor Drive, Parma, Ohio 44130.

STANLEY, MARJORIE T Occupation: Professor of Finance and Chairperson, Department of Finace and Decision Sciences, Texas Christian University. Education: B.A., University of Wisconsin; A.M., Ph.D., Indiana University. Address: 4009 Fairway Court, Arlington, Texas 76013.

STANLEY, R C Occupation: Artist, College Instructor. Education: A.A. Address: 30355 Morning View Drive, Malibu, California 90265.

STARK, MARTIN J Occupation: President, Oryx Corporation. Education: A.A., B.A. Address: 60 Riverside Drive, #1D, New York, New York 10024.

STARKER, JANOS Occupation: Concert Solo Cellist. Education: Attended Franz Liszt Academy, Hungary; Honorary Doctor of Music, Chicago Conservatory 1961, Cornell College 1978, East-West University 1982, Williams College 1983.

STARKERMAN, RUDOLF Occupation: Professor of Mechanical Engineering, U.N.B. Education: Doctor of Science Technology. Address: 172 Riverview Drive, Fredericton, CDN E38 5Y1.

STARNES, WILLIAM H JR Occupation: Research Chemist, AT&T Bell Laboratories. Education: B.S. honors, Ph.D. Address: 123-E Jerome Street, Roselle Park, New Jersey 07204.

STASIAK, MARILYN FELICIA Occupation: Symphony General Manager. Education: B.A. cum laude, M.A., M.F.A. Address: 620 Lewis Street, De Pere, Wisconsin 54115.

STATES, CAPEL CARLISLE Occupation: Creative Director, Advertising. Education: B.A. Marketing, Boston University. Address: 1870 Commonwealth Avenue, Boston, Massachusetts 02135.

STATON, KNOTEL LEE Occupation: Author/ President, Pacific Christian College. Education: B.A., M.Div. Address: 959 Oakdale, Corona, California 91720.

STAUFFER, HELEN WINTER Occupation: Professor of English, Kearney State College. Education: B.A., Kearney State College; Ph.D., University of Nebraska. Address: 808 West 24th Street, Kearney, Nebraska 68847.

STAVINOHA, WILLIAM B Occupation: Professor, Department of Pharmacology, U.T.H.S.C.S.A. Education: B.S., M.S., Ph.D. Address: 3910 Tupelo, San Antonio, Texas 78229.

STAVIS, BARRIE Occupation: Playwright, Historian. Education: Attended Columbia University. Address: 70 East 96th Street, New York, New York 10128.

STEBINS, JANET H (deceased) Occupation:

Former Corporate Executive, Lecturer.

STEELE, CHARLES WILLIAM Occupation: Consultant, Vocational Rehabilitation, Law Administration. Education: A.B. 1927, M.A. 1929, University of Missouri; M.S., Harvard University, 1931. Address: 1 Wakefield Street, Lewiston, Maine 04240.

STEEN, PATRICIA JEANE WAUGH Occupation: Educational Diagnostician. Education: B.A., North Texas State University, 1973; M.Ed., West Texas State University, 1976. Address: 2603 South Van Buren, Amarillo, Texas 79109.

STEFFEN, SHARRON V Occupation: Transmission Maintenance Assistant. Education: College Studies. Address: 960 Brickner Road, College Place, Washington 99324.

STEFFENHAGEN, RONALD A Occupation: Professor. Education: B.A., M.S.A., Ph.D. Address: 167 Curtis Avenue, Burlington, Vermont 05401.

STEIN, PAUL MARC Occupation: Physiologist, Chairman, Scientist, Educator. Education: B.S. Life Sciences, M.S. Physiology and Pharmacology, Ph.D. Physiology. Address: 139 North Ashland Avenue, Evanston, Illinois 60202.

STEIN, RITA F Occupation: Administration. Education: B.S., R.N., M.S., Ph.D. Address: 4808 Dorkin Court, Indianapolis, Indiana 46254.

STEINBERG, ELLIS PHILIP Occupation: Director Chemistry Division, Argonne National Laboratory. Education: S.B. 1941, Ph.D. 1947. Address: 194 Westwood Drive, Park Forest, Illinois 60466.

STEINEGER, JOHN F JR Occupation: Attorney. Education: B.S., J.D. Address: 6400 Valley View Road, Kansas City, Kansas 66111.

STEINGRABER, FRED G Occupation: Chief Operating Officer. Education: M.B.A., University of Chicago; B.S., University of Indiana. Address: 615 Warwick Road, Kenilworth, Illinois 60043.

STEINHEIDER, JAMES H Occupation: Senior Vice President. Education: B.S., University of Missouri, 1971. Address: 14318 West 89th, Lenexa, Kansas 66215.

STEINKRAUS, WARREN E Occupation: Professor. Education: A.B., S.T.B., Ph.D., L.H.D. Address: 89 Sheldon Avenue, Oswego, New York 13126.

STEINMANN, JOHN COLBURN Occupation: Architect. Education: B.Arch, University of Illinois, 1964; Postgraduate, Illinois Institute of Technology. Address: 4316 106th Place Northeast, Kirkland, Washington 98033.

STELLER, DEBORAH HASSELO Occupation: Administrator. Education: B.S., M.Ed., Ed.D. Address: 1813 West Main, Princeton, West Virginia 24740.

STELLERS, THOMAS J Occupation: Director of Administrative Services, Mahoning County Schools. Education: B.S.Ed., M.Ed., Ph.D. Address: 2405 Vollmer Drive, Youngstown, Ohio 44511-1951.

STELZER, IRWIN M Occupation: Economist. Education: Ph.D., M.A., Cornell University; B.A., New York University. Address: 884 Oenoke Ridge Road, New Canaan, Connecticut 06840.

STELZIG, EUGENE L Occupation: Associate Professor. Education: B.A., B.A., A.M., M.A., Ph.D. Address: 6892 Bailey Road, Groveland, New York 14462.

STEMBER, MARILYN L Occupation: Associate Professor. Education: B.S., M.S., M.A., Ph.D. Address: 345 Dahlia Street, Denver, Colorado 80220.

STENGARD, ADAIR MARIE Occupation: Acquisition Analyst. Education: B.S., University of

Maryland. Address: 3618 Castle Terrace, Silver Spring, Maryland 20904.

STENQUIST, LEE BORG Occupation: University Administrator. Education: M.B.A., University of Utah; B.S., Brigham Young University. Address: 1489 East 1100 North Logan, Utah 84321.

STENZEL, DAVID BENTHEIM Occupation: Professor. Education: B.A., Georgetown University; M.A., Ph.D., University of California-Berkeley. Address: 761 East Tuolumne Road, Turlock, California 95380.

STEORTS, NANCY HARVEY Occupation: Chairman. Education: B.S., Syracuse University, 1959. Address: 5606 Chesterbrook Road, Bethesda, Maryland 20816.

STEPHENS, JOHN F Occupation: Instructor. Education: B.S. Address: 14970 Lindsay, Detroit, Michigan 48227.

STEPHENS, LOWNDES F Occupation: Associate Professor. Education: Ph.D., M.A., B.A. Address: 308 Townes Road, Columbia, South Carolina 29210.

STEPP, JOHN R Occupation: Director. Education: Ph.D., M.B.A., B.S. Address: 3rd and Constitution Avenue, Northwest, N5677, Washington, D.C. 20216.

STERLING, KEIR BROOKS Occupation: Command Historian. Education: B.S. 1963, M.A. 1965, Ph.D. 1973, Columbia University. Address: 2030 Castleton Road, Darlington, Maryland 21034.

STERN, BARBARA B Occupation: Assistant Chairman. Education: B.A., M.A., Ph.D., M.B.A. Address: 160 East 84th Street, New York, New York 10028.

STERN, DANIEL H Occupation: Professor. Education: B.S., M.S., Ph.D., University of Illinois. Address: 4312 West 111th Terrace, Leawood, Kansas 66211.

STERN, PAULA Occupation: Senior U.S. International Trade Commissioner. Education: B.A., Goucher College, 1967; M.A., Harvard University, 1969; M.A. 1970, M.A.L.D. 1970, Ph.D. 1976, Fletcher School of Law and Diplomacy. Address: Washington, D.C.

STERN, PHYLLIS NOERAGER Occupation: Professor. Education: D.N.Sc., M.Sc., B.Sc. Address: Dalhousie University, Halifax, NS B3H 3J5.

STERNBERGER, STEPHEN J Occupation: Vice President. Education: B.S. Education 1971, C.L.U. 1980. Address: 9210 North Tacoma, Indianapolis, Indiana 46240.

STERNS, PATRICIA M Occupation: Attorney and Counsellor at Law. Education: B.A., J.D. Address: Suite 519, Luhrs Building, Eleven West Jefferson, Phoenix, Arizona 85003.

STETTEN, DeWITT JR Occupation: Senior Scientific Advisor. Education: M.D., Ph.D. Address: 2 West Drive, Bethesda, Maryland 20814.

STEVENS, BARBARA Occupation: Vice President. Education: Sioux Falls College. Address: 909 East 34th Street, Sioux Falls, South Dakota 57105.

STEVENS, ROBERT I Occupation: Independent Consultant. Education: B.A., Rutgers University. Address: 3551 Carrollton Avenue, Wantagh, New York 11793.

STEVENSON, EVERETT E Occupation: Professor. Education: B.S., M.Ed., Ph.D., Ohio State University. Address: 4792 Cole Road, Memphis, Tennessee 38117.

STEVENSON, JOSIAH IV Occupation: Director of Development, Boston Symphony Orchestra. Education: A.B., Dartmouth College; M.B.A., Ames Tuck School of Business Administration. Address: Spring Pond Road, Box 422, Norwich, Vermont 05055.

STEVENSON, NORA CARROLL Occupation: Research Assistant. Education: B.A., M.S., M.M. Address: 34 Monument, Bennington, Vermont 05201.

STEVENSON, T T B Occupation: Medical Anthropologist. Education: B.S. Address: 84 Sumpwams Avenue, Babylon, New York 11702.

STEVER, MARGO TAFT Occupation: Poet. Education: A.B., Radcliffe College, 1972; Ed.M., Harvard Graduate School of Education, 1974. Address: 157 Millard Avenue, North Tarrytown, New York 10591.

STEWART, ARTHUR VAN Occupation: Assistant Dean. Education: B.S., M.Ed., D.M.D., Ph.D. Address: 6101 Tidewater Court, Prospect, Kentucky 40059.

STEWART, BARBARA J Occupation: Chief Executive Officer, B. J. Stewart Advertising and Public Relations. Education: Attended Wright Junior College, University of California-Los Angeles. Address: 423 Vista Flora, Newport Beach, California 92660.

STEWART, DORIS M Occupation: Professor. Education: B.S., M.S., College of Puget Sound; Ph.D., University of Washington. Address: 1100 Raven Drive, Baltimore, Maryland 21227.

STEWART, DUDLEY M JR Occupation: Psychiatrist. Education: B.S., M.D. Address: 1302 Constantinople Street, New Orleans, Louisiana 70115.

STEWART, ELIZABETH VICTORIA Occupation: Leader, Committees D.C.M.A., D.C.L.N.; Member, Legislative Committee, Long Term Care Council. Education: Diploma 1933, R.N. 1935, Freed Men's Hospital School of Nursing; B.S.N.E., The Catholic University of America, 1945; M.S., University of Maryland, School of Nursing, 1971. Address: 77 Watkins Park Drive, Upper Marlboro, Maryland 20772.

STEWART, ELLA PHILLIPS Occupation: Pharmacist. Education: Ph.D., School of Pharmacy, University of Pittsburgh. Address: 2700 Pelham Road, Toledo, Ohio 43606.

STEWART, JOHN JUNIOUS Occupation: Educator. Education: Ed.D. Vocational Administration, 1984. Address: 1182 Sharonton Drive, Stone Mountain 30083.

STICKEL, TIMOTHY P Occupation: Student. Education: B.S. Address: 266A Hillcrest Road, Boonton, New Jersey 07005.

STICKLER, JOHN COBB Occupation: Publisher. Education: Graduate, The Putney (Vermont) School, 1955; B.A. Sociology with honors, Yale University, 1959. Address: 8300 North La Cholla Boulevard, Tucson, Arizona 85741.

STIEGHORST, JUNANN J Occupation: Seed Company Co-Owner. Education: B.A., M.A., University of Oklahoma; Graduate Studies. Address: 2070 Foothills Road, Golden, Colorado 80401.

STILES, GERALD EARL Occupation: President. Education: Ph.D., M.A., B.S. Address: 66 Prior Farm Road, Duxbury, Massachusetts 02332.

STILES, LORREN JR Occupation: Test Pilot. Education: B.S., U.S. Air Force; M.S., University of Southern California. Address: 131 Quaker Farms Road, Oxford, Connecticut 06483.

STILGENBAUER, ROBERT M Occupation: Quality Assurance Engineer. Education: College Studies. Address: 1660 Edgecliffe Drive, Los Angeles, California 90026.

STILL, JOHN L Occupation: Director. Education: B.S., Davidson College; M.A., Peabody; Ph.D., Florida State University. Address: 2312 Jones Drive, Dunedin, Florida 33528.

STINCHCOMB, THOMAS GLENN Occupation: Professor of Radiation Physics, DePaul University. Education: B.S., Heidelberg College, 1944; S.M. 1948,

Ph.D. 1951, University of Chicago. Address: 429 D Grant Place, Chicago, Illinois 60614.

STINE, ANNA MAE Occupation: Vice President. Education: B.S., M.S., Address: 215 Haddon Commons, Haddonfield, New Jersey 08033.

STINNETT, D MITCHELL Occupation: Cardio-Thoracio Surgeon. Education: M.D. Address: Route 5, Box 139-A, Joplin, Missouri 64801.

STINSON, KARL B Occupation: Environmental Engineer. Education: B.S. Engineering, 1971; M.S. Environmental Engineering, 1975. Address: 1721 Arrowhead Drive, Oakland, California 94611.

STINSON, SUE Occupation: Writer. Education: B.S., North Texas University. Address: 324 Evelyn Drive, Garland, Texas 75042.

STIRLING, RAYMOND MARTIN Occupation: Importer. Education: B.A., M.S., C.S.U.L.B. Address: Route 2 Box 165, Ruckersville, Virginia 22968.

STOCKTON, CARL R Occupation: Academic Dean. Education: B.A., Missouri; S.T.B., Boston; D.Phil., Oxford. Address: 6740 Yellowstone Parkway, Indianapolis, Indiana 46217.

STOCKTON, M J Occupation: Educator. Education: B.A., M.A., Ed.D. Address: 1528 N.E. 51st, Terrace, Kansas City, Missouri 64118.

STOCKWELL, DOROTHEA BOUTWELL Occupation: Psychotherapy. Education: B.S., M.Ed., C.A.G.S. Address: Rural Delivery 2 Box 196A, West Brattleboro, Vermont 03501.

STOESSEL, CAROLE JEAN Occupation: Physician, Concert Pianist, Antique Doll Dealer. Education: A.B. magna cum laude; M.D., Bowman Gray School of Medicine. Address: 329 South Fulton Street, Salisbury, North Carolina 28144.

STOKES, ERIC Occupation: Composer, Conductor, Musician. Education: B.M., Lawrence College, 1952; M.M., New England Conservatory, 1956; Ph.D., University of Minnesota, 1964. Address: 72 Pleasant Street, Minneapolis, Minnesota 55408.

STOKES, JOAN BRAZER Occupation: Publicist. Education: A.A. Address: 675 Kensington Place, Fort Lauderdale, Florida 33305.

STOKES, JONE C Occupation: Retired. Address: 7119 Westchester Drive, Temple Hills, Maryland 20748.

STOLBA, K MARIE Occupation: Musicologist. Education: A.A., B.A., M.A., Ph.D. Address: 5621 Joyce Avenue, Fort Wayne, Indiana 46818.

STOLEN, STEVEN L Occupation: Administrator. Education: B.M., Simpson College; M.M., University of Michigan. Address: 921 A Dyrtle Drive, Salem, Virginia 24153.

STOLTZFUS, BEN F Occupation: University of Professor. Education: B.A., Doctor of Letters, Amherst College; M.A., Middlebury College; Ph.D., University of Wisconsin. Address: 2040 Arroyo Drive, Riverside, Ohio 92506.

STOLZBERG, MARK ELLIOTT Occupation: Psychologist. Education: B.A., M.A., Ph.D. Address: 3 Seabrook Court, Stony Brook, New York 11790.

STONE, CARLETON GOSHEN Occupation: Artist, Art Teacher. Address: Box 81, East Baldwin, Maine 04024.

STONE, LAWRENCE H Occupation: President. Education: B.Che., M.Ch.E., M.B.A. Address: 258 Rivervale Road, Rivervale, New Jersey 07675.

STONE, ROBERT E Occupation: Bank Loan Officer. Education: B.S. Address: 1002 Stanwood Drive, Lebanon, Ohio 45036.

STONER, RICHARD BURKETT Occupation: Vice Chairman. Education: B.S., Indiana University, 1941;

J.D., Harvard University, 1947. Address: Post Office Box 290, Columbus, Indiana 47202.

STOTHERS, DAVID M Occupation: Professor/ Research Director, Laboratory of Ethnoarchaeology, The University of Toledo. Education: B.A., McMaster University, 1969; M.A., University of Toronto, 1971; Ph.D., Case Western Reserve University, 1974. Address: Laboratory of Ethnoarchaeology, The University of Toledo, Toledo, Ohio 43606.

STOTLAR, SUZANNE C Occupation: Physicist. Education: B.S. Address: 1618 Camino Uva, Los Alamos, New Mexico 87544.

STOTMEISTER, KEVIN S Occupation: Business Executive. Education: B.S. Civil Engineering, M.S., M.B.A. 1985. Address: 10911 Lakeshore Drive East, Carmel, Indiana 46032.

STOTT, KENHELM WELBURN JR Occupation: General Curator Emeritus. Education: B.A. Address: Apartment 402, 2300 Front Street, San Diego, California 92101.

STOTZ, ROBERT EDWARD Occupation: Health Educator. Education: B.A., M.P.H. Address: 2343 Fernview Street, Simi Valley, California 93065.

STOWE, RALPH SHIRLEY Occupation: Expert Witness, Author, Businessman, Carpenter, Pilot, Computer Programmer, Draftsman, Electrician, Inventor, Lecturer, Physician, Professor. Education: Diploma, Joliet Junior College, 1966; B.S., Illinois Institute of Technology, 1970; B.S. 1975, D.C. 1975, National College of Chiropractic; Diploma, National-Lincoln School of Postgraduate Education, 1975; B.S. 1980, M.S. and Ph.D. 1983, Clayton University. Address: 2431 Plainfield Road, Joliet, Illinois 60435.

STRAIN, JOHN WILLARD Occupation: Aerospace Company Executive. Education: B.A., University of Northern Iowa, 1952. Address: 626 Oneida Drive, Sunnyvale, California 94087.

STRANDHAGEN, ADOLF G Occupation: Research Professor, College of Engineering, University of Notre Dame. Education: B.S., M.S., Ph.D., University of Michigan. Address: 611 Edgewater Drive, South Bend, Indiana 46618.

STRAUB, CHESTER J Occupation: Lawyer/Willkie Farr and Gallagher. Education: B.A., St. Peter's College; LL.D., University of Virginia School of Law. Address: 35 Prescott Avenue, Bronxville, New York 10708.

STRAUSS, ROBERT P Occupation: Professor of Economics and Public Policy. Education: A.B. Economics with honors, University of Michigan, 1966; M.A., Ph.D. Economics, University of Wisconsin, 1970. Address: 1541 Asbury Place, Pittsburgh, Pennsylvania 15217.

STREETEN, PAUL PATRICK Occupation: Director/Professor. Education: M.A., Hon. LL.D., Aberdeen; B.A., M.A., D.Litt., Oxon. Address: 21 Penniman Road, Brookline, Massachusetts 02146.

STRETTON, MARTHA SHAVER Occupation: Technical Writer and Student. Education: B.S. (in progress), Pace University. Address: 71 Aiken Street, Norwalk, Connecticut 06851.

STRICKMAN, ARTHUR E Occupation: Chairman of the Board, Chief Executive Officer. Education: B.A. Address: 291 Vista Drive, Jericho, New York 11753.

STRINGHAM, JUDITH MITCHELL Occupation: Corporate Secretary, Treasurer, Trustee. Education: B.S., Cornell University, 1961; M.S., State University of New York and New Paltz, 1964. Address: 10 Dogwood Hill Road, Wappingers Falls, New York 12590.

STROCK, HERBERT L Occupation: Motion Picture Producer/Director. Education: A.B., M.A.

Address: 1630 Hilts Avenue, Los Angeles, California 90024.

STROESSNER, ROBERT JOSEPH Occupation: Curator of New World Art. Education: B.F.A., University of Denver. Address: 811 South Downing Street, Denver, Colorado 80209.

STROMAN, SAMUEL DAVID Occupation: Professor. Education: A.B., South Carolina State College, 1950; M.A., Howard University, 1964; M.S., University of Wisconsin-Milwaukee, 1972; Ph.D., The American University, 1976; Studies at the United States Army Command and General Staff College and Other Military Schools. Address: Post Office Box 1601, South Carolina State College, Orangeburg, South Carolina 29117.

STROMWALL, EVA Occupation: Clinical Psychologist. Education: A.B. cum laude, Radcliffe College, 1933; M.A. Psychology, Columbia University, 1934. Address: 235 Whitman Street, Bridgewater, Massachusetts 02324.

STRONG, MAURICE F Occupation: Chairman of the Board, C.D.I.C. Education: 23 Honorary Degrees. Address: 532 Tsawwassen Beachroad, Delta, B.C., Canada V4M 2J3.

STROPE, RALPH MORGAN Occupation: Manager, The Kroger Company. Education: B.S. Mathematics, West Virginia Institute of Technology. Address: 2302 Fidling Road, Charleston, South Carolina 29407.

STROUT, LILIA DAPAZ Occupation: Associate Professor, University of Puerto Rico, Mayaguez Campus. Education: M.A. Comparative Literature, Ph.D. Spanish. Address: Post Office Box 5608, College Station, Mayaguez, Puerto Rico 00709.

STRUGGS, CALLIE FOSTER Occupation: Director, Department of Health and Human Services. Education: M.A. Urban Studies, B.B.A. Address: 2129 Kessler Court, Dallas, Texas 75208.

STUART, ALLAN Occupation: Educational Consultant. Education: B.S., M.A., D.P.A. Address: 129 Peachtree Lane, Roslyn Heights, New York 11577.

STUART, JAMES R Occupation: Chief Engineer, Orbital Sciences Corporation. Education: B.S. Physics 1968, M.S.E.E. 1972, M.S.O.R. 1977, Ph.D. Engineering 1979. Address: 1300 Meadowbrook Road, Altadena, California 91001.

STUBBLEFIELD, ROBERT D Occupation: Research Chemist. Education: B.S. Address: 4134 North Chelsea Place, Peoria, Illinois 61614.

STUDDERT, STEPHEN MARK Occupation: Consultant. Education: B.S. Address: 10204 Country View Court, Vienna, Virginia 22180.

STUDLEY, HELEN ORMSON Occupation: Artist, Poet, Writer, Educator, Designer. Education: Attended Pat Stevens School, Los Angeles College. Address: 5020 Hameltine Avenue, Sherman Oaks, California 91423.

STURGEON, THEODORE Occupation: Writer. Address: 3050 Hayden Bridge Road, Springfield, Oregon 97477.

STURM, FRED GILLETTE Occupation: Professor of Philosophy, Chair of Department, University of New Mexico; Honorary Lifetime Professor of Foreign Languages and Literatures, Shaanxi Teachers University, People's Republic of China; Editor-in-Chief, *Journal of Chinese Studies*; Member Board of Directors, American Association for Chinese Studies; Fellow, International Centre for Asian Studies; Fellow, Royal Asiatic Society; Director, Institute for Pueblo Indian Studies of the Indian Pueblo Cultural Center. Education: A.B. (Hons.) Philosophy, Allegheny College; M.Div., Union Theological Seminary; A.M., University of Rochester; Ph.D., Columbia University. Address: 7709 Midge Northeast, Albuquerque, New Mexico 87109.

STUTZMAN, THOMAS CHASE Occupation: Attorney at Law. Education: B.A., University of California-Santa Barbara, 1972; J.D., University of Santa Clara, 1975. Address: 3164 Linkfield Way, San Jose, California 95135.

STYBEL, LAURENCE J Occupation: Business College Professor. Education: Ed.D., Harvard University. Address: 525 California Street, Newton, Massachusetts.

SUBRAMONY, DORASWAMY Occupation: Sales Representative. Education: M.S., M.S., M.B.A. Address: 69 Treble Cove Road, North Billerica MAO 1862.

SUDDITH, ROBERTA LUCILLE Occupation: Registered Nurse. Education: Lutheran Hospital School of Nursing. Address: 9720 Hosler Road, Leo, Indiana 46765.

SUELFLOW, AUGUST ROBERT Occupation: Director, Concordia Historical Institute. Education: B.D. (M.Div.) 1946, S.T.M. 1947, D.D. 1967, Concordia Seminary. Address: 7249 Northmoor, St. Louis, Missouri 63105.

SUFFET, IRWIN HENRY Occupation: Professor. Education: B.S., M.S., Ph.D., Brooklyn College. Address: 403 Waring Street, Elkins Park, Pennsylvania 19117.

SUGIHARA, JAMES M Occupation: Dean. Education: Ph.D, University of Utah, 1947. Address: 1001 Southwood Drive, Fargo, North Dakota 58103.

SUINN, RICHARD M Occupation: Professor. Education: Ph.D., M.A., B.A. Address: 808 Cheyenne Drive, Fort Collins, Colorado 80525.

SUKONECK, HARRIET Occupation: Director. Education: Ph.D. 1971, M.A. 1968, University of Southern California; B.A., Rutgers University, 1966. Address: 7541 Stewart Avenue, Los Angeles, California 90045.

SULEIMAN, MICHAEL W Occupation: Professor. Education: B.A., M.S., Ph.D. Address: 427 Wickham Road, Manhattan, Kansas 66502.

SULLINGER, WILLIAM STANCIL Occupation: Minister. Education: B.A., M.R.E. Address: 1118 South Killingsworth, Bolivar, Missouri 65613.

SULLIVAN, BARBARA PETERSON Occupation: Associate Financial Consultant. Education: Boston University, Eastern Montana College. Address: 977 Southeast 27th Street, Gresham, Oregon 97030.

SULLIVAN, BETTY ANN Occupation: Homemaker. Education: Executive Secretarial. Address: Route 1, Box 3667, Shenandoah, Virginia 22849.

SULLIVAN, DONALD J Occupation: Justice. Education: B.A., Iona College, 1951; J.D., Brooklyn Law School, 1954. Address: 22 Throggs Neck Boulevard, Bronx, New York 10465.

SULLIVAN, JOANN MARIE Occupation: Medical Laboratory Director. Education: B.S. Address: Post Office Box 7, Agana, Guam 92690.

SULLIVAN, LAWRENCE W Occupation: President. Education: A.B., J.D. Address: 47 Meetinghouse Circle, Needham, Massachusetts 02192.

SULLIVAN, RICHARD F Occupation: Senior Research Associate. Education: B.A., Ph.D., University of Colorado. Address: 23 Upper Oak Drive, San Rafael, California 94903.

SULTANIK, KALMAN Occupation: Executive Co-President. Education: Colombia University. Address: 120 East 81st Street, New York, New York 10028.

SULZBERGER, ROBERTA ZECHIEL Occupation: Writer/Producer, Motion Pictures, Other Audiovisual Aids. Education: A.B., Heidelberg College, 1935; M.A. English Literature, University of Chicago, 1936. Address: 2785 Jackson Street, San Francisco, California 94115.

SULZER, ALEXANDER J Occupation: Research Microbiologist. Education: B.A., M.Sc., Ph.D., D.M.C. (Honorary). Address: 3711 Canadian Way, Tucker, Georgia 30084.

SUMMERS, ANTHONY J Occupation: Publisher, Editor, Writer. Education: A.B. English Literature. Address: 5662 Marquette Street, St. Louis, Missouri 63139.

SUMMERS, MARSHA JOY Occupation: Administrator I. Education: A.A., B.A., M.A. Address: 438 Skyline Drive, Daly City, California 94015.

SUN, ROBERT Z J Occupation: President. Education: B.S., E.E., University of Pennsylvania. Address: 116 North 3rd Street, Gaston, Pennsylvania 18042.

SUNDEM, GARY L Occupation: Professor. Education: B.A., Carleton University, 1967; M.B.A. 1969, Ph.D. 1971, Stanford University. Address: 307 36 Avenue East, Seattle, Washington 98112.

SUNDERLAND, DAVID KENDALL Occupation: Real Estate Developer. Education: B.A., Dartmouth College, 1952. Address: 3103 Springridge Drive, Colorado Springs, Colorado 80906.

SUNDT, THORALF M JR Occupation: Professor and Chairman, Department of Neurosurgery, Mayo Clinic. Education: B.S. Medicine, M.D. Neurosurgery. Address: 1406 Weatherhill Court, Southwest, Rochester, Minnesota 55902.

SUNSTEIN, MICHAEL A Occupation: Chief Executive Officer. Address: 2548 Brust Court, El Cajon, California 92021.

SUNTAG, CHARLES Occupation: Management Consultant. Education: B.Chem 1942, M.S. Address: 1065 Cutspring Road, Stratford, Connecticut 06497.

SUPERNAK, JANUSZ C Occupation: Associate Professor. Education: B.Sc., M.S. Civil Engineering, Ph.D. Address: 2400 Chestnut Street, Philadelphia, Pennsylvania 19103.

SURACI, PATRICK J Occupation: Clinical Psychologist. Education: Ph.D., New School for Social Research, 1981. Address: 8 Gramercy Park South, New York, New York 10003.

SURI, TEJ P S Occupation: Certified Public Accountant. Education: M.B.A., C.P.A., Chartered Accountant, N.A.S.D. License. Address: 13 Lafferty Drive, Cherry Hill, New Jersey 08002.

SUTNICK, ALTON I Occupation: Dean of Medical School. Education: M.D. Address: 2135 St. James Place, Philadelphia, Pennsylvania 19129.

SUTHERLAND, KERMIT A Occupation: Prayer Breakfast Coordinator, Executive Ministries. Address: 645 Lemke Drive, Placentia, California 92670.

SUTHERLAND, MARY S Occupation: College Professor. Education: M.P.H., Ed.D., W.S., B.S. Address: 2007 B Bradford Court, Tallahassee, Florida 32303.

SUTHERLAND, PAUL HOWARD Occupation: Financial Investment and Retirement Planning. Education: Registered Principal; Graduate, L.U.T.C. Address: Route 1 Box 72, Suttons Bay, Michigan 49682.

SUTTER, CAROLYN SUE Occupation: General Manager. Education: B.S., Calvin College, 1964; M.S., Western Michigan University, 1972; M.P.A., California State University-Long Beach, 1982. Address: 3270 Chestnut Avenue, Long Beach, California 90806.

SUTTON, DAVID F Occupation: Director. Education: B.S., Oberlin College. Address: 2411 Greenwood Avenue, Wilmette, Illinois 60091.

SUTTON, GEORGE H Occupation: Certified Management Consultant. Education: B.A. Address: 17 Long Mountain, New Milford, Connecticut 06776.

SUTTON, MARCELLA FRENCH Occupation: Interior Designer/Premises Officer. Education: B.S. Professional Arts. Address: 22639 Mulholland Drive, Woodland Hills, California 91364.

SUTTON, PHILIP D Occupation: Private Practice Psychology. Education: Ph.D. Psychology, University of Utah, 1979. Address: Box 810, Nederland, Colorado 80466.

SUYEMATSU, KIYO Occupation: Music Librarian and Music Teacher. Education: B.Mus., M.Mus., M.A. Address: 220 Thayer Avenue, Mankato, Minnesota 56001.

SUYENAGA, ELSIE S Occupation: Educator, Pearl City Neighborhood Board Member, Pearl City Community Association Member. Education: B.A. Address: 2381 Anihinihi Street, Pearl City, Hawaii 96782.

SUZUKI, HIDETARD Occupation: Concert Master. Education: Curtis Institute of Music. Address: 430 West 93rd, Indianapolis, Indiana 46260.

SWAMY, SRIKANTA M N Occupation: Dean. Education: B.Sc., D.I.I.Sc., M.Sc., Ph.D. Address: 275 Des Landes, St. Lambert, Que, Canada J451V9.

SWAN, HARRY KELS Occupation: Curator. Education: B.S., M.E. Address: 32 Elizabeth Street, South Bound Brook, New Jersey 08880.

SWANGO, MAXINE MAY Education: B.S., West Virginia Wesleyan College; Graduate Classes, North Virginia University. Address: 843 Baier Street, St. Albans, West Virginia 25177.

SWANSON, MARY LINN Occupation: Orthopedic/Geriatric Clinical Nurse Specialist. Education: B.S.N., M.S.N. Address: 511 Vale Avenue North, Rockford, Illinois 61107.

SWARTSEL, MARK E Occupation: Real Estate Sales/Development. Education: B.S., B.A., University of Florida. Address: 6024 Casey Drive, New Port Richey, Florida 33553.

SWEENEY, JAMES E Occupation: U.S. Air Force Officer. Education: B.S., Eastern Michigan; M.A., University Northern Colorado. Address: 313 Campus Drive, Belleville, Illinois 62221.

SWEENEY, JAMES LEE Occupation: Professor. Education: S.B., Massachusetts Institute of Technology; Ph.D., Stanford University. Address: 1020 Continental Drive, Menlo Park, California 94305.

SWEITZER, HARRY P Occupation: Clergyman, Pastor Emeritus (Retired). Education: B.A., M.Div., D.D. Address: 1392 Wasatch Drive, Salt Lake City, Utah 84108.

SWHIER, CLAUDIA V Occupation: Partner. Education: B.A., Yale University, 1972; J.D., Harvard Law School, 1975. Address: 7216 Chablis Court, Indianapolis, Indiana 46278.

SWIFT, GAYLE C Occupation: Director. Education: B.S., M.S. Address: 9332 Coronet Avenue, Westminister, California 92683.

SWIFT, HUMPHREY HATHAWAY Occupation: President. Education: A.B., University of North Carolina. Address: 38 Cottage Street, Hinghan, Virginia 02043.

SWIFT, RICHARD N Occupation: Professor. Education: A.B. 1943, A.M., Ph.D., Harvard University. Address: 72 Barrow Street, Apartment 3-N, New York, New York 10014.

SWIGNOSKI, MARY E Occupation: Professor. Education: M.S.W., Marywood College. Address: 15 Westway, Clinton, New Jersey 08809.

SWIHART, JOHN M Occupation: Vice President. Education: B.S., Bowling Green State University, 1947. Address: 6825 83rd Avenue, Southeast, Mercer Island, Virginia 98040.

SWIRSKY, JESSICA R Occupation: Rehabilitation Researcher. Education: B.A., Northwestern University; M.A., The University of Michigan. Address: 300 Edwards Street, Roslyn Heights, New York 11577.

SWITALA, WILLIAM J Occupation: Supervisor. Education: B.A., M.A., Ph.D. Address: 5306 Greenridge Drive, Pittsburgh, Pennsylvania 15236.

SWOGGER, HUGH T Occupation: Vocational Teacher Educator. Education: B.S. 1961, M.Ed. 1963, Ed.D. 1976.

SWOPES, REGINA Occupation: Composer, Record Producer. Education: B.A. Economics. Address: 833 North LeClaire, Chicago, Illinois 60651.

SWOVICK, MELVIN JOSEPH Occupation: Forensic Chemist. Address: 345 Folkstone Court, Troy, Michigan 48098.

SYKES, BOBBY WYATT Occupation: Behavioral Consultant. Education: A.A., B.A., M.A., Ph.D. Address: 1735 Laird Court, Rio Rancho, New Mexico 87124.

SYLVA, JULIA ELIZABETH Occupation: Attorney at Law. Education: B.A., J.D., Loyola Law School. Address: 9371 Bird Circle, Westminister, Pennsylvania 92683.

SZCEZESNIAK, ALINA SURMACKA Occupation: Principal Scientist. Education: Bachelor of Arts, Doctor of Science. Address: 22 Wilson Block, Mt. Vernon, New York 10552.

SZEGHO, EMERIC Occupation: Attorney. Education: University of Cernauti; J.D., University of Cluj, Rumanian Bar Association. Address: 215 Ross Avenue, Cambridge Avenue, Pennsylvania 19403.

SZEKELY, DEBORAH Occupation: Founder/President, Golden Door, Inc.; President, Council of Women's Services. Address: 3232 Dove Street, San Diego, California 92103.

SZÉLL, THOMAS R M Occupation: Head of Science Department. Education: Dr.Nat., Dr.Tech., C.Sc., D.Sc. Address: 157 Hudson Avenue, Tenafly, New Jersey 07670.

SZOTT, FRAN S Occupation: Vice President, Manager, Szott's of Peru. Education: Attended Illinois State University, Chicago School of Interior Design. Address: 4 Creek Bed Trail, Peru, Illinois 61354.

SZPREJDA, EVELYN A Occupation: International Marketing Executive. Education: Business Administration/Marketing, College of St. Thomas. Address: 121 South Washington Avenue #1310, Minneapolis, Minnesota 55401.

SZUHAY, JOSEPH A Occupation: Chairman. Education: Ph.D., M.S., B.S. Address: 66 Woodland Way, Clarks Summit, Pennsylvania 18411.

SZYCHER, MICHAEL Occupation: Vice President Research. Education: Ph.D. Cardiac Physiology. Address: 2 Durham Drive, Lynnfield, Massachusetts 01940.

T

TABOR, CURTIS HAROLD JR Occupation: Professor, Librarian, Evangelist. Education: A.A., B.A., M.A., M.Div., M.L.S. Address: 154 Kelly Lane, Thonotosassa, Florida 33592.

TABOR, DORIS DEE Occupation: Professor of Teacher Education. Education: Ed.D. 1968, M.A. 1958, University of Nebraska. Address: 6000 Stearns, Long Beach, California 90815.

TAFT, SETH C Occupation: Lawyer. Education: B.A., Yale College, 1943; LL.B., Yale Law School, 1948. Address: 9 Pepper Ridge Road, Cleveland, Ohio 44124.

TAITANO, JOHN RAY Occupation: Physician; President, Family Medical Clinic; President, Guam Memorial Hospital Medical Staff. Education: M.D. Address: Family Medical Clinic, Post Office Box 4651, Agana, Guam 96910.

TAKAKI, MELVIN H Occupation: Dentist, President of City Council. Education: B.A., D.D.S., F.A.C.D., F.R.S.H. Address: 401 LaVista Road, Pueblo, Colorado 81005.

TAKAMURA, MASAHIRO Occupation: President, Marusan Shokai. Education: Doctor of Economics. Address: 13908 Bethpage Lane, Wheaton, Maryland 20906.

TAKASHI, FUKUSHIMA Occupation: Professor of Economics, Department of Economics, State University of New York-Albany. Address: 60 Alden Court, Delinar, New York 12054.

TALBOT, BERNARD Occupation: Deputy Director, National Institute of Allergy and Infectious Diseases. Education: M.D., Ph.D. Address: 9508 Forest Road, Bethesda, Maryland 20814.

TALCOTT, STEVEN ROGER Occupation: Resource Specialist Teacher. Education: B.A., Upper Iowa University; M.A., California State University. Address: 7902 Rhine Drive, Huntington Beach, California 92647.

TALLEY, MARIAN Y Occupation: Executive Director, Creative Educators. Education: B.S., M.A., Ph.D. Address: 2727 Ninth Street, Riverside, California 92507.

TALLEY, RONDA CAROL Occupation: Coordinator, Assessment/Placement Services. Education: B.S. Early Childhood Education, Western Kentucky University, 1973; M.Ed. Special Education 1974, Ed.S. Administration and Supervision of Special Education Programs 1976, University of Louisville; Ph.D. School Psychology, Indiana University, 1979. Address: 9104 Hurstwood Court, Louisville, Kentucky 40222.

TALLEY-MORRIS, NEVA BENNETT Occupation: Lawyer, Educator, Author. Education: Bachelor of Arts magna cum laude, Ouachita University, 1930; Master of Education, University of Texas, 1938; Postgraduate Education and Pre-Law, University of Texas, 1939-42. Address: 722 West Markham Street, Little Rock, Arkansas 72201.

TAMBS, LEWIS A Occupation: U.S. Ambassador to Colombia. Education: B.S.I.E., M.A., Ph.D. Address: American Embassy, Bogota, APO Miami, Florida 34038.

TAMBURINI, JOSEPH URBAN Occupation: Professional Engineer. Education: M.S. Civil/ Environmental Engineering. Address: 9223 Fern Way, Golden, Colorado 80403.

TAMRES, MILTON Occupation: Professor of Chemistry, Department of Chemistry, University of Michigan. Education: B.A., Brooklyn College, 1943; Ph.D., Northwestern University, 1949. Address: 1307 Brooks Street, Ann Arbor, Michigan 48109.

TAN, CHOR WENG Occupation: Dean, School of Engineering. Education: B.S., M.S., Ph.D. Address: 85 Columbia Avenue, Berkeley Heights, New Jersey 07912.

TANJA, JON J Occupation: Pharmacist, Educator. Education: B.S. Pharmacy, M.S. Hospital Pharmacy. Address: 641 Thorp, Auburn, Alabama 36830.

TANNEN, STEPHEN DANIEL Occupation: President, Etonic Inc. Education: B.S., Cornell University; M.B.A., Columbia University. Address: 163 Hampshire Road, Wellesley Hills, Massachusetts 02181.

TANNENWALD, ROBERT Occupation: Economist. Education: B.A., Dartmouth College; Ph.D., Harvard University. Address: 6 Clifton Road, Newton, Massachusetts 02106.

TANNER, MARTHA B Occupation: Attorney. Education: L.L.B., Doctor of Jurisprudence. Address: 421 East Hildebrand, San Antonio, Texas 78212.

TANNER, WILLIAM M Occupation: Student, Professional Singer. Education: B.A. Psychology. Address: 156 Hart Avenue, Athens, Georgia 30606.

TAPIA, JOHN R Occupation: Professor Emeritus, Fort Lewis College.

TAPPAN, SANDRA H Occupation: Psychotherapist, Dance Executive. Education: B.A., Trinity College; M.S., University of Vermont. Address: 22 Rugg Street, St. Albans, Vermont 05478.

TARLOW, ARTHUR LEE Occupation: Attorney. Education: B.S., J.D., A.A. Address: 1222 Northwest Old Quarry Road, Portland, Oregon 97229.

TARR, JAMES L Occupation: Art Director. Education: College Studies. Address: 721 South 11th Avenue, St. Charles, Illinois 60174.

TATA, GIOVANNI Occupation: Museum Curator, Archaeologist. Education: B.S. cum laude 1977, M.A. 1980, Brigham Young University; Graduate Certificate, University of Utah. Address: Post Office Box 8414, Salt Lake City, Utah 84108.

TATE-OWENS, FERNANDA GALE Education: M.A., B.A. Address: 1704 A Brockett, High Point, North Carolina 27260.

TATYREK, ALFRED FRANK Occupation: Chemical Engineer. Education: B.S. Chemistry. Address: 27 Orchard Road, Maplewood, New Jersey 07040.

TAUTENHAHN, GUNTHER Occupation: Composer, Author. Address: 1534 3rd Street, Manhattan Beach, California 90260.

TAWNEY, MELVIN L Occupation: Management Consultant. Education: B.S. Business Administration, Kansas State University. Address: 6402 Del Monte #17, Houston, Texas 77057.

TAYBACK, MATTHEW Occupation: Medical Educator, Administrator. Education: A.B., A.M., Sc.D. Address: 109 St. Albans Way, Baltimore, Maryland 21212.

TAYLOR, B ELDON Occupation: Criminologist. Education: D.D., M.Sc.D., Ph.D. Address: Post Office Box 7116, Salt Lake City, Utah 84107.

TAYLOR, CHARLES CLAYTON Occupation: Choral Director. Education: A.B., West Virginia Wesleyan College. Address: Route 4 Box 68, Murphysboro, Illinois 62966.

TAYLOR, DUNCAN PAUL Occupation: Neuropharmacologist, Bristol-Myers Company. Education: B.S. Chemistry, Ph.D. Biochemistry. Address: 112 Ryan Lane, Evansville, Indiana 47712.

TAYLOR, DON L Occupation: Bank President.

Education: B.B.A. Address: 27100 Shananagi Lane, Waukesha, Wisconsin 53186.

TAYLOR, ELIZABETH CARR Occupation: Library, Media Specialist. Education: B.A., Murray State University; M.L.S., Peabody College of Vanderbilt. Address: Route 1, Highway 68E, Cadiz, Kentucky 42211.

TAYLOR, ERNEST A JR Occupation: Electrical Engineer. Education: B.S.E.E., Georgia Institute of Technology, 1948. Address: 22012 Cleveland Avenue, Decatur, Alabama 35661.

TAYLOR, GEORGE WILLIAM Occupation: President, Princeton Research Associates, Inc. Education: B.E., Ph.D., D.Eng. Address: 305 Dodds Lane, Princeton, New Jersey 08540.

TAYLOR, LISA SUTER Occupation: Director, Cooper-Hewitt Museum. Education: D.F.A., Parsons School of Design. Address: 1115 Fifth Avenue, New York, New York 10028.

TAYLOR, LYNN BOGGESS Occupation: Associate Dean of Students, Director of Counseling. Education: B.A., Western Michigan University; M.Ed., Kent State University. Address: 1066 DeLeone Drive, Kent, Ohio 44240.

TAYLOR, SHARON KAY Occupation: President, Owner, Sharon K. Taylor and Associates. Education: B.A. Journalismm, M.S. Communications, San Diego State University. Address: 5033 Montessa Street, San Diego, California 92124.

TAYLOR, STEPHEN L Occupation: Lawyer. Education: B.A., Semo University; J.D., University of Missouri. Address: 801 Vernon, Sikeston, Missouri 63801.

TAYLOR, THEMAN RAY Occupation: Associate Professor, History. Education: A.A., B.A., M.A., Ph.D. History. Address: 1808 Clara Drive, Conway, Arkansas 72032.

TCHERNEV, DIMITER IVANOV Occupation: President and Owner, The Zeopower Company; President, Mesa-Tchernev, Inc. Education: Dipl.Ing., Technical University, 1953; Ph.D., Massachusetts Institute of Technology, 1965. Address: 9 Woodman Road, Chestnut Hill, Massachusetts 02167.

TEACHWORTH, ANNE Occupation: Director, Gestalt Institute of N.O. Education: Fellowship Degree, Gestalt Institute of Houston. Address: 6708 Schouest Street, Metairie, Louisiana 70003.

TEAL, MARY D Occupation: College Professor, Eastern Michigan University. Education: B.S., M.Mus., Ph.D. Address: 2671 Bedford Road, Ann Arbor, Michigan 48104.

TEARE, MARALYN L Occupation: Marriage and Family Counselor, Private Practice, Clinical Institute of Psychiatry, University of Southern California Medical School. Education: B.S., M.S., M.F.C.C. Address: Post Office Box 1386, Ojai, California 93023.

TEBBETTS, CHARLES EASTMAN Occupation: Director, Hypnotism Training Institute of Washington. Education: College Studies. Address: 7900 236th Street Southwest, #3, Edmonds, Washington 98020.

TEERE, HAROLD BENTON JR Occupation: Marketing Professor, Consultant. Education: B.S. Business Administration, M.B.A. Address: 711 Clovis Drive, Durange, Colorado 81301.

TEETS, JOHN WILLIAM Occupation: Chairman and Chief Executive Officer, The Greyhound Corporation. Education: Attended the University of Illinois. Address: 5303 Desert Park Lane, Scottsdale, Arizona 85253.

TEEVAN, RICHARD C Occupation: Professor of Psychology, Researcher. Education: B.A., M.A., Ph.D.

Address: 1400 Washington Avenue, Albany, New York 12222.

TEGELER, DONALD MAURICE SR Occupation: Consultant, Employee Benefits. Education: B.A. Economics. Address: 216 Elm Court, Libertyville, Illinois 60048.

TEICHERT, CARLOS Occupation: Director, Quality Fisher Cheese Company. Education: B.A., University of Mississippi; M.S., Mississippi State University. Address: 464 Richards Road, Columbus, Ohio 43214.

TEJADA, ELIZABETH A HAYES Occupation: Interior Designer. Education: B.A. Psychology/ Economics. Address: 4700 Aliso, Northeast, Albuquerque, New Mexico 87110.

TELFORD, DONALD McCREA Occupation: College Mathematics Instructor. Education: B.S., Kansas State University, 1930; M.S., East Tennessee State University, 1971. Address: 2952 Adrain Avenue, Largo, Florida 33540.

TELLER, EDWARD Occupation: Senior Research Fellow, Hoover Institution; Consultant, Lawrence Livermore National Laboratory. Education: Ph.D., University of Leipzig, 1931. Address: Hoover Institution, Stanford, California 94305.

TEMIANKA, HENRI Occupation: Artistic Director, California Chamber Symphony. Education: Curtis Institute of Music. Address: 2915 Patricia, Los Angeles, California 90064.

TEMPLER, DONALD I Occupation: Psychologist. Education: A.B., M.A., Ph.D. Address: 1350 M Street, Fresno, California 93721.

TEN BRINK, HELEN D Occupation: Associate Professor, West Virginia Wesleyan College. Education: B.S., P.H.N., Master Public Health. Address: 105 Pocahontas Street, Buckhannon, West Virginia 26201.

TENENBAUM, ALLEN Occupation: Psychologist. Education: Ph.D., University of California. Address: 663 Fifth Avenue, New York City, New York 10022.

TENNANT, FOREST SEARLES JR Occupation: Executive Director, Community Health Projects, Inc. Education: A.A., B.A., M.D. Address: 1744 Aspen Village Way, West Covina, California 91791.

TENNANT, FRANK ARTHUR Occupation: Professor Public Relations and Journalism. Education: M.S. Journalism 1953, B.A. Political Science 1950, University of California-Los Angeles. Address: 1779 North 2nd Avenue, Upland, California 91786.

TENNEN, LESLIE I Occupation: Attorney. Education: B.A. with distinction, University of Arizona, 1973; Attended Hebrew University, Jerusalem, 1975; J.D., University of Arizona, College of Law. Address: 4717 East 2nd Street, Tucson, Arizona 85711.

TEPPER, ANDREW STEPHEN Occupation: Software Designer. Education: M.Math., University of Waterloo, 1978; B.S.E.E., Massachusetts Institute of Technology, 1972; Attended Drexel University. Address: 926 Amarillo Avenue, Palo Alto, California 94301.

TEPPER, NANCY BOXLEY Occupation: Attorney. Education: LL.B., Harvard Law School, 1958; B.A., Radcliffe College, 1953. Address: 331 Vista Suerte, Newport Beach, California 92660.

TERADA, HARRY T Occupation: Optometrist. Education: O.D., B.S. Address: 5383 Manauwea Street, Honolulu, Hawaii 96821.

TERRELL, BEVERLY JOLLY Occupation: Human Services Supervisor I. Education: B.S. Education. Address: 2186 Carnes Avenue, Memphis, Tennessee 38114.

TERRES, JOHN K Occupation: Writer/Editor,

Lecturer, Field Naturalist. Education: Special University Studies. Address: 635 Cheese Spring Road, New Canaan, Connecticut 06840.

TERRY, DAVID RAY Occupation: Assistant Commissioner for Higher Education. Education: M.S., Brigham Young University; Ph.D., University of Illinois. Address: 5432 South 800 East, South Ogden, Utah 84405.

TERRY, EDWARD ALLISON JR Occupation: Civil Engineer. Education: B.S.C.E. Address: 10 Madison Mills Court, Baltimore, Maryland 28228.

TERRY, HELEN Occupation: Personnel Manager, Civil Service Examiner. Education: B.A., The Evergreen State College, 1978. Address: 7108 N.W. 2nd Avenue, Vancouver, Washington 98665.

TERRY, REESE S Occupation: Vice President, Technical Resources. Education: B.S.E.E., M.S.E.E. Address: 2703 Glenn Lakeo Lane, Missouri City, Texas 77459.

TERRY, ROGER L Occupation: College Professor, Hanover College; Psychologist. Education: A.B., Yale University, 1962; M.S., Auburn University, 1964; Ph.D., University of Missouri, 1968. Address: 708 East Main Street, Madison, Indiana 47250.

TERZIAN, SHOHIG SHERRY Occupation: Director, Mental Health Information Service. Education: A.B., Radcliffe College; M.S., Columbia University. Address: 11740 Wilshire Boulevard, Los Angeles, California 90025.

TESCH, STEPHANIE THORPE Occupation: Curriculum/Staff Development Director. Education: B.A. 1959, M.Ed. 1977. Address: 2105 North 8th, Pasco, Washington 99301.

TESENY, PAUL ANTHONY Occupation: Programmer Analyst. Address: R.D. #4, Box 149, Quakertown, Pennsylvania 18951.

TEVIS, BETTY A Occupation: Health Educator. Education: B.A., B.S., M.A., Ph.D. Address: 96201 Bryson, Dallas, Texas 75238.

THACKER, BARBARA JEWELL Occupation: Resource Specialist. Education: A.A., B.A., M.A. Address: 1818 Cougar Lane, Clovis, California 93612.

THAL, LAWRENCE S Occupation: Optometrist. Education: B.S., B.S., O.D., M.B.A. Address: 216 Amherst Avenue, Kensington, California 94708.

THAMS, MARGIE LOUISE Occupation: Manager, Travel Ventures. Education: Certificate, 1983. Address: 2220 Park, Newport, Apartment 215, Newport Beach, California 92660.

THARP, ROLAND G Occupation: Professor, University of Hawaii. Education: B.A., M.A., Ph.D. Address: 3349 B Andai, Honolulu, Hawaii 96822.

THEIN, ANTHONY P Occupation: Chairman/ Professor of Music, Mayville State College. Education: B.A., M.M., Ph.D. Address: 343 3rd Avenue Northeast, Mayville, North Dakota 58257.

THEINER, ERIC CHARLES Occupation: Clinical Psychologist. Education: B.S. 1957, M.A. 1960, Ph.D. 1966. Address: 61 Bellfair Drive, Memphis, Tennessee 38104.

THEIS, ROBERT P Occupation: Director of Business and Financial Services. Education: M.B.A., B.S., University of Scranton. Address: 15 Grandview Drive, Hughestown, Pennsylvania 18640.

THEOBALD, WILLIAM LOUIS Occupation: Director, Pacific Tropical Botanical Garden. Education: B.S., M.S., Ph.D. Address: Post Office Box 381, Lawai, Hawaii 96765.

THEODORE, ATHENA R Occupation: Sociologist, Professor of Sociology. Education: B.S.Ed., M.Ed., M.A., Ph.D. Address: 27 Turning Mill Road, Lexington, Massachusetts 02173.

THEROUX, MARJORIE E Occupation: Educator, Political Activist. Education: B.S. Address: 8 Belleview Boulevard, #102, Belleair, Florida 33516.

THIELKE, FREDERICK LOWELL Occupation: Dental Student, School of Dentistry. Education: B.S.C.E. Address: 147 Glenora Drive, Martinez, Georgia 30907.

THIERET, JOHN W Occupation: University Professor. Education: B.S., M.S., Utah State University; Ph.D., University of Chicago. Address: 4129 Beiting Drive, Alexandria, Kentucky 41001.

THIMOTHEOSE, KADAKAMPALLIL GEEVARGHESE Occupation: Executive Director, Central Therapeutic Services, Inc. Education: M.A. Sociology, M.A. Psychology, M.A. History, Ph.D. Psychology, C.S.W., C.A.C. Address: 21701 Parklawn, Oak Park, Michigan 48237.

THOMAN, RICHARD S Occupation: Professor Emeritus. Education: B.A., University of Colorado; M.A., Ph.D., University of Chicago. Address: 3425 Oakes Drive, Hayward, California 94542.

THOMAS, ARTHUR LOUIS Occupation: Editor Market Research. Education: A.B., Columbia College, 1951; Ph.D., Princeton University, 1956. Address: 20 Brookside Drive 3D, Greenwich, Connecticut 06830.

THOMAS, BARBARA N Occupation: Director, Katherine Gibbs. Education: B.S. Address: 1500 Locust Street #4001, Philadelphia, Pennsylvania 19102.

THOMAS, BARBARA S Occupation: President, Samuel Montagu Holdings, Inc. Education: B.A., J.D. Address: 35 Sutton Place, New York, New York 10022.

THOMAS, CHARLES W Occupation: Professor, Political Consultant. Education: B.S., M.A., Ph.D. Address: 610 Bradford Road, El Cajon, California 92021.

THOMAS, GARNETT JETT Occupation: Administrative Officer and Chief Accountant, Mississippi State University Agricultural and Forestry Experiment Station. Education: B.S. Address: 114 Grand Ridge Drive, Starkville, Mississippi 39759.

THOMAS, GEORGE Occupation: Medical Doctor. Education: M.D. Address: 7803 19th Avenue Drive, Bradenton, Florida 33529.

THOMAS, GEORGELLE Occupation: Professor of Psychology. Education: B.A., Queens College; M.S., Ph.D., University of Georgia. Address: Route 7, Greenbriar #36, Statesboro, Georgia 30458.

THOMAS, GRACE FERN Occupation: Physician Specialist in Psychiatry. Education: B.S., M.A. Biochemistry, M.A. Religion, M.D. Address: 2001 La Jolla Court, Modesto, California 95350.

THOMAS, JESSIE LEE Occupation: Counselor. Education: B.A., M.Ed., Ed.S. Address: 409 First Street, Natchez, Mississippi 39120.

THOMAS, JIMMY L Occupation: V.P. Financial Services and Treasurer. Education: B.S., University of Kentucky; M.B.A., Columbia University. Address: 13 New England Drive, Rochester, New York 14618.

THOMAS, JOSEPH E Occupation: Psychologist. Education: Ph.D. Address: 16 West 731 89th Place, Hinsdale, Illinois 60521.

THOMAS, M DONALD Occupation: Consultant. Education: Ed.D., Litt.D. Address: 860 18th Avenue, Salt Lake City, Utah 84103.

THOMAS, MAHLON WAYNE Occupation: Educator (English). Education: B.S. and M.A. Education. Address: Post Office Box 113, Bardwell, Kentucky 42023.

THOMAS, PEGGY RUTH Occupation: Supply Management, Contract Consultant. Education:

University of Oklahoma, Southwestern State College. Address: SRA 85-T, 6001 Barry, Anchorage, Alaska 99516.

THOMAS, PETER D Occupation: Professor, English and Humanities. Education: M.A., Oxon University. Address: 620 Sheridan, Sault Ste. Marie, Michigan 49783.

THOMAS, PHILIP R Occupation: Consultant. Education: B.Sc., M.Sc. Physics, Ph.D. Engineering. Address: Route 1, Box 181, Ethel, Louisiana 70730.

THOMAS, RICHARD V Occupation: Justice, Wyoming Supreme Court. Education: B.S. with honors Business Administration, University of Wyoming, 1954; LL.B. with honors, University of Wyoming Law School, 1956; LL.M. Taxation, New York University School of Law, 1961. Address: 212 West Pershing Boulevard, Cheyenne, Wyoming 82001.

THOMAS, ROBERT C Occupation: Professor of Sculpture. Education: B.A., M.F.A. Address: 38 San Mateo Avenue, Goleta, California 93117.

THOMAS, ROBERT EDWIN Occupation: Executive Director, Wyoming Church Coalition. Education: A.B., Boston University; B.D., M.Div., Vanderbilt University. Address: 1925 Hyview Drive, Casper, Wyoming 82604.

THOMAS, ROY POOTHICOTE Occupation: Physician. Education: M.D. (American Specialty Board Certified). Address: 8516 Wedgewood, Burridge, Illinois 60521.

THOMAS, RUTH G Occupation: Professor. Education: B.S. 1965, M.A. 1975, Ph.D. 1977. Address: 900 Edgewater Avenue West, St. Paul, Minnesota 55112.

THOMAS, STEPHEN NAYLOR Occupation: Author, College Professor. Education: A.B., Harvard University, 1964; Ph.D., Massachusetts Institute of Technology, 1968. Address: 2809 Boyer Avenue East, Seattle, Washington 98102.

THOMASON, MICHAEL GARY Occupation: Professor of Computer Science, University of Tennessee. Education: B.S., Clemson University; M.S., Johns Hopkins University; Ph.D., Duke University. Address: 8032 Hayden Drive, Knoxville, Tennessee 37919.

THOMASON, STEPHEN C Occupation: President. Education: M.S., B.S. Address: 7521 Meade Way, Westminster, Colorado 80030.

THOMASON, TOM W Occupation: Artist, Jewelry Designer. Education: B.F.A., University of New Mexico. Address: 615 16th Street, Northwest, Albuquerque, New Mexico 87104.

THOMPSON, ALLEN L Occupation: Data Processing Training Executive. Education: B.S. Accounting. Address: 25 Seven Hills Drive, Boulder, Colorado 80302.

THOMPSON, DAMON LEON Occupation: Professor of English. Education: B.F.A., M.F.A., University of Iowa. Address: 638 Fourth Avenue, Williamsport, Pennsylvania 17701.

THOMPSON, DAVID RUSSELL Occupation: Professor, Agricultural Engineering and Food Science. Education: B.S., M.S., Ph.D. Address: 1711 Skillman Avenue, Roseville, Minnesota 55113.

THOMPSON, EDWARD T Occupation: Editor in Chief. Education: B.S., Massachusetts Institute of Technology, 1949. Address: Guard Hill Road, Bedford, New York 10506.

THOMPSON, FRANK J Occupation: Attorney. Education: B.S.E.E., LL.B. Address: 1090 Galloping Hill Road, Fairfield, Connecticut 06430.

THOMPSON, FREDDIE ELAINE Occupation:

Dance Instructor/Educator. Education: B.A. Address: 12226 South Western Avenue, Los Angeles, California 90301.

THOMPSON, HENRY O Occupation: Clergy, Teacher. Education: B.Sc., M.Div., Ph.D., M.Sc. Education, M.A. Educational Psychology. Address: 7 University Mews, Philadelphia, Pennsylvania 19104.

THOMPSON, JACK MANSFIELD JR Occupation: Mechanical Engineer. Education: B.S., Master of Engineering, Cornell University. Address: 39 Mound Street, Milford, Ohio 45150.

THOMPSON, JOHN R Occupation: Professor, Department of Psychology, Oberlin College; Clinical Psychologist. Education: B.A., M.A., Ph.D. Address: 254 Elm, Oberlin, Ohio 44074.

THOMPSON, JULIA A Occupation: Physicist. Education: Ph.D. 1969, M.S. 1967, Yale University; B.A., Cornell College, 1964. Address: 5872 Ellsworth Avenue, Pittsburgh, Pennsylvania 15232.

THOMPSON, JOSEPH WARREN Occupation: Physician/Surgeon; President, Missouri Society of General Practitioners. Education: B.S., D.O. Address: 2342 East Royal Court, St. Louis, Missouri 63131.

THOMPSON, LARRY R Occupation: Special Assistant to the President, Ohio State University. Education: J.D. summa cum laude, M.S., B.A. Address: 2533 Bryden Road, Columbus, Ohio 43209.

THOMPSON, LAURENCE CASSIUS Occupation: Professor of Linguistics (Retired). Education: Ph.D., Yale University. Address: 959 Koae Street, Honolulu, Hawaii 96816.

THOMPSON, LOIS JEAN Occupation: Counselor, Industrial Psychologist. Education: Ed.D. Counselor Education, M.A., B.A. Address: 340 Aragon, Los Alamos, New Mexico 87544.

THOMPSON, MARION ELIZABETH Occupation: Professor, International Broadcasting. Education: B.A. 1943, M.A. 1960, Ph.D. 1971, University of Wisconsin. Address: 4 Mirick Lane, Wilbraham, Massachusetts 01095.

THOMPSON, MARK E Occupation: Finance Manager, Coast-to-Coast Stores, Northern Division. Education: B.S. Commercial Economics, South Dakota State University. Address: 2015 Derdull Drive, Brookings, South Dakota 57006.

THOMPSON, MARYBELLE Occupation: Clinical Laboratory Manager; Program Director, School of Medical Technology. Education: B.S., M.A. Address: West 3313 Fairway Drive, Coeur d'Alene, Idaho 83814.

THOMPSON, RICHARD EARL Occupation: Artist-American Impressionist. Education: Attended Chicago Academy of Fine Arts, American Academy of Art, Chicago Art Institute. Address: Richard Thompson Gallery, 80 Maiden Lane, San Francisco, California 94108.

THOMPSON, SHIRLEY JEAN Occupation: Epidemiologist. Education: Ph.D. Address: 4514 Sylvan Drive, Columbia, South Carolina 29206.

THOMPSON, SYDNEY E Occupation: Cultural Engineer. Address: 2100 Martin Luther King Jr. Way, Berkeley, California 94704.

THOMS, PAUL E Occupation: Director of Curriculum. Education: B.M., M.M. Address: 128 South D Street, Hamilton, Ohio 45013.

THORGEIRSSON, SNORRI S Occupation: Medical Officer and Chief, Laboratory of Experimental Oncology. Education: M.D., Ph.D., Address: 9305 Kingsley Avenue, Bethesda, Maryland 20205.

THORN, JOHN PATTERSON Occupation: Psychologist. Education: A.S., B.A., M.A., Ph.D. Address: Post Office Box 2463, Jackson, Wyoming

83001.

THORNDAL, NANCY H Occupation: Vocational Education Administrator. Education: B.S., North Dakota State University, 1953. Address: 1111 First Street North, J6, Bismarck, North Dakota 58501.

THORNE, JOHN R Occupation: Chairman, The Enterprise Corporation of Pittsburgh. Education: B.S., Brown University, 1947; M.S., University of Pittsburgh, 1949; M.I.A., Graduate School of Industrial Administration, 1952. Address: Furnace Run, Laughlintown, Pennsylvania 15655.

THORNE, ROBERT D Occupation: Vice President and Controller, United States Gypsum Company. Education: B.S., M.B.A., Northwestern University; C.P.A., Illinois. Address: 1409 Burr Oak Road, Hinsdale, Illinois 60521.

THORNTON-TRUMP, W E (TED) Occupation: Inventor, Business Entrepreneur; President, Trump, Inc. Education: Attended the University of British Columbia, University of Southern California (affiliate). Address: Box 3342, Spanish Cove, Lillian, Alabama 36549.

THORSTEINSSON, GUDNI Occupation: Staff Physician, Medical Director. Education: M.D., M.S. Address: 2020 Telemark Court, Rochester, Minnesota 55901.

THRASH, SARA ARLINE Occupation: Professor of Education, St. Leo College. Education: B.A., M.A., Ed.S., Ph.D. Address: 4200 14th Way Northeast, St. Petersburg, Florida 33703.

THRASH, WILLARD MARK Occupation: Minister. Education: B.A., M.A., M.Div. Address: 4200 14 Way N.E., St. Pete, Florida 33703.

THRESHMAN, GEORGE T Occupation: Professional Sales Representative, Pharmaceuticals. Education: A.B., A.A.S., B.A., M.B.A. Address: 61 East Avenue, Milford, Connecticut 06460.

THURBER, STEVEN DAVID Occupation: Clinical Psychologist. Education: B.S., M.S., Ph.D., Postdoctoral Diploma. Address: 1200 Eagle Hills Way, Eagle, Idaho 83616.

THURMAN, RICHARD LEE Occupation: Professor. Education: Ph.D., M.S. Education, B.S. Education. Address: 12272 Weleba, St. Louis, Missouri 63121.

THURMOND, JANICE MATHIS Occupation: Attorney. Education: J.D., University of Georgia, 1980; B.A., Duke University, 1975. Address: Post Office Box 1262, Athens, Georgia 30603.

THURSTON, ETHEL HOLBROOKE Occupation: Director, 2 Animal Protection Societies. Education: Ph.D. Music History, New York University; Student of Nadia Boulanger. Address: 175 West 12th Street, #16G, New York, New York 10011.

THYGERSON, ALTON L Occupation: University Professor. Education: B.S., M.H. Education, Ed.D. Address: 3300 Mohican Lane; Provo, Utah 84604.

TIANO, JUDITH JORDAN Occupation: Registered Nurse, Director of Nursing Education. Education: B.S.N., University of Cincinnati; M.Ed., Xavier University, 1974. Address: 723 Brightridge Drive, Bridgeport, West Virginia 26330.

TICK, EDWARD BRYAN Occupation: Psychotherapist, Writer. Education: B.A., M.A., Ph.D. Address: Red Rick Road, Box 113, East Chatham, New York 12060.

TIDEIKSAAR, REIN Occupation: Educational Coordinator. Education: Doctoral in Gerontology. Address: 555 Main Street, New York, New York 10044.

TIEMEYER, HOPE JOHNSON Occupation: President, The Mail Way Advertising Co. Education: A.B. Address: 2786 Little Dry Run Road, Cincinnati, Ohio 45244.

TIEN, CHANG-LIN Occupation: Educator/ Professor, Department of Engineering, University of California-Berkeley. Education: B.S., M.M.E., M.A., Ph.D. Address: 1451 Olympus Avenue, Berkeley, California 94708.

TILDEN, LORRAINE FREDERICK Occupation: News Writer. Education: A.A., B.A., M.A., Ph.D. Address: 351 Oakdale Drive, Claremont, California 91711.

TILLINGHAST, MURIEL K Occupation: Community Preventive Service Program, Administrator. Education: B.A., M.A. Address: 550 Carlton Avenue, Brooklyn, New York 11238.

TILLMAN, CELESTINE Occupation: Associate Professor, Chemistry Department, Southern University. Education: B.S., Southern University, 1955; M.S., Howard University, 1957. Address: 10761 South Gibbens Drive, Baton Rouge, Louisiana 70807.

TILLY, LOLA CREMEANS Occupation: Emeritus Professor of Home Economics, University of Alaska. Education: B.A. 1920, M.S. 1920, University of Illinois; Doctorate of Humanities, University of Alaska, 1963. Address: 665 10th Avenue, #304, Fairbanks, Alaska 99701.

TILY, STEPHEN B Occupation: Trust Company Executive. Education: B.A., Washington and Jefferson College, 1960. Address: 523 Pugh Road, Strafford, Pennsylvania 19087.

TIMMINS, WILLIAM F Occupation: Painter, Fine Arts. Education: Attended Art Student's League, Grand Central Art School. Address: Post Office Box 5685, Carmel, California 93921.

TINAJERO, ROBERTO JOSE Occupation: Interpreter. Education: U.L.C.I., Ph.D. Religion. Address: 99 Miller Circle, El Paso, Texas 79915.

TING, ER YI Occupation: Physician. Education: M.D. Address: 224 Highwood Avenue, Tenafly, New Jersey 07670.

TINKER, ROSE MARIE Occupation: Director Social Services. Education: B.S. History and Journalism, Murray State University. Address: 777 Southland Drive, Radcliff, Kentucky 40160.

TIPTON, DOROTHY V Occupation: Partner in Business; Musician. Education: High School. Address: 9485 Southwest Inglewood Street, Portland, Oregon 97225.

TIPTON, HARRY B Occupation: Physician. Education: B.A., University of Colorado; M.D., University of Colorado. Address: Hillcrest Drive, Lander, Wyoming 82520.

TITSWORTH, TOBIE R III Occupation: Vice President for Continuing and Technical Education, Rogers State College. Education: B.S. 1967, M.S. 1973, Ed.D. 1976, Oklahoma State University. Address: 1461 Paradise Park, Claremore, Oklahoma 74017.

TIWANA, NAZAR HAYAT Occupation: Librarian. Education: B.A., Cambridge University; M.A., University of Chicago. Address: 2620 West Pratt Boulevard, Chicago, Illinois 60695.

TOBIAS-TURNER, BESSYE Occupation: Assistant Professor English and Speech, Writer (Poet Laureate International). Education: A.B. English, Rust College; M.A. English, M.A. Speech, Columbia University; Ph.D. Literature, World University. Address: 829 Wall Street, McComb, Mississippi 39645.

TODD, IAN ALEXANDER Occupation: Associate Professor, Brandeis University. Education: B.A., Ph.D. Address: 20 Deacon Hunt Drive, Acton, Massachusetts 01720.

TOENJES, DON A Occupation: Agriculturist, University of California Cooperative Extension. Education: B.S. Address: Route 1, Box 1551A, Orland, California 95963.

TOGNONI, HALE C Occupation: Professional Engineer, Lawyer. Education: B.E.G.E. 1948, LL.B. 1953. Address: 1525 West Northern, Phoenix, Arizona 85021.

TOKAYER, MARVIN Occupation: Author/ Director, North Shore Hebrew Academy. Education: B.A., B.R.E., M.H.L., Ph.D., Rabbi. Address: 9 Stony Run Road, Great Neck, New York 11023.

TOLBERT, WILLIAM AUSTIN Occupation: Research Engineer. Education: B.S. Civil Engineering, M.S. Architectual Engineering. Address: 6762 Xenon Drive, Arvada, Colorado 8004.

TOLES, GEORGE EDWARD JR Occupation: Owner, Advertising Agency. Education: B.A. Speech, Master of Television. Address: 6905 191st Place Southwest, Lynnwood, Washington 98036.

TOLLEFSON, KENNETH D Occupation: Professor of Anthropology. Education: B.A., M.A., M.Div., Ph.D. Address: 807 West Barrett, Seattle, Washington 98119.

TOLLEFSON, ROBERT J Occupation: Professor of Religion and Philosophy. Education: B.S.E.E., B.D., Th.M., Ph.D. Address: 1305 Shoreway, Storm Lake, Iowa 50588.

TOM, KATHLEEN E Occupation: Student. Education: M.B.A./J.D. Student, University of Southern California; B.S., B.U.A.D. Address: 315 Obispo #12, Long Beach, California 90814.

TOMARKEN, ANNETTE H Occupation: European Center Coordinator, Oxford. Education: B.A., Ph.D. Address: 326 West Vine Street, Oxford, Ohio 45056.

TOMIKAWA, SANDRA AKIKO Occupation: Department of Education Psychologist. Education: M.A., Ph.D. Address: 99-650 Allpoe Drive, Alea, Hawaii 96701.

TOMLINSON, H PAT Occupation: Professor. Education: B.S., Louisiana State University; M.A., University of Arkansas. Address: 6828 Apona Diamondhead, Bay Street Louis, Mississippi 39520.

TOMLINSON, JOAN HOUGH HARRINGTON Occupation: Speech Pathologist, Bay St. Louis, Mississippi. Education: B.A., M.Ed., Post-Master's Work, Northwestern State University of Louisiana; Doctoral Work, Texas Woman's University. Address: 435 Longleaf Road, Shreveport, Louisiana 71106.

TONE, YASUNAO Occupation: Artist. Education: B.A. Japanese Literature. Address: 307 West Broadway, New York, New York 10013.

TONELLI, EDITH A Occupation: Professor, Department of Art, University of California, Los Angeles. Address: B.A., M.A., Ph.D. Address: 17321 Castellammare Drive, #1, Pacific Palisades, California 90272.

TOORENAAR, JACALYN SUE Occupation: Production Director. Education: A.A. Liberal Arts, 1971; B.A. Journalism, 1973. Address: 1405 Marshall Street, Redwood City, California 94063.

TORNDAL, NANCY HERBISON Occupation: Educational Equality Coordinator for State Board for Vocational Education. Education: B.S. Address: 221 Avenue B West, Bismarck, North Dakota 58501.

TORRANCE, ELLIS PAUL Occupation: Studies of Creative, Gifted and Future Behavior. Address: 185 Riverhill Drive, Athens, Georgia 30606.

TORRES, EUGENIO Occupation: Controls Engineer, Certified Manufacturing Engineer. Education: A.E.E., A.E.E. Address: 2501 Longmeadow Northwest, Grand Rapids, Michigan 49504.

TORRES AYBAR, ANA MARIA Occupation: Special Services Director, Catholic University. Education: M.A.S. Guidance and Counseling, Ed.D. Address: Jardines Fagot, Calle 3 #E15, Ponce, Puerto Rico 00731.

TOTH, JULIEANA Occupation: Director of Medical Surgical Nursing. Education: M.S.N. Address: 2435 McKinley #29, El Paso, Texas 79930.

TOTH, MARIAN DAVIES Occupation: Author, Educator (Supervisor Language Arts, Reading). Education: B.A., M.A., Ed.D. Address: 310 Chamounix Road, Saint Davies, Pennsylvania 19087.

TOTTON, CARL ALLEN II Occupation: Administrator, Counselor, Educator. Education: B.S. Counseling, California State University-Los Angeles, 1978; M.S. Counseling, 1980. Address: 10632 Burbank Boulevard, North Hollywood, California 91601.

TOURTELLOTTE, WALLACE WILLIAM Occupation: Chief, Neurology Service, VA Wadsworth Medical Center. Education: Ph.B. 1945, B.S. 1945, Ph.D., M.D. Address: 1140 Tellem Drive, Pacific Palisades, California 90272.

TOWNE, DOROTHEA ALICE III Occupation: Chiropractic Doctor and Educator. Education: B.A., D.C., B.S. Address: East 508 Eaton Avenue, Spokane, Washington 99218.

TOWNSEND, DARLENE A Occupation: University Administrator. Education: Ph.D., M.A., B.A. Address: Southeast 515 Dexter, Pullman, Washington 99163.

TOYE, HELEN Occupation: Artist, Writer. Education: B.A., M.A. Address: 8208 Plum Street, New Orleans, Louisiana 70118.

TOYOMURA, DENNIS T Occupation: Architect. Address: 2602 Manoa Road, Honolulu, Hawaii 96822.

TRAAEN, TERESA J Occupation: Director, J.T.P.A. Program. Education: B.A., M.A. Address: 6626 East Oak Street, Scottsdale, Arizona 85257.

TRACEY, WILLIAM RAYMOND Occupation: President, Human Resources Enterprises of Cape Cod, Inc. Education: Ed.D., Ed.M., B.S. Education. Address: 54 Evergreen Street, South Yarmoth, Massachusetts 02664.

TRACK, GERHARD Occupation: Music Director, Conductor, Composer. Education: M.M., M.S., B.A. Address: 130 Baylor, Pueblo, Colorado 81005.

TRACY, LOIS BARTLETT Occupation: Painter, Writer, Lecturer. Education: A.B., Master's Degree, Michigan State University. Address: 580 Artist Avenue, Englewood, Florida 33533.

TRACY, MARILYN L Occupation: Speech Pathologist, Owner Tracy Graphics. Education: B.S., M.A. Address: Route #131, St. George, Maine 04857.

TRACZ, RICHARD FRANCIS Occupation: Professor of English. Education: A.B., M.A. Address: 1400 North State Parkway, Chicago, Illinois 60610.

TRAHAN, PHILIP JOSEPH Occupation: Student. Address: 5794 Main Street, Trumbull, Connecticut 06611.

TRAHEY, NANCY MARIE Occupation: Supervisory Chemist, United States Department of Energy, New Brunswick Laboratory. Education: B.S./ B.A. Chemistry. Address: 7513 Farmingdale Drive, Apartment #406, Darien, Illinois 60559.

TRAKIMAS, RAYMOND DOMINIC Occupation: Management Consultant, Price Waterhouse. Education: B.S.I.E., M.B.A. Finance. Address: 671 Stolle Road, Elma, New York 14059.

TRANQUILLO, MARY DORA Occupation: Program Coordinator. Education: B.F.A., M.A. Address: 34 Turnstone Drive, Clearwater, Florida 33519.

TRAUSCH, THOMAS V Occupation: Artist. Education: B.F.A. Graphic Design. Address: 507 West Third Street, Woodstock, Illinois 60098.

TRAVIS, CRAIG M Occupation: Finance Consultant. Education: B.A. Public Relations. Address: 1914 Emory Street, San Jose, California 95126.

TRAYNOR, KENNETH Occupation: College Professor. Education: B.A., M.A., Ph.D. Address: 339 South Street, Clarion, Pennsylvania 16214.

TREESE, DARLENE ANN Occupation: Gifted Resource Teacher, Counselor, Writer, Hypnotherapist, Motivational Speaker. Address: 1825 West Ocotillo 40, Phoenix, Arizona 85015.

TREFTS, ALBERT SHARPE Occupation: Engineering Consultant. Education: Mechanical Engineering 1952, Administration 1953, Cornell University. Address: 20101 Malvern Road, Shaker Heights, Ohio 44122.

TREFTS, DOROTHY E Occupation: Manager, Computer Software Firm. Education: B.A., Wellesley College, 1975; M.B.A., Harvard Business School, 1978. Address: 254 Commonwealth Avenue #2, Boston, Massachusetts 02116.

TRELEASE, FRANK J III Occupation: Consulting Water Engineer. Education: B.S.C.E., M.S.C.E. Address: 3228 Locust Drive, Cheyenne, Wyoming 82001.

TRENT, DARRELL M Occupation: U.S. Ambassador to the European Civil Aviation Committee. Education: A.B., M.B.A. Address: Post Office Box 2349, Wilmington, Delaware 19899.

TRENT, JOHN BRABSON Occupation: Vice President, Stifel Nicolaus, Inc. Education: B.A., M.A. Ph.D. Address: 70 Fair Oaks, St. Louis, Missouri 63124.

TRENT, NELLIE JANE Occupation: Psychologist, Private Practice in Gerontology. Education: B.A., M.A. Address: 70 Fair Oaks, St. Louis, Missouri 63124.

TRENT, RAYMOND CARSON RAY Occupation: Entertainer. Education: Real Estate, Insurance. Address: Box 162, Denver City, Texas 79323.

TRIANDIS, HARRY CHARALAMBOS Occupation: University Professor. Education: Bachelor of Engineering, M.Com., Doctor of Philosophy. Address: 1 Lake Park, Champaign, Illinois 61820.

TRIBBE, FRANK CALVERT Occupation: Writer, Editor, Researcher, Lecturer. Education: LL.B., LL.M. Address: 134 Donna-Gail Drive East, Penn Laird, Virginia 22846.

TRIMM, MICHAEL DAVID Occupation: Quality Control Engineer, Hyster Corporation. Education: B.S. Mechanical Engineering (in progress). Address: Post Office Box 383, Vernon, Alabama 35592.

TRIPLEHORN, CHARLES A Occupation: Professor of Entomology. Education: B.S, M.S., Ohio State University; Ph.D., Cornell University. Address: 3943 Medford Square, Columbus, Ohio 43220.

TRIPP, RUSSELL MAURICE Occupation: President, SKIA Corporation, Medical Instruments Manufacturer. Education: Geological Engineer, Master Geophysical Engineering, Colorado School of Mines; Sc.D., Massachusetts Institute of Technology. Address: 15231 Quito Road, Saratoga, California 95070.

TROELL, HENRY NEIL Occupation: Government Agency Official. Education: B.B.A., University Texas-Austin; A.A., San Antonio College. Address: Route 2, Box 93, Manor, Texas 78653.

TROST, EILEEN BANNON Occupation: Attorney, McDermott, Will & Emery. Education: B.A., Shimer College, 1972; J.D., University of Minnesota, 1976. Address: 65 Waverly Avenue, Clarendon Hills, Illinois 60514.

TROUT, BOBBI EVELYN Occupation: Retired Businessman. Education: Attended University of Southern California. Address: 7512 Vieja Castilla Way, Carlsbad, California 92008.

TRUAX, DONALD ROBERT Occupation: Professor of Mathematics. Education: B.A., University of Washington, 1951; M.A., University Washington, 1953; Ph.D., Stanford, 1955. Address: 2323 University Street, Eugene, Oregon 97403.

TRUE, CHARLES W JR Occupation: Genealogist, Editor, Publisher. Education: B.S., Texas College of Arts and Industries, 1941. Address: 9324 McFall Drive, El Paso, Texas 79925.

TRUJILLO, PAUL EDWARD Occupation: Lecturer. Education: B.S.E.E. 1976, M.S.E.E. 1984. Address: Box 396, Peralta, New Mexico 87042.

TRULIO, JOHN G Occupation: B.S., Harvard University; M.A., Ph.D., Columbia University. Address: 2551 Pesquera Drive, Los Angeles, California 90049.

TRYBUL, THEODORE N Occupation: Engineer. Education: B.S., M.S., D.Sc. Address: 4037 Via Marina, Marina, Del Rey, California 90291.

TSAU, WEN SHIUNG Occupation: Project Engineer, Inspector. Education: M.S. Civil Engineering, University of Wyoming. Address: Post Office Box 2012 (516 Fossil Butte Drive), Kemmerer, Wyoming 83101-1901.

TSE, FRANCIS LAI-SING Occupation: Senior Scientist and Unit Head, Drug Metabolism Section. Education: B.S., M.S., Ph.D., University of Wisconsin-Madison. Address: 9-Q Dorado Drive, Convent Station, New Jersey 07961.

TSOULFANIDIS, NICHOLAS Occupation: Professor. Education: B.S., M.S., Ph.D. Address: Route 6, Box 523, Rolla, Maryland 65401.

TSUDA, ROY T Occupation: Dean of Graduate School and Research, Professor, University of Hawaii. Education: B.A., M.S., Ph.D. Address: Maria N. Aragon Street, Chalan Pago, Guam 96910.

TU, KUO-CH'ING Occupation: Associate Professor of Chinese, Department of Eastern Languages, University of California-Santa Barbara. Education: Ph.D. Address: 415 Mills Way, Goleta, California 93117.

TUCHMAN, MAURICE SIMON Occupation: Librarian, Book Appraiser. Education: B.A., B.H.L., M.L.S., D.A. Address: T6 Duffield Road, Auburndale, Massachusetts 02166.

TUCKER, C DELORES Occupation: National President, Federation of Democratic Women. Address: 6700 Lincoln Drive, Philadelphia, Pennsylvania 19119.

TUCKER, CAROLYN C Occupation: Public Relations. Education: B.A., De Pauw University. Address: 5329 White Marsh Lane, Indianapolis, Indiana 46226.

TUCKER, DONALD M Occupation: Music, Conductor, Director, Educator, Tenor. Education: B.A., M.A. Music Education. Address: 1615 Southeast Malden Street, Portland, Oregon 97202.

TUCKER, FLORENCE DENSLOW Occupation: Human Resource Manager, Federal Government. Education: B.M.E. Music Education, M.S. Counseling, Ed.D. Human Resource Development. Address: 4701 Kenmore Avenue, Alexandria, Virginia 22304.

TUCKER, GORDON CHARLES JR Occupation: Archaeological Consultant. Education: B.A., M.A.,

Ph.D. Address: 920 South 8th Street, Montrose, Colorado 81401.

TUFTE, MARILYN J Occupation: Professor of Biology, Department of Biology, University of Wisconsin-Platteville. Address: 980 Hillcrest Circle, Platteville, Wisconsin 53818.

TUGGLE, FRANCIS DOUGLAS Occupation: Dean, Jesse H. Jones Graduate School of Administration, Rice University. Education: Ph.D., M.S., Carnegie Mellon; S.B., Massachusetts Institute of Technology. Address: 2628 Sunset Boulevard, Houston, Texas 77005.

TULLY, WILLIAM J Occupation: President, All American Financial Services. Education: B.A., J.D., M.B.A., Ph.D. Address: 634 East Yale Street, Ontario, California 91764.

TURCO, LEWIS L Occupation: Public School Administrator (Assistant Superintendent of Schools). Education: B.S., Education Specialist, Michigan State University; M.A., University of Michigan. Address: 1612 North State, Big Rapids, Michigan 49307.

TUREL, STANLEY PETER Occupation: Safeguards Analyst. Education: B.S. Chemistry, M.B.A. Address: 8721 Wandering Trail Drive, Potomac, Maryland 20854.

TURK, RUDY H Occupation: Museum Director. Education: B.S. Education, M.A. Address: 2113 East Huntington Drive, Tempe, Arizona 85282.

TURKAT, DAVID M Occupation: Psychologist. Education: B.A., M.A., Ph.D. Address: 3221 I Post Woods Drive, Atlanta, Georgia 30339.

TURNAGE, ELMA DOLORES W Occupation: Teacher of Preschool Handicapped Children. Education: B.S., Whitworth College; M.Ed., University of Southern Mississippi. Address: Route 3, Box 76, Liberty, Mississippi 39645.

TURNBULL, WILLIAM Occupation: Architect. Education: B.A. 1956, M.F.A. 1959, Princeton University. Address: Pier 1½, The Embarcadero, San Francisco, California 94111.

TURNER, ARTHUR EDWARD Occupation: Co-Founder, Northwood Institute. Education: B.S., Alma College, 1952; M.Ed., Wayne State University, 1954; Hu.D., Colegio Americano de Quito, 1968; LL.D., Ashland College, 1968. Address: 4608 Arbor Drive, Midland, Michigan 48640.

TURNER, BARBARA BUSH Occupation: Assistant Professor of Physiology, Department of Physiology, College of Medicine, East Tennessee State University. Address: 2814 Steven Drive, Johnson City, Tennessee 37601.

TURNER, BRUCE A Occupation: Dirctor of Human Resources. Education: B.S., M.A. Address: 417 East 57th Street #12C, New York City, New York 10022.

TURNER, CARL JEANE Occupation: International Business Consultant. Education: B.S. Education, B.S.E.E., M.B.A., Ph.D. Address: GSD/GIC, 600 West John Street, Hicksville, New York 11802.

TURNER, EUGENE ANDREW Occupation: Executive. Education: Columbia Business School. Address: 8312 Sierra Drive, Muncie, Indiana 47302.

TURNER, GLADYS T Occupation: Social Worker. Education: B.A., M.S.W. Address: 1107 Lexington Avenue, Dayton, Ohio 45407.

TURNER, JESSIE JR Occupation: Assistant Director of Bands, Alabama State University. Education: B.S. Music Education, Master Music Education. Address: 50 South Lewis Street, Montgomery, Alabama 36107.

TURNER, LEAF Occupation: Theoretical Physicist.

Education: A.B., M.S., Ph.D. Address: 3112 Villa Street, Los Alamos, New Mexico 87544.

TURNER, MARGUERITE ROSE COWLES Occupation: Library Director. Education: B.A., M.L.S., M.A. Address: 202 South Gaston Street, Kings Mountain, North Carolina 28086.

TURNER, ROBERT L Occupation: General Manager. Education: B.M., M.M. Address: 2829 Avis Court, Yorktown Heights, New York 10598.

TURNER, WELD W Occupation: Industrial Psychologist. Education: B.S., M.S., Ph.D. Address: 601 East Rosery Road, Apartment 3905, Largo, Florida 33540.

TUROCZY, CHERYL L Occupation: Program Administrator. Education: B.A. Psychology, M.Ed. Human Services. Address: 1975 Sherry Lane, Twin Falls, Idaho 83301.

TUTHERLY, LOIS R Occupation: Author; Medical Transcriptionist; Assistant Professor, C.H.C.C. Address: B.S., University of Hartford; M.S., Central Connecticut State University; C.A.G.S., University of Connecticut. Address: 21 Orchard Road, Windsor, Connecticut 06095.

TUTTLE, DANIEL W JR Occupation: University Faculty. Education: A.B., M.A., Ph.D. Address: 14 Akilolo Street, Honolulu, Hawaii 96821.

TUTTLE, LINDA L Occupation: Owner, Broker, Earl Keim Accent Real Estate. Education: Real Estate Certificate. Address: 10901 200th Avenue, Tustin, Maryland 49688.

TUTTLE, WILLIAM M JR Occupation: Professor of History, University of Kansas. Education: B.A., Denison University, 1959; M.A. 1964, Ph.D. 1967, University of Wisconsin. Address: 21 Winona Avenue, Lawrence, Kansas 66044.

TWINING, SALLY SHINEW Occupation: Assistant Professor of Biochemistry. Education: B.S., M.A., Ph.D. Address: 715 Huron, Oostburg, Wisconsin 53070.

TWIST, JOSEPH A Occupation: Strategic Business Unit Manager. Education: B.S. Pharmacy, M.B.A. Address: 12 Cambridge Drive, Sparta, New Jersey 07871.

TWIST, OLIVER PHILIP Occupation: Actor, Singer, Entrepreneur, Oliver Industries Incorporated. Education: B.F.A., Georgetown University; Ph.D., Yale University; D.F.A., Notre Dame University.

TWITCHELL, HANFORD MEAD Occupation: Vice President, Printing Firm. Education: Attended Princeton University. Address: Post Office Box 1200, Huntington, Indiana 46750.

TYLER, JOANNA ARMIGER Occupation: Psychologist. Education: B.A. Psychology, M.A. Psychology, Ph.D. Human Development Psychology. Address: 9647 Green Moon Path, Columbia, Maryland 21046.

TYNER, MAX RAYMOND Occupation: Clergyman, Businessman. Education: B.L.S., University of Oklahoma. Address: 6213 North 17th Street, McAllen, Texas 78501.

TYRE, LEMUEL F Occupation: Vice President, Customer Financial Relations. Education: B.S. Accounting, 1965. Address: 59 Longwood Drive, Naugatuck, Connecticut 06770.

TYRRELL, KARINE Y Occupation: Technical Writer in Computer Systems. Education: Hon. B.A., M.A., Ph.D. Address: 9405 East Bluestem, Wichita, Kansas 67207.

TYSON, HELEN FLYNN Occupation: Budget Analyst. Education: Specialized Studies. Address: 4900 North Old Dominion Drive, Arlington, Virginia 22207.

U

UDA, ROBERT T Occupation: Chairman, President and Chief Executive Officer, Apollo Systems Technology, Inc. Education: B.S. Aerospace Engineering, M.S. Astronautics. Address: 19544 Delight Street, Canyon Country, California 91351.

UDELL, BUDD A Occupation: Chairman Department of Music, University of Florida. Education: B.Mus., M.Mus.Ed., Doctor Musical Arts in Composition. Address: 315 Southwest 84th Terrace, Gainesville, Florida 32607.

UEBEL, KATHLEEN ANN Occupation: Private Music Teacher. Education: B.A. 1978, University New Hampshire. Address: 5 Landmark Lane, Pittsgord, New York 14534.

UHLIR, G ANN Occupation: Dean. Education: B.S., M.A., Ed.D. Address: 1901 Highland Park Circle, Denton, Texas 76201.

UHLMAN, HELENE C Occupation: Environmentalist. Education: Address: 1532 West 4th Place, Hobart, Indiana 46342.

ULISSE, PETER JAMES Occupation: Associate Professor. Education: A.B., Providence College; M.A., University of Virginia. Address: 65 Rivercliff Drive, Devon, Connecticut 06460.

ULLMAN, EDWIN FISHER Occupation: Vice President. Education: B.A., Reed College, 1952; M.S. 1954, Ph.D. 1956, Harvard University. Address: 135 Selby Lane, Atherton, California 94025.

ULLMAN, PIERRE LIONI Occupation: Professor. Education: B.A., Yale University; M.A., Columbia University; Ph.D., Princeton University. Address: 749 East Beaumont Avenue, Milwaukee, Wisconsin 53217.

ULRICH, WALTER E Occupation: Deputy Commissioner. Education: LL.B., John Marshall School of Law, 1948. Address: 8 Pasadena Drive, Hamilton Township, New Jersey 08619.

UMBER, NOVALINE PIERCE Occupation: Pharmacist. Education: B.A., B.S. Address: 2204 Northfield, Coffeyville, Kansas 67337.

UMBERGER, DOROTHY R Occupation: Postmaster. Education: A.A.S. summa cum laude, Business Management. Address: Route 1, Box 29, Ceres, Virginia 24318.

UMHOLTZ, CLYDE ALLAN Occupation: Manager. Education: B.S., University of Illinois, 1969; M.S., University of Mississippi, 1972; D.B.A., Memphis State University, 1983. Address: 3580 Hanna Drive, Memphis, Tennessee 38128.

UNDERHILL, PATRICIA Occupation: Director. Education: B.A., M.A., Ph.D. Address: 371 Pedretti, Cincinnati, Ohio 45238.

UNDERWOOD, JANE H Occupation: Assistant Vice President. Education: Ph.D 1964, M.A. 1962, B.A. 1960, A.A. 1957. Address: 2228 East 4th Street, Tucson, Arizona 85719.

UNDERWOOD, ROBERT C Occupation: Justice. Education: A.B., LL.B., J.D. Address: 11 Kent Drive, Normal, Illinois 61761.

UNGAR, TAMÁS G Occupation: Head, Piano Faculty, Department of Music, T.C.U. Education: Doctor of Music; L.Mus.A. D.S.C.M., Australia. Address: 4216 Bilglade Road, Fort Worth, Texas 76109.

UNIACKE, CHARLES ALLYN Occupation: Professor of Optometry and Physiological Optics, Ferris State College, College of Optometry. Education: B.S., M.S., O.D., Ph.D. Address: 19400 Seneca Lane, Big Rapids, Michigan 49307.

UPTON, LEE Occupation: College Instructor. Education: B.A., M.F.A. Address: 123 Lansing Station Road, Lansing, New York 14882.

URBAN, ELIZABETH ANN Occupation: Administrative Director. Education: High School Graduate. Address: 1509 Highway 46 South, New Braunels, Texas 78130.

URBAN, WALTER J Occupation: Research Psychoanalyst. Education: Ph.D. Address: 6320 Drexel Avenue, Los Angeles, California 90048.

URBANOWICZ, CLARENT MARIE Occupation: Instructor. Education: B.A., M.A. Address: 2901 Cope John Paul Drive, Chicago, Illinois 60632.

URBELIS, KATHLEEN Occupation: Vice President. Education: B.A., M.B.A. Address: Post Office Box 583, Diablo, California 94528.

UREDA, KATHLEEN ANN Occupation: Professional Speaker. Education: B.A., University of California at Los Angeles. Address: 648 University Avenue, Los Altos, California 94022.

URKA, MARTIN C Occupation: Natural Resource Specialist, U.S.D.I., Bureau of Indian Affairs. Education: Graduate, Agricultural Institute, Michigan State University, 1948; Additional Studies. Address: 3854 Monte Vista Avenue, Cedar City, Utah 84720.

URRY, VERN WILLIAM Occupation: Personnel Research Psychologist. Education: Ph.D., Purdue University, 1970; M.S. 1962, B.A. 1955, University of Utah. Address: 3301 Accolade Drive, Clinton, Maryland 20735.

USPRICH, CELIA Occupation: Academic. Education: Ph.D. Address: 20-63 43 Street, Astoria, New York 11105.

UTGAARD, MERTON B Occupation: Director. Education: B.A., Valley City State College; M.M.Ed., University; Ed.D., University of Northern Colorado. Address: Highview Estates, Bottineau, North Dakota 58318.

UTHE, ELAINE F Occupation: Professor. Education: Ph.D., University of Minnesota; M.A., Catholic University of America; B.A., Marycrest College. Address: 899 Lynkaylee, Waterloo, Iowa 50701.

UTLEY, ANTHONY JOHN Occupation: President, Penn-West Securities and Company/Stock Brokerage. Education: B.A. American History, Muhlenberg College. Address: Post Office Box 2982, Park City, Utah 84060.

V

VACEK, JAMES L Occupation: Physician, Director of Cardiovascular Research, Department of Medicine/ S.G.H.M., Keesler Medical Center. Education: B.S. Mathematics, M.D. Address: 3537 Courtney Circle, Ocean Springs, Mississippi 39564.

VACHON, GLORIA I Occupation: Classical Artist. Address: 1 Park Avenue, Fairfield, New Jersey 07006.

VADLEJCH, JAN B JR Occupation: Director Southwest Europe, Quadrex Corporation. Education: M.S. Mechanical Engineering. Address: c/o Quadrex Corporation, 1700 Dell Avenue, Campbell, California 95008.

VAGNEUR, KATHRYN O Occupation: Certified Public Accountant and Management Consultant. Education: B.S. Mathematics, M.S. Agricultural Business Management. Address: 14725 Jones Road, Peyton, Colorado 80831.

VAIL, ILONA M M Occupation: Clinical Psychologist, Professional Practice. Education: Ph.D. Address: 12732 Gibralter Drive, San Diego, California 92128.

VALANCE, MARSHA JEANNE Occupation: Consultant. Education: A.B., M.L.S. Address: 861 Mercury, Geneseo, Illinois 61254.

VALDEZ, LINDA A Occupation: Executive Vice President. Education: B.S. Business Administration 1968, M.P.A. Studies, University of Colorado-Boulder; Special Graduate Program, University of California-Berkeley; Marketing Management Certificate, University of Southern California, 1978; Management Certificate, Northeastern University, 1980. Address: 6517 Honey Hill, San Antonio, Texas 78229.

VALENTINE, RALPH SCHUYLER Occupation: Research Director. Education: Ph.D., M.S., B.S. Address: 7242 Via Mimosa, San Jose, California 95135.

VALLEN, JEROME J Occupation: Dean. Education: B.S., M.Ed., Ph.D. Address: 1744 Ottawa, Las Vegas, Nevada 89110.

VALONE, KATHERINE G Occupation: Elementary School Teacher. Education: B.S.Ed., B.A., University of Chicago. Address: 10716 South La Crosse Avenue, Oak Lawn, Illinois 60453.

VAMOS, MARA SOCEANU Occupation: Professor. Education: M.A., Ph.D., Brown University. Address: 11 Fifth Avenue, New York, New York 10003.

VAN ALLEN, VERONICA ELAINE Occupation: Executive Vice President. Education: B.E. Address: 2024 Ardley Court, North Palm Beach, Florida 33408.

VAN BLARICOM, DONALD P Occupation: Chief of Police. Education: B.A., University of Washington; Master of Public Service, Seattle University; Graduate, 85th Session FBI National Academy; F.A.A. Licensed Commercial Airplane and Glider Pilot. Address: Post Office Box 1768, Bellevue, Washington 98009.

VAN BOER, BERTIL HERMAN JR Occupation: Assistant Professor of Music. Education: Ph.D., University of Uppsala; M.A., University of Oregon; B.A. University of California-Berkeley. Address: 263 South 200 East, Springville, Utah 84663.

VANCE, VICKIE LYNN Occupation: Free-Lance Journalist. Education: A.A. Business Communications. Address: 2041 U.S. 31 North, Petoskey, Michigan 49770.

VANDE KEMP, HENDRIKA Occupation: Clinical Psychologist, Academic. Education: B.A., M.S., Ph.D. Address: 1671½ Loma Vista, Pasadena, California 91104.

VAN DEN HAAG, ERNEST Occupation: Professor, Jurisprudence and Public Policy, Fordham University. Education: M.A., State University of Iowa; Ph.D., New York University. Address: 118 West 79th Street, New York, New York 10024.

VANDERKAMP, JOHN Occupation: Dean and Professor, College of Social Science, University of Guelph. Education: B.Ec.Sc., M.B.A., Ph.D. Address: 27 Lynwood Place, Guelph, Ontario, Canada.

VANDERLINDE, ALBERT Occupation: Dean, School of Vocational Studies, Alfred State College. Education: B.S., M.A., Ph.D. Address: 52 Hills Street, Wellsville, New York 14895.

VanDERSAL, WILLIAM R Occupation: Writer. Education: B.A., Reed College; M.S., Ph.D., University of Pittsburgh. Address: 8101 Greenspring Avenue, Baltimore, Maryland 21208.

VANDERWERFF, LYLE LLOYD Occupation: Professor of Religion, Northwestern College; Minister. Education: B.A., Hope College, 1956; M.Div., Western Seminary, 1959; M.Th., Princeton Seminary, 1961; Ph.D., University of Edinburgh, 1968. Address: 506 Zuider Zee Drive, Orange City, Iowa 51041.

VAN DER WYK, JACK A Occupation: Percussionist, Oakland Symphony; Percussion Teacher, Music and Arts Institute of San Francisco, Holy Names College. Education: B.A., University of Southern California. Address: 6857 Armour Drive, Oakland, California 94611.

VAN DE WATER, JOHN RANDOLPH Occupation: Attorney at Law, Management Consultant, Long Beach, California. Education: Bachelor of Arts, Doctor of Law. Address: 2062 Mount Shasta Drive, San Pedro, California 90732.

VanDUYN, ROBERT GERALD Occupation: Consultant on Education Development and Management; Partner, Private Business. Education: B.A. 1934, M.A. 1939, Ball State University; Graduate Studies, Harvard University, Columbia University; Ph.D., University of Chicago, 1953; Attended Danish Folk School, Copenhagen. Address: 21 West 88th Street, New York, New York 10024.

VAN DYKE, MARC DAVID Occupation: Office Manager. Education: B.S. Education. Address: 3670 South Walnut Street Road, Bloomington, Indiana 47401.

VAN DYKE, WILLIAM ADOLPHUS JR Occupation: Aerospace Engineer. Education: B.S. Mathematics/Physics, M.E.A. Engineering Administration. Address: 2991 Summit Drive, Ijamsville, Maryland 21754.

VANEK, GARY M Occupation: Liquor Control Commissioner. Education: B.A., M.A. Address: 419 Englewood, Royal Oak, Michigan 48073.

VANESS, MARGARET H Occupation: Artist, Consultant, Instructor. Education: Master's Degree. Address: 17128 2nd Avenue, Southwest, Seattle, Washington 98166.

VAN HORSSEN, RONALD DARRELL Occupation: President, Mobile Technology, Los Angeles, California. Education: Bachelor of Science honors Chemical Engineering, South Dakota School of Mines and Technology, 1973; Master of Science Industrial Administration, Carnegie-Mellon University, 1977. Address: 2716 Ocean Park Boulevard, Suite 3006, Santa Monica, California 90405.

VAN HOUTEN, GENE STEVEN Occupation: Manager of Industrial Engineering, Products Group Operations, Sunkist Growers, Inc. Education: A.S. Electronics Research and Design, A.A. Industrial Supervision, Riverside City College. Address: 5042 Red

Bluff Road, Riverside, California 92503.

VANICEK, PETR Occupation: Professor of Geology, University of New Brunswick. Education: Dipl. Ing. Geodesy, Ph.D. Mathematics Physics. Address: 180 Charing Crescent, Fredericton, Northeast, Canada.

VAN IMPE, JACK LEO Occupation: National Television Minister. Education: Th.D., D.D., Th.D., D.Lit., LL.D., D.S.T., Ph.D., D.R.E., D.S.Lit. Address: Post Office Box J, Royal Oak, Michigan 48068.

VAN KIRK, DONALD JOHN Occupation: Professional Forensic Engineer. Education: B.S., B.S.E.E., M.S.E.M., M.B.A. Address: 23917 Rockford, Dearborn, Michigan 48124.

VANMORGAN, JACQUE GRACE Occupation: Pastorial Minister to the Handicapped, Roman Catholic Arch-Diocese of Los Angeles; Substitute Teacher. Education: B.S., M.A., Doctorate in Theology (in progress). Address: 2626 South Manhattan Place, #207, Los Angeles, California 90018.

vanNOORDAN, KATHERINE Occupation: Sculptor, Teacher, Personnel Consultant. Education: B.F.A., Syracuse University. Address: 420 Pilgrim Lane, Stratord, Connecticut 06497.

VAN OOSBREE, CHARLYNE NELSON Occupation: Librarian. Education: B.A. English, M.A. Library Science. Address: 339 East Market, Warrensburg, Missouri 64093.

VAN SCHAACK, ERIC Occupation: Professor and Chairman, Fine Arts Department, Colgate University. Education: A.B., Dartmouth College, 1953; Ph.D., Columbia University, 1969. Address: 25 Madison Street, Hamilton, New York 13346.

VAN SCHAIK, PETER H Occupation: Associate Deputy Administrator, U.S.D.A.-A.R.S.-Western Region. Education: B.S.A., M.S.A., Ph.D. Address: 414 East Fairmont Avenue, Fresno, California 93704.

VAN SCHILFGAARDE, JAN Occupation: Director, Rocky Mountain Area, Agricultural Research Service. Education: B.S. 1949, M.S. 1950, Ph.D. 1954, Iowa State University, Agricultural Engineering and Soil Physics. Address: 12075 Glenwood Avenue, Colton, California 92324.

VAN VELDHUIZEN, PHILIP A Occupation: Professor. Education: B.S., M.S. Address: Post Office 81577, Fairbanks, Arkansas 99708.

VAN VELZER, VERNA J Occupation: Research Librarian. Education: B.S. Library Science, M.L.S. Address: 404B Laguna Way, Palo Alto, California 94306.

VAN WEEZENDONK, FRANKLIN MICHAEL Occupation: Corporate Vice President and General Manager, Lighting Systems. Education: B.A. Marketing, Doctorate Economics, Doctorate Law. Address: 639 Twin Rivers Drive, North East Windsor, New Jersey 08520.

VÁRGAS, ARMANDO JR Occupation: Recreation Coordinator. Education: B.A. 1976, M.P.A. 1983. Address: 1520 West Windsor, Tucson, Arizona 85705.

VARGHESE, PHILIP LESLIE Occupation: Assistant Professor. Education: B.Tech., M.S., Ph.D. Address: University of Texas at Austin, Department of Mechanical Engineering, Austin, Texas 78712.

VARMA, MAN MOHAN Occupation: Scientist. Education: Ph.D. Address: 704 Chichester Lane, Silver Springs, Maryland 20906.

VASIS, ANTHONY CHARLES Occupation: Associate Professor. Education: B.S., M.S., M.Ed. Address: 6083 North Albany, Chicago, Illinois 60659.

VASTBINDER, EARL EDWARD Occupation: Chairman, Department of Allied Health, Trevecca Nazarene College. Education: B.S., M.D., M.Sc. Address: 889 Lakemont Drive, Nashville, Tennessee 37220.

VAUDRIN, DONNA M Occupation: Supervisor. Education: Ed.D. 1983, M.A. 1970, B.S. 1968. Address: 14217 12th Avenue, Southwest, Seattle, Washington 98166.

VAUGHN, HOWARD BEECHER Occupation: Industrial Arts Teacher. Education: B.Ed., University of Miami; M.A., University Western Kentucky. Address: 5815 Southwest 19th Street, Miami, Florida 33155.

VAUGHN, JACQUELINE B Occupation: President, Chicago Teachers Union, Local #1. Education: B.E. Kindergarten Primary, 1956; M.E. Special Eduction, E.M.H., 1965. Address: 1169 South Plymouth Court, Chicago, Illinois 60605.

VAUGHN, PEARL HENDERSON Occupation: Professor. Education: B.S., M.S. Address: 6102 Emery Drive, Chattanooga, Tennessee 37421.

VAUGHN, RICHARD C Occupation: Professor of Industrial Engineering, Iowa State University. Education: B.A., M.I.E. Address: 1222 Ridgewood Avenue, Ames, Iowa 50010.

VAUGHN, RUTH WOOD Occupation: Professional Author/Playwright. Education: B.A., M.A., Ph.D. Address: Box 1565, Bethany, Oklahoma 73008.

VEATCH, ELIZABETH WILSON Occupation: Fellowship Officer, I.A.F. Education: B.A., Indiana University; M.S.F.S., Georgetown University. Address: 6711 D Washington Boulevard, Arlington, Virginia 22213.

VECCHIO, ROBERT P Occupation: Associate Professor. Education: B.S., M.A., Ph.D. Address: 52173 Brookview, South Bend, Indiana 46556.

VEGA, JOSE GUADALUPE Occupation: Certified Psychologist. Education: B.A., Pan American University, 1975; M.A. 1976, Ph.D. 1979, University of Denver. Address: 4239 Blueflax, Pueblo, Colorado 81001.

VEGA, MIQUEL Occupation: Social Worker, Veterans Administration Center. Education: Bachelor of Social Science, Master Social Work, Accredited Certified Social Worker (A.C.S.W.). Address: 220 Gandara Avenue, Rio Piedras, Puerto Rico 00925.

VEGA, ROY DAVID Occupation: Director of Public Safety. Education: B.A. Political Science, University of Santa Clara. Address: 433 Meadow Drive (Post Office Box 4159), Pagosa, Colorado 81157.

VELARDO, JOSEPH THOMAS Occupation: Molecular Biologist/Endocrinologist; Medical Curriculum Specialist and Writer. Education: A.B., University North Colorado; S.M., Miami University; Ph.D., Harvard University. Address: Southwest Corner Wilson Road and Cherry Lane, Old Grove East, Lombard, Illinois 60148.

VELLA, RUTH A Occupation: Real Estate Broker. Education: Certified Residential Broker. Address: 23 Tenby Chase Drive, Newark, Delaware 19711.

VELZY, DAVID WALTER Occupation: Supervisor. Education: B.S., Ohio State University, 1975. Address: 162 West Weber Road, Columbus, Ohio 43202.

VENDITTO, JAMES JOSEPH Occupation: Division Engineer. Education: B.S., University of Oklahoma. Address: 2211 Live Oak, Portland, Texas 78374.

VÉR, ISTVÁN L Occupation: Principal Consultant. Education: Ph.D., M.S., B.S. Address: 10 Glen Road, Lexington, Massachusetts 02173.

VERBRUGGE, CALVIN J Occupation: Research Chemist. Education: B.A., Calvin College. Ph.D., Purdue University. Address: 1031 Ohio Street, Racine, Wisconsin 53405.

VERDUIN, JOHN RICHARD JR Occupation: Professor of Education, Department of Educational Leadership, Southern Illinois University-Carbondale. Education: B.S., University of Albuquerque; M.A., Ph.D., Michigan State University. Address: 107 North Lark Lane, Carbondale, Illinois 62901.

VER EECKE, WILFRIED Occupation: Professor. Education: License, Ph.D., Leuven; M.A., Georgetown University. Address: 4100 Nebraske Avenue, N.W., Washington, D.C. 20016.

VERGASON, GLENN A Occupation: Professor. Education: M.Ed., Ed.D. Address: 4412 Mink Livsey Road, Lithonia, Georgia 30058.

VERNICE, MARY MAKOVIC Occupation: Member of Religious Order, Professor of Education, Curriculum Consultant. Education: B.S.Ed., M.A., Ph.D. Address: 4545 College Road, Cleveland, Ohio 44121.

VERNON, CAROLE SAXTON Occupation: Special Education Teacher. Education: B.S., M.S. Address: 1287 West Avenue, Buffalo, New York 14213.

VERZINO, WILLIAM JOHN JR Occupation: Assistant Professor. Education: B.S., M.S., Ph.D. Address: 1840 Camino Mora, Los Alamos, New Mexico 87544.

VESCE, THOMAS EUGENE Occupation: Full Professor Foreign Languages, Mercy College. Education: B.A. cum laude, Manhattan College; M.A., Ph.D., Fordham University; M.A., Western Connecticut State University. Address: 98 Hidden Hollow Lane, Millwood, New York 10546.

VESSENES, PETER Occupation: Senior Marketing Executive. Education: B.A. Communications. Address: 14 Apple Hill Circle, Madison, Wisconsin 53717.

VEST, H GRANT JR Occupation: Professor and Head. Education: B.S., M.S., Ph.D. Address: Route 5, Box 1603, College Station, Texas 77840.

VETTER, RICHARD J Occupation: Radiation Physics, Mayo Clinic. Education: B.S. 1965, M.S. 1967, Ph.D. 1969. Address: 523 17th Street Southwest, Rochester, Minnesota 55902.

VIA, SHEREE Occupation: Medical Social Worker. Education: B.A. Address: 331 Poplar Street, Apartment E-1, Danville, Virginia 24541.

VICIAN, ELIZABETH OVERGAARD Occupation: Psychologist. Education: Doctor of Philosophy, Master of Arts, Bachelor of Arts. Address: 3718 Redwood Circle, Palo Alto, California 94306.

VIDA, LOUISA KRAMER Occupation: Personnel Administrator. Education: B.A., Marymount Manhattan College, 1973; M.A., Manhattan College, 1976; C.A.S. 1982, P.D 1982, Ed.D. (in progress), Hofstra University. Address: 19 Lilac Drive, Syosset, New York 11791.

VIDAILLET, CARIDAD MERCEDES Occupation: Law Student. Education: B.A., University of Oklahoma. Address: 919 Hickory Lane, Ardmore, Oklahoma 73401.

VIDOSIC, JOSEPH PAUL Occupation: Regents Professor. Education: M.E., M.S., Stevens Institute of Technology; Ph.D., Purdue University. Address: Rural Delivery 1, Box 224, Cooperstown, New York 13326.

VIERA, GRELA Occupation: Satellite Office Manager. Education: A.A. Miami Dade Community College; Postgraduate, University of Florida, Florida International University. Address: 4409 Berkshire Manor Drive, #1323, Tampa, Florida 33614.

VIERAS, FRANK Occupation: Nuclear Medicine Physician. Education: M.D. Address: Malcolm Grow U.S.A.F. Medical Center, Andrews, A.F.B., D.C. 20331.

VIGLIANTE, SZYDLOWSKI MARY F Occupation: Novelist. Education: B.A., State University of New York. Address: 92 B Columbia Turnpike, Rensselaer, New York 12144.

VILARDI, AGNES FRANCINE Occupation: Real Estate Broker. Education: Certified Dental Assistant and Real Estate Broker. Address: 18982 Vila Terrace, Yorba Linda, California 92686.

VILLARREAL, FERNANDO MARIN Occupation: Attorney. Education: J.D., B.B.A. Address: 2731 Old Robinson Road, Waco, Texas 76706.

VILLARREAL, HERMES Occupation: Bank Teller. Education: B.B.A. Address: 3000 Norma Avenue, McAllen, Texas 78501.

VILLHARD, VICTOR J Occupation: Captain, United States Air Force; Aeronautical Engineer. Education: B.S., Parks College, 1979; M.S., A.F.I.T., 1980. Address: 4743 Daybreak Circle S., Colorado Springs, Colorado 80917.

VINCENT, CLARE Occupation: Museum Curator. Education: A.B., College of William and Mary; M.A., New York University. Address: 326 East 85th Street, New York, New York 10028.

VINKOVETSKY, YAKOV A (deceased) Occupation: Former Artist, Geologist, Philosopher. Education: Ph.D. Geology. Address: 4331 Wigton, Houston, Texas 77096.

VIRGIL, ROBERT C Occupation: Professional Counselor. Education: B.A., M.S. Address: 209 Moffat Street, Brooklyn, New York 11207.

VIRGO, JULIE CARROLL Occupation: Executive Director. Education: M.B.A. 1983, Ph.D. 1974, M.A. 1964, University of Chicago; A.L.A.A. Librarianship. Address: 60 East Scott Street, Chicago, Illinois 60610.

VIRK, MUHAMMAD YAQUB Occupation: Management Specialist. Education: B.A., M.A., Ph.D., M.B.A. Address: Post Office Box 1022, Rolla, North Dakota 58367.

VISCO, SUSAN J Occupation: Psychologist. Education: Ph.D. Address: 438 Essex Street, Saugus, Massachusetts 01906.

VISSER, AUDRAE EUGENIE Occupation: English Teacher. Education: M.A., University of Denver; B.S., South Dakota State University. Address: Rural Route 1 Box 108 A, Elkton, South Dakota 57026.

VITALIANO, DONALD F Occupation: Associate Professor. Education: B.B.A. 1963, Ph.D. 1969, City University of New York. Address: 1600 Jacob Street, Troy, New York 12180.

VITE, BRADLEY S Occupation: Fine Arts Dealer. Education: B.L.S., Hillsdale University. Address: 1838 Greenleaf, Elhart, Indiana 46514.

VIVANTE, ARTURO Occupation: Writer. Education: B.A., M.D. Address: Box 817, Wellfleet, Massachusetts 02667.

VOEGE, HERBERT WALTER Occupation: Professor of Accounting and Finance, School of Business, Ferris State College. Education: B.Sc. summa cum laude, M.B.A., Ph.D, C.P.A., C.C.A. Address: 12891 Sixteen Mile Road, Rodney, Michigan 49342.

VOEGE, JANIS MACKEY Occupation: University Professor of Home Economics, Central Michigan University. Education: B.S., M.A., Ph.D. Address: 12891 Sixteen Mile Road, Rodney, Michigan 49342

VOELCKER, HUNCE Occupation: Poet. Education: A.B., Villanova University. Address: Box 11 Duncans Mills, California 95430.

VOGAN, SARA Occupation: Novelist. Education:

Stegner Writing Fellowship, Stanford University, 1979-80; M.F.A. Creative Writing, University of Iowa, 1978; Master's Work in English, West Virginia University, 1971-73; B.S. Journalism, West Virginia University, 1969. Address: 2559 29th Avenue, San Francisco, California 94116.

VOGEL, STEVE GREGORY Occupation: Group Controller. Education: B.A., M.B.A., Lehigh University; C.P.A. Address: 543 Adams Lane, Delaware, Ohio 43015.

VOGELPOOL, ANTHONY P Occupation: Manufacturing Company Executive. Education: B.S., Boston University, 1964; Postgraduate, Northeastern University, 1965. Address: 7896 Red Fox Drive, Manlius, New York 13104.

VOGELS, WALTER ALFONS Occupation: Professor. Education: Ph.D., S.T.D., S.S.L. Address: 252 Argyle Avenue, Ottawa, Ontario, Canada K2P 189.

VOGELSANG, BARBARA ANN Occupation: Assistant Professor. Education: M.S. Business Education. Address: 211 Dillon, Mankato, Minnesota 56001.

VOGET, FRED W Occupation: Retired Professor. Education: B.A., University of Oregon, 1936; Ph.D., Yale University, 1948. Address: 106 Osage Drive, Post Office Box 87, Edwardsville, Illinois 62025.

VOLCKHAUSEN, WILLIAM A Occupation: Executive Vice President. Education: B.A., Princeton University; M.A., University of California-Berkeley; J.D., Harvard University. Address: 262 President Street, Brooklyn, New York 11231.

VOLKERT, DORIS CAMPBELL Occupation: Professor. Education: B.S., Pennsylvania State University; M.S., University of Pittsburgh. Address: 2031 New Bedford Road, Spring Lake Heights, New Jersey 07762.

VOLKHARDT, JOHN MALCOLM Occupation: Consultant. Education: A.B., Brown University. Address: 1530 Palisade Avenue, Fort Lee, New Jersey 07024.

VOLKMAR, LLOYD BAKER Occupation: Clergyman. Education: B.A., B.D., Th.M., Ph.D. Address: 3205 Reno Road, Fort Worth, Texas 76116.

VOLPÉ, ROBERT Occupation: Professor. Education: M.D., F.R.C.P., F.A.C.P. Address: 3 Daleberry Place, Don Mills, Ontario M3B 2A5 Canada.

VOLZ, MICHAEL G Occupation: Public Health Chemist. Education: B.S., Ph.D. Address: 1130 Brighton Avenue, Albany, California 97406.

VON MAKNASSY, HARRO Occupation: Executive. Education: B.A., Rand Graduate Institute for Policy Studies; M.B.A., Wuerzburg. Address: 745 Fifth Avenue, New York, New York 10151.

VON RHEINWALD EVA Occupation: Doctor of Medicine. Education: B.A., M.A., Ph.D. Address: 6908 D Round Tree Drive, Las Vegas, Nevada 89128.

VORIES, EUGENE C Occupation: President, Top Line Supply Company. Education: Mesa College, Xavier University. Address: Post Office Box 2201, Grand Junction, Colorado 81502.

VOYLES, JIMMY P Occupation: Vice President. Education: A.A., B.A., M.A., Ph.D. Address: Post Office Box 268, Ailey, Georgia 30410.

VRAJICH, NICK Occupation: College Professor. Education: B.V.E., M.A., Ph.D. Address: 745 Evans Road, San Luis Obispo, California 93401.

VREEMAN, JERRY H Occupation: Radio and Television Broadcaster, Minister. Education: B.A., M.Div., Th.M. Address: 3664 Washington, Lansing, Illinois 60438.

VRSIC, PAVLA GABRIEL FRANK Occupation: Student. Education: B.S., Brigham Young University. Address: Jarvis Christian College, Hawkins, Texas 75765.

VUCHIC, VUKAN R Occupation: University Professor. Education: Dipl. Ing., Belgrade University; M.Eng., Ph.D., University of California at Berkeley. Address: 222 Moylan Avenue, Moylan, Pennsylvania 19065.

W

WACHTER, KENNETH W Occupation: Asociate Professor, Demography and Statistics. Education: B.A. Harvard University, 1964; M.A., Oxford, 1971; Ph.D., Cambridge, 1974. Address: Box 270, The Sea Ranch, California 25497.

WADDINGTON, BETTE HOPE Occupation: Violinist. Education: A.B., University of California. Address: 2800 Olive Street, St. Louis, Missouri 63103.

WADDOUPS, RAY O Occupation: Engineer. Education: Ph.D. Address: 1510 East Gable, Mesa, Arizona 85204.

WADE, BEN F Occupation: Provost of the College. Education: B.A., M.Div., St.M., M.S., Ph.D. Address: 112 West College Street, Bridgewater, Virginia 22812.

WADE, JULIA HOWARD Occupation: Interior Designer. Education: B.A. Address: 412 Baxter Lane, San Augustine, Texas 75972.

WADE, PAULINE L Occupation: Owner, Antique and Craft Shop. Education: B.S. Home Economics Education. Address: 17 Marlin Road, South Harwich, Massachusetts 02661.

WAGNER, ANDREW JAMES Occupation: Meteorologist. Education: B.A., Wesleyan University, 1956; M.S., Massachusetts Institute of Technology, 1958. Address: 7007 Beverly Lane, Springfield, Virginia 22150.

WAGNER, EDWIN E Occupation: Professor of Psychology, University of Akron. Education: B.A., M.A., Ph.D. Address: 76 North Revere Road, Akron, Ohio 44313.

WAGNER, GREGORY ALAN Occupation: Licensed Psychologist. Education: B.A., M.A., Ph.D. Address: 17302 Park Avenue, Sonoma, California 95476.

WAGNER, LOIS HYRT (CROW) Occupation: (Retired) Investor, Writer, Religious Scientific Study Group Leader, Director. Education: B.Ed. 1933, M.Ed. 1952, University of California-Los Angeles; General Secondary Credential, University of Redlands; Graduate, Marriage Counselling, Institute of Family Relations; Ordained Minister. Address: 455 East Ocean Boulevard, Apartment 316, Long Beach, California 90802.

WAGNER, ROMAN FRANK Occupation: Chartered Financial Consultant, C.L.U., C.P.C.U. Education: B.S. Business Administration, M.S. Financial Services. Address: 1120 A Aspen Court, Kohler, Wisconsin 53044.

WAGNER, WILLIAM STUART JR Occupation: Vice President, Sales. Education: B.S. Business Management and Administration. Address: Rural Route 2, Box 219A, Chariton, Iowa 50049.

WAIHEE, JOHN Occupation: Lieutenant Governor. Education: Graduate, Hawaiian Mission Academy; Graduate, Andrews University; Additional Studies, Central Michigan University; Law Degree, University of Hawaii Law School.

WAITE, THOMAS J Occupation: Director of Communications. Education: B.A. English. Address: 54 Carleton Street, Newton, Massachusetts 02158.

WAKIM, JUDITH H Occupation: Professor and Chairperson, Department of Nursing, Austin Peay State University. Education: B.S.N., M.S.N., Ed.D. Address: 1743 Cedarcroft, Clarksville, Tennessee 37043.

WAKOSKI, DIANE Occupation: Writer in Residence. Education: B.A. English, University of California, 1960. Address: 607 Division, East Lansing, Michigan 48823.

WALBROEHL, GORDON S Occupation: Physician. Education: A.B., M.D. Address: 3186 Suburban Drive, Dayton, Ohio 43432.

WALCHARS, JOHN Occupation: Writer, Lecturer, Counsellor. Education: M.A. Liberal Arts, Innsbruck University. Address: Campion Center, Weston, Massachusetts 02193.

WALCOTT, CYNTHIA ANN Occupation: Product Manager. Education: R.N., New England Baptist Hospital School of Nursing. Address: 72 Prescott Drive, Chelmsford, Massachusetts 01863.

WALCOTT, OLIVER G Occupation: Hospital Administrator. Education: B.A. Address: 545 South 9th Avenue, Mount Vernon, New York 10550.

WALDERA, GERALD JOSEPH Occupation: College Professor, Chairperson Social and Behavioral Science Division, Dickinson State College; North Dakota State Senator. Education: B.S., M.S., North Dakota State University; Postgraduate Studies, University of Denver. Address: 942 9th Avenue West, Dickinson, North Dakota 58601.

WALDRON, ACIE CHANDLER Occupation: Professor, Ohio State University; Coordinator, North Central Region Pesticide Impact Assessment Program. Education: B.S., Brigham Young University, 1957; M.S. 1959, Ph.D. 1961, The Ohio State University. Address: 4220 Lyon Drive, Columbus, Ohio 43220.

WOLFERS, ELSIE ELIZABETH Occupation: Author, Artist, Lecturer. Education: Attended University of Pittsburgh, Carnegie Institute. Address: 97 Wexley Way, San Carlos, California 94070.

WALKER, ANGUS LIGHTFOOT Occupation: Chairman, Executive Committee. Education: Engineering Degree. Address: 784 Park Avenue, New York, New York 10021.

WALKER, CAROLYN KAY Occupation: Artist. Education: B.S. Address: 643 Chestnut Street, Colorado City, Texas 79512.

WALKER, CHARLOTTE E Occupation: Coordinator Special Services, Mental Health. Education: M.A., University of Chicago. Address: 25 Skyland Drive, Greenville, South Carolina 29607.

WALKER, DONALD E Occupation: District Superintendent, College District. Education: Ph.D., M.TH., A.B. Address: 7276 Caminito Carlotta, San Diego, California 92120.

WALKER, DONNA L Occupation: Assistant Professor. Education: B.A., M.A. Ed.D. Address: 2416 South 13th #116, Temple, Texas 76501.

WALKER, DONNA RAE (BOYD) Occupation: Co-Owner, Tax and Accounting Business. Address: 4804 Burning Tree Drive, Baytown, Texas 77521.

WALKER, HENRY A JR Occupation: Chairman of the Board, Amfac, Inc. Education: Attended Harvard University; Columbia University, School of Business. Address: Post Office Box 3230, Honolulu, Hawaii 96801.

WALKER, JANET RICHARDSON Occupation: Human Services Administrator. Education: B.A., University of Illinois; M.A., University of Evansville. Address: 126 West North Street, Grayville, Illinois 62844.

WALKER, JESSE MARSHALL Occupation: Director of Associational Missions. Education: A.B., Th.M., D.Min. Address: Route 1, #3 Staff Village, Dublin, Virginia 24084.

WALKER, KEITH ALLEN Occupation: Vice President Research. Education: B.A., College of Wooster, 1970; Ph.D., Yale University, 1940. Address: 8233 Sunbonnet, Fair Oaks, California 95628.

WALKER, LINDA KATHRYN Occupation: Rehabilitation Counselor, Production Foreman. Education: B.S. Vocational Rehabilitation. Address: 1109 Dorothy Lane, Billings, Montana 59015.

WALKER, LORNA ANN Occupation: Nutritional Consultant. Education: B.S., M.T., M.A. Address: 11091 Northwest 21st Court, Sunrise, Florida 33322.

WALKER, OLYN McCLINTON Occupation: Thoracic, Cardiovascular Surgeon. Education: B.S., M.D. Address: 4568 South Laredo Street, Aurora, Colorado 80015.

WALKER, ROBERTA RUTH Occupation: Associate Professor Emeritus. Education: B.A., M.A. Address: 224 Paso Noble, El Paso, Texas 79912.

WALKER, U OWEN Occupation: Engineer. Education: Bachelor of Engineering, Yale University. Address: Post Office Box 1224, Albuquerque, New Mexico 87103.

WALKER, WILLIAM OLIVER JR Occupation: Professor of Religion and Chairperson Department of Religion, Trinity University. Education: B.A., Austin College; M.Div., Austin Presbyterian Theological Seminary; M.A., University of Texas. Address: 315 Cloverleaf Avenue, San Antonio, Texas 78284.

WALL, CELIA JO Occupation: Librarian. Education: B.A., M.S., M.A. Address: 1908A Westwood Drive, Murray, Kentucky 42071.

WALL, GENEVIEVE Occupation: Attorney. Education: J.D. Address: 24232 Barquero Drive, Mission Viejo, California 92691.

WALL, ISABELLE LOUISE WOOD Occupation: Wall Clergywoman, Author. Education: Attended Appalachian State Teachers College, Draughn's Business College, Lee College, Franklin Institute, High Point College. Address: 3231 High Point Road, Winston-Salem, North Carolina 27107.

WALL, VIRGINIA B Occupation: English Teacher, Chillicothe High School. Education: B.S. Education, Master's Degree Education. Address: 1707 Jackson, Chillicothe, Missouri 64601.

WALLACE, CAROL CONLEY Occupation: Graduate Nurse. Education: A.A. Nursing. Address: Route 2, Box 16-K, Sharon, Tennessee 38255.

WALLACE, DEBORAH SUE Occupation: Associate Professor. Education: B.S.Ed., M.A., Ph.D. Address: 2727 Godby Road, College Park, Georgia 30349.

WALLACE, DON JR Occupation: Professor of Law. Education: B.A., Yale University, 1953; LL.B., Harvard University, 1957. Address: 2800 35th Street, Northwest, Washington, D.C. 20007.

WALLACE, GARY ROE Occupation: Chemical Officer, U.S. Army. Education: B.S. Animal Science, Tarleton State University, 1977. Address: Bar W Ranch Box 180, Bluff Dale, Texs 76433.

WALLACE, JENNIFER DIANNE Occupation: Consultant. Education: B.A., Specialist Degree. Address: 522 North Pine, Lansing, Michigan 48933.

WALLACE, JOEL K Occupation: Hospital Chaplain. Education: B.A., M.Div., D.Min. Address: 1148 Park Place, West Carrollton, Ohio 45449.

WALLACE, MARTHA REDFIELD Occupation: President, Redfield Associates. Education: B.A., M.A. Address: 435 East 52, New York, New York 10022.

WALLACE, ROBERT BRUCE Occupation: Professor of Psychology and Biology. Education: B.A., M.A., Ph.D. Address: 48 Avonwood Road, Avon, Connecticut 06117.

WALLACE, ROBERT E Occupation: Chief Scientist, Office of Earthquakes, Volcanoes and Engineering, U.S. Geological Survey. Education: B.S.,

Northwestern University; M.S., Ph.D., California Institute of Tehchnology. Address: 240 Cervantes Road, Portola Valley, California 94025.

WALLACE, SHARON A Occupation: Dean, School of Home Economics. Education: B.S., M.S., Ph.D. Address: 70 Redstone, Reno, Nevada 89512.

WALLACE, SHARON LORETTA Occupation: Educational Specialist. Education: B.S., M.A. Address: 5406 Gantry Drive, Montgomery, Alabama 36108.

WALLACE, SONJA YVETTE Occupation: Student. Address: 412 Avenue, Talladega, Alabama 35160.

WALLBANK, STANLEY T Occupation: Attorney-at-Law. Education: A.B. 1917, LL.B. 1981, University of Colorado. Address: 2800 South University Boulevard #131, Denver, Colorado 80210.

WALLER, JERRY J Occupation: Agronomist. Education: B.S., M.S. Address: 2103 Pamela, Temple, Texas 76502.

WALLIS, BEN A JR Occupation: Attorney, Rancher. Education: B.B.A., J.D., University of Texas. Address: 13623 Inwood Park, San Antonio, Texas 78216.

WALLS, BETTY L WEBB Occupation: Psychologist. Education: R.N., B.A., M.A., Ph.D. Address: 8019 Kenwood, Kansas City, Missouri 64131.

WALLS, FRANCINE ELIZABETH Occupation: Library Director. Education: M.A. English, Master of Librarianship. Address: 3305 Vittoria Way #25, Newberg, Oregon 97132.

WALLS, JOSEPH KYLE Occupation: Executive Director, Arts and Humanities Council. Education: B.F.A., M.F.A. Address: Post Office Box 2604, Baton Rouge, Louisiana 70821.

WALSH, HOWARD BENJAMIN Occupation: Chairman, Private Industry Council. Education: University of Maryland, U.S. Navy Postgraduate School, Claremont Graduate School. Address: 48 Alston Place, Santa Barbara, California 93108.

WALSH, SARA ELIZABETH Occupation: Assistant Professor, University of Houston. Education: B.S., M.S. Address: 9023 Gaylord #102, Houston, Texas 77024.

WALTER, JOHN P Occupation: Professor, Computer Information Systems. Address: 1240 Seventeenth Street, Hermosa Beach, California 90254.

WALTER, JOSEPH D Occupation: Engineer, Scientist/Research Director. Education: B.S., M.S., Ph.D. Address: 343 Barnstable Road, Akron, Ohio 44313.

WALTER, NOLA J Occupation: Real Estate Executive. Address: 825 Barland Street, Eau Claire, Wisconsin 54701.

WALTERS, DOROTHY M (DOTTIE) Occupation: Publisher, Author, Speaker, News/Magazine Editor, Certified Speaking Professional, President and Founder of 4 Corporations. Education: High School Diploma. Address: 18825 Hicrest Road, Glendora, California 91740.

WALTERS, SUMNER ELIOT Occupation: Judge, Van Wert County Common Pleas Court. Education: A.B. 1971, J.D. 1974, Ohio Northern University. Address: Rural Route 5, Box 140, Van Wert, Ohio 45891.

WALTERS, SUMNER J Occupation: Municipal Judge. Education: J.D. Address: Route 2, Box 40, Ohio City, Ohio 45874.

WALTON, CAROL A (KARA) Occupation: Self-Employed, Social Science Researcher, Consultant. Education: Ph.D., University of California-Berkeley. Address: 242 West 123, New York, New York 10027.

WALTON, DIANA CLAIRE Occupation: Security/Safety Consultant; Security Manager. Education: B.A. Political Science, B. Police Science and Administration. Address: 6030 Manor Place, Everett, Washington 98203.

WALTON, JAMES STEPHEN Occupation: Research Scientist, Biomedical Science Department, GM Research Laboratories. Address: 692 Bolinger, Rochester, Michigan 48063.

WALTON, ORTIZ MONTAIGNE Occupation: Sociologist, Musician. Education: B.S., M.A., Ph.D. Address: 1129 Bancroft Way, Berkeley, California 94702.

WALTZ, KENNETH N Occupation: Ford Professor of Political Science. Education: A.B., M.A., Ph.D. Address: 70 Oak Ridge, Berkeley, California 94705.

WALTZ, THOMAS WILLIAM Occupation: Economist. Education: B.S., Ph.D., Northwestern University. Address: 2438 39th Place Northwest, Washington, D.C. 20007.

WALTZER, HERBERT Occupation: Professor of Political Science, Miami University (Ohio); Author; Consultant. Education: B.A. 1951, M.A. 1954, Ph.D. 1959, New York University. Address: 3 Bull Run Drive, Oxford, Ohio 45056.

WALZER, HAROLD LAURENCE Occupation: Computer Company Executive. Address: 5008 East Thomas Road #609, Phoenix, Arizona 85018.

WANG, CHIA PING Occupation: Research Physicist, Professor. Education: B.Sc., M.Sc., Ph.D. Address: 28 Hallett Hill Road, Weston, Massachusetts 02193.

WANG, GEORGE CHUNG Occupation: Professor, Editor. Education: B.S., M.A., M.B.A., Ph.D. Address: 1609 Via Zurita Poles Verdes Estate, California 90274.

WANG, JOSEPH S Occupation: Professor of New Testament. Education: B.S., B.D., Th.M., Ph.D. Address: 216 South Lexington Avenue, Wilmore, Kentucky 40390.

WANG, LAWRENCE KONGPU Occupation: Research Director. Education: B.S. 1962, M.S.C.E. 1965, M.S. 1967, Ph.D. 1972. Address: 43 Cloverfield Drive, Loudonville, New York 12211.

WANG, LEON RU-LIANG Occupation: Professor of Civil Engineering. Education: D.S. Address: 3706 Quail Drive, Norman, Oklahoma 73069.

WARD, CELESTE F Occupation: Principal Monticello Elementary Education. Education: B.S., M.S., M.S. Address: Route 1, Box 1051, Silver Creek, Mississippi 39663.

WARD, CHESTER V Occupation: Banker. Address: 704 Euclid, Alton, Illinois 62002.

WARD, CONNIE MICHELE Occupation: Assistant Professor, Counselor. Education: Ph.D., M.A., B.A. Address: 1405 North Crossing Way, Decatur, Georgia 30033.

WARD, DONALD E Occupation: Associate Professor of Psychology and Counseling. Education: B.A., M.S., Ph.D. Address: 2002 Countryside Drive, Pittsburgh, Kansas 66762.

WARD, HOWARD L Occupation: Periodontist, Professor of Periodontics, Assistant Dean. Education: B.A., D.D.S., M.A. Higher Education. Address: 150 Central Park South, New York, New York 10019.

WARD, SANDRA MILLER Occupation: Registered Nurse, Director of Nursing. Education: M.S.N. Address: 907 Darren Drive, Portsmouth, Virginia 23701.

WARD, SUZANNE FOWLER Occupation: Registered Nurse. Education: M.A., Master of Nursing Candidate. Address: 1 North Star #104, Marina Del Rey, California 90291.

WARE, CHARLES JEROME Occupation: Special Assistant to the Chairman. Education: B.A. 1970, J.D. 1975. Address: 7158 Peace Chimes Court, Columbia, Maryland 21045.

WARE, PINKIE CRAFT Occupation: Manager, Toccoa Symphony. Education: A.B. Music Education, Diploma Piano. Address: Box 532, Toccoa, Georgia 30577.

WARMBRUNN, JOAN STRONG Occupation: Writer, Musician. Education: A.B., M.A. Address: 107 Ramona Road, Menlo Park, California 94025.

WARNER, W KEITH Occupation: Professor of Sociology. Education: Ph.D., Cornell University; M.S., B.S., Utah State University. Address: 899 East 2730 North, Provo, Utah 84604.

WARREN, FOREST GLEN Occupation: Agricultural Consultant. Education: B.S., M.S., Ph.D. Address: 603 North 50 West, Valparaiso, Indiana 46383.

WARREN, THOMAS B Occupation: Author and Minister. Education: B.A., M.A., M.A., Ph.D. Address: Post Office Box 49118, Algood, Tennessee 38501.

WARRICK, ALAN EVERETT Occupation: Judge. Education: B.A., J.D. Address: 509 Burleson, San Antonio, Texas 78202.

WARSAW, IRENE Occupation: Retired Vice President and Trust Officer, Peoples National Bank and Trust Company of Bay City; Poet. Education: Honorary Degree, Doctor of Letters, Saginaw Valley State College. Address: 888 North Scheurmann Road, Essexville, Michigan 48732.

WARSHAVSKY, BELLE Occupation: Reading Specialist. Education: B.B.A., M.S.E., Ph.D. Address: 35 Cooper Drive, Great Neck, New York 11023.

WARLUFT, DAVID JONATHAN Occupation: Library Director, Professor. Education: B.A., M.A., M.Div., M.S. Address: 7328 Rural Lane, Philadelphia,

WASHBURN, STEWART ALEXANDER Occupation: Certified Management Consultant, Lakeville, Massachusetts. Education: Bachelor of Arts, Saint John's College-Annapolis, 1951. Address: Off Old Main Street, Lakeville, Massachusetts 02346.

WASS DE CZEGE, ALBERT Occupation: Writer, Editor, Publisher. Education: Ph.D. Address: Route 1, Box 59, Astor, Florida 32002.

WASSERMAN, JERRY Occupation: Management Consultant. Education: B.A. Mathematics, M.A. Mathematics, M.S. Electrical Engineering. Address: 11 Winthrop Road, Lexington, Massachusetts 02173.

WATANABE, NANCY A Occupation: Literary Comparatist. Education: M.A., Ph.D. Comparative Literature, B.A. French, B.A. English. Address: 1216 South Plum, Seattle, Washington 98144.

WATANABE, RONALD K Occupation: President, Principal Broker, Mid-Pacific Resorts Management, Inc. Address: 225 Queen Street, #17-C, Honolulu, Hawaii 96813.

WATERMAN, SHEREEN H Occupation: Registrar, Curriculum Director, Educator, Devic Representative. Education: B.A. Elementary Education Science, M.A. Counseling and Educational Psychology, Sp.E. Curriculum. Address: 290 Country Club Gardens MHP, Santa Fe, New Mexico 87501.

WATERS, THOMAS LYLE Occupation: College Teacher, Siena College. Education: B.E. Electrical Engineering, M.S. Systems Management, M.E. Education, Ph.D. Address: Post Office Box 459, West Sand Lake, New York 12196.

WATERWASH, JAMES S Occupation: Executive Vice President, Bulova Systems and Instruments

Corporation. Education: B.S.I.E., M.B.A. Address: 31 Gedney Esplanade, White Plains, New York 10605.

WATKINS, DANE HANSEN Occupation: Property Mangement/State Senator. Education: B.A. Political Science, University of Utah. Address: 2242 South Boulevard, Idaho Falls, Idaho 83402.

WATKINS, ELOISE Occupation: Nurse Epidemiologist. Education: R.N., B.A., B.S., M.P.H. Address: 140 Summer Street, Arlington, Massachusetts 02174.

WATKINS, JOHN BARR III Occupation: Assistant Professor of Pharmacology and Toxicology, Medical Sciences Program, Indiana University. Education: B.A. 1975, M.S. 1977, Ph.D. 1979. Address: Evermann Apartment 236, Bloomington, Indiana 47401.

WATSON, JACK H JR Occupation: Attorney (Partner). Education: B.A. English Literature, Vanderbilt University, 1960; LL.B., Harvard Law School, 1966. Address: 4092 Columns Drive, Marietta, Georgia 30067.

WATSON, LITA LEA Occupation: Employment Company Executive. Education: Graduate, Public Schools, Lovettsville, Virginia. Address: 594 Turnabout Road, Orange, California 92669.

WATSON, RONALD G Occupation: Chairman and Professor of Art, Department of Art, Texas Christian University. Education: B.F.A., M.F.A. Address: 1615 Arch Adams #220, Fort Worth, Texas 76107.

WATSON, THOMAS S JR Occupation: Certified Public Accountant. Education: M.B.A. Address: 2555 Pennsylvania Avenue, Northwest, Washington, D.C. 20037.

WATTENBERG, MARTIN P Occupation: Professor of Political Science, University of California-Irvine. Education: Ph.D., The University of Michigan, 1982. Address: 240 Nice Lane, 105, Newport Beach, California 92663.

WATTS, BARRY A Occupation: Executive Director, Warm Springs Center. Education: B.A. Religion, M.S. Psychology. Address: 2624 Ballantyne Lane, Eagle, Idaho 83616.

WATTS, LOWELL H Occupation: Director International Extension and Training, Colorado State University. Education: B.S., M.S. Address: 1521 Hillside Drive, Fort Collins, Colorado 80524.

WAXER, EDWARD PAUL Occupation: Executive Amateur and Professional Sports. Education: B.S. Physical Education and History. Address: 5600 Southwest 78 Street, Miami, Florida 33143.

WAWRZYNIAK, CAROL ANN Occupation: Assistant to the Governor's Trade Representative. Education: B.A. Political Science and Public Administration. Address: Route 3, Foley, Minnesota 56329.

WAYNE, JUNE C Occupation: Artist, Painter, Printmaker, Designer. Education: Doctor of Fine Arts. Address: 1112 North Tamarind Avenue, Los Angeles, California 90038.

WEATHERFORD, MATTIE CAROLYN Occupation: Executive Director, Woman's Missionary Union, S.B.C. Education: A.B., Florida State University; M.R.E., New Orleans Baptist Theological Seminary. Address: 1591 Vestridge Circle, Birmingham, Alabama 35216.

WEAVER, ALLEN D Occupation: Professor of Physics Emeritus, Northern Illinois University. Education: Ph.D. Science Education, New York University. Address: 591 Garden Road, DeKalb, Illinois 60115.

WEAVER, NOEL THOMAS Occupation: Vocal Director, Rowan Company; Soloist, Lexington Singers. Education: B.S., M.S., Morehead State University. Address: 171 A 11 Clearfield, Kentucky 40313.

WEBB, BERNICE LARSON Occupation: University Professor. Education: A.B., M.A., Ph.D., The University of Kansas. Address: 159 Whittington Drive, Lafayette, Louisiana 70503.

WEBB, ROBERT MICHAEL Occupation: Ophthalmologist. Education: B.S., M.D. Address: 412 Pinewood Avenue, Troy, New York 12180.

WEBER, CLARENE A Occupation: Professor Emeritus. Education: Ph.D., M.A., A.B. Address: 491 North Eagleville Road, Storrs, Connecticut 06368.

WEBER, DARRELL JACK Occupation: Professor of Botany. Education: Ph.D., University of California. Address: 560 East Robin, Orem, Utah 84057.

WEBER, RICHARD B Occupation: Professor of English. Education: B.A., M.A., Ph.D. Address: 42 Peconic Trail, Riverhead, New York 11901.

WEBER, ROBERTS BARSOTTI Occupation: Parent Education Coordinator. Education: M.S. Child Development, B.A. Political Science. Address: 236 Northwest 28th Street, Corvallis, Oregon 97330.

WEBSTER, BURNICE HOYLE Occupation: Physician, Thorocologist. Education: B.A., M.D., Dc.D., Ph.D., S.T.D., D.C.E., D.D. Address: 2315 Valley Brook Road, Nashville, Tennessee 37215.

WEBSTER, EDWARD H Occupation: Research Chemist. Education: B.S., University of Delaware. Address: 2 Swallow Circle, Newark, Delaware 19711.

WEBSTER, ROY C Occupation: Public Relations Account Supervisor. Education: B.A. Journalism, University of Washington, 1960; Attended Boston University, San Jose State University. Address: 309 Lee Street, Santa Cruz, California 95060.

WEBSTER, THOMAS GLENN Occupation: Professor of Psychiatry, George Washington University Medical Center. Education: A.B., M.D. Address: 8506 Woodhaven Boulevard, Bethesda, Maryland 20817.

WEED, MARY THEOPHILOS Occupation: College Teacher, Psychologist. Education: A.B., University of Miami, 1953; M.A., University of Chicago, 1960. Address: 5534 South Harper, Chicago, Illinois 60637.

WEEKS, ALBERT LOREN Occupation: Teacher, Journalist. Education: M.A., Ph.D. Address: 37 Washington Square West, New York, New York 10011.

WEEKS, RAMONA M Occupation: Editor, Writer. Education: B.A. English. Address: 326 West Dobbins Road, Phoenix, Arizona 85041.

WEGMAN, EDWARD J Occupation: Head, Mathematical Science Division, Office of Naval Research. Education: B.S., M.S., Ph.D. Address: 10821 Burr Oak Way, Burke, Virginia 22015.

WEGNER, PATRICIA ANN Occupation: Genealogical Researcher, Writer. Education: M.S. (in progress). Address: 1129 Webster, Fairmont, Minnesota 56031.

WEHLBURG, ALBERT F C Occupation: Lighting Designer, University of Florida. Education: A.A., B.A., M.A., Sp.Ed., Ed.D. Address: 1771 Southwest 35th Avenue, Gainesville, Florida 32608.

WEHNER, ALFRED PETER Occupation: Biomedical Scientist. Education: D.D.S., Sc.D., Cand.Med. Address: 312 Saint Street, Richland, Washington 99352.

WEHR, HERBERT MICHAEL Occupation: Administrator Laboratory Services Division, Oregon Department of Agriculture. Education: B.S., M.S.,

Ph.D. Address: 2180 Irene Court, Salem, Oregon 97302.

WEHRINGER, CAMERON KINGSLEY Occupation: Attorney. Education: B.A., Amherst College; J.D., New York Law School. Address: 556 Main Street, New York, New York 10044.

WEHRMAN, ELIZABETH A Occupation: College Professor in Music Education. Education: B.A., M.M.Ed., Ph.D. Address: 40 North Yorktown Road, Macomb, Illinois 61455.

WEIDENBAUM, MURRAY L Occupation: Director, Center for the Study of American Business. Education: B.B.A., M.A., M.P.A., Ph.D., LL.D. Address: 709 South Skinker, St. Louis, Missouri 63105.

WEIDER, JOSEPH Occupation: Publisher. Address: 131 South Hudson Avenue, Los Angeles, California 90004.

WEIL, FRANK A Occupation: Attorney. Education: A.B. 1953, J.D. 1956, Harvard University. Address: 1516 28th Street, Northwest, Washington, D.C. 20007.

WEINBERGER, CHARLES B Occupation: Professor, Chemical Engineering. Education: B.S., M.S.E., Ph.D. Address: 3451 Midvale Avenue, Philadelphia, Pennsylvania 19129.

WEINBERG, NORMAN L Occupation: President, Norman L. Weinberg Associates. Education: B.S., M.B.A., New York University. Address: 105 North Franklin Turnpike, Ho-Ho-Kus, New Jersey 07423.

WEINHOLD, BARRY K Occupation: Professor of Education, University of Colorado. Education: B.S., Millersville University, 1959; Ph.D., University of Minnesota, 1968. Address: 11030 Thomas Road, Colorado Springs, Colorado 80908.

WEINSTEIN, NORMAN JACOB Occupation: President, Recon Systems, Inc. Education: B.Ch.E., M.Ch.E., Ph.D. Address: 105 Reimer Street, Somerville, New Jersey 08876.

WEINSTOCK, HELENE SUZETTE KARLIN Occupation: Psychotherapist, Marriage, Family Counselor. Education: A.A., A.B., M.A., C.Phil., M.A. Address: Post Office Box 2051, Huntington Beach, California 92708.

WEISBERG, ROBERT F Occupation: President, Midland Chemical Laboratory; Educator. Education: B.A., B.S., M.Ph., M.B.A., Ph.D. Address: 102 Slater Avenue, Providence, Rhode Island 20406.

WEISBROD, KEN J Occupation: Chairman, Ken Weisbrod Productions, Inc. Address: 22304-3 Devonshire Street, Chatsworth, California 91311.

WEISS, DAVIDA S Occupation: Consultant, Time Management and Human Productivity. Education: B.A., M.A. Address: 79 Old Shore Hills Road, Shore Hills, New Jersey 07078.

WEISS, LOUIS ISRAEL (LOU) Occupation: Marketing Research Consultant. Address: 784 Barracuda Way, Lagunda Beach, California 92651.

WEISS, STEVEN ALAN Occupation: Executive, Television/Motion Picture Industry. Education: A.A., Los Angeles City College, 1964; B.S., University of Southern California, 1966; M.S., Northwestern University, 1967; J.D., La Salle Extension University, 1970. Address: 4137 North Sunset Lane, Channel Islands, California 93030.

WEISS, THEODORE RUSSELL Occupation: Professor of English, Creative Writing; Poet, Editor. Education: A.B., Columbia University. Address: 26 Hoslet Avenue, Princeton, New Jersey 08540.

WEISS, VLADIMIR STANLEY Occupation: Engineering Executive. Education: B.Sc. English, 1954; M.Sc. English, 1956 and 1957. Address: 69 Maplewood

Road, Mississippi, Ontario L5G 2M7 Canada.

WEISSBLUTH, MITCHEL Occupation: Professor of Applied Physics, Stanford University. Education: B.A., M.A., Ph.D. Address: 820 Pine Hill Road, California 94305.

WEISSENT, ALEXANDER B Occupation: Professional Sports Agent, Representative. Education: B.A., Harvard University, 1973; M.B.A., University of Chicago, 1976. Address: 1415 North Dearborn Parkway, Chicago, Illinois 60610.

WEISSMAN, RONEE FREEMAN Occupation: Speech Pathologist, Vice-President, Owner, Director. Education: B.A. Speech Education, 1973; M.A. Speech Pathology, 1978. Address: 517 Almena Avenue, Ardoley, New York 10502.

WEITZEL, AL R Occupation: Chairperson, Speech Communication Department, San Diego State University. Education: Ph.D., University of Southern California. Address: Post Office Box 15936, San Diego, California 92115.

WELBURN, RON (RONALD) G Occupation: Writer, Poet, Music Critic. Education: B.A., Lincoln University; M.A., Ph.D. Address: Post Office Box 692, Guilderland, New York 12084.

WELCH, JENNIFER ANN MILLER GROSE Occupation: Poet, Administrator, Teacher. Education: Ohio State University. Address: 2384 Hardesty Drive, South, Columbus, Ohio 43204.

WELCH, WALTER ANDREW JR Occupation: Aeronautical Lawyer, Commercial Pilot. Education: B.S.A.S., J.D. Address: Post Office Box 9696, Marina del Rey, California 90291.

WELDON, JAMES THOMAS Occupation: Holistic Health Care Specialist. Education: B.A., Master of Psychophysiology, Doctor of Nutrition. Address: 4725 Baylor Court, Saginaw, Michigan.

WELISCH, SOPHIE ANNA Occupation: Professor of History. Education: B.A., M.A., Ph.D. Address: 2 Hughes Street, Congers, New York 10920.

WELLHOEFER, BETTY JANE Occupation: Accounting Analyst, First Wisconsin National Bank of Eau Claire. Education: B.B.A. Business Finance. Address: Route 3, Stratford, Wisconsin 54484.

WELLMAN, GAIL EUNICE Occupation: Advertising and Sales Executive. Education: B.A., Queens College, 1959. Address: 410 Northwest 65th Terrace, Margate, Florida 33063.

WELLS, COY LEE Occupation: Associate Professor, Criminal Justice. Education: B.G.S., M.P.A., M.S., Ph.D. Address: 1643 Burnwood Road, Baltimore, Maryland 21239.

WELLS, DONALD T Occupation: Chief Financial Officer. Education: University of Kentucky, B.S. Finance and Marketing. Address: 7517 Spring Valley, Dallas, Texas 75240.

WELLS, ERNEST HATTON Occupation: Consulting Engineer and Scientist. Education: B.S.E.E., D.Sc. Address: 712 Kilkenny Street, Northwest, Huntsville, Alabama 35805.

WENBERG, BURNESS G Occupation: Registered Dietitian, Human Ecology, Michigan State University. Education: B.S., M.S., Certification as Registered Dietitian (R.D.) Address: 2608 Rockwood, East Lansing, Michigan 48823.

WENDELL, LEILAH B Occupation: Fine Artist, Author, Poet, Researcher. Education: High School Diploma, Medical Laboratory Citation. Address: 70 Middlesex Avenue, Oakdale, New York 11769.

WENGLOWSKI, GARY MARTIN Occupation: Partner, Director of Economic Research, Goldman Sachs and Company. Education: A.M., B.S., Ph.D.

Address: 85 Broad Street, New York, New York 10007.

WENTZ, DEBRA L Occupation: Financial Analyst in Venture Capital. Education: Ph.D., M.A., B.A. Address: 35 Corvell Street, Lambertville, New Jersey 08540.

WERA, ANNE R Occupation: Music Specialist, Administration Research. Education: Ph.D., D.A., M.M., M.A., B.A. Address: 2688 Marywood Drive, Dubuque, Iowa 52001.

WERRIES, E DEAN Occupation: President and Chief Operating Officer, Fleming Companies, Inc. Education: University of Kansas. Address: 3216 Rolling Stone Road, Oklahoma City, Oklahoma 73120.

WERT, JONATHAN MAXWELL JR Occupation: Manager, Organization and Management Services. Education: Ph.D. 1974, M.S. 1968, B.S. 1966, University of Alabama. Address: 916 Town Lane, Port Royal, Pennsylvania 17082.

WERTZ, DOROTHY CORBETT Occupation: Associate Professor of Social and Behavioral Science. Education: Ph.D. 1966, A.M. 1961, A.B. 1958, Harvard University. Address: Box 95, Westport Point, Massachusetts 02791.

WESCHLER, ANITA Occupation: Sculptor, Painter. Address: 136 Waverly Place, New York, New York 10014.

WESCOTT, ROGER WILLIAMS Occupation: Professor of Anthropology. Education: M.Litt., Ph.D. Address: 11 Green Hill Road, Madison, New Jersey 07940.

WESELY, DONALD R Occupation: State Senator. Education: B.A., University of Nebraska-Lincoln. Address: 2828 North 54th, Lincoln, Nebraska 68504.

WESLEY, THERESSA GUNNELS Occupation: Writer, Director of Writing Laboratory, University of Arkansas-Pine Bluff. Address: 14508 Sara Lynn Drive, Little Rock, Arkansas 72206.

WEST, DOROTHY ANNE Occupation: Compliance Consultant, Pupil Appraisal, EBR Schools. Education: B.S., M.Ed., Louisiana State University. Address: 976 Baird Drive, Baton Rouge, Louisiana 70808.

WEST, GWENETH LUCRETIA Occupation: Costume Designer, Associate Professor of Theatre, University of Florida. Education: B.A. Education, M.F.A. Theatrical Design. Address: 1809 Southwest 67 Terrace, Gainesville, Florida 32607.

WEST, JULIAN RALPH Occupation: Photographer, Community Service. Education: B.L.S., University of Oklahoma. Address: 1955 Tamarind Avenue #14, Hollywood, California 90068.

WEST, RICHARD Occupation: Director. Address: Post Office Drawer 1904, Biloxi, Mississippi 39530.

WEST, ROBERT P Occupation: Orthodontist. Education: D.D.S., M.S. Address: 2502 Quail Creek, Independence, Missouri 64055.

WESTBROOK, ARLEN RUNZLER Occupation: Clinical Social Worker. Education: M.S., M.S.W. Address: R.D. 1 Box 95, Voorheesville, New York 12186.

WESTBROOK, CARL U SR Occupation: City Councilman. Education: B.S.A.E., M.S. Address: Post Office Box 1003, Athens, Texas 75751.

WESTPHAL, LARRY EDWARD Occupation: Research Economist and Chief, Productivity Division, The World Bank. Education: B.A. summa cum laude, Occidental College, 1964; Ph.D. Economics, Harvard University, 1969. Address: 6912 Baylor Drive, Alexandria, Virginia 22307.

WETTEREAU, RICHARD BROADWAY Occupation: Editor and Writer. Education: B.A., Columbia University, 1954. Address: Post Office Box 189, Manhasset, New York 11030.

WHALEN, JOHN P Occupation: Educator. Education: A.B., S.T.L., M.A., S.T.D., J.D. Address: 1614 Parham Road, Silver Spring, Maryland 20903.

WHARTON, WILLIAM POLK JR Occupation: Consulting Psychologist. Education: B.A., M.A., Ph.D. Address: 415 North Main, Meadville, Pennsylvania 16335.

WHEALEY, ROBERT H Occupation: Associate Professor of History. Education: B.A., M.A., Ph.D. Address: 14 Oak Street, Athens, Ohio 45701.

WHEELER, ASHER L Occupation: Attorney. Education: A.B., University of Georgia; J.D., Harvard Law School. Address: 3030 West Lane Keys, Northwest, Washington, D.C. 20007.

WHEELER, RICHARD O Occupation: President, Chief Executive Officer, Winrick International. Education: B.S., M.S., Ph.D. Address: Route 3, Morrilton, Arkansas 72110.

WHEELER, RICHARD WESLEY Occupation: Director, Christian Life Christian Program. Education: M.A. Education, Doctorate Program. Address: Post Office Box 5858, Lynnwood, Washington 98036.

WHEELOCK, ARTHUR K JR Occupation: Curator of Dutch and Flemish Paintings. Education: B.A., Williams College; Ph.D., Harvard University. Address: 3418 Rodman Drive, Northwest, Washington, D.C. 20008.

WHITE, C EDWARD Occupation: Associate Professor of English, Minister. Education: B.A., M.A. Address: 122 Apache Drive, Searcy, Arkansas 72143.

WHITE, CHARLES B Occupation: Psychologist, Gerontologist, Professor. Education: B.A., M.A., Ph.D. Address: 14203 Modesta Place, San Antonio, Texas 78247.

WHITE, DONALD J Occupation: Dean Graduate Arts and Science, Associate Dean of Faculties, Boston College. Education: B.S., Boston College, 1943; M.A. 1946, Ph.D. 1949, Harvard University. Address: 25 Pilgrim Road, Milton, Massachusetts 02186.

WHITE, ELLA ELIZABETH Occupation: Research Administration. Education: B.S., Southern University, 1970; M.M., Miami University, 1971; Ph.D., Kansas State University, 1976. Address: 3003 Van Ness Street, Northwest, Washington, D.C. 20008.

WHITE, FRANKIE L Occupation: Display Advertising Salesperson, Hyde Park Herald Newspaper. Education: B.A., University of Illinois, Chicago Circle. Address: 5200 South Blackstone, #609, Chicago, Illinois 60615.

WHITE, IRMA REED Occupation: Writer, Librarian. Education: B.A., M.A. Address: 545 Del Price Court, Saint Louis, Missouri 63124.

WHITE, JOHN J III Occupation: Physicist. Education: B.S. 1960, Ph.D. 1965, P.E. 1976. Address: 4865 Arthur Place, Columbus, Ohio 43220.

WHITE, RAYMOND GENE Occupation: Administrator, Veterinary Medicine. Education: B.S., M.S., D.V.M. Address: 1320 Twinridge, Lincoln, Nebraska 68510.

WHITE, ROBERT J Occupation: Professor of Neurological Surgery. Education: M.D., Ph.D. Address: 2895 Lee Road, Shaker Heights, Ohio 44120.

WHITE, ROY C Occupation: U.S. Air Force, Commander. Education: B.S. Economics, M.A. Public Administration. Address: Route 1, Box 503, Bladenboro, North Carolina 28320.

WHITEHEAD, ARDELLE COLEMAN Occupation: Advertising/Public Relations Executive, Phoenix, Arizona. Education: Bachelor of Science Education.

Address: 337 East Pierson Street, Phoenix, Arizona 85012.

WHITEHEAD, MARVIN DELBERT Occupation: Plant Pathologist, Mycologist. Education: B.S., M.S., Ph.D. Address: 817 Clifton Road, Northeast, Atlanta, Georgia 30307.

WHITEMAN, BETTY BLUE Occupation: Retired Teacher. Education: Teacher's Certificate, 1933. Address: Post Office Box 218, Richey, Montana 59259.

WHITENER, DEAN KENNETH Occupation: Accountant. Education: A.B. Business Administration, Central Wesleyan College, 1974; Attended Carnegie Mellon University 1981, University of Kentucky College Business Management Institute 1976. Address: Post Office Box 1080, Central, South Carolina 29630.

WHITESEL, J WARREN Occupation: Lawyer. Education: J.D. 1948, LL.M. 1950, George Washington University; M.B.A., University of Chicago, 1964. Address: 5313 Grand, Western Springs, Illinois 60558.

WHITFIELD, BENJAMIN HATCH JR Occupation: Insurance Agent. Education: B.A. 1969, M.A. 1973, Ambassador College. Address: 1315 Date Street, Rawlins, Wyoming 82301.

WHITFIELD, VALLIE JO Occupation: Writer, Publisher and Realtor. Education: A.A., B.A. Address: 1841 Pleasant Hill Road, Pleasant Hill, California 94523.

WHITFORD, WALTER G Occupation: Professor of Biology, New Mexico State University. Education: B.A. 1961, Ph.D. 1964, University of Rhode Island. Address: 4210 Tesota, Las Cruces, New Mexico 88001.

WHITMAN, LONA G Education: High School Diploma. Address: Route 1, Finger, Tennessee 38334.

WHITLEY, NANCY O'NEIL Occupation: Professor of Radiology. Education: M.D. 1957. Address: Harper House #1411, Cross Keys, Baltimore, Maryland 21210.

WHITNEY, VIRGINIA KOOGLER Occupation: Educator. Education: B.A., M.Ed. Address: 502 Orchard Street, Aztec, New Mexico 87410.

WHITTEMORE, OSGOOD J Occupation: Professor of Ceramic Engineer and Director of Mineral Institute. Education: B.S., M.S., Cer.E. (Professional). Address: 10015 Lakeshore Boulevard, Northeast, Seattle, Washington 98125.

WHITWER, GLEN STERLING Occupation: Management Consultant. Education: M.B.A., Harvard University, 1972; B.S., University of Nebraska, 1966. Address: 8502 Grubb Road, Chevy Chase, Maryland 20815.

WICKLUND, LEE A Occupation: School Administrator. Education: B.Ed., Chicago State University; M.Ed., Loyola University; D.Ed., University of Oregon. Address: 206 Hillcrest Drive, North Bend, Oregon 97459.

WICKWIRE, PAT NELLOR Occupation: Consultant in Management and Education. Education: B.A., University of Northern Iowa; M.A., University of Iowa; Ph.D., University of Texas-Austin. Address: 2900 Amby Place, Hermosa Beach, California 90254.

WIDEMAN, CYRILLA H Occupation: University Professor and Researcher. Education: B.S., M.S., Ph.D. Address: 446 Richmond Park East, Cleveland, Ohio 44143.

WIDMAN, DALE POULNOT Occupation: Retailing Executive Vice President. Education: A.B., Duke University. Address: 90 King Street, Charleston, South Carolina 29401.

WIEBE, KATIE FUNK Occupation: Educator, Tabor College; Writer. Education: B.A., M.A. Address: 103 East B, Hillsboro, Kansas 67063.

WIEMANN, MARION RUSSELL JR Occupation: B.S. Professional Training in Microscopy, Certificates. Address: Post Office Box E, Chesterton, Indiana 46304.

WIENER, DANIEL N Occupation: Psychologist. Education: B.A., M.A., Ph.D. Address: 1225 LaSalle Avenue, Minneapolis, Minnesota 55403.

WIERBICKI, EUGEN Occupation: Head of Food Irradiation Research, Food Safety Laboratory, U.S. Department of Agriculture, Eastern Regional Research Center. Education: M.S., Ph.D. Address: 100 Albemarle Drive, Penilyn, Pennsylvania 19422.

WIITA, THOMAS A Occupation: President, Motion Control, Inc. Education: A.B. 1971, M.B.A. 1975, Harvard College. Address: 467 South 1200 East, Salt Lake City, Utah 84102.

WILBUR, LESLIE CLIFFORD Occupation: Professor. Education: B.S.M.E., M.S. Address: 32 Walnut Street, Post Office Box 97, Berlin, Massachusetts 01503.

WILCOX, JOHN CAVEN Occupation: Managing Director, Georgeson and Company, Inc. Education: B.A., M.A., J.D., LL.M. Address: 190 Riverside Drive, New York, New York 10024.

WILCOX, KENNETH R Occupation: Advertising, Design Communications Consultant. Address: 19 Nye Road, Gastonbury, Connecticut 06033.

WILCOX, RAND R Occupation: Associate Professor of Psychology, University of Southern California. Education: B.A., M.A., Ph.D. Address: 820 Wilson Place, Santa Monica, California 90405.

WILD, MICHAEL J Occupation: Medical Equipment Distributor. Education: B.S. Pharmacy. Address: 32 Seven Oaks Circle, Holmdel, New Jersey 07733.

WILDE, ALAN Occupation: Professor of English and Graduate Chairman. Education: B.A., M.A., Ph.D. Address: 410 Clarksville Road, Princeton Junction, New Jersey 08550.

WILDMAN, SUZANNE B Occupation: Composer, Educator, Republic Town Committee. Education: A.B. Classics, Stanford University; A.B., Vocal Artist, San Francisco Conservatory of Music. Address: 27 Pine Street, Manchester, Massachusetts 01944.

WILKERSON, ANNIE LOUISE WALKER Occupation: Retired Educator, Writer. Address: 1061 Harrison Boulevard, Gary, Indiana.

WILKERSON, CLAYTON DUKE Occupation: Dean, Turner Theological Seminary, I.T.C. Education: B.A., Morris Brown College; Master of Sacred Theology, I.T.C.; Doctor of Sacred Theology, Emory University. Address: 2822 Engle Road, Atlanta, Georgia 30318.

WILKINS, DERRICK L Occupation: High School Senior. Education: High School. Address: Post Office Box 265, Roper, North Carolina 27970.

WILKINS, JAMES RAYMOND Occupation: President, Reed Stenhouse, Ltd. Education: Associate of Insurance Institute of America and Insurance Institute of Canada. Address: Post Office Box 182, Seba Beach, Alberta, Canada T0E 2B0.

WILKINSON, CONNIE SUE Occupation: Nurse Teacher. Education: B.A., M.A. Address: 1709-C West Chase Avenue, Chicago, Illinois 60626.

WILKINSON, DEHLIA RAE Occupation: County Extension Agent-Agriculture. Education: B.S. Animal Science, Master of Agriculture/Agriculture Economics. Address: 10107 Westview Drive, #229, Houston, Texas 77043.

WILKINSON, MAURICE GILLIAN Occupation: Family Physician. Education: B.S., M.D. Address: Box 805, Shiner, Texas 77984.

WILKINSON, THOMAS L JR Occupation: Senior Project Director. Education: B.S., Master of Commerce. Address: 6908 Park Avenue, Richmond, Virginia 23226.

WILKINSON, WILLIAM EDWARD Occupation: Assistant Professor. Education: B.S.N., M.P.H., Dr.P.H., R.N.C. Address: 1709-C West Chase Avenue, Chicago, Illinois 60626.

WILLEMS, ARNOLD LEE Occupation: Head and Professor. Education: Ed.D., 1971, M.A., 1968, B.A., 1964. Address: 1810 Barratt, Laramie, Wyoming 82070.

WILLIAMS, BARBARA ELIZABETH WOMACK Occupation: School Guidance Counselor. Education: B.A., M.ED., American University. Address: 5556 McVitty Road, Southwest, Roanoke, Virginia 24018.

WILLIAMS, CHARLES MOLTON Occupation: Mortgage Banking Executive. Education: B.S., Washington and Lee University, 1952; Graduate, University of Alabama. Address: 3924 Royal Oak Drive, Birmingham, Alabama 35243.

WILLIAMS, CHARLES SAMUEL Occupation: Lecturer. Education: B.S., Arizona State University. Address: 4013 49th Street, Lubbock, Texas 79413.

WILLIAMS, CHERIE A DAWSON Occupation: Associate Professor. Education: B.S., M.A., Ed.D. Address: 5420 East 113th Place South, Tulsa, Oklahoma 74137.

WILLIAMS, DAVID L Occupation: Principal, Colonel White High School. Education: B.S., M.S. Education. Address: 3826 West Second Street, Dayton, Ohio 45417.

WILLIAMS, DAVID R JR Occupation: Chairman, Williams Technologies, Inc. Education: B.S., Yale University. Address: 6697 South Evanston Circle, Tulsa, Oklahoma 74136.

WILLIAMS, DAVID RUSSELL Occupation: Educational Administrator. Education: B.A., M.A., Columbia University; Ph.D., University of Rochester. Address: 295 Central Parkway, #2, Memphis, Tennessee 38111.

WILLIAMS, DOUGLAS Occupation: Management Consultant. Education: A.B., Cornell University, 1934; M.B.A., Harvard University, 1936. Address: Post Office Box 941, Carefree, Arizona 85377.

WILLIAMS, FRANK J Occupation: Attorney and Counsellor at Law. Education: B.A. Government and History, J.D. Law, Boston University. Address: R.F.D. Hope Valley Road, Hope Valley, Rhode Island 02832.

WILLIAMS, GERALD WALTER Occupation: Sociologist. Education: B.S. Sociology, M.S. General Studies Social Science, Ph.D. Sociology. Address: 3972 Oak Street, Eugene, Oregon 97405.

WILLIAMS, HATTIE KAY Occupation: Coordinator of Black Ministries, Shalom House, Paxton, Massachusetts. Education: Doctor of Humanities, Anne Maria College. Address: 4604 Lake Park, Chicago, Illinois 60653.

WILLIAMS, HAZEL PEARSON Occupation: Handicraft Consultant. Education: Student, University of Southern California, University of California-Los Angeles Extension. Address: 300 West Norman Avenue, Arcadia, California 91006.

WILLIAMS, IOLA M Occupation: Councilwoman. Education: Attended Harvard University, Kennedy School of Government, Program for Senior Executives in State and Local Government, 1980. Address: 801 North First Street, San Jose, California 95110.

WILLIAMS, JON E Occupation: Clinical and Health Psychologist; Clinical Director of Psychology, University of Maryland. Education: B.A. Sociology, Fulbright Scholar Sociology, M.Div. Psychiatry and Religion, M.S. and Ph.D. Clinical Psychology. Address: 1705 South Harbor Lane, Annapolis, Maryland 21401.

WILLIAMS, JOYCE E Occupation: Associate Professor of Sociology, Texas Woman's University. Education: Ph.D., Washington University. Address: 165 North Old Orchard Lane, #2022, Lewisville, Texas 75067.

WILLIAMS, NANCY J Occupation: National Program Manager, Adolph Coors Company. Education: B.B.A. Marketing. Address: 11081 Conifer Mountain Road, Conifer, Colorado 80433.

WILLIAMS, PATRICK NEHEMIAH Occupation: Commissioner of Agriculture. Education: Bachelor's Degree. Address: R.F.D. 2, Box 10461, Kingshill, St. Croix, Virgin Islands 00850.

WILLIAMS, PAUL OSBORNE Occupation: Professor of English, Novelist. Education: B.A., M.A., Ph.D. Address: Route #1, 4 Dogwood Lane, Elsah, Illinois 62028.

WILLIAMS, RICHARD CHARLES Occupation: Computer Programmer/Analyst. Education: B.A. Sociology/Mathematics, State University of New York. Address: 5 Dogwood Hill, Wappingers Falls, New York 12590.

WILLIAMS, STEPHEN O'BANNON Occupation: Private Practice, Holistic Nutritional Medicine. Education: Doctorate, Ph.D., Doctor of Divinity. Address: 455 Martins Court, Lilburn, Georgia 30247.

WILLIAMS, THEODORE E Occupation: Business Executive. Education: B.S.E. (M.E.). Address: 435 North Layton Way, Los Angeles, California 90049.

WILLIAMS, VICTOR R Occupation: President, Starboard Oil Company. Education: B.S. Petroleum Engineering, University of Texas, 1954; M.B.A., Harvard University, 1961. Address: 11851 Durrette Drive, Houston, Texas 77024.

WILLIAMS, WILLIE Occupation: Professor of Physics, Lincoln University. Education: B.S. Physics, M.S. Physics, Ph.D. Physics, Iowa State University. Address: 351 West Baltimore, West Grove, Pennsylvania 19390.

WILLIAMS, WILLIE LeTHAIT Occupation: Assistant Director of Financial Aid. Education: B.S. 1973, M.S. 1974. Address: 224 Lake Placid Drive, Bonaire, Georgia 31005.

WILLIAMSON, DOROTHY J Occupation: Artist, Educator, Leader. Education: M.A., Additional Studies. Address: 4053 21st Avenue South, Minneapolis, Minnesota 55407.

WILLIAMSON, EUNICE T Occupation: Family and Consumer Sciences Advisor. Education: B.S., M.P.H. Address: Post Office Box 55092, Riverside, California 92517.

WILLING, ROBERT NELSON Occupation: Episcopal Priest, Archdeacon of New York. Education: B.A. Philosophy, Hobart College, 1957; M.Div., Nashotah House. Address: Upper Boiceville Road, Boiceville, New York 12412.

WILLIS, MEREDITH SUE Occupation: Novelist, Educator. Education: M.F.A., Columbia University; B.A., Barnard College. Address: 317 Sixth Avenue, Brooklyn, New York 11215.

WILLISCROFT, BEVERLY R Occupation: Attorney. Education: B.A. Music, 1967; J.D. Law, 1977. Address: 1233 B Pine Creekway, Concord, California 94520.

WILLISCROFT, ROBERT GROVER Occupation: Head NOAA Diving Pacific, Author. Education: B.S., University of Washington, 1969; M.S. 1981, Ph.D. 1983, California Coast University. Address: 341 112th

Southeast, Bellevue, Washington 98004.

WILLMANN, CAMILLA CLAUDIA Occupation: Tax Preparation Executive. Education: Diploma, Basic Intermediate and Advanced, Greenville College, 1940-41, 1969-71; Attended University of Illinois 1947-79, University of Missouri 1975-79; Enrolled Agent, I.R.S. Address: Route 2, Pocahontas, Illinois 62275.

WILLOUGHBY, EARNEST DWIGHT Occupation: Government Official. Education: B.S. 1955, Postgraduate Studies, Wayne State University. Address: 15945 Curtis Avenue, Detroit, Michigan 48235.

WILMETH, DON B Occupation: Chairman Department of Theatre Arts, Professor Theatre Arts and English, Brown University. Education: B.A. 1961, M.A. 1962, Ph.D. 1964. Address: 525 Hope Street, Providence, Rhode Island 02906.

WILSON, ARTHUR JESS Occupation: Clinical Psychologist. Education: B.S., M.A., Ph.D., LL.B., J.D. Address: 487 Park Avenue, Yonkers, New York 10703.

WILSON, CHARLES WILLIAM Occupation: Private Practice, Psychiatry and Medical Hypnosis. Education: B.A., Wichita University, 1938; M.D., Kansas University, 1942; Intern, Harper Hospital, Detroit, Michigan, 1942-43; Resident Physician Neurology, University Hospitals, 1946-47; Resident Physician Psychiatry, Central State Hospital, 1964-67. Address: 4655 Basque Drive, Santa Maria, California 93455.

WILSON, DEIRDRE TERRY-LYNNE Occupation: Director, Academy of Ballet. Education: A.A., Grossmont College, 1977; B.A. Clinical Psychology, Antioch University, 1979; M.A. Counseling and Guidance 1984, M.Ed. Counseling, Washington State University; Doctoral Student. Address: Northeast 1050 B Street, Pullman, Washington 99163.

WILSON, DONALD A Occupation: Land Boundary Consultant. Education: B.S. Forestry, University of Maine, 1965; M.S. Forest Resources, University of New Hampshire, 1967. Address: R.F.D. Lamprey Road, East Kingston, New Hampshire 03827.

WILSON, FRANCES PRESHIA Occupation: Registered Nurse, Psychiatric Nurse, Psychotherapy Researcher. Education: B.A., Graduate Nurse. Address: 4655 Basque Drive, Santa Maria, California 93455.

WILSON, GEORGE WILTON Occupation: Professor, Economics and Business Administration, School of Business, Indiana University. Education: B.Comm., M.A. Economics, P.L.D. Economics. Address: 2325 Woodstock, Bloomington, Indiana 47401.

WILSON, GREGORY B Occupation: Associate Professor, Department Basic and Clinical Immunology and Microbiology, Medical University South Carolina; Consultant. Education: Ph.D. Address: 421 McCants Drive, Mount Pleasant, South Carolina 29464.

WILSON, HELEN PAXTON-GIBBENS Occupation: Secretary/Treasurer, Rational Alternatives, Inc. Education: A.A., Bachelor of Arts, B.L.S., Master of Arts, Doctor of Philosophy. Address: 1 Vista Grande Drive, Santa Fe, New Mexico 87501.

WILSON, IRENE K Occupation: Author, *Wildflowers of the Mind*; Poet; Writer. Address: 9 Foster Road, Lexington, Massachusetts 02173.

WILSON, JAMES WOODROW JR Occupation: Salesperson. Education: B.B.A., M.Ed., Ed.D. Address: Route 3, Box 37, Royston, Georgia 30662.

WILSON, KAREN Occupation: Management Consultant, Author, Speaker. Education: B.A., University of Illinois; M.B.A., Pepperdine University. Address: 18001-A Skypark South, Irvine, California 92714.

WILSON, KEITH CHARLES Occupation: Poet-in-Residence, Professor of English, New Mexico State University. Education: B.S., U.S. Naval Academy; M.A., University of New Mexico. Address: 1500 South Locust, Las Cruces, New Mexico 88001.

WILSON, LLOYD LEE Occupation: General Secretary, Friends General Conference (Quakers). Education: B.S. 1969, M.S. 1977, Massachusetts Institute of Technology. Address: Route 2, Box 57H, Barboursville, Virginia 22923.

WILSON, MARY LEE Occupation: Clinical Nurse Specialist. Education: B.S., M.S., Nursing. Address: 4 Dartmouth Drive, Little Rock, Arkansas 72204.

WILSON, NICHOLAS JON Occupation: Wildlife Artist. Address: 1600 West Mesa Drive, Payson, Arizona 85541.

WILSON, ROBERT L Occupation: Associate Professor of English, Shawnee State College; Poet. Education: B.S., Kent State University; M.Ed., Xavier University; Ph.D., Florida State University. Address: 2816 Tanglewood Drive, Wheelersburg, Ohio 45694.

WILSON, SODONIA M Occupation: Director of Special Programs and Services, Contra Costa College; Financial Vice President, San Francisco Board of Education. Education: A.S., B.A., M.A., Ph.D. Address: 540 Darien Way, San Francisco, California 94127.

WILTSHIRE, RAYMOND S Occupation: Executive Director, Oak Ridge National Laboratories. Education: B.E.E. 1952, M.B.A. 1976. Address: 107 Davidson Lane, Oak Ridge, Tennessee 37830.

WIMMER, GLEN ELBERT Occupation: Semi-Retired, Professional Engineer and Management Consultant. Education: B.S., M.S. Mechanical Engineering, M.B.A. Business Administration. Address: 3839-48 Vista Campana South, Oceanside, California 92056.

WINDELS, CAROL ELIZABETH Occupation: Assistant Professor of Plant Pathology, Northwest Experiment Station, University of Minnesota. Education: B.A. 1970, M.S. 1972, Ph.D. 1980. Address: 1211 Mill Street, Crookston, Minnesota 56716.

WINDHEIM, PAUL Occupation: Executive, Textiles. Education: B.A., M.A., University of Pennsylvania. Address: 132 Hagen Road, Newton Centre, Massachusetts 02159.

WINDSOR, OLIVER DUANE Occupation: University Professor, Rice University. Education: B.A., Rice University, 1969; A.M. 1975, Ph.D. 1978, Harvard University. Address: 5803 West Bellfort, Houston, Texas 77035.

WING, MARY C Occupation: Physician. Education: B.S. 1968, M.D. 1973. Address: Post Office Box 60087, Fairbanks, Arkansas 99706.

WING, ROSE E Occupation: Retired Federal Government Employee. Education: B.A., University of Tennessee-Knoxville. Address: 4014 Chappewa Place, Atlanta, Georgia 30319.

WINGATE, PAUL D Occupation: President and Chief Executive Officer, Hamden Steel and Aluminum Corporation. Education: B.S.M.E., University of Michigan. Address: 30 Swarthmore Street, Hamden, Connecticut 06517.

WINIKOW, ARNOLD Occupation: Pharmacy Procurement Manager, New York City Health and Hospital Corporation. Education: B.S., Doctor of Pharmacy. Address: 62 Sutin Place, New York, New York 10977.

WINKELMANN, JOHN PAUL Occupation: Executive Director, National Catholic Pharmacists Guild of the U.S. Education: B.S., St. Louis University

College of Arts and Sciences; B.S. Pharmacy, St. Louis College of Pharmacy. Address: 1012 Surrey Hills Drive, St. Louis, Missouri 63117.

WINKLER, AGNIESZKA M Occupation: President, Commart Advertising, Inc. Education: B.A., M.A., M.B.A. Address: 4701 Patrick Henry Drive, #7, Santa Clara, California 95050.

WINKLER, SHELDON Occupation: Dental Educator and Researcher. Education: B.A., D.D.S., Certificate in Prosthodontics. Address: 1224 Liberty Bell Drive, Cherry Hill, New Jersey 08003.

WINN, CYNTHIA Occupation: Educator. Education: B.S. Vocational Home Economics Education, M.A. Home Economics Education. Address: 7250 South Gaylord Street, #E, Littleton, Colorado 80122.

WINNEGRAD, MARK HARRIS Occupation: Investigator, New York City Department of Transportation. Education: B.A., M.L.S., M.A. Address: 1450 Parkchester Road, Bronx, New York 10462.

WINSKI, LOUISE F Occupation: Staff Biologist, Safety Assessment. Education: B.Sc. Medical Technology, Philadelphia College of Pharmacy and Science. Address: 1090 Bayless Place, Eagleville, Pennsylvania 19403.

WINTERS, JOANN SOMMERVILLE Occupation: Director, Patient Education, United Hospital Center, Inc. Education: B.S., M.S. Cell Physiology, Doctorate Health Education. Address: 406 Second Avenue, Nutter Fort, West Virginia 26301.

WIRTSCHAFTER, IRENE N Occupation: Tax Consultant. Education: B.C.S., Columbus University, 1942; Real Estate Appraiser, Philadelphia Board of Realtors. Address: 1825 Minutemen Causeway, Cocoa Beach, Florida 32931.

WISEMAN, STANLEY Occupation: Professor, Manager/Owner Company. Education: B.A., M.A., LL.B., Ph.D. Address: 8039 La Jolla Shores Drive, California 92037.

WISEMAN, T JAN Occupation: Executive Vice President, American Society of Farm Managers and Rural Appraisers. Education: J.B.S., University of Wisconsin; M.S. Education, C.A.S., Northern Illinois University. Address: 950 South Cherry Street, Ste. G-16, Denver, Colorado 80222.

WISNIOSKI, STANLEY W JR Occupation: Professor of Criminal Justice, Crime Justice Institute, Broward Community College. Education: B.S. Law Enforcement, M.Ed., Doctorate in Crime Justice Administration. Address: Rural Route #1, Post Office Box 242-G, Boca Raton, Florida 33434.

WISTISEN, MARTIN J Occupation: Agribusiness Executive. Education: B.S., M.B.A, Ph.D. Address: 178 Orchard Way, Richland, Washington 99352.

WITHAM, WILLIAM TASKER Occupation: Professor of English Emeritus, Indiana State University. Education: B.A., Drew University, 1936; M.A., Columbia University, 1940; Ph.D., University of Illinois, 1961. Address: 2323 Washington Avenue, Terre Haute, Indiana 47803.

WITHERUP, TERRENCE L Occupation: Business Counselor. Education: B.S. Computer Science, M.B.A. Finance. Address: 307 Cane Ridge Road, Antioch, Tennessee 37013.

WITORSCH, PHILIP Occupation: Clinical Professor of Medicine, George Washington University; Medical Director, Center for Environmental Health. Education: A.B., M.D. Address: 11033 Powder Horn Drive, Potomac, Maryland 20854.

WITT, LOUISE SCHAUB Occupation: Author, Publisher, Consultant. Education: Associate's Degree. Address: 4324 West 70 Terrace, Prairie Village, Kansas 66208.

WITT, RICHARD ALLEN Occupation: Insurance Company Investment Officer, Mutual of Omaha. Education: B.S.B.A. summa cum laude 1974. Address: 4936 South 98th Street, Omaha, Nebraska 68127.

WITTIG, SUSAN Occupation: Educational Administrator. Education: B.A., University of Illinois, 1967; Ph.D., University of California-Berkeley, 1972. Address: Southwest Texas State University, Marcos, TExas 78667.

WITTLER, JANET MARIE Occupation: Editor, Writer, Teacher. Education: M.A. English. Address: Post Office Box 205, Hopewell, New Jersey 08525.

WOELFLE, ARTHUR W Occupation: Business Executive. Education: B.S., University of Buffalo; International Management, University of Lucerne, Switzerland; Attended Northwestern University Graduate School of International Management. Address: 335 Woodley Road, Winnetka, Illinois 60093.

WOELPER, ALEXANDER ELLIOTT Occupation: Environmental Engineer. Education: B.S. Civil Engineering, M.A. Education. Address: U.S.A.E.H.A., R.D. 5, Box 121, Fort McPherson, Georgia 30330.

WOGSLAND, DANIEL K Occupation: Farmer, State Senator. Education: B.S. Agriculture Economics, North Dakota State University. Address: R.R. 1, Box W-8, Hannaford, North Dakota 58448.

WOHL, EMANUEL Occupation: Insurance Broker-Agent, Securities Broker-Dealer. Education: B.S., City College of New York; M.S., New York University; LL.B., LaSalle Extension University. Address: 3150 Rochambeau Avenue, New York, New York 10467.

WOHL, RICHARD HENRY Occupation: Registered Physical Therapist. Education: B.S. Physical Therapy. Address: 1700 Northwest Avenue, Minot, North Dakota 58701.

WOJCIECHOWSKA, MAIA (a.k.a. RODMAN) Occupation: Writer. Education: College Studies. Address: Post Office Box 304, Oakland, New Jersey 07436.

WOLD, ROBERT M Occupation: Optometrist. Education: A.A., B.S., O.D., M.S. Address: 627 Mission Court, Chula Vista, California 92010.

WOLF, ARTHUR H Occupation: Museum Director. Education: B.A., University of Nebraska, 1975; M.A., University of Arizona, 1977. Address: Post Office Box 1242, Taos, New Mexico 87571.

WOLF, GERTRUDE O Occupation: Librarian. Education: B.A. English, Brooklyn College, 1944. Address: 40-04 157 Street, Flushing, New York 11354.

WOLF, HARRY S Occupation: Supervisor Documentation, Westinghouse. Education: B.F.A. Address: 1190 West Northern Parkway, Baltimore, Maryland 21210.

WOLF, JOAN SILVERMAN Occupation: Assistant Professor, Department of Special Education, University of Utah. Education: B.S., M.A., Ph.D. Address: 4512 Bruce Street, Salt Lake City, Utah 84124.

WOLFE, ESTEMORE ALVIS Occupation: Educational Consultant and Vice President/Secretary, Wright Mutual Insurance Company. Address: B.S., M.Ed., M.A., D.Ed., Lh.D., Litt.D. Address: 2995 East Grand Boulevard, Detroit, Michigan 48202.

WOLFE, STEPHEN DOUGLAS Occupation: Rancher. Education: B.S. Animal Science. Address: Route 1 Box 135A, Wallowa, Oregon 97885.

WOLFF, FRANK JOSEPH III Occupation: Assistant Superintendent, Occupational and

Continuing Education, Nassau Technological Center. Education: B.S., M.S., Cornell University. Address: 45 Willoughby Path, East Northport, New York 11731.

WOLFSON, MURRAY Occupation: Professor of Economics, Oregon State University. Education: B.S., M.S., Ph.D. Address: Route 1, Box 292, Corvallis, Oregon 97330.

WOLFSON, ROBERT A Occupation: Physician. Education: A.B., M.D. Address: 16-5 Foxwood Drive, Pleasantville, New York 16570.

WOLLE, JOAN M Occupation: Health Educator/ Administrator. Education: B.A., M.P.H., Ph.D. Address: 207 Third Avenue, Southeast, Glen Burnie, Maryland 21601.

WOLLMAN, LEO Occupation: Physician, Author. Education: B.S., M.S., M.D., Ph.D. (Hon.), D.Sc. (Hon.). Address: 4505 Beach 45 Street, Brooklyn, New York 11224.

WOLMAN, BENJAMIN B Occupation: Editor-in-Chief, International Encyclopedia of Psychiatry, Psychology, Psychoanalysis and Neurology. Education: M.A. 1932, Ph.D. 1935, University of Warsaw. Address: 10 West 66 Street, New York, New York 10023.

WOLOTKIEWICZ, MARIAN M Occupation: President, Barrister Publishing, Inc. Education: B.A., Mount Holyoke College; J.D., Suffolk University. Address: 21 Dunster Drive, Stow, Massachusetts 01775.

WOLPE, HOWARD E Occupation: Member of Congress. Education: Ph.D. African Studies, Massachusetts Institute of Technology. Address: 1527 Longworth HOB, Washington, D.C. 20515.

WOLVERTON, NEWTON ELLIS Occupation: President, Wolverton and Company Limited. Education: B.Comm. Address: 534 Burrard Street, Vancouver, B.C. Canada V6C 2J9.

WOO, DAVID V Occupation: Nuclear Medicine Researcher/Radiopharmacologist. Education: B.S., M.S., Ph.D. Address: 119 Helm Way, Downington, Pennsylvania 19335.

WOOD, ARLETTA RENEE Occupation: President, Affiliated Enterprises, Inc., Booking Agency. Education: Attended Howard University, Montgomery College. Address: 2418 Homestead Drive, Silver Spring, Maryland 20902.

WOOD, CHARLES E Occupation: Physician. Education: M.D., F.A.C.O.G. Address: 5092 Alcova Road, Box 2, Casper, Wyoming 82604.

WOOD, CORINNE SHEAR Occupation: Professor, Department of Anthropology, California State University-Fullerton. Education: Ph.D. Address: 2769 Craig Circle, Fullerton, California 92635.

WOOD, DONALD DIXON Occupation: Dean of Students. Education: A.B., B.D., Th.D. Historical Theology. Address: Box 485 CWC, Central, South Carolina 29630.

WOOD, F CAROL Occupation: Director, Los Angeles County Area Agency on Aging. Education: B.A., M.S.W. Address: 2552 Benedict Canyon Drive, Beverly Hills, California 90210.

WOOD, FAY S Occupation: Vice President Sales and Marketing, Qutentech Electronics Corporation. Education: B.A. English. Address: 61-20 Grand Central Parkway, Forest Hills, New York 11375.

WOOD, LINCOLN JACKSON Occupation: Aerospace Engineer and University Professor. Education: B.S., Cornell University; M.S., Ph.D., Stanford University. Address: 4929 Ocean View Boulevard, La Canada Flintridge, California 91011.

WOOD, REGA Occupation: Editor Medieval Texts. Education: B.A., Reed College, 1968; M.A. 1971, Ph.D. 1975, Cornell University. Address: 123 North 17th Street, Olean, New York 14760.

WOOD, SANDRA ELAINE Occupation: Systems Analyst/Programmer. Education: B.A. cum laude Business Administration/Management, Lynchburg College; Certified Professional Secretary Rating. Address: Post Office Box 303, Big Island, Virginia 24526.

WOODARD, BLONDENA SABRINA Occupation: Accountant, Tico and Associates, Inc. Education: Bachelor of Science, Virginia State University, 1976; Master of Arts, Southern Connecticut State College, 1977; Master of Arts, Virginia State University, 1981. Address: 501 Montour Drive, Richmond, Virginia 23236.

WOODHOUSE, JOHN FREDERICK Occupation: President and Chief Executive Officer, Sysco Corporation. Education: M.B.A., Harvard University, 1955; B.A., Wesleyan University. Address: 650 Ramblewood Road, Houston, Texas 77079.

WOODROW, JAMES EUGENE Occupation: Environmental/Analytical Chemist, Department of Environmental Toxicology, University of California-Davis. Education: B.A. Chemistry, University of California; M.S. Chemistry, San Jose State University. Address: 738 West Cross Street, Woodland, California 95695.

WOODRUFF, JOSEPH F Occupation: Retired Research Manager. Education: B.S., Honorary D.Sc., Capital University. Address: 3437 Central Avenue, Middletown, Ohio 45042.

WOODS, DELMA MARIA PRIOLEAU Occupation: Psychologist. Education: Bachelor of Science, Master of Science. Address: 1106 Woodhaven Drive, Charleston, South Carolina 29407.

WOODS, MARGARET S Occupation: Professor Emeritus, Seattle Pacific University. Education: B.A., M.Ed. Address: 1206 West Leisure Street, Box 485, Coupeville, Washington 98239.

WOODWARD, HARRY H JR Occupation: Social Welfare Administrator. Education: A.B., M.A. Address: 1332 Sunview Lane, Winnetka, Illinois 60093.

WOOLEY, BETTY ANN Occupation: Horse Rancher, Poet. Address: Post Office Box 1905, Fontana, California 92335.

WORD, AMOS JARMAN III Occupation: Project Architect, The Ritchie Organization. Education: B.Arch., Auburn University. Address: 101 Gillon Drive, Birmingham, Alabama 35209.

WORKER, GEORGE F JR Occupation: Superintendent of Imperial Valley Field Station, Agronomist. Education: B.S., Colorado State University, 1949; M.S., University of Nebraska, 1953. Address: 1004 East Holton Road, El Centro, California 92243.

WORTHEN, BLAINE RICHARD Occupation: Professor and Head, Department of Psychology, Utah State University. Education: B.S. 1960, M.S. 1965, Ph.D. 1968. Address: 175 Quarter Circle Drive, Logan R.F.D., Utah 84321.

WRAY, JOHN LAWRENCE Occupation: Vice President, Computer Systems Division, Quadrex Corporation. Education: B.S., University of Missouri; M.S., Stanford University. Address: 14961 Haun Court, Saratoga, California 95070.

WRENN, MARY S Occupation: Principal. Education: M.S. Address: Post Office Box 2232, East St. Louis, Illinois 62202.

WRENTMORE, ANITA KAY Occupation: Mathematics Instructor. Education: B.S., M.S.,

Mathematics. Address: 103 Ramona Avenue, Newark, Ohio 43055.

WRIGHT, AMOS JASPER Occupation: Clinical Librarian, University of Alabama-Birmingham. Education: B.A. 1973, M.L.S. 1982. Address: 2208 Chapel Hill Road, Birmingham, Alabama 35216.

WRIGHT, JOHN MacNAIR JR Occupation: Lieutenant General, U.S. Army (Retired). Education: B.S., M.B.A., M.S. International Affairs. Address: 3813 Acapulco Court, Irving, Texas 75062.

WRIGHT, KENNETH L Occupation: Psychologist. Education: B.A., University of Washington, 1941; M.A., University of Southern California, 1957; Ph.D., San Gabriel College, 1958. Address: 3720 3rd Avenue, San Diego, California 92103.

WRIGHT, KENNETH LEE Occupation: Program Manager, Executive and Organization Development. Education: B.A., M.Ed., M.S. Address: 5944 Burnside Landing Drive, Burke, Virginia 22015.

WRIGHT, ROBERT G Occupation: Professor, Writer, Consultant. Education: B.S., M.B.A., Ph.D. Address: 4304 Admirable Drive, Palos Verdes Peninsula, California 90274.

WU, DAISY YEN Occupation: Consultant, Obesity Research Center, Nutrition and Metabolism Unit. Education: B.A., M.A. Address: 449 East 14 Street, New York, New York 10009.

WU, HAI Occupation: Engineer. Education: Ph.D. Address: 50150 Hanford Road, Canton, Michigan 48187.

WU, KONRAD T Occupation: Assistant Professor of Chemistry, State University of New York-Old Westbury. Education: Ph.D., State University of New York-Albany, 1976. Address: 6 Mitchel Court, Hicksville, New York 11801.

WU, LI PEI Occupation: President and Chief Executive Officer, General Bank. Education: M.B.A. Address: SRA Box 807, Anchorage, Alaska 99502.

WU, YING VICTOR Occupation: Research Chemist. Education: B.S. Chemistry, Ph.D. Physical Chemistry, Massachusetts Institute of Technology. Address: 7026 North Manning, Peoria, Illinois 61614.

WUHL, CHARLES MICHAEL Occupation: Physician/Psychiatrist. Education: M.D. Address: 769 Harristown Road, Glen Rock, New Jersey 07452.

WUNDER, GENE CARROLL Occupation: Professor of Marketing, Ball State University. Education: B.B.A., M.B.A., Ph.D. Address: 9 Redbud Lane, Muncie, Indiana 47302.

WUNDERLICH, ALFRED L Occupation: Head, Department of Painting, Head Department of Printmaking. Education: B.F.A., M.F.A., Yale University. Address: 18 William Ellery Place, Providence, Rhode Island 02904.

WYAND, MARTIN JUDD Occupation: Professor of Economics, Department of Economics, University of Denver. Education: B.A. 1953, M.A. 1954, Pennsylvania State University; J.S., University of Denver, 1969; Ph.D., University of Illinois, 1964. Address: 15740 East Greenwood Drive, Aurora, Colorado 80013.

WYATT, F KENT Occupation: President, Delta State University. Education: B.S. Education, Delta State University, 1956; M.Ed. Mathematics, University of Southern Mississippi, 1960; D.Ed. Administration and Supervision, University of Mississippi, 1970; Advanced Study, Harvard University, 1975.

WYATT, RICHARD JED Occupation: Physician, N.I.M.H.-St. Elizabeths Hospital, Washington, D.C. Education: M.D. Address: 7601 Glenbrook Road, Bethesda, Maryland 20814.

WYCHE, MARY GREEN Occupation: Chairperson Health, Physical Education and Recreation Department, Delaware State College. Education: B.S., M.Ed., Ph.D. Address: 600 Carriage Lane, Dover, Delaware 19901.

WYDLER, HANS ULRICH Occupation: International Lawyer. Education: B.S. 1944, B.M.E. 1947, B.I.E. 1949, Ohio State University; M.S., Massachusetts Institute of Technology, 1948; LL.B., Harvard Law School, 1951.

WYLIE, C ELAINE Occupation: Financial Analyst, Hella North America. Education: Graduate, Illinois Bankers School; B.B.A.; M.B.A. Address: Box 407, Fairfield, Illinois 62837.

WYNDEWICKE, KIONNE ANNETTE Education: B.S. Social Science, I.S.N.Y.-M.E.D. National College of Education. Address: 533 East 33rd Place, Chicago, Illinois 60616.

WYSLOTSKY, IHOR Occupation: Engineer. Education: Mechanical Engineer. Address: 6133 Forest Glen, Chicago, Illinois 60646.

WYSONG, EARL M JR Occupation: Professor/Consultant. Education: B.A., M.B.A., D.B.A. Address: 213 Farmgate Lane, Silver Spring, Maryland 20904.

Y

YAFFE, JAMES Occupation: Writer, College Professor. Education: B.S., Yale University, 1948. Address: 1215 North Cascade, Colorado Springs, Colorado 80903.

YALOW, ROSALYN SUSSMAN Occupation: Medical Investigator. Education: Ph.D., University of Illinois. Address: 3242 Tibbett Avenue, Bronx, New York 10463.

YAMANE, STANLEY J Occupation: Optometrist. Education: B.S., O.D. Address: 98-336 Kaonohi Street, Aiea, Hawaii 96701.

YAMATO, KEI C Occupation: International Business Consultant. Education: J.D., B.A. Address: Post Office Box 781, Honolulu, Hawaii 96808.

YAMAUCHI, KENT T Occupation: Clinical Psychology. Education: Ph.D. Address: Post Office Box 20022, South Lake Tahoe, California 95706.

YAMINS, J L Occupation: Consultant. Education: Attended Amherst College; Massachusetts Institute of Technology Graduate School of Chemistry. Address: P.O. Box 150, Freeport, New York 11520.

YANCY, PRESTON M Occupation: College Teacher. Education: Ph.D., M.S.S., M.H., B.A. Address: Post Office Box 25583, Richmond, Virginia 23260.

YANKOWITZ, SUSAN Occupation: Playwright, Novelist. Education: B.A., M.F.A. Address: 205 West 89 Street, New York, New York 10024.

YANNOPOULOS, KAITY (KATHERINE) Occupation: Pathologist. Education: Doctor of Medicine. Address: 105 Newmarket Road, Garden City, New York 11530.

YARBRO, CLAUDE L JR Occupation: Life Scientist. Education: B.A., Ph.D. Address: 147 Alger Road, Oak Ridge, Tennessee 37830.

YARLING, CHARLES BYRON Occupation: Senior Staff Engineer. Education: B.A. Math, B.S.E.E. Address: 1146 West Grandview, Mesa, Arizona, 85201.

YATES, EDWARD CARSON JR Occupation: Aerospace Engineer, Chief Scientist. Education: B.M.E., M.E.M., M.A.E., Ph.D. Address: 3800 Chesapeake Avenue, Hampton, Virginia 23669.

YEATS, ALVICE WHITEHURST Occupation: Professor of English (Retired). Education: B.A., M.A., Ph.D. Address: 725 Adams Street, Beaumont, Texas 77705.

YEATS, HELEN F Occupation: Retired Professor of Modern Languages, Angelo State University. Education: B.A., West Texas State University; M.A., Ph.D., University of Mexico. Address: Box 56, Roby, Texas 79543.

YEDOWITZ, ANNE MARIE Occupation: Florist. Education: B.A. Address: 171 Hunter Avenue, Yonkers, New York 10704.

YEH, HSU-CHONG Occupation: Associate Professor of Biology, Director of Diagnostic Ultrasound and Abdominal Computer Tomography, Department of Radiology, Mount Sinai Hospital. Education: M.D., College of Medicine, National Taiwan University. Address: 24 Jefferson Avenue, Tenafly, New Jersey 07670.

YELLEN, JANET LOUISE Occupation: Professor of Business Adminstration, University of California-Berkeley. Education: A.B., Brown University, 1967; Ph.D., Yale University, 1971. Address: 683 San Luis Road, Berkeley, California 94707.

YESSIS, MICHAEL Occupation: Professor of Physical Education; Writer; Editor/Publisher, *Soviet Sports Review*. Education: Ph.D. Address: P.O. Box 2878, Escondido, California 92025.

YOCUM, JOHN EMERSON Occupation: President, The Best of Video, Inc. Education: B.A., M.B.A. Address: Post Office Box 11607, Phoenix, Arizona 85061.

YOKELL, MICHAEL D Occupation: Principal, Economics; Consultant. Education: B.Sc. Physics, Ph.D. Economics. Address: 3010 Regis Drive, Boulder, Colorado 80303.

YOO, JANG HEE Occupation: Professor of Economics, Virginia Commonwealth University. Education: Ph.D. Economics. Address: 3219 Nuttree Woods Drive, Midlothian, Virginia 23113.

YOPCONKA, NATALIE ANN CATHERINE Occupation: Professor/Distributor. Education: B.S. Business Administration/Personnel and Industrial Relations, M.B.A. Information Technology. Address: 7401 New Hampshire Avenue, #1115, Hyattsville, Maryland 20783.

YORK, E T JR Occupation: Educator, Chancellor Emeritus, State University Systems of Florida; Chairman, Board for International Food and Agriculture Development, Washington. Education: B.S., M.S., Ph.D. Address: 7911 Southwest 36 Avenue, Gainesville, Florida 32608.

YORK, JOAN E S Occupation: Counselor/Therapist. Education: B.A., M.Ed. Address: 138 Sanhican Drive, Trenton, New Jersey 08618.

YOUNG, ANNA BETHEL Occupation: Educational Consultant. Education: B.S., M.Ed., Ed.D. Address: 117 North Sickels Street, Philadelphia, Pennsylvania 19139.

YOUNG, ARTHUR Occupation: Economist, Author. Education: A.B. 1910, LL.D. 1937, Occidental College; Ph.D. magna cum laude, Princeton University, 1914; LL.B., George Washington University, 1927. Address: 142 Cambridge Avenue, Claremont, California 91711.

YOUNG, AURELIA NORRIS Occupation: President, J. C. Maxwell Broadcasting, Inc. Education: B.S., M.Mus., D.Mus. (Honorary). Address: 3760 Brinkley Drive, Jackson, Mississippi 39213.

YOUNG, CLYDE WILLIAM Occupation: Professor of Music, Wayne State University. Education: B.S. Education, M.Mus. Organ, Ph.D. Musicology, M.S. Library Science. Address: 498 Barrington Road, Grosse Pointe Park, Michigan 48130.

YOUNG, DOUGLAS ALBERT JR Occupation: Commercial Real Estate Broker. Education: B.A. Address: 7430 Mercier, Kansas City, Missouri 64114.

YOUNG, DOUGLAS PARKER Occupation: Professor of Higher Education, University of Georgia. Education: B.A., M.A., Ed.D. Address: 220 Pine Forest Drive, Athens, Georgia 30606.

YOUNG, EUGENE C Occupation: School Specialist, Department of Education, State of Florida. Education: M.S. Educational Administration. Address: 1812 Aaron Drive, Tallahassee, Florida 32303.

YOUNG, FLORENCE Occupation: Oriental Rug Expert, Restorer, Appraiser; World Traveler and Lecturer; Real Estate Broker; Nebraska State President, National League of American Pen Women; Guild Board Member, Playhouse, Symphony, Opera, Morning Musicale, Omaha Woman's Club. Education: Attended the University of Nebraska-Omaha. Address: 503 South 67 Avenue, Omaha, Nebraska 68106.

YOUNG, JOSEPH L Occupation: Program Director, National Science Foundation. Education: B.A., Yale University, 1962; Ph.D., Stanford University, 1966. Address: 5905 McKinley Street, Bethesda, Maryland 20817.

YOUNG, HOPE THREADGILL Occupation: Psychotherapist, Program Coordinator, University of Colorado-Colorado Springs. Education: M.A. Counseling and Student Personnel Psychology. Address: 3785 Windmill Court, Colorado Springs, Colorado 80907.

YOUNG, JOSEPH EARNEST Occupation: Associate Professor of Art History; Director, Harry Wood Art Gallery; Art Critic, Scottsdale Daily Progress. Address: 8455 East Bonnie Rose Avenue, Scottsdale, Arizona.

YOUNG, M JAMES Occupation: Professor/Director of Theatre, Wheaton College. Education: B.A., M.A., Ph.D. Address: 829 South Main Street, Wheaton, Illinois 60187.

YOUNG, PAMELA R Occupation: Family Therapist/Social Worker. Education: B.A., M.S.W. Address: 401 East 86th Street, New York, New York 10028.

YOUNGBLOOD, GENE A Occupation: Southern Baptist Evangelist. Education: B.A., M.Div., D.Min. Address: 2998 Bernice Court, Jacksonville, Florida 32217.

YOUNGBLOOD, RONALD F Occupation: Professor of Old Testament and Hebrew, Bethel Theological Seminary West. Education: B.A., B.D., Ph.D. Address: 4747 College Avenue, San Diego, California 92115.

YOUNGLOVE, RUTH ANN Occupation: Artist, Watercolors. Education: B.E., University of California-Los Angeles, 1932. Address: 1180 Yocum Street, Pasadena, California 91103.

YOUNT, DAVID EUGENE Occupation: Professor of Physics, Department of Physics and Astronomy, University of Hawaii. Education: B.S., California Institute of Technology, 1957; M.S. 1959, Ph.D. 1963, Stanford University. Address: 2505 Correa Road, Honolulu, Hawaii 96822.

YOUNTS, SANFORD EUGENE Occupation: Vice President, University of Georgia. Education: B.S., M.S., Ph.D. Address: 150 Devereaux Drive, Athens, Georgia 30606.

YOUST, DAVID B Occupation: Executive Director, Career Development Council, Inc. Education: B.S., M.S., Ph.D. Address: 126 East Second Street, Corning, New York 14830.

YUDAIN, SIDNEY Occupation: Newspaper Publisher/Editor. Address: 4901 Potomac Avenue, Northwest, Washington, D.C. 20007.

YURICK, ANN M Occupation: Nurse Educator. Education: B.S.M., M.A., Ph.D. Address: 4670 Marjorie Drive, Murrysville, Pennsylvania 15668.

YUTHAS, LADESSA J Occupation: Professor of Reading, Metro State College. Education: B.S., C.S.U.; M.S., Purdue University; Ph.D., University of Colorado. Address: 495 West 4th Avenue Drive, Broomfield, Colorado 80020.

Z

ZABIK, MARY ELLEN Occupation: Professor, Department Food Science and Human Nutrition, Michigan State University. Education: B.S., M.S., Ph.D. Address: 5300 Barton, Box 326, Williamston, Michigan 48895.

ZABOROWSKI, ROBERT RONALD JOHN MARIA Occupation: Provincial Archbishop, Prime Bishop. Education: Student, LaSalle Extension University; D.D. 1971, J.C.D. 1974, S.T.D., Ph.D. 1976, St. Ignatius Bishop and Martyr Old Catholic Seminary. Address: Mariavite Old Catholic Church, Province of North America, Administrative Center, 2803 Tenth Street, Wyandotte, Michigan 48192-4994.

ZACK, GEORGE Occupation: Music Director/Conductor. Education: B.M., M.M, Ph.D. Address: 237 Woodspoint Road, Lexington, Kentucky 40502.

ZAHAVY, REUVAIN Occupation: Instructor, Queensborough Community College of City University of New York. Education: B.A., M.S., M.A. Address: 210 East 68 Street, New York, New York 10021.

ZAHRASTNIK, NINO Occupation: CAD Specialist, Mechanical Engineering Department, University of Texas-Austin. Education: B.S., M.S. Mechanical Engineering. Address: Mechanical Engineering Department, University of Texas, Austin, Texas 78712.

ZAIDI, MAHMOOD A Occupation: Professor and Director of Graduate Study, University of Minnesota. Education: B.A. (Hon.), M.A., University of California-Los Angeles; Ph.D., University of California-Berkeley. Address: 528 North Mississippi River Boulevard, St. Paul, Minnesota 55104.

ZAKIM, GERALD Occupation: Chemical Company Executive, Construction Consultant. Education: B.S., Clemson University, 1951; University of Wisconsin Engineering Extension. Address: 8 Nottingham Road, P.O. Box 2124, Wayne, New Jersey 07470.

ZAKIN, JACQUES LOUIS Occupation: Professor and Chairman, Department of Chemical Engineering, Ohio State University. Education: Bachelor of Chemical Engineering, M.S. Chemical Engineering, Doctor of Engineering Science. Address: 6550 Evening Street, Worthington, Ohio 43085.

ZALESKI, MAREK BOHDAN Occupation: Professor of Microbiology, Department of Microbiology, State University of New York. Education: M.D., Dr.Med.Sci. Address: 95 Willow Green, Tomawanda, New York 14150.

ZAMPIELLO, HELEN S Education: A.S., Western Connecticut State University, 1974. Address: Woodbury Road, Washington, Connecticut 06793.

ZAMPIELLO, RICHARD S Occupation: Executive, Copper Industry. Education: B.A., M.B.A. Address: Woodbury Road, Washington, Connecticut 06793.

ZANES, GEORGE W Occupation: Chief Executive Officer, Zanes and Associates, Inc. Education: B.S., University of New Hampshire. Address: 7000 Boulevard East, Guttenberg, New Jersey 07093.

ZANES, RUTH LEE Occupation: Marketing Consultant. Education: B.A. Psychology, Graduate Studies. Address: 7000 Boulevard East, Guttenberg, New Jersey 07093.

ZARANKA, WILLIAM F Occupation: Poet; Director, Creative Writing Program, University of Denver. Education: B.A., M.A., Ph.D. Address: 2105 South Fillmore Street, Denver, Colorado 80210.

ZARISKI, BIRDINE ADELSTEIN Occupation: Chairman, Rating Board, Veterans Administration. Education: A.B., J.D. Address: 2312 Calumet Court, Lincoln, Nebraska 68502.

ZASTOUPIL, MARK ALAN Occupation: Engineering Manager, Doric Foods Corporation. Education: B.S.I.E., University of Wisconsin, 1973; Business Management Diploma, LaSalle Extension University, 1976. Address: P.O. Box 1184, Mt. Dora, Florida 32757.

ZATZ, IRVING J Occupation: Structural Engineer, Princeton University, Plasma Physics Laboratory. Education: B.S. 1975, Master of Engineering 1976, Cornell University. Address: 20 Debbie Lane, East Windsor, New Jersey 08520.

ZEFFREN, EUGENE Occupation: Vice President, Research and Development, Helene Curtis Industries, Inc. Education: A.B., Washington University, 1963; M.S. 1965, Ph.D. 1967, University of Chicago. Address: 3 Bristol Court, Lincolnshire, Illinois 60015.

ZEHRING, JOHN WILLIAM Occupation: Vice President for Development. Education: B.A., M.A., M.R.E., M.Div. Address: 90 Saratoga Avenue, Bangor, Maine 04401.

ZEIGER, JEFFREY B Occupation: Assistant Professor of Recreation and Park Administration, University of Wyoming. Education: B.A., M.A., Ed.D. Address: 415 South 14th Street, Laramie, Wyoming 82070.

ZELAZO, NATHANIEL K Occupation: President and Chairman of the Board, Astronautics Corporation of America. Education: B.A., B.S.M.E., Honorary Doctor of Engineering. Address: 1610 North Prospect, Milwaukee, Wisconsin 53202.

ZELMAN, VLADIMIR Occupation: Professor of Anesthesiology and Neurosurgery, Director of Neuroanesthesia, University of Southern California School of Medicine. Education: M.D. Address: 1015 18th Street, #1, Santa Monica, California 90404.

ZEPPONI, ALEX J Occupation: Civil Engineer. Education: B.S. Address: 37 Stetson Road, Ringwood, New Jersey 07456.

ZEYBEKOGLU, ILHAN Occupation: Architect. Education: M.Arch., Harvard University; Dipl. Ing. Arch., University of Stuttgart, Germany, 1965. Address: 452 Beacon Street, Boston, Massachusetts 02115.

ZIBBELL, DAVID RICHARD Occupation: Manufacturing Company Executive. Education: B.E.E., Rensselaer Polytechnic Institute, 1961; M.S. Industrial Management, Massachusetts Institute of Technology, 1963; B.S. Accounting Equivalent; New Jersey Accountancy Qualifying Certificate, 1983; Certified Public Accountant. Address: 7255 Crescentville Boulevard, Pennsauken, New Jersey 08110.

ZIBRUN, S MICHAEL Occupation: Chief Executive Officer, S. Michael Associates, Ltd. Education: B.A. Business Administration, Elmhurst College; M.B.A., Illinois Benedictine College. Address: 346 South 48th Avenue, Bellwood, Illinois 60104.

ZIEMBA, THADDEUS S Occupation: Accountant. Education: B.B.A., M.B.A. Address: 12 Canterbury Road, New Hartford, New York 13413.

ZIMMER, JONATHAN E Occupation: Executive Director of ACTION-Houring, Inc. Education: B.A. Philosophy and Religion, Boston University, 1964; M.P.A., University of Pittsburgh. Address: 2020 Carriage Hill Road, Allison Park, Pennsylvania 15101.

ZIMMERMAN, FRANCES HOWELL Occupation: Instructor (Staff Trainer). Education: B.A. Fine Arts.

Address: 9706 Hayes, Overland Park, Kansas 66212.

ZIMMERMAN, JOHN W Occupation: Management Consultant. Education: B.S., University of Tennessee, 1951; M.B.A., University of Wisconsin, 1952. Address: 11 Old Orchard Lane, Princeton, New Jersey 08540.

ZIMMERMAN, TONI ORTNER Occupation: College Instructor, Writer. Education: B.A., Hofstra University; M.A., Western Connecticut State University. Address: Bell Hollow Road, Putnam Valley, New York 10579.

ZINNES, HARRIET F Occupation: Professor of English, Queens College. Education: B.A., M.A., Ph.D. Address: 25 West 54 Street, New York, New York 10019.

ZITKO, H JOHN Occupation: President and Board Chairman, World University and World University Roundtable; International Secretariat, Tucson, Arizona. Education: Doctor of Divinity, Golden State University, 1949. Address: 711 East Blacklidge Drive, Tucson, Arizona 85719.

ZODIKOFF, HOWARD P Occupation: Accounting Firm Executive. Education: B.S., Columbia University, 1963. Address: 36 Windgate Drive, New City, New York 10976.

ZOFFER, H J Occupation: Dean, Graduate School of Business, University of Pittsburgh. Education: B.B.A., M.A., Ph.D., C.P.C.U. Address: 5620 Aylesboro Avenue, Pittsburgh, Pennsylvania 15217.

ZOGBY, JOHN J Occupation: National Field Representative, American-Arab Anti-Discrimination Committee; Master's Degree, Syracuse University. Address: 18 Springate Street, Utica, New York 13502.

ZOMMERS, G JURIS Occupation: Interior Designer. Education: B.S., University of Washington-Seattle, 1962. Address: 459 Shannon Drive, Bainbridge Island, Washington 98110.

ZOOK, AMY JO Occupation: Writer, Lecturer, Educator. Education: B.A., Wittenberg; M.A., West Virginia. Address: 3520 State Route 56, Mechanicsburg, Ohio 43044.

ZOOK, MARY ANN Occupation: College Music Teacher, Hartwick College; Pianist. Education: B.S. Music Education, Pennsylvania State University; M.M. Piano, Indiana University. Address: 4 East Street, Oneonta, New York 13820.

ZOPPO, JEROME J Occupation: Sex Therapist, School Psychologist. Education: M.Ed., D.Ed. Address: 244 Fort Lee Road, Leonia, New Jersey 07605.

ZSIGMOND, ELEMER K Occupation: Professor, Department of Anesthesiology, University of Illinois Medical School. Education: M.D., University of Budapest, 1955. Address: 6609 North LeRoy Avenue, Chicago, Illinois 60646.

ZUCKERMAN, J J Occupation: Professor, Department of Chemistry, University of Oklahoma; Researcher; Author, *Basic Organometallic Chemistry*, Others. Education: B.S., University of Pennsylvania, 1957; A.M. 1959, Ph.D. 1960, Harvard University; Ph.D., University of Cambridge, 1962. Address: Department of Chemistry, 620 Parrington Oval, Room 111, Norman, Oklahoma 73019.

ZUKER, RAYMOND FREDERICK Occupation: Dean of Admissions and Financial Aid, Admissions Office, Pomona College. Education: A.B., M.Ed., Ph.D. Address: 542 West 12th Street, Claremont, California 91711.

ZULICH, MICHAEL JOSEPH Occupation: Systems Consultant. Education: B.S. Engineering, M.B.A. Finance. Address: 3656 Johnson Avenue, Riverdale, New York 10467.

ZUSSMAN, BERNARD MAURICE Occupation: Physician, Allergy and Clinical Immunology. Education: B.S., College of tne University of New York, 1925; M.A., Columbia University, 1926; M.D., New York University College of Medicine, 1980. Address: 321 Greenway Road, Memphis, Tennessee 38117.

ADDENDUM

BILBOW, JAMES ROBERT Occupation: Police Officer. Education: Associate in Aeronautical Engineering, Pennsylvania Institute of Technology, 1956; University of California Extension Course in Space Technology, 1960-61; Professional Certificate in Law Enforcement Science 1975, Certificate in Narcotics Investigation 1976, Certificate in Arson Investigation 1977, Certification in Police Management 1980, Certificate in Organized Crime 1980, American Police Academy. Address: 628 North Lemon Street, Media, Pennsylvania 19063.

CARO, CHARLES C Occupation: Microcomputer Company Executive, International Consultant. Education: B.A. Social Science, 1973; M.A. Political Science, 1976. Address: 1607 Deleon, Tampa, Florida 33606.

CORIATY, GEORGE MICHAEL Occupation: General and Chancellor for Melkites (Greek Catholic) in Canada. Education: Attended University of Boston, University of Montreal, Colombia Pacific University, St-Sauvuer du Liban; Licence en Theologie; Doctorate Socio-psychology; Doctorate Political Science. Address: 329 Avenue Viger, Montreal, Quebec, Canada H2X 1R6.

GIZA, MARIE THERESA Occupation: Intermediate Grade School Teacher. Education: B.A., College of Notre Dame of Maryland, 1953; M.A., The Catholic University of America, 1960; C.A.S.E. 1972, M.S. 1982, Johns Hopkins University; Russian Scholar, Georgetown University, 1963-64; N.D.E.A. Fellowship, Kutztown State Teachers College, 1956; Attended on Scholarship Catholic University of Lublin (Poland), Jagiellonian University (Poland), Mikotaj Copernicus University (Poland); Scholar, University of Oslo. Address: 1723 Bank Street, Baltimore, Maryland 21231.

GOODMAN, JULIUS Occupation: Nuclear Engineer/Theoretical Physicist. Education: M.S. Theoretical Physics, State University, Odessa, U.S.S.R., 1958; Ph.D. Theoretical Physics, Institute Nuclear Physics, Tashkent, U.S.S.R., 1962; Honorary Degree Nuclear Physics, Institute of Technology, Odessa, U.S.S.R., 1965. Address: 1630 Via Linda, Fullerton, California 92633.

GRAY, ROLAND FRANCIS Occupation: Professor of Education, University of British Columbia. Education: A.B., M.Ed., U.N.H.; Ph.D., University of California. Address: 15282 19th Avenue, #305, Surrey, B.C. Canada V4A 1X6; 4418 Victoria Drive, Friday Harbor, Washington 98250.

HANSEN, KATHRYN GIBBON Occupation: Writer. Education: B.Sc. Education, DePaul University, 1942; Ed.M., Loyola University, 1946; Middle and Upper Grade, Chicago Teacher's College, 1936; Advanced Adult Education, University of Chicago, 1947-48; Sociology Studies, George Willimams College, 1950; Attended the Art Institute of Chicago, 1937, 1948, 1949. Address: 2240-O Via Puerta, Laguna Hills, California 92653.

HUCK, LARRY R Occupation: President, Northwest Manufacturers' Association. Education: Attended Washington Technical Institute, Enmonds Community College, Seattle Community College. Address: 14203 Northeast 10th Place, Bellevue, Washington 98007.

LATTIMER, AGNES DOLORES Occupation: Pediatrician. Education: A.B., Fisk University, 1949; M.D., The Chicago Medical School, 1954; Intern, Cook County Hospital, 1954-56; Resident, Pediatrics, Michael Reese Hospital, 1956-58. Address: 2138 East 75th Street, Chicago, Illinois 60649.

LEE, ELEANOR GAY Occupation: Artist. Address: 15 Gramercy Park, New York, New York 10003.

OSWALD, LORI JO Occupation: Free-lance Writer, Music Teacher. Education: A.A. Social Science, B.M. Address: Post Office Box 6929, Anchorage, Alaska 99502-0929.

MAGEE, ALBERT A JR Occupation: Broker and Owner, Magee's Realty, Long Beach, California. Education: B.S., Southern University and A. & M.C.; Graduate Work in Education and Counseling, California State University-Long Beach; M.S., University of Southern California-Los Angeles. Address: 1886 West Willow Street, Long Beach, California 90810.

PEMBERTON, JANETTE E Occupation: Associate Professor. Education: D.A., Catholic University of America. Address: 4404 Sunflower Drive, Rockville, Maryland 20853.

PEMBERTON, S MACPHERSON Occupation: Member, National Advisory Board, American Security Council; Chairman, Metric Education Planning Committee, U.S. Department of Education. Education: B.A., M.A., Ph.D. Address: 4404 Sunflower Drive, Rockville, Maryland 20853.

RIGGS, LARRY W Occupation: Professor, University of Hawaii. Education: B.A., M.A., Ph.D. Address: 864A Aalapapa Drive, Kailua, Hawaii 96734.

ROBERTSON, THOMAS DONNELL Occupation: Director of Community Services. Education: B.A., B.S., A.M.B.A. Address: 664 MacDonough Street, Brooklyn, New York 11233.

SANDERS, DANIEL S Occupation: Dean, Professor and Director, International Programs. Education: B.A. Social Sciences, Ceylon; Postgraduate Diploma Social Work Administration, Wales; M.S.W., Ph.D. Social Work, University of Minnesota. Address: 1807 Vancouver Place, Honolulu, Hawaii 96822.

TSANG, N F Address: 28796 Adobe Court, Hayward, California 94542.

YAKIN, PAUL M Occupation: Clinical Psychologist, Executive Director, Bridgeport Mental Health Center, Ltd. Education: B.S. Psychology, University of Wisconsin, 1953; M.A. Clinical Psychology, Indiana University, 1955; M.A. Personality and Psychopathology, University of Chicago, 1970; Registered Psychologist, State of Illinois, 1965. Address: 4800 South Lake Shore Drive, Apartment 1302 S., Chicago, Illinois 60615.

BIOGRAPHIES OF
DISTINGUISHED YOUNG AMERICANS

A

ABBOTT, DAVID CHARLES Occupation: Director of Children's Ministry; Student. Education: B.A.; Attending New Orleans Baptist Theological Seminary. Address: Route 1, Box 62-B, Wilmer, Alabama 36587.

ABRAMOFF, JACK A Occupation: Chairman, College Republican National Committee; Chairman, U.S.A. Foundation. Education: B.A. magna cum laude English, Brandeis University. Address: 8708 First Avenue, #902, Silver Spring, Maryland 20910.

AGUILERA, RAYMOND OTTO Occupation: Student. Education: Attending Lewis University. Address: 1724 West Melrose, Chicago, Illinois 60657.

AKIYAMA, JULIE S Occupation: Doctoral Graduate Student. Education: B.A., M.A., Doctorate (in progress). Address: 1147 South Windsor Boulevard, Los Angeles, California 90019.

ALDERMAN, AMELIA ANNE Occupation: Senior Resident Physician in Psychiatry, J.H.M.H.C., University of Florida. Education: A.B., M.D. Address: 4411 Northwest 29th Terrace, Gainesville, Florida 32605.

ALDERMAN, LOUIS CLEVELAND III Occupation: Computer Systems Technical Support Engineer, Hewlett Packard Company, Computer Support Division. Education: A.A. Electrical Engineering, Middle Georgia College, 1975; Bachelor Electrical Engineering, Georgia Institute of Technology, 1977. Address: 3011 Falling Brook Drive, Kingwood, Texas 77345.

ALDERMAN, ROBERT EDWARD JR Occupation: Student. Education: Student Agricultural Education, University of Florida; A.A., Hillsborough Community College. Address: 2801 North 76th Street, Tampa, Florida 33619.

ALEXANDER, ALPHA VERNELL Occupation: Athletic Administrator. Education: B.A., The College of Wooster; M.A., Ed.D., Temple University. Address: 870 North 28th Street, Apartment 216, Philadelphia, Pennsylvania 19130.

ALEXANDER, RONALD E Occupation: Student. Education: B.A. Political Science. Address: Route 2, Box 31, Salem, South Carolina 29676.

ALLEGRETTI, EDWARD PHILIP Occupation: Student. Education: Attending San Jose State University. Address: 12500 Poppy Lane, San Jose, California 95127.

ALLEN, KERRY LYN Occupation: Speech Pathologist, Trigg County Middle School. Education: B.S. 1981, M.S. 1982, Western Kentucky University. Address: Route 2, Cadiz, Kentucky 42211.

ALLEN, ROGER CRAIG Occupation: Student. Education: Degree Political Science/Economic Management, Ohio Wesleyan University. Address: 279 Grandview Avenue, Piscataway, New Jersey 08854.

ALLEN, SHELLEY M Occupation: Student. Address: Route 3, Box 713, Selmer, Tennessee 38375.

ALLGOR, RONALD D Occupation: Vocal Music Specialist/Teacher. Education: B.A., Augsburg College. Address: 315 Washington Street, Monticello, Minnesota 55362.

ALLINGER, ILENE S Occupation: Student, Production Director of Gardner-Webb Sign Language Choir. Education: Student, Gardner-Webb College. Address: 4780 Lexington Road, Athens, Georgia 30605.

ALLISON, KENNETH RAY Occupation: Student. Education: Attending Vanderbilt University. Address: 6004 Chrisbin Drive, Columbus, Georgia 31909.

ALLISON, LYNDA M Occupation: Publicity Manager, Public Relations Department, The Commercial Bank. Education: B.A. Journalism and Communications, Brenau College. Address: 1005 Buckingham Circle, Atlanta, Georgia 30327.

ALTENHOF, SHIRLEY ELAINE Occupation: Law Student. Education: B.S. Agricultural Economics cum laude, Texas A&M University; Law Student, Texas Tech University. Address: Route 2, Box 687, New Braunfels, Texas 78130.

AMISTAD, FELINO ANTHONY R II Occupation: Securities Investor, Account Manager. Education: A.B., Stanford University. Address: 44201 Arapaho Avenue, Fremont, California 94538.

ANDERSON, DEBORAH KAY Education: B.A. Music Education, Master's Degree Religious Education. Address: Post Office Box 308, South Bridge Street, Enterprise, Kansas 67441.

ANDERSON, RICHARD E Occupation: Student. Education: Degree in Electrical Engineering (in progress). Address: Box 140, Highway 5904, Woston, Wyoming 82731.

ANDREWS, RICHARD G Occupation: Assistant United States Attorney. Education: B.A., Haverford College, 1977; J.D., University of California, 1981. Address: 844 King Street, Wilmington, Delaware 19801.

ANSCHUTZ, LUCY ANN Occupation: Graduate Student. Education: B.A. magna cum laude 1983, Graduate Studies Clinical Psychology, Fort Hays State University. Address: Post Office Box 190, Russell, Kansas 67665.

ANTOLIN, STANISLAV Occupation: Research Assistant. Education: B.Sc. Materials Engineering. Address: 627 Minnesota Street, Pittsburgh, Pennsylvania 15217.

ARBOGAST, CYNTHIA JEANNE Occupation: Student. Education: Attending Prince George's Community College. Address: 64 Circle Avenue, Indian Head, Maryland 20640.

ARBUCKLE, PAUL DOUGLAS Occupation: Aerospace Engineer, NASA-Langley. Education: B.S. Aerospace Engineering. Address: 107 Maple Road, Newport News, Virginia 23602.

ARCHER, JACKIE D Occupation: Secretary, Flat Top Insurance Agency. Education: A.S. Legal Secretarial Science. Address: 105 Vine Street, Princeton, West Virginia 24740.

ARMBRISTER, DENISE L Occupation: Student. Education: Attending College. Address: Rural Route 1, Zurich, Kansas 67676.

ARMBRUSTER, TRACEY LEE Occupation: Student. Education: Attending Centre College of Kentucky. Address: 53 Hillsdale Drive, Louisville, Kentucky 40220.

ARNOLD, CHERYL ANN Education: B.S. Dietetics. Address: 25 South Boxwood, O'Fallon, Missouri 63366.

ARNOVITZ, TAMARA KAY Occupation: Student. Address: Route #2, Berea, Kentucky 40403.

ARTMANN, CHARLIE WILLIAM Occupation: Experimentalist, CIBA-Geigy Corporation. Education: B.A. and M.Ag., Mississippi State University; M.B.A., Delta State University, 1985. Address: 927 West Lynn Circle, Greenville, Mississippi 38701.

ASH, DON A Occupation: Student. Education: Attending Jonesboro Senior High School. Address: 681 Flint River Road, Apartment 34-E, Jonesboro, Georgia 30236.

ASHLEY, SAUNDRA LYNN Occupation: Enlisted in the United States Air Force. Education: High School

Diploma. Address: 9367 Heitts Chapel Road, Ripley, Ohio 45167.

ATCHLEY, ANTHONY A Occupation: Graduate Student. Education: B.A., M.S., Ph.D. (in progress), University of Mississippi. Address: Box 3835, University, Mississippi 38677.

AYERS, BOBBY G Occupation: College Student. Address: Star Route, Double Springs, Alabama 25553.

B

BACON, DOUGLAS RICHARD Occupation: Medical Student. Education: B.A. History, B.S. Medicinal Chemistry. Address: 5101 Clearview Drive, Williamsville, New York 14221.

BAER, BARBARA SUE Occupation: Pre-Medical Student. Education: Degree in Pre-Medicine (in progress). Address: 345 South North Street, Maugansville, Maryland 21767.

BAGLEY, MARY CAROL Occupation: Instructor/Professional Writer. Education: B.A., M.A. Address: 12539 Falling Leaves Court, St. Louis, Missouri 63141.

BAILEY, JOE EDWARD Occupation: Salesperson. Education: B.B.A. 1984. Address: Post Office Box 1085, San Juan, Texas 78589.

BAILEY, JOHN S Occupation: College Student. Education: B.A. (in progress), Averett College. Address: 2435 Kingston Road, Northwest, Roanoke, Virginia 24017.

BAKER, CHARLOTTE M Occupation: Student. Education: B.S. Physical Education. Address: Route 2, Box 2618, Auburndale, Florida 33823.

BAKER, SHEILA LEA Occupation: Licensed Vocational Nurse. Education: Vocational Nursing and Associates of Science. Address: 431 Walnut, Ranger, Texas 76470.

BAKER, TRACY THOMAS Occupation: Student. Education: Degree in Accounting (in progress), LaSalle College. Address: 50 East Knight Avenue, Collingswood, New Jersey 08108.

BAKKO, MARK THOMAS Occupation: Certified Public Accountant, Student. Education: B.S. Business Administration, Master of Business Taxation. Address: 9119 13th Avenue South, Bloomington, Minnesota 55420.

BALDRIDGE, SCOTT ALAN Occupation: Church Representative to Bogota, Colombia, Church of Jesus Christ of Latter-Day Saints. Address: 1358 Woodside Drive, San Luis Obispo, California 93401.

BALL, JILL RAE Occupation: College Student. Education: B.S. Business Administration (in progress), Georgetown College. Address: Rural Route 1, Worthville, Kentucky 41908.

BALLINGER, VIRGINIA P Occupation: Teacher's Aid/Student. Education: A.A., B.A. (in progress). Address: 1151 Arthur Street, Orlando, Florida 32804.

BANICK, PAUL DAVID Occupation: Medical Student. Education: B.S. Chemistry, B.S. magna cum laude. Address: 6 San Hill Road, Stanhope, New Jersey 07874.

BARBER, JANICE ANN Occupation: Respiratory Therapy. Education: Student, C.R.T.T. Program. Address: 2300 Taft Circle, #276, Baytown, Texas 77520.

BARBOUR, CATHY ANN Occupation: Registered Nurse. Education: B.S.N. Address: 1139 North Church Street, Apartment B-4, Greensboro, North Carolina 27401.

BARKER, MARK HUDSON Occupation: Student. Education: Attending University of Tennessee-Knoxville. Address: 121 Westwood Drive, Clinton, Tennessee 37716.

BARNES, SANDRA ANN Occupation: College Student. Education: B.A., Master of Social Science. Address: Route 2, Box 161, Columbia, Mississippi 39429.

BARRETTE, JEANNINE R Occupation: Inside Salesperson, Corp Brothers. Education: B.A. Psychology, 1981. Address: 1097 Mendon Road, Woonsocket, Rhode Island 02895.

BARTOLOMEO, RICK C Occupation: Gary City Councilman, Chief Probation Officer, Lake County Court, Division I. Address: 4742 Adams, Gary, Indiana 46408.

BARTYLLA, JAMES ROBERT Occupation: Bank Accountant. Education: B.B.A. Accounting. Address: West 220, South 3731 Hidden Court, Waukesha, Wisconsin 53186.

BARTYLLA, THOMAS EDWARD Occupation: Student. Education: Attending University of Wisconsin-Milwaukee. Address: West 220, South 3731 Hidden Court, Waukesha, Wisconsin 53186.

BATCHELOR, PATRICIA ANN Occupation: Paysheet Data Entry Operator. Education: Accounting Tech., Indiana Business College. Address: 68 East Grove, Lot 1, Morocco, Indiana 47963.

BATSON, INDIRA TAVIRA Occupation: Student, Volunteer Teacher. Education: Attending Brooklyn College. Address: 1156 Troy Avenue, Brooklyn, New York 11203.

BATTEN, JULIA VAN Occupation: Doctoral Student; Gifted Mentorship Director, University of Georgia. Education: B.A. Psychology, M.A. Special Education, Ph.D. Educational Psychology (in progress). Address: 835-B Hill Street, Athens, Georgia 30605.

BAUER, VIRGINIA ANN Occupation: Nurse, United States Air Force Regional Hospital, March Air Force Base. Education: B.S. Nursing. Address: 512 Kerrwood Road, Pittsburgh, Pennsylvania 15215.

BAUGHN, LISA RENEE Occupation: Student. Address: 6390 Duquesne Drive, Pensacola, Florida 32504.

BAUGHMAN, WILLIAM ALLEN Occupation: Counselor, Individual and Family. Education: B.A. Psychology, Behavioral Science, M.Ed. Community Counseling. Address: 6078 Cherokee Valley Lane, Lithonia, Georgia 30058.

BAUMER, KIMBERLY A Occupation: Salesperson, IBM. Education: B.A. Communication Arts. Address: Post Office Box U-278 U.S.A., Mobile, Alabama 36688.

BEAN, MICHAEL CHRIS Occupation: Programmer/Analyst, Science Applications, Inc. Education: B.S. Computer Science, Middle Tennessee State University. Address: 910 Willowbrook Drive #1, Huntsville, Alabama 35802.

BEASLEY, MARK STEVEN Occupation: Police Communications Operator. Education: B.S. (in progress). Address: 821 Stockell Street, Nashville, Tennessee 37207.

BEASLEY, WILLIAM A Occupation: Educator/Consultant, Department of Educational Psychology, University of Georgia. Education: B.A. Psychology, M.Ed. Educational Psychology, Ed.D. Education of the Gifted (in progress). Address: 185 Tuxedo Road, Athens, Georgia 30606.

BECHMAN, ANITA MARIE Occupation: College Student. Address: 1707 Monroe Street, Covington, Kentucky 41014.

BECHT, MERI B Occupation: Electrical Engineer. Education: Bachelor of Science Electrical Engineering, Bachelor of Science Comp. Engineering. Address: 1004 Dolores, St. Louis, Missouri 63132.

BECHTOLD, MADELINE MICHELLE Occupation: Student. Education: B.A. German, 1984. Address: 640 Sweetbriar Branch, Longwood, Florida 32750.

BECK, JULIE RENEE Occupation: Student. Education: Bachelor Arts and Sciences (in progress). Address: Route 3, Box 347, Montpelier, Ohio 43543.

BECK, SCOTT DOUGLAS Occupation: Graphic

Designer. Education: Attending Washburn University. Address: 10222 Northwest 70th, Silver Lake, Kansas 66539.

BECKER, BRIAN L Occupation: Student. Education: Attending George Washington University. Address: 10081 Dudley Drive, Ijamsville, Maryland 21754.

BECKER, MICHAEL ELIAS Occupation: Aeronautical Engineer. Education: B.S. Aircraft Maintenance Engineering. Address: 214 West Pitman, O'Fallon, Missouri 63366.

BECKMAN, VAUGHN F Occupation: Graduate Student; High School Teacher, Lanakila Baptist Schools, Waipahu, Hawaii. Education: B.S., M.A., Liberty Baptist College. Address: R.F.D. Box 643, Deer Isle, Maine 04627.

BEFORT, JAKE J Occupation: Secondary Teacher. Education: B.S. Mathematics. Address: Box 101, Rexford, Kansas 67753.

BEGNAUD, WANDA HEBERT Occupation: Assistant Professor-Dietitian, University Southwestern Louisiana. Education: B.S., M.S., R.D. Address: 110 Karen Drive, Lafayette, Louisiana 70503.

BEHRENS, BRETT ALLEN Occupation: Photographer. Education: B.A., Arizona State University. Address: 2060 Wilkins Avenue #20, Napa, California 94558.

BEISH, LEONARD CHARLES Occupation: Student. Education: B.A. Computer Science, Messiah College, 1984. Address: R.D. #5, Bloomsburg, Pennsylvania 17815.

BELL, JOHN M Occupation: Student. Education: B.A. Marketing (in progress). Address: 214 Hannings Lane, Martin, Tennessee 38238.

BELL, LIZABETH LEIGH Occupation: Student. Education: B.A. Biochemistry (in progress). Address: 3828 Rockhill Road, Birmingham, Alabama 35223.

BELL, LOUISE HELEN Occupation: Assistant to the President's Personal Photographer, The White House. Education: B.A., Washington and Jefferson College. Address: 3246 Q Street, Northwest, Washington, D.C. 20007.

BELZER, JUDITH ANN Occupation: Accountant. Education: B.A. Business Administration, Mid-America Nazarene College. Address: 600 South Harrison, Apartment 62, Olathe, Kansas 66061.

BENESON, DAVID ELLIOTT Occupation: Podiatrist, Foot Specialist. Education: Doctor of Podiatric Medicine, Ohio College of Podiatric Medicine. Address: 24320 Kipling, Oak Park, Michigan 48237.

BENNETT, JOHN REAGAN Occupation: Student. Education: Attending California University of Pennsylvania. Address: 507 Union Street, Brownsville, Pennsylvania 15417.

BENNETT, JOY LYNN Occupation: Student. Education: B.S. Accounting. Address: Route 1, Box 273, Lost Creek, West Virginia 26385.

BENNETT, NEAL SCOTT Occupation: College Student. Education: Attending Texas Lutheran College. Address: Route 1 Box 135 B, Stockdale, Texas 78160.

BERGER, JOY SUSANNE Occupation: Graduate Student, Musician/Teacher. Education: B.M. Piano Performance, Sanford University. Address: S.B.T.S. Box 548, Louisville, Kentucky 40280.

BERGER-BRUNN, ANITA R Occupation: Physical Therapist. Education: B.S., L.P.T., M.A. Address: 26-31 Warren Road, Apartment E, Fair Lawn, New Jersey 07410.

BERNHARDT, DARCY GWEN Occupation: Student. Education: Attending Pepperdine University. Address: Route 1, Imperial, Nebraska.

BERNSTEIN, ELLEN Occupation: Registered Nurse, Intensive Care Unit, Maryland Institute for Emergency Medical Service Systems-The Shock Trauma Center. Education: B.S. Nursing (honors), M.S. Trauma/Critical Care and Nursing Administration (in progress). Address: 4607 Horizon Circle, #204, Baltimore, Maryland 21208.

BERRY, JIMMY DARRELL Occupation: Student. Education: Attending Stephen F. Austin State University. Address: Route 2, Box 41-A, Linden, Texas 75563.

BERRY, MARILYN DIANE Occupation: Peace Corps Volunteer in Marine Fisheries. Education: B.S. Environmental Biology, Heidelberg College. Address: 1046 Sharon-Copley Road, Wadsworth, Ohio 44281.

BERTASI, RICHARD S Occupation: Student. Education: B.A. International Relations, 1984. Address: 17 Maple Avenue South, Westport, Connecticut 06880.

BESHARA, HELEN MARIE Occupation: Student. Education: Attending Pepperdine University. Address: 4099 Fairway Drive, Canfield, Ohio 44406.

BESWICK, JEFFREY WILLIAM Occupation: Student. Education: B.A. Political Science/Economics 1984. Address: 7144 Heatherwood Drive, Jenison, Michigan 49428.

BETTI, GERALD L Occupation: College Student. Education: High School Diploma. Address: 26 Old Mill Road, Jermyn, Pennsylvania 18433.

BICE, VESTA D Occupation: Founder and Director, Reach Out to Texas Deaf. Address: Post Office Box 1886, Har L, Texas 78551.

BIFULCO, ANNA MARIE Occupation: Student. Education: B.S. Biology, Saint Joseph's College. Address: 448 Eldert Lane, Brooklyn, New York 11208.

BISSETTE, WANDA DIANNE Occupation: Student. Education: Attending Atlantic Christian College. Address: Route 2 Box 305D, Middlesex, North Carolina 27557.

BISSINGER, LAURENCE WAYNE Occupation: Computer Systems Engineer. Education: B.S.B.A., University of North Dakota, 1980. Address: 8-05 Pheasant Hollow Drive, Plainsboro, New Jersey 08536.

BIVENS, GYNA M Occupation: Public Information Manager. Education: B.A. Communication/Radio, Television, Film. Address: 500 North Santa Rosa #713, San Antonio, Texas 78207.

BIXLER, MARTHA ELIZABETH Occupation: Attending U.M.B.C. Address: 223 Balto Annap Boulevard, Severna Park, Maryland 21146.

BLACKLIDGE, FRANKIE LEE Occupation: Student. Education: A.A., New Mexico State University. Address: 212 Baldwin Avenue, Belen, New Mexico 87002.

BLAIR, TERRY L Occupation: Director of Bands and Choral Activities, Albany High School. Education: B.M.E. cum laude, Central Methodist College, 1983. Address: 101 South 7th, Albany, Missouri 64402.

BLATT, B DANIEL Occupation: Student; Chairman, Massachusetts College Republican Union. Education: B.A. Candidate, Williams College. Address: SU Box 2661, Williams College, Williamstown, Massachusetts 01267.

BLAZAR, CYNTHIA G Occupation: Bookstore Manager, Chapman College. Education: B.S. Business Administration. Address: 1645 Riverview Avenue, Orange, California 92665.

BOATMAN, JEFFERY P Occupation: College Student. Education: B.S. Computer Engineering (in progress). Address: Post Office Box 2347, Spartanburg, South Carolina 29304.

BODINE, PETER VanNEST Occupation: Graduate Student. Education: B.S. Biology; Graduate Student, Temple University School of Medicine. Address: 6603 McCallum Street, Philadelphia, Pennsylvania 19119.

BOGGS, DANNY LEE Occupation: Group Buyer/Personnel Director. Education: B.S. Business Administration. Address: 31630 9th Place Southwest, Federal Way, Washington 98023.

BOKOVOY, JOANNA LYNN Education: B.S. Elementary Education/Biology, A.S. (R.N.) Nursing, M.P.H. Health Education. Address: 310 Oakhill Drive, Keene, Texas 76059.

BOLDEN, ALAN SCOTT Occupation: Legislative Aid to Georgia Legislative Black Caucus. Education: B.A. Political Science, Morehouse College. Address: 521 South Joliet, Joliet, Illinois 60436.

BOLGER, CHARLES JR Occupation: Senior Technical (Computer) Specialist, Free-lance Technical Writer. Education: M.S., University of Pennsylvania; B.B.A., Temple University. Address: 1518 Robinson Avenue, Willow Grove, Pennsylvania 19090.

BOLIN, STEVEN JOSEPH Occupation: Student/Soccer Player. Education: Degree in Economics (in progress), Benedictine College. Address: 7516 South Pierce Court, Littleton, Colorado 80123.

BOLTON, SHAWN MARK Occupation: Pre-Veterinary Medicine Student. Education: Attending College. Address: 1102 West Main, Henderson, Tennessee 38340.

BOND, RUTH G Occupation: Legal Secretary. Education: General Business Administration, Sam Houston State University. Address: 1107 University Avenue, Huntsville, Texas 77340.

BONINE, DARRELL W Occupation: Salesman. Education: B.A. Computer Science (in progress). Address: Route 1 Box 264B, California, Missouri 65018.

BONNER, PAMELA MARIE COSENTINO Occupation: Fisheries Biologist, Microbiologist Technician. Education: B.S. Wildlife Biology, M.S. Fisheries Biology. Address: 546½ Orion Street, Metairie, Louisiana 70005.

BOOKOUT, CRAIG LEWIS Occupation: Physician. Education: M.D., Marshall University, 1983. Address: 427 East Cambridge Avenue, Greenwood, South Carolina 29646.

BOREN, SANDRA ANN Occupation: Student. Education: Student Speech and Drama. Address: 3951 East Edgerton, Cudahy, Wisconsin 53110.

BORJON, KIMBERLY ANNE Occupation: Southern California Jurisdiction Sweetheart, Order of DeMolay; Student. Address: 38461 Carolside, Palmdale, California 93550.

BORONSTEIN, TRACY Occupation: Student. Education: M.Ed. (in progress), Austin College. Address: 1185 Sailfish, Hitchcock, Texas 77563.

BOSS, ANN ELISE Occupation: Student. Education: Attending Middle Tennessee State University. Address: 713 Westside Drive, Tullahoma, Tennessee 37388.

BOSTIC, HEUGUETTE Occupation: Student. Education: B.S. Computer Engineering, Clemson University, 1984. Address: Route 3 Box 860, Moncks Corner, South Carolina 29461.

BOUDREAU, DEBORAH L Occupation: Director, National Development Council. Education: B.A. Urban Affairs, University of Connecticut. Address: 3030 Wisconsin Avenue, Washington, D.C. 20016.

BOVE, LEONARD FRANCIS Occupation: Musician/Composer. Address: 446 West 10th Street, Erie, Pennsylvania 16502.

BOWARD, MARJORIE ANN Occupation: Special Education Teacher. Education: B.A. Early Childhood Elementary and Special Education. Address: 4905 Earlston Drive, Bethesda, Maryland 20816.

BOWDISH, FANNIE BETH Occupation: Student. Education: Law Enforcement Photography Certificate, C.J. Degree. Address: Rural Route 1, Leonard, Missouri 63451.

BOWEN, SARA MARGARET Occupation: Doctoral Student. Education: B.S.Ed. Special Education; M.Ed. School Psychology; Doctoral Student School Psychology, University of Georgia. Address: 121 B Mark Twain Circle, Athens, Georgia 30605.

BOWEN, YVONNE RENA Occupation: Clerical/Deputy Clerk. Education: Graduate, Barbizon School of Modeling; Diploma, Associate Schools, Inc. Address: Route 1 Box 196, Crittenden, Kentucky 41030.

BOWIE, PAMELA KAYE Occupation: Graduate Teaching Fellow, Sociology Department, T.W.U. Education: B.S. 1982, Master's Degree (in progress). Address: Route 4, Box 171, Tyler, Texas 75703.

BOWRING, TAMII LEIGH Occupation: Bookkeeper. Education: College Studies, Biology/Business. Address: 21042 Hickory Street, Brooksville, Florida 33512.

BOYER, DOUGLAS WILLIAM Occupation: Student. Education: Attending Messiah College. Address: 59 Wooley Road, West Milford, New Jersey 07480.

BOYETTE, KATRINA MARCIA Occupation: Student. Education: B.B.A. Computer Information Systems (in progress), Delta State University. Address: 316 Southwest Avenue, Durant, Mississippi 39063.

BRAACKEN, DEBRA J Occupation: High School Student. Address: Post Office Box 2205, Venice, Florida 33595.

BRANNING, DONNA JEANNE Occupation: Student. Education: Attending College of Charleston. Address: 109 Marion Street, Batesburg, South Carolina 29006.

BRASHER, JERRY WAYNE Occupation: Industrial Engineer. Education: B.S. Industrial Engineering, A.A. Engineering, A.S. Design Technology. Address: 13615 Tara Oak Drive, Houston, Texas 77065.

BRAWLEY, JAMIE BLANCHE Occupation: Student. Education: Attending Kent State University. Address: 4655 County Line Road, Newton Falls, Ohio 44444.

BRAY, JERRY MARK Occupation: College Republican State Chairman. Education: B.A. Political Science/History (in progress). Address: Box 245, First Street, Hackensack, Minnesota 56452.

BRAZIEL, MARTEN LEIGH Occupation: Student. Education: B.Mus. magna cum laude; M.M. Voice; Student Accounting/German, West Berlin. Address: 4521 Candletree Circle, Indianapolis, Indiana 46254.

BREED, JANET C DEATON Occupation: Educator, Student. Education: B.S. Education, Baylor University; Master's Degree (in progress), Houston Baptist University. Address: 9330 Synott #408N, Houston, Texas 77099.

BRETT, TRACY LYN Occupation: Student. Education: Attending Chowan College. Address: 414 Holly Hill Road, Murfreesboro, North Carolina 27855.

BREWTON, JACKIE L Occupation: Supervisor, Promotion Payment Office, Procter & Gamble. Education: B.A. Business Administration, Furman University. Address: 1735 Carrahen Avenue, Cincinnati, Ohio 45237.

BRIDGES, SHERRI LEIGH Occupation: Manager, Mooresville Swimming Pool. Education: Student,

Winthrop College. Address: 781 Pinewood Circle, Mooresville, North Carolina 28115.

BRISTER, MARK ALLEN Occupation: Minister. Education: B.A., M.Div., Ph.D. Address: 626 North Park Place, Bolivar, Missouri 65613.

BRITT, VALERIE J Occupation: Registered Nurse. Education: B.S. Biology, Boston College; Nursing Diploma, Orange Memorial SON; R.N; L.P.N.; B.S.N. (in progress), Rutgers University. Address: 314 16th Avenue, Newark, New Jersey 07103.

BROCATO, CHERYL LYNN Occupation: Industrial Engineer, Duke Power Company. Education: B.S. Industrial Engineering. Address: 4609 J Colony Road, Charlotte, North Carolina 28226.

BROOKS, BARBARA ANN Occupation: Student. Education: Attending Potomac State College. Address: 113 Main Street, Post Office Box 470, Ridgeley, West Virginia 26753-0470.

BROOKS, JAMES RICHARD Occupation: Student. Education: Associate Degree Commercial Design, Fairmont State College. Address: 113 Main Street, Ridgeley, West Virginia 26753.

BROOKS, TED DANIEL Occupation: Graduate Student. Education: B.S., Graduate Student Agricultural Economics, Texas A&M University. Address: 1301 Harvey Road, #404, College Station, Texas 77840.

BROOME, SHARON GAIL Occupation: Graduate Student. Education: M.A. Spanish, M.S. Psychology (in progress). Address: 5 Christian Place, Gulfport, Mississippi 39503.

BRORSEN, ANN JONNINE Occupation: Registered Nurse, Tucson Medical Center. Education: A.S. 1977, B.S. summa cum laude 1984, State University of New York at Albany; A.D.M., Pima Community College, 1981; B.S.M., University of Phoenix, 1984. Address: 6501 East Golf Links, Tucson, Arizona 85730.

BROSS, JAMES B JR Occupation: Student Government President, Central Wesleyan College; Part-time Public Accountant. Education: B.A. Accounting, Business Administration and Psychology, 1984. Address: Thomas Lane, Box 497 CWC, Central, South Carolina 29630.

BROSSOIT, JOYCE LYNN (OTT) Occupation: Assistant Hall Director, Student. Education: B.A. Biology, Education Certificate, 1984. Address: 11900 Southwest 116, Tigard, Oregon 97223.

BROTZ, STEPHEN MATTHEW Occupation: New Jersey Chairman, College Republicans. Education: B.S. (in progress). Address: 65 Mountain Avenue North, Plainfield, New Jersey 07060.

BROWN, DARRYL DeWYNN Occupation: Student. Address: Rural Route 1 Box 158, Laurel, Indiana 47024.

BROWN, GREGORY DEAN Occupation: Houseparent, Quakerdale Children's Home; Freelance Photographer. Education: A.A.A. Photography. Address: Box 217, Union, Iowa 50258.

BROWN, JOSELYN Occupation: Law Student. Education: B.A. Criminal Justice, Notre Dame College. Address: Route 1 Box 215, Orwell, Ohio 44076.

BROWN, LaJUAN Occupation: Expanded Duties Dental Assistant, Certified Dental Assistant. Education: E.D.D.A., C.D.A. Address: Route 1, Apollo Drive, Mt. Washington, Kentucky 40047.

BROWN, LAURIE LYNNE Occupation: Nurse. Education: B.S. Nursing, Medical College of Georgia School of Nursing. Address: 4460 Rivoli Drive, Macon, Georgia 31210.

BROWN, MICHAEL WAYDE Occupation: Electrician/Auto Mechanic. Education: A.A.S., Tri-Cities State Technical Institute, 1980. Address: Route 1 Box 271, Telford, Tennessee 37690.

BROWN, PATRICIA DENEICE Occupation: Graduate Assistant. Education: B.A., M.A., Alabama State University. Address: 457 Maury Street, Montgomery, Alabama 36104.

BROWN, TYRONE KURT Occupation: College Student. Education: Attending College. Address: 604 Shiloh Circle, Douglas, Georgia 31533.

BRUMMUND, FRANCINE ANN Occupation: College Student/Job Service Interviewer. Education: Bachelor of University Studies (Communications). Address: 3402 15 Avenue, Southwest, Suite 206, Fargo, North Dakota 58103.

BRUNI, JEFFREY SCOTT Occupation: Student. Education: Attending Gulfport High School. Address: 5100 Quincy Avenue, Gulfport, Mississippi 39501.

BRUNNER, SANDRA KAY Occupation: Enlisted United States Air Force. Address: 148 Brunner Lane, Beaver, Ohio 45613.

BRUNY, KEVIN WILLIAM Occupation: Management Trainee, Retailing. Education: B.A. Psychology. Address: 108 Ash Avenue, Moundsville, West Virginia 26041.

BRYSON, CHRISTOPHER D Occupation: Student. Education: High School Diploma. Address: 104 Elberta Drive, Lexington, South Carolina 29072.

BUCCHERI, SANTO Occupation: Medical Student, Eastern Virginia Medical School. Education: B.S. Chemistry, B.S. Biology. Address: 128 Freeman Street, Hartford, Connecticut 06114.

BUCKNER, JAMES RUSSELL Occupation: College Music Teacher, Music Department, Quincy College. Education: B.Mus., M.Mus. Address: Music Department, Quincy College, Quincy, Illinois 62301.

BUDILO, PAVEL ANDREJ Occupation: Student. Address: 1122 East Greenville Drive, West Covina, California 91790.

BULLA, JEFFERSON DAVIS III Occupation: Architectural Student. Education: B.S. Architecture, Master's Degree (in progress). Address: 300 Jefferson Drive, Graham, North Carolina 27253.

BULLARD, TRACEY L Occupation: Student. Education: B.B.A. (in progress). Address: Route 1, Cincinnati, Iowa 52549.

BUNCH, MELANIE ANNE Occupation: Student. Education: Degree in Business Administration (in progress), East Carolina University. Address: 1706 East Fourth, Greenville, North Carolina 27834.

BURCH, BEBE JILL Occupation: Student. Education: Attending Berry College. Address: 1993 Kunuga Drive, Jonesboro, Georgia 30236.

BURCH, CHARLES JR Occupation: Accountant. Education: B.S. Accounting, North Carolina A&T University. Address: 15215 Blue Ash Drive, #123, Houston, Texas 77090.

BURCH, DEBORAH LYNN Occupation: Student. Education: B.S. (in progress). Address: 5345 DuBois, Toledo, Ohio 43615.

BURCK, PETER WARREN Occupation: Student. Education: B.A. Geology (in progress), Princeton University. Address: 1138 Clinton, Oak Park, Illinois 60304.

BURKE, BRIAN E Occupation: Government Employee. Education: B.S. Political Science. Address: 53 Logan Way, South Boston, Massachusetts 02127.

BURKE, PATRICIA ANN Occupation: Attorney, Interstate Commerce Commission. Education: B.A., University of Notre Dame, 1976; J.D., Catholic University of America, 1979. Address: 1600 South East

Street, #636, South Arlington, Virginia 22202.

BURT, ANN L Occupation: Student. Education: Associate Degree, Legal Assistant. Address: 608 Oxford Oaks Lane, Oxford, Michigan 48051.

BURT, BARBARA JEAN (JEANIE) Occupation: Nursing Instructor, Baptist System School of Nursing. Education: B.S.N., Harding University, 1979; M.S.M. (in progress). Address: 622 Newcastle, Sherwood, Arkansas 62116.

BURTON, MICHAEL RAY Occupation: College Student, Park Ranger (summers). Education: B.A. History/B.A. English, Trinity University, 1985. Address: 1339 Engel, Lawrence, Kansas 66044.

BUSCH, ANN M HERBAGE Occupation: Registered Nurse, Stanford University Hospital. Education: B.S. Nursing. Address: 330 North Mathilda, Apartment #302, Sunnyvale, California 94086.

BUSHART, CHARLES RAE Occupation: Computer Programmer, Assistant DP Manager. Education: Bachelor's Degree in Computer Science. Address: 12556 South Stoney Creek, Maybee, Michigan 48159.

BUTLER, KEITH ROBERT Occupation: Taxidermist, Meat Cutter, Cabinet Crafter. Education: Meat Services. Address: 1375 9th Street, Ogden, Utah 84404.

BUTTI, THOMAS A Occupation: Chiropractor. Education: B.S., D.C. Address: 5 Seminary Avenue, Yonkers, New York 10704.

BUTTRY, JOHN DAVID Occupation: Student. Education: Attending Central State University. Address: 11117 Northwest 116th, Yukon, Oklahoma 73099.

BUTZ, DONALD J Occupation: Research Scientist, Ordnance. Education: B.S. Aeronautical and Astronautical Engineering. Address: 100 East Frambes Avenue, B-4, Columbus, Ohio 43201.

BYERS, SPERLYNN RVENOID Occupation: Student, Intern Electrical Engineering. Education: Attending University of Kansas. Address: 1300 North 44th Street, Kansas City, Kansas 66102.

C

CACHERIS, WILLIAM P Occupation: Research Assistant; Graduate Student. Education: B.A. Chemistry; Attending Florida State University. Address: 16633 South Clover, Tinley Park, Illinois 60477.

CADE, JAMES E Occupation: Dentist; Assistant Professor, Louisiana State University School of Dentistry. Education: B.A. Biology, D.D.S., Certificate in Oral Pathology. Address: 2614 Gadsden Street, Kenner, Louisiana 70062.

CADENA, HECTOR FABIO Occupation: Adjunct Lecturer; Teacher. Education: B.A., Queens College, C.U.N.Y. Address: 143-06 Barclay Avenue, Flushing, New York 11355.

CAIN, DANIELLE RAE Occupation: Student. Education: B.A. (in progress), Villanova University. Address: 308 Oak Avenue, Sharon Hill, Pennsylvania 19079.

CAIN, MARY CATHERINE Occupation: Student. Education: B.A., M.S. Psychology; Attending University of South America. Address: Route 4, Box 424, Cole Circle, Mobile, Alabama 36608.

CALDWELL, MELISSA BRIDGES Occupation: Senior Nursing Student. Education: Attending University of North Carolina at Greensboro. Address: 2428G Holden Road, Greensboro, North Carolina 27407.

CALFY, DOYLE WAYNE Occupation: Student. Education: B.S. International Trade; Attending Texas Tech University. Address: 306 Cheyenne, Canadian, Texas 79014.

CALLAHAM, KATHLEEN L Occupation: Director of Cooperative and Continuing Education. Education: B.S. Communications, M.A. Occupational and Adult Education (in progress). Address: 1212 West School Street, Claremore, Oklahoma 74017.

CALLAHAN, AMY KATHERINE Occupation: A.D. Nursing Student. Address: 2814 Ridgeland Drive, Jackson, Mississippi 39212.

CALLARI, CHARLES KIRBY Occupation: Student; IBM Intern. Education: B.S. Address: 155 Woodbine Avenue, Staten Island, New York, New York 10314.

CAMPBELL, ALVIN T III Occupation: Graduate Student. Education: B.A. Computer Science, University of Texas; Graduate Student (Ph.D.). Address: 3107 Salem Court, Sugar Land, Texas 77478.

CAMPBELL, BRADLEY J Occupation: Student; International Trustee, Key Club International. Education: High School Diploma. Address: 86 Pusey Boulevard, Brantford, Ontario, Canada N3R 2S5.

CAMPBELL, CARL DAVID Occupation: Oil Company Executive. Education: B.B.A., University of Oklahoma. Address: 4101 Northwest Expressway CB-16-253, Oklahoma City, Oklahoma 73116.

CAMPBELL, JAMES ROBERT JR Occupation: President, Campbell Motor Company. Education: Attending Southern Methodist University. Address: 1809 Arrow Lane, Garland, Texas 75042.

CAMPBELL, LISA RENEE Occupation: Student. Education: High School Diploma, B.S. Physical Education (in progress), J.M.U. Address: Route 1, Box 121, Mount Crawford, Virginia 22841.

CANFIELD, DAVID WILLIAM Occupation: Resident in Anesthesiology. Education: D.D.S., M.S. Oral Biology. Address: 5819 Los Arcos Way, Buena Park, California 90620.

CANNON, CYNTHIA A Occupation: Student

(U.K.). Education: High School Diploma. Address: 116 Cornelison Road, Richmond, Kentucky 40475.

CANTRELL, FREDERICK JOHN Occupation: Student. Education: Studying Marketing and Finance. Address: Route 13, Ingram Lane, Knoxville, Tennessee 37918.

CANTU, ORALIA SELENNA Occupation: Student. Education: Attending Freer High School. Address: 601 Huisaeh, Post Office Box 867, Freer, Texas 78357.

CAPPAERT, STEVEN MICHAEL Occupation: Student. Education: B.S. Commerce; Master of Accountancy (in progress). Address: 3411-11th Avenue A, Moline, Illinois 61265.

CARDA, JUANITA MARIE Occupation: Computer Operator. Education: A.A.S. Address: 1622 Grayson, Hobbs, New Mexico 88240.

CARLOCK, JON THOMPSON Occupation: Student. Education: Attending Bethel College. Address: 122 Netherland, Oak Ridge, Tennessee 37830.

CARLSON, RICKY LEE Occupation: Student. Education: B.S. Chemical Engineering. Address: Rural Route 1, Erwin, South Dakota 57233.

CARMICHAEL, LAWRENCE RAY Occupation: Law Student. Education: Associate in Communications, Bachelors in Business Administration. Address: 105 Gover Street, Somerset, Kentucky 42501.

CAROUTHERS, STEPHANIE ELAINE Occupation: Telecommunicator. Education: Bachelor of Science Speech Pathology and Audiology. Address: 1106 Frederick Street, Shelby, North Carolina 28150.

CARPENTER, SHEILA R Occupation: Instructor in Horse Riding. Education: Bachelor of Arts in Communications, Judson College. Address: 23 Ridgewood, Hilton Head, South Carolina 29928.

CARR, DANIEL L Occupation: Sports Editor, News-Herald. Education: B.S. Communications, University of Tennessee, 1976. Address: Route 4, Box 5A, Louden, Tennessee 37774.

CARREON, SHARON D Occupation: Computer Operator. Address: 2515 5th Avenue North, Texas City, Texas 77590.

CARROLL, RICKY L Occupation: Student; National Park Employee, Mammoth Cave National Park. Education: B.A. Communications, 1984. Address: Route 2, Box 242, Smith's Grove, Kentucky 42171.

CARTER, MARSHA ARLENE Occupation: Student. Education: B.S. English Education. Address: Post Office Box 342, Faison, North Carolina 28341.

CARUSO, EDWARD ANTHONY Occupation: Student. Education: B.S. Commerce, Rider College, 1984. Address: 1083 Glen Oak Drive, Yardley, Pennsylvania 19067.

CASEY, BRIAN K Occupation: Student. Education: Attending University of Virginia, S.V.C.C. Address: R.F.D. 1, Box 83, Swords Creek, Virginia 24649.

CASLIN, BELINDA Occupation: Student. Education: High School; Attending Summer College. Address: 318 Whitmore Avenue, Dayton, Ohio 45417.

CASON, REGINA TISA Occupation: Student. Education: B.S. Chemistry/Business. Address: 10537 South Rhodes, Chicago, Illinois 60628.

CASSEL, SUSIE L Occupation: Student. Education: Degree in Psychobiology and English (in progress). Address: 1362 Santa Cruz Court, Chula Vista, California 92010.

CASTAGNA, MARGARET ANN Occupation: Student. Education: B.A., California State University at Northridge, 1984. Address: 273 Mar Vista Drive, Vista, California 92083.

CASTRO, VINCENT EDWARD Occupation: Student. Education: B.S., St. Joseph's College, 1984. Address: 460 Grand Street, New York, New York 10002.

CATALDO, CHET WILLIAM Occupation: Pastor, Olatle General Baptist Church. Education: B.A. Religion, M.A. Religious Studies. Address: 331 North Olatheview Road, Olathe, Kansas 66061.

CATANIA, ANTHONY JR Occupation: Student. Education: B.S. (in progress), University of Miami. Address: 9290 Northwest 19th Place, Sunrise, Florida 33322.

CAUTHEN, RANDOLPH Occupation: Writer; Technical Director. Education: B.A. Address: 906 Butte Street, Claremont, California 91711.

CAZEAUX, ISABELLE ANNE-MARIE Occupation: Professor and Chairman, Music Department, Bryn Mawr College. Education: B.A., M.A., M.S., Ph.D., Licence d'Enseignement, 1ere medaille. Address: 415 East 72nd Street, New York, New York 10021.

CECHINI, CYNTHIA ROSE Occupation: Management Consultant in Construction. Education: B.A. Business Administration, M.B.A. Finance and Marketing. Address: 12890 West 16th Drive, Golden, Colorado 80401.

CECHINI, JEFFREY J Occupation: Student. Education: Chemical Engineering Degree (in progress), Attending University of Colorado. Address: 12890 West 16th Drive, Golden, Colorado 80401.

CHANDLER, CAROLE-ANN E Occupation: Senior Financial Analyst, J. Henry Schroder Bank and Trust Company. Education: B.S. Finance, St. John's University. Address: 115 Euston Road, Garden City, New York 11530.

CHAPLEY, LINDA A Occupation: Freelance Photographer; Writer. Education: B.S. Marketing and Media Production. Address: 24 Pert Street, Trumbull, Connecticut 06611.

CHAPMAN, JEFF W Occupation: Student. Education: Attending Brookland Cacye High School. Address: 3145 Woodsen Circle, West Columbia, South Carolina 29169.

CHAPMAN, NANCY ELIZABETH Occupation: Student; Instructor. Education: B.A. Business Administration (in progress). Address: 3145 Woodsen Circle, West Columbia, South Carolina 29169.

CHAPMAN, PAMELA M Occupation: Teacher. Education: B.A. Biology, Wesleyan University; A.A. with honors, Hartford College. Address: 44 Kilbourne Avenue, New Britain, Connecticut 06053.

CHAPMAN, WILLIAM WARREN Occupation: Senior Bank Examiner, Missouri Division of Finance. Education: B.S. Accounting, Business Administration, Economics, Political Science, Communications. Address: 1410 East Seminole, Springfield, Missouri 65804.

CHEW, SERENE SIOK CHENG Occupation: Graduate Student. Education: B.B.A., Chaminade University; M.S., University of Oregon. Address: 16th, Fifth Avenue, Singapore 1026.

CHILDRESS, CHARLIE JR Occupation: Wing Defensive Systems Officer, United States Air Force. Education: M.S. Operations Management, University of Arkansas; B.S. Electrical Engineering, United States Air Force Academy. Address: 36 West 22nd, Merced, California 95340-3907.

CHILDRESS, CONNIE A Occupation: Student Nurse. Education: Attending U.T.C.H.S. Address: 6282 Quince, Memphis, Tennessee 38119.

CHOI, YOON MEE Occupation: Student. Education: Attending, University of California at Irvine. Address: 52 Red Rock, Irvine, California 92714.

CHOLEWCZYNSKI, WALTER MICHAEL Occupation: Student. Education: Associate of Arts, 1983; Bachelor of Arts, 1984; Attending University of Maryland. Address: 5535-1 Green Mountain Circle, Columbia, Maryland 21044.

CHRISTIAN, CAROL J Occupation: Instructor of Physical Education, Eastern Kentucky University. Education: B.S., M.A., Rank I in School Administration. Address: 200 Patchen Drive, #102, Lexington, Kentucky 40502.

CHUN, ADA TERESA Occupation: Student. Education: B.A. (in progress), Yale University. Address: 1049 Oakdale Lane, Arcadia, California 91006.

CHURCH, AUDREY PUCKETT Occupation: Librarian, Central Senior High School. Education: B.A., Bridgewater College. Address: Route 1, Box 25-B, Keysville, Virginia 23947.

CHURCHWELL, JAMES TRACY Occupation: Electrician. Education: High School Diploma. Address: Route 1, Box 256, Adamsville, Tennessee 38310.

CIANCIOSI, VANDA Occupation: Freelance Italian Interpretor and Translator, Berlitz Translation Service. Education: B.A. French, St. Joseph's University. Address: 663 North 65th Street, Philadelphia, Pennsylvania 19151.

CICOVSKY, GEORGETTE JOANN Occupation: Activity Therapist; Student. Education: Attending University of Illinois at Chicago. Address: 5918 South Francisco, Chicago, Illinois 60629.

CLARK, BONNIE LEIGH Occupation: Radio Personality. Education: M.A., Bowling Greek State University; B.S. magna cum laude, A.A., The Defiance College. Address: 1104 Oakwood Avenue, Bryan, Ohio 43506.

CLARK, JAMES M Occupation: Real Estate Developer and Financier, The Spectrum Group, Kilburn Vacation-Homeshare, Inc., and Bajan Resorts, Inc. Education: B.S., University of the State of New York; M.B.A. Real Estate and Finance, Ph.D. Real Estate, Columbia Pacific University. Address: Salt Lake City, Utah.

CLARK, JEROME Occupation: Commercial Artist and Designer. Address: 4921 Theodore Avenue, St. Louis, Missouri 63115.

CLARK, JESS TODD Occupation: National Youth Representative, Boy Scouts of America. Education: Attending High School. Address: 4467 Frances Drive, Delray Beach, Florida 33445.

CLARK, JULIA V Occupation: Science Education Professor, Howard University. Education: Ed.D., Rutgers Univesity, 1980; M.Ed., University of Georgia, 1968; B.S., Fort Valley State College, 1960. Address: 5101 River Road #208, Bethesda, Maryland 20816.

CLARK, SHELLY LEIGHTON Occupation: Professional Performing Artist (Vocalist). Education: College Preparatory Diploma. Address: 40 Evans Street, Dorchester, Massachusetts 02124.

CLARKE, STEPHANIE A Occupation: Elementary School Teacher. Education: B.S. Education. Address: O.E.H.C. Building 31, Apartment 271, St. Thomas, Virgin Islands 00801.

CLAYTON, LESLIE JOE Occupation: Electrical Design Engineer. Education: B.S. Electrical Engineering. Address: 9455 Skillman #1711, Dallas, Texas 75243.

CLAYTON, VICTORIA Occupation: Librarian/ Videographer. Education: B.A., M.A., M.L.S. Address:

41-13 10th Street, L.I.C., New York 11101.

CLENDENIN, BILLY JOE Occupation: Student. Education: Attending West Virginia University in Mechanical Engineering. Address: Box 734, West Logan, West Virginia 25601.

CLOWNEY, WANDA DENISE Occupation: Student. Education: B.S.N. (in progress). Address: 2121-C Clemson Court, Kannapolis, North Carolina 28081.

COAD, MICHAEL DAVIS Occupation: Graduate Student in Chemistry. Education: B.S. Chemistry; A.C.S. Approved. Address: 202 B. Montclair, College Station, Texas 77840.

COBB, KENDRA LEIGH Occupation: Assistant Buyer, J. W. Robinson's. Education: B.A. Industrial Psychology and Psycholinguistics. Address: 404 Garfield, Ste. 16, Pasadena, California 91101.

COCHRAN, SHERI PAULETTE Occupation: Student. Education: Attending Jacksonville State University. Address: 314 East Jule Peek Avenue, Cedartown, Georgia 30125.

COCO, JOSEPH JEFFREY Occupation: Student. Education: B.M.E.; Attending Villanova University. Address: Shady Drive, R.D. 2, Moscow, Pennsylvania 18444.

COLE, DUNELL MARIE Occupation: Dietary Aide, Lebanon Community Hospital. Address: 910 10th Street, #23, Lebanon, Oregon 97355.

COLEMAN, DUDLEY MICHAEL Occupation: Pilot; Rancher. Education: Pilot's Training. Address: Post Office Box 178, Ackerly, Texas 79713.

COLEMAN, EARL ROBERT Occupation: USAF Telecommunications. Address: Route 2, Box 1, Packens, West Virginia 26230.

COLEMAN, KATHRYN E Occupation: Registered Nurse, Traveling Nurse Corps. Education: Associate Degree in Technical Nursing. Address: Route 3, Box 472C, Aiken, South Carolina 29801.

COLLADO, DAISY Occupation: Product Development Assistant, Revlon, Inc. Education: A.A.S. Fashion, Buying and Merchandising; B.S. Marketing. Address: 105 Pinehurst Avenue, New York, New York 10033.

COLLINS, JENNIFER HEATHER Occupation: Publications Director, Texas Woman's University. Education: B.S. Journalism, Texas Woman's University. Address: 1800 Teasley Lane #114, Denton, Texas 76205.

COMFORT, DERRICK MARK Occupation: Administrative Assistant. Education: Distinguished Honor Graduate, U.S. Army Infantry Officers Basic Course, Ft. Benning, Georgia, 1983. Address: 525 Chesapeake Avenue, Stevensville, Maryland 21666.

COMFORT, PAUL WILLIAM Occupation: Student. Education: Attending College. Address: 525 Chesapeake Avenue, Stevensville, Maryland 21666.

CONE, DEBORAH ANN Occupation: Student. Education: B.A. (in progress), Purdue University. Address: 2560 Delk Road, Apartment 0-11, Marietta, Georgia 30067.

CONGROVE, AUDREY MAE Occupation: Loan Processing Clerk. Education: Business Administration Accounting Diploma, Owensboro Junior College of Business. Address: 1736 ½ St. Mary's Avenue, Owensboro, Kentucky 42301.

CONLEY, BRIAN E Occupation: Firefighter; Emergency Medical Technician; Student. Education: Fire Science Degree; E.M.T. Address: 121 Riverview Park, Montgomery, West Virginia 25136.

CONLEY, ULYSSES Occupation: Resident Counselor and Student, Jackson State University.

Education: B.S. Environmental Health; M.P.A. (in progress). Address: Route 2, Box 47, Carrollton, Mississippi 38917.

CONN, L LUCILLE Occupation: Teacher, Rowan County High School. Education: B.A. Business Education, M.B.E., Rank I in Supervision. Address: Route 5, Whispering Pines, Morehead, Kentucky 40351.

CONNELL, NANCY CHARLENE Occupation: Student. Education: Attending University of Tennessee at Martin. Address: 2207 Dogwood Lane, Dyersburg, Tennessee 38024.

CONSTABLE, JULIA FRENCH Occupation: Student. Education: Attending High School. Address: 2737 Devonshire Place Northwest, Washington, D.C. 20008.

COOK, TAMARA JEANNETTE Occupation: Legal Assistant. Education: B.A. English. Address: 707 New Street, Graham, North Carolina 27253.

COOLEY, HAROLD R Occupation: Student. Education: B.A. (in progress), Southern Illinois University. Address: 531 Chisholm Trail, Wyoming, Ohio 45215.

COON, FRANCES GRACE Occupation: Student in Public Administration and Pre-law. Education: Attending Harding University. Address: Four Mile Village, Santa Rosa Beach, Florida 32459.

COOPER, ANGELA MICHELLE Occupation: Student. Address: 2429 LaClede Avenue, Paducah, Kentucky 42001.

COOPER, PAUL CONRAD Occupation: Student. Education: Attending Susquehanna University. Address: Selinsgrove, Pennsylvania 17870.

CORCORAN, JEROME CLARENCE Occupation: Student. Education: Bachelor's Degree in Water Resources (in progress), UW-Steven Point. Address: Post Office Box 37, West Brooklyn, Illinois 61378.

CORDER, BONNIE SUE Occupation: Graduate Student, Education of the Hearing Impaired. Education: B.A. Elementary Education, University of Denver; Attending University of Arizona. Address: 204 South Martin, Tucson, Arizona 85719.

CORPSTEIN, JOANNE Occupation: Student; Arizona State Chairman of the College Republicans. Education: Bachelor in Business Administration. Address: 4342 East Highlands Drive, Paradise Valley, Arizona 85253.

CORSELLO-EAMES, MARANATHA MARLENE Occupation: High School Teacher, Audio-Visual Supervisor. Education: A.A., B.A. Theatre, B.A. Communications. Address: 1249 Seabreeze Boulevard, Fort Lauderdale, Florida 33316.

CORWIN, KELLEY LINETTE Occupation: Student. Education: Attending University of Utah. Address: 1155 East 3005 #12, Salt Lake City, Utah 84102.

COSTANZO, RALPH MICHAEL Occupation: Student. Education: B.S. (in progress). Address: 8056 Emberly, Jenison, Michigan, 49428.

COTTRELL, FREDERICK L III Occupation: Student; State Chairman, Delaware College Republicans. Education: B.A. (in progress). Address: 1007 Darley Road, Wilmington, Delaware 19810.

COVERT, AIMEE Occupation: Student. Education: Attending California State University. Address: 816 Potomac Avenue, Sacramento, California 95833.

COX, DIETHRA DIANE Occupation: Doctor of Internal Medicine, Hurley Medical Center. Education: B.S., Millsaps College, 1978; M.D., Meharry Medical College, 1982. Address: 4133 Azalea Drive, Jackson,

Mississippi 39206.

COX, GINA LYNN Occupation: Student in Medical Technology. Education: Attending Clinch Valley College. Address: Post Office Box 28, Cedar Bluff, Virginia 24609.

COX, JAMES CLIFTON Occupation: Attorney. Education: B.A. summa cum laude; J.D. Address: 4871 Northeast 13th Terrace, Fort Lauderdale, Florida 33302.

COX, PATRICIA ELLEN Occupation: Administrative Officer. Education: B.S. Address: 1222 Linden Place Northeast, Washington, D.C. 20002.

COX, STEVEN S Occupation: Student. Education: Attending Borger High School. Address: 215 Garrett, Borger, Texas 79007.

COX, TAMMIE YOLANDA Occupation: Student. Education: B.S. Zoology. Address: Route 2, Box 192, Holly Grove, Arkansas 72069.

CRABTREE, BONI LOU Occupation: Resident Assistant; Student. Education: B.A. Interpersonal Communications. Address: Post Office Box 412, Warrensburg, Missouri 64093.

CRADDOCK, KIM ALLYSON Occupation: Student. Education: Attending High School. Address: 3920 River View Drive, Birmingham, Alabama 35243.

CRAVER, LISA ANNE Occupation: Student. Education: B.A., East Carolina University. Address: 125 Forest Park Drive, Thomasville, North Carolina 27360.

CRAWFORD, KOLON MALACILE Occupation: Pastor. Education: Business Administration, 1980; Master of Divinity (in progress). Address: Post Office Box 521, M.B.B.C., Watertown, Wisconsin 53094.

CRAWLEY, TINA FAITH Occupation: Student in Medical Social Work. Education: Attending University of Tennessee at Martin. Address: 6999 Loddon Cove, Memphis, Tennessee 38119.

CREASY, CANDYCE KELLY Occupation: Clerical Specialist I. Education: Arts and Sciences Degree, First Assembly Christian; Attended Bethel College. Address: 3704 Friar Tuck, Memphis, Tennessee 38111.

CRENSHAW, SHERYL DIANE Occupation: Student. Education: Attending High School. Address: 2511 Jester, Stafford, Texas 77477.

CREW, TRACEE J Occupation: Marketing Director, Eternal Word Television Network. Education: B.S. Journalism, Jeff. State Junior College; Attending University of Alabama at Birmingham. Address: 896 Twin Lake Drive, Birmingham, Alabama 35215.

CROOK, BECKY ANN Occupation: Industrial Engineer. Education: Bachelor of Industrial Engineering. Address: 461 Douglas Street, Janesville, Wisconsin 53545.

CROOKE, DARCELLE FRANCIS Occupation: Hand Therapist. Education: M.S. Occupational Therapy, Boston University. Address: 59 Grissing Court, Cedar Grove, New Jersey 07009.

CROWE, DONALD E JR Occupation: Student in Criminal Justice. Education: Attending University of Tennessee at Martin. Address: Post Office Box 1, Dickson, Tennessee 37055.

CROWE, TONYA LOUISE Occupation: Student. Address: 15952 S.R. 81, Dunkirk, Ohio 45836.

CRUZ, AIDA M Occupation: Student. Education: Bachelor Degree Biology, University of Puerto Rico; M.D. (in progress). Address: Victor Lopez #856, Santurce, Puerto Rico 00909.

CUMMINGS, WILMA JOHNSON Occupation: Registered Pharmacist. Education: B.S. Pharmacy. Address: 303 Fifth Street, Leland, Mississippi 38756.

CUMMINS, RHONDA D Occupation: Computer Operator; Student. Education: Attending East Texas State University. Address: 10305 Oak Creek Drive, Greenville, Texas 75401.

CUNNINGHAM, PAUL V Occupation: Student. Education: A.S. Business Administration, Westchester Community College, 1982; B.S., Clarkson College, 1984. Address: 74 Rockland Avenue, Yonkers, New York 10705.

CURRY, GLENDA LEE Occupation: Accounting and Secretarial Student; Waitress. Education: Attending Clackamas Community College. Address: 23250 South Day Hill Road, Estacada, Oregon 97023.

CURTH, MICHAEL E Occupation: Agent, John Hancock Company. Education: Attended The Ohio State University. Address: 803 East Main Street, Eaton, Ohio 45320.

CURTIS, ANNE LORENE Occupation: Student. Education: Attending University of South Alabama; Address: 456 Carolee Circle, Biloxi, Mississippi 39532.

CURTIS, JEFFREY NEVIUS Occupation: General Electric Sales Engineer. Education: B.A. Chemistry, B.A. Economics, University of Delaware. Address: 2411 Richland Avenue, Metairie, Louisiana 70001.

CUTLER, SANDRA JEANNE Occupation: Student. Education: B.S. Math (in progress), Muskingum College. Address: 410 4th Avenue, Warren, Pennsylvania 16365.

CUTRUBUS, TROY JAMES Occupation: Computer Specialist. Education: Weber State College. Address: 4850 South 354E., Post Office Box 3456, Ogden, Utah 84403.

D

DALMONT, KENT W Occupation: Student; Rancher. Education: Attending Oklahoma State University. Address: Route 1, Box 193, McAlister, Oklahoma 74501.

DAMASO, MICHELLE Occupation: General Electric Sales Representative. Address: 2255 Par Lane #219, Willoughby Hills, Ohio 44094.

DANCIL, ROCH M Occupation: Crisis Outreach Counselor. Education: B.A. Sociology. Address: Rural Route 2, Box 115, Kula, Hawaii 96790.

DANDO, R KEVIN Occupation: Writer; Public Relations. Education: B.A. Journalism. Address: Rural Route 8, West Prospect #5, Fort Collins, Colorado 80526.

D'ANGELO, VICTORIA SCOTT Occupation: Student. Education: Attending Columbia Business School. Address: 157 East 57th Street, New York, New York 10022.

D'ANNIBALLE, PRISCILLA L Occupation: Banking Officer, Mortgage Banking Department. Education: Bachelor of Business Education. University of Toledo, 1975. Address: 7962 Millford Drive, Sylvania, Ohio 43560.

DANSER, TIMOTHY LEE Occupation: Student. Education: Attending West Virginia University. Address: 117 Belmar Avenue, Morgantown, West Virginia 26505.

DARBY, JOSEPH BRANCH III Occupation: Writer; Lawyer. Education: LL.B., Harvard University; B.S., University of Illinois. Address: 17 Lloyd Road, Watertown, Massachusetts 02172.

DASSONVILLE, JOHN A Occupation: Student. Education: B.S. Computer Science, Baylor University. Address: 404 Sylvia, Longview, Texas 75604.

DAUBENSPECK, ANDREW DEAN Occupation: Student. Education: Attending University of Colorado. Address: 8630 West 46th Avenue, Wheat Ridge, Colorado 80033.

DAUGHERTY, KARLA K Occupation: Information Specialist. Education: B.B.A. cum laude, North Texas State University, 1982. Address: 106-A Pecan Valley, Granbury, Texas 76048.

DAVIDSON, JAMES BLAINE Occupation: Professor of Ocean Engineering. Education: B.S., U.S. Naval Academy; B.S.E.E., U.S. Naval Postgraduate School; M.S. Applied Physics-Acoustics, University of California at Los Angeles. Address: 1190 Southwest 11th Street, Boca Raton, Florida 33432.

DAVIS, CHARLES G Occupation: Student. Education: Attending Mississipi State University. Address: 8694 Yorktown Drive, Southaven, Mississippi 38671.

DAVIS, CINDY LEA Occupation: Owner, The Tin Shed Gift Shop. Education: Attending Texas Tech University. Address: Post Office Box 848, Plains, Texas 79355.

DAVIS, DOUGLAS BRADLEY Occupation: Employee Service-Accounting Department, Law Offices of Lemle, Kelleher, Kohlmeyer and Matthews. Education: A.A. Journalism; B.A. Art History and English. Address: 2833 St. Charles Avenue #32, New Orleans, Louisiana 70115.

DAVIS, ELISE LAWTON Occupation: Nursing Student. Education: Attending University of South Carolina. Address: 4418 Wedgewood Drive, Columbia, South Carolina 29206.

DAVIS, HOLLI JACKSON Occupation: Legal Secretary. Education: B.B.A. Finance. Address: 3311 Woodlawn Street, Hopewell, Virginia 23860.

DAVIS, JIM MILLER JR Occupation: Student. Education: Attending University of South Carolina. Address: 4418 Wedgewood, Columbia, South Carolina 29206.

DAVIS, LINDA GAIL DOSSETT Occupation: Student Nurse, Forrest General Hospital. Education: B.S. Nursing, 1984. Address: 209 South 24 Avenue, Hattiesburg, Mississippi 39401.

DAVIS, MAURICE ARNETT Occupation: Student. Education: Attending Lee High School. Address: 3812 J.F.K. Cr., Huntsville, Alabama 35811.

DAVIS, TIMOTHY SPENSER Occupation: Television Programming Executive. Education: B.S., Southern Illinois University, 1979. Address: 135 West 96 Street #88, New York, New York 10025.

DAWS, DEBORAH DENISE Occupation: Elementary School Teacher. Education: A.A., B.S. Address: 4940 Ridgewood Road, #O-1, Jackson, Mississippi 39211.

DAY, KEVIN DAVID Occupation: Sales Negotiator for AT&T Information Systems. Education: B.S. Business, Indiana University. Address: 582 Whispering Oaks, Nashville, Tennessee 37211.

DEALY, JOSEPH B Occupation: Student. Education: Attending Oregon State University. Address: Post Office Box 291, Corvallis, Oregon 97339.

DeBLASIO, PASQUALE BERNARD Occupation: Student; Computer Programer. Education: Associate Degree, Computer Science. Address: 132 Pennsylvania Avenue, Bridgeville, Pennsylvania 15017.

DECKER, FRANCES M Occupation: Criminal Justice Student. Address: Post Office Box 91, Holt, Missouri 64048.

DEES, BARRY NEIL JR Occupation: Tech. Marketing Representative. Education: B.B.A., M.B.A. Address: 617 Sleepy Hollow, Midlothien, Texas 76065.

DEIS, CARROLL L Occupation: Office Manager; Part-time Science Instructor. Education: A.S., Harcum Junior College; B.S., West Chester State College. Address: 45 South Wyoming Avenue, Ardmore, Pennsylvania 19003.

DE LA CRUZ, CAROLINA M Occupation: Student. Address: 342 Maple Street, Kearney, New Jersey 07032.

DE LAUNE, TRACIE JEANNANNE Occupation: Student. Address: Post Office Box 307, Clayton, Louisiana 71326.

DE LUCA, ROSE Occupation: Student. Education: B.A., LaSalle College, 1977; M.A., Boston College, 1979; Ph.D. (in progress), Brandeus University. Address: 145 Warren Street #8, Watertown, Massachusetts 02172.

DEL VILLAR, GEORGE Occupation: Medical Student. Education: A.A. Biology, Florida Keys Community College; B.A. Biology, Southampton College; M.D. (in progress). Address: 28 Dekalb Avenue, White Plains, New York 10605.

DEMICO, CAROL BROWN Occupation: Nursing Student. Education: B.S. Nursing (in progress), Duquesne University. Address: 630 North Neglly Avenue, Pittsburgh, Pennsylvania 15206.

DEMING, CARLA JONETT Occupation: Registered Nurse. Education: B.S. Biology; B.S. Nursing. Address: 2200 South Rock Road #1503, Wichita, Kansas 67207.

DEMING, RHONDA KAY Occupation: Special Education Student. Education: A.S. Education; B.S. Elementary Education. Address: 1123 West Blaine, Pratt, Kansas 67124.

DENNIS, FLORENCE CHARLOTTE Occupation:

Educator, Doctoral Candidate. Education: B.Sc. Secondary Education, M.Ed. Educational Administration, Ed.D. International Educational Development (Candidate). Address: 5300 Columbia Pike, Apartment 301, Arlington, Virginia 22204.

DENTICE, KIM L Education: B.B.A. Management. Address: 4539 Woodvalley Drive, Acworth, Georgia 30101.

D'ERCOLE, PATRICIA MARY Occupation: Suzuki Violin Specialist. Education: B.M.E. Address: 1000 College Avenue, Ladysmith, Wisconsin 54848.

DE SANTIS, ANTHONY QUINN Occupation: Student. Education: B.B.A., Stetson University, 1985. Address: 240 Otis Road, North Port, Florida 33596.

DESCH, MATTHEW J Occupation: Supervisor, Computer Engineering, AT&T. Education: B.S. Computer Science, Ohio State University; M.B.A. (in progress), University of Chicago. Address: 362 Brandon Avenue, Glen Ellyn, Illinois 60137.

D'ESPOSITO, LOUIS V Occupation: Student. Education: A.S., Westchester Community College, 1981; B.S., Clarkson College, 1982. Address: 57 Storer Avenue, Pelham, New York 10803.

DEVERS, CASH LESTER Occupation: Student. Education: Associate Degree, Claremore College; Attending Northeastern State University. Address: 18 North Cherokee, Pryor, Oklahoma 74361.

DeVORE, J CAROLINE Occupation: Student; Assistant to Director of Admissions. Education: B.S. Comp. Engineering (in progress), Lander College. Address: 712 Logan Court, Greenwood, South Carolina 29646.

DeVRIES, ROBERT S Occupation: Intern, Economic Development Corporation, City of Albion. Education: B.A., Albion College. Address: 215 Country Club Boulevard, Battle Creek, Michigan 49015.

DEWALD, HOWARD D Occupation: Student. Education: B.S. University of Wyoming, 1980; Ph.D. (in progress), New Mexico State University. Address: 215 South Mesquite Street, Apartment 13, Las Cruces, New Mexico 88001.

DILLON, MELISSA ANN Occupation: Student. Education: Associate Degree in Radiologic Technology (in progress). Address: 8040 Homeland Circle, Belews Creek, North Carolina 27009.

DI PIPPO, PHILIP ALBERT Occupation: Student. Education: B.A. (in progress). Address: 108 Arthur Street, Garden City, New York 11530.

DIVERSE DIZA, MARIE DENNISSE Occupation: Resident Level II in Pediatrics. Education: M.D. Address: BB11 Daisy Street, Alt de Boringuen Gardens, Rio Piedras, Puerto Rico 00926.

DIX, WILLIAM CLARK Occupation: Agricultural-Farm Operations Student. Education: Attending Iowa State University. Address: Rural Route 1, Janesville, Iowa 50647.

DIXON, JAMES WILLIAM JR Occupation: Student; Eagle Scout; President, Goldsboro, North Carolina, Stake Seminary; President, Stake Ad Hoc Committee for Youth. Education: Route 1, Box 253, Warsaw, North Carolina 28398.

DIXON, KAREN D Occupation: Housewife. Education: High School Graduate. Address: Box 91, Chase, Kansas 67524.

DIXSON, RODRIQURESS Education: B.S. Registered Nursing (in progress). Address: 917 Ouachita, El Dorado, Arkansas 71730.

DODD, PHILIP ADAM Occupation: Student. Address: Box 3514, Pinedale, California 93650.

DOGGETT, ANNIE M Occupation: Student. Education: Attending Howard University. Address: R.F.D. 1, Box 72C, Cape Charles, Virginia 23310.

DOIDGE, ROBERT J Occupation: Student, Data Processing Manager. Education: A.A. (in progress), B.S. (in progress), U.C.I. Address: 749 St. Anne's Drive, Laguna Beach, California 92651.

DOMINGUEZ, JOHN J Occupation: Medical Student. Education: B.S. summa cum laude, Pan American University; M.D. (in progress). Address: 337 South Washington, Mercedes, Texas 78570.

DONAHUE, KEITH D Occupation: General Contractor/Developer. Education: B.S. Business Administration; M.B.A. Finance. Address: 5006 Tyler Lane, Castro Valley, California 94546.

DONOVAN, J McCARTHY Occupation: Student. Address: 1321 D Illinois Avenue, Cape May, New Jersey 08204.

DONOVAN, RANDY CHARLES Occupation: Inorganic Laboratory Preparations. Education: Attending George Washington University. Address: 206 Perkins Street, Melrose, Massachusetts 02176.

DONOVAN, THERESA E Occupation: Therapeutic Recreation Specialist Consultant. Education: B.S.P.E. and B.A. Rehab., West Virginia Wesleyan; M.S.T.R., Virginia Polytechnic Institute and State University. Address: 1711 Whipple Drive, Apartment 17, Blacksburg, Virginia 24060.

DOODY, DANIEL W Occupation: Minister of Music and Youth. Education: B.S. Bible; B. Music. Address: Maple Court Apartment Building 3, Apartment 17, Keene, New Hampshire 03431.

DORROUGH, REBECCA L Occupation: Student. Education: Attending Southwestern Oklahoma State University. Address: Post Office Box 1409, Woodward, Oklahoma 73802.

DORSEY, ROBIN LEE Occupation: Architect; Fallout Shelter Analyst. Education: B.Arch. cum laude, 1982. Address: 525 Dunning Street, Williamsburg, Virginia 23185.

DOWELL, PEARL McLEAN Occupation: Associate Director of Settlement Hse. Education: B.S., M.S.Ed. Candidate. Address: 63 Mencel Circle, Bridgeport, Connecticut 06610.

DOWNING, GWENDOLYN Occupation: Surgical Assistant to Orthopedic Podiatrist. Education: A.A., 1980; B.S., 1981. Address: 1008 East Selma, Dothan, Alabama 36301.

DOYLE, CHRISTOPHER ROBERT Occupation: Student. Address: 3431 Arcadia Drive, Ellicott City, Maryland 21043.

DOYLE, JAMES ANDREW Occupation: National Convention Coordinator, The Pi Kappa Alpha Fraternity. Education: B.S. Zoology, Clemson University, 1980. Address: 577 University, Memphis, Tennessee 38112.

DOYLE, STEPHEN MICHAEL Occupation: Student. Education: Attending Loyola College. Address: 3431 Arcadia Drive, Ellicott City, Maryland 21043.

DRAKE, MALETA FREDONA Address: Route 2, Box 605, Travelers Rest, South Carolina 29690.

DRAUGHN, LISA CAROL Occupation: Student. Education: Attending Palm Beach Atlantic College. Address: 316 Glenn Road, West Palm Beach, Florida 33405.

DREBES, NANCY JOBERTA Occupation: Business Student. Education: B.S. (in progress), University of Missouri at Columbia. Address: Rural Route #3, Palmyra, Missouri 63461.

DREW, KATHY DIANE Occupation: Student. Education: B.S. Psychology; M.Ed. School Psychometry; Ph.D. Educational Psychology (in progress). Address: 512 Freeman Drive, Athens, Georgia 30601.

DRUM, KIMBERLY LEE Occupation: Junior Accountant. Education: A.B. Accounting, Lenior-Rhyne College. Address: Route 2, Box 521, Newton, North Carolina 28658.

DRUMMOND, LORI LYNN Occupation: Student. Education: B.A. English (in progress), Stetson University. Address: Box 7336, Stetson University, De Land, Florida 32720.

DUFF, JULIA GRACE Education: Bachelor of Music Educ.; S.E. Mo. State. Address: Post Office Box 66, Tamms, Illinois 62988.

DUKES, TERRY J Occupation: Pharmacy Student. Education: Doctor of Pharmacy. Address: 522 Smokey Drive, Loudon, Tennessee 37774.

DUMA, SCOTT LANCET Occupation: Midshipman, U.S. Naval Academy. Education: Attending U.S. Naval Academy. Address: 2410 Castlebridge Road, Midlothian, Virginia 23113.

DUNAWAY, NANCY ALICE Occupation: Pre-Dentistry Student. Education: Attending Union College. Address: 244 Cumberland Avenue, Barbourville, Kentucky 40906.

DUNN, JACQUELINE ANN Occupation: Administrator, Molloy College. Education: B.A. Art and Elementary Education; M.P.A. Candidate. Address: 69 Vassar Street, Garden City, New York 11530.

DUNN, TERENCE Occupation: Marketing Agent. Education: B.S., M.B.A. Address: 834 South Orange Grove Avenue, Los Angeles, California 90036.

DUPEE, LEIGH DE FOREST Occupation: Student. Address: South Stream Road, Bennington, Vermont 05201.

DUPLER, STEPHEN DOUGLAS Occupation: College Student. Education: Degree in Journalism (in progress). Address: 2250 Tent Road, Lancaster, Ohio 43130.

DURHAM, REBECCA LYNNE (BECKY) Occupation: Student. Education: Bachelor of Arts, Lander College, 1985. Address: Box 332, 5 Queens Court, Pickens, South Carolina 29671.

DUTSON, NATALIE Occupation: Student. Education: Attending Brigham Young University. Address: 625 South 500 West, Delta, Utah 84624.

DYKES, HART LEE Occupation: Student. Education: Attending High School. Address: 1719 Laurel Street, Bay City, Texas 77414.

E

EASON, KARLA MICHELLE Occupation: Internal Auditor, Dart & Kraft. Education: B.B.A. Accounting. Address: 3236 Concord Circle, Smyrna, Georgia 30080.

ECKES, KAREN CLARE Occupation: Contract Furniture Manufacturer's Representative. Education: B.A. Psychology/Marketing, Stetson University. Address: 1024 A Green Pine Boulevard, West Palm Beach, Florida 33409.

EDIRISINGHE, JANAKA Occupation: Industrial Engineer. Education: B.Sc. Industrial Engineering; M.Sc. Industrial Engineering. Address: 700-A, South Chapman Street, Greensboro, North Carolina 27403.

EDWARDS, MARY A Occupation: Student. Education: Attending College. Address: 322 Feezer, Covington, Tennessee 38019.

EGGERS, CYNTHIA ANNE Occupation: Student. Education: B.S. Earth Science-Meteorology (in progress). Address: 236 Printz Avenue, Essington, Pennsylvania 19029.

EIDSON, PAMELA LYNN Occupation: Student. Education: Attending University of Georgia. Address: Route 4, Box 532, Palatka, Florida 32077.

EIFE, MARGARET MEREDITH Occupation: Therapist. Education: B.A., University of Maryland; M.A., Lesley College. Address: 4425 35th Street Northwest, Washington, D.C. 20008.

ELDRIDGE, LAURETTA ALTHEA Occupation: Student. Education: Attending College. Address: 12346 "F" Street, Trona, California 93562.

ELLIOTT, VICTORIA BEARD Occupation: English, Drama and Speech Instructor. Education: B.A. Drama and Speech, Houston Baptist University, 1980; M.A. Drama, University of Houston, 1982. Address: 14114 Barryknoll, Houston, Texas 77079.

ELLIS, FRANCES Occupation: Controller. Education: B.B.A., Kennesaw College, 1984. Address: 3416 Sharon Drive, Powder Springs, Georgia 30073.

ELLIS, LUCINDA Occupation: Veterinary Student. Education: A.A.; B.S. Biology. Address: 1406 Southwest 12th Avenue, Gainesville, Florida 32601.

ELLIS, MICHAEL STEPHEN JR Occupation: Student. Education: Attending Williamsport Area Community College. Address: 1201 Arthur Road, Montoursville, Pennsylvania 17754.

ELMS, SELINA VALDRIE Occupation: Real Estate and Legal Secretary. Address: 119 West Curtis, Liberal, Kansas 67901.

ELROD, DIANA DEE Occupation: Nurse Extern. Education: B.S.R.N. Address: 1115 Chestnut Drive, Smithfield, North Carolina 27577.

ELZINGA, RONALD HARRIS Occupation: Educator, Northgate High School. Education: B.A.; Master Christian Studies; Teaching Credential. Address: 2236 Lomond Lane, Walnut Creek, California 94598.

ENDRESS, PAMELA JO Occupation: Court Reporter. Education: Associate Degree Legal Science. Address: Rural Route 1, Edelstein, Illinois 61526.

ENGELHARD, DIANE M Occupation: Student. Education: Attending University of Wisconsin at Steven's Point. Address: 4309 Janick Circle North, Stevens Point, Wisconsin 54481.

ENGLISH, FRANCINE LENORA Occupation: Student. Education: B.S. Business Administration, M.P.A. Public Administration. Address: Route 1, Box 266-A, Winnsboro, South Carolina 29180.

EPKE, COURTNEY K Occupation: Student. Education: Attending Creighton University. Address: 1228 McKaig Avenue, York, Nebraska 68467.

EPPENGER, WINFRED LINTON Occupation: Legal Redress Committee, NAACP. Education: General Equivelence Diploma, 1979. Address: 308 Kings View Drive, Nashville, Tennessee 37218.

ERWIN, KATE E Occupation: Audiology Student. Education: B.A. Communicative Disorders, University of Mississippi; M.S. Audiology (in progress). Address: Cove Apartments #H-8, Oxford, Mississippi 38655.

ESQUENAZI, ROBERT Occupation: Student. Education: B.A. Psychology. Address: Route 2, Box 564, Eagle Pass, Texas 78852.

ETZKORN, SHAWN CLEAON Occupation: Graduate Student. Education: A.B. summa cum laude, Washington University; Attending Washington University School of Architecture. Address: 237 Gremer, Edwardsville, Illinois 62025.

EVANS, ROBERT A Occupation: Student. Education: Attending University of Florida. Address: 300 Yampa Circle, Sacramento, California 95838.

EVENSON, JUNE ANN Occupation: High School Business Teacher. Education: B.S.Ed. Address: 232 Forest Avenue, Plymouth, Wisconsin 53073.

EVERSOLE, KELLYE A Occupation: Legislative Assistant, Senator David Boren. Education: B.A. Political Science, George Washington University. Address: 2603 Windbreak Drive, Alexandria, Virginia 22306.

F

FAIN, THOMAS ALTON JR Occupation: Public School Band Director. Education: B.S. Music, Lamar University. Address: 3400 Custer Road, #1106, Plano, Texas 75023.

FAIRCHILD, PAMELA BETH ELIZABETH Occupation: Student; Vice President, Fairchild and Company. Education: B.A., University of North Carolina, 1984; Law Student. Address: 9513 Ferry Harbour Court, Alexandria, Virginia 22309.

FAIRES, TRACY RANDALL Occupation: Self-Employed. Education: B.B.A. Marketing. Address: Post Office Box 1199, Edinburg, Texas 78539.

FALCONI, ALINA Occupation: Personnel/Payroll Officer. Education: B.S. Management, University of Illinois-Chicago Circle Campus. Address: 2715 South Kolin Avenue, Chicago, Illinois 60623.

FALCONI, CECILIA DEL ROSARIO Occupation: Student. Education: B.A. 1982, M.F.A. 1984, University of Illinois at Chicago. Address: 2715 South Kolin Avenue, Chicago, Illinois 60623.

FALCONI, FREDDY F Occupation: Artist and Quilter. Education: John Walsh School, West Town Workshop, Easter Seal Society Center. Address: 2715 South Kolin Avenue, Chicago, Illinois 60623.

FALWELL, JEAN A Occupation: Student. Address: 6023 Piedmont Place, Lynchburg, Virginia 24502.

FARRIOR, NATHAN Occupation: Assistant Branch Manager, Central Carolina Bank. Education: B.B.A. Address: 1755 Morehead Avenue, Durham, North Carolina 27707.

FARROW, GARY LEE Occupation: Co-operative Student, Ottawa County Engineers. Education: Attending University of Akron. Address: 8605 West Salem Carroll, Oak Harbor, Ohio 43449.

FARRUGGIA, DAVID JOSEPH Occupation: Captain, U.S. Army Military Police. Education: B.S. Criminology, M.S. Criminial Justice. Address: 1315 Cavern Trail, San Antonio, Texas 78245.

FAUST, CLARK WESLEY Occupation: Music Student. Education: Attending Southwest Texas State University. Address: 9 River Oaks Drive, New Braunfels, Texas 78130.

F.-CALIENES, NORA Occupation: Secretary/Teacher. Education: B.A. Foreign Language Education. Address: 526 West 114th Street, New York, New York 10025.

FEINSILVER, JULIE MARGOT Occupation: Ph.D. Candidate, Yale University. Education: M.A., M.Phil., Yale University. Address: 705 Mt. Pleasant, Ann Arbor, Michigan 48103.

FELDER, WILTRESS TYLER Occupation: Student. Education: Attending South Carolina State College. Address: 200 Middle Street, Bamber, South Carolina 29003.

FELICE, STEPHANY A Occupation: Cost Accounting Clerk, Accounting Student. Education: Associate Degree in Business Administration, Rochester Institute of Technology, 1984. Address: 43 Lyceum Street, Geneva, New York 14456.

FELS, HEIDEMARIE VERONIKA Occupation: Student. Address: 3508 East Smith Road, Bellingham, Washington 98226.

FERNANDEZ, NINA S Occupation: Librarian Technician. Education: A.A. Journalism, B.A. English. Address: 604 Royal Drive, Jacksonville, North Carolina 28540.

FERNANDEZ, RICHARD EDWARD Occupation: Student. Education: B.S. Chemistry, Loyola University; Ph.D. (in progress), University of South Carolina. Address: 3824 Motor Avenue #40, Culver City, California 90230.

FICTUM, BRUCE J Occupation: President, BJF Associates. Address: 2000 G Street, Lincoln, Nebraska 68510.

FIKE, SHEILA RENE Occupation: Student. Education: B.S. Elementary Education, Slippery Rock University. Address: 3581 Norland Circle, Norfolk, Virginia 23513.

FISHER, ROBIN LYNNE Occupation: Student. Education: Attending University of Mississippi. Address: 181 Horner Drive, Selmer, Tennessee 38375.

FITZ GERALD, RHONDA Occupation: Student. Education: Attending High School. Address: Route 1, Box 38, Falkville, Alabama 35622.

FIXICO, JO ANNA Occupation: Student. Education: Attending Marquette University. Address: 724 South Linden, Sapulpa, Oklahoma 74066.

FLINT, LAURIE ANN Occupation: Medical Student. Education: B.A. Chemistry. Address: 7113 Falcon Street, Annandale, Virginia 22005.

FLORIO, WILLIAM JOSEPH Occupation: Student. Education: Michigan State University; Doennen College. Address: 122 Church Street, Hoosick Falls, New York 12090.

FLOYD, HENRY BASCOM IV Occupation: Physician. Education: B.S. 1976; M.D. 1981. Address: 18 South Kings Highway, St. Louis, Missouri 63108.

FLOYD, STEPHANIE A Occupation: Teaching Assistant, University of Georgia. Education: B.A., Furman University; M.Ed., University of Georgia. Address: 290 Holman Avenue, Athens, Georgia 30606.

FONG, PAUL YEE Occupation: Student. Education: A.A. Address: 4431 Northeast 20th Avenue, Ft. Lauderdale, Florida 33308.

FORD, FELECIA LEE Occupation: Student. Education: Attending Howard College. Address: 424 Edwards, Big Spring, Texas 79720.

FOREMAN, PAMELA LEE Occupation: Student (Teacher). Education: B.S.E. Speech/Theatre/Secondary EMR Special Education. Address: Route 1, Box 238, Osage Beach, Missouri 65065.

FORGACS, LINDA MARY Occupation: Documentation Support Specialist. Education: B.A. English, 1981. Address: 1400 Regal Road, Clearwater, Florida 33516.

FOSHEE, CARLYN D Occupation: Administrative Assistant. Education: B.B.A. Address: 2223 8th, Galena Park, Texas 77547.

FOUSHEE, ADRIAN M Occupation: Student. Education: Attending College. Address: 3011 Nash Place, Southeast, Washington, D.C. 20020.

FOX, FRANCES JO Occupation: Student. Education: High School Diploma. Address: Post Office Box 450, Jellico, Tennessee 37762.

FOX, MARLA L Occupation: Commercial Loans and Mortgage Loans. Education: B.B.A. Management. Address: 285 Dark Hollow Road, Waynesburg, Pennsylvania 15370.

FOX, REBECCA JOYCE Occupation: Student. Education: B.A., University of Tennessee, 1984. Address: Post Office Box 450, Jellico, Tennessee 37762.

FRAME, MARSHA WIGGINS Occupation: Minister. Education: B.A. Christian Education; Master of Divinity. Address: 4711 Northwest 17 Place, Gainesville, Florida 32605.

FRANKE, MARY REBECCA Occupation: Elementary Music Teacher. Education: Bachelor of Music, 1983. Address: 1179 Fernwood Drive, Schnectady, New York 12309.

FRANKLIN, ANGELA WALKER Occupation: Graduate Student; Staff Psychologist, University Counseling Center. Education: B.A. Psychology, Furman University, 1981; M.A. Clinical Psychology 1983, Ph.D. (in progress), Emory University. Address: 1411 Reddington Lane, Norcross, Georgia 30093.

FRANKLIN, CARY JOHN Occupation: Musician, Composer/Conductor. Education: B.A., Macalester College. Address: 1973 Lincoln Street, Paul, Minnesota 55105.

FRANKLIN, SHERRY D Occupation: Student. Address: Post Office Box 4552, University, Mississippi 38677.

FRANTZ, PAUL L Occupation: Lawyer. Education: B.S., Montana State University; J.D., University of Montana. Address: 112 Sunset Boulevard, Bozeman, Montana 59715.

FRIEDLANDER, JANET A Occupation: Student. Education: B.S. Restaurant, Hotel and Institutional Management, Purdue University, 1984. Address: 2014 North Jackson, Waukegan, Illinois 60087.

FRISCH, MICHAEL BURNS Occupation: Assistant Professor of Clinical Psychology, Baylor University. Education: B.A.; M.A. and Ph.D. Clinical Psychology. Address: 2307 Gorman Avenue, Waco, Texas 76707.

FROEMMING, CARRIE LYNN Occupation: Dental Hygienist. Education: A.S. Health Science; B.S. Dental Hygiene. Address: 6227 West 34th Street #25, St. Louis, Minnesota 55416.

FRONABARGER, DEBORAH ANN Occupation: Student. Education: Mechanical Engineering Technology Student. Address: 615 Natchez Trace Drive, Lexington, Tennessee 38351.

FRYAR, ROBERT NORMAN Occupation: Student. Education: B.S. Animal Production, Tarleton State University. Address: Route Box 153C, Early, Texas 76801.

FUHRMAN, NICOLAS ANDREW Occupation: Student; Chairman, Wisconsin College Republicans. Education: Attending College. Address: 4778 Springbrook, Toledo, Ohio 43615.

FULGINITI, BRIAN G Occupation: Student. Education: B.A. (in progress), La Salle College. Address: 3339 Fairdale Road, Philadelphia, Pennsylvania 19154.

FUNK, MICHAEL D Occupation: Student. Education: Attending Illinois Wesleyan University. Address: Rural Route #2, Box 116, Manito, Illinois 61546.

FUSILLO, LISA ANN Occupation: Assistant Professor of Ballet; Master Teacher and Choreographer. Education: B.S., George Washington University; D.R.B.S.; M.A., Ph.D., Texas Woman's University. Address: 5532 Creekwood Drive #2035, Fort Worth, Texas 76109.

G

GABBARD, REBECCA S (BECKY) Occupation: Student, Part-time Bank Teller. Education: Attending Indiana University-Fort Wayne. Address: 7611 Hope Farm Road, Fort Wayne, Indiana 46815.

GABLE, KATHERINE REBEL Occupation: Student. Address: 10428 Kardwright Court, Gaithersburg, Maryland 20879.

GAETANO, MARIO A Occupation: Instructor of Music, Western Carolina University. Education: B.M., M.M. Address: Post Office Box 1090, Cullowhee, North Carolina 28723.

GAJEWSKI, KATHLEEN MARY Occupation: Student. Education: Attending Southwest Texas State University. Address: 502 Oakwood, North Braunfels, Texas 78130.

GALE, BRIAN DAVID Occupation: President, Pennsylvania Podiatric Medical Students Association. Education: B.A. Biology. Address: 8424 Sheraton Drive, Miramar, Florida 33025.

GALLAGHER, JAMES ROBERT Occupation: Farmer. Education: F.F.A. Farmer, Working American Farmer Degree. Address: Rt. 1, Maitland, Missouri 64466.

GALLUCCI, JOHN ARTHUR Occupation: Graduate Student in French Literature. Education: B.A., Williams College; Attending Yale University. Address: 20 Hughes Court, Glens Falls, New York 12801.

GANNAWAY, DEBORAH MAREL Occupation: Registered Nurse. Education: B.S.N., Vanderbilt University, 1982. Address: 2504 Noblecreek Drive, Northwest, Atlanta, Georgia 30327.

GARCIA, GAMALIEL M Occupation: Minister. Education: B.S. Business Administration. Address: 1722 27th Street, Yuma, Arizona 85364.

GARDNER, STEPHEN D Occupation: Senior Medical Research Associate. Education: B.A., M.S.P.H. Address: 3727 Greenleaf Circle, Number 202, Kalamazoo, Michigan 49008.

GARLATI, VALERIE ELAINE Occupation: Assistant Manager of Apartment Complex, Pre-School Teacher. Education: A.S. Education Technology, I.P.F.W. Address: 5701-C River Run Trail, Fort Wayne, Indiana 46825.

GARRISON, TOMMY MAX Occupation: Minister. Education: A.B., B.A., M.A., Candidate for M.T.H. Address: 111 Meadow Lane, Calhoun, Georgia 30701.

GARRITY, EDWARD R Occupation: Graduate Student, Materials Engineer. Education: B.S. Materials Engineering, Drexel University; Ph.D. (in progress). Address: 1756 Hillside Drive, Cherry Hill, New Jersey 08003.

GARVIN, ELEANOR J Occupation: Analyst, Southern Bell Telephone. Education: B.S. Accounting/Computer Science. Address: 2504 Crofton Way, Apartment C, Columbia, South Carolina 29206.

GELARDO, MARK SAMUEL Occupation: Teaching Assistant, University of Georgia. Education: B.A. Psychology; M.Ed. Learning Disabilities. Address: Post Office Box 407, Watkinsville, Georgia 30677.

GELDART, CRYSTAL LILLIAN RUTH Occupation: Student. Address: 1545 Oleander Drive, Avon Park, Florida 33825.

GEORGE, MARIAN LEIGH Occupation: Executive Secretary/Saleswoman. Education: Associate Degree in Secretarial Administration. Address: Box 222, White Stone, Virginia 22578.

GEORGE, ROY ALAN Occupation: Tissue Culture Specialist/Research Assistant, Oregon State University. Education: B.S. Biology, George Fox College. Address: 3930 Northwest Witham Hill Drive #136, Corvallis, Oregon 97330.

GEREDINE, LYNNE MICHELLE Occupation: B.A. Administration of Justice, M.A. Religious Education. Address: 3409 Indiana, Kansas City, Missouri 64128.

GIBBS, DONNA ANNETTE Occupation: Public Relations Director. Education: A.S. Address: Route 1, Box 76, Newton, Mississippi 39345.

GIDEON, ELLEN ELAYNE Occupation: Student. Education: Associate of General Education; Attending East Texas State. Address: Box 213, Palmer, Texas 75152.

GILBERT, SANDRA JANE Occupation: Student. Education: B.S. Business Management (in progress), University of Tennessee. Address: Route 1, Box 114, Darden, Tennessee 38328.

GILLAN, JENNIFER L Occupation: Student. Education: Attending Immaculate Heart Academy. Address: 40 Post Avenue, Hawthorne, New Jersey 07506.

GILLESPIE, SUSAN ANNETTE Occupation: Editorial Assistant, Harcourt Brace Jovanovich, Inc. Education: B.A. magna cum laude, Stetson University, 1983. Address: 424 West Oak Ridge Road #101, Orlando, Florida 32809.

GILLIAM, TERRI LYNN Occupation: Student. Education: B.M. Music Education; B.A. Music History, Ohio Wesleyan University. Address: 108 Frazier Street, Mingo Junction, Ohio 43938.

GILMORE, KAREN E Occupation: Systems Engineer Development Program-E.D.S. Education: B.S. Commerce. Address: 2616 Milton, Dallas, Texas 75205.

GLASER, LOUISE FERRIS Occupation: Student. Education: Attending College. Address: 20 Panoramic, Berkeley, California 94704.

GLASER, WILLIAM T Occupation: Student. Education: Attending Cornell University. Address: 1140 Grizzly Park, Berkeley, California 94708.

GLASS, RICHARD T Occupation: Personnel Representative. Education: B.A.; M.B.A. Real Estate. Address: 2366 Croyden Place, San Leandro, California 94577.

GLESNER, RONALD GLENN Occupation: Dairy Farmer. Education: Diploma, Big Spring High School. Address: R.D. #4, Box 465, Newville, Pennsylvania 17241.

GLOVER, CARLA O Occupation: Operations Director, WXEX TV. Education: B.S. Journalism. Address: 4630 Ripley Street, Davenport, Iowa 52806.

GOEBEL, JIL T Occupation: Product Marketing Planner. Education: B.B.A. Buxiness; M.B.A. Business/Marketing. Address: 750 State Street #317, San Diego, California 92101.

GOERZ, DAVID JONATHAN III Occupation: Student. Education: Attending University of California at Los Angeles. Address: 10938 Strathmore Drive, Los Angeles, California 90024.

GOLLEDGE, TERESA A Occupation: Air Midwest Airline Sales Representative. Education: High School Diploma; Attending College. Address: Route 1, Box 114C, Texico, New Mexico 88135.

GOLLEHON, GERALD G JR Occupation: Student. Education: Attending Embry-Riddle Aeronautical University. Address: Route 1, Box 33, Wilbur, Washington 99185.

GOOCH, JUANITA ANN Occupation: Legal Secretary. Education: Attended College. Address: 82

Henry Clay Road, Newport News, Virginia 23601.

GOODE, BRENDA ANN Occupation: Teacher. Education: B.S. Elementary Education. Address: 4618 La Paz, Pasadena, Texas 77504.

GOODWIN, LAURIE ANN Occupation: Nurse. Education: Bachelor's Degree in Nursing. Address: Route 3, Box 442, Lot 62, Cape Girardeau, Missouri 63701.

GORDON, GREGORY WALTER Occupation: Student. Education: Attending Abilene Christian University. Address: 1385 Edwards, New Braunfels, Texas 78130.

GORDON, RICHARD GLENN Occupation: Student. Education: Attending Rutgers University. Address: 309 Fourth Avenue, Belmar, New Jersey 07719.

GOSSARD, JULIA KAY Occupation: Elementary Teacher. Education: B.S. Elementary Education. Address: Rural Route #1, Box 106, Sheridan, Indiana 46069.

GRACIA, CARMEN MARIA Occupation: Chemical Engineering Student. Education: University of Puerto Rico. Address: I-1 7 Street Sans Souci, Bayamon, Puerto Rico 00619.

GRANT, MICHAEL DANIEL Occupation: Student. Education: B.S., Texas A & M University, 1984; Attending University of Texas Medical School at Houston. Address: 200 Prinz, San Antonio, Texas 78213.

GRANTHAM, DAVID C Education: Bachelor of Business Administration. Address: Route 1, Box 1768, Fort Valley, Georgia 31030.

GRECULA, DOROTHY MARIE Occupation: Student. Education: B.E. Electrical Engineering. Address: 237 Summit Avenue, Mingo Junction, Ohio 43938.

GRECULA, JOHN CHRISTOPHER Occupation: Medical Student. Education: B.S./M.D. (in progress), Youngstown State University and N.E.O.U.C.O.M. Address: 237 Summit Avenue, Mingo Junction, Ohio 43938.

GRECULA, MICHAEL JOSEPH Occupation: Medical Student. Education: B.S./M.D. (in progress), Kent State University and N.E.O.U.C.O.M. Address: 237 Summit Avenue, Mingo Junction, Ohio 43938.

GRECULA, MICHALEEN ANNETTE Occupation: Medical Student. Education: B.S. Chemistry. Education: Attending Ohio State University. Address: 237 Summit Avenue, Mingo Junction, Ohio 43938.

GREEN, JANE HELENE Occupation: Lab Instructor, Sul Ross State University. Education: B.S., 1981; A.T.R. Certificate, 1981. Address: 102 East Harriet, Alpine, Texas 79830.

GREEN, VIRGINIA K Occupation: Student. Education: B.S. Biology, Atlantic College. Education: 22650 McKenzie Street, Dowagiac, Michigan 49047.

GREENFIELD, LISA L Occupation: Residence Hall Coordinator, Florida State University. Education: B.A.; M.S. Higher Education (in progress). Address: Post Office Box U-4273, Tallahassee, Florida 32313.

GREENWOOD, JOHN MURRAY III Occupation:

Student. Education: B.A./B.S., University of Texas. Address: Post Office Box 728, El Campo, Texas 77437.

GREGO, NICHOLAS J Occupation: Physician; Educator. Education: Ph.D. Physiology; D.O. Address: 593 Wigard Avenue, Philadelphia, Pennsylvania 19128.

GREGORY, TEENA DENISE Occupation: Secretary of Community Development Office. Education: Bachelor's Degree in Business Management (in progress), Cumberland College. Address: Route 1, Box 196, Dixon Springs, Tennessee 37057.

GRIFFIN, LOVEY DEANE Occupation: Student. Education: Bachelor of Music Education. Address: 219 Nunn Street, Havelock, North Carolina 28532.

GRIFFITH, MARUIN SCOTT Occupation: College Student. Education: B.S. Accounting (in progress). Address: 618 Hunt Avenue, Trenton, New Jersey 08610.

GRIMES, KATHRYN ANN Occupation: Student. Address: Rural Route 2, Box 168, Mt. Pleasant, Tennessee 38474.

GRISSETT, NADINE I Occupation: Student. Education: B.S. Psychology; Attending Stetson University. Address: Post Office Box 1244, Winter Garden, Florida 32787.

GROB, DOUGLAS BENSON Occupation: University Student. Education: B.A./M.A. Candidate. Address: 675 West End Avenue, New York, New York 10025.

GROSS, KATHLEEN ANN Occupation: Medical Student. Education: B.S., Northern Illinois University. Address: 54 Sunset Drive, Streator, Illinois 61364.

GROSS, SUSAN MARIE Occupation: Special Education Teacher. Education: B.A. Address: Rural Route 2, Box 105A, Dunlap, Iowa 51529.

GROSS, TERRENCE MICHAEL Occupation: Student. Education: B.S. Biological Science, Northern Illinois University. Address: 54 Sunset, Streator, Illinois 61364.

GROVE, JEFFREY SCOTT Occupation: Student. Education: Attending Florida Southern College. Address: 13913 105th Avenue North, Largo, Florida 33544.

GRUDZINSKAS, MARY ELIZABETH Occupation: Assistant Contracts Manager, Department of Social Services. Education: A.S., Quinsigamond Community College. Address: 60 South Street, Worcester, Massachusetts 01604.

GUCKIAN, DONNA LYNN Occupation: Student. Education: M.B.A. (in progress). Address: 2347 Anna Avenue, Clearwater, Florida 33575.

GUENTHER, ANNE CHRISTINE Occupation: Student. Education: B.A. Telecommunications, Purdue University. Address: 1039 Park Avenue, New Haven, Indiana 46774.

GUTSCHENRITTER, DENISE LYNN Occupation: Educator. Education: Associate of Arts; Bachelor of Science in Education; Master of Science in Education. Address: Box 324, Fairfax, Missouri 64446.

GUTHRIE, TERESA ANN Occupation: Travel Consultant. Education: Diploma, Booker T. Washington High School. Address: 1604 R South Utica, Tulsa, Oklahoma 74104.

H

HAHN, NICHOLAS GEORGE JR Occupation: Certified Public Accountant, Coopers and Lybrand. Education: B.S.C. Accounting, De Paul University; M.B.A. (in progress), University of Chicago. Address: 300 Banbury Avenue, Elk Grove Village, Illinois 60007.

HAIRSTON, CORNELIA ANN Occupation: Treasurer, Progressive D.C. Chapter of F.E.W.; Accounting Technician, G.S.A. Address: 4810 Alabama Avenue, Southeast, Apartment #4, Washington, D.C. 20019.

HALL, DONALD NATHAN Occupation: Student. Address: 1500 Whitehall, Marion, South Carolina 29571.

HALL, DOSHIA EDITH Occupation: Student. Education: B.S., Morehead State University. Address: Post Office Box 384, Louisa, Kentucky 41230.

HALL, MAUREEN THERESE Occupation: Student. Education: B.A. Spanish and Bachelor of Journalism (in progress), University of Missouri at Columbia. Address: Route #2, Hannibal, Missouri 63401.

HALL, MICHAEL E Occupation: Medical Student. Education: B.S. Biology, Pittsburg State University; Associate in Bible, Grace College of the Bible; Attending University of Kansas School of Medicine. Address: Rural Route 3, Girard, Kansas 66743.

HALL, TRICIA H Occupation: Realtime Simulations Programer. Education: B.S. Mathematics. Address: 17 Cathy Drive, Newport News, Virginia 23602.

HALL, VIRGINIA LEIGH Occupation: Student. Education: A.S., Jeff State Junior College; Attending Auburn University. Address: Post Office Box 741, Talladega, Alabama 35160.

HALLMARK, KEZIA JANE Occupation: Graduate Student; Graduate Teachers Assistant. Education: B.A. German. Address: 3205 Porter Avenue, El Paso, Texas 79930.

HALLORAN, TAMMY A Occupation: Student. Education: Attending College. Address: 20613 Howard Drive, O'Fallon, Illinois 62269.

HALSEY, VICKY LYNN Occupation: Student. Education: Attending Wytheville Community College. Address: Route 1, Box 56, Max Meadows, Virginia 24360.

HALVORSON, RANDOLPH OWEN Occupation: Student. Education: Attending University of North Dakota. Address: Post Office Box 233, Tolna, North Dakota 58380.

HAMILTON, JACKIE DALE Occupation: Service, United States Navy. Education: High School Diploma. Address: Route 2, Box 323-C, Spiro, Oklahoma 74959.

HAMILTON, SANDRA LYNN Occupation: Student. Education: Attending University of Arkansas. Address: Route 2, Box 89A, Lincoln, Arkansas 72744.

HAMMOND, JANET LAMBERT Education: B.B.A. Marketing, Associate B.A., Associate Science/ Social Services. Address: 235 Freyer Drive, Marietta, Georgia 30060.

HANKS, MICHAEL L Occupation: Student. Education: Attending Brigham Young University. Address: 495 East 1010 South, Orem, Utah 84057.

HANNESTAD, PEGGY SUE Occupation: Radio Announcer. Education: Attending North Dakota State University. Address: 2909 3rd Street North, Fargo, North Dakota 58102.

HANSOM, TELA MARIA Occupation: Student. Education: Attending High School. Address: 3113 Montrose, Richmond, Virginia 23222.

HANSON, MARY MARGARET Occupation: Nursing Assistant. Education: High School Diploma; Attended Roanoke College. Address: 921 Marston Street, Salem, Virginia 24153.

HARGETT, RANDALL ALLEN Occupation: Process Engineer, 3M Corporation. Education: B.S. Chemical Engineering. Address: Post Office Box 804, Guin, Alabama 35563.

HARJO, SUSAN ARKEKETA Occupation: Graduate Student. Education: B.A. Journalism, M.A. Communication. Address: 1616 Alameda, A7, Norman, Oklahoma 73071.

HARKINS, MARY DOLORES Occupation: Student. Education: B.A. Philosophy; J.D. Candidate. Address: 9905 Belleview, Kansas City, Missouri 64114.

HARKINS, VICTORIA SMITH Occupation: Clinical Nurse Specialist, Mental Health Nursing, Vanderbilt School of Nursing. Education: B.S.N., M.S.N. Address: 4105 Aberdeen Road, Nashville, Tennessee 37205.

HARMAN, MARK E Occupation: Student. Education: Brigham Young University. Address: 5771 Highway 330, Box 366, Collbran, Colorado 81624.

HARMAN, MATTHEW E Occupation: Student. Education: Attending Brigham Young University. Address: 5771 Highway 330, Box 366, Collbran, Colorado 81624.

HARMAN, MICAH A Occupation: Student. Education: Attending Plateau Valley High School. Address: 5771 Highway 330, Box 366, Collbran, Colorado 81624.

HARMON, ANGELA GAY Occupation: Nursing Student. Education: A.S.; B.S. (in progress). Address: Route 1, Box 15A, Ahoskie, North Carolina 27910.

HARPER, BRADLEY DRAKE Occupation: Percussionist. Education: Attending University of Texas at Arlington. Address: 2118 Prestonwood Drive, Arlington, Texas 76012.

HARPER, CHRISTOPHER EARL Occupation: University Student. Address: 59 East Norwood, Memphis, Tennessee 38109.

HARPER, MICHELLE E Occupation: Lifeguard; Swimming Instructor; Theatre Employee. Education: Attending College. Address: 523 Paul Street, Harrisonburg, Virginia 22801.

HARRIMAN, CHERYL ALISA Occupation: Graduate Student. Education: B.S. Accountancy; Attending University of Central Florida. Address: 123 East Stuart Avenue, Lake Wales, Florida 33853.

HARRIS, CONNIE F Occupation: Sales Associate. Education: B.A. Business Administration. Address: 2207 South Schiller, Little Rock, Arkansas 72202.

HARRIS, ELIZABETH CLAUDIA Occupation: Student; Paraprofessional; Assistant Counselor. Education: B.S. Child Development and Family Relations. Address: Sunshine Canyon, Salina Star Route, Boulder, Colorado 80302.

HARRIS, JANA LYNN Occupation: Student. Education: A.A., Western Texas College. Address: Post Office Box 892, Ozona, Texas 76943.

HARRIS, SHEILA LA NAY Occupation: Student. Education: Attending Indiana University School of Music. Address: 3425 North Audubon Road, Indianapolis, Indiana 46218.

HARRIS, SHIRLEY D Occupation: Certified Public Accountant. Education: B.A. summa cum laude, University of West Florida, 1980; A.A. High Honors, Pensacola Junior College, 1979. Address: Route 3, Box 920, Jay, Florida 32565.

HARRIS, YVETTE WAYNE Occupation: Teacher.

Education: B.S. Education, Physical Education and English. Address: 241 Vine Street, Bluefield, West Virginia 24701.

HARRISON, C ROBERT JR Occupation: Student; Minister. Education: B.A. Address: Post Office Box 479, Glasgow, Kentucky 42141.

HARRISON, ROBERT DAVID (SKIP) Occupation: Computer Programmer and Operator. Education: Graduate, Texas Institute. Address: Lakewood Apartments, #N12, 303 Highway 1417 South, Sherman, Texas 75090.

HART, MELISSA GRACE Occupation: Student. Education: Attending Middle Tennessee State University. Address: Route 2, Box 206A, Watertown, Tennessee 37184.

HARTSOCK, DION ERIC Occupation: Assistant Manager, Haagen Dazs. Education: A.A. Hotel/Restaurant Management. Address: 3610 Northwest 21 Street, Laud Lakes, Florida 33311.

HARTZOG, DANIEL JEFFERSON Occupation: High School Student. Address: Post Office Box 127, Hilda, South Carolina 29813.

HARTZOG, GEORGE TERRANCE Occupation: High School Student. Address: Post Office Box 127, Hilda, South Carolina 29813.

HARTZOG, WENDY VIRGINIA Occupation: Student. Education: Attended Denmark Technical College, University of South Carolina. Address: Post Office Box 127, Hilda, South Carolina 29813.

HASTINGS, KAY LYNN Occupation: Teacher of Pre-primary Lab School. Education: B.S. Early Childhood Education; M.S. Early Childhood Education. Address: 11710 Fuqua #56, Houston, Texas 77034.

HATCH, BRIAN J Occupation: Financial Analyst. Education: B.S. Political Science; M.P.A. (in progress). Address: Post Office Box 81212, Salt Lake City, Utah 84108.

HATHAWAY, DOUGLAS W Occupation: Mechanical Engineer. Education: B.S. Engineering, Harvey Mudd College. Address: 845 Paularino #13108, Costa Mesa, California 92626.

HAUPT, KEVIN PAUL Occupation: Electrical Engineering Student. Address: 7 Fales Street, Randolph, Vermont 05060.

HAWKINS, KELVIN RAYNARD Occupation: Student, Kansas City Inroader. Education: Attending University of Missouri. Address: 4038 Indiana, Kansas City, Missouri 64130.

HAXTON, LORI ANN Occupation: Residence Life Programming Coordinator. Education: B.S., M.A. Address: Box 15006 Northern Arizona University, Flagstaff, Arizona 86011.

HAYNES, W LEIGHTON Occupation: Graduate Student. Education: B.A. Economics. Address: 1725 Orrington Avenue #729, Evanston, Illinois 60201.

HAZARD, SUSAN NANON Occupation: Bookkeeping Department Manager. Education: B.B.A. Accounting. Address: 855 South Irving Heights #114, Irving, Texas 75060.

HEARD, BRENDA MARIE Occupation: Graduate Student. Education: B.A. English and French, Stetson University. Address: 8632 Pinetree Drive, Seminole, Florida 33542.

HEASTON, JACQUELYN ANN Occupation: Student. Education: B.S. Address: 324 Bledsoe, Covington, Tennessee 38019.

HEATH, CYNTHIA DIANNE Occupation: Student. Education: Attending North Carolina A & T State University. Address: 113 Carver Road, Baltimore, Maryland 21222.

HECKERT, CONNIE K Occupation: Writer; Graduate Student. Education: A.A., B.A., M.A. Address: 5628 Appomattox Road, Davenport, Iowa 52806.

HEDGEPETH, BRUCE EDWARD Occupation: Graduate Student. Education: B.S. Psychology, Stetson University; Ph.D. Clinical Psychology (in progress), Emory University. Address: 3735 Wetherburn Drive, Clarkston, Georgia 30021.

HEISER, TIMOTHY ROBERT Occupation: Staff Accountant. Education: Bachelor Business Administration. Address: Box 125, Pleasanton, Kansas 66075.

HELICZER, SONYA BEATRICE Occupation: Student. Address: 3303 59th Avenue Southwest, Seattle, Washington 98116.

HENARD, MARK EDWARD Occupation: Student. Education: Liberal Arts Degree in Bible and Religion. Address: 6062 Leesburg Pike, Falls Church, Virginia 22041.

HENDERSON, JANET McCUISTON Occupation: Special Education Teacher. Education: Masters of Education-Interrelated/Learning Disabilities. Address: 2268 Boy Scout Camp Road, Gainesville, Georgia 30501.

HENDERSON, KATHLEEN MARTIN Occupation: Head Nurse Cardiac Surgery in the Operating Room. Education: Associate of Arts, Bachelor of Science in Nursing. Address: 324 North Florence Street, Maxton, North Carolina 28364.

HENDERSON, NELLIE ANN Occupation: Student. Education: Attending Queens College. Address: 324 North Florence Street, Maxton, North Carolina 28364.

HENDERSON, WILLIAM F Occupation: Center Manager, Hall County Parks and Recreation. Education: A.B.A., Reinhardt College; Attended Piedmont College; B.A. (in progress), North Georgia College.

HENDLER, STACEY ANNE Occupation: Student. Education: B.A. Communications, University of Houston, 1984. Address: 922 West Main Street, Houston, Texas 77006.

HENRY, MARY BRIGGS Occupation: Director, Editorial Office, Department of Radiology, Venderbilt University Medical Center. Education: B.A. Address: 180 Wallace Road, #V-19, Nashville, Tennessee 37232.

HENSHAW, IAN WILLIAM Occupation: Student. Education: B.S. Mechanical Engineering, 1984. Address: 126 Klein Road, Williamsville, New York 14221.

HERDA, ANTHONY MARK Occupation: Exchange Student to Sweden. Address: 2241 Villafont Way, Sacramento, California 95825.

HERMAN, SUSANNA JESSICA Occupation: Poet, Editor. Education: A.A., B.G.S.U. Address: 1005 North Grove, A-3, Bowling Green, Ohio 43402.

HERNANDEZ, MELBA "JEAN" Occupation: Field Service Coordinator, College Placement Council, Inc. Education: B.S., M.Ed. Address: 1405 North Locust #9, Denton, Texas 76201.

HESTER, JOHN R Occupation: Staff Member, Reagan-Bush '84; Student. Education: Attending College. Address: Route 2, Box 337, Sallis, Mississippi 39160.

HICKMAN, MICHAEL WESLEY Occupation: Educator. Education: B.A. History, M.A.T., University of North Carolina-Chapel Hill. Address: 102-H Ramsey Court, Cary, North Carolina 27511.

HICKS, JAMIE D Occupation: Accountant. Education: Attended Lane College, 1982. Address: 821 Boston Street, Memphis, Tennessee 38114.

HICKS, SHERRIE BERNAY Occupation: Student. Education: B.S.B.A., University of Arkansas, 1984. Address: 3706 Tulane Circle, Garland, Texas 75043.

HILDRETH, JOHNNY DAYTON Occupation: Student; Employee, Sears Roebuck, Receiving, Catalog. Education: Diploma, Mar Vista High School, 1981; Attending Patricia Stevens Fashion College. Address: 1470 California Street, Imperial Beach, California 92032.

HILGERT, JOHN ANDREW Occupation: Student, Conservative Activist. Address: 4223 Poppleton Avenue, Omaha, Nebraska 69105.

HILL, JAMES PIERCE JR (JIMMY) Occupation: Student. Education: B.A. Politics, Wake Forest University; M.A. Political Science, Appalachian State University. Address: Post Office Box 4881, Asheboro, North Carolina 27204-0488.

HILL, LISA KAREN Occupation: Student. Education: A.A., University of Florida; B.S. Ocean Engineering (in progress), Florida Atlantic University. Address: 100 Jackson Lane, Hendersonville, Tennessee 37075.

HILL, SANDRA LaTANYA Occupation: Musician, Church Organist, Piano Instructor. Education: Graduate (honors), Southwest McEvoy B; Attending Mercer University. Address: 871 Woodard Avenue, Macon, Georgia 31204.

HINDMAN, TIMOTHY WILLIAM Occupation: Student. Education: Attending University of Nebraska-Lincoln. Address: HC70, Box 45, Hay Springs, Nebraska 69347.

HINDS, AMY LYNN Occupation: Secretary. Education: Graduate, Auston's Modeling School. Address: 767 Crescent, AuGres, Michigan 48703.

HINDS, JENNIFER LEE Occupation: Sims Township Deputy Treasurer. Education: High School Diploma 1980. Address: 767 Crescent Drive, Point Lookout, Augres, Michigan 48703.

HINKAMPER, RICKY R Occupation: Student. Education: A.A. high honors; Attending Culver-Stockton College. Address: 1853 Maple Street, Quincy, Illinois 62301 .

HINTON, JOHNNY DEAN Occupation: Student. Education: B.A. Bible (in progress), Oklahoma Christian College. Address: Route 2, Box 268, Hardy, Arkansas 72542.

HINTON, TAMMY JUNE Education: B.S.E. English. Address: Route 2, Box 268, Hardy, Arkansas 72542.

HIPP, JOEY MAC Occupation: District Sales Manager. Education: B.S. Business Administration. Address: Route 2, Box 213, Wilmer, Alabama 36587.

HIRAYAMA, DAVID T Occupation: Student. Education: B.S. Computer Science/Electrical Engineering. Address: 2120 Bangor Way, Anaheim, California 92806.

HIRSCHFELD, LYNN A Occupation: Student. Education: Graduate, Madison West High School, 1981; Attending University of Wisconsin-Madison. Address: 6410 Masthead Drive, Madison, Wisconsin 53705.

HISSOM, JAMIE LYNNE Occupation: Student. Address: 995 Spanish Grove Drive, Richmond, Kentucky 40475.

HITE, ANNA FAYE MORRIS Occupation: Chairperson, Department of Nursing, Belmont College. Education: B.S.M. 1965, M.Ed. 1970, M.S.N. 1979, D.S.N. 1980. Address: 5025 Hillsboro Road 2M, Nashville, Tennessee 37215.

HOCHMAN, IRA JONATHAN Occupation: Computer Programmer/Consultant. Address: 17 Herbert Road, Worcester, Massachusetts 01602.

HODGE, GREGORY CHRISTOPHER Occupation: Student. Education: High School Diploma, Associate's Degree Electronic Engineering, Bachelor of Science in Electronic Engineering (in progress). Address: 162 Pond Street, Holbrook, Massachusetts 02343.

HODGE, ROBERT W Occupation: Musical Artist. Education: B.F.A. 2, California Institute of the Arts. Address: 209 Lorac Road, Williamsburg, Virginia 23185.

HODGES, SIMUEL WARD Occupation: Student. Education: A.S. Accounting; Attending East Carolina University. Address: 214 Spring Avenue, Murfreesboro, North Carolina 27855.

HOFFER, DAVID PAUL Occupation: Student/Computer Programmer. Education: Student, High School. Address: 14 Welland Road, Brookling, Massachusetts 02146.

HOFING, ILENE BESS Occupation: Student. Education: B.S. Address: 9 Hilltop Road, Trenton, New Jersey 08638.

HOKOANA, LENI MELEKA Occupation: Program Coordinator, Maui Kokua Services. Education: Bachelor of Social Work. Address: 663 Waiehu Beach Road, Wailuku, Hawaii 96793.

HOLBROOK, ROBERT DAVID Occupation: B.A. Psychology, King College, 1985. Address: Route 6, Box 684, Bristol, Virginia 24201.

HOLDER, ANDREW JOSEPH Occupation: Graduate Student. Education: B.S., Mobile College. Address: 214 39th Avenue, Apartment #1, Hattiesburg, Mississippi 39401.

HOLLAND, HOLLY ANN Occupation: Student. Education: Attending Texas A&M University. Address: 812 Northpine, Conroe, Texas 77301.

HOLLIDAY, HENRY HUNTER III Occupation: Banker, Bank and Finance, Colonial American National Bank. Education: A.A. Business Management. Address: 1214 Missouri Avenue, Salem, Virginia 24153.

HOLTZ, ALICE Occupation: Scientific Projects Coordinator. Education: B.A. Biology, Psychology, Education; Ph.D. Biology/Biochemistry. Address: 275 Fort Washington Avenue, New York, New York 10032.

HOOK, CARL CHRISTOPHER Occupation: Medical Student. Education: B.A. Chemistry, Greenville College; M.D. (in progress), University of Illinois College of Medicine. Address: 141 East Hoehn Street, Carlinville, Illinois 62626.

HOOKER, EUGENIA ANN Occupation: Graduate Student Sociology. Education: B.A. Sociology. Address: Broadmoor Apartments, I-48, West Columbia, South Carolina 29169.

HOOVER, LANNIE L (PYBURN) Occupation: Student. Education: Attending Texas Tech University. Address: 109 Marla Drive, Lafayette, Louisiana 70508.

HOPKINS, CHARLES STANFORD Occupation: Student. Education: Attending College Prep School. Address: 5425 Shirley Avenue, Tarzana, California 91356.

HOPKINS, JOHN L Occupation: Student. Education: B.A. Business (Decision Systems Analyst). Address: 5425 Shirley Avenue, Tarzana, California 91356.

HOPPER, JOHN W II Occupation: Financial Analyst. Education: B.A., Mount Union College; M.B.A., University of Pittsburgh. Address: 16 Hillcrest Drive, Apartment 4, Pittsburgh, Pennsylvania 15202.

HOPSTETTER, ROBERT A Occupation: Administrative Aide, Everite Knitting Mills. Education: B.S. Business Administration. Address: 22 Lehman Street, Lebanon, Pennsylvania 17042.

HORN, JOHN L Occupation: Engineer/Programmer. Education: B.S. Mechanical Engineering, Stanford University. Address: 2232 Blake, Berkeley, California 94704.

HORTON, JENISE LENONA Occupation: Student. Education: Degree in Social Work (in progress). Address: Post Office Box 551, Pittsboro, North Carolina 27312.

HOSCH, PATRICIA GARRETT Occupation: Student. Education: B.S. Finance. Address: Post Office Box 7569, Marietta, Georgia 30065.

HOTTE, KATHLEEN ROSANNA Occupation: Student. Education: B.S.A., University of Georgia, 1984. Address: Route 1, Box 390, Byron, Georgia 31008.

HOUSE, JAMES W Occupation: Computer Portal Teacher, University of Wyoming, University of Wyoming. Education: B.A. Address: Box 157, Elk Mountain, Wyoming 82324.

HOUSEHOLDER, GINA MARIE Occupation: Student. Education: Graduate, Williamsport High School, 1982; Attending Shepherd College. Address: 16 Plum Tree Lane, Williamsport, Maryland 21795.

HOUSER, KAREN YVONNE Occupation: Programmer/Analyst. Education: Associate Degree Computer Science. Address: 44 Pennsylvania Avenue, Watsontown, Pennsylvania 17777.

HOUSTON, WILLIE WALTER JR Occupation: Assistant Professor of Biology, Central State University. Education: B.S., Morehouse College; M.S., Ph.D., Atlanta University. Address: 1000 Frederick Drive, Xenia, Ohio 45385.

HOWARD, PAMELA FAITH Occupation: Nursing Student. Education: B.S.N., East Carolina University, 1984. Address: Route 2, Box 501, Richlands, North Carolina 28574.

HOWE, STEPHEN WILLIAM Occupation: Supervisor, Social Worker. Education: B.A., Lycoming College; M.S.W., University of Maryland. Address: 223 Stanmore Road, Baltimore, Maryland 21212.

HOWELL, LARRY ALAN Occupation: Realtor. Education: B.S. Marketing. Address: 1035 North Roosevelt Avenue, Liberal, Kansas 67901.

HOWIE, MARY Occupation: Radiology Supervisor. Education: B.A. English, Education; M.B.A. Business. Address: 11 Bennington Street, Lawrence, Massachusetts 01841.

HOWLAND, ELIZABETH I Occupation: Student. Education: Associate Degree Medical Technology. Address: 3076 Lindberg Avenue, Allentown, Pennsylvania 18103.

HUCH, DONNA LYNN Occupation: Student. Education: B.S. Mathematics/French. Address: 317 Lamar Avenue, Hattiesburg, Mississippi 39401.

HUEBNER, JOHN BURTON Occupation: Student. Education: Attending College. Address: 409 Summit Street, Monroeville, Indiana 46773.

HUERTA, BRENDA LEE Occupation: Owner, Servicio Capitalina en espanol. Address: 8811 Dawnridge Circle 101, Austin, Texas 78758.

HUEY, LISA MARIE Occupation: Student. Education: Attending Appalachian State University. Address: 1160 Pine Knolls Road, Kernersville, North Carolina 27284.

HUFFINE, SHERRIE ELAINE Occupation: Student. Education: A.S. Business Administration, Roane State Community College. Address: 310 West Outer Drive, Oak Ridge, Tennessee 37830.

HUGHES, LILLIE SUE Occupation: Optometric Assistant. Education: A.A. Business Management. Address: Post Office Box 215, Cadiz, Kentucky 42211.

HUGHES, MARY ELIZABETH Occupation: Student. Education: B.A., Mollay College; M.S., Hunter College; Ed.M., Ed.D. Candidate, Teacher's College, Columbia University. Address: 621 Elmont Road, Elmont, New York 11003

HUGHES, THOMAS W Occupation: Student. Education: Attending M.S.S. College. Address: Route 2, Box 416, Baxter Springs, Kansas 66713.

HUMPHREYS, MARY JEWELL Education: B.S.E. Address: Route 6, Box 203, Hot Springs, Arkansas 71901.

HUNT, JOHN WILLIAMSON JR Occupation: Supervisor of Hunting and Game Management. Education: B.A. Agriculture. Address: 905 Alturas Road, Bartow, Florida 33830.

HUNTER, SHARON K Occupation: Licensed Practical Nurse. Education: Associate L.P.N. Address: 450 South Mission, Colby, Kansas 67701.

HURBAN, PENNY G Occupation: Student. Education: A.B. Romance Languages (in progress). Address: 888½ Oglethorpe Avenue #16, Athens, Georgia 30605.

HURST, DEBRA LOUISE Occupation: Graduate Student. Education: Degree in Health and Physical Education (in progress). Address: 221 Beverly Drive, Lafayette, Louisiana 70503.

HURT, MELISSA BANE Occupation: Junior Accountant. Education: B.S. Accounting. Address: Route 2, Box 433, Saluda, South Carolina 29138.

HUSBAND, PHILLIP LYLE Occupation: College Student. Education: A.A., Meridian Junior College; B.B.A., Missisippi State University. Address: Route 4, Box 208, Meridian, Mississippi 39305.

I

IMMEL, CHRIS K Occupation: Student. Education: Attending Southwestern University. Address: Route 7, Box 110, Llano, Texas 78643.

INGRAM, MICHAEL L Occupation: College Student. Address: 1151 Sherwood Road, Paducah, Kentucky 42001.

INMAN, LISA GAYLE Occupation: Student. Education: Attending Western Carolina University. Address: Post Office Box 213, Raeford, North Carolina 28376.

INMAN, TAMMY JUNE Occupation: Educator. Education: B.S.E. English. Address: Route 2, Box 268, Hardy, Arkansas 72542.

IRBY, WILLIAM VAUGHN JR Occupation: Student. Education: Attending Troy State University. Address: 117 Starmount Drive, Valdosta, Georgia 31602.

IRIARTE, MATILDE D Occupation: Secretary; Student. Education: Bachelors Degree in Business Management and Marketing. Address: 8791 Southwest 54 Terrace, Miami, Florida 33165.

ISAAC-TIMMONS, DENISE PAULETTE Occupation: Registered Nurse; President, Praises Fine Hats and Accessories, Inc. Education: Associate of Arts, Associate of Science, Miami Dade Medical Center Campus. Address: 224 Southwest 4th Avenue, #5, Miami, Florida 33130.

IVEY, REBECCA MOODY Education: B.S. Business Education. Address: Route 2, Box 404, Mount Olive, North Carolina 28365.

J

JACKSON, CINDY KAY Address: 1701 Roman Road, Grand Prairie, Texas 75050.

JACKSON, SARA C Occupation: Assistant Professor Special Education, University of Southern Mississippi-Jackson County Campus. Education: B.A.E., M.Ed., Ed.D. Address: University of Southern Mississippi-Jackson County Campus, 1424 East Beach Boulevard, Gulfport, Mississippi 39503.

JACKSON, SHARON STOCKMAN Occupation: Research Technician, Bacterial Genetics. Education: A.S., B.S. Address: 911 Avenue K, #6, Galveston, Texas 77550.

JACKSON, SHEILA H Occupation: High School Student. Address: Route 3, Box 191, St. Pauls, North Carolina 28384.

JACKSON, WILLIAM ERICK Occupation: Chiropractor. Education: B.A., D.C. Address: 1857 South 31st, Kansas City, Kansas 66106.

JAGGARS, CINDY ANNETTE Occupation: Student. Education: Degree in Communications (in progress), Union University. Address: Route 2, Box 66, Ramer, Tennessee 38367.

JAMES, ABBE LOUISE Occupation: Student, University of Tennessee Martin. Education: Accounting. Address: 5064 Quince, Memphis, Tennessee 38117.

JAMES, ANDREA MARCIA Occupation: Student. Education: Attending Coker College. Address: 225 Rogers Road, Darlington, South Carolina 29552.

JAMESON, DOUGLAS SCOTT Occupation: Student. Education: Attending S.M.S.U. Address: 668 West Springfield Street, Aurora, Missouri 65605.

JANSEN, JULIE DAWN Occupation: Student. Education: Attending Illinois State University. Address: 304 Hemlock, Romeoville, Illinois 60441.

JASPER, SHAN CASSANDRA Occupation: Student. Education: Attending Miles College. Address: Post Office Box 626, Chattahoochee, Florida 32324.

JEFFREYS, MARGARET VILLAR (PEGGY) Occupation: Petroleum Landman. Education: College Graduate. Address: 1810 Old Government Street, Mobile, Alabama 36606.

JENKINS, JEFFREY VAN Occupation: Veterinary Student. Education: B.A., Southern Methodist University; D.V.M. (in progress). Address: 2010 Seaton Apartment 4, Manhatton, Kansas 66502.

JENKINS, SHARON RENEE Occupation: Model. Education: High School Diploma; Graduate, Barbizon Modeling School. Address: Route 1, Box 322-A½, Estill Springs, Tennessee 37330.

JENKINS, WILLIAM PHILIP Occupation: Student. Address: 2123 North Dayton, Chicago, Illinois 60614.

JENKINSON, KIM M Occupation: Student. Education: B.A. (in progress), University of Scranton. Address: 17 Marion Road, Montvale, New Jersey 07645.

JESTER, MICHAEL T Occupation: Vice President, Sierra Insurance Agency, Inc. Education: B.S., University of Delaware. Address: 927 Conquistador, Hanford, California 93230.

JETER, BILL W Address: Post Office Box 65, Davis, Oklahoma 73030.

JIMENEZ, ARACELI Occupation: Student. Education: A.A., Laredo Jnior College; B.S. Secondary Education (in progress), Laredo State University. Address: 3005 Salinas, Laredo, Texas 78040.

JOHNKOSKI, JOHN ANTHONY Occupation: Student. Address: 75 Magnolia, Battle Creek, Michigan 49017.

JOHNSON, ALECIA JAYNE Occupation: Music Teacher. Education: B.M. Voice; B.M.E. Choral. Address: 1805 West 18th, Little Rock, Arkansas 72202.

JOHNSON, CYNTHIA L Occupation: Student. Education: B.S.E., M.A. Speech Pathology; Attending George Peabody College for Teachers, Vanderbilt University. Address: 2003 Lucia Lane, Pine Bluff, Arkansas 71601.

JOHNSON, DAVID WILLIAM Occupation: Student. Education: B.A. Economics (in progress), Princeton University. Address: 5519 Firethorn Court, Cincinnati, Ohio 45242.

JOHNSON, FELICIA LYNETTE Occupation: High School Student. Address: 409 Park Ridge, Grand Prairie, Texas 75051.

JOHNSON, GREGORY ALAN Occupation: Student. Education: Attending College. Address: Apartment 47, Thomas Jefferson Court, Paducah, Kentucky 42001.

JOHNSON, HOWARD ARTHUR JR Occupation: Operations Research Analyst, EG&G Inter Tech, Inc. Education: B.A. Operations Research Analysis 1974, B.A. International Relations 1974, M.A. International Management 1984. Address: 309 Yacht Club Drive, Northeast, Fort Walton Beach, Florida 32548.

JOHNSON, JAMES KENNETH Occupation: Graduate Student. Education: B.S. Engineering; Attending North Carolina State University. Address: 101 Bremer Street, Fayetteville, North Carolina 28303.

JOHNSON, JOHANNA Occupation: Certified Nurses Assistant. Education: High School Graduate. Address: 9841 Clover Trail, Salinas, California 93907.

JOHNSON, LINDA S Occupation: Systems Designer. Education: B.A., Grambling State University. Address: 6826 Desert Rose, Houston, Texas 77086.

JOHNSON, LYNNE L Occupation: Neonatal Nurse Practitioner. Education: B.S.N. 1980, M.S.N. 1983. Address: 5859 C Ivy Knoll Court, Indianapolis, Indiana 46250.

JOHNSON, MARVA JEAN Occupation: Admissions Representative for Business Colleges. Education: B.S. Address: 2480 78th Avenue, Baton Rouge, Louisiana 70807.

JOHNSON, PAULA J Occupation: Teacher. Education: B.S. Education. Address: Route 640, Box 84, Cobham, Virginia 22929.

JOHNSON, RONALD EARL Occupation: Student. Education: Attending Central Wesleyan College. Address: 812 Driftwood Drive, Siler City, North Carolina 27344.

JOHNSON, SHERRY LYNN Occupation: Student. Education: Attending East Texas University. Address: 2214 Simmons Street, Kilgore, Texas 75662.

JOHNSON, SUSAN ANNE Occupation: Store Detective. Education: B.S. Political Science, 1985. Address: 1540 Oak Creek Drive Northeast, Marietta, Georgia 30066.

JOHNSON, TERRY GLEN Occupation: Student. Education: Attending IJE Junior College. Address: Route 1, Oklona, Mississippi 38860.

JOHNSON, WINNIE G Occupation: Speech and Language Specialist. Education: B.S. Speech, Language and Auditory Pathology. Address: 1024 Brandywine Lane, Rocky Mount, North Carolina 27801.

JOHNSTON, JEFFREY Occupation: Student. Education: Attending Troy State University. Address: Route 2, Box 53-A, Ariton, Alabama 36311-9802.

JOHNSTON, SHANNON SHERWOOD Occupation: Counselor; Teacher.

Education: B.A. magna cum laude. Address: 1709½ Bruce Drive, St. Simons Island, Georgia 31522.

JONES, AMANDA G Occupation: Librarian. Education: B.A. English; Masters, Library Science; 1 Year Bible Certificate. Address: 208 North Sparrow Road, Chesapeake, Virginia 23325.

JONES, AMY E Occupation: Student. Education: Attending Texas Tech University. Address: 1709 Crooks Court, Grand Prairie, Texas 75051.

JONES, ANGELA R Occupation: Graduate Student and Teacher's Assistant. Education: B.S. Music Education. Address: 709B Patty Drive, Maryville, Illinois 62062.

JONES, BARBARA LYNN Occupation: Licensed Physical Therapist. Education: B.S. Physical Therapy. Address: 4155 Essen Lane, #189, Baton Rouge, Louisiana 70809.

JONES, DAVID ERIC Occupation: College Student. Education: Attending Auburn University. Address: 505 Timberlane Avenue, Tullahoma, Tennessee 37388.

JONES, ETTA MAE Occupation: Outreach Worker, Female Group. Education: B.A., Graduate Studies (in progress). Address: 616 Hayes, Apartment #2, San Francisco, California 94102.

JONES, EVELYN ROJEAN Occupation: Professional Educator. Education: B.A. Human Relations; M.A. Theatre Management. Address: 1308 South Bruce, Monahans, Texas 79756.

JONES, FREDDA L Occupation: Student. Education: B.A. (in progress). Address: 606 North Elm, Comanche, Texas 76442.

JONES, JAMES LEONARD III Occupation: Student. Address: Post Office Box 421, Sylva, North Carolina 28779.

JONES, KAREN LYNETTE Occupation: Student. Education: B.A. (in progress). Address: 606 North Elm, Comanche, Texas 76442.

JONES, LINDA SWISHER Occupation: Executive Secretary. Education: Associate Degree in Applied Science. Address: 1226 B Bayside Drive, Treasure Island, California 94130.

JONES, RACHEL ELIZABETH Occupation: Employee, Gardner-Webb College. Education: B.S. Management/Information Systems, Gardner-Webb College. Address: Post Office Box 124, Boiling Springs, North Carolina 28017.

JOSEPH, DEBORAH ANN Occupation: Student. Education: Letters (Liberal Arts). Address: 214 South Oak, Sapulpa, Oklahoma 74066.

JOSEPH, DIANA MARIE Occupation: Lawyer. Education: B.A., J.D., University of Oklahoma. Address: 5837-D East University, Dallas, Texas 75206.

JOSEPHSON, DARYL CRAIG Occupation: Electrical Engineering Research and Development. Education: B.S. Electrical and Computer Engineering; B.A. Music Theory. Address: 230 Central Avenue, Lawrence, New York 11559.

JOSLIN, SHELEDIA YAVETTE Occupation: Student. Education: Attending College. Address: 3900 Kings Lane, Nashville, Tennessee 37218.

JOYNER, BYRON DAVID Occupation: Medical Student. Education: B.A. Biology, Princeton University; M.D. (in progress), Harvard University. Address: 380 East Drive, Oak Ridge, Tennessee 37830.

JUDD, DENNIS L Occupation: Attorney. Education: B.A. Political Science, 1978; J.D., 1981. Address: 402 East 1500 South, Naples, Utah 84078.

JUDGE, DEBRA ANN Occupation: Student. Education: Attending Concordia College. Address: 13927 Edbrooke Avenue, Riverdale, Illinois 60627.

JUDGE, MARLENE SUSAN Occupation: Student. Education: Attending Mercyhurst College. Address: 13927 Edbrooke Avenue, Riverdale, Illinois 60627.

JUMONVILLE, SUSAN LYNN Occupation: Student. Education: Attending California State University at Worthridge. Address: 8816 Whitaker, Sepulveda, California 91343.

JUROE, JONATHAN DAVID Occupation: Carpenter. Education: Attended College. Address: 369 Rob Way, Anaheim, California 92801.

K

KALAHA, LISA MARIE Occupation: Advertising Artist, Gann-Dawson Advertising. Education: B.A. Advertising, Marywood College, 1983. Address: 1023 Lincoln Street, Dickson City, Pennsylvania 18519.

KAMMER, ALICE A Occupation: Key Account Manager, Cosmetics and H.B.A., Del Laboratories, Inc. Education: B.S. Business Management and Marketing. Address: 1729-204 Gosnell, Vienna, Virginia 22180.

KANDYBOWICZ, IRENA M Occupation: Eligibility Technician for the State of Connecticut. Education: B.A. Social Work and Native American Studies. Address: 131 Vought Place, Stratford, Connecticut 06497.

KANTOR, LISA LYNN Occupation: Student; Math Tutor. Education: Attending Troy State University. Address: 117 Hilltop Drive, Troy, Alabama 36081.

KATAYAMA, SHARA GAYLE Occupation: Occupational Health Nurse R.N. Education: A.A. Nursing; B.A. Home Economics; M.A. Health Education. Address: 2255 West 15th Street, Los Angeles, California 90006.

KATZ, BERT Occupation: Management Trainee. Education: Sc.B. Mechanical Engineering, M.A. Economics, Brown University, 1983. Address: 338 East 78th Street, Apartment 1F, New York, New York 10021.

KEANE, DANIEL J Occupation: Research Participant, Argonne National Laboratory. Education: B.S. Physics, Stetson University. Address: Stetson University, Post Office Box 8013, Deland, Florida 32724.

KEARNS, JOHN MICHAEL Occupation: Student; Graduate Teaching Assistant. Education: B.A.; M.A. Address: 2243-A Sea View Avenue, Honolulu, Hawaii 96822.

KECK, KARLA MAY Occupation: Teacher. Education: B.S. Address: Route 1, Clay City, Illinois 62824.

KEEGAN, DENISE M C Education: B.A. Political Science, A.A. Business. Address: 6431 Rich Road Southeast, Olympia, Washington 98501.

KELLEY, ANGELA MARIE Occupation: Student. Education: B.S. Accounting, University of Tennessee at Martin, 1984. Address: Post Office Box 92, Oakland, Tennessee 38060.

KELLEY, KEVIN M Occupation: Student. Education: A.B. Molecular Biology/Zoology (in progress), University of California at Berkeley. Address: 223 Orchard Road, Orinda, California 94563.

KELLEY, PAULA RENEE Occupation: Electrical Engineering Technology Student. Address: Route 6, Box 83, Martin, Tennessee 38237.

KELLEY, STARLA KAYE Occupation: Music/ Mathematics Education Student. Address: 103 East Brookwood Circle, Ozark, Alabama 36360.

KELLY, DAVID ANTHONY Occupation: Student. Education: B.S., Political Science/Speech Candidate, University of Wisconsin-Oshkosh. Address: 2821 Embassy Row, Apartment 814, Speedway, Indiana 46224.

KELLY, KEVIN JAMES Occupation: Student. Education: B.A. Social Science, B.A. Spanish. Address: 1757 Southeast Dominic Avenue, Port St. Lucie, Florida 33452.

KELLY, LAURA JUNE Occupation: Student. Education: Degree Candidate, Horace Mann High School. Address: 325 Polk Street, Apartment 5A, N

Fonddulac, Wisconsin 54935.

KENNEDY, MARY R Occupation: Fast Food Operator, The Krystal Company. Education: Diploma, Barbizon Professional Modeling, 1982. Address: 304 Crestview Drive, Martinez, Georgia 30904.

KENNEDY, SHERRY Occupation: Business Education Teacher. Education: B.S. Business Education. Address: Route 1, Box 1346, Cross Hill, South Carolina 29332.

KENNEY, STEPHEN MARTIN Occupation: Evangelist. Education: A.A. Address: Post Office Box 444, Lobelville, Tennessee 37097.

KENNICOTT, CHERYL LYNN Occupation: Senior Customer Service Representative, Family Federal Savings. Education: B.A. History, Saginaw Valley State College. Address: 15635 West Townline Road, St. Charles, Michigan 48655.

KERLEY, JENNIE F Occupation: Account Executive. Education: B.S.B.A. Management. Address: 406-D Honey Locust Lane, Birmingham, Alabama 35209.

KERNER, HOWARD ALEX Occupation: Administrator; Instructor of English, Jefferson Community College. Education: B.A. 1971; M.A. 1972. Address: 422 College Heights #2, Watertown, New York 13601.

KETTENBURG, JUDITH SCOTT Occupation: Student. Education: Attending Oregon State University. Address: 415 Catalina Boulevard, San Diego, California 92106.

KHAN, SELINA Occupation: Student. Education: B.S. Computer Science (in progress). Address: Calle Uroyan, AD4, Mayaguez, Puerto Rico 00709.

KHAN, SHERREZA Occupation: Student. Address: Calle Uroyan, Mayaguez, Puerto Rico 00709.

KIBBLE-SMITH, BRIAN G Occupation: Senior Secretary, Law Student. Education: B.A. Address: 6127 West Cermak, Cicero, Illinois 60650.

KINBACK, KEVIN MICHAEL Occupation: Student. Education: B.S. Biology, B.S. Chemistry, King College. Address: 750 US 19 North, #70, Tarpon Springs, Florida 33589.

KING, CATHY LYNNE Occupation: Educator. Education: B.A./B.S., Judson College. Address: 2813 Hartmetz, Evansville, Indiana 47712.

KING, JOHN CAMERON Occupation: Student. Education: Attending University of Nevada-Reno. Address: Post Office Box 1516, Fernley, Nevada 89408.

KING, TAMMY LYNN Occupation: Student. Education: B.A./B.S. (in progress), Freed Hardeman College. Address: Route 2, Box 408, Selmer, Tennessee 38375.

KINGREN, JOHN FRED Occupation: Accountant. Education: B.S. with honors (summa cum laude). Address: 1156 Burdette Street, Roanoke, Alabama 36274.

KIRCHER, CARL C JR Occupation: Research Chemist. Education: B.S., University of Arizona; Ph.D., Michigan State University. Address: 500 South Madison, #7, Pasadena, California 91101.

KIRK, THOMAS D Occupation: Educator. Education: A.A., B.S. Address: 5045 Seminoe, Cheyenne, Wyoming 82009.

KIRKMAN, ALLEN JR Occupation: Instructor, Missile Crew Commander, United States Air Force. Education: B.S., North Carolina Central University; M.P.A., University of South Dakota. Address: 12 Anamosa Street, Rapid City, South Dakota 57701.

KITRELL, DANIEL THOMAS Occupation: Sales Representative. Education: B.S. Marketing/Speech Communication. Address: 3800 Green Heights Trail

Southwest, Prior Lake, Minnesota 55372.

KLEIN, CARA LYN Occupation: Miss Emmet-Dickinson County, 1983; Miss Teenworld, 1982; Miss Iowa Teenworld, 1981; Miss Iowa United Teenager, 1980. Education: Attending Iowa State University. Address: Box AG, Spirit Lake, Iowa 51360.

KLEINE, MARY CHRISTINE Occupation: Student, Farmer. Education: Attending the University of Missouri-Columbia. Address: Route 3, Box 81A, Troy, Missouri 63379.

KLINE, LINDA MANNIK Occupation: Psychology Graduate Student. Education: B.A. Psychology, University of Toledo, 1978; M.S. Psychology (in progress), Colorado State University. Address: 3717 South Taft Hill, #276, Fort Collins, Colorado 80526.

KLINK, MAXINE A Occupation: College Student. Education: B.S. Address: Route 1, Salisbury, Pennsylvania 15558.

KLOEWER, DENISE MARIE Occupation: Personnel Assistant. Education: A.A. Business. Address: Route 1, Box 275, Underwood, Iowa 51576.

KNIGHT, TRACY J Occupation: Doctor of Optometry (Optometrist). Education: B.S. Visual Science; O.D. Address: 5480 Illahee Road, Northeast, Bremerton, Washington 98310.

KNOLL, ALBERT B Occupation: Business/Government Relations. Education: A.B., Georgetown University; M.A., The Eagleton Institute/Rutgers University. Address: 311 Cherry Street, Philadelphia, Pennsylvania 19106.

KNUTSON, COLLEEN ELISE Occupation: Student. Education: Attending Roberts University. Address: Rural Route 1, Box 111, Hendricks, Minnesota 56136.

KOCERKA, CAROL ANN Occupation: Student. Education: B.S. Nursing. Address: 373 North Moreland Street, Bobtown, Pennsylvania 15315.

KOLLMAN, KEVIN WAYNE Occupation: Student. Address: 7013 18th Avenue, Kenosha, Wisconsin 53140.

KONDONASSIS, JOHN I Occupation: Student.

Education: B.M., Depauw University. Address: 512 Manor Drive, Norman, Oklahoma 73069.

KOONTZ, ELIZABETH DUNCAN Occupation: Retired Educator/Administrator, Consultant/Lecturer. Education: A.B., M.A., Honorary Doctorates (32). Address: 418 South Caldwell, Salisbury, North Carolina 28144.

KOPJOE, PAUL ROBERT Occupation: Drug and Alcohol Counselor, U.S.M.C. Education: Part-time Student, Eastern Carolina University. Address: 6014 Johnson Capel Road, Brentwood, Tennessee 37027.

KRITCHER, KAREN MARIE Occupation: Assistant Head Cashier. Education: A.S. Address: 312 Mitchell, Petoskey, Michigan 49770.

KROHN, JEFFREY SCOTT Occupation: Student. Education: Engineering. Address: 4685 Couma, St. Louis, Missouri 63128.

KRUPP, CORINNE MARIE Occupation: Indiana State College Republican Chairman. Education: B.A. Economics (in progress). 210 South Grant, Bloomington, Indiana 47401.

KRYJAK, MICHAEL ANTHONY Occupation: Researcher. Education: Certificate Fundamental Economics, Henry George Institute; Graduate Study Sociology of Organization, University of Leeds; B.A. honors Sociology, Schiller College, West Germany. Address: 32N Catherine Street, Shenandoah, Pennsylvania 17976.

KUCHEROV, MICHAEL FREDERICK Occupation: Student. Education: Attending College. Address: 5033 North 35th Street, Arlington, Virginia 22207.

KUENZLE, KATHYJO W Occupation: Kindergarten Teacher. Education: B.S. Elementary Education. Address: 748 Dace Lane, St. Louis, Missouri 63125.

KUNZWEILER, TIMOTHY P Occupation: Second Lieutenant, United States Air Force. Education: A.B. Radio/Television/Film, University of Missouri-Columbia. Address: 710 Highway C, St. Peters, Missouri 63376.

L

LaFAVE, DAWNICE J Occupation: Student. Education: A.A., Bismarck Junior College; Student, University of North Dakota. Address: 1123 Hillside Terrace, Bismarck, North Dakota 58501.

LANE, CANDY NELL Occupation: Student. Education: Attending College. Address: 406 Nola Lane, Pinehurst, Texas 77362.

LANE, SANDRA L Occupation: Assistant Payments Worker, Department of Social Services. Education: B.A. Social Science, 1980. Address: 180 Custer, Apartment 220, Sandusky, Michigan 48471.

LANEY, JANET LYNN Occupation: Avon Representative. Education: A.S. Address: 1166 North University Drive, Plantation, Florida 33322.

LANSFORD, ELIZABETH RHODES Occupation: Attorney-at-Law. Education: B.A. Accounting 1980, J.D. 1983, Texas Tech University. Address: 3005 Manioca Road, Lubbock, Texas 79401.

LANTIGUA, ADOLFO Occupation: Student. Education: Attending College. Address: 4230 Southwest 108 Avenue, Miami, Florida 33165.

LAPPE, DONNIE GENE Occupation: Attorney. Education: B.A., J.D. Address: 2111 Avenue C, Brownwood, Texas 76801.

LAPPE, RONNIE DEAN Occupation: Attorney/Justice of the Peace. Education: B.A.-B.A. 1977, J.D. 1980. Address: 2111 Avenue C, Brownwood, Texas 76801.

LASSITER, DARRYL D Occupation: Student. Education: Attending Alabama State University. Address: W. H. Benson Hall, Alabama State University, Montgomery, Alabama 36195.

LASTOVICA, ROBERT LOUIS Occupation: Veterinary Medical Student. Education: B.S. Animal Science. Address: Route 6, Box 6720, Belton, Texas 76513.

LAVIN, ANN W Occupation: Assistant to the Director, OPM. Education: B.A. Government, M.A. Candidate, George Washington University. Address: 1013 Maryland Avenue Northeast, Washington, D.C. 20002.

LAWLESS, ROBIN RENEE Occupation: Aspiring Opera Singer and Church Receptionist. Education: B.A. Music. Address: 522 Bird Road, Jacksonville, Florida 32218.

LAWSON, DANA ALEX Occupation: Attorney. Education: B.S. Political Science/Administration of Justice, 1980; J.D., 1983. Address: 1926 South Jefferson Street, Casper, Wyoming 82601.

LAWSON, MARK ALAN Occupation: Student. Education: B.S.E.E., 1984. Address: 379 North Perkins Road, Memphis, Tennessee 38117.

LAWSON, TAMI MARIA Address: Route 7, Box 430, Lenior City, Tennessee 37771.

LEACH, MARK RONALD Occupation: Graduate Student in Systems Engineering. Education: B.S. Systems and Control Engineering, M.S. (in progress), Case Western Reserve University. Address: 10206 Independence Boulevard, Apartment #22, Parma Heights, Ohio 44130.

LeBLANC, CARLA RAE CUTHBERTSON Occupation: Secretary, Northwest Community College. Education: Associate of Business. Address: 1027 Lane 9 Route 1, Powell, Wyoming 82435.

LEDGER, JOYCE SMITHERS Occupation: Programmer/Analyst. Education: B.B.A. Data Processing and Analysis, University of Texas at Austin. Address: 1205 East 32nd, Austin, Texas 78722.

LEE, AMELIA BETH Occupation: Registered Nurse. Education: B.S.N. Address: Route 2, Box 157-A, Benson, North Carolina 27504.

LEE, JANNA Occupation: Student. Education: A.A., Meridian Junior College, 1984. Address: Post Office Box 63, Enterprise, Mississippi 39330.

LEE, PAULA KAY Occupation: HERO Assistant State Advisor, Student. Education: Attending Devry Institute of Technology. Address: 5532 West Veenon Avenue, Phoenix, Arizona 85035.

LEE, VICTOR H Occupation: Law Student. Education: J.D. (in progress). Address: 3020 University Terrace, Northwest Washington, D.C. 20016.

LEGGETT, DAVID JOHN Occupation: Law Student. Education: B.A. History, Washington and Jefferson College. Address: 897 East Beau Street, Washington, Pennsylvania 15301.

LEHRICH, JEFFREY LLOYD Occupation: Executive Assistant, Cleveland Roundtable. Education: B.A. Political Science; Masters in Public Policy. Address: 17601 Winslow, Shaker Heights, Ohio 44120.

LeMASTER, SHERRY R Occupation: Vice-President of Development, Midway College. Education: B.S. Food Science and Technology, M.S. Higher Education Administration, University of Kentucky. Address: Highview Drive, Midway, Kentucky 40347.

LEMPESIS, COSTA P Occupation: Social Sciences Teacher; Coach. Education: B.A. Education. Address: 1334 Bryjo Place, Charleston, South Carolina 29407.

LEONARD, LEON J Occupation: Orthodontist. Education: D.M.D., M.S. Address: Tarheel Manor S-5, Carrboro, North Carolina 27510.

LEONARD, THOMAS NELSON Occupation: Programmer/Analyst. Education: B.S., West Liberty State; M.S., College of Graduate Studies. Address: 1568 Jackson Street, Charleston, West Virginia 25311.

LEONARD, YOLYNDA DENISE Occupation: Student. Education: Attending High School. Address: 1324 Ginsberg Drive, Daytona Beach, Florida 32014.

LEONG, DEBORAH J Occupation: Student. Education: B.S. Address: 134 High School Avenue, Cranston, Rhode Island 02910.

LEVIN, RENEE B Occupation: Graduate Student in Clinical Psychology. Education: A.B. Brown University; M.A. Emory University. Address: 1231 Clairmont Road-12D, Decatur, Georgia 30030.

LEVIN, SUSAN B Occupation: Student. Education: B.S. Education, 1979; M.A. Psychology-Family Therapy (in progress). Address: 8304 South Course #305, Houston, Texas 77072.

LEWIS, CAROL DEMETRIA Occupation: Secretary/Student. Education: Attending Devry Institute of Technology. Address: 703 South Catherine, Terrell, Texas 75160.

LEWIS, DONALD COWPERTHWAITE III Occupation: Student. Education: Attending University of Maine. Address: Post Office Box 1107, Bangor, Maine 04401.

LEWIS, KELI KRISTINE Occupation: Student and Office Assistant. Education: A.S., Bachelor of Education. Address: #7 Anderson Court, Newton, Kansas 67114.

LEWIS, KELVIN CABOT Occupation: Telecommunications Account Executive. Education: B.A. Business/Economics, Morehouse College. Address: 740-B Oakland Avenue Southeast, Atlanta, Georgia 30315.

LEWIS, ROBERTA MAYE Occupation: Owner, Berta's. Education: Cosmetology Degree. Address: Box 36, Centerville, Kansas 66014.

LIESS, MICHAEL THOMAS Occupation:

Student/Researcher. Education: B.S. (in progress). Address: 8702 Queen Elizabeth Boulevard, Annandale, Virginia 22003.

LINDGREN, CARL MATHIAS JR Occupation: Student. Education: B.S. Address: 19675-310th Street, Shafer, Minnesota 55074.

LINGLE, TAMARA JANE Occupation: Student. Education: B.S. Elementary Education. Address: 4730 Hillside, Lincoln, Nebraska 68506.

LINTON, LOUCINDY DENISE Occupation: Student. Education: High School Diploma. Address: 1010 West Indiana, Midland, Texas 79701.

LOCKRIDGE, MARGARET E Occupation: Student. Education: Attending College of the Ozarks. Address: Box 46, Everton, Arkansas 72633.

LOFERSKI, KAREN S Occupation: Lab Specialist In Chemistry and Computer Science. Education: B.S., M.S. Address: 1490 South Franklin Street, Christiansburg, Virginia 24073.

LOFTIN, RICHARD C Occupation: Firefighter-Emergency Medical Technician. Education: First Class Firefighters Diploma, Georgia Fire Academy. Address: Route 2, Franklin, Georgia 30217.

LOGAN, TERI KAY Occupation: Missionary. Education: B.S. Address: 1411 Southwest 67 Avenue, Apartment 16, Miami, Florida 33144.

LONG, ANGIE SUE Occupation: Clerk/Office Clothing Store; Student. Education: Attending College. Address: 3603 South 16th, Chickasha, Oklahoma 73018.

LONG, MARK ALEXANDER DIETTERICH Occupation: Clinical Psychologist. Education: Ed.D. Counseling Psychologist. Address: 404 Ridge Road, Apartment 4, Greenbelt, Maryland 20770.

LOPEZ, AMBROCIO Occupation: Professor, California Poly State University. Education: B.S., M.S., Ph.D. Address: 1327 Palm Street #D, San Luis Obispo, California 93401.

LOWENBORG, KIM ANNE Occupation: Student; Piano Teacher. Education: B.A. Music/Philosophy, 1984. Address: 8 Woodlawn Place, Lynbrook, New York 11563.

LUDGOOD, LASANDRA LAVETTE Occupation: Student. Education: Business Administration/ Marketing Degree (in progress), Livingston University. Address: 3820 Salem Street, Whistler, Alabama 36612.

LUTZ, KENDALL R Occupation: Client Support Representative and Marching Band Choreographer. Education: Attended Oakton Community College. Address: 1112 Westover, Schaumburg, Illinois 60193.

LYNCH, BRENDA VALERIE Occupation: Systems Analyst, Energistics Corporation. Education: Computer Science Student, George Mason University. Address: 5318 Queensberry Avenue, Springfield, Virginia 22151.

LYSFORD, VERN M Occupation: Controller, Econ, Inc. Education: B.A. Economics, University of Minnesota. Address: Post Office Box 273, Kennedy, Minnesota 56733.

M

MACEBUH, SANDY Occupation: Writer; Community Liaison. Education: Ph.D., M.A., B.A. Address: 1942 Deerpark Drive #48, Fullerton, California 92631.

MACKAY, JULIE ANNE Occupation: Attorney at Law. Education: B.A., University of Denver, 1978; J.D., Stanford University, 1981. Address: 2880 South Locust, Denver, Colorado 80222.

MADIANOS, LORETTE DESPINA Occupation: Graduate Student. Education: Graduate Student, Speech Pathology, Temple University. Address: 1081 Fox Chase Road, Jenkintown, Pennsylvania 19046.

MADISON, EDWARD III Occupation: Blood Bank Extern, Medical Student. Education: B.S. Pre-Medicine, Loyola University, 1984; Medical Student, Louisiana State University. Address: 2833 Magazine, Apartment 202, New Orleans, Louisiana 70115. ·

MAHARJAN, TULSI RAM Occupation: Graduate Student Advisor, School of Education, American University. Education: B.A., Skidmore University; M.A., Ph.D., American University. Address: 2030 F Street Northwest, Washington, D.C. 20006.

MALOTT, HEATHER LEIGH Occupation: Free Lance Artist. Education: Louisville School of Art. Address: R.R. 5, Box 119, Wabash, Indiana 46992.

MANIS, MARGARET JILL Occupation: Student; Bookkeeper. Education: A.S. Business Administration; A.S. Computer Science. Address: Post Office Box 758, Kingston, Tennessee 37763.

MANNING, CAROL ANN Occupation: Personnel Research Psychologist. Education: B.A., Drury College, 1976; M.S., University of Oklahoma, 1979; Ph.D., University of Oklahoma, 1982. Address: 3424 Northwest 19th Street, Oklahoma City, Oklahoma 73107.

MANZO, JAY ANTHONY Occupation: Student. Education: Attending Edward R. Murrow High School. Address: 39 8th Avenue, Brooklyn, New York 11217.

MAPLES, MARK ANDREW Occupation: Data Processor. Education: Attending S.M.S.U. Address: Route 2, Box 221, Rogersville, Missouri 65742.

MARASZEK, LISA L Occupation: Student. Education: B.S. Industrial Technology and Business (in progress). Address: Route 1, Box 187, Loganville, Wisconsin 53943.

MARBERT, MICHAEL CAIN Occupation: Student. Education: Attending University of South Carolina. Address: 1605 Pine Log Road, Aiken, South Carolina 29801.

MARCHBANKS, CHRISTOPHER LAYNE Occupation: Director of Marketing, Versi Craft Corporation. Education: Attended University of Texas. Address: 2025 Augusta #906, Houston, Texas 77057.

MAREADY, GREGORY A Occupation: Student. Education: High School Diploma. Address: Post Office Box 876, Wallace, North Carolina 28466.

MARINO, SUZANNE ELLEN Occupation: Nursing Student. Education: B.S.N. (in progress). Address: 1203 Salem Road, Burlington, New Jersey 08016.

MARK, BARBRA JILL Occupation: Nurse, Psychiatric Floor, Johns Hopkins Hospital. Education: B.A. Elementary Education, A.A. Nursing. Address: 853 West University Parkway, Baltimore, Maryland 21210.

MARKS, FRANCES Occupation: Obstetrics and Gynecology Resident, Columbia Presbyterian Medical Center. Education: B.S. 1978; M.D., Columbia, 1982.

Address: 2348 Linwood Avenue, Fort Lee, New Jersey 07024.

MARSHALL, PAUL EUGENE Occupation: Student. Education: Attending New Mexico State University. Address: Post Office Box 700, Thoreau, New Mexico 87323.

MARTI, DENISE CECILIA Occupation: Student. Education: Attending Georgetown Law School. Address: 3709 Wesley Loop Northwest, Olympia, Washington 98502.

MARTIN, BERTHA P Occupation: Student. Education: Attending University of New Mexico in Albuquerque. Address: Post Office Box 35, Cochiti, New Mexico 87041.

MARTIN, CHRISTINE LORENE Occupation: Student. Address: Route 4, Sulphur Springs, Texas 75482.

MARTIN, GLADYS M Occupation: Elementary School Counselor. Education: B.A. Business Education; M.A. Counseling. Address: Post Office Box 35, Cochiti Pueblo, New Mexico 87041.

MARTIN, THOMAS ALAN Occupation: Student. Education: Attending Pharmacy School, University of North Carolina-Chapel Hill. Address: 814 Rhodann Drive, Shelby, North Carolina 28150.

MARTIN, JEAN ELIZABETH (BETH) Occupation: Student Worker, Records Office, Lander College. Education: B.S. Business Administration/Accounting. Address: 177 Highland Drive, Greenwood, South Carolina 29646.

MASCHEK, JEAN MARIE Occupation: R.N.; Nursing Coordinator; Nursing Supervisor. Education: B.S. Nursing, University of Southern Mississippi. Address: 1501 Natchez Lane, La Place, Louisiana 70068.

MATER, DAVID ALLEN Occupation: Graduate Student in Public Administration. Education: B.A. Sociology. Address: 5426 Medmont Circle, Roanoke, Virginia 24018.

MATHEWS, MARSHALL RICK Occupation: Student. Education: B.A. Political Science. Address: 1950 East 70th Street, Chicago, Illinois 60649.

MATZKE, ANA CRISTINA Occupation: Student. Education: Certification in Chemistry and Chemistry/ Mathematics. Address: 405 Oyster Creek Court, Richwood, Texas 77531.

MAVITY, YOLANDE MICHELLE Occupation: United States National Team Member, Gymnastics. Address: 1013 Eastridge, Modesto, California 95355.

MAXWELL, JOSEPH L III Occupation: Student. Education: B.A. Psychology and English. Address: 5328 Runnymeade, Jackson, Mississippi 35211.

MAYFIELD, MICHAEL WADE Occupation: Student. Education: Attending Western Illinois University. Address: 1929 Honore Avenue, North Chicago, Illinois 60064.

McCALLA, TOMMY L Occupation: Educator, Student Affairs, Lander College. Education: B.S., Lander College, 1980. Address: 609 Bryte Street, Greenwood, South Carolina 29646.

McCHESNEY, SUSAN R Occupation: Associate School Psychologist and Graduate Student. Education: M.Ed.; Ed.S.; Attending University of Georgia. Address: 2000 Jefferson Place, Apartment 8, Athens, Georgia 30601.

McCLAMB, STANLEY HILTON Occupation: Housing Manager. Education: B.A. Religion and Philosophy. Address: 545 Liberty Square, Apartment 9, Durham, North Carolina 27707.

McCLOUD, DAVID LEE Occupation: Electrical Engineer, Teledyne Electronics. Education: A.A., B.S. in C.S. (in progress). Address: 1770 North Los Robles,

Pasadena, California 91104.

McCLOUD, SUSAN JoAN Occupation: Administrative Secretary/Choral Educator, California State Polytechnic University. Education: A.A. 1977, B.M. 1981, B.A. Psychology Candidate. Address: c/o 1770 North Los Robles, Pasadena, California 91104.

McCOLLUM, IRA WILLIAM Occupation: U.S. Congressman. Education: J.D., University of Florida, 1968; Address: 1010 Cathy Drive, Altamonte Springs, Florida 32714.

McCOMBS, HARRIET G Occupation: Assistant Professor, Yale University. Education: B.S. 1974, M.S. 1976, Ph.D. 1978. Address: 111 Park Street, New Haven, Connecticut 06511.

McCOURRY, JOSEPH MICHAEL Occupation: Security Officer. Education: B.A. Political Science. Address: 4628 North Ann Arbor, Oklahoma City, Oklahoma 73122.

McCRAW, VICKY LYNN Occupation: Student. Education: Attending University of North Carolina at Chapel Hill. Address: Route 1, Box 264, Elkin, North Carolina 28621.

McCRIMON, A DARLA Occupation: Student. Education: B.S. Psychology and Criminal Justice, University of Southern Mississippi, 1983. Address: Route 2, Box 32, Magnolia, Mississippi 39652/

McCUE, DAVID J Occupation: Senior Management Consultant. Education: B.S.C., Rider College; M.B.A., New York University. Address: 2270 Whitehorse-Hamilton Square Road, Hamilton Square, New Jersey 08690.

McCUEN, CHARLES GREGORY Occupation: Executive Trainee, Greenwood Motor Lines, Inc. Education: B.S. General Business 1983, B.S. Accounting 1984, Lander College. Address: 218 Kaye Drive, Greenwood, South Carolina 29646.

McCUISTON, MARY ANN Occupation: Psychologist. Education: B.S.Ed. Special Education 1978; M.Ed. School Psychology, 1979; Ph.D. (in progress). Address: 3211 Wrightsboro, Apartment L-4, Augusta, Georgia 30909.

McCULLAR, SHANE SCOTT Occupation: Student. Education: Attending University of Mississippi. Address: Post Office Box 411, Southaven, Mississippi 38671.

McDANIEL, DANNY H Occupation: Political Consultant. Education: A.A. Business Administration. Address: 1835 42nd Avenue, Vero Beach, Florida 32960.

McDANIEL, MIMI EVELYN Occupation: Secretary; Doctor's Assistant. Education: B.A. Address: 119 Marable Drive, Tuskegee, Alabama 36083.

McDANIELS, ANTHONY DERRICK Occupation: Respiratory Therapist/Minister. Education: A.A., B.R.E. Address: 17131 Northwest 10th Court, Miami, Florida 33169.

McDUFFIE, LYNN MARIE Occupation: Operator. Education: Undergraduate Mass Communicaiton. Address: 1050 Pleasant Hill Road, F-65, Nashville, Tennessee 37214.

McELHINNEY, TANA DEE Occupation: Psychologist, Primate Laboratory Research. Education: B.S. Psychology; M.S. Psychology (in progress); Attending University of South Alabama. Address: Post Office Box U-677, University of South Alabama, Mobile, Alabama 36688.

McGARY, JEFFREE LUCIEN Occupation: Student. Education: B.A., University of Southern California, 1984. Address: 9041 North Alpine Road, Stockton, California 95212.

McGUIGAN, BRIAN KEITH Occupation: Employed in the Construction Business; United States Marine. Education: High School Diploma. Address: Route 1, Box 235A, Bismarck, Arkansas 71929.

McKINNEY, CHERYL RENEE DAVIS Occupation: Cost and Inventory Clerk. Education: Bachelor of Science in Business Administration. Address: 1127 Elmore, Borger, Texas 79007.

McLAUGHLIN, JON STUART Occupation: Student. Education: Attending Rhodes College. Address: Post Office Box 392, Atoka, Tennessee 38004.

McMAHON, BRENDA JEAN Occupation: Student. Education: Attending University of Maryland. Address: 8405 Maryland Road, Pasadena, Maryland 21122.

McMILLAN, DARRYL JEROME Occupation: Student. Education: High School Diploma. Address: Post Office Box 61, Shannon, North Carolina 28386.

McNEIL, PORTER Occupation: Student. Education: B.A. Political Science/History, Macalester College, 1982; M.A. Candidate, Saugamon State University. Address: 4410 5th Avenue, Moline, Illinois 61265.

McSWEENEY, SHAWN DAVID Occupation: Student. Education: Attending Duke University. Address: 563 C Woodview Road, Barrington, Illinois 60010.

McWHORTER, JAMES MARK Occupation: Student. Education: Attending College. Address: Route 2, Box 64, Iowa Park, Texas 76367.

McWHORTER, TIMOTHY JOHN Occupation: Student. Education: Attending College. Address: Route 2, Box 64, Iowa Park, Texas 76367.

MEANS, LYDIA ANN Occupation: Student. Education: B.S. Education. Address: 310 North Street, Cuero, Texas 77954.

MEDCALF, ROBYN LYNNE Occupation: Student. Education: B.A. Psychology; M.S.W. (in progress). Address: 5609 College Avenue, Oakland, California 94618.

MEIER, JANNINE ANN Occupation: Secretary. Education: B.S. Education. Address: 5009 Buffalo, Odessa, Texas 79762.

MERRITT, JACQUELINE F Occupation: Typist; Student. Education: Attending College. Address: 1808 Cedar Lane, Nashville, Tennessee 37212.

MERRITT, JAMYE MARIE Occupation: Policyholder Servicer. Education: Attending College. Address: 1808 Cedar Lane, Nashville, Tennessee 37212.

MERRITT, MELISSA LYNN Occupation: Rotary Exchange Student. Education: Rotary Exchange Student, Lycee d'Orsay, Paris, France. Address: "Hollyberry," 15 Hidden Lane, Doylestown, Pennsylvania 18901.

MEZZACAPPA, CAROL ANN Occupation: Professional Dancer/Dance Instructor, Brooklyn College Prep Center. Education: B.S. Dance, Brooklyn College. Address: 1830 63rd Street, Brooklyn, New York 12204.

MILDENBERG, JUANITA M HOLLER Occupation: Chief, Master Planning Branch; Architect. Education: Bachelor of Architecture, Master of Architecture Urban Design. Address: 12305 Catoctin Spring Drive, Mt. Airy, Maryland 21771.

MILES, SOLOMON THOMAS JR Occupation: Student. Education: Attending Howard University. Address: 6426 6th Street Northwest, Washington, D.C. 20012.

MILLER, JACK BURION II Occupation: Electrical Contractor, Volunteer Fireman. Education: Associate in Electronic Engineering. Address: 307 Smith Avenue,

Cumberland, Kentucky 40823.

MINER, DAVID M Occupation: Student. Education: B.B.A. (in progress), Campbell University. Address: 101 Lake Street, Fuquay-Varina, North Carolina 27526.

MIRACLE, JOE Occupation: Vocational Rehabilitation Counselor. Education: B.A. Social Work; M.Ed. Vocational Rehabilitation Counseling. Address: 2550 West 8th #47, Odessa, Texas 79763.

MITCHELL, THECLA M Occupation: Tax Service Representative. Education: B.A. Political Science; Certificate, Paralegal Studies. Address: 829 Greenwood Avenue 3A, Brooklyn, New York 11218.

MOAK, CARLA JO Occupation: Student. Education: High School. Address: Route 4, Summit, Mississippi 39666.

MOHLMANN, ANDREA MICHELLE Occupation: Student. Education: High School Diploma. Address: 105 Princee Charles, Red Springs, North Carolina 28377.

MONCRIEF, LUTHER L Occupation: Student. Education: Attending College. Address: 108 Poplar Drive, Newton, Mississippi 39345.

MOORE, BARRY R Occupation: Student. Education: Attending Texas Tech University. Address: 2608 Maxwell, Midland, Texas 79705.

MOORE, KATHLEEN Occupation: Student. Education: Attending Alabama A&M University. Address: 6111 Belgrade Drive, Huntsville, Alabama 35810.

MOORE, MICHAEL STEVEN Occupation: Student. Education: Attending Samford University. Address: 505 Third Street, Andalusia, Alabama 36420.

MOORMAN, GARY L Occupation: Physician. Education: B.A. Biology, Ohio Northern University, 1976; D.O., Kirksville College of Osteopathic Medicine, 1980. Address: 2942 Shoreland, Toledo, Ohio 43611.

MORGAN, GARY L Occupation: Youth Minister. Education: Mt. Vernon Nazarene College. Address: 140 Greenwood, Hereford, Texas 79045.

MORRIS, DAVID R Occupation: Student. Education: Business and Political Science Degrees (in progress). Address: 140 Fairlawn Road, Topeka, Kansas 66606.

MORRIS, EDITH ANN Occupation: Student. Education: Attending College. Address: Post Office Box 217, Friars Point, Mississippi 38631.

MORRISON, GERALD W Occupation: Inventory Control. Education: A.A.S. Business Management-Supervision. Address: 5490 South 670 W Murray, Utah 84123.

MORRISON, SHARON NANETTE Occupation: Student. Education: Attending Georgia Southern College. Address: 1837 Fellowship Road, Box 38, Tucker, Georgia 30084.

MORROW, COLLEEN TOVE Occupation: Student. Education: Attending Ohio State University. Address: 402 Toledo Street, Elmore, Ohio 43416.

MORSE, CHARLES KENNETH Occupation: Student. Education: B.S. of E.E.E. (in progress). Address: 1144 College Street, Fargo, North Dakota 58102.

MOSCA-VILLAMIL, CARLOS J Occupation: Medical Student; Clinical Investigation. Education: B.S. Address: 305 Harvard Street, Rio Piedras, Puerto Rico 00927.

MOSER, JEFFERY RICHARD Occupation: Student; Artist; Writer. Education: Attending University of Minnesota. Address: Star Route Post Office Box 19, Wessington, South Dakota 57381.

MOSER-HORSLEY, MARY JO Occupation: Intensive Care Registered Nurse. Education: B.S. Nursing; Emergency Medical Technician. Address: 405 Euclid, Ft. Morgan, Colorado 80701.

MOSHONAS, TULA MICHELE Occupation: Student. Education: A.A. Business, University of Florida. Address: 2220 Southwest 34th Street, #248, Gainesville, Florida 32608.

MOSS, TANYA YVONNE Occupation: Student. Education: Attending University of Illinois at Chicago. Address: 1463 West 71st Place, Chicago, Illinois 60636.

MOTOBU, CHANA C Occupation: Student. Education: Attending Washington University at St. Louis. Address: 1695 Wailuku Drive, Hilo, Hawaii 96720.

MOTT, VIRGINIA N Occupation: Student. Education: Degree in Civil Engineering (in progress), Georgia Institute of Technology. Address: 2315 Hudson Drive, Lilburn, Georgia 30247.

MOUNT, MELINDA MARIE Occupation: Student. Education: Attending College. Address: Route 1, Friendship, Tennessee 38034.

MUELLER, STEVEN PAUL Occupation: Student. Education: Attending Christ College. Address: 201 Harvard Lane, Seal Beach, California 90740.

MULLEN, BRUCE DIEDRICH Occupation: Student. Education: Attending College of Charleston. Address: 705 Parish Road, Charleston, South Carolina 29407.

MURRAY, ELWYN GREY Occupation: High School Student. Address: Post Office Box 636, Rose Hill, North Carolina 28458.

MURRAY, WILLIAM BATTLE Occupation: Program Coordinator for Muscular Dystrophy Association. Education: B.A. Communication Arts Education, University of North Carolina-Greensboro. Address: 7101 Fernwood Street, Apartment 2721, Richmond, Virginia 23228.

MURSCH, PETRA IRMGARD HELENE Occupation: Doctor of Chiropractic. Education: D.C., 1983; Address: 21 Colonial Street, West Hartford, Connecticut 06110.

MUSIBAY, YAMILE Occupation: Student. Education: Attending Florida International University. Address: 9841 Southwest 20 Street, Miami, Florida 33165.

MUSSER, PAUL A Occupation: Missionary. Education: B.A. French. Address: 23 bvd. de la Corniche, 42700 Firminy, France.

MUSSO, MARK COLE Occupation: Speaker/Consultant. Education: A.A., B.B.A., M.B.A. Address: 2219 Jardine Drive, Wichita, Kansas 67219.

MUUS, PAUL MAGNER Occupation: Architectural Student. Education: B.A. 1983. Address: 500 8th Avenue Southeast, Minot, North Dakota 58701.

N

NAGY, JUDITH ELAINE Occupation: Inventory Control Agent. Education: B.S. Nursing (in progress). Address: 16849 Le Claire, Oak Forest, Illinois 60452.

NAKAMURA, JUDITH KAREN Occupation: Constituent Liaison for U.S. Senator Pete Domenici. Education: B.A. Political Science. Address: 3701 Juan Aldama Court, Rio Rancho, New Mexico 87124.

NAVIA, ALICIA S Occupation: Admissions Counselor, New York Institute of Technology. Education: B.A. Address: 594 Irving Street, Westbury, New York 11590.

NAZARIO, STEPHEN J Occupation: Medical Illustrator and Graphic Artist. Education: B.S. Biological Medical Illustration; B.S. Graphic Design. Address: 19628 East Bails Place, Aurora, Colorado 80017.

NEDRY, ROBERTA KATHLEEN Occupation: Corporate Marketing/Public Relations Executive; Account Executive. Education: B.S. Linguistics, University of California-Los Angeles. Address: 246 South Doheny Drive, Beverly Hills, California 90211.

NEELEY, GEORGE STEVEN Occupation: Law Student, Graduate Student. Education: B.S.B.A. Address: 9452 Meadow Ridge Drive, Cincinnati, Ohio 45241.

NEGRI, ANNE MARIE Occupation: Medical Technology Student, Salem Hospital. Education: B.S. (in progress). Address: 59 Superior Street, Lynn, Massachusetts 01902.

NELSON, ROBERT MELAND Occupation: Pediatrician. Education: Diploma, Deerfield Academy, 1970; B.A., Wesleyan University, 1974; M.Div., Yale Divinity School, 1980; M.D., Yale University School of Medicine, 1980; Intern Pediatrics 1980-81, Junior Assistant Resident Pediatrics 1981-82, Senior Assistant Resident Pediatrics 1982-83, Massachusetts General Hospital. Address: Dunster House, K-52, Harvard University, Cambridge, Massachusetts 02138.

NESPRAL, FRANK JOSEPH Occupation: Student, Bascom Palmer Eye Institute. Address: 333 Northwest 31 Avenue, Miami, Florida 33125.

NEUMANN, BRUCE E Occupation: Certified Public Acocuntant. Education: B.S. Business Administration. Address: 2526 Elliott Court, #191, Fort Mitchell, Kentucky 41017.

NEWELL, BENNIE LOUIS SR Occupation: Minister of Gospel/Mental Health Counselor. Education: B.A. Psychology, B.S. Religion. Address: 8471 Diana Avenue, #244, Riverside, California 92504.

NEWTON, KAREN JACINTHA Occupation: A.A.A./Sales Representative. Education: B.A. Theatre, M.A. Educational Media (in progress). Address: 802 Laverne Avenue, San Antonio, Texas 78237.

NEYMAN, JOHN EUGENE JR Occupation:
Administrator, Liberty Baptist College. Education: B.S., M.A. Address: 3302 Richmond Street, Lynchburg, Virginia 24501.

NICE, GARY ALAN Occupation: Student. Education: Attending W.S.U. Address: 2332 North 160 East, Wichita, Kansas 67228.

NILSSON-MACMURPHY, INGRID SUSANNE Occupation: Automated Data Processing Liaison Officer. Education: B.A. Business Administration, Multi-National Corporation/ European Marketing. Address: 1540 Ivy Street, Denver, Colorado 80220.

NIX, KENNETH DON Occupation: College Student. Address: Route 2, Box 183, Adamsville, Tennessee 38310.

NORCROSS, JOHN C Occupation: Research Fellow, Psychologist, Psychology Department, University of Rhode Island. Education: B.A., M.A., Ph.D. Address: Curtis Corner Road, R.D. 3, Peace Dale, Rhode Island 12879.

NORMAN, TANYA M Occupation: Bank Teller, First National Bank of Cobb County. Education: B.B.A. Management, 1984. Address: 2144 Ridge Wood Court, Marietta, Georgia 30066.

NORTHCUTT, LEE EDWIN Occupation: Church Organist/Choir Director, Student. Education: Attending Pfeiffer College. Address: 515 Lee Avenue, Wadesboro, North Carolina 28170.

NORTON, ELENA HOLLY Occupation: Student. Education: Associate's Degree (in progress), University of Bridgeport. Address: 632 Valley Brook Avenue, Lyndhurst, New Jersey 07071.

NOSWORTHY, DARLENE M Occupation: Dance Instructor, Butte College. Education: B.A. and M.A. Theater Arts and Dance, Community College Credential. Address: 14184 Creston Road, Magalia, California 95954.

NOTARO, GIACOMO (JACK) Occupation: Accountant. Education: B.S. Commerce/Accounting. Address: 192 McAdoo Avenue, Hamilton Square, New Jersey 08619.

NOVAK, JEAN E Occupation: Student. Education: B.S. Finance (in progress), West Virginia University. Address: Box 549, California, Pennsylvania 15419,

NULTY, MICHAEL JOSEPH Occupation: Community Activist. Education: High School Diploma, Advanced Accounting. Address: Post Office Box 846, San Francisco, California 94101.

NUNEZ, LOUIS EDWARD Occupation: Senior Aviation Underwriter. Education: Associate's Degrees in Management, Risk Management, Underwriting; B.B.A.; M.B.A. Address: 117 Bay 17th Street, Brooklyn, New York 11214.

NZEGWU, ANNE L N Occupation: Student, Government Comptroller. Education: Associate Degree in Accounting. Address: Texas Southern University, Box 865, Houston, Texas 77004.

O

OBENSHAIN, MARK DUDLEY Occupation: Student/Chairman, College Republican Federation of Virginia. Education: B.A. Degrees History and Economics, Virginia Polytechnic Institute and State University, 1984. Address: 25 Maxwell Road, Richmond, Virginia 23226.

O'BRIEN, GERALDINE ANNE Occupation: Underwriter, Personal Financial Security Division. Education: B.A. English with Elementary Education Teacher Training. Address: 299 11th Street, Brooklyn, New York 11215.

O'BRYAN, JAMES A Occupation: President, Just A Thought Amusement Corporation. Education: B.S., Boston University School of Public Communication. Address: Post Office Box 501, St. Thomas, Virgin Islands 00801.

O'CONNOR, CHRISTINE Occupation: Systems Analyst. Education: B.A. Mathematics. Address: 815 Palo Duro, Amarillo, Texas 79106.

O'CONNOR, THOMAS JAMES Occupation: Budget Accountant and Office of Management, N.E.O.B. Education: B.S. Accounting; M.T., St. Mary's College. Address: 5301 Essex Court, Alexandria, Virginia 22311.

ODEKU, LENORA F Occupation: Legislative Assistant. Education: B.A., Smith College, 1979. Address: 4806 Leland Street, Chevy Chase, Maryland 20815.

O'DONOGHUE, AILEEN A Occupation: Graduate Student. Education: A.A. 1978, B.S. 1981, Graduate Studies in Physics. Address: Box 3426 C/ S, Socorro, New Mexico 87801.

OFENGAND, GUNDA STEPHANIE Occupation: High School Student. Address: 720 Terrace Heights, Wyckoff, New Jersey 07481.

OGDEN, RICHARD W Occupation: Vice President, Credit Farmers P.C.A. Education: B.A. Agricultural Business. Address: 152 Woodcrest, Rolla, Missouri 55401.

O'HARA, SHEILA M Occupation: Textile Artist/ Weaver. Education: B.F.A. Textiles, California College of Arts and Crafts. Address: c/o Modern Master Tapestries, 11 East 57th Street, New York, New York 10022.

O'HAVER, PAMELA SUE Occupation: Secretary, The Fountain Trust Company. Education: A.S.

Accounting, B.S. (in progress). Address: 205 5th Street, Covington, Indiana 47932.

OLIVAS, ADOLF Occupation: Attorney and Counselor at Law. Education: B.A. Political Science, J.D. Address: 1385 Carriage Hill Lane, Suite 88, Hamilton, Ohio 45013.

OLIVER, F GREGORY Occupation: Student. Education: Attending Western Texas College. Address: Route 1, Box 119, Loraine, Texas 79532.

OLSON, ELIZABETH DENISE Occupation: College Student. Education: B.A., 1985. Address: 49 Boggess Street, Buckhannon, West Virginia 26201.

OLSON, WILLIAM T Occupation: Student. Education: Attending University of Utah. Address: 1705 East Browning Avenue, Salt Lake City, Utah 84108.

OPPERMAN, KIMBERLY ANNE Occupation: High School Student. Address: 101 Monte Video Drive, Seneca, South Carolina 29678.

ORTIS, JEIGH LYNN Occupation: Student. Education: Attending Louisiana State University. Address: 2457 Villaage Drive, Opeloosas, Louisiana 70570.

O'SULLIVAN, SEAN MICHAEL Occupation: Student. Education: Biology/Pre-Dentistry Degree (in progress). Address: 1417 Jan Drive, Wilmington, Delaware 19803.

OSWELL, NOREEN NOELLE Occupation: Student. Education: B.S. Biology; Attending Pennsylvania College of Podiatric Medicine. Address: 1076 Meade Avenue, Scranton, Pennsylvania 18508.

OTTEN, SYLVIE I Occupation: Professional Ballet Dancer, New York City Ballet; Dance Student. Education: Student, School of American Ballet, Scarsdale High School. Address: Stonehouse Road, Scarsdale, New York 10583.

OWEN, TIMOTHY A Occupation: Minister. Education: B.A., Southeastern College; Min.M., International Bible Institute. Address: Post Office Box 338, Ozark, Alabama 36361.

OWENS, EDDIE Occupation: Director Public Services, Wayland Baptist University. Education: B.A., Wayland Baptist University; M.A. Texas Tech University. Address: 3600 Red Oak Lane, Plainview, Texas 79072.

OWENS, JASON PAUL Occupation: Student. Address: 4019 Primrose, Paducah, Kentucky 42001.

OZMENT, D'ANN Occupation: Student. Education: Attending Texas A&M University. Address: 2108 Creekside Drive, Hillsboro, Texas 76645.

P

PACE, FRANKLIN WAYNE Education: A.A. Business Administration, Ferrum College; B.S., Old Dominion University; C.P.A. (in progress). Address: Route 3, Box 515, Mineral, Virginia 23117.

PADGETT, ELIZABETH LOYD Occupation: Student, Governor-Capital District Circle K. Education: B.S. Biology/Pre-Medicine, Master's Degree (in progress). Address: 1400 Kenmore Avenue, D3, Fredericksburg, Virginia 22401.

PAGE, PATRICIA A Occupation: Branch Support Assistant, IBM. Education: Attending University of Georgia. Address: 2360 West Broad Street, #V72, Athens, Georgia 30606.

PALANZO, DAVID ANTHONY Occupation: Certified Clinical Perfusionist. Education: B.S. Biology, Certificate Perfusion Technology. Address: 2540 Whippletree Drive, Harvey, Louisiana 70058.

PANKAU, VANESA ANN Occupation: Student. Education: B.B.A. Address: 1710 Gardenia, New Braunfels, Texas 78130.

PAPAGEORGE, CHRISTINE L Occupation: Nurse's Aid/Student. Education: B.S.N. (in progress). Address: 104 Rocky Hill Road, Hadley, Massachusetts 01035.

PARKER, CAROL JEAN Occupation: Student. Education: A.S. Pharmacy, East Central Junior College, 1984. Address: 1202 Kosciusko Road, Philadelphia, Mississippi 39350.

PARKER, DONNA MARIE Occupation: Bookkeeper. Education: B.S. Business Administration. Address: 616 F Street, Beckley, West Virginia 25801.

PARKER, HARRY B Occupation: Teaching Assistant, Ph.D. Candidate, University of Kansas. Education: M.A. Theatre 1982, Ph.D. Candidate, University of Kansas; B.F.A. Theatre, T.C.U. Address: 2331 Alabama, #5, Lawrence, Kansas 66044.

PARKS, TRENT ALLEN Occupation: Student. Education: Attending University of Nevada-Las Vegas. Address: 4200 Paradise Road, Las Vegas, Nevada 89109.

PARROTT, ELIZABETH A Occupation: Chiropractor. Education: B.A., D.C. Address: Post Office Box 706, 510 South 6th, Mayfield, Kentucky 42066.

PARSONS, JOHN SCOTT Occupation: Student. Education: B.S. Mathematics and Computer Science, California University of Pennsylvania, 1984. Address: Post Office Box 25, Beallsville, Pennsylvania 15313.

PATE, DEBBIE J Occupation: Student. Address: 4644 Tara Drive, Nashville, Tennessee 37215.

PATE, ELIZABETH LORENE Occupation: Student. Education: Attending David Lipscomb College. Address: 4644 Tara Drive, Nashville, Tennessee 37215.

PATE, TIMOTHY THOMAS Occupation: Teacher/Music Director. Education: B.S., David Lipscomb College; Advanced Diploma, Southeaster Singing School. Address: Route 2, Box 218, Bell Buckle, Tennessee 37020.

PATERNO, C PETER Occupation: College Student. Education: B.A. Economics, 1984. Address: Eckerd College, Post Office Box 855, St. Petersburg, Florida 33733.

PATERSON, ANDREA SUZANNE Occupation: Poet, Teacher. Education: B.A., M.A., English, University of Denver. Address: 258 South Dekker, Golden, Colorado 80401.

PATRAY, SHERRI L Occupation: Student.

Education: Degree in Political Science (in progress). Address: 3389 Carriage Lane, Lexington, Kentucky 40502.

PATRINELY, CHRIS E Occupation: Student. Address: 815 Lipton Drive, Newport News, Virginia 23602.

PATTERSON, ELWYN KENNETH Occupation: Banker, First Atlanta Corporation. Education: M.B.A. Finance, Atlanta University, 1980; B.S. Business, Southern Illinois University-Carbondale. Address: 2571 South Candler Road, C-16, Decatur, Georgia 30032.

PATTERSON, THERESA DEAN Occupation: Middle School Teacher, Fort Johnson Middle School. Education: B.S., Master's Degree (M.A.T.), Reading Specialist. Address: 1230 Teal Avenue, Charleston, South Carolina 29412.

PAUL, HOWARD ROGER Occupation: Parks and Outdoor Recreation Officer. Education: B.S., Colorado State University. Address: 12260 Orchard Road, Englewood, Colorado 80111.

PAULUS, MICHAEL JOHN Occupation: Economist. Education: B.A. Economics, History and Political Science. Address: 312 West 98th Street, New York, New York 10025.

PEARSON, DAWN I Occupation: Marital and Family Therapist. Education: B.S., M.A. Address: 12 Dunham Pond Road, Storrs, Connecticut 06268.

PEEPLES, PATRICIA JOYCE Occupation: Student. Education: Diploma, Starkville High School; Attending University of Mississippi Pharmacy School. Address: 242 Critz Street, Starkville, Mississippi 39759.

PELLEN, RITA M Occupation: Reference Librarian. Education: B.A., M.L.S. Address: 21597 Casa Monte Court, Boca Raton, Florida 33433.

PELLETIER, MARK DANIEL Occupation: Student. Education: B.A. Philosophy (in progress), Cardinal Newmann College. Address: 1700 East 56th Street, #1610, Chicago, Illinois 60637.

PEMBERTON, TAMMY JO Occupation: Student. Education: High School Diploma, Student Pre-Pharmacy. Address: Route 2, Box 394A, LaFollette, Tennessee 37766.

PENNINGTON, LORI CHOYCE Occupation: Graduate Student. Education: B.A. Human Services; Graduate Studies (in progress), The Citadel. Address: 3 Sawgrass Road, C-1, Charleston, South Carolina 29412.

PENNINGTON, ROBIN AMIE Occupation: Student. Education: Attending University of Georgia. Address: 211 North Avenue, #8, Athens, Georgia 30601.

PENNOCK, MARY IRENE Occupation: Educator, Macrobiotic Cook. Education: B.M., B.A. Address: Route 3, Sackets Harbour, New York 13685.

PERALES, RALPH Occupation: Engineer. Education: B.S. Industrial Engineering. Address: 562 West John Hand Road, Cedartown, Georgia 30125.

PERLMAN, SCOTT D Occupation: Law Student, Legislative Counsel Intern. Education: B.A. Biology, J.D. (in progress). Address: 6120 Riverside Boulevard, B-59, Sacramento, California 95851.

PERRY, RON B Occupation: Cadet, United States Air Force Academy. Education: B.S. Engineering Mechanics (in progress). Address: 2626 Prairie Dunes Place, Ontario, California 91761.

PETERS, BRIAN KEITH Occupation: Graduate Student. Education: B.A. Mathematics; Attending Indiana University. Address: 231 Scott Lane, Bowling Green, Kentucky 42101.

PETERSEN, ANNETTE JUANITA Occupation: Accountant. Education: B.S. Business Administration. Address: 6-456, Star Route 18, R1, Hamler, Ohio 43524.

PETERSEN, MARGA JOY Occupation: Student. Education: Associate's Degrees Arts and Sciences, Ricks College, 1980; B.S. Family Science, Brigham Young University, 1983; M.S. (in progress), Utah State University. Address: 778 Montana Avenue, Lovell, Wyoming 82431.

PETERSON, KENNETH ALLEN JR Occupation: Student. Education: Attending High School. Address: 3208 Phillips Avenue, Steger, Illinois 60475.

PETTRY, DANIEL KEITH Occupation: Pharmaceutical Salesperson, The Upjohn Company. Education: B.S. Biological Science, 1980; M.S. Biological Science, 1983. Address: Box 44, Daniels, West Virginia 25832.

PETTY, GINA A Occupation: Educator. Education: B.A. Spanish Education. Address: 2220 East Cayuga, Tampa, Florida 33610.

PHILLIPS, JEFFREY T Occupation: Student, Professional Musician, Teacher. Education: B.Mus. Education, Middle Tennessee State University, 1984. Address: 202 Hurst Drive, Old Hickory, Tennessee 37138.

PHILLIPS, SONIA ANN Occupation: Student. Education: B.S. Vertebrate Zoology (in progress), Memphis State University. Address: Route 1, Box 322, Adamsville, Tennessee 38310.

PICARD, HELENE MARIE Occupation: Dental Hygienist. Education: A.A.S. Dental Hygiene. Address: 1212 D Holik Drive, College Station, Texas 77840.

PIERSON, DEIRDRE KATHLEEN Occupation: Student. Education: B.C. Philosophy and German (in progress), Boston College. Address: 31 Ilford Avenue, North Arlington, New Jersey 07032.

PINO, MARLISYS C Occupation: Part-time Secretary, Student. Education: B.A. Business Administration (in progress). Address: 10919 Stroud, Houston, Texas 77072.

PIPER, CHERYL LEA Occupation: Student. Address: Post Office Box 428, Harrison, Nebraska 69346.

PLANCH, LAURIE MICHELE Occupation: Student. Address: 1919 Ventura Drive, Jackson, Mississippi 39204.

PLATT, WILLIAM RHODES Occupation: Student. Education: B.S. Agriculture. Address: Apartment J-16, University Courts, Martin, Tennessee 38237.

PLEW, GEORGE THOMAS Occupation: Assistant to the Bursar. Education: B.R.E., C.S.S. Address: 35 Bailey Road, Somerville, Massachusetts 02145.

PLOTNER, DENA JEAN Occupation: Sign-maker. Education: Associate's Degree Visual Arts, 1984. Address: 2302 Brookshire East, Champaign, Illinois 61821.

PLUNK, LISA ANNETTE Occupation: Student. Education: Attending Memphis State University. Address: Route 1, Box 165C, Stantonville, Tennessee 38379.

POKRANDT, HARRY RUDOLF Occupation: Student, S.F.U. Education: B.A. Address: 89 Bonnymuir Drive, West Vancouver V7S 1L1 Canada.

POMERANTZ, SHARON E Occupation: Reservation Sales Agent. Education: High School Diploma. Address: 7785 Southwest 86 Street, #E213, Miami, Florida 33143.

PONDER, ANNA KATHERYN Occupation: Student. Education: Attending Fisk University. Address: Fisk University, Nashville, Tennessee 37203.

POOLE, THELMA J Occupation: Student. Education: B.S. Education. Address: Route 1, Box 7A, Havelock, North Carolina 28532.

POPE, TAMERA ANNE Occupation: Student. Address: Route 2, Box 99, Martin, Tennessee 38237.

PORTER, KEVIN T Occupation: College Student. Education: Attending University of Missouri-Rolla. Address: 6804 Bales, Kansas City, Missouri 64132.

POSEY, STELLA LOUISE Occupation: Student. Education: A.A., East Central Junior College; Attending University of Southern Mississippi. Address: Route 1, Box 218-D, Forest, Mississippi 39074.

POTTEIGER, BRIAN DALE Occupation: Design Engineer. Education: B.S.M.E., Pennsylvania State University. Address: 115 North 4th Street, Hamburg, Pennsylvania 19526.

POTTER, RINDA VAE Occupation: Student. Education: A.A. Medical Tech., A.A. Business Administration, B.A. Accounting (in progress). Address: Star Route #1, Box 48, Jackhorn, Kentucky 41825.

POTTS, RAPHAEL EUGENE JR Occupation: Pre-Law Student. Education: Attending Drake University. Address: Route #3, St. Joseph, Missouri 64505.

POWELL, NANCY RUTH Occupation: Student. Address: 401 Guilford Road, Rock Hill, South Carolina 29730.

POWELL, RALPH W Occupation: Idaho State Police Officer. Education: Associate's Degree Criminal Law, Ricks College; B.S. Paralegal/Justice Administration, Brigham Young University. Address: 1690 West Overland, Meridian, Idaho 83642.

POWELL, SHERRY YVONNE Occupation: Student. Education: Attending Paducah Tilghman High School. Address: 1110 North 8th Street, Paducah, Kentucky 42001.

POWER, PATRICE A Occupation: Student. Education: B.B.A. (in progress). Address: 4911 Lambeth, San Antonio, Texas 78228.

PRICE, MARY PAULINE Occupation: Registered Occupational Therapist. Education: B.S. Occupational Therapy. Address: 2823 East 21st Place, Tulsa, Oklahoma 74114.

PRICE, TODD DUNCAN Occupation: Aerospace Engineer. Education: B.S. Aerospace Engineering. Address: 507 Forrest Road, Warsaw, North Carolina 28398.

PRINGLE, ERIC MARVIN Occupation: Reservoir Engineer. Education: B.S. Chemical Engineering. Address: 712 Boyd, Midland, Texas 79705.

PROCANICK, LISA MARIE Occupation: Student. Education: B.S. Accounting (in progress). Address: 103 Wynthrop Road, Solvay, New York 13209.

PROCHORENA, KAREN ANNETTE Education: B.S. Business Administration. Address: 420 Boston Post Road, East Lyme, Connecticut 06333.

PRUITT, CHERYL LYNN Occupation: Student. Education: Attending Rust College. Address: 2581 Monroe Street, Gary, Indiana 46407.

PURVIS, MICHAEL BERNARD Occupation: Graduate Student. Education: B.S. Chemistry, Appalachian State University, 1981; Ph.D. Chemistry (in progress), Virginia Polytechnic Institute and State University. Address: Rural Route 2, Box 55-A, Bennett, North Carolina 27208.

PURVIS, SHARON MECHELE Occupation: Kindergarten Teacher. Education: B.S. Elementary Education. Address: Route 2, Box 55-A, Bennett, North Carolina 27208.

PURYEAR, PAULA LYNN Occupation: High School Student. Education: Attending Leon High School. Address: 3228 Constellation Court, Tallahassee, Florida 32312.

PYNE, PHILIP SCHUYLER Occupation: Sales Representative. Education: Bachelor of Science, Ball State University. Address: 3131 Meetinghouse Road, #J-11, Boothwyn, Pennsylvania 19061.

Q

QUEEN, DEBRA NAPIER Occupation: Teacher/ Musician, Vocal and Piano. Education: A.S. and B.S. Music Education, M.A. School Administration.

Address: Post Office Box 247, Hillsboro, Alabama 35643.

QUINN, JOSEPH MARSHALL Occupation: Psychologist I. Education: A.S., Jefferson State Junior College; B.A., University of Southern Alabama. Address: 6665 Timbers Drive, Mobile, Alabama 36609.

R

RADEMACHER, PHILLIP ALLEN Occupation: Pilot Candidate, A.F.R.O.T.C., Student. Education: B.S.; Attending University of Arizona. Address: Post Office Box 1212, Parker, Arizona 85344.

RADIEL, BONNIE JUNE Occupation: Student. Address: Box 12, Sharon Springs, Kansas 67758.

RAGLAND, SHERMAN LEON II Occupation: Student. Education: B.A. Mass Communications (in progress). Address: 5470 Watercress Place, Columbia, Maryland 21045.

RALEY, JOHN CALVERT Occupation: Assistant Personnel Director. Education: B.S., Towson State University. Address: 4327 Hallfield Manor Drive, Baltimore, Maryland 21236.

RALSTON, JONI LeMOINE Occupation: Owner/Instructor, I Can Do School of Gymnastics; Student. Education: B.A. Psychology and Business Management, Anderson College; M.A. Experimental Psychology (in progress), Wichita State University. Address: 1740 South Oliver, Wichita, Kansas 67218.

RAMEY, MELINDA LOUISE Occupation: Educator. Education: B.A. Music. Address: 2230 Richmond, Houston, Texas 77098.

RAMIREZ, PETER PAUL Occupation: Student. Education: Attending Loyola College. Address: 7757 Cross Creek Drive, Glen Burne, Maryland 21061.

RATLEY, JEANIE R Occupation: Student. Address: 207 Stack Street, St. Pauls, North Carolina 28384.

READ, ELDEN LEON Occupation: Student. Education: Degree in Business Management (in progress), Brigham Young University. Address: 151 South 1000 East, Provo, Utah 84601.

READ, WILLIAM DAVID Occupation: Librarian, Media Specialist, Computer Coordinator, College of Education, Memphis State University. Education: A.A., B.S., Advance Graduate. Address: 3554 Dalebranch, #2, Memphis, Tennessee 38116.

RECHARD, ROBERT P Occupation: Civil Engineer, Sandia National Laboratories. Education: B.S., M.S., University of Wyoming. Address: 12721 Chandelle Northeast, Albuquerque, New Mexico 87112.

RECHEIGL, NANCY-ANN Occupation: Research Assistant. Education: B.S. Plant Science; M.S. Plant Pathology (in progress), Virginia Polytechnic Institute and State University. Address: 11 Wharton Street, Blacksburg, Virginia 24060.

REDDICK, M JAMES JR Occupation: Minister, Student. Education: A.A., B.A., M.Div. Address: Post Office Box 802, N.O.B.T.S., New Orleans, Louisiana 70126-9988.

REDDING, LISA LuELLEN Occupation: Sales Specialist, Hardee's, Princeton, Kentucky. Education: Attended Western Kentucky University, Henderson Community College. Address: Route 1, Box 44-A, Fredonia, Kentucky 42411.

REDMON, SONIA MARLENE Occupation: Student. Education: Attending Tennessee Technical University. Address: Route 2, Box B, Smithville, Tennessee 37166.

REDMOUNT, IAN H Occupation: Physicist, Postdoctoral Research Fellow. Education: B.S., M.S., Ph.D. Address: 411 Franklin Street, #702, Cambridge, Massachusetts 02139.

REECE, STEPHEN TAYLOR Occupation: Graduate Student, Classical Languages. Education: B.A., M.A. Address: 1054 Kalo Place, Honolulu, Hawaii 96826.

REES, WILLIAM SMITH JR Occupation: Graduate Student. Education: B.S. Chemistry, Texas Tech University, 1980; Graduate Studies Chemistry (in progress), University of California-Los Angeles. Address: 601 Westholme, #204, Los Angeles, California 90024.

REFOSCO, PAMELA MOORE Occupation: Music Teacher. Education: B.A. Music Education, West Liberty State College. Address: 190 Sugar Maple Circle, Washington, Pennsylvania 15301.

REID, CHARLES LEON Occupation: Graduate Student. Education: B.S. Psychology, M.S. Psychology, Psy.D. (in progress) Clinical Psychology. Address: Bishop House, Room 104, Rutgers College, New Brunswick, New Jersey 08903.

REID, KRISTI TERESA Occupation: Employee, Child Development Center; Student. Education: Attending College. Address: Route 2, Box 357-A, Taylorsville, North Carolina 28681.

REID, RONALD G Occupation: Student. Education: Attending Ripon College. Address: 2045 Menominee Drive, Oshkosh, Wisconsin 54901.

RENTMEESTERS, ELIZABETH A Occupation: Student. Education: B.S. 1976, M.S. 1978, M.B.A. 1984. Address: 1940 Mount Vernon Court, #6, Mountain View, California 94040.

RERES, JANET M Occupation: Elementary School Teacher. Education: B.A. English/Education. Address: 7420 10th Avenue, Brooklyn, New York 11228.

REX, DAVID L Occupation: Medical Student. Education: B.S. Biology and Chemistry, San Houston State University; Attending University of Texas Medical School. Address: 5315 Fredericksburg, San Antonio, Texas 28229.

RHODES, BARBARA ANN Occupation: Student. Education: Attending Marshall University. Address: Route 4, Box 299, Beckley, West Virginia 25801.

RICARD, GINA A Occupation: Student. Education: B.A. Humanities (in progress). Address: 1930 Foster, Memphis, Tennessee 38114.

RICARD, MICHELE TOURGEE Occupation: Student. Education: Attending LeMoyne-Owen College. Address: 1930 Foster Avenue, Memphis, Tennessee 38114.

RICCARDO, VICKI AVIS Occupation: Law Student. Education: B.A. Political Science; Master's Degree International Studies; Attending Arizona State University College of Law. Address: 8520 East Mackenzie Drive, Scotsdale, Arizona 85251.

RICE, ANDREW H Occupation: Podiatric Medical Student. Education: B.S. Biology. Address: 8 Douglas Drive, Norwalk, Connecticut 05850.

RICHARDSON, GREG DREXEL Occupation: Attorney, Assistant District Attorney. Education: B.A., University of Wisconsin-Whitewater; J.D., University of Wisconsin Law School. Address: 207 East Irving Avenue, #204, Oshkosh, Wisconsin 54901.

RICHARDSON, ORINTHIA FAY Occupation: Title IV-A Education Project Coordinator, Eastman Middle School. Education: B.A. English, A.A. General Education. Address: Route 1, Box 17, Hollister, North Carolina 27844.

RICHBERG, JAMES B Occupation: Graduate Research Assistant, Massachusetts Institute of Technology. Education: B.A., Ohio University, 1982. Address: 2601 Kirklyn Street, Falls Church, Virginia 22043.

RIDENOUR, DAVID ALLEN Occupation: State Chairman, Oregon College Republicans; Student. Education: B.S. Political Science, 1984. Address: Post

Office Box 170, Eagle Point, Oregon 97524.

RIDENOUR, ROBERT NEIL Occupation: Attorney. Education: J.D. Address: 1238 Elysian Park Avenue, Apartment G, Los Angeles, California 90026.

RIDLEY, KELLY ANN Occupation: Audit Intern, Arthur Young and Company. Education: Attending Arizona State University. Address: 1050 South Longmore, #100, Mesa, Arizona 85202.

RINDERLE, THERESA LYNN Occupation: Student. Address: 144 Lee Court, River Ridge, Louisiana 70123.

RING, ANITA M Occupation: Student, English Tutor. Address: Rural Route #2, Lyman, Nebraska 69352.

RINGLEY, MARTHA O Occupation: Student. Education: B.A. (in progress), College of the Ozarks. Address: Route 1, Box 112, New Blaine, Arkansas 72851.

ROBERTS, RHONDA KAY Occupation: Self-Employed Craftsman. Address: 207 Mill Road, Bisbee, Arizona 84603.

ROBERTS, ROSA L Occupation: Amway Distributor. Education: High School Diploma. Address: HC 61, Box 15A, Whitney, North Carolina 69367.

ROBINSON, ANNIE LAURIE Occupation: Student. Education: Attending University of Mississippi. Address: Post Office Drawer 737, West Point, Mississippi 39773.

RODGERS, DANIEL LEE Occupation: Student. Education: Attending College. Address: 122 Locust Street, Roselle Park, New Jersey 07204.

ROHACK, J JAMES Occupation: Chief Resident and Instructor, Internal Medicine, Department of Internal Medicine, University of Texas Medical Branch. Education: B.S. Psychology, M.D. Address: 104 Pompano, Galveston, Texas 77550.

ROMINE, JANICE I (NEWPORT) Occupation: Bookkeeper, Cashier, Attendant, Gas Station. Education: B.F.A.. Education (in progress). Address: Box 156, Lebanon, Nebraska 69036.

RONE, DEANNA LYNNE Occupation: Student. Education: Attending Memphis State University. Address: Route 1, Box 294, Burlison, Tennessee 38015.

RONGSTAD, JAMES PAUL Occupation: Accountant. Education: B.A. Business Administration/ Accounting. Address: 3792 Oakridge Lane, White Bear Lake, Minnesota 55110.

RONNE, ALLAN KENT Occupation: Mechanical Engineer, Program Manager. Education: M.S. Mechanical Engineering, Stanford University; B.S. Mechanical Engineering, University of Utah. Address: 1727 Woodland Avenue, #17, Palo Alto, California 94303.

ROPER, DAVID JAMES Occupation: Seminary Student. Education: B.S., Furman University; J.D., University of Chicago. Address: 500 Quincy Road, Seneca, South Carolina 29678.

ROQUEMORE, DEBORAH ANN Occupation: State Court Legal Secretary. Education: B.A. Political Science. Address: 4145 Fawn Lane, Smyrna, Georgia 30080.

ROSAMOND, ALICE MARIE Occupation: Student. Education: A.A. 1982, B.A. 1984, University of Arkansas-Little Rock. Address: 509 Blackstone Circle, North Little Rock, Arkansas 72118.

ROSE, LISA LEA Occupation: Student, Basketball Player. Education: Attending Everett Community College. Address: Star Route Box 66A, Darrington, Washington 98241.

ROSEN, DAVID PAUL Occupation: Marketing adn Promotion Coordinator, Temple University Press.

Education: B.A., Elmira College; M.A., Temple University. Address: 337 Lisbon, Buffalo, New York 14215.

ROSENTHAL, CARYN S Occupation: Business Student; Business Owner. Education: Attending Babson College. Address: 5 Heller Court, Edison, New Jersey 08817.

ROSS, JOHN FERRIS LOWE Occupation: Doctoral Candidate. Education: M.Sc.; L.S.E.; B.S. highest honors, University of North Carolina-Chapel Hill; Ph.D. Candidate, London School of Economics. Address: 2050 Stonebridge Lane, Charlotte, North Carolina 28211.

ROSS, ROBERT JAMES Occupation: Advertising Executive. Education: B.S., University of Illinois. Address: 12735 South Oak Park Avenue, Palos Heights, Illinois 60463.

ROSS, TERRI L Occupation: Student; Part-time Service Desk Employee, K-Mart. Education: Attended Fitchburg State College; Currently Attending Southeastern Massachusetts University. Address: 42 Orchard Street, Taunton, Massachusetts 02780.

ROTHROCK, PERRY C III Occupation: Student. Education: B.S. Zoology, University of Arkansas, 1984. Address: 812 Illinois, Blytheville, Arkansas 72315.

ROUSH, CLARK ALAN Occupation: Vocal Music Teacher. Education: B.A., Harding University; M.A., University of Iowa. Address: 401 Kennedy, Walnut, Iowa 51577.

ROVEN, GLEN P Occupation: Composer. Education: B.A., Columbia University. Address: 2166 Broadway, New York, New York 10024.

ROVENTO, ROSANN C Occupation: Graduate Student. Education: B.A., Caldwell College; Graduate Studies Sociology (in progress), Columbia University. Address: 409 70th Street, Guttenberg, New Jersey 07093.

ROWELL-SMITH, AUDREY VERA Occupation: Psychologist. Education: B.S. Psychology, M.Ed. Counseling, M.Div. Theology, Doctorate in Psychology (in progress). Address: 5326 Soldiers Home Road, Miamisburg, Ohio 45342.

ROY, JOHN THOMAS Occupation: Graduate Student. Education: B.S. Chemistry, Alderson-Broaddus College, 1980; Degree in Chemistry (in progress), Virginia Polytechnic Institute and State University. Address: 1600H Terrace View, Blacksburg, Virginia 24060.

ROY, JULANNE G Occupation: Special Assistant to the Department Head, Acquisitions Department, University Libraries, Virginia Polytechnic Institute and State University. Education: B.S. Business Management, Alderson-Broaddus College. Address: 1600 H Terrace View, Blacksburg, Virginia 24060.

RUARK, DEBRA ANN Occupation: Student, Residence Hall Counselor. Education: Occupational Home Economics Education. Address: Rural Route 1, Fillmore, Indiana 46128.

RUBIN, LAURENCE GLENN Occupation: Podiatric Medical School Student. Education: B.A. Zoology and Psychology. Address: 1025 Ledgewood Road, Mountain Side, New Jersey 07092.

RUBIO, IRMA MARIA Occupation: Student/ Medical Assistant. Education: B.Mus. Address: 8260 Northwest 185 Street, Miami, Florida 33015.

RUBLE, MARTHA ANN Occupation: Student. Education: Degree in Journalism-Media Sales (in progress), Eastern Kentucky University. Address: Route 5, Box 224, Shelbyville, Kentucky 40065.

RUBOW, DAVID GEORGE Occupation: Student, Abstracter of Land Titles. Education: B.A. Business

Administration (in progress), University of Iowa. Address: 1001 18th Avenue, Eldora, Iowa 50627.

RUDOLPH, JAMES Occupation: Doctoral Candidate. Education: B.A. Psychology and Sociology, M.A. Special Education, Doctoral Candidate Guidance and Counseling, Lehigh University. Address: 13108 Turquoise Northeast, Albuquerque, New Mexico 87123.

RUND, DOROTHY ANN Occupation: Student, Writer/Poet. Education: B.S. Administrative Studies. Address: 1008 North Acacia Rialto, California 92376.

RUNDE, EDDIE W Occupation: Student, Pre-Medicine. Address: Rural Route 2, Mexico, Missouri 65265.

RUSK, JOHN G Occupation: Student. Education: Attending St. Lawrence University. Address: Woodcrest Lane, Milton, New York 12547.

RUSSELL, ROBERT FOSTER Occupation: Student. Education: B.A., Emory and Henry College, 1981; M.B.A. (in progress), Colgate Darden Graduate School of Business Administration, University of Virginia. Address: 526-A Georgetown Road, Charlottesville, Virginia 22901.

RUTLAND, CHARLES JR Occupation: Certified Public Accountant. Education: B.S., Florida A&M University. Address: 7734 Holland Court, Arvada, California 80005.

RUTLAND, GRISELDA LaTREASE Occupation: Student. Education: Attending High School. Address: 1312 Moody Road, Warner Robins, Georgia 31903.

S

SAFFO, GINA MARIE Occupation: Student. Education: B.S. Biology, Allegheny College; Attending Pennsylvania College of Podiatric Medicine. Address: 900 Commonwealth Avenue, West Mifflin, Pennsylvania 15122.

SALIBA, RUSSELL M Occupation: Mechanical Engineer/Consumer Services Representative. Education: Bachelor of Mechanical Engineering. Address: 142 Delaronde Street, New Orleans, Louisiana 70174.

SAMS, DON H Occupation: President, Student Government Association. Education: B.S. Chemistry (in progress). Address: 4995 White Oak Street, Smyrna, Georgia 30080.

SANBORN, SCOTT MICHAEL Occupation: Assistant Bill Clerk, U.S. Senate. Education: Attending George Washington University. Address: 314 East Capitol Street, Northeast, Washington, D.C. 20003.

SANCHEZ, DONNA FELIS Occupation: Student. Education: Attending Ozona High School. Address: Post Office Box 1331, Ozona, Texas 76943.

SANDERS, DORIL Occupation: Educator/Coordinator. Education: A.A.S., Bachelor's Degree. Address: 501 East Choctaw Street, Magee, Mississippi 39111.

SANDERS, KEVIN SCHAUN Occupation: Law Student. Education: A.A., B.S. Address: 7381 Wendine Court South, Jacksonville, Florida 32244.

SANDERS, TERRI SUE Occupation: College Student. Address: 504 Fernwood, Toronto, Ohio 43964.

SANDHORST, LAURA LYNN Occupation: Student. Education: Attended Caldwell College; Currently Attending Linden Paralegal School. Address: 2276 Church Street, Rahway, New Jersey 07065.

SANDS, RAYMOND C III Occupation: Surveillance Systems Technician, Tropicana Hotel Casino. Education: B.A., Rutgers State University. Address: 1727 Haven Avenue, Ocean City, New Jersey 08226.

SATOVSKY, JAMES BENNETT Occupation: Dentist/Endodontist. Education: A.B., D.D.S., M.S. Address: 1201 South Ocean Drive, Hollywood, Florida 33019.

SATTERFIELD, THOMAS ALBERT Occupation: Courtesy Clerk, Student. Education: Attending University of Tennessee-Chattanooga. Address: 2589 Avalon Circle, Chattanooga, Tennessee 37415.

SAYADI, SUREYA ALI Occupation: Medical Technologist. Education: B.S. Mathematics and Science (Medical Technician). Address: 809 McHugh, Grafton, North Dakota 58237.

SCEARCE, MICHAEL JAY Occupation: Student. Education: B.A. English, Northeast Missouri State University, 1984. Address: 717 East Scott, Kirksville, Missouri 63501.

SCHAAF, ANNA MARIE Occupation: Student. Education: Attending College. Address: 8844 South Pleasant, Chicago, Illinois 60620.

SCHAEFER, ROSE A Occupation: Facility Head, Citizen's Bank of New Haven. Education: Associate Applied Science. Address: Rural Route #1, Box 11, New Haven, Missouri 63068.

SCHAFFER, MARY ANN Occupation: Speech/Language Pathologist. Education: B.S., M.S. Address: B-22 441 Harding Place, Nashville, Tennessee 37211.

SCHALDECKER, CARLA JEAN Occupation: Part-time Student, Shift Supervisor. Education: Associate of Arts in Accounting; Attending York College. Address: 1903 Grant Avenue, York, Nebraska 68467.

SCHECHTER, KENNETH JONATHAN Occupation: Student. Education: A.B., Stanford University; M.P.P.M. Candidate, Yale University. Address: Post Office Box 275, Moose, Wyoming 83012.

SCHENK, MICHELLE LAREE Occupation: Student. Education: B.A., Iowa State University, 1983. Address: Rural Route 2, Columbus Junction, Iowa 52638.

SCHIPPERT, KELLY ANN Occupation: Student. Education: Attending Hastings College. Address: 402 West 3rd, Alma, Nebraska 68920.

SCHLAFER, RACHEL ELISABETH Occupation: Interpreter for the Deaf, Minister of Music, Worker Preschool Deaf Program. Education: B.A. Music Education and Performance, Gardner Webb College. Address: 5315 Shadey Dell Trail, Knoxville, Tennessee 37914.

SCHNEIDER, CHARLES STEVEN Occupation: Film Director and Screenwriter. Education: B.A. Film, Pratt Institute. Address: 238 Washington Avenue, Brooklyn, New York 11205.

SCHNEIDER, PAMELA S Occupation: Student. Education: B.S. Chemical Engineering (in progress), University of Nebraska. Address: Route 3, Box 80, Minden, Nebraska 68959.

SCHOENWALD, SCOTT M Occupation: Student. Education: A.B. 1984. Address: 26 Cambridge Drive, Colonia, New Jersey 07067.

SCHOMER, SHERREE DEE Occupation: Occupational Therapy Student. Education: Attending College. Address: 748 East Main, Ravenna, Ohio 44266.

SCHULTZ, LORI ANN Occupation: Student. Education: Attending Chicago Medical School. Address: 132 Keith Avenue, Waukegan, Illinois 60085.

SCHWAGER, DAVID E Occupation: Chairman, College Republicans of Pennsylvania. Education: Attending Lafayette College. Address: 100 Third Avenue, Kingston, Pennsylvania 18704.

SCHWARZAUER, SUZANNE RENAE Occupation: Student. Address: Route 2, Box 685, Silver Creek, Mississippi 39663.

SCIOLARO, CHARLES MICHAEL Occupation: Doctor of Medicine. Education: B.A. 1980, M.D. 1984. Address: 8822 West 57th Street, Merriam, Kansas 66202.

SCIOLARO, SUSAN DIANE Occupation: Special Projects Accountant. Education: B.A. Address: 8822 West 57th Street, Merriam, Kansas 66202.

SCOTT, DEE ANN Occupation: District Manager. Education: B.A. Spanish. Address: 9311 North Tacoma Avenue, Indianapolis, Indiana 46240.

SCOTT, VIRGIL MIGUEL Occupation: New England Area Credit Manager. Education: B.A. magna cum laude Communications, Clark College, 1983. Address: 1096 Fountain Drive, Atlanta, Georgia 30314.

SEABROOK, MARCH EDINGS Occupation: Medical Student. Education: B.S. Biology, Wofford College; M.D. (in progress), University of South Carolina School of Medicine. Address: 1202 Rutledge Way, Anderson, South Carolina 29621.

SEAMANS, REGINA C Occupation: Teaching Assistant Special Education Resource Room. Education: Associate Social Sciences. Address: Turnpike Road, Box 130, Searsport, Maine 04974.

SEARS, JOHN MATTHEW Occupation: Student. Address: Route 2, Box 8, Clarksville, Arkansas 72830.

SECRIST, STEVEN RONALD Occupation: Student. Education: B.A. Economics. Address: 5236

Brassfield Drive, Olympia, Washington 98501.

SEEHAFER, JULIE JANE Occupation: Medical Technologist. Education: B.S. Biology, B.S. Medical Technology. Address: 2808 Huetter, Marshfield, Wisconsin 54449.

SEGOVIS, TERRY MORRIS Occupation: Youth Minister. Education: A.A. Address: 2536 Forbes Street, Jacksonville, Florida 32204.

SEIBRING, ANGEL RENEE Occupation: Legal Secretary. Education: Attending University of Florida. Address: 1817 Dodge Circle South, Melbourne, Florida 32935.

SEIDER, LYNN BETH Occupation: Computer Programmer. Education: B.B.A. Management Information Systems and Marketing. Address: 8434 West Lisbon Avenue, Apartment 1, Milwaukee, Wisconsin 53222.

SEKIYA, GENE HARUO Occupation: Student. Education: Attending California State University-Fresno. Address: 4736 North Bengston, Fresno, California 93705.

SELLERS, CRISTY JOY Occupation: Graduate Student in Robotics. Education: B.S. Industrial Engineering, Georgia Institute of Technology, 1983; Attending Purdue University. Address: 623 Hawkins Graduate House, West Lafayette, Indiana 47906.

SERGENT, SHEILA KAYE BLAIR Occupation: Clerk, Student. Address: Post Office Box 1614, Harlan, Kentucky 40831.

SEXTON, LISA A Occupation: Teacher of Hearing Impaired. Education: B.S. Special Education/Elementary Education, M.S. Counseling (in progress). Address: 5513 Hames Trace, Louisville, Kentucky 40291.

SHAFFER, BRENDA ANN Occupation: Assistant Editor, *The Green Tab*. Education: B.A. magna cum laude English, Waynesburg College. Address: 309 Spring Street, Greensburg, Pennsylvania 15601.

SHAMSID-DEEN, DARIAN AMEER Occupation: Electrical Engineer. Education: B.S. Electrical Engineering; A.A. Electrical Engineering. Address: 1133 West Desert Drive, Phoenix, Arizona 85041.

SHAMSID-DEEN, DORINDA MAHASIN Occupation: Student. Education: B.S. Marketing, 1984. Address: 113 West Desert Drive, Phoenix, Arizona 85041.

SHAMSID-DEEN, JAMEELAH CELINDA Occupation: Student. Education: Attending South Mountain High School. Address: 113 West Desert Drive, Phoenix, Arizona 85041.

SHAMSID-DEEN, KHADIJAH LARISA Occupation: Student. Education: Attending South Mountain High School. Address: 113 West Desert Drive, Phoenix, Arizona 85041.

SHAMSID-DEEN, MALIKAH CELINA Occupation: Student. Education: Attending South Mountain High School. Address: 113 West Desert Drive, Phoenix, Arizona 85041.

SHANAHAN, MICHAEL H Occupation: Associate, Eastech Management Company, Inc. Education: A.B., College of the Holy Cross; M.B.A., Harvard Business School. Address: 67 Mount Vernon Street, Boston, Massachusetts 02108.

SHAPIRO, MICHAEL S Occupation: Neuropsychology Intern. Education: B.S., M.Ed., Ph.D. (pending). Address: 3211 Wrightsboro Road, J-11, Augusta, Georgia 30909.

SHARBAUGH, GENE WALTER Occupation: United States Army Officer. Education: B.S. Accounting, Norwich University. Address: 608 Main Street, Freeland, Pennsylvania 18224.

SHEBROE, VALERIE LYNN Occupation: Assistant Director, Psychoeducational Clinic at California Psychological Services Center. Education: Doctoral Candidate Clinical Psychology, California School of Professional Psychology. Address: 701 North Rios Avenue, Solana Beach, California 92075.

SHELNUTT-LOFTIN, RITA J Occupation: Student, Private Piano Teacher. Education: B.Mus., West Georgia College. Address: Route 2, Box 109, Franklin, Georgia 30217.

SHELTON, ARLEN K Occupation: Student, Church Treasurer, Sunday School Teacher. Education: B.A., A.A. Social Science, A.A. Accounting (in progress). Address: 4051 Hazel Street, Marysville, California 95901.

SHEPPERD, REGINA LaLAINE Occupation: Student. Education: A.A. Business Education; Bachelor's Degree (in progress), University of Southern Mississippi. Address: 123 Reed Avenue, Louisville, Mississippi 39339.

SHERA, BRIAN EVAN Occupation: College Student. Education: B.S. Business Administration (in progress). Address: Rural Route #2, Laurel, Indiana 47024.

SHERMAN, LAURA LYNN Occupation: Student. Education: Attending the University of Texas-Austin. Address: Route 9, Box 9400, Midland, Texas 79703.

SHERR, JOSEPH SAMUEL Occupation: Graduate Student, Teaching Assistant, Mathematics Department, Emory University. Education: B.S. Mathematics and Chemical Physics, St. Andrews Presbyterian College; Attending Emory University. Address: 1700 Clairmont Way, Northeast, Atlanta, Georgia 30329.

SHIELDS, SUSAN JANE Occupation: Student. Education: Diploma, North American Correspondence Schools; Attending Pennsylvania State University. Address: Box 263, Hetzler Road, R.D. #1, Rochester Mills, Pennsylvania 15771.

SHMORHUN, MARK ALEXANDER Occupation: Graduate Student. Education: B.S. Chemical Engineering; M.S. Candidate, Drexel University, Department of National Engineering. Address: 4412 Locust Street, Philadelphia, Pennsylvania 19104.

SHULMAN, MARC DAVID Occupation: Student. Address: 5193 Duane Drive, Fayetteville, New York 13066.

SHURNEY, NINA TEQUILLA Occupation: Electronic Technician. Education: A.S. Electronics. Address: 607 Albert Court, Albany, Georgia 31701.

SIDWELL, TONY D Occupation: Outdoor Education Instructor. Education: A.A., Weatherford College; B.A., W.T.S.U. Address: 414 East 2nd, Texline, Texas 79087.

SILVA, GEORGE S Occupation: Computer Programmer/Analyst. Education: B.A. Mathematics, Stonehill College. Address: 10 Kingsbury Street, Needham, Massachusetts 02192.

SILVA ANSSARI, CARLA DENISE Occupation: Claims Analyst, INA. Education: A.A. Business Administration; B.S. Business Administration. Address: 1213 Kansas Avenue, Kansas City, Kansas 66105.

SILVERTOOTH, ANGY B Occupation: Student. Education: Attending David Lipscomb College. Address: Route 2, Box 198, Winchester, Tennessee 37398.

SIMMONS, MICHAEL JOSEPH Occupation: Student. Education: Pre-Medical Student, Loyola University of New Orleans. Address: 4716 Wilson Drive, Metairie, Louisiana 70003.

SIMMS, WESLEY WOODROW Occupation: Student. Education: Attending Valdosta State College. Address: 302 Fulwood Boulevard, Tifton, Georgia 31794.

SIMPSON, TERESA K Occupation: Student. Education: Attending Western Kentucky University. Address: Monterey Road, Route 6, Franklin, Kentucky 42134.

SKINNER, TAMATHA KAY Occupation: Student. Education: Attending East Ascension High School. Address: Post Office Box 704, Gonzales, Louisiana 70737.

SLATE, SUSAN M Occupation: Student. Education: Attending University of Montevallo. Address: 1809 Sunset Street, Hartselle, Alabama 35640.

SLY, BRIAN NELSON Occupation: Account Executive, Merrill Lynch. Education: B.S. Commerce, University of Virginia. Address: 601 Stockton #4, San Francisco, California 94108.

SMITH, ANTHONY WAYNE Occupation: Analytical Chemist. Education: A.A. Chemistry, B.S. Chemistry, M.S. Chemistry. Address: 1243 Bay Area Boulevard, #1805, Houston, Texas 77058.

SMITH, CAROLYN LEIGH Occupation: Student. Education: B.B.A. (in progress). Address: 1110 Lambuth, Jackson, Tennessee 38301.

SMITH, DENNIS WAYNE Occupation: Non-professional Actor. Education: High School Diploma. Address: Route #1, Box 63, Bethel Springs, Tennessee 38315.

SMITH, DWAYNE A Occupation: Director of College Relations, Central College. Education: B.A. English. Address: 542-B North Eshelman, McPherson, Kansas 67460.

SMITH, GEORGE NELSON Occupation: Law Student. Education: B.A. magna cum laude, Howard University; Attending University of Virginia School of Law. Address: 837-2 Copely III, Charlottesville, Virginia 22903.

SMITH, GREGORY R Occupation: College Student. Education: Attending Roberts Wesleyan College. Address: 210 Longmeadow Drive, Syracuse, New York 13205.

SMITH, KENNETH EDWARD Occupation: Aircraft Electrician. Education: High School Diploma. Address: Route 1, Box 256, Danville, Alabama 35619.

SMITH, MARK ALFRED Occupation: Marketing Representative. Education: B.S. Education, Northeastern University. Address: 59 School Street, Northboro, Massachusetts 01532.

SMITH, MICHAEL E Occupation: Student; Vice President, Pennsylvania Podiatric Medical Students Association. Education: B.S., Medical Student. Address: 43 Grant Avenue, Cresskill, New Jersey 07626.

SMITH, NOEL KATHARINE Occupation: Student. Education: Attending the University of Hartford. Address: 4 Dudie Drive, Newtown Square, Pennsylvania 19073.

SMITH, RICHARD JAMES Occupation: Student. Education: Attending Owego Free Academy. Address: 6 Clover Road, Apalachin, New York 13732.

SMITH, STEVE J Occupation: Accountant. Education: B.B.A., University of Georgia; A.B.A., Middle Georgia College. Address: 461 Forest Hill Road, Apartment 9F, Macon, Georgia 31210.

SMITH, TERESA BELL Occupation: Kindergarten Teacher. Education: B.A. Early Childhood Education. Address: 37 Kiker Street, Tallapoosa, Georgia 30176.

SMITH, THOMAS MICHAEL Occupation: Student. Education: B.S. Nursing (in progress), Wesleyan College. Address: 2329 Pleasant Avenue, Wellsburg, West Virginia 26070.

SMITH, TIMOTHY D Occupation: Student, Geologist Assistant. Address: 2200 South Rock Road, Wichita, Kansas 67207.

SMITH, YALE R Occupation: Physician, Student. Education: B.A. Chemistry; Attending Ross University School of Medicine. Address: 1405 Magee Avenue, Philadelphia, Pennsylvania 19111.

SMITHERS, DONNA M Occupation: Assistant State Auditor. Education: B.A. Accounting, University of Houston. Address: 2023 South Gessner, #P9, Houston, Texas 77063.

SMITHSON, ALYCE LOUISE Occupation: Registered Nurse. Education: B.S.N. 1980, M.S.N. 1984. Address: 4116 Astoria, Irving, Texas 75062.

SNELL, JEFFREY GLYN Occupation: Student. Education: Attending College of Southwest, Hobbs. Address: Star Route 4, Lamesa, Texas 79331.

SNOW, SANDI ELIZABETH Occupation: Registered Nurse. Education: B.S.N. Address: 66 Elmwood Drive, Apalachin, New York 13732.

SOLER, MAYRA MARIA Occupation: Student. Education: Attending University of Miami. Address: 4198 West 7th Lane, Hialeah, Florida 33012.

SOLLEY, GINA CARNES Occupation: Licensed Practical Nurse. Education: L.P.N., Pineville School for Practical Nurses. Address: Route 1, Box 440, Bimble, Kentucky 40915.

SOLOMONSON, MARK D Occupation: Respiratory Therapist. Education: A.A. Respiratory Therapy, B.A. Psychology. Address: 1106 5th Street Northwest, Austin, Minnesota 55912.

SOMMERFELD, JODY L Occupation: College Student. Address: HC #2 Box 16, Sharon Springs, Kansas 67758.

SORENSON, SCOTT PAUL Occupation: Educator. Education: B.A., M.A., Ph.D. Candidate. Address: 1807 2nd Avenue South, Minneapolis, Minnesota 55403.

SPEAKE, MELANIE CAROL Occupation: Representative of Alabama, "Citizens Washington Focus," National Resource and Development Conference, McCalls Creative Contest, 4-H National Congress; Sunday School Teacher; 4-H Leader; Church Organist. Education: Student, University of North Alabama; Attended Calhoun State Community College. Address: Route 1 Box 245, Mount Hope, Alabama 35651.

SPIELBERGER, JOAN ELLEN Occupation: Law Student. Education: B.A. International Relations; J.D. (in progress), College of William and Mary. Address: 104 Friars Court, Williamsburg, Virginia 23185.

STACY, DAVID CHRISTOPHER Occupation: Student. Address: 3164 North 51 Boulevard, Milwaukee, Wisconsin 53216.

STAFFORD, RONALD J Occupation: College Instructor, Professional Musician. Education: B.Mus. Address: 960 Sutton Court, Kansas City, Kansas 66103.

STALLARD, DONNA BENTON Occupation: Financial Aid Senior Clerk and Student. Education: A.A., Bachelor's Degree (in progress). Address: 9232 Adams Avenue, Jacksonville, Florida 32208

STAMATAKOS, THEODORE CONSTANTINE Occupation: Pre-medical Student. Education: Attending University of Michigan. Address: 2014 Yuma Trail, Okemos, Michigan 48864.

STANBACK, ROSALIND MARIE Occupation: Student. Education: B.S. Business Information and Support Systems (in progress), University of North

Carolina-Greensboro. Address: 1240 Bilmark Avenue, Charlotte, North Carolina 28213.

STANOS, PETER PARDEE Occupation: Student/ Biological Research. Address: 3661 Barber Drive, Canfield, Ohio 44406.

STARR, DAVID B Occupation: Assistant Sports Information Director, Iowa State University. Education: B.A., Simpson College. Address: 3000 Regency, Ames, Iowa 50010.

STATEN, BARBARA G LOVE Occupation: Research Intern. Education: B.S., M.Ed., Ed.Sp., Ph.D. Address: Post Office Box 1143, Mississippi State, Mississippi 39762.

STAVRO, STEVEN CRAIG Occupation: Student. Education: B.S. Biology, University of Georgia, 1984; M.Div. (in progress), Southern Baptist Seminary. Address: 5440 Huron Drive, Morrow, Georgia 30260.

STEELE, JAMES E Occupation: Psychotherapist. Education: B.A. Liberal Arts and Sciences. Address: 1745 North Keystone, Chicago, Illinois 60639.

STEELE, TIMOTHY HOWARD Occupation: Doctoral Student, University of Chicago. Education: B.Mus.Ed., M.Mus. Address: 6052 South Ingleside, Chicago, Illinois 60637.

STEIN, SANDRA SUE Occupation: Student. Education: Associate Arts and Sciences. Address: 906 West Kensington Drive, Peoria, Illinois 61614.

STEINBERG, IDA BRIDGETTE Occupation: Eligibility Counselor I, State of Tennessee, Department of Human Services-Family Assistance. Education: B.A., LeMoyne-Owen College, 1984. Address: 4574 Westmont, Memphis, Tennessee 38109.

STELLINGWERF, JUDY EILEEN Occupation: Student. Education: Attending Calvin College. Address: 8652 South Davista Drive, Whittier, California 90605.

STENGER, FREDONA EAMES Occupation: Nurse Educator; Past President, West Virginia University School of Nursing. Education: B.S.N., University of Virginia; M.S.N., Boston University. Address: 800 Stewart Street, Morgantown, West Virginia 26505.

STEPHENS, KENTON EDGAR Occupation: Research Chemist, Chemistry Department, University of Massachusetts. Education: B.S. summa cum laude, B.S. cum laude. Address: 100 Sand Hill Road, Amherst, Massachusetts 01002.

STEVENS, JANELL D Occupation: Student. Education: Attending University of South Dakota. Address: 2201 West 16, Sioux Falls, South Dakota 57104.

STEVENS, STEPHANIE JoANNE Occupation: Student Assistant, Lander College Admissions Office. Education: High School Diploma. Address: 113 Frances Street, Greenwood, South Carolina 29646.

STEWART, JAMES TERRENCE Occupation: Anti-Submarine Warfare Officer/Naval Officer. Education: B.S. Mechanical Engineering (distinction), U.S. Naval Academy. Address: 1125 Park Avenue, Port Hoeneme, California 93041.

STEWART, JULIE ANN Occupation: Engineering Assistant, Sugar Processing. Education: B.S. Chemical Engineering. Address: 181 Cascabel, Los Alamos, New Mexico 87544.

STEWART, LAWRENCE KEVIN Occupation: Assistant Manager, Southern Bell. Education: B.C. Civil Engineering, The Citadel. Address: 1212 Chadford Road, Irmo, South Carolina 29063.

STEWART, ROSEMARY ELLEN Occupation: First Lieutenant, United States Army Signal Corps. Education: B.S. General Engineering, United States

Military Academy. Address: 1125 Park Avenue, Port Hueneme, California 93041.

STILWAGNER, FRANK JOSEPH Occupation: Student. Education: Attending Illinois Wesleyan University. Address: 947 Robin Drive, Batavia, Illinois 60510.

STINNETT, TERESA LYNN Occupation: Admissions Secretary, Athens State College. Education: B.S. Business Administration, 1982. Address: Route 6, Box 375, Athens, Alabama 35611.

STIVER, KEITH WILLIAM Occupation: Recording Engineer. Address: 277 Calistoga Drive, Pittsburg, California 94565.

STORY, GLORIA MARIE (CINQUINA) Occupation: Analytical Laboratory Technician, Ivorydale Technical Center. Education: Associate's Degree Science Technology. Address: 5720 Winton Road, #508C, Cincinnati, Ohio 45232.

STRANGE, JO-RUTH Occupation: Educator, Business/Speech. Education: B.S., B.A., M.S. Address: 1502 Florence, Mansfield, Louisiana 71502.

STREPEK, EUGENE E Occupation: Banker, First National Bank of Chicago. Education: High School Diploma. Address: 2112 South 57th Court, Cicero, Illinois 60650.

STRICKLAND, WILLIAM GARRISON Occupation: Physician/Medical Research. Education: B.S., M.D., Ph.D. Address: 2703 B West Linden Avenue, Nashville, Tennessee 37232.

STRUWE, SARA A Occupation: President, Residence Hall Association. Education: Bachelor of Public Administration (in progress). Address: 2703 B West Linden Avenue, Nashville, Tennessee 37232.

STUBAT, MARJORIE CUNNINGHAM Occupation: Student/Researcher. Education: B.A., University of Florida; B.S., University of Southern Florida; Ph.D., University of North Carolina.

STUBBS, WILLIAM B III Occupation: Graduate Assistant. Education: B.A., Louisiana College; M.A. (in progres), Baylor University. Address: 1820 South 7th, #408, Waco, Texas 76706.

SUAU, LUIS ORLANDO Education: A.A., Miami Dade Community College. Address: 12300 190 Street, Miami, Florida 33177.

SULLIVAN, WESLA ANN Occupation: Student Body Vice President, University of Mississippi. Education: B.A. Address: Box 4192, University, Mississippi 38677.

SUMILAT, JAMES M Occupation: Medical Technologist. Education: B.S. Address: 25219 Davidson Street, San Bernardino, California 92408.

SUTHERLAND, SANDRA G Occupation: Assistant Manager. Education: B.B.A. Management. Address: 152 Hillview Drive, Berrien Springs, Michigan 49103.

SUTTON, JOHN C Occupation: Church Music Director. Education: A.A., B.A., Graduate Studies. Address: 2780 Skyline Drive, Corvallis, Oregon 97330.

SUTTON, SHARAN DIANN Occupation: Assistant Librarian, Reference Librarian, Director Conversion to Computerized Library System. Education: B.S., M.L.S. Address: Route 3, Box 223, Hedgesville, West Virginia 25427.

SWITZER, JANET DIANNE Occupation: Unit Secretary. Education: Attending East Central Oklahoma State University. Address: 2629 East 14th, Ada, Oklahoma 74820.

SZETO, YIM MOI Occupation: Student. Education: B.A., Midwestern State University, 1984. Address: 4518 Prince Edward, Wichita Falls, Texas 76308.

T

TAMPLEN, DAVID G Occupation: Student. Education: Degree in Architecture (in progress), Texas A&M University. Address: 421 Highway 30, #121, C.S., Texas 77840.

TANDY, SHARON VIRGINIA Occupation: Dean of Girls, Indianapolis Teen Challenge; Ministry. Education: B.Mus., B.Mus.Ed., B.A. Religious Education. Address: 2542 North Delaware, Indianapolis, Indiana 46205.

TATE, JAMES G Occupation: Student. Education: Attending University of Tennessee-Knoxville. Address: 914 Speed Street, Memphis, Tennessee 38107.

TATE-OWENS, FERNANDA GAYLE Education: B.A., Johnson C. Smith University; M.A., Iowa State University. Address: 2201 Severn #F101, Metairie, Louisiana 70001.

TAYLOR, DEBRA D Occupation: Paralegal Specialist, United States Department of Justice. Education: B.A., Sangamon State University, 1979. Address: 1100 North La Salle Drive, Chicago, Illinois 60610.

TAYLOR, GENE ANDREWS JR Occupation: Student. Education: Attending Hampden-Sydney. Address: Post Office Box 202, Boykins, Virginia 23827.

TAYLOR, PHILLIP Occupation: Data Processing Instructor, Groves High School; National Vice President, Future Business Leaders of America. Education: Attended Savannah State College, Draughons Business College. Address: 906 Carter Street, Savannah, Georgia 31401.

TAYLOR, TERRY DEAN Occupation: Student and Secretary. Education: Attending College. Address: 5473 Rappahannock, Memphis, Tennessee 38134.

TEEL, JOE DEWAYNE Occupation: Student. Education: Attending Oklahoma State University. Address: Post Office Box 21, Wayne, Oklahoma 73095.

THAGGARD, ANSON LEE Occupation: Student. Education: Attending East Central Junior College. Address: 432 Columbus Avenue, Philadelphia, Mississippi 39350.

THIEL, TIMOTHY D Occupation: Pharmacist/Student. Education: B.S. Pharmacy. Address: 2445 West Bancroft Street, Apartment 12, Toledo, Ohio 43607.

THOMAS, DEBRA ANN Occupation: Student. Education: Attending Brescia College. Address: Route #2, Lloyd Lane, Mt. Washington, Kentucky 40047.

THOMPSON, AMANDA YVETTE Occupation: Student. Address: 2500 Linkwood Place, Charlotte, North Carolina 28208.

THOMPSON, BOBBY GAINES JR Occupation: Student. Education: Attending University of Georgia. Address: 15 Post Oak Road, Greenville, South Carolina 29605.

THOMPSON, DANA LYNN Occupation: Certified Public Accountant. Education: B.S. Accounting. Address: 4109 South 19th Street, Tacoma, Washington 98405.

THOMPSON, DEWAYNE G Occupation: Instructor in Business. Education: B.S., M.B.A. Address: 5002 Cindy Circle, Cleveland, Tennessee 37311.

THOMPSON, DONALD LEE Occupation: Biologist, Veterans Administration Medical Center. Education: A.A.S., B.S. Address: 16 Valley View Drive, Vienna, West Virginia 26105.

THOMPSON, JOYCE MARIE BLEY Occupation: Elementary Public School Music Teacher, Private Piano Instructor. Education: B.A., Columbia College. Address: Post Office Box 65, Starr, South Carolina 29684.

THOMPSON, PERRY WALLACE Occupation: Student. Education: Attending University of Georgia. Address: 15 Post Oak Road, Greenville, South Carolina 29605.

THOMURE, SUSANNE F Occupation: Laboratory Professional. Education: B.S. Biology/Chemistry. Address: 206 Forestlake South, Longview, Texas 75605.

THORNLEY, CONNIE DALE Occupation: Music Performance Student (Voice). Education: B.A. Music (in progress). Address: 2609 Fort Drive, Suitland, Maryland 20746.

THURMON, KIMBERLY BOOTH Occupation: Student. Education: Attending Georgia Southern College. Address: Route 2, Box 206, Buck Creek Acres, Sylvonia, Georgia 30467.

TIERNEY, ELAINE Occupation: Student. Education: B.A. Address: 34-001 Buckman Hall, Gainesville, Florida 32612.

TIGUE, ANNIE M Occupation: National Bank Examiner. Education: B.S. Accounting. Address: 3000 Evangeline, Apartment 63-B, Monroe, Louisiana 71201.

TOBA, CLARICE KAYOKO Occupation: Student. Education: Attending University of Hawaii-Manoa. Address: 302 South Papa Avenue, Kahului, Hawaii 96732.

TOM, KATHLEEN E Occupation: Student. Education: Bachelor's Degree (in progress), University of Southern California. Address: 3115 South Orchard #308, Los Angeles, California 90007.

TOMASHPOL, KIM ANN Occupation: Student. Education: B.S. Journalism/Social Work (in progress). Address: 13749 Delaware, Apple Valley, California 92307.

TORRES, ALFREDO J Occupation: Student. Education: B.A. Computer Science. Address: 5204 Palisade Avenue, West New York, New Jersey 07093.

TOYAMA, LISA M Occupation: Student. Education: Attending Duke University. Address: 2905 Lake Forest Drive, Greensboro, North Carolina 27408.

TRACANNA, KIM L Occupation: Research Assistant, University of North Carolina-Greensboro. Education: B.S.Ed., Slippery Rock University; M.S. (in progress), University of North Carolina. Address: 172 East Katherine, Washington, Pennsylvania 15301.

TRAKIMAS, KATHLEEN MARIE Occupation: Student. Education: Attending Canisius College. Address: 671 Stolle Road, Elma, New York 14059.

TREAT, DENNIS LEE Occupation: Farmer, College Student. Education: A.A.; B.A. Education (in progress), Eastern Washington University. Address: Route 1, Box 143, Warren, Washington 98857.

TREAT, TAMMY A Occupation: Student. Education: A.A., Big Bend Community College; Attending E.W.U. Address: Route 1, Box 143, Warden, Washington 98857.

TREFTS, C ELIZABETH Occupation: Student. Education: Graduate cum laude, Laurel School; B.A. cum laude, Wellesley College; Master Medical Anthropology, Case Western Reserve University, 1983; Attending Dartmouth Medical School. Address: 20101 Malvern Road, Shaker Heights, Ohio 44122.

TRONCOSO, SERGIO ARTURO Occupation: Student. Education: B.A., Harvard University, 1983. Address: 9301 San Lorenzo, El Paso, Texas 79907.

TRUETNER, DEBRA DELORES Occupation:

Student; Junior Vice President, Leeson's Party Cakes, Inc. Address: 19460 Glenwood Road, Chicago Heights, Ilinois 60411.

TRUSS, SUSAN KIM Occupation: Student. Education: B.A. (in progress). Address: 98 Village Drive, Shelton, Connecticut 06484.

TSCHIDA, DENISE MARIE Occupation: Student of Audio Engineering. Education: Attending National Academy of Recording Arts and Sciences. Address: Post Office Box 93408, Memphis State University, Memphis, Tennessee 38152.

TSUKAMOTO, LISA Y Occupation: Student. Education: B.A. Political Science and American History (in progress). Address: 225 Hanamaulu Street, Honolulu, Hawaii 96825.

TUCKER, DANNY LEO Occupation: Assistant Pastor, Prison Corrections Corporal. Education: B.A. Music Education, Virginia State University. Address: 20885 River Terrace Road, Ettrick, Virginia 23803.

TUCKER, KATHY MARIE Occupation: College Student/Sales Clerk. Education: Attending College. Address: 5707 Whitby Road, Baltimore, Maryland 21206.

TURNAGE, KEITH ANTHONY Occupation: Student. Education: Attending Copiah-Lincoln Junior College. Address: Route 3, Box 76, Liberty, Mississippi 39645.

TUTTLE, DON WESLEY Occupation: Piano Tuner/Technician. Education: A.A. Music, B.A. Religion. Address: 112 Cheviot Drive, Kernersville, North Carolina 27284.

U

UBERTALLI, JAMES THOMAS Occupation: Student. Education: B.S. Biology. Address: 8 Claren Drive, Holyoke, Massachusetts 01040.

UDOH, MACAULAY A Address: 6003 Rampart #188C, Houston, Texas 77081.

ULEP, STACEY J Occupation: United States Army Airborne Engineer. Education: High School Diploma. Address: 66-531 Kaupe Road, Waialua, Hawaii 96791.

UMBERGER, LISA A Occupation: Vice President, DeGreen Corporation; Executive Director, Wealth Builder$; President, Golden Tierra Enterprises. Education: B.S. Music Education. Address: 1602 East Ocatillo Road, #205, Phoenix, Arizona 85016.

UMSTOTT, MARTHA LOUISE Occupation: Consultant; Doctoral Candidate. Education: A.B., College of William and Mary; Ed.S. and M.Ed., University of Virginia; Ph.D. (in progress), The American University. Address: 1225 Perry William Drive, McLean, Virginia 22101.

UNGAR, JILL A Occupation: Senior Vice President, Public Relations. Education: B.A. English, Skidmore College. Address: 220 East 73, New York, New York 10021.

UNGER, LANGDON S JR Occupation: Lawyer. Education: B.S. Accounting 1980, J.D. 1983. Address: 207 East Sherrod, Covington, Tennessee 38019.

URIBE, GEORGE Occupation: Student. Education: Degree in Finance/Marketing (in progress), DePaul University. Address: 11036 Avenue B, Chicago, Illinois 60617.

URQUHART, WANDA JOY Occupation: Student. Education: B.S. Address: 8585 North Port Washington Road, Milwaukee, Wisconsin 53217.

V

VAKACEGU, ILIESA LEDUA Occupation: College Student. Education: Degree in Mechanical Engineering (in progress), Memphis State University. Address: 3554 Dalebranch #2, Memphis, Tennessee 38116.

VANCE, VICKIE LYNN Occupation: Free-lance Journalist. Education: A.A. Business Communications. Address: 2041 U.S. 31 North, Petoskey, Michigan 48770.

VANN, ANGELA LEVELLE Occupation: Counselor, DeJarnette Center; Student. Education: B.A. Psychology; Ed.S. (in progress), James Madison University. Address: 1742 Englewood Drive, Apartment D-1, Staunton, Virginia 24401.

VAUGHAN, DONNA MARIE Occupation: Student, Botany Laboratory Instructor. Address: 1710 Old Marion Road, New Braunfels, Texas 78130.

VAZQUEZ, CARLOS ALFREDO Occupation: Supervisor, Industrial Engineering. Education: A.A., B.A. Address: 149 Carlisle, Miami Springs, Florida 33166.

VEAL, ANDREW JAMES Occupation: Tennis Professional. Education: B.S. Business Administration. Address: B4, Cokesbury Apartments, Greenwood, South Carolina 29646.

VEAL, DELICIA LYNN Occupation: Student. Education: B.A. Psychology/Christianity, Mercer University, 1983. Address: 200 Hobbins Drive, Dublin, Georgia 31021.

VEIN, LINDA FRAN Occupation: Student. Education: B.A. Biology (in progress), Douglass College. Address: 2575 Eleanor Terrace, Union, New Jersey 07083.

VICK, DANA JAMES (DAN) Occupation: Student. Education: B.A. Biopsychology, 1984. Address: 2114 Telemark Lane, Northwest, Rochester, Minnesota 55901.

VILLARREAL, RENE Occupation: Meat Laboratory Manager. Education: B.S. Meat Science, M.S. Food Science. Address: 629 West Durham, Raymondville, Texas 78580.

VILLARREAL, RUBEN Occupation: Student. Education: Degree in Meat Science (in progress), Sul Ross State University. Address: 108 North 11th, Box 6672, Sul Ross State University, Alpine, Texas 79830.

VINCIGUERRA, AMELIA MARIA Occupation: Student. Education: Attending Frostburg State College. Address: 6018 Suzanne Road, Waldorf, Maryland 20601.

VINCOLESE, KENNETH G Occupation: Attorney. Address: 683 Berkley, Elmhurst, Illinois 60126.

VINKLAREK, CYNTHIA ANN PERKINS Occupation: Graduate Student. Education: B.A. Psychology cum laude, Angelo State University, 1980; Attending Texas A&M University. Address: Post Office Box 1544, San Angelo, Texas 76902.

VOGLER, VALERIE DENISE Occupation: Student. Education: Diploma, Seminole High School, 1981. Address: Route A, Box 365, Lamesa, Texas 79331.

VOLOSHIN, MICHAEL D Occupation: Student. Education: Attending the University of Pittsburgh. Address: 520 Buch Avenue, Lancaster, Pennsylvania 17601.

VOSLER, DEBORAH L Occupation: Secondary Science Teacher, Volleyball Coach. Education: A.A., B.S., M.E. Address: 3306 Bevans, Cheyenne, Wyoming 82001.

VRSIC, PAVLA G F Occupation: Student. Education: B.S. Psychology (in progress). Address: Jarvis C.C., Hawkins, Texas 75765.

VURLICER, SANDRA Occupation: Student. Education: Degree in Secondary English Education (in progress), Rider College. Address: 40 Howard Drive, Manahawkin, New Jersey 08050.

W

WADE, JAMES ANTHONY Occupation: Student. Education: Attending University of Delaware. Address: 11 Hickory Lane, Dover, Delaware 19901.

WADE, SAMANTHA Occupation: Student. Address: Route 5, Box 279, Alexander City, Alabama 35010.

WAGNER, LORENE FAY Occupation: Student. Education: Attending University of Nebraska-Lincoln. Address: Rural Route #1, Chapman, Nebraska 68827.

WAGNER, LYNNETT MAE Occupation: Student. Education: Attending U.N.-L. College of Agriculture. Address: Rural Route 1, Post Office Box 109, Chapman, Nebraska 68827.

WAITSMAN, BONNIE MICHELE Occupation: Paramedic/Emergency Medical Services Communications Operator, Maryland Institute for Emergency Medical Services (Shock-Trauma). Education: B.S., U.M.B.C.; Attended University of Maryland Baltimore County. Address: 21 Lower Gate Court, Owings Mills, Maryland 21117.

WALBORN, ERIC D Occupation: Graduate Student, English Teaching Assistant. Education: B.A. English, Secondary Certificate, M.A. English. Address: R.D. #2, Clifton Springs, New York 14432.

WALKER, CHERYL LYNN Occupation: Student. Education: A.A., Cumberland College; Degree in Art (in progress), Cumberland University. Address: 425 Eastland Drive, Lebanon, Tennessee 37087.

WALKER, REBECCA LOUISE Occupation: Student. Education: B.S. Administrative Management. Address: 504 South Holden, Warrensburg, Missouri 64093.

WALKER, RONIT Z Occupation: Student. Address: 545 South Wyncourtney, Atlanta, Georgia 30328.

WALL, DAVID A E Occupation: Student, Laboratory Tutor, Teletypesetter. Education: B.S., DePaul University; University of Chicago. Address: 2100 Lincoln Park West, Chicago, Illinois 60614.

WALLACE, SUSAN C Occupation: Missionary. Education: B.A. Music. Address: Route 2, Box 305, Cherryville, North Carolina 28201.

WALSTEAD, MICHAEL G Occupation: Assistant Buyer/Department Manager. Education: B.A. Biology, B.A. Biology Education. Address: Post Office Box 3613, Federal Way, Washington 98063-3613.

WARD, JAMES INMAN JR Occupation: Midshipman/Student. Education: B.S.E.E. Address: 305 47th Street, Gulfport, Mississippi 39501.

WAREHAM, ROBERT M Occupation: Student. Education: Attending Jackson Heights High School. Address: R.R. #1, Whiting, Kansas 66552.

WARLICK, KATHY N Occupation: Registered Nurse. Education: A.S. Nursing. Address: Route 2, Kingston, Georgia 30145.

WASCHER, MICHAEL DAMON Occupation: San Diego Warehouse Manager, U.S. Radiator Company; Student. Education: Bachelor's Degree Industrial Psychology and Spanish (in progress). Address: 3993 Debbyann Place, San Diego, California 92154.

WATANABE, MAKITO Occupation: Student. Education: B.A. Address: 2563 Date Street, #202, Honolulu, Hawaii 96826.

WATERS, S J Occupation: Minister. Education: Grduate, Fruitland Baptist Bible Institute; B.A., Mars Hill College. Address: Route 1, Box 244B, Whittier, North Carolina 28789.

WATFORD, TAMMY YVONNE Occupation: Student. Education: Degree in Art and Broadcast Journalism, Troy State University. Address: 1209 Fairlane Drive, Dothan, Alabama 36301.

WATSON, GIRTHA LEE Occupation: Maintenance Management Specialist Officer. Education: B.S. Address: 5429 Gaines Street, Apartment 5, Davenport, Iowa 52806.

WATSON, N CAMERON Occupation: Puppeteer/Artist. Education: A.B. Philosophy, Yale University. Address: South Pamet Road, Truro, Massachusetts 02666.

WATTS, CLEAL T III Occupation: Fellow, Cornell Hospital, New York. Education: M.D., Cetec University. Address: Post Office Box 12227, Dallas, Texas 75225.

WATTS, KARLA ELIZABETH Occupation: Owner, Dance Studio. Education: Attending College. Address: 1901 Maple, Alva, Oklahoma 73717.

WAYNE, BRYAN MATTHEW Occupation: Physician, E.N.T., Baylor College of Medicine, Texas Medical Center. Education: B.S. Biology, Baylor University; M.D., U.T.H.S.C.-San Antonio. Address: 5401 Chimney, Suite 318, Houston, Texas 77081.

WEBB, JEROLYN YVETTE Occupation: Student. Education: Attending Dillard University. Address: 1621 Elm Street, Southwest, Birmingham, Alabama 35211.

WEBSTER, F ELAINE Occupation: Student. Education: A.S. Business Administration; Attending University of Alabama. Address: Post Office Box 366, Winfield, Alabama 35594.

WEED, MARY T Occupation: Clinical Psychologist, Part-time Private Practice; Assistant Professor of Psychology, Chicago City Colleges. Education: M.A., University of Chicago, 1960; B.A., University of Miami, 1953. Address: 5534 South Harper, Chicago, Illinois 60637.

WEEMSTRA, JANET MARIE Occupation: Dental Hygienist/Student. Education: A.S. Dental Hygiene, B.S. Allied Health (in progress). Address: R.D. #L, Box 33A, Sussex, New Jersey 07461.

WEGTER, JAMES JOHN Occupation: Laboratory Technician. Education: B.S., University of Wisconsin-Oshkosh. Address: W10544 Highway C, Deerbrook, Wisconsin 54424.

WELLEIN, GEOFFREY MICHAEL Occupation: Student. Education: Attending Mid-Pacific Institute. Address: 98-260 Ualo Street, #O2, Aiea, Hawaii 96701.

WENDEL, ELIZABETH DAWN Occupation: Student. Education: B.A. Administrative Management; B.A. Mass Communications; Attending Texas Lutheran College. Address: 115 Chase Drive, Portland, Texas 78374.

WENTZ, DAVID NORTHROP Occupation: Minister, United Methodist Church. Education: B.S. Systems Engineering, University of Virginia, 1976; M.Div., Melodyland School of Theology, 1981. Address: 5923 Woodville Road, Mt. Airy, Maryland 21771.

WERKHEISER, KIM MARGARET Occupation: Engineering Coordinator. Education: Math and Computer Science Degrees (in progress). Address: 225 East Broad Street, East Stroudsburg, Pennsylvania 18301.

WERNER, MARK JOHN Occupation: Student. Education: B.S. Accounting, DePaul University. Address: Rural Route 2, Box 69, Monee, Illinois 60449.

WESTCOTT, WILLIAM LEONARD Occupation: Pilot, United States Air Force. Education: B.S. Business Administration/Quantitative Analysis, 1979; M.B.A., 1981. Address: 920 25½ Avenue Northwest, Minot, North Dakota 58701.

WHITE, ELLA ELIZABETH Occupation: Research Administrator. Education: B.S. Music, M.M., Ph.D. Address: 2456 78th Avenue, Baton Rouge, Louisiana 70807.

WHITE, EMILY ANN Occupation: Transportation Industry Analyst. Education: B.A. 1977, M.B.A. 1979, University of Alabama. Address: 1600 South Eads Street, #613 South, Arlington, Virginia 22202.

WHITE, LINDA MARIE Occupation: Secretarial Position, Student. Education: A.S. Accounting. Address: Rural Route #3, Storm Lake, Iowa 50588.

WHITE, LORRIE CHRISTINE Occupation: Legal Secretary. Education: A.A., Mesa Community College. Address: Route 2, Box 118 J, Chandler, Arizona 85224.

WHITE, PRESTON HAYES Occupation: Administrative Assistant. Education: B.S. 1971, M.Ed. 1982. Address: 2456 78th Avenue, Baton Rouge, Louisiana 70807.

WHITE, RANDY DALE Occupation: Student; Second Lieutenant, United States Army Reserves. Education: High School Diploma. Address: Box 5685, Huntington, West Virginia 25703.

WHITE, SCOTT RAY Occupation: Student. Education: B.S. Mechanical Engineering (in progress). Address: 300 West Wall, Harrisonville, Missouri 64701.

WHITNEY, G WARREN Occupation: Student. Education: Attending College. Address: Post Office Box 60489, Fairbanks, Alaska 99706.

WHITT, MARCUS C Occupation: Advertising/Public Relations Director. Education: B.A. Speech Communication, M.A. Sociology. Address: 610 Frank Street, Paintsville, Kentucky 41240.

WICKMAN, CECILIA MARIE Occupation: Telemarketing Promotions Manager, Twin Circle Publishing Company. Education: A.A. Theatre Arts, B.A. Communication Arts. Address: 17631 Palora Street, Encino, California 91316.

WIDELL, MICHAEL ALAN Occupation: College Sudent; Announcer, KLYR Radio. Education: B.S. Business Management/Marketing, College of the Ozarks. Address: 39 Fountaine Drive, Clarksville, Arkansas 72830.

WIESTLING, YVONNE MARIE Occupation: Student. Education: Attending College. Address: 122 Holly Street, Hummelstown, Pennsylvania 17036.

WILKINS, RICHARD WAYNE Occupation: Student. Education: B. Mech. Eng. (in progress), Georgia Polytechnic Institute. Address: 831 Suburbian Road, Reisterstown, Maryland 21136.

WILLIAMS, CECILIA CATHERINE Occupation: Assistant to Congressman Michael D. Barnes. Education: B.A., University of Maryland. Address: 2905 Tapered Lane, Bowie, Maryland 20715.

WILLIAMS, CHRISTOPHER DALE Occupation: Student. Education: Attending Union University. Address: 315 Florence Drive, Selmer, Tennessee 38375.

WILLIAMS, EFELL Occupation: Director of Special Services. Education: B.S., Master's Degree. Address: 4006 Merrifield Drive, Selma, Alabama 36701.

WILLIAMS, JIMMY RUSSELL Occupation: Distribution Engineer, Alabama Power Company. Education: B.S. Electrical Engineering. Address: Post Office Box 98, Headland, Alabama 36345.

WILLIAMS, JOSEPH E JR Occupation: Director of Special Services, Livingston University. Education: Master's Degree Guidance and Counseling. Address: Station 17, Livingston, Alabama 35470.

WILLIAMS, JOYCE E Occupation: Associate Professor of Sociology, Texas Women's University. Education: B.A. Sociology, M.A., Ph.D. Address: 165 North Old Orchard Lane, #2022, Lewisville, Texas 75067.

WILLIAMS, LISA ELAINE Occupation: College Student. Education: B.S. Business Administration. Address: 101 Wares Drive, Weirton, West Virginia 26062.

WILLIAMS, REGINALD ROMERO Occupation: Student. Education: Degree in Geo-Science and Physics Meteorology (in progress). Address: 610 Gainesville, Memphis, Tennessee 38109.

WILLIAMSON, CONSTANCE JEAN Occupation: Assistant Stage Manager, University of Evansville and Evansville Dance Theatre. Education: Attending University of Evansville. Address: 245 Green, New Albany, Indiana 47150.

WILSON, ANNETTE Y Occupation: Senior Secretary/Cashier, Aetna Finance Company. Education: High School Diploma. Address: 622 Burgoyne Drive, Fayetteville, North Carolina 28304.

WILSON, DANIEL KEVIN Occupation: Senior Medical Student. Education: B.S. Chemistry. Address: Star Route, Rew, Pennsylvania 16744.

WILSON, DAWNITA JULIANNA Occupation: Student. Address: 1039 Park Avenue, Paducah, Kentucky 42001.

WILSON, DOUGLAS KEYES JR Occupation: Preacher, Student. Address: Route 10, Box 42, Franklin, North Carolina 28734.

WILSON, LARRY TIMOTHY Occupation: Student. Education: B.A. History and Government; Attending George Mason University School of Law. Address: 1510 South George Mason Drive, #12, Arlington, Virginia 22204.

WILSON, MARJORIE DENISE Occupation: B.S. Accounting; M.B.A. 1984. Address: 2401 Barclay Place, Ponca City, Oklahoma 74601.

WINDHAM, DWAYNE MARK Occupation: Student. Education: Attending Mississippi State University. Address: 2168 Monaco Street, Jackson, Mississippi 39204.

WINKLER, MAURY R Occupation: Student. Education: Attending Rugters College. Address: 484 West 43rd Street, Apartment 28-5, New York, New York 10036.

WINN, ALLICYN CHARISSE Occupation: Insurance Clerk. Education: Attending Alabama A&M University. Address: 487 Section Line Road, Gurley, Alabama 35748.

WISMANN, ROBERT BARCLAY Occupation: President, Administrative Assistant, Inc. Education: A.A., Moorpark College; E.A., Enrolled Agent. Address: 2527 O'Brien Circle, Camarillo, California 93010.

WITHROW, GREGORY BYRON Occupation: Pianist, Organist, Arranger. Education: B.M., M.B.A., M.Div. (in progress), M.Min. (in progress). Address: 115 East First Street, Silver Grove, Kentucky 41085.

WLASUK, PETER T Occupation: Student. Education: B.A., Yale University. Address: 111 Sunnyside Road, Syracuse, New York 13224.

WOHL, LAURA MUUS Occupation: Speech/Language Pathologist. Education: B.A., Creighton University; M.S., Idaho State University. Address: 1700 Northwest Avenue, Minot, North Dakota 58701.

WOHLSTEIN, KATHY LYNN Occupation: Voice Coach, Accompanist, Pianist. Education: B.Mus. (in progress). Address: 146 Whitman Avenue, West Hartford, Connecticut 06107.

WONG, CAROL JOAN MARIE Occupation: Student. Education: High School Diploma. Address: 23 Cardamon Drive, Orlando, Florida 32817.

WOOD, CAROL S Occupation: Student. Education: Attending Ripon College. Address: Route 2, Box 303A, Pilot Mountain, North Carolina 27041.

WOOD, RAYMOND DEAN Occupation: Carnation Territory Manager. Address: Route 2, Box 386 eee, Springfield, Louisiana 70462.

WOOD, RICHARD W Occupation: Student. Education: A.S. Address: Post Office Box 5, Wilburton, Oklahoma 74578.

WOODARD, PATSY CAROL Occupation: Student. Education: Attending East Carolina University. Address: Route 2, Box 68-A, Murfreesboro, North Carolina 27855.

WOODEN, WILLIAM CLAYTON II Occupation: Business Consultant. Education: B.S. Economics. Address: Post Office Box 4, Georgetown, Tennessee 37336.

WOODWARD, KAREN Occupation: Educator. Education: B.S. summa cum laude, Brigham Young University. Address: 1075 East 400 North, Orem, Utah 84057.

WOOSLEY, JEFFREY NATHAN Occupation: Student. Education: Attending Louisiana Tech University. Address: 9 Castle Hill Court, Little Rock, Arkansas 72207.

WORTH, RICHARD WAITE Occupation: Writer. Education: B.A. Address: 201 Pershing Avenue, Roselle Park, New Jersey 07204.

WRIGHT, DEBBIE LYNNE Occupation: Student. Address: 215 Horner Drive, Selmer, Tennessee 38375.

WRIGHT, DEBORAH KAYE Occupation: Elementary Teacher. Education: B.A. Elementary Education. Address: 1126 Haltown, San Antonio, Texas 78213.

WUNKER, FREDERICK J Occupation: Student, Life Sciences; Emergency Medical Technician, Terre Haute Regional Hospital; Medical Student. Education: B.A. 1984, Medical Student, Indiana State University. Address: 12 Park Lane, Terre Haute, Indiana 47803.

WURL, GARY D Occupation: Assistant Manager. Education: High School Diploma. Address: 2002 Airline #1405, Corpus Christi, Texas 78412.

Y

YASINITSKY, GREGORY WALTER   Occupation: Assistant Professor of Music, Washington State University. Education: M.A., B.M., San Francisco State University. Address: Northwest 1800 Hall Drive, Pullman, Washington 99163.

YATES, DEAN ROYAL   Occupation: Veterinary Student. Education: B.S. Animal Science, Veterinary Student, Texas A&M University.

YATES, GAYLYN DENISE   Occupation: Staff Accountant. Education: B.B.A. Address: 403 Longmire #103, Conroe, Texas 77306.

YOUNG, KIM L   Occupation: Student. Education: Attending Averett College. Address: 1326 30th Avenue, Vero Beach, Florida 32960.

YOUNG, STEVEN WAYNE   Occupation: Student. Education: B.B.A., Baylor University, 1984. Address: 18718 Prince William, Houston, Texas 77058.

YOUNGINER, JEFFREY G   Occupation: Graduate Student. Education: B.S. Psychology 1978, M.A. Sociology 1984. Address: 1415 Blossom Street, #139, Columbia, South Carolina 29201.

YURICEK, LAURA A   Occupation: Software Technical Director. Education: B.A. Address: 1400 Worcester Road, Apartment 7201, Framingham, Massachusetts 01701.

Z

ZABEL, DEBORAH MICHELLE Occupation: Student. Education: Attending Graceland College. Address: 710 Village Drive, Pittsburg, Kansas 66762.

ZALAR, MYLENE GUDRUN Occupation: Student; Assistant Dock Supervisor, Press-Enterprise Company. Address: 841 Kentwood Drive, Riverside, California 92507.

ZANNINI, GIAVANNA Occupation: Student. Education: B.A. Christian Education, 1984. Address: 442 Charlotte Circle, Jackson, Alabama 36545.

ZAWIERUCHA, CHRISTINA F M Occupation: High School English Teacher. Education: B.S. Education, M.S. Education. Address: 14 Wanda Avenue, Cheektowaga, New York 14211.

ZEDNIK, PETER GREGORY Occupation: Actor/Playwright. Education: M.A. Drama, University of Toronto, 1980. Address: 1154 Ritson Road South, Oshawa, Ontario, Canada L1H 5M1.

ZEITEB, JERROLD R Occupation: Resident in Surgery, University of Michigan Hospital. Education: B.S., M.S., University of Chicago. Address: 2068 Yorktown Road, Ann Arbor, Michigan 48105.

ZEITELS, SUSAN HATFIELD Occupation: Clinical Coordinator, Harper-Grace Hospitals; Doctor of Pharmacy, Assistant Professor, Wayne State University. Education: B.S., Pharm.D., University of Michigan. Address: 2068 Yorktown, Ann Arbor, Michigan 48105.

ZELEI, BERNADETTE VERONICA Occupation: Pre-Medical Student. Education: Attending Ohio State University. Address: 1019 Silvercrest Avenue, Southwest, Akron, Ohio 44314.

ZELLER, DIANE L Occupation: Staff Clerk, Computer Studies of Telephone Service Growth. Education: Associate Degree Business Management. Address: 824 Rabbit Lane, Reading, Pennsylvania 19606.

ZEMPLENY, KALMAN STEPHEN II Occupation: President and Chief Executive Officer, Wiz Communications. Education: B.B.A. International Business, 1984. Address: 13720 Riverside Drive, #308, Sherman Oaks, California 91423.

ZENOBIANS, ARA Occupation: Student. Education: B.A. Architecture (in progress), University of Southern California. Address: 6805 Golden West Avenue, Arcadia, California 91006.

ZIEBART, GEOFFREY CHARLES Occupation: Student. Education: Attending University of Wyoming. Address: Box 365 Spearfish Canyon, Spearfish, South Dakota 57783.

ZUEHLKE, SHEILA Occupation: Lieutenant, United States Air Force; Student. Education: B.S., United States Air Force Academy; M.A. (in progress), University of Hawaii. Address: EWC BX 1558 1777 East West Road, Honolulu, Hawaii 96848.

ADDENDUM

BELENCHIA, THERESA AMELIA Occupation: Director of Education, North Mississippi Retardation Center. Education: B.A. Communicative Disorders; Master of Speech Pathology. Address: 215 Williams Street, Oxford, Mississippi 38655.

BROBECK, KATHI R Occupation: Student. Education: B.A. Accounting. Address: 5370 South Locust, Meridian, Idaho 83642.

DIAZ, ELIZABETH Occupation: Salesperson. Education: B.B.A. Address: 310 East Van Week, Edinburg, Texas 78539.

HAYES, NANCY DIANE Occupation: Student. Education: B.S. Agricultural Economics (in progress), Texas A&M University. Address: 811 Itasca, Plainview, Texas 79072.

HOFFMAN, JANET LOUISE Occupation: Elementary Physical Education Teacher. Education: B.S. Elementary Education, Howard Payne University. Address: Post Office Boxx 245, Somerset, Texas 78069.

LIVERMORE, JILL DIANE Occupation: Shop Manager, Sette Publishing Company. Education: B.F.A. Printmaking, Arizona State University. Address: 1418 South Grandview, Tempe, Arizona 85281.

McKAMEY, DAWN L Occupation: Student. Education: A.A., Michigan Christian College; Degree in Child Development (in progress), Harding University. Address: Route 1, Box IVY-1, New Palestine, Indiana 40163.

NICKERSON, SCOTT PHILLIP Occupation: Student. Education: B.S. Electrical Engineering, 1984. Address: 73 Skylark Road, Portland, Maine 04103.

ORR, ARLINE ELIZABETH Occupation: Dental Assistant, Office Manager; School Board Member, District 152, Harvey, Illinois. Education: B.S. (in progress), Indiana State University. Address: 49 East 156th Street, Harvey, Illinois 60426.

ROBERT, ROBERT Occupation: Theology Student. Education: M.A. Theology, Ph.D. Theology (in progress). Address: 12, Frontenac E., St-Eruno, Quebec, Canada H3V 1B4.

ROTH, DUANE "DEWEY" A Occupation: Student, Minister to Youth. Address: 3288 Montana, Cincinnati, Ohio 45211.

SENNETT, JOHN PATRICK Occupation: Editor/ Student. Education: B.A. English, B.S. Electronics Engineering, University of Wisconsin-Madison. Address: 553 West Oakdale, #317, Chicago, Illinois 60657.

SMITH, SHARON M Occupation: Personnel Assistant. Education: A.A., B.A. Psychology (in progress). Address: 601 Pico Avenue, San Mateo, California 94403.

STICKEL, TIMOTHY P Occupation: Student. Education: B.S. Computer Science, 2-Year Accounting Certificate. Address: 266A Hillcrest Road, Booneton, New Jersey 07005.

STRAHLE, WILLIAM M Occupation: Doctoral Student. Education: B.S. Biological Engineering, M.A. Sociology, Doctoral Degree in Marketing (in progress). Address: 808 South Stull, Bloomington, Indiana 47401.

THIELKE, FREDERICK LOWELL Occupation: Dental Student. Education: B.S. Civil Engineering, D.M.D. (in progress). Address: 147 Glendora Drive, Martinez, Georgia 30907.

THRASH, WILLARD MARK Occupation: Minister. Education: B.A., M.A., M.Div. Address: 4200 14 Way Northeast, St. Petersburg, Florida 33703.

VIDAILLET, CARIDAD MERCEDES Occupation: Law Student. Education: B.A. honors, University of Oklahoma. Address: 919 Hickory Lane, Ardmore, Oklahoma 73401.

WALLACE, SONJA YVETTE Occupation: Student. Education: Degree in Art and Music (in progress). Address: 412 Avenue H, Talladega, Alabama 35160.

WILKINS, DERRICK L Occupation: High School Student. Address: Post Office Box 265, Roper, North Carolina 27970.

WRIGHT, RACHEL N O Occupation: Student. Education: B.S. Home Economics and Science, Elementary Education; M.S. Rehabilitative Counseling; Post-Master's Vocational Evaluation; Ph.D. (in progress), University of North Carolina. Address: Route 6, Box 377, Goldsboro, North Carolina 27530.

Appendix I

Roster of Life and Annual Members
The American Biographical Institute
Research Association

LIFE PATRONS

Allison, Frank
Aly, Said
Anderson, Vivian
Aragona, Guylaine
Aragona, Ronald
Au, Chang-Hung
Ayers, Anne
Barbour, Judy
Barcynski, Leon
Barnes, Melver
Barr, Nona
Baruwa, Abraham
Batal, A.
Baxter, Ruth
Bebawi, Girgis
Belisle, Lenore
Bell, Deanne
Benner, Richard
Benskina, Margarita
Berkey, Maurice
Blakely, Martha
Bohmfalk, Johnita
Bomkamp, Loraine
Boulton, Shauna
Break, Virginia
Carnevale, Dario
Carver, George
Cecconi-Bates, Augusta
Chambers, Lois
Chilton, Howard
Chin, Sue
Christensen, R.
Clark, James
Cole, Eddie-Lou
Collier, Richard
Cook, David
Cook, J.
Coriaty, George
Crause, Herman
Crihan, Herman
Croxton, Thomas
Dansby, Huddie
Davis, Alexander
Davis, Gordon
Davis, Robert
Dennison, Jerry
Denton, Thomas
Di Ponio, Concetta
DuBroff, Diana
Dumouchel, Anne
Duncan, Dyna
Duncan, Gertrude
Ellerbee, Estelle
Erwin, Jean
Everett, Thelma
Farmakis, George
Fergus, Patricia
Ferguson, Harry

Fisher, Mary
Follingstad, Henry
Ford, Gordon
Fox, Pauline
Fox, Vivian Estelle
Freeze, Elizabeth
Freund, E.
Gebo, Robert
Gershowitz, Sonya
Ghattas, Sonia
Giraudier, Antonio
Goh, Han
Gomez, Nelida
Goodman, Jess
Goulding, C.
Griffith, Reginald
Haas, Arthur
Hackett, William
Hanns, Christian
Hanson, Freddie
Harbani, Suharnoko
Harpster, V.
Harris, Louise
Harris, Thomas
Harrison, Winnie
Harz, Frances
Hatajack, Frank
Headlee, William
Heckart, Robert
Hendricks, Robert
Herren, Peter
Holland, Ray
Hornsby, J.
Houseal, Reuben
Houseal, Ruth
Howard, Adeline
Hubbard, L.
Huff, Cherry
Huff, Norman
Huraj, Helen
Ilo, Moses
Johnson, Rufus
Jordan, Lan
Kagey, F.
Kales, Robert
Karpen, Marian
Kaufman, Irene
Kerr, Catherine
King, Joseph
Kjartansson, Kristjan
Ko, Yih-Song
Kokenzie, Henry
Larde, Enrique
Laudenslager, Wanda
Leavitt, Charles
Lewis, Loraine
Long, Shirley
Lowry, Dolores

Malone, June
Manogura, Ben
Marchetti, Jean
Martin, Deborah Louise
Mashhour, Abdel-Hay
Mason, Madeline
Mathewson, Hugh
McCoy, Patricia
McCullough, Constance
McLaughlin, Sybil
Michna, Marienka
Miller, Virginia
Mills, George
Mills, William
Mitra, Gopal
Mobley, Herbert
Mollenhauer, Bernhard
Mooney, John
Moore, Dalton
Morahan, Daniel
Morgan, Branch
Mori, Marianne
Morrison, Francine
Music, Edward
Nazareno, Jose
Nicholls, James
Nikolai, Lorraine
Ogden, R.
O'Malley, William
O'Neal, Robert
Overby, George
Overby-Dean, Talulah
Pace, Jon
Parks, Anna
Payton, Ralph
Peachey, Christine
Pearson, Norman
Phillips, Karen
Phillips, Virginia
Pirkle, Estus
Plewinski, Gustaw
Plewinski, Teresa
Pollack, Stephen
Powell, Russell
Prichard, Thora
Puh, Chiung
Purvis, Mary
Puskarich, Michael
Raatz, Sherry
Rahimtoola, S.
Rasmussen, Helen
Rex, Lonnie
Reyman, Maria
Rhemann, Eugene
Richmond, John
Riemann, Wilhelmina
Roberts-Wright, Bessie
Robeson, Lillyan

Robinson, Ralph
Rodkiewicz, Czeslaw
Rodriguez, Beatriz
Rosenberg, Claire
Rowe, Iris
Rubly, Lucille
Sabella, Emmanuel
Savard, Lorena
Sawyer, Joseph
Seale, Ruth
Shah, Shirish
Sharif, Mohammed
Sheh, Violet
Simeck, Clyde
Smith, Norvel
Stein, David

Stevens, Myrtle
Stimach, Janet
Straub, Nellie
Stueper, Gustav
Sutton, Doris
Sweeney, James
Switaj, Lawrence
Szegho, Emeric
Tashiro, Noboru
Tekle, Atewerk
Thomas, William
Thompson, Andrew
Torres-Aybar, Francisco
Toutorsky, Basil
Urry, Vern
Van der Kuyp, Edwin

Vaughn, Pearl
Volpert, Don
Wainwright, Mary
Walden, Kathryn
Wlaker, Glynda
Waters, Raymond
Waters, Rowena
Webb, Rozana
Weinbaum, Eleanor
Whisenant, Mary
Wiemann, Marion
Williams, Annie
Williams, Melva
Williams, Yvonne
Wolanin, Sophie
Wolf, Joseph
Woods, Willie
Young, James

LIFE FELLOWS

Abba, Hilda
Abba, Raymond
Abrell, Ronald
Adetoro, J.
Al Bahar, Adnan
Al Seif, Khaled
Allen, Edgard
Allison, William
Ames, John
Amir-Moez, Ali
Anderson, Gordon
Anderson, Thelma
Anderson, Ursula
Aston, Katherine
Atkinson-Killian, Hulda
Attiah, Hassan
Averhart, Lula
Ayim, Emmanuel
Babajide, Solomon

Bair, Mary
Baker, Elsworth
Barbachano, Don
Bare, Jean
Baum, Carl
Beardmore, Glenn
Benebig, Roger
Bennett, Stefanie
Benson, Opral
Besche-Wadish, Pamela
Bethell, M.
Binford, Linwood
Bitters, Robert
Black, Larry
Blakeney, Roger
Bolton, Douglas
Bossert, Michael
Bourne, Geoffrey
Boyer, Theodore
Brame, Arden
Brown, Earle
Brown, F.
Bullard, Ethel
Bunnag, Srichitra
Burgess, Caroline
Burley-Allen, Madelyn
Burns, Maretta
Bush, Wendell
Bushbaum, Marianne
Campbell, Caroline
Carpenter, Charles
Carroll, Beatrice
Carson, William

Castro, Manfredo
Cauthen, Deloris
Chan, Kum Peng
Chang, Hong-Lou
Chang, Woo Joo
Char, Wai
Chisholm, William
Chretien, LaVerne
Chun, Sae-il M.D.
Ciancone, Lucy
Cintron, Emma
Clark, Fred
Clemente, Patrocinio
Cleveland, Hattye
Clift, Annie
Cohen, Irwin
Corniffe, Doris
Corsello, Lily
Couch, M.
Cullingford, Ada
D'Agostino, Ralph
Davis, Evelyn
Delphin, Jacques
Dillon, Robert
Doelle, Horst
Doherty, Elizabeth
Dolezal, Henry
Dorion, Robert
Dow, Marguerite
Drummond, Malcolm
D'Silva, Roby
Dunn, Helen
Dyer, Eileen
Eastland, Mary
Edwards, Angela
El-Sayeh, Ramzy
Emrick, Raymond
Enyi, Brown
Errazuriz, Rafael
Essenwanger, Oskar
Evans, Roymond
Fadahunsi, Samuel
Fairweather, Gladstone
Farley, Dorothy
Farrar, Margaret
Fawcett, James
Feist, Marian
Field, Elizabeth
Fink, Aaron
Francis, Mabel
Fries, Herluf
Frym, Janet

Fuchs, Helmuth
Gambrell, Mildred
Gan, Woon
Garcia, Henry
Gardine, Juanita
Garrison, Patricia
Gausman, Harold
Gauthier, Thomas
German, Fin
Gibson, Curtis
Gibson, Weldon
Glaze, Diana
Goerigk, Wolfgang
Goodman, Julius
Gospodaric, Mimi
Gossge-Blue, Edna
Gray, Dora
Greene, Sharon
Groeber, Richard
Guest, Bernette
Guyton, Suzanne
Haastrup, Adedokun
Hackney, Howard
Hale, Arnold
Hall, Wilfred
Hamilton, Madrid
Hammer, Jane
Hammons, Thomas
Hanf, James
Hanif, Akhtar
Hansen, Kathryn
Haritun, Rosalie
Hearn, Charles
Hedtke, Delphine
Hobdy, Frances
Holland, Ruby
Holmstrom, Gustaf
Hooper, Marjorie
Huck, Larry
Hui, Stephen
Hunter, Cannie
Huq, Syed
Hussaini, Hisham Rushdi
Huzurbazar, Vasant
Jacobsen, Parley
Jacobsen, William
Javed, Muhammad
Jensen, Helen
Johnston, Ruth
Jones, Bernard
Jordan, W.
Kaltenbach, Anneliese

Kanagawa, Robert
Kai, Anil
Karl, Dorothy
Kellogg, Bruce
Kelly, John
Kemp, Dorothy
Khan, Muzaffar
Kiehm, Tae M.D.
Kim, Un
King, Edwin
King, Helen
Kitada, Shinichi
Knaebel, Jeff
Knelson, Nelda
Koch, Frances
Kolb, Florence
Kolman, Laurence
Kong, Lim
Kraus, Pansy
Kritjanson, Harold
La Claustra, Vera
Landers, Newlin
Landers, Vernette
Le Cocq, Rhoda
Leeds, Sylvia
Lennox, William
Lim, Phillip
Lindberg, Elayne
Little, Florence
Littlejohn, Joan
Loening, Sarah
Long, Leonard
Lonneker, Arleen
Loper, Marilyn
Luahiwa, Judith
Lundell, Frederick
Lutzker, Edythe
Maass, Vera
Mabe, Ruth
MacLennan, Beryce
Magargal, Larry
Maigida, Umaru-Sanda
Malami, Alhaji
Malin, Howard
Manahan, Manny
Marais, Jan
Martin, James
Mason, Aretha
Massier, Paul
Masuda, Gohta
Matsumoto, Junji
McAdoo, Phyllis
McAvoy, Joseph
McCoin, John
McCormack, Grace
McNabb, Sue
Meldrum, Alex
Mellichamp, Josephine
Mello, Henry
Meskell, Una
Mestnik, Irmtraut
Meyer, G.
Miller, C.
Miller, Laverne
Miller, Robert
Mills, Rosemary
Min, Frank
Morler, Edward
Morris, Rich
Moseley, Laurice
Moses, Elbert
Mosonyi, Emil

Murayama, Makio
Naidu, Shrinivas
Naylor, Pleas
NeSmith, Vera
Nevel, Eva
Newbern, Captolia
Newman, Michele
Nichols, Thomas
Njoku, Rose
Norby, Alice
Northup, William
Novak, Lela
Nwankwo, Ochia
O'Dougherty, Pascual
Oh, May
Oien, Arthur
Okafor, Andrew
Okigbo, Pius
Oloruntoba, Barnabas
Opalka, Joyce
Osborn, Prime
Owelle, Frank
Oyeleye, Victor
Pai, Chung-Ruei
Pak, Chan
Palombo, Thomas
Parker, Lucy
Pasricha, Manohar
Pastor, Lucille
Perks, Barbara
Perry, Emma
Persch, Ruth
Peterson, Daniel
Philpott, Emalee
Pine, Charles
Pirs, Joze
Pollard, Joseph
Polley, Elizabeth
Porter, Michael
Prentice, Sartell
Price, Thomas
Putnam, Michael
Raddatz, Otto
Ragan, Bryant
Ramovs, Primoz
Regan, Helene
Reinhardt, Siegfried
Reynolds, Clayton
Richards, John
Richards, Novelle
Rifaat, Alsayed
Roberts, C.
Roberts, Josephine
Rodenburg, Carl
Rodkiewicz, Czeslaw
Rogers, Gayle
Rogers, Gifford
Roode, Johanna
Roth, Frederic
Rozenbaum, Najman
Ruas, Vitoriano
Rubly, Grant
Rutledge, Varian
Saheed, Mohammed
Sanders, Frances
Santiago, Margaret
Saxton, Beryl
Schabbel, Helen
Schirripa, Dennis
Schliephake, Erwin
Schwarzott, Wilhelm
Scott, Wilton

Sealy, Vernol
Sebastianelli, Mario
Seegar, Charlon
Segan, B.
Sewer, Pauline
Silvers, Morgan
Simpson, Jack
Singer, Jeanne
Slack, Florence
Slowik, Richard
Smith, Cecile
Snookal, Donald
Snyder, John
Soekanto, R.
Southward, B.
Speir, Kenneth
Sreenivas, Nanjappa
Steiner, A.
Stevens, Ben
Stewart, Elizabeth
Stewart, Roberta
Stilgenbauer, Robert
Stockton, Barbara
Stonebridge, Jerry
Stromillo, Mario
Stuhl, Oskar
Suleiman, Suleiman
Swamy, M.
Tabuena, Romeo
Talley-Morris, Neva
Tanzil, H. O. K.
Terao, Toshio
Tew, E.
Thomas, K.
Thomas, V.
Thomasson, Raymond
Todd, Vivian
Todres, Bernice
Torres, Rafael
Towne, Dorothea
Toyomura, Dennis
Tran, Quang
Tsau, Wen
Tulong, Joseph
Tung, Rosalie
Turk, Oscar
Turkay, Osman
Turyahikayo-Rugyema, Benon
Tyson, Helen
Umber, Anna
Vlachos, Estella
Voss, Arthur
Vukovic, Drago
Wallis, Ben
Walters, Helen
Walters-Godfree, Dorothy
Wanderman, Richard
Ward, William
Weber, Gertrude
Webster, Burnice
Welsh, Carol June
Whitfield, Vallie Jo
Wilhelm, Willa
Williams, Harvey
Willoughby, Clarice
Wilson, Jeanne
Woo, Po-Shing
Wrentmore, Anita
Wright, Jean
Wyslotsky, Ihor
Yee, Phillip
Yopconka, Natalie

LIFE ASSOCIATES

Breazeale, Morris
Dunlap, Estelle
Gaither, Dorothy
James, Shaylor
Lauer, Frances
McDowell, Margaret
Meeks, Elsie
Overton, Dean
Pasternak, Eugenia
Purcell, George
Sliwinski, M.
Small, Fay
Weaton, George

ANNUAL ASSOCIATES

Adewole, Olufunmilayo
Aldrich, Stephanie
Alexander, Samuel
Allen, Johnny
Amer, Nabil
Angus, J.
Baily, Doris
Banik, Sambhu
Basu, Debatosh
Beaman, Margarine
Bera, Sudhir
Bernard, Jonathan
Berresford, Brady
Bjornsson, Petur
Bjornsson, Sigurjon
Boim, Leon
Bomberger, Audrey
Bothwell, Shirley
Boykin, Frances
Bradley, Ramona
Brady, Bryan
Britton, Michael
Brod, Joseph
Brost, Eileen
Brott, Alexander
Brown, Edward
Brunale, Vito
Bryant, Sylvia
Burns, Marjorie
Campazzi, Betty
Capitol, Viola
Carter, Marion
Cassidy, Virginia
Cellini, William
Chappell, Mae
Chesney, Rose
Chor Fook Sin, Bill
Choun, Robert
Christensen, Don
Christias, Christos
Clark, Richard
Colston, Freddie
Corey, Margaret
Crafton-Masterson, Adrienne
Cucin, Robert
Dabbousi, M.
Davidson, Mabel
de Bettencourt Barbosa, Maria
de Brault, E.
Dean, Lloyd

DeJoia, Ruth
Dell, Margaret
Denktas, Raul
Deyton, Camilla
Dixon, Lawrence
Dossett, Betty
Downing, Everett
Drake, Josephine
Durbney, Clydrow
Dwyer, Marie
Engle, Patricia
Ester, Mary
Fales, DeCoursey
Fehrman, Cherie
Fenske, Virginia
Filos, Alberto
Forman, Ruth
Fuertes, Abelardo
Fuller, James
Fulling, Kay
Galamaga, Donald
Gallipeau, Joan
Garcia Olivero, Carmen
Gardner, Nord
Garnham, Frank
Gary, Gayle
Gibson, Jacquelyn
Gil del Real, Maria
Golton, Margaret
Goodstone, Geraldine
Gregory, Calvin
Groesbeck, E.
Gruber, Rosalind
Gugl, Wolfgang
Guy, Edward
Hagan, Paul
Hain, Violet
Hardy, Carole
Harris, Vander
Hartmann-Johnsen, Olaf
Hasumi, Toshimitsu
Havilland, Ben
Helgi, Johannes
Hemenway, Dorothy
Herring, Michael
Horswell-Chambers, Margaret
Howell, James
Hsu, Wen-ying
Hu, John
Hulsey, Ruth

Hunt, Edward
Ijiri, Yutaka
Jackson, Linda
Jamison, Maggie
Jeffrey, Margie
JemmottWilliams, Maxwell
Joannou, Michael
Jones, Myrtle
Joseph, Cuthbert
Kachel, Henry
Kane, Flora
Kang, Byung-Kyu
Kaplan, Richard
Kawano, Ietoshi
Keenan, Retha
Keroher, Grace
Kiddell, Sidney
Kihlstenius, Alf-Roger
Kjoss-Hansen, Bente
Kline, Tex
Klit, Erik
Knauf, Janine
Knepper, Eugene
Koehler, Isabel
Kopfler, Judith
Kraus, Mozelle
Ksiazek, Marilyn
Lair, Helen
Lane, Cynthia
Lang, Helmer
Larkin, Gertie
Lauterbach, Kathryn
Lawrie, Eileen
Leader, Harry
Learnard, James
Leba, Samuel
Lemire, David
Lester, William
Levandowski, Dr. Barbara
Lewis, Cecelia
Lim, Ho-Peng
Lim-Quek, Muriel
Littell, Bertha
Loret de Mola, Maria
MacLellan, Helen
Mader, Eileen
Mahaffey, Joan
Makinen, Kauko
Mallon, Thomas
Marcucci, Silvestro

Marshall, Patricia
Martin, Chippa
Martins, Micael
Masse, Louis
Mavros, Constantin
Mayer, Jacob
McCabe, Donald
McCune, Weston
McDowell, A.
Meghji, Mohamed
Melton, Ira
Mendieta, Marcelo
Messerlian, Zaven
Moore, Martha
Morgan, Clyde
Morris, William
Morse, Genevieve
Moutote, Daniel
Moya, Aury
Mozingo, Margaret
Muhlanger, Erich
Munson, Norma
Muss, Peter
Naouri, Issa
Neeper, Ralph
Nelson, Lorraine
Nelson, Robert
Nelson, Thomas
Newell, Virginia
Ney, Judy
Nicholson, Rosemary
Nicklin, Helen
Nicole, Christopher
None, B.
Norby, Alice
Norton, Alan
Nozaki, Masako
Nzegwu, Ifeanyi
Olsen, Virginia
Orata, Pedro
Oswald, Roy
Ovenstone, Irene
Papamichael, Anna
Parson, Erwin
Paschall, Amy
Patten, Clara
Patterson, E.
Perate, Hannah
Peterson, Constance
Peterson, Mary

Pilioko, Aloi
Pizer, Elizabeth
Poehner, Raymond
Posta, Elaine
Prydz, Svein
Pulliainen, Erkki
Pulliam, Paul
Rahming, Philip
Rao, A.
Reicher, Arthur
Reichle, Frederick
Reid, Douglas
Reifler, Henrietta
Reinl, Harry
Ringsdorf, W.
Ritter, Olive
Rogell, Irma
Rogers, Carol
Roney, Alice
Rughani, M.
Saleh, Mohamad
Salsbury, Barbara
Salter, Margaret
Sanchez, Juan
Sanford, Paul
Snataella, Irma
Schioldborg, Ragnhild
Scott, J.
Seltzer, Ronni
Seppala, Arvo
Shaw, Imara
Sheetz, Ralph
Shelton, Bessie
Shiffman, Max
Shragai, E.
Simmons, Troy
Slappey, Mary
Smith, Mary
Smythe-Wood, Ian
Sperry, S.
Sproll, Heinz
Staffeld-Madsen, Alfred
Stanat, Ruth
Stankovic, Milorad
Stanley, Sandra
Stephens, Rupert
Stevens, Grace
Stewart, Joan
Stiefel, Betty
Stoeger, Keith

Stottsberry, Teresa
Studley, Helen
Stuhl, Johannes
Sulaiman, Suliantono
Takino, Masiuchi
Tamari, Moshe
Tan, It-Koon
Taylor, John
Tekelioglu, Meral
Terpening, Virginia
Thomas, Peggy
Tipton, Dorothy
Tipton, Rains
Tisch, J.
Tompkins, James
Touw, J.
Tunick, Phyllis
Turner, Terrance
Tzafestas, S.
Ulrich, Walter
Varner, Barbara
Vilgrain, Jacques
Vinokooroff, Leonide
Waddington, Bette
Walker, Lorna
Wallace, Betty
Wallace, Deborah
Walton, Fernie
Warner, J.
Way, Tsung-To
Wayne, David
Webb, William
Welch, Fern
Wells, Marrion
White, Margaret
Wierbicki, Eugen
Wilford, Rowland
Wilkinson, George
Wilson, Reba
Winston, William
Wolfe, Janet
Womack, William
Wong, Robert
Wood, Sandra
Wright, Dana
Yanosko, Elizabeth
Yap, Meow
Zelner, Estelle
Zibrun, S.
Zimmerman, Richard

ABIRA FOUNDING MEMBERS

Acker, Louise
Bardis, Panos
Benton, Suzanne
Brownell, Daphne
Kalvinskas, John
Westerfield, Hilda
Williams, Patrick

Appendix II

EDITORIAL ADVISORY BOARD
The American Biographical Institute, Inc.

NATIONAL AND INTERNATIONAL DIVISIONS

MALCOLM S. ADISESHIAH, Ph.D.
79, Second Main Road, Gandhinagar, Adyar, Madras-20, India
Chairman, Madras Institute of Development Studies, India; Member of Parliament (Rajya Sabha), India

RONALD J. ARAGONA, D.C., Ph.C., L.P.A.B.I.
132 Webster Street, Manchester, New Hampshire 03104 USA
Executive Director, Founder, Developer, Chief of Staff, Head of Research, R.J. Aragona Cooperative Chiropractic Health Center

DAVID BABNEW, JR., Ph.D., L.L.D., F.A.C.H.A.
16260 West Trooon Circle, Miami Lakes, Florida 33014 USA
President, Management and Planning Associates; Researcher, Administrator, Counselor, Author

H. KENT BAKER, D.B.A., Ph.D.
5816 Edson Lane, Rockville, Maryland 20852 USA
Professor of Finance, Kogod College of Business Administration, The American University, Washington, D.C.

PANOS D. BARDIS, Ph.D., F.I.A.L., F.I.B.A.
Professor of Sociology, The University of Toledo, Toledo, Ohio 43606 USA
Editor and Book Review Editor, International Social Science Review; Editor in Chief and Book Review Editor, International Journals of World Peace

HOWARD N. BARON
Post Office Box 2349, Tampa, Florida 33601 USA
Vice President International and Managing Director, Seald-Sweet International, Inc., Executive in Management, Foreign Trade, Banking

JOHN W. BARRIGER
224 South Michigan Avenue, Chicago, Illinois 60604 USA
Director, Special Services, Corporate Communications Department, Santa Fe Industries, Inc.

LAURA ELIZABETH BEVERLY, F.A.B.I.
150 Washington Street, Apt. 6B, Hempstead, New York 11550 USA
Professor of Special Education, Board of Cooperative Educational Services, Nassau County, New York

Dr. JAI RATTAN BHALLA, F.R.I.B.A., F.I.I.A., F.V.I., H.F.A.I.A.
5, Sunder Nagar, New Delhi 110003, India
President, Council of Architecture, India, Indian Institute of Architects; Executive Council, National Institute of Urban Affairs, India

ASIT K. BISWAS, Ph.D.
76 Woodstock Close, Oxford OX2 8DD, England
Director, Biswas and Associates, Oxford, England

Dr. B, EVERARD BLANCHARD, Ph.D., D.D.
315 Dee Court, 'C', Bloomingdale, Illinois 60108 USA
President, Villa Educational Research Associates; Researcher, Educational Administrator, Author

IRVING BRAZINSKY, Sc.D., F.A.B.I.
6 Rustic Lane, Matawan, New Jersey 07747 USA
Process Development Manager, Foster Wheeler Energy Corporation; Researcher, Engineering Manager, Author, Educator

Dr. GEORGE BRUCE
25 Warriston Crescent, Edinburgh, EH3 5LB Scotland
Lecturer in Extra-Mural Studies, Edinburgh University, Scotland; Writer, Broadcaster

SYLVIA LEIGH BRYANT, F.I.B.A., A.M.A.B.I.
Route 5, Box 498A, Madison Heights, Virginia 24572 USA
Editor-Publisher, The Anthology Society; *Poet, Free-lance Writer, Consultant*

JUAN B. CALATAYUD, M.D., F.A.C.A.
1712 Eye Street, NW, Suite 1004, Washington, D.C. 20006 USA
Professor, George Washington University School of Medicine, Private Physician

JOSEPH PETER CANGEMI, Ed.D, F.A.C.A.
Psychology Department, Western Kentucky University, Bowling Green, Kentucky 42101 USA
Professor of Psychology, Western Kentucky University; Management Consultant, Researcher, Educator

C. EUGENE COKE, Ph.D., F.R.S.C., F.A.I.C., F.A.B.I., F.S.D.C., F.T.I., F.C.I.C.
26 Aqua Vista Drive, Ormond Beach, Florida 32074 USA
Chairman, Coke and Associate Consultants; Scientist, Author, Educator, International Authority on Man-Made Fibers

GROVER F. DAUSSMAN, P.E., Ph.D.
1910 Colice Road, SE, Huntsville, Alabama 35801 USA
Engineering Consultant; Former United States Government Engineer

GARTH WILFRED PRYCE DAVIES
11 Rue Charles De Gaulle, Cappellen/Olm 8322, Luxembourg
Head, European Networks Service, Commission of the European Communities

ELIAS D. DEKAZOS, Ph.D.
408 Sandstone Drive, Athens, Georgia 30605 USA
Plant Physiologist, R. Russell Agriculture Research Center

BERNARD T. DELOFFRE
2 Bis Villa Mequillet, 92200 Neuilly, France
Director General, Satel Conseil, Paris; Executive Secretary, European Consulting Satellite Organization, Paris

The Hon. Mr. Justice R. ELSE-MITCHELL, C.M.G.
2nd Floor, Northbourne House, 219 Northbourne Avenue, Canberra, ACT 2600 Australia
Chairman, Commonwealth Grants Commission

Mr. INGEMAR ESSEN
Eriksbergsgatan 16, S-114 30 Stockholm, Sweden
President, Swedish Federation of Trades, Industries and Family Enterprises

SANDRA FOWLER, F.A.B.I., L.A.A.B.I.
West Columbia, West Virginia 25287 USA
Associate Editor, Ocarina *and* The Album; *Editor, Publisher*

LORRAINE S. GALL, Ph.D., F.A.B.I.
Sandpiper Village, 1049 Anna Knapp Boulevard, Mt. Pleasant, South Carolina 29464 USA
President, Bacti-Consult Associates; Senior Microbiological Consultant, Private Business; Researcher, Space Scientist, Educator

JOSEPH B. GAVIN, Ph.D., S.J.
Campion College, University of Regina, 3769 Winnipeg Street, Regina S4S 0A2 Canada
President, Campion College, University of Regina, Regina, Canada

CARRIE LEIGH GEORGE, Ph.D., M.Div., Ed.S., M.A., D.Rel.
1652 Detroit Avenue, NW, Atlanta, Georgia 30314 USA
Research Associate and Assistant Professor of Curriculum and Instruction, Georgia State University; Ordained Clergywomen, Consultant, Researcher, Educator

ANTONIO GIRAUDIER, F.A.B.I., L.P.A.B.I.
215 East 68th Street, New York City, New York 10021 USA
Writer, Author, Poet, Artist, Musician

LEWIS DANIEL HOUCK, JR., Ph.D., L.F.I.B.A., F.A.B.I.
11111 Woodson Avenue, Kensington, Maryland 20795 USA
Project Leader for Economic Research Service, United States Department of Agriculture; Management Consultant, Author, Educator, Businessman

MOZELLE BIGELOW KRAUS, Ed.D., L.A.A.B.I.
The Willoughby, No. 925N, 5500 Friendship Blvd., Chevy Chase, Maryland 20815 USA
Private Psychology Practice, Psychotherapist

JOHN F. KURTZKE, M.D., F.A.C.P.
7509 Salem Road, Falls Church, Virginia 22043 USA
Vice Chairman and Professor of Nuerology, Georgetown Medical School, Washington D.C.; Neurologist, Epidemiologist, Consultant, Author

ENRIQUE ROBERTO LARDE, M.G.A., F.A.B.I.
Post Office Box 2922, Old San Juan, Puerto Rico 00903 USA
Director, South Continental Insurance Agency, Inc.; Director and President, Corporacion Insular de Seguros; Researcher, Business Executive

RUBY STUTTS LYELLS, L.H.D.
1116 Isiah Montgomery Street, Jackson, Mississippi 39203 USA
Federal Jury Commissioner, United States District Court, Southern District of Mississippi; Trustee, Prentiss Institute; Writer, Researcher, Librarian

KRISHNA SHANKAR MANUDHANE, Ph.D., F.A.B.I.
5211 Meadowview Avenue, North Bergen, New Jersey 07047 USA
Director of Technical Services, Zenith Laboratories, Inc., Northvale, New Jersey; Researcher

ROBERT C. McGEE, JR., F.A.B.I.
Box 29540, Richmond, Virginia 23229 USA
President, Swan Industries, Inc.; Business Executive, Aeronautical Engineer, Consultant, Administrator

ROD McKUEN
Post Office Box G, Beverly Hills, California 90213 USA
Poet, Composer-Lyricist, Author, Performer; President, Stanyan Records, Discus New Gramophone Society, Mr. Kelly Productions, Montcalm Productions, Stanyan Books, Cheval Books, Biplane Books, Rod McKuen Enterprises

HERBERT B. MOBLEY, Ph.D., D.D., S.T.D., L.P.A.B.I.
Post Office Box 165, Summit Station, Pennsylvania 17979 USA
Pastor Emeritus, St. Mark's (Brown's) United Church of Christ, Summit Station; Acting Pastor, St. Peter's United Church of Christ, Frackville, Pennsylvania

MAKIO MURAYAMA, Ph.D.
5010 Benton Avenue, Bethesda, Maryland 20814 USA
Research Biochemist, National Institute of Health

VIRGINIA SIMMONS NYABONGO, Ph.D.
935 34th Avenue North, Nashville, Tennessee 37209 USA
Professor Emeritus of French, Research, Tennessee State University; Researcher, Author, Educator

MIHAIL PROTOPAPADAKIS
Square Ambidrix 32, 1040 Brussels, Belgium
Deputy, European Parliament

ROLAND B. SCOTT, M.D.
1723 Shepherd Street, NW, Washington, DC 20011 USA
Distinguished Professor of Pediatrics and Child Health and Director, Sickle Cell Disease Center, Howard University; Educator, Administrator

SIR JAMES SIDNEY RAWDON SCOTT-HOPKINS, M.E.P.
2, Queen Anne's Gate, London, SW1H 9AA England
Member of the European Parliament

DR. CHOOMPOL SWASDIYAKORN
196 Phaholyothin Road, Bangkhen, Bangkok 10900 Thailand
Secretary-General, National Research Council of Thailand

HERBERT H. TARSON, Ph.D., F.A.B.I.
4611 Denwood Rod, La Mesa, California 92041 USA
Senior Vice President, National University, San Diego, California; Researcher, Educator

ANDREW B. THOMPSON, JR., F.A.B.I., L.P.A.B.I., L.F.I.B.A.
Post Office Box 3008, Montgomery, Alabama 36109 USA
President, National Pricing Service, Inc.

BASIL P. TOUTORSKY, D.Mus., L.P.A.B.I., F.A.B.I., L.F.I.B.A.
1720 16th Street, NW, Washington DC 20009 USA
Director, Toutorsky Academy of Music; Professor, Composer, Pianist

WALTER E. ULRICH
8 Pasadena Drive, Hamilton Township, New Jersey 08619 USA
Deputy Commissioner, New Jersey State Department of Human Services

AYIYAH W.M. VON NUSSBAUMER, Ph.D., D.Th.
11110 Hazen Road, Houston, Texas 77072 USA
Research Librarian, Published Author, Educator

ROGER LODGE WOLCOTT
4796 Waterloo Road, Atwater, Ohio 44201 USA
Former Specialist in Aeromechanical Research and Development; Engineering Department, Goodyear Aerospace Corporation, Akron; Secretary, The Lighter Than Air Society; Aviation Pioneer, Inventor, Association Executive